Genre Fairy Tale

MW00343096

Essential Question
What can you do to get the information you need?

The Bird of Truth

by James McNaughton
illustrated by Sandy Wong

CHAPTER 1
TWINS

One day, a poor fisherman was casting his net into the river when he saw something in the water. It was shining in the sun like a diamond.

He lifted it out of the water. It was a cradle made of crystal. In the cradle were twin babies, a girl and a boy. They were carefully wrapped in soft blankets. The babies looked up at him and smiled.

Filled with pity, the man took the babies and cradle home to his wife. She threw up her hands in despair. "We already have eight children!" she cried.

"We can't put them back and let them drift out to sea," replied her husband.

The woman's heart softened at the sight of them. "You're right," she sighed, "and ten can eat as cheaply as eight."

The orphaned twins grew up to be good and gentle. Their adoptive parents came to love them even more than their own children, who were jealous and argumentative.

The couple's other children picked on the twins. To escape their teasing, the two spent hours alone on the banks of the river. The twins often brought bread they'd saved from their breakfast to feed the birds. In return, the birds taught the two children to speak their language.

At first, learning a new way of speaking was very difficult, but the twins practiced whenever they could. Eventually they learned how to speak the language of birds.

The twins were kind and generous to their brothers and sisters. However, the other children continued to tease and taunt them. The eldest boy told them, "You think you're better than us, but at least we have a mother and father. You've only got the river, like the toads and frogs."

The poor twins didn't know what to say. The boy's insult made them very unhappy with their circumstances. They realized that their siblings would never accept them as part of the family, no matter how hard they tried. "We can't stay here any longer," they whispered to each other.

The next morning, the twins arose with the birds and set off to find their destiny.

CHAPTER 2
THE SWALLOWS

All day long, the twins walked along the river. They didn't see anyone else. By evening, the children were tired and hungry, but when they saw a small house ahead, their spirits rose. They imagined a warm and friendly welcome, a hot meal, and a comfortable bed. But their expectations were soon dashed. The house was dark and deserted.

The boy fought back hot tears. Trying to sound cheerful, he said, "At least we'll be able to lie down and sleep inside."

His sister smiled bravely. "Yes," she said after careful consideration. "We'll have a rest and decide what to do next."

They went inside and lay down in a corner to sleep. After they had been lying quietly for a while, some swallows flew in. The birds perched on the beams in the ceiling overhead. Unaware that the children knew their language, they began to chat freely. The swallows were a comforting presence, so the twins kept their eyes closed and listened.

"It sure is good to be back," said a swallow with a sigh.

"It's good to have you back," called the others happily.

"I tell you, life at the palace isn't all it's cracked up to be," said the first, who was sleeker than the other swallows.

"But wasn't it exciting seeing the king and hearing all the gossip?" asked another.

"Gossip?" said the first. "Birds don't like gossip!"

The birds all laughed, and the twins smiled at each other.

"So why did you leave?" asked one.

"It's peaceful here. There are too many cats in the palace! Enough about me, though—what's the news here?"

"Nothing ever happens here," said another. "Tell us the palace news!"

"Yes, yes," cried the others. "Tell us!"

When the country swallows had quieted down, the palace swallow began.

"You probably know that years ago, the king fell in love with a tailor's daughter. His nobles wanted him to choose a queen from one of their own daughters, so they tried to prevent the marriage. The king didn't listen to their protests. He went ahead with the wedding anyway. A few months later, the king went away to war. When he returned, the nobles told him that the queen had given birth to twins, but they had both died. They told the king that his wife was sick with grief and had shut herself in a tower in the mountains."

"Was that the truth? Were the twins dead?" asked the country swallows.

"Of course not!" replied the palace swallow. "The babies were alive. The nobles didn't want any heirs to the throne, so they imprisoned the queen and told the gardener to kill the babies. The gardener couldn't do it. Instead, he put them in a crystal cradle, then he laid it in the river. The babies were found by a fisherman, who raised them as his own."

STOP AND CHECK

What do the children learn from the swallows?

CHAPTER 3
THE BIRD OF TRUTH

When the twins heard about the crystal cradle, they gasped in astonishment. Their adoptive parents had told them the story of how they were found. "I can't believe it!" whispered the girl to her brother.

"If we hadn't learned the language of the birds, we might never have found out," he replied.

One of the country swallows said, "Why don't the children return to their father and set their mother free?"

"They won't be able to prove who they are," said the palace swallow. "The only way things can ever be put right is if the king consults the Bird of Truth. But she's trapped in a castle. A giant keeps her locked in a large cage with the Birds of Bad Faith. They make so much noise that she cannot be heard."

"Where is this castle?" cried the swallows.

"I don't know," replied the palace swallow sadly.

"Oh dear, oh dear, oh dear," said the birds.

The twins knew what they had to do.

At daybreak, the twins set off to find the giant's castle. They wanted to free the Bird of Truth. The countryside became bleaker and lonelier, but there was still no sign of the castle. They threw themselves to the ground in despair. Suddenly, they heard movement in the tree above them. It was a turtledove.

"Oh dove," the boy cried, using the bird's language, "please help us. We need to find the castle where the Bird of Truth is caged."

"Follow the wind," said the dove. "Today it's blowing toward the castle. If it pities you, it will blow steadily."

They thanked the bird and followed the wind. It blew and blew, guiding the children until they came to a large and gloomy castle. The doors were wide open, but the children still hesitated. The castle was as quiet as a grave. They were very frightened. Unsure of what to do next, they hid behind a lone olive tree near the castle door.

"What shall we do?" the boy asked the girl.

"What shall you do?" repeated an owl that was sitting above them in the tree.

The twins leaped for joy and said softly in the bird's language, "We've come to free the Bird of Truth. How should we do it?"

"There is an aviary in the great courtyard," said the owl. "It is filled with many brightly colored birds. Each one will call to you, saying it is the Bird of Truth. Be sure to ignore them. They are the Birds of Bad Faith. Take only the small white bird hidden in a corner. Now go while the giant is asleep, for he sleeps only 15 minutes a day!"

The twins ran quickly through the open doors and into the great courtyard. There they saw an enormous aviary. As soon as they stepped inside, the birds began to make a deafening noise. Peacocks, parrots, ravens, and all sorts of other birds called out. The birds all claimed to be the Bird of Truth.

The twins ignored the uproar. They walked among the birds until they found a small white bird in a corner.

The Bird of Truth was hemmed in by crows. The girl reached down and picked up the bird.

"Thank you, children. I have been waiting for someone to set me free," she said.

The girl gently placed the Bird of Truth inside her jacket. Then the twins ran as fast as they could out of the aviary and through the castle gates, followed by the screams of the Birds of Bad Faith.

Terrified that the giant would be awakened by the noise, the children kept running until the castle was out of sight.

News that the Bird of Truth was free spread throughout the kingdom. This made the king's wicked nobles and courtiers nervous. They were afraid she would reveal the truth about the queen and their children to the king. So they set traps to catch her and trained eagles and falcons to hunt her.

CHAPTER 4
TOGETHER AGAIN

The king spent most of his time alone in the palace. He didn't get much news. Usually he only heard what the nobles wanted him to hear. But this rumor was so strong that even the king knew about it. He proclaimed that whoever found the Bird of Truth should bring her to him immediately.

The twins heard about the king's proclamation and headed straight for the palace. However, at the entrance, the courtiers stopped them.

All of a sudden, the Bird of Truth flew out of the girl's jacket and into the king's chamber through an open window. She bowed respectfully. "Your Majesty, I am the Bird of Truth," she said. "The boy and girl who brought me here are being held at the gate by your courtiers."

The king ordered the children to be brought to him at once, and he asked them for an explanation.

"Please, Your Majesty," said the girl, "the Bird of Truth will explain everything."

And so the Bird of Truth told the king about the nobles' wicked plot and how they had imprisoned the queen and tried to kill his children.

When the king learned that he'd been misled, he took the twins, and together they hurried to the tower where the queen was imprisoned.

The queen was as pale as marble, but when she saw her husband and children, the color returned to her face, and she became as beautiful as ever.

"It's so good to see you," she said to the king. "Why did you wait so long?"

The king looked shocked. "Every month I received a letter from you telling me to stay away."

"The nobles lied to you," she said. "I wrote every day, asking you to come."

The king wiped away tears as he embraced the queen and their children. "No one will ever separate us again."

When the royal family returned to the city, they were greeted by cheering crowds. A great banquet was held in celebration. The fisherman and his wife sat in a position of honor next to the grateful king and queen. The wicked nobles fled the kingdom and never returned. And so it was that the family was reunited and lived happily ever after.

STOP AND CHECK

How are the twins reunited with their parents?

Respond to Reading

Summarize

Use important details from *The Bird of Truth* to summarize how the twins learned important information. Your graphic organizer may help you.

Event	→	Outcomes
	→	
	→	
	→	
	→	

Text Evidence

1. What features of the story tell you that *The Bird of Truth* is a fairy tale? GENRE

2. How are the events in Chapter 2 similar to and different from the events in Chapter 3? COMPARE AND CONTRAST

3. What does the simile "quiet as a grave" on page 9 mean? SIMILE

4. Write about the events that happened after the twins were born and the events that helped them return to their parents. Use details from the text to help you compare and contrast the events. WRITE ABOUT READING

Compare Texts

Read about talking animals who are on a quest.

The Singers of Bremen

There was a donkey who worked for a man, carrying sacks of flour from the mill. After many years of hard labor, the donkey's strength began to fail. One day, he overheard his master telling another man that the donkey was too old to work. After careful consideration, the donkey decided to run away to the nearby town of Bremen. He thought he could find a job as a singer when he got there.

On the road to Bremen, the donkey met a dog who looked very sad. The dog explained that he had become too weak to hunt, and his master was going to replace him.

"Don't worry," said the donkey, "I'm going to Bremen to become a singer. Come along and be a singer too."

illustrated by Philip Webb

17

The dog liked this plan, and they walked on together. On the way, they met a cat who was too tired to catch rats. Then they met a rooster about to be cooked for Sunday dinner. The donkey told them both that they were fine singers. He said there would be plenty of work for them all in Bremen.

When night fell, the animals had still not arrived in Bremen. It seemed that they would have to sleep in the woods. The donkey and dog lay under a tree, and the cat curled up on a branch. The rooster flew up to the top of the tree, where it was safest for him to sleep. From his perch, he could see a light in the distance. He called down to his friends and told them what he saw.

"Let's get a closer look," said the donkey. "We might find somewhere more comfortable to spend the night."

They all set off in the direction of the light. Soon they came to a house. The donkey was the tallest, so he looked in the window.

"Well, what do you see?" asked the cat.

"A gang of robbers eating a huge feast," said the donkey.

"We're all hungry," said the dog. "That meal is just what we need."

The donkey consulted his companions to figure out how they could get the robbers out of the house. After much discussion, they came up with a plan.

The donkey placed his front hooves on the windowsill. The dog got up on the donkey's back. Then the cat jumped up on top of the dog. Finally, the rooster flew up and perched on the cat's head.

Then they began to perform their music. The donkey brayed, the dog howled, the cat yowled, and the rooster crowed. The robbers leaped up in fright. They thought it was a monster. They fled from the house and disappeared into the woods.

The four friends went inside. They feasted as if they hadn't eaten for a month. The robbers were so afraid that they never returned. And the four singers of Bremen were so comfortable in the house that they never left.

Make Connections

How did the animals find out what was happening in the house? ESSENTIAL QUESTION

Why do the characters in these two stories go on their quests? TEXT TO TEXT

19

Focus on Genre

Fairy Tales The plot of a fairy tale often requires a character to carry out a difficult quest or a set of tasks to achieve a goal. They can be helped or tricked by people, animals, or objects that use special powers to do incredible things, such as transform themselves.

In a fairy tale, the good characters always win over the bad ones to live "happily ever after."

Read and Find In *The Bird of Truth*, the kind, gentle twins are treated badly by the fisherman's children.

The twins learn to speak bird language, which helps them to learn about their true parents. Their quest is to find the Bird of Truth, who is able to tell the king what happened to the queen and their children.

The twins and their parents live happily ever after.

Your Turn

Think about another fairy tale that you have read or heard. Retell the fairy tale, copying the style and features of the fairy tales in this book. Remember to use a plot that sets tasks or challenges for the main character. Include other people, animals, or objects that can help—or trick!—this character by using special powers.

ISBN 978-0-266-63513-0
PIBN 10989829

This book is a reproduction of an important historical work. Forgotten Books uses
state-of-the-art technology to digitally reconstruct the work, preserving the original format
whilst repairing imperfections present in the aged copy. In rare cases, an imperfection in
the original, such as a blemish or missing page, may be replicated in our edition. We do,
however, repair the vast majority of imperfections successfully; any imperfections that
remain are intentionally left to preserve the state of such historical works.

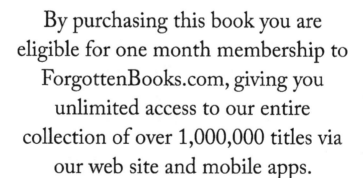

MESSAGE

FROM THE

PRESIDENT OF THE UNITED STATES

TO

THE TWO HOUSES OF CONGRESS

AT THE COMMENCEMENT OF THE

FIRST SESSION OF THE FORTY-THIRD CONGRESS,

WITH THE

REPORTS OF THE HEADS OF DEPARTMENTS

AND

SELECTIONS FROM ACCOMPANYING DOCUMENTS.

EDITED BY

BEN: PERLEY POORE,

CLERK OF PRINTING RECORDS.

WASHINGTON:
GOVERNMENT PRINTING OFFICE.
1873.

Prepared in accordance with the following provisions of "An act to re
regulate the printing of public documents, and for other purposes," appro
1864:

Be it enacted by the Senate and House of Representatives of the United Stat
in Congress assembled, That hereafter, instead of furnishing manuscript
documents usually accompanying their annual reports to each House of C
heads of the several Departments of Government shall transmit them, on
first day of November in each year, to the Superintendent of Public Print
cause to be printed the usual number, and, in addition thereto, one thousa
the use of the Senate and two thousand copies for the use of the House of
tives. And that it shall be the duty of the Joint Committee on Printing
some competent person, who shall edit and select such portions of the d
placed in their hands as shall, in the judgment of the committee, be d
popular distribution, and to prepare an alphabetical index to the same.

    •   •   •   •   •

SEC. 3. *And be it further enacted,* That it shall be the duty of the heads of
Departments of Government to furnish the Superintendent of Public Pi
copies of their respective reports on or before the third Monday in Nove
year.

SEC. 4. *And be it further enacted,* That it shall be the duty of the Super
Public Printing to print the President's message, the reports of the head
ments, and the abridgment of accompanying documents prepared under t
of the Joint Committee on Public Printing, suitably bound; and that, in
the number now required by law, and unless otherwise ordered by eith
Congress, it shall be his duty to print ten thousand copies of the same fc
the Senate, and twenty-five thousand copies for the use of the House, as
the same to the proper officer of each House, respectively, on or before the
nesday in December following the assembling of Congress, or as soon t
practicable.

ＥＳＳＡＧＥ

OF

OF THE UNITED STATES.

presentatives :

nce the submission of my last message to
ng the latter part of it—been an eventful
idst of great national prosperity a finan-
has brought low fortunes of gigantic pro-
ip has almost ceased to exist, especially in
finally, the capture upon the high seas of a
or a time threatened the most serious con-
he public mind from one end of the coun-
happily, now is in the course of satisfac-
both nations concerned.

d States, however, with most of the other
dly and cordial. With France, Germany,
European powers; with Brazil and most
lica, and with Japan, nothing has occurred
ecial notice. The correspondence between
d various diplomatic representatives in or
mitted herewith.

ongress, as expressed in its joint resolution
t, and in accordance with the provisions of
of "practical artisans," of "scientific men,"
ners" were authorized to attend the exposi-
ners on the part of the United States. It is
med the object which Congress had in view
olution, "in order to enable the people of the
e in the advantages of the international ex-
agriculture, manufactures, and the fine arts
take pleasure in adding that the American
a gratifying number of diplomas and of

conference was held at Vienna for the pur-

Prepared in accordance with the following provisions of "An act to expedite and regulate the printing of public documents, and for other purposes," approved June 25, 1864:

Be it enacted by the Senate and House of Representatives of the United States of America in Congress assembled, That hereafter, instead of furnishing manuscript copies of the documents usually accompanying their annual reports to each House of Congress, the heads of the several Departments of Government shall transmit them, on or before the first day of November in each year, to the Superintendent of Public Printing, who shall cause to be printed the usual number, and, in addition thereto, one thousand copies for the use of the Senate and two thousand copies for the use of the House of Representatives. And that it shall be the duty of the Joint Committee on Printing to appoint some competent person, who shall edit and select such portions of the documents so placed in their hands as shall, in the judgment of the committee, be desirable for popular distribution, and to prepare an alphabetical index to the same.

     *   *   *   *   *   *   *

SEC. 3. *And be it further enacted,* That it shall be the duty of the heads of the several Departments of Government to furnish the Superintendent of Public Printing with copies of their respective reports on or before the third Monday in November in each year.

SEC. 4. *And be it further enacted,* That it shall be the duty of the Superintendent of Public Printing to print the President's message, the reports of the heads of Departments, and the abridgment of accompanying documents prepared under the direction of the Joint Committee on Public Printing, suitably bound; and that, in addition to the number now required by law, and unless otherwise ordered by either House of Congress, it shall be his duty to print ten thousand copies of the same for the use of the Senate, and twenty-five thousand copies for the use of the House, and to deliver the same to the proper officer of each House, respectively, on or before the third Wednesday in December following the assembling of Congress, or as soon thereafter as practicable.

MESSAGE

OF

THE PRESIDENT OF THE UNITED STATES.

To the Senate and House of Representatives:

The year that has passed since the submission of my last message to Congress has—especially during the latter part of it—been an eventful one to the country. In the midst of great national prosperity a financial crisis has occurred that has brought low fortunes of gigantic proportions; political partisanship has almost ceased to exist, especially in the agricultural regions; and finally, the capture upon the high seas of a vessel bearing our flag has for a time threatened the most serious consequences, and has agitated the public mind from one end of the country to the other. But this, happily, now is in the course of satisfactory adjustment, honorable to both nations concerned.

The relations of the United States, however, with most of the other powers continue to be friendly and cordial. With France, Germany, Russia, Italy, and the minor European powers; with Brazil and most of the South American republics, and with Japan, nothing has occurred during the year to demand special notice. The correspondence between the Department of State and various diplomatic representatives in or from those countries is transmitted herewith.

In executing the will of Congress, as expressed in its joint resolution of the 14th of February last, and in accordance with the provisions of the resolution, a number of " practical artisans," of " scientific men," and of " honorary commissioners" were authorized to attend the exposition at Vienna as commissioners on the part of the United States. It is believed that we have obtained the object which Congress had in view when it passed the joint resolution, "in order to enable the people of the United States to participate in the advantages of the international exhibition of the products of agriculture, manufactures, and the fine arts to be held at Vienna." I take pleasure in adding that the American exhibitors have received a gratifying number of diplomas and of medals.

During the exposition a conference was held at Vienna for the purpose of consultation on the systems prevailing in different countries for the protection of inventions. I authorized a representative from the Patent-Office to be present at Vienna at the time when this conference was to take place, in order to aid, as far as he might, in securing any possible additional protection to American inventors in Europe. The report of this agent will be laid before Congress.

It is my pleasant duty to announce to Congress that the Emperor of China, on attaining his majority, received the diplomatic representatives of the western powers in person. An account of these ceremonies, and of the interesting discussions which preceded them, will be found in the documents transmitted herewith. The accompanying papers show that some advance, although slight, has been made during the past year toward the suppression of the infamous Chinese cooly-trade. I recommend Congress to inquire whether additional legislation be not needed on this subject.

The money awarded to the United States by the tribunal of arbitration at Geneva was paid by Her Majesty's government a few days in advance of the time when it would have become payable according to the terms of the treaty. In compliance with the provisions of the act of March 3, 1873, it was at once paid into the Treasury, and used to redeem, so far as it might, the public debt of the United States; and the amount so redeemed was invested in a five per cent. registered bond of the United States for fifteen million five hundred thousand dollars, which is now held by the Secretary of State, subject to the future disposition of Congress.

I renew my recommendation, made at the opening of the last session of Congress, that a commission be created for the purpose of auditing and determining the amounts of the several " direct losses growing out of the destruction of vessels and their cargoes " by the Alabama, the Florida, or the Shenandoah, after leaving Melbourne, for which the sufferers have received no equivalent or compensation, and of ascertaining the names of the persons entitled to receive compensation for the same, making the computations upon the basis indicated by the tribunal of arbitration at Geneva; and that payment of such losses be authorized to an extent not to exceed the awards of the tribunal at Geneva.

By an act approved on the 14th day of February last, Congress made provision for completing, jointly with an officer or commissioner to be named by Her Britannic Majesty, the determination of so much of the boundary-line between the territory of the United States and the possessions of Great Britain as was left uncompleted by the commissioners appointed under the act of Congress of August 11, 1856. Under the provisions of this act the northwest water-boundary of the United States has been determined and marked in accordance with the award of the Emperor of Germany. A protocol and a copy of the map upon which the line was thus marked are contained in the papers submitted herewith.

I also transmit a copy of the report of the commissioner for marking the northern boundary between the United States and the British possessions west of the Lake of the Woods, of the operations of the commission during the past season. Surveys have been made to a point four hundred and ninety-seven miles west of the Lake of the Woods, leaving about three hundred and fifty miles to be surveyed, the field-work of which can be completed during the next season.

The mixed commission organized under the provisions of the treaty of Washington for settling and determining the claims of citizens of either power against the other arising out of the acts committed against their persons or property during the period between April 13, 1861, and April 9, 1865, made its final award on the 25th day of September last. It was awarded that the Government of the United States should pay to the government of Her Britannic Majesty, within twelve months from the date of the award, the sum of $1,929,819 in gold. The commission disallowed or dismissed all other claims of British subjects against the United States. The amount of the claims presented by the British government, but disallowed or dismissed, is understood to be about $93,000,000. It also disallowed all claims of citizens of the United States against Great Britain which were referred to it.

I recommend the early passage of an act appropriating the amount necessary to pay this award against the United States.

I have caused to be communicated to the government of the King of Italy the thanks of this Government for the eminent services rendered by Count Corti as the third commissioner on this commission. With dignity, learning, and impartiality he discharged duties requiring great labor and constant patience, to the satisfaction, I believe, of both governments. I recommend legislation to create a special court, to consist of three judges, who shall be empowered to hear and determine all claims of aliens upon the United States arising out of acts committed against their persons or property during the insurrection. The recent reference under the treaty of Washington was confined to claims of British subjects arising during the period named in the treaty; but it is understood that there are other British claims of a similar nature, arising after the 9th of April, 1865, and it is known that other claims of a like nature are advanced by citizens or subjects of other powers. It is desirable to have these claims also examined and disposed of.

Official information being received from the Dutch government of a state of war between the King of the Netherlands and the Sultan of Acheen, the officers of the United States who were near the seat of the war were instructed to observe an impartial neutrality. It is believed that they have done so.

The joint commission under the convention with Mexico of 1868 having again been legally prolonged, has resumed its business, which, it is hoped, may be brought to an early conclusion. The distinguished representative of Her Britannic Majesty at Washington has kindly consented, with the approval of his government, to assume the arduous and responsible duties of umpire in this commission, and to lend the weight of his character and name to such decisions as may not receive the acquiescence of both the arbitrators appointed by the respective governments.

The commissioners appointed pursuant to the authority of Congress to examine into the nature and extent of the forays by trespassers from that country upon the herds of Texas, have made a report, which will be submitted for your consideration.

The Venezuelan government has been apprised of the sense of Congress in regard to the awards of the joint commission under the convention of 25th April, 1866, as expressed in the act of the 25th of February last.

It is apprehended that that government does not realize the character of its obligations under that convention. As there is reason to believe, however, that its hesitancy in recognizing them springs in part at least from real difficulty in discharging them in connection with its obligations to other governments, the expediency of further forbearance on our part is believed to be worthy of your consideration.

The Ottoman government and that of Egypt have latterly shown a disposition to relieve foreign consuls of the judicial powers which heretofore they have exercised in the Turkish dominions, by organizing other tribunals. As Congress, however, has by law provided for the discharge of judicial functions by consuls of the United States in that quarter under the treaty of 1830, I have not felt at liberty formally to accept the proposed change without the assent of Congress, whose decision upon the subject, at as early a period as may be convenient, is earnestly requested.

I transmit herewith for the consideration and determination of Congress an application of the republic of Santo Domingo to this Government to exercise a protectorate over that republic.

Since the adjournment of Congress the following treaties with foreign powers have been proclaimed: A naturalization convention with Denmark; a convention with Mexico for renewing the claim commission; a convention of friendship, commerce, and extradition with the Orange Free State, and a naturalization convention with Ecuador.

I renew the recommendation made in my message of December, 1870, that Congress authorize the Postmaster-General to issue all commissions to officials appointed through his Department.

I invite the earnest attention of Congress to the existing laws of the United States respecting expatriation and the election of nationality by individuals. Many citizens of the United States reside permanently abroad with their families. Under the provisions of the act approved February 10, 1855, the children of such persons are to be deemed and taken to be citizens of the United States, but the rights of citizenship are not to descend to persons whose fathers never resided in the United States.

It thus happens that persons who have never resided within the United States have been enabled to put forward a pretension to the protection of the United States against the claim to military service of the government under whose protection they were born and have been reared. In some cases even naturalized citizens of the United States have returned to the land of their birth, with intent to remain there, and their children, the issue of a marriage contracted there after their return, and who have never been in the United States, have laid claim to our protection, when the lapse of many years had imposed upon them the duty of military service to the only government which had ever known them personally.

Until the year 1868 it was left embarrassed by conflicting opinions of courts and of jurists to determine how far the doctrine of perpetual allegiance derived from our former colonial relations with Great Britain was applicable to American citizens. Congress then wisely swept these doubts away by enacting that "any declaration, instruction, opinion order, or decision of any officer of this Government which denies, restricts, impairs, or questions the right of expatriation, is inconsistent with the fundamental principles of this Government." But Congress did not indicate in that statute, nor has it since done so, what acts are deemed to work expatriation. For my own guidance in determining such questions, I required (under the provisions of the Constitution) the opinion in writing of the principal officer in each of the Executive Departments upon certain questions relating to this subject. The result satisfies me that further legislation has become necessary. I therefore commend the subject to the careful consideration of Congress, and I transmit herewith copies of the several opinions of the principal officers of the executive department, together with other correspondence and pertinent information on the same subject.

The United States, who led the way in the overthrow of the feudal doctrine of perpetual allegiance, are among the last to indicate how their own citizens may elect another nationality. The papers submitted herewith indicate what is necessary to place us on a par with other leading nations in liberality of legislation on this international question. We have already in our treaties assented to the principles which would need to be embodied in laws intended to accomplish such results. We have agreed that citizens of the United States may cease to be citizens, and may voluntarily render allegiance to other powers. We have agreed that residence in a foreign land, without intent to return, shall of itself work expatriation. We have agreed in some instances upon the length of time necessary for such continued residence to work a presumption of such intent. I invite Congress now to mark out and define when and how expatriation can be accomplished; to regulate by law the condition of American women marrying foreigners; to fix the status of children born in a foreign country of American parents residing more or less permanently abroad, and to make rules for determining such other kindred points as may seem best to Congress.

In compliance with the request of Congress I transmitted to the American minister at Madrid, with instructions to present it to the Spanish government, the joint resolution, approved on the 3d of March last, tendering to the people of Spain, in the name and on the behalf of the American people, the congratulations of Congress upon the efforts to consolidate in Spain the principles of universal liberty in a republican form of government.

The existence of this new republic was inaugurated by striking the fetters from the slaves in Porto Rico. This beneficent measure was followed by the release of several thousand persons illegally held as slaves in Cuba. Next, the captain-general of that colony was deprived of the power to set aside the orders of his superiors at Madrid, which had pertained to the office since 1825. The sequestered estates of American citizens, which had been the cause of long and fruitless correspondence, were ordered to be restored to their owners. All these liberal steps were taken in the face of a violent opposition directed by the reactionary slaveholders of Havana, who are vainly striving to stay the march of ideas which has terminated slavery in Christendom, Cuba only excepted. Unhappily, however, this baneful influence has thus far succeeded in defeating the efforts of all liberal-minded men in Spain to abolish slavery in Cuba, and in preventing the promised reform in that island. The struggle for political supremacy continues there.

The pro-slavery and aristocratic party in Cuba is gradually arraigning itself in more and more open hostility and defiance of the home government, while it still maintains a political connection with the republic in the peninsula; and although usurping and defying the authority of the home government, whenever such usurpation or defiance tends in the direction of oppression or of the maintenance of abuses, it is still a power in Madrid, and is recognized by the government. Thus an element more dangerous to continued colonial relations between Cuba and Spain than that which inspired the insurrection at Yara— an element opposed to granting any relief from misrule and abuse, with no aspirations after freedom, commanding no sympathies in generous breasts, aiming to rivet still stronger the shackles of slavery and oppression—has seized many of the emblems of power in Cuba, and, under professions of loyalty to the mother country, is exhausting the resources of the island, and is doing acts which are at variance with those principles of justice, of liberality, and of right, which give nobility of character to a republic. In the interests of humanity, of civilization, and of progress, it is to be hoped that this evil influence may be soon averted.

The steamer Virginius was on the 26th day of September, 1870, duly registered at the port of New York as a part of the commercial marine of the United States. On the 4th of October, 1870, having received the certificate of her register in the usual legal form, she sailed from the port of New York, and has not since been within the territorial jurisdiction of the United States. On the 31st day of October last, while sailing under the flag of the United States, on the high seas, she was forcibly seized by the Spanish gun-boat Tornado, and was carried into the port of Santiago de Cuba, where fifty-three of her passengers and crew were inhumanly, and, so far at least as relates to those who were citizens of the United States, without due process of law, put to death.

It is a well-established principle, asserted by the United States from the beginning of their national independence, recognized by Great Britain and other maritime powers, and stated by the Senate in a resolution passed unanimously on the 16th of June, 1858, that "American vessels on the high seas in time of peace, bearing the American flag, remain under the jurisdiction of the country to which they belong; and therefore any visitation, molestation, or detention of such vessel by force, or by the exhibition of force, on the part of a foreign power, is in derogation of the sovereignty of the United States."

In accordance with this principle the restoration of the Virginius, and the surrender of the survivors of her passengers and crew, and a due reparation to the flag, and the punishment of the authorities who had been guilty of the illegal acts of violence, were demanded. The Spanish government has recognized the justice of the demand, and has arranged for the immediate delivery of the vessel, and for the surrender of the survivors of the passengers and crew, and for a salute to the flag, and for proceedings looking to the punishment of those who may be proved to have been guilty of illegal acts of violence toward citizens of the United States, and also toward indemnifying those who may be shown to be entitled to indemnity. A copy of a protocol of a conference between the Secretary of State and the Spanish minister, in which the terms of this arrangement were agreed to, is transmitted herewith.

The correspondence on this subject with the legation of the United States in Madrid was conducted in cipher and by cable, and needs the verification of the actual text of the correspondence. It has seemed to me to be due to the importance of the case not to submit this correspondence until the accurate text can be received by mail. It is expected shortly, and will be submitted when received.

In taking leave of this subject for the present, I wish to renew the expression of my conviction, that the existence of African slavery in Cuba is a principal cause of the lamentable condition of the island. I do not doubt that Congress shares with me the hope that it will soon be made to disappear, and that peace and prosperity may follow its abolition.

The embargoing of American estates in Cuba; cruelty to American citizens detected in no act of hostility to the Spanish government; the murdering of prisoners taken with arms in their hands; and, finally, the capture upon the high seas of a vessel sailing under the United States flag and bearing a United States registry have culminated in an outburst of indignation that has seemed for a time to threaten war. Pending negotiations between the United States and the government of Spain on the subject of this capture, I have authorized the Secretary of the Navy to put our Navy on a war footing, to the extent, at least, of the entire annual appropriation for that branch of the service, trusting to Congress and the public opinion of the American people to justify my action.

CONSTITUTIONAL AMENDMENTS.

Assuming from the action of the last Congress, in appointing a " Committee on Privileges and Elections," to prepare and report to this Congress a constitutional amendment to provide a better method of electing the President and Vice-President of the United States, and also from the necessity of such an amendment, that there will be submitted to the State legislatures, for ratification, such an improvement in our Constitution, I suggest two others for your consideration :

First. To authorize the Executive to approve of so much of any measure passing the two Houses of Congress as his judgment may dictate, without approving the whole, the disapproved portion, or portions, to be subjected to the same rules as now, to wit, to be referred back to the house in which the measure, or measures, originated, and if passed by a two-thirds vote of the two houses, then to become a law without the approval of the President. I would add to this a provision that there should be no legislation by Congress during the last twenty-four hours of its sitting, except upon vetoes, in order to give the Executive an opportunity to examine and approve or disapprove bills understandingly.

Second. To provide, by amendment, that when an extra session of Congress is convened by Executive proclamation, legislation during the continuance of such extra session shall be confined to such subjects as the Executive may bring before it, from time to time, in writing.

The advantages to be gained by these two amendments are too obvious for me to comment upon them. One session in each year is provided for by the Constitution, in which there are no restrictions as to the subjects of legislation by Congress. If more are required, it is always in the power of Congress, during their term of office, to provide for sessions at any time. The first of these amendments would protect the public against the many abuses, and waste of public moneys, which creep into appropriation bills, and other important measures passing during the expiring hours of Congress, to which, otherwise, due consideration cannot be given.

TREASURY DEPARTMENT.

The receipts of the Government from all sources for the last fiscal year were $333,738,204, and expenditures on all accounts $290,345,245, thus showing an excess of receipts over expenditures of $43,392,959. But it is not probable that this favorable exhibit will be shown for the present fiscal year. Indeed, it is very doubtful whether, except with great economy on the part of Congress in making appropriations, and the same economy in administering the various departments of Government, the revenues will not fall short of meeting actual expenses, including interest on the public debt.

I commend to Congress such economy, and point out two sources where, it seems to me, it might commence, to wit, in the appropriations for public buildings in the many cities where work has not yet been commenced; in the appropriations for river and harbor improvement in those localities where the improvements are of but little benefit to general commerce, and for fortifications.

There is a still more fruitful source of expenditure, which I will point out later in this message. I refer to the easy method of manufacturing claims for losses incurred in suppressing the late rebellion.

I would not be understood here as opposing the erection of good, substantial, and even ornamental buildings by the Government wherever such buildings are needed. In fact, I approve of the Government owning its own buildings, in all sections of the country, and hope the day is not far distant when it will not only possess them, but will erect in the capital suitable residences for all persons who now receive commutation for quarters or rent at Government expense, and for the Cabinet, thus setting an example to the States which may induce them to erect buildings for their Senators. But I would have this work conducted at a time when the revenues of the country would abundantly justify it.

The revenues have materially fallen off for the first five months of the present fiscal year from what they were expected to produce, owing to the general panic now prevailing, which commenced about the middle of September last. The full effect of this disaster, if it should not prove a " blessing in disguise," is yet to be demonstrated. In either event it is your duty to heed the lesson, and to provide by wise and well-considered legislation, as far as it lies in your power, against its recurrence, and to take advantage of all benefits that may have accrued.

My own judgment is that, however much individuals may have suffered, one long step has been taken toward specie payments; that we can never have permanent prosperity until a specie basis is reached; and that a specie basis cannot be reached and maintained until our exports, exclusive of gold, pay for our imports, interest due abroad, and other specie obligations, or so nearly so as to leave an appreciable accumulation of the precious metals in the country from the products of our mines.

The development of the mines of precious metals during the past year and the prospective development of them for years to come, are gratifying in their results. Could but one-half of the gold extracted from the mines be retained at home our advance toward specie payments would be rapid.

To increase our exports, sufficient currency is required to keep all the industries of the country employed. Without this, national as well as individual bankruptcy must ensue. Undue inflation, on the other hand, while it might give temporary relief, would only lead to inflation of prices, the impossibility of competing in our own markets for the products of home skill and labor, and repeated renewals of present experiences. Elasticity to our circulating medium, therefore, and just enough of it to transact the legitimate business of the country, and to keep all industries employed, is what is most to be desired. The exact medium is specie, the recognized medium of exchange the world over. That obtained, we shall have a currency of an exact degree of elasticity. If there be too much of it for the legitimate purposes of trade and commerce, it will flow out of the country. If too little, the reverse will result. To hold what we have and to appreciate our currency to that standard, is the problem deserving of the most serious consideration of Congress.

The experience of the present panic has proven that the currency of the country, based as it is upon the credit of the country, is the best that has ever been devised. Usually in times of such trials, currency has become worthless, or so much depreciated in value as to inflate the values of all the necessaries of life as compared with the currency. Every one holding it has been anxious to dispose of it on any terms. Now we witness the reverse. Holders of currency hoard it as they did gold in former experiences of a like nature.

It is patent to the most casual observer that much more currency, or money, is required to transact the legitimate trade of the country during the fall and winter months, when the vast crops are being removed, than during the balance of the year. With our present system the amount in the country remains the same throughout the entire year, resulting in an accumulation of all the surplus capital of the country in a few centers when not employed in the moving of crops, tempted there by the offer of interest on call loans. Interest being paid, this surplus capital must earn this interest paid with a profit. Being subject to "call," it cannot be loaned, only in part at best, to the merchant or manufacturer for a fixed term. Hence, no matter how much currency there might be in the country, it would be absorbed, prices keeping pace with the volume, and panics, stringency, and disasters would ever be recurring with the autumn. Elasticity in our monetary system, therefore, is the object to be attained first, and next to that, as far as possible, a prevention of the use of other people's money in stock and other species of speculation. To prevent the latter it seems to me that one great step would be taken by prohibiting the national banks from paying interest on deposits, by requiring them to hold their reserves in their own vaults, and by forcing them into resumption, though it would only be in legal-tender notes. For this purpose I would suggest the establishment of clearing-houses for your consideration.

To secure the former many plans have been suggested, most, if not all, of which look to me more like inflation on the one hand, or compelling the Government, on the other, to pay interest, without corresponding benefits, upon the surplus funds of the country during the seasons when otherwise unemployed.

I submit for your consideration whether this difficulty might not be come by authorizing the Secretary of the Treasury to issue, at any time, to national banks of issue, any amount of their own notes below a fixed percentage of their issue, say forty per cent., upon the banks depositing with the Treasurer of the United States an amount of Government bonds equal to the amount of notes demanded, the banks to forfeit to the Government, say four per cent. of the interest accruing on the bonds so pledged during the time they remain with the Treasurer, as security for the increased circulation, the bonds so pledged to be redeemable by the banks at their pleasure, either in whole or in part, by returning their own bills for cancellation to an amount equal to the face of the bonds withdrawn. I would further suggest for your consideration the propriety of authorizing national banks to diminish their standing issue at pleasure, by returning for cancellation their own bills and withdrawing so many United States bonds as are pledged for the bills returned.

In view of the great actual contraction that has taken place in the currency, and the comparative contraction continuously going on, due to the increase of population, increase of manufactories, and all the industries, I do not believe there is too much of it now for the dullest period of the year. Indeed, if clearing-houses should be established, thus forcing redemption, it is a question for your consideration whether banking should not be made free, retaining all the safeguards now required to secure bill-holders. In any modification of the present laws regulating national banks, as a further step toward preparing for resumption of specie payments, I invite your attention to a consideration of the propriety of exacting from them the retention, as a part of their reserve, either the whole or a part of the gold interest accruing upon the bonds pledged as security for their issue. I have not reflected enough on the bearing this might have in producing a scarcity of coin with which to pay duties on imports to give it my positive recommendation. But your attention is invited to the subject.

During the last four years the currency has been contracted, directly, by the withdrawal of three per cent. certificates, compound-interest notes, and "seven-thirty" bonds outstanding on the 4th of March, 1869, all of which took the place of legal tenders in the bank reserves to the extent of sixty-three million dollars.

During the same period there has been a much larger comparative contraction of the currency. The population of the country has largely increased. More than twenty-five thousand miles of railroad have been built, requiring the active use of capital to operate them. Millions of acres of land have been opened to cultivation, requiring capital to move the products. Manufactories have multiplied beyond all precedent in the same period of time, requiring capital weekly for the payment of wages and for the purchase of material; and probably the largest of all comparative contraction arises from the organizing of free labor in the South. Now every laborer there receives his wages, and, for want of savings-banks, the greater part of such wages is carried in the pocket or hoarded until required for use.

These suggestions are thrown out for your consideration, without any recommendation that they shall be adopted literally, but hoping that the best method may be arrived at to secure such an elasticity of the currency as will keep employed all the industries of the country, and prevent such an inflation as will put off indefinitely the resumption of specie payments, an object so devoutly to be wished for by all, and by none more earnestly than the class of people most directly interested—those who "earn their bread by the sweat of their brow." The decisions of Congress on this subject will have the hearty support of the Executive.

In previous messages I have called attention to the decline in American ship-building, and recommended such legislation as would secure to us our proportion of the carrying-trade. Stimulated by high rates and abundance of freight, the progress for the last year in ship-building has been very satisfactory. There has been an increase of about three per cent. in the amount transported in American vessels over the amount of last year. With the reduced cost of material which has taken place, it may reasonably be hoped that this progress will be maintained, and even increased. However, as we pay about $80,000,000 per annum to foreign vessels for the transportation to a market of our surplus products, thus increasing the balance of trade against us to this amount, the subject is one worthy of your serious consideration.

"Cheap transportation" is a subject that has attracted the attention of both producers and consumers for the past few years, and has contributed to, if it has not been the direct cause of, the recent panic and stringency.

As Congress, at its last session, appointed a special committee to investigate this whole subject during the vacation, and report at this session, I have nothing to recommend until their report is read.

There is one work, however, of a national character, in which the greater portion of the East and the West, the North and the South, are equally interested, to which I will invite your attention.

The State of New York has a canal connecting Lake Erie with tide-water on the Hudson River. The State of Illinois has a similar work connecting Lake Michigan with navigable water on the Illinois River, thus making water-communication inland, between the East and the West and South. These great artificial water-courses are the property of the States through which they pass, and pay toll to those States. Would it not be wise statesmanship to pledge these States that if they will open these canals for the passage of large vessels the General Government will look after and keep in navigable condition the great public highways with which they connect, to wit, the overslaugh on the Hudson, the Saint Clair Flats, and the Illinois and Mississippi Rivers? This would be a national work; one of great value to the producers of the West and South in giving them cheap transportation for their produce to the sea-board and a market; and to the consumers in the East in giving them cheaper food, particularly of those articles of food which do not find a foreign market, and the prices of which, therefore, are not regulated by foreign demands. The advantages of such a work are too obvious for argument. I submit the subject to you, therefore, without further comment.

In attempting to regain our lost commerce and carrying-trade, I have heretofore called attention to the states south of us offering a field where much might be accomplished. To further this object I suggest that a small appropriation be made, accompanied with authority for the Secretary of the Navy to fit out a naval vessel to ascend the Amazon River to the mouth of the Madeira; thence to explore that river and its tributaries into Bolivia, and to report to Congress at its next session, or as soon as practicable, the accessibility of the country by water, its resources, and the population so reached. Such an exploration would cost but little; it can do no harm, and may result in establishing a trade of value to both nations.

In further connection with the Treasury Department I would recommend a revision and codification of the tariff laws, and the opening of more mints for coining money, with authority to coin for such nations as may apply.

WAR DEPARTMENT.

The attention of Congress is invited to the recommendations contained in the report of the Secretary of War herewith accompanying.

The apparent great cost of supporting the Army is fully explained by this report, and I hope will receive your attention.

While inviting your general attention to all the recommendations made by the Secretary of War, there are two which I would especially invite you to consider: First, the importance of preparing for war in time of peace by providing proper armament for our sea-coast defenses. Proper armament is of vastly more importance than fortifications. The latter can be supplied very speedily for temporary purposes when needed; the former cannot. The second is the necessity of re-opening promotion in the staff corps of the Army. Particularly is this necessity felt in the Medical, Pay, and Ordnance Departments.

At this time it is necessary to employ "contract surgeons" to supply the necessary medical attendance required by the Army.

With the present force of the Pay Department it is now difficult to make the payments to troops provided for by law. Long delays in payments are productive of desertions and other demoralization, and the law prohibits the payment of troops by other than regular Army pay masters.

There are now sixteen vacancies in the Ordnance Department, thus leaving that branch of the service without sufficient officers to conduct the business of the different arsenals on a large scale if ever required.

NAVY DEPARTMENT.

During the past year our Navy has been depleted by the sale of some vessels no longer fit for naval service, and by the condemnation of others not yet disposed of. This, however, has been more than compensated for by the repair of six of the old wooden ships, and by the building of eight new sloops of war, authorized by the last Congress. The building of these latter has occurred at a doubly fortunate time. They are about being completed at a time when they may possibly be much needed, and the work upon them has not only given direct employment to thousands of men, but has no doubt been the means of keeping open establishments for other work at a time of great financial distress. Since the commencement of the last month, however, the distressing occurrences which have taken place in the waters of the Caribbean Sea, almost on our very sea-board, while they illustrate most forcibly the necessity always existing that a nation situated like ours should maintain in a state of possible efficiency a navy adequate to its responsibilities, has at the same time demanded that all the effective force we really have shall be put in immediate readiness for warlike service. This has been and is being done promptly and effectively, and I am assured that all the available ships and every authorized man of the American Navy will be ready for whatever action is required for the safety of our citizens or the maintenance of our honor. This, of course, will require the expenditure in a short time of some of the appropriations which were calculated to extend through the fiscal year, but Congress will, I doubt not, understand and appreciate the emergency, and will provide adequately, not only for the present preparation, but for the future maintenance of our naval force. The Secretary of the Navy has, during the past year, been quietly putting some of our most effective monitors in condition for service, and thus the exigency finds us in a much better condition for work than we could possibly have been without his action.

POST-OFFICE DEPARTMENT.

A complete exhibit is presented, in the accompanying report of the Postmaster-General, of the operations of the Post-Office Department during the year. The ordinary postal revenues for the fiscal year ended June 30, 1873, amounted to $22,996,741.57, and the expenditures of all kinds to $29,084,945.67. The increase of revenues over 1872 was $1,081,315.20, and the increase of expenditures $2,426,753.36.

Independent of the payments made from special appropriations for mail-steamship lines, the amount drawn from the general Treasury to meet deficiencies was $5,265,475. The constant and rapid extension of our postal service, particularly upon railways, and the improved facilities for the collection, transmission, distribution, and delivery of the mails, which are constantly being provided, account for the increased expenditures of this popular branch of the public service.

The total number of post-offices in operation, on June 30, 1873, was 33,244, a net increase of 1,381 over the number reported the preceding year. The number of presidential offices was 1,363, an increase of 163 during the year. The total length of railroad mail-routes at the close of the year was 63,457 miles, an increase of 5,546 miles over the year 1872. Fifty-nine railway post-office lines were in operation June 30, 1873, extending over 14,866 miles of railroad-routes, and performing an aggregate service of 34,925 miles daily.

The number of letters exchanged with foreign countries was 27,459,185, an increase of 3,096,685 over the previous year, and the postage thereon amounted to $2,021,310.86. The total weight of correspondence exchanged in the mails with European countries exceeded 912 tons, an increase of 92 tons over the previous year. The total cost of the United States ocean-steamship service, including $725,000 paid from special appropriations to subsidized lines of mail-steamers, was $1,047,271.35.

New or additional postal conventions have been concluded with Sweden, Norway, Belgium, Germany, Canada, Newfoundland, and Japan, reducing postage rates on correspondence exchanged with those countries; and further efforts have been made to conclude a satisfactory postal convention with France, but without success.

I invite the favorable consideration of Congress to the suggestions and recommendations of the Postmaster-General for an extension of the free-delivery system in all cities having a population of not less than ten thousand; for the prepayment of postage on newspapers and other printed matter of the second class; for a uniform postage and limit of weight on miscellaneous matter; for adjusting the compensation of all postmasters not appointed by the President, by the old method of commissions on the actual receipts of the office, instead of the present mode of fixing the salary in advance upon special returns: and especially do I urge favorable action by Congress on the important recommendations of the Postmaster-General for the establishment of United States postal savings depositories.

Your attention is also again called to a consideration of the question of postal telegraphs, and the arguments adduced in support thereof, in the hope that you may take such action in connection therewith as in your judgment will most contribute to the best interests of the country.

DEPARTMENT OF JUSTICE.

Affairs in Utah require your early and special attention. The Supreme Court of the United States, in the case of Clinton vs. Englebrecht, decided that the United States marshal of that Territory could not lawfully summon jurors for the district courts; and those courts hold that the territorial marshal cannot lawfully perform that duty, because he is elected by the legislative assembly and not appointed as provided for in the act organizing the Territory. All proceedings at law are practically abolished by these decisions, and there have been but few or no

NAVY DEPARTMENT.

During the past year our Navy has been depleted by the sale of some vessels no longer fit for naval service, and by the condemnation of others not yet disposed of. This, however, has been more than compensated for by the repair of six of the old wooden ships, and by the building of eight new sloops of war, authorized by the last Congress. The building of these latter has occurred at a doubly fortunate time. They are about being completed at a time when they may possibly be much needed, and the work upon them has not only given direct employment to thousands of men, but has no doubt been the means of keeping open establishments for other work at a time of great financial distress.

Since the commencement of the last month, however, the distressing occurrences which have taken place in the waters of the Caribbean Sea, almost on our very sea-board, while they illustrate most forcibly the necessity always existing that a nation situated like ours should maintain in a state of possible efficiency a navy adequate to its responsibilities, has at the same time demanded that all the effective force we really have shall be put in immediate readiness for warlike service. This has been and is being done promptly and effectively, and I am assured that all the available ships and every authorized man of the American Navy will be ready for whatever action is required for the safety of our citizens or the maintenance of our honor. This, of course, will require the expenditure in a short time of some of the appropriations which were calculated to extend through the fiscal year, but Congress will, I doubt not, understand and appreciate the emergency, and will provide adequately, not only for the present preparation, but for the future maintenance of our naval force. The Secretary of the Navy has, during the past year, been quietly putting some of our most effective monitors in condition for service, and thus the exigency finds us in a much better condition for work than we could possibly have been without his action.

POST-OFFICE DEPARTMENT.

A complete exhibit is presented, in the accompanying report of the Postmaster-General, of the operations of the Post-Office Department during the year. The ordinary postal revenues for the fiscal year ended June 30, 1873, amounted to $22,996,741.57, and the expenditures of all kinds to $20,084,945.67. The increase of revenues over 1872 was $1,081,315.20, and the increase of expenditures $2,426,753.36.

Independent of the payments made from special appropriations for mail-steamship lines, the amount drawn from the general Treasury to meet deficiencies was $5,265,475. The constant and rapid extension of our postal service, particularly upon railways, and the improved facilities for the collection, transmission, distribution, and delivery of the mails, which are constantly being provided, account for the increased expenditures of this popular branch of the public service.

The total number of post-offices in operation, on June 30, 1873, was 33,244, a net increase of 1,381 over the number reported the preceding year. The number of presidential offices was 1,363, an increase of 163 during the year. The total length of railroad mail-routes at the close of the year was 63,457 miles, an increase of 5,546 miles over the year 1872. Fifty-nine railway post-office lines were in operation June 30, 1873, extending over 14,866 miles of railroad-routes, and performing an aggregate service of 34,925 miles daily.

The number of letters exchanged with foreign countries was 27,459,185, an increase of 3,096,685 over the previous year, and the postage thereon amounted to $2,021,310.86. The total weight of correspondence exchanged in the mails with European countries exceeded 912 tons, an increase of 92 tons over the previous year. The total cost of the United States ocean-steamship service, including $725,000 paid from special appropriations to subsidized lines of mail-steamers, was $1,047,271.35.

New or additional postal conventions have been concluded with Sweden, Norway, Belgium, Germany, Canada, Newfoundland, and Japan, reducing postage rates on correspondence exchanged with those countries; and further efforts have been made to conclude a satisfactory postal convention with France, but without success.

I invite the favorable consideration of Congress to the suggestions and recommendations of the Postmaster-General for an extension of the free-delivery system in all cities having a population of not less than ten thousand; for the prepayment of postage on newspapers and other printed matter of the second class; for a uniform postage and limit of weight on miscellaneous matter; for adjusting the compensation of all postmasters not appointed by the President, by the old method of commissions on the actual receipts of the office, instead of the present mode of fixing the salary in advance upon special returns; and especially do I urge favorable action by Congress on the important recommendations of the Postmaster-General for the establishment of United States postal savings depositories.

Your attention is also again called to a consideration of the question of postal telegraphs, and the arguments adduced in support thereof, in the hope that you may take such action in connection therewith as in your judgment will most contribute to the best interests of the country.

DEPARTMENT OF JUSTICE.

Affairs in Utah require your early and special attention. The Supreme Court of the United States, in the case of Clinton vs. Englebrecht, decided that the United States marshal of that Territory could not lawfully summon jurors for the district courts; and those courts hold that the territorial marshal cannot lawfully perform that duty, because he is elected by the legislative assembly and not appointed as provided for in the act organizing the Territory. All proceedings at law are practically abolished by these decisions, and there have been but few or no fully invite your attention to the reports of the Secretary of the Interior and Commissioner of Patents on this subject.

The business of the General Land-Office exhibits a material increase in all its branches during the last fiscal year. During that time there were disposed of, out of the public lands, 13,030,606 acres, being an amount greater by 1,165,631 acres than was disposed of during the preceding year. Of the amount disposed of 1,626,266 acres were sold for cash; 214,940 acres were located with military land-warrants; 3,793,612 acres were taken for homesteads; 653,446 acres were located with agricultural-college scrip; 6,083,536 acres were certified by railroads; 76,576 acres were granted to wagon-roads; 238,548 acres were approved to States as swamp-lands; 138,681 acres were certified for agricultural colleges, common schools, universities, and seminaries; 190,775 acres were approved to States for internal improvements; and 14,222 acres were located with Indian scrip. The cash receipts during the same time were $3,408,515.50, being $190,415.50 in excess of the receipts of the previous year. During the year 30,488,132 acres of public land were surveyed, an increase over the amount surveyed the previous year of 1,037,193 acres, and, added to the area previously surveyed, aggregates 616,554,895 acres which have been surveyed, leaving 1,218,443,505 acres of the public land still unsurveyed.

The increased and steadily increasing facilities for reaching our unoccupied public domain, and for the transportation of surplus products, enlarges the available field for desirable homestead locations, thus stimulating settlement and extending year by year in a gradually increasing ratio the area of occupation and cultivation.

The expressed desire of the representatives of a large colony of citizens of Russia to emigrate to this country, as is understood, with the consent of their government, if certain concessions can be made to enable them to settle in a compact colony, is of great interest, as going to show the light in which our institutions are regarded by an industrious, intelligent, and wealthy people, desirous of enjoying civil and religious liberty; and the acquisition of so large an immigration of citizens of a superior class would, without doubt, be of substantial benefit to the country. I invite attention to the suggestion of the Secretary of the Interior in this behalf.

There was paid during the last fiscal year for pensions, including the expense of disbursement, $29,185,289.62, being an amount less by $984,050.98 than was expended for the same purpose the preceding year. Although this statement of expenditures would indicate a material reduction in amount compared with the preceding year, it is believed that the changes in the pension-laws at the last session of Congress will absorb that amount the current year. At the close of the last fiscal year there were on the pension-rolls 99,804 invalid military pensioners and 112,088 widows, orphans, and dependent relatives of deceased soldiers, making a total of that class of 211,892; 18,266 survivors of the war of 1812, and 5,053 widows of soldiers of that war pensioned under the act of Congress of February 14, 1871, making a total of that class of 23,319; 1,430 invalid Navy pensioners, and 1,770 widows, orphans, and dependent relatives of deceased officers, sailors, and marines of the Navy, making a total of Navy pensioners of 3,200, and a grand total of pensioners of all classes of 238,411, showing a net increase during the last fiscal year of 6,182. During the last year the names of 16,405 pensioners were added to the rolls, and 10,223 names were dropped therefrom for various causes.

The system adopted for the detection of frauds against the Government in the matter of pensions has been productive of satisfactory results, but legislation is needed to provide, if possible, against the perpetration of such frauds in future.

The evidently increasing interest in the cause of education is a most encouraging feature in the general progress and prosperity of the country, and the Bureau of Education is earnest in its efforts to give proper direction to the new appliances and increased facilities which are being offered to aid the educators of the country in their great work.

The ninth census has been completed, the report thereof published and distributed, and the working force of the bureau disbanded. The Secretary of the Interior renews his recommendation for a census to be taken in 1875, to which subject the attention of Congress is invited The original suggestion in that behalf has met with the general approval of the country, and even if it be not deemed advisable at present to provide for a regular quinquennial census, a census taken in 1875, the report of which could be completed and published before the one hundredth anniversary of our national independence, would be especially interesting and valuable, as showing the progress of the country during the first century of our national existence. It is believed, however, that a regular census every five years would be of substantial benefit to the country, inasmuch as our growth hitherto has been so rapid that the results of the decennial census are necessarily unreliable as a basis of estimates for the latter years of a decennial period.

DISTRICT OF COLUMBIA.

Under the very efficient management of the governor and the board of public works of this District, the city of Washington is rapidly assuming the appearance of a capital of which the nation may well be proud. From being a most unsightly place three years ago, disagreeable to pass through in summer in consequence of the dust arising from unpaved streets, and almost impassable in the winter from the mud, it is now one of the most sightly cities in the country, and can boast of being the best paved.

The work has been done systematically, the plans, grades, location of sewers, water and gas mains being determined upon before the work was commenced, thus securing permanency when completed. I question whether so much has ever been accomplished before in any American city for the same expenditures. The Government having large reservations in the city, and the nation at large having an interest in their capital, I recommend a liberal policy toward the District of Columbia, and that the Government should bear its just share of the expense of these improvements. Every citizen visiting the capital feels a pride in its growing beauty, and that he too is part owner of the investments made here.

I would suggest to Congress the propfiety of promoting the establishment in this District of an institution of learning, or university of the highest class, by the donation of lands. There is no place better suited for such an institution than the national capital. There is no other place in which every citizen is so directly interested.

CIVIL-SERVICE REFORM.

In three successive messages to Congress I have called attention to the subject of "civil-service reform."

Action has been taken so far as to authorize the appointment of a board to devise rules governing methods of making appointments and promotions, but there never has been any action making these rules, or any rules, binding, or even entitled to observance where persons desire the appointment of a friend, or the removal of an official who may be disagreeable to them.

To have any rules effective they must have the acquiescence of Congress as well as of the Executive. I commend, therefore, the subject to your attention, and suggest that a special committee of Congress might confer with the civil-service board during the present session for the purpose of devising such rules as can be maintained, and which will secure the services of honest and capable officials, and which will also protect them in a degree of independence while in office.

Proper rules will protect Congress, as well as the Executive, from much needless persecution, and will prove of great value to the public at large.

I would recommend for your favorable consideration the passage of an enabling act for the admittance of Colorado as a State in the Union. It possesses all the elements of a prosperous State, agricultural and mineral, and, I believe, has a population now to justify such admission. In connection with this I would also recommend the encouragement of a canal for purposes of irrigation from the eastern slope of the Rocky Mountains to the Missouri River. As a rule, I am opposed to further donations of public lands for internal improvements, owned and controlled by private corporations, but in this instance I would make an exception. Between the Missouri River and the Rocky Mountains there is an arid belt of public land from three hundred to five hundred miles in width, perfectly valueless for the occupation of man, for the want of sufficient rain to secure the growth of any product. An irrigating-canal would make productive a belt, as wide as the supply of water could be made to spread over, across this entire country, and would secure a cordon of settlements, connecting the present population of the mountain and mining regions with that of the older States. All the land reclaimed would be clear gain. If alternate sections are retained by the Government, I would suggest that the retained sections be thrown open to entry under the homestead laws, or sold to actual settlers for a very low price.

I renew my previous recommendation to Congress for general amnesty. The number engaged in the late rebellion yet laboring under disabilities is very small, but enough to keep up a constant irritation. No possible danger can accrue to the Government by restoring them to eligibility to hold office.

I suggest for your consideration the enactment of a law to better secure the civil rights which freedom should secure, but has not effectually secured, to the enfranchised slave.

U. S. GRANT.

EXECUTIVE MANSION, *December* 1, 1873.

Protocol of the conference held at the Department of State, at Washington, on the 29th of November, 1873, between Hamilton Fish, Secretary of State, and Rear-Admiral Don José Polo de Bernabé, envoy extraordinary and minister plenipotentiary of Spain.

The undersigned having met for the purpose of entering into a definitive agreement respecting the case of the steamer Virginius, which, while under the flag of the United States, was, on the 31st day of October last, captured on the high seas by the Spanish man-of-war Tornado, have reached the following conclusions:

Spain, on her part, stipulates to restore forthwith the vessel referred to, and the survivors of her passengers and crew, and on the 25th day of December next to salute the flag of the United States. If, however, before that date Spain should prove to the satisfaction of the Government of the United States that the Virginius was not entitled to carry the flag of the United States, and was carrying it, at the time of her capture, without right and improperly, the salute will be spontaneously dispensed with, as in such case not being necessarily requirable; but the United States will expect, in such case, a disclaimer of the intent of indignity to its flag in the act which was committed.

Furthermore, if on or before the 25th of December, 1873, it shall be made to appear to the satisfaction of the United States that the Virginius did not rightfully carry the American flag and was not entitled to American papers, the United States will institute inquiry, and adopt legal proceedings against the vessel, if it be found that she has violated any law of the United States, and against any of the persons who may appear to have been guilty of illegal acts in connection therewith: it being understood that Spain will proceed, according to the second proposition made to General Sickles, and communicated in his telegram read to Admiral Polo on the 27th instant, to investigate the conduct of those of her authorities who have infringed Spanish laws or treaty obligations, and will arraign them before competent courts and inflict punishment on those who may have offended.

Other reciprocal reclamations to be the subject of consideration and arrangement between the two governments; and in case of no agreement, to be the subject of arbitration if the constitutional assent of the Senate of the United States be given thereto.

It is further stipulated that the time, manner, and place for the surrender of the Virginius, and the survivors of those who were on board of her at the time of her capture, and also the time, manner, and place for the salute to the flag of the United States, if there should be occasion for such salute, shall be subject to arrangement between the undersigned, within the next two days.

HAMILTON FISH.
JOSÉ POLO DE BERNABÉ.

REPORT

OF

THE SECRETARY OF THE TREASURY.

TREASURY DEPARTMENT,
Washington, D. C., December 1, 1873.

SIR: In compliance with the provisions of law, I have the honor to submit to Congress the following report:

RECEIPTS, &C., FOR FISCAL YEAR ENDING JUNE 30, 1873.

The moneys received and covered into the Treasury during the fiscal year ended June 30, 1873, were—

From customs	$188, 089, 522 70
From internal revenue	113, 729, 314 14
From sales of public lands	2, 882, 312 38
From tax on circulation and deposits of national banks	6, 830, 037 67
From repayment of interest by Pacific Railway Companies	514, 206 04
From customs' fines, penalties, &c.; labor, drayage, storage, &c	1, 966, 469 36
From sales of Indian trust lands	818, 246 58
From fees, (consular,) letters patent, homestead, &c.	1, 877, 221 67
From proceeds of sales of Government property	1, 637, 283 15
From marine-hospital tax	333, 003 03
From steamboat fees	259, 092 56
From direct tax	315, 254 51
From profits on coinage	489, 134 62
From tax on seal-skins	252, 181 12
From miscellaneous sources	2, 184, 394 25
Total ordinary receipts	322, 177, 673 78
Premium on sales of coin	11, 560, 530 89
Total net receipts	333, 738, 204 67
Balance in Treasury June 30, 1872, including $3,047 80 received from "unavailable"	106, 567, 404 74
Total available cash	440, 305, 609 41

The net expenditures by warrants during the same period were—

For civil expenses..............................	$19,348,521 01
For foreign intercourse..........................	1,571,362 85
For Indians....................................	7,951,704 88
For pensions......,............................	29,359,426 86
For military establishment, including fortifications, river and harbor improvements, and arsenals.....	46,323,138 31
For naval establishment, including vessels and machinery, and improvements at navy yards........	23,526,256 79
For miscellaneous, civil, including public buildings, light-houses, and collecting the revenue..........	52,408,226 20
For interest on the public debt...................	104,750,688 44
For premium on bonds purchased.................	5,105,919 99
Total, exclusive of the public debt...........	290,345,245 33

Redemption of the principal of the debt, exclusive of the certificates of deposit issued under act of June 8, 1872, for the redemption of which a like amount of United States notes was set apart and held as a special deposit..................$50,498,335 58

Outstanding certificates of deposit mentioned above, added to the principal of the debt and to the cash balance in the Treasury........... 31,730,000 00

Leaving net disbursements on account of loans.....	18,768,335 58
	309,113,580 91

Balance in the Treasury June 30, 1873.$99,462,028 50
To which add special deposit of legal-tender notes for redemption of certificates of deposit, added above... 31,730,000 00

Total cash balance July 1, 1873..............	131,192,028 50
Total.......................................	440,305,609 41

By the foregoing statement it will be seen that the

net revenues for the fiscal year were.............	$333,738,204 67
And the ordinary expenses.......................	290,345,245 33
Leaving a surplus revenue of.................	43,392,959 34

Which has been applied to the reduction of the debt, as follows:

Reduction of principal account, exclusive of certificates of deposit	$50, 498, 335 58
Decrease of cash in the Treasury, exclusive of special deposit of United States notes for redemption of certificates of deposit, as compared with June 30, 1872	7, 105, 376 24
Reduction in debt	43, 392, 959 34

This statement treats solely of the principal of the debt. By the monthly debt statement of the public debt, into which enter the accrued interest, interest due and unpaid, and the cash in the Treasury, as ascertained on the day of publication, as well as the principal of the debt, the reduction of the debt during the past year amounted to $43,667,630 05; and the total reduction from March 1, 1869, to November 1, 1873, has been $383,629,783 39, the annual saving of interest resulting therefrom being $27,432,932 04.

RECEIPTS, &c., FOR FIRST QUARTER OF FISCAL YEAR ENDING JUNE 30, 1874.

The receipts during the first quarter of the current fiscal year were—

From customs	$49, 195, 403 68
From sales of public lands	573, 768 07
From internal revenue	25, 640, 454 41
From tax on circulation, &c., of national banks	3, 490, 743 66
From repayment of interest by Pacific Railways	198, 970 56
From customs' fines, &c	438, 514 21
From consular, patent, and other fees	503, 941 12
From proceeds of Government property	303, 765 32
From miscellaneous sources	1, 507, 931 21
Net ordinary receipts	81, 853, 492 24
From premium on sales of coin	2, 350, 818 34
From Government of Great Britain—payment of the award of the tribunal of arbitration at Geneva	15, 500, 000 00
Total receipts	99, 704, 310 58
Balance in Treasury June 30, 1873	131, 192, 028 50
Total available	230, 896, 339 08

The expenditures during the same period were as follows:

For civil and miscellaneous expenses, including public buildings, light-houses, and collecting the revenues	$17,372,293 60
For Indians	2,008,715 19
For pensions	8,698,156 58
For military establishment, including fortifications, river and harbor improvements, and arsenals	13,795,053 48
For naval establishment, including vessels and machinery and improvements at navy yards	9,792,451 57
For interest on the public debt, including Pacific Railway bonds	37,051,907 79
Total, exclusive of the principal and premium on public debt	88,718,578 21

Premium on purchased bonds	$1,301,946 78	
Award by Geneva tribunal, investment account	15,500,000 00	
Net redemption of the public debt	32,986,828 91	
		49,788,775 69

Total net expenditures	138,507,353 90
Balance in Treasury September 30, 1873	92,388,985 18
Total	230,896,339 08

Owing to the large proportion of the interest on the public debt maturing July 1, the amount paid out on that account during the first quarter of the year is more than half as much as will be required for the next nine months, and although it enters into the expenses of this quarter, it is properly chargeable to a longer period of time. Many other expenditures are greater also during the first than any subsequent quarter, by reason of the necessity of supplying disbursing officers with money under new appropriations which became available on the first of July.

For the remaining three-quarters of the current fiscal year it is estimated that the receipts will be—

From customs	$111,000,000 00
From sales of public lands	1,500,000 00
From internal revenue	60,000,000 00
From tax on national banks	3,200,000 00
From Pacific railways	300,000 00
From customs' fines, &c.	800,000 00

From consular, patent, and other fees..............	$1,300,000 00
From sales of public property......................	1,000,000 00
From miscellaneous sources......................	2,000,000 00
Total..................................	187 100,000 00

For the same period it is estimated that the expenditures will be—

For civil expenses..............................	$15,250,000 00
For foreign intercourse..........................	1,100,000 00
For Indians.....................................	6,500,000 00
For pensions...................................	21,780,000 00
For military establishment	34,000,000 00
For naval establishment	18,000,000 00
For miscellaneous, civil, including public buildings..	34,000,000 00
For interest on the public debt...................	70,000,000 00
Total..................................	200,630,000 00

This will leave a deficiency in the revenues of $13,530,000.

ESTIMATES FOR FISCAL YEAR ENDING JUNE 30, 1875.

It is estimated that the receipts for the fiscal year ending June 30, 1875, will be—

From customs..................................	$180,000,000 00
From sales of public lands.......................	2,500,000 00
From internal revenue...........................	108,000,000 00
From tax on national banks......................	6,200,000 00
From Pacific railways	500,000 00
From customs' fines, &c..........................	1,500,000 00
From consular, patent, and other fees..............	1,500,000 00
From sales of public property.....................	1,500,000 00
From miscellaneous sources......................	4,000,000 00
Total..................................	305,700,000 00

It is estimated that the expenditures for the same period will be—

For civil expenses..............................	$19,500,000 00
For foreign intercourse..........................	3,350,000 00
For Indians.....................................	7,000,000 00
For pensions...................................	30,480,000 00
For military establishment, including fortifications, river and harbor improvements, and arsenals	50,000,000 00

For naval establishment, including vessels and machinery and improvements at navy yards $23,000,000 00

For miscellaneous, civil, including public buildings, light-houses, and collecting the revenues 54,067,144 00

For interest on the public debt 98,000,000 00

For interest on Pacific Railway bonds 3,875,000 00

For sinking fund 29,918,856 00

Total 319,191,000 00

The estimates received from the several Executive Departments are as follows:

Legislative $3,961,405 62
Executive 17,805,674 90
Judicial 3,409,750 00
Foreign intercourse 3,347,304 00
Military 34,881,618 10
Naval 19,251,935 86
Indians 6,765,779 61
Pensions 30,480,000 00
Public works 33,168,287 10
Postal service 6,811,363 00
Miscellaneous 10,704,381 12
Permanent 16,926,890 49
Interest on public debt 97,798,080 00
Interest on Pacific Railway bonds 3,877,110 72
Sinking fund 29,918,856 00

Total 319,198,736 82

The book of estimates, now ready to be laid before Congress, thoroughly prepared under the immediate supervision of Mr. C. F. Conant, chief of the warrant division of the Secretary's office, whose watchful care, industry, and judgment have made it a work of great accuracy, will prove to be of the utmost convenience to committees and members.

The several tables which form part of this report furnish details of the accounts of the Department.

THE REVENUES AND ESTIMATES.

On account of the alterations in the tariff laws, effected by the acts of May 1 and June 6, 1872, adding tea and coffee and other articles to the free list, and the reduction of duties on other merchandise, as well as by the removal of a considerable amount of internal revenue taxation, the receipts have fallen off for the year ending June 30, 1873, much below those of previous years, as was anticipated.

Since the close of that year the recent severe financial and commercial crisis has caused an additional and unexpected diminution in the revenues during part of September and the whole of October and November.

But it is gratifying to find that, in this period of the greatest commercial embarrassment, the receipts in coin from customs have been greater than the proportionate amount required for the same period to meet the interest on the public debt and all other expenditures which are payable in coin.

For the remainder of the year the currency payments will be much larger than the ordinary currency receipts without the sale of gold. The revenues have already fallen off sufficiently to make it important and necessary to exercise the greatest economy in appropriations and expenditures for the future. And should there not be a revival of business at an early day, and an increase in the receipts over those of the past two and a half months, additional means will be required to meet expenses. Should such be the case, I recommend additional taxation, judiciously laid, so as to be the least burdensome upon the people and the business of the country, rather than a resort to borrowing money and increasing the public debt.

In the estimates for the next nine months, as well as for the next fiscal year, the probable effect of the financial and business derangement has been somewhat taken into account; but, as it is yet too early to determine its full effect upon the future revenues, or to estimate when and to what extent they will be restored to their former amounts, these estimates are subject to future contingencies, which, during the next few months, Congress will be better able to take into account and to judge of than it is possible to do at this time.

In any event, I earnestly commend every reduction in the appropriations which may be found possible, to the end that the economy which the people, suffering under the present embarrassment in business, are everywhere disposed to make, may be shared and encouraged by the Government through their public servants.

REFUNDING THE PUBLIC DEBT.

Under arrangements made by my immediate predecessor in January last, the refunding of the public debt has been successfully continued, and is still progressing in precisely the same manner as previous negotiations were conducted. Subscriptions have been made to the new five per cent. funded loan to the extent of eighty-four and a half million dollars, and the proceeds are applied, as fast as subscriptions mature, to the redemption of an equal amount of five-twenty bonds bearing six per cent. interest.

In addition to that amount, the fifteen and a half million dollars received from Great Britain in payment of the Geneva award, under the first article of the Treaty of Washington, have been used to redeem so far the outstanding public debt bearing six per cent. interest, and an amount equal to the debt so redeemed has been invested in five per cent. bonds of the funded loan, and a registered bond therefor has been issued to the Secretary of State, in trust, to be held subject to the future disposition of Congress, according to the provisions of the act of March 3, 1873.

When the subscriptions above mentioned shall have matured there will have been thus effected since January last a conversion of the debt bearing six per cent. interest into the new five per cent. loan, one hundred million dollars, making an annual saving of interest to the amount of one million dollars. And the whole amount converted into this loan since the passage of the refunding act will be three hundred million dollars, reducing the annual interest charge three million dollars.

The credit of the United States has not stood higher since the close of the rebellion than it does at the present time, and it is believed that the refunding of the six per cent. debt at a lower rate of interest can be still further continued.

LOAN OF 1858.

Under the provisions of the act of June 14, 1858, as amended by the act of March 3, 1859, (chap. 82, sec. 6,) the then Secretary of the Treasury contracted a loan of twenty million dollars, for part of which registered bonds were issued " redeemable at the pleasure of the United States at any time after the expiration of fifteen years after the 1st of January, 1859;" and for the balance, and much larger part, coupon bonds were issued " payable at any time after the 1st day of January, 1874, on presentation and surrender of the certificate at the Treasury of the United States."

It will be perceived that the two classes of bonds differ materially in phraseology as to the option of payment after January 1, 1874, but I am unable to discover, either from the act itself or from the records of the Department, that any difference in the contracts was intended, and it is presumed that the variation in language of the two classes of bonds was wholly accidental. Since the passage of the act of June 30, 1864, authorizing the Secretary of the Treasury to issue registered bonds of any loan in exchange for coupon bonds of the same loan, the coupon bonds of this loan to the amount of about four million dollars have been exchanged into the registered bonds, and the amount of each class now outstanding is $6,255,000 registered, and $13,745,000 coupon.

It is understood that some holders of the coupon bonds have regarded them as payable on the first of January next or at any time after that date, at their option. Applications have been made to the Department for the privilege of exchanging coupon bonds for five per cent. bonds of the funded loan, which exchange the Secretary of the Treasury has now no authority to permit.

No appropriation has been made, either in the act authorizing the loan or in any subsequent act, for the payment of the principal, and no provision of law exists for determining the pleasure of the United States as to the time of payment of either class of bonds.

The attention of Congress is thus called to this loan with the recommendation that such action in relation thereto may be taken, before the 1st day of January next, as Congress may deem wise and just.

THE BANKS, THE FINANCIAL CRISIS, AND THE CURRENCY.

The prevailing practice, not only of national banks, but of State banks and private bankers, of paying interest on deposits attracts currency from all parts of the country to the large cities, and especially to New York, the great financial centre. At seasons of the year when there is comparatively little use for currency elsewhere, immense balances accumulate in New York, where, not being required by the demands of legitimate and ordinary business, they are loaned on call at a higher rate of interest than that paid to depositors and are used in speculation.

Every year, at the season when the demand sets in from the West and South for currency to be used in payment for and transportation of their agricultural products, there occurs a stringency in the money market arising from the calling in of such loans to meet this demand.

· Until this year, though annually creating some embarrassment, this demand has been met without serious difficulty.

During the past summer, anticipating the usual autumn stringency, the Treasury Department sold gold while the market price was high, currency abundant, and bonds for sale in the market were scarce,

and while there was a surplus of gold in the Treasury, and thereby
accumulated about fourteen million dollars of currency with the view
of using the same or such part thereof as might be necessary in the
purchase of bonds for the sinking fund at times during the autumn
and winter when they could be bought at a price not above par in
gold, or in meeting demands upon the Treasury, as circumstances
should require.

This year there was a great demand for currency to pay for the
heavy crops of a bountiful harvest, for which the European countries
offered a ready market. The suspension of certain large banking
houses, the first of which occurred on the 18th day of September,
alarmed the people as to the safety of banks and banking institutions
in general. Suddenly there began a rapid calling in of demand loans
and a very general run on the banks for the withdrawal of deposits.
Entire confidence was manifested in United States notes and even in
national-bank notes, and they were drawn wherever they could be
obtained and were largely hoarded with as much avidity as coin was
ever hoarded in times of financial distress when that was the circulating medium of the country. The banks found themselves unable to
meet the demands upon them, currency in circulation became exceedingly scarce, and the business of the country became greatly embarrassed.

In this condition of things, great pressure was brought to bear upon
the Treasury Department to afford relief by the issue of United States
notes. The first application came from a number of gentlemen in New
York, suggesting that no measure of relief would be adequate that did
not place at the service of the banks of that city twenty millions of
dollars in United States notes, and asking that the assistant treasurer
at New York should be authorized to issue to those banks that amount
of notes as a loan upon a pledge of clearing-house certificates secured
by ample collaterals, and for which certificates all the banks were to ·
be jointly and severally responsible. This proposition was declined,
it being clearly not within the duty or the authority of the Treasury
Department, under any provisions of law, thus to employ the public
money.

Exchange on Europe having fallen to unusually low rates, and indeed having become almost unsaleable in the market, to the embarrassment of our foreign and domestic trade, applications were made to the
Secretary of the Treasury to use the money in the Treasury in the purchase of exchange. The Treasury Department having no occasion to
do this for its own use, and no necessity for transferring funds to
Europe, was compelled to decline this proposition, which, if accepted,

would have put the Department in the position of becoming a dealer in exchange, a position clearly inconsistent with its duties.

Subsequently the New York Produce Exchange made a proposition to accomplish the same result in a different form, and also requested, as others had before, that the Secretary should pay at once the twenty-million loan of 1858, to which the following reply was made:

> TREASURY DEPARTMENT,
> *Washington, September 30, 1873.*

SIR: Your letter of the 29th inst., covering two resolutions of the New York Produce Exchange, has been received and the subject-matter fully considered.

The resolutions are as follows:

"WHEREAS the critical condition of the commercial interests of the country requires immediate relief by the removal of the block in negotiating foreign exchange; therefore be it

"*Resolved*, That we respectfully suggest to the Secretary of the Treasury the following plans for relief in this extraordinary emergency:

"*First.* That currency be immediately issued to banks or bankers, upon satisfactory evidence that gold has been placed upon special deposit in the Bank of England, by their correspondents in London, to the credit of the United States, to be used solely in purchasing commercial bills of exchange.

"*Second.* That the President of the United States and the Secretary of the Treasury are respectfully requested to order the immediate prepayment of the outstanding loan of the United States due January 1, 1874."

While the Government is desirous of doing all in its power to relieve the present unsettled condition of business affairs—as has already been announced by the President—it is constrained, in all its acts, to keep within the letter and spirit of the laws, which the officers of the Government are sworn to support, and they cannot go beyond the authority which Congress has conferred upon them. Your first resolution presents difficulties which cannot be overcome. It is not supposed that you desire to exchange coin in England for United States notes in New York at par. If your proposition is for the Government to purchase gold in England, to be paid for in United States notes at the current market rate in New York, it would involve the Government in the business of importing and speculating in gold, since the Treasury has no use for coin beyond its ordinary receipts, and would be obliged to sell the coin so purchased at a price greater or less than was paid for it. If your object is to induce the Treasury Department to loan United States notes to banks in New York upon the pledge and deposit in London of gold, it is asking the Secretary of the Treasury to loan the money of the United States upon collateral security for which there is no authority in law. If the Secretary of the Treasury can loan notes upon a pledge of coin he can loan them upon a pledge of other property in his discretion, as he has recently been requested to do, which would be an extraordinary power as well as a most dangerous business to engage in, and which my judgment would deter me from undertaking, as the Secretary of the Treasury, even if by any stretch of construction I might not find it absolutely prohibited by law. The objections already mentioned to your first resolution are so insuperable and conclusive that it is unnecessary for me to refer to the many practical difficulties which would arise if an attempt should be made to comply with your request. Your second resolution calls for the payment at once of the loan of 1858, or the bonds commonly called "Fives of 1874." Upon a thorough investigation I am of opinion that Congress has not conferred upon the Secretary of the Treasury power to comply with your request in that particular, and in this opinion the law officers of the Government concur. Under these circumstances you will perceive that, while I have great respect for the gentlemen comprising the New York Produce Exchange, I am compelled, by my views of the law and of my duty, to respectfully decline to adopt the measure which your resolutions propose.

I have the honor to be, very respectfully,

WM. A. RICHARDSON,
Secretary of the Treasury.

The Chamber of Commerce of Charleston, South Carolina, petitioned for the transfer of currency to that city, and the purchase with it, at that point, of exchange on New York, to aid those engaged in forwarding the cotton crop to the market. The following letter was sent in answer to this petition:

TREASURY DEPARTMENT,
October 3, 1873.

SAMUEL Y. TUPPER, Esq.,
President Chamber of Commerce, Charleston, S. C.:

I have the honor to acknowledge the receipt of the memorial of the Charleston, South Carolina, Chamber of Commerce, addressed to the President of the United States, and referred to this Department, which, after reciting the present stringency in the money market and the difficulty of obtaining currency, requests "that the sum of five hundred thousand dollars be placed and maintained on deposit with the assistant treasurer at Charleston, to be used by him in the purchase of New York exchange from the banks."

To comply with the request it would be necessary for the Treasury Department to send currency by express to Charleston from time to time, and to buy with it exchange on New York in competition with private bankers.

Should this request be granted a hundred other places in the country might, with equal propriety, ask for the same relief, and if all such requests were impartially granted, the Department would find itself engaged in an extensive exchange business, fixing and regulating the rate of exchange between different places in the country, and the public money, raised by taxation only for the purpose of carrying on the Government, would be employed to a very large amount in a business which Congress has not given the Secretary of the Treasury any authority to engage in.

With a due regard to the proper management of the Treasury Department, within the provisions of law, I have felt it to be my duty to decline all similar propositions from other places, and your request must, therefore, receive the same response.

I have the honor to be, very respectfully, yours,

WM. A. RICHARDSON,
Secretary of the Treasury.

The Executive Department of the Government was anxious to do everything in its power, under the law, and with due regard to the protection of the Treasury and the maintenance of public credit, to allay the panic and to prevent disaster to the legitimate commercial and industrial interests of the country; but it was found impossible to afford the relief in any of the many forms in which that relief was asked. It was decided, therefore, to adopt the only practicable course which seemed to be open to it, the purchase of bonds for the sinking fund to such an extent as the condition of the Treasury would allow, and thus release a considerable amount of currency from its vaults. Purchases of bonds were commenced on the morning of the 20th of September, and were continued until the 24th, when it became evident that the amount offering for purchase was increasing to an extent beyond the power of the Treasury to accept, and the purchasing was closed after bonds to the amount of about thirteen million dollars had been bought, and without the use of any part of the forty-four millions of United States notes, generally known as the reserve.

It should be stated that in the excitement there were many persons in the city of New York who insisted with great earnestness that it was the duty of the Executive to disregard any and all laws which stood in the way of affording the relief suggested by them—a proposition which indicates the state of feeling and the excitement under which applications were made to the Secretary of the Treasury to use the public money, and which, it is scarcely necessary to add, could not be entertained by the officers of the Government to whom it was addressed.

These facts are recited in order to lay before Congress, and place on record in a concise form, exactly what the Treasury Department was asked to do, and what it did, in the late financial crisis.

The currency paid out of the Treasury for bonds did much to strengthen many savings banks, and to prevent a panic among their numerous depositors, who began to be alarmed, and had there developed an extended run upon those useful institutions, it would inevitably have caused widespread disaster and distress. It also fortified other banks, and checked the general alarm to some extent. But the loss of confidence in the value of a great amount of corporate property which immediately followed the failure of banking houses connected with largely-indebted corporations, the distrust of the solvency of many other institutions, the doubt as to the credit of firms and individuals whose business was supposed to be greatly extended, and the legitimate effect thereof in disturbing the business of the country, could not be avoided by any amount of currency which might be added to the circulation already existing.

Confidence was to be entirely restored only by the slow and cautious process of gaining a better knowledge of true values and making investments accordingly, and by conducting business on a firmer basis, with less inflation and more regard to real soundness and intrinsic values.

There can be no doubt that the practice by banks of allowing interest on deposits payable on demand is pernicious, and fraught with danger and embarrassment to borrower and lender, as well as to the general business interests.

Deposits payable on demand should be limited to that surplus which individuals require over and above their investments, and no part of that from which they expect an income. Such deposits are comparatively stable in average amount, and constitute a healthy basis for banking purposes within proper limits, which prudent bankers know how to determine.

But if deposit accounts are employed as temporary investments, the interest attracts a large amount of money to those cities where such interest is paid, and where speculation is most active, at seasons when as much profit thereon cannot be secured elsewhere. With the first return of activity in legitimate business these temporary investments are called in, and jeopardize in their sudden withdrawal the whole business of the banks, both affecting the legitimate depositors on the one hand by excitement and distrust, and on the other creating a condition of things in which the borrowers on call are also unable to respond. The banks have borrowed their money of depositors on call. They have loaned it on call to speculators, who by its use have contributed to inflate the prices of the stocks or merchandise which have been the subject of their speculations. The speculator wants it to carry the stocks till he can dispose of them without a loss. This he is unable to do in a stringent money market. The banks, their depositors, and the borrowers, all want it at the same time, and of course a stringency is developed which spreads distress throughout the country.

The system creates immense amount of debts payable on demand, all of which thus suddenly and unexpectedly mature at the first shock of financial or commercial embarrassment in the country, and at the very time when most needed by debtors and when they are least able to respond.

There is no safety for corporations or individuals whose capital employed is wholly or mostly borrowed on call. Many savings banks were protected from ruin in the recent financial excitement by availing themselves of provisions in their rules requiring sixty days or other periods of notice before paying depositors, thus making all their deposits payable on time. Every cautious and well-managed savings in stitution has such a rule among its by-laws.

Without attributing the stringency in the money market, which is experienced every autumn and occasionally at other seasons of the year, solely to this practice of paying interest upon deposits in the large cities, it is evident that, when money is less needed in legitimate business, the practice encourages overtrading and speculation, always detrimental to the best interests of the country, and the bad effects of which upon those interests become more apparent, and the disaster more widespread, when the necessary contraction begins to be felt.

I recommend that national banks be prevented from paying interest on deposits, or that they be restricted and limited therein, either by direct prohibition, by discriminating taxation, or otherwise.

While legislation by Congress cannot prevent State banks and private bankers from continuing the practice, it can prevent national banks from becoming involved in, and instrumental in producing, the embarrassments and difficulties to which it necessarily leads.

The national banks, organized by law of Congress and having relations with the Government in the issue of circulating notes, ought to be the most cautious and safe banking institutions of the country, and should be kept aloof from all hazardous business which it is not possible to prevent sanguine, venturesome, and speculative individuals from engaging in, at the risk of their capital and their credit.

With a fixed amount of circulation of bank notes and of United States legal-tender notes not redeemable in coin, and with gold above par in currency, there must be each year times of redundancy and times of scarcity of currency, depending wholly on the demand, no method existing for increasing the supply.

With a circulating medium redeemable in coin, a redundancy is corrected by the export, and a scarcity by the import of specie from other countries.

There is a prevailing sentiment that more elasticity should be given to the volume of the currency, so that the amount in circulation might increase and diminish according to the necessities of the business of the country. But the difference of opinion on this subject is so great, and the real difficulties attending its solution are so numerous, that, without discussing any of the multitude of plans which have been presented to the public through the press and otherwise, I earnestly commend to the wisdom of Congress a careful and thorough consideration of this important subject, rendered more obviously important by the present embarrassed condition of large business interests which have suffered by the recent financial crisis; and that, in such inquiry, avoiding further inflation of the issue of irredeemable legal-tender notes, the most desirable of all financial results to be attained, namely, a permanent return to the sound basis of specie payments, and a gold standard to which all our paper issues shall be made of equal value, shall be the aim.

To allow national banks to use part of their reserves at seasons of the greatest pressure, under proper restrictions and regulations, would afford some flexibility.

Rigid statute laws applied to all banks, at all seasons, and in all places alike, often prove an embarrassment and injury when they conflict with economic principles and the laws of trade and business, which are stronger than legislative enactments, and cannot be overthrown thereby. Associated banks at the several redemption cities named in the banking law, which are the great controlling centres of business, might do much to give steadiness and safety, if they were authorized, through properly constituted boards or committees of their own officers, to exercise a large discretion in the use of their reserves, in the rate of interest to be charged at different seasons and under different circumstances, and in other matters, within limits prescribed by law.

Should it be deemed necessary or expedient to temporarily enlarge the paper-money circulation in cases of great emergency, provision may be made to permit the national banks, under certain circumstances and to a limited extent, to increase their note circulation by a pledge of United States bonds, bearing no interest while so pledged, or subjecting the banks to special taxation upon the circulating notes obtained thereon, or upon such other terms that it would be for their interest to recall the notes and redeem the bonds at the earliest possible day after the pressure and their necessities should have ceased.

But any large augmentation of the issue of United States legal-tender notes in time of peace would not only be a departure from that "declaration of public policy and pledge of the public faith to the national creditors," made in the act of June 30, 1864, that the total amount of such notes shall never exceed four hundred million dollars, as well as from that more solemn pledge contained in the first act of the Forty-first Congress, "to make provision at the earliest practicable period for the redemption of United States notes in coin," but would postpone the day of specie payments and render it more difficult to attain in the distant future, unsettle confidence in our national finances, and be a serious detriment to public credit at home and abroad.

There can be no doubt that during the eight years since the rebellion there has been a growing desire among the people to restore the paper circulation to a specie standard, and that any steps taken to accomplish that object will be received with general favor.

It is not possible to resume and maintain specie payments with so large an amount of notes in circulation, and so small an amount of gold in the country. The volume of currency must be reduced or that of coin greatly increased. Should the national banks be prohibited from selling the coin received by them as interest upon bonds pledged to secure circulation, retaining the same in whole or in part in reserve, or loaning it in the discount of bills and notes payable in coin, as Congress might prescribe, there would be a gradual accumulation of gold in the banks, which would do something towards preparing for resumption. This, with a constant increase of coin in the Treasury, undertaken with the approval of Congress, would ere long lead to the desired result, when other conditions required for the maintenance of specie payments should become favorable.

The acts of Congress of February 25, 1862, July 11, 1862, and March 3, 1863, together authorize the issue of four hundred million dollars of United States notes, in addition to fifty million dollars of such notes reserved for the purpose of securing prompt payment of temporary-loan deposits, and the act of June 30, 1864, contains these words: "nor shall the total amount of United States notes issued, or to be issued, ever exceed four hundred millions of dollars, and such additional sum not exceeding fifty millions of dollars, as may be temporarily required for the redemption of temporary loan."

The temporary loans referred to in the foregoing acts having been redeemed, the maximum amount of United States notes which, under existing laws, can now or hereafter be issued, is four hundred million dollars.

Between the 31st of August, 1865, when the amount of United States notes outstanding was at its highest point, and the 4th of February, 1868, there was a gradual contraction of the amount in actual circulation, limited by the act of February 12, 1866, to not more than ten million dollars within the then next six months, and thereafter not more than four million dollars in any one month. On the 4th of February, 1868, Congress passed an act suspending further reduction of the currency, when the amount outstanding was three hundred and fifty-six million dollars, and that sum is now the minimum limit of issue. But the law authorizing the issue of the maximum of four hundred million dollars has never been repealed, and has uniformly been held by the Treasury Department and the law officers thereof to be in full force. In view of the uncertainty which exists in public sentiment as to the right of the Secretary of the Treasury to issue United States notes in excess of the minimum, and the conflict of opinion as to the policy of doing so, conceding that he has that right under the law, I respectfully recommend that Congress shall set these questions at rest by a distinct enactment.

Until that is done, whenever there is a stringency in the money market there will continue to be a pressure upon the Treasury Department, by those who favor a policy of expansion, to increase the issue of notes to the maximum, by the purchase of bonds or otherwise; while, on the other hand, those who conceive that the public interests will be better served thereby will bring equal pressure to keep the issue down to the minimum.

Assuming that it is the settled policy of Congress, as declared in the act of June 30, 1864, above cited, that the total amount of United States notes, *issued and to be issued,* shall never exceed four hundred million dollars, I am of opinion that it would be unwise to *require* the amount in actual circulation to be kept up to the maximum or to any amount above the present minimum. The Treasury, depending principally upon the receipts from customs and internal taxation, without the power of borrowing or otherwise increasing its resources, with liabilities created by congressional appropriations which must be met in currency to the extent of nearly two hundred million dollars a year, ought always to have a large reserve upon which it can draw to meet the ordinary demands upon it in case of emergencies, when the revenues suddenly and unexpectedly diminish by reason of a national calamity or financial derangement, which from time to time are liable to occur in all nations.

Such a reserve is also rendered necessary by the fact that the fractional currency authorized to be issued to the amount of fifty million dollars, now in actual circulation to the extent of more than forty million dollars, is redeemable in United States notes at the option of the holders.

In order that there may be no misunderstanding as to the circumstances under which the amount between the minimum and the maximum may be issued, and, that it may not be issued for the purpose of inflating the paper currency of the country, I recommend that it be declared a reserve to be issued temporarily when the ordinary demands upon the Treasury shall require it, and in payment of such demands and for the redemption of fractional currency; the amount so issued to be returned to the reserve as soon as the condition of the Treasury shall warrant it, and that the purchase of bonds shall be forbidden so long as the outstanding United States notes shall exceed the minimum fixed by the act of February 4, 1868.

I believe that such a reserve, so restricted, would be a proper and reasonable protection against any contingencies whereby the revenues of the country might temporarily be diminished, and would give no reasonable cause to fear permanent inflation. As it ought not to be the business of the Treasury Department to increase and diminish the amount of legal-tender notes from time to time, according to the condition of the money market, and for the sole purpose of affecting that market, I think it would be unwise to authorize the reserve to be issued except for the purposes and in the manner which I have suggested.

NATIONAL BANK NOTES.

In the general appropriation act for the fiscal year ending June 30, 1874, the following special appropriation is made, in addition to the usual annual appropriation for making and issuing the national currency:

"For replacing the worn and mutilated circulating notes of national banking associations, and for engraving and preparing, in such manner and on such paper and of such form and design as the Secretary of the Treasury may prescribe, new circulating notes for such associations to replace notes of a design and denomination now successfully counterfeited, six hundred thousand dollars: *Provided*, That each of said national banking associations shall reimburse the Treasury the costs of the circulating notes furnished under this provision."

The operation of this clause must be very limited without further legislation. The making of new plates and replacing notes seem to be restricted to those of denominations which have been successfully counterfeited, and it is found that the only one that can be thus considered is the ten-dollar note, although the two and the twenty-dollar notes have been counterfeited to some extent. A plate has been made for the ten-dollar note, but as the proviso in this clause requires banking associations to reimburse the Treasury for the cost thereof, few banks are inclined to order them while they can continue to have notes of other denominations printed from the old plates without cost to themselves, under the provisions of the general banking law.

I recommend that the proviso in the clause above cited be repealed, or that banks be required to pay for all new notes furnished them, whether printed from new or old plates.

The soiled and mutilated condition of the circulating notes of national banks now in use makes it a matter of necessity that something should be done to redeem the same and to supply their places with new currency, to the end that all the notes which the people are obliged to take and use as money may be clean and whole. Several methods to accomplish this result have been carefully considered, but no plan seems to be feasible without the active co-operation of the banks themselves, assisted by such congressional enactments, as may be required for that purpose, which are earnestly recommended.

EXPORTS AND IMPORTS.

During the fiscal year ending June 30, 1873, the value of merchandise imported into the United States was $642,029,539, as against $626,595,077 for the previous year.

An analysis shows an increase in the imports of merchandise admitted duty free, in raw materials and in some articles of necessity, while in some articles of luxury there was a reduction.

The increase in the importation of coffee was $6,164,339, and in tea, $1,522,519, in addition to the amounts in bond July 1, 1872, and which were withdrawn therefrom during the year. Coffee was so withdrawn for consumption to the value of $16,901,126, and tea to the value of $18,024,217. There was an increase, also, in the importation of copper and copper manufactures of $1,818,488; soda and salts, $1,719,408; tin in plates, $2,681,222; hides and skins, $1,427,784; furskins, $188,170; melado, $2,656,138; wood and manufactures thereof, $2,141,766; earthenware, $745,140; manufactures of cotton, $9,893,870.

There was a decrease in silk goods, $5,723,582; precious stones, $182,905; fruits, $713,203; fancy goods, $278,577; fine linen, laces, and other manufactures of flax, $1,054,115; as well as in some articles of a different class, such as barley, $440,626; opium and extracts thereof, $128,839; leather and leather goods, $1,829,917; wool, $8,105,114.

The gold value of the exports of merchandise from the United States was $522,478,802, as against $444,177,586 for the previous year.

There was an increase in certain articles exported as follows, the value being stated in currency:

Cotton, $47,201,672; wheat, $12,537,194; wheat flour, $1,425,980; bacon and hams, $13,895,545; pork, $884,727; lard, $1,068,196; cheese,

$2,745,092; oils, $7,256,514; wood and manufactures thereot, $3,878,930; manufactures of iron, $2,372,725; coal, $952,449; drugs and chemicals, $575,050; hides and skins, $2,159,845; furs and fur-skins, $382,545; leather and leather goods, $1,621,465; in live animals, $259,731.

The export of gold and silver in excess of the imports was $63,127,637, as against $66,133,845 for the previous year.

The balance of trade in merchandise has been largely against the United States for many years, and the country has exported during the twenty years ending with the last fiscal year gold and silver to the extent of more than a thousand million dollars over and above the amount imported.

For some months past, and especially in the months of October and November, the export trade in merchandise has greatly increased, and, owing to the disturbance of financial affairs and other causes, the importation of goods has largely diminished, so that the balance of trade at present is in favor of the United States; and gold and silver have flowed into the country during the past two months at a rate more rapid than ever before, except in the year 1861, when, for the whole year, the excess of imports over exports was $16,548,531; and for the past twenty years there has been no other single year in which there has been an excess of imports of gold and silver over the exports.

The condition of the carrying trade with foreign countries, though exhibiting a large adverse balance, shows some slight gains, with prospects of still further improvement. Of the exports and imports during the past year, twenty-seven per cent. were carried in United States vessels—a gain of three per cent. over the previous year.

The increase in ship-building in the country is decided. Official numbers were awarded by the Bureau of Statistics to 1,699 vessels of the aggregate tonnage of 313,743 tons, while, during the year preceding, the addition to our mercantile marine was only 38,621 tons. Since the close of the fiscal year still greater activity has prevailed in the ship-yards on the Atlantic seaboard. From the 1st of July to the 1st of November documents have been issued to 1,288 completed vessels of 181,000 tons in all, while such returns as have been received, incomplete as they are, indicate that there were building in October last 386 vessels of the tonnage of 177,529 tons; including 69 steamers with a tonnage of 67,007 tons, of which 18 iron steamers with an aggregate of 38,492 tons are in course of construction on the Delaware.

In view of the high price of iron and coal and the recent advance in the cost of labor in Europe, together with the superior tensile strength of American ship-plates, as proved by actual experiments, there is reasonable encouragement to expect that this branch of industry will make rapid strides of progress, to the great advantage of the commerce, trade, and financial strength of the country.

The following table shows the amount of merchandise imported or taken out of bond at the places therein named since the passage of the act of June 6, 1872, authorizing the importation free of duty of certain articles actually used for ship-building:

Port.	Value.	Duties remitted.	Duties estimated.	Duties to be collected.	Vessels built.	Vessels repaired.
New York	$173,626 00	$36,992 00		$1,306 13	2	
Boston	139,246 00	37,646 86	$10,317 06	Duties remitted, but vessel engaged in coasting trade more than three months in one year, hence duties accrued.	4	47
Philadelphia	2,768 00	894 48				
Portland	15,403 00	4,687 67			5	1
Bath	56,666 00	4,743 92			17	2
Total	387,709 00	84,864 93	10,347 06	1,306 13	28	50
Duties estimated		10,347 06				
		95,211 99				

Nothing, except a sound financial system, is more important to the welfare of the country than that of turning and retaining the balance of trade in favor of the United States, by a healthy stimulation of the agricultural and manufacturing industry of the country, the reduction in the cost of production at home, and of the transportation of merchandise from the interior to the seaboard, and the building of ships and vessels to do the carrying trade, now mostly in the hands of the people of other countries; and no legislation should be neglected which may assist the industrious people of our country in attaining those most desirable results.

With the balance of trade in favor of the United States a return to specie payments may be easily reached, and, when reached, may be maintained if such wise financial measures are adopted as will prevent overtrading, extravagance, and speculation, and encourage economy, industry, thrift, and only well-directed and prudent enterprises—conditions as essential to the prosperity of nations as to individuals.

CUSTOMS, COMMERCE, AND NAVIGATION.

The attention of Congress is invited to the necessity of a revision and codification of existing tariff laws. Duties on imports are now imposed under fourteen principal statutes relating to classification and rates, besides twenty other acts or resolutions modifying or affecting tariff acts, all passed between March 1, 1801, and March 4, 1873, to which must be added the very numerous customs revenue laws enacted prior to March, 1861, and remaining either wholly or partially in force.

Under these various enactments, questions relating to the proper assessment of duties constantly arise. There is often a direct conflict between different statutes, and occasionally between two or more provisions of the same statute, while single provisions are frequently held to embrace different meanings. These differences can be settled only by arbitrary interpretations or by adjudications in court. As a necessary consequence, protests against the payment of duties exacted by collectors of customs and appeals to this Department, based on such protests, are of daily occurrence, while suits brought by the Government to collect unpaid duties, or by individuals to recover back duties paid, crowd the calendars of our courts.

The number of statutory appeals to the Secretary of the Treasury on tariff questions during the last fiscal year was four thousand seven hundred and thirty-one, exclusive of miscellaneous cases or applications for relief, numbering five thousand and sixty-five.

The onerous duties imposed upon the Department, the vexatious delays to individuals, and the expense of litigation to all concerned, resulting from this state of affairs, are obvious. The following remedies are suggested for adoption, in a general revision of the tariff laws:

First. The abandonment of distinctions based upon commercial usage. In other words, the material of which an article is composed instead of it commercial designation, where a particular material forms the sole or chief element of value, should control its classification, and the rate of duty consequently imposed, whether ad valorem or specific.

Second. The abandonment of "charges and commissions" as an element of dutiable value. The revenue from this source, while uncertain and comparatively trifling in amount, is a fruitful source of embarrassment and complaint in the liquidation of duties. Its continued exaction is therefore not desirable.

Third. The repeal of all provisions of law for what are commonly known as "damage allowances," or proportionate abatements of duties on merchandise injured during the voyage of importation. These vary at different ports, exceeding at some by ten or fifteen per cent. those made at others in like cases. In many instances the extent of damage can be only approximately determined, while in others there is room to suspect fraudulent practices, and, in all, the operation of the system is unfavorable to the honest importer as well as to the Government. I therefore recommend its entire abolition—a measure which would place all importers on an equality in this respect, while there would result to them only the extra expense of insurance on the duties, in addition to that upon the foreign cost of the goods.

Many articles upon which duties are now levied, and which do not come in competition with those of the manufacture or production of this country, are imported in such small quantities that the duties collected thereon are insignificant and do not compensate for the cost of collection. I suggest that all such articles be added to the free list.

The fees prescribed by law for services upon the northern frontier connected with the execution of the laws relating to navigation and the collection of the revenue from customs are different from those upon the coast, and it is questionable whether such difference does not constitute a violation of the constitutional provision prohibiting the giving of a preference by any regulation of commerce or revenue to the ports of one State over those of another; and a revision and equalization of such fees are recommended.

A tonnage tax is now levied on all American sailing vessels engaged in the foreign trade, and on all sailing vessels of other nationalities. It is not imposed upon American vessels engaged in the coasting trade. Steamships of foreign nationality, in some cases, are subject to the tonnage tax; in others, they are exempt by old treaty stipulations only recently carried into effect. But all American steam-vessels arriving from foreign countries are subject to the tax. In consideration of the fact that this tax was entirely abolished on all vessels for more than thirty years and only resorted to as a war measure in 1862, and that those engaged in the coasting trade were again relieved from this burden by recent enactments, I recommend that this tax be wholly abolished.

The Department has found difficulty in the administration of the act of February 18, 1793, relating to the enrolment and license of vessels, with reference to its application to canal-boats and similar craft designed to be chiefly employed on the internal waters of States. From a period immediately subsequent to the passage of the act down to a comparatively recent date, the Department uniformly held that such boats, exceeding five tons burden, were liable to be enrolled and licensed. During the term of my immediate predecessor the question was thoroughly considered, and the liability to enrolment and license was held to attach to this class of vessels only when they emerged from the internal waters of a State into the navigable waters of the United States. But even this modified view of their liability has been contested on the ground that such boats are not included in the provisions of the enrolment act. The growth of inland commerce and the necessities of trade have, of late years, led not only to a large increase in the number of canal boats, but also to their more frequent egress into navigable waters.

Hence it becomes more and more for the interest of the numerous owners of this species of property to claim entire exemption from the burdens imposed by the coasting laws, or incidental to an enforcement thereof, while the Department has no option but to administer the law. It is, therefore, important that the status of this class of vessels should be definitely fixed by such legislation as the case requires.

Rivers and harbors which have been dredged by the Government at great expense are often made the receptacle of ballast thrown from vessels, by which the channels become filled and navigation impeded. There is much necessity for a law to prevent this practice, making it a penal offence to deposit, in such channels or harbors, ballast or other matter by which their value as such is lessened.

The general regulations of this Department, issued in 1857, and partially revised in 1868–'69, having become to some extent obsolete, and in many respects deficient, have been completely revised and adapted to existing laws, special pains being taken to make the arrangement of topics convenient, and the text of the regulations simple, comprehensive, and concise. It is believed that this revision, an edition of which will be issued at an early date, will materially aid customs and other officers in the performance of their duties.

REORGANIZATION OF CUSTOMS DISTRICTS.

I invite the attention of Congress to the propriety of reorganizing the customs collection districts on the Atlantic coast, seventy-nine in number.

The establishment of many of these districts dates back to a period when the conditions determining their importance, relative to the commerce of the country, were entirely different from those existing at the present time. In some, the expenses of collecting the revenue exceed the amount collected, and the consolidation of such districts with others may be advisable. At the same time, it must be remembered, that the effective administration of the revenue system often requires the services of customs officers at points where few or no duties are collected. The judicious disposition of a force for the prevention of smuggling is indispensable to the collection of the revenue from imports, especially where the extent of coast affords opportunities for the clandestine introduction of dutiable merchandise. I would therefore suggest such action as may lead to a reduction of the number of districts, and a consequent reduction of expenses, without affecting the convenience of importers or the safety of the revenue.

4 Ab

INTERNAL REVENUE.

The following statement shows the increase and decrease from each general source of internal revenue for the fiscal years ended June 30, 1872, and June 30, 1873, as appears from the report of the Commissioner of Internal Revenue:

Sources.	Increase.	Decrease.
Spirits	$2,623,855 42	
Tobacco	650,132 57	
Fermented liquors	1,086,439 34	
Penalties	19,447 98	
Banks and bankers		$457,197 68
Adhesive stamps		8,474,943 75
Articles and occupations formerly taxed but now exempt		12,723,244 53
Total	4,389,875 31	22,055,385 96

It will be seen that there has been an increase in the receipts for taxes on spirits, tobacco, fermented liquors, and from penalties.

The decrease in the receipts from banks and bankers is due principally to that provision in the act of June 6, 1872, which raises the exemption of all sums deposited in savings banks, &c., in the name of one person, from $500 to $2,000.

The repeal of all stamp taxes imposed under Schedule B, act of June 30, 1864, except that of two cents on bank checks, drafts, or orders, took effect October 1, 1872, and has caused a falling off from that source.

The class of articles and occupations formerly taxed but now entirely exempt includes incomes, gas, and other sources of taxation on lists repealed prior to the act of June 6, 1872, and the receipts from these sources constantly and rapidly diminish.

In accordance with the provisions of the act of December 24, 1872, the offices of assessors and assistant assessors of internal revenue have been abolished, and all their final accounts approved by the Commissioner of Internal Revenue and referred to the accounting officers. The number of these officers varied according to the exigencies of the service, being greatest in 1868, when there were three thousand and forty-three, of which two hundred and forty-one were assessors; since which time the number had, up to the taking effect of the act above referred to, been reduced about one-half.

The system of collecting taxes by stamps, and without assessments, has been found to give general satisfaction. Since its application to special taxes they have been collected more promptly and thoroughly, and a more gratifying and healthy increase in the receipts therefrom is apparent.

The old assessment lists have been disposed of in a large number of the collection districts, and the aggregate amount held as collectible thereon does not exceed $450,000.

REVENUE MARINE AND LIFE-SAVING SERVICE.

A marked improvement has been made during the past year in the Revenue Marine Service. The number of vessels boarded and examined, and the number of those reported for violation of revenue laws, and of those assisted in distress, as well as the number of lives saved through the agency of the revenue cutters, is largely in excess of like service performed during any previous year. The character of the service has been elevated by rigid professional examinations. Ten old vessels have been thoroughly repaired and three new ones have been built. There are now employed twenty-eight steamers and six sailing vessels, and these are better adapted to the service required of them than were the vessels formerly in use. Three new steam-vessels are constructing and will go into commission next spring. With the addition of a new steamer for the Columbia river and vicinity, it is believed that this branch of the service will be in a condition to answer the demands upon it, economically and efficiently, for many years to come.

I desire to renew the recommendations heretofore submitted to Congress that the navy-pension laws be made applicable to the officers and seamen of the Revenue Marine, and that provision be made for a retired list of officers. These measures are demanded to aid in promoting efficiency, and in justice to meritorious officers and seamen whose lives are spent in the performance of hazardous public service.

From the appropriation of $100,000 " for the establishment of new life-saving stations on the coast of the United States," twenty-one new stations are in process of erection upon the coasts of Maine, New Hampshire, Massachusetts, Virginia, and North Carolina. Of these, ten will be ready for occupancy by the first of February next, and the others at a later period in the season. Arrangements are also being made for the establishment of two other stations. No provision of law exists for the two additional superintendents which these new stations render necessary, nor for keepers and crews for the same. It is recommended that early authority be given for the employment of such persons.

Although during the past year marine disasters have been unusually numerous, it is gratifying to be able to state, that upon the coasts provided with life-saving stations, which are the most dangerous upon the seaboard, the loss of life and property has been exceedingly slight.

The wreck reports from the various stations show that since the last annual report of the Secretary of the Treasury, thirty-two vessels have been driven ashore upon these coasts by stress of weather, valued, with their cargoes, at $832,230, on which the loss was only about $220,000.

The number of lives imperilled was two hundred and thirty-five, of which number, but a single life was lost.

In accordance with the directions of the act of March 3, 1873, measures have been taken to ascertain "at what points on the sea and lake-coasts of the United States the establishment of life-saving stations would best subserve the interests of commerce and humanity," and a report on the subject will be transmitted to Congress during the session.

For the purpose of recognizing and encouraging the services of the keepers and crews of the stations, in the performance of the perilous duties they are frequently called upon to undertake in rescuing the shipwrecked, it is recommended that a system of rewards be adopted in the shape of medals of honor, to be distributed to such of them as may particularly distinguish themselves by special or notable acts of gallantry or daring, resulting in the rescue of persons from imminent danger. Such rewards might be properly extended even beyond the life-saving service, and bestowed upon any others who may have made extraordinary exertions, at their own peril, in saving life in marine disasters. Similar rewards are bestowed in foreign countries, where life-saving institutions exist, and are considered prizes worth the most adventurous efforts.

THE COAST SURVEY.

The important service of the Coast Survey under this Department has been prosecuted with vigor and usefulness. The changeable character of many of our harbors and most frequented coastwise passages calls for constant watchfulness, to maintain the charts and aids to navigation as correct indicators of the actual channels. Work has been prosecuted on portions of the coast heretofore surveyed, and examinations and resurveys have also been made at Boston, New York, Philadelphia, Baltimore, San Francisco, and many other harbors, as well as in the great thoroughfare between Nantucket and Monomoy. Twenty-five new charts are reported as published during the year. The publication of a "Coast Pilot," or printed sailing directions for harbors and coastwise navigation, has been commenced, which, with the annual predictions of tides, will complete and digest for ready use the information laid down on the charts. Much interest has been manifested in the extension of the great triangulation lines across the continent; and the system, steadily pursued, will in time, at a small annual expense, supply the frame-work for an accurate map of the whole country.

LIGHT-HOUSES.

I have frequently attended the meetings of the Light-House Board, and have been much impressed with the importance of the work under its control, and the efficiency with which it has been conducted.

Our Light-House Establishment is now larger than that of any other country in the world, extending with its lights and beacons over more than ten thousand miles of coast and shore, maintaining, at the close of the last fiscal year, five hundred and twenty-one light-houses, thirty-five powerful signals operated by engines driven by steam or hot air, twenty-one light-ships, three hundred and sixty-four day or unlighted beacons, and twenty-eight hundred and thirty-eight buoys.

During the past summer the Board, with my approval, directed its Engineer Secretary, Major Elliot, of the Corps of Engineers of the Army, to make an inspection of the light-house systems of Europe, with a view of improving our own by the introduction of such modifications as have been found useful there. His report has been made, and the practices in other countries which differ from our own will be duly considered by the Board, with a view to the adoption of such as will render still more efficient the light-house system under its control.

At some of the most important points on the French and English coasts, electric and gas light-houses have been placed, and I recommend that the Treasury Department be authorized to make experiments in the same direction, by applying to two of our most important stations, on towers already constructed, one electric and one gas light, of most powerful character.

MINTS.

The Mint Bureau, established by the act of February 12, 1873, was organized on the 1st of April, when the coinage act became operative. Doctor H. R. Linderman was appointed director; and, under his able and energetic management, the operations of the mints and assay offices have been efficiently conducted, and a more speedy and systematic rendition of the bullion accounts effected. At the request of the Department, he has obtained valuable information on various technical and scientific points connected with the coinage, by which the transaction of business has been greatly facilitated.

The coinage during the fiscal year ending June 30, 1873, was as follows:

Gold coinage	$35,249,337 50
Silver coinage	2,945,795 50
Minor coinage	494,050 00
Total	38,689,183 00

During the same period, the value of bars manufactured was as follows:

Fine gold	$7,439,843 78
Unparted gold	8,485,602 35
Total gold	15,925,446 13
Fine silver	$3,149,372 64
Unparted silver	8,442,711 84
Total silver	11,592,084 48
Total gold and silver bars	$27,517,530 61

The reduction of the coinage charge from one-half to one-fifth of one per cent. has been followed by an increased coinage, and prevented, to a considerable extent, the export of gold bullion—its value for coinage in this country having thereby been brought nearly to its mint value in London, where it is coined without charge. Some further advantages would no doubt follow the adoption by this country of the free-coinage system as to gold. I recommend the repeal of the charge for coining gold, and also the charge imposed for copper used for alloy, as being an inconvenient item in estimating the coinage value of gold.

With the view to prevent the export of gold coins, authority should be given for keeping in the Treasury, when its condition will admit of the same, a supply of fine gold bars bearing the mint stamp of fineness, weight, and value, and for exchanging such bars for coin. They would always be preferred to coin for export, and gold coins of full weight would be retained in the country, instead of being selected for export.

The repeal or modification of that part of the coinage act which requires gold coins to be excluded from the benefit of the half per cent. abrasion limit, unless they have been in circulation for certain prescribed periods, is recommended, on the ground that in the daily transactions of the custom-houses it cannot be carried into effect.

The subsidiary silver coins being manufactured by the Government on its own account, and the seigniorage or difference between the bullion and nominal value of such coin realized by it, provision should be made for redeeming in kind such pieces as have become unduly worn from long circulation. This is done in other countries which, like ours, have adopted the gold standard and demonetized silver.

The recent fall in the price of gold, together with the depreciation in the market value of silver, as compared with gold, which has been going on for some time, has enabled the Director to coin silver, to be paid out instead of United States notes to advantage. Availing himself of this opportunity, the Director caused to be purchased as much silver bullion as could be conveniently used in giving employment to the mints, when not engaged in the more important business of coining gold, and the same was so coined and paid out.

During the last few years, our subsidiary silver coins have been sent in considerable amounts to Central and South America, where it is understood they circulate as full-valued coins. It would be better for us to manufacture coin according to standards and values legally prescribed by those countries, than to encourage the export of our subsidiary coin, which is intended for home circulation.

In connection with this subject, it should be stated, that applications have been received from some of the South American governments to supply them with coins of their own standards. These applications could not be granted for want of lawful authority. As an act of comity to friendly States who have no facilities for coinage, and for commercial reasons, it is recommended that authority be granted for the execution of coinage of other countries, when it can be done at our mints without interfering with home demands for coin.

No coinage has been executed at the New Orleans Mint since the year 1861, but the machinery, with inconsiderable exceptions, is still there, and reported to be in good condition. As that section of the country will, at no distant period, require a large supply of coin, estimates for the amount required, to place the mint in condition for coining operations, and for its support during the next fiscal year, have been submitted, and, it is hoped, will receive the favorable consideration of Congress.

Under the provisions of the coinage act, depositors receive in stamped bars from assay offices, where refining is not done, the identical bullion deposited by them, and are subjected to heavy discounts in converting the bars into coin or currency. These interior assay offices would become much more useful to the mining interests, if authority were given to the Secretary of the Treasury to issue coin certificates for the net value of such bars.

MARINE HOSPITALS.

The relief operations of the Marine Hospital Service embraced at the close of the last fiscal year ninety-one customs districts, and showed an increase of twelve per cent., as compared with the year preceding. and nearly thirty-seven per cent. since the passage of the act of June 30, 1870, under which the service is now administered. Medical and surgical attendance was furnished to thirteen thousand five hundred and twenty-nine seamen. The hospital at Chicago has been completed, and a site has been selected for the pavilion hospital authorized at the last session of Congress to be erected at San Francisco. The recommendations contained in the last annual report of my predecessor as to hospitals at New York and Pittsburg are renewed, and Oyster Island is suggested as an eligible site for that at New York.

Instead of costly alterations and repairs to the hospitals at Detroit, Cleveland, Louisville, and Portland, the Supervising Surgeon proposes, for sanitary and other reasons, that comparatively inexpensive wooden pavilion wards be built on the grounds adjoining, and only such expenditures be made upon the present buildings as may be necessary to fit them for administrative purposes.

The recommendation is also renewed as to the use for hospital purposes of wooden pavilion structures, of simple design and comparatively small cost, which may be destroyed and renewed when their continued occupancy renders them unhealthy. In these views I fully concur.

PUBLIC BUILDINGS.

In the annual report of the Secretary of the Treasury for 1872, the attention of Congress was called to the fact that very large sums of money would be needed for the completion of buildings begun or authorized, and it was recommended that, with the exception of pavilion hospitals and a building for the accommodation of the Bureau of Engraving and Printing and the surplus files of the Treasury Department, no new work should be authorized. Contrary to this recommendation, Congress, while making no appropriation for the building last named, authorized the commencement of seventeen new buildings and the purchase of sites for several others. This legislation, together with the work previously commenced, has imposed an unprecedented and extraordinary amount of labor upon the Supervising Architect's office, and has rendered it necessary to submit estimates in an aggregate sum much larger than I think should be expended in any one year.

It is highly important to limit the erection of public buildings to such as are imperatively demanded by the necessities of the public service, and where suitable temporary accommodations cannot be provided at a reasonable cost. While it is no doubt true that all buildings authorized to be erected are needed and their early completion would be desirable, those in the larger cities where permanent buildings are imperatively demanded for the proper transaction of business should have the preference. With the present organization of the Supervising Architect's office, it does not seem practicable in a single year to commence or properly supervise the construction of all the buildings authorized by Congress.

In this connection I desire to refer to the labor performed by that office, and the magnitude of the business committed to its charge.

There are one hundred and fifteen buildings finished and occupied for federal purposes, which are by law placed under the charge of the Treasury Department, consisting of Treasury buildings, custom-houses, court-houses, post offices, appraisers' stores, warehouses, marine hospitals, mints, and assay offices. The Supervising Architect's office has, by direction of the Secretary of the Treasury, the supervision of the repair and supply of these buildings with furniture, heating apparatus, safes, vaults, fuel, lights, water, &c. Most of these buildings require more or less repairs every year, and thirty of them are now undergoing extensive repairs and remodelling, several to an extent involving as much time and attention as the erection of new buildings. The office is also charged with the construction of all new buildings erected under the Treasury Department, and is now engaged in the construction of seventeen such new buildings, and also the new State, War, and Navy Department in this city, and the new jail for the District of Columbia.

The expenditures during the past year were $9,039,698 76, and the balances of appropriations standing to the credit of that office on July 1, 1873, amounted to $14,774,573 00.

Congress has provided for the erection of twenty new buildings not yet commenced, plans for six of which are now being prepared; sites have been secured for eleven, and negotiations are in progress for the purchase of the remaining nine.

The Supervising Architect's office has also the renting of buildings and office-rooms for the use of the various officers of the Treasury Department throughout the country at places where there are no public buildings, or where such buildings are insufficient. The number now occupied is two hundred and twenty-six, which are located in every State in the Union, except Kansas and Arkansas, and in five of the Territories, at a total annual rental of $190,488 25.

Great credit is due to the Supervising Architect and his subordinates for the able, faithful, and economical manner in which they have conducted the vast business submitted to their immediate supervision.

NEW YORK CUSTOM-HOUSE.

The great extent and rapid increase of the commerce of the port of New York, where are collected about sixty-seven per cent. of all the duties levied on imported goods, has already rendered the custom-house accommodations there quite insufficient. With the certain increase of business which this port must attain in the future, and with the prospect of its becoming more and more an exchange centre for other countries, it is a matter of the first importance to select, at an early day, a site for a new custom-house on a larger scale, together with the buildings needed in connection therewith, where the situation, convenience, and accommodations will be adequate to the requirements and worthy of the position of this great mart. The expense of erecting the building may well be extended over a series of years. The present custom-house lot may be sold to advantage, when no longer required, in part reimbursement of the expense. I earnestly commend this subject to the consideration of Congress.

THE SEAL ISLANDS.

Valuable reports have recently been made by Captain Charles Bryant, agent, and Mr. Henry W. Elliott, assistant agent of the Treasury Department, at the seal islands of Alaska, in respect to the geography of the islands, the condition of the inhabitants, and the habits of the seals. They concur in the opinion that the law of July 1, 1870, providing that of the one hundred thousand seals to be taken annually, the proportion of one-quarter from St. George Island is altogether too large for the number of seals now frequenting that island, making it necessary, in order to obtain the full complement, to kill seals too small to afford first-class skins. They think the proportion between the two islands should be eighty-five thousand from St. Paul, and fifteen thousand from St. George. I am of opinion that the law of July 1, 1870, above referred to, should be so altered that the proportion to be taken from the separate islands may be fixed by the Treasury Department, and changed from time to time as the course of the seals may render it necessary.

LOUISVILLE AND PORTLAND CANAL.

In the "act making appropriations for the repair, preservation, and completion of certain public works on rivers and harbors, and for other purposes," approved March 3, 1873, the following appropriations and provisions are made:

"For completing the Louisville and Portland canal, one hundred thousand dollars; and the Secretary of the Treasury is authorized and directed to assume, on behalf of the United States, the control and management of the said canal, in conformity with the terms of the joint resolution of the Legislature of the State of Kentucky, approved March 28, 1872, at such time and in such manner as in his judgment the interests of the United States, and the commerce thereof, may require; and the sum of money necessary to enable the Secretary of the Treasury to carry this provision into effect is hereby appropriated: *Provided*, That after the United States shall assume control of said canal, the tolls thereon on vessels propelled by steam shall be reduced to twenty-five cents per ton, and on all other vessels in proportion."

The resolution of the State of Kentucky recites the facts that all the stock of the canal company belongs to the United States except five shares owned by the directors, that the property of the company is subject to a mortgage to secure bonds therein mentioned, and that the company may owe other debts, and directs the Louisville and Portland Canal Company to surrender the canal and all the property connected therewith to the government of the United States upon the terms and conditions therein specified, the sixth and last of which is "that the government of the United States shall before such surrender discharge said mortgage and pay all debts due by said canal company, and purchase the stock of said directors."

The United States, by repeated acts, have manifested the intention of taking possession of this canal and maintaining it for the benefit and improvement of the navigation of the Ohio river, and the importance of consummating that intention at as early a day as possible is apparent. As long ago as 1855 the United States had become the owners of all the shares in the company except the five shares held at the request of the then Secretary of the Treasury by the directors, to enable them to retain their offices and keep up the corporate organization and the management of the business of the company. Since that time Congress has at different times made appropriations and expenditures for enlarging and improving the canal to the amount of more than a million dollars, for which the Treasury has never been reimbursed.

Recognizing the great benefit which would accrue to the commerce of the country bordering on the Ohio river, by the United States taking possession of the canal and reducing the tolls thereon, steps were taken to ascertain the debts of the company, and to devise a plan for carrying into effect the provisions of the appropriation act above cited.

It is found that the unsecured floating debt of the company, after deducting cash on hand, is not large, and may be easily ascertained and paid, and that the five shares of stock may be obtained of the directors by paying therefor one hundred dollars per share, with interest from February 9, 1864.

In addition to these debts, there are outstanding eleven hundred and seventy-two bonds of the company, of $1,000 each, with coupons attached, bearing six per cent. interest, payable semi-annually. Of these bonds, $373,000 will mature January 1, 1876; $399,000 will mature January 1, 1881; and $400,000 will mature January 1, 1886. While the resolutions of the State of Kentucky require that these bonds shall all be paid, and the mortgage discharged before the surrender of the canal to the United States, and the bonds do not all mature until the year 1886, and are supposed to be distributed among a great number of unknown holders, the difficulty of carrying into effect the provision of Congress may be readily seen.

If Congress would authorize the Secretary of the Treasury, with the consent of the State of Kentucky, to take possession of the canal upon paying the floating debts of the company, purchasing the five shares of stock, and assuming the payment of the bonds secured by the mortgage when matured, with authority to purchase them at any time previously, as circumstances would warrant, one great obstacle in the way of accomplishing this most desirable result would be removed, and the cost thereof might be distributed over a period of several years.

While this subject was under consideration a communication was received from the president of the company, under date of July 9, 1873, informing the Department that "the Louisville and Portland Canal Company has been sued in the Louisville Chancery Court, by the devisees of Colonel John Campbell, for nearly all the land owned by the company."

This suit, which is now pending, and is understood to involve the title to all or nearly all the land through which the canal runs, has so changed the aspect of affairs, that I deemed it the part of prudence, within the discretion intrusted to my judgment, to expend no money towards paying the debts of the company until these facts should be laid before Congress for its consideration and action thereon.

REPORTS OF BUREAU OFFICERS.

The several reports of the different bureau officers to accompany this report, to wit: those of the First and Second Comptrollers, Commissioner of Customs; the First, Second, Third, Fourth, Fifth, and

Sixth Auditors; Treasurer, Register, Director of the Mint, Chief of the Bureau of Statistics, Solicitor of the Treasury, Superintendent of the Coast Survey, the Light-house Board, Supervising Architect, and Commissioner of Internal Revenue, with that of the Comptroller of the Currency, are respectfully commended to the consideration of Congress, as showing the extent and condition of the business of the Department in all its numerous branches, and the faithfulness, industry, and integrity with which the same has been conducted during the past year by all persons employed in the service.

WILLIAM A. RICHARDSON,
Secretary of the Treasury.

Hon. SPEAKER OF THE HOUSE OF REPRESENTATIVES.

TABLES ACCOMPANYING THE REPORT.

TABLE A.—*Statement of the net receipts (by warrants) during the fiscal year ended June 30, 1873.*

CUSTOMS.

Quarter ended September 30, 1872	$57, 729, 540 27	
Quarter ended December 31, 1872	39, 501, 519 96	
Quarter ended March 31, 1873	49, 902, 018 67	
Quarter ended June 30, 1873	40, 866, 443 80	
		$188, 069, 522 70

SALES OF PUBLIC LANDS.

Quarter ended September 30, 1872	797, 324 57	
Quarter ended December 31, 1872	670, 821 88	
Quarter ended March 31, 1873	641, 558 38	
Quarter ended June 30, 1873	772, 607 55	
		2, 882, 312 38

INTERNAL REVENUE.

Quarter ended September 30, 1872	34, 169, 047 22	
Quarter ended December 31, 1872	25, 066, 701 30	
Quarter ended March 31, 1873	24, 262, 778 30	
Quarter ended June 30, 1873	29, 230, 787 32	
		113, 729, 314 14

DIRECT TAX.

Quarter ended September 30, 1872	....	
Quarter ended December 31, 1872	272, 687 02	
Quarter ended March 31, 1873	42, 567 49	
Quarter ended June 30, 1873	....	
		315, 254 51

TAX ON CIRCULATION, DEPOSITS, ETC., OF NATIONAL BANKS.

Quarter ended September 30,'1872	3, 307, 238 69	
Quarter ended December 31, 1872	72, 150 01	
Quarter ended March 31, 1873	3, 427, 084 71	
Quarter ended June 30, 1873	23, 364 26	
		6, 830, 037 67

REPAYMENT OF INTEREST BY PACIFIC RAILWAY COMPANIES.

Quarter ended September 30, 1872	119, 093 73	
Quarter ended December 31, 1872	177, 973 84	
Quarter ended March 31, 1873	179, 405 33	
Quarter ended June 30, 1873	37, 733 14	
		514, 206 04

CUSTOMS, FINES, PENALTIES, AND FORFEITURES.

Quarter ended September 30, 1872	103, 787 30	
Quarter ended December 31, 1872	45, 294 59	
Quarter ended March 31, 1873	613, 928 45	
Quarter ended June 30, 1873	406, 505 04	
		1, 169, 515 38

FEES.

Consular, letters-patent, steamboat, and land :

Quarter ended September 30, 1872	479, 306 03	
Quarter ended December 31, 1872	373, 161 48	
Quarter ended March 31, 1873	484, 668 88	
Quarter ended June 30, 1873	540, 085 28	
		1, 877, 221 67

PROCEEDS OF SALES OF GOVERNMENT PROPERTY.

Quarter ended September 30, 1872	$336, 801 84	
Quarter ended December 31, 1872	544, 442 56	
Quarter ended March 31, 1873	138, 665 10	
Quarter ended June 30, 1873	577, 353 50	$1, 637, 262 13

MISCELLANEOUS SOURCES.

Quarter ended September 30, 1872	1, 346, 257 47	
Quarter ended December 31, 1872	1, 083, 825 43	
Quarter ended March 31, 1873	939, 256 97	
Quarter ended June 30, 1873	1, 753, 666 27	
		5, 134, 686 14
Total receipts, exclusive of loans and premium on coin		333, 177, 673 78

Premium on sales of coin:

Quarter ended September 30, 1872	2, 438, 736 91	
Quarter ended December 31, 1872	2, 567, 127 50	
Quarter ended March 31, 1873	2, 946, 726 72	
Quarter ended June 30, 1873	3, 509, 939 67	
		11, 460, 530 89
Total net receipts		333, 734, 204 67
Balance in Treasury June 30, 1872, (including $4,047.40 received from "unavailable")		106, 567, 404 74
Total		440, 305, 609 41

TABLE B.—*Statement of the net disbursements (by warrants) during the fiscal year ended June 30, 1873.*

CIVIL.

Congress	$7, 251, 832 46	
Executive	6, 896, 567 13	
Judiciary	3, 896, 131 77	
Government of Territories	271, 985 38	
Sub-treasuries	340, 530 92	
Public land-offices	414, 135 19	
Inspection of steam-vessels	321, 917 50	
Mints and assay-offices	185, 499 68	
Total civil list		$19, 348, 582 62

FOREIGN INTERCOURSE.

Diplomatic salaries	376, 862 69
Consular salaries	416, 973 86
Contingencies of consulates	93, 063 75
Relief and protection of American seamen	5, 235 04
American and Mexican claims commission	20, 212 90
American and Spanish claims commission	14, 030 70
American and British claims commission	184, 679 64
Tribunal of arbitration at Geneva	62, 216 82
Expenses of the Japanese embassy	730 00
Capitalization of Scheldt dues	66, 584 00
Return of consular receipts	3, 040 54
War expenses in Madrid, Paris, Berlin, and London	2, 303 63
International Exposition at Vienna	111, 146 29
Survey of boundary between the United States and British possessions	75, 000 00
Contingent and miscellaneous	139, 270 15
Total foreign intercourse	1, 571, 380 65

MISCELLANEOUS.

Mint establishment	629, 483 65
Branch-mint buildings	392, 857 43
Coast Survey	852, 824 75
Light-House Establishment	1, 905, 570 96
Building and repairs of light-houses	1, 700, 718 61
Refunding excess of deposits for unascertained duties	3, 190, 192 00
Refunding duties on tea and coffee	257, 231 82
Drawbacks on certain articles imported into district of Chicago	192, 155 95
Payments for coins, nickels, &c., destroyed at Chicago	370, 813 24
Revenue-cutter service	995, 308 84
Building revenue-cutters	138, 592 40
Life saving service	212, 383 08
Custom-houses, court-houses, post-offices, &c.	6, 941, 039 97
Furniture, fuel, &c., for public buildings under Treasury Department	409, 362 45
Repairs and preservation of public buildings under Treasury Department	414, 822 16
Collecting customs revenue	7, 079, 743 42
Debenture and drawbacks under customs laws	1, 211, 710 90
Refunding duties erroneously or illegally collected	134, 552 08
Marine hospital establishment	398, 230 02
Marine hospital, Chicago, Illinois	62, 482 04
Distributive shares of fines, penalties, and forfeitures	608, 156 74
Assessing and collecting internal revenue	5, 337, 194 83
Punishing violations of internal-revenue laws	35, 648 40
Internal-revenue stamps	329, 727 70

Refunding duties erroneously or illegally collected	$630, 708 28
Internal-revenue allowances and drawbacks	134, 293 84
Redemption of internal-revenue stamps	215, 414 03
Mail-steamship service	725, 000 00
Deficiencies in revenue of Post-office Department	4, 765, 475 00
Refunding proceeds of captured and abandoned property	1, 980, 679 26
Collection of captured and abandoned property	84, 459 50
Expenses national loan	2, 806, 863 94
Expenses refunding national debt	54, 736 83
Expenses national currency	181, 654 84
Suppressing counterfeiting and frauds	125, 608 73
Contingent expenses independent treasury	96, 377 15
Public buildings and grounds in Washington	1, 920, 197 26
Re-imbursement District of Columbia for repairs on avenues, &c	1, 294, 535 75
Capitol extension, dome repairs, &c	87, 222 04
Extension of Capitol grounds	731, 199 15
State, War, and Navy Department buildings	1, 609, 233 24
Columbian Institute for Deaf and Dumb	124, 000 00
Government Hospital for the Insane	206, 800 00
Charitable institutions in Washington	188, 013 32
Metropolitan police	205, 175 78
Support of sixty transient paupers	12, 000 00
Surveys of public lands	1, 128, 060 13
Repayment for lands erroneously sold	32, 486 27
Proceeds of swamp-lands to States	3, 799 96
Five per cent. fund, &c., to States	237, 624 01
Expenses of eighth and ninth censuses	103, 282 44
Penitentiaries in the Territories	37, 345 20
Payments under relief acts	265, 851 61
Unenumerated items	22, 435 90
Total miscellaneous	852, 408, 226 20

INTERIOR DEPARTMENT.

Indians	7, 951, 704 88
Pensions	29, 359, 426 86
Total Interior Department	37, 311, 131 74

MILITARY ESTABLISHMENT.

Pay Department	3, 513, 840 88
Commissary Department	2, 521, 837 81
Quartermaster's Department	14, 512, 010 30
Ordnance Department	2, 091, 063 22
Medical Department	346, 214 53
Military Academy	66, 505 77
Expenses of recruiting	107, 564 00
Contingencies	396, 813 04
Signal service	350, 500 00
Refugees, freedmen, and abandoned lands	178, 796 74
Bounties to soldiers	10, 445, 014 77
Re-imbursing States for raising volunteers	758, 110 31
Military organizations in Kansas	324, 439 37
Claims of loyal citizens for supplies	927, 910 19
Payments under relief acts	353, 155 96
Forts and fortifications	1, 997, 589 56
Improvements of rivers and harbors	6, 321, 880 49
Re-imbursing Kentucky for militia during the rebellion	525, 258 72
Suppressing Indian hostilities in Montana Territory	425, 000 00
Allowance for reduction of wages under eight-hour law	158, 632 56
Total military establishment	46, 323, 138 31

NAVAL ESTABLISHMENT.

Pay and contingent of the Navy	6, 587, 607 24
Marine Corps	1, 171, 872 59
Navigation	339, 511 65
Ordnance	1, 158, 923 19
Provisions and clothing	2, 767, 721 33
Medicine and surgery	254, 811 46
Equipment and recruiting	1, 837, 156 42
Construction and repairs	4, 546, 057 54
Steam-engineering	1, 682, 009 00
Yards and docks	2, 463, 022 59
Payments under relief acts	341, 195 34
Surveying Isthmus of Darien for ship-canal	5, 009 00
Surveying Isthmus of Tehuantepec and Nicaragua	13, 074 39
Miscellaneous	358, 204 05
Total naval establishment	23, 525, 256 79
Interest on the public debt	104, 750, 688 44
Total net disbursements exclusive of premium and principal of public debt	285, 239, 325 34
Premium on bonds purchased	5, 105, 919 99
Redemption of the public debt	18, 768, 335 58
	23, 874, 255 57
Total net disbursements	309, 113, 580 91
Balance in Treasury, June 30, 1873	131, 192, 028 50
Total	440, 305, 609 41

D.—*Statement of the net receipts (by warrants) for the quarter ended September 30, 1873.*

RECEIPTS.

Customs	$49,195,403 68
Sales of public lands	573,768 07
Internal revenue	25,640,454 41
Tax on circulation, deposits, &c., of national banks	3,490,743 66
Repayment of interest by Pacific railway companies	198,970 56
Customs fines, penalties, and fees	438,514 21
Consular, letters-patent, homestead, and land fees	503,941 12
Proceeds of sales of Government property	303,765 32
Miscellaneous	1,507,931 21
Premium on sales of coin	2,350,818 34
Total ordinary receipts, exclusive of loans	84,204,310 58
Payment by the British government of the award of the tribunal of arbitration at Geneva	15,500,000 00
Total net receipts	99,704,310 58
Balance in Treasury June 30, 1873	131,192,028 50
Total	230,896,339 08

E.—*Statement of the net disbursements (by warrants) for the quarter ended September 30, 1873, civil and miscellaneous.*

Customs		$5,558,157 45
Internal revenue		1,249,656 67
Diplomatic service		399,592 17
Judiciary		821,297 12
Interior, (civil)		1,209,538 30
Treasury proper		8,030,614 16
Quarterly salaries		103,437 73
Total civil and miscellaneous		17,372,293 60
Indians	$2,008,715 19	
Pensions	8,698,156 58	
Military establishment	13,795,053 48	
Naval establishment	9,792,451 57	
Interest on public debt	37,051,907 79	
		71,346,284 61
Total net ordinary expenditures		88,718,578 21
Premiums on purchase of bonds	1,301,946 78	
Award of Geneva Tribunal, investment account	15,500,000 00	
Excess of net redemptions of loans over receipts	32,986,828 91	
		49,788,775 69
Total net expenditures		138,507,353 90
Balance in Treasury September 30, 1873		92,388,985 18
Total		230,896,339 08

5 Ab

TABLE F.—*Statement of outstanding principal of the public debt of the United States on the 1st of January of each year from 1791 to 1843, inclusive, and on the 1st of July of each year from 1844 to 1873, inclusive.*

Year.	Amount.
1791	$75,463,476 52
1792	77,227,924 66
1793	80,352,634 04
1794	78,427,404 77
1795	80,747,587 39
1796	83,762,172 07
1797	82,064,479 33
1798	79,228,529 12
1799	78,408,669 77
1800	82,976,294 35
1801	83,038,050 80
1802	80,712,632 25
1803	77,054,686 30
1804	86,427,120 88
1805	82,312,150 50
1806	75,723,270 66
1807	69,218,398 64
1808	65,196,317 97
1809	57,023,192 09
1810	53,173,217 52
1811	48,005,587 76
1812	45,209,737 90
1813	55,962,827 57
1814	81,487,846 24
1815	99,833,660 15
1816	127,334,933 74
1817	123,491,965 16
1818	103,466,633 83
1819	95,529,648 28
1820	91,015,566 15
1821	89,987,427 66
1822	93,546,676 98
1823	90,875,877 28
1824	90,269,777 77
1825	83,788,432 71
1826	81,054,059 99
1827	73,987,357 20
1828	67,475,043 87
1829	58,421,413 67
1830	48,565,406 50
1831	39,123,191 68
1832	24,322,235 18
1833	7,001,698 83
1834	4,760,082 08
1835	37,513 05
1836	336,957 83
1837	3,308,124 07
1838	10,434,221 14
1839	3,573,343 82
1840	5,250,875 54
1841	13,594,480 73
1842	20,601,226 28
1843	32,742,922 00
1844	23,461,652 50
1845	15,925,303 01
1846	15,550,202 97
1847	38,826,534 77
1848	47,044,862 23
1849	63,061,858 69
1850	63,452,773 55
1851	68,304,796 02
1852	66,199,341 71
1853	59,803,117 70
1854	42,242,222 42
1855	35,586,956 56
1856	31,972,537 90
1857	28,699,831 85
1858	44,911,881 03
1859	58,496,837 88
1860	64,842,287 88
1861	90,580,873 72
1862	524,176,412 13
1863	1,119,772,138 63
1864	1,815,784,370 57
1865	2,680,647,869 74
1866	2,773,236,173 69

REPORT OF THE SECRETARY OF THE TREASURY.

TABLE F.—*Statement of outstanding principal of the public debt, &c.—Continued.*

Year.	Amount.
1867	$2,678,126,103 87
1868	2,611,687,851 19
1869	2,588,452,213 94
1870	2,480,672,427 81
1871	2,353,211,332 32
1872	2,253,251,328 78
1873	*2,234,482,993 20

* In the amount here stated as the outstanding principal of the public debt, is included the certificates of deposit outstanding on the 30th June, issued under act of June 8, 1872, amounting to $31,730,000, for which a like amount in United States notes was on special deposit in the Treasury for their redemption, and added to the cash balance in the Treasury. These certificates, as a matter of accounts, are treated as a part of the public debt, but being offset by notes held on deposit for their redemption, should properly be deducted from the principal of the public debt in making comparison with former years. (See note at foot of Table O, page 6.)

TABLE G.—*Statement of the receipts of the United States from March 4, 1789, to June*

Year.	Balance in the Treasury at commencement of year.	Customs.	Internal revenue.	Direct tax.	Public lands.	Miscellaneous.
1791		$1,599,473 09				$10,478 10
1792	$973,905 75	3,413,070 85	$208,942 81			9,918 65
1793	783,444 51	4,255,306 56	337,705 70			21,410 88
1794	753,661 69	4,801,065 28	274,089 62			53,277 97
1795	1,151,924 17	5,588,461 26	337,755 36			28,317 97
1796	516,442 61	6,567 94	475,289 60		$4,836 13	1,028,415 78
1797	888,995 42	7,549 65	575,491 45		83,580 60	286,130 29
1798	1,021,899 04	7,061 93	644,337 03		11,963 11	58,192 81
1799	617,451 43	6,449 31	779,136 44			46,187 56
1800	2,161,867 77	9,532 73	809,396 55	$734,223 97	443 75	152,719 10
1801	2,623,311 99	10,778 93	1,048,033 43	534,343 38	167,726 06	343,649 15
1802	3,295,391 00	12,245 74	621,898 89	206,565 44	188,628 02	1,500,505 16
1803	5,020,607 64	10,417 61	215,179 69	71,879 20	165,675 69	131,945 44
1804	4,825,811 60	11,098,565 33	50,941 29	20,198 44	487,526 79	139,075 53
1805	4,037,005 26	12,936,487 04	21,747 15	21,882 91	540,193 80	40,382 39
1806	3,999,388 99	14,667,698 17	20,101 45	55,763 86	765,245 73	51,121 76
1807	4,538,123 80	15,845,521 61	13,051 40	34,732 56	466,163 27	38,550 62
1808	9,643,850 07	16,363,550 58	8,190 23	19,159 21	647,939 06	21,822 85
1809	9,941,809 96	227,	4,034 29	7,517 31	442,252 33	62,162 57
1810	3,848,056 78	8,583,	7,430 63	12,448 68	696,548 82	84,476 94
1811	2,672,276 57	13,313,222 73	2,295 95	7,666 66	1,040,237 53	59,211 22
1812	3,502,305 80	8,958,	4,903 06	859 22	710,427 78	126,165 17
1813	3,862,217 41	224,	4,755 04	3,605 52	835,655 14	271,571 00
1814	5,196,542 00	998,	1,682,984 82	2,219,497 36	1,135,971 09	164,399 81
1815	1,727,848 63	282,942 22	4,678,059 07	2,162,673 41	1,287,959 28	285,282 64
1816	13,106,592 88		5,124,708 31	4,253,635 09	1,717,985 03	273,782 35
1817	22,033,519 19		2,678,100 77	1,834,187 04	1,991,226 06	109,761 60
1818	14,989,465 48	17,176,385 00	955,270 20	264,333 36	2,606,564 77	57,617 71
1819	1,478,526 74	20,283,608 76	229,593 63	83,650 78	3,274,422 78	57,098 68
1820	2,079,992 38	15,005,612 15	106,260 53	31,586 82	1,635,871 61	61,338 44
1821	1,198,461 21	13,004,447 15	69,027 63	29,349 05	1,212,966 46	152,589 43
1822	1,681,592 24	17,589,761 94	67,665 71	20,961 56	1,803,581 54	452,957 19
1823	4,237,427 55	19,088,433 44	34,242 17	10,337 71	916,523 10	141,129 84
1824	9,463,922 81	17,878,325 71	34,663 37	20,101 96	984,418 15	127,603 60
1825	1,946,597 13	20,098,713 45	25,771 35	2,330 45	1,216,090 56	130,451 81
1826	5,201,650 43	23,341,331 77	21,589 93	6,638 76	1,393,785 09	94,588 66
1827	6,358,686 18	19,712,283 29	19,885 68	2,626 90	1,495,845 26	1,315,729 63
1828	6,668,286 10	23,205,523 64	17,451 54	2,218 81	1,018,308 73	65,126 49
1829	5,972,435 81	22,681,965 91	14,502 71	11,335 05	1,517,175 13	112,648 35
1830	5,755,704 79	21,922,391 39	12,160 62	16,980 59	2,329,356 14	73,227 77
1831	6,014,539 75	24,224,441 77	6,933 51	6,791 13	3,210,815 48	584,124 05
1832	4,502,914 45	28,465,237 24	11,630 65	394 12	2,623,381 03	270,410 61
1833	2,011,777 55	29,032,508 91	2,759 00		3,967,682 55	470,096 67
1834	11,702,905 31	16,214,957 15	4,196 09	19 80	4,857,600 69	480,812 32
1835	8,892,858 42	19,391,310 59	10,459 48	4,263 33	14,757,600 75	759,972 13
1836	26,749,803 96	23,409,940 53	370 00	734 79	24,877,179 86	2,945,808 93
1837	46,708,436 00	11,169,290 39	5,493 84	1,647 70	6,776,236 52	7,001,444 30
1838	37,327,252 69	16,158,800 36	2,467 27		3,730,945 66	6,410,348 45
1839	36,891,196 94	23,137,924 81	2,553 32	755 22	7,361,576 40	979,939 06
1840	33,157,503 68	13,499,502 17	1,682 25		3,411,818 63	2,587,112 99
1841	29,963,163 46	14,487,216 74	3,261 36		1,365,627 42	1,004,054 75
1842	28,685,111 08	18,187,908 76	495 00		1,335,797 52	451,995 97
1843	30,521,979 44	7,046,843 91	103 25		898,158 18	283,695 98
1844	39,186,284 74	26,183,570 94	1,777 34		2,059,939 80	1,075,419 70
1845	36,742,829 62	27,528,112 70	3,517 12		2,077,022 30	361,453 68
1846	36,194,274 81	26,712,667 87	2,897 26		2,694,452 48	289,950 13
1847	38,261,959 65	23,747,864 66	375 00		2,498,355 20	220,808 30
1848	33,079,276 43	31,757,070 96	375 00		3,328,642 56	612,610 69
1849	29,416,612 45	28,346,738 82			1,688,959 55	683,379 13
1850	32,827,082 69	39,668,686 42			1,859,894 25	2,064,308 21
1851	35,871,753 31	49,017,567 92			2,352,305 30	1,185,166 11
1852	40,158,353 25	47,339,326 63			2,043,239 58	464,249 40
1853	43,338,860 02	58,931,865 52			1,667,084 99	988,081 17
1854	50,261,901 09	64,224,190 27			8,470,798 39	1,105,352 74
1855	48,591,073 41	53,025,794 21			11,497,049 07	827,731 40
1856	47,777,672 13	64,022,863 50			8,917,644 93	1,116,190 81
1857	49,108,229 80	63,875,905 05			3,829,486 64	1,259,920 88
1858	46,802,855 00	41,789,620 96			3,513,715 87	1,352,029 13
1859	35,113,334 22	49,565,824 38			1,756,687 30	1,454,596 24
1860	33,193,248 60	53,187,511 87			1,778,557 71	1,088,530 25
1861	32,979,530 78	39,582,125 64			870,658 54	1,023,515 31
1862	30,963,857 83	49,056,397 62		1,795,331 73	152,203 77	915,327 97
1863	46,965,304 87	69,059,642 40	37,640,787 95	1,485,103 61	167,617 17	3,741,794 38
1864	36,523,046 13	102,316,152 99	109,741,134 10	475,648 96	588,333 29	30,291,701 86
1865	134,433,738 44	84,928,260 60	209,464,215 25	1,200,573 03	996,553 31	25,441,556 00

* For the half year from Jan

30, 1873, *by calendar years to* 1843, *and by fiscal years (ending June* 30) *from that time.*

Year.	Dividends.	Net ordinary receipts.	Interest.	Premiums.	Receipts from loans and Treasury notes.	Gross receipts.	Unavailable.
1791		$4,409,951 19			$361,391 34	$4,771,342 53	
1792	$8,028 00	3,669,960 31			5,102,498 45	8,772,458 76	
1793	38,500 00	4,652,923 14			1,797,272 01	6,450,195 15	
1794	303,472 00	5,431,904 87			4,007,950 78	9,439,855 65	
1795	160,000 00	6,114,534 59	$4,800 00		3,396,424 00	9,515,758 59	
1796	160,000 00	8,377,529 65	42,800 00		390,000 00	8,740,329 65	
1797	80,960 00	8,622,780 99			70,000 00	8,758,780 99	
1798	79,920 00	7,900,495 80	78,675 00		200,000 00	8,179,170 80	
1799	71,040 00	7,546,813 31			5,000,000 00	12,546,813 31	
1800	71,040 00	10,848,749 10			1,565,229 24	12,413,978 34	
1801	88,800 00	12,935,330 95	10,125 00			12,945,455 95	
1802	39,960 00	14,995,793 95				14,995,793 95	
1803		11,064,097 63				11,064,097 63	
1804		11,826,307 38				11,826,307 38	
1805		13,560,693 20				13,560,693 20	
1806		15,559,931 07				15,559,931 07	
1807		16,398,019 26				16,398,019 26	
1808		17,060,661 93				17,060,661 93	
1809		7,773,473 12				7,773,473 12	
1810		9,384,214 28			2,750,000 00	12,134,214 28	
1811		14,422,634 09				14,422,634 09	
1812		9,801,132 76			12,837,900 00	22,639,032 76	
1813		14,340,409 95	300 00		26,184,135 00	40,524,844 95	
1814		11,181,625 16	85 79		23,377,826 00	34,559,536 95	
1815		15,696,916 82	11,541 74	$32,107 64	35,220,671 40	50,961,237 60	
1816		47,676,985 66	68,665 16	686 09	9,425,084 91	57,171,421 82	
1817	202,426 30	33,099,049 74	267,819 14		466,723 45	33,833,592 33	
1818	525,000 00	21,585,171 04	412 62		8,333 00	21,593,936 66	
1819	675,000 00	24,603,374 37			2,291 00	24,605,665 37	
1820	1,000,000 00	17,840,669 55		40,000 00	3,000,824 13	20,881,493 68	
1821	105,000 00	14,573,379 72			5,000,324 00	19,573,703 72	
1822	297,500 00	20,232,427 94				20,232,427 94	
1823	350,000 00	20,540,666 26				20,540,666 26	
1824	350,000 00	19,361,212 79			5,000,000 00	24,381,212 79	
1825	367,500 00	21,840,858 02			5,000,000 00	26,840,858 02	
1826	402,500 00	25,260,434 21				25,260,434 21	
1827	420,000 00	22,966,363 96				22,966,363 96	
1828	455,000 00	24,763,629 23				24,763,629 23	
1829	490,000 00	24,827,627 38				24,827,627 38	
1830	490,000 00	24,844,116 51				24,844,116 51	
1831	490,000 00	28,526,820 82				28,526,820 82	
1832	490,000 00	31,867,450 66				31,867,450 66	$1,889 50
1833	474,985 00	33,948,426 25				33,948,426 25	
1834	234,349 50	21,791,935 55				21,791,935 55	
1835	506,480 82	35,430,087 10				35,430,087 10	
1836	292,674 67	50,826,796 08				50,826,796 08	
1837		24,954,153 04			2,992,989 15	27,947,142 19	63,288 35
1838		26,302,561 74			12,716,820 86	39,019,382 60	
1839		31,482,749 61			3,857,276 21	35,340,025 82	1,458,782 93
1840		19,480,115 33			5,589,547 51	25,069,662 84	37,469 25
1841		16,860,160 27			13,659,317 38	30,519,477 65	
1842		19,976,197 25			14,808,735 64	34,784,932 89	11,188 00
1843		8,231,001 26		71,700 83	12,479,708 36	20,782,410 45	
1844		29,320,707 78		666 60	1,877,181 35	31,198,555 73	
1845		29,970,105 80				29,970,105 80	28,251 90
1846		29,699,967 74				29,699,967 74	
1847		26,467,403 16		22,365 91	28,872,399 45	55,308,168 52	30,000 00
1848		35,698,699 21		37,080 00	21,256,700 00	56,992,479 21	
1849		30,721,077 50		487,065 48	28,588,750 00	59,796,892 98	
1850		43,592,889 82		10,550 00	4,045,950 00	47,649,388 88	
1851		52,555,039 33		4,264 22	203,400 00	52,762,704 25	
1852		49,846,815 60			46,300 00	49,893,115 60	
1853		61,587,031 68		22 50	16,350 00	61,603,404 18	103,301 37
1854		73,800,341 40			2,001 67	73,802,343 07	
1855		65,350,574 68			800 00	65,351,374 68	
1856		74,056,699 24			200 00	74,056,899 24	
1857		68,965,319 57			3,900 00	68,969,219 57	
1858		46,655,365 96			24,717,300 00	70,372,665 96	
1859		52,777,107 92		709,357 72	28,287,500 00	81,773,965 64	15,408 34
1860		56,054,599 83		10,008 00	20,776,800 00	76,841,407 83	
1861		41,476,299 49		33,630 90	41,861,709 74	83,371,640 13	
1862		51,919,261 09		68,400 00	529,692,460 50	581,680,121 59	11,110 81
1863		112,004,945 51		602,345 44	776,682,361 57	889,379,652 52	6,001 01
1864		243,412,971 20		21,174,101 01	1,128,873,945 36	1,393,461,017 57	9,210 40
1865		322,031,158 19		11,683,446 89	1,472,224,740 85	1,805,939,345 93	6,095 11

nary 1, 1843, to June 30, 1843.

TABLE G.—*Statement of the receipts of the United States*

Year.	Balance in the Treasury at commencement of year.	Customs.	Internal revenue.	Direct tax.	Public lands.	Miscellaneous.
1866	$22,383,627 40	$172,046,623 90	$309,226,813 42	$1,974,754 12	$665,031 03	$69,696,344 20
1867	162,017,000 73	176,417,810 88	306,087,337 43	4,200,233 70	1,163,555 76	15,037,326 15
1868	133,676,237 60	164,464,599 56	191,087,589 41	1,788,145 85	1,348,715 41	17,745,403 30
1869	128,308,662 67	180,048,426 63	158,356,460 86	765,685 61	4,020,344 34	13,997,338 6
1870	163,701,035 76	194,538,374 44	184,899,756 49	329,388 49	3,350,481 83	12,942,118 9
1871	177,604,116 51	206,270,408 05	143,098,153 63	580,355 37	2,388,646 68	22,093,541 21
1872	138,019,122 15	216,370,286 77	130,642,177 72		2,575,714 19	15,106,051 23
1873	134,666,091 63	188,089,569 70	113,729,314 14	315,254 51	2,882,312 38	17,161,270 45
		3,205,738,606 18	1,606,191,933 19	27,354,286 83	192,771,488 60	682,734,388 67

from March 4, 1789, to June 30, 1873, &c.—Continued.

Year.	Dividends.	Net ordinary receipts.	Interest.	Premiums.	Receipts from loans and Treasury notes.	Gross receipts.	Unavailable.
1866	....	$519,949,564 38	....	$38,083,055 68	$712,851,553 05	$1,270,884,173 11	$172,094 29
1867	....	462,846,679 92	....	27,787,330 35	640,426,910 29	1,131,060,920 56	721,827 93
							2,675,918 19
1868	....	376,434,453 82	....	29,203,629 50	625,111,433 20	1,030,749,516 52	
1869	....	357,186,256 09	....	13,755,491 12	238,678,081 06	609,691,828 27	*2,070 73
1870	....	395,959,833 87	....	15,295,643 76	285,474,496 00	696,729,973 63	
1871	....	374,431,104 94	....	8,892,839 95	268,768,523 47	659,092,468 36	*3,396 18
1872	....	364,694,229 91	....	9,412,637 65	305,047,054 00	679,153,921 56	*18,228 33
1873	....	322,177,673 78	....	11,560,530 89	214,931,017 00	548,669,221 67	*3,047 80
	99,790,136 29	5,749,093,476 31	$485,224 45	188,984,958 83	7,614,519,112 38	13,553,082,771 97	2,649,175 13

vailable, and since recovered and charged to his account.

TABLE II.—*Statement of the expenditures of the United States from March 4, 1789, to June*

Year.	War.	Navy.	Indians.	Pensions.	Miscellaneous.
1791	$632,804 03	....	$27,000 00	$175,813 88	$1,083,971 61
1792	1,100,702 09	....	13,648 85	109,243 15	4,672,664 38
1793	1,130,249 08	....	27,282 83	80,087 81	511,451 61
1794	2,639,097 59	$61,408 97	13,042 46	81,399 24	730,350 76
1795	2,480,910 13	410,562 03	23,475 68	68,673 22	1,378,920 66
1796	1,260,263 84	274,784 04	113,563 98	100,843 71	801,847 58
1797	1,039,402 46	382,631 89	62,396 58	92,256 97	1,259,422 62
1798	2,009,522 30	1,381,347 76	16,470 09	104,845 33	1,139,524 94
1799	2,466,946 98	2,858,081 84	20,302 19	95,444 03	1,039,391 09
1800	2,560,878 77	3,448,716 03	31 22	64,130 73	1,337,613 22
1801	1,672,944 08	2,111,424 00	9,000 00	73,533 37	1,114,768 45
1802	1,179,148 25	915,561 87	94,000 00	85,440 39	1,462,929 40
1803	822,055 85	1,215,230 58	60,000 00	62,902 10	1,842,635 76
1804	875,423 93	1,189,832 75	116,500 00	80,092 80	2,191,009 43
1805	712,781 28	1,597,500 00	196,500 00	81,854 59	3,768,599 73
1806	1,224,355 34	1,649,641 44	234,200 00	81,875 53	2,890,137 01
1807	1,288,085 91	1,722,064 47	205,425 00	70,500 00	1,697,897 51
1808	2,900,834 40	1,884,067 80	213,575 00	82,576 04	1,423,285 61
1809	3,345,772 17	2,427,758 80	337,503 84	87,833 54	1,215,803 79
1810	2,294,323 94	1,654,244 20	177,625 00	83,744 16	1,101,144 99
1811	2,032,828 19	1,965,566 39	151,875 00	73,043 82	1,367,291 40
1812	11,817,798 24	3,959,365 15	277,845 00	91,402 10	1,683,088 21
1813	19,652,013 02	6,446,600 10	167,358 28	86,989 91	1,724,435 61
1814	20,350,806 86	7,311,290 60	167,394 86	90,164 36	2,208,089 70
1815	14,794,294 22	8,660,000 25	530,750 00	69,656 06	2,898,870 47
1816	16,012,096 80	3,908,278 30	274,512 16	188,804 15	2,989,741 17
1817	8,004,236 53	3,314,598 49	319,463 71	297,374 43	3,518,936 76
1818	5,622,715 10	2,953,695 00	505,704 27	890,719 90	3,835,839 54
1819	6,506,300 37	3,847,640 42	463,181 39	2,415,939 85	3,067,211 41
1820	2,630,392 31	4,387,990 00	315,750 01	3,208,376 31	2,592,021 94
1821	4,461,291 78	3,319,243 06	477,005 44	242,817 25	2,223,121 54
1822	3,111,981 48	2,224,458 98	575,007 41	1,948,199 40	1,967,996 28
1823	3,096,924 43	2,503,765 83	380,781 82	1,780,588 52	2,022,093 99
1824	3,340,939 85	2,904,581 56	429,987 90	1,499,326 59	7,155,308 81
1825	3,659,914 18	3,049,083 86	724,106 44	1,308,810 57	2,748,544 89
1826	3,943,194 37	4,218,902 45	743,447 83	1,556,593 83	2,600,177 79
1827	3,948,977 88	4,263,877 45	750,624 88	976,138 86	2,713,476 58
1828	4,145,544 56	3,918,786 44	705,084 24	850,573 57	3,676,052 64
1829	4,724,291 07	3,308,745 47	576,344 74	949,594 47	3,082,234 68
1830	4,767,128 88	3,239,428 63	622,262 47	1,363,297 31	3,237,416 04
1831	4,841,835 55	3,856,183 07	930,738 04	1,170,665 14	3,084,646 10
1832	5,446,034 88	3,956,370 29	1,352,419 75	1,184,422 40	4,577,141 45
1833	6,704,019 10	3,901,356 75	1,802,980 93	4,589,152 40	5,716,945 99
1834	5,696,189 38	3,956,260 42	1,003,953 20	3,364,285 00	4,404,728 85
1835	5,759,156 89	3,864,939 06	1,706,444 48	1,951,711 32	4,229,698 33
1836	11,747,345 25	5,807,718 23	5,037,022 88	2,882,797 96	5,243,279 72
1837	13,682,730 80	6,646,914 53	4,348,036 19	2,672,160 45	9,893,370 23
1838	12,897,224 16	6,131,580 53	5,504,191 34	2,156,057 29	7,160,064 76
1839	8,916,995 80	6,182,294 25	2,528,917 28	3,142,750 51	5,725,990 89
1840	7,095,267 23	6,113,896 89	2,331,794 86	2,603,562 17	5,995,398 96
1841	8,801,610 24	6,001,076 97	2,514,837 12	2,388,434 51	6,490,881 45
1842	6,610,438 02	8,397,242 95	1,199,099 68	1,578,931 33	6,775,094 61
1843	2,908,671 95	3,727,711 53	578,371 00	839,041 12	3,902,713 09
1844	5,218,183 66	6,498,199 11	1,256,532 39	2,032,008 99	5,645,183 04
1845	5,746,291 28	6,297,177 89	1,539,351 35	2,400,788 11	5,911,780 94
1846	10,413,370 58	6,455,013 92	1,427,420 64	1,811,097 56	6,711,263 80
1847	35,840,000 33	7,900,635 76	1,430,411 30	1,744,883 63	6,885,609 33
1848	27,688,334 21	9,408,476 02	1,252,296 81	1,227,496 48	5,650,651 55
1849	14,558,473 26	9,786,705 92	1,374,161 55	1,328,867 64	12,883,334 24
1850	9,687,024 58	7,904,724 66	1,663,591 47	1,866,886 02	16,043,763 34
1851	12,161,965 11	8,880,581 87	2,829,801 77	2,293,377 22	17,888,992 18
1852	8,521,506 19	8,918,842 10	3,043,576 04	2,401,858 78	17,504,171 45
1853	9,910,498 49	11,067,789 53	3,880,494 12	1,756,306 80	17,463,009 01
1854	11,722,282 87	10,790,096 32	1,550,339 55	1,232,665 00	26,672,144 04
1855	14,648,074 07	14,327,065 11	2,772,990 78	1,477,612 33	24,090,023 33
1856	16,963,160 51	14,074,834 64	2,644,263 97	1,296,229 65	31,794,038 87
1857	19,159,150 87	12,651,604 61	4,354,418 87	1,310,380 58	34,565,498 77
1858	25,679,121 63	14,053,264 64	4,978,266 18	1,219,768 30	26,400,016 49
1859	23,154,720 53	14,690,927 90	3,490,534 53	1,222,222 71	23,797,544 49
1860	16,472,202 72	11,514,649 83	2,991,121 54	1,100,802 32	27,977,978 30
1861	23,001,530 67	12,387,156 52	2,865,481 17	1,034,599 73	23,327,287 31
1862	389,173,562 29	42,640,353 09	2,327,948 37	852,170 47	21,345,069 50
1863	600,314,411 82	63,261,235 31	3,152,032 70	1,078,513 36	23,108,382 37
1864	690,391,048 66	85,704,963 74	2,629,975 97	4,985,473 90	27,572,216 87

    * For the half year from June

1873, by calendar years, to 1843, and by fiscal years (ending June 30) from that time.

Year.	Net ordinary expenditures.	Premiums.	Interest.	Public debt.	Gross expenditures.	Balance in Treasury at the end of the year.
1791	$1,919,589 52	....	$1,177,863 03	$699,984 23	$3,797,436 78	$973,905 75
1792	5,896,258 17	....	2,373,611 28	693,050 25	8,962,920 00	783,444 51
1793	1,749,070 73	....	2,097,859 17	2,633,048 07	6,479,977 97	753,661 69
1794	3,545,299 00	....	2,752,523 04	2,743,771 13	9,041,593 17	1,151,924 17
1795	4,362,541 72	....	2,947,059 06	2,841,639 37	10,151,240 15	516,442 61
1796	2,551,303 15	....	2,839,347 68	2,577,126 01	6,367,776 84	888,995 42
1797	2,836,110 52	....	3,172,516 73	2,617,250 12	8,625,877 37	1,021,899 04
1798	4,651,710 42	....	2,955,875 90	976,032 09	8,583,618 41	617,451 43
1799	6,480,166 72	....	2,815,651 41	1,706,578 84	11,002,306 97	2,161,867 77
1800	7,411,369 97	....	3,402,601 04	1,138,563 11	11,952,534 12	2,623,311 99
1801	4,981,669 90	....	4,411,830 06	2,879,876 98	12,273,176 94	3,295,391 00
1802	3,737,079 91	....	4,239,172 16	5,294,245 24	13,270,497 31	5,020,697 64
1803	4,002,824 24	....	3,949,462 36	3,306,697 07	11,258,983 67	4,825,811 60
1804	4,452,858 91	....	4,185,048 74	3,977,206 07	12,615,113 72	4,037,005 26
1805	6,357,234 62	....	2,657,114 22	4,583,969 63	13,598,309 47	3,999,388 99
1806	6,080,209 36	....	3,308,968 26	5,572,018 64	15,021,196 26	4,538,123 80
1807	4,984,572 89	....	3,369,578 48	2,938,141 62	11,292,292 99	9,643,850 07
1808	6,504,338 85	....	2,557,074 23	7,701,288 96	16,762,702 04	9,941,809 96
1809	7,414,672 14	....	2,866,074 90	3,586,479 26	13,867,226 30	3,848,056 78
1810	5,311,082 92	....	3,163,671 09	4,835,241 12	13,309,994 49	2,672,276 57
1811	5,592,604 86	....	2,585,435 57	5,414,564 43	13,592,604 86	3,502,305 80
1812	17,829,498 70	....	2,451,272 57	1,998,349 88	22,279,121 15	3,862,217 41
1813	28,082,396 92	....	3,599,455 22	7,508,668 22	39,190,520 36	5,196,542 00
1814	30,127,686 28	....	4,593,239 04	3,307,304 90	38,028,230 32	1,727,848 63
1815	26,953,571 00	....	5,990,090 24	6,638,832 11	39,582,493 35	13,106,592 88
1816	23,373,432 58	....	7,822,923 34	17,048,139 59	48,244,495 51	22,033,519 19
1817	15,454,609 92	....	4,536,282 55	20,886,753 57	40,877,646 04	14,989,465 48
1818	13,808,673 78	....	6,209,954 03	15,086,247 59	35,104,875 40	1,478,526 74
1819	16,300,273 44	....	5,211,730 56	2,492,195 73	24,004,199 73	2,079,992 32
1820	13,134,530 57	....	5,151,004 32	3,477,489 96	21,763,024 85	1,198,461 21
1821	10,723,479 07	....	5,126,073 79	3,241,019 83	19,090,572 69	1,681,592 24
1822	9,827,643 51	....	5,172,788 79	2,676,160 33	17,676,592 63	4,237,427 55
1823	9,784,154 59	....	4,922,475 40	607,541 01	15,314,171 00	9,463,922 81
1824	15,330,144 71	....	4,943,557 93	11,624,835 83	31,898,538 47	1,946,587 13
1825	11,490,459 94	....	4,366,757 40	7,728,587 38	23,585,804 72	5,201,650 43
1826	13,062,316 27	....	3,975,542 95	7,065,539 24	24,103,398 46	6,358,686 18
1827	12,653,095 65	....	3,486,071 51	6,517,596 88	22,656,764 04	6,668,286 10
1828	13,296,041 45	....	3,098,800 60	9,064,637 47	25,459,479 52	5,972,435 81
1829	12,641,210 40	....	2,542,843 23	9,860,304 77	25,044,358 40	5,755,704 79
1830	13,229,533 33	....	1,912,574 93	9,443,173 29	24,585,281 55	6,014,539 75
1831	13,864,067 90	....	1,373,748 74	14,800,629 48	30,038,446 12	4,502,914 45
1832	16,516,388 77	....	772,561 50	17,067,747 79	34,356,698 06	2,011,777 55
1833	22,713,755 11	....	303,796 87	1,239,746 51	24,257,298 49	11,702,905 31
1834	18,425,417 25	....	202,152 98	5,974,412 21	24,601,982 44	8,892,858 42
1835	17,514,950 28	....	57,863 08	328 20	17,573,141 56	26,749,803 96
1836	30,868,164 04	....	....	....	30,868,164 04	46,708,436 00
1837	37,243,214 24	....	....	21,822 91	37,265,037 15	37,327,252 69
1838	33,849,718 08	....	14,996 48	5,590,723 79	39,455,438 35	36,891,196 94
1839	26,496,948 73	....	399,833 89	10,718,153 53	37,614,936 15	33,157,503 68
1840	24,139,920 11	....	174,598 08	3,912,015 62	28,226,533 81	29,963,163 46
1841	26,196,840 29	....	284,977 55	5,315,712 19	31,797,530 03	28,685,111 08
1842	24,361,336 59	....	773,549 85	7,801,990 09	32,936,876 53	30,521,979 44
1843	11,256,508 60	....	523,583 91	338,012 64	12,118,105 15	39,186,284 74
1844	20,650,108 01	....	1,833,452 13	11,158,450 71	33,642,010 85	36,742,829 62
1845	21,895,369 61	$18,231 43	1,040,458 18	7,536,349 49	30,490,408 71	36,194,274 81
1846	26,418,459 59	....	842,723 27	371,100 04	27,632,282 90	38,261,959 65
1847	53,501,569 37	....	1,119,214 72	5,600,067 65	60,520,851 74	33,079,276 43
1848	45,227,454 77	....	2,390,765 88	13,036,922 54	60,655,143 19	29,416,612 45
1849	38,933,542 61	82,863 81	3,565,535 78	12,804,478 54	56,386,422 74	32,827,082 69
1850	37,165,990 09	....	3,782,393 03	3,636,335 14	44,604,718 26	35,871,753 31
1851	44,054,717 66	69,713 19	3,696,760 75	654,912 71	48,476,104 31	40,158,353 25
1852	40,389,954 56	170,063 42	4,000,297 80	2,152,293 05	46,712,608 83	43,338,860 02
1853	44,078,156 35	420,498 64	3,665,832 74	6,412,574 01	54,577,061 74	50,261,901 09
1854	51,967,528 42	2,877,818 69	3,070,926 69	17,556,896 95	75,473,170 75	48,591,073 41
1855	56,316,197 72	872,047 39	2,314,464 99	6,662,065 86	66,164,775 96	47,777,672 13
1856	66,772,527 64	325,379 90	1,953,822 37	3,614,618 66	72,726,341 57	49,108,229 80
1857	68,041,143 70	363,572 39	1,593,265 23	3,276,606 05	71,274,587 37	46,802,855 00
1858	72,330,437 17	574,443 08	1,652,055 67	7,505,250 82	82,062,186 74	35,113,334 22
1859	66,355,950 07	....	2,637,649 70	14,685,043 15	83,678,642 92	33,193,248 60
1860	60,056,754 71	....	3,144,120 94	13,854,250 00	77,055,125 65	32,979,530 78
1861	62,616,055 78	....	4,034,157 30	18,737,100 00	85,387,313 08	30,963,857 83
1862	456,379,896 81	....	13,190,344 84	96,097,322 09	565,667,563 74	46,965,304 87
1863	694,004,575 56	....	24,729,700 62	181,081,635 07	899,815,911 25	36,523,046 13
1864	811,283,679 14	....	53,685,421 69	430,572,014 03	1,295,541,114 86	134,433,738 44

ary 1, 1843, to June 30, 1843.

TABLE H.—*Statement of the expenditures of the United*

Year.	War.	Navy.	Indians.	Pensions.	Miscellaneous.
1865	$1,030,690,400 06	$122,617,434 07	$5,039,360,71	$16,347,621 34	$42,929,352 10
1866	283,154,676 06	43,265,662 00	3,295,729 32	15,605,549 52	40,613,114 17
	3,569,620,312 28	717,551,816 39	163,399,211 42	119,607,656 01	643,604,534 33
	*2,621,780 07	*77,992 17	*53,286 61	*9,737 87	*712,709 90
1867	3,572,260,098 25	717,629,808 56	103,492,498 03	119,617,393 88	644,321,382 05
1868	95,234,415 63	31,034,011 04	4,642,531 77	29,006,531 71	31,110,229 78
1869	123,246,648 62	25,775,502 72	4,100,682 32	23,782,386 78	32,030,662 67
1870	78,501,990 61	20,000,737 97	7,042,923 06	28,476,621 78	26,174,081 59
1871	57,655,675 40	21,780,229 87	3,407,938 15	32,346,202 17	42,127,461 36
1872	35,799,991 82	19,431,027 21	7,426,997 44	34,443,894 88	60,481,916 85
1873	35,372,157 20	21,349,809 90	7,061,728 12	32,331,602 76	60,984,737 64
	46,382,138 31	23,526,256 79	7,951,704 88	29,359,426,90	71,342,110 08
	4,044,284,109 94	680,427,404 15	145,057,004 47	313,489,889 82	1,052,949,728 04

* Outstanding

NOTE.—This statement is made from warrants paid by the Treasurer up to June 30, 1866. The balance in the Treasury June 30, 1873, by this statement, is $159,293,673.41, from which should be 30, 1873, $131,192,008.50.

States from March 4, 1789, *to June* 30, 1873—Continued.

Year.	Net ordinary expenditures.	Premiums.	Interest.	Public debt.	Gross expenditures.	Balance in Treasury at the end of the year.
1865	$1,217,704,199 28	$1,717,900 11	$77,395,090 30	$609,616,141 68	$1,906,433,331 37	$33,933,657 83
1866	385,954,731 43	58,476 51	133,067,624 91	690,263,249 10	1,139,344,081 95	165,301,654 76
	5,159,771,550 43	7,611,003 56	502,689,519 27	2,374,677,103 12	8,037,749,170 38	
	*4,481,566 24	....	*2,888 48	*100 31	*4,484,555 03	*4,484,555 03
1867	5,157,253,116 67	7,611,003 56	502,692,407 75	2,374,677,203 43	8,042,233,731 41	160,817,099 73
1868	292,947,733 87	10,813,349 38	143,781,591 91	735,536,980 11	1,093,079,655 27	198,076,537 09
1869	229,915,088 11	7,001,151 04	140,424,045 71	692,549,685 88	1,069,889,970 74	158,936,082 87
1870	190,496,354 95	1,674,680 05	130,694,242 80	261,912,718 31	584,777,996 11	183,781,985 76
1871	164,421,507 15	15,996,555 60	129,235,498 00	393,254,282 13	702,907,842 88	177,604,116 51
1871	157,583,827 58	9,016,794 74	125,576,565 93	399,503,670 65	691,680,858 90	138,019,122 15
1872	153,201,856 19	6,958,266 76	117,357,839 72	405,007,307 54	682,525,270 21	134,666,001 85
1873	180,488,636 90	5,105,919 99	104,750,688 44	233,699,352 58	524,044,597 91	159,293,673 41
	6,436,308,121 42	64,177,721 12	1,394,512,880 26	5,496,141,200 63	13,391,139,923 43	

warrants.

outstanding warrants are then added, and the statement is by warrants *issued* from that date. The deducted the amount deposited with the States, $28,101,644.91, leaving the net available. balance, June

TABLE I.—*Statement of the differences between the several accounts showing the outstanding principal of the public debt, with an explanation thereof, so far as the examination of the accounts has progressed.*

The statement of receipts (Table G) shows the amount which has been covered into the Treasury, as derived from loans and Treasury notes, from the organization of the Government to and including June 30, 1873, to have been............................ $7,614,519,112 36
The statement of expenditures (Table H) shows the payments from the Treasury for the redemption and purchase of loans and Treasury notes for the same period to have been............................ 5,496,141,200 63

Showing the principal outstanding by these tables, June 30, 1873............... 2,118,377,911 73
The *actual* outstanding principal, at that date, as shown by Tables F and O, and by the debt statement of July 1, 1873, was............................ 2,234,482,993 20

Showing............................ 116,105,081 45

more outstanding and unpaid principal by the debt statement, and by Tables F and O, than by the receipts and expenditures, Tables G and H.

This difference of $116,105,081.45 is thus explained: The following stocks were issued in payment of various debts and claims, but in the transaction no money ever came into the Treasury. When the stock matured it was paid out of the general funds then in the Treasury. This showed an expenditure where there had been no corresponding receipt, and, of course, a statement of the debt made from the receipts and expenditures on account of loans and Treasury notes would not be correct unless these items were added to the receipt side of the account. This cannot be done until legislation has been had authorizing it:

French farmers-general loan	$153,689 50
French loan of eighteen million livres	3,367,000 00
Spanish loan of 1781	174,017 12
French loan of ten million livres	1,815,000 00
French loan of six million livres	1,088,000 00
Balance of supplies due France	94,338 16
Dutch loan of 1782	2,000,000 00
Dutch loan of 1784	800,000 00
Debt due foreign officers	186,988 75
Dutch loan of 1787	400,000 00
Dutch loan of 1788	400,000 00
Interest due on the foreign debt	1,771,496 90
Domestic debt of the Revolution, *estimated*	63,918,475 44

The above are the details (so far as the progress of the examination has developed them) of the item in the finance report of 1871, (page 20,) "Revolutionary debt, *estimated, $76,000,000*."

Mississippi-purchase stock	4,282,151 12
Louisiana-purchase stock	11,250,000 00
Washington and Georgetown debt assumed by the United States	1,500,000 00
United States Bank subscription stock	7,000,000 00
Six per cent. Navy stock	711,700 00
Texas-purchase stock	5,000,000 00
Mexican indemnity stock	303,573 92
Bounty-land scrip	333,075 00
Tompkins fraud in loan of 1798	1,000 00

The following amounts represent the discounts suffered in placing the loans named; only the money actually received was covered into the Treasury. The difference between this and the face value of the stock issued was the discount. To make the receipts and expenditures on the loan accounts correct, these discounts should be credited to the loans as receipts and charged to a discount account. This also requires legislation to enable it to be done:

Loan of 1796	10,000 00
Loan of February, 1813	2,100,377 43
Loan of August, 1813	996,561 93
Ten-million loan of 1814	1,963,895 25
Six-million loan of 1814	1,076,626 97
Undesignated stock of 1814	93,869 93
Loan of March, 1815	566,620 93
Loan of February, 1861	2,019,776 10

The foregoing are the details of the difference of $116,105,081.45, so far as the examination of the public-debt accounts has progressed. There still remains to be explained............................ 942,633 83
Which is the resultant error arising out of differences yet to be discovered and reconciled. The full details of this item can only be given after the accounts have all been examined and corrected, and the amount of it may be increased or diminished when the examination of the domestic debt of the Revolution shall have shown what *its* true amount is. This examination is still being continued, for the purpose of perfecting the records.

Total............................ 116,105,081 45

TABLE K.—*Statement showing the condition of the sinking-fund, from its institution in May, 1869, to and including June 30, 1873.*

THE SECRETARY OF THE TREASURY IN ACCOUNT WITH SINKING-FUND.

Dr.

Date	Item	Amount	Total
July 1, 1868..	To ¼ of 1 per cent. on the principal of the public debt, being for the three months from April 1 to June 30, 1868	$4,539,219 63	
June 30, 1869.	To interest on $6,691,000, being amount of principal of public debt purchased during fiscal year 1869 on this account	196,590 00	
	Balance to new account	672,080 23	
			7,397,889 86
July 1, 1869..	To 1 per cent. on the principal of the public debt on June 30, 1869, $2,588,452,213.94	25,884,592 14	
June 30, 1870.	To interest on $6,691,000, amount of redemption in 1869	321,460 00	
	To interest on $29,151,900, amount of principal of public debt purchased during fiscal year 1870 on this account	1,254,897 00	
			27,660,679 14
July 1, 1870..	To balance from last year	744,711 80	
July 1, 1870.	To 1 per cent. on the principal of the public debt on June 30, 1870, $2,460,672,427.81	24,806,724 29	
June 30, 1871.	To interest on redemption of 1869, $6,691,000	321,460 00	
	To interest on redemption of 1870, $29,151,900	1,689,114 00	
	To interest on $29,936,250, amount of principal of public debt purchased during fiscal year 1871 on this account	1,357,264 50	
			29,319,274 58
July 1, 1871..	To balance from last year	257,474 38	
June 30, 1872.	To 1 per cent. on the principal of the public debt on June 30, 1871, $2,353,211,332.59	23,532,113 32	
	To interest on redemption of 1869, $6,691,000	321,460 00	
	To interest on redemption of 1870, $29,151,900	1,689,114 00	
	To interest on redemption of 1871, $29,936,250	1,706,175 00	
	To interest of redemption of $32,618,450, amount of principal of public debt purchased during fiscal year 1872 on this account	2,059,385 50	
	To balance to new account	2,683,891 46	
			32,679,553 60

Cr.

Date	Item	Amount	Total
June 30, 1869.	By amount of principal purchased, $6,691,000, including $1,000 donation, estimated in gold	$7,261,437 30	
	By accrued interest on the amount of purchases in 1869	136,392 56	
			7,397,889 86
July 1, 1869..	By balance from last year	672,080 23	
June 30, 1870.	By amount of principal purchased, $29,151,900, estimated in gold	25,893,143 57	
	By accrued interest on account of purchases in 1870	351,003 54	
	By balance to new account	744,711 80	
			27,660,679 14
June 30, 1871.	By amount of principal purchased, $29,936,250, estimated in gold	28,694,017 73	
	By accrued interest on account of purchases in 1871	367,782 53	
	By balance to new account	257,474 38	
			29,319,274 58
June 30, 1872.	By amount of principal purchased, $32,618,450, estimated in gold	32,248,645 22	
	By accrued interest on account of purchases in 1872	430,908 38	
			32,679,553 60

TABLE K.—Statement of the condition of the sinking-fund, &c.—Continued.

Dr.			Cr.	
July 1, 1872...	To 1 per cent. on the principal of the public debt on June 30, 1872, $1,353,251,254.78	$8,532,513 24	July 1, 1872... By balance from last year	$2,853,891 46
June 30, 1873.	To interest on redemption of 1869, $2,691,000	221,449 00	June 30, 1873. By amount of principal purchased, $23,678,000, estimated in gold	22,457,562 83
	To interest on redemption of 1870, $26,151,900	1,963,114 00	By accrued interest on account of purchases in 1873	322,385 43
	To interest on redemption of 1871, $29,936,250	1,736,175 00		
	To interest on redemption of 1872, $22,618,459	1,457,107 00		
	To interest on redemption of $23,678,000, amount of principal of public debt purchased during fiscal year 1873 on this account	1,725,961 50		
	To balance to new account	1,431,538 00		
		31,673,839 74		31,673,839 74

TABLE L.—*Statement showing the purchases of bonds on account of the sinking-fund during each fiscal year from its institution in May, 1869, to and including June 30, 1873.*

Year ended—	Principal redeemed.	Premium paid.	Net cost in currency.	Net cost estimated in gold.	Interest due at close of fiscal year.	Accrued interest paid in coin.	Balance of interest due at close of fiscal year.
JUNE 30, 1869.							
Five-twenties of 1862	$1,621,000 00	$253,892 84	$1,874,892 84	$1,349,970 08	$16,210 00	$7,394 60	$8,825 40
Five-twenties of March, 1864	70,000 00	111,725 00	181,725 00	57,552 88	700 00	218 63	481 37
Five-twenties of June, 1864	1,051,000 00	161,946 45	1,212,946 45	873,552 61	10,510 00	1,470 43	9,039 58
Five-twenties of 1865	485,000 00	74,960 00	559,960 00	367,566 99	4,650 00	2,683 54	1,966 46
Consols, 1865	461,000 00	73,736 88	534,736 88	367,903 98	13,630 00	689 54	13,400 96
Consols, 1867	4,718,000 00	749,909 98	5,467,909 98	3,946,966 11	141,540 00	116,033 33	25,507 65
Consols, 1868	305,000 00	49,448 50	354,448 50	256,653 90	9,150 00	9,173 98	976 02
Total	8,691,000 00	1,374,850 67	10,065,850 67	7,261,437 30	196,590 00	136,368 56	60,197 44
JUNE 30, 1870.							
Five-twenties of 1862	3,542,050 00	493,479 42	4,035,529 42	3,953,099 51	160,919 50	45,994 49	114,925 01
Five-twenties of March, 1864	85,000 00	15,742 87	100,742 87	75,658 54	5,350 00	1,080 99	4,269 01
Five-twenties of June, 1864	3,971,400 00	506,189 91	4,477,589 91	3,647,628 99	165,834 00	49,946 00	115,888 00
Five-twenties of 1865	2,790,250 00	361,731 43	3,151,985 43	2,606,636 90	105,257 50	37,113 53	68,143 97
Consols, 1865	11,332,250 00	1,454,778 37	12,996,998 37	10,631,726 97	495,491 50	145,518 99	349,903 91
Consols, 1867	5,682,550 00	661,763 73	6,744,313 73	5,309,810 90	302,734 50	65,111 51	236,623 99
Consols, 1868	348,500 00	53,363 95	401,963 95	308,573 16	19,380 00	5,238 73	14,141 27
Total	28,151,900 00	3,767,053 68	31,898,953 68	25,863,143 57	1,254,897 00	351,003 54	903,893 46
JUNE 30, 1871.							
Five-twenties of 1862	2,792,950 00	297,607 56	3,090,557 56	2,680,909 05	145,975 00	36,657 80	109,317 30
Five-twenties of March, 1864	29,500 00	2,277 90	31,777 90	29,590 88	1,940 00	388 15	851 65
Five-twenties of June, 1864	3,967,350 00	340,529 63	4,307,879 63	3,847,189 42	201,375 00	51,703 46	149,671 54
Five-twenties of 1865	6,768,600 00	574,923 00	7,343,523 00	3,525,231 42	331,933 50	92,929 58	239,673 98
Consols, 1865	10,222,200 00	830,949 79	11,073,149 79	9,782,367 78	592,117 00	109,455 99	412,661 72
Consols, 1867	6,103,000 00	541,559 41	6,644,609 41	5,800,618 37	331,598 00	76,745 99	274,789 07
Consols, 1868	53,600 00	4,784 61	57,364 61	49,797 81	3,096 00	5,572 13	3,585 87
Total	29,936,250 00	2,542,631 20	28,478,881 20	28,694,017 73	1,557,964 50	367,782 53	1,189,461 97

TABLE 1.—*Statement showing the purchases of bonds on account of the sinking-fund during each fiscal year from its institution, &c.—Continued.*

Year ended—	Principal redeemed.	Premium paid.	Net cost in currency.	Net cost estimated in gold.	Interest due at close of fiscal year.	Accrued interest paid in coin.	Balance of interest due at close of fiscal year.
JUNE 30, 1872.							
Five-twenties of 1862	$6,417,850 00	$764,055 91	$7,181,905 91	$6,345,391 98	$457,849 00	$73,179 43	$332,669 57
Five-twenties of March, 1864	127,100 00	14,939 03	142,039 03	120,123 46	8,894 00	1,332 70	7,555 30
Five-twenties of June, 1864	3,604,650 00	438,656 16	4,043,306 16	3,573,225 63	246,001 50	57,449 40	188,551 70
Five-twenties of 1865	3,635,900 00	436,989 46	4,072,889 46	3,594,747 85	246,569 00	37,817 37	208,744 63
Consols, 1865	11,789,900 00	1,435,999 46	13,225,899 46	11,660,785 69	707,334 00	149,848 21	554,085 79
Consols, 1867	6,939,900 00	852,600 15	7,792,500 15	6,883,777 39	417,334 00	108,497 92	309,046 08
Consols, 1868	65,850 00	9,951 63	83,801 63	84,595 08	5,151 00	1,366 93	3,764 03
Total	32,618,450 00	3,953,050 34	38,553,500 34	32,948,645 22	2,059,325 60	430,908 39	1,628,417 19
JUNE 30, 1873.							
Five-twenties of 1862	7,137,100 00	925,783 87	8,062,883 87	7,069,542 58	431,450 50	101,960 57	329,489 93
Five-twenties of March, 1864	50,000 00	7,372 50	57,372 50	49,789 91	3,500 00	813 70	2,686 30
Five-twenties of June, 1864	3,741,150 00	480,684 37	4,221,634 37	3,715,211 92	223,270 50	42,216 46	181,054 04
Five-twenties of 1865	1,924,650 00	250,835 93	2,810,485 93	1,943,449 80	190,986 50	93,744 47	96,282 03
Consols, 1865	10,768,250 00	1,371,187 17	12,139,437 17	10,686,617 09	644,085 00	143,039 31	501,035 60
Consols, 1867	4,462,100 00	1,533,610 69	4,985,710 69	4,372,781 76	984,136 00	69,632 51	194,493 49
Consols, 1868	619,550 00	81,983 44	701,533 44	617,140 34	37,173 00	6,948 60	29,224 40
Total	28,678,000 00	3,671,259 17	38,369,258 17	28,457,589 83	1,735,681 50	392,385 43	1,333,496 06
Grand total	129,075,600 00	15,370,644 08	163,346,444 08	132,354,606 65	6,760,956 50	1,678,472 46	5,115,486 04

TABLE M.—*Statement showing the purchase of bonds in excess of the amount required for the sinking-fund during each fiscal year from the commencement of the purchases in May, 1869, to and including June 30, 1873.*

Year ended—	Principal redeemed.	Premium paid.	Net cost in currency.	Net cost estimated in gold.	Interest due at close of fiscal year.	Accrued interest paid in coin.	Balance of interest due at close of fiscal year.
JUNE 30, 1870.							
Five-twenties of 1862	$9,975,250 00	$1,438,465 74	$11,413,715 74	$9,926,361 36	$502,456 55	$110,968 99	$391,487 56
Five-twenties of March, 1864	597,400 00	116,951 00	714,351 00	532,072 21	40,948 00	9,621 13	31,326 87
Five-twenties of June, 1864	11,742,700 00	1,767,653 37	13,510,353 37	10,680,518 91	599,697 55	146,031 16	443,666 39
Five-twenties, 1865	7,620,350 00	1,102,967 36	8,723,317 36	7,051,018 61	329,437 85	94,005 47	224,432 38
Consols, 1865	36,118,900 00	5,242,087 61	41,360,297 61	32,725,094 63	1,861,918 50	483,633 72	1,378,284 78
Consols, 1867	18,436,800 00	2,922,445 22	21,349,245 22	16,374,250 02	1,037,797 00	206,748 91	830,978 79
Consols, 1868	2,105,500 00	364,879 14	2,470,379 14	1,869,116 40	121,495 00	22,141 27	100,353 73
Total	86,566,200 00	12,955,449 44	99,541,649 44	78,309,437 46	4,494,660 45	1,074,149 95	3,410,530 50
JUNE 30, 1871.							
Five-twenties of 1862	7,695,250 00	725,443 91	8,420,693 91	7,517,631 86	315,665 00	88,115 14	227,749 86
Five-twenties of March, 1864	100,500 00	10,869 85	111,369 85	100,135 51	1,335 00	196 94	1,138 06
Five-twenties of June, 1864	7,145,950 00	637,670 36	7,863,620 36	6,968,994 28	280,772 50	88,675 68	192,097 48
Five-twenties, 1865	9,117,730 00	677,459 15	9,995,599 15	8,875,458 67	362,211 00	90,147 01	272,063 99
Consols, 1865	24,476,800 00	2,348,715 50	26,825,515 50	23,917,430 49	969,468 00	355,520 04	633,901 96
Consols, 1867	10,741,550 00	1,011,485 32	11,753,035 32	10,430,837 44	478,047 00	153,991 14	324,055 86
Consols, 1868	163,600 00	16,802 01	180,402 01	139,625 18	6,813 00	2,780 76	4,032 34
Total	59,441,400 00	5,648,436 50	65,069,836 50	57,969,533 42	2,433,525 50	779,186 05	1,654,339 45
JUNE 30, 1872.							
Five-twenties of 1862	12,394,000 00	1,359,618 69	13,723,618 69	12,317,468 38	334,467 00	132,389 84	222,097 16
Five-twenties of March, 1864	34,000 00	6,549 90	60,549 90	53,884 81	1,020 00	389 92	630 08
Five-twenties of June, 1864	4,299,550 00	493,186 15	4,791,736 15	4,279,333 48	104,153 50	46,636 00	57,527 41
Five-twenties, 1865	1,968,400 00	208,329 93	2,077,629 93	1,858,868 91	40,336 00	16,649 98	32,886 04
Consols, 1865	7,909,700 00	959,620 72	8,908,320 72	7,975,883 64	237,501 00	153,887 37	81,613 63
Consols, 1867	705,750 00	95,671 84	800,821 84	703,446 24	21,285 00	13,956 70	7,339 30
Consols, 1868	8,950 00	1,170 36	10,120 36	6,919 01	283 50	186 94	96 56
Total	27,210,350 00	3,166,450 59	30,376,800 59	27,098,083 47	769,266 00	366,096 93	402,179 18

6 Ab

TABLE M.—*Statement showing the purchases of bonds in excess of the amount required for the sinking-fund during each fiscal year, &c.—Continued.*

Year ended—	Principal redeemed.	Premium paid.	Net cost in currency.	Net cost estimated in gold.	Interest due at close of fiscal year.	Accrued interest paid in coin.	Balance of interest due at close of fiscal year.
JUNE 30, 1873.							
Five-twenties of 1862	$3,068,300 00	$455,488 12	$3,587,788 12	$3,068,586 79	$113,440 00	$58,369 39	$37,070 61
Five-twenties of March, 1864	6,300 00	956 16	7,256 16	6,182 53	198 00	4 14	193 86
Five-twenties of June, 1864	1,915,450 00	272,520 16	2,187,970 16	1,985,085 70	63,666 00	98,376 00	77,990 61
Five-twenties, 1865	550,700 00	78,273 53	628,973 53	543,974 43	16,990 00	6,390 43	10,599 57
Consols, 1865	2,579,700 00	385,648 53	2,965,348 53	2,354,176 08	58,391 00	82,828 07	44,549 12
Consols, 1867	897,500 00	121,083 50	998,313 50	946,313 88	33,717 00	4,229 17	18,568 12
Consols, 1868	302,300 00	47,386 30	349,686 30	307,654 88	9,046 00	4,670 48	4,400 12
Total	8,059,900 00	1,991,497 65	10,905,907 65	8,098,660 00	301,090 00	131,189 76	168,642 06
Grand total	168,941,750 00	53,061,766 18	205,363,516 18	178,574,639 95	7,997,560 95	2,333,045 08	6,654,980 37

NOTE.—This and the preceding table show the entire amount of bonds purchased from the commencement of the purchases to and including June 30, 1873. In this connection attention is invited to the note at the end of Table N.

TABLE N.—*Statement showing the purchases of bonds from May, 1869, to September 30, 1873.*

Date of purchase.		Opening price of gold.	Principal.	Amount paid.	Currency value of interest accrued on bonds bought "flat."	Net cost.	Net cost estimated in gold.	Average rate of premium on each purchase.	Average cost in gold of each purchase.	Average rate of premium on total purchases to date.	Average cost in gold of total purchases to date.
1869.											
May	12	138¼	$1,000,000 00	$1,155,070 00	$2,504 36	$1,152,565 64	$838,177 36	15.26	83.29		
	19	142	70,000 00	81,718 00		81,718 00	57,548 45	16.74	82.21		
	19	142	1,000,000 00	1,168,512 10		1,168,512 10	822,895 85	16.85	82.29		
	27	139¾	1,000,000 00	1,153,581 50		1,153,581 50	826,940 14	15.36	82.69	15.84	82.72
June	3	138⅛	1,000,000 00	1,164,058 90	711 78	1,164,770 68	842,510 43	16.46	84.25		
	10	138⅝	1,000,000 00	1,161,967 00		1,161,967 00	838,208 84	16.20	83.82		
	16	138	1,000 00	1,155 00		1,155 00	836 44	15.50	83.64		
	17	138¼	1,000,000 00	1,152,950 00		1,152,950 00	833,960 21	15.30	83.40		
	23	137⅛	1,620,000 00	1,870,402 50		1,870,402 50	1,364,012 76	15.46	84.20		
	26	137⅜	1,000,000 00	1,158,228 25		1,158,228 25	842,347 82	15.82	84.23	15.82	83.55
July	1	137⅜	1,000,000 00	1,158,098 75		1,158,098 75	842,253 63	15.81	84.22		
	3	137	3,000,000 00	3,496,474 00		3,496,474 00	2,552,170 80	16.54	85.07		
	9	136	3,000,000 00	3,518,044 00		3,518,044 00	2,586,797 06	17.27	86.23		
	14	137⅜	3,000,000 00	3,607,622 90		3,607,622 90	2,626,113 19	20.25	87.54		
	15	137	1,000,000 00	1,201,850 00		1,201,850 00	877,262 77	20.18	87.73		
	21	135⅛	3,000,000 00	3,600,028 80		3,600,028 80	2,664,281 12	20.00	88.81		
	28	136⅜	3,000,000 00	3,604,859 00		3,604,859 00	2,640,922 34	20.16	88.03		
	29	135⅝	1,000,000 00	1,201,570 55		1,201,570 55	885,134 84	20.16	88.51	17.85	85.93
August	4	136	2,000,000 00	2,431,136 80		2,431,136 80	1,787,600 59	21.56	89.38		
	11	135½	2,000,000 00	2,422,036 27		2,422,036 27	1,787,462 12	21.10	89.37		
	12	135⅛	1,000,000 00	1,198,931 70		1,198,931 70	887,376 00	19.89	88.73		
	18	133	2,000,000 00	2,378,781 81		2,378,781 81	1,788,557 75	18.94	89.43		
	25	133¼	2,000,000 00	2,389,539 01		2,389,539 01	1,793,275 07	19.48	89.66		
	26	133⅞	1,000,000 00	1,196,247 80		1,196,247 80	893,555 78	19.63	89.36	18.48	86.87
September	1	133⅜	2,000,000 00	2,401,991 00		2,401,991 00	1,800,930 46	20.10	90.05		
	8	136	2,000,000 00	2,356,000 00		2,356,000 00	1,732,352 94	17.80	86.62		
	9	135⅞	1,000,000 00	1,183,972 53		1,183,972 53	871,368 92	18.40	87.14		
	15	136⅛	2,000,000 00	2,369,639 55		2,369,639 55	1,740,782 04	18.48	87.04		
	22	137⅞	2,000,000 00	2,337,657 62		2,337,657 62	1,697,029 12	16.88	84.85		
	23	141⅝	1,000,000 00	1,165,548 50		1,165,548 50	822,962 17	16.55	82.30		
	25	133⅜	3,000,000 00	3,537,158 16		3,537,158 16	2,647,078 14	17.91	88.24		
	29	133⅝	3,000,000 00	3,473,533 12		3,473,533 12	2,599,463 51	15.78	86.65	18.38	86.91
October	6	130	2,000,000 00	2,319,139 18		2,319,139 18	1,783,953 22	15.96	89.20		
	7	131⅛	1,000,000 00	1,159,945 10		1,159,945 10	884,610 18	15.99	88.46		
	7	131⅛	*153,500 00	178,187 69		178,187 69	135,891 47	16.08	88.53		
	13	130⅛	2,000,000 00	2,318,883 53		2,318,883 53	1,782,043 06	15.94	89.10		
	20	130	2,000,000 00	2,314,079 00		2,314,079 00	1,780,060 77	15.70	89.00		

Table N.—Statement showing the purchases of bonds from May, 1869, to September 30, 1870—Continued.

Date of purchase.	Opening price of Gold.	Principal.	Amount paid.	Currency value of premium received on bonds sold.	Net cost.	Net cost of purchase.	Amount rate of premium.	Cost of purchase rate per day.	Average rate of premium paid.
1869.									
October 31									
November 3									
4									
5									
10									
17									
24									
December 1									
8									
15									
22									
30									
1870.									
January 5									
11									
13									
19									
27									
February 10									
11									
24									
March 3									
10									
17									
24									
30									
April 7									
13									

	2	113⅞	1,000,000 00	1,078,778 18		1,078,778 18	951,513 28	7.88	95.15		
	27	113¼	1,000,000 00	1,100,490 79		1,100,490 79	966,409 45	10.05	96.64		
	30	114½	*345,400 00	390,847 25	7,826 85	383,080 40	333,423 63	10.69	96.53		
	30	114¼	*758,800 00	859,029 25	18,099 70	840,929 55	732,038 78	10.82	96.47	15.10	89.36
May	5	114⅞	2,000,000 00	2,215,447 70		2,215,447 70	1,932,778 80	10.77	96.64		
	12	115⅛	*1,850 00	2,074 31	3 85	2,070 46	1,794 55	11.92	97.00		
	12	115⅜	1,000,000 00	1,118,370 86		1,118,370 86	969,335 52	11.84	96.93		
	19	114⅝	2,000,000 00	2,230,611 87		2,230,611 87	1,943,888 34	11.53	97.19		
	26	114¼	1,000,000 00	1,108,910 71		1,108,910 71	970,600 18	10.89	97.06	14.90	89.76
June	2	114⅛	2,000,000 00	2,223,786 41		2,223,786 41	1,942,171 53	11.19	97.11		
	9	113¼	1,000,000 00	1,109,976 64		1,109,976 64	977,959 99	11.00	97.79		
	16	113⅝	2,000,000 00	2,217,755 94		2,217,755 94	1,960,447 24	10.89	98.02		
	23	111⅛	1,000,000 00	1,104,612 10		1,104,612 10	989,574 11	10.46	98.96		
	30	111⅜	2,000,000 00	2,218,005 71		2,218,005 71	1,987,015 19	10.90	99.35	14.63	90.31
July	7	112⅛	1,000,000 00	1,107,000 00		1,107,000 00	987,290 97	10.70	98.73		
	11	115¼	*690,400 00	758,749 60		758,749 60	659,065 88	9.90	95.46		
	11	115¼	*1,683,150 00	1,848,423 98		1,848,423 98	1,605,580 00	9.82	95.39		
	14	112⅝	2,000,000 00	2,182,332 89		2,182,332 89	1,933,406 77	9.12	96.67		
	21	121⅜	1,000,000 00	1,070,136 00		1,070,136 00	878,961 81	7.01	87.90		
	28	121⅜	2,000,000 00	2,162,085 83		2,162,085 83	1,777,665 64	8.10	88.88	14.29	90.52
August	4	121⅜	1,000,000 00	1,085,712 21		1,085,712 21	891,735 41	8.57	89.17		
	11	116¼	2,000,000 00	2,191,414 93		2,191,414 93	1,885,089 11	9.57	94.25		
	18	116⅝	1,000,000 00	1,097,329 29		1,097,329 29	939,896 61	9.73	93.99		
	25	117⅞	2,000,000 00	2,181,093 02		2,181,093 02	1,850,344 02	9.05	92.52	14.07	90.62
September	1	116⅞	1,000,000 00	1,091,038 65		1,091,038 65	937,519 78	9.10	93.75		
	8	114	3,000,000 00	3,272,957 77		3,272,957 77	2,871,015 58	9.10	95.70		
	15	114⅝	2,000,000 00	2,183,503 11		2,183,503 11	1,909,073 76	9.18	95.45		
	22	113⅞	3,000,000 00	3,281,789 74		3,281,789 74	2,881,922 93	9.39	96.06		
	29	113⅜	2,000,000 00	2,177,057 86		2,177,057 86	1,911,796 14	8.85	95.59	13.71	90.98
October	6	113	2,000,000 00	2,174,300 26		2,174,300 26	1,924,159 52	8.72	96.21		
	13	113¼	2,000,000 00	2,170,465 37		2,170,465 37	1,906,006 91	8.52	95.30		
	20	112⅞	2,000,000 00	2,170,236 48		2,170,236 48	1,922,690 12	8.51	96.13		
	27	112	2,000,000 00	2,165,529 30		2,165,529 30	1,933,808 30	8.28	96.68	13.44	91.24
November	3	110⅞	1,000,000 00	1,077,698 19		1,077,698 19	973,090 92	7.77	97.31		
	3	110⅞	*245,850 00	265,173 81		265,173 81	239,434 59	7.86	97.39		
	3	110⅞	*542,250 00	584,808 61	8 06	584,800 55	528,036 61	7.85	97.39		
	10	110⅞	1,000,000 00	1,072,263 90		1,072,263 90	971,473 52	7.23	97.15		
	17	113	1,000,000 00	1,064,972 36		1,064,972 36	942,453 42	6.50	94.25		
	25	112	1,000,000 00	1,065,650 15		1,065,650 15	951,473 35	6.56	95.15	13.25	91.39
December	1	110⅝	1,000,000 00	1,064,917 08		1,064,917 08	969,636 91	6.49	96.26		
	8	110⅞	1,000,000 00	1,063,854 32		1,063,854 32	961,676 22	6.38	96.17		
	15	111⅛	1,000,000 00	1,065,972 75		1,065,972 75	958,177 75	6.60	95.82		
	22	110⅝	1,000,000 00	1,064,459 26		1,064,459 26	962,293 06	6.45	96.22		
	29	110⅞	1,000,000 00	1,064,473 95		1,064,473 95	961,150 29	6.45	96.11	13.05	91.53
1871.											
January	4	110⅞	2,000,000 00	2,147,345 03		2,147,345 03	1,938,911 99	7.37	96.96		
	11	111	1,000,000 00	1,074,257 50		1,074,257 50	967,799 55	7.43	96.78		
	18	110⅞	2,000,000 00	2,144,457 32		2,144,457 32	1,938,409 49	7.22	96.92		
	25	110⅝	1,000,000 00	1,074,651 96		1,074,651 96	971,436 80	7.46	97.14	12.85	91.72
February	1	111⅛	2,000,000 00	2,173,985 90		2,173,985 90	1,943,227 62	8.70	97.16		
	8	111⅜	2,000,000 00	2,175,643 46		2,175,643 46	1,946,884 53	8.78	97.34		

TABLE N.—*Statement showing the purchases of bonds from May, 1869, to September 30, 1873—Continued.*

Date of purchase.	Opening price of gold.	Principal.	Amount paid.	Currency value of interest accrued on bonds bought "flat."	Net cost.	Net cost estimated in Gold.	Average rate of premium on each purchase.	Average cost in gold of each purchase.	Average rate of premium on total purchases to date.	Average cost in gold of total purchases to date.
1871.										
February 15							9.91	94.16	12.68	91.99
21							9.59	94.19		
March 1							8.99	94.39		
8							8.89	94.61		
15							8.94	94.71	12.52	96.34
22							9.16	94.08		
29							8.17	94.78		
April 5							8.65	94.98		
12							9.59	94.68		
19							10.57	94.66	12.41	92.71
26							10.78	94.47		
May 3							11.06	94.43		
10							11.16	94.38		
17							11.43	94.77		
24							11.31	94.61	12.35	93.04
31							11.58	94.96		
June 7							11.49	94.67		
14							11.67	94.96		
21							13.94	94.67	12.34	93.16
28							12.36	94.96		
July 5							12.97	94.98		
12							12.91	94.97		
19							12.09	94.30		
26							11.99	94.15	12.34	93.96
August 2							12.31	94.98		
9							12.56	94.69		
16							13.20	94.13		
23							13.34	94.49	12.36	93.33
30							13.18	94.78		
September 6							13.13	94.67		
13							11.72	97.13	12.36	92.29
20										
27										
October 4										
11										

1872.

TABLE L.—*Statement showing the purchases of bonds on account of the sinking-fund during each fiscal year from its institution, &c.*—Continued.

Year ended—	Principal redeemed.	Premium paid.	Net cost in currency.	Net cost estimated in gold.	Interest due at close of fiscal year.	Accrued interest paid in coin.	Balance of interest due at close of fiscal year.
JUNE 30, 1872.							
Five-twenties of 1862	$6,417,850 00	$764,035 21	$7,181,905 21	$6,345,391 98	$487,849 00	$75,179 43	$332,669 57
Five-twenties of March, 1864	127,100 00	14,959 03	142,039 03	126,123 46	8,894 00	1,338 70	7,555 30
Five-twenties of June, 1864	3,604,650 00	438,656 16	4,043,306 16	3,573,223 63	246,001 50	57,449 60	188,551 70
Five-twenties of 1865	3,635,300 00	436,838 70	4,072,038 70	3,594,747 85	246,568 00	37,817 37	208,744 63
Consols, 1865	11,788,900 00	1,436,989 46	13,225,889 46	11,660,785 69	707,334 00	149,248 21	558,085 79
Consols, 1867	6,939,900 00	833,600 15	7,792,500 15	6,863,777 39	417,534 00	108,497 19	309,046 08
Consols, 1868	83,850 00	9,931 63	93,801 63	84,595 02	5,151 00	1,386 93	3,764 03
Total	32,616,450 00	3,935,050 34	36,553,500 34	32,248,645 22	2,059,323 50	430,908 38	1,628,417 12
JUNE 30, 1873.							
Five-twenties of 1862	7,137,100 00	925,783 87	8,062,883 87	7,069,542 58	431,430 50	101,960 57	329,469 93
Five-twenties of March, 1864	50,000 00	7,372 50	57,372 50	49,780 91	3,500 00	213 70	2,686 30
Five-twenties of June, 1864	3,741,150 00	480,684 37	4,221,834 37	3,715,911 22	223,270 50	42,216 46	181,054 04
Five-twenties of 1865	1,939,850 00	250,635 93	2,210,465 93	1,943,468 93	120,986 50	23,744 47	96,592 03
Consols, 1865	10,768,250 00	1,371,187 17	12,139,437 17	10,668,617 09	646,085 00	145,069 34	501,025 66
Consols, 1867	4,402,100 00	553,610 89	4,955,710 89	4,373,781 76	284,126 00	69,632 51	194,493 49
Consols, 1868	619,550 00	81,983 44	701,533 44	617,140 34	37,173 00	8,948 40	28,224 60
Total	28,678,000 00	3,671,258 17	28,349,258 17	99,457,562 83	1,725,881 50	392,385 43	1,333,496 05
Grand total	192,075,000 00	15,270,844 08	143,346,444 08	122,554,606 65	6,793,956 50	1,678,672 46	5,115,456 04

TABLE M.—*Statement showing the purchases of bonds in excess of the amount required for the sinking-fund during each fiscal year from the commencement of the purchases in May, 1869, to and including June 30, 1873.*

Year ended—	Principal redeemed.	Premium paid.	Net cost in currency.	Net cost estimated in gold.	Interest due at close of fiscal year.	Accrued interest paid in coin.	Balance of interest due at close of fiscal year.
JUNE 30, 1870.							
Five-twenties of 1862	$9,975,250 00	$1,439,465 74	$11,413,715 74	$9,126,361 36	$502,456 55	$110,968 99	$391,487 56
Five-twenties of March, 1864	597,400 00	116,951 00	714,351 00	532,072 21	40,948 00	9,621 13	31,326 87
Five-twenties of June, 1864	11,742,700 00	1,767,653 37	13,510,353 37	10,680,518 21	589,697 53	146,031 12	443,666 39
Five-twenties, 1865	7,680,350 00	1,102,967 36	8,783,317 36	7,051,018 61	328,437 85	94,005 47	234,432 38
Consols, 1865	36,118,900 00	5,242,087 61	41,360,297 61	32,775,094 65	1,801,918 50	481,633 72	1,278,284 78
Consols, 1867	18,496,800 00	2,932,445 22	21,349,245 22	16,374,250 02	1,037,797 00	206,748 21	830,978 79
Consols, 1868	2,105,500 00	364,879 14	2,470,379 14	1,869,116 40	123,495 00	23,141 27	100,353 73
Total	86,596,900 00	12,955,449 44	99,541,649 44	78,308,437 46	4,434,680 45	1,074,149 93	3,410,530 50
JUNE 30, 1871.							
Five-twenties of 1862	7,695,250 00	725,443 91	8,420,693 91	7,517,031 86	315,865 00	88,115 14	227,749 86
Five-twenties of March, 1864	100,500 00	10,869 25	111,369 25	100,135 51	1,335 00	196 94	1,138 06
Five-twenties of June, 1864	7,145,950 00	637,670 36	7,783,620 36	6,968,994 28	290,772 50	89,675 02	192,097 48
Five-twenties, 1865	9,117,750 00	877,459 15	9,995,209 15	8,875,459 67	362,811 00	90,147 01	272,663 99
Consols, 1865	24,476,800 00	2,348,715 50	26,825,515 50	23,917,450 48	988,489 00	355,590 04	633,391 96
Consols, 1867	10,741,550 00	1,011,485 32	11,753,035 32	10,430,837 44	478,047 00	153,991 14	324,055 86
Consols, 1868	163,600 00	16,862 01	180,462 01	159,625 18	6,813 00	2,780 76	4,032 24
Total	59,441,400 00	5,648,438 50	65,089,838 50	57,969,533 42	2,433,525 50	779,186 05	1,654,339 45
JUNE 30, 1872.							
Five-twenties of 1862	12,364,000 00	1,359,618 69	13,723,618 69	12,317,898 38	334,467 00	132,389 84	222,097 16
Five-twenties of March, 1864	54,000 00	6,549 90	60,549 90	53,884 81	1,020 00	389 92	630 08
Five-twenties of June, 1864	4,299,550 00	495,186 15	4,794,736 15	4,279,333 48	104,153 50	46,626 09	57,527 41
Five-twenties, 1865	1,868,400 00	209,239 93	2,077,639 93	1,854,868 91	42,536 00	16,649 96	25,886 04
Consols, 1865	7,909,700 00	999,620 72	8,909,320 72	7,875,863 64	237,501 00	153,887 37	81,613 63
Consols, 1867	705,750 00	95,071 84	800,821 84	703,446 24	21,285 00	13,956 70	7,329 30
Consols, 1868	8,950 00	1,170 36	10,120 36	8,918 01	283 50	186 94	96 56
Total	27,210,350 00	3,166,450 59	30,376,800 59	27,099,083 47	768,996 00	366,086 92	402,179 18

TABLE M.—*Statement showing the purchases of bonds in excess of the amount required for the sinking-fund during each fiscal year, &c.*—Continued.

Year ended—	Principal redeemed.	Premium paid.	Net cost in currency.	Net cost estimated in gold.	Interest due at close of fiscal year.	Accrued interest paid in coin.	Balance of interest due at close of fiscal year.
JUNE 30, 1873.							
Five-twenties of 1862	$3,082,200 00	$435,588 12	$3,527,788 12	$3,052,989 79	$113,440 00	$56,369 39	$57,070 61
Five-twenties of March, 1864	6,300 00	955 16	7,255 16	6,162 53	198 00	4 14	193 86
Five-twenties of June, 1864	1,915,450 00	272,520 18	2,187,970 18	1,895,085 70	65,666 50	28,276 89	37,389 61
Five-twenties, 1865	550,700 00	78,273 53	628,973 53	543,974 45	18,560 00	8,229 43	10,330 57
Consols, 1865	2,279,700 00	385,646 53	2,665,346 53	2,354,176 05	68,391 00	25,908 86	42,482 14
Consols, 1867	597,250 00	131,063 53	988,313 53	848,313 40	23,717 50	4,533 17	19,184 33
Consols, 1868	302,200 00	47,366 90	349,586 90	297,634 98	9,066 00	5,970 68	3,095 12
Total	9,003,500 00	1,391,677 65	10,394,397 65	8,090,495 90	301,039 00	131,132 76	169,946 24
Grand total	189,941,750 00	23,061,766 18	205,203,516 18	173,274,050 55	7,987,540 95	2,330,545 58	5,656,995 37

NOTE.—This and the preceding table show the entire amount of bonds purchased from the commencement of the purchases to and including June 30, 1873. In this connection attention is invited to the note at the end of Table N.

TABLE N.—*Statement showing the purchases of bonds from May, 1869, to September 30, 1873.*

Date of purchase.	Opening price of Gold.	Principal.	Amount paid.	Currency value of Interest accrued on bonds bought "flat."	Net cost.	Net cost estimated in Gold.	Average rate of premium on each purchase.	Average cost in Gold of each purchase.	Average rate of premium on total purchases to date.	Average cost in Gold of total purchases to date.
1869.										
May 12	139¼	$1,000,000 00	$1,135,070 00	$2,504 36	$1,132,565 64	$958,177 36	15.26	83.59		
18	142	70,000 00	81,718 10		81,718 10	57,546 45	16.74	59.31		
19	142	1,000,000 00	1,168,513 10		1,168,513 10	992,895 85	16.85	82.99	15.84	82.78
27	139¼	1,000,000 00	1,153,581 50	711 78	1,153,581 50	996,940 14	15.36	82.69		
June 3	138½	1,000,000 00	1,164,770 00		1,164,770 00	996,510 43	16.48	84.25		
10	139	1,000,000 00	1,161,067 00		1,161,067 00	988,999 84	16.99	83.54		
16	185		1,135,000 00		1,135,000 00	933,998 91	13.50	83.40		
17	187½	1,000,000 00	1,132,590 00		1,132,590 00	1,004,011 68	15.30	84.90		
21	187¼	1,000,000 00	1,676,506 75		1,676,506 75	1,364,347 68	15.66	84.20	15.89	83.55
26	187	1,000,000 00	1,135,606 00		1,135,606 00	992,179 60	15.81	84.86		
July 3	186	3,000,000 00	3,404,471 00		3,404,471 00	2,925,737 65	14.57	87.07		
9	136	1,000,000 00	3,516,044 00		3,516,044 00	677,208 77	16.94	87.58		
14	187	1,000,000 00	1,301,850 00		1,301,850 00	1,301,113 12	17.97	88.66		
15	186	2,000,000 00	2,000,669 00		2,000,669 00	695,113 19	20.35	88.51		
21	184	2,000,000 00	2,601,570 53		2,601,570 53	677,208 77	20.00	89.08		
28	184	2,000,000 00	1,601,128 97		1,601,128 97	1,644,951 34	20.16	88.51		
29	181	2,000,000 00	1,301,570 53		1,301,570 53	685,134 64	20.16	88.58		
August 4	188	2,000,000 00	2,426,130 00		2,426,130 00	1,767,498 12	21.56	89.37		
11	184½	2,000,000 00	2,196,561 97		2,196,561 97	1,787,392 94	21.10	89.05	17.85	85.93
12	185	2,000,000 00	2,378,781 61		2,378,781 61	1,785,687 73	18.69	88.43		
25	186	2,000,000 00	2,194,947 80		2,194,947 80	1,893,533 78	18.94	89.66		
September 1	188	2,000,000 00	2,356,591 00		2,356,591 00	1,840,930 46	19.63	90.05		
9	134½	1,000,000 00	1,185,972 53		1,185,972 53	671,366 99	19.16	86.62		
15	187½	2,000,000 00	2,309,639 55		2,309,639 55	1,671,782 04	18.40	67.14		
22	141½	1,000,000 00	337,657 62		337,657 62	1,697,029 12	18.48	87.04	18.48	86.67
23	185½	1,000,000 00	1,185,548 16		1,185,548 16	1,697,074 14	16.55	84.85		
25	140½	2,000,000 00	3,537,158 16		3,537,158 16	282,982 17	17.91	82.30		
October 6	180	2,105,530 00	3,472,533 19		3,472,533 19	2,986,463 51	15.78	84.65		
7	184½	1,000,000 00	1,319,139 18		1,319,139 18	684,610 18	15.96	88.46		
13	130½	125,530 00	159,945 10		159,945 10	135,581 47	15.94	88.53		
20	130	1,000,000 00	178,187 89		178,187 89	1,752,043 08	16.08	89.10		
		$36,000,000 00	$2,314,070 00		2,314,070 00	1,780,080 77	15.70	89.00	18.36	86.91

TABLE N.—*Statement showing the purchases of bonds from May, 1869, to September 30, 1873*—Continued.

Date of purchase.		Opening price of gold.	Principal.	Amount paid.	Currency value of interest accrued on bonds bought "flat."	Net cost.	Net cost estimated in gold.	Average rate of premium on each purchase.	Average cost in gold of each purchase.	Average rate of premium on total purchases to date.	Average cost in gold of total purchases to date.
	1869.										
October	21	130¼	$1,000,000 00	$1,152,000 00		$1,132,000 00	$885,308 50	15.90	88.53		
	27	130⅛	2,000,000 00	2,292,600 00		2,292,600 00	1,761,814 38	14.63	88.09	17.80	87.20
November	3	127⅞	2,000,000 00	2,257,255 21		2,257,255 21	1,768,662 26	12.86	88.43		
	4	126⅝	1,000,000 00	1,126,843 74		1,126,843 74	889,906 21	12.68	88.99		
	4	126½	1,000,000 00	1,129,090 29		1,129,090 29	891,680 39	12.91	89.17		
	5	126¼	*201,370 00	227,580 43	$167.43	227,413 00	179,773 12	12.97	89.31		
	5	126⅛	*433,000 00	492,158 94	2,917 87	480,941 07	386,751 83	12.99	89.32		
	10	126⅞	2,000,000 00	2,259,000 00		2,230,000 00	1,780,492 61	12.95	89.02		
	17	127⅛	2,000,000 00	2,256,513 69		2,256,513 69	1,775,035 35	12.83	88.75		
	17	127½	1,000,000 00	1,129,039 02		1,129,039 02	888,132 95	12.90	88.81		
	24	126½	3,000,000 00	3,382,483 67		3,382,483 67	2,671,260 54	12.75	89.04	16.97	87.48
December	1	122¼	2,000,000 00	2,206,992 21		2,206,992 21	1,807,158 41	10.35	90.36		
	2	122¼	1,000,000 00	1,102,659 61		1,102,659 61	901,971 06	10.27	90.20		
	8	123	2,000,000 00	2,248,236 56		2,248,236 56	1,818,583 78	12.41	90.93		
	13	121⅞	2,000,000 00	2,239,710 90		2,239,710 90	1,830,598 97	11.98	91.98		
	16	121½	1,000,000 00	1,118,412 34		1,118,412 34	919,557 94	11.84	91.96		
	22	120¼	2,000,000 00	2,215,985 83		2,215,985 83	1,844,733 96	10.80	92.24		
	27	119⅞	2,000,000 00	2,220,427 12		2,220,427 12	1,852,285 40	11.02	92.61		
	30	119¼	1,000,000 00	1,110,507 80		1,110,507 80	926,388 15	11.05	92.64	16.13	86.20
	1870.										
January	5	119⅞	2,000,000 00	2,246,595 03		2,246,595 03	1,876,071 01	12.33	93.80		
	11	122⅛	*431,700 00	517,400 49		517,400 49	422,367 75	14.54	93.51		
	11	122¼	*1,342,550 00	1,539,826 93	32 58	1,539,794 35	1,256,971 98	14.69	93.63		
	13	121⅞	1,000,000 00	1,141,010 09		1,141,010 00	932,137 79	14.10	93.81		
	19	121¼	2,000,000 00	2,281,553 49		2,261,553 49	1,877,823 45	14.08	93.89		
	27	123	1,000,000 00	1,142,872 27		1,142,872 27	936,780 53	14.29	93.68	15.94	88.55
February	10	120⅞	1,000,000 00	1,126,500 00		1,126,500 00	932,919 25	12.65	93.30		
	11	120⅛	50,000 00	56,325 00		56,325 00	46,888 66	12.65	93.78		
	24	117⅞	1,000,000 00	1,115,764 80		1,115,764 80	948,577 94	11.57	94.86		
	24	117⅜	1,000,000 00	1,117,488 85		1,117,488 85	930,043 86	11.75	95.04	15.79	88.73
March	2	116⅝	1,000,000 00	1,107,377 50		1,107,377 50	951,559 61	10.74	95.16		
	10	111	1,000,000 00	1,067,347 35		1,067,347 35	961,574 19	6.73	96.16		
	17	112	1,000,000 00	1,067,480 27		1,067,480 27	953,107 39	6.75	95.31		
	24	112¾	1,000,000 00	1,060,440 34		1,060,440 34	942,613 63	6.04	94.26		
	30	111⅝	1,000,000 00	1,069,965 26		1,069,965 26	958,411 41	7.00	95.64	15.49	89.04
April	7	112	1,000,000 00	1,070,874 91		1,070,874 91	955,870 46	7.08	95.59		
	13	112⅝	1,000,000 00	1,073,983 37		1,073,983 37	954,985 99	7.39	95.48		

TABLE N.—*Statement showing the purchase of bonds from May, 1869, to September 30, 1873.*—Continued.

18	112⅝	4,000,000 00	4,414,343 08	....	4,414,343 08	3,915,160 16	10.36	97.88	....	....
18	112⅜	50,000 00	55,160 00	....	55,160 00	48,982 39	10.32	97.84	....	....
25	111⅛	2,000,000 00	2,217,901 51	....	2,217,901 51	1,986,981 84	10.89	99.35	12.31	93.83
November 1	112	1,000,000 00	1,113,421 29	....	1,113,421 29	994,138 15	11.34	99.41	....	....
8	111⅜	1,000,000 00	1,114,150 87	....	1,114,150 87	998,119 48	11.41	99.81	....	....
15	111½	21,100 00	23,452 74	....	23,452 74	21,081 11	11.11	99.88	....	....
21	110⅝	1,000,000 00	1,107,389 47	....	1,107,389 47	999,900 20	10.74	99.99	12.30	93.90
December 6	109⅞	517,450 00	568,325 56	....	568,325 56	517,247 38	9.83	99.96	....	....
13	109½	43,700 00	47,734 84	....	47,734 84	43,693 21	9.24	99.99	....	....
20	108¾	81,000 00	88,083 15	....	88,083 15	80,996 00	8.74	99.99	....	....
27	108¾	240,550 00	260,908 91	....	260,908 91	240,469 04	8.46	99.97	12.28	93.91
1872.										
January 4	109⅛	566,200 00	617,775 00	....	617,775 00	566,116 84	9.11	99.99	....	....
18	109	899,750 00	978,713 38	....	978,713 38	897,908 18	8.78	99.80	12.27	93.95
February 1	109¼	1,000,000 00	1,091,919 01	....	1,091,919 01	994,914 81	9.19	99.49	....	....
15	110¼	1,000,000 00	1,092,584 13	....	1,092,584 13	991,006 01	9.26	99.10	....	....
29	110⅛	1,000,000 00	1,091,388 34	....	1,091,388 34	984,341 23	9.14	98.43	12.23	94.02
March 14	110¼	1,000,000 00	1,092,821 91	....	1,092,821 91	992,346 80	9.28	99.23	....	....
28	110⅜	1,000,000 00	1,095,961 25	....	1,095,961 25	998,943 37	9.40	99.89	12.21	94.05
April 3	109⅞	1,000,000 00	1,097,435 25	....	1,097,435 25	998,883 41	9.74	99.88	....	....
10	110⅛	1,000,000 00	1,100,721 08	....	1,100,721 08	998,396 46	10.07	99.84	....	....
17	110⅝	2,000,000 00	2,213,295 42	....	2,213,295 42	1,996,207 82	10.66	99.81	....	....
24	111⅞	263,850 00	294,794 93	....	294,794 93	263,503 85	11.73	99.87	12.18	94.15
May 1	112¼	691,650 00	776,203 34	....	776,203 34	691,495 18	12.22	99.98	....	....
6	113⅛	5,000 00	5,640 00	....	5,640 00	4,963 70	12.80	99.27	....	....
8	113⅜	4,000,000 00	4,519,795 84	....	4,519,795 84	3,977,818 12	12.99	99.44	....	....
15	114	3,000,000 00	3,395,896 68	....	3,395,896 68	2,978,795 34	13.19	99.29	....	....
22	113⅜	2,000,000 00	2,267,116 41	....	2,267,116 41	1,993,069 37	13.36	99.65	....	....
29	113⅝	2,000,000 00	2,274,174 67	....	2,274,174 67	1,997,079 84	13.71	99.85	12.22	94.38
June 5	114⅝	825,950 00	945,245 28	....	945,245 28	824,641 46	14.44	99.84	....	....
12	114	47,850 00	54,486 79	....	54,468 79	47,795 42	13.87	99.88	....	....
19	113⅞	921,900 00	1,047,373 04	....	1,047,373 04	919,756 79	13.61	99.77	....	....
26	113⅝	1,084,400 00	1,227,634 17	....	1,227,634 17	1,082,808 53	13.22	99.85	12.24	94.44
July 3	113⅜	300,850 00	342,155 19	....	342,155 19	300,795 77	13.73	99.98	....	....
10	113⅜	511,750 00	581,975 72	....	581,975 72	511,627 81	13.72	99.98	....	....
17	114⅛	1,000,000 00	1,144,063 85	....	1,144,063 85	999,182 40	14.41	99.92	....	....
24	114⅛	47,900 00	53,956 89	....	53,956 89	47,123 92	14.32	99.84	....	....
31	115½	1,000,000 00	1,146,469 17	....	1,146,489 17	995,864 64	14.65	99.59	12.26	94.49
August 7	115¼	2,000,000 00	2,296,663 19	....	2,296,663 19	1,992,766 31	14.83	99.64	....	....
7	115½	7,000 00	8,038 80	....	8,038 80	6,975 10	14.84	99.64	....	....
14	114⅝	1,000,000 00	1,145,208 63	....	1,145,208 63	998,003 16	14.52	99.80	....	....
21	114½	34,300 00	38,996 39	....	38,996 39	34,132 50	13.69	99.51	....	....
22	114½	5,000 00	5,683 00	....	5,683 00	4,974 18	13.66	99.48	....	....
28	113	1,000,000 00	1,123,616 18	....	1,123,616 18	994,350 60	12.36	99.44	12.29	94.57
September 4	113½	1,000,000 00	1,123,204 81	....	1,123,204 81	992,888 23	12.32	99.29	....	....
11	113	1,000,000 00	1,112,251 60	....	1,112,251 60	984,293 45	11.23	98.43	....	....
18	114½	3,000,000 00	3,343,130 94	....	3,343,130 94	2,926,154 00	11.44	97.54	....	....
25	113⅝	1,000,000 00	1,120,993 75	....	1,120,993 75	986,573 14	12.10	98.66	12.27	94.64
October 2	114⅜	3,000,000 00	3,369,121 78	....	3,369,121 78	2,945,680 25	12.30	98.19	....	....
7	113	5,000,000 00	5,641,797 44	....	5,641,797 44	4,992,741 10	12.84	99.85	....	....
16	112⅝	94,100 00	106,178 24	....	106,178 24	94.067 11	12.84	99.97	....	....

TABLE N.—*Statement showing the purchases of bonds from May, 1869, to September 30, 1873*—Continued.

Date of purchase.		Opening price of gold.	Principal.	Amount paid.	Currency value of interest accrued on bonds bought "flat."	Net cost.	Net cost estimated in gold.	Average rate of premium on each purchase.	Average cost in gold of each purchase.	Average rate of premium on total purchases to date.	Average cost in gold of total purchases to date.
1872.											
October	23	113¼	$1,100,000 00	$1,126,635 51	....	$1,126,635 51	$995,930 89	12.66	99.50	....	....
	30	112⅞	359,250 00	403,657 23	....	403,657 23	358,203 54	12.36	99.99	12.29	94.79
November	6	112⅝	428,400 00	478,902 16	....	478,902 16	426,632 90	11.79	99.59	....	....
	13	113¼	1,000,000 00	1,126,009 23	....	1,126,009 23	992,078 62	12.60	99.21	....	....
	20	113¼	2,000,000 00	2,250,861 59	....	2,250,861 59	1,989,711 90	12.54	99.48	....	....
	26	112⅞	489,150 00	551,216 06	....	551,216 06	488,883 42	12.69	99.95	12.29	94.85
December	4	112⅛	560,600 00	631,947 79	....	631,947 79	560,485 64	12.73	99.98	....	....
	26	111⅞	417,950 00	466,978 08	....	466,978 08	417,877 48	11.73	99.98	12.29	94.86
1873.											
January	8	111⅛	20,850 00	23,297 79	....	23,297 79	20,818 14	11.74	99.99	....	....
	15	112	197,600 00	221,278 24	....	221,278 24	197,569 86	11.98	99.98	....	....
	22	113¼	516,400 00	584,824 36	....	584,824 36	514,606 91	13.25	99.67	....	....
	29	114	169,350 00	192,613 81	....	192,613 81	168,959 48	13.74	99.77	12.29	94.69
February	5	113⅜	518,250 00	587,510 76	....	587,510 76	516,492 98	13.36	99.66	....	....
	12	114⅛	1,000,000 00	1,138,246 72	....	1,138,246 72	997,368 43	13.82	99.74	....	....
	19	114⅝	1,000,000 00	1,137,351 75	....	1,137,351 75	992,237 07	13.74	99.22	....	....
	26	114⅝	1,000,000 00	1,137,509 59	....	1,137,509 59	991,293 76	13.75	99.13	12.31	94.94
March	5	115	1,000,000 00	1,135,731 04	....	1,135,731 04	987,592 21	13.57	98.76	....	....
	12	115⅛	500,000 00	567,161 07	....	567,161 07	492,648 05	13.43	98.53	....	....
	19	115⅛	1,000,000 00	1,133,941 25	....	1,133,941 25	983,896 96	13.39	98.39	....	....
	20	115⅜	3,800 00	4,332 00	....	4,332 00	3,750 49	14.00	98.70	....	....
	26	116	500,000 00	572,335 00	....	572,335 00	493,392 25	14.47	98.68	12.32	94.97
April	9	118	500,000 00	574,095 97	....	574,095 97	486,522 01	14.82	97.30	....	....
	23	117¼	500,000 00	575,915 67	....	575,915 67	491,186 07	15.18	98.24	12.33	94.98
May	7	117⅜	500,000 00	578,944 55	....	578,944 55	493,243 49	15.79	98.65	....	....
	21	117½	500,000 00	579,840 14	....	579,840 14	493,480 97	15.97	98.70	12.34	95.00
June	4	118	500,000 00	581,790 70	....	581,790 70	493,042 97	16.36	98.61	....	....
	18	115⅜	500,000 00	578,032 20	....	578,032 20	498,841 17	15.61	99.77	12.35	95.01
July	16	116	207,850 00	240,737 77	....	240,737 77	207,532 56	15.83	99.85	12.36	95.01
August	13	115⅜	15,500 00	17,843 60	....	17,843 60	15,462 51	15.12	99.89	12.36	95.01
September	17	111⅛	55,850 00	61,944 08	....	61,944 08	55,660 07	10.91	99.66	....	....
	20	111⅛	11,702,100 00	12,963,682 93	....	12,963,682 93	11,658,748 70	10.78	99.53	....	....
	20	111¼	47,000 00	52,036 40	....	52,036 40	46,776 09	10.73	99.52	....	....
	20	111⅛	741,150 00	817,011 04	....	817,011 04	734,341 95	10.24	99.09	....	....
	26	111⅛	161,000 00	178,365 73	....	178,365 73	160,238 86	10.78	99.53	....	....
Total		....	363,253,800 00	363,018,330 71	$30,940 98	362,981,463 79	307,702,907 64	....	....	12.17	95.10

RECAPITULATION BY LOANS.

Five-twenties of 1862	$54,139,350 00	$62,955,548 50	$938 14	$62,954,610 36	$54,136,633 87	12 10	96 43
Five-twenties of March, 1864	1,118,800 00	1,307,208 39	18 48	1,307,185 91	1,059,967 67	16 74	91 98
Five-twenties of June, 1864	41,459,750 00	48,903,964 34	4,094 39	48,789,940 02	41,492,330 61	12 30	95 47
Five-twenties of 1865	35,982,300 00	40,015,596 19	53 49	40,015,329 71	34,599,031 08	11 39	96 12
Consols, 1865	118,965,550 00	133,457,305 57	24,983 68	133,432,321 89	115,374,317 08	12 18	95 33
Consols, 1867	69,931,980 00	70,983,372 67	744 92	70,982,627 75	59,668,585 27	12 94	93 42
Consols, 1868	4,794,050 00	5,510,347 03	91 90	5,510,255 15	4,451,149 06	14 94	92 85
Total	326,253,800 00	363,013,332 71	30,848 98	362,061,463 79	307,702,907 64	13 57	95 19

NOTE.—The bonded debt of the United States has been reduced by the amount of these bonds, which have ceased to bear interest and have been cancelled and destroyed. This statement does not include the six per cent. bonds converted into fives, par for the redemption of past-due and called securities, which have also ceased to bear interest and have been cancelled and destroyed. These items marked (*) are the bonds bought with the proceeds of the interest collected on the bonds previously purchased. These "interest-purchases" were discontinued after the passage of the act of July 14, 1870, (16 Statutes, 272,) authorizing the refunding of the national debt and directing the cancellation and destruction of the bonds purchased. All bonds, whether purchased, redeemed, or received in exchange for other bonds bearing a lower rate of interest, either before or since the date of that act, have ceased to bear interest, and the annual interest-charge has been reduced by the amount of interest that would have been payable on the first two classes, and the difference in rate on the last class, but for such redemption, purchase, or exchange.

TABLE O.—*Statement of the various descriptions of public debt of the United States, June 30, 1848.*

	Length of loan.	When redeemable.	Rate of interest.	Price at which sold.	Amount author-ized.	Amount issued.	Amount out-standing.
... DEBT.							
Unclaimed dividends upon a debt created prior to 1846, and the principal and interest of the redeemable debt created during the war of 1812 and up to 1837.	......	On demand	5 and 6 per cent.	...			
TREASURY NOTES PRIOR TO 1846.							
The act of October 12, 1837, (5 Statutes, 201,) May 21, 1838, (5 Statutes, 228,) March 31, 1840, (5 Statutes, 370,) February 15, 1841, (5 Statutes, 411,) January 31, 1842, (5 Statutes, 469,) August 31, 1842, (5 Statutes, 581,) and March 3, 1843, (5 Statutes, 614,) authorized the issue of Treasury notes in various amounts, and with interest at rates named therein from 1 mill to 6 per centum per annum.	1 and 2 years	1 and 2 years from date	1 mill to 6 per cent.	Par ...			
TREASURY NOTES OF 1846.							
The act of July 22, 1846, (9 Statutes, 39,) authorized the issue of Treasury notes in such sums as the exigencies of the Government might require; the amount outstanding at any one time not to exceed $10,000,000, to bear interest at not exceeding 6 per centum per annum, redeemable one year from date. These notes were receivable in payment of all debts due the United States, including customs duties.	1 year	1 year from date.	6 per cent ..	Par ...	$10,000,000 00		
MEXICAN INDEMNITY.							
A proviso in the civil and diplomatic appropriation act of August 10, 1846, (9 Statutes, 94,) authorized the payment of the principal and interest of the fourth and fifth installments of the Mexican indemnity due April and July, 1844, by the issue of stock, with interest at 5 per centum, payable in five years.	5 years......	April and July, 1849.	5 per cent ..	Par ..		$303,573 92	
TREASURY NOTES OF 1847.							
The act of January 28, 1847, (9 Statutes, 118,) authorized the issue of $23,000,000 Treasury notes, with interest at not exceeding 6 per centum per annum, or the issue of stock for any portion of the amount, with interest at 6 per centum per annum. The Treasury notes under this act were redeemable at the expiration of one or two years, and the interest was to cease at the expiration of sixty days' notice. These notes were receivable in payment of all debts due the United States, including customs duties.	1 and 2 years	After 60 days' notice.	6 per cent ..	Par	$27,000,000 00		

LOAN OF 1847.

The act of January 28, 1847, (9 Statutes, 118,) authorized the issue of $23,000,000 Treasury notes, with interest at not exceeding 6 per centum per annum, or the issue of stock for any portion of the amount, with interest at 6 per centum per annum, re-imbursable after December 31, 1867. Section 14 authorized the conversion of Treasury notes under this or any preceding act into like stock, which accounts for the apparent overissue.

BOUNTY-LAND SCRIP.

The 9th section of February 11, 1847, (9 Statutes, 125,) authorized the issue of land-warrants to soldiers of the Mexican war, or scrip, at the option of the soldiers, to bear 6 per centum interest per annum, redeemable at the pleasure of the Government, by notice from the Treasury Department. Interest ceases July 1, 1849.

TEXAS INDEMNITY STOCK.

The act of September 9, 1850, (9 Statutes, 447,) authorized the issue of $10,000,000 stock, with interest at 5 per centum per annum, to the State of Texas, in satisfaction of all claims against the United States arising out of the annexation of the said State. This stock was to be redeemable at the end of fourteen years.

TREASURY NOTES OF 1857.

The act of December 23, 1857, (11 Statutes, 257,) authorized the issue of $20,000,000 in Treasury notes, $6,000,000 with interest at not exceeding 6 per centum per annum, and the remainder with interest at the lowest rates offered by bidders, but not exceeding 6 per centum per annum. These notes were redeemable at the expiration of one year, and interest was to cease at the expiration of sixty days' notice after maturity. They were receivable in payment of all debts due the the United States, including customs duties.

LOAN OF 1858.

The act of June 14, 1858, (11 Statutes, 365,) authorized a loan of $20,000,000, with interest at not exceeding 5 per centum per annum, and redeemable any time after January 1, 1874.

LOAN OF 1860.

The act of June 22, 1860, (12 Statutes, 79,) authorized a loan of $21,000,000, (to be used in redemption of Treasury notes,) with interest at not exceeding 6 per centum per annum, redeemable in not less than ten nor more than twenty years.

Term	Redeemable	Interest	Rate	Amount authorized	Amount issued	Outstanding
20 years	January 1, 1868.	6 per cent	Par	23,000,000 00	22,207,000 00	1,650 00
Indefinite	July 1, 1849.	6 per cent	Par	Indefinite	....	3,600 00
14 years	January 1, 1865.	5 per cent	Par	10,000,000 00	5,000,000 00	174,000 00
1 year	60 days' notice.	5 and 5½ per cent.	Par	20,000,000 00	20,000,000 00	2,000 00
15 years	Jan. 1, 1874.	5 per cent	Par	20,000,000 00	20,000,000 00	20,000,000 00
10 years	Jan. 1, 1871.	5 per cent	Par	21,000,000 00	7,022,000 00	10,000 00

Table Q.—*Statement of the outstanding principal of the public debt, &c.*—Continued.

	Length of loan.	When redeemable.	Rate of interest.	Price at which sold.	Amount authorized.	Amount issued.	Amount outstanding.
LOAN OF FEBRUARY, 1861, (12 Statutes, 129.) The act of February 8, 1861, (12 Statutes, 129,) authorized a loan of $25,000,000, with interest at not exceeding 6 per centum per annum, redeemable in not less than ten nor more than twenty years from the date of the act.	10 or 20 yrs.	Jan. 1, 1881	6 per cent	Par	$25,000,000 00	$18,415,000 00	$18,415,000 00
TREASURY NOTES OF 1861. The act of March 2, 1861, (12 Statutes, 178,) authorized a loan of $10,000,000, with interest at not exceeding 6 per centum per annum, redeemable on three months' notice after July 1, 1871, and payable July 1, 1881. If proposals for the loan were not satisfactory, authority was given to issue the whole amount in Treasury notes, with interest at not exceeding 6 per centum per annum. The same act gave authority to substitute Treasury notes for the whole or any part of loans authorized at the time of the passage of this act. These notes were to be received in payment of all debts due the United States, including customs duties, and were redeemable at any time within two years from the date of the act.	2 years.... / 60 days....	2 years after date, / 60 days after date.	6 per cent	Par	$22,468,100 00 / 12,896,350 00	$33,364,480 00	3,120 00
OREGON WAR DEBT. The act of March 2, 1861, (12 Statutes, 198,) appropriated $2,800,000 for the payment of expenses incurred by the Territories of Washington and Oregon in the suppression of Indian hostilities in the years 1855 and 1856. Section 4 of the act authorized the payment of these claims in bonds redeemable in twenty years, with interest at 6 per centum per annum.	20 years....	July 1, 1881	6 per cent	Par	2,800,000 00	1,090,850 00	945,000 00
LOAN OF JULY AND AUGUST, 1861, (1881s.) The act of July 17, 1861, (12 Statutes, 259,) authorized the issue of $250,000,000 bonds, with interest at not exceeding 7 per centum per annum, redeemable after twenty years. The act of August 5, 1861, (12 Statutes, 313,) authorized the issue of bonds, with interest at 6 per centum per annum, payable after twenty years from date, in exchange for 7.30 notes issued under the act of July 17, 1861. Now of such bonds were to be issued for a sum less than $500, and the whole amount of them was not to exceed the whole amount of 7.30 notes issued under the above act of July 17. The amount issued in exchange for 7.30s was $18,321,000.	20 years....	July 1, 1881	6 per cent	Par	250,000,000 00	{50,000,000 00 / 139,381,000 00}	{189,381,350 00}
OLD DEMAND NOTES. The act of July 17, 1861, (12 Statutes, 259,) authorized the issue of $50,000,000 Treasury notes, not bearing interest, of a less denomination	....	On demand....	None	Par	60,000,000 00	60,000,000 00	79,967 50

than fifty dollars and not less than ten dollars, and payable on demand by the assistant treasurers at Philadelphia, New York, or Boston. The act of August 5, 1861, (12 Statutes, 313,) authorized the issue of these notes in denominations of five dollars; it also added the assistant treasurer at Saint Louis and the designated depositary at Cincinnati to the places where these notes were made payable. The act of February 12, 1862, (12 Statutes, 338,) increased the amount of demand notes authorized $10,000,000.

SEVEN-THIRTIES OF 1861.

The act of July 17, 1861, (12 Statutes, 259,) authorized a loan of $250,000,000, part of which was to be in Treasury notes, with interest at 7 3-10 per centum per annum, payable three years after date.

				Rate		Payable	Term
		140,094,750 00	140,094,750 00	7 3-10 per ct.	Par	August 19 and October 1, 1864.	3 years

FIVE-TWENTIES OF 1862.

The act of February 25, 1862, (12 Statutes, 345,) authorized a loan of $500,000,000 for the purpose of funding the Treasury notes and floating debt of the United States, and the issue of bonds therefor, with interest at 6 per centum per annum. These bonds were redeemable after five and payable twenty years from date. The act of March 3, 1864, (13 Statutes, 13,) authorized an additional issue of $11,000,000 of bonds to persons who subscribed for the loan on or before January 21, 1864. The act of January 28, 1865, (13 Statutes, 425,) authorized an additional issue of $4,000,000 of these bonds and their sale in the United States or Europe.

				Rate		Payable	Term
283,625,600 00	514,771,800 00	515,000,000 00		6 percent.	Par	May 1, 1867.	5 or 20 years.

LEGAL-TENDER NOTES.

The act of February 25, 1862, (12 Statutes, 345,) authorized the issue of $150,000,000 United States notes, not bearing interest, payable to bearer at the Treasury of the United States, and of such denomination, not less than five dollars, as the Secretary of the Treasury might deem expedient; $50,000,000 to be in lieu of demand notes authorized by the act of July 17, 1861; these notes to be a legal tender. The act of July 11, 1862, (12 Statutes, 532,) authorized an additional issue of $150,000,000 United States Treasury notes, of such denominations as the Secretary of the Treasury might deem expedient, but no such note should be for a fractional part of a dollar, and not more than $35,000,000 of a lower denomination than five dollars; these notes to be a legal tender. The act of March 3, 1863, (12 Statutes, 710,) authorized an additional issue of $150,000,000 United States notes, payable to bearer, of such denominations, not less than one dollar, as the Secretary of the Treasury might prescribe; which notes were made a legal tender. The same act limited the time at which Treasury notes might be exchanged for United States bonds to July 1, 1863. The amount of notes authorized by this act were to be in lieu of $100,000,000 authorized by the resolution of January 17, 1863, (12 Statutes, 822.)

				Rate		Payable	Term
336,000,000 00	915,490,031 00	450,000,000 00		None	Par	On demand.	

TABLE O.—*Statement of the out-standing principal of the public debt, &c.*—Continued.

	Length of loan.	When redeemable.	Rate of interest.	Price at which sold.	Amount authorized.	Amount issued.	Amount outstanding.
TEMPORARY LOAN. The act of February 25, 1862, (12 Statutes, 346,) authorized temporary loan not exceeding $25,000,000, for not less than thirty days, with interest at 5 per centum per annum, payable after ten days' notice. The act of March 17, 1862, (12 Statutes, 370,) authorized the increase of temporary loan deposits to $50,000,000. The act of July 11, 1862, (12 Statutes, 532,) authorized a further increase of temporary loan deposits to $100,000,000. The act of June 30, 1864, (13 Statutes, 218,) authorized a further increase of temporary loan deposits to not exceeding $150,000,000, and an increase of the rate of interest to not exceeding 6 per centum per annum, or a decrease of the rate of interest on ten days' notice, as the public interest might require.	Not less than 30 days.	After 10 days' notice.	4, 5, and 6 per cent.	Par	$150,000,000 00	....	$78,560 00
CERTIFICATES OF INDEBTEDNESS. The act of March 1, 1862, (12 Statutes, 352,) authorized the issue of certificates of indebtedness to public creditors who might elect to receive them, to bear interest at the rate of 6 per centum per annum, and payable one year from date, or earlier, at the option of the Government. The act of May 17, 1862, (12 Statutes, 370,) authorized the issue of these certificates in payment of disbursing officers' checks. The act of March 3, 1863, (12 Statutes, 710,) made the interest payable in lawful money.	1 year	1 year after date.	6 per cent	Par	No limit.	$561,753,241 65	5,000 00
FRACTIONAL CURRENCY. The act of July 17, 1862, (12 Statutes, 592,) authorized the use of postal and other stamps as currency, and made them receivable in payment of all dues to the United States less than five dollars. The fourth section of the act of March 3, 1863, (12 Statutes, 711,) authorized the issue of fractional notes in lieu of postal and other stamps and postal currency, made them exchangeable in sums not less than three dollars for United States notes, and receivable for postage and revenue stamps, and in payment of dues to the United States, except duties on imports, less than five dollars; and limited the amount to $50,000,000. The fifth section of the act of June 30, 1864, (13 Statutes, 220,) authorized an issue of $50,000,000 in fractional currency, and provided that the whole amount of these notes, outstanding at any one time, should not exceed this sum.	....	On presentation.	None	Par	50,000,000 00	283,685,683 45	44,709,105 64
LOAN OF 1863. The act of March 3, 1863, (12 Statutes, 709,) authorized a loan of $900,000,000, and the issue of bonds, with interest at not exceeding six per centum per annum, and redeemable is not less than ten nor more than forty years, principal and interest payable in coin. The act of June 30, 1864, (13	17 years	July 1, 1881	6 per cent	Average premium of 4.13.	75,000,000 00	75,000,000 00	75,000,000 00

Statute, 212,) repeals so much of the preceding act as limits the authority thereunder to the current fiscal year, and also repeals the authority altogether except as relates to $75,000,000 of bonds already advertised for.

Description							
ONE-YEAR NOTES OF 1863. The act of March 3, 1863, (12 Statutes, 710,) authorized the issue of $400,000,000 Treasury notes, with interest at not exceeding six per centum per annum, redeemable in not more than three years, principal and interest payable in lawful money, to be a legal tender for their face value.	1 year	1 year after date.	5 per cent	Par	400,000,000 00	44,520,000 00	84,635 00
TWO-YEAR NOTES OF 1863. The act of March 3, 1863, (12 Statutes, 710,) authorized the issue of $400,000,000 Treasury notes, with interest at not exceeding six per centum per annum, redeemable in not more than three years, principal and interest payable in lawful money, to be a legal tender for their face value.	2 years	2 years after date.	5 per cent	Par	400,000,000 00	166,480,000 00	57,450 00
COIN-CERTIFICATES. The fifth section of the act of March 3, 1863, (12 Statutes, 711,) authorized the deposit of gold coin and bullion with the Treasurer or any assistant treasurer, in sums not less than $20, and the issue of certificates therefor in denominations the same as United States notes; also authorized the issue of these certificates in payment of interest on the public debt. It limits the amount of them to not more than 20 per centum of the amount of coin and bullion in the Treasury, and directs their receipt in payment for duties on imports.		On demand	None	Par	Indefinite	562,776,400 00	39,460,000 00
COMPOUND-INTEREST NOTES. The act of March 3, 1863, (12 Statutes, 709,) authorized the issue of $400,000,000 Treasury notes, with interest at not exceeding six per centum per annum, in lawful money, payable not more than three years from date, and to be a legal tender for their face value. The act of June 30, 1864, (13 Statutes, 218,) authorized the issue of $200,000,000 Treasury notes, of any denomination not less than $10, payable not more than three years from date, or redeemable at any time after three years, with interest at not exceeding seven and three-tenths per centum, payable in lawful money at maturity, and made them a legal tender for their face to the same extent as United States notes: $177,045,770 of the amount issued was in redemption of 5 per cent. notes.	3 years	June 10, 1867, & May 15, 1868.	6 per cent, comp'nd.	Par	400,000,000 00	266,595,440 00	479,400 00
TEN-FORTIES OF 1864. The act of March 3, 1864, (13 Statutes, 13,) authorized the issue of $200,000,000 bonds, at not exceeding six per centum per annum, redeemable after five and payable not more than forty years from date, in coin.	10 or 40 years.	March 1, 1874.	5 per cent	Par to 7 per c't. prem.	200,000,000 00	194,117,300 00	194,567,300 00

TABLE O.—*Statement of the outstanding principal of the public debt, &c.*—Continued.

	Length of loan.	When redeemable.	Rate of interest.	Price at which sold.	Amount authorized.	Amount issued.	Amount outstanding.
FIVE-TWENTIES OF MARCH, 1864. The act of March 3, 1864, (13 Statutes, 13,) authorized the issue of $200,000,000 bonds, at not exceeding six per centum per annum, redeemable after five and payable not more than forty years from date, in coin.	5 or 20 years.	Nov. 1, 1869	6 per cent	Par		$2,882,500 00	$2,291,700 00
FIVE-TWENTIES OF JUNE, 1864. The act of June 30, 1864, (13 Statutes, 218,) authorized a loan of $400,000,000, and the issue therefor of bonds redeemable not less than five nor more than thirty (or forty, if deemed expedient) years from date, with interest at not exceeding 6 per centum per annum, payable semi-annually in coin.	5 or 20 years.	Nov. 1, 1869	6 per cent	Par	$400,000,000 00	125,561,300 00	66,819,300 00
SEVEN-THIRTIES OF 1864 AND 1865. The act of June 30, 1864, (13 Statutes, 218,) authorized the issue of $200,000,000 Treasury notes, of not less than $10 each, payable at not more than three years from date, or redeemable at any time after three years, with interest at not exceeding 7 3-10 per centum per annum. The act of March 3, 1865, (13 Statutes, 468,) authorized a loan of $600,000,000, and the issue therefor of bonds or Treasury notes. The notes to be of denominations not less than $50, with interest in lawful money at not more than 7 3-10 per centum per annum.	3 years.	Aug. 15, 1867. June 15, 1868. July 15, 1868.	7 3-10 per ct.	Par	800,000,000 00	829,992,500 00	274,100,000 00
NAVY PENSION FUND. The act of July 1, 1864, (13 Statutes, 414,) authorized the Secretary of the Navy to invest in registered securities of the United States so much of the Navy pension fund in the Treasury January 1 and July 1 in each year as would not be required for the payment of naval pensions. Section 2 of the act of July 23, 1868, (15 Statutes, 170,) makes the interest on this fund 3 per centum per annum in lawful money, and confines its use to the payment of naval pensions exclusively.	Indefinite.		3 per cent	Par	Indefinite	14,000,000 00	14,000,000 00
FIVE-TWENTIES OF 1865. The act of March 3, 1865, (13 Statutes, 468,) authorized the issue of $600,000,000 of bonds or Treasury notes in addition to amounts previously authorized; the bonds to be for not less than $50, payable not more than forty years from date, or after any period not less than five years from date, payable in coin, at not exceeding 6 per centum interest, payable semi-annually.	5 or 20 years.	Nov. 1, 1870	6 per cent	Par	900,327,250 00	200,327,880 00	155,467,450 00

CONSOLS OF 1865.

bearing obligations into bonds authorized by it. The act of April 12, 1866, (14 Statutes, 31,) construed the above act to authorize the Secretary of the Treasury to receive any obligations of the United States, whether bearing interest or not, in exchange for any bonds authorized by it, or to sell any of such bonds, provided the public debt is not increased thereby.

The act of March 3, 1865, (13 Statutes, 468,) authorized the issue of $600,000,000 of bonds or Treasury notes in addition to amounts previously authorized; the bonds to be for not less than $50, payable not more than forty years from date of issue, or after any period not less than five years; interest payable semi-annually, at not exceeding 6 per centum per annum when in coin, or 7 3-10 per centum per annum when in currency. In addition to the amount of bonds authorized by this act, authority was also given to convert Treasury notes or other interest-bearing obligations into bonds authorized by it. The act of April 12, 1866, (14 Statutes, 31,) construed the above act to authorize the Secretary of the Treasury to receive any obligations of the United States, whether bearing interest or not, in exchange for any bonds authorized by it, or to sell any of such bonds, provided the public debt is not increased thereby.

CONSOLS OF 1867.

The act of March 3, 1865, (13 Statutes, 468,) authorized the issue of $600,000,000 of bonds or Treasury notes in addition to amounts previously authorized; the bonds to be for not less than $50, payable not more than forty years from date of issue, or after any period not less than five years; interest payable semi-annually, at not exceeding 6 per centum per annum when in coin, or 7 3-10 per centum per annum when in currency. In addition to the amount of bonds authorized by this act, authority was also given to convert Treasury notes or other interest-bearing obligations into bonds authorized by it. The act of April 12, 1866, (14 Statutes, 31,) construed the above act to authorize the Secretary of the Treasury to receive any obligation of the United States, whether bearing interest or not, in exchange for any bonds authorized by it, or to sell any of such bonds, provided the public debt is not increased thereby.

CONSOLS OF 1869.

The act of March 3, 1865, (13 Statutes, 468,) authorized the issue of $600,000,000 of bonds or Treasury notes in addition to amounts previously authorized; the bonds to be for not less than $50, payable not more than forty years from the date of issue, or after any period not less than five years; interest payable semi-annually, at not exceeding 6 per centum per annum, when in coin or 7 3-10 per centum per annum when in currency. In addition to the amount of bonds authorized by this act, authority was also given to convert Treasury notes or other interest-bearing obligations into bonds authorized by it. The act of April 12,

5 or 20 years	July 1, 1870	6 per cent	Par	332,998,950 00	332,998,950 00	206,861,560 00
5 or 20 years	July 1, 1872	6 per cent	Par	379,609,350 00	379,616,050 00	315,014,550 00
5 or 20 years	July 1, 1873	6 per cent	Par	42,539,350 00	42,539,350 00	38,335,500 00

TABLE O.—*Statement of the outstanding principal of the public debt, &c.*—Continued.

	Length of loan.	When redeemable.	Rate of interest.	Price at which sold.	Amount authorized.	Amount issued.	Amount outstanding.
THREE PER CENT. CERTIFICATES.	Indefinite	On demand	3 per cent	Par	$75,000,000 00	$85,155,000 00	$20,000 00
CERTIFICATES OF INDEBTEDNESS OF 1870.	5 years	Sept. 1, 1875	4 per cent	Par	678,362 41	678,362 41	678,000 00
FUNDED LOAN OF 1881.	10 years	May 1, 1881	5 per cent	Par	500,000,000 00	200,000,000 00	200,000,000 00

1866, (14 Statutes, 31,) construed the above act to authorize the Secretary of the Treasury to receive any obligation of the United States, whether bearing interest or not, in exchange for any bonds authorized by it, or to sell any of such bonds, provided the public debt is not increased thereby.

THREE PER CENT. CERTIFICATES.

The act of March 2, 1867, (14 Statutes, 558,) authorized the issue of $50,000,000 in temporary loan certificates of deposit, with interest at 3 per centum per annum, payable in lawful money on demand, to be used in redemption of compound-interest notes. The act of July 25, 1868, (15 Statutes, 183,) authorized $25,000,000 additional of these certificates for the sole purpose of redeeming compound-interest notes.

CERTIFICATES OF INDEBTEDNESS OF 1870.

The act of July 8, 1870, (16 Statutes, 197,) authorized the issue of certificates of indebtedness, payable five years after date, with interest at 4 per centum per annum, payable semi-annually, principal and interest, in lawful money, to be hereafter appropriated and provided for by Congress. These certificates were issued, one-third to the State of Maine, and two-thirds to the State of Massachusetts, both for the use and benefit of the European and North American Railway Company, and were in full adjustment and payment of any and all claims of said States or railway company for money expended (or interest thereon) by the State of Massachusetts on account of the war of 1812-'15.

FUNDED LOAN OF 1881.

The act of July 14, 1870, (16 Statutes, 272,) authorizes the issue of $200,000,000 at 5 per centum, and $1,000,000,000 at 4½ per centum, principal and interest payable in coin of the present standard value, at the pleasure of the United States Government after ten years; for the 5 per cents; after fifteen years, for the 4½ per cents; and after thirty years, for the 4 per cents. These bonds to be exempt from the payment of all taxes or duties of the United States, as well as from taxation in any form by or under State, municipal, or local authority. This act is amended by the act of January 20, 1871, (16 Statutes,) in order of dates and numbers, beginning with each class last dated and numbered. Interest to cease at the end of three months from notice of intention to redeem. The act of January 28, 1871, (16 Statutes, 386,) increased the amount of 5 per cents to $20,000,000, provided the total amount of bonds issued shall not exceed the amount originally authorized, and authorizes the interest on any of these bonds to be paid quarterly.

CERTIFICATES OF DEPOSIT.

The act of June 8, 1872, (17 Statutes, 336,) authorizes the deposit of United States notes without interest by banking associations in sums not less than $10,000, and the issue of certificates therefor in denominations of not less than $5,000, which certificates shall be payable on demand in United States notes, at the place where the deposits were made. It provides that the notes so deposited in the Treasury shall not be counted as a part of the legal reserve, but that the certificates issued therefor may be held and counted by the national banks as part of their legal reserve, and may be accepted in the settlement of clearing-house balances at the places where the deposits therefor were made, and that the United States notes for which such certificates were issued, or other United States notes of like amount, shall be held as special deposits in the Treasury, and used only for the redemption of such certificates.

Indefinite	On demand	None........ Par ...... No limit...	57,160,000 00	31,720,000 00

2,234,682,993 90

TABLE 1.—Statement of 30-year 6 per cent. bonds (interest payable January and July) issued to the several Pacific Railway companies, under the acts of July 1, 1862, (12 Statutes, 492,) and July 2, 1864, (13 Statutes, 359.)

Railway companies.	Amount of bonds outstanding.	Amount of interest accrued and paid to date, as per preceding statement.	Amount of interest due, as per Register's schedule.	Total interest paid by the United States.	Repayment of interest by transportation of mails, troops, &c.	Balance due the United States on interest account, deducting repayments.	Balance of accrued interest due the United States on interest account.	Total amount of interest due the United States from Pacific Railway companies.
On July 1, 1865:								
Central Pacific	$1,324,000 00		$37,740 00	$37,740 00				$37,740 00
Kansas Pacific								
Union Branch Union Pacific								
Western Pacific								
Sioux City and Pacific								
	1,324,000 00		37,740 00	37,740 00				37,740 00
On January 1, 1866:								
Central Pacific	2,362,000 00	$37,740 00	35,056 83	92,796 83				92,796 83
Kansas Pacific	640,000 00		6,417 53	6,417 53				6,417 53
Union Pacific								
Western Branch Union Pacific								
Western Pacific								
Sioux City and Pacific								
	3,002,000 00	37,740 00	61,474 36	99,214 36				99,214 36
On July 1, 1866:								
Central Pacific	3,002,000 00	92,796 83	63,160 03	175,965 86				175,965 86
Kansas Pacific	1,280,000 00	6,417 53	33,026 56	39,444 06				39,444 06
Union Pacific	1,600,000 00		19,917 09	19,917 09				19,917 09
Western Branch Union Pacific								
Western Pacific								
Sioux City and Pacific								
	6,042,000 00	99,214 36	136,119 68	235,397 04				235,397 04
On January 1, 1867:								
Central Pacific		175,965 86	111,677 84	287,665 37				287,665 37
Kansas Pacific		39,444 06	33,146 84	14,883 74				14,883 74
Union Pacific		19,917 09	97,733 65	117,677 74				117,677 74
Union Branch Union Pacific			16,098 74					

	Bonds issued						
Western Pacific	11,002,000 00	253,327 04	274,879 74	510,206 78		510,206 78	510,206 78
Sioux City and Pacific							
On July 1, 1867:							
Central Pacific	4,602,000 00	987,603 37	126,334 50	494,337 87	22,949 07	401,468 90	401,468 90
Kansas Pacific	3,300,000 00	94,639 93	76,654 29	173,985 22	27,414 40	145,840 82	145,840 82
Union Pacific	5,380,000 00	117,673 74	167,886 87	285,499 61		985,499 61	985,499 61
Central Branch Union Pacific	980,000 00	10,099 74	22,408 75	32,508 49		32,508 49	32,508 49
Western Pacific	390,000 00		8,306 03	8,306 03		8,306 03	8,306 03
Sioux City and Pacific	14,702,000 00	510,206 78	363,650 44	903,637 23	50,293 47	853,543 75	853,543 75
On January 1, 1868:							
Central Pacific	6,074,000 00	694,337 87	145,613 83	569,951 70	29,899 07	540,052 63	540,052 63
Kansas Pacific	4,680,000 00	173,985 22	192,580 26	285,865 48	146,933 96	146,920 92	146,920 92
Union Pacific	8,160,000 00	985,499 61	210,325 50	476,081 69	949,191 92	225,889 91	225,889 91
Central Branch Union Pacific	1,980,000 00	62,533 99	9,600 00	62,533 99		62,533 99	62,533 99
Western Pacific	390,000 00	8,306 03		17,506 03		17,506 03	17,506 03
Sioux City and Pacific	90,714,000 00	903,637 23	518,081 87	1,492,519 00	428,026 31	994,492 78	994,492 78
On July 1, 1868:							
Central Pacific	7,080,000 00	569,951 70	185,641 16	755,592 86	36,949 07	718,643 79	718,643 79
Kansas Pacific	6,090,000 00	235,865 48	165,258 16	461,123 64	266,367 71	194,755 93	194,755 93
Union Pacific	12,987,000 00	476,081 69	588,383 86	764,455 75	594,633 03	983,808 72	983,808 72
Central Branch Union Pacific	1,600,000 00	62,533 99	46,974 27	109,808 26		109,808 26	109,808 26
Western Pacific	390,000 00	17,506 03	9,600 00	27,406 03		27,405 03	27,405 03
	1,112,000 00	19,603 76	19,603 76	19,603 76		19,603 76	19,603 76
Sioux City and Pacific	29,089,000 00	1,492,519 00	715,671 21	2,138,190 30	698,169 81	1,314,020 49	1,314,020 49
On January 1, 1869:							
Central Pacific	16,694,000 00	755,592 86	347,193 73	1,102,786 59	46,158 10	1,056,628 49	1,056,628 49
Kansas Pacific	6,303,000 00	461,123 64	184,580 43	645,723 09	368,406 97	277,316 12	277,316 12
Union Pacific	24,075,000 00	764,455 73	548,109 77	1,312,808 52	719,214 87	594,550 65	594,550 65
Central Branch Union Pacific	1,600,000 00	109,808 26	48,000 00	157,808 26		157,808 26	157,808 26
Western Pacific	1,380,000 00	27,446 03	9,600 00	37,006 03		37,006 03	37,006 03
Sioux City and Pacific	1,112,000 00	19,603 76	33,360 00	52,963 76	16 27	52,947 49	52,947 49
	50,097,000 00	2,138,190 30	1,171,662 93	3,310,053 23	1,133,796 21	2,176,257 04	2,176,257 04

TABLE P.—*Statement of amount of 6 per cent. bonds (interest payable January and July) issued to the several Pacific Railway companies, &c.*—Continued.

Railway companies.	Amount of bonds outstanding.	Amount of interest accrued and paid to date as per preceding statement.	Amount of interest due, as per Register's schedule.	Total interest paid by the United States.	Repayment of interest by transportation of mails, troops, &c.	Balance due the United States on interest account, deducting repayments.	Balance of accrued interest due the United States on interest account.	Total amount of interest due the United States from Pacific Railway companies.
On July 1, 1869:								
Central Pacific	$25,789,000 00	$1,102,786 29	$616,429 59	$1,719,216 18	$72,656 99	$1,646,549 19		$1,646,549 19
Kansas Pacific	6,303,000 00	645,782 09	189,260 07	834,813 09	546,569 10	288,243 99		288,243 99
Union Pacific	25,990,000 00	1,312,765 52	784,104 37	2,081,909 89	906,446 11	1,175,463 78		1,175,463 78
Central Branch Union Pacific	1,600,000 00	157,908 86	46,000 40	205,908 96		902,317 47		902,317 47
Western Pacific	1,640,000 00	44,606 03	9,600 00	44,606 03		44,606 03		44,606 03
Sioux City and Pacific	1,329,320 10	52,983 76	43,514 93	96,596 69	16 27	96,492 42		96,492 42
	58,638,300 00	3,316,033 25	1,674,766 99	4,994,682 14	1,396,189 96	3,453,632 98		3,453,632 98
On January 1, 1870:								
Central Pacific	25,891,000 00	1,719,216 18	772,528 98	2,491,744 38	116,765 86	2,374,978 40		2,374,978 40
Kansas Pacific	6,303,000 00	834,813 09	189,860 08	1,024,960 09	631,994 99	392,678 10		392,678 10
Union Pacific	27,075,000 00	2,081,909 89	408,889 08	2,489,780 83	1,107,427 54	1,784,303 31		1,784,303 31
Central Branch Union Pacific	1,600,000 00	205,908 96	48,000 00	253,908 96	5,351 98	946,305 34		946,305 34
Western Pacific	1,646,000 00	44,606 03	28,682 73	73,288 76		73,288 76		73,288 76
Sioux City and Pacific	1,658,300 00	96,506 69	48,849 60	145,336 29	329 40	144,966 89		144,966 89
	64,135,320 00	4,984,822 14	1,465,010 37	6,479,832 51	1,861,069 71	5,018,742 80		5,018,742 80
On July 1, 1870:								
Central Pacific	25,891,000 00	2,491,744 38	770,023 98	3,261,767 84	164,054 17	3,097,713 67	$155,730 40	3,253,444 07
Kansas Pacific	6,303,000 00	1,024,960 09	149,000 08	1,312,950 09	664,359 12	398,633 18	98,717 38	2,491,851 55
Union Pacific	27,075,000 00	2,691,729 83	621,641 80	3,713,371 03	1,360,576 67	2,453,794 18	67,767 43	2,491,851 55
Central Branch Union Pacific	1,648,000 00	253,908 96	57,908 68	301,686 96	7,401 98	294,285 77	17,657 43	312,983 77
Western Pacific	1,970,300 00	73,288 76	44,506 68	131,107 36		131,107 36	4,971 71	125,473 07
Sioux City and Pacific	1,668,300 00	145,336 29		194,907 89		189,811 81	4,134 50	193,966 01
	64,457,300 00	6,679,802 51	1,935,529 96	8,215,245 49	2,145,799 16	6,669,557 33	279,202 01	6,949,059 34
On January 1, 1871:								
Central Pacific	25,891,000 00	3,261,767 84	776,439 88	4,029,197 84	241,654 17	3,794,329 14	231,995 81	4,125,334 95
Kansas Pacific	6,303,000 00	1,312,963 09	195,860 96	1,459,469 09	633,324 43	633,324 43	54,670 68	
Union Pacific	27,075,000 00	2,713,371 03	617,658 08	3,564,088 98		344,309 22	164,320 32	3,177,917 17
Central Branch Union Pacific	1,668,300 00	301,686 96						

Western Pacific	1,970,000 00	131,197 36	59,100 00	190,297 36	8,981 93	182,016 11	10,568 00	192,614 90
Sioux City and Pacific	1,628,320 00	194,207 69	48,849 60	243,057 49	396 06	242,661 41	15,762 43	258,423 84
	64,618,632 00	8,815,345 49	1,938,564 96	10,753,910 45	2,460,818 94	8,293,091 51	640,035 97	8,933,127 48
On July 1, 1871:								
Central Pacific	25,881,000 00	4,038,197 84	776,430 00	4,814,627 84	343,266 90	4,471,360 94	419,753 57	4,921,114 51
Kansas Pacific	6,303,000 00	1,402,083 09	189,090 00	1,591,173 09	857,330 93	733,842 16	76,932 82	810,774 98
Union Pacific	27,236,512 00	4,530,466 41	817,095 36	5,347,561 77	1,755,303 15	3,592,258 62	289,874 27	3,882,132 89
Central Branch Union Pacific	1,600,000 00	349,808 96	48,000 00	397,808 96	9,276 92	388,531 34	46,725 32	435,256 66
Western Pacific	1,970,000 00	190,297 36	59,100 00	249,397 36	8,281 25	241,116 11	16,370 52	257,492 63
Sioux City and Pacific	1,628,320 00	243,057 49	48,849 60	291,907 09	401 88	291,505 21	23,515 13	315,020 34
	64,618,632 00	10,753,910 45	1,938,564 96	12,692,475 41	2,973,861 03	9,718,614 38	903,177 63	10,621,792 01
On January 1, 1872:								
Central Pacific	25,881,000 00	4,814,627 84	776,430 00	5,591,057 84	422,556 33	5,168,501 51	595,998 12	5,764,499 63
Kansas Pacific	6,303,000 00	1,591,173 09	189,090 00	1,780,263 09	927,889 30	852,433 79	100,272 17	952,705 96
Union Pacific	27,236,512 00	5,347,561 77	817,095 36	6,164,657 13	1,964,830 08	4,199,807 05	402,429 92	4,602,236 97
Central Branch Union Pacific	1,600,000 00	397,808 96	48,000 00	445,808 96	9,276 92	436,531 34	59,783 02	496,314 36
Western Pacific	1,970,000 00	249,397 36	59,100 00	308,497 36	9,350 25	299,147 11	24,078 92	323,226 03
Sioux City and Pacific	1,628,320 00	291,907 09	48,849 60	340,756 69	401 88	340,354 81	32,965 74	373,330 55
	64,618,632 00	12,692,475 41	1,938,564 96	14,631,040 37	3,334,264 76	11,296,775 61	1,215,497 19	12,512,272 80
On July 1, 1872:								
Central Pacific	25,895,190 00	5,591,057 84	777,318 93	6,368,376 07	527,025 99	5,841,350 08	766,646 68	6,606,249 36
Kansas Pacific	6,303,000 00	1,780,263 09	189,090 00	1,969,353 09	973,904 69	995,448 40	128,982 25	1,123,710 65
Union Pacific	27,236,512 00	6,164,657 13	817,095 36	6,981,752 49	2,181,989 43	4,799,763 06	537,973 92	5,337,736 98
Central Branch Union Pacific	1,600,000 00	445,808 96	48,000 00	493,808 96	15,339 95	477,968 64	74,538 93	552,507 57
Western Pacific	1,970,560 00	308,497 36	59,131 98	367,679 34	9,339 60	358,299 69	33,775 70	392,104 79
Sioux City and Pacific	1,628,320 00	340,756 69	48,849 60	389,606 29	885 60	388,780 69	44,165 12	432,945 81
	64,633,512 00	14,631,040 37	1,939,535 17	16,570,575 54	3,708,934 78	12,861,640 76	1,585,613 50	14,447,254 26
On January 1, 1873:								
Central Pacific	25,895,190 00	6,368,376 07	776,553 60	7,144,929 67	614,057 06	6,530,872 61	963,722 26	7,494,595 87
Kansas Pacific	6,303,000 00	1,969,353 09	189,090 00	2,158,443 09	1,067,179 03	1,091,264 06	160,631 78	1,251,895 84
Union Pacific	27,236,512 00	6,981,752 49	817,095 36	7,798,847 85	2,996,875 90	5,501,971 95	696,737 82	6,198,709 77
Central Branch Union Pacific	1,600,000 00	493,808 96	48,000 00	541,808 96	17,714 49	594,093 84	91,093 42	615,187 26
Western Pacific	1,970,560 00	387,670 34	59,116 80	426,796 14	9,350 52	417,445 89	45,538 64	462,984 73
Sioux City and Pacific	1,628,320 00	389,606 29	48,849 60	438,455 89	885 69	437,630 20	57,153 49	494,783 69
	64,633,512 00	16,570,575 54	1,938,705 36	18,509,280 90	4,006,009 35	14,503,878 55	2,014,878 61	16,518,157 16

TABLE P.—Statement of 30-year 6 per cent. bonds (interest payable January and July) issued to the several Pacific Railway Companies, &c.—Continued.

Railway companies.	Amount of bonds outstanding.	Amount of interest accrued and paid to date, as per preceding statement.	Amount of interest due, as per Register's schedule.	Total interest paid by the United States.	Repayments of interest by transportation of mails, troops, &c.	Balance due the United States on interest account, deducting repayments.	Balance of accrued interest due the United States on interest account.	Total amount of interest due to the United States from Pacific Railway Companies.
On July 1, 1873.								
Central Pacific	$25,885,120 00	$7,144,929 67	$776,553 60	$7,921,483 27	$725,037 15	$7,196,446 12	$1,186,138 37	$8,382,584 49
Kansas Pacific	6,303,000 00	2,158,443 09	189,090 00	2,347,533 09	1,082,193 36	1,265,337 73	197,874 38	1,463,212 11
Union Pacific	27,236,512 00	7,729,847 85	817,083 36	8,614,943 21	2,363,019 67	6,522,923 34	681,985 16	7,114,191 70
Central Branch Union Pacific	1,600,000 00	341,608 95	48,000 00	384,408 95	13,451 98	371,155 94	108,589 94	690,686 98
Western Pacific	1,970,560 00	486,786 14	59,116 80	545,912 94	9,367 00	476,545 94	59,408 03	535,973 96
Sioux City and Pacific	1,628,320 00	438,433 89	48,849 60	487,305 40	4,089 72	482,435 77	71,947 61	554,383 39
	64,623,512 00	18,509,280 50	1,508,703 36	20,447,986 36	4,202,140 82	16,924,845 44	2,306,186 48	18,731,031 92

TABLE Q.—*Returns, by award of the United States Court of Claims, of proceeds of property seized as captured or abandoned under the act of March 12, 1863, paid from July 1, 1872, to June 30, 1873.*

Date.	To whom paid.	Amount.
1872.		
July 2	Dominick O. Grady's executors, John Quinlan *et al*..............	$68, 268 60
3	Asher Ayres...........................	34, 604 08
6	William W. Worthington	42, 904 83
8	Daniel L. Ferguson	15, 343 88
10	Melvin B. Wilbur	1, 098 63
	Eide F. Torck................	1, 278 91
	William and Robert McIntyre	4, 830 15
	Simon Queyrouze's administrator	14, 592 00
	William H. Greene...................	10, 549 15
11	James Cantwell........	10, 131 87
	George W. Anderson............	5, 863 78
	Alexander Abrams............	1, 490 13
	Daniel H. Baldwin	12, 252 18
	William Hunter...................	3, 311 40
	Theodore B. Marshall and George S. Marshall	13, 907 88
	Levi De Witt and Richard Morgan............	11, 358 93
	James K. Reilly	9, 934 20
	James J. Waring................	2, 483 55
17	William Lightfoot and David Flanders	13, 411 17
19	Henry C. Freeman's administrator	55, 134 81
	Esadore Cohn	5, 775 00
	James W. and Harvey W. Lathrop............	8, 795 67
	Samuel F. O'Neil..........	2, 980 26
	John Stevenson..............	1, 891 27
	E. E. Simpson *et al.*, administrators of John A. Simpson	12, 630 42
	Ezekiel E. Simpson............	28, 380 13
20	Erastus Henry................	5, 504 02
22	John C. Schreiner & Sons	7, 119 51
23	Herman Parker's administratrix	5, 976 80
24	Elie Coté, for use of J. C. Martin *et al*......	9, 871 91
26	Desiré Godet...........	5, 760 00
27	Lawrence de Give.............	2, 255 30
Aug. 1	Andrew Low	450, 580 19
	Henry A. Richmond's administratrix and Samuel Wilmot	18, 493 46
	Edward Padelford's executors	12, 323 73
	Chandler H. Smith	25, 166 64
	Albert Johnson's executrix, for use of Martin Tally..........	421 96
	Adolph B. Weslow	5, 463 81
5	Anthony Fernandez	19, 537 96
7	Edwin Parsons and George Parsons.........	17, 219 28
	Edward Padelford's executors *et al*....	25, 565 85
	Michel Castille	18, 240 00
8	Julius Witkowski	92, 547 00
10	Edwin M. Price................	68, 712 93
12	William B. Adams.........	21, 396 02
	Abraham Backer............	42, 652 37
	Luke Christie................	4, 470 39
	John R. Wilder	15, 227 00
	Lovell & Lattimore	5, 296 42
	William Lattimore	662 28
	Edward Lovell................	6, 439 29
	Aaron Wilbur's executor...........	16, 888 14
	Alfred Austell	12, 385 88
	Alexander Oldham...........	7, 000 00
	Herman Bulwinkle.............	8, 218 03
13	Henry and Isaac Meinhard...........	10, 148 85
	Simon Witkowski.............	19, 537 26
14	William Lindon............	1, 729 97
17	Ralph Meldrim.............	2, 566 33
1873.		
Feb. 17	John S. Daniel's administratrix............	67, 258 23
19	Hibernia Armstrong.............	16, 780 00
April 26	Hugh Carlisle and George S. Henderson.......	43, 232 00
May 14	James C. Terry, survivor of Terry & Carnes	32, 460 39
15	Henry Cobia's executors...........	107, 126 63
	Octavus Cohen	10, 784 75
21	Samuel Meinhard, Isaac M. Frank, and Abraham Epstein........	24, 180 47
24	Ake Henry	12, 345 75
29	William Markham...........	5, 891 99
June 2	Isaac Rosenheim	14, 201 73
	Antoine Caire, for use of Thomas C. Payan...........	36, 096 00
6	Virginia Sheftall	4, 179 22
	John S. Rogers.............	7, 889 85
	John A. Douglass	6, 136 53
	John M. Cooper	6, 570 38
	William H. Hunter and John Gammel...........	3, 506 60
	William W., and Nelly K. Gordon...........	3, 013 27
	John and Margaret Richards..........	1, 970 21

TABLE Q.—*Returns, by award of the United States Court of Claims, &c.*—Continued.

Date.	To whom paid.	Amount.
1873. June 6	Henry D. Headman	$695 37
	William H. Starke	44,939 77
	Jacob Stern..	1,380 74
	Karl M. Oppenheimer	3,782 65
	Stern & Oppenheimer	4,907 31
	Edwin Bates...	10,687 46
11	Horatio N. Spencer..	4,545 21
	Robert Hunter...	1,894 62
	Rufus C. Barkley	5,227 60
	Charles Deignan	912 31
	Stephen N. Boone	1,930 60
12	Aaron Champion...	7,013 30
	George H. Linstedt..	2,085 32
	Lowell T. Whitcomb	2,549 60
	James Reed, for use of Benoni G. Carpenter...................	8,415 24
23	John J. Gardner...	9,402 60
	Zenon J. Broussard..	15,744 60
24	Jules Perrodin	64,532 60
27	David W. Davis..	651 65
	Augustus W. Eckel	781 90
	George J. Huthmacher	1,633 63
28	Cornelius Donato..	960 60
	James Snipes	65 16
	Thaddeus Kelley's administrator	4,170 30
	Total...	1,960,189 96

TABLE R.—*Awards of the United States Court of Claims of proceeds of property seized as captured or abandoned under the act of March 12, 1863, decreed but not paid during the fiscal year ended June 30, 1873.*

Date of decree.	Name of claimant.	Amount awarded.
Feb. 10, 1873	John M. Powell	$1,994 77
March 3, 1873	Michael Slattery	320 55
March 31, 1873	Thomas W. Keyn's administrators	1,172 97
	Abraham B. Matthews	16,130 34
	Samuel G. Cabell	20,513 61
	Mary Hunter, executrix of James Hunter	4,375 00
	John L. Hardee, executor of Noble A. Hardee	103,856 86
April 14, 1873	Thomas and Catharine McDermott	595 99
April 21, 1873	Emma P. Sykes	3,352 36
	Jean M. Lupeyre	9,955 66
May 5, 1873	Charles Wilson et al	4,032 59
May 19, 1873	Henry D. Weed and George Cornwell	249,437 18
	William M. Wilson	9,625 00
	Alfred L. Tyler	88,892 31
	Dwight Lathrop	5,610 56
	Carl William Heinsula	40,747 83
	Edward W. Marshall, John N. Beach, and Sidney Root	31,033 41
	Andrew J. Miller	29,553 42
May 26, 1873	William J. Poitevent	1,631 27
	William Battersby	87,013 67
	William Battersby and Thomas S. Metcalf's executor	487,242 07
	William Battersby and Octavus Cohen	7,880 86
	William Battersby and Andrew Low	3,940 43
	Charles Green	155,554 89
	William W. Cones	92,596 40
June 2, 1873	Abraham A. Solomons	4,733 97
	William J. Jenkins, executor of Eliza Hans Chaplin	9,432 12
	William J. Hill	18,769 50
	Oakley H. Bynum	4,405 87
	John McMahon, administrator of James Cody	4,598 58
	Henry Skipwith, executor of Eliza Hardesty	27,339 56
	Samuel Houston	2,595 47
	Gazaway B. Lamar	579,343 51
	Lucy C. Murphy	6,593 00
	Freeman Burr	6,336 00
	The Home Insurance Company	35,529 58
	The Southern Insurance and Trust Company	27,176 15
	John F. Pargoud	15,266 81
	Martin Tally	678 72
	Frederick A. Kimch, administrator of John Scudder	9,503 39
	Daniel O'Connor, for the use of Joseph B. Stewart	2,317 90
	John L. Villalonga	90,389 89
	Henry Brigham et al	876 65
	Samuel C. McPherson's executrix	7,680 00
	Leon Lippman, survivor of M. and L. Lippman	4,025 00
	Matilda Johnson	15,195 52
	James Sheppard	42,908 32
	Howell W. Wright	1,620 10
	Edward P. Scott, executor of Isaac Scott	9,029 49
	Edward P. Scott, executor of Isaac Scott	18,234 52
	Edward P. Scott, executor of Isaac Scott	62,942 15
June 4, 1873	James N. Cartwright	14,193 00
	J. Wesley Vick	1,356 10
	Clarissa Ashford, executrix of James P. Ashford	23,569 43
	Charles Hill	37,695 95
	Warren R. Dent	17,923 90
	Augustus P. Wetter, trustee of Margaret Telfair	8,941 83
	Matthew Malsch	8,218 80
	Brittain M. Odom	6,392 40
	John B. Moncure	6,638 11
	J. A. Martin, administrator of James B. Johnson	34,813 70
	R. A. Rutherford and N. S. Rector	4,109 40
	A. B. Christian, administrator of J. B. Christian	7,685 75
	Total	2,635,096 94

PAPERS

ACCOMPANYING

REPORT OF THE SECRETARY OF THE TREASURY.

REPORT OF THE COMMISSIONER OF INTERNAL REVENUE.

TREASURY DEPARTMENT,
OFFICE OF INTERNAL REVENUE,
Washington, November 7, 1873.

SIR: I have the honor to transmit herewith the tabular statements made up from the accounts of this Office, which the Secretary of the Treasury is required to lay before Congress, as follows:

Table A, showing the receipts from each specific source of revenue, and the amounts refunded in each collection district, State, and Territory of the United States, for the fiscal year ended June 30, 1873.

Table B, showing the number and value of internal revenue stamps ordered monthly by the Commissioner, the receipts from the sale of stamps, and the commissions allowed on the same; also the number and value of stamps for special taxes, tobacco, cigars, snuff, distilled spirits, and fermented liquors, issued monthly to collectors during the fiscal year ended June 30, 1873.

Table C, showing the territorial distribution of internal revenue from various sources in the United States for the fiscal years ended June 30, 1864, 1865, 1866, 1867, 1868, 1869, 1870, 1871, 1872, and 1873.

Table D, showing the aggregate receipts from each collection district, State, and Territory, for the fiscal years ended June 30, 1863, 1864, 1865, 1866, 1867, 1868, 1869, 1870, 1871, 1872, and 1873.

Table E, showing the total collections from each specific source of revenue for the fiscal years ended June 30, 1863, 1864, 1865, 1866, 1867, 1868, 1869, 1870, 1871, 1872, and 1873.

Table F, showing the ratio of receipts from specific sources to the aggregate of all collections for the fiscal years ended June 30, 1864, 1865, 1866, 1867, 1868, 1869, 1870, 1871, 1872, and 1873.

Table G, an abstract of reports of district attorneys concerning suits and prosecutions under the internal revenue laws, during the fiscal year ended June 30, 1873.

Table H, an abstract of seizures of property for violation of internal revenue laws during the fiscal year ended June 30, 1873.

The aggregate receipts from all sources, exclusive of the direct tax upon lands and the duty upon the capital, circulation, and deposits of national banks, for the fiscal year ended June 30, 1873, were $114,075,456.08. This amount includes sums refunded and allowed on drawbacks.

The amount of drawback allowed during the last fiscal year was as follows:

On spirits	$33,700 20
On tobacco	1,959 30
On general merchandise	16,686 81
Total	52,346 31

The amount of tax abated on spirits destroyed under act of May 27, 1872, was $27,855.

There were refunded during the last fiscal year for taxes illegally assessed and collected $618,667.77.

SPIRITS.

The following statement shows the receipts from the several sources relating to distilled spirits for the fiscal years ended June 30, 1872 and 1873, together with the increase and decrease from each source:

Sources.	Receipts for fiscal year 1872.	Receipts for fiscal year 1873.	Increase.	Decrease.
Spirits distilled from apples, peaches, or grapes	$544, 848 83	$2, 014, 645 60	$1, 469, 796 77	
Spirits distilled from materials other than apples, peaches, or grapes	32, 572, 940 16	41, 116, 419 18	8, 543, 479 02	
Wine made in imitation of champagne	20 00	3, 531 90	3, 511 90	
Rectifiers	*319, 504 20	371, 456 72	51, 952 52	
Dealers, retail liquor	4, 028, 604 93	5, 016, 904 10	988, 299 17	
Dealers, wholesale liquor	*727, 651 92	781, 663 82	54, 011 90	
Manufacturers of stills	1, 391 66	1, 393 26	1 60	
Stills or worms manufactured	4, 260 00	3, 280 00		$980 00
Stamps for distilled spirits intended for export		7, 081 50	7, 081 50	
Stamps, distillery warehouse	290, 264 00	148, 418 80		141, 845 20
Stamps, rectifiers'	367, 424 00	186, 100 60		181, 323 40
Stamps, wholesale liquor dealers'	139, 602 75	73, 767 00		65, 835 75
Excess of gaugers' fees	4, 118 93	520 83		3, 598 10
Articles and occupations relating to spirits formerly taxed but now exempt	*10, 474, 884 96	2, 374, 188 45		8, 100, 696 51
Total	49, 475, 516 36	52, 099, 371 78	11, 118, 134 38	8, 494, 278 96

Aggregate increase, $2,623,855.42.

* This amount, $10.474,884.96, includes $636,200.71 tax on rectifiers producing in excess of 200 barrels per year; $1,337,911.71 on sales of liquors in excess of $25,000 (including other merchandise) per annum; $2,010,986.53, per diem tax on distilleries, and $6,489,786.01 distillers' special and barrel tax, all of which taxes were included in the report for last year on page VII under their appropriate headings, but which taxes were repealed by act of June 6, 1872, and are now therefore presented in one amount.

The increase in the receipts from the gallon tax on distilled spirits was $10,013,276; and from the special tax of rectifiers and dealers in liquor, $1,094,264; making a total increase from these sources of over $11,000,000. The tax on distilled spirits was raised from 50 to 70 cents per gallon August 1, 1872. To this fact is due the large increase in the receipts from this source. The large increase in the receipts from special taxes is doubtless owing in great part to the earlier and more thorough collection of special taxes since the introduction of the present system of paying them by stamps. A part of this $11,000,000 increase was, however, offset by the loss of nearly $400,000 during the last year by the reduction of the value of stamps for spirits, other than tax-paid stamps, from 25 cents to 10 cents each, under act of June 6, 1872; and by the further loss of a little over $8,000,000 by the repeal, under the same act, of certain taxes relating to spirits, leaving a balance of a little more than two and a half millions as the increase in the receipts from all sources relating to spirits.

PRODUCTION OF SPIRITS DURING FISCAL YEAR ENDED JUNE 30, 1873.

Taxable gallons.

Total production from materials other than fruit 68, 236, 567
Total production from fruit 2, 914, 800

Total 71, 151, 367

The following tabular statement shows the distribution of distilleries in the various States and Territories:

Statement showing the number of distilleries registered and operated during the fiscal year ended June 30, 1873.

States and Territories.	Grain.		Molasses.		Fruit.		Total number registered.	Total number operated.
	No. registered.	No. operated.	No. registered.	No. operated.	No. registered.	No. operated.		
Alabama	3	1			74	57	77	3
Arkansas					21	18	21	18
California	8	6			231	194	228	200
Connecticut	5	5			125	125	130	130
Delaware					77	77	77	77
Florida	1	1					1	1
Georgia	3	3			646	629	649	632
Idaho	2	2					2	2
Illinois	43	43			84	80	127	123
Indiana	24	28			157	148	185	176
Iowa	4	4			14	14	18	18
Kansas	7	2					7	2
Kentucky	178	163			714	706	892	869
Louisiana	4	4			16	1	20	5
Maine			1	1			1	1
Maryland	8	8			118	95	126	103
Massachusetts	2	2	7	7	54	28	63	4
Michigan	2	2					2	2
Minnesota								
Mississippi					7	7	7	7
Missouri	24	20			205	185	229	205
Montana	1	1					1	1
Nebraska	1	1					1	1
Nevada								
New Hampshire			1	1	2	2	3	3
New Jersey	2	2			200	189	202	191
New Mexico					5	5	5	5
New York	14	13	1	1	121	116	136	130
North Carolina	30	33			1,699	1,696	1,728	1,729
Ohio	61	51			70	69	131	120
Oregon					3	3	3	3
Pennsylvania	87	78	2	2	129	115	218	195
Rhode Island			1	1			1	1
South Carolina					142	138	142	124
Tennessee	48	40			666	657	714	697
Texas	2				25	21	27	21
Utah								
Vermont					10	10	10	10
Virginia	21	20			1,424	1,401	1,445	1,421
Washington	2	1			1	1	3	2
West Virginia	1	1			264	162	265	163
Wisconsin	10	9					11	9
Total	611	563	13	13	7,325	6,948	7,949	7,504

From the above table it appears that during the last fiscal year 7,325 fruit distilleries were registered, and 6,948 operated; and that of the distilleries other than fruit, 624 were registered, and 556 operated.

The following statement shows the number of grain and molasses distilleries in operation at the beginning of each month during the fiscal year ended June 30, 1873:

Months.	Number of distilleries.		Capacity of grain distilleries.		Capacity of molasses distilleries.		Total spirit-producing capacity.
	Grain.	Molasses.	Bushels.	Gallons.	Gallons.	Spirits.	
July..................	158	8	58, 813	209, 506	11, 209	9, 567	219, 163
August................	144	7	41, 037	136, 921	11, 323	9, 624	146, 545
September............	150	10	49, 988	174, 536	15, 613	13, 270	187, 806
October..............	196	10	61, 928	214, 960	15, 896	13, 510	228, 470
November.............	227	9	71, 992	249, 481	15, 132	12, 862	262, 343
December.............	260	9	73, 234	229, 832	11, 608	9, 866	239, 698
January..............	301	10	77, 465	268, 197	12, 261	10, 422	278, 619
February.............	352	10	78, 503	271, 824	14, 390	12, 291	284, 115
March................	378	9	74, 535	255, 645	13, 631	11, 585	267, 230
April................	402	9	71, 514	241, 604	9, 877	8, 395	249, 999
May..................	309	10	53, 652	181, 860	10, 950	9, 324	191, 184
June.................	301	10	58, 607	203, 110	11, 304	9, 109	212, 219

	Gallons.	Gallons.
Quantity of distilled spirits in bond July 1, 1872, at 50 cents..............		10, 103, 392
Quantity of distilled spirits produced during the year ended June 30, 1873, at 50 cents.................................	5, 359, 013	
Quantity of distilled spirits produced during the year ended June 30, 1873, at 70 cents.................................	62, 877, 554	
		68, 236, 567
Quantity of distilled spirits withdrawn on payment of tax, at 50 cents..	14, 885, 340	
Quantity of distilled, spirits withdrawn on payment of tax, at 70 cents..	48, 086, 073	
		62, 971, 413
Quantity of distilled spirits exported, at 70 cents......................		625, 944
Quantity allowed by special credits, at 50 cents		45, 664
Quantity of distilled spirits withdrawn for scientific purposes, at 70 cents.		2, 865
Quantity on which the tax has been abated under the act of May 27, 1872, at 50 cents		43, 925
Quantity remaining in bond July 1, 1873, at 50 cents	487, 476	
Quantity remaining in bond July 1, 1873, at 70 cents	14, 162, 672	
		14, 650, 148
1,732,686 gallons of the quantity reported as remaining in bond have been removed on export bonds and proofs of landing, not yet presented, so that the quantity actually in warehouse is		12, 917, 462
Quantity removed for export during the year, including the quantity accounted for..		2, 358, 630

The tax collected on spirits withdrawn from warehouse during the fiscal year 1872 was $32,457,235.50. The tax collected on spirits withdrawn from warehouse during the fiscal year 1873 was $41,102,921.10. The tax on spirits withdrawn for export during the fiscal year 1873 was $1,651,041. If the tax had been collected on spirits withdrawn for export during the fiscal year 1873, as was the case during the fiscal year 1872, the receipts for the fiscal year 1873 would have been increased $1,651,041; thus swelling the receipts from spirits withdrawn from bond for the fiscal year 1873 to $42,753,962.10.

A comparative statement, therefore, of the receipts on account of all spirits withdrawn from bond for the two years, under like circumstances, would show an increase of $10,296,726.60, or over 31 per cent., in the receipts of the fiscal year 1873 over those for the preceding fiscal year.

The act of June 6, 1872, authorizing the withdrawal of spirits from distillery warehouse for export, without payment of the tax, has been in operation since the 1st of August, 1872, under the regulations of this Office approved by the Secretary of the Treasury:

Number of rectifiers in business July 1, 1873	1, 347
Number of distillery warehouses in existence July 1, 1872.....................	385
Number of distillery warehouses in existence July 1, 1873.....................	581
Number of distillery store keepers in assignment July 1, 1873..................	625
Number of distillery store keepers in commission July 1, 1873..................	1, 104

IMITATION WINES.

The tax received on imitation wines during the year ended June 30. 1873, was $3,531.90.

FERMENTED LIQUORS.

The tax received on fermented liquors, at $1 per barrel, for the years 1872 and 1873 was $8,009,969.72 and $8,910,823.83 respectively.

The number of brewers engaged in the manufacture of fermented liquors during the fiscal year ended June 30, 1873, was 3,554, distributed as follows: Alabama, 5; Arizona, 15; Arkansas, 1; California, 301: Colorado, 44; Connecticut, 31; District of Columbia, 18; Delaware, 3; Dakota, 5; Florida, 3; Georgia, 7; Idaho, 15; Illinois, 210; Indiana. 158; Iowa, 174; Kansas, 55; Kentucky, 53; Louisiana, 17; Maine, 8; Maryland. 74; Massachusetts, 49; Michigan, 202; Minnesota, 132; Mississippi, 3; Missouri, 130; Montana, 31; Nebraska, 23; Nevada, 41; New Hampshire, 5; New Jersey, 81; New Mexico, 8; New York, 481; North Carolina, 2; Ohio, 296; Oregon, 34; Pennsylvania, 500; Rhode Island, 6; South Carolina, 4; Tennessee, 7; Texas, 50; Utah, 29; Vermont 2; Virginia, 10; Washington Territory, 15; West Virginia, 21; Wisconsin. 280; Wyoming, 15.

The number of breweries reported for 1872 was 3,421.

The increase in the receipts of the last over the preceding year will be seen to be, in number of breweries 133, in aggregate of tax paid $900,854.11, and average per brewery of $165.86.

But this comparison does not afford a full and fair exhibit of the increased productiveness of the country in this branch of our manufactures, or of the increased efficiency of the improved means employed by this Office for securing the tax imposed thereon.

The number of breweries given for the year ended June 30, 1873, comprise all the tax-paying breweries, which had been in operation for any portion of that year. This is true, also, of the number given for the year 1872. But within the fiscal year ended June 30, 1873, in portions of the country the sale of fermented liquors was prohibited by State enactments, and numbers of breweries were thus cut short, by other than business causes, of the time within the year during which they would otherwise have continued to operate, and the production of those continuing to manufacture in the States referred to has been materially lessened.

TOBACCO.

The total receipts from tobacco for the fiscal year ended June 30, 1873, were $34,386,303.09. Compared with the total receipts for the fiscal year ended June 30, 1872, the following results are shown:

Year ended June 30, 1873, tobacco manufactured, of all descriptions, taxed at 20 cents per pound.......	$22, 217, 127 93	
Snuff, taxed at 32 cents per pound	1, 082, 048 60	
Tobacco, &c., taxed at 32 cents per pound, old collections......................................	94, 270 22	
Tobacco, &c., taxed at 16 cents per pound, old collections......................................	4, 411 47	
		$23, 397, 858 22
Year ended June 30, 1872, tobacco manufactured, snuff, &c., taxed at 32 cents per pound..................	18, 674, 569 26	
Tobacco, smoking, &c., taxed at 16 cents per pound...	5, 896, 206 33	
		24, 570, 775 59
Showing a decrease of collections on manufactured tobacco of all descriptions of............................		1, 172, 917 37

Year ended June 30, 1873, cigars, cheroots, and cigarettes............ $8,940,391 48
Year ended June 30, 1872, cigars, cheroots, and cigarettes............ 7,566,156 86

Showing an increase on cigars, &c., of............................ 1,374,234 62

Year ended June 30, 1873, received from sale of export
    stamps, at 25 cents $175 00
Export stamps, at 10 cents............................. 5,419 60
                                                                    $5,591 60
Year ended June 30, 1872, received from sale of export stamps........ 53,576 25

Decrease from sale of export stamps................................ 47,981 65

Year ended June 30, 1873, received from dealers in leaf tobacco...... $118,517 74
Year ended June 30, 1872, received from dealers in leaf tobacco...... 260,487 62

Decreased collections from dealers in leaf tobacco.................. 141,969 88

Year ended June 30, 1873, received from dealers in manufactured to-
    bacco, &c.. $1,663,552 02
Year ended June 30, 1872, received from dealers in manufactured to-
    bacco, &c.. 1,102,357 89

Increased collections from dealers in manufactured tobacco, &c...... 561,194 13

Year ended June 30, 1873, received from special taxes of tobacco and
    cigar manufacturers....................................... $165,091 27
Year ended June 30, 1872, received from special taxes of tobacco and
    cigar manufacturers....................................... 182,816 31

Decreased collections from special taxes of tobacco and cigar manu-
    facturers.. 17,725 04

Year ended June 30, 1873, collected from special taxes of peddlers of
    tobacco, under the act of June 6, 1872......................... $50,694 96

Year ended June 30, 1873, collected from sales of cigars, leaf and
    manufactured tobacco, and upon the penal sum of bonds of tobacco
    manufacturers, taxes which had accrued prior to June 30, 1872..... $44,602 80

Giving a grand total as above of $34,386,303.09, and showing an increase in the total receipts from the manufacture and sale of tobacco, snuff, and cigars, in all their forms, over the receipts from the same sources for the preceding fiscal year, of $650,132.57.

PRODUCTION OF MANUFACTURED TOBACCO.

The quantity of tobacco represented by the collection of taxes, as above, during the year ended June 30, 1873, is as follows:

	Pounds.
Tobacco of all descriptions, taxed at 20 cents per pound................	111,095,640
Snuff, taxed at 32 cents per pound.....................................	3,381,402
Tobacco, taxed at 32 cents per pound..................................	294,594
Tobacco, taxed at 16 cents per pound.................................	27,572
Tobacco, &c., exported directly from manufactories...................	8,177,107

Total in pounds.. 122,906,315
Deducting the quantity stored in bonded warehouses June 30, 1872, and
    withdrawn during the year on payment of tax, together with the quan-
    tity on which taxes were collected which had accrued prior to July 1,
    1872, to the amount of... 6,525,381

And we have a balance of,... 116,440,934

8 Ab

pounds as the actual product of the year, so far as such products have been reported to this Office, and showing an increase over the annual production reported for the preceding fiscal year of 9,180,079 pounds.

The number of cigars, cheroots, &c., on which taxes were collected during the fiscal year ended June 30, 1873, was 1,807,034,646, showing an excess over the number reported for the preceding fiscal year of 279,328,674.

The act of June 6, 1872, established a uniform rate of tax on all descriptions of chewing and smoking tobacco of 20 cents per pound, instead of the previous rates of 16 and 32 cents per pound, leaving the rate of tax on snuff at 32 cents per pound, as provided by the act of July 20, 1868. This was an average reduction of 22½ per cent. upon the rates at which the taxes for the previous fiscal year had been collected. But, notwithstanding this large reduction in the average rate of tax, the decrease of collections under the new ate of 20 cents per pound on all descriptions of tobacco, both chewing and smoking, is only a small fraction over 4 per cent., or, more exactly, 4$\frac{1}{10}$ per cent. During the fiscal year ended June 30, 1873, the unprecedented quantity of 114,789,20b pounds of tobacco in its various manufactured forms reached taxation, being a quantity in excess of the preceding fiscal year of 19,579,889 pounds.

A part of this increase is owing to increased consumption, which undoubtedly keeps pace with the annual increase of population. A part may be due to the fact that after the closing out of the bonded warehouses a portion of the surplus stock which previously had been stored in them, awaiting a demand for consumption before the tax was paid, was during the last year placed upon the market, tax paid in anticipation of its demand. But by far the greater portion of this increase, in my opinion, to an amount not less than 15,000,000 pounds, is directly due to the fact that the act of June 6, 1872, which went into operation at the beginning of the last fiscal year, imposed a heavier tax on the sale of leaf tobacco, where such sales were made to persons who purchased leaf tobacco for direct consumption in an unmanufactured state, thus requiring the consumer to pay about the same amount of tax to the Government on the tobacco he consumed, whether in the manufactured or unmanufactured form. As between the two classes of tobacco, the tax being equal, or nearly so, the consumer does not hesitate to give the preference, in almost every case, to the manufactured article.

As shown by the figures given, the result of this legislation has been to increase largely the returns of manufactured tobacco, thus showing that the business of the manufacturers has been also largely increased. It has at the same time freed them from an unjust and an unequal competition with dealers in unmanufactured tobacco. It has enabled the Government to make a large reduction in the rate of tax, (22½ per cent.,) thereby cheapening the article to general consumers, while at the same time no material reduction has been made in the revenue derived directly from chewing and smoking tobacco.

Equally favorable have been the results upon the legitimate cigar trade of the additional provisions relating to leaf tobacco. They have been alike protective to the interests both of the Government and the honest cigar manufacturers. Under the present law none but legally authorized cigar manufacturers can purchase leaf tobacco to be made into cigars. The leaf dealer who shall sell leaf tobacco to an unauthorized manufacturer or maker of cigars, to be illicitly worked up without the payment of the Government tax, which was largely practiced prior to the present stringent enactments on that subject, renders himself liable to a special tax of $500, in addition to penalties. It is estimated that not less than $500,000 of the increased collections upon cigars during the last fiscal year are due directly to the practical operation of these provisions on that branch of the tobacco business, and to that extent has the legitimate cigar trade, as well as the Government, been benefited.

EXPORTATION OF MANUFACTURED TOBACCO.

Apprehensions were entertained by parties favoring the continuance of the former system of export bonded warehouses, that there would be a large falling off in the quantity of manufactured tobacco shipped to foreign countries under the present system. These predictions, however, have not been verified by the actual results, which show, that notwithstanding some considerable time was required fully to inaugurate the change, and to familiarize shippers with all the details of the law and regulations under which such shipments are now made, instead of there being any falling off, there was an actual increase of some 544,064 pounds of exported tobacco during the last fiscal year.

The reports made to this Office of such shipments show the following results:

	Pounds.
Year ended June 30, 1873, exported of tobacco in warehouses, June 30, 1872	1,932,937.75
Exported directly from manufactories	8,177,107.75
Total exports for the year	10,110,045.50
Year ended June 30, 1872	9,565,981.00
Showing an increase of	544,064.50

It has been the aim of this Office to render every facility in its power to the exporters of manufactured tobacco, and to that end it has endeavored to make the rules and regulations governing such exportations no more exacting than the safety of the revenue should require, and to reduce the expenses of exporters on account of export stamps, inspection fees, &c., to the minimum sum that the efficiency of the service would allow, in order to promote as much as possible this branch of our foreign trade.

UNIFORM TAX.

The consolidation of the different rates of tax on different classes of chewing tobacco has seemed to realize in practice all that the friends of this measure predicted of good results. No branch of the business seems to have experienced any inconvenience, or suffered any diminution in the amount of business formerly done under a graded tax, in consequence of such uniform tax. Not only has there been a large increase generally in the production and sale of manufactured tobacco, but it is believed that this increased business has been done with a reasonable amount of profit to the manufacturer. The law in its present operation is thought to act equally and impartially. Its requirements have become better understood. There has been a more general acquiescence in these requirements during the last fiscal year than ever before. There have been fewer violations of law and regulations, fewer seizures, and fewer prosecutions reported.

Abstract of cases compromised.

The whole number of cases compromised, as provided under section 102, act of July 20, 1868, during the fiscal year ended June 30, 1873, was 492.

Amount of tax accepted...	$182,376 10
Assessed penalty fixed by law..	1,872 56
Specific penalty in lieu of fines, penalties, and forfeitures................	77,921 33
Total amount received by compromises............................	262,169 99

Abstracts of reports of district attorneys for the fiscal year 1873.

SUITS COMMENCED.

Number of criminal actions	2,315
Number of civil actions in personam......................................	631
Number of actions in rem...	271
Whole number commenced..	3,217

SUITS DECIDED IN FAVOR OF UNITED STATES.

Number of criminal actions	150
Number of civil actions in personam......................................	378
Number of actions in rem...	316
Total number of suits decided in favor of United States..............	1,644

SUITS DECIDED AGAINST THE UNITED STATES.

Number of criminal actions	411
Number of civil actions in personam......................................	34
Number of actions in rem...	50
Total number of suits decided against the United States..............	495

SUITS SETTLED OR DISMISSED.

Number of criminal actions	1,315
Number of civil actions in personam......................................	125
Number of actions in rem...	116
Total number of suits settled or dismissed	1,556

SUITS PENDING JULY 1, 1873.

Number of criminal actions	3,930
Number of civil actions in personam......................................	1,221
Number of actions in rem...	474
Total number of suits pending July 1, 1873......................	5,625

Amount of judgments recovered by United States in suits in criminal actions...	$154,296 90
Amount of judgments recovered by United States in suits in civil actions in personam...	1,476,346 23
Amount collected on judgments and paid into court in suits in criminal actions...	38,493 97
Amount collected on judgments and paid into court in suits in civil actions in personam..	291,514 81
Amount collected on judgments and paid into court in actions in rem or proceeds of forfeiture...	73,953 45

Abstract of seizures.

Seizures of property for violation of internal revenue law during the fiscal year ended June 30, 1873, were as follows:

45,531 gallons of distilled spirits, valued at	$58,231 95
702 barrels of fermented liquors, valued at	3,486 87
210 pounds of snuff, valued at	16 50
41,885 pounds of tobacco, valued at	18,853 95
796,069 cigars, valued at	15,029 55
Miscellaneous property, valued at	193,587 50
Total value of seizures	289,206 32

The following table shows the receipts from all sources other than spirits and tobacco for the last two fiscal years, with the increase and decrease from each source:

Sources.	Receipts fiscal year 1872.	Receipts fiscal year 1873.	Increase.	Decrease.
FERMENTED LIQUORS.				
Fermented liquors, tax of $1 per barrel on	$8,009,969 72	$8,910,823 83	$900,854 11	
Brewers' special tax	248,528 74	304,650 21	56,121 47	
Dealers in malt liquors		100,463 80	109,463 80	
Total	8,258,498 46	9,324,937 84	1,066,439 38	
BANKS AND BANKERS.				
Bank deposits	3,643,272 19	3,009,302 79		$633,969 40
Bank capital	976,092 13	736,950 05		239,142 08
Bank circulation	8,864 82	24,778 62	15,913 80	
Total	4,698,229 14	3,771,031 46	15,913 80	873,111 48
Adhesive stamps	16,177,320 60	7,702,376 85		8,474,943 75
Penalties	442,205 12	461,653 06	19,447 94	
Articles and occupations formerly taxed but now exempt	19,053,006 53	6,329,782 00		12,723,224 53

The decrease in receipts from banks and bankers and adhesive stamps is due to legislation approved June 6, 1872. The class entitled "Articles and occupations formerly taxed but now exempt," includes certain taxes on old lists repealed prior to June 6, 1872, with the tax on income and gas. The aggregate receipts for the last fiscal year exceeded my estimate by $4,075,456.08.

It is estimated that the total receipts for the current fiscal year will be $100,000,000. This estimate will of course be affected somewhat by the continuance, or otherwise, of the present financial embarrassment. It is not thought that any material loss will ensue from the amounts of taxes received from the personal consumption of spirits or tobacco should the financial trouble continue; but a loss would undoubtedly be felt in the amount of spirits used chemically and in the mechanic arts.

SCHEDULE C.

The correspondence of this Office during the past year developed the fact that a contrariety of opinion and practice existed among the officers and tax-payers in relation to taxable articles under Schedule C. To secure uniformity of practice and, as far as possible, the proper collections from that source of revenue, a pamphlet containing the various rulings of this Office from 1863 to 1873 in regard to stamp duties on medicines and cosmetics was issued to the local officers, with instructions to place a copy in the hands of every dealer and druggist. The awakened attention thus secured already gives evidence of a healthy effect, and cannot fail to materially increase the revenue from that source should it remain unrepealed.

THE NEW SYSTEM.

The act of December 24, 1872, provided for the abolition of the offices of assessor and assistant assessor on or before the 30th day of June, 1873. Immediately upon the passage of the act, preparations were begun in the Office for this radical change. Regulations had to be revised and reprinted and general instructions prepared as to the method to be pursued in closing up the assessing offices and turning over their effects either to the Commissioner or the collectors. To avoid embarrassment from failures to transfer the offices, which would probably occur in some instances if the change was delayed until the last day (July 1) under the act, it was determined to make it, as far as practicable, on the 20th day of May. On that date a large proportion of the assessing offices were finally closed, and their papers and property turned over, a part to this Office and a part to the collectors. The assessment lists, by virtue of which, since the organization of the internal revenue system in 1862, the vast sums collected were authorized, and by which all refunding claims, either by Congress or the Commissioner, are tested, were shipped by express to this Office, and required over one thousand large boxes to contain them. The lists have been carefully sorted and filed for the future daily use which is demanded of them. Under the full and explicit instructions prepared and distributed by this Office the change was quietly and systematically made. The outgoing officers, with scarcely an exception, laid off their official garments gracefully, commending the simplicity and economy of the incoming system. The few districts that were not ready at that date, through accident or otherwise, were prepared for the change by the 30th of June, 1873, and the first day of the current fiscal year found the old system gone and the new in operation. Two hundred and twenty-eight assessors, 240 clerks, and 1,010 assistant assessors were thus finally discharged from the service at a large annual saving to the national Treasury, as shown below.

The law which abolished the office of assessor, authorized and required the Commissioner to make the various inquiries, determinations, and assessments of taxes which had been made by these officers; accordingly such monthly assessment lists are now so made up, and transmitted to the collectors of the various districts. It was soon found that the receipts of collectors, for their lists, reached this Office earlier than when prepared by the local assessing officers. This is doubtless largely due to the fact that all these assessments are prepared at one point, and by the same hands, thus avoiding the delays and controversies referred to in the report of last year, incident to the varied " interpretations of two or three hundred unassociated minds." The receipts of special taxes (licenses) show particularly the beneficial effects of the changes wrought by the new law.

The collections from spirits and tobacco have been hereinbefore treated at large under their respective heads.

In the report of this Office made last year, in which the new system was proposed, it was asserted that a large saving per annum, in expenses, might be expected if the system was adopted. The following figures will show its annual saving in comparison with the old system which it supplanted, and the plan (act of June 6, 1872) of reducing to eighty districts, which was repealed before it had been inaugurated:

The appropriations for assessing and collecting the internal revenue for the
  fiscal year ended June 30, 1873, were, (including $1,500,000 for salaries
  and expenses of gaugers and store keepers)............................. $6,200,000
Appropriations for the fiscal year 1874, (including $1,500,000 for salaries
  and expenses of gaugers and store keepers)............................. 4,600,000
                                                                          _____
  Difference.. 1,600,000

The estimate for the fiscal year 1874, based on the reduction to eighty districts, was $5,062,827, or $537,173 less than the appropriation for the fiscal year 1873.

The plan adopted in lieu of the eighty-district plan, to wit, abolishing the offices of assessors and assistant assessors, reduced the expenses $1,062,827 lower than the estimated reduction under the eighty-district plan, and $1,600,000 lower than the appropriation for 1873, under the old system.

The estimates for the fiscal year 1875 show a further reduction of $9,458, or $1,609,458 less than the appropriation for the fiscal year 1873, and $1,072,285 less than the estimate for 1874, based on the eighty-district plan.

It was thought at first that an additional clerical force would be needed in this Office in view of the increased labor under the act of December 24, 1872, but diligence and an enthusiastic application to their new duties on the part of the existing clerical forces have obviated such supposed necessity. For a considerable part of the past summer a number of the clerks were employed several hours each day after the regular business hours in executing and adjusting the new system. This gratuitous labor was cheerfully performed, and is deserving of special commendation.

SALARIES.

The change under the law dispensing with assessors and assistant assessors made a re-organization of the collecting forces necessary, and required a small average increase of allowance for collecting expenses. The assessing had cost more than the collecting in about the proportion of three to two. To make the saving anticipated under the new system, and at the same time to insure a sufficient force to superintend and collect the revenue of the country, it was concluded to regulate the expenses, as a general thing, by the following rule: aggregate the entire expense of assessing and collecting in the respective districts for the past year under the old plan, divide that by two, and allow the result respectively to each district. This gives a slight average increase to the collectors for expenses to compensate them for the additional labor and responsibility, and yet makes sure the large saving heretofore noticed. It is very desirable that Congress should fix definitely the pay of the leading local officers—collectors. Under the present system, special and controlling allowances have to be made in all cases, the districts arranging themselves into two classes, each of which requires allowance, but for contrary reasons: First, when the collections are small and the salary and commissions are not large enough to personally compensate the collector, and at the same time afford him sufficient means to employ a proper subordinate force. Second, when the collections are so large that, with the maximum salary ($4,500) allowed the collector, there would be more realized, in addition to his personal salary, than would be proper to be expended on subordinates. In the first class we give additional aid to secure the due enforcement of the law. In the second we withhold certain amounts to prevent the lavish and unnecessary expenditure of money.

It will at once be seen that this is a most delicate responsibility. It involves the measuring of men's services, which is always embarrassing, and urges a conflict between this department and its chief subordinates on the most tender point, next to character—that of moneyed interest. On the one hand, the subordinate officer is apt to think that he has been unfairly dealt with, while, on the other, the controlling officer is fearful that he may have been too free with that portion of the public purse intrusted to him.

It is urgently desired that Congress should fix by law the exact compensation of collectors, and the following schedule, based upon collections, is respectfully submitted as one that would fairly compensate them:

Collectors collecting not over $50,000 per annum, salary $2,500
Collectors collecting over $50,000 and not exceeding $250,000, salary 3,000
Collectors collecting over $250,000 and not exceeding $500,000, salary 3,500
Collectors collecting over $500,000 and not exceeding $750,000, salary $4,000
Collectors collecting over $750,000 and not exceeding $1,000,000, salary 4,500
Collectors collecting over $1,000,000, salary 5,000

Starting with a sum ($2,500) none too large, it would seem, for one who gives a bond ranging from $50,000 to $100,000, and who is responsible in the matter of due diligence for all the taxes of his district, as well as the honesty of his subordinates, and concluding with an amount ($5,000) strikingly small for the annual care, as is the case in a number of instances, of six or seven millions of the public money, it is hoped that this recommendation will receive congressional favor and early pass into the law.

The act of June 6, 1872, reduced the number of supervisors from twenty-five to ten, thus more than doubling the area of their districts but leaving their compensation $3,000 per annum, the same as before. Under these circumstances I recommend that the salary of supervisors be fixed at $4,000 per annum. The duties of these officers are of great importance to the service and involve constantly pressing and grave responsibilities. In some of their districts the performance of duty is frequently attended with personal danger, and in all it demands constant travel and exposure. Their individual districts average in square miles a territory one-fifth larger than Austria, or nearly as large as the whole of Great Britain and France together.

With the general service so much reduced in its numbers of employés and yearly expenses, with the responsibility of the remaining officers so largely increased, it is respectfully suggested that the above slight increase of expenditure can be well afforded.

REVISION AND COMPILATION OF THE LAWS.

During the year a revision of the internal revenue laws in force, as provided for in section 45, act of June 6, 1872, has been prepared and published, and generally distributed to Congress and the revenue service. This work has been conveniently arranged for reference by placing, as far as possible, all the law on each subject of taxation under its appropriate title; all obsolete or repealed law is eliminated, amendments are incorporated in their proper places, and a full and proper index accompanies the whole. It meets a want long felt, substantially aids the efforts of those charged with the execution of the laws, and will materially simplify the labor of Congress when considering amendments thereto. The two gentlemen in this Office, appointed by you to perform this work have accomplished it in addition to their regular duties, the larger portion of it after office hours, and, in accordance with precedent, I would recommend that they be suitably compensated.

ADDITIONAL RECOMMENDATIONS.

Section 44 of the act of June 6, 1872, provided, in effect, that all claims for the refunding of taxes alleged to have been erroneously assessed or collected must be presented to the Commissioner, and all suits or proceedings to recover such taxes must be brought "within two years next after the cause of action accrued and not after." It provided, however, as to claims which had accrued prior to the passage of the act, (June 6, 1872,) that the presentation thereof to the Commissioner, or the bringing of action thereon in the courts, must be done within one year from the last mentioned date.

As must always occur on the taking effect of any statute of limitation, some meritorious claims have doubtless been barred by the act above mentioned which might have been presented, but through neglect, indifference, or otherwise, were not. It would seem reasonable, however, to assume that few, if any, cases of actual hardship to tax-payers failed of presentation within the year given for that purpose.

On the other hand, it is quite probable that the statute has barred very many claims which, with a *prima-facie* appearance of legality, were in fact without merit, either in law or equity, but which it would have been difficult for the Government to disprove, owing to the recent change of system, under which many of our oldest officers have necessarily left the service.

I would repeat the suggestion contained in my report of November 21, 1871, that "section 44 of the act of July 20, 1868, should be amended by making the minimum penalty smaller, such penalty being now a fine of not less than $1,000, with not less than six months' imprisonment. The undue severity of this punishment would seem to be obvious as applied to the offenses of carrying on the business of a retail or wholesale liquor-dealer, rectifier, or manufacturer of stills, ' without having paid the special tax' in cases wherein no intent to defraud exists; the omission arising from ignorance of the law, or other circumstances not fraudulent, yet constituting no legal excuse under the terms of the section. The practical effect of providing so disproportionate a punishment for these offenses is to discourage complaints, defeat convictions, and induce suspensions of sentence, in many cases in which some moderate punishment should be enforced, as well to vindicate the law as to secure future compliance with its requirements."

The repeal of all documentary stamp duties under Schedule B, except that of two cents on bank checks, drafts, or orders, by the act of June 6, 1872, left many stamps in the hands of dealers and others throughout the country, for which they had no use; and such as have been presented to this office have been redeemed or exchanged, under the provisions of section 161 of the act of June 30, 1864, as amended by section 41 of the act of June 6, 1872.

The amount so redeemed and exchanged from October 1, 1872, to October 1, 1873, was $473,844.44.

As it is believed that the public have now had a sufficient notification of the willingness of the Government to redeem or exchange such stamps as might be presented, accompanied by satisfactory evidence that they had not been used, I would recommend such legislation by Congress as will limit the time to July 1, 1874, within which documentary stamps issued under Schedule B of a greater denomination than two cents may be presented for redemption, under section 161 of the act of June 30, 1864, as amended by section 41 of the act of June 6, 1872.

The suggestions made in my last annual report that the amendment of June 6, 1872, to section 59 of the act of July 20, 1868, relating to the special taxes of dealers in liquors, should be made more explicit, were fully met by the carefully drawn House bill No. 4069, entitled "An act to correct an error in section 13 of the act of June 6, 1872, and to amend certain sections of other acts relating to internal revenue." That bill passed the House of Representatives on the 3d day of March last, but unfortunately failed of being acted on by the Senate, solely, it is understood, for want of time in which to consider it. It is very important that the same or a similar bill should be enacted as soon as practicable.

Respectfully,

J. W. DOUGLASS,
Commissioner.

Hon. WILLIAM A. RICHARDSON,
Secretary of the Treasury.

REPORT OF THE COMPTROLLER OF THE CURRENCY.

TREASURY DEPARTMENT,
OFFICE OF THE COMPTROLLER OF THE CURRENCY,
Washington, November 28, 1873.

SIR: I have the honor to submit for the consideration of Congress, in compliance with section sixty-one of the national currency act, the following report:

The first national bank, under the act of February 25, 1863, was organized in Philadelphia June 20, 1863,* and the first circulating notes were issued December 21 of the same year. Since that time 2,129 national banks have been organized, 32 of which have failed, and 117 gone into voluntary liquidation by a vote of two-thirds of the shareholders, under section 42 of the act. During the last year 68 banks have been organized, 11 have failed, and 21 have gone into voluntary liquidation, leaving 1,980 in existence on November 1, 1873.

---

* The first proceedings in the Congress of the United States in reference to the establishment of a bank were June 21, 1780, at which time a committee of three was appointed to confer with the inspectors and directors of the proposed bank, which committee, on June 22, 1780, reported as follows:

Whereas a number of patriotic citizens of Pennsylvania have communicated to Congress a liberal offer on their own credit, and by their own exertions, to supply and transport 3,000,000 rations, and 300 hogsheads of rum, for the use of the Army, and have established a bank for the sole purpose of obtaining and transporting the said supplies with the greater facility and dispatch; and whereas on the one hand the associators, animated to this laudable exertion by a desire to relieve the public necessities, mean not to derive from it the least pecuniary advantage; so, on the other, it is just and reasonable that they should be fully re-imbursed and indemnified: Therefore,

Resolved unanimously, That Congress entertain a high sense of the liberal offer of the said associators to raise and transport the beforementioned supplies for the Army, and do accept the same as a distinguished proof of their patriotism.

Resolved, That the faith of the United States be, and the same hereby is, pledged to the subscribers to the said bank, for their effectual re-imbursement in the premises.

The proposed bank of 1780 was completed by the act of incorporation of 1781 of the Bank of North America. This bank was converted from a State bank to a national bank December 8, 1864.

The following table exhibits the resources and liabilities of the national banks at the close of business September 12, the date of their last regular report—the returns from New York City, from other redemption cities, and from the remaining banks being given separately:

	New York City. 48 banks.	Other redemption cities.* 1-1 banks.	Country banks. 1,767 banks.	Aggregate. 1,076 banks.
Resources.				
Loans and discounts	$199,160,557 79	$302,223,070 82	$478,549,345 61	$940,223,304 22
Overdrafts	162,450 04	594,439 05	3,209,914 63	3,946,812 12
U. S. bonds to secure circulation	33,870,100 00	89,591,050 00	264,809,250 00	388,330,400 00
U. S. bonds to secure deposits	650,000 00	3,026,000 00	11,129,000 00	14,805,000 00
U. S. bonds and securities on hand	3,352,400 00	1,707,400 00	3,765,050 00	8,824,850 00
Other stocks, bonds, and mortgages	4,552,797 40	4,736,037 68	14,420,199 45	23,709,034 53
Due from redeeming and reserve agents		32,279,436 51	63,854,624 15	96,134,120 66
Due from other national banks	15,740,765 99	10,976,806 44	14,696,017 59	41,413,620 06
Due from other banks and bankers	2,077,886 04	3,335,722 30	6,609,850 07	12,022,873 41
Real estate, furniture, and fixtures	8,469,864 33	8,601,588 75	17,590,310 13	34,661,623 21
Current expenses	905,022 11	2,380,410 80	3,699,404 08	6,985,436 99
Premiums	786,179 60	1,689,840 56	5,356,773 62	7,752,843 87
Checks and other cash items	2,074,729 53	1,906,842 91	7,466,300 80	11,433,913 22
Exchanges for clearing-house	67,897,740 69	21,024,262 84		88,920,003 53
Bills of other national banks	2,615,583 00	4,955,579 00	8,502,644 00	16,076,806 00
Bills of State banks		11,211 00	15,826 00	27,037 00
Fractional currency	335,394 32	535,538 90	1,432,841 04	2,302,774 26
Specie	14,585,810 55	3,210,970 07	2,071,688 83	19,868,469 45
Legal-tender notes	21,468,530 00	24,569,405 00	46,279,722 00	92,347,683 00
U. S. certificates of deposit	10,810,000 00	7,530,000 00	2,250,000 00	20,610,000 00
Clearing-house certificates	175,000 00			175,000 00
Totals	389,406,310 48	489,356,098 65	951,784,836 40	1,830,627,845 53
Liabilities.				
Capital stock	70,235,000 00	127,164,985 00	293,672,631 00	491,072,616 00
Surplus fund	21,923,211 45	32,470,516 75	65,920,771 00	120,314,499 20
Undivided profits	11,210,470 03	12,764,472 21	30,540,189 52	54,515,131 76
National bank notes outstanding	27,492,342 00	77,800,560 00	233,794,897 00	339,081,799 00
State bank notes outstanding	146,525 00	207,127 00	835,201 00	1,188,853 00
Dividends unpaid	203,979 69	390,700 03	875,868 26	1,402,547 89
Individual deposits	167,512,669 74	172,065,102 29	283,107,794 96	622,685,563 99
U. S. deposits	296,877 39	1,496,322 71	6,036,117 63	7,829,327 73
Deposits of U. S. disbursing officers	40,297 13	1,396,783 51	6,731,509 49	8,698,560 13
Due to national banks	72,257,760 95	43,649,016 01	17,765,945 64	133,672,732 94
Due to other banks and bankers	18,113,050 50	15,469,278 24	5,715,819 36	39,298,148 14
Notes and bills rediscounted		1,349,053 54	4,638,454 78	5,987,512 36
Bills payable	62,125 30	3,272,799 24	2,145,629 42	5,480,554 00
Totals	389,406,310 48	489,356,098 65	951,784,836 40	1,830,627,845 53

* The redemption cities, in addition to New York, are: Boston, Albany, Philadelphia, Pittsburgh, Baltimore, Washington, New Orleans, Louisville, Cincinnati, Cleveland, Chicago, Detroit, Milwaukee, Saint Louis and San Francisco.

DISTRIBUTION OF THE CURRENCY.

The act of February 25, 1863, and the subsequent acts of June 3, 1864, and March 3, 1865, authorize the issue of three hundred millions of circulating notes to national banks to be organized under the provisions of those acts, one hundred and fifty millions of which were required to be "apportioned to associations in the States, in the District of Columbia and the Territories, according to representative population, and the remainder among associations formed in the several States, the District of Columbia and the Territories, having due regard to the existing capital, the resource and business of each State, District, and Territory."

The whole amount of currency authorized by these acts was issued to national banks during the four years following.

The following table exhibits the apportionment of the whole amount of circulation authorized by law ($354,000,000) to the different States and Territories, upon the basis of population and wealth as given in the census returns of 1870, together with the amount outstanding and authorized, and the excess and deficiency:

States and Territories.	Apportionment on population.	Apportionment on wealth.	Aggregate apportionment.	Outstanding and authorized circulation.	Excess.	Deficiency.
Maine	$2,677,812	$2,053,200	$4,031,018	$8,029,252	$3,998,234	
New Hampshire	1,461,134	1,446,840	2,947,934	4,624,525	1,676,547	
Vermont	1,517,376	1,380,600	2,897,976	6,932,030	4,034,054	
Massachusetts	6,669,869	12,549,300	19,220,169	59,523,671	40,284,442	
Rhode Island	997,747	1,752,300	2,750,047	13,385,840	10,635,793	
Connecticut	2,467,152	4,566,600	7,033,752	17,994,648	10,960,896	
Total Eastern States	16,011,120	23,789,800	39,790,920	110,499,966	70,699,046	
New York	20,118,813	34,267,400	53,386,213	60,976,006	2,589,793	
New Jersey	4,150,382	5,540,100	9,690,482	11,036,880	1,327,408	
Pennsylvania	16,167,317	22,425,900	38,593,217	42,055,781	3,462,564	
Delaware	573,873	566,400	1,140,273	1,296,615	156,342	
Maryland	3,584,651	3,787,800	7,372,451	9,252,847	1,880,396	
Total Middle States	44,604,036	70,587,600	115,191,636	124,608,139	9,416,503	
District of Columbia	604,520	743,470	1,347,990	1,530,091	182,131	
Virginia	5,624,642	2,407,200	8,031,842	3,902,342		$4,128,900
West Virginia	2,029,041	1,115,100	3,144,141	2,360,307		783,834
North Carolina	4,918,022	1,539,900	6,457,922	1,419,300		4,638,622
South Carolina	3,239,045	1,221,300	4,460,345	2,319,500		2,140,845
Georgia	5,435,587	1,575,300	7,010,887	2,365,603		4,645,382
Florida	861,846	265,500	1,127,346	90,000		1,037,346
Alabama	4,576,646	1,185,900	5,762,546	1,541,133		4,221,413
Mississippi	3,700,529	1,220,000	4,630,529	5,876		5,033,653
Louisiana	3,236,983	1,830,900	5,230,703	3,646,870		1,583,843
Texas	3,757,640	928,100	4,685,740	920,160		3,764,780
Arkansas	2,223,936	920,400	3,144,336	192,405		2,951,861
Kentucky	6,064,027	3,557,700	9,621,727	7,657,900		1,963,827
Tennessee	5,777,114	2,238,200	8,715,318	3,341,736		5,373,582
Missouri	7,901,509	7,557,900	15,459,409	6,476,193		8,983,216
Total Southern and Southwestern States.	60,150,411	29,098,800	89,249,211	34,160,304	182,131	51,271,034
Ohio	12,234,726	13,151,100	25,385,826	23,876,370		$1,509,456
Indiana	7,714,871	7,469,400	15,184,271	14,706,415		477,856
Illinois	11,659,230	12,496,200	24,155,430	17,824,209		6,331,221
Michigan	5,435,357	4,230,300	9,665,657	7,485,043		2,180,614
Wisconsin	4,841,403	4,141,800	8,983,203	3,254,316		5,728,887
Iowa	5,481,681	4,230,300	9,711,981	5,674,985		4,036,996
Minnesota	2,018,445	1,345,200	3,363,645	3,330,414		33,231
Kansas	1,672,754	1,115,100	2,787,854	1,825,496		962,358
Nebraska	544,582	407,100	951,682	809,500		142,182
Total Western States	51,622,459	48,546,500	100,202,959	78,785,148		21,423,811
Nevada	195,052	177,000	372,052	11,864		360,188
Oregon	417,377	300,900	718,277	225,000		493,277
California	2,571,783	3,752,400	6,324,183		232,103	6,324,183
Colorado	192,953	193,900	386,853	528,955	232,103	
Utah	396,396	55,500	446,896	419,829		67,037
Idaho	68,852	35,400	104,252	90,000		14,252
Montana	94,540	68,500	163,040	232,000	68,960	
Wyoming	41,855	35,400	77,255	72,800		4,455
New Mexico	421,742	194,700	616,442	270,000		346,442
Arizona	44,334	17,700	62,034			62,034
Dakota	65,086	35,400	100,486	45,000		55,486
Washington	103,904	88,500	198,464			198,464
Total Pacific States and Territories	4,611,974	4,938,300	9,550,274	1,924,664	301,063	7,926,648
Grand total of States and Territories	177,000,000	177,000,000	354,000,000	333,968,249	40,589,742	80,621,493

The following table exhibits the number of banks organized, the number closed and closing, and the number in operation, with their capital, amount of bonds on deposit, and circulation issued, redeemed, and outstanding, in each State and Territory, on the 1st day of November, 1873:

States and Territories.	Banks organized.	Closed and closing.	In operation.	Capital paid in.	Bonds on deposit.	Circulation issued.	Circulat'n redeemed.	Circulat'n outstanding.
Maine	65	2	63	$9,540,000	$8,880,750	$10,392,100	$2,392,854	$8,029,252
New Hampshire	43	1	42	5,165,000	5,165,000	5,967,755	1,343,250	4,624,505
Vermont	44	2	42	8,555,012	7,736,000	8,909,960	1,977,980	6,932,630
Massachusetts	220	3	217	91,342,000	67,346,750	83,956,110	24,432,439	59,523,671
Rhode Island	62		62	20,504,800	14,981,700	18,044,800	4,699,960	13,345,840
Connecticut	83	3	80	25,324,620	20,306,800	24,530,980	6,556,342	17,994,648
Total Eastern States	517	11	506	160,291,632	124,415,000	151,861,751	41,571,785	110,466,966
New York	321	45	276	110,654,601	40,025,150	98,504,160	37,592,154	60,974,006
New Jersey	63	1	62	13,965,350	12,300,650	14,394,875	3,371,955	11,026,920
Pennsylvania	213	11	202	53,510,240	47,446,740	57,510,680	15,454,909	42,055,771
Delaware	11		11	1,523,185	1,453,200	1,756,515	459,900	1,296,615
Maryland	34	1	33	13,640,203	10,291,250	12,822,540	3,575,693	9,232,847
Total Middle States	642	58	584	193,286,689	140,706,050	185,202,780	60,504,641	124,660,139
District of Columbia	8	4	4	1,652,000	1,670,000	2,294,100	764,009	1,530,091
Virginia	28	6	22	4,185,000	3,926,000	4,229,800	607,458	3,582,342
West Virginia	19	2	17	2,506,000	2,571,600	3,169,200	808,893	2,360,307
North Carolina	16		16	2,100,000	1,830,100	1,836,160	147,360	1,684,800
South Carolina	12		12	4,170,000	2,425,000	2,229,540	53,040	2,176,500
Georgia	15	2	13	2,785,000	2,726,400	2,649,200	373,645	2,275,635
Florida	10	1	9	1,549,300	1,430,000	1,477,800	187,767	1,290,033
Mississippi	2	2				66,000	60,194	5,876
Louisiana	11	3	8	5,220,000	4,000,000	4,345,340	729,470	3,615,870
Texas	8		8	985,000	840,000	1,007,000	251,540	755,460
Arkansas	3	1	2	305,000	915,000	272,700	80,205	192,495
Kentucky	37	1	36	8,263,700	7,709,850	8,178,645	1,136,745	7,041,970
Tennessee	25	1	24	3,520,401	3,249,750	3,665,510	573,504	3,088,606
Alabama	11	5	36	9,345,300	6,695,350	8,126,055	1,908,622	6,217,433
Total Southern and Southwestern States	231	30	201	45,836,701	39,242,050	43,617,180	7,902,462	35,744,718
Ohio	149	12	168	29,035,000	26,187,750	31,572,610	7,948,240	23,624,370
Indiana	97	5	92	17,611,900	16,277,300	18,949,620	4,413,605	14,536,015
Illinois	144	7	137	20,443,000	18,010,000	20,149,450	4,323,391	16,346,059
Michigan	80	3	77	9,765,500	7,865,050	8,892,570	1,675,167	7,217,363
Wisconsin	52	7	45	3,640,000	3,434,350	4,365,700	1,242,844	3,122,816
Iowa	84	9	75	6,017,000	5,909,050	7,115,675	1,751,810	5,363,865
Minnesota	34	2	32	4,173,700	3,509,250	3,851,250	706,376	3,144,914
Kansas	25	1	20	1,975,000	1,765,000	1,740,135	202,609	1,537,496
Nebraska	11	1	10	905,000	940,000	886,200	94,700	791,500
Total Western States	708	46	662	94,062,000	83,906,500	98,222,880	22,552,992	75,664,459
Nevada	1	1				131,700	119,836	11,864
Oregon	1		1	250,000	250,000	275,500	25,500	225,000
Colorado	3		3	625,000	440,000	562,720	46,725	175,795
Utah	4	1	3	500,000	450,000	554,500	144,673	419,829
Idaho	1		1	100,062	100,000	110,600	29,620	80,000
Montana	6	1	5	450,000	245,000	262,300	10,300	252,000
Wyoming	2		2	125,000	40,000	54,000		54,000
New Mexico	2		2	200,000	200,000	289,800	19,800	270,000
Nevada	1		1	50,000	50,000	45,000		45,000
Washington								
Total Pacific States and Territories	25	3	22	2,250,000	2,015,000	2,261,120	417,462	1,843,600
Grand Total of States and Territories	2,129	147	1,975	495,736,022	390,314,600	441,196,161	132,745,222	348,550,949
OLD BANKS.								
Massachusetts	1	1				120,000	120,000	
California	5		5	3,990,000	2,537,500	2,074,600	44,600	2,030,000
Total	6	1	5	3,290,000	2,537,500	2,194,600	164,600	2,030,000

The act of July 12, 1870, authorized an additional issue of fifty-four millions of dollars, and provided that such notes should be issued to banking associations organized or to be organized in those States and Territories having less than their proportion under the apportionment contemplated by the act of March 3, 1865, and that the bonds deposited with the Treasurer of the United States to secure the additional circulation should be of any description of United States bonds bearing interest in coin. It also provided that a new apportionment of the increased circulation should be made as soon as practicable, based upon the census of 1870, and for the cancellation monthly of three per cent. certificates equal in amount to the national bank notes issued—the last of these certificates having been finally redeemed during the present year. Of this additional circulation, authorized by the act of July 12, 1870, there was issued to November 1, 1871, $24,773,260; in the year ending November 1, 1872, $16,220,210; in the year ending November 1, 1873, $7,357.17; leaving, at the date of this report, still to be issued to banks already organized, and in process of organization, $5,649,051.

The act of July 12, 1870, further provides that when the fifty-four millions of additional circulation "shall have been taken up," "the Comptroller of the Currency shall, as additional circulation may be required by the banks having less than their proportion, make a requisition for such an amount, commencing with the banks having a circulation exceeding one million of dollars in States having an excess of circulation, and withdrawing their circulation in excess of one million of dollars, and then proceeding *pro rata* with other banks having a circulation exceeding three hundred thousand dollars in States having the largest excess of circulation, and reducing the circulation of such banks in States having the greatest proportion in excess, leaving undisturbed any States having a smaller proportion until those in greater excess shall have been reduced to the same grade, and continuing thus to make the reduction provided for by this act until the full amount of twenty-five millions provided for shall be withdrawn; and the circulation so withdrawn shall be distributed among the States and Territories having less than their proportion, so as to equalize the same."

In accordance with the provisions of this section, it will be the duty of the Comptroller, as soon as the necessary bonds shall have been deposited to secure the small amount of additional circulation not already issued or "taken up," to proceed to make requisitions upon banks organized in the States which have an excess. It will probably be the duty of the Comptroller during the next three months to make requisitions as provided for by this act upon banks already organized in States which are in excess, for an amount equal to the aggregate amount of circulation called for by the applications on file from the States which are deficient. These requisitions will be made upon the banks located in the following States and cities:

Four in the city of New York $5,013,600
Thirty-seven in the city of Boston 13,250,000
Twenty-one in the State of Massachusetts 2,659,000
Seventeen in the city of Providence 2,518,000
Fifteen in the State of Connecticut 1,185,000

This will reduce to $1,000,000 the circulation of all banks in the city of New York having an excess over that amount, and the circulation of all banks in Massachusetts and Rhode Island to $300,000. If these banks do not return the amount of circulation within one year after the

* The amount of three per cent. certificates outstanding on July 1, 1870, was $45,545,000

requisition is made upon them, it is made the duty of the Comptroller of the Currency to sell at public auction, upon twenty days' notice, the bonds deposited by such associations as security for said circulation equal in amount to the circulation to be withdrawn, and not returned in compliance with the requisition. With the proceeds of the bonds the Comptroller is required to redeem the notes of these banking associations as they come into the Treasury. The notes of these banks are so scattered through the whole country that it will be impracticable for them to return their circulation without an expense not contemplated by the act; and it will, therefore, be for the interest of the banks to provide the Comptroller of the Currency with the requisite amount of legal-tender notes with which to redeem their circulation as it comes into the Treasury. To this extent the act may be executed; but the notes to be redeemed will not come to the Treasury for redemption to any considerable amount, and therefore but a small proportion of the twenty-five millions will be placed at the disposal of the Comptroller for redistribution to the banks of the South and West. The result will, therefore, be great embarrassment to the banks to whom the currency has already been issued, without providing any relief for organizations elsewhere, as contemplated by the act. The Comptroller, therefore, repeats the recommendation contained in his previous report, that section six of the act of July 12, 1870, be repealed, and that twenty-five millions additional circulation be authorized to be issued and distributed among the States, as heretofore provided.

The Comptroller also renews his recommendation that the law be so amended that national banks may be organized without circulation, upon the deposit of $10,000 of United States bonds with the Treasurer, instead of the deposit of one-third of the paid-up capital, as now required. He also recommends that banks already organized without circulation may be authorized to withdraw the bonds now on deposit in excess of $10,000, and that banks desiring to reduce their circulation may deposit legal-tender notes for that purpose and withdraw a proportionate amount of bonds.

The following comparative table exhibits the amount of circulation issued under State laws previous to the establishment of the national banking system, and the amount authorized by Congress; the ratio of bank circulation in each State in 1862, and the amount now issued, in proportion to capital and wealth, and the per capita of circulation in 1862, and the per capita of circulation authorized by Congress:

Comparative table, exhibiting by States the bank circulation,* the amount per capita, and the ratio of circulation to wealth and to capital, previous to the organization of the national banking system and in 1873.

States and Territories.	Bank circulation.		Circulation per capita.		Ratio of circulation to wealth.		Ratio of circulation to capital.	
	1862.	1873.	1862.	1873.	1862.	1873.	1862.	1873.
					Per ct.	Per ct.	Per ct.	Per ct.
Maine	85,499,478	84,051,252	$10 53	$12 41	2.4	2.3	91.3	95.
New Hampshire	1,192,034	4,624,525	12 46	14 53	2.6	1.8	83.3	74.
Vermont	5,621,851	6,932,630	17 81	20 97	4.6	2.9	132.7	93.
Massachusetts	28,957,630	50,525,671	23 52	40 31	3.5	2.8	42.6	64.
Rhode Island	6,413,404	13,395,840	36 73	61 29	1.7	4.5	30.7	51.
Connecticut	13,842,758	17,994,648	30 08	33 48	3.1	2.3	63.5	78.
Total Eastern States	65,516,155	110,449,906	20 90	31 69	3.5	2.7	51.7	68.
New York	30,182,819	60,976,006	10 10	13 01	2.1	0.9	26.8	24.
New Jersey	8,173,305	11,026,840	12 16	12 17	1.7	1.1	99.4	78.
Pennsylvania	27,649,501	42,055,781	9 53	11 94	1.9	1.1	105.8	76.
Delaware	678,340	1,296,615	6 04	10 37	1.5	1.3	176.2	63.
Maryland	6,649,030	9,252,847	9 68	11 85	1.8	1.4	54.9	63.
Total Middle States	82,372,091	124,606,130	9 97	12 82	2.0	1.0	53.1	66.
District of Columbia		1,530,091		11 63		1.2		86.
Virginia	19,817,148	3,902,342	12 41	3 18	2.5	1.0	180.2	69.
West Virginia		2,390,207		5 34		1.3		93.
North Carolina	5,218,500	1,819,300	5 26	1 70	1.1	0.7	66.3	86.
South Carolina	6,089,636	2,319,500	8 65	3 29	1.1	1.1	40.7	67.
Georgia	9,311,724	2,365,635	7 86	2 00	1.3	0.9	58.9	82.
Florida	116,270	90,000	83	48	0.1	0.2	97.3	84.
Alabama	5,055,228	1,541,133	5 24	1 55	1.0	0.8	101.5	83.
Mississippi		5,876		01		0.0		80.
Louisiana	8,876,519	3,646,470	12 51	5 02	1.5	1.1	51.0	68.
Texas		930,980		1 11		0.6		51.
Arkansas		192,495		40		0.1		98.
Kentucky	9,035,724	7,637,900	7 82	5 74	1.3	1.3	65.5	84.
Tennessee	4,540,906	3,341,736	4 09	2 66	0.9	0.7	127.4	83.
Missouri	4,037,277	6,476,193	3 42	3 76	0.8	0.5	33.9	64.
Total Southern and Southwestern States	71,098,406	38,160,308	6 17	2 91	1.1	0.8	66.3	77.
Ohio	9,057,837	23,876,370	3 87	8 98	0.7	1.1	150.6	81.
Indiana	6,702,890	14,706,415	5 02	8 75	1.3	1.2	150.9	83.
Illinois	619,246	17,824,399	36	7 02	0.1	0.9	31.4	75.
Michigan	131,067	7,163,043	17	6 32	0.0	1.0		75.
Wisconsin	1,643,390	3,253,316	2 12	3 06	0.6	0.5	58.9	69.
Iowa	1,249,000	5,674,385	1 85	4 75	0.5	0.8	136.5	91.
Minnesota	198,491	3,380,414	1 15	7 57	0.4	1.5	62.4	80.
Kansas	2,770	1,825,496	61	5 01	0.0	1.0	5.2	75.
Nebraska		869,500		6 28		1.2		63.
Total Western States	19,684,564	78,785,148	2 49	7 09	0.6	1.0	123.4	78.
Nevada		11,864		24				66.
Oregon		225,000		2 47		0.4		58.
California								
Colorado		538,395		13 52		2.6		72.
Utah		419,820		4 81		2.6		86.
Idaho		80,000		6 60		1.1		90.
Montana		222,000		12 24		1.7		63.
Wyoming		74,000		3 06		1.0		82.
New Mexico		270,000		2 91		0.9		88.
Arizona								
Dakota		15,000		3 17		0.7		80.
Total Pacific States and Territories		1,924,688		1 82		0.2		78.
Grand total of States and Territories	238,671,210	373,985,280	7 50	9 18	1.5	1.2	58.9	83.

* The circulation of the State banks in the year 1862 has been obtained from page 219 of the report of the Secretary of the Treasury on the condition of the banks at the commencement of the year 1862. The returns from Delaware, Maryland, Louisiana, Tennessee, and Kentucky were not complete. The aggregate amount of State bank circulation reported at that time was much greater than at any previous period.

† Outstanding and authorized circulation. ‡ Outstanding circulation.

FREE BANKING.

The restraining law of the State of New York (act of April 21, 1818) provided that " it shall not be lawful for any person, association of persons, or body-corporate, from and after the 1st day of August next, to keep any office of deposit for the purpose of discounting promissory notes, or for carrying on any kind of banking business or operations which incorporated banks are authorized by law to carry on, or issue any bills or promissory notes, as private bankers, unless thereunto specially authorized by law."

This law placed the whole banking interests of the country in the hands of a few chartered institutions, and was, in its effects, a grievous monopoly.   Most of the States of the Union organize, by special act of legislature, trust companies, savings-banks, and other corporations.   The Bank of England, and the private and joint-stock banks of England, organized prior to 1844, possess the right to issue circulation, and no such right has been granted to other organizations since that year.   All such favored institutions are monopolies.   But it cannot be said that the national banks of the United States are monopolies, in the same sense of the word.   The organization of national banks has, from the beginning, been open to all, and until the amount of circulation authorized by Congress was exhausted, all applications for the organization of such institutions with circulation, accompanied by proper indorsements certifying to the means and character of the applicants, were considered and granted, and the aggregate of circulation for which applications are now on file in this Office, the consideration of which has been postponed, does not exceed ten millions of dollars.   That the banks which were first organized were profitable to their shareholders is conceded; and it is a cause of congratulation that the surplus earnings of those years are husbanded in a surplus fund of more than one hundred and twenty millions of dollars, as a protection to depositors and creditors, in anticipation of times of panic and disaster.   The statistics we present show that the earnings of the banks, of late years, have not been excessive, and in many cases much less than the earnings and dividends which the shareholders of manufacturing, railroad, and other corporations realize from capital invested.   If the national banking system, under which one or more national banks have been organized in almost every city and thriving village in the Union, and where the earnings of business men and the savings of the people can be deposited with a greater degree of safety than under any previous system, is in any sense a monopoly, it is not the fault of the system, but an evil which arises from the existing state of the currency; and it is believed that the national banking system is in every sense less a monopoly than any national system of banking ever before devised.

The system is considered a monopoly because it is supposed that large profits are derived from the privilege of issuing circulating notes which are limited in amount.   The act of March 12, 1870, authorized an additional issue of fifty-four millions of dollars of national bank notes, but the whole amount has not yet been issued, chiefly for the reason that in the States to which the amount was assigned there is but little profit in the issue of such notes, as will be seen hereafter.   But to the erroneous belief that a large profit accrues from circulation to organizations of this kind, the demand for what is termed free banking may, to a large extent, be attributed.   The restraining act of the State of New York, as has been seen, prohibited individuals and associations from carrying on the business of banking without first obtaining special

9 AB

charters from the legislature. This law was repealed about thirty years after its passage, not without encountering bitter opposition. In the year following the repeal, the general banking system of the State of New York was authorized—a system based on the deposit of securities, with redemption at a fixed rate of discount, and it is probable that the term " free banking" originated chiefly from the fact that it superseded the monopoly which preceded it. The signification of the phrase " free banking," however, as now used, is not clearly defined, for there is nothing in this country to-day more free than banking. Every individual or association of individuals throughout the country has the right to negotiate promissory notes, drafts, and bills of exchange, to receive deposits, to loan money upon personal or real estate security, and to transact almost every kind of business pertaining to legitimate banking.

There is little doubt that the term " free banking" is, by many persons, understood to mean the unrestricted issue of bank-notes to any association of persons organizing a national bank and depositing the required amount of United States bonds as security; but there are few persons who have given any considerable attention to this subject who would be willing to advocate the unrestricted issue of national bank notes to an amount equal to the public debt.

It is probable that a more satisfactory definition of free banking would be, an issue of paper money which shall be promptly redeemed at the commercial center of the country. Such a currency may be divided into three classes—(1) an unsecured circulation, redeemable at par by the bank, or its agent in some designated city ; (2) a secured circulation, redeemable at its own counter at par, and at the commercial center at a fixed rate of discount ; and (3) a circulation exchangeable at par for lawful money at its own counter, and by its agent appointed for that purpose.

The currency of the New England States previous to the war is a fair example of the first class. That system was generally known as the " Suffolk system," because the Suffolk Bank, at Boston, compelled the redemption of the notes of the New England Banks at its own counter at par. The system, however, was not free, but a monopoly, as banks could only be organized under special charters obtained from the legislatures of the six New England States. This circulation was not required to be secured by any deposit pledged for that purpose, and the failure of banks in some of the New England States, which not infrequently happened, almost always resulted in great loss, not only to the creditor, but to the bill-holder. The Suffolk Bank, at Boston, forced the redemption of the notes at par at its own counter, by a system of assorting and returning the notes to the place of issue, but the same notes were invariably at a discount of one-eighth per cent. in New York. The notes of these banks were therefore neither safe nor exchangeable at par in coin at the chief commercial center.

The New York State system of free banking is an example of the second class of currency, and the only system of free banking which has ever been successfully maintained ; and it is probable that the more thoughtful advocates of what is termed free banking propose that circulation shall be issued and redeemed under the national-currency act upon a similar plan.

Taking for granted that the advocates of free banking base their arguments upon the success of the system authorized in that State by the act of April 18, 1838, it may be well to contrast the condition of the currency and of the public debt at the time of the inauguration of that system, at the commencement of the war, and at the present time.

The currency of the State of New York first issued was secured by stocks of the different States, and by bonds and mortgages deposited by corporations with the comptroller of the State. Subsequently, by various amendments, the law was so changed as to provide for the issue of circulation based entirely upon the bonds of the United States and of the State of New York, and that was the basis at the time of the breaking out of the war. The debt of the State of New York at the time of the inauguration of the system was $11,256,152, and the debt of the United States was $10,434,221, and all these bonds were above par in the market. In 1860, the funded debt of the State of New York was $34,140,238 and the funded debt of the United States $44,794,092.* The laws authorizing the issue of circulating notes were more numerous than the States and Territories of the Union, and the rates of discount in the New York market upon the bank-notes issued and in general circulation varied from one-eighth of one per cent. to one and one-half per cent. discount, while many bank-notes that had a local circulation were quoted at from 5 to 10 per cent. discount. The notes of the New York and New England banks, only, circulated throughout the whole Union, like the national bank currency of to-day.

The funded debt of the United States is to-day more than eighty times as great as were the combined debts of the United States and of the State of New York in 1838, and it is about twenty-one times greater than was their combined debt in 1860. The United States then issued coin, only, as currency. Now the national bank notes and the legal-tender notes are about twenty times the amount of the circulation of the State of New York at that time, and more than three and one-half times the amount of the circulation authorized at that time by all of the States of the Union.†

The amounts of the funded debt and of the currency are therefore entirely changed, and it is by no means evident that what was a good thing for the State of New York in 1860 is, in 1873, a good thing for the whole United States.

The New York State law authorized the issue of bank-notes to all associations organized under its provisions, at the face value of United States and New York State six per cent. bonds deposited, and to this feature of the law the Bank of England and the national-currency act are indebted for those excellent provisions which insure absolute security to the bill-holder.

But this law did not authorize an unrestricted issue of bank-notes. It required that the bank-notes issued to an association should be redeemed at its own counter, and by its agent in New York, Albany, or Troy, at a discount. Practically the notes were redeemed at the agency, and not at the counters of the bank. Redemption was the cardinal principle of the law, and it was expected that this principle of redemption would prevent an issue of circulation which should exceed the requirements of business. Redemption in the New York law meant discount. It was to be a redemption in specie, and was founded upon the avowed principle that specie was worth more, and was more desirable to hold, than the circulating notes authorized. But in order that there should be no mistake, the law itself provided that the discount upon the circulating notes at the redemption agencies should be one-fourth of one per cent. If a law had been passed by Congress at that time for the redemption of the gold coin in silver coin, or for the redemption of the silver coin in copper coin, such a law

---

* In addition to the funded debt proper there were $19,795,611 of Treasury notes outstanding.

† Circulation in 1860 was $207,102,000.

would have been a dead letter, (for the reason that gold coin is known to be of greater intrinsic value in the market than silver coin, and the silver of greater intrinsic value than copper,) though each of these coins is a legal tender to an amount fixed by law. In order to have a proper system of redemption, it is necessary that the thing to be redeemed shall be known to be worth less than the thing in which it is to be redeemed; and this principle was legalized by the New York State legislature, when it provided that the bank-note should be worth, in the city of New York, one-quarter of one per cent. less than the gold coinage of the United States. If forty millions of dollars, therefore, were issued,* its value at the moment of issue was $100,000 less than $40,000,000. If the circulation were redeemed three times a year, there would be $300,000 of loss on one side, and $300,000 of gain on the other side. The gain was, as a general rule, divided between the bank which issued the money and the banks which redeemed the same, while the country merchant, the manufacturer and the jobber in the great cities, experienced the loss. But the circulation of the State of New York was known to be so much safer, and the discount so much less, than the circulation of any other State of the Union, that the discount was hardly noticed, while the loss upon the notes of most of the other States of the Union was from four to six times as great. The result was, as might have been expected, that the notes were not fulfilling their function of a circulating medium, but were being sent forward, not for the purpose of obtaining specie, but to be exchanged one for the other at the clearing-house, in order to provide a fund in New York for the redemption of other notes, and also to provide exchange at a profit of from one-quarter to one and a quarter per cent. The amount of exchange thus gained by the bankers and brokers, and the amount of exchange lost by the people in these transactions, cannot be computed, but there is no doubt that it amounted, annually, to millions of dollars.

The average amount of specie held by the New York State banks for ten years previous to the year 1860, was $17,565,006.10.‡

1851	8,978,918	1858	23,597,211
1852	13,301,356	1859	22,997,782
1853	13,384,410	1860	24,582,249
1854	10,792,429		
1855	15,921,467		175,650,061
1856	18,510,835		
1857	14,370,434	Yearly average	17,565,006

Of this amount about one-eighth, say $2,200,000, was held by the country banks in their vaults, and the balance, seven-eighths, say $15,300,000, was held in New York City. If from this amount should be deducted the coin belonging to banks and persons residing outside of the State of New York, and the amount represented by checks payable in coin, it would be found that the amount of circulating notes issued in the State of New York was, on an average, for ten years at least, five times the amount of specie on deposit for the purpose of redeeming their notes.

The amount of national bank notes now authorized to be issued is $354,000,000, and of legal-tender notes, $356,000,000; so that the amount of legal-tender money, in which the national bank notes are now redeemable, is nearly identical with that of such notes, though slightly in excess. If the national banking law were so amended as to require the redemp-

* The circulation of New York State was $39,182,819.
‡ Specie held by the New York State banks from 1851 to 1860. (Report of Superintendent of Banking Department of the State of New York, January 1, 1861, page 79.)

tion of the national bank notes in the legal-tender notes at one-fourth of one per cent. discount, as in the New York State law, instead of at par, as provided in the national-currency act, and the national banks of the whole country would agree to such a provision of the law, the prompt redemption of the national bank notes would be insured; but the redemption of this vast amount of circulating notes, if redeemed but once a year, would result in a loss to the people of the United States of $900,000; if the notes were to be redeemed four times annually, $3,600,000; and if redeemed six times annually, $5,400,000. A system of redemption of this kind would also at once increase the rate of exchange from the rate of one-tenth of one per cent. now existing at most periods of the year between the different cities of the Union, to from one-half per cent. to one per cent., thus restoring, to a considerable degree, the condition of the exchange at the time of the inauguration of the national banking system, and causing an annual loss to the people of millions of dollars. Such a system would, however, undoubtedly result in the return of the notes of the national banks, at certain seasons of the year when they were not needed, to the vaults of the country banks, to be paid out when the demand for currency increased. Such a system would also give, what is exceedingly desirable at the present time, elasticity to the currency.

The profit upon the circulation of national banks organized in the Southern and Western States during the past year, did not much exceed one per cent. for the country banks, and was less than one-half per cent. in the redemption cities, as will be shown more fully hereafter. Under such a condition of things, with so small a margin of profit to be derived from the issue of circulating notes, there would be little demand for circulation, and consequently but little danger in throwing the doors wide open for the issue of circulating notes to any association properly organized that might desire such circulation; but with the reduction of the value of the bonds, and the approximation of the value of the bank-note to the value of specie, the profit would increase, and with the increase of profit the demand for the issue of additional bank-notes would also increase; so that under such a system the issue of bank-notes would have a continual tendency to lessen the value of the paper dollar, and prevent its approximation to the value of the gold dollar, and all ideas of specie payment might forever be abandoned:

In order to insure the prompt redemption of the national bank notes, the amount issued must be so much increased that the notes will be, say, at one-eighth of one per cent. discount, and this would probably not be accomplished until an addition should be made to the present circulation of one hundred millions of dollars. The same result would follow from the reduction of the volume of legal-tender notes simultaneously with the increase of the issues of the bank-notes; but Congress has so frequently refused to diminish the amount of legal-tender notes, that, in the opinion of the Comptroller, any general system of free banking, accompanied with redemption, must be postponed until the resumption of specie payment.

The Comptroller, in order to avoid any misapprehension of his views upon this subject, desires to state that he is not an advocate of any permanent system of currency usually known as an irredeemable currency. He belives, however, that the people of this country will not, and ought not to, submit to the higher rates of exchange prevailing previous to the war, and that any amendment to the national-currency act which shall result in restoring such high rates of exchange will also result in the downfall of a system of banking which, it is believed, will yet become the most satisfactory and complete of any ever established.

During the past year, so far as his observation has extended, the national bank note has been rarely at any perceptible discount for legal-tender notes in the city of New York; and during the late panic no distinction was made by the people between legal-tender notes of the United States and national bank notes. Both were alike hoarded as being the most desirable of all things to hold, and it is probable that when specie payments shall be resumed, the faith of the people will be so well established in the safety of the currency of the banks that no such general system of redemption will be required as was necessary for the unsafe currency issued by the different States previous to the war.

If the circulation should become redundant, as is sometimes the case with the silver coinage, and the national bank notes be at a discount for legal-tender notes, it will be only necessary for the surplus to be presented to the agencies in the city of New York, where more than two-thirds of the circulation is now redeemable, in order to restore the equilibrium; for it is to be hoped that previous to the return to specie payments some system will be adopted which will give abundant elasticity to the currency without increasing the expense and burden of general redemption, and without the loss resulting from the high rates of exchange which have always prevailed under previous systems.

RESERVE.

The advocates of a free-banking law are also advocates of the repeal of the chief restrictions of the national currency act, and particularly of the provision which requires the keeping of a certain amount of money as reserve against liabilities. They claim that the directors and managers of the banks, and not the legislature which enacts the law or the officer who executes it, are the best judges of the amount of money to be loaned, and the amount to be held on hand for the protection of their creditors; that the Government should be careful to protect the bill-holder from loss, but the depositor or other creditor may safely be allowed to protect himself. They further maintain that such laws prevent the banks from extending accommodations to legitimate business interests, which, consequently, suffer on account of the lack of such accommodations. In some instances this may be true, but such laws are passed not so much for the benefit of those persons who conduct their business on sound principles as for that class or association of persons which has but little experience in the method of transacting a legitimate business. If the law be correct in principle, it will be found not to interfere with the rights of those persons who understand the true theory of business, but its tendency will be to prevent abuses on the part of those who would otherwise take risks which a prudent and careful man would avoid.

Any association of persons may organize a bank under the provisions of the national currency act. If private citizens wish to transact business in accordance with their own judgment, they can avail themselves of the privilege by conducting a private business. If other citizens prefer to organize corporations under an act of Congress which imposes restrictions designed for the public good, who shall object? The privilege is open to both, and each can decide without prejudice or hindrance. A private banker solicits and obtains business on the strength of his good name, and it is well understood that the funds placed in his hands are to be used at his discretion, the depositors relying upon his business sagacity and judgment; but if corporations desire to organize under the authority and seal of a great nation, care should be exercised that the authority obtained shall not be abused.

During the past few years great corporations have been organized by authority of law, with the advantages of immense subsidies, but almost wholly without restrictions, the law-making power having been led to believe that the corporations authorized would contribute as much to the public good as to their own profit. But it has been found that overgrown corporations are conducted in defiance of the rights of the shareholders, and with little regard to the comfort, wants, and profit of the people, but chiefly for the benefit of the few officers and directors; and the whole country is now aroused to the mistaken legislation which has placed the highways of the nation under the control of a few men, without reserving such salutary restrictions as should compel the common carrier to deliver the products of the land to the market for a fair remuneration; and it is the great economical problem of the day how to correct a monstrous evil, which would have been under complete control if the proper restrictions had at first been provided and enforced.

The officers and directors of stock companies which have a good reputation are too apt to forget that they are but the servants of the shareholders, and that the poorest shareholder is entitled to information in reference to its affairs. The Bank of Amsterdam is said to have been bankrupt for fifty years prior to the announcement of its failure, yet it continued business for a half century upon the strength of the name and character it had built up; and many individuals and corporations are to-day supposed to be possessed of large wealth, whose affairs, if carefully scrutinized, would be found to exhibit the reverse. If banks are to be organized under the authority of law, and intrusted with the earnings of the people, it is right that legislators shall require them to loan the savings of the people upon real estate security of twice the value of the loan; and if the banks are organized for commercial purposes, it is right that they should be prohibited from loaning money upon real estate, and be required to loan money chiefly to business men upon commercial paper; and depositors have a right to expect that the contract which the law provides between them and the bank shall be enforced. If the law provides for a proper security for circulation, and at the same time defines the kind of security in which deposits shall be invested, it is as important to know that the contract with the depositor will be fulfilled, as well as the contract with the bill-holder. It is the business of such corporations to receive the money of the people, and first of all to fulfill their legal obligations with their creditors, rather than to attempt to follow the vagaries and manipulations of the stock-board, or assume to regulate the rate of interest on the street. While the law permits banking corporations to use a certain portion of the deposits of each creditor, and realize a profit therefrom, it provides also that they shall keep a certain other portion of such deposits on hand for the prompt payment of the creditor whenever it shall be demanded. The correctness of this principle of law is evident, but the difficulty is to ascertain the exact amount necessary to keep on hand. The reckless banker or director would loan it all, and frequently not to his neighbors for the purpose of facilitating legitimate transactions, but to himself, for use in some enterprise which promises well, but results in ruin. The prudent banker invests carefully the savings of his neighbors, and studies their wants, holding an ample fund at his command for all emergencies. The law properly provides that all the assets of a bank, even including the furniture, shall first be applied to the payment of the creditors, the shareholders having a right only to the balance which may remain after the payment of every cent of indebtedness. If the law is so careful to protect the interests of the depositors, it is also just that it should provide restrictions to that end, and devise methods of ascertaining frequently whether these restrictions are strictly observed. The amount of the capital of the shareholder may be small, and the amount of the capital furnished by the depositor may be many times as great, so that the risk of the shareholder is by no means as great as that of the depositor.

The capital and surplus of the London and Westminster Bank of England belonging to the shareholders is fifteen millions of dollars, while the average capital, in the shape of deposits contributed by its creditors, is one hundred and twenty millions of dollars. Three national banks in the city of New York, with a capital and surplus belonging to the shareholders of ten millions of dollars, had, previous to the late crisis, deposits contributed by their creditors equal to fifty millions of dollars; and a late report from a savings bank in this country, on file in this Office, exhibits a capital belonging to shareholders of but $25,000, while the capital contributed by the depositors was $1,000,000. The capital contributed by the depositors in the first instance, that of the English bank, was eight times that contributed by the shareholders; in the second instance, that of the three New York banks, five times, and in the case of the savings bank forty times. The necessity of restrictions to govern corporations holding such large proportionate amounts of credits could not be better illustrated.

The banks of England, of Scotland, and of other countries of Europe, are managed by men who have had long experience in that branch of business, and their experience is handed down from generation to generation to their successors, and the organization of a corporation to conduct the business of banking by men untried in that particular profession or calling would be looked upon with disfavor, and meet with no success. But in this country, under the provisions of the act, any association of persons may organize a bank; and it is no uncommon occurrence for applications to be received for that purpose from persons who have had little or no experience in banking, but who desire to organize under the national currency act, because it is believed that an organization under that act will give to the shareholders a character and credit which they could not obtain if they should attempt to conduct a private banking business.

It is said that the restriction in reference to reserve should be removed from circulation, for the reason that the circulation is already safe beyond a peradventure. This is undoubtedly true, for the security of the circulation rests not alone upon the bonds which are deposited, but also upon the total assets of the bank, the personal liability of the shareholders, and, finally, upon the guarantee of the Government that in any event the face value of the note shall be paid. The absolute certainty of the full payment of the notes is therefore assured. But the question is not whether a reserve shall be held which shall insure the *payment*, merely, of the note, for that is unnecessary, but what amount of reserve shall be held by the banks to insure the *prompt* payment of all their liabilities? The percentage of reserve could be fixed relatively to the capital if the amount of the liabilities were in all cases proportionate to the amount of capital, which, as is well known, is not the case. The question is not what percentage should be held upon capital, upon deposits, or upon circulation, but what amount of reserve should be held to protect the demand-liabilities of the bank; and the experience of years can alone determine that proportion.

A recent writer* on English banking, who has been extensively quoted in this country, has stated that the provision of the national cur-

_____

* "Lombard Street," by Walter Bagehot.

rency act requiring a fixed proportion of reserve to liabilities is not the proper standard for a bank reserve, for the reason that a fixed proportion " will sometimes err by excess, and sometimes by defect," and that " the near approach to the legal limit of reserve would be a sure incentive to panic." He says that " the very essence and principle in the American system is faulty;" but in the final summing up of his argument in reference to the reserve which the Bank of England should hold, he gives it as his opinion that the bank " ought *never* to keep less than £11,000,000, or £11,500,000, of reserve on hand, and that in order not to be below £11,500,000, the bank must begin to take precautions when the reserve is between £14,000,000 and £15,000,000, for experience shows that between £2,000,000 and £3,000,000 may probably enough be withdrawn from the bank's store before the right rate of interest is found which will attract money from abroad, and before that rate has had time to attract it." Again he says, " I should say that at the present time the mind of the monetary world would become feverish and fearful if the reserve of the banking department of England went below £10,000,000." This proportion is equal to more than one-third of the average liabilities of the Bank of England, and is more than eight per cent. in excess of the amount required by the national currency act.

When this distinguished economist asserts that the Bank of England " ought *never* to keep less than £11,000,000 " on hand, and that " the monetary world would become feverish and fearful if the reserve in the bank department of the Bank of England went below £10,000,000," and at the same time that the rule of reserve required by the national currency act " will sometimes err by excess and sometimes by defect," the mind of the searcher after the truth in reference to the principles which should govern legislation upon this subject is bewildered, and will look in vain for light to the abstruse legislation and management of the Bank of England, and to the dark statistics which emanate semi-annually from the parlors of the London joint-stock banks.

The requirement that the reserve shall be proportional to the liabilities is based on the conviction that the amount of the reserve should be dependent on, or have some definite relation to, the varying amount of the liabilities; and the opposite view, to wit, that the reserve should have no such relation, but should be a fixed quantity, entirely independent of and undisturbed by changes in the amount of liabilities, appears to be in conflict with sound principles, and is at variance with the practice, when untrammeled, of the leading and safer banking institutions both of this country and of Europe.[*]

Bank of England deposits and reserve, compiled from the London Economist.

Date.	Deposits.	Banking reserve.	Rate of discount.	Per cent. of reserve.
	£	£	Per cent.	
July 30	24, 403, 984	12, 423, 352	3½	.50. 9
August 6	23, 673, 965	11, 996, 907	....	.50. 6
August 13	24, 989, 30	12, 713, 623	....	.52. 9
August 20				.53. 9
August 27	25, 601, 351	13, 318, 865	....	.51. 8
September 3	27, 501, 06	12, 760, 283	....	.46. 2
September 10	29, 080, 53	13, 177, 780	....	.46. 9
September 17	29, 416, 360	13, 346, 813	....	.45. 3
September 24	29, 456, 519	13, 238, 507	4	.44. 9
October 1	29, 040, 400	9, 954, 181	5	.34. 2
October 8	27, 544, 764	9, 115, 152	....	.33. 0
October 15	24, 747, 665	7, 861, 036	6	.31. 7
October 22	22, 961, 415	8, 109, 529	7	.35. 2
October 29	22, 530, 271	8, 435, 447	8	.37. 5
November 6	22, 357, 428	8, 071, 288	9	.36. 1

But it is claimed that the Bank of England is required to hold the large amount of reserve because it holds in its vaults the reserve, not only for its own dealers, but also of the joint-stock banks of England, whose combined deposits are three times as great as all the deposits of the Bank of England; and that, therefore, the Bank of England must at all times be ready, not only to pay the demands of its creditors, but also to extend loans to the other institutions in times of panic. The joint-stock banks of England are not, however, entirely deficient in reserve, for it is found upon reference to the statistics of the London and Westminster Bank for 1867, published by the same author, that this bank, with a capital of £2,000,000 and a surplus of £1,000,000, had at that time deposits of £13,889,021; cash on hand, £2,226,441, and government securities amounting to £3,572,797. This bank, which is the largest joint-stock bank in England, and second only to the Bank of England itself, held therefore at that time six per cent. of its liabilities in cash, and more than 25 per cent. in addition in available resources, while many other of the leading joint-stock banks of England continually hold in available resources a still greater amount, as may be seen from the following table:

Table of reserve, &c., of the ten principal joint-stock banks of London, on June 30, 1873, compiled from the London Economist of October 18, 1873, (supplement.)

Number.	Banks.	Capital and surplus.	Cash deposits.	Reserve.			Proportion of reserve to liabilities.		
				Cash.	Stock investments.	Total.	June 30, 1873.	Dec. 31, 1872.	June 30, 1873.
							Per ct.	Per ct.	Per ct.
1	London and Westminster	£3,600,000	£29,383,420	£3,795,639	£3,259,851	£7,055,490	24.90	26.4	42.3
2	London Joint Stock	1,673,840	17,401,319	2,218,816	1,060,000	3,298,816	16.95	14.32	13.6
3	Union	1,500,000	14,371,016	5,143,934	2,255,825	7,414,819	35.43	30.93	54.0
4	City	750,000	3,050,046	923,402	500,823	931,989	31.54	30.	35.0
5	Imperial	540,000	2,253,567	471,949	98,746	560,695	25.0	24.0	35.0
6	Alliance	940,000	1,821,563	665,028	758,176	723,184	39.70	36.90	34.3
7	Consolidated	876,125	2,988,705	834,029	208,402	1,082,431	35.54	32.90	34.9
8	Central	109,000	689,014	159,165		159,165	25.79	42.77	28.3
9	London and Southwest ru	172,680	729,479	179,219		179,219	24.57	43.71	22.0
10	London and County	1,500,000	17,821,259	5,195,143	1,647,498	6,842,641	38.96	37.40	41.3
	Total	11,501,651	88,751,925	19,295,411	8,991,065	28,286,149	31.97	32.54	31.00

a Cash in hand and at the Bank of England.
b Government stock and exchequer bills.
c Consols new 3 per cents, and reduced at 90.
d Embraces £1,754,516 cash in the bank, £951,292 cash in Bank of England and £2,191,115 cash lent at call.
e Government stock, exchequer bills, debentures, &c.
f Cash in hand at Bank of England, and at call.
g Exchequer bills, East India debentures, and government securities.
h Consols, India debentures and city bonds.
i Investments in consols &c.
j New 3 per cents, and other government stocks.
k Cash in hand and at call.
l Cash on hand at head office and branches and with Bank of England, cash at call and at notice covered by securities.
Government and guaranteed stocks.
From the London Economist of March 1, 1873, page 84.

It is well known that the funds of the English government are the most readily convertible of any in the markets of the world, and that while English consols* can at all times be purchased at a moderate discount, (92,) they can also at all times be converted into a coin at a smaller loss than any other securities upon the market. The joint-stock banks of England, therefore, have a final resource in which their reserves can be invested with the certainty of conversion at any moment. The Bank of England thus holds continually a reserve of about one-third of the amount of its average liabilities, while the joint-stock banks of England continually hold in available reserve a still greater proportionate amount in cash and government securities; and it is no answer to the proposition under discussion to say that the conversion of the consols held by the English joint-stock banks into coin would have the effect at once to reduce the reserves of the Bank of England, for the money-market of London is, as we have been taught to believe, the money-market of the world, to which is attracted the capital of all nations by the simple process of raising the rate of interest.

The national currency act requires that the country banks shall hold 6 per cent., the redemption cities 12½ per cent., and the New York City banks 25 per cent. of their liabilities in cash, making an aggregate of cash reserve of from 13 to 15 per cent. The remainder of the reserve required to be held by the country banks may be on deposit with the banks in the redemption cities, while that of the redemption cities may be on deposit in the city of New York.

These large accumulations in the redemption cities, and in the banks of the city of New York, are to a large extent invested in call loans, the banks in the redemption cities and in the city of New York having no resource like the joint-stock banks of England in which to place their surplus of reserves, which can be readily converted in the markets of the world into coin, if occasion shall require; and it can hardly be doubted that if the surplus means of the country banks, which were invested in call-loans by their city correspondents, had been invested in funds convertible into cash upon demand, the disastrous results of the late panic would have been largely avoided.

The crisis was caused in a great degree by the desire of the country banks to withdraw their balances from the city banks; first, because in the month of September the amount on deposit with the city banks was needed for the legitimate purposes of trade; and secondly, because the country banks, foreseeing and fearing the return of the experience of previous years, thought it safer to withdraw their balances at once. When the reserves of the New York City banks became alarmingly reduced by the drafts of their country correspondents, the only resource left to the city banks was to convert their call-loans, amounting to some $60,000,000; but these, if paid at all, were paid in checks upon the associated banks, and the latter found, the next morning, at the clearing-house, that, although a portion of their liabilities had been reduced by the payment of call-loans, they were in the aggregate no richer in currency than on the previous day. Suspension followed; but if the surplus of the country banks had been to a considerable extent invested in Government certificates, the drafts upon the city banks would have been proportionately less; and if the surplus fund of the city banks had likewise been held in such certificates, the avails of such certificates would have

* Since the year 1850 the English consols (three per cents,) have ranged in price from 99¼ (in 1851) to 87¼ (in 1866.) The average price has, however, during that period been above 92; a rate which indicates the borrowing power of the government to be about 3¼ per cent. per annum.

been quietly withdrawn from the Treasury, and the banks would have found themselves possessed of ready means with which to supply the demands of their dealers.

It is said that the issue of such certificates would facilitate the withdrawal of legal-tender notes for speculative purposes, but the assistant treasurer in New York could hardly fail to be advised of the deposit of large amounts of money with himself for illegitimate purposes, and a provision of law similar to the one already in force, forfeiting the amount of money on deposit, and directing the prosecution of such offenders, would effectually prevent such transactions.

The issue of a Government certificate for the use of all the banks of the country, to be counted as a certain portion of their reserve, was recommended as follows in my last annual report:

The reserves of the nineteen hundred national banks located elsewhere than in the city of New York are held to a great extent in that city. For most of the time during the past year an amount equal to more than one-fifth of the capital of all these national banks has been held on deposit by the national banks of the city of New York to the credit of their correspondents. In many cases these credits amount to twice the capital of the bank with which they are deposited; in other cases the amount of deposits is three, four, and even five times the capital, which amount has been attracted thither largely by the payment of interest on deposits. The failure of one of these New York City banks in a time of monetary stringency would embarrass, if not ruin, many banks in the redemption cities, and, in turn, the country correspondents of these banks would suffer from the imprudence of the New York bank, which would be responsible for wide-spread disaster.

In times of excessive stringency loans are not made by such associations to business men upon commercial paper, but to dealers in speculative securities, upon short time, at high rates of interest; and an increase of call-loans beyond the proper limit is more likely to afford facilities for unwarrantable stock speculations than relief to legitimate business transactions.

The variations in the liabilities requiring reserve in the banks of the city of New York are very great. The banks outside of New York, during the dull season, send their surplus means to that city for deposit upon interest, to await the revival of business. The banks in the city of New York, at such periods of the year, have no legitimate outlet for these funds, and are, therefore, threatened with loss. The stock board takes advantage of this condition of affairs, speculation is stimulated by the cheapness of money, and a market is found for the idle funds upon doubtful collaterals, and the result is seen in the increased transactions at the clearing-house, which, during the past year, exceeded thirty-two thousand millions of dollars, or an average of more than one hundred millions of dollars daily—not one-half of which was the result of legitimate business; the total amount of transactions being greater than that of the bankers' clearing-house of the city of London. The evil arises largely from the payment by the banks of interest on deposits, an old-established custom which cannot easily be changed by direct legislation. A considerable portion of these deposits would remain at home if they could be used at a low rate of interest, and made available at any time upon the return of the season of active business. No sure investment of this kind is, however, open to the country banks, and the universal custom is to send forward the useless dollars, from vaults comparatively insecure, to their correspondents in the city, where they are supposed to be safer, and at the same time earning dividends for shareholders. A Government issue, bearing a low rate of interest, to be counted as a certain proportion of the reserve, and an increase of the amount which the country banks are required to keep on hand, is the proper remedy for such a state of things. Such an investment need not result in inflation, for the currency invested would be in the possession of the Government. If the currency is held, the objection is the loss of interest to the Government; but this loss would be no more than a just rebate upon the six millions of dollars of taxation annually paid by the banks to the Government, at a time when almost every kind of internal taxation has been discontinued. Such a reduction of taxation should not be grudgingly made, if the result shall be to give elasticity to the currency, to strengthen and steady the money market, to give additional security to seven hundred millions of dollars belonging to depositors by retaining in the vaults of the banks a large amount of funds for legitimate business purposes, which would otherwise be thrown upon the stock board to unsettle values throughout the country, and alternately increase and depress the price of every commodity.

The recommendation for the issue of these certificates, to be counted as a certain portion of the reserve, is renewed.

The same certificates could also be issued to a large extent as a safe investment for laboring men and others desiring such an investment for earnings. If such certificates were issued in amounts of $50 they would at once be recognized as the safest possible temporary investment, and the Government would soon ascertain by experience what proportions of such certificates could be safely invested in the 6 per cent. bonds of the United States, thus saving the interest upon the funds in which the earnings of the laboring man were invested, and conferring a permanent benefit upon its humblest citizens.

The returns made to the clearing-house association of the weekly average of reserve of the national banks for each week since the first of January last, show that the provision referred to has been generally observed, and the exceptions to the rule have not been among banks of old established reputation, whose experience is entitled to great weight, but among banks more recently organized, which have been ambitious to obtain business and are willing to assume risks for that purpose.*

The rule requiring a reserve was adopted by the voluntary action of the clearing-house association of the city of New York, previous to the passage of the national currency act. At a meeting of bank officers, representing forty-two of the forty-six banks of the city of New York, held at the rooms of the clearing-house association in March, 1858, it was agreed "to keep on hand *at all times* an amount of coin equivalent to not less than 20 per cent. of our net deposits of every kind, which shall be made to include certified checks and other liabilities, except circulating notes, deducting the daily exchanges received from the clearing-house." This resolution was adopted five years previous to the passage of the national currency act, and its phraseology is not unlike the provisions of that act in reference to reserves to be held by the national banks of New York City. The resolution did not provide for a reserve on circulation, for the reason that the circulation of the city banks was at that time redeemable at par in coin; so that no action was necessary in

* *Statement of the weekly average percentage of reserve held by the New York City banks, as reported to the clearing-house.*

Week ending—	Average percentage of national banks.	Average percentage of State banks.	Average percentage of all.	Week ending—	Average percentage of national banks.	Average percentage of State banks.	Average percentage of all.
1873.				1873.			
Jan. 4	26.32	18.21	25.61	May 17	27.53	19.57	26.85
11	27.25	19.96	25.61	24	27.03	20.00	26.43
18	27.60	19.31	26.85	31	27.61	18.50	26.82
25	27.46	19.00	26.71	June 7	29.70	21.34	29.00
Feb. 1	26.56	17.59	25.77	14	30.28	20.87	29.50
8	26.75	16.99	25.54	21	30.34	20.80	29.51
15	24.93	17.90	24.32	28	30.07	21.25	30.14
21	24.78	16.88	24.10	July 5	31.78	19.09	30.72
Mar. 1	25.57	16.97	24.84	12	31.42	20.91	30.58
8	25.56	17.61	24.89	19	30.87	21.10	30.04
15	25.53	16.63	24.78	26	30.95	21.54	30.12
22	25.50	17.26	24.80	Aug. 2	30.59	19.83	28.67
29	25.34	16.95	24.62	9	30.18	21.42	28.42
Apr. 5	23.83	15.97	23.16	16	30.39	20.24	28.46
12	24.43	17.38	23.82	23	28.28	18.52	27.43
19	25.02	17.69	24.39	30	27.94	18.84	27.15
26	25.17	18.93	24.65	Sept. 6	27.67	17.62	24.95
May 3	25.51	19.03	25.87	13	24.44	18.35	23.89
10	27.32	19.54	26.67	20	23.55	17.95	23.03

From the weekly average percentage of the State banks is excluded the weekly average percentage of the Bank of America and the Manhattan Company, the former of which was invariably and the latter usually in excess of 25 per cent.

respect to the reserve to be held upon circulating notes. From that time to the passage of the national currency act the resolution was generally observed, and since the passage of the act neither the New York clearing-house association nor the clearing-house association of any city has requested the repeal of such restrictions. On the contrary, the New York association has repeatedly refused to modify the rule by agreeing that national bank notes, which by the law can be used in payment of debts to each other, may be so employed.

The national currency act requires that the national banks "shall at all times have on hand" the reserve required in lawful money, and the advocates of a repeal of the reserve laws insist that, under this provision, the national banks are absolutely prohibited from using these reserves at any time. The provision requiring that a reserve shall be kept on hand at all times, was intended to protect the depositor, and to keep the bank in funds for the purpose of responding at all times to the demands of its creditors. This is evident from the fact that the bank is required, when its reserves become deficient, to cease discounting and making dividends until the amount of the reserve shall be restored. The word "reserve" is used, as has been suggested, in the same sense as it is used in an army, and "the fact that a military commander cannot be definitely instructed when he may employ his reserve force, is not regarded as a reason why that important portion of the army organization should be abandoned, or be reduced in number or efficiency." To claim that a bank cannot redeem its own notes upon presentation, and cannot pay the checks of its depositors on demand if the payment of such debts shall intrench upon its reserves, is equivalent to declaring that the national currency act was intended to provide for the destruction of the very institutions it had created. From the first organization of the system to the present time, the uniform decisions have been that the object of the reserve is to enable the bank at all times to pay its debts. In times of panic the depositors of a bank, and not its officers and directors, are its masters; and it is absurd to maintain that a bank, liable at such times to be called upon to pay its debts, would, if there were no reserve laws, loan upon commercial paper, at the risk of almost certain failure and disgrace, the money which belongs to its creditors.

While the Comptroller concedes that experience may hereafter justify a modification of the provisions of the act in this respect, he is clearly of the opinion, in view of the lessons to be derived from the late suspension of currency payment in New York, that he would not be warranted in recommending any change at present, except the offer of inducements, as already stated, to the banks of the country to hold a larger proportion of their reserve in their own vaults, in certificates which can be readily converted into cash when the funds of the depositor are demanded.

If the certificates should, however, be issued as proposed, the reserve of the country banks and the reserve of banks in the redemption cities (other than New York) may with propriety be reduced, the amount required to be kept on hand being largely increased; while the banks in the city of New York should still be required to keep on hand 25 per cent., (one half in certificates, if desired,) subject to a reduction at any time by the Comptroller, with the concurrence of the Secretary, upon the recommendation of the clearing house. Upon the return to specie payments and the funding of the United States debt into bonds bearing a low rate of interest, the reserve now required may be very much reduced and perhaps altogether dispensed with.

A table in the appendix, which has been compiled from the regular reports to this office, exhibits the percentage of reserve held by the national banks of the country for the past five years, and shows that in every State, and in the principal cities of the Union, they have been found, in almost every instance, to hold in the aggregate an amount of reserve considerably beyond the requirements of the law.

THE PANIC OF 1873.

The monetary crisis of 1873 may be said to have had its beginning in New York City on September 8, by the failure of the Warehouse Security Company, and of two houses which had left their regular business to embark in enterprises foreign thereto, which were followed on the 13th by the failure of a large firm of stock-brokers. On the 18th and 19th two of the largest banking-houses in the city, well known throughout the country, and which were interested in the negotiations of large amounts of railroad securities, also failed; and on the 20th of the same month the failures of the Union Trust Company, the National Trust Company, the National Bank of the Commonwealth, and three other well-known banking-houses were announced. On the same day the New York Stock Exchange, for the first time in its existence, closed its doors, and they were not again opened for a period of ten days, during which period legal-tender notes commanded a premium over certified checks of from one-fourth of one per cent. to three per cent. An active demand for deposits commenced on the 18th, and increased rapidly during the 19th and 20th, chiefly from the country correspondents of the banks; and their drafts continued to such an extent, "calling back their deposits in a medium never before received," that the reserves of the banks were alarmingly reduced.

The "call loans," amounting to more than sixty millions of dollars, upon which the banks relied to place themselves in funds in such an emergency, were entirely unavailable, because the means of the borrowers, upon the realization of which they depended to repay their loans were, to a great extent, pledged with the banks. These collaterals could in ordinary times have been sold, but at that moment no market could be found except at ruinous sacrifices. Had there been a market, the payments would have been made in checks upon the associated banks, which would not have added to the general supply of cash. A meeting of the clearing house association was called, and on Saturday evening, September 20, the following plan for facilitating the settlement of balances at the clearing house was unanimously adopted:

In order to enable the banks of this association to afford such additional assistance to the business community, and also for the purpose of facilitating the settlement of the exchanges between the banks, it is proposed that any bank in the clearing-house association, may, at its option, deposit with a committee of five persons, to be appointed for that purpose, an amount of its bills receivable, or other securities to be approved by said committee, who shall be authorized to issue therefor to said depositing bank certificates of deposit, bearing interest at seven per cent. per annum, in denominations of five and ten thousand dollars, such as may be desired, to an amount not in excess of seventy-five per cent. of the securities or bills receivable so deposited. Except when the securities deposited shall consist of either United States stocks or gold certificates, the certificates of deposit may be issued upon the par value of such securities.

These certificates may be used in settlement of balances at the clearing-house for a period not to extend beyond the first of November proximo, and they shall be received by creditor banks during that period daily, in the same proportion as they bear to the aggregate amount of the debtor balances paid at the clearing house.

The interest which may accrue upon these certificates shall, on the 1st day of November next, or sooner, should the certificates all be redeemed, be apportioned amæg the banks which shall have held them during that time.

The securities deposited with the committee, as above named, shall be held by the as a special deposit, pledged for the redemption of the certificates issued thereon.

The committee shall be authorized to exchange any portion of said securities for a equal amount of others, to be approved by them, at the request of the depositing bank, and shall have power to demand additional security, either by an exchange or an increased amount, at their discretion.

The amount of certificates which this committee may issue as above shall not exceed ten million dollars.

This arrangement shall be binding upon the clearing-house association when assented to by three-fourths of its members.

The banks shall report to the manager of the clearing-house every morning at 1 o'clock the amount of such certificates held by them.

That, in order to accomplish the purposes set forth in this arrangement, the legal tenders belonging to the associated banks shall be considered and treated as a common fund, held for mutual aid and protection, and the committee appointed shall have power to equalize the same by assessment, or otherwise, at their discretion.

For this purpose a statement shall be made to the committee of the condition of each bank on the morning of every day, before the commencement of business, which shall be sent with the exchanges to the manager of the clearing-house, specifying the following items:

1st. Amount of loans and discounts.
2d. Amount of loan certificates.
3d. Amount of United States certificates of deposit and legal-tender notes.
4th. Amount of deposits, deducting therefrom the amount of special gold deposits.

The suspension of currency payments followed and was at first confined to the banks of New York City, but afterward extended to other large cities because the New York banks could not respond to the demands of their correspondents in those cities, and these, in turn, could not respond to the demands of *their* correspondents. Exchange on New York, which would otherwise have commanded a slight premium, was at a discount, and to a considerable extent unavailable. The suspension of the banks in other leading cities, almost without exception, therefore followed, and their partial or entire suspension continued for forty days, until confidence was in a measure restored by the resumption of the New York City banks on the first day of November.

Although predictions had been made of the approach of a financial crisis, there were no apprehensions of its immediate occurrence. On the contrary there were in almost every direction evidences of prosperity. The harvest was nearly or quite completed, and the bins and granaries were full to overflowing. The manufacturing and mining interests had also been prosperous during the year, and there was good promise that the fall trade, which had opened, would be as large as during previous years. The value of the cereals, potatoes, tobacco, and hay for 1872, is estimated by the Department of Agriculture at $1,324,385,000. It is supposed that the value of these products for the present year, a large portion of which was at this time ready for sale and awaiting shipment to market, will not vary materially from the above-mentioned estimate of last year. An estimate based upon the census returns of 1869 gives the probable aggregate value of the marketable products of industry for that year as $4,056,000,000, and a similar estimate upon the same basis, and upon returns to the Agricultural Department, gives an increase of $1,788,000,000 for 1873 over the amount for 1868.

It is not the province of the Comptroller to explain the causes which led to this suspension. In order to enter upon such an explanation it would be necessary to obtain comparative data for a series of years in reference to the imports and exports, the products of industry, the issue of currency and other evidences of debt, and, in fact, a general discussion of the political economy of the country. The immediate cause of the crisis is, however, more apparent. The money market had become overloaded with debt, the cost of railroad construction for five years past being estimated to have been $1,700,000,000, or about $340,000,000 annually; while debt based upon almost every species of property—State, city, town, manufacturing corporations, and mining companies—had been sold in the market. Such bonds and stocks had been disposed of to a considerable extent in foreign markets, and so long as this continued the sale of similar securities was stimulated, and additional amounts offered. When the sale of such securities could no longer be effected abroad, the bonds of railroads and other enterprises of like nature which were in process of construction were thus forced upon the home market, until their negotiation became almost impossible. The bankers of the city of New York, who were burdened with the load, could not respond to the demands of their creditors, the numerous holders of similar securities became alarmed, and the panic soon extended throughout the country.

The present financial crisis may, in a great degree, be attributed to the intimate relations of the banks of the city of New York with the transactions of the stock-board, more than one-fourth, and in many instances nearly one-third, of the bills-receivable of the banks, since the late civil war, having consisted of demand loans to brokers and members of the stock-board, which transactions have a tendency to impede and unsettle, instead of facilitating, the legitimate business interests of the whole country. Previous to the war the stock-board is said to have consisted of only one hundred and fifty members, and its organic principle was a strictly commission business, under a stringent and conservative constitution and by-laws. The close of the war found the membership of the stock-board increased to eleven hundred, and composed of men from all parts of the country, many of whom had congregated in Wall street, adopting for their rule of business the apt motto of Horace, "Make money; make it honestly if you can; at all events make money."* The law of the State of New York, restricting the operations of the stock-board, which had been retained on the statute-book since 1813,† had, unfortunately, been repealed in 1858, so that its members and manipulators were enabled to increase their operations to a gigantic scale.

---

* *Rem facias; rem,*
Si possis, recte; si non, quocunque modo rem.

† "All contracts, written or verbal, for the sale or transfer of any certificate or other evidence of debt, due by or from the United States, or any separate State, or any share or interest in the stock of any bank, or of any company incorporated under any law of the United States, or of any individual State, shall be absolutely void, unless the party contracting to sell or transfer the same shall, at the time of making such contract, be in the actual possession of the certificate or other evidence of such debt, share or interest, or be otherwise entitled in his own right, or be duly authorized by some person so entitled, to sell or transfer the said certificate of debt, share or interest so contracted for.

"All wagers concerning the price or prices, present or future, of any part of any debt due by or from the United States, or any separate State, or of any share or interest in the stock of any bank or other company incorporated under the laws of the United States, or any individual State, or of any certificate or other evidence of any such debt or part of such debt, or of any such share or interest, shall be void.

"Every person who shall pay or deliver any money, goods or thing in action, by way of premium or difference, in pursuance of any contract or wager in the two last sections declared void, and his personal representatives may recover such money, goods, or other thing in action, of and from the party receiving the same and his personal representatives."

Passed February 25, 1813. (Page 706, revised statutes of New York, vol. 1, second edition.) Repealed laws of New York, page 251, eighty-first session, 1858.

10 Ab

The quotations of the stock-board are known to be too frequently fictions of speculation, and yet these fictions control the commerce and business of a great country, and their influence is not confined to this country, but extends to other countries, and seriously impairs our credit with foreign nations. The fictitious debts of railroads and other corporations which they have bolstered up, and which have obtained quotations in London and other markets of the world, have now been reduced to a more proper valuation, or stricken from the list.

Whether the Congress of the United States or the legislature of the State of New York may not re-enact a law reviving similar restrictions with great benefit to the true business interests of all parties is respectfully submitted.

Many measures of reform are proposed in order that the lessons of the crisis may not be lost, and others be led hereafter to repeat similar errors. Unity of action among the leading banks of the great cities will do more to reform abuses than any congressional enactment : for. unless such corporations shall unite and insist upon legitimate methods of conducting business, the laws of Congress in reference thereto will be likely soon to become inoperative—such enactments being observed in their true spirit by the few, while the many evade them and thus invite a repetition of similar disasters.

If, however, the banks are disinclined to unite for such a purpose, the legislation required of Congress will be such as will induce associations outside of the city of New York to retain in their vaults such funds as are not needed at the commercial center for purposes of legitimate business.

The following table, exhibiting the condition of the banks in New York City in the month of October for four years past, has been prepared for purposes of comparison with the statement of September 12, of the present year, which is also given :

Resources.	October 9, 1869.	October 8, 1870.	October 7, 1871.	October 5, 1872.	September 12, 1873.
	54 banks.	54 banks.	54 banks.	50 banks.	48 banks.
Loans on U. S. bonds on demand					
Other st'ks, b'ds, &c., on dem'd					
Loans payable in gold					
Loans, all other					
Overdrafts					
Bonds for circulation					
Bonds for deposits					
U. S. bonds on hand					
Other stocks and bonds					
Due from national banks					
Due from State banks					
Real estate, furniture, & fixtures					
Current expenses					
Premiums paid					
Cash items					
Clearing house exchanges					
National bank notes					
Fractional currency					
Coin					
Gold Treasury notes					
Legal tender notes					
Three per cent. certificates					
U. S. certificates of deposit					
Clearing house certificates					

Liabilities.	October 9, 1869.	October 8, 1870.	October 2, 1871.	October 3, 1872.	September 12, 1873.
	54 banks.	54 banks.	54 banks.	50 banks.	48 banks.
Capital stock	$73,218,100 00	$73,435,000 00	$73,235,000 00	$71,285,000 00	$70,235,000 00
Surplus fund	17,768,667 71	18,835,699 19	19,468,615 20	20,878,877 81	21,923,211 45
Undivided profits	10,964,277 76	10,039,181 42	10,388,683 51	11,049,162 36	11,210,470 03
National bank circulation	34,683,075 00	32,945,080 00	30,632,976 00	28,070,951 00	27,482,342 00
State bank circulation	243,974 00	235,959 00	226,479 00	189,575 00	146,525 00
Dividends, unpaid		236,800 65	265,569 71	261,830 46	203,979 60
Individual deposits—currency	136,680 848 70	127,991,339 01	141,091,424 39	117,740,902 19	111,463,264 04
gold				6,170,566 20	12,101,731 10
Certified checks	52,580,265 47	37,680,570 53	44,670,638 56	63,827,794 36	42,695,185 81
Cashiers' checks	1,282,332 26	1,389,457 01	801,358 43	778,720 10	1,259,481 79
United States deposits	253,692 98	241,961 99	4,073,218 32	238,003 15	296,877 39
Deposits of U. S. disb'g officers				3,213 37	40,207 13
Due to other national banks	50,005,913 23	55,947,435 65	76,701,443 53	60,580,921 60	72,257,769 25
Due to State banks and bankers	12,901,946 14	16,225,168 70	20,630,052 21	14,852,270 01	18,113,050 50
Notes and bills rediscounted			61,500 00		
Bills payable				30,825 14	62,125 39
Total	390,563,093 35	375,152,133 15	422,345,958 95	395,976,719 78	389,486,310 48

Reserve, 24.4 per cent.

The following totals exhibit similar data, compiled from the returns of the country banks of New England, the Middle, and the Western and Northwestern States.

States.	Items.	September 12, 1873.	October 13, 1873.	November 1, 1873.
NEW ENGLAND STATES.				
Maine	Loans	$154,407,121	$150,841,262	$148,291,782
New Hampshire	Circulation	68,746,627	83,454,774	83,288,566
Vermont	Deposits	61,912,935	55,830,697	52,795,563
Massachusetts	Balance due to banks	3,230,941	2,994,069	552,117
Rhode Island	Due from redeeming agents	18,969,598	13,411,621	12,625,176
Connecticut	Legal-tenders	19,956,979	11,517,756	11,431,217
	Specie	360,786	304,187	339,634
MIDDLE STATES.				
New York	Loans	150,137,621	142,085,003	138,273,174
New Jersey	Circulation	65,416,519	65,871,069	65,976,343
Pennsylvania	Deposits	102,671,101	80,636,682	85,907,955
Delaware	Balance due to banks	1,226,981	1,869,819	
Maryland	Due from redeeming agents	21,428,875	14,015,227	12,024,641
	Legal tenders	13,541,549	14,782,708	14,949,860
	Specie	430,944	301,930	357,335
WESTERN STATES.				
Ohio				
Indiana	Loans	123,654,884	116,833,970	111,549,204
Illinois	Circulation	59,659,474	60,253,336	60,475,650
Michigan	Deposits	92,856,762	75,541,162	70,772,060
Wisconsin	Balance due to banks			
Iowa	Due from redeeming agents	17,993,614	8,029,701	7,984,507
Minnesota	Legal tenders	14,085,011	16,341,748	16,709,236
Kansas	Specie	246,003	217,680	275,521
Nebraska				

The Comptroller, in order to obtain statistics of the condition of the banks during the late panic, as well as just previous to its commencement, issued a circular calling upon all the national banks for reports on October 13, the day on which the banks of the city of New York held the smallest amount of legal-tender notes during the late crisis, and on November 1, the day on which the banks resumed currency payments. The aggregates of these statements for each State and the redemption cities will be found in full in the appendix to this report, as will also a statement exhibiting in detail the average amount of loans, circulation, deposits, specie, and legal-tender notes of each of the associated banks of New York City for the week ending September 20, 1873, and the aggregates as reported to the clearing-house for the week ending November 22. From all these returns the following comparative statement of the banks in New York City at different dates has been prepared:

	September 13, 1873.	September 20, 1873.*	October 13, 1873.	November 1, 1873.	November 22, 1873.
Loans	$199,160,888		$179,135,030	$169,164,529	$27,957,79
Circulation	27,484,342	$27,151,600	27,851,906	27,885,612	
Deposits	99,952,097	167,184,000	89,664,948	92,581,997	138,025,9
Balance due to banks	72,552,765		38,390,118	36,911,568	
Legal tenders	34,278,530	29,607,200	6,517,230	15,684,452	25,390,6
Specie	14,585,811	16,119,400	10,031,470	11,499,457	14,529,3

* Averages as reported to clearing-house, for week ending at the date mentioned.

Some of the special reports were not received until during the present week, and the abstracts were therefore so lately completed that the Comptroller can only refer the inquirer to these curious and interesting statistics of the condition of the banks of the country during the month of the panic, without any extended comments.*

INTEREST ON DEPOSITS.

In my last annual report I referred briefly to the evils resulting from the payment of interest upon deposits, and my predecessors have frequently referred more at length to the same subject. The difficulty has been that the proposed legislation by Congress upon the subject would apply only to the national banks. The effect of such legislation would be to bring State banks and savings banks, organized by authority of the different States, in direct competition with the national banks in securing the accounts of correspondents and dealers; the national banks would be desirous of retaining their business, and the more unscrupulous would not hesitate to evade the law by offering to make collections throughout the country free of charge, to buy and sell stocks without commission, and to rediscount paper at low rates. The proposed action of the clearing-house in the city of New York, if adopted by the clearing-houses of the principal cities of the Union, would do more to prevent the payment of interest on deposits than any congressional enactment. But the evils resulting from the payment of interest upon deposits are by no means confined to the city banks. It may be safely said that this custom, which prevails in almost every city and village of the Union, has done more than any other to demoralize the business of banking. State banks, private bankers, and associations under the guise of savings banks, everywhere, offer rates of interest upon deposits which can

* Since writing the above the following statement has been prepared, showing the whole amount of national-bank currency, legal-tender notes, and fractional currency issued up to October 13 and November 1, 1873:

	October 13.	November 1.
National-bank currency	$350,809,056	$350,882,581
Legal-tender notes	339,566,888	360,602,29
Fractional currency	16,689,191	17,876,14
Totals	756,315,135	729,161,22
Deduct amounts held by the Treasury and by the banks	116,496,997	128,140,72
Which will leave unaccounted for	639,818,138	631,030,51

After making due allowance for the currency held by State and savings-banks, trust companies, and private bankers, these are larger amounts than can be supposed to have been in the pockets of men or the tills of small dealers. But it may be left to the ingenious in such matters to divine what portion thereof was hoarded by the timid, the ignorant, or the covetous.

not safely be paid by those engaged in legitimate business. National banks, desirous of retaining the business of their dealers, also make similar offers, and the result is, not only the increase of the rates of interest paid to business men, but, as a consequence, investments in unsecured loans, bringing ultimate loss both upon the shareholders of the bank and the depositors. The kind of legislation needed is that which shall apply to all banks and bankers alike, whether organized under the national currency act or otherwise. A law prohibiting the payment of interest on deposits by the national banks will have little effect, unless followed by similar legislation under authority of the different States, and there is little hope that such legislation can be obtained. The national currency act, which was passed during the war, provided for a tax of one-half of one per cent. upon all deposits, and, subsequently, internal revenue legislation extended this tax to all deposits made with State banks and individual bankers. If legislation prohibiting the payment of interest on deposits shall be proposed, I recommend that this law be so amended as to repeal this tax, so far as it applies to demand deposits, and that an increased rate of taxation be imposed uniformly upon all deposits which, either directly or indirectly, are placed with banks and bankers with the offer or expectation of receiving interest. Such legislation, if rigidly enforced, would have the effect, not only of reducing the rate of interest throughout the country, but at the same time preventing the illegitimate organization of savings-banks—which organizations should be allowed only upon the condition that the savings of the people shall be carefully and prudently invested, and the interest arising therefrom, after deducting reasonable expenses, distributed from time to time to the depositors, and to no other persons whatsoever.

CERTIFICATION OF CHECKS.

The act of March 3, 1869, authorizes the appointment of a receiver "if any officer, clerk, or agent of any national bank shall certify any check drawn upon said bank, unless the person or company drawing the said check shall have on deposit in said bank at the time said check is certified an amount of money equal to the amount specified in such check."

Receivers have been appointed during the past year, for the National Bank of the Commonwealth of New York and the New Orleans National Banking Association, for violations of this act; and it is the intention of the Comptroller to hereafter rigidly enforce this act whenever he is satisfied of such violation.

PROFIT ON CIRCULATION; TAXATION, EARNINGS, AND DIVIDENDS.

It is asserted that the national banks should be subject to greater taxation than other capital because they derive large profits from the issue of their circulating notes. In general terms it is stated that the profit derived by the national banks from such circulation is between five and six per cent. in gold interest upon the amount of the bonds on deposit with the Treasurer, bearing that rate of interest payable in coin. Nothing could be more erroneous. The banks hold an average reserve of more than one hundred millions of legal-tender notes, which is equivalent to a loan to the Government without interest. They also hold of United States bonds, purchased at a premium, $42,471,000 in excess of the circulation issued, which they are required to keep on deposit with the Treasurer of the United States as security for circulation, and from which they derive no profit except the annual interest paid to all holders of such bonds. Large amounts of United States six per cent. bonds held by the banks have also from time to time been voluntarily surrendered by them to the Government and five per cent. bonds taken in exchange.

The only national banks authorized to be organized under the act of July 12, 1870, were banks to be located in States which had received less than their proportion of circulation, as provided by the act. During a large portion of the past year, five per cent. bonds issued by the Government have been at a premium in the market of fifteen per cent. A national bank organized in the city of Chicago deposits with the Treasurer $100,000 of five per cent. bonds, costing $115,000 in currency. Upon these bonds the bank receives from the Government $5,000 interest in gold, which, with the premium thereon, would amount to $5,750. It also receives in circulation $90,000, and is required to keep twenty-five per cent. of that amount on hand as reserve, leaving $67,500, from which it would derive an income, at ten per cent., of $6,750; and from this must be deducted a tax of one per cent. ($900) upon the amount of circulation issued, leaving an income of $5,850, which, if added to the interest received from the bonds, would amount to $11,600. If the $115,000 had been invested in bonds and mortgages bearing ten per cent. interest, it would net annually $11,500, leaving a profit of $100 to the bank for circulation during the year, and a loss of $15,000 premium upon the bonds at the date of their maturity. The profits of a country bank located in the West or South, with interest at ten per cent., adopting the same calculation, would be a little more than one per cent., and of a bank located in the city of New York, with interest at seven per cent., about 1¼ per cent.; and of a country bank located in the East, with interest at seven per cent., less than 2¼ per cent. The earnings upon capital invested in United States bonds upon which circulation is issued, would not, in the city of New York, exceed the profits of an investment returning an income of 8½ per cent., and in a country bank in the East they would be but little more than on an investment earning nine per cent.

The national banks, prior to May 1, 1871, paid to the Commissioner of Internal Revenue a license or special tax of $2 on each $1,000 of capital, and an income tax on net earnings to December 31, 1871. The special or license tax from May 1, 1864, to May 1, 1871, amounted to $5,322,088.43; the income tax from March 1, 1869, to September 1, 1871, amounted to $5,539,289.17. The national banks also pay the following taxes to the Treasurer of the United States: one per cent. annually on circulation outstanding; one-half of one per cent. annually upon deposits; and one-half of one per cent. annually upon capital not invested in United States bonds. These taxes are payable semi-annually.

The following table exhibits the amount of taxes collected by the Treasurer, annually, from the organization of the system to January 1, 1873:

Year	Circulation.	Deposits.	Capital.	Aggregate.
1864	$287,740 45	$112,953 99	$355,631 63	$756,348 07
1865	1,351,150 52	2,106,480 51	316,829 01	3,784,460 27
1866	2,638,306 45	2,042,674 72	320,545 29	5,457,616 56
1867	2,934,685 63	2,514,540 66	414,800 42	5,764,365 20
1868	2,955,394 60	2,657,215 91	299,186 21	5,911,734 74
1869	2,946,168 02	2,325,571 87	349,147 97	5,620,887 86
1870	2,911,341 51	2,894,480 26	341,588 67	6,017,460 24
1871	3,092,595 56	4,027,767 26	385,247 07	7,505,612 21
1872	3,282,597 46	3,111,889 45	418,863 75	6,846,360 60
Totals	22,460,332 00	21,736,765 17	2,871,909 02	47,069,665 19

The national banks are required by the act of March 3, 1869, to make semi-annual returns to this office of their dividends and earnings. From these returns the following table has been compiled, exhibiting the aggregate capital and surplus, total dividends, and total earnings of the national banks, with the ratio of dividends to capital, dividends to capital and surplus, and earnings to capital and surplus for each half year, commencing March 1, 1869, and ending September 1, 1873.

Period of six months ending—	No. of b'nks.	Capital.	Surplus.	Total dividends.	Total net earnings.	RATIOS.		
						Dividends to capital.	Divid'nds to capital and surplus.	Earnings to capital and surplus.
						Per ct.	Per ct.	Per ct.
Sept. 1, 1869.	1,481	$401,650,802	$84,105,848	$21,767,831	$29,221,184	5.42	4.50	6.04
Mar. 1, 1870.	1,571	416,366,991	86,118,210	21,479,005	28,906,934	5.16	4.37	5.77
Sept. 1, 1870.	1,601	425,317,104	91,630,620	21,080,343	26,813,885	4.96	4.08	5.19
Mar. 1, 1871.	1,665	426,690,165	94,679,401	22,905,150	27,243,162	5.18	4.24	5.91
Sept. 1, 1871.	1,693	445,999,264	98,286,791	22,195,279	27,315,311	4.96	4.07	5.09
Mar. 1, 1872.	1,750	450,693,706	99,431,243	22,859,836	27,508,539	5.07	4.16	5.00
Sept. 1, 1872.	1,852	465,676,023	105,161,942	23,827,289	30,572,691	5.12	4.17	5.36
Mar. 1, 1873.	1,912	475,917,683	114,257,288	24,826,061	31,926,478	5.22	4.21	5.41
Sept. 1, 1873.	1,955	488,100,951	118,113,848	24,855,029	33,122,000	5.09	4.09	5.46

This table shows that the dividends of the national banks upon an average for a series of years, have been about ten per centum per annum, while the dividends upon capital and surplus, which is the true ratio, have been less than nine per cent.* As the law now stands, the

* The following statement of the ten principal joint-stock banks of London, including their branches, exhibiting the capital, reserve, deposits, net profits, and dividends of each for the half year previous to July 1, 1873, has been compiled from balance-sheets of the banks published in the London Economist of October 18, 1873 :

No.	Banks.	Capital and surplus.	Total deposits and acceptances.	Net profits.	Proportion of net profits to capital.	Amount of dividends for half year.	Proportion of dividend to capital.			
							June 30, 1873.	December 31, 1872.	June 30, 1872.	December 31, 1871.
					pr ct. pr an.		pr ct. pr an.	pr ct. pr an.	pr ct. pr an.	pr ct. pr an.
1	London and Westminster..........	£3,000,000	£29,548,770	£241,098	24.10	£300,000	20	*20	*20	*18
2	London Joint Stock..	1,673,849	17,404,319	139,867	23.31	120,000	20	25	20	25 5-6
3	London and County.	1,800,000	20,936,233	169,384	24.23	100,000	20	20	20	19
4	Union	1,500,000	18,028,531	137,910	22.96	127,500	20	20	20	20
5	City	750,000	6,154,383	49,509	16.50	30,000	10	10	10	9
6	Imperial	740,000	2,919,237	46,634	13.82	27,000	8	8	8	6
7	London and Southwestern..........	172,680	758,314	7,101	8.54	4,985	6	6	5	5
8	Consolidated........	876,125	3,258,035	68,895	16.47	36,000	9	8	8	7½
9	Central	109,000	669,018	8,004	16.00	4,000	8	8	8	6
10	Alliance	940,000	2,336,440	34,520	8.63	28,000	7	7	6	5
	Total..........	11,561,654	102,013,280	903,922	20.62	677,485	15†	......	......	......
	Bank of England, August 31, 1873...	17,580,000	129,080,534	785,221	10.80	764,039	10	10		

* From the London Economist of March 15, 1873, page 84.
† Public and other deposits September 11, 1873.

The statistics of the Bank of England and its dividends were obtained from the report of the Bank of England published in the Economist for September 13, 1873. The usual dividends of this bank are 10 per cent. per annum, but the amount has varied for some years past from 8 to 13 per cent.

national banks are subject to a tax of one per cent. per annum upon circulation, of one-half of one per cent. upon the average amount of deposits, and one-half of one per cent. upon the average amount of capital stock beyond the amount invested in United States bonds. The taxation on deposits was essentially a "war-tax," such a duty never having been, as is believed, before imposed upon the banks of any country. While almost every other species of property and investment escape taxation upon its full valuation, the data for the taxation of the national banks can always be obtained from their reports; so that a tax is derived from this species of investment at a much greater ratio than that derived from capital otherwise invested. The result of such excessive taxation is to increase the rate of interest which is paid by the borrower, for the same reason that an internal-revenue tax upon the products of the manufacturer is paid, not by the manufacturer, but by the consumer. The Comptroller is of opinion that justice to all parties requires the repeal of the provision imposing a tax upon deposits, unless, in the judgment of Congress, interest-bearing certificates shall be issued as recommended, which may be counted as a certain portion of the reserve to be kept on hand; in which event it is believed that the taxation derived from deposits will much more than liquidate the interest derived from such certificates.

An additional table in the appendix exhibits in a concise form the ratio of dividends to capital, dividends to capital and surplus, and earnings to capital and surplus, of the national banks in every State of the Union and in the redemption cities, semi-annually, from March 1, 1869, to September 1, 1873.

INSOLVENT BANKS.

Since the last annual report, receivers have been appointed for eleven national banks, (seven of which failed during the late financial crisis,) as follows:

Name and location.	Appointment of receiver.	Capital stock.	Claims proved.	Dividends.	Cash on hand.
				Per ct.	
Scandinavian National Bank, Chicago, Ill.	Dec. 12, 1873	$250,000	$240,810	25	$16,337
Wallkill National Bank, Middletown, N. Y.	Dec. 31, 1872	175,000	153,309	75	15,392
Crescent City National Bank, New Orleans, La.	Mar. 18, 1873	500,000	606,751	....	131,343
Atlantic National Bank, New York, N. Y.	Apr. 28, 1873	300,000	521,526	....	107,479
First National Bank of Washington, D. C.	Sept. 19, 1873	500,000	*1,655,785	50	.....
National Bank of the Commonwealth, New York	Sept. 22, 1873	750,000	*791,036	....	153,309
Merchants' National Bank, Petersburgh, Va.	Sept. 25, 1873	400,000	1,092,346	....	12,782
First National Bank of Petersburgh, Va.	Sept. 25, 1873	280,000	*176,614	....	8,925
First National Bank of Mansfield, Ohio.	Oct. 18, 1873	100,000	*177,207	....	8,350
New Orleans National Banking Association, La.	Oct. 23, 1873	600,000	*662,182	....	7,953
First National Bank of Carlisle, Pa.	Oct. 21, 1873	50,000	68,960	....	1,844
Total		3,825,000	6,097,849	....	.....

*Estimated amount of claims.

The failure of all of these banks may be attributed to the criminal mismanagement of their officers, or to the neglect or violation of the act on the part of their directors. The officers of two of these banks have been arrested; one has been convicted, and the other is undergoing trial: while the president of the first bank which failed during the year left the country on the pretext of visiting some of the foreign shareholders of the bank for the purpose of inducing them to subscribe for additional stock, but did not, of course, return upon the announcement of the failure of the bank.

Dividends have been declared in favor of the creditors of these banks as follows:

Scandinavian National Bank, Chicago	25 per cent.
Wallkill National Bank, Middletown, N. Y	75 per cent.
Atlantic National Bank, New York City	55 per cent.
First National Bank, Washington, D. C	30 per cent.

During the year dividends have been declared as follows upon banks which had previously failed:

First National Bank, Selma, Ala	35 per cent.
National Unadilla Bank, Unadilla, N. Y	32 per cent.
First National Bank, Bethel, Conn	28 per cent.
National Bank of Vicksburg, Miss	35 per cent.
First National Bank, Rockford, Ill	25 per cent.
First National Bank of Nevada, Austin, Nev	15 per cent.
Eighth National Bank, New York	10 per cent.
First National Bank, Fort Smith, Ark	100 per cent.

Assessments will soon be made upon the shareholders for deficiency, and, if not paid, suits will be brought to collect such deficiency from the shareholders of The Farmers and Citizens' National Bank of Brooklyn and The Eighth National Bank of New York. Similar suits will be promptly brought against the shareholders of the other banks as soon as the deficiency shall be ascertained. The receivers of The Ocean National Bank of New York, The Wallkill National Bank of Middletown, N. Y., The Atlantic National Bank of New York, The First National Bank of Washington, D. C., The National Bank of the Commonwealth, New York, The First National Bank of Mansfield, Ohio, and The First National Bank of Carlisle, Pa., encourage me to believe that the creditors will be paid in full in the course of the next year. No effort will be spared on the part of the Comptroller to collect promptly the assets of these insolvent banks, and return, if possible, the full amount to the creditors. In many cases creditors grow impatient, and attribute great neglect to the Comptroller and the receiver, when the delay in the payment of dividends has been caused by protracted litigation which could not be avoided, and which has been continued for the benefit of the creditors. It is believed, however, that no other system of banking previous to the organization of the national banking system has been so successful in converting assets and making prompt dividends to creditors.

Attorney-General Akerman gave an opinion, September 9, 1871, that the United States was not entitled to precedence for moneys deposited in national banks beyond the amount of security on deposit with the Treasurer. This decision has recently been confirmed by the present Attorney-General, and approved by the Secretary of the Treasury, and under that decision dividends have been declared during the past year in favor of the creditors of The First National Bank of Selma, Ala., and The National Bank of Vicksburg, Miss. A dividend in favor of the creditors of The First National of New Orleans is still delayed, on account of a claim of the Government consisting of a balance of $221,769 unpaid upon a check of a former assistant treasurer of the United States upon the bank; but there is some encouragement to believe that the claim may be settled without further litigation, and a dividend of 25 per cent. be soon declared.

At the time of the failure of The First National Bank of New Orleans, bills of exchange were outstanding, drawn upon the Bank of Liverpool, amounting to about $280,000. Proceedings in chancery were commenced in England by the holders of these bills to recover, upon the theory that there had been a specific appropriation of funds to pay the several bills as they were issued. The decision of the vice-chancellor was in favor of the holders of the drafts. The receiver appealed to the Lord High Chancellor, and three judges with him sitting pronounced elaborate opinions, reversing the vice-chancellor's decision and decreeing the payment of the money to the receiver. Two of the claimants appealed to the House of Lords, and this appeal has recently been dismissed with costs, after six years' litigation from the lowest to the highest chancery tribunal in England.

The Comptroller desires to call the attention of Congress to the necessity for some legislation authorizing him to appoint receivers of national banks, for insolvency, when such insolvency shall become evident from the protest of the drafts of such associations, or otherwise, if, after due examination shall have been made, the assets of the association are found not sufficient to liquidate its debts. The Comptroller also desires to call the attention of Congress to the fact that where suits are brought for the forfeiture of the charter of a bank, as provided in section 53 of the act, no provision exists for the appointment of a receiver when the charter is determined and adjudged forfeited by the United States court before whom the suit is required to be brought by the Comptroller. It is desirable that prompt measures should be taken for forcing weak banks into liquidation, under section 42 of the act, when it is believed that the officers and directors will honestly wind up the affairs of such banks, and that full authority should be given to appoint a receiver in all cases where the forfeiture of the charter is adjudged. Provision should also be made, after full payment of all the debts of the association, for placing the remaining assets in the hands of an agent appointed by the shareholders of the bank, and discharging the Comptroller and the receiver, by virtue of such legislation, from all further responsibility. Provision should also be made for the investment of the funds on deposit with the Treasurer in interest-bearing securities, when dividends are delayed by reason of protracted litigation.

Criminal prosecutions will be brought against officers and directors of national banks for violations of the law, whenever such prosecutions can, in the opinion of the Solicitor, be maintained.

The Comptroller has been subjected to some criticism during the late crisis because the indebtedness of private bankers to national banks has been found in some instances to exceed one-tenth of the capital of the bank. Section 29 of the act as it now stands does not prohibit deposits payable on demand from being made with private bankers or State banks. An amendment to this section of the act was prepared by the Comptroller, and was introduced and referred to the proper committee during the last session of Congress, which provided "that the total liabilities to any association, of any person, or of any company, corporation, or firm, (not including the liability of one national bank to another national bank,) including in the liabilities of a company or firm the liabilities of the several members thereof, shall at no time exceed one-tenth part of the aggregate amount of the capital stock of such association actually paid in, and its surplus fund." The Comptroller urgently recommends the passage of this amendment.

Tables giving statistics in reference to insolvent national banks will be found in the appendix.

SAVINGS BANKS, TRUST AND LOAN COMPANIES, AND STATE BANKS ORGANIZED UNDER STATE LAWS.

The act of Congress approved 19th February, 1873, requires the Comptroller of the Currency "to report annually to Congress, under appro priate heads, the resources and liabilities, exhibiting the condition of banks, banking companies, and savings-banks, organized under the laws of the several States and Territories; such information to be obtained by the Comptroller from the reports made by such banks, banking companies, and savings-banks to the legislatures or officers of the States and Territories. And where such reports cannot be obtained the deficiency shall be supplied from such other authentic sources as may be available."

Savings institutions.

In obedience to this command the Comptroller reports that he has encountered a full measure of the difficulties and disappointments in his way which are intimated in the last clause of his instructions. The deficiency of official reports is shown by the fact that he has been able to obtain, in form for use, the condition of these institutions in only eight of the thirty-seven States in the Union and the District of Columbia, and none at all from the nine Territories. The inaccuracy and incompleteness of many of these official returns will show how unavailing have been his efforts to comply with the requisitions of the act. Only about twenty-eight of the States have made any reply to his applications for the required information, and ten of this number answer that they have none to give; ten of them make such returns, but in such form that they cannot be put into satisfactory statements. They afford no clear exhibit of either the whole number of these State institutions, or any means of balancing their resources and liabilities. To do something like justice to the reports received from the several States they may be divided into four classes.

First. The official returns which this office has been able to put into a regular form.

Second. Those of the States which do not afford either comprehensive or satisfactory exhibits of the number and condition of their State banks, savings-banks, and trust and loan companies, distinctively.

Third. Those which answer through their executive authorities that they can make no reports whatever.

Fourth. Those from which no answers of any kind have been received.

The first class consists of the six New England States, New York, New Jersey, and the District of Columbia. The reports of these have been found capable of general tabulation, and fairly obtained balances of resources and liabilities. The statement in detail will be found in the appendix.

Savings institutions of the first class.

The following noteworthy particulars pertain to the savings-banks of these States, exclusive of the District of Columbia.*

1st. They are old Eastern States, geographically contiguous, and in general have their business and banking institutions tolerably well or-

---

* The District of Columbia is not embraced in the following comparative statements for the reason that thirty-four branches of the Freedmen's Savings and Trust Company, distributed throughout sixteen States, are reported from the central office as of the District of Columbia; and it may be noted here that thirty-two of these branches are located in the old slave States, and their aggregate deposits at June, 1873, were $3,522,712

While those of the two old free States were 505,927

Total 4,028,639

ganized; and they observe more respect to the just claim of the community for publicity of their affairs than do the monetary institutions of other divisions of the Union.

2d. The magnitude of their deposits, as they are given at the close of the year 1872—aggregating, for the eight States, $663,244,179, while the deposits of the national banks of the same States at about the same date stood at $360,399,206—the deposits of these savings-banks bearing the proportion to those of the national banks nearly as 65 to 37. The deposits of the savings-banks of the six New England States, taken alone, at the close of 1872, amounted to $349,395,377, while those of the national banks of the same States, at the same time, were but $100,498,415; or they stood as 77.66 to 22.34, respectively, which is nearly 3½ to 1.

Again, the relative numbers were then 406 savings-banks, and of the national banks 449. The aggregate population of New England in the autumn of 1872 may be stated at 3,628,855. The number of open depositor accounts is given at 1,109,995, which is equal to 30½ per cent. of the entire population. Connecticut reports, for January 1, 1873, the number of depositors in her savings-banks at 39 per cent. of the population. The whole amount of the deposits at this date averaged to each person in the State $127.50, and to each depositor $340. The average amount to the credit of each depositor in the six New England States was $315.73.

The interest and dividend paying investments of the savings-banks of these six States amounted to $340,556,997, which is equal to 97.16 per cent. of the aggregate deposits, and their cash on hand was $5,913,127,* or 1.69 per cent. of their liabilities to the depositors. The character of these investments will be seen in the appendix. The rates of interest or dividends paid to the depositors will appear, so far as they could be obtained, in the same tabular statement. The average rate of interest, for some of these States, is not given in their summary statements, and it was found impossible to calculate it from reports of the individual banks. It should be understood, also, that the stated

---

* To explain an apparent discrepancy between the aggregate amount of "cash on hand" in the savings-banks of the six New England States and that found in the tabular statement of the appendix, it must be observed that the summaries or aggregates of the resources and liabilities of these banks, made by the bank superintendents of the several States, are adopted in all the cases in which such summaries are made. But the summaries in all the New England States, except Massachusetts, treat "deposits in banks" as "cash on hand." The propriety of such aggregations is doubtful, or a matter of construction, and, deferring so far to the judgment of the State superintendents their figures have been accepted in the foregoing calculations. But if "cash on hand" were separated from "deposits in banks," the proportion to the amount of deposits would stand thus:

Cash on hand in the six New England States, $3,286,719; equal to 0.94 per cent. of their aggregate deposits, or liability to their depositors; while, if their "deposits in banks" are included, the total would be $5,913,127; equal to 1.69 per cent.

So, with the corresponding account of the single State of Connecticut, hereafter given at $1,567,354, "cash on hand" would be reduced to $27,256, excluding the amount of the "deposits in banks," or to 1.20 per cent. instead of 2.28 per cent. of the liabilities to the depositors. It may be added that the "cash on hand" in the New York savings-banks stands at $3,795,396—equal to 1.33 per cent. of the deposits; but if their "deposits in banks" are added, the "cash" will be $16,328,893, or 5.72 per cent. of their liabilities to their depositors.

Again, it is to be noted that in a number of instances, greatly affecting the accuracy of the division in the tabular statement of the cash-account in all the States of our first class, except New York and Massachusetts, no separation of these two classes of funds is made in the summaries of the State reports, and this office has been obliged to accept an undistinguishing aggregate: all of which suggests the necessity of a uniform formula of reports.

amount of "deposits," in some cases, means the amount "due depositors," including accrued interest.

An approximate idea of the business done by these New England
savings-banks may be derived from the report of those of Connecticut
for January 1, 1873.

Their deposits at that date amounted to............... $68,523,397

Their real estate securities were....................... $43,174,015
Personal and collateral................................ 9,495,819
Bonds and stocks 16,423,662

Total investments........................... 69,093,496

Total assets 71,271,395

Cash on hand $1,567,334=2.28 % of deposits.

The rate of increase in the business of the New England savings-
banks is also indicated by an increase of the deposits of Connecticut
on January 1, 1873, over those of January 1, 1872, amounting to
$5,805,583 upon $62,717,814, or 9¼ per cent. for the year.

At the end of the year 1872 the loans and discounts of the New England savings-banks, amounting to $251,668,764, exceeded those of the
national banks of the same States, at the same time, by the sum of
$21,608,411, or 9¼ per cent.

The States of New England, with New York and New Jersey, are here
selected as the best representatives of the savings-bank system, as it existed
and is reported at the latest dates; and the deposits, loans, and discounts
of the national banks; are taken, for the purpose of comparison, at the
nearest corresponding date, (3d of October, 1872.) Nearly all of these
State institutions make their returns to the State authorities but once a
year, and that so late in the year that those for the present year cannot
be received in time to be embodied in this report. For the purpose of
exhibiting the relative amount of the deposits in the savings-banks of
the States of the first class, and affording some measure of their magnitude and business importance, those of the national banks in the same
States have been given. A comparison of the condition of similar institutions in the United Kingdom of Great Britain and Ireland may help
in forming a judgment of their value and force in the business of the
community.

In the old savings-banks of the United Kingdom there were, on No
vember 30, 1872, open depositors' accounts, 1,425,147. In the post-
office savings-banks on December 31, 1872, 1,442,448.

The amount due to depositors in the former............ £39,680,652
The amount due to depositors in the latter.............. 19,318,339

Total 58,998,991

An average to each depositor of £20 12s. Thus we have for the number
of the depositors of New England, New York, and New Jersey 2,044,640.
Total deposits, $663,244,179, and an average of $324.45 to each depositor; while in the United Kingdom the number of depositors was
2,867,595; total deposits, $286,145,107, and an average of $99.91 to each
depositor.

In view of the enormous disparity in the total and average amounts
of deposits here exhibited, the question arises whether all the deposits

in the New England savings-banks, or what portion of them, are *savings*, and what amount are merely mercantile accounts—a question for the solution of which the reports afford no safe data. It has, however, been estimated that not more than 30 per cent. are actual savings.

Savings-banks of the second class of State reports.

Many of these returns, under the name of "savings-banks," *show capital paid in and dividends paid to stockholders*. These, in constitution and operation, seem to differ in nothing from ordinary banks of discount and deposit. A distinctive description of savings institutions is given in section 110 of the internal-revenue act, as amended by the act of July 13, 1866, in these words:

Associations or companies known as provident institutions, savings-banks, saving-funds, or savings institutions, having *no capital stock*, and doing no other business than receiving deposits, to be loaned or invested for the sole benefit of the parties making such deposits, without profit or compensation to the association or company.

Justice Field, of the Supreme Court of the United States, gave full effect to this distinctive definition, in the case of *The German Saving and Loan Society* versus *George Oulton*, in April, 1871, at a circuit court held for the district of California. Governed by this legislative and judicial definition, the Comptroller, in this report, excludes from the class of savings-banks, without regard for the names assumed, all banks which report capital stock or dividends to stockholders.

General deficiency of savings-banks' reports in States of our second class.

Some of these States require by their laws and charters annual or semi-annual reports to be made to the State authorities, which the authorities do not publish in any of their statistical reports. In other States such reports of the individual banks are allowed to be made to their county or supreme courts, and are inaccessible to the Comptroller. Some of these banks report only to their depositors, in accordance with their own by-laws. For an instance of the impossibility of obtaining full and satisfactory statements, the reply to the Comptroller's inquiries of the president of one of the largest, most legitimate, and soundest of the savings-banks of Philadelphia, may be properly quoted, so far as this point is concerned. He says, "We have no printed reports." The importance of this bank is shown in his answer, by letter, that "it now has near 45,000 depositors and about twelve million dollars." It is probable that many of the savings-banks individually publish their annual statements in the newspapers of their respective towns and cities, but it is certain that they cannot be found registered officially with the financial officers of their respective States.

Savings-banks of the District of Columbia.

On the 26th page of the Comptroller's Annual Report for 1872 will be found his recommendation to Congress for the repeal, so far as it applies to the organization of savings-banks, of the fourth section of the act of 1st June, 1870, which provides "for the creation of corporations in the District of Columbia by general law." He repeats his recommendation for the repeal, for the reasons given in his last report, and for the enactment in its stead of a general law with judicious provisions and restrictions.

Third class of States

From whose executive officers answers to the Comptroller's letters of inquiry have been received. Extracts from a few of such replies will suffice to explain the large deficiency of the summaries of this report:

The governor of Virginia says: "Banks (except of circulation) are authorized to be organized under our general laws, and they are not required by law to make any reports whatever, except such as may be required by the financial officers of the Government for the purposes of taxation."

The governor of West Virginia replies: "There are banks of discount and deposit in the State organized and chartered under a general law. * * * * There is no provision in our statutes requiring such banks to make reports to any officer of the State, consequently none are made."

The governor of Arkansas answers: "There is no law requiring State banks and savings-banks to make a report of their condition to the State authorities, and, therefore, I am unable to furnish you with the information desired."

The secretary of state of Missouri says: "Banks and savings associations may be organized under a general statute, and are required to publish semi-annual statements," but adds, "that no report on their condition is made by any State authority."

The governor of California answers: "Associations may be formed, under general laws, for the deposit of gold and silver, but no reports are made either to the legislature or to any State officers."

The secretary of state of Alabama says: "There are savings-banks incorporated by special acts of the general assembly, but I am not prepared now to name them, or to direct your attention to the particular statutes creating them," and adds, "There is no provision made that I am apprised of requiring savings-banks to make any report to the State authorities." And an officer of one of the national banks of that State, to whom application was made for the required statistics, says: "With respect to two of the State banks in one of the cities, even the stockholders and a majority of the directors can get no information as to the stock and business generally. With regard to the others, the information can only be obtained by a demand made by one having the legal authority to make it."

The governor of Mississippi answers: "While the laws of the State authorize the establishment of banks and savings institutions, they do not require them to make reports to the State authorities."

The governor of Kansas says: "Savings institutions are authorized, and required, to publish statements of their condition in their county papers, and to deposit copies in the state department." but adds, "There are no published State reports upon the subject."

Altogether, ten of the States whose officers have made replies to the applications of the Comptroller are of a like tenor and import with those above cited. In all of the States of this class there is common newspaper evidence of the existence of State banks, savings-banks, and trust and loan companies, but no such comprehensive or specific statements of their condition and business as would serve any of the purposes of this report.

States and Territories of the fourth class.

From these, embracing twelve States and nine Territories, no reports or answers to his inquiries have been received.

Trust and loan companies.

These companies are usually organized, by special State statutes, in the large cities. Their capitals, deposits, and business are quite large in amount. Generally, if not always, they are not required to report to the State authorities, but under the orders of one or other of the court. Some of these occur at long intervals, and are probably published in the newspapers; but even when so published they are by no means full, and furnish but little available information. For instance, one of the largest of these institutions has published but one report in the year, and that report contains only a statement of its assets, without any mention of the amount due to its depositors, or of any of its liabilities.

The bank superintendent of New York, in reply to an inquiry in reference to these institutions, says, (under date of 31st July, 1873:) "The trust companies of New York are peculiarly situated. Some are under the supervision of the bank department; some are under the control of the comptroller of the State; but the great majority of them are under no sort of supervision. * * * This class of corporations (meaning the last described) has multiplied rapidly during the last few years. * * * I am not able to furnish a copy of the charter of any of these companies." Some reports of such companies have been received, but the number is obviously so few in proportion to the whole that any attempted report of them for the whole country would be not only useless but possibly delusive, and for this reason they are now wholly omitted.

State banks.

In the appendix will be found a statement of the condition of such State banks as have furnished reports which could be cast into regular form. The deficiencies in the number and the details of the reports received are so obvious that the Comptroller deems it unavailing to attempt any generalization of their contents, other than is given in the tabular statement referred to.

In accordance with the legislative and judicial definition of savings-banks proper, all those State institutions entitling themselves "savings-banks," but reported as having capital stock, are, for the purposes of classification, treated in the tabular statement as banks of discount and deposit.

It deserves to be noted here that the returns of the State banks of New York are at once full, and properly distinguished from the savings institutions. They exhibit the condition of the State banks upon the 12th of September, 1873, the same day as the date of the last regular returns of the national banks.

The Comptroller has great pleasure in acknowledging the courtesy and promptitude of the executive and financial officers of the majority of the States, in making such replies to his inquiries as were within their power. In view of the paucity of the information furnished, it should be remembered that this is the first call made upon them by any officer of the Federal Government. They were thus, in many instances, unprepared to furnish such statements of their monetary institutions as were required of them: and it may be added that they were not long enough apprised of the requisition made upon them, or sufficiently assured of the generality of the investigation, to put the financial machinery of their respective States in operation for the purpose. But now, fully acquainted with the nature and importance of the investigation, it may be expected that in the coming year a greatly better and more serviceable collection of statistics will be supplied.

Upon reflection, it will be clearly understood that the proposed collection of information concerning the money institutions of the several States, like the inquiries of the Census Department of the General Government, seeks only to inform the people of the condition of their organized agencies of commercial and business exchanges. It is also respectfully submitted that the members of Congress, and of the State legislatures, and the officers of the States, may exert their influence to obtain the passage of such laws as will give us, in the next year, a full and thoroughly useful presentment of the vast money agencies not within the legal control of this office.

SPECIE AND SURPLUS.

The following table will exhibit the amount of specie held by the national banks at the dates mentioned—the coin, coin-certificates, and checks payable in coin, held by the national banks of the city of New York, being stated separately for a period of six years. The old reports of the State banks included in the item of "specie," checks payable in coin, and it is known that such checks composed a considerable proportion of the amount reported as specie, and it is believed that no true exhibit of the actual amount of coin held by the banks of the city of New York has been presented previous to the preparation of this table :

Date.	Held by national banks in New York City.				Held by other national banks.	Aggregate.
	Coin.	U. S. coin certificates.	Checks payable in coin.	Total.		
Oct. 5, 1868..	$1,608,623 24	$6,390,140	$1,536,353 66	$9,625,116 90	$3,378,506 49	$13,003,713 39
Jan. 4, 1869..	1,902,769 48	18,038,590	2,348,140 49	22,289,429 97	7,337,320 29	29,626,750 26
April 17, 1869..	1,652,575 21	3,720,040	1,469,826 64	6,842,441 85	3,102,090 30	9,944,532 15
June 12, 1869..	2,542,533 96	11,953,680	975,015 82	15,471,229 78	2,983,860 70	13,455,090 48
Oct. 9, 1869..	1,792,740 73	16,897,900	1,013,948 72	19,704,589 45	3,297,816 38	23,002,405 83
Jan. 22, 1870..	6,100,036 29	28,501,460	2,190,644 74	36,898,141 03	11,457,242 69	48,345,383 72
Mar. 24, 1870..	2,647,008 39	21,872,480	1,069,094 30	25,580,482 69	11,507,060 75	37,096,543 44
June 9, 1870..	2,942,400 24	18,660,920	1,163,905 88	22,767,226 12	8,332,211 66	31,099,437 78
Oct. 8, 1870..	1,607,742 91	7,533,900	3,994,006 42	13,135,649 33	5,324,362 14	18,460,011 47
Dec. 28, 1870..	2,268,521 96	14,065,540	3,748,126 87	20,080,248 83	6,227,002 76	26,307,251 59
Mar. 18, 1871..	2,982,155 61	13,090,730	3,829,881 64	19,911,757 25	5,857,409 39	25,769,166 64
April 29, 1871..	2,047,930 71	9,845,080	4,382,107 24	16,275,117 95	6,456,909 07	22,732,027 02
June 10, 1871..	2,249,408 06	9,161,160	3,680,854 92	15,091,422 98	4,833,532 18	19,924,955 16
Oct. 2, 1871..	1,121,869 40	7,590,260	1,163,628 44	9,875,757 84	3,377,240 33	13,252,998 17
Dec. 16, 1871..	1,454,930 73	17,354,740	4,255,631 39	23,065,302 12	6,529,997 44	29,595,299 56
Feb. 27, 1872..	1,490,417 70	12,341,060	3,117,100 90	16,948,578 60	8,559,246 72	25,507,825 32
April 19, 1872..	1,898,650 74	10,102,400	4,718,364 25	16,646,423 99	7,787,475 47	24,433,899 46
June 10, 1872..	3,782,909 64	11,412,160	4,219,419 52	19,414,489 16	4,842,154 98	24,256,644 14
Oct. 3, 1872..	920,767 37	5,454,580	....	6,375,347 37	3,854,409 42	10,229,756 79
Dec. 27, 1872..	1,306,091 05	12,471,940	....	13,778,031 05	5,269,305 40	19,047,336 45
Feb. 28, 1873..	1,958,759 86	11,530,790	....	13,499,549 86	4,279,123 67	17,777,673 53
April 25, 1873..	1,344,940 93	11,743,310	....	13,088,250 93	3,780,557 81	16,868,808 74
June 13, 1873..	1,442,087 71	22,139,000	....	23,581,177 71	4,368,009 01	27,950,086 72
Sept. 12, 1873..	1,063,200 55	13,522,610	....	14,585,810 55	5,282,658 90	19,868,469 45

The surplus of the national banks now amounts in the aggregate to more than $120,000,000, which is a perpetual and increasing fund, to which losses and bad debts may be charged. The act limits the liabilities of any association, person, company, or firm, for money borrowed, to one-tenth of the capital paid in. It is recommended that this limit be extended to fifteen per cent. of capital and surplus, for banks located in the redemption cities, and one-tenth of capital and surplus for the other banks.

SHINPLASTERS.

In my last report 1 called the attention of Congress to the issue of bills of credit by the State of Alabama, which issues are prohibited by

11 Ab

section 10, article 1, of the Constitution of the United States; and also to the issue of unauthorized currency by various corporations in the South, and the necessity of legislation to prevent this abuse. The issue of such unauthorized currency is increasing in various directions. Railroad corporations in the Southern States have been issuing, for some years past, notes for circulation, of different denominations, many of which are similar to the following:

$10.   CENTRAL RAILROAD BANK.   SAVANNAH, GA.: FARE-TICKET.   I.
Good for the fare of two passengers one hundred and twenty-five miles.
The Central Railroad and Banking Company of Georgia.   Savannah, Dec. 1, 1871.

——— ———,   President.
      Superintendent.

I am informed that these issues are redeemed by the railroad company, and that quite extensive arrangements are being made by manufacturing companies and corporations to issue similar devices. Such circulation is also being issued by the mining corporations of Lake Superior, and by "Zion's Commercial Co-operative Institution" in Salt Lake City. Similar issues are also made for circulation in the State of Maine, which purport to be drawn on (or by) parties residing at Saint Stephen, New Brunswick. Issues of this character will be likely to increase in the present anomalous condition of the currency, unless Congress shall legislate them out of existence by inflicting such penalties, or assessing such taxes, as will deter the corporations in question from engaging in such illegitimate practices. A carefully prepared bill to remedy this evil was submitted to Congress during its last session, and its passage is urgently recommended.

SPECIAL DEPOSITS.

The abuses arising from the receiving by the national banks of what are termed "special deposits," are growing more and more numerous. The common law classifies the duties of bailee as follows : He is bound to extraordinary diligence in those contracts for bailments where he alone receives benefit, as in the case of loans; he must observe ordinary diligence in those bailments which are beneficial to both parties, and is responsible for gross negligence in those bailments which are only for the benefit of the bailor. Special deposits which are received on deposit from the dealer of a bank are almost entirely of the latter class. Such deposits consist chiefly of bonds in packages or in tin trunks, which are deposited in the vaults of the bank for safe-keeping, by those persons who are accustomed to make deposits and transact other business with the bank. The bank would prefer to decline such deposits, but the custom having been long established, they dislike to refuse. In the case of the Ocean National Bank, seven different suits have arisen, each of which presents different questions, and all of which it is thought will be carried to the highest court, thus inflicting protracted litigation at the expense of the creditors or the shareholders of the bank, which could easily have been avoided had the national currency act contained a specific provision in reference to such deposits. The robbery of the Ocean National Bank took place previous to its suspension, and by that robbery its own bonds, as well as those of its correspondents, were stolen, and the bank therefore exercised the same prudence in caring for the deposits of its dealers as for its own. But if it can be shown that the bank did not exercise the greatest degree of diligence in the protection of its own property, a jury will in most cases find a verdict involving, not only the loss of the assets of the corporation, but also the property of its dealers, which has been left entirely for the convenience of the depositor, and not for the profit or benefit of the bank. Similar litigation is likely to arise in the settlement of the affairs of all insolvent national banks. In the large cities there is no necessity, since the establishment of safe-deposit companies, for the deposit of such packages with the banks; and it would relieve the banks of the cities from a burden were a law passed prohibiting the receipt by them of such deposits. Country banks cannot, however, without some provision of law, relieve themselves from the duty of receiving such deposits, and I recommend, therefore, the passage of an act, which shall provide that "no national bank shall be liable to make good any deficiency which may hereafter arise in any special deposit made with any national bank, unless a receipt shall be produced by the owner of such deposit, in which the liability of the bank shall be distinctly stated." Such an act can work no injustice, for the depositor will take good care, at the time of leaving the deposit, to obtain a receipt from the bank which shall explicitly state the liability; and if he choose to make a special deposit without such acknowledgment, he will do so, understanding at the time that the deposit is placed in the bank solely at his own option, for his own convenience, and at his own risk.

MUTILATED CURRENCY.

The following table exhibits the number and amount of national bank notes, of each denomination, which have been issued and redeemed since the organization of the system, and the number and amount outstanding November 1, 1873:

Denomination.	Number.			Amount.		
	Issued.	Redeemed.	Outstanding.	Issued.	Redeemed.	Outstanding.
1	15, 524, 189	9, 891, 606	5, 632, 583	$15, 524, 189 00	$9, 891, 606 00	$5, 632, 583 00
2	5, 195, 111	3, 120, 723	2, 074, 388	10, 390, 222 00	6, 241, 446 00	4, 148, 776 00
5	34, 894, 456	9, 141, 963	25, 752, 493	174, 472, 280 00	45, 709, 815 00	128, 762, 465 00
10	12, 560, 309	2, 573, 070	9, 987, 329	125, 603, 990 00	25, 730, 700 00	99, 873, 290 00
20	3, 608, 219	653, 671	2, 955, 148	72, 164, 380 00	13, 061, 420 00	59, 102, 900 00
50	559, 722	168, 976	390, 746	27, 986, 100 00	8, 448, 800 00	19, 537, 300 00
100	416, 500	144, 057	272, 533	41, 650, 000 00	14, 405, 700 00	27, 253, 300 00
500	10, 496	9, 658	6, 838	8, 248, 000 00	4, 829, 000 00	3, 419, 000 00
1, 000	5, 148	4, 530	618	5, 148, 000 00	4, 530, 000 00	618, 000 00
	72, 780, 330	25, 707, 654	47, 072, 676	481, 196, 161 00	132, 848, 487 00	348, 347, 674 00
Deduct for fragments of notes lost or destroyed					3, 275 30	
Add for fragments of notes lost or destroyed						3, 275 30
					132, 845, 211 70	348, 350, 949 30

NOTE.—Amount of gold notes outstanding not included in the above, $2,030,000.

From the organization of the system, in 1863, to November 1, 1873, $132,845,211, or more than one-third of the whole amount outstanding, has been returned to the Treasury for destruction, as follows:

Previous to November 1, 1865	$175, 490
During the year ending October 31, 1866	1, 050, 382
During the year ending October 31, 1867	3, 401, 423
During the year ending October 31, 1868	4, 602, 825
During the year ending October 31, 1869	8, 603, 729
During the year ending October 31, 1870	14, 305, 689
During the year ending October 31, 1871	24, 344, 047
During the year ending October 31, 1872	30, 211, 720
During the year ending October 31, 1873	36, 433, 171
Additional amount of notes of banks in liquidation destroyed by the Treasurer of the United States	9, 716, 735
Total amount destroyed	132, 845, 211

During the past year $36,433,171 of national bank notes have bee:
returned to the Treasury for destruction, which is more than one-tenth of
the whole amount of circulation.

The amount of legal-tender notes and the amount of national bank
notes in circulation are about equal. The whole issue of the national
bank notes is, however, continually in circulation, while more than one-
third of the legal-tender notes is held permanently by the national
banks as reserve. The national bank notes are redeemable only by the
banks issuing them, or at their redeeming agencies, while the legal
tender notes are all redeemable at the Treasury of the United States.
If the national banks are not in as good condition as the legal-tender
notes, the reason is evident. But if the bank notes should be carefully
assorted by the different treasurers, assistant treasurers, and depositories of the United States, and transmitted to the redeeming agencies
in the city of New York, where more than two-thirds of the national
bank notes are redeemable, the worn and mutilated notes would soon be
replaced by new notes issued from this office. Section 39 of the act
provides that no association shall "pay or put in circulation the notes
of any bank or banking association which shall not at any such time be
receivable at par on deposit and in payment of debts by the association so paying out or circulating such notes; nor shall it knowingly pay
out or put in circulation any notes issued by any bank or banking association which at the time of such paying out or putting in circulation
is not redeeming its circulating notes in lawful money of the United
States." I recommend that the return of such notes to the Treasury
for redemption be authorized at the expense of the United States, the
amount necessary for this purpose to be appropriated from the tax on
circulation already paid by the banks. The effect of such an authorization will be to return to the Treasury the outstanding notes of all
banks which have failed and are in liquidation, amounting to $5,246.938,
which may be issued thereafter to the States which have less than
their proportion.

The Comptroller has received many letters from officers of national
banks, suggesting that a division be organized in his office for the assorting and redemption of the mutilated currency of the national banks,
the expense to be borne *pro rata*, by the banks whose notes are transmitted to this office for that purpose. The Comptroller will willingly
undertake the work of purifying the bank currency now in circulation,
if the proper force shall be placed at his command, and will endeavor
to re-imburse to the Treasury the expense thereof by assessment upon
such national banks as shall avail themselves of the privilege.

The present arrangement for burning notes to ashes, as required by
section 24 of the act, is very unsatisfactory, the law having evidently
contemplated that the burning should take place in the Treasury building.
I recommend that an appropriation be made to test by experts the practicability of, and to authorize the purchase of suitable machinery for,
grinding to pieces mutilated notes, thus utilizing the paper material
now lost, amounting in value to thousands of dollars annually.

NEW NATIONAL BANK NOTES.

The "act making appropriations for sundry civil expenses of Government for the fiscal year ending June 30, 1871," contained the following provision :

For replacing the worn and mutilated circulating notes of national banking associations, and for engraving and preparing, in such manner and on such paper and of such

form and design as the Secretary of the Treasury may prescribe, new circulating notes for such associations to replace notes of a design and denomination now successfully counterfeited, six hundred thousand dollars: *Provided*, That each of said national banking associations shall re-imburse the Treasury the costs of the circulating notes furnished under this provision.

Section 41 of the currency act provided that the plates and special dies to be prepared by the Comptroller of the Currency for the printing of such circulating notes, shall be under his control and direction, "and the expenses necessarily incurred in executing the provision of this act respecting the procuring of such notes, and all other expenses of the Bureau, shall be paid out of the proceeds of the taxes or duties now or hereafter to be assessed on the circulation, and collected from associations organized under this act." The tax to which reference is made is a semi-annual tax of one-half of one per cent., required to be paid to the Treasurer of the United States, semi-annually, in the months of January and July; and, under this provision, $22,460,332 have been collected and paid into the Treasury since the organization of the system, as provided by law. The section of the appropriation bill referred to was passed without report from any committee, and no recommendation was ever made by the Treasury Department for the authorization of a new issue of national bank notes at the expense of the national banks. The engraving of the new notes will involve an expense of more than $1,000,000; and if new notes are to be issued in place of those already issued, the expense will amount probably to not less than $2,000,000. The national banks maintain that the expense of the new issue should be paid out of the taxes already exacted; and they insist that there is no necessity for the issue of a new set of notes at the present time; and that if the Government shall decide upon such an issue, the expense should be defrayed, not by themselves, but from the tax already collected, as provided by section 41 of the act.

An additional reason why the expense of printing new notes for the banks should be borne by the Government is that the Government receives the benefit of all lost and worn-out notes not finally returned for redemption, and the amount to be finally realized from this source alone is estimated to be much greater than the amount required to be expended in the replacing of worn-out notes.

The following extract from a letter of a well-known Boston cashier, who has had great experience as secretary of the association of banks for the suppression of counterfeiting, expresses the sentiments of the national banks in reference to the proposed issue of new notes.:

There has been no counterfeit on any of the notes of this bank to my knowledge; and the amount of counterfeit notes of other banks presented to this bank for redemption or examination, say for the past year, has been very small. I should not estimate it at more than $250. In fact the amount reported from all sections of the country would not seem to warrant, in any degree, the legislation by Congress—act of March 3, 1873—authorizing new plates for national bank circulation at the expense of said institutions. So far as my knowledge extends, there is a universal feeling against a new issue of national bank circulation. My opinion is that it is a mistaken policy to engrave a new set of plates for bank notes. The present issue has been so little tampered with that only two or three plates of individual banks have been at all successfully counterfeited, and those plates are well known, and have already done all the harm they can do, as the public has become well educated as to the genuineness of the present national bank circulation.

Now, if a new issue is made, the public have got to be educated as to the genuineness of the new issue, which will take a long time, and then keep posted on two sets of plates instead of one; and my belief still further is that the new plates will be the first to be counterfeited, because the least known, and then the policy about to be adopted would require you to immediately issue a *third* set of plates, and so on. As secretary of the "Association of Banks for the Suppression of Counterfeiting," my experience of twenty years, in causing the detection and conviction of parties for the crime of counterfeiting bank notes, would lead me to say, without any hesitation, that the best policy for the Government to pursue would be to protect the present issue to the best of its ability, in preference to making any new one.

I hope, therefore, that Congress will repeal the act of March last.

I recommend that the section in the appropriation bill referred to be repealed, or so amended as to provide that the expense of such notes shall be paid by the Government. The appropriation for the issue of new notes would not result, as is supposed, in the issue of new notes in place of the worn-out and mutilated notes now in circulation, for the reason that such notes must be returned to the Treasury by the banks themselves for destruction, and the notes would not be likely to be so returned if the expense for engraving and printing were to be borne by the banks, instead of being paid out of the taxes already collected and appropriated for that purpose.

Previous to the organization of the national banking system, counterfeit bank notes of more than three thousand different designs were in circulation. These notes were retired and the national bank notes issued in their place, and during the last ten years the notes of but thirty-seven banks, located in but nine States of the Union, have been counterfeited, and only forty-three plates, of the whole six thousand plates which have been engraved, have been counterfeited. The correct policy is undoubtedly to prevent the counterfeiting of the notes now in circulation, instead of introducing new notes upon which the counterfeiter may practice his art; and correspondence with all the banks whose notes have been counterfeited shows that, so far from counterfeiting being on the increase during the last two or three years, the number of notes counterfeited has sensibly diminished.

A method, both simple and practicable, exists, by which the issue of such counterfeit notes can be readily prevented, and that is by the withdrawal from circulation of such denominations of the genuine notes of national banks as have been counterfeited. Counterfeit two-dollar notes have appeared upon only ten banks, and the whole amount of genuine notes issued to these banks is but $60,000. Counterfeit twenty-dollar notes upon only eleven different national banks have appeared, and the whole amount of genuine twenty-dollar notes issued to these banks is, say, $800,000. It is plain that, if an appropriation be made, to be paid from the tax on circulation already collected from the banks, sufficient to offer a premium of one-half of one per cent. upon these notes when presented to the Treasury for redemption, most of the genuine notes would soon be retired, after which all genuine notes (except when presented to the Treasury or to the bank issuing them for redemption would be refused along with the counterfeits. No additional notes of these denominations would thereafter be issued to the banks upon which counterfeits are known to exist. The Comptroller is confident that an appropriation of, say, $10,000 would withdraw from circulation all the genuine issues which have been counterfeited, and that an annual appropriation of $1,000 thereafter would be sufficient to prevent the abuse.

EXAMINATIONS.

During the recent panic the Comptroller has endeavored to obtain, as far as possible, examinations of all national banks which have been considered in a weak or insolvent condition, and he desires to return his thanks to the efficient corps of examiners who have made prompt examinations and returns to him of the condition of such banks in all parts of the country. It is not to be supposed that the short time usually spent in the examination of a national bank will be sufficient, in all cases, to detect bad management or defalcations. If the directors of national banks, to whom are confided the interests of shareholders, neglect their duties, it is not to be expected that an examiner shall, in a single day, detect and correct the abuses of a year. A number of days is required for the thorough examination of a national bank of any considerable business, and if it is expected that the reports to this office shall detect and expose defalcations, and other violations of law, the means should be provided for defraying the expenses of more frequent and thorough examinations. The necessary expense can be levied and collected from the banks, if they shall be found delinquent; but if, upon examination, it shall be found that the investigation was unnecessary, then the expense should be paid out of a fund to be placed at the disposal of the Comptroller for that purpose.

AMENDMENTS.

Carefully-prepared bills were in possession of the proper committees during the last session of Congress, providing, (1) for the consolidation of national banks; (2) defining the duties of receivers; (3) providing for the organization of national banks without circulation, upon the deposit of ten thousand dollars of bonds with the Treasurer of the United States, instead of the deposit of one-third of the capital, as now required; (4) for the repeal of section 4 of the act of June 17, 1870, providing for the organization of savings-banks in the District of Columbia; (5) for the prevention of the issue of unauthorized currency; (6) prohibiting the deposit of more than ten per cent. of the capital with any private banker, or any person or association other than a national banking association; (7) requiring the word "counterfeit," or "altered," or "illegal," to be stamped on all counterfeit or unauthorized issues. A recommendation was also made for the issue of Government securities, bearing a low rate of interest, to be held by the national banks as part of their reserve, and for a provision of law requiring a larger proportion of cash to be kept on hand; and the attention of Congress is specially called to the necessity of prompt legislation upon these several subjects, for the proper consideration of which it is to be regretted that the brevity of the session did not afford sufficient time.

THE OFFICE.

The recent panic has required from the Comptroller unusual and exhausting duties, and if he has been in any measure successful in fulfilling these duties, he is in a large measure indebted to the employés of the office for a faithful performance of duty. In other offices in the Treasury Department, compensation in addition to the salaries provided by law is given. This additional compensation is, to a great extent, merited, and the business of the Department could not be properly and efficiently conducted without it. Many of the employés of this office, however, perform far greater labor and have much greater responsibility in the examination of reports, the preparation of letters, and the counting and return of large amounts of money, than others who receive additional compensation; and the Comptroller therefore recommends that additional compensation be appropriated, for distribution to those employés who render the most efficient and responsible service. Such an appropriation will have the effect to promote and encourage industry and efficiency in the public service, and will be in consonance with the spirit of the civil service recommended by the President.

The library of the Comptroller is very deficient in works on political economy and banking, and he recommends that an annual appropriation be provided, out of which books on finance and of reference upon financial subjects may be purchased.

THE APPENDIX.

Special attention is called to the carefully-prepared tables contained in the appendix, exhibiting the aggregate resources and liabilities of all the national banks, yearly, for the last eleven years; showing their condition during the present year, for five different periods, arranged by States and redemption cities, and separate statements of every bank of the Union upon the twelfth day of September ultimo; also exhibiting the different kinds of funds held as reserve; also showing for twenty-seven different dates, during the years 1868–'73, the percentage of reserve to circulation and deposits of the national banks in each of the redemption cities; the dividends and earnings of the national banks, by States and cities, semi-annually, from March 1, 1869, to September 1, 1873; also exhibiting, by States and redemption cities, the ratios of dividends to capital, dividends to capital and surplus, and earnings to capital and surplus of the national banks, semi-annually, from March 1, 1869, to September 1, 1873; together with lists of insolvent banks, and banks which have gone into voluntary liquidation, and the amounts and different kinds of United States bonds deposited with the Treasurer as security for circulating notes. The appendix also contains tables arranged by States and redemption cities, together with the aggregates, compiled from special reports of the national banks on October 13, the day on which the banks of the city of New York held the smallest amount of legal-tender notes during the late crisis, and on November 1, the day on which these banks resumed currency payments; also a statement exhibiting in detail the average amount of loans, circulation, deposits, specie, and legal-tender notes of each of the associated banks of New York City for the week ending September 20, and the aggregates for the week ending November 22; also statement of the condition of the State banks and savings-banks organized under the laws of the different States of the Union, so far as they could be obtained from official sources. A table of contents will be found on the succeeding page.

JOHN JAY KNOX,
Comptroller of the Currency.

Hon. JAMES G. BLAINE,
Speaker of the House of Representatives.

REPORT OF THE FIRST COMPTROLLER OF THE TREASURY.

TREASURY DEPARTMENT, FIRST COMPTROLLER'S OFFICE,
November, 1873.

SIR: The following report, which embraces the operations of this office during the fiscal year ending June 30, 1873, is respectfully submitted.

The number of warrants examined, countersigned, entered upon blotters, and posted into ledgers was as follows, viz:

Treasury proper	2,054
	222
	1,704
	2,149
	4,777
	7,036
	2,010
	4
	5,703
War	833
Navy pay	1,443
Navy proper	168

Interior civil 2,289
Interior pay 1,995
Interior repay... 205
Appropriation... 155
Customs, (covering)... 1,392
Land, (covering) 928
Internal revenue, (covering) 2,902
Miscellaneous, (covering).. 6,841
Miscellaneous repay, (covering) 1,527

The following accounts were received from the First and Fifth Auditors of the Treasury, and the Commissioner of the General Land-Office, and revised and certified, viz:

Judiciary, embracing the accounts of United States marshals for their fees and for the expenses of the United States courts, of the United States district attorneys, and of the commissioners and clerks of the United States courts 2,201

Diplomatic and consular, embracing the accounts arising from our intercourse with foreign nations, expenses of consuls for sick and disabled seamen, and of our commercial agents in foreign countries............................... 1,868

Public lands, embracing the accounts of the registers and receivers of land offices, and surveyors-general and their deputies, and of lands erroneously old... 2,710

Steamboats, embracing accounts for the expenses of the inspection of steam-vessels, and salaries of inspectors 329

Mint and its branches, embracing the accounts of gold, silver, and cent coinage, of bullion, of salaries of the officers, and general expenses........... 124

Public debt, embracing the account of the Treasurer of the United States, and the accounts of Assistant Treasurers for the redemption of United States stocks and notes, and for the payment of the interest on the public debt.... 713

Public printing, embracing accounts for printing, for paper, and for binding.. 84

Territorial, embracing accounts for the legislative expenses of the several Territories, and all the expenses incident to their government................ 373

Congressional, embracing accounts for salaries, for contingent expenses, and for other expenses of the United States Senate and House of Representatives.. 111

Internal revenue collectors' accounts of the revenue collected, the expenses of collecting the same, their own compensation, and the expenses of their offices.. 3,011

Internal revenue assessors' accounts for the expenses of levying the taxes, and for their own compensation... 1,066

Internal revenue stamp-agents' accounts for the sale of stamps................ 133

Internal revenue miscellaneous accounts for salaries and incidental expenses of supervisors, surveyors, detectives, &c..................................... 3,254

Miscellaneous, embracing accounts for the contingent expenses of all the Executive Departments at Washington, the salaries of judges, district attorneys, marshals, territorial officers, &c... 1,919

Number of letters written from this office on official business................. 11,505

Number of receipts given by collectors for tax-lists examined, registered, and filed... 2,912 .

Number of requisitions examined, entered, and reported, viz:
    Diplomatic and consular.. 698
    Collectors of internal revenue... 2,688
    United States marshals... 289
    United States depositaries... 153

The above details furnish but a portion of the duties appertaining to this office. In addition thereto must be added the examination, registering, and filing of official bonds; the examination, filing, and registering of all powers of attorney for the collection of interest, and the collection of money due to public creditors from the Department; the examination and decision of applications for the re-issue of securities in place of those lost or destroyed, and a variety of miscellaneous business occurring daily, which it is impossible to enumerate.

The business of the office continues steadily to increase, as the aggregate of the items stated in the table above is 7,642 greater than in the year immediately preceding, but the work has been carried on promptly and efficiently.

I commend the persons employed in the office for their faithfulness and efficiency. Many of them merit a higher rate of compensation than they now receive, not only because of their attention to business but because, also, of the important and responsible duties devolved upon them, which they discharge to my satisfaction.

Respectfully submitted.

R. W. TAYLER,
Comptroller.

Hon. WILLIAM A. RICHARDSON,
Secretary of the Treasury.

REPORT OF SECOND COMPTROLLER OF THE TREASURY.

TREASURY DEPARTMENT.
Second Comptroller's Office, October 31, 1873.

Sir: I have the honor to submit the following detailed statement of the business operations of this Office for the fiscal year ending June 30, 1873.

The aggregate number of accounts of disbursing officers and agents which have been received, as well as those which have been finally adjusted, is as follows.

From—	Received.	Revised.	Amount.
Second Auditor	3,742	3,779	$63, 616, 000 0
Third Auditor	4,441	2,504	170, 851, 720 34
Fourth Auditor	383	561	23, 288, 673 34
Total	8,568	6,934	237, 096, 683 68

The above accounts have been duly entered, revised, and the balances found thereon certified to the Secretary of the Department in which the expenditure has been incurred, viz, those from the Second and Third Auditors to the Secretary of War, (excepting the accounts of Indian agents, which are certified to the Secretary of the Interior,) and those from the Fourth Auditor to the Secretary of the Navy.

Character of accounts.	Received	Revised.	Amount.
FROM THE SECOND AUDITOR.			
Embracing accounts of disbursing officers of the War Department for collecting, organizing, and drilling volunteers.	29	33	$2, 052, 517 2
Paymasters' accounts for the pay of officers and the pay and rations of soldiers of the Army.	1,113	1,164	34, 809, 614 17
Special and referred accounts	699	699	1, 176, 00 00
Accounts of Army recruiting-officers for clothing, equipments, and bounty to recruits, &c.	132	137	1, 444, 384 83
Ordnance, embracing the accounts of disbursing officers of the Ordnance Department, for arsenals, armories, armaments for fortifications, arming militia, &c.	177	177	2, 1 45, 200 00
Indian Department: Accounts of Indian agents, including the pay of Indian annuities, presents to Indians, expenses of holding treaties, pay of interpreters, pay of Indian agents, &c., and the settlement of personal claims for miscellaneous services of agents and others in connection with Indian affairs.	1,127	1,110	13, 507, 479 23
Medical and hospital accounts, including the purchase of medicines, surgical instruments, hospital stores, the claims of private physicians for services, and surgeons employed under contract.	323	323	225, 2 9 42
Contingent expenses of the War Department, including expenses for military civil service, secret service, &c.	77	77	73, 000 24
Freedmen's Bureau: Pay and bounty	13	13	1, 571, 074 43
Soldiers' Home	24	24	301, 254 60
National Volunteer Asylum	12	12	382, 341 22
Total	3,742	3,779	63, 616, 000 47

Character of accounts.	Received.	Revised.	Amount.
FROM THE THIRD AUDITOR.			
Quartermasters' accounts for transportation of the Army, and the transportation of all descriptions of Army supplies and ordnance, and for the settlement of personal claims for services in the Quartermasters' Department.	2,815	1,177	$45,307,879 00
Commissaries' accounts for rations or subsistence of the Army, and for the settlement of personal claims for services in the Commissary Department.	1,131	1,136	5,936,243 78
Accounts of pension-agents for the payment of military pensions, including the entries of the monthly reports of new pensioners added to the rolls, and the statements from the Commissioner of Pensions respecting the changes arising from deaths, transfers, &c., and for pension claims presented for adjustment.	210	199	27,476,730 61
Accounts of the Engineer Department for military surveys, the construction of fortifications, for river and harbor surveys and improvements.	71	65	9,793,004 10
Signal service	1	1	134,742 05
Accounts for the relief of freedmen and refugees	13	16	603,160 00
Total	4,241	2,594	170,251,759 54
FROM THE FOURTH AUDITOR.			
Marine Corps accounts: 1st, quartermasters of the Marine Corps, embracing accounts for the expenses of officers' quarters, fuel, forage for horses, attendance on courts-martial and courts of inquiry, transportation of officers and marines, supplies of provisions, clothing, medical stores and military stores for barracks, and all incidental supplies for marines on shore; 2d, accounts of paymasters of the Marine Corps for pay of the officers and the pay and rations of the marines.	6	5	528,691 92
Paymasters of the Navy: Accounts for the pay and rations of officers and crew of the ship, supplies of provisions, of clothing, and repairs of vessels on foreign stations.	412	407	4,480,382 70
Paymasters at navy-yards: Accounts for the pay of officers on duty at navy-yards, or on leave or absence, and the pay of mechanics and laborers on the various works.	26	25	5,389,838 75
Paymasters acting as navy agents: Accounts for their advances to paymasters, purchases of timber, provisions, clothing, and naval stores.	106	96	8,785,615 83
Navy pension agents' accounts for the payment of pensions of officers and seamen, &c., of the Navy, and officers and privates of the Marine Corps.	32	24	539,780 24
Financial agent of the Navy Department	3	4	3,504,668 70
Total	585	561	23,228,978 14
Naval prize-lists	6	5	....
CLAIMS REVISED DURING THE YEAR.			
Soldiers' pay and bounty...	13,628	13,023	1,595,052 16
Sailors' pay and bounty...	1,561	1,027	427,144 09
Prize-money...............	495	495	398,813 12
Quartermasters' stores under the act of July 4, 1864; property lost, or destroyed, or captured, &c., under the act of March 3, 1849; rent of buildings and land for the use of the Army, and for other miscellaneous military claims against the War Department.	4,864	4,809	2,035,246 62
Oregon and Washington Territory war claims, including Montana Indian war claims of 1867.	503	503	450,317 53
Claims of States for enrolling, subsisting, clothing, supplying, arming, equipping, paying, and transporting their troops in defense of the United States.	12	12	1,582,085 72
Subsistence	234	234	76,299 27
Total	21,302	21,362	6,495,551 51
Referred cases................................	3,172	3,172	....

Settlements for the fiscal year ending June 30, 1873...................................... 6,934
Accounts on hand at the commencement of the fiscal year, July 1, 1872............................. 1,952
Accounts on hand at the close of the fiscal year, June 30, 1873................................. 3,586
Letters written on official business.. 1,078

Number of requisitions recorded during the year.

Requisitions.	War.	Navy.	Interor
Accountable	1,665	1,218	6
Refunding	724	136	5
Settlement	3,860	308	1 bd
Transfer	156	49	6
Total	6,465	1,611	18

Number of contracts, classified as follows :

Quartermaster's Department..................................... 72
Engineer Department 32
Indian Department 15
Ordnance 7
Navy Department 12
Adjutant-General. 11
Leases 1
Commissary of Subsistence 32
Official bonds filed 14

BIENNIAL EXAMINATION OF PENSIONERS.

There is one large item of expenditure occurring in the accounts subject to the revision of this Office to which I respectfully call your special attention, with a view to suggest legislation on the subject. It is the expense of the medical and surgical examinations of invalid pensioners required by the second section of the law of March 3, 1859, (11 Stat. 439,) to be made biennially. Not less than $200,000 are expended biennially in fees to examining-surgeons, beside many incidental charges, and the reductions of pensions from previous rates will not exceed an average of $10,000. If the law requiring biennial examinations should be repealed, some of the invalids on the roll would undoubtedly receive more than their disability would warrant; but it is bad economy to spend nearly a quarter of a million of dollars to guard against a possible loss of $10,000. In addition to the direct pecuniary saving which would be effected by the repeal of the law, the adjustment of the accounts of the disbursing pension-agents would thereby be facilitated, much time and labor being now spent in verifying reductions made during a period for which the accounts have been settled and subsequently called up on appeal.

The aggregate annual sum paid to pension-agents for compensation alone amounts to more than half a million of dollars, to say nothing of contingent expenditures, the keeping of accounts between the Assistant Treasurer and nearly sixty agencies, the transmission, monthly, to the Treasury, by express, of unwieldy packages, and other similar items.

Since the law of July 8, 1870, (sec. 2, 16 Stat., 194,) pensioners have all been paid directly by check, payment to attorneys being prohibited except in cases of pensioners residing in foreign countries.

It is not seen why *one* general agency at the seat of Government, near the Pension Office, where errors could readily be corrected, and a more thorough supervision exercised, might not be as effective and convenient as the numerous agencies now existing, at less than a tenth of their present cost. A check mailed from Washington would reach most of the pensioners nearly as soon as one sent from either of the agencies. No additional expenditure would be required for separate rolls, as duplicate rolls, the property of the Government, and containing the post-office address of every pensioner in the United States, are now at the agencies. The process of issuing duplicate checks, also, under the law of April 19, 1871, (17 Stat., 4,) to replace those lost or stolen, would be much simplified if all pensions were payable from one disbursing office, and that at the seat of Government.

Respectfully submitted.

J. M. BRODHEAD,
Comptroller.

Hon. WM. A. RICHARDSON,
Secretary of the Treasury.

REPORT OF THE COMMISSIONER OF CUSTOMS.

TREASURY DEPARTMENT,
Office of Commissioner of Customs, September 22, 1873.

SIR: I submit herewith, for your information, a statement of the work performed in this Office during the fiscal year ending 30th June, 1873.

The number of accounts on hand July 1, 1872, was	238
The number of accounts received from the First Auditor during the year	6,443
	6,681
Number of accounts adjusted during the year	6,298
Number of accounts adjusted, returned to the First Auditor, during the year	30
	6,318
Number of accounts on hand June 30, 1873	363

The amounts paid into the Treasury of the United States from sources the accounts of which are settled in this Office, are as follows:

On account of customs	$188,089,522 70
On account of fines, penalties, and forfeitures	1,169,515 38
On account of steamboat inspections	259,092 56
On account of labor, drayage, and storage	475,741 37
On account of Marine-Hospital tax	333,003 03
The amount of fees earned by collectors	611,525 44
	190,938,400 48

And there was paid out of the Treasury—

On account of expenses of collecting the revenue from customs	$7,079,743 42
On account of refunding excess of deposits	3,705,067 97
On account of debentures	1,176,055 18
On account of public buildings	3,748,780 28
On account of construction and maintenance of lights	2,910,857 64
On account of construction and maintenance of revenue-cutters	1,133,901 37
On account of distributive shares of fines, penalties, and forfeitures	626,156 74
On account of marine-hospital service	398,778 69
On account of life-saving stations	212,383 08
On account of miscellaneous accounts	117,468 80
	21,109,193 17

The number of estimates received	2,669
The number of requisitions issued	2,572
The amount involved in said requisitions	$12,785,721 15
The number of letters received	9,305
The number of letters written	10,368
The number of letters recorded	9,946
The number of returns received and examined	5,983
The number of oaths examined and registered	4,786
The number of appointments registered	3,629
The average number of clerks employed	26
The amount involved in this statement	$224,833,314 80

The statement of transactions under the bonded-warehouse regulations for the year will be prepared and transmitted as soon as all the
necessary returns shall have been received.

Very respectfully,

W. T. HAINES,
Commissioner of Customs.

Hon. W. A. RICHARDSON,
Secretary of the Treasury.

REPORT OF THE FIRST AUDITOR.

TREASURY DEPARTMENT,
First Auditor's Office, September 18, 1873.

SIR: In obedience to your request of the 7th ultimo, I have the hon-
or to submit the following statement of the business transactions of this
Office for the fiscal year ending June 30, 1873:

Accounts adjusted.	Number of accounts.	Amount.
RECEIPTS.		
Collectors of customs	1,407	$222,423,38
Collectors under steamboat act	799	346,48
Mints and assay-offices	111	59,352,88
Fines, penalties, and forfeitures	673	1,008,88
Wages of seamen forfeited	8	
Marine-hospital money collected	1,436	354,68
Official emoluments of collectors, naval officers, and surveyors received	1,043	596,88
Moneys received from captured and abandoned property	9	54,88
Treasurer of the United States for moneys received	5	918,382,88
Records of sales of public property	2	44,88
Moneys received on account of deceased passengers	34	3,88
Miscellaneous receipts	1	38
	5,582	1,302,849,38
DISBURSEMENTS.		
Expenses of collecting the revenue from customs	1,297	6,536,62
Official emoluments of collectors, naval officers, and surveyors	1,096	1,613,62
Excess of deposits for unascertained duties	143	2,567,36
Debentures, drawbacks, bounties, and allowances	196	583,88
Light-house establishment	315	640,88
Marine-hospital service	785	381,30
Revenue cutter disbursements	469	817,98
Additional compensation to collectors, naval officers, and surveyors	2	38
Distribution of fines, penalties, and forfeitures	217	522,48
Accounts for duties illegally exacted, fines remitted, judgments satisfied, and net proceeds of unclaimed merchandise paid	1,474	1,163,38
Judiciary expenses, embracing accounts of United States marshals, district attorneys, commissioners, and clerks, rent of court-houses, support of prisoners, &c.	2,420	4,289,38
Mints and assay-offices	111	57,301,68
Territorial accounts, embracing salaries of officers and legislative expenses	75	168,30
Salaries of the civil list paid directly from the Treasury	1,307	364,68
Disbursements on account of captured and abandoned property	9	34,370
Defense of suits in relation to captured and abandoned property	11	67,68
Treasurer of the United States for general expenditures	5	362,009,38
Salaries and mileage of members of the Senate and House of Representatives	1	443,38
Salaries of officers of the Senate	1	122,88
Contingent expenses of the Senate	32	341,57
Salaries of officers of the House of Representatives	9	369,68
Contingent expenses of the House of Representatives	40	212,88
Survey of the coast of the United States	22	601,88
Redemption of the public debt, including principal, premium, and interest	117	36,277,68
Payment of interest on the public debt	282	109,862,88
Certificates of deposit in currency redeemed	4	21,643,68
Reimbursement of the Treasurer of the United States for United States national bank notes, legal-tender notes, fractional currency, and gold certificates destroyed by burning	44	141,310,68
Construction of the State, War, and Navy Department	4	1,314,88
Construction of court-houses and post-offices	74	2,981,70
Construction of custom-houses	164	1,895,88

Accounts adjusted.	Number of accounts.	Amounts.

DISBURSEMENTS—Continued.

Accounts adjusted.	Number of accounts.	Amounts.
Construction of marine hospitals	86	$56,212 31
Construction and repair of light-houses	330	1,397,941 70
Construction of heating-apparatus for public buildings	6	65,635 11
Fuel, lights, and water for public buildings	38	170,900 41
Repairs and preservation of public buildings	102	274,822 54
Furniture and repairs of same	15	146,635 57
Government Hospital for the Insane	9	170,608 10
Providence Hospital, for care, support, and medical treatment of transient paupers	12	12,000 00
Maryland Institution for the Blind	4	1,703 17
National Association for Colored Women	2	5,955 29
Humane Society of Massachusetts	4	8,412 29
Columbia Hospital for Women and Lying-in Asylum, and other charities	4	43,958 40
Public printing and binding	73	1,734,216 40
Supervising and local inspectors of steam-vessels, for traveling and incidental expenses	332	44,958 46
Salaries of same	3	122,376 82
Disbursing clerks, for salaries of the several Departments of the Government at Washington	275	5,033,845 77
Contingent expenses of said Departments	389	1,149,018 29
Salaries of United States assistant treasurers, United States depositaries, and the employés in their respective offices	54	319,059 12
Expenses of national loan	30	1,799,123 36
Commissioner of Public Buildings and Grounds	42	405,428 06
Washington aqueduct	10	129,480 92
Expenses of Department of Agriculture	54	213,408 63
Warehouse and bond accounts	748	
Preserving life and property from shipwreck	54	225,178 32
Payments to District of Columbia for improvements around buildings and reservations belonging to the United States	5	2,637,565 56
New jail, District of Columbia	3	50,784 57
Expenses of board of health	1	39,300 00
Geological survey of Territories and mining statistics	13	103,028 07
Bringing the electoral vote from the several States and Territories	2	18,103 25
Extension of Government grounds	3	661,878 63
Building and ground for reform-school	1	30,000 00
United States Capitol extension	6	67,777 69
Heating Hall of House of Representatives	1	12,724 95
Construction of pneumatic tube	2	10,350 00
Salaries of custodians and janitors of public buildings	5	54,806 56
Expenses, &c., for detection of persons engaged in counterfeiting the coin and currency of the United States	6	137,093 79
Contingent expenses Independent Treasury	35	30,477 49
Outstanding liabilities paid	94	26,499 84
Judgments of the Court of Claims paid	173	2,483,112 02
Purchase of rebel records	5	79,957 50
Salaries of civil service commission	2	1,208 95
Miscellaneous accounts	911	10,683,963 10
Total	**14,474**	**1,416,198,007 42**

Reports and certificates recorded	12,433
Letters written	2,339
Letters recorded	2,339
Acknowledgments of accounts written	10,571
Powers of attorney for collecting interest on the public debt registered and filed	5,138
Requisitions answered	605
Judiciary emolument accounts registered	474
Total	**33,989**

It may be proper to state, so as to prevent misconception, that this report does not exhibit the amounts of receipts from the sources named, or expenditures on account of the subjects specified, actually accruing within the fiscal year, but simply these amounts as shown by the accounts examined and adjusted during the year.

The business of the Office has been kept up, as far as practicable, with the means within its control, and is now in a satisfactory condition. Embarrassment and delays, however, have arisen from tardiness in filling vacancies which have occurred under the present system of making appointments.

I take pleasure in commending the clerks and other employés now in the Office generally for the fidelity and alacrity with which they have discharged their assigned duties.

Very respectfully,

D. W. MAHON,
Auditor.

Hon. WM. A. RICHARDSON,
Secretary of the Treasury.

REPORT OF THE SECOND AUDITOR.

TREASURY DEPARTMENT,
Second Auditor's Office, November 1, 1873.

SIR : I have the honor to transmit herewith the annual report of this Office for the fiscal year ending June 30, 1873, showing in detail the condition of business in each division at the commencement of the year, its progress during the year, and its condition at the end thereof.

BOOK-KEEPER'S DIVISION.

The following statement exhibits the amount and nature of the work performed by this division during the year:

Requisitions registered, journalized, and posted.

On what account drawn.	No.	Amount.
DEBIT REQUISITIONS.		
Payments on account of the Pay Department	263	$13,847,435 73
Payments on account of the Ordnance Department	233	2,277,706 65
Payments on account of the Medical Department	230	440,179 00
Payments on account of the Quartermaster's Department	3	41,964 33
Payments from appropriations under control of the Adjutant General's Department	64	194,137 16
Payments from appropriations under control of the Secretary of War	81	347,483 56
Payments from the appropriation under control of the General of the Army	2	5,000 00
Payments to the National Home for Disabled Volunteer Soldiers	12	402,581 12
Payments to the Soldiers' Home	25	483,462 56
Payments to the Treasurer United States on account of Internal Revenue fund	5	113,736 21
Payments under special acts of relief by Congress	21	96,562 86
Payments on account of the Indian Department	1,364	7,920,652 77
Total payments	2,293	26,040,841 95
TRANSFER.		
Requisitions issued for the purpose of adjusting appropriations:		
Transferring amounts from appropriations found to be chargeable to such as are entitled to credit on the books of the Second Auditor's Office	18	28,256,538 06
Transferring amounts as above to the books of the Third Auditor's Office	77	483,874 63
Transferring amounts as above to the books of the First Auditor's Office	2	453 33
Transferring amounts as above to the books of the Register's Office	31	11,409 64
Total transfer	128	28,752,275 66
Aggregate debits	2,421	54,793,117 61
CREDIT REQUISITIONS.		
Deposit.		
In favor of Pay Department		1,368,787 04
In favor of Ordnance Department		22,810 98
In favor of Medical Department		6,568 09
In favor of Adjutant-General's Department	196	6,323 11
In favor of Quartermaster's Department		299 45
To the credit of appropriations under control of the Secretary of War		27,016 92
To the credit of the appropriation under control of the General of the Army		186 11
In favor of Indian Department	22	127,813 27
Total deposit	218	1,560,704 97

Requisitions registered, journalized, and posted—Continued.

On what account drawn.	No.	Amount.
Counter.		
Requisitions issued for the purpose of adjusting appropriations:		
Transferring amounts to appropriations entitled to credit from appropriations found to be chargeable on the books of the Second Auditor's Office	18	$28, 256, 538 06
Transferring amounts as above from appropriations on the books of the Third Auditor's Office to the books of the Second Auditor's Office	22	4, 763 99
Total counter	40	28, 261, 302 05
Aggregate credits	258	29, 822, 007 02
Aggregate debits and credits	2, 679	84, 615, 124 61
Deducting the credits from the debits shows the net amount drawn out to be	....	24, 971, 110 30
AFPROPRIATION WARRANTS.		
Credits.		
In favor of appropriations of Pay Department		24, 191, 515 52
In favor of appropriations of Ordnance Department		2, 260, 781 96
In favor of appropriations of Medical Department		683, 000 00
In favor of appropriations of Adjutant-General's Department	9	125, 580 00
In favor of appropriations under control of Secretary of War		567, 200 00
In favor of appropriation under control of the General of the Army		5, 000 00
In favor of the appropriations of the Indian Department	49	5, 742, 671 65
Under special acts of relief by Congress	5	27, 641 48
Total credits	63	33, 598, 390 61
Debits.		
Surplus fund warrants	2	1, 173, 583 94
Total debits	2	1, 173, 583 94
Aggregate debits and credits	65	34, 767, 974 55
Excess of credits over debits	....	32, 416, 806 67

CONDENSED BALANCE-SHEET OF APPROPRIATIONS

	War Department.	Indian Department.
Credit.		
Balance to credit of all appropriations on the books of this office June 30, 1872	$26, 500, 606 16	$9, 994, 765 05
Amount credited by appropriation warrants during fiscal year ending June 30, 1873	27, 844, 698 61	5, 747, 692 00
Amount credited by deposit and transfer requisitions during same period	29, 550, 605 45	271, 401 57
Amount credited through Third Auditor's Office to appropriations used in common by both offices	989, 539 80	....
Total	84, 865, 470 02	15, 943, 856 62
Debit.		
Amount debited to appropriations by Surplus Fund warrants during fiscal year ending June 30, 1873	1, 001, 315 54	174, 268 40
Amount drawn from appropriations by requisitions during same period	46, 562, 622 82	8, 230, 204 79
Amount drawn through Third Auditor's Office from appropriations used in common by both offices during same period	1, 426, 154 40	....
Balance remaining to the credit of all appropriations on books of this office June 30, 1873	35, 893, 176 96	7, 539, 385 43
Total	84, 865, 470 02	15, 943, 856 62

12 Ab

SETTLEMENTS MADE.

The following settlements incidental to the work of this division was made during the year:

On what account.	No.	Amount.
Transfer settlements for the adjustment of appropriations................	5	$42,027,673
Miscellaneous settlements..........	5	24,596
Total..................	10	64,991,633

SETTLEMENTS ENTERED.

Paymasters'..	2
Recruiting	15
Ordnance	3
Medical	4
Contingencies of the Army, and of the Adjutant-General's Department	5
Soldiers' Home..	1
National Home for Disabled Volunteer Soldiers................	1
Charges and credits to officers for overpayments, refundments, &c............	8
Charges to disbursing officers for canceled checks	1
Arrears of pay..	1
Proceeds of Government property....................	1
Special acts of relief by Congress....................	1
Transfers to the credit of disbursing officers on books of the First and Third Auditors' Offices....................	3
Transfer settlements for adjustment of appropriations on books of Second Auditor's Office....................	
Indian	3
Miscellaneous	4
Claims, war..	23
Claims, Indian	8
Total	2,03

Twenty-five transcripts of accounts were prepared for suit; 872 certificates as to the indebtedness or non-indebtedness of officers having claims against the United States were given to the Second and Third Auditors' officers; and 823 letters were written during the year.

PAYMASTERS' DIVISION.

The number of accounts examined and settlements made in this division was 2,021, as follows:

Paymasters' accounts audited and reported to the Second Comptroller	1,03
Old settlements of paymasters' accounts revised....................	36
Charges raised against officers on account of overpayments................	32
Charges raised against officers on account of double payments..........	17
Credits to officers for overpayments refunded	7
Credits to officers for double payments refunded	7
Lost checks paid under act of February 2, 1872	1
Transfers to books of Treasurer's office on account of "outstanding liabilities," (act May 2, 1866)....................	2
Paymasters' accounts balanced and closed....................	88
Paymasters' accounts finally adjusted on which balances remain due the United States	5
Transfers to books of Third Auditor....................	7
Miscellaneous	9
Total	2,03

The amounts involved in the above are as follows:

Paymasters' accounts.. $27,116,621 39

Amount of fines by sentence of courts-martial, forfeitures by desertion, arrears of pay, and bounties disallowed, found to have accrued to the benefit of the National Home for Disabled Volunteer Soldiers under existing laws, and paid to the president of said home by requisition on the Treasury, as follows:

1872.

August 2..	$2,013 69
September 3..	30,762 69
October 3...	14,964 73
November 1...	53,521 04
December 3..	36,545 31

1873.

January 3..	33,097 24
February 4...	38,639 50
March 6..	66,482 44
April 3...	36,942 42
May 3..	24,929 94
June 3..	26,756 29
June 30...	34,896 28

$399,551 57

Amount of fines, forfeitures, &c., for the support of the Soldiers' Home, found to be due in the examination of paymasters' accounts, and paid to said Soldiers' Home in accordance with the act of Congress of March 2, 1859, as follows:

1872.

August 2..	$18,095 05
September 3..	32,335 16
October 3...	30,156 73
November 1...	17,337 26
December 3..	31,113 12

1873.

January 3..	28,625 83
February 4...	21,779 30
March 6..	15,775 73
April 3...	26,726 33
May 3..	39,843 17
June 3..	29,621 71
June 30...	22,477 73

313,887 12

Amount credited to the Treasurer of the United States on account of tax on salaries.. 102,912 97

Amount transferred from the appropriation for "pay of the Army" to that for "ordnance, ordnance stores and supplies," on account of deductions from the pay of officers and ordnance and ordnance stores, in accordance with paragraph 1380, revised Army Regulations of 1863.. 17,147 53

Amount transferred from the appropriation for "Pay of the Army" to that of the Subsistence Department on the books of the Third Auditor's Office, on account of deductions from the pay of soldiers for tobacco, pursuant to General Orders No. 63, War Department, Adjutant-General's Office, June 11, 1867... 191,497 76

Amount transferred to the books of the Third Auditor's Office, on account of stoppages against officers for subsistence stores, quartermaster's stores, transportation, &c.. 1,343 96

Amount charged to officers on account of overpayments 19,158 24

Amount charged to officers on account of double payments 38,093 28

Amount credited to officers on account of overpayments refunded...... 3,907 15

Amount credited to officers on account of double payments refunded... 4,318 17

Amount deposited by paymasters to close their accounts, being balances due United States on final settlement....................................... 15,905 75

Amount of balances found due paymasters and paid them to close accounts 2,922 33

Amount paid to civilians under the "reconstruction acts"............... 269 56

Amount of "lost checks" paid in accordance with the act of February
2, 1872 .... $4.36 3
Amount transferred to the books of the Treasurer's Office, on account of
"outstanding liabilities," (act May 2, 1866) 1.81 2
Miscellaneous credits 11,74 2

Total 29,245.69 6

Accounts of paymasters on hand June 30, 1872 1,13
Draft rendezvous accounts on hand June 30, 1872 5
Accounts of paymasters received during the year 3

Total 1.65

Accounts of paymasters audited and reported to the Second Comptroller during
the year 1.6

Accounts of paymasters on hand unexamined June 30, 1873 6
Draft rendezvous accounts under examination June 30, 1873 5

Total number of accounts on hand June 30, 1873 6

Since the last report the accounts of forty-three paymasters have been
closed and certificates of non-indebtedness issued. The accounts of
thirty-five paymasters have been finally revised on which there is due
the United States $76,541, and the accounts of twelve paymasters have
been prepared for suit, the balances due the United States aggregating
$541,447.87.

Number of letters written, 36,889.

MISCELLANEOUS DIVISION.

The following statement shows the number of money accounts on
hand in this division at the commencement of the fiscal year, the number received and settled during the year, and the number remaining
unsettled at the close of the year, together with the expenditure embraced
in the settlements.

Number of accounts on hand June 30, 1872 .... 1.49
Number of accounts received during the year 2.37

Total 4.66
Number of accounts settled during the year 2.96

Number remaining unsettled June 30, 1873 .... 1.69

The amounts involved in the above settlements are as follows:

Ordnance, medical, and miscellaneous:
Ordnance Department $1,378,992 01
Medical Department 175,622 48
Expended by disbursing officers, out of Quartermaster's
fund, not chargeable to said fund, but to certain appro-
priations on the books of this Office 32,890 95
Purchase of property of the Green Bay and Mississippi
Canal Company 115,000 00
Expenses of arbitration between the United States and
the Green Bay and Mississippi Canal Company 13,512 32
Bronze equestrian statue of Lieut. Gen. Winfield Scott 19,750 00
Expenses of military convicts 56,003 84
Contingencies of the Army 32,684 22
Proceeds on sale of real and personal property of J. Led-
yard Hodge 11,041 36

Medical and surgical history and statistics	$2,195 57
Freedmen's Hospital and Asylum	43,165 75
Medical Museum and Library	7,390 66
Trusses for disabled soldiers	6,939 74
Contingencies of the Adjutant-General's Department	4,668 09
Expenses of the Commanding General's Office	2,237 82
Expenses of recruiting	1,017 95
Appliances for disabled soldiers	934 50
Pay of the Army	932 50
Providing for the comfort of sick and discharged soldiers	947 75
Medals of honor	15 00
Collecting, drilling, and organizing volunteers	3 23
Relief of Joseph Harmon, act April 28, 1870	359 54
Relief of heirs of Capt. B. R. Perkins, act May 29, 1872	1,738 00
Relief of Mary M. Clark, act June 8, 1872	1,902 00
Relief of legal representatives of the late George T. Wiggins, act June 8, 1872	1,080 00
Relief of Andrew J. Jamison, act June 8, 1872	190 00
Relief of heirs of Lieut. Col. H. M. Woodyard, act June 10, 1872	1,099 07
Relief of Samuel Hitchcock, act December 20, 1872	861 56
Relief of Capt. Lyman J. Hissong, act January 23, 1873	375 50
Act authorizing the Secretary of the Treasury to settle and pay the accounts of Col. J. F. Jaques, act February 12, 1873	6,719 00
Relief of R. H. Pratt, act February 17, 1873	200 00
Relief of Charles Trichler, act February 19, 1873	300 00
Relief of Henry E. Janes, act February 27, 1873	295 00
Relief of Ethan A. Sawyer, act March 3, 1873	5,000 00
Relief of Thomas L. Tutt & Co., act March 3, 1873	2,795 78
Relief of William Bayne, trustee, act March 3, 1873	2,550 00
Relief of Dr. W. J. C. Duhamel, act March 3, 1873	600 00
Relief of Aaron B. Fryear, act March 3, 1873	500 00
Relief of Peter J. Butchell, act March 3, 1873	314 05
Relief of B. H. Randall, act March 3, 1873	300 00
Relief of Julia P. Lyncie, act March 3, 1873	274 40
Relief of Eli H. Janett, act March 3, 1873	150 29
	———— $1,968,183 01

Regular recruiting:

Expenses of recruiting	231,002 73
Bounty to volunteers and regulars	25 00
Contingent expenses of the Adjutant-General's Department	1 50
Pay of the Army	210 93
Subsistence of officers	171 00
Medical and hospital department	124 25
Pay in lieu of clothing for officers' servants	9 42
	———— 231,544 83

Volunteer recruiting:

Collecting, drilling, and organizing volunteers	142,197 38
Bounty to volunteers and regulars	2,488 08
Draft and substitute fund	28,574 65
Pay of the Army	130 90
Subsistence of officers	112 20
Medical and hospital department	6 90
Pay in lieu of clothing for officers' servants	5 50
	———— 173,515 61

Local bounty:

Pay of two and three-year volunteers	1 423 45

Freedmen's Bureau accounts:

Number received during the year	146
Number settled during the year	64
Number on hand June 30, 1873	82
Amount involved in settlement of Freedmen's Bureau accounts	8,541,725 08
Total	10,916,391 98

Six hundred paymasters' accounts were examined for the requisite data as to double payments to officers, and two hundred and nine double payments were discovered and reported to the paymasters' division, in which charges are raised against officers on this account. Several of the clerks ordinarily engaged on this work are now auditing the accounts of General Oliver O. Howard, late Commissioner of the Freedmen's Bureau.

Number of letters written, 1,838.

INDIAN DIVISION.

General report of the Indian division for the fiscal year ending June 30, 1873:

Money accounts of agents on hand June 30, 1872	??
Property accounts of agents on hand June 30, 1872	??
Claims on hand June 30, 1872	??
Money accounts of agents received during the year	??
Property accounts received during the year	??
Claims received during the year	??
Total	3,63?
Money accounts of agents audited during the year	??
Property accounts examined during the year	??
Claims settled during the year	??
Total	2,27?
Money accounts of agents on hand June 30, 1873	7??
Property accounts of agents on hand June 30, 1873	3??
Claims on hand June 30, 1873	1
Total number of accounts, &c., on hand June 30, 1873	1,??
Amount involved in money accounts audited	$3,598,43? ?
Amount involved in claims settled	4,730,749 3?
Total	8,329,19? ??

The copying incident to the business of this division, including a report to Congress of the receipts and expenditures of the Indian Department during the fiscal year, extended to 1,630 pages of folio-post and 463 pages of foolscap.

Number of letters written, 1,665.

PAY AND BOUNTY DIVISION.

The following tabular statements exhibit in detail the operation of the two branches of this division during the year, together with the condition of the business both at the commencement and close of the year.

EXAMINING BRANCH.

The work performed by the examining branch of this division is exemplified by the five following tables:

Claims in cases of white soldiers.

Additional bounty, act July 28, 1866, and amendments.

Date	Original claims — Whole number examined	Number found correct	Number found incomplete and suspended	Number rejected	Number of duplicate applications found	Suspended claims — Whole number examined	Number completed by additional evidence received	Number again suspended; additional evidence insufficient	Number rejected	Total number of claims examined	Number of letters written
1872											
July	563	93	315	81	74	366	100	208	58	929	1,962
August	826	346	291	99	90	732	217	516	99	1,578	2,531
September	513	61	345	46	61	663	209	404	65	1,178	1,990
October	295	40	186	8	61	951	216	570	132	1,246	1,782
November	380	55	179	100	53	699	210	401		1,079	2,946
December	457	31	291	131	44	920	253	568	120	1,407	3,351
1873											
January	700	44	317	139	189	1,492	275	1,009	99	2,129	2,989
February	760	21	577	166	136	1,081	296	707	120	1,781	2,665
March	686	16	383	161	197	1,321	216	905	226	2,007	2,783
April	588	16	380	206	44	1,048	175	675	157	1,636	2,617
May	221	6	116	67	33	1,300	231	699	137	1,521	3,504
June	410	51	211	93	63	1,576		1,308		1,966	
Total	6,396	781	3,323	1,291	974	12,101	2,767	8,050	1,284	18,470	28,479

Arrears of pay and original bounty.

Date	Original claims — Whole number examined	Number found correct	Number found incomplete and suspended	Number rejected	Number of duplicate applications found	Suspended claims — Whole number examined	Number completed by additional evidence received	Number again suspended; additional evidence insufficient	Number rejected	Total number of claims examined	Number of letters written
1872											
July	359	91	140	11	187	1,056	142	848	66	1,415	1,397
August	396	53	190	30	151	1,618	229	1,257	182	2,014	2,686
September	692	137	372	46	157	1,408	173	1,196	109	2,100	2,149
October	614	57	456	8	113	1,189	195	904	90	1,803	2,163
November	784	90	526	141	97	1,201	173	891	137	1,985	2,810
December	495	22	983	112	98	1,427	209	1,106	112	1,922	2,588
1873											
January	843	15	457	134	267	2,150	129	1,759	262	2,993	4,006
February	1,255	18	989	172	176	1,397	158	1,175	64	2,632	3,701
March	644	96	327	147	144	2,176	284	1,810	148	2,980	4,133
April	717	96	382	183	135	2,549	256	2,113	180	3,966	4,551
May	946	111	359	58	137	1,906	220	1,572	104	2,439	3,787
June	759		388	139	111	2,055	302	1,647	106	2,814	3,903
Total	8,084	468	4,709	1,154	1,783	20,132	2,420	16,208	1,504	28,216	37,465

Bounty-claims under the act of April 22, 1872.

Date.	Original claims.					Suspended claims.				Total number of claims examined.	Number of letters written
	Whole number examined.	Number found correct.	Number found incomplete and suspended	Number rejected.	Number of duplicate applications found.	Whole number examined.	Number completed by additional evidence received.	Number again suspended; additional evidence incomplete.	Number rejected.		
1872.											
July	3,966	517	3,054	252	143	3,906	607	3,005	203	7,872	4
August	493	11	297	77	108	4,818	1,359	3,039	420	5,311	4
September	493	79	300	50	64	3,503	1,149	2,083	251	3,996	5
October	46	1	6	.....	39	2,871	840	1,982	49	2,917	3
November	453	50	186	143	44	1,473	402	622	451	1,924	3
December	151	13	55	48	35	1,464	417	826	221	1,615	2
1873.											
January	239	20	78	91	41	1,120	240	630	250	1,350	2
February	236	25	135	40	36	1,209	274	737	198	1,445	2
March	144	24	55	34	35	1,045	246	613	186	1,150	1
April	120	13	56	27	24	633	163	363	134	771	1
May	55	8	25	11	11	732	194	406	132	787	1
June	19	9	52	24	13	445	100	257	94	543	1
Total	6,450	770	4,299	797	593	23,261	5,990	14,544	2,747	29,780	32

Claims in cases of colored soldiers, including both arrears of pay and bounties.

Date.	Original claims.					Suspended claims.				Total number of claims examined.	Number of letters written.
	Whole number examined.	Number found correct.	Number found incomplete and suspended	Number rejected.	Number of duplicate applications found.	Whole number examined.	Number completed by additional evidence received.	Number again suspended; additional evidence incomplete.	Number rejected.		
1872.											
July	93	4	84	5	.....	949	124	749	76	1,042	1
August	270	1	105	164	.....	1,043	144	836	63	1,313	1
September	43	.....	35	8	.....	833	121	647	65	876	4
October	82	3	66	13	.....	745	103	608	34	827	5
November	45	.....	41	4	.....	738	50	654	34	751	4
December	102	2	90	10	.....	724	65	649	10	826	4
1873.											
January	148	1	121	24	2	848	79	724	45	996	1
February	94	.....	78	16	.....	732	36	677	25	826	4
March	94	.....	85	9	.....	875	93	703	79	1,001	4
April	126	1	120	5	.....	947	117	774	56	1,073	1
May	59	.....	46	13	.....	841	131	637	73	900	2
June	34	4	28	2	.....	650	74	494	82	684	3
Total	1,193	16	899	273	2	9,935	1,146	8,152	637	11,125	15

Bounty claims in cases of colored soldiers, under the act of March 3, 1873.

Date.	Original claims.					Suspended claims.				Total number of claims examined.	Number of letters written.
	Whole number examined.	Number found correct.	Number found incomplete and suspended.	Number rejected.	Number of duplicate applications found.	Whole number examined.	Number completed by additional evidence received.	Number again suspended; additional evidence incomplete.	Number rejected.		
1873.											
April	195	7	94	94	......	268	14	150	104	463	......
May	118	1	68	49	......	630	28	390	212	748	......
June	150	2	122	26	......	1,078	152	689	237	1,228	......
Total	463	10	284	169	......	1,976	194	1,229	553	2,439	......

SUMMARY.

Date.	Whole number examined.	Number found correct.	Number found incomplete and suspended.	Number rejected.	Number of duplicate applications found.	Whole number examined.	Number completed by additional evidence received.	Number again suspended; additional evidence incomplete.	Number rejected.	Total number of claims examined.	Number of letters written.
1872.											
July	4,981	635	3,593	349	404	6,277	973	4,811	493	11,258	7,819
August	1,985	381	883	372	349	8,931	1,939	5,648	644	10,216	14,992
September	1,741	277	1,052	150	262	6,409	1,645	4,240	524	8,150	10,674
October	1,037	81	714	29	213	5,756	1,454	4,064	238	6,793	8,391
November	1,632	125	925	388	194	4,111	850	2,568	693	5,743	8,805
December	1,235	68	699	291	177	4,555	931	3,129	495	5,790	8,449
1873.											
January	1,921	82	943	388	508	5,540	741	4,122	677	7,461	10,488
February	2,265	64	1,459	394	348	4,425	743	3,296	386	6,690	9,662
March	1,572	66	849	351	306	5,417	859	4,031	527	6,989	9,838
April	1,746	49	972	522	203	5,465	765	4,075	625	7,211	10,300
May	999	40	614	164	181	5,409	758	3,904	747	6,408	9,442
June	1,451	177	811	286	177	5,810	859	4,295	656	7,261	11,195
Total	22,565	2,045	13,514	3,684	3,322	67,405	12,517	48,183	6,705	89,970	120,055

SETTLING BRANCH.

The work performed by the settling branch during the year is shown by the annexed tables:

Claims in cases of white soldiers.

Date.	Additional bounty, act of July 28, 1866.					Arrears of pay, &c., act of July 22, 1861.				
	Number of claims.				Amount involved.	Number of claims.				Amount involved.
	Received.	Allowed.	Rejected.	Whole number disposed of.		Received.	Allowed.	Rejected.	Whole number disposed of.	
1872.										
July	425	125	28	153	$14,100 00	746	223	40	263	$33,518 10
August	346	106	150	256	8,283 00	744	126	225	351	16,897 86
September	331	167	65	232	17,450 00	607	178	50	228	29,012 65
October	243	164	2	166	19,676 93	572	217	1	218	29,413 33
November	239	187	210	397	18,900 00	445	145	75	220	30,408 87
December	281	165	100	265	17,150 00	549	192	75	267	37,268 64
1873.										
January	1,395	273	50	323	27,840 00	1,183	230	20	250	29,804 86
February	1,356	464	29	493	40,460 91	925	232	20	252	26,943 73
March	664	351	100	451	36,540 67	660	238	32	320	39,715 03
April	229	358	300	658	37,648 53	567	390	102	492	73,581 39
May	223	262	220	482	27,109 75	569	336	200	536	42,057 40
June	219	346	113	459	35,612 00	475	385	102	487	52,129 02
Total	5,951	2,968	1,367	4,335	300,771 79	8,042	2,942	942	3,884	440,810 84

Bounty claims under the act of April 22, 1872.

Date.	Number of claims.				Amount involved.
	Received.	Allowed.	Rejected.	Whole number disposed of.	
1872.					
July	722	656	40	696	$60,628 10
August	474	914	250	1,164	97,040 00
September	1,432	604	130	724	60,700 00
October	243	437	3	440	43,700 00
November	220	1,186	205	1,391	110,785 62
December	163	793	175	968	73,667 01
1873.					
January	222	522	40	562	56,010 12
February	230	421	70	491	50,868 63
March	140	461	150	611	46,821 31
April	117	327	100	427	41,402 39
May	68	332	334	666	35,196 09
June	64	133	200	333	13,300 06
Total	4,115	6,786	1,687	8,473	690,189 33

Claims in cases of colored soldiers, including both arrears of pay and bounties.

Date.	Number of claims.				Amount involved.
	Received.	Allowed.	Rejected.	Whole number disposed of.	
1872.					
July	99	133	49	182	$21,139 66
August	253	83	96	179	14,371 51
September	32	15	62	77	3,170 49
October	96	55	4	59	7,943 68
November	96	84	97	181	15,672 32
December	102	149	41	188	22,573 74
1873.					
January	120	143	23	166	21,998 17
February		138	27	165	22,732 25
March	95	139	50	189	96,846 59
April	1,651	137	113	250	23,392 64
May	2,692	137	47	204	28,841 61
June	1,835	147	30	177	24,538 02
Total	7,071	1,378	639	2,017	253,213 68

SUMMARY.

Date.	Number of claims.				Amount in- volved.	Number of letters written.
	Received.	Allowed.	Rejected.	Whole number disposed of.		
1872.						
July	1,992	1,137	157	1,294	$129,388 86	11,123
August	1,817	1,229	721	1,950	136,592 37	1,305
September	2,422	964	297	1,261	110,333 14	1,853
October	1,154	873	10	883	100,733 94	1,267
November	1,000	1,602	587	2,189	175,896 81	1,922
December	1,095	1,297	391	1,688	150,659 35	1,634
1873.						
January	2,920	1,168	133	1,301	135,583 15	1,831
February	2,511	1,255	146	1,401	141,065 52	1,981
March	1,559	1,239	332	1,571	149,963 60	1,508
April	2,564	1,212	615	1,827	176,014 95	2,058
May	3,552	1,087	801	1,888	133,244 85	2,056
June	2,593	1,011	445	1,456	125,579 10	1,151
Total	25,179	14,074	4,635	18,709	1,664,985 64	29,689

Consolidated statement showing the operations of the entire division for the fiscal year ending June 30, 1873.

Data.	Number of claims.				Amount in- volved.	Number of letters written.	Number of certificates issued.
	Received.	Allowed.	Rejected, including plicates.	Whole number disposed of.			
1872.							
July	1,992	1,137	1,402	2,539	$129,388	18,942	1,000
August	1,817	1,229	2,096	3,325	136,592	16,297	854
September	2,422	964	1,239	2,903	110,383	12,527	1,127
October	1,154	873	484	1,357	100,733	9,658	903
November	1,000	1,602	1,862	3,464	175,896 86	10,727	1,595
December	1,095	1,297	1,354	2,651	150,659 83	10,083	909
1873.							
January	2,920	1,168	1,704	2,872	135,583 15	12,319	1,569
February	2,511	1,255	1,274	2,529	141,065 52	11,643	1,153
March	1,559	1,239	1,516	2,755	149,963 60	11,346	1,468
April	2,564	1,212	1,960	3,172	176,014 95	12,358	1,400
May	3,552	1,087	1,893	2,980	130,244 85	11,498	1,232
June	2,593	1,011	1,562	2,573	125,579 10	12,346	1,032
Total	25,179	14,074	18,346	32,420	1,664,985 64	149,744	14,262

In addition to the foregoing there were made in this division twelve settlements on account of fines, forfeitures, stoppages, &c., against soldiers of the Regular Army, upon which the sum of $22,845.89 was paid to the treasurer of the Soldiers' Home, in accordance with the acts of Congress of March 3, 1851, and March 3, 1859, making the total number of settlements 14,086, and the total disbursements $1,687,831.53.

Number of claims under act of July 28, 1866, (white,) on hand June 30, 1872.... 7,321
Number of claims for arrears of pay and original bounty (white) on hand June 30, 1872.... 19,337
Number of colored claims on hand June 30, 1872.... 4,171
Number of bounty claims under act of April 22, 1872, on hand June 30, 1872... 11,183

Total number of claims on hand June 30, 1872.... 42,012 .

Number of claims under act of July 28, 1866, (white,) on hand June 30, 1873.. ...

Number of claims for arrears of pay and original bounty on hand June 30. 1873. ...

Number of colored claims on hand June 30, 1873............................... ....

Number of bounty claims under act of April 22, 1872, on hand June 30, 1873.... ...

    Total number of claims on hand June 30, 1873........................ ....

The condition of the claims on hand is shown by the following statement :

Number of claims suspended awaiting evidence to be filed by claimants or their
attorneys ....

Number of claims ready for settlement......................................

Number of claims unexamined June 30, 1873.................................

    Total...

PROPERTY DIVISION.

The subjoined statement shows the progress and condition of business
in this division :

Number of property returns of officers on hand June 30, 1872..................

Returns of ordnance, ordnance stores, &c., received during the year ....

Returns of clothing, camp, and garrison equipage received during the year....

    Total ....

Number of returns settled during the year..................................

Number of returns on hand June 30, 1873..................................

Number of certificates of non-indebtedness issued to officers................

Amount charged to officers for property not accounted for...............$18,115

Number of returns registered...

Number of letters written..

Number of letters recorded...

Thirty-one thousand one hundred and ninety-seven property returns
rendered by volunteer officers in previous years, but not heretofore
reported, have been settled under the provisions of the act of June 20,
1870.

DIVISION OF INQUIRIES AND REPLIES.

The work performed in this division during the year is as follows:

Number of inquiries on hand unanswered June 30, 1872......................

Number received during the year, as per detailed statement below ....

    Total ....

Number of inquiries answered during the year.............................

Number of inquiries on hand unanswered June 30, 1873.....................

Officers making inquiry.	Number received.	Number answered.
Adjutant-General	7,276	4,16
Paymaster-General	708	74
Quartermaster General	105	16
Commissary General of Subsistence...	107	16
Commissioner of Pensions	750	72
Third Auditor	1,392	1,58
Fourth Auditor	886	9
Paymasters' division, local bounty cases..................................	12,949	16,78
Paymasters' division, deserter's cases	14,360	16,73
Miscellaneous	1,809	1,74
Total..	39,979	42,39

Rolls and vouchers copied for the Adjutant-General and Paymaster-General.. 1,113
Rolls and vouchers copied for preservation in this office...................... 219
Rolls and vouchers partially copied and traced for preservation in this office.. 2,259
Signatures verified... 2,610
Letters written.. 22,737

A large amount of miscellaneous business devolved upon this division, such as the copying of affidavits, final statements of enlisted men, letters, and other documents, in which 2,244 pages of foolscap were used.

DIVISION FOR THE INVESTIGATION OF FRAUD.

During the year 5,276 cases have been under investigation and prosecution by this division. Abstracts of facts have been prepared in 240 cases; 527 have been finally disposed of, and 83 prepared for suit and prosecution through the various United States district courts. The amounts recovered by suit and otherwise are as follows:

Amount recovered by draft, certificate of deposit, and current funds, in cases of white soldiers, and turned into the Treasury to be credited to the proper appropriations.. , 070 09
Amount recovered in cases of colored soldiers, principally through the agency of the Freedmen's branch of the Adjutant-General's Office, and turned into the Treasury for appropriate credit...................... 41,644 68
Amount wrongfully withheld by claim agents, and secured to the rightful owners by the interposition of this office.............................. 7,297 42
Amount of disbursing-officers' checks recovered and cancelled.............. 1,000 00
Amount of judgments recovered, but not yet satisfied...................... 10,277 17
Amount secured by stoppages and offset................................... 560 35
Amount of checks secured from the Indian Office, being on account of bounty to Indian Home Guards, and properly cancelled.............. 1,660 40
Amount recovered and turned over to Army paymasters.................. 115 07

Total... 71,625 18

To which should be added—
Amount of fines imposed by United States courts in criminal cases....... 750 00
Bond of indemnity on hand... 1,700 00

74,075 18

There are now under examination and investigation 4,749 cases, involving forgery, fraud, unlawful withholding of money, overpayments, &c., as follows:

Fraudulent and contested claims in cases of white soldiers, in which settlements had been made prior to notice of fraud or contest........................... 1,187
Fraudulent and contested unsettled claims in cases of white soldiers.......... 626
Alleged fraudulent claims awaiting the decision of United States courts....... 80
Cases involving overpayments to ex-officers of the Army and volunteers...... 207
Fraudulent and contested claims in cases of colored soldiers in which settlements had been made prior to notice of fraud or contest.................... 1,153
Unsettled claims in cases of colored soldiers involving fraud in the marriage evidence... 146
Unsettled contested claims in cases of colored soldiers...................... 294
Unsettled claims in cases of colored soldiers in which evidence of heirship is believed to have been manufactured by claim agents and their abettors.... 974
Claims in cases of Indian Home Guards in which fraud is alleged............ 25
Miscellaneous cases.. 57

Total 4,749

Number of claims on hand June 30, 1872..................................... 4,381
Number of claims received during the year.................................. 895

Total 5,276
Number of claims finally disposed of during the year...................... 527

Number of claims on hand June 30, 1873................................... 4,749
Number of letters written....................................... 4,814

In addition to the foregoing cases there is a large number of letters and informal complaints relating to fraudulent transactions, which are held as caveats against the persons complained of until cases of a similar nature, now pending in the courts, shall have been finally determined. It will be observed by the exhibit of this division that there is a further increase of labor, although the result of the past year's operations is highly satisfactory, especially in the prosecution of suits and recovery of money. Since the transfer of the Freedmen's Bureau to the Adjutant-General's Department, many irregularities and dishonest practices of some of the officers lately employed by that Bureau have been discovered, necessitating much labor and care in the examination of certain claims, vouchers, and accounts. Much credit is due to the officers of the War Department who now have the management of the Freedmen's Bureau affairs, the Solicitor of the Treasury, and the United States district officers for their earnest co-operation with this office in the discovery and punishment of wrongs, and in protecting the Government and its wards. With the continued aid of these officers it is anticipated that the fraudulent practices in the bounty-claim business will soon be suppressed, and the ends of justice rapidly answered.

ARCHIVES DIVISION.

The following are the details of the work performed by this division:

Number of accounts received from the Paymaster-General................... 556
Number of accounts on file awaiting settlement 634
Number of confirmed settlements received from the Second Comptroller verified, briefed, and transferred to permanent files—
    Paymasters'....................................... 261
    Indian.. 1,047
    Miscellaneous 1,371
                                      2,679
Number of paymasters' settlements re-examined 581
Number of settlements withdrawn and returned to files 2,602
Number of vouchers withdrawn and returned to accounts 58,872
Number of abstracts of accounts bound in covers......................... 225
Number of duplicate bounty vouchers examined for certificates of payment... 16,085
Number of mutilated muster and pay-rolls repaired 19,919
Number of letters written 789

REGISTRY AND CORRESPONDENCE DIVISION.

The record of the work pertaining to this division is as follows:

Number of letters received.. 30,365
Number of letters written 42,467
Number of letters recorded 2,355
Number of letters referred to other bureaus............................. 1,983
Number of dead letters received and registered 3,275
Number of miscellaneous vouchers received, stamped, and distributed........ 103,749
Number of letters, with additional evidence in the case of suspended claims, received, briefed, and registered.. 25,902
Number of pay and bounty certificates examined, registered, and sent to the Paymaster-General, in accordance with joint resolution April 10, 1869...... 12,855
Number of claims received, briefed, and registered 31,284
Number of pay and bounty certificates examined, registered, and mailed 14,262
Number of reports calling for requisitions sent to the War Department....... 440

For convenience of reference, and for the purpose of showing at a glance the various classes of accounts settled in the Office, and the number of each class received, disposed of, and remaining on hand, I annex the following :

Consolidated statement.

Description of accounts.	On hand June 30, 1872.	Received during the year.	Disposed of during the year.	On hand June 30, 1873.	Amount involved in settlements.	Number of letters written.
Paymasters........................	1,127	556	1,033	650	$27,532,170 94	36,880
Indian agents.....................	780	825	887	718	3,596,438 87	
Indian agents.....................	729	544	400	873		1,665
Indian claims.....................	60	925	984	1	4,730,749 34	
Bounty, arrears of pay, &c	42,011	25,179	32,420	34,771	1,664,985 64	149,744
Ordnance, medical, and miscellaneous..					1,968,183 01	
Regular recruiting					931,544 83	
Volunteer recruiting	1,828	2,197	2,567	1,458	173,515 61	1,838
Claims for return of local bounty					1,422 45	
Freedmen's Bureau accounts.......	....	146	64	82	6,541,725 08	
Ordnance and Quartermaster's Department.)	16,855	3,194	10,578	9,401	....	3,778
Soldiers' Home...................	....	24	24	....	336,733 01	....
National Home...................	....	12	12	....	399,551 57	....
Total...................	63,391	33,532	48,969	47,954	49,179,021 35	193,914

Besides the number of letters stated in the above table, there have been written 71,630 relating to the miscellaneous business of the Office, making a total of 265,544, or 62,886 in excess of the correspondence of last year.

The average number of clerks employed during the year was 272.

The following statements and reports were prepared and transmitted during the year :

Annual report to the Secretary of the Treasury of the transactions of the Office during the fiscal year.

Annual statement of the recruiting fund, prepared for the Adjutant-General of the Army.

Annual statement of the contingencies of the Army, prepared for the Secretary of War.

Annual statement of the clerks and other persons employed in this Office during the year 1872, or any part thereof, showing the amount paid to each on account of salary, with place of residence, &c., in pursuance of the eleventh section of the act of August 12, 1842, and resolution of the House of Representatives of January 13, 1846, transmitted to the Secretary of the Treasury.

Monthly tabular statement showing the business transacted in the Office during the month, and the number of accounts remaining unsettled at the close of the month, transmitted to the Secretary of the Treasury.

Monthly report of absence from duty of employés of this Office, with reasons therefor, transmitted to the Secretary of the Treasury.

Pay-rolls, upon which payment was made to the employés of this Office, prepared semi-monthly.

It affords me great pleasure to say that the results accomplished during the year have been satisfactory.

The showing in the number of settlements made, especially of claims for pay and bounty, has not been as large as in preceding years, for the reason that more than half of the unsettled claims upon the registers of the Office, at the commencement of the year, have been accumulating during the last ten years, have been suspended from time to time in cause, and, owing to peculiarities in their character, require great care in their treatment, and involve a large amount of investigation and correspondence. A special effort is being made to dispose of them in such a manner as to secure the rights of the Government and of the claimants.

Claims under recent laws are promptly settled, and if there should be no large class of claims created by new legislation it is believed that during the current year the clerical force upon this branch of work will be materially reduced.

While there has been no lack of official courtesy toward this office, one of the principal obstacles to the prompt dispatch of business has been the difficulty of obtaining necessary information from other offices, in consequence of their inability to furnish it. On the 3d of July last a letter was addressed to this office from the Adjutant-General, acknowledging the fact that there was then in that office over six thousand unanswered requests from this, for statements of service in the cases of enlisted men of the volunteer army, and stating that "This delay arises from the fact that the clerical force is not sufficient to keep up the current work, and at the same time keep in a proper state of preservation the muster-rolls from which the information called for is obtained." Its effect upon the business of this office is a cause of regret, which it is hoped will be promptly removed by Congress.

The conduct of the clerical force of this office is entitled to high commendation. Their ability and faithful discharge of their duties have been marked and constant, and leave nothing to be desired.

I am, sir, very respectfully,

E. B. FRENCH, *Auditor.*

Hon. Wm. A. Richardson,
  Secretary of the Treasury.

REPORT OF THE THIRD AUDITOR.

Treasury Department,
  Third Auditor's Office, September 16, 1873.

Sir: In compliance with instructions from your office and the requirements of law, I have the honor to transmit herewith the following report of business operations of this office for the fiscal year ending June 30, 1873.

BOOK-KEEPER'S DIVISION.

The duties devolving upon this division are, in general, to keep the appropriation and money accounts of the office.

The annexed statement of the financial operations of the office during the fiscal year ending June 30, 1873, exhibits the amounts drawn on specific appropriations, except those under direction of the Chief of Engineers of the Army, which are aggregated and entered under the general heading, "Engineer Department." It also shows the repayments into the Treasury for the same period.

The average number of clerks engaged in this division during the period embraced in this report has been nine, and that number now constitutes the active force of the division.

The number of requisitions drawn on the Secretary of the Treasury by the Secretaries of War and of the Interior for the fiscal year ending June 30, 1873, was 1,651, amounting to $61,693,170.22, as follows, viz:

Requisitions drawn by the Secretary of War and the Secretary of the Interior.

Appropriations	Advances to officers and agents to be accounted for during the fiscal year.	Claims paid during the fiscal year.	Second Auditor.	Third Auditor.	Fourth Auditor.	Interior Department.	Special referrers.	Total.
Quartermaster's Department, regular supplies	4,346,342 34	647,630 06	441 52	82,787 44				5,197,992 90
Incidental expenses, Quartermaster's Department	1,301,500 31	49,404 34	173 40	702 79				1,431,363 70
Barracks and quarters	1,485,162 15	293,626 58	136 70	32 40				1,706,456 82
Army transportation	4,330,754 24	924,652 93	1,748 52	10,302 87		855 30		5,290,914 84
Officers' transportation		1,546 07						1,546 07
Cavalry and artillery horses	214,273 54	87,030 93						301,304 44
Purchase of stores	10,040 00	231 93						10,291 93
Clothing of the Army	470,973 84	10,543 38		225,000 00				106,521 12
Preservation of clothing and equipage	150,000 00							150,000 00
Contingencies of the Army	777 75							777 75
National cemeteries	338,707 31	398 00		138,917 85				47,823 16
Construction and repair of hospitals	44,329 51							44,329 51
Allowance for reduction of wages under eight-hour law	59,674 55							59,674 55
Expenses of sales of stores and materials	848 43							842 43
Transportation of Isano volunteer soldiers	1,000 00							1,000 00
Commutation of rations to prisoners of war	2,000 00							2,000 00
Extension of military reservation, Camp Mohave	14,919 00							14,919 00
Telegraph for military purposes				17,230 36				17,230 36
Purchase, construction, and maintenance of steam rams		120 66		14,428 27				14,548 58
Supplying arms and munitions of war to loyal citizens, &c				945 38				945 38
Keeping, transporting, and supplying prisoners of war		10 00		257,488 11				257,498 11
Payment of members of certain military organizations, Kansas City Guard								
Defraying expenses of minute-men, &c., in Pennsylvania, Maryland, Ohio, Indiana, and Kentucky		938 50						938 50
Refunding to States expenses incurred in suppressing the rebellion		738,110 31		28,792 32				98,702 35
Reimbursing Kentucky expenses incurred in suppressing the rebellion		593,334 72						738,110 31
Reimbursing Kansas expenses incurred in suppressing the rebellion		336,887 37						593,334 72
Suppressing Indian hostilities in the Territory of Montana	435,000 00							336,817 37
Gun-boats on western rivers								435,000 00
Reimbursing cadets for losses incurred by fire		6,818 89		43,409 98				43,404 28
Claims of loyal citizens for supplies, &c., southern claims		927,910 19						6,818 89
Payment to loyal citizens of Loudoun County, Virginia, &c		61,621 13						927,910 19
Services of Oregon and Washington volunteers, &c	5	17,131 66						61,621 13
Pay of Oregon and Washington volunteers, &c		9,591 00						17,131 66
Capture of Jefferson Davis		2,051 00						9,051 00
Horses, &c., lost act of March 3, 1849		98,975 75						98,975 75
Sundry engineer appropriations	8,260,678 35	5,159 75		2,109 21				297,678 31
Signal service	12,500 00							12,500 00
Observation and report of storms	238,000 00							338,000 00
Current and ordinary expenses Military Academy	63,043 00							63,043 00

13 AD

Requisition drawn by the Secretary of War and the Secretary of the Interior—Continued.

Appropriations.	Advances to officers and agents during the next fiscal year.	Claims paid during the fixed year.	Second Auditor's.	Third Auditor's.	Fourth Auditor's.	Interior Department.	Special officers.	Total.
				TRANSFERS.				
Miscellaneous items and incidental expenses, Military Academy	$15,699 00							$15,699 00
Buildings and grounds, Military Academy	17,550 00							17,550 00
Support of Bureau of Refugees, Freedmen, &c								46,971 95
Subsistence of the Army	2,846,971 50	$12,971 95		$34,000 00				2,957,641 11
Pensions, Army	30,239,115 33	80,789 13	$1,646 85	14,257 62				30,339,217 75
Pensions to widows and others		102 00		30,179 68				12,414 55
Pensions to survivors of war of 1812		1,294 57		664 43				12,696 68
Pensions to invalids		12,321 36		1,221 68	$612 32			1,533 51
		101 03						
Act for the relief of Thomas D. West							200 00	
Act for the relief of John W. Phelps							355 00	
Act for the relief of S. B. Mitchell and others							2,322 47	
Act for the relief of Harriet Spring							2,510 07	
Act for the relief of Albert Grant							40,906 43	
Act for the relief of Thomas B. Stewart and Alexander McConn							1,443 36	
Act for the relief of Omaha National Bank							1,503 96	
Act for the relief of Thomas F. Spencer							100 00	
Act for the relief of Charles H. Thompson							3,100 00	
Act for the relief of Theodore Adams							112,740 78	
Act for the relief of Harriet W. Pond							1,000 00	
Act for the relief of Beverly R. Betts and others							1,980 16	
Act for the relief of Minerva Lewis, administratrix							7,000 00	
Act for the relief of William Webster, of Maine							4,598 53	
Act for the relief of Orville J. Jennings							8,132 93	
Act for the relief of William Spence							24,390 90	
Act for the relief of Mary Low							4,000 00	
Act for the relief of Horace Tyler							30,964 53	
Act for the relief of George Reber							707 15	
Act for the relief of Warren & Moore							252 56	
Act for the relief of James E. Peyton							1,644 42	
Act for the relief of Heirs of Thomas Lawson							4,670 00	
Act for the relief of Milo Pratt							2,000 00	
Act for the relief of Charles H. Mallory & Co., New York							4,160 50	
Act for the relief of Levi J. Burnell							104 50	
Act for the relief of Margaret Merklien							400 00	
Total	$35,772,220 87	$8,003,640 95	4,357 05	$82,655 83	117 32		$66,911 70	36,013,190 93

Nineteen thousand dollars advanced out of the appropriation for capturing expedition, title permits.

The number of credit and counter requisitions drawn by the Secretaries of War and of the Interior on sundry persons in favor of the Treasurer of the United States is 697, on which repayments into the Treasury during the fiscal year ending June 30, 1873, were made through the Third Auditor's Office, as follows, viz:

Deposits	$2,145,112 12
Canceled requisitions	110 00
Second Auditor's transfers	480,711 12
Third Auditor's transfers	856,450 05
Fourth Auditor's transfers	4,133 73
Interior Department transfers	991 58
War Department transfers	80 12
Total	3,487,588 72

NOTE.—The aggregate amount of $5,626,733.26 standing to the credit of twenty-nine "specific appropriations" respectively, has been carried to the surplus fund by warrant No. 151, dated June 30, 1873.

The following statement shows, in a tabular form, the principal items of business transacted in this Office during the fiscal year ending June 30, 1873, and the number and amount of unsettled accounts and claims on hand:

Description of accounts.	Number of accounts remaining on hand June 30, 1872. Monthly and quarterly.	Number of accounts received in fiscal year ending June 30, 1873. Monthly and quarterly.	Number of accounts settled in fiscal year ending June 30, 1873. Monthly and quarterly.	Amount involved.	Number of accounts unsettled June 30, 1873. Monthly and quarterly.	Amount involved.
Quartermasters' money	832	3,783	3,467	$29,065,636 80	1,148	$3,456,919 06
Quartermasters' property	3,867	3,667	7,255		279	
Commissaries' money	417	1,059	1,143	4,372,779 33	331	674,479 26
Refugees, Freedmen, and Abandoned Lands	10	4	14	118,198 14		
Pension agents' money	645	711	795	33,926,556 19	561	16,150,003 20
Engineers' money	75	203	216	8,826,443 56	62	4,595,787 47
Signal-officers' money	80	26	97	297,229 52	9	192,650 21
Signal-officers' property		102	102			
Total	5,926	9,555	13,091	76,606,833 54	2,390	25,071,839 20
Montana war-claims		136	136	409,785 52		
Claims for horses lost	5,150	238	413	73,033 93	5,004	919,037 52
steamboats destroyed	69	3	4	37,183 00	68	556,493 70
Oregon war	842	129	146	17,503 05	825	69,664 61
miscellaneous	6,786	6,016	4,750	4,419,908 00	8,032	4,658,224 32
State war	6	6	8	1,701,418 28	4	290,160 68
Total	12,862	6,548	5,457	6,658,831 78	13,953	6,483,640 89

QUARTERMASTERS' DIVISION.

The accounts of quartermasters cover a varied range of money disbursements and property accountability, embracing disbursements for barracks, quarters, hospitals, store-houses, offices, stables, forage, and transportation of all Army supplies, Army clothing, camp and garrison equipage; the purchase of cavalry and artillery horses, fuel, forage, straw, material for bedding, stationery; hired men; per diem to extra-duty men; of the pursuit and apprehension of deserters; of the burial of officers and soldiers; of hired escorts; of expresses, interpreters, spies and guides; of veterinary surgeons, and medicines for horses; of supplying posts with water, and generally the proper and authorized expenses for the movements and operations of an army, not expressly assigned to any other department. The "returns" are an account of the disposition made of all property paid for by the Quartermaster's Department, (except clothing, camp and garrison equipage, which are accounted for to the Second Auditor.)

The tabular statement herewith exhibits in a condensed form the results of the labors of the force employed in this division:

	Money accounts.		Property returns.	Supplemental settlements.		
	No.	Amount involved.		Property.	Money.	Amount involved.
On hand per last report	832	$17,863,150 52	3,867	....	....	....
Received during the fiscal year........	3,783	14,661,395 34	3,667	2,492	2,379	$10,152,684 70
Total............................	4,615	32,524,545 86	7,534	2,492	2,379	10,152,684 70
Reported during the fiscal year	3,467	29,065,626 80	7,255	2,492	2,379	10,152,684 70
Remaining unsettled..................	1,148	3,458,919 06	279	....	....	....
Total	4,615	32,524,545 86	7,534	2,492	2,379	10,152,684 70

	Signal-accounts.			Total	
	Property.	Money.	Amount involved.	No.	Amount involved.
On hand per last report	....	80	$207,102 88	4,779	$18,070,253 40
Received during the fiscal year..................	102	26	282,776 85	12,449	25,096,856 89
Total..	102	106	489,879 73	17,228	43,167,110 29
Reported during the fiscal year	102	97	297,229 52	15,792	39,515,541 02
Remaining unsettled	....	9	192,650 21	1,436	3,651,569 27
Total	102	106	489,879 73	17,228	43,167,110 29

Number of letters written, 8,292; average number of clerks employed, 69½.

Number of vouchers examined, 533,192, and pages of manuscript written, 13,874.

The above table exhibits in a concise form the principal items of labor performed by the clerical force employed in this division, and shows also the number of accounts remaining unsettled at the end of the fiscal year, and the amount involved in such unsettled accounts.

It will be seen that 832 quartermaster accounts, involving $17,863,150.52, and 80 signal-officers' accounts, involving $207,102.88, total, $18,070,253.40, remained on hand June 30, 1872; that 3,783 quartermaster accounts, involving $14,661,395.34, and 26 accounts of signal-officers, involving $282,776.85, total, $14,944,172.19, were received from the proper military bureaus; that 3,467 quartermaster accounts, involving $29,065,626.80, and 97 accounts of signal-officers, involving $297,229.52, total, $29,362,856.32, were settled during the fiscal year, leaving 1,148 quartermaster accounts and 9 accounts of signal-officers, involving $3,651,569.27, remaining on hand unadjusted. There were also 2,379 supplemental money-statements made, involving $10,152,684.70, making a grand total of $39,515,541.02

adjusted by this division during the year.   A reference to prior reports will show that the unsettled accounts remaining on hand ($3,651,569.27) is a smaller amount than remained on hand at the close of any fiscal year subsequent to the year ending June 30, 1860.   Of these accounts a large portion have been examined and are ready to be reported to the Second Comptroller, as soon as settlements of the same disbursing officers' accounts, now in that office, shall be returned to this office.   A careful examination shows that 2,206 settlements, made in this office, of the money accounts of disbursing officers of the Quartermaster's Department, are now in the Second Comptroller's Office awaiting the official action of that office.

The number of letters sent from this division was 8,292, against 17,444 sent during 1872.   Letters on official business are prepared at considerable cost to the Government, and, while care has been taken to answer promptly all communications requiring replies, it is deemed important that only those should be written which are absolutely required for the proper discharge of the administrative duties of the office.

The best results obtained in the year just closed will be found in the "supplemental money-settlements."   These settlements are based generally on explanations, or corrected vouchers, furnished by disbursing officers in answer to objections raised against their accounts.   The amount involved in these settlements, it will be seen, was $10,152,684.70 during the year just closed.

Of the vast number of "Returns of quartermaster stores," rendered during the rebellion, only about forty remain unadjusted, and of that number the larger portion were rendered by officers who were subsequently dismissed the service for fraudulent transactions in connection with their accountability to the Government, and who have not consequently been permitted to receive the benefit of the liberality displayed by Congress to faithful officers in the passage of the acts of June 23, 1870, and June 7, 1872, authorizing allowances for losses of funds, &c.

SUBSISTENCE DIVISION.

This division audits the accounts of all commissaries and acting commissaries of subsistence in the Army, whose duties are to purchase the provisions and stores necessary for the feeding of the Army, and see to their proper distribution.   These commissaries render monthly money-accounts, with proper vouchers, for disbursements of the funds intrusted to them, together with a provision-return, and vouchers showing the disposition of provisions and stores purchased and received during each month.   These accounts are received monthly through the office of the Commissary General of Subsistence, and are every six months (or oftener if the officer ceases to disburse) examined and audited in this division, and the money accounts and vouchers, together with a certified statement of their condition, referred to the Second Comptroller of the Treasury for his decision thereon.   Upon their receipt back from the Comptroller with the statement approved, the officers are then officially notified of the result of said examinations and are called upon by this office to adjust or explain any omissions or errors that may have been discovered.   The money and provision accounts, together with vouchers and papers belonging thereto, are, after examination, placed in the settled files of this division for future reference, and remain permanently in the custody of this office.

Annual report of the Subsistence Division for the fiscal year ending June 30, 1873.

| | Subsistence accounts. | | | Refugees, Freedmen & Abandoned Land accs. | |
| | Money accounts. | | Provision returns. | Money accounts. | |
	No.	Amount involved.		No.	Amount involved.
On hand per last report, June 30, 1872	417	$301,941 83	405	10	$4,832 8
Received during fiscal year	1,059	4,545,316 76	1,043	4	42,26 8
Total	1,476	5,047,258 59	1,448	14	119,79 4
Audited during fiscal year	1,145	4,372,779 33	1,120	14	119,49 5
Remaining on hand June 30, 1873	331	674,479 26	328	......	....

Number of vouchers examined, 57,252; difference-sheets written, 738; letters written, 1,090; queries answered, 1,105; average number of clerks, 7.

ENGINEER DIVISION.

This division is employed in the examination of the accounts of the officers and agents of the Engineer Department, who, under direction of the Chief of Engineers of the Army, (except the superintendent of the Military Academy at West Point, whose disbursements are directed by the Inspector-General,) disburse moneys out of various appropriations—now 248 in number—made from time to time by Congress for works of a public nature, which may be classed under the following general heads, viz:

The purchase of sites and materials for, and construction and repairs of, the various fortifications throughout the United States;

Construction and repairs of roads, bridges, bridge-trains, &c., for armies in the field;

Surveys on the Atlantic and Pacific coasts;

Examination and surveys of the northern and western lakes and rivers;

Construction and repairs of breakwaters;

Repairs and improvement of harbors, both on sea and lake coasts;

Improvement of rivers and purchase of snag and dredge boats for the same; and

The expenses of the Military Academy at West Point.

The average number of clerks employed in the division for the year ending June 30, 1873, was 4.25, and the transactions of the division for the same period are shown by the following statement, viz:

| | Accounts. | | Number of reports referred to Inspector |
	Number of quarters.	Amount involved.	
On hand per last report, June 30, 1872	75	$4,918,071 84	.....
Received during the year	203	8,504,149 19	.....
Total ...	278	13,422,221 03	
Reported during the year	216	8,856,443 56	5
Remaining on hand	62	4,565,777 47	.....
Total ...	278	13,422,221 03	5

Number of letters written, 612.

The business of this division is well up, as will be seen by the following : Of the accounts on hand four are for disbursements made in 1871, thirty-four in 1872, and the remainder in 1873.

STATE WAR-CLAIMS DIVISION.

The duties of this division embrace the settlement, under the various acts and resolutions of Congress relating thereto, of all claims of the several States and Territories for the costs, charges, and expenses properly incurred by them for enrolling, subsisting, clothing, supplying, arming, equipping, paying, and transporting their troops employed by the United States in aiding to suppress the recent insurrection against the United States.   Also, Indian and other border invasions.

	Original accounts.		Suspended accounts.		Montana war claims.	
	No.	Amount.	No.	Amount.	No.	Amount.
On hand June 30, 1872	6	$661,457 91	76	$4,178,936 51		
Received during the fiscal year ending June 30, 1873	6	1,320,121 15	3	657,921 80	136	$409,785 52
Total	12	1,981,579 96	79	4,836,858 31	136	409,785 52
Reported during the fiscal year ending June 30, 1873	8	1,701,419 28	22	84,984 40	136	409,785 52
Balance remaining June 30, 1873	4	280,160 68	57	4,751,873 91		

Number of official letters written during the year, 89.
Number of clerks employed during the year, 3.

CLAIMS DIVISION.

The duties of this division embrace the settlement of claims of a miscellaneous character arising in the various branches of service in the War Department, growing out of the purchase or appropriation of supplies and stores for the Army ; the purchase, hire, or appropriation of water-craft, railroad stock, horses, wagons, and other means of transportation : the transportation contracts of the Army ; the occupation of real estate for camps, barracks, hospitals, fortifications, &c. ; the hire of employés, mileage, court-martial fees, traveling expenses, commutations, &c. : claims for compensation for vessels, railroad-cars, and engines, &c., lost in the military service : claims growing out of the Oregon and Washington war of 1855 and 1856, and other Indian war claims ; claims of various descriptions under special acts of Congress, and claims not otherwise assigned.

The following statements show the business transacted in this division during the fiscal year ending June 30, 1873, and the condition of the business at the commencement and at the end thereof :

Miscellaneous claims.

	No.	Amount claimed.
On hand June 30, 1872	6786	$41,681,774 57 [*]
Received during the year	6036	$4,867,418 01 [†]
Total	12822	$9,479,193 18 [‡]
Disposed of	4720	$4,819,908 86
Total on hand June 30, 1873	8052	$4,659,284 32 [§]

[*] This is the amount claimed in 5,462 cases, the amounts claimed in the others (1,324) not being stated.
[†] This is the amount claimed in 5,766 cases, the amounts claimed in the others (270) not being stated.
[‡] This is the amount claimed in 4,667 cases, the amounts claimed in the others (53) not being stated.
[§] This is the amount claimed in 6,561 cases, the amounts claimed in the others (1,491) not being stated.

Annual report of the Subsistence Division for the fiscal year ending June 30, 1873.

	Subsistence accounts.			Refugees, Freedmen, and Abandoned Land accounts	
	Money accounts.		Provision returns.	Money accounts.	
	No.	Amount involved.		No.	Amount involved.
On hand per last report, June 30, 1872	417	$501,941 83	405	10	$49,802 62
Received during fiscal year	1,059	4,545,316 76	1,043	4	64,396 42
Total.............................	1,476	5,047,258 59	1,448	14	118,198 14
Audited during fiscal year	1,145	4,372,779 33	1,120	14	118,198 14
Remaining on hand June 30, 1873	331	674,479 26	328		

Number of vouchers examined, 57,252; difference-sheets written, 738; letters written, 1,090; queries answered, 1,105; average number of clerks, 7.

ENGINEER DIVISION.

This division is employed in the examination of the accounts of the officers and agents of the Engineer Department, who, under direction of the Chief of Engineers of the Army, (except the superintendent of the Military Academy at West Point, whose disbursements are directed by the Inspector-General,) disburse moneys out of various appropriations—now 248 in number—made from time to time by Congress for works of a public nature, which may be classed under the following general heads, viz:

The purchase of sites and materials for, and construction and repairs of, the various fortifications throughout the United States;

Construction and repairs of roads, bridges, bridge-trains, &c., for armies in the field;

Surveys on the Atlantic and Pacific coasts;

Examination and surveys of the northern and western lakes and rivers;

Construction and repairs of breakwaters;

Repairs and improvement of harbors, both on sea and lake coasts;

Improvement of rivers and purchase of snag and dredge boats for the same; and

The expenses of the Military Academy at West Point.

The average number of clerks employed in the division for the year ending June 30, 1873, was 4.25, and the transactions of the division for the same period are shown by the following statement, viz:

	Accounts.		Number of supplemental settlements.
	Number of quarters.	Amount involved.	
On hand per last report, June 30, 1872	75	$4,918,071 84	....
Received during the year	203	8,504,149 19	....
Total...	278	13,422,221 03	....
Reported during the year............................	216	8,806,443 56	36
Remaining on hand	62	4,595,777 47	....
Total...	278	13,422,221 03	36

Number of letters written, 612.

The business of this division is well up, as will be seen by the following: Of the accounts on hand four are for disbursements made in 1871, thirty-four in 1872, and the remainder in 1873.

STATE WAR-CLAIMS DIVISION.

The duties of this division embrace the settlement, under the various acts and resolutions of Congress relating thereto, of all claims of the several States and Territories for the costs, charges, and expenses properly incurred by them for enrolling, subsisting, clothing, supplying, arming, equipping, paying, and transporting their troops employed by the United States in aiding to suppress the recent insurrection against the United States. Also, Indian and other border invasions.

	Original accounts.		Suspended accounts.		Montana war claims.	
	No.	Amount.	No.	Amount.	No.	Amount.
On hand June 30, 1872	6	$661,457 81	76	$4,178,936 51		
Received during the fiscal year ending June 30, 1873	6	1,320,121 15	3	657,921 80	136	$409,785 52
Total	12	1,981,578 96	79	4,836,858 31	136	409,785 52
Reported during the fiscal year ending June 30, 1873	8	1,701 418 28	22	84,984 40	136	409,785 52
Balance remaining June 30, 1873	4	280,160 68	57	4,751,873 91		

Number of official letters written during the year, 89.
Number of clerks employed during the year, 3.

CLAIMS DIVISION.

The duties of this division embrace the settlement of claims of a miscellaneous character arising in the various branches of service in the War Department, growing out of the purchase or appropriation of supplies and stores for the Army; the purchase, hire, or appropriation of water-craft, railroad stock, horses, wagons, and other means of transportation; the transportation contracts of the Army; the occupation of real estate for camps, barracks, hospitals, fortifications, &c.; the hire of employés, mileage, court-martial fees, traveling expenses, commutations, &c.; claims for compensation for vessels, railroad-cars, and engines, &c., lost in the military service; claims growing out of the Oregon and Washington war of 1855 and 1856, and other Indian war claims; claims of various descriptions under special acts of Congress, and claims not otherwise assigned.

The following statements show the business transacted in this division during the fiscal year ending June 30, 1873, and the condition of the business at the commencement and at the end thereof:

Miscellaneous claims.

	No.	Amount claimed.
On hand June 30, 1872	6786	*$4,890,774 57
Received during the year	6036	†4,887,418 61
Total	12822	‡9,678,193 18
Disposed of	4759	‖4,419,908 86
Total on hand June 30, 1873	8052	§4,658,284 32

* This is the amount claimed in 5,402 cases, the amounts claimed in the others (1,324) not being stated.
† This is the amount claimed in 5,766 cases, the amounts claimed in the others (270) not being stated.
‡ This is the amount claimed in 4,667 cases, the amounts claimed in the others (93) not being stated.
‖ This is the amount claimed in 6,561 cases, the amounts claimed in the others (1,491) not being stated.

Number of letters written during the year in all the branches, 262.

Washington and Oregon Indian war claims 1855 and 1856.

	No.	Amount claimed
On hand June 30, 1872	842	*$6,372
Received during the year	129	7,00 a
Total	971	3,64
Disposed of	146	3,35
On hand June 30, 1873	825	50,00

* This is the amount claimed in 405 cases, the amounts claimed in the others (437) not being stated.
† This is the amount claimed in 49 cases, the amounts claimed in the others (80) not being stated.
‡ This is the amount claimed in 29 cases, the amounts claimed in the others (117) not being stated.
§ This is the amount claimed in 425 cases, the amounts claimed in the others (400) not being stated.

Lost vessels, &c., Act March 3, 1849.

	Number.	Amount claimed.	Amount allowed
On hand June 30, 1872	69	$560, 873 07	
Received during the year	3	32, 803 63	
Total	72	593, 676 70	
Disposed of	4	37, 183 00	$32,03 0
On hand June 30, 1873	68	536, 493 70	

HORSE-CLAIMS DIVISION.

This division is engaged in settling claims for compensation for the loss of horses and equipage sustained by officers or enlisted men while in the military service of the United States, and for the loss of horses, mules, oxen, wagons, sleighs, and harness while in said service by impressment or contract.

The number of claims received and docketed during the year is 251, in which the aggregate amount claimed is $60,501.63. The number settled and finally disposed of during the same period (including those received prior as well as during the year) is 413, in which the aggregate amount claimed is $73,033.93, and on which the aggregate amount allowed is $58,437.69.

There have been during the year 389 briefs made; 2,669 claims examined and suspended; 1,703 letters received and docketed, and 4,95 letters written.

The following table presents the condition of the business of this division at the commencement and close of the fiscal year, as well as its progress through the year:

	Number.	Amount.	Number.	Amount
Claims on hand June 30, 1872			5, 150	$60,62 6
Claims received during the year			251	60,50 6
Claims reconsidered during the year			7	1,38 6
Total			5, 417	992,73 3
Claims allowed during the year	369	$58, 437 69		
Rejected on same		8, 445 PM		
Amount claimed		65, 883 57		
Claims disallowed during the year	44	6, 150 36		
Deduct as finally disposed of during the year			413	72,03 6
Claims on hand June 30, 1873			5, 004	919,67 3

The adjustment of this class of claims grows more difficult every year as the lapse of time between the accruing and settlement of them increases, and it necessarily requires more work and longer time to complete the evidence, and, therefore, the same number of clerks settle a less number of claims each succeeding year.

I have again to invite your attention to the fact that quite a considerable number of very meritorious claims are on file in this division for the allowance of which no statute provision is made. These claims are as equitable as any of those specified in the act of March 3, 1849, and it is recommended that the first section of that act be amended so as to provide payment for all losses of horses and equipage that are incident to the service, as suggested in my report for the year 1870.

PENSION DIVISION.

The duties of this division embrace the settlement of all accounts which pertain to the payment of Army pensioners throughout the United States.

The name of each pensioner, his rank, rate, date of commencement, increase, reduction, transfer, remarriage, death, and expiration, whether by limitation under existing laws or on account of the disability having ceased, is recorded in a roll-book for each agency prepared for such purpose. An account is kept with each pension agent, charging him, under the proper appropriation bond, and fiscal year, with all moneys advanced for the payment of pensioners. Each agent pays the amount of pension due on vouchers properly executed, with duplicate receipts attached, signed by the person entitled thereto; and in the margin of the receipt is the number and date of the check issued. At the end of each month the agent forwards his account direct to this office, with abstract and vouchers of payments made, and, upon receipt thereof, the account is primarily examined, compared, acknowledged, and placed in the unsettled files for audit.

Each voucher is afterward carefully examined, and the payment made is entered on the roll-book opposite the pensioner's name.

The account, when audited, is reported to the Second Comptroller for his revision and approval, which, when completed, is returned to this office. The agent is then duly notified of any and all errors, and the account placed in the settled files, where it permanently remains.

In case of any defalcation, this office prepares the papers necessary for suit, and transmits the same to the Second Comptroller, "who directs the prosecution."

Under act July 8, 1870, pensioners are paid quarterly, instead of semi-annually, as theretofore, which more than doubles the labor in the examination and auditing of the accounts.

Act July 12, 1870, requires all accounts to be audited by fiscal years, and the balance unexpended to be covered into the Treasury. So far as it relates to these accounts I think it one of the best laws enacted.

Act February 14, 1871, granted pensions to the survivors of the war of 1812 who served sixty days, and to the widows who married prior to the treaty of peace. The number added to the roll under this act is 23,319.

Act June 8, 1872, amended the act June 6, 1866, which granted disabled soldiers fifteen, twenty, and twenty-five dollars per month, so that now they are entitled to receive eighteen, twenty-four, and thirty-one and twenty-five hundredths dollars per month. The number receiving the above increase is 15,505.

Act March 3, 1873, to revise, amend, and consolidate the pension laws, necessitates the change and increase of a great many pensioners.

Number of pensioners on the rolls at present:

Revolutionary, half-pay, act 1848, &c .... |.:
Invalid act July 14, 1862, &c .... %.~
Widows and others, not including children.................................. ||: —
War of 1812, act February 14, 1871...................... :: .:

    Total.. :::.:

Pensioners who have received artificial limbs...................... 1.%:
Pensioners who have received commutation in lieu thereof.................. % ::
Amount appropriated to pay Army pensions for the fiscal year ending
   June 30, 1873.. $::, ::::, ::: :
Amount drawn from the Treasury to pay pensions during the year.... ::, ::::, ::: :
Balance in the Treasury... : ::: :
Amount paid to pensioners during the fiscal year ending June 30, 1873,
   as appears from the accounts rendered, and more fully from the tabu-
   lar statement herewith....................................... ::, ::::, ::: :
The unexpended balance will be refunded and covered into the Trea-
   sury.. 1, ::::, ::: :

The following tabular statement shows the amount of business disposed of during the fiscal year ending June 30, 1873:

	Number.	Amount involved.
Accounts on hand June 30, 1872......................	645	$21, 314, 92
Accounts received during the year........................	711	28, 724, 78
Total......................................	1,356	50, 071, 39
Accounts reported during the year......................	795	33, 913, 33
Accounts remaining unsettled......................	561	16, 159, 06
Total......................................	1,356	50, 673, 39

The accounts on file unsettled, although many are already in hand,
are divided as follows, viz:

Accounts of 1872.. ::
Accounts of 1873.. :::

    Total.. :::

Pensioners recorded, increased, restored, and re-issued...................... ::,:::
Pensioners transferred .... : :::
Pension-vouchers examined...................... :::,:::
Payments entered.................................. :::,:::
Pages of abstract added.................................. :::,:::
Pages of difference and miscellaneous copied...................... :,:::
Copies of surgeon's certificates of examination furnished Commissioner of Pen-
   sions in increase-cases...................... 1,:::

Seventy-two special settlements were made, (the number not being in
cluded in the tabular statement above,) mostly old accounts, finally
closed, some of which had remained unsettled many years.

The force in this division during the year numbered 47 clerks and :
copyists.

It is my desire that the work of this division shall be brought up to
current work. The changes that constantly occur at the agencies, and
the errors made, should be discovered as soon as possible, so that steps
can be taken to have the accounts adjusted and closed at once.

By a constant, careful, and sometimes personal examination of the
accounts of agents who have been out of office some time, I have succeeded in collecting many thousands of dollars which were heretofore
considered as total loss.

The following tabular statement exhibits the amount paid at the several agencies during the year ending June 30, 1873:

State.	Agency.	Agent.	Artificial limbs.	Invalids.	Act of February 14, 1871.	Widows and others.	Total.
Arkansas	Little Rock	James Coates	$20 00	$17,463 38	$1,289 09	$74,804 61	$113,637 08
Do	do	A. D. Thomas		2,219 10	2,519 10	10,011 01	16,399 43
Connecticut	Hartford	D. C. Rodman	736 90	131,283 71	31,606 13	268,794 11	435,420 87
California	San Francisco	H. C. Bennett	1,001 89	34,989 84	9,170 41	21,189 09	66,351 23
District of Columbia	Washington City	David C. Cox	2,794 75	257,759 61	240,493 56	271,656 43	741,704 35
Delaware	Wilmington	E. D. Porter	125 00	27,463 83	3,134 39	41,897 79	72,591 01
Indiana	Fort Wayne	Hiram Iddings	709 63	167,497 52	20,250 82	244,643 38	453,100 77
Do	Indianapolis	C. W. Browne	1,834 45	349,305 79	59,341 02	332,925 71	943,476 57
Do	do	W. H. H. Terrill	550 00	106,168 34	13,302 37	152,011 49	271,992 99
Illinois	Madison	Mark Tilton	693 40	137,900 90	28,246 51	250,101 46	417,141 59
Do	Chicago	Daniel Blakely	1,959 30	381,732 90	34,744 88	331,287 65	768,744 73
Do	Quincy	B. M. Prentiss	500 00	183,232 49	26,685 18	224,740 99	437,358 66
Do	Springfield	William Jayne		4,427 31	1,343 97	9,922 12	15,693 40
Do	do	S. H. Jones	709 30	109,990 67	1,807 04	316,083 27	408,590 32
Do	do	J. H. Moore	430 00	60,891 03	7,989 29	79,900 18	149,220 50
Do	Salem	James S. Martin	337 00	131,644 48	18,701 18	265,233 85	415,916 51
Do	do	W. E. McMackin	503 33	120,414 03	15,626 07	243,112 55	379,656 22
Iowa	Des Moines	B. F. Gue	200 00	33,091 59	6,131 13	50,189 18	89,611 90
Do	Fairfield	D. B. Wilson	775 00	83,779 98	12,038 62	122,403 70	219,017 30
Do	Marion	J. B. Young	518 47	137,333 61	20,195 87	193,353 15	351,401 13
Kansas	Topeka	Charles B. Lines	432 47	144,315 49	17,464 58	208,118 21	370,370 75
Kentucky	Lexington	A. H. Adams	1,317 45	135,019 60	9,448 90	250,664 79	396,163 30
Do	Louisville	W. D. Gallagher	406 88	66,610 40	61,899 34	250,664 79	379,681 38
Do	do	R. M. Kelley	575 00	65,999 03	41,886 09	181,560 49	289,770 61
Louisiana	New Orleans	R. H. Isabelle	150 00	68,105 83	37,433 97	164,588 34	270,276 14
Maine	Augusta	F. M. Drew	1,150 00	30,899 72	40,319 78	46,129 07	119,647 98
Do	Bangor	S. B. Morison	505 00	138,998 72	33,636 34	280,689 75	330,082 84
Do	Portland	George L. Beal	413 85	138,417 08	14,633 85	305,601 44	446,395 85
Massachusetts	Boston	Charles A. Phelps	2,278 50	175,144 43	38,706 86	233,965 71	1,384,191 87
Maryland	Baltimore	Harrison Adreon	1,118 30	327,044 81	55,667 67	799,599 69	375,971 94
Michigan	Detroit	Arnold Kinchen	1,095 88	194,647 92	35,686 67	192,284 44	785,901 69
Do	do	Samuel Post	600 00	290,100 01	35,839 22	468,686 66	389,529 16
Do	Grand Rapids	Thomas Foote	977 30	162,274 76	17,674 62	128,490 38	224,354 64
Missouri	Macon City	William C. Ebert	1,125 00	97,770 11	12,446 07	129,161 96	404,527 94
Do	Saint Louis	James Lindsay	1,005 00	131,878 38	46,662 93	299,690 71	485,358 17
Do	do	A. R. Easton	130 00	132,490 73	9,340 77	64,419 90	109,691 30
Minnesota	Saint Paul	E. McMurtrie	351 71	35,490 73	9,159 76	146,490 43	276,735 99
Mississippi	Vicksburgh	John T. Rankin	168 53	117,983 07	38,690 88	44,137 56	65,088 24
New Hampshire	Concord	Alvah Smith	237 80	6,389 10	38,590 80	221,388 97	431,388 24
New York	Portsmouth	D. J. Vaughan	341 90	176,708 94	9,568 83	70,751 16	121,629 22
Do	Albany	S. H. H. Parsons	6,349 38	41,017 94	165,149 91	771,467 19	1,499,013 77
Do	Canandaigua	L. M. Drury	3,278 36	555,777 50	146,423 30	668,753 49	1,377,632 72
Do	Brooklyn	John Hall	655 00	558,177 54	46,748 38	146,135 50	385,423 96
Do	New York City	L. L. Doty	1,466 73	69,863 68	32,782 84	146,135 50	316,644 64
Do	do	S. B. Dutcher	2,089 00	114,766 18	67,197 34	167,625 69	760,393 84
New Jersey	Trenton	James F. Rusling	929 00	233,061 76	59,998 66	303,028 53	590,026 97

	Agency	Agent	Artificial limbs	Invalids	Act of February 14, 1871.	Widows and others.	Total.
North Ca...	Raleigh	Charles H. B...	166 85	15,362 32	45,339 97	73,923 71	134,216 10
Nebraska	Omaha	... R. Caldwell		39,447 62	2,614 66	19,699 31	53,150 64
New Me...	Santa Fé	E. W. Little	50 00	3,651 40	146 03	2,933 73	6,999 13
Ohio	Cincinnati	Charles E. Brown	4,300 60	475,766 89	87,261 21	667,759 68	1,225,081 61
Do	Cleveland	Seth M. Barker	1,919 70	317,373 25	64,150 27	376,202 82	759,746 04
Do	Columbus	John A. Norris	1,549 62	298,991 85	76,536 64	454,171 12	831,240 47
Oregon	Oregon City	Henry Warren		5,182 30	3,753 31	4,414 42	13,400 00
Pennsylvania	Philadelphia	H. G. Sickel	11,009 62	922,059 10	96,746 45	10,601 24	1,078,559 65
Do	do	D. R. B. Nevin			50,244 71	1,267,799 97	1,338,044 66
Do	Pittsburgh	James McGregor	2,494 85	364,940 85	61,620 76	471,022 63	920,158 69
Rhode Island	Providence	Charles R. Bruyton	7,300 00	47,622 10	8,161 44	97,328 66	154,433 84
Tennessee	Knoxville	D. T. Boynton	40 40	91,277 71	62,403 60	301,550 57	455,019 28
Do	Nashville	William J. Stokes	184 62	26,061 62	13,742 41	125,631 03	233,589 07
Do	do	W. Y. Elliott		5,676 99	19,779 11	31,298 45	54,461 35
Vermont	Burlington	J. L. Barstow	685 40	83,034 31	18,613 67	123,016 68	225,390 07
Do	Montpelier	Stephen Thomas	1,106 70	114,699 64	96,716 93	141,683 68	284,199 26
Virginia	Richmond	Andrew Washburn	100 00	29,463 19	186,029 31	52,505 90	367,088 43
West Virginia	Wheeling	T. M. Harris	1,757 93	154,267 32	73,360 64	279,769 11	311,374 50
W. ...	La Crosse	John A. Kellogg	505 16	63,616 01	6,479 11	94,674 62	107,974 93
Do	Milwaukee	Edward Ferguson	1,383 38	176,543 59	13,370 86	590,175 13	453,432 86
Do	Madison	Thomas Reynolds	535 00	191,357 76	16,102 57	196,673 79	334,668 12
Washington Ter.	Vancouver	S. W. Brown		3,698 11	759 99	1,105 92	5,654 02
Total			74,036 33	10,379,954 62	2,782,976 45	15,521,885 53	26,956,859 95

COLLECTION DIVISION.

. The following statement shows the work of this division during the months named:

Month.	Delinquents recorded.	Entries on register.	Special cases.			Letters written.
			Number of cases examined.	Vouchers examined.	Accounts referred to.	
1872.						
July	330	123	162	672	294	102
August	470	89	162	627	291	194
September	226	140	100	328	137	65
October		194				52
November	76	207	80	554	200	78
December	80	153	226	1,792	444	124
1873.						
January	93	164	263	3,696	433	253
February		256	335	6,883	479	222
March		146	117	2,148	317	220
April		188	379	7,193	449	169
May		141	250	7,126	476	149
June	31	131	307	7,542	308	217
Total	1,306	1,932	2,381	38,531	3,828	1,847

Number of cases reported for suit, 2.

BOUNTY-LAND AND PENSION DIVISION, WAR OF 1812.

During the fiscal year ending 30th of June, 1873, 11,201 pension claims, act of February 14, 1871, have been examined and returned to the Commissioner of Pensions for his action.

Seven hundred and fifty-one bounty-land claims have been examined and reported to the Commissioner of Pensions.

Four hundred and thirty-nine letters have been written on subjects connected with the war of the Revolution and the war of 1812.

The work of the division is up to date, so that the mails of the day may be answered on the succeeding day.

There are ten lady copyists assigned to this office, and this number seems to be sufficient for the discharge of the duties required of them. The number of pages of difference-sheets copied was 4,585; compared, 4,675. The number of pages of miscellaneous papers copied was 6,226; compared, 9,813; letters copied, 4,062; compared, 6,879; total pages copied, 14,873; compared, 21,367; names indexed, 27,514; money difference-sheets registered and copied, 698; property difference-sheets registered and copied, 349; engineer difference-sheets registered and copied, 44; miscellaneous papers copied, 1,039.

The number of settlements added to the files during the fiscal year is 10,226, viz: settlements certified by Second Comptroller—accounts of disbursing quartermasters, 1,276; of commissaries, 1,238; of agents for paying pensions, 183; of engineer officers, 57; of officers of Freedmen's Bureau, 13; miscellaneous claims, 2,661; and returns of quartermasters' property, 4,798; total, 10,226. The quantity of matter now on the files is enormous, being estimated at 125 tons in weight. Another room, containing 3,300 feet of shelving, has been assigned to this office, and it is probable that this is all that will be required this year. The pension accounts will, for the next ten years, probably require more room than all others. The large file-room has been furnished with extinguisher, and great care is taken to guard against fire. The files are in good condition, and, I am glad to say, the men in charge of them are careful and attentive to the trust committed to them.

The act of Congress approved June 23, 1870, to authorize the settlement of the accounts of officers of the Army and Navy for lost funds, vouchers, and property during the war of the rebellion, and extended for two years by the act of June 7, 1872, will expire by limitation June 23, 1874. It is believed that within the period covered by the extension all the urgent cases requiring relief under said acts will be adjudicated.

Nearly one year remains during which said acts will be available, though it is impossible to say whether these acts will afford sufficient time to enable all worthy claimants under them to take advantage of the relief they afford.

It is suggested that a general law might with propriety be recommended for the favorable action of Congress, giving the accounting officers, in conjunction with the proper military bureaus having administrative action on the accounts and returns, equity jurisdiction for a limited amount, to enable them to close accounts without recourse to Congress for a special act of relief in each particular case. In this connection it may not be improper to ask attention to the report from this office for the fiscal year ending June 30, 1868, showing statement of balances standing to the debit of officers arising out of advances made between May, 1792, and July 1, 1815, (Finance Report, 1868, pages 75–127 inclusive.) These balances are generally for small amounts, and the accounts have stood open on the books since 1815—nearly sixty years. As there does not appear to be any probability that any portion of the money thus charged will ever be recovered, I respectfully renew the recommendation made in that report, and refer to it now as an additional reason for granting the equity jurisdiction above suggested.

Claims for services rendered in the Quartermaster's Department, and filed under the law known as the eight-hour law, act of May 18, 1872, and the President's proclamation of May 19, 1869, have been received. Much difficulty has been experienced in fixing upon a proper basis on which settlements can be made. It seemed necessary that all claims accruing under the act should be received before action should be taken on any of them. This course appeared to be necessary for the reason that owing to the fact that Army officers frequently changed their stations, and the name of a claimant was liable to appear on the rolls of two or more officers for the same service. In this way unintentional errors were liable to be made. To avoid confusion and liability to errors of this sort, it was deemed best to have each chief quartermaster forward the rolls of claimants for reduced pay, and also request them to notify this office in cases where no just claims under said act exist.

All the rolls have not yet reached this office, but as soon as they shall be received, settlements will be made promptly, and little if any delay is anticipated in their final adjustment.

During the year nearly all of the claims made by employés of the Engineer Corps, under the act of May 18, 1872, known as the "Eight-hour law," and numbering several thousand, have been adjusted, and disbursing officers are now engaged in paying the men entitled to extra compensation under that law. The number of claimants and the total amount paid cannot yet be ascertained, owing to the fact that the approved rolls are in possession of the different disbursing officers and will not be forwarded to this office until the men are paid.

The experience of each new year demonstrates more clearly the necessity of a limitation upon the time within which claims may be presented to the Executive Departments. Congress has deemed it wise to make a limitation in respect to claims presented to the Commissioners of Claims and the Court of Claims; and there is, I believe, no State in the Union which has not made such provision in respect to suits between individuals. The Government needs such protection much more than an individual, for the latter generally has such personal knowledge of his business as will put him upon his guard when fraud is attempted against him, while the Government transacts its immense business entirely through agents or officers, whose stations are often changed. Frequently its agents or officers, after quitting its service, are not disposed to neglect their private pursuits to bestow time and labor gratuitously in protecting the Government from imposition; and often, when they have the disposition, lapse of time will so impair their recollections that they can give no information of value. Every day's experience shows how difficult it frequently is to procure on behalf of the Government definite and reliable evidence in respect to ancient transactions on which stale claims are founded.

Under such circumstances it is comparatively easy for claimants, by ex-parte evidence secured at their own leisure, and with no check of cross-examination, to bolster up demands which are either wholly unfounded or grossly exaggerated.

A proper limitation would seem to be three years from the time when the claim accrued, with one year after the passage of the act in case of claims which accrued more than two years previous to the passage of the act. If it be thought that this is allowing but a short period for the adjustment of such claims, it should be considered that the creditor of the Government always knows where to find his debtor, and that the debtor is always willing and able to pay just demands.

I invite your attention particularly to claims under the act of March 2, 1861, which provided for payment of expenses incurred in the Indian hostilities in Oregon and Washington Territories in the years 1855-'56. Seventeen years have passed since the close of the war, and during more than twelve years the law has been in force authorizing the adjustment of the claims. Very few claims are now being presented, and it seems advisable that only a short period—say one year—should be longer allowed for presentation of claims under this act.

I take great pleasure in bearing testimony to the general faithfulness, industry, and fidelity displayed by the clerks employed in this office during the past year, and trust the day is not far distant when the labors they have performed for the Government will be properly appreciated by Congress, and a fair increase of the inadequate compensation allowed in some cases will be granted.

It is not creditable to the Government that faithful and useful clerks in the Auditors' offices who perform identical duties of equal responsibility with others, should be more meagerly paid than the clerks in offices which have been recently reorganized. It is true that the salaries of the former were long since fixed, and have not been changed, but justice and fair-dealing alike require that this inequality should be promptly corrected, and I trust this matter will receive early attention.

Respectfully submitted.

ALLAN RUTHERFORD,
Auditor.

Hon. WILLIAM A. RICHARDSON,
Secretary of the Treasury.

accounts will. for the next ten years, probably require more room than all others. The large file-room has been furnished with extinguishers, and great care is taken to guard against fire. The files are in good condition, and, I am glad to say, the men in charge of them are careful and attentive to the trust committed to them.

The act of Congress approved June 23, 1870, to authorize the settlement of the accounts of officers of the Army and Navy for losses of funds, vouchers, and property during the war of the rebellion, and extended for two years by the act of June 7, 1872, will expire by limitation June 23, 1874. It is believed that within the period covered by the extension all the urgent cases requiring relief under said acts will be adjudicated.

Nearly one year remains during which said acts will be available, though it is impossible to say whether these acts will afford sufficient time to enable all worthy claimants under them to take advantage of the relief they afford.

It is suggested that a general law might with propriety be recommended for the favorable action of Congress, giving the accounting officers, in conjunction with the proper military bureaus having administrative action on the accounts and returns, equity jurisdiction for a limited amount, to enable them to close accounts without recourse to Congress for a special act of relief in each particular case. In this connection it may not be improper to ask attention to the report from this office for the fiscal year ending June 30, 1868, showing statement of balances standing to the debit of officers arising out of advances made between May, 1792, and July 1, 1815, (Finance Report, 1868, pages 75-127 inclusive.) These balances are generally for small amounts, and the accounts have stood open on the books since 1815—nearly sixty years. As there does not appear to be any probability that any portion of the money thus charged will ever be recovered, I respectfully renew the recommendation made in that report, and refer to it now as an additional reason for granting the equity jurisdiction above suggested.

Claims for services rendered in the Quartermaster's Department, and filed under the law known as the eight-hour law, act of May 18, 1872, and the President's proclamation of May 19, 1869, have been received. Much difficulty has been experienced in fixing upon a proper basis on which settlements can be made. It seemed necessary that all claims accruing under the act should be received before action should be taken on any of them. This course appeared to be necessary for the reason that owing to the fact that Army officers frequently changed their stations, and the name of a claimant was liable to appear on the rolls of two or more officers for the same service. In this way unintentional errors were liable to be made. To avoid confusion and liability to errors of this sort, it was deemed best to have each chief quartermaster forward the rolls of claimants for reduced pay, and also request them to notify this office in cases where no just claims under said act exist.

All the rolls have not yet reached this office, but as soon as they shall be received, settlements will be made promptly, and little if any delay is anticipated in their final adjustment.

During the year nearly all of the claims made by employés of the Engineer Corps, under the act of May 18, 1872, known as the "Eight-hour law," and numbering several thousand, have been adjusted, and disbursing officers are now engaged in paying the men entitled to extra compensation under that law. The number of claimants and the total amount paid cannot yet be ascertained, owing to the fact that the proved rolls are in possession of the different disbursing officers and not be forwarded to this office until the men are paid.

accounts will, for the next ten years, probably require more room than all others. The large file room has been furnished with extinguishers, and great care is taken to guard against fire. The files are in good condition, and, I am glad to say, the men in charge of them are careful and attentive to the trust committed to them.

The act of Congress approved June 23, 1870, to authorize the settlement of the accounts of officers of the Army and Navy for losses of funds, vouchers, and property during the war of the rebellion, and extended for two years by the act of June 7, 1872, will expire by limitation June 23, 1874. It is believed that within the period covered by the extension all the urgent cases requiring relief under said acts will be adjudicated.

Nearly one year remains during which said acts will be available, though it is impossible to say whether these acts will afford sufficient time to enable all worthy claimants under them to take advantage of the relief they afford.

It is suggested that a general law might with propriety be recommended for the favorable action of Congress, giving the accounting officers, in conjunction with the proper military bureaus having administrative action on the accounts and returns, equity jurisdiction for a limited amount, to enable them to close accounts without recourse to Congress for a special act of relief in each particular case. In this connection it may not be improper to ask attention to the report from this office for the fiscal year ending June 30, 1868, showing statement of balances standing to the debit of officers arising out of advances made between May, 1792, and July 1, 1815, (Finance Report, 1868, pages 75–127 inclusive.) These balances are generally for small amounts, and the accounts have stood open on the books since 1815—nearly sixty years. As there does not appear to be any probability that any portion of the money thus charged will ever be recovered, I respectfully renew the recommendation made in that report, and refer to it now as an additional reason for granting the equity jurisdiction above suggested.

Claims for services rendered in the Quartermaster's Department, and filed under the law known as the eight-hour law, act of May 18, 1872, and the President's proclamation of May 19, 1869, have been received. Much difficulty has been experienced in fixing upon a proper basis on which settlements can be made. It seemed necessary that all claims accruing under the act should be received before action should be taken on any of them. This course appeared to be necessary for the reason that owing to the fact that Army officers frequently changed their stations, and the name of a claimant was liable to appear on the rolls of two or more officers for the same service. In this way unintentional errors were liable to be made. To avoid confusion and liability to errors of this sort, it was deemed best to have each chief quartermaster forward the rolls of claimants for reduced pay, and also request them to notify this office in cases where no just claims under said act exist.

All the rolls have not yet reached this office, but as soon as they shall be received, settlements will be made promptly, and little if any delay is anticipated in their final adjustment.

During the year nearly all of the claims made by employés of the Engineer Corps, under the act of May 18, 1872, known as the "Eight-hour law," and numbering several thousand, have been adjusted, and disbursing officers are now engaged in paying the men entitled to extra compensation under that law. The number of claimants and the total amount paid cannot yet be ascertained, owing to the fact that the approved rolls are in possession of the different disbursing officers and will not be forwarded to this office until the men are paid.

The experience of each new year demonstrates more clearly the necessity of a limitation upon the time within which claims may be presented to the Executive Departments. Congress has deemed it wise to make a limitation in respect to claims presented to the Commissioners of Claims and the Court of Claims; and there is, I believe, no State in the Union which has not made such provision in respect to suits between individuals. The Government needs such protection much more than an individual, for the latter generally has such personal knowledge of his business as will put him upon his guard when fraud is attempted against him, while the Government transacts its immense business entirely through agents or officers, whose stations are often changed. Frequently its agents or officers, after quitting its service, are not disposed to neglect their private pursuits to bestow time and labor gratuitously in protecting the Government from imposition; and often, when they have the disposition, lapse of time will so impair their recollections that they can give no information of value. Every day's experience shows how difficult it frequently is to procure on behalf of the Government definite and reliable evidence in respect to ancient transactions on which stale claims are founded.

Under such circumstances it is comparatively easy for claimants, by *ex-parte* evidence secured at their own leisure, and with no check of cross-examination, to bolster up demands which are either wholly unfounded or grossly exaggerated.

A proper limitation would seem to be three years from the time when the claim accrued, with one year after the passage of the act in case of claims which accrued more than two years previous to the passage of the act. If it be thought that this is allowing but a short period for the adjustment of such claims, it should be considered that the creditor of the Government always knows where to find his debtor, and that the debtor is always willing and able to pay just demands.

I invite your attention particularly to claims under the act of March 2, 1861, which provided for payment of expenses incurred in the Indian hostilities in Oregon and Washington Territories in the years 1855-'56. Seventeen years have passed since the close of the war, and during more than twelve years the law has been in force authorizing the adjustment of the claims. Very few claims are now being presented, and it seems advisable that only a short period – say one year – should be longer allowed for presentation of claims under this act.

I take great pleasure in bearing testimony to the general faithfulness, industry, and fidelity displayed by the clerks employed in this office during the past year, and trust the day is not far distant when the labors they have performed for the Government will be properly appreciated by Congress, and a fair increase of the inadequate compensation allowed in some cases will be granted.

It is not creditable to the Government that faithful and useful clerks in the Auditors' offices who perform identical duties of equal responsibility with others, should be more meagerly paid than the clerks in offices which have been recently reorganized. It is true that the salaries of the former were long since fixed, and have not been changed, but justice and fair-dealing alike require that this inequality should be speedily corrected, and I trust this matter will receive early attention.

ectfully submitted.

ALLAN RUT   ,
                    ditor.

WILLIAM A. RICHARDSON,
Secretary of the Treasury.

A.—*Statement of the expenses of all missions abroad, &c.*—Continued.

No.	Mission.	Salary.	Conti en-cies	Loss by exchange.	Total
	ITALY				
31	George P. Marsh, minister	$6,000 00	$6,281 89		
32	G. W. Wurts, secretary of legation	1,800 00			
		9,800 00	6,281 89		$16,081 89
	JAPAN.				
33	C. E. DeLong, minister	12,000 00	966 77	1,034 90	
34	E. DeLong Berry, secretary of legation	2,500 00		204 59	
35	N. E. Rice, interpreter	2,500 00		204 86	
		17,000 00	966 77	1,444 35	18,311 12
	LIBERIA.				
36	M. J. Turner, minister	3,507 00	298 24	40 40	3,845 64
	MEXICO.				
37	T. H. Nelson, minister	12,000 00	1,286 82		
	P. Bliss, secretary of legation	1,800 00			
		13,800 00	1,286 82		15,086 82
	NETHERLANDS.				
39	C. T. Gorham, minister	7,500 00	438 24		7,938 24
	PARAGUAY AND URUGUAY.				
40	J. L. Stevens, minister	11,250 00	122 46	310 50	11,682 96
	NICARAGUA.				
41	C. N. Riotte, minister	6,758 24	236 08		6,994 50
	RUSSIA.				
42	J. L. Orr, late minister	3,356 16			
43	E. Schuyler, chargé d'affaires	6,495 92	880 87		
		9,852 08	880 87		10,732 95
	SALVADOR.				
44	T. Biddle, minister	7,500 00	190 42		7,690 42
	SPAIN.				
45	D. E. Sickles, minister	12,000 00	6,596 65	306 32	
46	A. A. Adee, secretary of legation	1,800 00			
		13,800 00	6,596 65	306 32	20,702 97
	SWEDEN.				
47	C. C. Andrews, minister	7,500 00	804 75	370 71	8,675 46
	SWITZERLAND.				
48	H. Rublee, minister	7,500 00	304 46		7,804 46
	TURKEY.				
49	George H. Boker, minister	7,500 00	4,214 79	155 58	11,870 37
	VENEZUELA.				
50	William A. Pile, minister	1,875 00	84 10		1,959 10
	CENTRAL AMERICAN STATES.				
51	George Williamson, minister	2,439 56	66 20		2,505 76
	UNITED STATES OF COLOMBIA.				
52	Thomas F. Wallace, chargé	1,944 80			1,944 80

A.—*Statement of the expenses of all missions abroad, &c.*—Continued.

No.	Mission.	Salary.	Contingencies.	Loss by exchange.	Total.
	UNITED STATES DISPATCH AGENT.				
53	B. F. Stevens.............	$2,000 00	$20,032 50	....	$22,032 50
	Total..	325,795 95	57,579 99	$9,231 47	392,607 41
	UNITED STATES BANKERS, LONDON.				
54	Clews, Habicht & Co..............................	....	....	1,112 39	355,334 50

REMARKS.

9. Inclusive of salary while receiving instructions and for transit.
17. Salary while acting as chargé.'
24. Private amanuensis and cable dispatches included in contingencies; accounts for first and second quarter of 1873 not received.
31. Accounts for first and second quarter of 1873 not received—$6,000—for moving legation from Florence to Rome, included in contingent expenses.
50. No accounts received for three quarters.
53. Amount of contingencies not included in total of the other accounts, as they already contain the same.

B.—*Statement of consular fees, consular salaries and emoluments to officers, and loss by exchange for the fiscal year ended June 30, 1873.*

Consulates, consular agencies, &c.	Salary and emoluments.	Fees.	Loss.	Remarks.
Acapulco.................	$2,000 00	$1,132 27	....	
Aguas Calientes...........	....	....	....	No returns.
Aix-la-Chapelle..........	1,875 00	2,187 50	....	Accounts for second quarter 1873 not received.
Cologne............	491 50	491 50	....	Inclusive only of first quarter, 1873. Returns incomplete.
Alexandria.............	4,290 76	437 07	$80 62	Inclusive of salary of consular clerk.
Algiers...............	1,500 00	52 50	119 39	
Alicante...............	175 27	175 27	....	Inclusive only of third quarter 1872 and second quarter 1873. No returns for other quarters.
Amoor River..........	250 00	10 30	....	No returns received since September 30, 1872.
Amoy..............	3,000 00	2,594 14	373 45	
Amsterdam...........	1,000 00	1,182 71	....	
Nieuwediep..........	135 23	135 23	....	
Ancona..............	68 26	68 26	....	
Antigua..............	....	....	....	No returns.
Antwerp.............	2,500 00	2,846 18	....	
Apia................	1,000 00	141 05	214 72	
Archangel............	....	....	....	No returns.
Aspinwall............	2,760 83	3,930 29	....	Inclusive of transit salary.
Augsburg............	131 25	131 25	....	Returns for first and second quarters 1873, not received.
Aux Cayes..........	500 00	678 11	....	Reports from agencies not received.
Bahia..............	750 00	705 44	....	Accounts for second quarter 1873 not received.
Bangkok............	3,000 00	144 75	713 81	
Barbadoes...........	1,587 28	1,587 28	....	No returns received from agencies.
Barcelona...........	1,500 00	288 76	57 78	
Tarragona..........	301 20	301 20	....	
Barmen.............	2,000 00	6,751 00	198 63	Inclusive of additional compensation allowed when fees reach $4,000.
Crefeld.............	1,902 59	3,185 50	....	
Dusseldorf..........	1,142 00	1,142 00	....	
Basle..............	2,000 00	3,309 50	86 99	
Olten..............	2,010 68	2,840 00	....	
Batavia.............	1,000 00	923 29	....	Report from agency not received.
Bathurst............	77 18	77 18	....	Return for second quarter 1873 not received.
Bay of Islands........	1,000 00	630 94	17 21	
Christchurch........	80 41	80 41	....	
Beirut..............	2,000 00	143 92	113 79	Returns from agencies incomplete.
Belfast.............	2,164 84	10,713 73	....	Inclusive of instruction salary.
Ballymena..........	329 00	329 00	....	
Belize..............	530 18	530 18	....	
Bergen.............	116 50	116 50	....	No returns from agencies.
Berlin.............	4,006 40	9,295 50	....	

B.—*Statement of consular fees, consular salaries and emoluments to officers, &c.*—Continued.

Consulates, consular agencies, &c.	Salary and emoluments.	Fees.	Loss.	Remarks.
Bilbao	$2,500 00	$11,480 02		No returns.
Birmingham	1,768 50	1,808 25		
Leicester	1,222 00	1,222 00		
Kidderminster	1,009 50	1,009 50		
Redditch	985 00	985 00		
Wolverhampton	43 50	43 50		
Bogota	218 00	218 00		
Bombay	2,000 00	6,561 44	$29 18	
Bordeaux	118 90	118 00		
Pau	22 00	22 00		
Bayonne	3,015 47	14,951 00		Accounts for second quarter 1873 not received.
Bradford				
Bremen	3,000 00	3,400 50		
Geestemunde	2,000 00	2,369 48		
Brindisi	1,500 00	21 25	75 51	No report from agency.
Bristol	1,200 36	1,200 36		
Gloucester	383 08	383 08		No returns.
Worcester				
Brunswick	2,494 50	2,494 50		
Brussels	3,701 14	4,182 50		
Bucharest				Do.
Buenaventura				Do.
Buenos Ayres	2,192 25	4,267 90		
Gadiz	1,500 00	1,542 67	11 58	
Cairo	89 00	80 00		Return for second quarter 1873 not received.
Calcutta	6,845 75	5,553 79		Returns from agencies incomplete. Inclusive of transit salary.
Callao	3,500 00	3,592 48		
Camargo	195 98	195 98		
Canea	1,000 00		100 00	
Canton	4,000 00	1,353 37	414 63	No reports received from the agencies.
Cape Haytien	1,000 00	694 94		Returns from agencies incomplete.
Cape Town	1,000 00	485 17	36 35	
Port Elizabeth	542 36	542 36		
Cardiff	2,859 02	2,859 02		
Llanelly	37 50	37 50		
Milford Haven	10 15	10 15		
Newport	459 92	459 92		
Swansea	195 92	195 92		
Carlsruhe	2,259 75	2,259 75		
Mannheim	759 50	759 50		
Kehl	322 50	322 50		
Carrara	590 00	590 00		
Carthagena, United States of Colombia	500 00	400 84		
Carthagena, Spain				No returns.
Ceylon	1,000 00	639 96		
Chee-Foo	858 31	858 31		
Chemnitz	1,164 84	4,154 50		Accounts for first and second quarters 1873 not received.
Chihuahua	108 00	108 00		Inclusive of first and second quarters 1873 only. The returns for third and fourth quarters 1872 not received.
Chin-Kiang	3,000 00	3,147 15	131 78	
Christiania	204 00	204 00		
Ciudad Bolivar	230 50	230 50		Returns for first and second quarters 1873 not received.
Clifton	2,000 00	5,063 00		Inclusive of additional compensation allowed when fees reach $3,000.
St. Catharines	278 50	278 50		
Coaticook	2,000 00	6,341 75	7 25	Do.
Lineboro	1,721 00	1,721 00		
Hereford	270 00	270 00		
Potton	147 50	147 50		
Stanstead	347 50	347 50		
Georgeville	98 00	98 00		
Cobija				No returns.
Colonia	11 42	11 42		No returns from agency. Account second quarter 1873 not received.
Comayagua and Tegucigalpa				No returns.
Amapala	165 98	165 98		Returns for third and fourth quarters 1872 not received.
Constantinople	3,000 00	339 75	263 44	
Copenhagen	332 00	332 00		
Coquimbo				No returns.
Caldera				Do.
Cork	2,600 00	1,156 96		
Waterford	47 57	47 57		

B.—*Statement of consular fees, consular salaries and emoluments to officers, &c.*—Continued.

Consulates, consular agencies, &c.	Salary and emoluments.	Fees.	Loss.	Remarks.
Corunna	$75 88	$75 88		No returns from agencies.
Curaçoa	2,249 47	2,249 47		
Bonaire	104 76	104 76		Return for first quarter 1873 not received.
Cyprus	500 00		$32 50	Accounts for first and second quarters 1873 not received.
Demerara	2,000 00	2,513 09		
Drain				No returns.
Dresden	4,238 65	5,245 73		
Dublin	2,257 62	2,257 62		
Dundee	2,000 00	7,572 28	5 47	
Aberdeen	1,030 75	1,030 75		
Elsinore	375 00	3 00	18 60	Inclusive only of the third quarter 1872; vice-consul in charge not a citizen of United States.
Falmouth	442 07	442 07		
Scilly Islands				No fees.
Fayal	750 00	461 54		
Flores	98 71	98 71		
Graciosa	6 00	6 00		
St. Jorge	23 95	23 95		
St. Michael	94 74	94 74		
Terceira	22 88	22 88		
Florence	2,252 50	2,252 50		No returns from agency.
Foo-Chow	3,500 00	1,330 71	353 30	
Fort Erie	1,500 00	2,382 50		
Port Rowan	562 50	562 50		Partial returns.
Port Stanley and St. Thomas	317 00	317 00		
Frankfort-on-the-Main	3,000 00	3,980 50		
Funchal	1,500 00	154 68	67 24	
Gaboon	1,000 00	3 00		
Galatz				No returns.
Gaspe Basin				No fees.
Geneva	1,500 00	1,541 90	3 92	
Genoa	1,500 00	1,564 91	4 82	
Milan	339 25	339 25		
Ghent	262 50	262 50		
Gibraltar	1,500 00	831 06		
Glasgow	3,000 00	11,803 30		
Goderich	1,408 33	761 77		
Stratford	2,012 50	2,012 50		
Gottenburg				No returns.
Grand Bassa	26 83	26 83		Return for fourth quarter 1872 not received.
Guadeloupe	857 82	857 82		No return from agency.
Guatemala	703 00	703 00		Returns from agencies not received.
Guayaquil	562 50	415 90		Account for fourth quarter 1872 not received.
Guaymas	1,000 00	833 26		
Guerrero	160 00	160 00		
Hakodadi	2,500 00	436 06	252 23	
Halifax	2,000 00	3,803 01	5 06	Returns from agencies not received.
Hamburg	2,000 00	9,998 35	132 97	
Harburg	1,844 25	1,844 25		
Lubec	55 78	55 78		
Kiel	41 50	41 50		
Cuxhaven				No fees.
Hamilton, Bermuda	2,462 82	2,462 82		
St. George's	359 53	359 53		Return for fourth quarter 1872 not received.
Hamilton, Canada	2,844 70	4,366 00		
Paris	932 50	932 50		
Hankow	3,000 00	1,348 56	439 86	
Kin-Kiang	721 24	721 24		
Havana	8,000 00	23,815 97		Inclusive of salary of two consular clerks.
San Juan de los Remedios	893 15	893 15		
Havre	6,000 00	5,839 30	10 30	
Dunkirk	263 82	263 82		
Brest	225 00	225 00		
Rouen	201 97	201 97		
Dieppe	85 63	85 63		
Cherbourg	20 00	20 00		
Honfleur				
Helsingfors	15 49	15 49		Inclusive only of third and fourth quarter 1872; the other quarters' returns not received.
Hobart Town				No returns.
Hong-Kong	2,625 00	9,195 14		Accounts for second quarter 1873 not received.
Jerusalem	1,500 00	44 00	153 57	
Kanagawa	3,000 00	5,684 59	305 22	
Kingston, Jamaica	2,000 00	1,937 77	7 83	
Black River	103 45	103 45		

B.—*Statement of consular fees, consular salaries and emoluments to officers, &c.*—Continued.

Consulates, consular agencies, &c.	Salary and emoluments.	Fees.	Loss.	Remarks.
Falmouth	$26 50	$26 50		
Montego Bay	145 12	145 12		
Port Antonia	83 31	83 31		
Grand Caymans	35 95	35 95		
Old Harbor	11 38	11 38		
Han-la-Mar	48 14	48 14		
Kingston, Canada	1,500 00	1,297 00		
Bellville	1,938 50	1,938 50		
Napanee	843 50	843 50		
Picton	329 50	329 50		
Gananoque	60 95	60 25		
Laguayra	1,185 00	441 75		Accounts for second quarter 1873 not received.
Laguna				No returns.
Lambayeque	85 18	85 18		Return for second quarter 1873 not received
Lanthala	750 00	27 40	$108 32	Accounts for second quarter 1873 not received.
La Paz, Bolivia				No returns.
La Paz, Mexico	677 10	677 10		
San José	61 50	61 50		
La Rochelle	1,656 59	349 50	38 81	Inclusive of instruction and transit salaries.
Cognac	1,616 50	689 00		
Limoges	1,383 50	1,383 50		
Rochefort	107 50	107 50		
La Union	508 84	508 84		
Leeds	1,000 08	1,162 49	08	Accounts for first and second quarters 1873 not received.
Huddersfield	1,000 00	3,160 50		Returns for first and second quarters 1873 not received.
Hull	246 16	246 16		Do.
Leghorn	1,500 00	1,902 94	2 35	
Leipsic	3,000 00	7,777 75		Inclusive of consular clerks' salary and additional compensation when fees reach $3,000.
Leith	3,137 49	3,508 62		
Dunfermline	1,955 00	1,955 00		
Liege	1,468 50	1,468 50		
Lisbon	1,500 00	540 93	96 40	Returns from agencies not received.
Liverpool	9,270 37	34,210 57		Inclusive of instruction and transit salaries.
Saint Helena	2,043 38	3,946 00		
London	7,500 00	51,444 03		
Ramsgate	29 00	29 00		Returns imperfect.
Dover	2 00	2 00		Do.
Londonderry	495 50	495 50		
Ludwigshafen	1,751 00	1,751 00		
Lyons	2,981 32	9,730 53	851 95	Inclusive of consular clerk's salary from April 1, 1873, to June 30, 1873.
Saint Etienne	2,056 30	3,143 00		
Malaga	1,500 00	1,680 50	13 07	
Almeria Malaga	295 00	295 00		No fees received at the other agencies.
Malta	1,500 00	138 89	71 63	
Manchester	3,000 00	29,905 72		
Manila	1,350 18	1,350 18		No returns from agencies
Matzanillo, Mexico	555 91	555 91		
Maracaibo	1,192 06	1,192 96		
Maranham	1,000 00	173 46	5 20	
Marseilles	4,923 99	3,802 33	9 15	Inclusive of instruction and transit salaries.
Cette	1,201 21	1,201 21		
Toulon	35 35	35 35		
Matamoras	2,000 00	826 00		
Santa Cruz Point	2,002 50	2,430 00		
Matanzas	2,840 00	4,991 86		
Cardenas	1,000 00	4,727 70		
Nagua la Grande	1,500 00	2,430 91		
Mayence	2,812 00	3,351 50		Accounts for expenses incomplete.
Mazatlan	1,276 93	1,276 93		
Medellin				No returns.
Melbourne	4,000 00	2,414 77	29 01	
Port Adelaide	81 15	81 15		Inclusive only from April 14, 1873, to June 30, 1873.
Merida	110 50	110 50		Do.
Progreso	131 93	131 93		
Messina	1,500 00	2,556 01		
Catania	70 22	70 22		
Syracuse	11 37	11 37		
Gioja				No fees
Mexico	1,000 00	390 50		
Mier	149 50	149 50		Return for fourth quarter 1872 not received.
Minatitlan	929 94	929 94		No returns from agency.

B.—*Statement of consular fees, consular salaries and emoluments to officers, &c.*—Continued.

Consulates, consular agencies, &c.	Salary and emoluments.	Fees.	Loss.	Remarks.
Monterey	$34 00	$31 00		Returns for fourth quarter 1872 and first quarter 1873 not received; no returns from agencies.
Montevideo	1,911 00	884 44	$13 62	Inclusive of instruction and transit salaries.
Montreal	4,060 00	5,901 87		
Lachine	1,139 50	1,139 50		
Hemmingford	469 50	469 50		
Three Rivers	367 00	367 00		
Sorel	226 00	226 00		
Moscow	13 00	13 00		Returns for first and second quarters 1873 not received.
Mozambique				No returns.
Munich	1,500 00	1,277 50	27 93	
Nagasaki	3,000 00	731 51	350 69	
Nantes	1,500 00	323 82	31 75	
L'Orient	77 50	77 50		
Saint Nazaire	98 96	98 96		
Naples	1,500 00	1,458 31		
Castelamare	288 50	288 50		
Nassau	2,000 00	1,292 23		
Harbor Island	287 17	287 17		
Governor's Harbor	294 90	294 90		
Green Turtle Bay	49 79	49 79		
San Salvador	84 20	84 20		
Inagua	40 66	40 66		
Newcastle-upon-Tyne	1,500 00	1,721 00		
Carlisle	795 00	795 00		
Hartlepool	587 92	587 92		
Sunderland	582 27	582 27		
New-Chwang	160 68	160 68		
Nice	1,500 00	482 00	44 18	
Mentone	120 00	120 00		
Ningpo	773 61	773 61		
Nuevo Laredo	728 50	728 50		
Nuremberg	4,007 97	6,452 22		
Bamberg	1,099 50	1,099 50		
Oaxaca	4 00	4 00		Returns for first and second quarters 1873 not received.
Odessa	2,000 00	78 00	287 18	
Taganrog	134 50	134 50		
Rostoff	21 50	21 50		
Omoa and Truxillo		193 00	99 60	Returns incomplete.
Oporto	1,761 07	193 00	99 60	Inclusive of instruction and transit salaries. No fees received at the agencies.
Osaka and Hiogo	3,692 95	2,368 84	105 63	Inclusive of transit salary.
Ostend				No returns.
Padang				No returns.
Palermo	1,611 26	1,753 20		Inclusive of instruction salary.
Marsala	51 05	51 05		
Licati	52 21	52 21		
Girgenti	98 24	98 24		
Trapani	147 40	147 40		
Panama	3,500 00	3,105 50		
Para	896 73	1,810 56		Accounts for second quarter 1873 not received. Inclusive of instruction and transit salaries.
Paramaribo	1,774 03	1,774 03		
Paris	8,000 00	52,416 00		Inclusive of salary of three consular clerks.
Calais	213 00	213 00		Returns incomplete.
Lille	88 00	88 00		Do.
Paso del Norte	595 15	78 50		Inclusive of instruction and transit salaries.
Payta	500 00	314 52		
Pernambuco	2,000 00	1,458 21	64 57	Returns from agencies incomplete.
Picton	375 00	427 78		Returns incomplete.
Piedras Negras	277 00	277 00		Returns for first and second quarters 1873 not received.
Piræus	980 50	12 00		
Syra	17 72	17 72		
Plymouth	171 85	171 85		
Brixham	99 90	99 90		
Dartmouth	4 00	4 00		
Guernsey	22 00	22 00		
Jersey	54 00	54 00		
Port Louis, Mauritius	2,651 10	360 58	106 90	Inclusive of instruction salary.
Port Mahon	1,039 78	3 50	44 94	Returns incomplete.
Port Said	2,000 00	29 50	103 52	No returns received from agencies.
Port Sarnia	1,500 00	1,468 00		
London	1,415 75	1,415 75		
Port Stanley	500 00	96 55		Accounts for first and second quarters 1873 not received.

B.—*Statement of consular fees, consular salaries and emoluments to officers, &c.*—Continued.

Consulates, consular agencies, &c.	Salary and emoluments.	Fees.	Loss.	Remarks.
Prague..................	$1,250 00	$2,083 00	....	Accounts for expenses not received; no returns of fees for first and second quarters 1873.
Prescott................	1,500 00	1,313 00	$1 86	
Ottawa	1,786 54	2,319 00		
Brockville.........	1,343 00	1,343 00		
Morrisburg	756 50	756 50		
Cornwall..........	492 00	492 00		
Prince Edward Island...	1,500 00	717 57	7 00	
Georgetown	42 74	42 74		
Cascumpec	60 00	60 00		
Summerside	94 00	94 00		
Puerto Cabello	1,184 33	1,184 33		
Quebec	1,500 00	1,027 34	4 95	
Rheims................	1,695 00	1,695 00		
Riga	....	....		No returns.
Rio Grande do Sul......	833 33	367 22		Accounts for second quarter 1873 not received.
Rio Hacha.............	....	....		No fees.
Rio de Janeiro..........	9,046 13	6,750 80	1 12	Inclusive of allowance, by act of Congress approved December 17, 1872, to Vice-Consul Cordeiro.
Rio Negro	....	....		No returns.
Rome	1,890 21	375 50	43 29	Returns incomplete.
Rosario	461 40	461 40		
Rotterdam............	2,000 00	1,880 42	22 89	
Scheidam	1,979 50	1,979 50		
Flushing	2 00	2 00		
Rabanilla.............	....	....		No returns.
San Andres	122 45	122 45		Return for first quarter 1873 not received.
San Dimas	....	....		No returns.
San José	....	....		Do.
Port Limon	....	....		Do.
Punta Arenas.....	....	....		Do.
San Juan del Norte....	3,035 00	413 30		Inclusive of instruction and transit salaries.
San Juan del Sur	2,000 00	377 66		
San Juan, P. R	2,000 00	706 31		
Ponce	1,464 62	1,464 62		
Mayaguez........	1,401 73	1,401 73		
Guayama	497 90	497 90		
Arecibo	379 03	379 03		
Fajardo	225 28	225 28		Returns for third quarter 1872 not received.
Aquadilla	64 85	64 85		Returns for fourth quarter 1872 and first quarter 1873 not received.
Naguabo	196 92	196 92		
San Luis Potosi.........	....	....		No fees for third quarter 1872; no other returns received.
San Salvador..........	42 50	42 50		Returns for first and second quarters 1873 not received.
La Libertad	191 58	191 58		Do.
Santa Cruz...........	1,500 00	113 90		Returns from agency incomplete.
Santa Martha..........	589 87	589 87		
Santander.............	44 00	44 00		Return for first quarter 1873 not received.
Gijon	8 12	8 12		Do.
Santiago, Cape Verde ...	582 50	131 92	47 84	Accounts for second quarter 1873 not received.
Santiago de Cuba.......	2,500 00	863 25		
Baracoa..........	971 71	971 71		
Guantanamo	375 91	375 91		
Manzanillo	373 31	373 31		
Santa Cruz	2 90	2 90		
Santos	175 25	175 25		
Seville	757 39	757 39		
Seychelles............	1,500 00	143 93	67 68	
Shanghai............	5,197 70	10,807 35		Inclusive of salary of consular clerk.
Sheffield	4,354 46	9,482 75		
Nottingham	2,118 26	7,943 50		
Sierra Leone	151 08	151 08		Return for second quarter 1873 not received.
Singapore.............	2,500 00	1,301 92	102 51	
Penang	144 86	144 86		
Smyrna	2,000 00	1,444 55	61 77	
Sonneberg............	3,854 47	6,404 75		
Sonsonate............	299 54	299 54		Returns for third quarter 1872 not received.
Southampton..........	2,000 00	499 50		
Portsmouth	36 00	36 00		
Weymouth	19 50	19 50		
Cowes	56 00	56 00		
Spezia	1,500 00	5 00	† 112 99	
St. Bartholomews.....	....	....		No returns.
St. Catharine's.........	1,500 00	107 68		

B.—*Statement of consular fees, consular salaries and emoluments to officers, &c.*—Continued.

Consulates, consular agencies, &c.	Salary and emoluments	Fees.	Loss.	Remarks.
St. Christopher	$59 56	$59 56		No returns for first quarter 1873
St. Domingo	1,500 00	534 38		
St. Helena	1,500 00	728 87	$17 90	
St. John's, Canada	1,500 00	2,841 50		
Stanbridge	1,072 50	1,072 50		
Frelighsburg	314 00	314 00		
Sutton	209 50	209 50		
St. John's, Newfoundland	445 46	445 46		No returns from agencies.
St. John, New Brunswick	3,706 93	5,956 46	6 30	
St. Stephen's	1,172 72	1,172 72		
St. Andrew's	347 92	347 92		
St. George	384 82	384 89		
St. McAdam	297 53	297 53		
St. Merimichi	65 60	65 60		
Fredericton	368 00	368 00		
St. Mare	444 32	444 32		
St. Martin	457 69	457 69		
St. Eustatius	11 76	11 76		No returns for first and second quarters 1873.
St. Paul de Loando	1,000 00			No returns.
St. Pierre, Martinique				Do.
Fort de France				Inclusive only of third and fourth quarters 1872. Other quarters not received.
St. Pierre, Miquelon	97 87	97 87		
St. Petersburg	1,000 00	460 50	70 13	Accounts for first and second quarters 1873 not received.
St. Thomas	4,000 00	2,364 50		
Stettin	1,224 78	304 44	36 94	Inclusive of instruction and transit salaries.
Königsburg	195 25	195 25		
Danzig	30 75	30 75		
Memel	15 50	15 50		
Swinemünde	5 00	5 00		
Stockholm	592 08	592 08		No returns from agencies.
Stuttgart	2,000 00	3,012 75	20 43	Inclusive of additional compensation allowed when fees reach $3,000.
Swatow	3,500 00	667 50	470 67	
	1,249 96	1,249 96		
	759 29	759 29		
Tabasco	602 86	129 56		Inclusive of instruction and transit salaries.
Tahiti	1,000 00	653 10		
Talcahuano	1,000 00	366 66		
Tamatave	2,000 00	32 86	213 65	
Tampico	1,919 83	578 61		
Tuxpan	141 53	141 53		
Tangier	3,000 00	20 00	100 50	
Tomato				No fees.
Teneriffe	288 54	288 54		
Las Palmas	198 25	198 25		
Tien-Tsin	3,500 00	776 13	534 72	
Toronto	2,000 00	4,210 00		Inclusive of additional compensation allowed when fees reach $3,000.
Port Hope	2,042 76	2,237 00		
Coburg	1,014 00	1,014 00		
Guelph	783 50	783 50		
Whitley	112 50	112 50		From May 8 to June 30, 1873.
Trieste	2,000 00	1,416 37		
Fiume	19 48	19 48		
Trinidad de Cuba	2,671 70	579 23		Inclusive of instruction salary.
Cienfuegos	2,230 47	2,536 71		
Trinidad, (island)	433 36	433 36		
Tripoli	3,000 00	1 00	191 52	
Tumbez	500 00	145 13	9 68	
Tunis	3,000 00	17 00		
Tunstall	2,000 00	7,610 02		Inclusive of additional compensation allowed when fees reach $3,000.
Turk's Islands	2,000 00	447 11	60 50	
Cockburn Harbor	185 81	185 81		
Salt Cay	273 52	273 52		
Valencia	634 61	2 00	12 40	Returns incomplete
Valparaiso	3,000 00	2,463 40		
Venice	750 00	425 34	30 11	
Vera Cruz	3,500 00	1,712 67		
Victoria	2,725 00	2,867 36		
Vienna	1,500 00	5,304 50	79 40	Adjustment of salary not yet effected.
Brunn	325 50	325 50		
Pesth	249 50	249 50		
Windsor, Nova Scotia	1,000 00	573 76		
Windsor, Canada	1,500 00	2,617 25		
Chatham	1,024 50	1,024 50		
Wallaceburg	879 00	879 00		
Winnipeg	1,500 00	534 10		

B.—*Statement of consular fees, consular salaries and emoluments to officers, &c.—*Continued

Consulates, consular agencies, &c.	Salary and emoluments.	Fees.	Loss.	Remarks.
Zacatecas	$6 00	$6 00	....	Inclusive only of first and second quarters 1873; third and fourth of 1872 not received.
Zante	16 50	16 50	....	
Cephalonia	30 00	30 00	....	Returns for first and second quarters 1873 not received.
Patras...............	140 00	140 00	....	Return for second quarter 1873 not received.
Zanzibar	1,390 81	207 14	$196 20	Inclusive of transit salary.
Zurich	2,000 00	3,359 50	....	Inclusive of additional compensation allowed when fees reach $3,000.
St. Gall	2,000 00	2,917 25	....	
Total............	539,441 32	746,594 89	9,156 24	

RECAPITULATION.

Total fees received.. $746,594 89
Salaries, &c., to officers... $539,441 32
Loss by exchange.. 9,156 24

                    548,597 56

  Excess of fees over salaries and loss by exchange........................ 197,997 33

B 1.—*Expenditures on account of sundry appropriations from July 1, 1872, to June 30, 1873, as shown by adjustments in this Office.*

For interpreters to the consulates in China, Japan, and Siam.............. $8,502 52
For salaries of the marshals of the consular courts in Japan, including
 that at Nagasaki, and in China, Siam, and Turkey 3,890 88
For rent of prisons for American convicts in Japan, China, Siam, and Turkey. 11,751,13
For expenses of the consulates in the Turkish dominions, viz: Interpreters,
 guards, and other expenses of the consulates at Constantinople, Smyrna,
 Candia, Alexandria, Jerusalem, and Beirut.............................. 4,261 50

C.—*Statement showing the amount expended by the consular officers of the United States for the relief of American seamen, the money received by said officers for extra wages, &c., and the loss by exchange incurred by them during the fiscal year ended June 30, 1873, as shown by the accounts settled in this Office.*

Consulate.	Expended.	Received.	Loss by exchange.
Acapulco......................	$2,138 94	$22 85	$4 29
Amoy	111 38	33 37	13 52
Amsterdam	....	126 00	....
Antigua	225 00	....	....
Antwerp	111 80	777 18	....
Apia	289 00	165 00	31 68
Aspinwall	1,138 80	143 20	....
Aux Cayes, Hayti	501 20	....	....
Bangkok	47 69	....	....
Barbadoes..................	309 59	103 35	....
Barcelona	12 90	....	....
Batavia	2,825 25	175 45	222 96
Bay of Islands, New Zealand.	888 35	644 49	17 42
Belize, Honduras	21 00	....	....
Bermuda	307 96	284 00	....
Bombay	50 38	71 92	....
Bremen	403 20	354 48	....
Bristol	110 38	123 63	....
Buenos Ayres	784 84	573 28	....
Cadiz	620 12	121 70	13 33
Calcutta	85 00	655 31	....
Callao......................	4,038 00	3,580 03	....
Cardiff	137 80	81 80	....
Constantinople	31 39	....	64
Cape Town	13 64	....	....
Comayagua	60 25	....	....
Cork	65 32	592 38	....
Corunna	38 25	....	....
Demerara	35 56	100 44	....
Dundee, Scotland...........	557 88	....	....
Elsinore....................	86 44	....	....
Fayal......................	3,326 07	1,188 69	....
Falmouth, England..........	304 49	....	....
Port Erie, Canada..........	62 00	....	....
Genoa......................	7 12	31 66	....

C.—*Statement showing the amount expended by the consular officers, &c.*—Continued.

Consulate.	Expended.	Received.	Loss by exchange.
Gibraltar	$284 61	$43 35	
Glasgow		50 00	
Guayaquil	1,219 34	120 00	
Guaymas		13 20	
Hakodadi	42 50	263 50	
Halifax	76 35		
Hamburg	46 70	818 05	$16 79
Havana	362 75	2,025 69	
Havre	678 20	110 75	11 82
Hong-Kong	819 06	574 20	
Honolulu	729 75	891 25	
Kanagawa	108 00	346 11	
Kingston, Jamaica	305 29	229 29	5 12
Laguayra	16 74		
Leghorn		80 00	
Leith, Scotland		656 63	
Liverpool	750 86	34,428 70	
London	1,133 53	1,280 50	
Londonderry	8 51		24
Malaga	1,805 13	34 00	39 76
Madagascar	20 00	30 94	
Manila	1,134 25	325 83	
Manchester	20 00		
Manzanillo, Mexico		125 00	
Marseilles	386 15	75 00	
Matanzas	97 00	278 75	
Matamoras	78 00		
Mauritius	659 62	120 00	24 49
Melbourne	621 50	735 84	5 61
Montevideo	369 41	92 64	
Nagasaki		146 85	
Nassau, Bahamas	3,701 16	175 05	
Naples	36 05	81 00	
Newcastle, England	140 55	715 00	3 68
Osaca and Hiogo	110 00		19 22
Panama	1,829 35	1,339 70	
Paramaribo	668 40		
Paris	15 44		
Payta	4,040 48	840 00	
Pernambuco, (steamship Erie burned at sea)	6,170 18	45 00	731 44
Plymouth, England	240 62		
Quebec	8 50		
Rio de Janeiro		827 14	
Rio Grande do Sul, Brazil	531 39	110 00	
Santiago, Cape Verde Islands	733 45	143 25	65 74
Santiago de Cuba	209 50		
Seychelles	525 00	92 17	18 10
Saint Catharine's, Brazil	72 56	20 00	
Saint Helena	139 26	577 38	
Seville		33 34	
Singapore	742 55	1,687 78	
Swatow	66 50	193 17	
Shanghai	50 82	301 72	
Sydney, Australia	486 26	1,449 62	
Saint John, New Brunswick	35 50	174 75	
Saint Pierre, Miquelon	93 70		
Saint Thomas, West Indies	1,423 57	150 00	
Tahiti	1,825 98		
Talcahuano	3,347 64	145 00	
Tampico	31 92		
Teneriffe	581 95	128 93	47 24
Tien-Tsin, China		40 00	
Toronto	10 00		
Trieste	14 78	36 53	
Trinidad de Cuba	32 60		
Trinidad Island	111 51		
Valparaiso	138 70	386 61	
Vera Cruz	199 13	63 80	
Victoria, Vancouver's Island	43 50	120 00	
Zanzibar	12 00		
Total	59,950 46	64,312 13	1,314 05

RECAPITULATION.

Amount expended by consuls for relief of seamen	$59,950 46
Amount expended by consuls for loss in exchange	1,314 05
Amount paid for the passage of destitute seamen, (see Schedule D)	11,019 91
Total amount of expenditures	72,284 42
Amount of extra wages, &c., received by consuls	64,312 13
Excess of expenditures over receipts	7,972 29

R.—*Statement of consular fees, consular salaries and emoluments to officers, &c.*— Continued

Consulates, consular agencies, &c.	Salary and emoluments.	Fees.	Loss.	Remarks.
Zacatecas	$6 00	$6 00		Inclusive only of first and second quarters 1873; third and fourth of 1873 not received.
Zante	16 50	16 50		
Cephalonia	30 00	30 00		Returns for first and second quarters 1873 not received.
Patras	140 00	140 00		Return for second quarter 1873 not received.
Zanzibar	1,390 81	207 14	$198 20	Inclusive of transit salary.
Zurich	2,000 00	3,359 50		Inclusive of additional compensation allowed when fees reach $3,000.
St. Gall	2,000 00	2,917 25		
Total	539,441 39	746,594 89	9,156 24	

RECAPITULATION.

Total fees received.. $746,594 89
Salaries, &c., to officers................................. $539,441 32
Loss by exchange.. 9,156 24
                                                          548,597 56

Excess of fees over salaries and loss by exchange........... 197,997 33

B 1.—*Expenditures on account of sundry appropriations from July 1, 1872, to June 30, 1873, as shown by adjustments in this Office.*

For interpreters to the consulates in China, Japan, and Siam.............. $8,502 52
For salaries of the marshals of the consular courts in Japan, including that at Nagasaki, and in China, Siam, and Turkey.................... 3,890 88
For rent of prisons for American convicts in Japan, China, Siam, and Turkey. 11,751 13
For expenses of the consulates in the Turkish dominions, viz: Interpreters, guards, and other expenses of the consulates at Constantinople, Smyrna, Candia, Alexandria, Jerusalem, and Beirut.................... 4,261 50

C.—*Statement showing the amount expended by the consular officers of the United States for the relief of American seamen, the money received by said officers for extra wages, &c., and the loss by exchange incurred by them during the fiscal year ended June 30, 1873, as shown by the accounts settled in this Office.*

Consulate.	Expended.	Received.	Loss by exchange.
Acapulco	$2,138 94	$22 85	$4 29
Amoy	111 38	33 37	13 52
Amsterdam		126 00	
Antigua	225 00		
Antwerp	111 80	777 18	
Apia	259 00	165 00	31 68
Aspinwall	1,138 80	143 20	
Aux Cayes, Hayti	501 20		
Bangkok	47 69		
Barbadoes	309 59	103 55	
Barcelona	12 90		
Batavia	2,825 25	175 45	222 90
Bay of Islands, New Zealand	888 35	614 42	17 42
Belize, Honduras	21 00		
Bermuda	367 96	283 00	
Bombay	50 38	71 92	
Bremen	403 30	351 48	
Bristol	110 38	153 64	
Buenos Ayres	784 84	573 26	
Cadiz	620 12	181 79	10 33
Calcutta	85 00	655 31	
Callao	4,038 00	3,580 03	
Cardiff	137 80	81 80	
Constantinople	31 39		63
Cape Town	13 68		
Comayagua	60 85		
Cork	65 32	592 38	
Corunna	38 25		
Demerara	35 58	100 44	
Dundee, Scotland	557 88		
Elsinore	86 44		
Fayal	3,326 07	1,188 62	
Falmouth, England	304 49		
Fort Erie, Canada	62 00		
Genoa	7 12	31 66	

C.—*Statement showing the amount.expended by the consular officers, &c.*—Continued.

Consulate.	Expended.	Received.	Loss by exchange.
Gibraltar	$284 61	$43 35	
Glasgow		50 00	
Guayaquil	1,219 34	120 00	
Guaymas		13 20	
Hakodadi	42 50	263 50	
Halifax	76 35		
Hamburg	26 70	818 95	$16 79
Havana	362 75	2,025 60	
Havre	678 20	110 75	11 82
Hong-Kong	819 06	574 20	
Honolula	729 75	891 25	
Kanagawa	108 00	348 11	
Kingston, Jamaica	305 20	229 20	3 12
Laguayra	16 74		
Leghorn		80 00	
Leith, Scotland		656 63	
Liverpool	750 86	34,428 70	
London	1,133 53	1,280 50	
Londonderry	8 51		24
Malaga	1,805 13	34 00	30 76
Madagascar	20 00	30 94	
Manila	1,134 25	385 83	
Manchester	20 09		
Manzanillo, Mexico		125 00	
Marseilles	386 15	75 00	
Matanzas	97 00	278 75	
Matamoras	78 00		
Mauritius	659 62	120 00	24 49
Melbourne	621 50	755 84	5 64
Montevideo	369 41	92 64	
Nagasaki		146 85	
Nassau, Bahamas	3,701 16	175 05	
Naples	36 05	81 00	
Newcastle, England	140 55	715 00	3 68
Osaca and Hiogo	110 00		12 22
Panama	1,829 35	1,339 70	
Paramaribo	668 40		
Paris	15 44		
Payta	4,040 48	840 00	
Pernambuco, (steamship Erie burned at sea)	6,170 18	45 00	731 44
Plymouth, England	240 02		
Quebec	8 50		
Rio de Janeiro		827 14	
Rio Grande do Sul, Brazil	531 39	110 00	
Santiago, Cape Verde Islands	733 45	143 25	65 74
Santiago de Cuba	909 50		
Seychelles	525 00	92 17	18 10
Saint Catharine's, Brazil	72 56	20 00	
Saint Helena	139 26	577 38	
Seville		33 34	
Singapore	742 55	1,687 78	
Swatow	66 50	193 17	
Shanghai	50 82	301 72	
Sydney, Australia	486 26	1,449 02	
Saint John, New Brunswick	35 50	174 75	
Saint Pierre, Miquelou	93 70		
Saint Thomas, West Indies	1,423 57	150 00	
Tahiti	1,835 98		
Talcahuano	3,347 64	445 00	
Tampico	31 92		
Teneriffe	581 95	128 93	47 24
Tien-Tsin, China		40 00	
Toronto	10 00		
Trieste	14 78	36 53	
Trinidad de Cuba	32 60		
Trinidad Island	111 54		
Valparaiso	138 70	386 64	
Vera Cruz	199 13	63 80	
Victoria, Vancouver's Island	43 50	120 00	
Zanzibar	12 00		
Total	59,950 46	64,312 13	1,314 05

RECAPITULATION.

Amount expended by consuls for relief of seamen $59,950 46
Amount expended by consuls for loss in exchange 1,314 05
Amount paid for the passage of destitute seamen, (see Schedule D) 11,019 91

Total amount of expenditures 72,284 42
Amount of extra wages, &c., received by consuls 64,312 13

Excess of expenditures over receipts 7,972 29

Statement showing the expenses of assessing the internal-revenue taxes in the several collection-districts.

District	Compensation.	Clerk-hire.	Stationery.	Printing and advertising.	Postage and express.	Rent of assessors.	Survey of distilleries.	Compensation of subalterns, &c.	Compensation of store-keepers.	Total.
Alabama	$3,378 91	$3,402 80	$220 86	$12 00	$53 04	$399 66	$118 45	$19,334 32	$1,378 00	$30,546 04
Arizona	9,218 40	1,514 50	10 00		9 00	300 00		780 00		3,257 36
Arkansas	5,463 85	6,993 84	169 82	53 72	75 70	985 86	102 00	8,789 89	7,355 00	16,331 36
California	12,059 88	5,964 58	430 51	90 63	215 49	2,744 16		35,622 69		67,439 64
Colorado	6,300 69	775 91	79 80	17 50	31 50	2,450 33	19 80	3,012 63	6,838 00	7,149 88
Connecticut	7,644 83	8,966 58	173 76	1 50	144 46	508 53		17,463 16		35,985 58
Dakota	7,407 94				5 00			1,729 88		4,164 56
Delaware	2,373 71	1,235 60	61 00		37 00			3,012 69		9,048 93
District of Columbia	2,541 00	1,000 00	44 65	9 50	8 00	373 00	58 65	4,499 61		6,007 51
Florida	2,881 00	1,000 00	337 66	93 50	151 86	300 00		7,197 53	1,018 00	10,759 10
Georgia	5,348 59	5,335 78	581 88		361 04	1,134 63		37,128 89	2,239 00	66,283 30
Idaho	1,675 00	139 00	58 76		469 34	300 00	74 05	4,231 21		196,372 93
Illinois	62,842 47	11,964 10	431 68	5 30	913 45	271 17	596 90	58,012 61	59,763 00	97,372 53
Indiana	35,307 68	5,191 94	406 41	29 00	213 57	918 86	83 80	94,907 98	27,655 50	34,313 56
Iowa	11,983 65	2,950 60	208 44	37 90	179 71	332 00	130 93	14,523 54	4,274 00	10,991 51
Kansas	1,709 82	1,081 29	192 94		411 78	352 00	949 93	52,689 84	517	51,610 78
Kentucky	29,960 35	11,139 93	765 61	7 95	31 71	565 00	69 50	25,089 25	159,110 30	18,373 30
Louisiana	9,401 64	1,000 00	92 94	23 50	48 69	280 43		9,346 89	10,983 20	70,368 40
Maine	6,421 73	4,964 43	79 63	11 75	27 00	706 37	47 50	37,346 66	13,607 16	117,079 86
Maryland	13,000 24	11,506 90	276 63	23 50	92 84	429 40	18 00	54,546 44	10,765 00	13,657 58
Massachusetts	25,009 16	1,044 90	937 69	11 75	144 15	3,047 40		9,890 39		29,314 99
Minnesota	2,699 47	3,779 71	44 68	19 00	181 91	1,047 81	5 00	19,341 13	1,678 00	30,385 99
Michigan	7,044 39	2,998 11	249 39	16 50	299 44	1,687 38	64 90	34,783 89		64,922 81
Mississippi	5,573 75	7,611 11	517 06	43 10	797 50	66 92	922 64	5,804 35	16,634 35	4,922 61
Missouri	1,675 00	750 00	84 00		17 00	449 30		5,610 33	145 00	5,280 13
Montana	2,125 68	835 00	30 00		35 22	179 17		2,317 45	1,402 32	10,151 68
Nebraska	1,771 51	602 00	84 81		27 00	257 74		5,865 64		5,280 30
Nevada	4,335 04	1,315 00	71 82	3 00	76 11	815 68	40 45	44,362 00	1,044 00	17,046 85
New Hampshire	14,995 00	6,738 23	57	27 00	191 14	189 86		4,651 00	1,328 00	70,612 66
New Jersey	2,398 34	394 99	5 50		14	139 41		298,159 67	27,690 00	7,606 34
New Mexico	66,100 53	41,357 29	463 99	47 50	1,095 11	9,143 49	86 29	57,753 90	13,005 84	376,653 64
New York	16,656 64	7,446 99	412 53	16 23	291 07	1,014 69	44 00	85,023 22	66,438 00	96,911 44
North Carolina	64,129 11	16,726 72	1,091 62	67 41	433 58	3,499 53	87 70	5,247 01	221,301 63	7,063 57
Ohio	2,312 94	68 00	63 34		47 44	297 00	30 50	4,887 01		7,065 57
Oregon	47,278 16	23,376 39	1,179 27	105 14	603 37	4,229 61	315 66	143,855 78	69,924 94	295,386 44
Pennsylvania	2,998 56	1,584 39	118 65		17 89	177 47		10,339 53	971 23	16,715 35
Rhode Island	2,323 84		68		90 41	301 79		11,344 31		18,989 56
South Carolina	14,669 57	7,634 06	317 73	3 00	198 68	1,589 92	330 41	24,227 36	21,542 00	73,081 67
Tennessee										

Texas									
Utah									
Vermont									
Virginia			13,644 00						
Washington									
West Virginia			1,528 00						
Wisconsin			10,488 00						
Wyoming									
Total	2,722,480 06	564,850 18	1,975,336 93	4,376 36	46,453 69	9,810 08	687 99	14,608 91	229,085 56	587,904 16

Statement showing the expenses of collecting the internal-revenue taxes in the several collection-districts, &c.

District.	Compensation.	Stationery and blank-books.	Postage.	Express and dep. money.	Advertising.	Total expenses of collecting.	Expenses of administering office.	Assessments.	Collections.
Alabama	$28,251 73	$29 35	$366 19	$8 29	$269 50	$29,075 96	$29,410 08	$30,935 78	$102,494 75
Arizona	3,498 91	2 50	53 99		117 50	3,672 90	1,905 38	19,633 16	14,238 87
Arkansas	13,814 90	33 28	243 14	40 00	145 00	14,336 32	6,293 97	398,965 83	94,963 85
California	62,799 64	492 62	877 21	3,099 77	682 38	67,946 63	41,932 78	3,908,419 00	2,376,044 88
Colorado	8,174 93	61 32	99 30	19 00	131 00	8,466 15	3,674 93	74,069 92	76,971 56
Connecticut	20,910 88	126 52	422 39	38 92	119 93	21,606 96	3,680 36	1,034,335 78	973,984 97
Dakota	2,179 47		33 00	10 63	97 12	2,320 94	673 81	11,123 28	7,134 90
Delaware	6,814 44	51 29	141 60		13 62	7,020 92	2,389 51	459,162 37	429,403 34
District of Columbia	4,834 25	51 82	71 00	57 89		5,014 67	1,893 55	156,962 58	133,481 38
Florida	6,969 98	71 80	176 57			7,173 35	4,076 58	198,674 18	143,568 30
Georgia	27,949 12	325 62	535 30	30 31	330 00	29,142 10	33,552 63	692,038 63	491,151 31
Idaho	3,874 12	11 90	39 90	292 30	161 50	4,289 73	1,382 18	73,476 98	18,698 50
Illinois	95,757 77	1,333 21	1,661 32	192 61	795 63	99,742 54	45,434 67	19,175,493 14	16,607,333 48
Indiana	66,996 61	449 10	1,329 74	48 53	973 89	69,837 82	27,692 43	7,429,378 15	5,742,309 71
Iowa	27,395 98	46 24	1,238 68	58 57	453 43	29,820 20	10,741 96	1,136,667 77	945,597 17
Kansas	5,178 10	99 25	187 50		337 00	5,464 85	2,935 52	181,531 01	104,789 67
Kentucky	67,346 83	843 17	1,495 81	640 75	37 20	70,723 56	26,795 16	7,231,973 01	5,368,226 98
Louisiana	27,593 97	163 33	62 59	106 84	133 56	27,964 24	17,857 19	1,553,125 57	1,317,660 55
Maine	13,577 74	132 64	376 39	9 63	225 41	14,233 17	2,729 84	276,754 30	914,983 49
Maryland	30,023 65	307 53	434 04	61 40	29 64	31,031 03	16,983 77	3,145,031 38	2,668,463 88
Massachusetts	60,101 84	460 53	697 93	64 07	339 64	62,284 76	29,493 78	4,249,320 73	3,773,817 92
Michigan	28,869 87	253 73	599 63	90 53	116 34	14,060 76	8,312 32	2,308,744 51	1,985,180 47
Minnesota	12,844 11	131 38	324 64	27 53	422 17	14,009 83	12,985 51	260,791 43	297,794 37
Mississippi	41,024 18	228 73	491 82	39 45	338 55	42,133 43	26,947 18	277,989 40	108,794 89
Missouri	41,616 22	286 27	1,961 82	161 60	737 47	47,562 28	26,947 12	4,643,916 12	3,407,800 44
Montana	6,941 16	13 60	39 00		71 50	7,065 98	5,590 00	79,702 31	36,173 15
Nebraska	12,180 67	141 68	399 92	13 56	303 53	12,831 29	9,510 12	532,091 92	305,273 35
Nevada	9,315 00	37 31	121 98	24 63	271 31	9,771 25	7,737 11	84,063 01	63,237 18
New Hampshire	12,141 20	139 63	320 93	11 75	73 13	12,698 63	2,951 98	364,337 08	281,300 14
New Jersey	36,626 83	396 34	545 80	180 66	303 35	37,984 98	17,417 80	2,915,343 08	626,051 08
New Mexico	6,253 43	83 90	61 64	28 52	80 00	6,507 74	3,969 12	38,133 87	42,821 43
New York	214,022 04	1,962 34	3,256 27	270 22	1,061 45	220,572 39	113,599 30	20,600,524 66	19,296,630 43
North Carolina	48,987 85	647 63	790 12	115 74	308 00	50,849 35	33,309 15	1,702,029 86	1,433,161 74
Ohio	117,512 67	1,357 59	1,661 57	191 42	832 65	121,557 91	51,783 74	18,085,140 52	14,671,961 93
Oregon	5,798 60	53 66	83 00		9 75	5,917 31	2,970 97	106,106 747 36	7,545,427 98
Pennsylvania	131,720 61	1,015 93	2,172 10	179 30	901 51	139,005 27	59,428 31	9,030,423 70	7,345,427 91
Rhode Island	9,095 12	28 98	72 00	6 40	66 85	9,278 75	3,073 04	368,389 39	334,552 17
South Carolina	17,368 20	299 39	422 35	38 60	457 35	18,223 12	4,689 04	327,251 65	160,500 38
Tennessee	43,996 21	586 59	521 76	90 80	207 19	45,342 49	20,049 70	1,144,292 51	697,307 19
Texas	35,031 03	303 64	580 47	1,803 10	53 15	38,231 61	20,654 77	454,036 93	306,699 91
Utah	6,850 01	55 63	223 82	61 47	74 10	7,275 62	2,665 50	56,141 33	51,591 95
Vermont		43 55	296 72	11 37	74 31		*668 82	107,301 11	74,001 79
Virginia	58,338 62	74 65	1,111 53	172 18	366 73	60,623 43	33,022 92	2,703,053 45	7,313,015 56

Washington............................	5,857 27	19 08	86 00	91 53	28 00	6,109 66	3,341 83	62,797 11	14,798 21
West Virginia..........................	15,084 38	208 62	320 55	60	257 00	15,894 35	3,680 08	630,649 37	453,008 18
Wisconsin.............................	63,763 60	306 14	514 77	16 15	165 50	24,651 45	11,978 36	2,394,021 02	1,846,028 71
Wyoming..............................	2,570 38	28 25	50 60	27 24	30 00	2,715 47	1,035 84	13,785 13	11,112 99
Grand total.........................	1,590,697 66	16,051 93	27,031 37	8,195 53	13,499 57	1,585,476 98	780,540 49	123,945,980 47	165,238,480 45

REPORT OF THE SIXTH AUDITOR.

OFFICE OF THE AUDITOR OF THE TREASURY
FOR THE POST-OFFICE DEPARTMENT,
October 18, 1873.

SIR : I have the honor to submit the following report of the business operations of this office for the fiscal year ended June 30, 1873. My annual report to the Postmaster-General, now in course of preparation, will exhibit in detail the financial transactions of the Post-Office Department for the past fiscal year.

A comparison of the tables and statements of the present report with those contained in my report for the fiscal year ended June 30, 1872, shows a large increase of business in each division of this Bureau, especially in that of the money-order division.

EXAMINING DIVISION—BENJAMIN LIPPINCOTT, PRINCIPAL EXAMINER.

This division receives and audits the quarterly accounts-current of all post-offices in the United States. It is divided into four subdivisions, viz, the opening-room, the stamp-rooms, the examining corps proper, and the error-rooms.

1. *The opening-room.*—All returns, as soon as received, are opened, and if found in order according to regulations are entered on the register, carefully folded and tied, and then forwarded to the stamp-rooms.

The number of quarterly accounts-current received during each quarter of the fiscal year ended June 30, 1873, was as follows :

Third quarter, 1872... 30,816
Fourth quarter, 1872 31,659
First quarter, 1873.. 31,962
Second quarter, 1873........................... 32,170

       Total... 126,607

2. *The stamp-rooms.*—The quarterly returns received from the opening-room are divided alphabetically among eight stamp-clerks, whose duties consist in comparing the stamp-statements of the postmasters in the accounts-current with their own books and the returns made to them from the stamp-division of the finance office, whence stamp-orders are issued and receipts for the same received and forwarded to the stamp-clerks. The returns thus approved or corrected are passed to the examiners. All accounts from offices of the first and second classes are passed through the various subdivisions of the office in advance of other returns, so that they may reach the chief examiner and his assistants with as little delay as possible.

The number of accounts examined and settled by the stamp-clerks for each quarter of the fiscal year ended June 30, 1873, was as follows :

Third quarter, 1872.. 30,743
Fourth quarter, 1872... 31,358
First quarter, 1873.. 31,464
Second quarter, 1873... 31,574

       Total... 125,139

3. *The examining corps proper* is composed of seventeen clerks, among whom the returns received from the stamp-rooms are divided by sections, each comprising several States or parts of States.

The average number to each section is about 1,700. After the exam ination of the accounts-current and the stamp-account, reviewing and refooting the transcript of mails received, and examining all vouchers belonging to that portion of the work, the balance is drawn on all accounts of the third, fourth, and fifth classes. The returns thus examined and completed are forwarded to the registering division to be entered upon its books.

The number of accounts examined and sent to the registering division for the fiscal year ended June 30, 1873, was as follows:

Third quarter, 1872... 30,743
Fourth quarter, 1872... 31,358
First quarter, 1873.. 31,464
Second quarter, 1873.. 31,574

    Total.. 125 139

The error-rooms contain five clerks, who review and re-examine the error-accounts received from the registering division, and forward to each postmaster a copy of his account, as stated by him, and as audited and corrected by this office.

The number of accounts so corrected and copied for the fiscal year ended June 30, 1873, was as follows:

Third quarter, 1872.. 8,503
Fourth quarter, 1872... 5,809
First quarter, 1873.. 5,870
Second quarter, 1873.. 5,511

    Total.. 25,693

Each subdivision reports weekly to the chief examiner, and monthly through that officer to the chief clerk, the progress of the work, so that the exact amount of labor done by each clerk is clearly ascertained.

All vouchers relative to allowances made by the Post-Office Department for clerk-hire, lights, fuel, rent, stationery, &c., at post-offices of the first and second classes, are forwarded at the beginning of each quarter to the chief examiner and his assistant for examination. A statement is then prepared, showing the vouchers received, the amount allowed and the amount suspended, when found to be in excess of the allowance.

On receipt of the returns from the examiners these accounts are received, and the amount allowable added, and the balance drawn by the chief examiner.

The number of post-offices of the first and second classes which have received allowances for clerk-hire, rent, &c., was 350.

The number of offices of the second class having an allowance for clerk-hire only, was 180.

The number of offices having an allowance for clerk-hire to aid in separating the mails, (independent of the number above stated,) was 445.

Total number of offices of all classes receiving allowances, and approved by the chief examiner, was 975.

The expense-accounts of the offices of the first and second classes were regularly entered by the chief examiner and his assistant on the expense-register, and show quarterly the amount of vouchers received, amount allowed, and amount suspended, copies of which were forwarded to each postmaster.

Attached to the examining division is a corresponding clerk, whose duty consists in corresponding with postmasters relative to errors in their accounts-current and in making day-book entries, &c.

The amount involved in the settlement of the quarterly accounts-current of postmasters during the fiscal year was as follows:

Third quarter, 1872	$5,413,821 91
Fourth quarter, 1872	5,663,617 80
First quarter, 1873	5,913,128 68
Second quarter, 1873	5,891,087 33
Total	22,881,055 72

The labors of the examining division for the fiscal year ended June 30, 1873, have been fully completed. All accounts received in proper form have been examined and passed to the registering division. At no period has the work been more perfect in all its details. Not only has there been a decided improvement in the preparation of returns by postmasters, particularly those of first and second class offices, but, by judicious changes in the office, the efficiency of the examining corps has been greatly increased.

REGISTERING DIVISION—F. I. SEYBOLT, PRINCIPAL REGISTER.

This division receives from the examining division the quarterly accounts-current of postmasters, and re-examines and registers them, placing each item of revenue and expenditure under its appropriate head; noting also, in books prepared for the purpose, corresponding with each register, the amount of letter-postage and stamps reported as remaining on hand in each account. The same books also show the proper amount of newspaper-postage and box-rents chargeable to, and compensation allowed, each office contained therein, and afford a complete check in the settlement of each account.

Upon this division thirteen clerks are employed, and during the fiscal year the number of accounts registered, and amounts involved therein, were as follows:

Third quarter, 1872	31,012	$5,439,393 94
Fourth quarter, 1872	31,548	5,691,418 39
First quarter, 1873	31,818	5,936,597 81
Second quarter, 1873	31,754	5,910,517 46
Total	126,132	22,977,927 60

The number of changes of postmasters, establishment, re-establishment, discontinuance, and change of name of post-offices reported from the appointment office during the fiscal year, and noted by the registers, was as follows:

Third quarter, 1872	2,104
Fourth quarter, 1872	2,359
First quarter, 1873	2,888
Second quarter, 1873	3,621
Total	10,972

The work of this division is fully up to the requirements of the office, the quarterly accounts current received from every office having been registered to the 30th of June, 1873, the footings and recapitulations made, and the books prepared for the registration of the accounts for the quarter ending September 30, 1873.

BOOK-KEEPER'S DIVISION—F. B. LILLEY, PRINCIPAL CLERK.

To this division is assigned the duty of keeping the ledger-accounts of the Department, embracing postmasters, late postmasters, contractors, late contractors, and accounts of a general, special, and miscellaneous nature.

This work requires the services of fifteen clerks, who are employed as follows, viz: One principal book-keeper, in charge of the division and ledger of general accounts; one assistant principal, in charge of cash-book, deposit-book, stamp-journal, ledger of warrants and deposits, and day-book entries on reports approved by the Auditor; one clerk, in charge of the transfer-journal and miscellaneous duties; nine book-keepers of postmasters' accounts, and three of contractors' accounts.

The auxiliary books prepared in this and other divisions, and from which the postings are made quarterly, are as follows: 13 registers of postmasters' quarterly returns, 35 pay-books, 9 journals, 1 register of warrants, 3 registers of Postmaster-General's drafts, 1 stamp-journal, 1 cash-book, 1 deposit-book, 1 Auditor's draft-book, 1 transfer-journal, 1 money-order transfer-book, 12 registers of mail-messenger and special-mail service, 1 route-agent's book, 1 letter-carrier's book, 1 special agent's fare-book; total, 82 books.

The system of transferring debit and credit balances of payments to contractors, of Auditor's drafts counter-credited, &c., embodied one year ago in the transfer-journal, has worked well in practice, enabling the book-keepers to get the items on their ledgers from thirty to sixty days sooner than by the old method of day-book and journal.

Accounts of the first, second, and third classes, and all contractors' accounts, are balanced quarterly; all others at the end of the fiscal year.

* * * * * *

The work of the division is in a most satisfactory condition, and fully up to the requirements of the office.

* * * *

STATING DIVISION—WILLIAM H. GUNNISON, PRINCIPAL CLERK.

The general postal accounts of present and late postmasters are in charge of this division. The number of clerks employed is fifteen.

During each quarter the accounts of present postmasters at offices of the first, second, and third classes, and those of the fourth and fifth classes showing debit balances of $10 or more, have been stated for the preceding quarter from the earliest records made in the office in time to send special instructions for rendering accounts, and for paying the amounts due the United States at the close of the current quarter. The items of the remaining accounts have been stated as soon as they could be obtained from the ledgers. Statements of such of them as showed debit balances of $1 or more, when stated and balanced with the ledgers (as usual) to the close of the last fiscal year, were sent to postmasters, with special instructions, before December 31, 1872.

The accounts of late postmasters have been revised *monthly* to secure the earliest possible adjustment, and all such accounts have been fully stated to the latest dates, in advance of the time usually allowed, that the results may be used in the annual report of the office to the Postmaster-General.

Special attention has been given to cases showing neglect or failure to comply with the instructions, especially those relating to indebtedness.

The addition of one clerk, and the reduction of the work on several of the sections, has partially removed the inequality formerly existing, and has promoted the general efficiency of the division.

Reference to the following statements will show the increase in the number of the accounts during the year, and also in the miscellaneous work of the division. It is only just to say that the accounts were never in so good a condition as at the present time.

Statement of the number of the general accounts of present postmasters, the increase in the number, and the classification of the offices, for the fiscal year ended June 30, 1873.

Number of section.	States and Territories.	Draft-offices. First, second, and third classes.	Draft-offices. Fourth and fifth classes.	Deposit-offices. First, second, and third classes.	Deposit-offices. Fourth and fifth classes.	Collection-offices. First, second, and third classes.	Collection-offices. Fourth and fifth classes.	Special offices. Fourth and fifth classes.	Number in each State and Territory.	Number in each State or Territory.	Increase in each State and Territory.	Increase in each section.	Number of accounts of first, second, and third classes in each section.	Number of accounts of fourth and fifth classes in each section.
1	Maine	5	3	8	120	11	680	37	864					
	New Hampshire	7	....	8	52	8	337	12	424					
	Vermont	10	4	2	76	7	365	16	480		7			
	Massachusetts	12	1	39	119	41	504	20	736	2,504	29	36	158	2,346
	Total	34	8	57	367	67	1,886	85						
2	New York, A to S	31	....	34	403	71	1,628	227		2,394		21	138	2,256
	Total	31		34	403	71	1,628	227						
3	Pennsylvania, A to R	9	1	36	135	41	2,097	13		2,332		55	86	2,246
	Total	9	1	36	135	41	2,097	13						
4	Wisconsin	2	....	8	81	36	973	70	1,170		25			
	West Virginia	1	....	2	25	5	612	14	659		31			
	Rhode Island	2	....	4	10	4	80	2	102					
	Connecticut	8	....	14	92	18	281	26	429	2,360	8	64	104	2,256
	Total	13		28	198	63	1,946	112						
5	North Carolina	2	....		51	7	843	22	925		86			
	South Carolina	1	....	4	16	7	359	7	394					
	Georgia	2	....	2	42	18	513	41	616		54			
	Alabama	1	....	4	65	9	618	16	713	2,650	35	175	57	2,593
	Total	6		10	174	41	2,333	86						
6	Kansas	1	....	8	79	23	697	70	878		89			
	Minnesota	2	....	6	54	10	631	58	761		39			
	Alaska		....		3				3		*1			
	Arizona		....			2	31		33		4			
	Colorado	1	....	3	9	5	122	10	150		16			
	Dakota		....		7	2	80	6	95		17			
	Idaho		....		1	2	53	2	58		14			
	Montana		....		1	4	79	10	94		2			
	New Mexico		....			2	46		48		2			
	Utah		....		8	3	143	12	166		10			
	Washington		....		3	2	114	10	129		13			
	Wyoming		....	2	17		4	6	29	2,444	3	208	78	2,366
	Total	4		19	182	55	2,000	184						
7	Ohio	11	....	10	182	76	174	89	2,089		19			
	Oregon		....		6	5	197	22	230		14			
	Nevada		....	1	10	7	49	10	77	2,396	5	38	110	2,286
	Total	11		11	198	88	1,967	121						
8	Illinois	6		26	455	89	1,187	27	1,780		36			
	New Jersey	2		17	87	23	467	23	619	2,408	24	60	162	2,246
	Total	8		43	542	111	1,654	50						
9	California			5	82	17	492	31	627		35			
	Missouri			3	71	40	1,188	141	1,443	2,070	*38	*3	65	2,005
	Total			8	153	57	1,680	172						

* Decrease.

Statement of the number of the general accounts of present postmasters, &c.—Continued.

Number of section.	States and Territories.	Draft-offices. First, second, and third classes.	Draft-offices. Fourth and fifth classes.	Deposit-offices. First, second, and third classes.	Deposit-offices. Fourth and fifth classes.	Collection offices. First, second, and third classes.	Collection offices. Fourth and fifth classes.	Special offices. Fourth and fifth classes.	Number in each State and Territory.	Number in each State and Territory.	Increase in each State and Territory.	Decrease in each section.	Number of accounts of first, second, and third classes in each section.	Number of accounts of fourth and fifth classes in each section.
10	Texas	2	....	1	75	17	654	9	758	....	79	....	....	....
	Mississippi	..	....	15	93	4	393	6	511	....	45	....	....	....
	Kentucky	3	....	..	107	19	825	53	1,007	2,276	17	141	61	2,225
	Total	5	....	16	275	40	1,872	68	....	....	....	....	....	....
11	Virginia	2	....	1	79	19	1,113	40	1,274	....	88	....	....	....
	Maryland	..	....	6	34	6	509	13	568	....	6	....	....	....
	New York, T to Z	2	....	5	66	13	267	25	378	....	7	....	....	....
	Nebraska	1	....	..	43	7	398	54	433	2,653	60	161	62	2,591
	Total	5	....	12	222	45	2,237	132	....	....	....	....	....	....
12	Delaware	1	....	1	9	2	87	1	101	....	7	....	....	....
	District of Columbia	..	....	2	..	..	3	..	5	....	*2	....	....	....
	Indiana	10	....	9	81	36	1,238	71	1,445	....	3	....	....	....
	Pennsylvania, S to Z	4	....	8	55	15	612	12	706	2,257	39	47	88	2,169
	Total	15	....	20	145	53	1,940	84	....	....	....	....	....	....
13	Iowa	16	....	9	136	38	1,108	50	1,360	....	82	....	....	....
	Michigan	11	....	7	101	47	912	34	1,113	2,473	6	88	128	2,395
	Total	27	....	16	237	85	2,020	84	....	....	....	....	....	....
14	Tennessee	3	....	2	109	12	739	92	957	....	25	....	....	....
	Arkansas	2	....	..	19	3	520	37	581	....	9	....	....	....
	Florida	1	....	3	9	1	160	7	181	....	31	....	....	....
	Louisiana	..	....	1	18	5	276	18	318	2,037	33	198	33	2,004
	Total	6	....	6	155	21	1,695	154	....	....	....	....	....	....

* Decrease.

Number of general postal accounts first, second, and third classes............ 1,328
Number of general postal accounts fourth and fifth classes................. 31,926

Whole number of general postal accounts for fiscal year..................... 33,254
Whole number of general postal accounts for fiscal year ended June 30, 1872 . 32,065

Increase during fiscal year.......... 1,189
Increase during fiscal year ended June 30, 1872............................. 1,741

Statement showing the number of changes, and the condition of general postal accounts of late postmasters for and during the fiscal year ended June 30, 1873.

Changes reported to this office weekly by the First Assistant Postmaster-General, recorded for the fiscal year.	Third quarter, 1872.	Fourth quarter, 1872.	First quarter, 1873.	Second quarter, 1873.	Total number during the year.
Established	454	370	493	591	1,908
Re-established	130	132	157	140	559
Discontinued	269	266	219	306	1,060
New bonds	79	176	248	383	886
Miscellaneous, removals, resignations, &c.	1,319	1,567	2,179	1,865	6,930
Total	2,251	2,511	3,296	3,285	11,343

Number of section.	Number of accounts of late postmasters adjusted on each section.	Number of accounts of late postmasters unadjusted on each section.	Number of section.	Number of accounts of late postmasters adjusted on each section.	Number of accounts of late postmasters unadjusted on each section.
1	200	236	8	546	458
2	300	279	9	223	452
3	181	400	10	515	468
4	394	720	11	614	452
5	623	476	12	452	480
6	777	558	13	568	535
7	439	363	14	608	577

Number of late accounts adjusted for the fiscal year............................ 6,523
Number of late accounts unadjusted for the fiscal year 5,994

Total 12,517
Number of late accounts adjusted for the fiscal year 1872 3,262
Number of late accounts unadjusted for the fiscal year 1872 4,776
                                      8,038

Increase 4,479

Miscellaneous statements.	Third quarter, 1872.	Fourth quarter, 1872	First quarter, 1873.	Second quarter, 1873	Total.
Letters received..................................	*	482	558	511	1,551
Letters written, correspondence in special cases	123	262	166	118	609
General accounts, circulars, &c., received	*	*	1,250	1,500	1,750
Circulars sent in answer to letters received, and in special cases..	889	442	606	715	2,672
Reports made to Post-Office Department—delinquencies.........	90	43	243	157	533

* No record.

COLLECTING DIVISION—E. J. EVANS, PRINCIPAL CLERK.

The duties of this division are to collect balances due from late and present postmasters throughout the United States, and to attend to the final settlement of the same.

The number of clerks employed is twenty, apportioned as follows:

On Correspondence, 4. Their duties are to correspond in relation to postmasters', late postmasters', and contractors' accounts, with a view to the collection of balances due to the Department, and to submit, for suit, accounts of defaulting late postmasters and contractors.

On Drafts, 1. His duties are to locate and issue drafts for the collection of balances due by postmasters and contractors; record the same in the draft-register, and to report to the Post-Office Department for payment all balances due to late postmasters, and record the same in a book kept for that purpose.

On Changes, 1. His duties are to record all changes of postmasters reported to this office from the Post-Office Department; to enter and file drafts paid; to record all accounts of late postmasters in the book of balances; and to state the final action thereon.

On Letter-books, 2. Their duties are to record all letters written, and address and transmit the same, together with all circulars received by them from the corresponding clerks.

On Miscellaneous, 1. His duties are to examine and compare with the ledgers all accounts of late postmasters, and close the same as "un-collectible" or by "suspense," and to assist in the preparation of the annual report to the Postmaster-General.

On Copying, 14. Their duties are to copy all accounts of postmasters and others, and transmit the same in their respective circulars; to copy changes of postmasters; to prepare salary-books of the various post-offices in the country; to assist in the adjustment of salaries, and to furnish a portion of the material for the United States Official Register.

The regulation of the Department requiring current business to be dispatched on the day received is observed by the division generally, but particularly by the gentlemen on correspondence.

* * * * * * *

LAW DIVISION—J. BOZMAN KERR, PRINCIPAL CLERK.

To this division is assigned the duty of preparing for suit, and trans-mitting to the Department of Justice, accounts of late postmasters and contractors who fail to pay their indebtedness to the United States upon the drafts of the Department.

The number of accounts and accompanying papers certified for suit during the fiscal year was as follows:

Quarter ended September 30, 1872	35	$19,545 32
Quarter ended December 31, 1872	20	10,806 02
Quarter ended March 31, 1873	26	15,412 25
Quarter ended June 30, 1873	30	9,950 37
Total	111	55,714 56

Amount of collections on judgments, including interest.................. $25,338 34

All accounts received from the collecting division have been prepared for suit and sent to the Department of Justice.

FOREIGN-MAIL DIVISION—ISAAC W. NICHOLLS, PRINCIPAL CLERK.

This division has charge of all postal accounts between the United States and foreign governments, and making up the accounts of steam-ship companies for ocean transportation of mails when not paid by subsidy.

* * * * * * *

Amounts reported for payment of balances due foreign governments on settlement of the accounts for the quarters named, together with the cost in currency,

To—	Quarter ended.	Amount in gold.
United Kingdom of Great Britain and Ireland	June 30, 1871	$14,982 13
	Sept. 30, 1871	15,589 26
	Dec. 31, 1871	13,242 14
	Mar. 31, 1872	16,550 71
	June 30, 1872	14,222 12
	Sept. 30, 1872	13,782 05
Total		88,369 41
Costing, in currency		93,370 67
German Union	Sept. 30, 1871	31,189 47
	Dec. 31, 1871	27,205 67
	Mar. 31, 1872	33,371 23
	June 30, 1872	27,624 66
	Sept. 30, 1872	25,268 33
	Dec. 31, 1872	27,283 62
	Mar. 31, 1873	33,056 24
Total		208,602 22
Costing, in currency		228,869 29

Amounts reported for payment of balances due foreign governments, &c.—Continued.

To—	Quarter ended.	Amount.
Belgium	June 30, 1871	$1,533 24
	Sep. 30, 1871	1,580 65
	Dec. 31, 1871	1,815 74
	Mar. 31, 1872	2,034 96
	June 30, 1872	1,917 38
	Sept. 30, 1872	1,974 55
	Dec. 31, 1872	1,937 35
Total		12,817 92
Costing, in currency		14,508 69
Denmark, for extra national postage	Mar. 31, 1872 } 412 05	
	June 30, 1872 }	
	Sept. 30, 1872	707 90
	Dec. 31, 1872	787 69
Total....................................		1,907 64
Costing, in currency		2,388 98
Total amount reported		311,175 19
Costing, in currency		349,137 03

The following amounts have been paid, in gold, by the governments named:

By—	Quarter ended.	Amount.
Switzerland...	Mar. 31, 1872	$1,958 65
	June 30, 1872	1,941 44
	Sept. 30, 1872	3,401 64
	Dec. 31, 1872	2,084 94
Total		9,385 67
Netherlands...	Mar. 31, 1872	359 60
	June 30, 1872	678 04
	Sept. 30, 1872	587 10
	Dec. 31, 1872	1,032 31
Total		2,657 05
Italy...	Dec. 31, 1871	1,142 56
	Mar. 31, 1872	1,523 82
	June 30, 1872	1,037 05
	Sept. 31, 1872	507 50
Total		4,210 93
Total amount received, in gold.................		16,253 65

PAY DIVISION—A. E. BOONE, PRINCIPAL CLERK.

This division has in charge the settlement and payment of all accounts for transportation of the mails, including railroad companies, steamboat companies, and other mail-contractors, special mail-carriers, mail-messengers, railway postal clerks, route-agents, special agents, letter-carriers, and all miscellaneous payments.

To this division is also assigned the registration of all warrants and drafts countersigned by the Auditor, and the custody of the archives pertaining to all branches of the office.

Accounts of contractors settled during the fiscal year ending June 30, 1873.

Quarter.	Number.	Amount.
In the quarter ended September 30, 1872............................	7,288	$3,087,195 98
In the quarter ended December 31, 1872...........................	7,370	3,377,008 65
In the quarter ended March 31, 1873..............................	7,315	3,475,339 50
In the quarter ended June 30, 1873...............................	7,362	3,534,011 66
Total...	29,336	13,473,555 79
Foreign mail accounts settled in the fiscal year	153	1,054,053 89
Collection orders sent out to postmasters:		
In the quarter ended September 30, 1872...........................	24,728	639,435 48
In the quarter ended December 31, 1872...........................	24,884	767,579 18
In the quarter ended March 31, 1873..............................	24,856	838,427 94
In the quarter ended June 30, 1873...............................	25,997	768,521 49
Total...	100,465	3,013,962 99
Mail-messenger service:		
Accounts settled during the fiscal year:		
In the quarter ended September 30, 1872...........................	3,057	121,387 04
In the quarter ended December 31, 1872...........................	3,259	125,462 45
In the quarter ended March 31, 1873..............................	3,285	136,850 38
In the quarter ended June 30, 1873...............................	3,308	130,416 21
Total...	12,909	514,116 08
Warrants issued by the Postmaster-General and countersigned by the Auditor, passed, and registered:		
In the quarter ended September 30, 1872...........................	1,767	2,283,812 32
In the quarter ended December 31, 1872...........................	1,975	2,457,098 47
In the quarter ended March 31, 1873..............................	2,119	2,484,144 32
In the quarter ended June 30, 1873...............................	2,108	2,485,695 63
Total...	7,969	9,710,750 74
Drafts issued by the Postmaster-General and countersigned by the Auditor, passed, and registered:		
In the quarter ended September 30, 1872...........................	4,676	706,541 83
In the quarter ended December 31, 1872...........................	4,703	634,915 33
In the quarter ended March 31, 1873..............................	4,904	764,188 43
In the quarter ended June 30, 1873...............................	4,615	649,246 04
Total...	18,896	2,754,891 63
Railway postal clerks, route, and other agents:		
In the quarter ended September 30, 1872...........................	1,835	433,123 63
In the quarter ended December 31, 1872...........................	1,880	447,841 58
In the quarter ended March 31, 1873..............................	2,067	465,955 61
In the quarter ended June 30, 1873...............................	2,224	483,973 56
Total...	8,006	1,830,894 38
Miscellaneous accounts:		
In the quarter ended September 30, 1872...........................	143	207,469 46
In the quarter ended December 31, 1872...........................	167	227,383 17
In the quarter ended March 31, 1873..............................	208	283,543 11
In the quarter ended June 30, 1873...............................	169	283,699 90
Total...	687	10,002,095 64
Accounts of letter-carriers:		
In the quarter ended September 30, 1872...........................	1,587	54,204 09
In the quarter ended December 31, 1872...........................	1,782	359,402 62
In the quarter ended March 31, 1873..............................	1,649	352,826 21
In the quarter ended June 30, 1873...............................	1,589	353,342 21
Salary of special agent paid out of appropriation for letter-carriers.............	....	2,720 35
Total...	6,607	1,422,495 48
Accounts of special mail-carriers:		
In the quarter ended September 30, 1872...........................	1,452	12,018 71
In the quarter ended December 31, 1872...........................	1,442	12,134 52
In the quarter ended March 31, 1873..............................	1,437	12,932 35
In the quarter ended June 30, 1873...............................	1,464	12,217 80
Total...	5,795	49,303 38
Accounts of special agents:		
In the quarter ended September 30, 1872...........................	195	46,771 26
In the quarter ended December 31, 1872...........................	221	55,894 12
In the quarter ended March 31, 1873..............................	196	50,579 05
In the quarter ended June 30, 1873...............................	215	55,912 53
Total...	827	209,086 96

MONEY-ORDER DIVISION—JOHN LYNCH, PRINCIPAL CLERK.

Number.

Domestic money-order statements received, examined, and registered during the fiscal year, as follows:

Quarter ended September 30, 1872	34,942
Quarter ended December 31, 1872	33,183
Quarter ended March 31, 1873	33,180
Quarter ended June 30, 1873	33,174
Total	134,479

British international money-order statements received, examined, and registered during the fiscal year:

Quarter ended September 30, 1872	9,714
Quarter ended December 31, 1872	11,088
Quarter ended March 31, 1873	11,088
Quarter ended June 30, 1873	11,088
Total	42,978

Swiss international money-order statements received, examined, and registered during the fiscal year:

Quarter ended September 30, 1872	1,963
Quarter ended December 31, 1872	1,812
Quarter ended March 31, 1873	1,812
Quarter ended June 30, 1873	1,812
Total	7,399

German international money-order statements received, examined, and registered during the fiscal year:

Quarter ended December 31, 1872	6,012
Quarter ended March 31, 1873	6,012
Quarter ended June 30, 1873	6,012
Total	18,036

	Number.	Amount.
Domestic money-orders issued during the fiscal year	3,355,686	$57,516,214 69
British international money-orders issued during the fiscal year	69,592	1,364,476 32
Swiss international money-orders issued during the fiscal year	2,801	78,313 93
German international money-orders issued during the fiscal year	19,454	420,722 12
Domestic money-orders paid, received, examined, assorted, checked, and filed during the fiscal year	3,314,818	56,900,351 23
British international money-orders paid, received, examined, assorted, checked, and filed during the fiscal year	10,486	215,087 01
Swiss international money-orders paid, received, examined, assorted, checked, and filed during the fiscal year	600	16,809 58
German international money-orders paid, received, examined, assorted, checked, and filed during the fiscal year	11,613	310,108 26

Certificates of deposit registered, compared, and entered during the fiscal year:

	Number.	Amount.
Quarter ended September 30, 1872	40,427	
Quarter ended December 31, 1872	42,576	
Quarter ended March 31, 1873	46,119	
Quarter ended June 30, 1873	46,184	
Total	175,306	49,049,503 28

Transfers registered compared and filed during the fiscal year:

	Number.	Amount.
Quarter ended September 30, 1872	1,746	
Quarter ended December 31, 1872	1,712	
Quarter ended March 31, 1873	1,504	
Quarter ended June 30, 1873	1,747	
Total	6,709	$1,202,186 68

Drafts registered during the fiscal year:

	Number.	Amount.
Quarter ended September 30, 1872	2,313	
Quarter ended December 31, 1872	2,663	
Quarter ended March 31, 1873	2,373	
Quarter ended June 30, 1873	2,720	
Total	10,069	5,002,715 00

* * * * * * *

In concluding this report I am gratified to say that the work performed by the employés in my Bureau has been done with alacrity and promptness, and, I think, to the satisfaction of the Post-Office Department and the public generally. To the energy and efficiency of my chief clerk, Mr. J. M. McGrew, and the heads of the divisions, I am greatly indebted for these results.

Very respectfully, your obedient servant,

J. J. MARTIN,
Auditor.

Hon. WILLIAM A. RICHARDSON,
Secretary of the Treasury.

REPORT OF THE TREASURER.

TREASURY OF THE UNITED STATES,
WASHINGTON, *November* 1, 1873.

SIR: For the thirteenth time since I came in charge of this office, it has become my duty, by virtue of statutory law and of Departmental regulations, to make a full and correct exhibit and statement to the Secretary of the Treasury of the actual condition of the Treasury of the United States, as it truly appeared from the books of this office at the close of business on the thirtieth day of June, one thousand eight hundred and seventy-three.

The statements and tables hereto appended will fully exhibit not only the actual condition of this office at the close of the fiscal year on the aforesaid day, but its movement for the year preceding; and show the actual amount of moneys received, and from what sources received, and the actual amount of disbursements, and for what purposes disbursed, in said fiscal year.

I have also taken the liberty to make such suggestions as have occurred to me in regard to the future conduct and management of the office; and have perhaps gone beyond what is expected or required of me, by making some remarks in regard to the currency and the finances of the country.

If therein I have transgressed, I hope for forgiveness therefor.

On comparing the tables of "*Receipts*" and of "*Expenditures*," that appear at the beginning of the appendix, hereto annexed, with the like tables in my report of the preceding year, it will appear that there has been a large falling off in the receipts, amounting to $28,280,764.07 on *Customs*, and to $16,912,863.58 on *Internal Revenue*.

This decrease in the revenue is mainly due to the great reduction of taxation in both of these, the main sources of national income, that was made by the last Congress, which was demanded by the people, and has received their sanction and approval.

But, unfortunately, it will also appear from further inspection, that the expenditures are largely in excess of those for the preceding year. This increase of expenditures is mainly due to the large appropriations made by the last Congress in excess of the estimates made by the several Executive Departments of the Government. The falling off of the receipts, and the increase of expenditures, have put a check upon the rate per annum at which the public debt was paid off in preceding years. These facts combined make an interesting subject for reflection, the study of which will make a good guide, if not a warning, to Congresst and the administrative officers as well, of the course that should be pursued in the future. Either taxation must be increased, an expedient that can hardly be thought of, or the appropriations must be kept largely below the receipts. Otherwise the rapid reduction of the public debt will be arrested, if not abandoned.

INTERCHANGEABILITY OF UNITED STATES NOTES AND BONDS.

Few, if any, believe that the volume of the circulating medium, as fixed by law, stands at an amount that is exactly right. The people are divided into two parties, holding directly opposite opinions; the one, judging from the difficulty of procuring sufficient money, at certain seasons of the year, to move the crops and other products, contending that there should be a large increase; the other, knowing that at other times there is a plethora of currency that for the time being drives men into the wildest speculations, insisting that the volume of the circulating medium should be greatly reduced, through which speculations would be checked, and a return to specie payments thereby be speedily and easily assured.

Now, both are, from their respective stand-points, entirely correct; and yet, paradoxical as it may seem, both are wrong.

It must be obvious to all who have an interest in, and who have watched the course of, the business and financial relations of the country, that there are times when the real wants of the country demand and there should be an increase of currency; and that there are other times, when the safety of all legitimate business requires that it should be largely reduced. What is really needed is a currency so flexible as to, at all times, accommodate itself to the real business wants of the whole country.

The greatest objection to an exclusively metallic currency is its want of elasticity. That there are regularly recurring times when the wants of legitimate trade require an expansion of the circulating medium to an amount much greater than is necessary at other times, is a fact that is patent to all observing business men. When the times arrive for the purchase of the crops and other products of the country, and for their transportation from the interior to the sea-board and a market, immense amounts of currency are imperatively demanded for the purpose, which, when the mission is accomplished, are not wanted for any legitimate purposes of trade and commerce; and therefore seek, for the time being, other channels of profitable use. Unfortunately, not being needed as a medium for the interchange of values, this then redundancy of the currency is driven into channels of wild speculation in fancy stocks and visionary enterprises. Here it is stranded; and when again needed for the real wants of the people, for the proper transaction of the business of the country, it cannot be had, and the staple commodities and crops that then seek a market are hindered and kept back, through which all classes of people are injured and damaged.

It has, perhaps, not occurred to every one who has not studied the subject, that during the suspension of specie payments, and when the amount of paper money is limited to a certain sum, as ours is, by law, the rigidity or want of flexibility and elasticity of such currency is greater, and consequently more injurious to the interest of the people than a metallic currency can possibly be. Coin always flows to the countries where it is appreciated and most wanted. So, in case of need, it would flow in from other countries in exchange for our surplus products. An irredeemable paper currency, on the contrary, is confined exclusively to the country that issues it; and when the amount is fixed and unalterable, for all the year round, the effect is that at certain times of the year, as is the case now, it is altogether insufficient for the genuine purposes of trade and commerce, and for bringing forward the great staples of the country, wherewith to pay our debts and enrich the country by bringing the balance of trade in our favor.

At other seasons of the year nothing like the legally fixed quantity of currency is needed; neither can it be used for any legitimate purposes. At such times the holders, naturally desirous to "turn an honest penny," finding all the legitimate avenues of trade closed, either engage in speculations themselves, or place their money at interest with corporations and individuals, who too often use it for purposes that, in point of morality, are but little removed from ordinary gambling and downright swindling.

Partially by the force and more by the abuse of law, the arrangement between the country banks and those located in cities, where the redemption of the circulating notes of national banks is required to be made, has originated nearly all the evils that have, from time to time, deranged the business and financial affairs of the country. Banks, in certain locations, are permitted by law to have their redemption agencies in interior cities. These, in turn, have theirs in the large cities on the Atlantic coast, principally in the city of New York. Certain amounts of the legal-tender reserves of the interior banks are permitted by law to be deposited with their redemption agencies. This forms a nucleus around which larger amounts, above what is required for the reserve deposits, accumulate. For all these deposits interest is allowed. In times of partial stagnation of business, which always occur at certain seasons of the year, money accumulates in country banks. These banks being unable, at those times, to make more profitable use of their funds, send them to their redemption agencies in order to make and receive interest thereon. The city banks, particularly those in the city of New York, are thus flooded with money at the very time, and for the reason that there is then no legitimate use for it anywhere. The city banks being obliged to pay interest on these enormous deposits, look around for some profitable employment of these funds. They find it most convenient, for their present interest, to loan them on notes subject to call, with all kinds of stocks as collaterals. Soon the times change, the business season returns, and money, in large amounts, is now required to move the crops and staple commodities that seek a market. The

16 Ab

money being locked up, or perhaps swamped in disastrous schemes and wild speculations, cannot be had for the purposes of legitimate trade and commerce that then so much need it, and for the want thereof these languish, to the great injury of the people of the whole country.

For these notorious evils a remedy should be found and interposed. In looking over the whole ground, no scheme has presented itself that would be so likely to accomplish the end in view as the authorization by Congress of the issue of a certain amount of legal-tender notes, that could at all times be converted into a currency interest-bearing stock of the United States, and for which the holder of such stock so authorized could at pleasure at any time receive legal-tender notes, with the accrued interest, from the day of issue of such stock to the day of its redemption. It is believed that a rate of interest no higher than $3\frac{65}{100}$ per cent. will be high enough to absorb the desired amount of the circulation when not needed for commercial purposes, and low enough to force the return of the bonds in exchange for legal-tender notes at the times when the business wants of the country shall require more currency.

This rate of interest, being just one cent a day for the use of one hundred dollars, would be popular with the masses of the people, because of the ease with which interest could be computed on any amount for the known number of days that a bond may have run. It is very probable that the legally authorized amount of four hundred million dollars of legal-tender notes need not be increased in order to carry out this scheme; and it is more than likely that under the then changed condition of the currency, with no tendency to go into wild projects and stock speculations, the minimum amount of three hundred and fifty-six million dollars would, on account of its being readily obtained in exchange for the proposed stocks, be sufficient for the easy transaction of the legitimate business of the country at times when commercial wants shall need the largest amount. It is believed that with this new attribute of the legal-tender notes, the parties who are now so clamorous for more paper currency will become satisfied that no more is needed; and that those who believe that it is mischievously redundant and a hinderance to the resumption of specie payments, will have opportunity to judge of the correctness of their preconceived opinions.

In addition to the urgent economical reasons, there are strong moral ones why the legal-tender notes should again be made to be convertible into United States stocks. The first issues of these notes bore the following legend upon their backs: "This note is a legal tender for all debts, public and private, except duties on imports and interest on the public debt, *and is exchangeable for United States six per cent. twenty years' bonds*, redeemable at the pleasure of the United States after five years."

These notes, so indorsed, were issued by virtue of and in accordance with the acts of February 25, 1862, and of July 11, 1862. By the act of March 3, 1863, the right of the holders of these notes to so convert them was made to cease and determine on the first day of July then following. The disavowal by the Government of this obligation was, no doubt, influenced by the fact that on the day of the passage of the last-named act gold was quoted at 171 per cent. It was a war measure, and was considered as a thing necessary to be done, at a time when the life of the republic was in peril. On no other ground could such an act be justified. There is no longer any such necessity, and it would seem to be but fair and just that the attribute of the convertibility of these notes into a stock of the United States should be restored. The privilege of the reconvertibility of the stock into notes would, perhaps, be an equivalent for the lower rate of interest that it is now proposed to allow, below that fixed by former laws. Should the national banks be permitted to hold the proposed new bonds in part, or for the full amount of the legal-tender reserves required of them by existing laws, it would go far to prevent the pernicious practice on their part of paying interest on deposits.

This practice has been, and will continue to be, unless inhibited by force of law, the main source of all the financial troubles that have of late years disturbed and damaged all the business relations of the country. Banks were created for the purpose of loaning money, for the more easy transaction of business, and not for the purpose of borrowing it for purposes of speculation, and thus blocking the channels of legitimate trade and commerce. So long as they confine themselves to this, their legitimate business, they benefit themselves and the community as well. But the moment they reverse the machinery and become borrowers instead of lenders of money, they not only put their own interests in peril, but they become instruments of great danger to everybody within their influence.

This practice on the part of national banks of paying interest on deposits, and especially that of one bank allowing interest on the deposits of another, whether they be permitted to hold the proposed bonds as a part of their reserves or not, should be forbidden by law, under the severe penalty of the forfeiture of their charters.

Objection will, no doubt, be made to the new attribute proposed to be given to the legal-tender notes, on the ground that interest will have to be paid on that part of them which will be represented by the proposed stock. The minimum amount of legal-tender notes, $356,000,000, is now a loan from the people to the Government without interest. Should the plan proposed be adopted, it is believed that at times the part of these notes represented by stocks would amount to $150,000,000, and that at other times it would not be more than one-half that amount. This would bring the average amount at interest to about $112,000,000. If the maximum of $400,000,000, authorized by law, should be issued, it would reduce the amount on the difference of interest to be paid by $44,000,000, being an average of $68,000,000 on which interest would have to be paid. This at 3$\frac{65}{100}$ per cent. would amount to $2,482,000 per annum.

The whole circulation issued by the Government, including the fractional currency, would then be about four hundred and forty million dollars, on which the interest at five per cent. would be twenty-two million dollars. Deducting the amount of currency interest that would probably be paid on the contemplated new bonds as aforesaid, it would still leave over nineteen and a half million of dollars as the saving of gold interest by reason of this large loan by the people to the Government, on which the latter pays no interest. The apparent loss of less than two and a half million dollars in currency to the people, who would hold the stock, would be a mere trifle as compared with the great gain that would accrue to the whole country in consequence of the better circulating medium that would be introduced, and which, it is believed, would protect them in the future from "corners" of all kinds, and from financial convulsions like the one that has just now swept over the whole country like a tornado. This could not have happened had there been an elastic and flexible, instead of our present rigid and unyielding, currency. There is scarce a doubt but this financial revulsion has cost the people in the aggregate hundreds of millions of dollars, to say nothing of the loss of revenue to the Government.

There are, no doubt, those who suppose it to be their interest to have money matters remain as they now are, who prefer a state of suspension and unsettled values to the resumption of specie payments and a fixed standard for the measure of exchangeable commodities, on the ground that a return to specie payments would make money scarce, and thus produce a great shrinkage in all values. These may dismiss their fears. An irredeemable currency, fixed as to amount, rigid, like ours, makes an uncertain measure of commodities, while a circulating medium that is elastic, with gold for the standard, insures one that is more uniform and equitable for both buyer and seller. Besides, resumption would not necessarily reduce the volume of paper money; but it would certainly increase the aggregate circulation of the country by the amount of gold and silver coin that would thereby be added to it. Expansion, rather than contraction, would be a much likelier consequence as the result of the resumption of specie payments.

Should, however, the maximum of legal-tender notes authorized by law be found to be inadequate and insufficient to prevent the brigands and banditti who infest our money-marts, and who at times conspire against the public weal by " *lock-ups*," making money scarce when most needed for business purposes, thereby robbing whole communities to enrich themselves, the Secretary of the Treasury might be authorized by law, in such case, or at any other time, when the exigencies of the Treasury may require the same, to issue an additional limited amount of such convertible legal-tender notes in exchange for any United States six per cent. stocks, allowing on and paying on such six per cent. stocks, on such exchange, the average price borne by them on actual sales thereof in the open stock-market in the city of New York for the three business days next preceding such purchase and exchange.

Should this become necessary and be done, the saving of interest on the six per cent. bonds would probably more than equal the interest that would be paid on the new bonds, into which legal-tender notes are to be made convertible, as hereinbefore proposed; thus not only making the interest on the public debt less than would otherwise be paid, but making a part of it payable in currency to our own people at home, instead of in gold to foreigners abroad.

The Postmaster-General has done me the honor to consult with me in regard to a scheme that he proposes to recommend to Congress, for the passage of a law authorizing the creation of a United States savings institution, under the joint management of the Post-Office and the Treasury Departments. By this plan, which, in some shape, has been adopted in Great Britain and in other countries, all persons will be enabled to deposit with postmasters in all parts of the country amounts of money for which, when received at the Treasury, will be issued to them currency interest-bearing bonds of a like character as hereinbefore described. As this would change a large amount of the indebtedness of the nation from six per cent. gold interest-bearing bonds to others bearing a lower rate of interest, payable in currency, thus making a great saving to the nation, and, at the same time, giving to all the people, who choose to avail themselves of its benefits, a place of safe deposit where they will be able to receive interest on their surplus means, and as it will be an auxiliary and a help in the project before indicated for the improvement of the currency, the plan commends itself strongly to my judgment as one that would not only be of great benefit to the individual depositors, who would at all times be able to receive their deposits, with the accrued interest, but to the people of the whole country as well.

Should the plans herein proposed go into operation, they would, no doubt, on the one hand, arrest the wild schemes of visionaries, who contract large debts abroad, for which there is a continuous drain on this country for the payment of the interest, on their unproductive undertakings, and on the other hand would facilitate the early and rapid transportation of the staple products of the country to the sea-board, for exportation to a foreign and profitable market. Both combined would soon bring the balance of trade largely in our favor. After which it would require no statutory enactments to enforce a return to specie payments. The natural laws of trade and commerce will, under such circumstances, bring about the desired resumption in a way peculiar to themselves; and the transition from a state of suspension, to that of honest specie payments, will be so easy, that the world will wonder why it did not take place before.

With a paper currency as proposed, secured as ours is, that will at all times adjust and accommodate itself to the real business wants of the country, and made still more elastic by the return to specie payments, and thus being at all times convertible into coin at the pleasure of the holder, the country will possess a circulating medium superior to that of any that has ever been known to any nation of the earth.

DISBURSING-OFFICERS' CHECKS.

The act of Congress, passed May 2, 1866, entitled "An act to facilitate the settlement of the accounts of the Treasurer of the United States, and to secure certain moneys to the people of the United States, or to the persons to whom they are due, and who are entitled to receive the same," has relieved this office of numerous accounts, some of which had remained on the books of the Treasurer for forty years. By the operation of this law, all moneys represented by these accounts that had remained unchanged for three years or more on the books of the Treasury, or any of the offices thereof, were covered into the Treasury by warrant to an appropriation account denominated "outstanding liabilities." The workings under this law have been satisfactory to all persons claiming payment on drafts and checks. There has been no difficulty in the way of persons entitled to receive pay therefor, such payment being made upon the statement of accounts in their favor by the First Auditor.

Occasionally claim is made that credit be given to a disbursing officer, on the settlement of his accounts, on outstanding checks issued by him on which he may have before received a credit on the receipt taken on the delivery of the checks. If allowed, the officer would thus receive two credits for one payment. In order to obviate this difficulty, and to remove all doubt as to whom the credit is due, it is suggested that the heads of the different Departments of the Government may be asked to issue orders to all their disbursing officers who make payments by checks on the Treasury, or on any of the officers thereof, requiring the disbursing officers, in such cases, to place the number of the check upon the receipt received therefor, and the number of the receipt upon the check given in payment for the same. If this cannot be done by departmental regulations, then it is suggested that Congress may be asked to amend the act aforesaid, or to pass such a new law as will compel all disbursing officers who make payments by checks on the Treasury to conform to the above-mentioned regulations.

OUTSTANDING UNITED STATES CURRENCY.

The amount of outstanding national currency at the close of the fiscal year was as follows:

Legal-tender notes	$356,000,000 00	
Deduct amount on hand	6,392,771 00	
		$349,607,229 00
Fractional currency	44,799,365 44	
Deduct amount on hand	6,799,847 71	
		38,089,517 73
Demand notes	79,967 50	
One-year notes	88,705 00	
Two-year notes	28,200 00	
Coupon two-year notes	31,250 00	
Compound-interest notes	499,780 00	
		727,902 50
Total amount of currency outstanding		388,424,649 23

From this amount there should be allowed a large margin for notes of all kinds that have been destroyed and lost, and that will never be presented for redemption. The following table exhibits the amount of the fractional currency of the first issue, commonly known as "postage currency," outstanding at the end of each of the fiscal years for ten years from 1864 to 1873, both inclusive, and also shows the amount redeemed and the percentage of redemptions in each of the ten years mentioned.

The figures of the table show that in the year 1864 the amount of this currency then outstanding was $14,842,335; of this amount there was redeemed in the next fiscal year $4,903,747.34, being at the rate of 33 per cent., or very nearly one-third of the whole amount outstanding at the beginning of the year.

After that the falling off of the amount of redemptions is shown to be very great. By inspection of the last column of the table it will be seen that while the decrease of redemptions in the next year was twenty-nine per cent., it has been running down with highly accelerated speed from year to year until, for the year closing with the thirtieth of June last, the actual redemptions on the amount outstanding was a trifle less than one-third of one per cent. These facts would seem to indicate that nearly the whole of this issue, originally amounting to $20,215,635, that still exists, has been redeemed, and that probably about four million dollars has been destroyed, and can be fairly deducted from the actual circulation of the fractional currency, and that the national indebtedness is reduced by that amount.

This is, to be sure, an extreme case. It is not probable that the same rate of loss will obtain in the case of any of the other issues of the Government. This particular fractional currency was all issued between August 21, 1862, and October 10, 1863, in a period of less than fourteen months, in the early part of the rebellion, at which time it was extensively used for the payment of troops in the field, in the States then in a state of insurrection, when and where, no doubt, the greater part of that which remains unredeemed was lost.

Table showing the decrease in outstanding fractional currency, from year to year, of the first issue, commonly known as postage-currency.

For year ending—	Amount outstanding.	Actual decrease.	Rate per cent. of decrease.
1863	$20,215,635 00		
June 30, 1864	14,842,335 00	$5,373,300 00	.265
June 30, 1865	9,938,387 66	4,903,747 34	.330
June 30, 1866	7,041,279 78	2,897,307 88	.291
June 30, 1867	5,497,538 93	1,543,740 85	.219
June 30, 1868	4,881,095 27	616,443 66	.112
June 30, 1869	4,605,712 52	275,382 75	.056
June 30, 1870	4,476,999 87	128,712 65	.028
June 30, 1871	4,414,025 04	62,974 83	.0140
June 30, 1872	4,391,299 09	22,725 95	.0050
June 30, 1873	4,376,979 15	14,319 94	.0032

In high contrast to this stand the redemption and percentage of the outstanding circulation of the old demand notes. These are the other extreme, and the redemption has been greater, and is nearer to the full amount issued than that of any of the issues of United States currency. These notes were all issued within the space of one and a half years prior to December 31, 1862. This thorough and quick redemption is due to the fact that they have always been receivable for customs duties, and have for many years been redeemed in gold.

Gold was at a premium of thirty-three per cent. and upward when the legal-tender notes were substituted in their stead, thus making three demand notes equal to four legal-tender notes of like denominations. These notes were always the equivalent of gold. This, with their short term of circulation, accounts for the small amount left outstanding.

Sixty million dollars of these notes, of the denominations of fives, tens, and twenties, were issued, all of which, except $79,967.50, were redeemed at the close of the fiscal year, being only about one and a third of one per cent. left outstanding, while the outstanding part of the first issue of the fractional currency is over twenty-one and one-half of one per cent. on the whole amount issued.

CONDITION OF THE CURRENCY.

The various offices of the Treasury, located in all the principal cities of the country, afford to the holders of mutilated and defaced currency, of all the kinds issued by the United States, facilities to have the same exchanged for new currency of like kinds. The Department offers additional inducements for such exchanges by paying the express charges, both ways, on the transportation of old currency to the Treasury, and on the new in return for the same. In this way all the issues of the legal-tender notes, and of the fractional-currency as well, are kept in tolerably good condition. Not so with the issues of the national banks; these have no such facilities, and no motive for making such exchanges. The consequence is that the larger part of the notes of these banks is in a most wretched condition, many of them being totally unfit for circulation. Section 23 of the national-currency act provides that these notes "shall be received at par in all parts of the United States in payment of taxes, excises, public lands, and all other dues to the United States, except for duties on imports, and also

for all salaries, and other debts and demands owing by the United States to individuals, corporations, and associations, within the United States, except interest on the public debt and in redemption of the national currency." Under this provision of law the national bank notes are received, in large numbers and amounts, in payment of taxes and dues, by the assistant treasurers, designated depositaries, and national banks designated as such depositaries, in the various places all over the United States where these officers are located. These officers, finding that the holders of drafts and checks on their offices refuse to receive these notes on account of their worn and ragged condition, send them as transfers of funds by express from their offices to the Treasury.

Here, because no other disposition can be made of them, they are assorted at considerable expense and with much labor, and sent, so assorted, to the offices of the assistant treasurers, designated depositaries, and national banks designated as such depositaries, in the cities where the banks that issued such notes, or their redemption agencies, are respectively located, thus incurring a second expense for their transportation, besides the loss of interest for three months' time from the date of their original receipt until the time they can be converted into funds fit to be used in payment of dues from the Government. The cost of two transportations by express, the necessary expenses incurred for clerk hire, and other incidental expenses attending their assorting and preparation for transportation to the various banks and agencies, and the interest on the amount for the time consumed in converting them into currency that can be used, amounts to more than two per cent.

The amount of legal-tender notes outstanding, as by the
   books of this office, on November 1, 1872, was...... $360,566,764
On the third of October of the same year,
   the national banks and their agencies
   held of these notes as their reserves required by law........................ $102,074,104
And there was in the offices of the Treasury, exclusive of special deposits for
   certificates 6,392,771
                                          ────────── 108,466,875
                                                      ──────────
Leaving the actual circulation at 252,099,889
On the day first named the circulation of the national
   banks amounted to................................ 340,943,170
The exchange of legal-tender notes for the year preceding, counted up in individual notes, was............ 14,221,291
That of the national banks, for the same time, deducting 568,512 notes of banks in liquidation, for which no
   new notes were issued, amounted to only............ 5,688,868

These figures, when compared with the respective issues outstanding, and on the supposition that like amounts represent like numbers of notes, would indicate that the United States had replaced one note in every seventeen and a half, and the national banks only one note in sixty.

Some idea may be formed from this statement of the relative condition of the two kinds of currency. The consequence is, that many of the notes of the banks are so badly worn, torn, dirty, and defaced, that even experts are often in doubt and unable to correctly judge of their genuineness, making it always a risk, often ending in loss to take them.

Some remedy must be found for the correction of this evil. Unless the banks can be induced to provide for the prompt retirement of such of their notes as are and may become unfit for circulation, Congress should be asked for the passage of a law compelling them to do so, or to authorize some arrangement through which the exchange of new for old and defaced notes of all the national banks can be made through the instrumentality of the Treasury Department.

I feel sure that you will be able to devise some plan that Congress will, on your recommendation, enact into a law that will work a perfect cure of the evil complained of.

Discount on mutilated currency.

Formerly, under and by virtue of Treasury regulations, deductions were made from the par face value of all United States notes and fractional currency, for the proportional part that was missing from any note returned to the Treasury for redemption. While the old rules continued in force, the deductions so made amounted to the large sum of $227,044.14. This source of revenue, if so it may be called, has now entirely ceased; and it is feared that frauds are being perpetrated. A great clamor was raised by persons who desired to commit frauds. Newspapers, whose editors and managers did not understand the frauds that were attempted to be practiced by so manipulating like notes as to compel the redemption of a larger from a smaller number, joined the rogues in the unreasonable clamor, through which the Department was induced to change the rule. Under the old regulations, the penalties collected for deductions, proportioned to the missing parts of mutilated notes deterred evil-minded persons from mutilating the currency. Under the new rules discounts ceased, and the practice of mutilation has largely increased. Some penalty is necessarily required to arrest the evil. The national banks have their protection in section 58 of the "act to provide a national currency, secured by a pledge of United State bonds."

It is therein enacted: "That every person who shall mutilate, cut, deface, disfigure, or perforate with holes, or shall unite or cement together, or do any other thing to any bank-bill, draft, note, or other evidence of debt, issued by any such association, or shall cause or procure the same to be done with intent to render such bank-bill, draft, note, or other evidence of debt unfit to be re-issued by said association, shall, upon conviction, forfeit fifty dollars to the association who shall be injured thereby, to be recovered by action in any court having jurisdiction." Such a law, as far as it is applicable, with an additional clause declaring it forgery to mutilate any United States notes with the intent of making a greater from a smaller number of such notes, has now, under the changed rules and regulations, become necessary for the protection of the public interest. But even such a law would not be as effective to prevent frauds, nor as profitable, as were the old Treasury regulations, which imposed the penalty on the instant, in every case, and which worked admirably in everything except for the interest of swindlers bent upon defrauding the Government and people by getting more notes redeemed than were issued.

It is therefore most respectfully recommended that the former rules and regulations, in regard to the redemption of United States notes and fractional currency from which parts may be missing, may be again put in force, or that Congress may be asked to pass such a law as may, at least in part, prevent, in this regard, frauds upon the Treasury.

CONCLUSION.

The business of the office has been regularly performed by the officers, clerks, and other employés belonging to it, to the satisfaction of the public doing business with them, and it really affords me great pleasure to commend them for their industry and zeal in the performance of their official duties.   In this connection I desire to reiterate my often-repeated expressions of opinion, in my reports of former years, that the employés of this office, through whose hands pass millions upon millions of money, receive a compensation lower than that paid for like, but less responsible, services in banks or the offices of business men.   I am sure that they earn and deserve to receive better pay from the Government that they serve so faithfully.   Notwithstanding their inadequate pay, not one of the hundreds employed in this office has, since my last report, taken a cent from the money that is always within their reach.   Through their vigilance others have not been able to steal.   I congratulate with you that not one cent has been lost to the Treasury within the fiscal year or since, through any fault of any one connected with this office.

I have the honor to be your obedient servant,

F. E. SPINNER,
Treasurer of the United States.

Hon. WM. A. RICHARDSON,
Secretary of the Treasury.

List of papers in Appendix.

A. General Treasury.
B. Post-Office Department.
C. National Banks.
D. United States Paper Currency.
E. Redemptions.
F. Statistical Destructions.
G. Coin Certificates.
H. Three per cent. Certificates.
I. Temporary-loan Certificates.
K. Certificates of Deposit, act of June 8, 1872.
L. Certificates of Indebtedness.

M. Treasury-notes of 1861.
N. Seven-thirties of 1861, and of 1864 and 1865.
O. Retirement of Five-twenty Bonds.
P. Interest.
Q. Payments by Checks.
R. Employés.
S. Official Correspondence.
T. Receipts and Payments of Assistant Treasurers.
U. Receipts and Payments of Designated Depositaries.

Receipts and expenditures by warrants.

The books of the Office were closed June 30, 1873, after the entry of all moneys received and disbursed on authorized warrants, as follows:

Receipts.

From—	Net.	Repayments.	Counter-warrants.	Totals.
Loans	$214,931,017 00			$214,931,017 00
Customs	188,089,522 70			188,089,522 70
Internal Revenue	113,729,314 14			113,729,314 14
Lands	2,882,312 38			2,882,312 38
Miscellaneous	29,037,055 45	$2,023,227 38	$286,840 95	31,346,123 78
War		2,264,035 12	29,402,654 11	31,666,689 23
Navy		990,788 14	2,752,791 26	3,743,579 40
Interior		1,464,545 48	208,862 26	1,673,407 74
	548,660,221 67	6,742,596 12	32,650,148 58	588,061,966 37
Late United States depositary, Galveston, Texas, formerly credited as unavailable				2,033 32
Balance from June 30, 1872				106,551,641 24
				694,615,640 93

Expenditures.

On account of—	Net.	Repayments.	Counter-warrants.	Totals.
Customs	$21,109,193 17	$607,630 39	$120,799 17	$21,837,022 73
Internal Revenue	6,700,118 47	216,630 29	21,851 91	6,938,600 07
Interior	37,311,131 74	1,464,545 48	208,862 26	38,984,539 48
Interior, civil	7,046,659 77	38,383 61	2,817 58	7,087,860 96
War	46,323,138 31	2,264,035 12	29,402,654 11	77,989,827 54
War, civil	9,340 23	11,134 03		20,474 26
Navy	23,526,256 79	990,788 14	2,752,791 26	27,269,836 19
Treasury	32,581,539 81	493,863 22	88,252 47	33,163,655 50
Diplomatic	1,572,762 85	133,727 45	48,909 34	1,755,399 64
Quarterly salaries	589,451 35			589,451 35
Judiciary	3,719,044 41	190,504 39	753 48	3,910,302 28
Public Debt	343,555,961 01	331,354 00	2,457 00	343,889,772 01
	524,044,597 91	6,742,596 12	32,650,148 58	563,437,342 61
Amount allowed Treasurer United States by act of March 3, 1873				161 00
Balance June 30, 1873				131,178,137 32
				694,615,640 93

NOTE.—The above balance in the Treasury June 30, 1873, differs from that of the Secretary and Register $161, the amount allowed the Treasurer as above, not yet credited by those officers.

Moneys advanced to disbursing officers, in excess of the amounts required for disbursement, are returned to the Treasury and carried to the credit of the appropriation from which they were drawn by repay covering-warrants.

Counter-warrants represent moneys returned to appropriations, which moneys had previously been expended on some other account.

REPORT OF THE REGISTER.

TREASURY DEPARTMENT,
Register's Office, November 1, 1873.

SIR: I have the honor to submit my annual report of the operations of this bureau for the fiscal year ending June 30, 1873.

The business of the office has been transacted during the last year with a less number of clerks than for quite a number of years past, although the work has not, in any of the divisions, materially diminished, while in some respects it has increased.

The organization of the bureau remains as at the date of my last report, and I take occasion to acknowledge my obligations to the assistant register and the chiefs of the several divisions, for their efficient co-operation in conducting the business of the office.

The clerks have performed their various duties satisfactorily, and generally merit commendation for efficiency and punctuality. The book-keepers of the various loan, appropriation, and personal ledgers deserve special mention for their efficiency, and the willingness with which they have performed extra work out of office hours in order to keep up the work of their respective desks when occasion required it.

To this bureau is committed the custody of very important and valuable files connected with the most important business transactions of the Government; it, therefore, becomes my duty to state that the accumulation of files has become so great as to fill the rooms allotted for this purpose, and it has become necessary to deposit a very large quantity of them in the south corridor, where they are inconvenient for reference, exposed to loss and mutilation, and also causing much inconvenience by obstructing the passage-way. The safety of these valuable papers requires that other rooms be provided and allotted for the use of the files, and I would respectfully urge its necessity upon your attention.

It is to be hoped that some arrangement may be made by which more room can be appropriated for this purpose.

A detailed statement of the business transacted in each division will be found under its proper head.

LOAN DIVISION—HARTWELL JENISON, CHIEF OF DIVISION.

The total number of coupon and registered bonds issued during the fiscal year was 68,067.

The total number of coupon and registered bonds canceled, 298,047.

The amount of bonds issued during the year was as follows:

Original issue	$45,191,900 00
Coupon bonds converted into registered	12,622,200 00
Transfers of registered stock	97,416,550 00
Total issue	155,230,650 00

The amount of coupon and registered bonds canceled was as follows:

Coupon bonds exchanged for registered	$12,622,200 00
Registered bonds transferred	97,416,550 00
Coupon and registered bonds redeemed, as per records of this office	139,103,600 00
Total canceled	249,142,350 00
Amount of canceled coupon bonds entered upon numerical registers, and turned over to the burning-committee for destruction	$122,902,650 00

The vault-account shows that there was on hand July 1, 1872:

Coupon	$81,015,650 00
Registered	715,159,400 00

Received during the year from the Bureau of Engraving and Printing:

Coupon	20,527,500 00
Registered	142,157,950 00
Total	958,860,500 00

Issued during the year:

Coupon	$29,925,950 00
Registered	125,304,700 00

Canceled and delivered to the committee for destruction:

Coupon	37,900 00
Registered	103,036,450 00

In hands of European agent for issue July 1, 1873:

Coupon	27,596,000 00
Registered	4,208,650 00

On hand, July 1, 1873:

Coupon	43,683,300 00
Registered	624,767,550 00
Total	958,860,500 00

Statement showing the number of cases, number and amount of registered and coupon bonds issued and canceled, during the fiscal year ending June 30, 1871.

Loans.	Direct issues.			ISSUED. Exchanges.			Transfers.			Total issue.
	No. of cases.	Bonds issued.	Amount.	No. of cases.	Bonds issued.	Amount.	No. of cases.	Bonds issued.	Amount.	Amount.
1847										
1848										
1850										
1858										
1860							18	53	$837,000	$837,000
1861, February 8				8	14	$92,000	218	479	1,315,000	1,315,000
Oregon war	2	2	$150				94	315	155,000	155,000
1861, July 17				79	203	245,150	885	3,300	11,318,150	11,463,433
1862				57	130	243,300	278	1,707	7,981,100	8,324,400
1863			34	29	67	157,000	438	1,429	4,619,550	4,747,550
1864—5-20s							16	304	1,414,900	1,414,900
1864—10-40s				217	614	1,734,450	694	2,789	12,974,050	14,708,500
1864, June 30				52	156	160,750	530	1,706	9,789,200	9,949,950
1865				30	106	148,600	345	1,682	5,793,900	5,941,700
Consols of 1865				968	657	1,853,550	639	2,816	9,467,900	10,721,500
Consols of 1867				330	914	1,222,600	1,047	4,301	14,586,550	15,810,650
Consols of 1868	2	2	1,500	125	296	973,500	191	540	1,735,000	2,665,500
Pacific Railroad loans							455	4,433	12,714,000	12,714,000
Five per cent. fund, 1881s	334	39,043	43,190,250	396	1,959	6,400,300	287	1,971	3,438,900	53,119,750
Total	338	39,047	43,191,900	1,530	3,446	12,622,990	5,600	21,574	97,416,550	155,930,650

Statement showing the number of cases, number and amount of registered and coupon bonds issued and canceled, &c.—Continued.

Loans.	CANCELED.							
	Redemptions.			Exchanges.		Transfers.		Total canceled.
	No. of cases.	Bonds canceled.	Amount.	No. of bonds.	Amount.	No. of bonds.	Amount.	Amount.
1847	3	12	$84,900					$84,900
1848								
1850						52	$257,000	857,000
1858								
1860								
1861, February 8				52	$83,000	529	1,252,000	4,335,000
Oregon war				529	245,120	449	156,000	156,000
1861, July 17	8,772	194,082	100,385,620	468	942,300	3,769	1,212,150	11,453,300
1862				184	127,600	3,083	7,091,100	108,682,530
1863	5	22	57,800	388		1,273	4,619,930	4,797,540
1864—5-20s				4,324	1,734,430	3,588	1,414,500	1,472,700
1864—10-40s	91	7,861	7,019,300	273	160,730	2,194	12,974,020	14,708,080
1864, June 30	64	2,377	4,324,530	197	148,900	1,960	5,799,800	17,989,320
1865	62	93,508	90,381,500	2,388	1,922,530	4,088	5,793,800	10,176,520
Consols of 1865	73	8,971	5,964,900	5,524	1,922,900	1,066	9,467,000	31,083,000
Consols of 1867	44	1,787	915,500	713	972,500	366	1,666,500	21,673,000
Consols of 1868						460	1,723,000	3,811,000
Pacific Railroad loans						12,714	12,714,000	12,714,000
Five per cent. fund, 1881s						1,537	3,433,500	9,993,500
Total	9,157	240,715	139,103,600	24,503	18,632,300	32,929	97,416,550	249,142,350

NOTE AND COUPON DIVISION—LEWIS D. MOORE, CHIEF OF DIVISION

The following consolidated statement exhibits the character and amount of work performed by this division during the fiscal year ending June 30, 1873:

Statement of Treasury notes, bonds, and coupons.

Notes, bonds, &c.	Authorizing act.	Number of pieces.	Total amount.
Treasury notes and gold certificates (upper halves) counted, assorted, arranged, registered, and examined:			
One-year 5 per cent	March 3, 1863	131	$8, 650
Two-year 5 per cent	March 3, 1863	948	21, 030
Three-year 6 per cent	March 3, 1863, and June 30, 1864	4, 578	121, 750
Gold certificates	March 3, 1863	27, 402	45 154, 300
Three-year 7 3-10 per cent	July 17, 1861, June 30, 1864, and March 3, 1865.	637	72, 000
Total		33, 730	45, 377, 730

Statement of Treasury notes, bonds, and coupons.

Notes, bonds, and coupons.	Authorizing act.	Number of pieces.	Total amount.	Coupons attached.
Five-twenty and other bonds registered, examined, scheduled, compared, and delivered to committee:				
Exchanged, transferred, and redeemed	March 3, 1863	5, 630	$3, 375, 550	$190, 316
Do	March 3, 1864	25, 958	11, 265, 000	1, 230, 247
Do	June 30, 1864	21, 821	14, 604, 000	580, 687
Do	March 3, 1865	45, 020	17, 751, 100	719, 669
Do	Consols of 1865	84, 279	43, 564, 450	2, 948, 247
Do	Consols of 1867	108, 491	40, 934, 900	3, 444, 054
Do	Consols of 1868	15, 881	5, 211, 950	539, 671
Do	Funded loan of 1881	28, 660	26, 192, 800	1, 070, 238
Total		315, 740	162, 899, 750	9, 973, 129

Interest on registered bonds received, registered, and examined.

	Authorizing act.	Number of pieces.	Total amount.
Coin checks	Funded loan of 1881	10, 998	$9, 627, 768 32

Of coupons detached from notes and bonds there were counted, assorted, and arranged numerically 4,021,590; registered, 4,366,362; and examined and compared, 7,896,624.

Schedule of the total number and amount of notes, bonds, and coupons received in this division

Notes, bonds, and coupons.	Authorizing act.	Number of pieces.	Amount.
One-year 5 per cent. Treasury notes	March 3, 1863	1, 739, 013	$11, 431, 410 00
Two-year 5 per cent. Treasury notes	March 3, 1863	232, 356	16, 454, 800 00
Two-year 5 per cent. Treas'y notes, (coupon).	March 3, 1863	432, 637	140, 958, 350 00
Three-year 6 per cent. Treasury notes	March 3, 1863	179, 955	11, 959, 889 00
Three-year 6 per cent. Treasury notes	June 30, 1864	5, 425, 091	247, 462, 300 00
Gold certificates	March 3, 1863	365, 991	374, 506, 700 00
Coin checks, (registered interest)	Funded loan of 1881	10, 998	9, 627, 768 32
Seven-thirty Treasury notes	July 17, 1861	485, 500	110, 075, 300 00
Seven-thirty Treasury notes	June 30, 1864	1, 223, 408	289, 908, 150 00
Seven-thirty Treasury notes	March 3, 1865	880, 408	330, 927, 250 00

Schedule of the total number and amount of notes, bonds, and coupons, &c.—Continued.

Notes, bonds, and coupons.	Authorizing act.	Number of pieces.	Amount.
Seven-thirty Treasury notes	March 3, 1865	996,463	$198,874,300 00
Coupon interest 6 per cent	April 15, 1842	42,268	1,904,540 00
Coupon interest 5 per cent	March 3, 1843	96,657	860,925 00
Coupon interest 6 per cent	March 31, 1848	222,212	7,664,010 00
Coupon interest 5 per cent	September 9, 1850, Texan indemnity stock.	106,850	2,671,250 00
Coupon interest 5 per cent	June 14, 1858	432,923	10,823,075 00
Coupon interest 5 per cent	June 22, 1860	26,317	657,925 00
Coupon interest 6 per cent	February 8, 1861	146,131	4,383,930 00
Coupon interest 6 per cent	March 2, 1861, Oregon war debt.	89,149	1,320,671 00
Coupon interest 7 3-10 per cent	July 17, 1861	2,326,702	23,652,303 22½
Coupon interest 6 per cent	July 17 and August 5, 1861	2,141,358	45,073,678 00
Coupon interest 6 per cent	February 25, 1862	13,656,728	214,455,029 50
Coupon interest 6 per cent	March 3, 1863	642,991	13,740,536 00
Coupon interest 5 per cent	March 3, 1863	878,742	7,167,893 75
Coupon interest 6 per cent	March 3, 1864	1,792,850	30,534,092 00
Coupon interest 6 per cent	June 30, 1864	1,290,017	26,700,879 50
Coupon interest 7 3-10 per cent	June 30, '64, and March 3, '65	12,834,267	123,315,039 92½
Coupon interest 6 per cent	March 3, 1865	2,246,561	51,965,509 00
Coupon interest 6 per cent	Consols of 1865	5,235,336	78,063,842 00
Coupon interest 6 per cent	Consols of 1867	6,207,341	82,849,789 00
Coupon interest 6 per cent	Consols of 1868	643,485	7,933,156 50
Coupon interest 5 per cent	Funded loan of 1881	708,092	5,075,922 07
Coupon interest 4 per cent	July 8, 1870	3,377	67,540 00

Bonds.	Authorizing act.	Number of pieces.	Amount.	Coupons attached.
6 per cent. bonds	March 31, 1848	6,800	$6,191,000	69,250
5 per cent. bonds	June 14, 1858	5,158	5,158,000	66,552
5 per cent. bonds	June 22, 1860	1,731	1,731,000	7,548
6 per cent. bonds	February 8, 1861	4,006	4,006,000	112,863
6 per cent. bonds	July 17 and August 5, 1861	98,531	73,435,800	2,824,476
6 per cent. bonds	February 25, 1862	110,002	67,456,150	3,545,123
6 per cent. bonds	March 3, 1863	46,876	35,625,150	1,409,387
5 per cent. bonds	March 3, 1864	176,930	100,930,100	10,283,462
6 per cent. bonds	June 30, 1864	103,945	79,712,150	3,532,736
6 per cent. bonds	March 3, 1865	76,570	50,004,700	2,638,109
6 per cent. bonds	Consols of 1865	227,506	133,623,350	6,726,749
6 per cent. bonds	Consols of 1867	221,511	85,065,300	7,413,292
6 per cent. bonds	Consols of 1868	29,485	11,390,050	1,049,075
5 per cent. bonds	Funded loan of 1881	58,660	26,102,800	1,070,273

NOTE AND FRACTIONAL CURRENCY DIVISION—CHARLES NEALE, CHIEF OF DIVISION.

Statement showing the number of notes and amount of fractional currency, Treasury notes, and national bank notes (of such banks as are broken or have gone into voluntary liquidation) counted, examined, canceled, and destroyed by burning during the fiscal year, viz:

	Number of notes.	Amount.
Legal-tender, new issue	5,648,477	$38,607,550
Legal-tender, series 1869	8,211,963	19,253,400
Demand notes	851	7,085
National bank notes	492,199	3,441,205
Fractional currency, third issue	2,400,000	531,200
Fractional currency, fourth issue	138,600,000	20,877,600
Fractional currency, fourth issue, second series	25,600,000	12,800,000
Total	180,953,490	95,518,050

Amount of notes counted, examined, canceled, and destroyed during the fiscal year ending June 30, 1872 .... $100,073,738

During the fiscal year ending June 30, 1873 95,518,050

    Decrease 4,555,688

Number of notes counted, examined, canceled, and destroyed during the fiscal year ending June 30, 1872 159,160,301

During the fiscal year ending June 30, 1873 180,953,480

    Increase 21,793,179

TONNAGE DIVISION—W. P. TITCOMB, CHIEF OF DIVISION.

The tonnage employed in foreign trade has increased 19,493 tons, and the tonnage employed in coastwise trade has increased 233,668 tons.

The total increase of tonnage, including that employed in fisheries, is 258,280 tons, as shown in the following table:

	1872.		1873.	
	Vessels.	Tons.	Vessels.	Tons.
Registered..........	2,699	1,410,647	2,759	1,423,288
Enrolled and licensed	28,415	3,027,099	29,913	3,272,738
Total..........	31,114	4,437,746	32,672	4,696,026

The comparison of the various classes of vessels is as follows:

	1872.		1873.	
	Vessels.	Tons.	Vessels.	Tons.
Sailing-vessels	17,655	2,325,375	17,949	2,383,801
Steam-vessels	3,753	1,111,552	4,015	1,156,443
Canal-boats	8,085	704,713	8,970	820,328
Barges	1,621	296,106	1,738	335,454
Total	31,114	4,437,746	32,672	4,696,026

The proportion of the steam tonnage of the country employed in foreign trade is 16.7 per centum.

The increase in the aggregate tonnage of the country during the year—1,558 vessels, 258,280 tons—is made up as follows: the sailing tonnage has increased 294 vessels, 58,426 tons: the steam tonnage, 262 vessels, 44,891 tons; the canal-boat tonnage, 885 vessels, 115,615 tons, and the barge tonnage, 117 vessels, 39,348 tons.

SHIP-BUILDING.

The amount of tonnage built during the year exceeds that of any year since 1865.

It is attributable to two causes—the unusually great, if not unprecedented, losses by sea, and the fact that, owing to the advance in prices of labor and materials abroad, the cost of American-built ships is now but slightly greater than that of the best British.

The total number of vessels built during the past two fiscal years, with the tonnage of each class, is shown below:

	1872.		1873.	
	Vessels.	Tons.	Vessels.	Tons.
Sailing-vessels	645	76,291	804	144,629
Steam-vessels	292	62,210	402	88,011
Canal-boats	538	46,017	835	78,288
Barges	168	24,534	230	48,318
Total	1,643	209,052	2,271	359,246

The increase of tonnage built over the preceding year was, therefore, 628 vessels, 150,194 tons.

The tonnage of vessels built during the last two years, within the several grand divisions of the country, is shown below:

	1872.	1873.
	Tons.	Tons.
Atlantic and Gulf coasts	125,820	212,661
Pacific coast	2,276	5,475
Northern lakes	44,612	92,445
Western rivers	36,344	48,650
Total	209,052	379,246

The number of iron vessels built during the year is 26, tonnage, 26,548 tons, which are all steam-vessels.

Of the foregoing three were ocean steamers of the largest class, built for foreign trade. Below is shown the iron tonnage built in the country since 1868:

Iron tonnage built.

	1868.	1869.	1870.	1871.	1872.	1873.
Sailing-vessels	None	1,039	679	2,067	None	None.
Steam-vessels	2,801	3,545	7,602	13,112	12,766	26,548
Total	2,801	4,584	8,281	15,179	12,766	26,548

THE FISHERIES.

The tonnage engaged in the fisheries during the past two years is as follows:

	1872		1873.	
	Vessels.	Tons.	Vessels.	Tons.
Cod and mackerel	2,385	97,506	2,453	109,514
Whale fisheries	217	51,408	182	44,755

The tonnage employed in the cod and mackerel fisheries seems to be steadily increasing.

The following table shows the amount of tonnage employed in the cod and mackerel fisheries, with the percentage belonging in each State:

State.	Tonnage.	Per cent.
Massachusetts	54,180	49.5
Maine	16,196	13.2
Connecticut	1,104	6.8
New York	1,751	1.6
California	1,155	1.1
Rhode Island	1,051	1.0
New Hampshire	852	0.8
Total	109,514	100

The amount of tonnage employed in the whale-fisheries has decreased during the last year. The whole amount on the 30th day of June, 1873, was 187 vessels, 44,785 tons, which shows a decline of 30 vessels, 6,823 tons, as follows:

Ports.	1872.		1873.	
	Vessels.	Tons.	Vessels.	Tons.
New Bedford	166	44,320	161	38,901
New London	19	3,113	19	2,952
Barnstable	19	1,671	18	1,502
Edgartown	4	1,206	3	945
Nantucket	3	467		
San Francisco	2	132	2	132
Salem and Beverly	2	348	1	117
Sag Harbor	2	261	1	116
Total	217	51,608	187	44,755

Of the above, 87 per cent. belongs at New Bedford.

Complete tables, showing the various classes of tonnage, will be found in the appendix to this report.

DIVISION OF RECEIPTS AND EXPENDITURES—J. H. BEATTY, CHIEF OF DIVISION.

The following statement exhibits the work of this division for the year:

The number of warrants issued during the year for civil, diplomatic, miscellaneous, internal revenue, and public debt expenditures and repayments was. 23,689
In the preceding year 19,951

Increase 3,738

The number of warrants issued for receipts from customs, lands, internal revenue, direct tax, and miscellaneous sources was 11,861
In the preceding year 11,330

Increase 531

The number of warrants issued for payments and repayments in the War, Navy, and Interior (Pensions and Indian) Departments was 10,303
In the preceding year 8,185

Increase 2,118

The number of drafts registered was 37,170
In the preceding year 34,604

Increase 2,566

The number of journal pages required for the entry of accounts relating to the civil, diplomatic, internal revenue, miscellaneous and public debt receipts and expenditures was 1,509
In the preceding year 1,236

Increase 273

The number of certificates published for settlement of accounts was 10,772
In the preceding year 10,464

Increase 308

The number of accounts received from the offices of the First and Fifth Auditors and Commissioner of the General Land-Office was 21,497
In the preceding year 24,448

Decrease 2,951

RECEIPTS AND EXPENDITURES.

' In accordance with the standing order of, the House of Representatives of December 30, 1791, and the act of Congress of August 26, 1842, the Secretary of the Treasury is required to prepare an accurate statement of the receipts and expenditures, of the United States for each fiscal year, to be laid before the House of Representatives within the first week of the session next following. It is required that this statement shall distinguish "the amount of the receipts of each State or district, and from each officer therein, in which statement shall also be distinguished the expenditures which fall under each head of appropriation." This statement has heretofore been made up from the audited accounts of the Treasurer, but as these accounts do not reach this office for nearly two years, owing to the great increase of the business of the Department occasioned by the late war, the statement is herewith submitted for the last fiscal year, the expenditures being made up from *warrants issued*. It will differ from the actual expenditures by the amount of warrants outstanding, which cannot be obtained until the Treasurer's accounts are settled by the accounting officers, when the detailed statement will be compiled.

I remain, with great respect, your obedient servant,

JOHN ALLISON,
Register.

Hon. WM. A. RICHARDSON,
Secretary of the Treasury.

REPORT OF THE DIRECTOR OF THE MINT.

OFFICE DIRECTOR OF THE MINT,
Treasury Department, Washington, D. C., November 1, 1873.

SIR : The second section of the coinage act of 1873 provides that the Director of the Mint shall have general supervision of all Mints and Assay-offices, and make an annual report to the Secretary of the Treasury of their operations at the close of each fiscal year. In compliance with this provision of law, I have the honor to submit the following report of the operations of the Mints and Assay-offices for the fiscal year ending June 30, 1873.

The operations of the Mints and Assay-offices from July 1, 1872, to March 31, 1873, inclusive, were conducted under the provisions of the mint and coinage laws in force prior to April 1, 1873, the day on which the coinage act took effect—after which they were conducted under the provisions of the new law. The two periods of time referred to constitute the fiscal year for which the operations are now reported.

The amount of gold and silver deposits and purchases, coins struck, and stamped-bars manufactured, during the fiscal year, was as follows:

DEPOSITS.

Gold... $59,937,429 45
Silver.......................... .... 12,317,389 43

Total amount received and operated upon..................... 72,254,818 88

Deducting redeposits, bars made and issued by one institution and deposited at another, the deposits were—

Gold... $57,704,385 88
Silver............................ ....   9,145,398 43

Total.................. .... 66,849,714 31

COINAGE.

	Pieces.	Value.
Gold	1,824,420	$35,249,357 50
Silver	11,774,250	2,945,795 50
Minor coinage	18,925,000	494,030 00
Total	32,523,670	38,689,183 00

BARS.

Fine gold	$7,554,956 86	
Unparted gold	12,940,659 25	20,495,616 11
Fine silver	3,034,259 56	
Unparted silver	3,987,654 94	7,021,914 50
Total gold and silver		27,517,530 61

The distribution of the gold and silver bullion deposited and purchased, including redeposits, was as follows:

MINT, UNITED STATES, PHILADELPHIA.

Gold deposits (including abraded coin)	$18,674,185 64
Silver deposits and purchases	2,756,879 24
Total	21,431,064 88

MINT, UNITED STATES, SAN FRANCISCO.

Gold deposits	17,659,472 58
Silver deposits and purchases	170,405 92
Total	17,829,878 50

MINT, UNITED STATES, CARSON CITY.

Gold deposits	5,004,536 69
Silver deposits and purchases	4,243,320 66
Total	9,247,857 35

MINT, UNITED STATES, DENVER, COLO.

Gold deposits	804,903 80
Silver deposits	13,465 08
Total	818,368 88

UNITED STATES ASSAY-OFFICE, NEW YORK.

Gold deposits	17,680,028 95
Silver deposits and purchases	5,130,815 60
Total	22,810,844 55

UNITED STATES ASSAY-OFFICE, CHARLOTTE, N. C.

Gold deposits	10,572 39
Silver deposits	160 24
Total	10,732 63

UNITED STATES ASSAY-OFFICE, BOISE CITY, IDAHO.

Gold deposits	103,729 40
Silver deposits	2,342 69
Total	106,072 09

The coinage at the different mints for the fiscal year was as follows :

MINT, UNITED STATES, PHILADELPHIA.

Denomination.	Pieces.	Value.
GOLD.		
Double-eagles	880, 925	$17, 644, 500 00
Eagles	825	8, 250 00
Half-eagles	1, 105	5, 525 00
Three-dollars	25	75 00
Quarter-eagles	1, 625	4, 062 50
Dollars	2, 525	2, 525 00
Total gold	888, 330	17, 664, 937 50
SILVER.		
Dollars	964, 150	964, 150 00
Half-dollars	1, 938, 050	969, 025 00
Quarter-dollars	616, 850	154, 212 50
Dimes	3, 986, 850	398, 685 00
Half-dimes	2, 822, 850	141, 142 50
Three-cents	850	25 50
Total silver	10, 329, 600	2, 627, 240 50
MINOR COINAGE.		
Five-cents	7, 048, 000	352, 400 00
Three-cents	1, 144, 000	34, 320 00
One-cent	10, 733, 000	107, 330 00
Total minor coinage	18, 925, 000	494, 050 00
Total coinage	30, 142, 930	20, 786, 228 00

MINT, UNITED STATES, SAN FRANCISCO.

Denomination.	Pieces.	Value.
GOLD.		
Double-eagles	830, 600	$16, 612, 000 00
Eagles	14, 000	140, 000 00
Half-eagles	36, 000	180, 000 00
Quarter-eagles	14, 000	35, 000 00
Total gold	894, 600	16, 967, 000 00
SILVER.		
Dollars	9, 700	9, 700 00
Half-dollars	37, 000	18, 500 00
Quarter-dollars	64, 000	16, 000 00
Dimes	160, 000	16, 000 00
Half-dimes	686, 000	34, 300 00
Total silver	956, 700	94, 500 00
Total coinage	1, 851, 300	17, 061, 500 00

MINT, UNITED STATES, CARSON CITY.

Denomination.	Pieces.	Value.
GOLD.		
Double-eagles	25, 450	$509, 000 00
Eagles	5, 640	56, 400 00
Half-eagles	10, 400	52, 000 00
Total gold	41, 490	617, 400 00
SILVER.		
Dollars	3, 300	3, 300 00
Half dollars	424, 500	212, 250 00
Quarter dollars	16, 600	4, 150 00
Dimes	43, 550	4, 355 00
Total silver	487, 950	224, 055 00
Total coinage	529, 440	841, 455 00

The bars made and issued at the Mints and Assay-offices were as follows:

MINT, UNITED STATES, PHILADELPHIA.

Fine gold bars	$62,025 41
Fine silver bars	116,046 51
Total	178,071 92

MINT, UNITED STATES, SAN FRANCISCO.

Unparted gold bars	7,554,785 61
Unparted silver bars	63,810 01
Total	7,618,595 62

MINT, UNITED STATES, CARSON CITY.

Fine gold bars	$115,113 08
Unparted gold bars	4,455,056 90
	4,570,169 98
Unparted silver bars	3,920,511 07
	8,490,681 05

MINT, UNITED STATES, DENVER.

Unparted gold bars	$16,028 08
Unparted silver bars	1,317 80
Total	$17,345 88

UNITED STATES ASSAY-OFFICE, NEW YORK.

Fine gold bars	7,377,818 37
Fine silver bars	2,918,213 05
Total	10,296,031 42

UNITED STATES ASSAY-OFFICE, CHARLOTTE.

Unparted gold bars	10,572 39
Unparted silver bars	160 24
Total	10,732 63

UNITED STATES ASSAY-OFFICE, BOISE CITY.

Unparted gold bars	104,216 27
Unparted silver bars	1,855 82
Total	106,072 09

The amount in bars transmitted from the United States assay-office, New York, to the Mint at Philadelphia for coinage, during the fiscal year, was—

Gold	$1,158,612 53
Silver	2,576,712 91
Total	3,735,325 44

Compared with the previous year there was an increase of $19,892,762.22 in gold deposits, $539,498.19 in silver deposits and purchases, and $210,290 in minor coinage.

EARNINGS AND EXPENDITURES.

The following summary exhibits the earnings and expenditures of the mints and assay offices:

EARNINGS.

Mints and Assay-offices	Coinage charge.	Parting and other charges.	Gain by coinage of silver, subsidiary coin.	Minor coinage, profits.	Sale of, by-products and old materials.	Proceeds of unexportable gold, fractions, assay clips.	Surplus bullion, melter and refiner.	Received from residue, dust, &c., and sweepings.	Profits from manufacture and sale of medals, proof, and specimen coins.	Assays of ores.	Total earnings.
Philadelphia	$12,350 51	$2,267 22	$27,093 50	$227,376 42	$618 14			$17,339 46	$3,721 70		$333,127 49
San Francisco	46,442 34	6,685 10	4,614 71		388 53		$17,423 57	1,382 73			66,403 27
Carson City	4,926 15	29,432 85	14,568 40		3,037 92						66,944 14
Denver		1,693 00									9,405 75
New-York		66,561 69			11,300 91	$1,025 76	11,452 61				90,677 67
Charlotte		325 87						69 18			335 87
Boise City		206 30								276 50	565 38
Total	63,719 00	107,173 13	44,776 61	227,376 42	15,344 88	1,025 76	12,675 18	18,791 30	3,721 70	276 50	476,249 57

* Amount which would have accrued to the Mint at Philadelphia if the coinage charge had been deducted on light gold coin received during fiscal year, $63,621.72.

EXPENDITURES.

| Mints and Assay-offices | Ordinary account. | | | Cent-coinage account. | | | | | | Difference between assay value of sweeps and amount realized from sale thereof. | Total expenditures. |
	Salaries.	Wages.	Contingent.	Ores and coins.	Freight.	Incidentals.	Cent metals.	Wages.	Wastage.		
Philadelphia	$35,027 08	$124,462 23	$34,721 71	$329 56	$4,028 01	$67,700 49	$32,795 01	$116,677 16	$27,668 43	$2,711 46	$473,891 29
San Francisco	29,715 00	189,999 66	58,434 03						11,630 37	456 45	300,420 96
Carson City	19,746 70	66,364 00	30,495 00						1,958 62	437 42	131,051 84
Denver	6,720 00	21,335 00	34,707 61							457 41	30,329 44
New-York	20,641 00	72,500 00	2,210 00							3,728 41	131,639 00
Boise City	4,380 00	3,998 00	565 57								9,168 85
Charlotte	4,700 00										3,587 00
Total	118,830 44	444,003 39	186,792 71	329 56	4,028 01	67,700 49	32,795 01	116,677 16	41,257 41	7,333 71	1,065,439 21

Before the coinage act took effect the expenses of wages, materials, and incidentals incurred in the manufacture of bronze and copper-nickel alloy coins were defrayed out of the gain arising from the issue of such coin in exchange for United States currency at par. These expenses have since been and will in future be paid from the regular appropriations made for the support of the Philadelphia Mint, and the money received in exchange for the minor coins, with the exception of the amount necessary to pay the expenses of transporting the coin, will be covered from time to time into the Treasury of the United States.

REDEMPTION OF MINOR COINS.

The following statements exhibit the amount of minor coins redeemed, re-issued, and exchanged under the acts of March 3, 1871, and coinage act of 1873.

REDEEMED.

Period.	Denomination and kind.	Pieces.	Value.
From March 27, 1871 to June 30, 1873.	Copper one-cent pieces............	3,549,739	$35,495 39
	Nickel one-cent pieces............	15,737,046	157,370 46
	Bronze one-cent pieces............	14,338,206	143,382 06
	Bronze two-cent pieces............	6,483,470	129,669 40
	Nickel three-cent pieces............	1,532,896	45,986 88
	Nickel five-cent pieces............	9,190,790	459,539 50
	Total........................	50,831,987	971,444 09

RE-ISSUED.

Period.	Denomination and kind.	Pieces.	Value.
From August 24, 1871, to June 30, 1873.	Bronze one-cent pieces...........	13,966,030	$139,660 30
	Bronze two-cent pieces............	3,466,884	69,337 68
	Nickel three-cent pieces............	1,464,875	43,946 25
	Nickel five-cent pieces...........	9,057,215	452,860 75
	Total........................	27,955,004	705,804 98

EXCHANGED.

(One denomination of minor coins for another.)

Period.	Denomination and kind.	Pieces.	Value.
During fiscal year ending June 30, 1873.	Nickel one-cent pieces..	4,304	$43 04
	Bronze one-cent pieces............	3,464	34 64
	Bronze two-cent pieces............	3,308	66 16
	Nickel three-cent pieces............	904	27 12
	Nickel five-cent pieces............	2,785	139 25
	Total........................	14,765	310 21

The tables exhibiting various details in relation to the coinage and the sources from whence the bullion was derived, are appended to this report.

In the tables of previous reports bars were included as coin, and the amount of coinage, as stated, consequently appeared to be largely in excess of the value of the coins issued. These tables have been reconstructed, and, as now presented, give the coinage and bars separately.

Some corrections in the former statements of gold of domestic production were also found to be necessary, in consequence of the deposits at the San Francisco mint having been, since 1870, twice credited, viz:

First. As deposits received from individuals.

Second. After being melted and sent to the San Francisco refinery for the parting operation, they were again treated as deposits when returned to the mint.

The proper deductions, as far as the data could be obtained, have been made, and the total deposits of domestic bullion now approximate to the actual amount received.

HISTORY OF THE COINAGE.

This being the first annual report under the coinage act, it appears to be proper to give a short outline of the history of the Mint and coinage, and to refer briefly to the money of account and various questions connected with metallic money.

The Mint was, by the act of April 2, 1792, established "for the purpose of a national coinage," at Philadelphia, that city then being the seat of Government. By the same act it was provided that the money of account should be expressed in dollars or units, dimes or tenths, cents or hundredths, and mills or thousandths; and that all accounts in the public offices, or proceedings in the courts of the United States, should be kept and had in conformity therewith. Although the ideal unit of the colonial money of account was originally called a pound, the "Spanish dollar" was for many years before the establishment of the present form of government the money of commerce and practical monetary unit, and, whether obligations were discharged in gold, silver, or paper money, a certain number of Spanish dollars constituted, specifically or by implication, the standard or measure of value. This had much to do with the selection in 1792 of the dollar as the monetary unit.

By the act referred to, provision was also made for the issue of gold, silver, and copper coins. The gold coins were to be rated at 24.75 grains of pure gold to the dollar, and the silver coins at 371¼ grains to the dollar or unit: the relative value of the two metals being declared in the same law to be as 15 to 1. These standards were continued down to 1834, when an act was passed reducing the pure gold from 24.75 to 23.20 grains to the dollar.

By the act of January 18, 1837, the fineness of the gold was increased about three-fourths of one thousandth by changing from the standard of .899225 to 900 thousandths, which increased the pure gold to the dollar from 23.20 to 23.22 grains, at which it still remains.

By this act the fineness of both the gold and silver coins was fixed at 900 thousandths. The silver dollar weighed 412½ grains troy, and the gold was issued at the rate of 25.8 per dollar in value, the actual gold dollar coin not being authorized, however, until 1849. The relation of the metals, therefore, was almost exactly 16 to 1.

The quantity of pure silver in the dollar, as originally fixed, was not changed from the date of its issue down to April 1, 1873, when it was discontinued; but the weight of the coins of less denomination was reduced from 412½ to 384 grains standard per dollar of nominal value by the act of February 21, 1853, which fixed the weight of the half-dollar at 192 grains, and the quarter-dollar, dime, and half-dime at one-half, one-fifth, and one-tenth of the said half dollar.

The standard weight of these latter coins was, by the coinage act of 1873, increased to 385.8 grains to the dollar, composed of two half-dollars, four quarter-dollars, and ten dimes, and corresponding in weight and fineness with the five-franc silver coin of the Latin states of Europe. These coins are issued at the rate of $1.24414 per standard ounce, 803¾ ounces giving coins of the nominal value of $1,000.

The coinage act, in effect, abolished the silver dollar of 412½ grains troy, (371¼ grains pure silver,) and declared the gold dollar of 25.8 grains, nine-tenths fine, (23.22 grains pure gold,) the unit of value, and thus legally established gold as the sole standard or measure of value. The issue of the copper coin commenced in 1793, silver in 1794, and gold in 1795.

Branch Mints were established in 1835 at New Orleans, La., Charlotte, N. C., and Dahlonega, Ga.; in 1854 at San Francisco, and in 1870 at Carson City, Nev. An Assay-office was established at New York in the year 1854; Denver, Colo., in 1864; and at Boise City, Idaho, in 1872.

These establishments were not distinct institutions, but branches of the Mint, managed by superintendents who were subject to the general control of the Director of the Mint at Philadelphia. Originally the Director made his report direct to the President of the United States, but in time the former became, by the provisions of several acts, subject to the control of the Secretary of the Treasury.

The coinage was conducted under this organization down to the 1st of April, 1873, when the new law became operative, and which established the Mints and Assay-offices as a bureau of the Treasury Department, placed the several institutions upon substantially an equal basis, and brought them under the general supervision of the chief officer of the bureau. Under other provisions of the same act the office of treasurer of the Mint was abolished, and the receiving and custody of all deposits, as well as the disbursing of all moneys, and keeping and rendition of accounts, formerly vested in that officer, devolved upon the superintendent; the Director of the Mint under the old law taking the title and assuming the duties of Superintendent of the Mint at Philadelphia.

MANUFACTURE OF MINOR COINS, MEDALS, AND WORKING-DIES.

The manufacture of the minor coins (bronze and copper-nickel alloys) is confined by law to the Mint at Philadelphia. The working-dies from originals only authorized are also to be made there, and when new devices or coins are authorized, the engraver must, if required by the Director, prepare the devices, models, molds, and matrices or original dies for the same; power, however, is given the Director to employ temporarily for that purpose artists not connected with the Mint.

MINT BUREAU.

Notwithstanding the inconveniences arising from the want of an appropriation for its support, the new bureau has been effectively organized, and the operations and business of the Mints and Assay-offices are being conducted under its direction in a satisfactory manner.

MOTTOES ON OUR COINS.

The law requires the motto "E Pluribus Unum" to be placed upon certain of the gold and silver coins, and provides that the Director of the Mint, with the approval of the Secretary of the Treasury, may cause the motto "In God we trust" to be inscribed upon such coins as shall admit of the same. The placing of "E Pluribus Unum" on the coins is therefore obligatory, and was accordingly observed in the preparation of the original dies for the trade-dollar. The motto "In God we trust" also appears upon that coin.

The additional motto cannot be placed upon either the obverse or reverse of the gold and silver coins, other than the trade-dollar, without excluding the motto "In God we trust," or rendering a new arrangement of devices, legends, and inscriptions necessary. It does not appear desirable to discontinue the motto last referred to, or incur the inconvenience and expense which would attend a new arrangement of devices. Moreover, the coins with a motto on the obverse, or an additional one on the reverse, would appear over-dressed. It will therefore be advisable to place the additional motto upon the periphery or rim of the coins.

Having concluded, after due examination of the subject, that the substitution of raised lettters on the gold coin in place of the present reeded edge would prevent, in a great measure, the splitting, filing, and filling of the coins for fraudulent purposes, I referred the subject of the preparation of the necessary machinery for that purpose to the officers of the Philadelphia Mint, also to a private engraver, who are now engaged upon the work. In connection with this question, I called for a report of the result of some experiments which were made at the Mint at Philadelphia in the year 1860, and which had for their object the better protection of the gold coins by making them thinner, and slightly concave on both sides. An elaborate report upon the subject from the assayer at Philadelphia has been received, and will be found attached to this report.

The question will be further considered, and the necessary experiments made to determine what measures will be most likely to afford complete protection, if possible, against fraudulent reduction of the weight of the coins.

Gold coin being the standard or measure of value, their protection from natural abrasion, and especially against fraudulent diminution, is a matter of the utmost importance. Sufficient time should therefore be taken to carefully examine the subject, and no alterations should be made without due consideration and the advantages of which are not clearly determined.

These observations are made with a view to explain what otherwise might be considered as a tardiness in complying with the requirements of law in respect to placing the additional motto upon the coins.

MANUFACTURE OF MEDALS.

Proper regulations for the manufacture of medals at the Mint at Philadelphia, which institution has the custody of the national and other medal-dies, and possesses the necessary machinery for the purpose, have been prescribed and are now in force.

These regulations were necessary, inasmuch as prior to the 1st of April last no statutory provision authorizing the striking of medals existed, the business having been carried on since the year 1856 under departmental authority only.

RECOINAGE OF ABRADED GOLD COINS.

The fourteenth section of the coinage act provides that the gold coins shall be receivable at the United States Treasury at their denominational value when not reduced by natural abrasion more than one-half per centum below the standard weight prescribed by law, after a circulation of twenty years, as shown by the date of coinage; a ratable proportion being allowed for less periods of circulation. It also authorized the recoinage of all pieces in the Treasury the weight of which should be found below the limit of wear.

Under this section, and the provisions of a previous act, about $27,000,000 were melted, of which $14,021,550.70 were recoined during the fiscal year. The recoinage of the balance has since been going on.

It is estimated that of the coin now in the Treasury there are about five millions which will require to be renovated. The difference between the nominal and intrinsic value of the amount recoined was about $73,549.30. The recoinage embraced nearly all the abraded gold coin in the country, other than those in circulation on the Pacific coast, and which it is estimated do not exceed $2,000,000. A proper provision should be made for calling in the light coins still in circulation, especially in view of the general renovation which has been made. The loss from natural abrasion should be defrayed by the Government and not by the last holder, for the reason that it has occurred while the coins were performing the function of a circulating medium. This principle has been fully recognized in the recent coinage laws of the German Empire, Denmark, Sweden and Norway. Provision should of course be made for excluding coins which may have been artificially reduced in weight or violently injured, and the reception of worn coins should be confined to the Mints, where all necessary precautions against receiving fraudulently reduced coins can be effectively observed.

In explanation of what might otherwise be considered an unusually large number of pieces found to be below the prescribed limit of abrasion, it should be stated there has not been a recoinage of gold in this country since that which followed the change of standard in 1834, and that in the very large exports of coin since the suspension of specie payments in 1861 the unworn coin were selected for that purpose and the light or worn pieces excluded.

After the present recoinage shall have been completed, the expense of keeping the gold coin in good condition will not probably exceed a few thousand dollars per annum. It should be added, in connection with this subject, that, in practice, the provisions of law as to periods of time of circulation cannot be enforced, and that it would be better to leave this point to departmental regulations.

NEW MINT AT SAN FRANCISCO.

The new mint edifice which has been for some time past in course of construction at San Francisco is about completed, and the work of fitting up the necessary machinery, fixtures, and apparatus has been commenced under the supervision of a competent superintendent, and will it is expected, be finished by the 1st of July, 1874.

When completd, this will be one of the best appointed Mints in the world, and will reflect much credit on Supervising Architect Mullet, who designed it and under whose direction it has been erected. It was at one time considered unnecessarily large, but in fitting it up with a refining and coining capacity equal to the present demand it has been found necessary to occupy the entire building.

MINT EXAMINATIONS.

Some important questions of a chemical and metallurgical character having arisen with regard to various mint manipulations of the precious metals, a series of experiments to determine the same were made at the Philadelphia Mint, in the latter part of the fiscal year, under the supervision of Professor R. E. Rogers. The results obtained were conclusive on several points, and will be of value in future minting operations.

Professor Rogers also visited San Francisco for the purpose of determining what process would be most advantageous to adopt for the refining and parting of the precious metals at the new mint in that city, and to prepare plans and drawings for the same. An able report upon this subject, in which the sulphuric-acid process is recommended for adoption, and submitting plans and estimates for fitting up the same, has been received.

The mint at Carson, Nev., and assay-offices at Denver, Colo., and Boise City, Idaho, were examined during the summer by R. J. Stevens, esq., formerly superintendent of the mint at San Francisco, and who reported those institutions as in a satisfactory condition.

EARNINGS AND EXPENDITURES.

In order that you may be fully advised in relation to the cost of operating the Mints and Assay-offices, a detailed statement of the expenditures and receipts of the several establishments is incorporated in this report.

The law requires that the charges to the depositor for the several operations necessary to bring bullion to the proper condition for coinage shall equal, but not exceed, the expenses thereof, including labor, materials, wastage, and use of machinery. There is some difficulty in complying strictly with this provision of law, arising mainly from the unequal distribution of the bullion to the different establishments. For example, all minor coinage, the principal recoinage of gold and silver, and the greater portion of the subsidiary silver coinage is done at the Philadelphia Mint, while the amount of bullion refined and parted there is quite small. Now the ratio of expenses in operating on bullion depends, to a considerable extent, on the amount operated upon within a given time. If the amount be large, the expenses will be less proportionately than if a smaller amount is treated. We are, therefore, compelled to aim at a fair average, and fix the charges accordingly. The present rates of charges are, I am satisfied, as low as can be properly fixed under the law. Our true policy is to be liberal with respect to these charges for the purpose of affording every proper encouragement to the gold and silver mining interests of the country. We should not, however, enter into competition, in the general sense of that term, with private refining establishments, but rather afford them every reasonable encouragement, especially when they are so located that the Government assay or determination of value, as well as accountability for the bullion, can be preserved to depositors. With respect to the expenses of the Mints, it should be stated that it never was intended that they should be self-sustaining, and that prior to 1853 no charge for the coinage of either gold or silver was imposed; the evident intention of the framers of the original mint law having been to invite foreign bullion and coin to the Mint for coinage. In the year above stated a law was enacted authorizing and requiring a coinage charge of one-half per cent. to be imposed, which continued in force down to the 1st of April, 1873, when the new coinage act took effect, reducing the charge to one-fifth of one per cent.

London has been for many years, and still continues to be, the principal bullion market of the world, and the advantages commercially and otherwise derived from the receipt and distribution of the greater portion of the precious-metal product are and have been very great, and so well convinced were the financiers of Great Britain as to the advantages of the free coinage system, that the effort made in the House of Commons a few years ago to practically abolish it by exacting a seigniorage from the gold coin, was, through their opposition, overwhelmly defeated.

The reasons for a free coinage of gold are simple and direct, and are briefly stated as follows:

1st. By throwing the cost of coinage on the depositor, the cost of production is correspondingly increased.

2d. The coining value of gold is lowered, which tends to repel it from the Mint and encourage its export. For the same reason it repels foreign gold.

3d. It is unjust to the depositor, as he pays the entire expense of coinage, in which the whole public are as much interested as himself. Coinage of the standard metal is indispensable to the public, and the expense should accordingly be contributed by all.

It should also be stated that, under the coinage act, the melting of bullion to bring it to a condition for determining by assay the proportion of gold and silver contained, or the "fineness," as it is termed in mint language, is made a subject of charge to the depositor, and will bring to the Treasury a sum approximating somewhat to that accruing from the coinage charge. The imposition of this new charge should be considered an additional argument for abolishing the coinage charge. It is not subject to the same objection, for the reason that a charge for melting is made in London.

INTRODUCTION OF THE CHLORINATION PROCESS FOR REFINING AND PARTING AT THE PHILADELPHIA MINT.

Arrangements have been made for the introduction and use at the Philadelphia Mint of the chlorination process of Professor Miller of the Australian mint, for refining and parting the precious metals, and is expected to be in operation in the course of another month.

The process is an economical and, in other respects, desirable one for separating silver from gold of high fineness, and for expelling small percentages of base metals occasionally present in gold, which, if not eliminated, renders it brittle and unfit for coinage. It is, however, inferior to the sulphuric-acid process for treating gold largely combined with silver, such, for example, as the bullion from the great Comstock lode in Nevada, which constitutes at the present time more than one-third of our total annual production.

COINAGE FOR SOUTH AMERICAN GOVERNMENTS.

Applications for the manufacture of silver and token-coins are occasionally received from some of the governments of South America, and declined, for the reason that by law none but United States coin can be issued from our mints. When the new mint at San Francisco shall have been completed, and especially if operations be resumed at New Orleans, our capacity will be sufficient to undertake occasional coinages for other countries. There can be no objection to authorizing such coinages as can be made at times when our mints are not fully employed in meeting the home demands for coin. It would be a friendly act to countries not possessing the facilities for manufacturing their own coin, as well as of some advantage to our commerce. The coins should, of course, be of the legal standards of the governments applying for them, and bear their prescribed devices and inscriptions.

In connection with this subject it should be stated that for several years past considerable amounts of United States subsidiary silver-coin have been exported to, and are now in circulation in, Central America and portions of South America. It would certainly be better to manufacture coin to be issued by those countries as their own than to encourage the exportation thence of our overvalued silver coins, a part of which sooner or later will return to us, and probably worn to an extent rendering their withdrawal from circulation and replacing with new coins necessary.

Overvalued or subsidiary coins, as they are generally termed, are not properly " coins of commerce," being intended for internal circulation in the country issuing them, and, having a higher nominal than bullion value, are inexportable, until expelled by inferior currency.

VALUATION OF FOREIGN COINS AND PAR OF EXCHANGE.

The first section of the act of March 3, 1873, entitled " An act to establish the custom-house valuation of the sovereign or pound sterling of Great Britain, and to fix the par of exchange," provides that "The value of foreign coin, as expressed in the money of account of the United States, shall be that of pure metal of such coin of standard value," and that " the values of the standard coins in circulation of the various nations of the world shall be estimated annually by the Director of the Mint, and proclaimed on the 1st day of January by the Secretary of the Treasury."

The Department having construed this section to require invoices of foreign merchandise at our custom-houses to be converted into the money of account of the United States (for the purpose of levying duties) on the basis of established standards instead of the values given to the various coins representing the same, by different acts of Congress, and which were based on the assay of coins more or less reduced in weight, and therefore not representing the values they were originally intended to denote, it became necessary to obtain authentic information in relation to the units of foreign moneys of account, and the quantity of pure metal declared by law to represent the same. A circular calling for this information was, soon after the organization of this Bureau, addressed through the State Department to all our representatives in foreign countries. The opportunity was embraced to ask also for information on various points connected with the coinage of metals and production of bullion. Replies from thirty-five governments have been received, and extracts therefrom will be found in the appendix to this report. These papers furnish a fund of valuable information, not to be found elsewhere in this country, and when the remaining countries are heard from, the entire list should be printed for the use of the different Departments of the Government.

It is proper to state that the earlier acts of Congress fixing the custom-house valuation of certain foreign coins were passed at a time when such coins were receivable for duties, and as they were more or less worn, their valuation on the basis of their actual average content of pure metal was necessary in order to protect the Treasury from loss in collecting the revenue. But the case is now different; foreign coins no longer being receivable for customs. In view of these facts the new law very properly makes it obligatory, after the 1st of January, 1874, to deal with established standards, and not the actual or bullion value of coins representing them.

Accordingly, when a foreign invoice is to be converted into the money of account of the United States, the quantity of pure gold declared by law to represent the monetary units respectively of the two countries will be the basis of computation.

From what is above stated it will at once be seen that under laws yet in force, the various foreign monetary units are undervalued, and that since the worn coins formerly representing them are no longer receivable in the payment of customs duties, the reform contemplated by the act referred to is necessary and proper.

It is expected that the change in the existing mode of computing and quoting sterling exchange will lead to the correct quotation of United States securities in London. Under the present system, which is a relic of colonial days, the par of a dollar is quoted in London at 91½, whereas in all fairness the quotation should be 100. The subject will no doubt receive the careful and ready attention of the proper parties in London, and our securities soon be quoted, as all others are, upon the actual and not a fictitious or technical par.

Notwithstanding the new basis for converting foreign moneys of account into that of the United States, accurate information in relation to the actual average weight, fineness, and value of such foreign coins as are known to our commerce, will be found useful for many purposes. Statements embracing the principal coins of the world, and exhibiting the results of their careful assay, (under the instructions of this Office,) at the Philadelphia Mint, are therefore given in the appendix of this report.

Occasional assays of foreign coins will in future be made at the San Francisco Mint, and Assay-office, New York, as well as at Philadelphia, and the results given annually in the Director's report.

GOLD THE STANDARD OR MEASURE OF VALUE; SILVER SUBSIDIARY.

The experiences of different countries, our own included, have conclusively shown that the double or alternate standard of gold and silver, at fixed rates, is subject to derangement from variations in the relative value of the two metals, and that the steady value of the money-unit, which is a matter of great importance, can only be maintained by making one of the precious metals the standard or measure of value, and assigning a subordinate position as to coinage for the other.

Gold being less variable than silver, and of superior value, has been adopted as the standard by all countries which have reformed their monetary laws during the last four years. The list embraces Japan, Germany, the United States of America, Denmark, and Sweden and Norway. Great Britain adopted the gold standard in the year 1816, and still continues it.

France, Belgium, Italy, Switzerland, and Greece still adhere to the double standard, but it is represented, so far as silver is concerned, by only one denomination of full-valued and unlimited legal-tender coin, viz, the five-franc piece; all other silver coins being overvalued or subsidiary, and of limited tender. The double standard of the countries last referred to was, when adopted, based on the assumption that 15½ ounces of silver were equal in value to 1 ounce of gold. Since that proportion was fixed, however, silver has declined to a rate which gives the relative market-value of the two metals as nearly 16½ to 1.

Holland, it is understood, is about to change from silver to the gold

18 Ab

standard, being forced to do so on account of the depreciation of silver and the consequent advance in the rate of exchange on countries of the gold standard. The same reason will gradually bring the remaining silver-standard countries to the gold standard. It therefore appears that the double standard must necessarily be a failure, and that its abandonment by all civilized countries is merely a question of time and convenience.

The passing from the double standard of gold and silver and from silver to gold by the nations cannot be completed without some embarrassments financially and otherwise. The United States prepared for the adoption of the gold standard in 1853 by demonetizing all silver coins of less denomination than the dollar. The latter coin being undervalued by the reduction of the gold coinage in 1834, was melted down or exported as fast as coined, and thus left the way clear for the adoption, without any embarrassment whatever, of the gold standard in 1873.

The countries adopting gold as the sole measure of value have, as a necessary consequence, assigned a subsidiary position for silver. This system increases the use of gold as money, and decreases that of silver for the same purpose; or, in other words, enhances the value of the one, and depreciates that of the other. While the demand for gold for coinage has materially increased, large quantities of silver hitherto in circulation as standard money in Germany, Denmark, and Sweden and Norway, and constituting treasury and bank reserves in those countries, will, by the substitution of the gold standard, be thrown on the market as bullion, and aid in its further depreciation.

It will be well to refer at this point to the price of silver bullion in London, during the decade ending with the year 1872. The able and interesting British Mint report for 1872 gives the yearly average mint-price of silver in the years 1863 to 1872, inclusive, as follows:

1863.	1864.	1865.	1866.	1867.	1868.	1869.	1870.	1871.	1872.
d. 61 1·2	d. 61 1·4	d. 61	d. 61 7·8	d. 60 3·4	d. 60 7·8	d. 60 5·16	d. 60 1·2	d. 60 7·16	d. 60 5·16

The price in London is now 58⅞ pence per ounce, British standard, (925 thousandths fine,) showing a decline since 1863 of 2⅜ pence, equal to about 5¼ cents per ounce, or about 4⅛ per cent.

India has for many years past been the principal market for silver, its circulation now being equal to a thousand millions of dollars. The demand from that market, however, has fallen off during the last ten years to the extent of several millions, the decline being due principally to the fall in the price of cotton, soon after the close of the late civil war in this country. Prior to the commencement of the war the United States was the principal source of England's cotton supply. When hostilities commenced India soon became the chief source of supply. When peace was declared and the cotton of the United States poured into England, the sales of India cotton in 1866 realized but half the money of the previous year, and the price of silver in London fell from 62¼ to 60 pence. In the year 1864 about one hundred millions of silver were sent from Europe to India.

In view of the foregoing facts, and the large annual production of this metal from the mines of the United States and Mexico, it is evident that Congress acted wisely in establishing gold as the sole standard of value.

The coinage act assigns a subsidiary position for silver, by providing for its issue in coin having a higher nominal than intrinsic value, limiting it as a legal tender to $5, and placing the issue under the control of the Government. These coins are issued at the rate of 124.414 cents per standard ounce, and the difference between that amount and the price paid for a standard ounce of silver bullion is the gain or seigniorage realized by the Government, and out of which it defrays the expenses of coinage and distribution. The seigniorage will of course vary with the market-price of silver, and with the mode of payment, i. e. whether in gold or subsidiary silver coin.

Silver coins have been issued at San Francisco and Carson since the 1st of April last in payment for silver contained in gold deposits, and being sufficient to meet the local demand for subsidiary coin, it has not been necessary to purchase silver for that purpose and pay for it in gold. The price paid for silver at those Mints has been 118 cents per ounce. When the coinage law went into effect the subsidiary silver coin on the Pacific coast were from 2 to 3 per cent. discount, as compared with gold, and caused much inconvenience, especially to the laboring classes and retail dealers. The discount has since declined to less than 1 per cent., and will no doubt soon disappear. I need scarcely add that as gold and silver coin constitute the circulating medium in California, Oregon, and Nevada, the issue of subsidiary silver coin by the Mints in that section should be restricted to the limit contemplated by law.

The twenty-eighth section of the coinage act provides that for two years after the passage of the act, "silver coins shall be paid out at the Mint in Philadelphia, and the Assay-office, New York, for silver bullion purchased for coinage, under such regulations as may be prescribed by the Secretary of the Treasury."

Under the above authority silver bullion has been purchased and paid for in subsidiary silver coin at the Philadelphia Mint, and Assay-office, New York, at 120 cents per standard ounce, the price having been reduced from 122½ cents to that rate by you in March last. The coins thus issued were, it is understood, sent to Texas, or exported to Central and South America, and where it is supposed they are now in circulation. These rates have since been reduced to 116 cents per standard ounce at San Francisco and Carson, and 118 at New York and Philadelphia, payable in silver coin.

The authority for issuing subsidiary silver coin in payment for silver bullion purchased for such coinage will expire on the 12th of February, 1875. The bullion for the purpose of supplying the coin will then be purchased from time to time at gold rates, and paid for in gold coin, the Government re-imbursing itself for the outlay with the gold coins received in exchange for the silver coin. This mode of issuing subsidiary silver is undoubtedly the true one in countries where gold is the standard, and the circulating medium consists of coin with bank or treasury notes as auxiliary to and convertible at par into coins of the standard metal.

In the mean time it is quite certain that the depreciation of silver and appreciation of United States currency will, before long, enable the Government to purchase silver bullion with gold, coin it on its own account, and pay out the resulting silver coins at their nominal value. At the present rate for silver and premium on gold, the operation would net the Treasury about 10 per cent. This plan could not, it is believed, do injury to any interest, but would be productive of much benefit to the precious metal mining interests and business of the country at large, and should be adhered to until specie payments shall have been resumed on a substantial basis; after which these coins should be issued only in exchange at par for gold coins, and thus restrict the issue to the actual requirements of the public for the purposes for which such coins are intended. To recapitulate, we have—

1st. Gold as the sole standard or measure of value issued in coins the intrinsic and denominational value of which correspond. Such coins are a legal tender in any sum.

2d. Silver as subsidiary to gold issued in coins the denominational value of which exceeds their bullion value, and are a legal tender in any sum not exceeding $5. They are manufactured on Government account only and paid out as follows:

1. The Government purchases from time to time silver bullion at its market-value in gold, for manufacture into coins of less denomination than the dollar, and issues them in exchange for gold coins at par, in sums of not less than $100. The difference between the price paid for the bullion and the rate at which it is issued in coin is the gain or seigniorage to the Government, less the expense of manufacture and distribution. Being exchangeable only for gold coin, the issue will consequently be limited to the actual requirements of the public for change. This plan is adapted to times of specie payment.

2. The Government purchases silver bullion, and pays for it in subsidiary silver coins, in which case the seigniorage is in effect divided with the seller of the bullion, provided he is able to pass them off at their nominal or tael value in this country in times of specie payment, or in other countries where coin constitutes the circulating medium. This mode of issue was authorized, for a limited period, to enable the coin to be exported to countries having respectively dollars of different values as the monetary unit, and expires, as before stated, by limitation of law on the 13th of February, 1875.

3. Purchases of silver bullion are made at gold value, and manufactured, on Government account, into subsidiary coins, which are paid out at the discretion of the Treasury Department and according to its convenience. In this last, as in the first case, the full seigniorage is realized by the Government.

The mode of issue last described is adapted for the condition of things which must necessarily precede the resumption of specie payments, and can be made available from time to time according to the market-value of silver and the price of gold compared with United States currency. When the market is depressed and prices rule low the Government may increase the silver-bullion fund of the Mints, transfer the coin manufactured from it to the Treasury, and pay it out at its discretion and convenience. It is the only system under which, until the resumption of specie payments, the Treasury can realize the full seigniorage on the subsidiary silver coin, which it should do in accordance with a well-established principle and the practice of other countries in respect to the manufacture and issue of such coins. For several years past the seigniorage realized by the Government upon the coinage of silver was only 2¼ cents per standard ounce, out of which the expense of manufacturing and distributing the coin was defrayed. In the European states the seigniorage on subsidiary coin is from 10 to 15 per cent.

A communication from the Superintendent of the Philadelphia Mint, presenting some interesting and useful information (obtained through a correspondence with the Master of the mint at Calcutta) in relation to the amount of silver in circulation in India, will be found in the appendix.

INTERNATIONAL COINAGE.

The subject of international coinage continues to be agitated by the friends of monetary reform, but no substantial progress appears to have been made in the direction of a general assimilation of the principal coinages of the world.

The United States adheres to the dollar, Great Britain to the pound sterling, and the states of the Latin monetary union (France, Belgium, Switzerland, and Italy) to the franc.

Germany has provided for a new money of account, with the mark as the unit, and which is represented by fine gold of the value in United States money of 23.82 cents. Denmark, Sweden, and Norway have established a new money of account with the crown as the unit, and represented by fine gold of the value of 26.798 cents in United States money.

These diverse moneys of account, to which the price of all commodities has been or will be adjusted, cannot be brought into harmony unless all adopt one of the foregoing, or a new money of account, and that does not appear probable. All, therefore, that can be reasonably expected to result from the frequent discussions of the subject is that gold (and the nine-tenths standard for coinage) will be universally adopted as the measure of value and money of commerce, together with a reasonable but uniform tolerance or variation from standard in the manufacture and issue of coins, and a limit of wear from the attrition of circulation; the first being necessary on account of the impracticability of making all the pieces of exactly the same weight and fineness, and the latter to avoid frequent recoinages. Provision should also be made for keeping the coins within the prescribed limits of abrasion by replacing those worn below it with new coins at the expense of the public treasury, and if there be charges for coinage, these should be uniform. Gold would then be the universal measure of value, and coins made from it, to represent the moneys of account, would be approximately of the same value by weight; gold being as to gold unchangeable in value, and of the same quality wherever produced.

In this connection it is gratifying to note that Germany, Denmark, Sweden, and Norway have in their recent coinage laws conformed to the above-stated requirements.

The advantages of any proposed unification of moneys involving alteration in the quantity of fine gold now representing the dollar of account should be decided and well determined before the United States would be justified in adopting it, especially as the funded loan is by law expressly payable in gold coin of the present standard, and it should be further added that the alterations of standard moneys, weights and measures to which the public have long been accustomed are grave matters, and should be undertaken only when imperatively required as a matter of public utility.

A convention of the friends of monetary reform was recently held at Vienna, and copies of its proceedings have, through the courtesy of Minister Jay and the State Department, been sent to this Office, and will receive due attention.

INCREASE OF COINAGE.

A gratifying increase of business at the San Francisco and Philadelphia Mints, and Assay-office, New York, took place immediately on and after the coinage act became operative, and which has recently been greatly augmented in consequence of large importations of foreign coin and bullion, and the almost total cessation of bullion exports. Arrangements have been made to promptly meet all demands upon the Mints for coin. As a general thing, deposits have been paid for within two days after they were made. This additional work has necessarily increased the expenses for wages and materials, and will render deficiency appropriations necessary.

Some idea of the increase of operations may be formed, when it is stated that the coinage of gold during the month of October approximated in value $14,000,000.

INCREASING DEMAND FOR GOLD.

The gradual adoption of the gold standard, and consequent demonetization of silver, will of course be followed by an increase in the value of gold, or what is the same thing, a decrease in the price of articles measured by it. Indeed it is quite certain that this effect is already perceptible in some portions of Europe. Be that as it may, however, it is safe to assume that Germany will soon have substituted three hundred millions of gold for silver heretofore used as standard money, and that Denmark, Sweden; and Norway will require nearly as much more in consequence of changing their standard from silver to gold. Now, add to the foregoing the requirements of France and the United States in the near future, and it will be readily understood that gold must appreciate in value.

It is true that the mines of the world produce annually about one hundred millions of gold; but in considering this as a stock to be drawn upon for coinage, it must be remembered that the consumption of gold in the arts has largely increased during the last twenty-three years, and now approximates to about twenty-five millions per annum.

It is not within the province of this report to consider or discuss the bearing of the above-stated facts upon financial questions, and I will therefore dismiss the subject with the remark that countries, however wealthy and prosperous, cannot, even with the aid of bills of exchange, maintain an exclusively metallic currency, and that the use of paper money as an auxiliary to and convertible into coin is more likely to increase than diminish in the future. A more extensive use of subsidiary coin than heretofore is also probable. In support of this latter view reference is made to the fact that during the year 1872 the subsidiary silver coinage of Great Britain amounted to about $6,000,000, all for home circulation, and in a country which was previously well stocked with coin. The French subsidiary coin for the same year amounted to about $7,000,000.

AMOUNT OF COIN IN THE COUNTRY.

The coin, except as to the Pacific coast States and Territories, being as a general thing in the Treasury and banks, the present time is a favorable one for estimating the amount of gold and silver coin in the country. From the most reliable data obtainable, the gold coin is estimated at $135,000,000, and subsidiary silver $5,000,000—total, $140,000,000. The silver coin is principally in circulation in California, Oregon, Nevada, Idaho, Arizona, and Texas.

The increase to the stock of coin in this country has been at a very fair rate since the 1st of April last, and the indications are that although there may be occasional exportations, it will gradually go on until an amount sufficient to enable the country to safely resume specie payments is reached. This much-desired result, however, will depend upon conditions which cannot here be discussed.

TEST ASSAYS OF THE COINAGE.

Pursuant to law a certain number of pieces are taken, indiscriminately, from every delivery of coins made by the Coiner to the Superintendent, sealed up and placed in a box securely closed by two different locks, the keys of which are respectively in the custody of the Superintendent and Assayer, so that neither officer can have access to it without the presence of the other.. In the month of February, annually, the pieces reserved from the coinage of the previous year are tested as to legal weight and fineness by the Assay Commission.

As the annual assay or trial of the coinage takes place after the coin has been issued, any error that might have occurred would not be discovered in time for its prompt correction. It has, therefore, been deemed proper, as a precautionary measure, to direct monthly assays of the coinage to be made. These assays have been conducted at the Philadelphia Mint, and the results found entirely satisfactory. Arrangements will soon be perfected to have these test assays made by one Mint upon another.

Although no difficulties are anticipated, it is well to have these tests made, for the reasons already stated, and especially in view of the fact that the limit of variation from the standard fineness of the gold coinage was reduced by the coinage act from two ounces to one ounce in a thousand; that is to say, the standard being 900 parts pure metal to 100 of alloy, the pure metal must not fall below 899 or exceed 901 parts in a thousand. Moreover, it should be stated that, of late years, a small percentage of base metals is to be found either chemically or mechanically combined with gold and silver bullion, resulting from lode or vein mining, particularly in the base-metal region of Eastern Nevada, and if not entirely eliminated in the refining operation, such bullion, when alloyed with copper to bring it to the standard for coinage, occasionally presents anomalies which render accurate mixture in melting more difficult than bullion containing no base or refractory metals.

From the facts above stated, it will be seen that not only is it necessary to take the precaution of test assays, but that our assayers and their assistants must be well qualified for the business.

PROPOSED RESUMPTION OF COINAGE AT NEW ORLEANS.

By your direction, the amount believed to be necessary to place the Mint at New Orleans in condition for coinage operations, and for its support during the fiscal year, was included in the estimates of appropriations for the Mints and Assay-offices. Should the necessary appropriations be obtained for that purpose, the establishment can probably be put in operation in about three months' time, and afterward usefully employed in the manufacture of stamped bars and coinage of silver..

TRADE-DOLLAR.

The trade-dollar of silver authorized by the coinage act is designed expressly for export, and has no fixed value as compared with gold. It is in no proper sense a monetary standard or unit of account, and is not included or referred to when the silver coins for home use are spoken of; the latter being purposely overvalued, as before stated, to retain them in circulation. Having been made a legal tender in limited amounts, it may eventually, if the price of silver relative to gold falls sufficiently, to some extent enter into home circulation, but its export value will always be in excess of that of the subsidiary silver coin, its bullion value or quantity of pure metal being about 8¼ per cent. in excess.

The issue of the trade-dollar was not commenced until nearly a month after the close of the fiscal year. It has been shipped to some extent to China and Japan, but we have not, as yet, received any account of its reception in those empires. It will no doubt require a year or two for its successful introduction there.

COMPENSATION OF MINT OFFICERS.

I deem it my duty to call your attention to the fact that the salaries allowed the officers of Mints and Assay-offices are inadequate. They were fixed at their present rates several years ago when the expenses of living were much lower than at the present time, and are insufficient to afford a respectable living.

The officers intrusted with the preparation of the coinage must be men of character, education, and fair ability. Their duties requiring all their time, the compensation should be placed at a rate which will render it unnecessary for them to engage in any private business. The present occupants are well qualified for their respective positions, the most of them having held them for a number of years, and acquired valuable experience. I respectfully urge that you will give this subject a fair consideration, to the end that the salaries referred to may be increased to an amount corresponding to the character of the service rendered.

Acknowledgments are due to the Secretary of the Treasury and other officers of the Department for the steady support given the Director in the organization of the Mint Bureau, also to the officers, assistants, and clerks of the several Mints and Assay-offices, together with the clerks of the Bureau, for faithful and efficient discharge of their responsible duties.

I must, in conclusion, express my satisfaction that, though we have several hundred employés performing various duties connected with the mintage of the precious metals, not a single case of embezzlement has come to our knowledge during the year, and we have good reasons for believing that none have occurred.

The regulations for the transaction of business at the Mints and Assay-offices are of the strictest character, requiring not only a record to be kept, but vouchers taken and given, and periodically rendered to the accounting officers of the Treasury through this Office, for every transaction involving the transfer of bullion, coin, or medals, and the receipt and payment of all moneys.

I am, sir, very respectfully,

H. R. LINDERMAN,
Director of the Mint.

Hon. WILLIAM A. RICHARDSON,
Secretary of the Treasury.

REPORT OF THE CHIEF OF THE BUREAU OF STATISTICS.

TREASURY DEPARTMENT,
Bureau of Statistics, November 4, 1873.

SIR: The Chief of the Bureau of Statistics has the honor of submitting the following report of its operations during the fiscal year ended June 30, 1873:

CLERICAL FORCE.

Clerical force of the Bureau at the close of the year, in addition to the chief clerk, consisted of thirty-one male and eight female clerks, who were employed as follows:

Division.	Names of chiefs.	Number of clerks.		
		Male.	Female.	Total.
Examination	J. N. Whitney	5		5
Compilation	Thomas Clear	12	2	14
Tonnage and immigration	L. F. Ward	5	1	6
Registry of merchant marine	J. B. Parker	4	1	5
Translation and revision	A. W. Angerer	2		2
Publication and miscellaneous	James Ryan	2	1	3
Library and files	E. T. Peters	1	1	2
Stationery, pay, property, and copying	J. D. O'Connell	1	1	2

In addition to the female clerks above designated, one has charge of the correspondence and postal arrangements.

At the present time the clerical force consists of one chief clerk, Mr. E. B. Elliott, who is a member of the Civil Service Commission; thirty-three male and eight female clerks, two of the former being assigned from the office of the Secretary of the Treasury.

WORK OF THE BUREAU.

It is impossible to furnish a tabular statement of the nature and extent of the work performed in the Bureau, owing to its peculiar and varied character.

Division of examination.—The following embraces a part of the work performed in this division:

Number of pages of letters written........................... 4,899
Acknowledgments of letters written........................... 2,241
Acknowledgments of statements written....................... 4,384
Statements called for.. 639
Statements examined... 18,470
Statements corrected by correspondence...................... 1,275

The work in this division includes a critical and elaborate examination of the monthly and quarterly returns from the various custom-houses. During the past year it has also aided the chief officers of the Bureau in the classification of countries and of articles imported, and in the revision of the customs regulations pertaining to the Bureau, and has prepared books of record and blanks for statements of customs statistics.

Compilation.—This division is divided into sections, embracing, respectively, statistics of home consumption, indirect and *in transitu* trade, and of merchandise warehoused and withdrawn from warehouse. No statement can be presented which will give an adequate idea of the amount of careful and intelligent labor performed by the clerks employed in the compilation of the statistics of commerce.

Immigration and navigation.—A considerable part of the work of this division consists in compiling the statistics of navigation, which have been largely increased by their publication monthly instead of quarterly, as formerly.

The importance of obtaining and publishing accurate statistics, not only of the ages, sexes, and ports of arrival, but of the nationalities and occupations of the large and increasing numbers of immigrants, has imposed additional duties on this division. Special efforts have been made by the undersigned to induce greater accuracy on the part of those who originally record the data, so that the compilations published by the Bureau may be full and trustworthy. The importance to our country of this annual inflow of foreign-born citizens requires more than ordinary care in the presentation of the facts.

NUMBERING OF VESSELS, TONNAGE, ETC.

Besides assigning official numbers to vessels, this division has expended a considerable amount of labor in carefully searching previous records to avoid duplication of entries, also in filling up and forwarding notices to the owners, and in entering the awards as well upon a manuscript list as upon the permanent records of the office. The compiling, copying, proof-reading, and distribution of the last annual "List of Merchant Vessels," and the usual compilations for the monthly and annual reports of the Bureau, with a variety of miscellaneous work, fully occupied the remaining time of the clerks of this division.

A statement showing the number of vessels and amount of tonnage belonging to the different customs districts of the United States on the 30th of June, 1873, geographically classified, is appended to this report, [marked A.] The aggregate tonnage of the country was 4,468,046 tons, and 31,684 vessels, a net increase over that at the close of the preceding fiscal year of 318,013 tons, or 7⅞ per cent., and 1,836 vessels, or 6¼ per cent.

Revision and translation.—The revision of the large amount of statistics compiled for publication, as well as in response to calls for information, is a work of considerable magnitude.

The statistical publications of various countries in continental Europe, received periodically by this Bureau, contain information of great value, which requires translation previous to publication. The Bureau is also enriched by the occasional receipt of information clothed in foreign languages, the translation of which increases the work of the division.

Publication, property, and miscellaneous.—A detailed mention of the variety of work performed in these divisions would occupy too much space. It is sufficient to say that the duties of the clerks so employed are onerous and responsible. The abolition of the franking privilege has imposed considerable additional labor upon the clerk in charge of the mails, who, in consequence, is required to carefully weigh and affix the requisite stamps, not only upon the letters sent, but upon the large number of blanks supplied to custom-houses, and also upon the monthly reports and other publications and documents sent by mail to all parts of the United States as well as to foreign countries.

Library.—Special efforts have been made by the librarian and his assistant to render the library increasingly useful.

The removal of the Bureau to another building at the close of the last fiscal year has afforded more room for the proper arrangement and classification of the books, documents, and newspapers, and consequently rendered them more easy of reference. The system of marking and indexing the chief items of interest in the various newspapers, magazines, and other periodicals on file, enables the Bureau to furnish to members of Congress and others much information not otherwise easy to be obtained. Continuous efforts will be made to procure, by exchange and otherwise, all publications of foreign governments which possess statistical value, as well as all similar publications issued by the governments of the States of our Union. From both these sources the library has received considerable additions during the past year, and a few valuable but inexpensive works have also been purchased. As our system of exchanges is extended, the number of valuable publications annually received from foreign governments will doubtless be largely increased.

PUBLICATIONS OF THE BUREAU.

Monthly reports of commerce and navigation.—The monthly reports of this Bureau have, as heretofore, been regularly published, and 3,000 copies distributed, a few hundred of which are sent to foreign countries. They have been compiled at the earliest date after the receipt and correction of the returns, and, no doubt, have been printed with as much dispatch as the arrangements of the Congressional Printing-Office would permit.

While regretting the delay occasioned by awaiting the returns from the remoter districts of our widely extended country, as well as by the frequently occurring necessity of writing to custom-house officers for corrected returns, the undersigned is unwilling to purchase greater celerity of publication at the expense of either completeness or accuracy in the monthly statements of our trade.

Though not so promptly published as the trade reports of some European countries, yet for accuracy of statement the statistics of commerce and navigation as issued by this Bureau may safely challenge comparison with those issued by any other government.*

Annual report of commerce, immigration, and navigation.—The volume for the fiscal year 1872 was compiled and sent to press at the usual period, but considerable delay in the publication occurred, as hereto-

---

* As an example of the recognition by the press of the importance of the work performed by the Bureau, and the value of its publications, it may not be improper to present a portion of an article which recently appeared in one of the leading commercial papers of New York, the Economist and Dry Goods Reporter, in its issue of November 22, 1873, as follows:

THE NATIONAL BUREAU OF STATISTICS.—The importance of this department of our Federal Government cannot be too highly appreciated by the commercial and manufacturing interests of the world, when they view the vast amount of labor necessary in compiling and condensing so much valuable information in such a small compass as its reports so ably testify. With a chain of sea-ports extending from the most eastern point in Maine down to Key West, thence along the Gulf coast to Mexico, across the Isthmus to California, and up the Pacific coast to the newly-acquired territory of Alaska, in all some four thousand miles; then gathering its reports from a territory of nearly three million square miles of area; considering all the difficulties that lie in the way, such as minute correspondence and tardiness of postal conveniences, we cannot but compliment the Bureau upon its efficiency, and the rapidity with which its work is given to the public. The monthly statements, which are transcripts of the various branches that come under its supervision, are, however, much later, and are at times of untold value to those engaged in the foreign trade. Its report for the fiscal year ended June 30, 1873, is a document of unusual interest to every business man of whatever nature, as it shows at a glance the entire amount of our trade with other nations, both as buyer and seller, besides giving many other statistics of great interest.

fore. The statements for the fiscal year 1873 have been compiled and sent to the Congressional Printer, and every effort will be made to furnish the volume to Congress early in the ensuing session.

The demand from nearly all the governments of the world for copies of this volume, as well as for the other publications of this Bureau and of the Department, induces the earnest recommendation that an increased number be authorized. Giving, as it does, in detail, our trade with each foreign country, as well as the trade of each customs-district, this annual possesses great value, not only to the statesmen, legislators, and commercial men of this country, and to our ministers and consuls abroad, but to foreign governments, who of late are urgently desirous of an interchange of statistical publications. As the report is not stereotyped, and additional copies cannot, therefore, be obtained after the meeting of Congress, a requisition has been made for two hundred extra copies of the volume now in press, to be sent abroad. It is urgently recommended that Congress authorize the publication of 1,000 copies in addition to the 300 now printed for the use of the Departments. In comparison with the large cost of the composition of 800 pages of rule and figure work, the expense of paper, press-work, and covers for that additional number would be small indeed.

List of merchant-vessels of the United States.—The fifth annual statement of " vessels registered, enrolled, and licensed under the laws of the United States, designating the class, name, and place of registry," as well as the official number and signal letters awarded to each vessel, was prepared, and 2,500 copies published for distribution to the officers of customs, the masters of vessels engaged in the foreign trade, and the principal ship-owners, as well as to the commanders of United States war-vessels. The value of this list has been enhanced by the insertion therein of a carefully prepared "code list," giving the signal letters assigned to all sea-going vessels, arranged in their regular alphabetical order without regard to the initial letter of the names of the vessels. Ship-masters can, by reference to it, obtain the name, tonnage, and home port of any vessel exhibiting her signals at sea. This volume also includes a list of vessels belonging to the United States Navy, giving their rate, guns, tonnage, mode of propulsion, and station of each ; also, a list of the vessels belonging to the revenue marine, giving, in addition to the information as to ships of war, the date and place of building, and the number of officers and men.

Special report on immigration.—Ten thousand copies of this report having been printed in the German, and the same number in the French language, for gratuitous distribution in the countries where those languages are spoken, the undersigned has forwarded the former by steamship to Bremen, Hamburg, and other German ports, and the latter chiefly to Havre and Antwerp, from which places they have been conveyed to the interior of Germany, Austria, Switzerland, France, and Belgium. No funds being available to pay for their transmission to the remote villages and rural districts of the countries named, a limited number has been distributed by the consuls of the United States, and a larger number by the agents of steamship lines, who, being interested in the increase of emigration to the United States, willingly forward at their own expense from New York, and distribute them in remote portions of the continent, thus affording such information in regard to our country as may be necessary for those persons who contemplate emigration from their native country.

Probably no emigrants from continental Europe have been more valued or more warmly welcomed than those who have come from Scandinavian countries. As translations of the report have been published in the German and the French languages, it seems not only proper, but in a high degree desirable, that the natives of those northern countries should be supplied with information in their own tongue in regard to the United States. Yielding to a request which has for several years been pressed with great urgency, a translation of the report into the Swedish language has been made, and will be submitted, at an early day, through you to Congress, with the recommendation that 5,000 copies be printed for distribution in Scandinavian countries.

An urgent demand has also been made for the translation of the report into the Slavic tongue, which is spoken not only in Russia and Poland, but in Bohemia, Silesia, and Moravia—countries from which streams of emigration would flow to the United States if the necessary information were supplied to those contemplating removal from their native soil.

The English edition of ten thousand copies, printed by order of Congress for gratuitous distribution in the United Kingdom of Great Britain and Ireland, is nearly exhausted, and a further issue of five thousand copies of the report, with a map of the United States, is urgently recommended. As the report has been stereotyped, the cost of paper, press-work, and stitching would be small in amount. At no period has the demand for this document been more urgent than at present, and at no time have the benefits resulting from its circulation in that country been so marked as in the recent past. The number of male immigrants from England, Scotland, and Wales during the last fiscal year was almost exactly the same as in the preceding one, (being 51,121 in 1872, and 51,144 in 1871,) and yet the increase in the skilled occupations of the adults over 1871 was 2,681. The greatest increase was exhibited in the following trades: Blacksmiths, an increase of 92; boiler-makers, 36; brick-makers, 31; cabinet-makers, 48; carpenters, 376, and joiners, 534; dyers, 22; gardeners, 107; jewelers, 46; manufacturers, 93; masons, 726; millers, 60; miners, 549; molders, 82; painters, 179; plumbers, 98; printers, 61; saddlers, 30; shoemakers, 160; spinners, 120; tailors, 38, weavers, 316; and wheelwrights, 74.

The immigrants from England included also many small farmers and some professional and business men, bringing with them ready money to invest in United States lands and in farm stock. Indeed, the inquiries of parties who desire to purchase lands, either for themselves or for small companies of intending emigrants, have been so extensive as to considerably increase the correspondence of the Bureau.

The total number of persons of foreign birth who in the year ended June 30, 1873, decided to make the United States their future home is 459,803, of whom 275,792 were males, and 184,011 females, being an increase of 54,997, or 13¼ per cent., over the immigration of the fiscal year 1872. The largest increase from any country was 25,734, or 18⅓ per cent., from Germany; while from England the excess over the previous year was 5,037, or 7¼ per cent.; and from Ireland, 8,612, or 12¼ per cent. The increase from France was nearly 59 per cent., being 9,317 in 1872, and 14,798 in 1873. If the average value of an immigrant, as stated by the undersigned in the report above referred to, be $800, the economical value of this addition to our population in the past year amounts to $367,842,400. It is respectfully submitted that so large an augmentation of our national wealth will justify the expenditure of a sum sufficient for the diffusion of such information as will serve to increase the volume of this tide of immigration.

BUREAU OF IMMIGRATION.

In the special report prepared by the undersigned, containing information for those who contemplate emigration to the United States, the question was asked, "What are the duties of the Government toward the immigrant?" In reply it was stated that the affording him adequate protection was one of these duties, and that it was alike called for by considerations of humanity and the dictates of sound policy.

The "act to encourage immigration," approved July 4, 1864, having expired by limitation, no such office as Commissioner of Immigration exists; and some of the duties pertaining to such an office have devolved upon the Chief of this Bureau. The information for immigrants, published in the report already referred to, was obtained and compiled by him; while the statistics of immigration have for a number of years past been regularly compiled and published quarterly instead of annually, as was previously done, and with great accuracy and fullness of detail. The Chief of this Bureau has therefore been regarded by many as discharging the functions of Commissioner of Immigration, and correspondence, especially from Europe, has been addressed to him as such.

Considering the important bearing of immigration on national welfare, it would seem to be the duty of the Government to the nation, as well as to the immigrant, to afford the latter all possible protection from the moment he leaves his native shore until he reaches his destination in the West or South. This subject has already occupied the attention of Congress, and, during the last two sessions of that body, it has had under consideration bills authorizing the creation of a national bureau of immigration. The failure to enact such a law as would provide for the proper discharge of our obligations toward the scores of thousands who annually bring to our shores their contributions of strength and skill to swell the wealth of the nation, has not arisen from any hostility to such a measure, or even from apathy, but from certain defects in the particular bills proposed; and it is believed to be quite practicable to prepare a measure which will embrace all essential provisions and at the same time command the approval of a large majority of both houses of Congress.

If, however, objection should be made on the score of expense, it is respectfully submitted that, at the cost of a few additional clerks and a slight increase in incidental expenses, the Chief of this Bureau could perform all the duties which would devolve upon a Commissioner of Immigration with a separate bureau. Many of these duties are already familiar to the undersigned, and to some of the officers and clerks of the Bureau, and, if imposed, they would be cheerfully undertaken, and performed with a hearty interest in the object contemplated in their imposition.

INTERNATIONAL STATISTICAL CONGRESS.

It was mentioned in the last report that the Chief of this Bureau was an official delegate to the international statistical congress which held its eighth session at Saint Petersburg in August, 1872. As that period is embraced within the fiscal year just closed, it may not be inappropriate to again refer briefly to his participation in the work of that congress, especially as he was chiefly engaged in the important sections, respectively, of commerce and industry. In the former he was a member of the committee charged with the preparation of a plan for the uniform nomenclature and classification for international purposes of mercantile commodities to be adopted in the published statements of external commerce, and also in the records of the movement of merchandise by railways and on navigable waters. The report of the committee on this subject was approved and recommended by the section, and subsequently adopted by the congress, but although considerably modified at the instance of the undersigned, neither the classification, nor in every respect the recommendations meet his entire approval. As the recommendations of the congress are to be submitted to the bureaus of statistics of the different countries in order that the latter may examine them and suggest. amendments or corrections, it is believed that the congress at its next session will be able to remove all objectionable features and unite upon a plan which will meet the approval of the leading statisticians in all the countries represented.

In the section on industry much time was also devoted to the preparation of a uniform. classification, for international purposes, of the various elements which enter into industrial statistics.

For full information on the action of the congress on the subjects above indicated, as well as on various others which likewise engaged its attention, reference is made to the report of the official delegates from the United States Government, which will shortly be presented to Congress by the President.

While the importance of the establishment of the international statistical congress, and of the direct benefits resulting from its labors and investigations, will receive due attention in that report, it is not improper here to allude to the incidental advantages derived by this Bureau from the attendance of its chief at the last session of that body. The presence, for the first time, of an official delegate who, at the same time, represented the Bureau, brought the latter directly to the attention of the European statisticians, and opportunities were afforded for presenting to their notice the scope and character of its labors; and though of far more recent origin, and possessing fewer facilities for the prosecution of its work than the bureaus of the leading nations of Europe, it received a cordial recognition as one of the most prominent of the agencies devoted to the advancement of the work which the congress had in view. The Bureau has since received from the chiefs of sister organizations, as well as from other statisticians of Europe, many attentions not previously accorded, while it has been enriched by the receipt of a largely increased number of valuable official publications, and of papers prepared especially for the undersigned, all of which will be of service in compiling statistics of foreign countries for publication.

STATISTICS OF LABOR.

The following extract from the report of last year, in reference to an investigation of the labor question in Europe, is again submitted:

" During his visit to Europe the undersigned employed his time, before and after the meeting of the international statistical congress, in investigating the cost and condition of labor in those branches which compete with similar industries in the United States. Although such an investigation formed no part of his duties, either as delegate to the congress, or as Chief of the Bureau of Statistics, and although no funds were provided by the Treasury to defray the expenses necessarily incurred in obtaining the desired information, yet as such *data* were called for by a large number of members of Congress, and sought with avidity by the public, he charged himself with this task and personally visited the most important manufacturing localities in Great Britain, Belgium, and Germany. In England he visited Liverpool, Birkenhead, Birmingham,

Wolverhampton, Sheffield, Manchester, Halifax, Bradford, Leeds, Nottingham, and other places in their vicinity, as well as the 'black country,' and other iron-producing regions.   In Scotland the iron-ship building works on the Clyde, and the manufactories of Glasgow and Dundee, occupied his chief attention.   On the continent he visited Antwerp, Brussels, Liege, Seraing, Huy, Namur, Charleroi, and Jumet, in Belgium ; Aix-la-Chapelle, Cologne, Dusseldorf, Eberfeld, Barmen, Essen, and the coal and iron districts in its vicinity, in Rhenish Prussia ; Chemnitz, Dresden, and Leipsic, in Saxony, with Berlin, Frankfort, and other Prussian cities ; also a number of smaller places in the several countries named.   Among the most prominent industries examined on the continent may be mentioned the renowned steel-works of Mr. Krupp, at Essen ; the iron and machine works of the John Cockerill Company, at Seraing ; the paper-mills at Huy, and other places ; the glass, iron, and coal productions of the Charleroi district ; and the various manufactories in and near Chemnitz.

"In France, owing to the unsettled state of the labor market, but few facts were obtained, and those chiefly in Paris, Lyons, and in those districts in the northern part of that country in which the textile fabrics and iron are chiefly produced.

"In Russia the chief towns visited were St. Petersburg, Cronstadt, Moscow, Nijni-Novgorod, and Warsaw, none of which, except St. Petersburg and Moscow, have important industries.   Russia iron, the superior quality of which is universally known, being manufactured in a remote portion of Europe, the cost of production is not easily ascertained.

"From many other parts of continental Europe information relative to the cost of labor and of subsistence was obtained through correspondence.

"The inquiries made in the places named embraced not only the rates of wages and the weekly earnings of male and female employés in the various industries pursued, but the cost of the chief articles of subsistence, the weekly expenditures for food, room-rent, &c., and the condition and habits of the working people as to health, comfort, education, and temperance.

"Owing to the recent decided advance in the cost of labor in Europe, the statistics published on this subject were rendered comparatively valueless.   If it were deemed important that the rates of wages which ruled during the past season, and which still prevail, be ascertained, extraordinary means must be resorted to ; and it is manifest that the desirable result could only be accomplished through personal investigation and inquiry.   The obtaining of such information was necessarily attended with difficulties, but these had to be met and surmounted.   If the *data* thus personally obtained, at no small cost of labor and money, be not so full as may be desired, they are as a whole more accurate, and consequently more trustworthy than can be gathered from other sources.

"The information already in the possession of the undersigned, supplemented by the facts which may yet be obtained from Europe and America, will be compiled at as early a period as his official engagements will permit."

Owing to the pressure of official duties, and health impaired thereby, the undersigned has made but little progress in the compilation of the work above indicated ; it will, however, be completed and submitted to Congress before the close of the ensuing session.

The delay has enabled him to obtain more recent *data* from the places which he visited last year, as well as to gather information from other towns in Europe and from the British possessions in America. To increase the value of the work it is his intention to present statements of the cost of labor in this country, but the rates paid during the present exceptional condition of our industries would not fairly represent the state of the American labor market, and hence a short delay may be advantageous, by enabling him to collect statistics on this subject after the present financial troubles shall have passed by.

SALARIES OF OFFICERS.

In testifying to the industry and efficiency of the clerks and other employés of this Bureau, the undersigned again invites attention to the insufficient salaries paid to the chiefs of division and other officers. Such exhaustive and responsible labors justly entitle them to a larger compensation than the salaries of clerks of the fourth class.

PRICES OF STAPLE ARTICLES.

Statements showing the prices of staple articles in the New York market at the beginning of each month, in the ten years from 1864 to 1873, inclusive, are appended to this report, (marked B.)

Very respectfully, yours,

EDWARD YOUNG,
Chief of Bureau.

Hon. WILLIAM A. RICHARDSON,
Secretary of the Treasury.

REPORT OF THE SOLICITOR.

DEPARTMENT OF JUSTICE,
OFFICE OF THE SOLICITOR OF THE TREASURY,
Washington, D. C., November 13, 1873.

SIR: I have the honor to transmit, herewith, seven tabular statements, exhibiting the amount, character, and results of the litigation, under the direction of this office, for the fiscal year ending June 30, 1873, so far as the same are shown by the reports received from the United States attorneys for the several districts. These tables embrace, respectively—

1. Suits on custom-house bonds.
2. Suits on transcripts of accounts of defaulting public officers, excepting those of the Post-Office Department, adjusted by the accounting officers of the Treasury Department.
3. Post-office suits, embracing those against officers of the Post-Office Department, and cases of fines, penalties, and forfeitures for violation of the postal laws.
4. Suits for the recovery of fines, penalties, and forfeitures under the customs revenue and navigation laws.
5. Suits against collectors of customs, and other agents of the Government, for refund of duties, and acts done in the line of their official duty.
6. Suits in which the United States is interested, not embraced in the other classes.
7. A general summary or abstract of all the other tables.

19 Ab

An examination of this summary will show that the whole number of suits commenced within the year was 2,715, of which—

160 were of class 1, for the recovery of..	$422, 220 47
59 were of class 2, for the recovery of..	1,206, 936 55
364 were of class 3, for the recovery of..	48, 249 18
331 were of class 4, for the recovery of..	4, 151, 944 67
794 were of class 5.	
1, 007 were of class 6, for the recovery of..	1, 928, 817 72

Making a total sued for, as reported, of............................ 7, 758, 168 69

Of the whole number of suits brought, 632 were decided in favor of the United States; 27 were adversely decided; 748 were settled and dismissed; in 6 penalties were remitted by the Secretary of the Treasury; leaving 1,302 still pending.

Of those pending at the commencement of the year, 600 were decided for the United States; 72 were decided adversely; 824 were settled and dismissed; and in 41 penalties were remitted by the Secretary of the Treasury.

The entire number of suits decided or otherwise disposed of during the year was 2,950; the whole amount for which judgments were obtained, exclusive of decrees *in rem*, was $1,526,992.85; and the entire amount collected from all sources was $1,861,467.26.

The following tables exhibit a comparative view of the litigation of the last year, and the next preceding one:

Date.	Aggregate sued for.	Aggregate in judgments for the United States.	Collected.	Decided for the United States.	Decided against the United States.	Settled and dismissed.	Remitted.	Pending.	Total number of suits brought.
	In suits commenced during the fiscal years ending June 30, 1872, and June 30, 1873.								
June 30, 1872..	$8, 567, 185 11	$397, 949 89	$478, 450 65	593	23	258	12	968	1, 854
June 30, 1873...	7, 758, 168 59	203, 335 50	778, 232 17	632	27	748	6	1, 302	2, 715

Date.	Aggregate of judgments in old suits.	Decided for the United States.	Decided against the United States.	Settled and dismissed.	Collections in old suits.	Total number of suits disposed of.	Total number of judgments in favor of the United States.	Whole amount of judgments.	Whole amount collected.
	In suits commenced prior to the fiscal years ending June 30, 1872, and June 30, 1873.						Proceedings in all suits.		
June 30, 1872..	$544, 415 85	357	73	858	$521, 971 76	2, 184	950	$942, 365 67	$1, 000, 423 41
June 30, 1873..	1, 323, 657 35	600	72	824	1, 083, 215 09	2, 950	1, 232	1, 526, 992 85	1, 861, 467 26

I am, very respectfully,

E. C. BANFIELD,
Solicitor of the Treasury.

Hon. WILLIAM A. RICHARDSON,
Secretary of the Treasury.

REPORT OF THE SUPERINTENDENT OF THE UNITED STATES COAST SURVEY.

COAST-SURVEY OFFICE,
Washington, D. C., September 18, 1873.

SIR: I have the honor to transmit, in advance of final reports from the field, an abstract showing the sites of work on the Atlantic, Gulf, and Pacific coasts of the United States, in which surveying parties have been engaged in the course of the present year. In the northern sections work will be continued until the approach of cold weather, when the parties will resume the survey of the southern coast. My detailed report will be prepared after the transfer of the parties.

The field operations of the year will be recapitulated in geographical order. Parties now on the coast of Maine are engaged in the survey of Mount Desert Island and the adjacent hydrography; on the shores of Eggemoggin Reach; on the coast near Castine; on the islands in that vicinity, including those of Isle-au-Haut Bay; and on the Penobscot above Belfast; supplementary work has been done in the upper part of Casco Bay, and in Portland Harbor; points have been determined by triangulation in New Hampshire; special observations are in progress near North Adams, Mass., for the determination of terrestrial gravity; and others at Cambridge for finding the longitude of points in the interior of the United States; off-shore hydrography is continued near George's Bank; in-shore soundings near Nantucket; and tidal observations have been constantly recorded at North Haven, Penobscot Bay, and at the United States navy-yard, Boston. The harbors between Portland and New York have been further examined for the preparation of final sailing-directions. Field work is advancing on the coast of Rhode Island west of Point Judith; special observations in hydrography, including those relating to tides and currents, are in progress in New York Harbor; field-work on the south side of Long Island; on the shores of Raritan River, New Jersey; on the shores of Lake Champlain with adjacent soundings; and station-marks of triangulation in the vicinity of New York have been examined with reference to their preservation. Determinations have been made for latitude, longitude, and the magnetic elements at Port Jervis, N. Y. Barnegat light-house has been connected with the primary triangulation which passes from New York to the head of Chesapeake Bay; coast topography has been prosecuted between Barnegat and Absecom; hydrography to the northward of Little Egg Harbor, and in the Delaware River at New Castle. Reconnaissance has been continued westward from Harper's Ferry, W. Va., for points in the geodetic connection between the Atlantic and Western coasts.

The harbors of the Chesapeake have been specially examined with reference to sailing-directions; the survey of James River, Virginia, has advanced above Warwick River entrance; that of Elizabeth River has been completed; latitude has been determined at a station on Knott's Island, Virginia; the survey has been continued in Currituck, Pamplico, and Core Sounds, including Pungo and Chowan Rivers, with observations for the latitude of a station near Ocracoke Inlet. Further southward the operations of the year include Cape Fear River to Wilmington, N. C.; the coast of South Carolina between Little River and Winyah entrance; the coast south of Winyah Bay; parts of Coosaw River and of Port Royal Island; latitude at Saint Simon's Island, Georgia; the survey of Halifax River and the adjacent coast below Matanzas Inlet, Florida; and the extension of hydrography in the vicinity of the Florida reef.

On the Gulf coast the operations of the year include Tampa Bay; the coast between Cedar Keys and Ocilla River, and between Saint George's Sound and Dickerson's Bay; the Gulf approaches to Apalachicola; the vicinity of the Atlanta base-line, Georgia; Chandeleur Sound, Louisiana; the Mississippi River from Jesuit Bend to New Orleans; the east branch of Galveston Bay; and Espiritu Santo, Saint Joseph's, and Aransas Bays, Texas.

Points in the geodetic connection between the Atlantic and Western coasts have been occupied in Missouri, Wisconsin, and Colorado, and now each State and Territory of the Union, along the belt which includes the thirty-ninth parallel, has at least one point accurately determined in latitude and longitude.

The plan of field and hydrographic work on the Western coast, and in the prosecution of which parties have been or are now engaged, comprises hydrographic developments in the vicinity of San Diego; the coast of California near Newport and San Juan Capistrano; Catalina Harbor; Port Hueneme, San Buenaventura, Santa Barbara, Santa Rosa Island; the coast north and south of Port Conception; reconnaissance between Santa Barbara and Monterey; the coast between Point Sal and San Luis Obispo Bay; north of Piedras Blancas; San Francisco entrance and approaches; latitude, longitude, azimuth, magnetic elements, coefficient of refraction, and observations on the tides and currents at stations north and south of San Francisco; deep-sea soundings near Falmouth Shoal; development of the Cordell Bank; field-work on the coast north of Mendocino Bay; south of Bear River; soundings between Cape Mendocino and Rocky Point, and off-shore from Crescent City reef; the coast north of Mack's Arch; soundings off the Orford Reef; extension of the survey of Columbia River and of Shoalwater Bay; Budd's Inlet; Puget Sound; and geographical reconnaissance of the coast, including special surveys of the harbors of Alaska.

The work in the Coast-Survey Office, embracing the computation of observations, the drawing, engraving, and publication of maps and charts, has kept pace with the operations in the field. Nineteen charts, engraved on copper, have been completed, twenty-three continued, and six new ones commenced, in addition to which six preliminary charts have been published by means of the photolithographic process, which greatly expedites the publication of new material. In the drawing division sixty-three charts have been worked upon, being either completed or brought up to the date of the survey. Fourteen thousand copies of copper-plate charts, and fifty-three hundred of lithographic charts have been printed, and nearly as many issued to sales-agents, and to different departments of the Government, chiefly the Navy and Revenue Marine. Tide-tables for all ports in the United States for the year 1874 have been computed and issued. The preparation of a "Coast Pilot," or Sailing Directions for all the Harbors, and the Coastwise Navigation between Eastport, Me., and Newport, R. I., has been completed, and that much-needed work is now ready for publication. The important matter of reproducing the original topographical maps, which exist only in a single copy, has received continued attention, and satisfactory results have been obtained by the comparatively inexpensive process of photo-lithography. It is proposed to proceed with the reproduction of these maps as fast as the means can be applied to that object.

Respectfully submitted.

BENJAMIN PEIRCE,
Superintendent United States Coast Survey.

Hon. W. A. RICHARDSON,
Secretary of the Treasury.

REPORT OF THE LIGHT-HOUSE BOARD.

TREASURY DEPARTMENT,
OFFICE OF THE LIGHT-HOUSE BOARD,
Washington, November 24, 1873.

SIR: I have the honor to transmit herewith the annual report of the Light-House Board for the fiscal year ending June 30, 1873.

Very respectfully,

JOSEPH HENRY, *Chairman.*

Hon. W. A. RICHARDSON, *Secretary of the Treasury.*

[1.]

TREASURY DEPARTMENT,
OFFICE OF THE LIGHT-HOUSE BOARD,
Washington, D. C., October 14, 1873.

Hon. W. A. RICHARDSON, *Secretary of the Treasury :*

SIR: The following report of the operations of this Board during the last year is respectfully submitted:

No part of the executive branch of the Government includes more diversified duties or involves greater responsibilities than the Light-House Establishment.

The character of the aids which any nation furnishes the mariner in approaching and leaving its shores marks, in a conspicuous degree, its advancement in civilization. Whatever tends to facilitate navigation, or to lessen its dangers, serves to increase commerce, and hence is of importance not only to the dwellers on the seaboard, but to the inhabitants of every part of the country. Whoever has surplus products of industry to dispose of has a pecuniary interest in the improvement of commerce.

Every shipwreck which occurs enhances the cost of transportation, and, therefore, affects the interests of the producer. But it is not alone in view of its economical effects that the light-house system is to be regarded. It is a life-preserving establishment, founded on the principles of Christian benevolence. None can appreciate so well the value of a proper system of this kind as he who has been exposed for weeks and perhaps months to the perils of the ocean, and is approaching in the darkness of night perhaps a lee shore. He looks then, with anxious gaze, for the friendly light which is to point the way amid treacherous rocks and sunken shoals to a haven of safety. Or it may be in mid-day, when observations cannot be had, the sun and coast being hid by dense fogs, such as imperil navigation on our northern and western coasts. He then listens with breathless silence for the sound of the fog-trumpet which shall insure his position and give him the desired direction of his course.

With that entire confidence which is inspired by a perfect light-house system the alternatives of life and death, of riches and poverty, are daily hazarded; and therefore it is of the first importance that the signals, whether of light or sound which indicate the direction of the course, and the beacons which mark the channel, shall be of the most improved character, and that they be under the charge of intelligent, efficient, and trustworthy attendants. But, above all, one maxim should ever be observed, namely, perfect regularity of exhibition of every signal from night to night and from year to year. A light, for example, which has been regularly visible from a tower, it may be for years, cannot be suffered to fail for a single night, or even for a single hour, without danger of casualties of the most serious character. A failure of such a light to send forth its expected ray, is, as it were, a breach of a solemn promise, which may allure the confiding mariner to an untimely death or a disastrous shipwreck.

In view of these facts our Government early established a light-house system, which, though simple and inexpensive at first, has since been extended and improved to meet the wants of an increasing commerce and the unrivaled resources of the country. It has been maintained with an enlightened liberality which indicates a just appreciation of its importance.

The magnitude of the light-house system of the United States may be inferred from the following facts: First, the immense extent of the coast which, from the St. Croix River, on the boundary of Maine, to the mouth of the Rio Grande, in the Gulf of Mexico, includes a distance of over 5,000 miles; on the Pacific coast a length of about 1,500 miles; on the great northern lakes about 3,000 miles, and on inland rivers about 700 miles, making a total of more than 10,000 miles. Secondly, the magnitude of the system is exhibited by the fact that nearly every square foot of the margin of the sea throughout the whole extent of 5,000 miles along the Atlantic and Gulf coast is more or less illuminated by light-house rays, the mariner rarely losing sight of one light until he has gained another. Thirdly, the same fact is illustrated by the number of signals now in actual existence as exhibited in the following table:

TOTAL SIGNALS FOR THE ENTIRE ESTABLISHMENT.

Light-houses and lighted beacons...	591
Light-houses and lighted beacons finished and lighted during the year ending July 1, 1873	29
Light-ships...	21
Fog-signals, operated by steam or hot-air engines	35
Day or unlighted beacons	363
Buoys in position..	2,632

To carry on so extended a system necessarily requires a carefully-devised organization, based upon the history of all that has been recorded in regard to the subject, and a series of efficient officers and trained assistants.

The duties which belong to the light-house system involve the most varied knowledge and practical skill, a thorough acquaintance with the wants of commerce, engineering abilities of high order, with scientific acquirements, which shall appreciate the value of every new discovery that may find an application in the improvement of signals, and the ability to make or direct such investigations as may from time to time be found desirable. To insure these requisites the organization of the light-house system includes, first, a Light House Board, consisting of two officers of the Navy, two engineer officers of the Army, and two scientific civilians, with the addition of an officer of the Navy and an engineer officer of the Army as secretaries, who are also members of the Board. Secondly. It also includes twelve inspectors from the Army or Navy, and as many engineer officers from the Army, who have united charge of the twelve districts into which the coast is divided. The Light-House Board, having charge of the supervision of the whole system, is divided into five committees, to each of which special duties are assigned. These committees are on finance, engineering, floating aids, lighting, and experiments. It is the duty of each member of the Board to render himself intimately acquainted with the details of the business intrusted to his care, as well as to keep himself informed, as far as possible, of the condition of the general system. For this purpose, as well as that of insuring the proper working of the establishment in the several districts, it is advisable that he should make, from time to time, inspection of light-houses at various points on the coast. The inspector of each district is required to visit, at stated intervals, each light-house within his jurisdiction after completion by the engineers, to correct any delinquencies on the part of the keepers, and to supply oil and other materials necessary to the efficient maintenance of the signals, and finally to inform the engineer as to any repairs which may be required. The district engineers, as well as the engineer officers of the board, find full employment for all the theoretical knowledge and practical skill they possess in the surveys of new sites, making studies for the construction of new permanent aids to navigation, many of them on submarine sites in exposed positions, in planning and rearing the towers, and in fitting up the lenticular apparatus.

The scientific portion of the Board is at present composed of the Superintendent of the Coast Survey and the director of the Smithsonian Institution; to the first of whom is referred the duty of fixing the precise latitude and longitude of the various positions on the coast, in furnishing exact surveys of harbors, channels, &c., as well as the data for determining the position of light-houses, and, in the case of the present incumbent, of solving any mathematical problem of unusual complexity which may arise in the course of the varied discussions of the Board. The duty of the second civilian mentioned has been to examine and report upon the improvements in the lighting apparatus, the different materials for illumination, and on the efficiency of fog-signals.

The naval and engineer secretaries are the principal executive officers, who carry on the routine duties of the establishment during the intervals of the meetings of the Board.

In order that the members of the Board from different departments of the Government may co-operate harmoniously with each other, the whole system is placed under the Secretary of the Treasury. This organization of the light-house system was adopted after much deliberation, founded upon a very able report made by Lieutenant (now Admiral) Jenkins, who had been appointed to investigate the light-house systems of Europe. It has now been in operation upward of twenty years, and has in that time been prosecuted with the most satisfactory results in the way of increasing the number of stations, in the economy of materials, and improvement in signals.

It is true that it is sometimes suggested that the light-house system might be better managed by a single department of the Government, but this we think it not difficult to disprove were this the place to enter into a discussion of the subject. It may be sufficient to observe that the old system, for which this was substituted, was managed by a single individual and his assistants as a bureau of the Treasury Department, with results which were far from being satisfactory.

The system requires the co-operation of officers of the Army and Navy, who by their special training are well fitted for the work to which they are respectively assigned, and of whom the Government has their commission and their official reputation as a guarantee against pecuniary loss and delinquency in a faithful discharge of duties. It has also been said that the light-house system is of a practical character, and, therefore, does not require the aid of high science. But in regard to this, it may be observed that the present system of light-house apparatus, now in use in every part of the civilized world, was invented and introduced into practice in its minutest details by a man of abstract science, the celebrated Fresnel, who shared with Young, of England, the invention of the undulatory theory of light, and its application to all the phenomena of optics.

The light apparatus introduced by the Board as a substitute for that previously in use is principally that of the French system. But the Board have been from the first alive to the introduction of improvements, and have carefully considered every suggestion and tested every invention which gave promise of greater economy or efficiency. Instead of sperm-oil, which was first employed, they have introduced, at one-third of the cost, lard-oil, and with this a required modification of the lamps, particularly those of the larger kind, in order that the oil may be burned at a higher temperature, especially in the northern portions of the United States. But the greatest improvement which has been introduced is that relative to fog-signals, indispensable aids to navigation, especially on the northeastern and western portions of our coast. At first these signals were principally confined to bells, weighing in some cases from 2,000 to 2,500 pounds. These were rung by winding up a weight which in its descent gave motion to a hammer striking the bell. In regard to this signal, an improvement has been introduced, by which an expenditure of about one-tenth of the power produces an equal effect. Bells are still used in cases where the signal is required to be heard only at a comparatively small distance, but in most cases much more powerful instruments are required, such as are founded on what is called resonance, in which the air itself is the resounding body as well as the conductor of sound. These instruments are of three kinds: first, the ordinary locomotive whistle, much enlarged in size and somewhat modified in form, and blown by steam from a high-pressure tubular boiler; second, the reed-trumpet actuated by air condensed in a reservoir by the power of a caloric engine; third, the syren-trumpet, operated by steam from a boiler sustaining a pressure of from 50 to 70 pounds per square inch. The sound from these instruments is many times more powerful than that from the largest bells.

A difficulty in carrying out the present system is the frequent change in the officers of districts, and the still more frequent change in the keepers of the stations.

The duties of the inspector and engineer are so special that it requires a considerable time to become perfectly familiar with them, and the experience which is gained by an individual is lost to the Government by his recall to the Army or Navy, and the substitution in his place of another officer, who has to pass through a similar training before he can render the best service. In regard to light-keepers, the most efficient and faithful men, who from years of practice have acquired the skill necessary to a proper discharge of their duties, have been in many cases changed by collectors of customs for new men, for no other reason than to give place to some political favorite. It is hoped that the application of the civil-service reform to the employment of light-keepers will be of material benefit to the general service.

The Light-House Board, during the past year, desirous of acquainting itself minutely with any improvements which of late years may have been introduced into the light-house service in Europe, obtained the sanction of the honorable the Secretary of the Treasury to commission Major Elliot, of the Corps of Engineers of the Army and engineer-secretary of the Board, to visit Europe and report upon everything which he might observe relative to light-house apparatus and the management of light-house systems. He has lately returned, after having gathered information which will prove of importance in its appli cation in our country, as will be evident from his preliminary report.

*   *   *   *   *   *   *

[3.]

CONDITION AND OPERATIONS OF THE LIGHT-HOUSE SYSTEM DURING THE FISCAL YEAR 1872-'73.

Light-houses, light-ships, fog-signals, day-beacons, and buoys belonging to the United States Light-House Establishment on the 1st of July, 1873.

ATLANTIC COAST AND STRAIT OF FLORIDA.

Light-houses and lighted beacons	332
Light-houses and lighted beacons finished and lighted during the year ending July 1, 1873	18
Light-ships	20
Fog-signals, operated by steam or hot-air engines	20
Day or unlighted beacons	344
Buoys in position	2,368

COAST OF THE GULF OF MEXICO.

Light-houses and lighted beacons	52
Light-houses and lighted beacons finished and lighted during the year ending July 1, 1873	2
Light-ships	1
Fog-signals, operated by steam or hot-air engines	2
Day or unlighted beacons	16
Buoys in position	135

PACIFIC COAST.

Light-houses and lighted beacons	26
Light-houses and lighted beacons finished and lighted during the year ending July 1, 1873	1
Light-ships	0
Fog-signals, operated by steam or hot-air engines	6
Day or unlighted beacons	1
Buoys in position	89

NORTHERN AND NORTHWESTERN LAKES.

Light-houses and lighted beacons	181
Light-houses and lighted beacons finished and lighted during the year ending July 1, 1873	8
Light-ships	0
Fog-signals, operated by steam or hot-air engines	7
Day or unlighted beacons	2
Buoys in position	246

It has ever been the endeavor of the Light-House Board to conduct the system under its charge with a strict regard to economy, with a view to obtaining the greatest amount of efficiency with a given expenditure of means. For this purpose frequent visits have been made to different parts of the coast, and a rigid enforcement of rules and regulations has been insisted on, holding officers and light-keepers personally responsible for the strict performance of duty.

Under the several names of the twelve geographical divisions or districts into which the coast of the United States is divided, will be found a detailed statement of the condition, changes, and work which has been done during the year. From these statements it will be seen that although the various signals at different stations are generally in such a condition of efficiency as to meet the wants of navigation, still there are many new lights called for by commerce, and many stations at which repairs and reconstructions are imperiously demanded. Indeed, in these respects the wants of the service are constantly recurring, since buildings, however well made at the time of their construction, are subject to the deteriorating influence of the weather, as well as the more immediate destructive effects of equinoctial storms and the occasional recurring commotions of the sea of almost irresistible violence.

In regard to the general estimates for repairs of light-houses, for supplies (including oil, &c.,) for light-ships, and for buoys, the Board has to say that it has always been the custom of this Office, in preparing the annual estimates for supporting the existing and authorized aids to navigation, and the construction of new ones, to make as close a calculation of items, quantities, and prices as the information at hand would allow, and to endeavor to so manage the disbursements as at all times to have ample funds available to supply any losses and repair any damage, however serious, to which this service is so peculiarly liable during the winter months.

For repairs and incidental expenses of light-houses we have estimated $250,000, an increase of $25,000 over the amount estimated last year, which experience during the last year has shown to be necessary.

For expenses of fog-signals we have estimated an increase of $10,000, on account of the extension of this branch of the service.

For the salaries of light-keepers the estimate is $599,400, and the increase is owing to the increase in the number of light-keepers authorized by the appropriations for new lights. There are in actual employment and required for new lights appropriated for, 999 light-keepers, and the average pay authorized by law is $600 per annum.

For supplies of light-houses the estimate is $395,350, and the increase is due, as above, to the increased number of lights authorized by law.

For the expenses of light-ships the estimate is $234,087.50, and an increase of $16,355 over the appropriation of last year, which experience has shown to be insufficient.

For expenses of buoyage our estimate is $350,000, and the increase is due to the increased demand for these aids to navigation, decay of those in use, and losses by ice and storm.

During the last fiscal year the following changes have occurred in the board : Rear-Admirals Bailey and Walke, having retired, were succeeded by Commodore Foxhall A. Parker and Capt. John Lee Davis. Commodore Parker was, in turn, succeeded by Rear-Admiral Charles H. Davis.

Rear-Admiral Boggs, the naval secretary, retired and was succeeded by Commander John G. Walker. The other members of the board, viz, Professor Henry, Generals Humphreys and Barnard, Professor Peirce, and Major Elliot, remain as at the date of the last annual report.

[4.]

List of light-houses finished and lighted between July 1, 1872, and July 1, 1873.

Name of station.	Locality.	When lighted.
Burnt-Coat Harbor, range or leading lights, (two).	Swan Island, off-coast of Maine......................	August 15, 1872.
Newburyport, inner range or leading lights, (two).	Harbor of Newburyport, Merrimac River, Massachusetts.	June 1, 1873.
Wood End......................	Entrance to harbor of Provincetown, Cape Cod, Massachusetts. Harbor of refuge.	November 20, 1872.
Bullock's Point	On a shoal in Providence River, Rhode Island, off Bullock's Point.	November 1, 1872.
Sabin's Point	On a shoal in Providence River, off Sabine's Point, Rhode Island.	November 1, 1872.
Blackwell's Island *........	North end of Blackwell's Island, near Hell Gate, East River, New York.	September 15, 1872.
West Point †............	On Gee's Point, (West Point,) Hudson River, New York.	October 1, 1872.
Esopus Meadows †........	On a shoal in Hudson River, between Poughkeepsie and Rondout, New York.	August 26, 1872.
Barber's Point............	On Barber's Point, west side of Lake Champlain, New York.	Opening of navigation in the spring of 1873.
Mispillion	On Delaware Bay, near mouth of Mispillion River...	June 15, 1873.
" The Thimble "........,....	On "The Thimble" shoal, entrance to Hampton Roads, Virginia.	October 10, 1872.
Love Point	On a shoal off Love Point, Chesapeake Bay, mouth of Chester River, Maryland.	August 15, 1872.
Body's Island ;............	On Body's Island, sea-coast of North Carolina........	October 1, 1872.
Sullivan's Island range or leading lights, (two).†	On Sullivan's Island, north side of entrance to harbor of Charleston, South Carolina.	July 15, 1872.
Saint Simon's	On Saint Simon's Island, entrance to Saint Simon's Sound, sea-coast of Georgia.	September 1, 1872.
Dame's Point............	On a shoal in Saint John River, Florida	July 15, 1872.
Mobile Point ;............	On Mobile Point, east side of entrance to harbor of Mobile, Alabama.	February 15, 1873.
Bolivar Point ;............	On Bolivar Point, north side of entrance to Galveston Bay, Texas.	November 15, 1872.
Cleveland †............	Cleveland, Ohio, Lake Erie	Opening of navigation in the spring of 1873.
Gibraltar †............	Mouth of Detroit River, Michigan, Lake Erie........	Do.
Pentwater ....;	On pier at harbor of Pentwater, Lake Michigan, Michigan.	June 20, 1873.
Racine......................	On pier at entrance to harbor of Racine, Lake Michigan, Wisconsin.	September 5, 1872.
Milwaukee	On pier at entrance to harbor of Milwaukee, Lake Michigan, Wisconsin.	October 30, 1872.
Grassy Island, (two)	At each end of canal into mouth of Fox River, Green Bay, Wisconsin.	....
Pigeon Point............	On Pigeon Point, sea-coast of California............	November 15, 1872.

* Erected and maintained by city of New York.
† Reconstructed.
; Reconstructed. Destroyed during the rebellion.

[5.]

FIRST DISTRICT.

The first district extends from the northeastern boundary of the United States (Maine) to and including Hampton Harbor, N. H., and includes all aids to navigation on the coasts of Maine and New Hampshire.

Inspector.—Commander Thomas O. Selfridge, United States Navy, to September 13, 1872; Commander W. K. Mayo, United States Navy, from September 13, 1872, to June 30, 1873; Commander W. N. Allen, United States Navy, present inspector.

Engineer.—Lieut. Col. James C. Duane, Corps of Engineers, Bvt. Brig Gen., United States Army.

In this district there are:

Light-houses and lighted beacons.. 51
Light-houses finished and lighted during the year ended July 1, 1873............. 2
Light-houses, for which appropriations were available, but which were not finished on July 1, 1873...... 2

Light-ships.. 0
Fog-signals operated by steam or hot-air engines.................................. ⁻
Day or unlighted beacons... 46
Buoys actually in position... 391
Spare-buoys for relief... 221
Tender (steamer) Myrtle for construction and repair; also used in second district,
 and tender Iris, (inspector's tender) 2
Tender (sail) schooner Wave (for repairs) also used in second district............. 1

The following numbers, which precede the names of stations, correspond with those of the light-house list of the Atlantic, Gulf, and Pacific
coasts of the United States, issued January 1, 1873.

LIGHT-HOUSES AND LIGHTED BEACONS.

6. *Nash's Island, off the mouth of Pleasant River, Maine.*—A new lantern, parapet, and deck have been made.

15-16. *Burnt-Coat Harbor, (range lights.)*—This new station was
completed and lighted for the first time on the 15th of August, 1872.
Both of the lights are white, the rear, fourth order, dioptric, 75 feet
above sea-level; the front, fifth order, dioptric, 42 feet above sea-level,
and are 100 feet apart, on a course NE ¾ N. The towers are of brick,
square in plan; the keeper's dwelling is of wood, and all of the buildings
are white. The station is located on the north side of the entrance to
the harbor.

34. *Monhegan, Monhegan Island.*—An appropriation for new house for
the keeper is recommended at this station.

40. *Seguin, off mouth of Kennebec River, Maine.*—A 10-inch steam-whistle
fog-signal has been established at this station, and is arranged to give
blasts of 8 seconds at intervals of 52 seconds. The work on the new
parapet and decks for the lantern is in progress. The exterior woodwork of the keeper's dwelling has been repainted.

42-43. *Cape Elizabeth, west side of entrance to Casco Bay, &c., Portland
Harbor, Maine.*—An appropriation was made last year for rebuilding the
western tower; the foundation and basement have been constructed,
and the iron-work for the tower is nearly ready.

45. *Portland Breakwater, in Portland Harbor, Maine.*—This structure
will be completed this year; during the course of its construction a light
has been exhibited from a temporary wooden tower, located at the outer
extremity of the pier. As soon as the breakwater is completed it will
be necessary to occupy the pier-head by a permanent tower, and an appropriation is asked for this purpose.

46. *Wood Island, west side of entrance to Saco River, Maine.*—A fog-bell
tower, with Stevens's striking-apparatus, and a cast-steel bell, weighing
1,315 pounds, has been established, and considerable repairs to the station have been made.

REPAIRS.

At each of the following-named light-stations there have been made
repairs and renovations more or less extensive during the year.

1. *Saint Croix river*, on Dochet's Island, in Saint Croix river, Maine.
2. *West Quoddy Head*, southwest side of entrance to Passamaquoddy
Bay, Maine.
3. *Little River*, west side of entrance to Little River Harbor, Maine.
4. *Libby Island*, entrance to Machias Bay, Maine.
5. *Moose-Peak*, west side of entrance to Bay of Fundy, Maine.
7. *Narraguagus*, west side of Narraguagus Bay, Maine.
8. *Petit Menan*, south end of Petit Menan Island, Maine.
9. *Prospect Harbor*, east side of entrance to the harbor.

10. *Winter Harbor*, west side of entrance to the harbor.
11. *Mount Desert Rock*, off Mount Desert, Maine.
12. *Baker's Island*, off Mount Desert, Maine.
13. *Bear Island*, off Cranberry Islands, Maine.
14. *Bass Harbor Head*, east side of entrance to Bass Harbor, Maine.
17. *Eggemoggin*, north side of east entrance to Eggemoggin Reach, Maine.
18. *Saddleback Ledge*, in Isle au Haute Bay, Maine.
19. *Heron Neck*, west side of entrance to Carver's Harbor, Maine.
20. *Deer Island Thoroughfare*, south side of west entrance to the thoroughfare.
21. *Eagle Island Point*, west side of Isle au Haute Bay, near the head.
22. *Pumpkin Island*, south side of west entrance to Eggemoggin Reach, Maine.
23. *Matinicus Rock*, entrance to Penobscot Bay, Maine.
25. *White Head*, west side of entrance to Muscle Ridge Channel, Penobscot Bay, Maine.
26. *Owl's Head*, south side of entrance to Rockland Harbor, Maine.
27. *Brown's Head*, east side of west entrance to Fox Island Thoroughfare, Maine.
28. *Negro Island*, entrance to Camden Harbor, Maine.
29. *Grindel's Point*, north side of entrance to Gilkey's Harbor, Maine.
30. *Dice's Head*, north side of entrance to Castine Harbor, Maine.
31. *Fort Point*, west side of entrance to Penobscot River, Maine.
32. *Tenant's Harbor*, south side of the entrance to the harbor.
33. *Marshall's Point*, east side of entrance to Herring Gut Harbor, Maine.
35. *Franklin Island*, west side of entrance to George's River, Maine.
36. *Pemaquid Point*, east entrance to John's Bay, Maine.
37. *Burnt Island*, west side of entrance to Townsend Harbor, Maine.
38. *Hendrick's Head*, east side of mouth of river Sheepscot, Maine.
39. *Pond Island*, west side of entrance to river Kennebec, Maine.
41. *Halfway Rock*, in Casco Bay, Maine.
44. *Portland Head*, west side of entrance to Portland Harbor, Maine.
45. *Portland Breakwater*, on the outer end of the breakwater in Portland Harbor, Maine.
47. *Goat Island*, north side of entrance to Cape Porpoise Harbor, Maine.
48. *Boone Island*, off York Harbor, Maine.
49. *Whale's Back*, east side of entrance to Portsmouth Harbor, New Hampshire.
50. *Portsmouth Harbor*, west side of entrance to the harbor.
51. *Isle of Shoals*, off Portsmouth, New Hampshire.

The following-named light-stations require repairs to be made during the current and ensuing year:

3. *Little River*, west side of entrance to harbor of Little River, Maine.
4. *Libby Island*, entrance to Machias Bay, Maine.
5. *Moose Peak*, on Moosepeak Head, Maine.
6. *Nash's Island*, west end of Moose Peak Reach, Maine.
18. *Saddleback*, in Isle au Haut Bay, Maine.
23. *Matinicus Rock*, off Penobscot Bay, Maine.
26. *Owl's Head*, west side of Muscleridge channel, Penobscot Bay, Maine.
34. *Monheigan Island*, off George's Islands, Maine.
40. *Seguin*, off mouth of river Kennebec, Maine.

LIGHT-SHIPS.

There are no light-ships in the first district.

FOG-SIGNALS OPERATED BY STEAM OR HOT-AIR ENGINES.

West Quoddy Head.—Ten-inch steam-whistle.
Petit Menan.—Ten-inch steam-whistle.
Matinicus Rock.—Twelve-inch steam-whistle.
White Head.—Ten-inch steam-whistle.
Monhegan.—Six-inch steam-whistle.
Seguin.—Ten-inch steam-whistle.
Cape Elizabeth.—Ten-inch steam-whistle.
Portland Head.—Second-class Daboll air-trumpet.
All of the above are in good condition.

At the *House Island Depot*, Portland Harbor, Maine, experiments with and tests of steam and air fog-signals, boilers, air-tanks, and engines have been made during the last year.

DAY OR UNLIGHTED BEACONS.

Names and positions of the day or unlighted beacons:
Jerry's Point, Portsmouth Harbor, New Hampshire.—Iron.
South Beacon, Portsmouth Harbor, New Hampshire.—Stone.
North Beacon, Portsmouth Harbor, New Hampshire.—Wooden mast.
Willey's Ledge, Portsmouth Harbor, New Hampshire.—Iron spindle.
York Ledge off River York, Maine.—Iron spindle.
Fishing Rocks, Kennebunkport, Maine.—Iron spindle broken off, spar buoy substituted.
Stage Island Monument, entrance to Saco River, Maine.—Stone tower 40 feet high.
Sharp's Rocks, entrance to Saco River, Maine.—Iron socket and wooden shaft; socket broken off, spar-buoy substituted.
Ram Island Ledge, (new,) east side of main entrance to Portland Harbor, Maine.—Wooden tripod 50 feet high.
Back Cove Beacon, Portland Harbor, Maine.—Pile beacon.
White Head Ledge, in White Head passage to Portland Harbor, Maine.—Iron spindle, slightly bent.
Trott's Rock, in White Head passage to Portland Harbor, Maine.—Iron spindle broken off, will be replaced with a new one.
Mark Island Monument, Casco Bay, Maine.—Stone tower 50 feet high, in good condition.
Black Jack Rock, entrance Kennebec River, Maine.—A new hole has been drilled in the rock, and a wrought-iron spindle will be set.
Seal Rock, Kennebec River, Maine.—Iron spindle, copper cylinder.
Lee's Rock, Kennebec River, Maine.—Iron socket, wooden shaft, socket broken, spar-buoy substituted.
Ram Island Ledge, Kennebec River, Maine.—Iron socket, wooden shaft.
Winslow's Rocks, Kennebec River, Maine.—Iron socket, wooden shaft, socket broken off, spar-buoy substituted.
Ames' Ledge, Kennebec River, Maine.—Iron socket, wooden shaft.
Beef Rock, Kennebec River, Maine.—Iron socket, wooden shaft.
Lime Rock, Back River, Maine.—Iron socket, wooden shaft.
Carleton's Ledge, Back River, Maine.—Iron socket, wooden shaft.
Clough's Rock, Sheepscot River, Maine.—Iron socket, wooden shaft.
Merrill's Ledge, Sheepscot River, Maine.—Iron socket, wooden shaft.
Yellow Ledges, Penobscot Bay, Maine.—Iron shaft, copper cylinder.

Garden Island Ledge, Penobscot Bay, Maine.—Iron shaft, copper cylinder and one ball, shaft good, lower part of cylinder partially broken away and ball gone.

Otter Island Ledge, Penobscot Bay, Maine.—Iron shaft, copper cylinder and two balls, shaft bent, lower part of cylinder partially broken away, and one ball gone.

Ash Island Point, Penobscot Bay, Maine.—Holes have been drilled in the ledge, and a tripod will be erected.

Dodge's Point Ledge, Penobscot Bay, Maine.—Wooden shaft attached to stump of iron spindle.

Potterfield Ledge, Penobscot Bay, Maine.—Stone beacon.

Lowell's Rock, Penobscot Bay, Maine.—Iron spindle and cage.

Seal's Ledge, Penobscot Bay, Maine.—Iron spindle and cage.

Harbor Ledge, Penobscot Bay, Maine.—Stone beacon.

Shipyard Ledge, Penobscot Bay, Maine.—Iron spindle broken off, not necessary.

Fiddler's Ledge, Penobscot Bay, Maine.—Stone beacon.

Northeast Ledge, Camden Harbor, Maine.—Iron spindle.

Morse's Point Ledge, Camden Harbor, Maine.—Iron spindle.

Hosmer's Ledge, Castine Harbor, Maine.—Stone monument.

Steel's Ledge, Belfast Harbor, Maine.—Stone beacon.

Fort Point Ledge, Penobscot River, Maine.—Stone beacon.

Odom's Ledge, Penobscot River, Maine.—Stone beacon.

Buck's Ledge, Penobscot River, Maine.—Iron beacon.

Center Harbor Ledge, Eggemoggin Reach, Maine.—Iron socket, wooden shaft.

Ship and barges, Blue Hill Bay, Maine.—Iron socket, wooden shaft.

Bunker's Ledge, Mount Desert, Maine.—Stone beacon.

Half-Tide Ledge, Narraguagus Harbor, Maine.—Iron socket, wooden shaft.

Norton's Reef, Pleasant River, Maine.—Iron tripod, shaft, and ball.

Snow's Rock, Moosepeak Reach, Maine.—Iron socket, wooden shaft.

Gilchrist's Rock, Moosepeak Reach, Maine.—Iron shaft and ball.

Western Bar, Lubec Narrows, Maine.—Wooden crib filled with stone.

The Ledge, Saint Croix River, Maine.—Wooden crib filled with stone.

All of these beacons are in good condition except where it is otherwise specified.

Steps have been taken to substitute spindles for buoys in the following places, viz:

Stone's Rock, Old York River.

Cow Island Ledge, Casco Bay.

Lower Basket Island Ledge, Casco Bay.

Gooly Ledge, Casco Bay.

Hodsdon's Ledge, Sheepscot River.

Basket Island Ledge, Casco Bay.

Hypocrite Ledge, near Damiscove Island.

Egg Rock, George's River.

Goose Rock, Fox Island.

Iron Point Ledge, Fox Island.

Inner Ledge, Isle au Haute.

Colby's Ledge, Merchant's Row.

Scrag Island Ledge, Merchant's Row.

Drunkard's Ledge, Penobscot Bay.

Trafton's Island Ledge, Millbridge.

Jordan's Delight Ledge, Narraguagus.

Bunker's Ledge, Mount Desert.

BUOYS.

New buoys have been placed to mark the following dangers, viz:

Burnt Coat Harbor, Maine.

John's Island Ledge.
Heron Island Ledge.
Gooseberry Island Ledge.
Hat Island Reef.

Lubec Narrows, Maine.

Lower Buoy.
Upper Buoy.

Machias Bay, Maine.

Cross Island Ledge.
Thornton Point Ledge.
Seal Cove Ledge.
Sea-shore Ledge.
Foster's Island Ledge.

Rockland Harbor, Maine.

North end of Southern Ledge.
South end of South Ledge.
Railway Ledge.
Ninety-eight new buoys have been used to supply losses during the year.

DEPOT.

A buoy-depot is at present located upon House Island, near Fort Scammel, Portland Harbor, upon land belonging to the War Department, which is now needed by the engineer in charge of the construction of fortifications at that point.

Notice has been given that the depot must be removed, and an appropriation of $15,000 is recommended for the purchase of a site and the erection of a wharf and the necessary buildings.

[6.]

SECOND DISTRICT.

Extends from Hampton Harbor, New Hampshire, to include Gooseberry Point, entrance to Buzzard's Bay, and embraces all the aids to navigation on the coast of Massachusetts.

Inspector.—Commander George H. Perkins, United States Navy.

Engineer.—Lieut. Col. James C. Duane, Corps of Engineers, brevet brigadier-general United States Army.

In this district there are:

Light-houses and lighted beacons 61
Light-houses finished and lighted during the year ending July 1, 1873........... 3
Light-houses for which appropriations were available, but which were not finished on the 1st of July, 1873.. 0

Light-ships, (in position) 8
Light-ships, (for relief) 2
Fog-signals, operated by steam or hot-air engines 4
Day or unlighted beacons.. 51
Buoys actually in position... 508
Spare buoys, for relief and to repair losses..................................... 414
Tender-steamer Verbena, inspector's tender................................... 1

The following numbers, which precede the names of stations, correspond with those of the light-house list of the Atlantic, Gulf, and Pacific coasts of the United States, issued January 1, 1873 :

LIGHT-HOUSES AND LIGHTED BEACONS.

54, 55. *Newburyport, upper harbor.*—Two range-lights to guide up the river Merrimack to the city of Newburyport have been established in the same position as the private lights heretofore maintained by subscription, and were lighted June 1, 1873. The front light is on an iron tower, conical in form, 14 feet 6 inches high, located on Bayley's new wharf, and the focal plane is 25 feet above the sea. The rear light is about 350 feet W. ¼ S. from the front light, on a brick tower, pyramidal in form, 32 feet high, and the focal plane is 47 feet above the sea.

64, 65. *Baker's Island, south side of northerly entrance to Salem Harbor, Massachusetts.*—A frame dwelling for the assistant keeper has been erected and the light-house land partially refenced with posts and pickets.

78. *Race Point, Cape Cod, Massachusetts.*—A 12-inch steam-whistle has been established, and is arranged to give two blasts of 4 seconds' duration each, with an interval of 8 seconds between them, followed by an interval of 44 seconds. A frame engine-house 12 feet by 24 feet, and fuel, water-sheds and tanks have been erected.

79. *Wood End, Cape Cod, Massachusetts.*—This new light-station was completed and lighted for the first time on the night of the 20th of November, 1872. The tower is of brick, pyramidal in form, and is painted brown. The focal plane is 34 feet above the ground and 45 feet above the sea. The lens is of the fifth order of the system of Fresnel, illuminating the entire horizon, and will show a red light flashing every 15 seconds, which can be seen in clear weather from the deck of a vessel 10 feet above the sea at a distance of eleven nautical miles. The exterior of the lantern, railing, and deck, and all of the iron-work at the top of the tower, are painted black. The keeper's dwelling is of wood; one and a half stories high; painted cream-color, and is placed northeastward of the tower.

80. *Long Point, Cape Cod, Massachusetts.*—A new keeper's dwelling and tower has become indispensable at this station, the beach having changed to such an extent as to leave the foundation of the present building exposed. The piles on which the present building is supported are decayed, and the entire structure in danger of being carried off by a heavy storm.

84. *Cape Cod Highlands, Truro, Massachusetts.*—A first-class Daboll trumpet has been established at this station, and is arranged to give blasts of 8 seconds' duration, with intervals between them of 30 seconds. A frame engine-house, 12 feet by 24 feet, and fuel-shed, have been erected. Some repairs have been made.

85, 86, 87. *Nauset Beach, at Eastham, Cape Cod, Massachusetts.*—Fourth-order lenses have been substituted in the places of the 6th at this station. The dwelling-house should be enlarged, or a small cottage built for the accommodation of the assistant keeper, as the building now occupied is entirely too small.

20 Ab

91. *Monomoy, southern extremity of Cape Cod, Massachusetts.*—The importance of establishing a powerful light at this point was urged in the last annual report. The present light is insufficient, and the necessity of furnishing a more efficient aid to the navigation of this great thoroughfare, cannot be exaggerated. The last annual report of the Light-House Board contains the following statement in relation to increasing the efficiency of this light:

Monomoy Point.—The light at this station, which is of the fourth order, on a tower about 40 feet high, was originally intended as a guide to Old Stage Harbor. The harbor has been filled with sand and cannot now be entered, and the light is therefore of no further use for that purpose. But, inasmuch as nearly all vessels (both steamers and sailing) plying between New York and the eastern ports pass this point, and have now no other guide than the light-ships, which cannot be seen a sufficient distance, it is considered a matter of the greatest importance that this light should be replaced by one of sufficient power to guide vessels safely through this intricate passage. For this purpose, there is recommended a second-order fixed light, varied by red flashes, for which an estimate is submitted.

95. *Sankaty Head, on southeast side of Nantucket, Mass.*—The tower and buildings require extensive repairs, and a new lantern is necessary, and a special estimate therefor is submitted.

108. *Edgartown, north side of the harbor.*—Extensive repairs have been made at this station.

—. *East Chop, Martha's Vineyard, east entrance to Holmes's Hole Harbor, Massachusetts.*—A light has been maintained for several years at this point by the subscription of the owners of steamships and by other private individuals. As there is no doubt as to the utility of the light, it is recommended that an appropriation for erecting a fourth-order light be made.

112. *Sow and Pigs, entrance to Vineyard Sound and Buzzard's Bay.*—The western entrance to Vineyard Sound is now marked by a light-ship anchored off the Sow and Pigs Ledge. A second-order light placed on this point would not only furnish a better guide to vessels entering the sound, but would be a saving of expense by enabling both the light-ship and the Cuttyhunk light to be dispensed with.

REPAIRS.

At each of the following-named light-stations there have been made repairs and renovations more or less extensive during the year:

56 and 57. *Ipswich*, entrance to Ipswich Harbor, Massachusetts.

58. *Annisquam*, entrance to Annisquam Harbor, Massachusetts.

59. *Straitsmouth*, north side of Cape Ann, Massachusetts.

62. *Eastern Point*, east side of entrance to Gloucester Harbor, Massachusetts.

63. *Ten-Pound Island*, Gloucester Harbor, Massachusetts.

66. *Hospital Point*, Beverly, Massachusetts.

67. *Fort Pickering*, Salem, Massachusetts.

68. *Derby Wharf*, Salem, Massachusetts.

69. *Marblehead*, south side of entrance to Marblehead Harbor, Massachusetts.

70. *Egg Rock*, off Nahant, Massachusetts.

71. *Minot's Ledge*, entrance to Boston Bay, Massachusetts.

72. *Boston*, north side of main entrance to Boston Harbor, Massachusetts.

73. *Narrows*, entrance to Boston Harbor, Massachusetts.

74. *Long Island Head*, Boston Harbor, Massachusetts.

75, 76. *Plymouth*, entrance to Plymouth Harbor, Massachusetts.
77. *Duxbury Pier*, entrance to Plymouth Harbor, Massachusetts.
81. *Mayo's Beach*, head of Wellfleet Bay, Massachusetts.
82. *Billingsgate Island*, near Wellfleet, Massachusetts.
83. *Sandy Neck*, entrance to Barnstable Harbor, Massachusetts.
88, 89. *Chatham*, west side of Chatham Harbor, Massachusetts.
90. *Pollock Rip*, light-ship, off Chatham, Massachusetts.
92. *Shovelful Shoals*, light-ship, off Chatham, Massachusetts.
93. *Handkerchief*, light-ship, Vineyard Sound, Massachusetts.
94. *Nantucket*, (Great Point,) northeast point of Nantucket, Massachusetts.
96. *South Shoal*, light-ship, off Nantucket, Massachusetts.
97. *Gay Head*, west point of Martha's Vineyard Island, Massachusetts.
98. *Brant Point*, entrance Nantucket Harbor, Massachusetts.
99. *Nantucket Range Beacon*, Nantucket Harbor, Massachusetts.
100, 101. *Nantucket Cliff Range Beacons*, near Nantucket Harbor, Massachusetts.
102. *Bass River*, entrance to Bass River, Massachusetts.
103. *Bishop & Clerk's*, Vineyard Sound, Massachusetts.
104. *Hyannis*, entrance Hyannis Harbor, Massachusetts.
105. *Cross Rip*, light-ship, off Nantucket, Massachusetts.
106. *Cape Poge*, near Edgartown, Massachusetts.
107. *Succonnessett*, light-ship, Vineyard Sound, Massachusetts.
109. *Holmes' Hole*, (west chop,) entrance to Holmes' Hole Harbor, Massachusetts.
110. *Nobsque Point*, entrance to Wood's Hole Harbor, Massachusetts.
111. *Tarpaulin Cove*, on Naushon Island, Vineyard Sound, Massachusetts.
113. *Hen and Chickens*, light-ship, entrance to Buzzard's Bay, Massachusetts.
114. *Cuttyhunk*, entrance to Buzzard's Bay, Massachusetts.
115. *Dumpling Rock*, Buzzard's Bay, Massachusetts.
116. *Clark's Point*, entrance to New Bedford Harbor, Massachusetts.
117. *Palmer's Island*, New Bedford Harbor, Massachusetts.
118. *Ned's Point*, entrance to Mattapoisett Harbor, Massachusetts.
119. *Bird Island*, Buzzard's Bay, Massachusetts.
120. *Wing's Neck*, entrance to Sandwich Harbor, Massachusetts.

The following-named light-stations require repairs to be made during the current and ensuing years:

60. *Cape Ann*, Massachusetts.
80. *Long Point*, (Cape Cod,) entrance to Provincetown Harbor, Massachusetts.
91. *Monomoy*, southern point of Cape Cod, Massachusetts.
95. *Sankaty Head*, island of Nantucket, Massachusetts.
97. *Gay Head*, western end of Martha's Vineyard, Massachusetts.
114. *Cuttyhunk*, entrance to Buzzard's Bay, Massachusetts.

LIGHT-SHIPS.

Although none of the light-ships in this district have parted their moorings, or met with any serious accidents during the past year, yet more extensive repairs have been required than perhaps ever before in a single year, eight out of the whole number (ten) having been taken into port for that purpose. With the exception of Vineyard Sound they are all now in excellent order.

90. Pollock Rip, off Chatham, Massachusetts. This vessel has been put in complete order during the year at a total expense of $1,258.66.

92. Shovelful, on Shovelful Shoal, off Chatham, Massachusetts. This vessel has been thoroughly repaired at an expense of $5,287.26.

93. "Handkerchief," on Handkerchief Shoal, in Vineyard Sound, Massachusetts. This vessel has been extensively repaired and refitted at an expense of $6,800, and is now in perfect order.

96. Nantucket, New South Shoals, twenty-one miles S. S. E. from the island of Nantucket. Has had no repairs during the year, and is in good condition.

105. "Cross Rip," off Cross Rip Shoal, in Nantucket Sound, Massachusetts. Early in December last the windlass of this vessel was started, in a severe gale, and it was found necessary to take her to New Bedford. Upon examination the vessel was found to be very rotten in her timbers and planking, and to require very extensive repairs, which were made at an expense of $12,393.79.

107. Succonnessett, between Succonnessett and Eldridge Shoals, Nantucket Sound. The repairs of this vessel, which were in progress at the date of the last annual report, were completed within the estimate, and the vessel returned to her station, for which she is well adapted, though much smaller than the other light-vessels in the district. The expense of the repairs was $4,707.63.

112. Vineyard Sound, off Sow and Pigs Rocks, western entrance to Vineyard Sound, Massachusetts. This vessel requires considerable repairs, at an estimated expense of $3,000.

113. Hen and Chickens, western side of entrance to Buzzard's Bay, Massachusetts. This vessel was taken to New Bedford last autumn, and some necessary repairs made, at an expense of $775.15.

Reliefs No. 9 and 24. Necessary repairs were made to these vessels during the year, at an expense of $1,527.00.

FOG-SIGNALS OPERATED BY STEAM OR HOT-AIR ENGINES.

Cape Ann.—Twelve-inch steam-whistle.
Boston.—First-class Daboll air-trumpet.
Race Point.—Twelve-inch steam-whistle.
Cape Cod.—First-class Daboll air-trumpet.
All of the above are in good condition.

FOG-SIGNALS ON LIGHT-SHIPS IN VINEYARD SOUND.

The entire commerce by sea between the East and New York and the South passes through Vineyard Sound, and depends on the light-ships at "Pollock Rip," on the eastern, and the "Sow and Pigs Reef," at the western entrance, to guide them in entering and leaving the sound. In foggy weather these lights are not available and many disasters occur in consequence.

The Board therefore earnestly recommend that an appropriation of $10,000 be granted for the purpose of putting fog-signals in these vessels, which may be operated by steam or hot air.

DAY OR UNLIGHTED BEACONS.

Names and positions of the day or unlighted beacons in the second district:

Old Cock, Buzzard's Bay, Massachusetts.—Iron spindle 86 feet high; cage at top.

Egg Island, Buzzard's Bay, Massachusetts.—Granite cone with iron spindle and vane.

Range Beacon, Fairhaven, Massachusetts.—Iron triangular pyramid 40 feet high.

Cormorant Rocks, entrance Mattapoisett Harbor, Buzzard's Bay, Massachusetts.—Iron spindle; cage at top.

Lone Rocks, entrance Wood's Hole, Massachusetts.—Iron spindle; cage at top,

Collier's Ledge, Centreville Harbor, Vineyard Sound, Massachusetts.—Granite base, iron spindle, ball, and vane.

Great Rock, west of Point Gammon, Vineyard Sound, Massachusetts.—Iron spindle; cage at top.

Hyannis Breakwater, Massachusetts.—Wooden spindle, four arms; cask at top.

Sunken Pier, Bass River Bar, Massachusetts.—Wooden spindle; cask at top.

Spindle Rock, entrance to Edgartown Harbor, Massachusetts.—A new iron spindle 12 feet high, with cask at top, surmounted by a spindle and vane, has been erected in place of the one which was carried away by the ice.

Billingsgate Shoal, Massachusetts.—Old site; timber beacon, with masts and slats.

Egg Island Rock, entrance to Wellfleet Harbor, Massachusetts.—Wooden spindle; cask at top.

Duxbury Beacon, Massachusetts.—Square granite, and granite post at top.

Breakwater Beacon, Massachusetts.—Square granite, with wooden spindle and cage.

Hogshead Beacon, Massachusetts.—Iron spindle, with arm, cask, and cage at top.

North Beacon, entrance to Scituate Harbor, Massachusetts.—Iron spindle, with two rounds.

South Beacon, entrance to Scituate Harbor, Massachusetts.—Iron spindle, with two lozenges.

Londoner, off Thatcher's Island, Cape Ann, Massachusetts.—Iron spindle with cage at top.

Point Alderton, Boston Bay, Massachusetts.—Square granite pyramid with cone at top.

False Spit, Boston Bay, Massachusetts.—Granite base, with iron spindle and cage at top.

Spit Beacon, Boston Bay, Massachusetts.—Square granite pyramid.

Nix's Mate, Boston Harbor, Massachusetts.—Square granite base, with octagonal wooden pyramid.

Great Farm Bar, Boston Bay, Massachusetts.—Square granite base and granite cone, with iron spindle and cage at top.

Deer Isle Point, Boston Bay, Massachusetts.—Square granite pyramid.

Bird Island, Boston Bay, Massachusetts.—Iron spindle, cage at top.

Sunken Island, Boston Bay, Massachusetts.—Granite base, with wooden spindle and cage at top.

Pig Rocks, Boston Bay, Massachusetts.—Granite pyramid, with wooden spindle and cage at top.

Half-tide Rock, entrance to Swampscot Harbor, Massachusetts.—A wrought-iron spindle 23 feet high, with cask at top, painted red, has been set in place of the wooden shaft.

Cat Island, entrance to Salem Harbor, Massachusetts.—Wooden spindle, with cask at top.

Marblehead Rock, entrance to Marblehead Harbor, Massachusetts.—Granite, conical, with wooden spindle.

Little Aqua-Vitæ, entrance to Salem Harbor, Massachusetts.—Granite, with wooden spindle and cage at top.

Great Aqua-Vitæ, entrance to Salem Harbor, Massachusetts.—Granite, with wooden spindle and cage at top.

Hardy's Rock, entrance to Salem Harbor, Massachusetts.—Wooden spindle, with two triangles at top.

Bowditch Beacon, entrance to Salem Harbor, Massachusetts.—This beacon has been rebuilt of granite on the old site; it is a triangular pyramidal structure, surmounted by a mast and cage; the sides at the base are 16 feet; at top 7 feet; height of masonry, 30 feet, to top of cage, 45 feet. The wooden mast and cage are painted black.

Halfway Rock, off Marblehead, Massachusetts.—Granite beacon. It has been nearly destroyed.

Little Haste Beacon, entrance to Salem Harbor, Massachusetts.—Wooden mast, with cask at top.

Abbott's Monument, entrance to Salem Harbor, Massachusetts.—Square granite, with wooden mast and cask at top.

Monument Bar, entrance to Beverly Harbor, Massachusetts.—Square granite, wooden mast, cage at top.

Ram's Horn Beacon, entrance to Beverly Harbor, Massachusetts.—Square granite, wooden mast.

Lobster Rocks, Beverly Harbor, Massachusetts.—Stone, with wooden spindle.

Black Rock, Gloucester Harbor, Massachusetts.—Iron spindle with cage at top.

Harbor Rock Beacon, Gloucester Harbor, Massachusetts.—Iron spindle with ball and cage at top.

Five-Pound Island Beacon, Gloucester Harbor, Massachusetts.—Granite base with iron spindle and ball at top.

Lobster Rock, Annisquam Harbor, Massachusetts.—Square granite beacon. Has been rebuilt.

Lane's Point, Annisquam Harbor, Massachusetts.—Square wooden beacon.

Point Neck Rocks, Entrance to Essex Harbor, Massachusetts.—Iron spindle, with ball at top.

Black Rocks, Newburyport Harbor, Massachusetts.—A stone pier, 15 feet square and 15 feet high, has been erected in the place of the iron spindle, and will be surmounted by a wooden pyramid painted red.

North Pier, Newburyport Harbor, Massachusetts.—Wooden crib filled with stone.

South Pier, Newburyport Harbor, Massachusetts.—Wooden crib filled with stone.

Dry Salvages, off Cape Ann, Massachusetts.—Holes have been drilled in this ledge and a day mark is being erected.

Harding's Ledge, Boston Bay, Massachusetts.—Holes are being drilled in this ledge; when completed a day mark will be erected.

BUOYS.

Owing to the want of another tender for buoy purposes it was found impossible to care for the buoys as thoroughly as desirable, and another tender will be sent as soon as possible to assist in the work of the district. Thirty-one spar buoys and nine iron buoys have been lost by ice and other causes during the year.

DEPOTS.

Cohasset, Massachusetts.—The buoy depot at Cohasset for the northern part of the district was temporarily adopted in its present position from motives of economy, the ground belonging to this establishment, and the sheds which had been used by the stone cutters and other workmen employed in the construction of Minot's Ledge light-house, serving for buoy sheds, but it was never intended that the location should be a permanent one, the channel of approach being very narrow, crooked, and shoal, and freezing early in the season, cutting off access to the depot by the tenders and causing great inconvenience.

For these reasons the sheds and wharf have not been repaired and as they are now fast going to decay it is not thought advisable to expend more money upon them. In view of the unfitness of this location, an appropriation is asked for the purpose of transfering the depot to Lovell's Island in Boston Harbor, which belongs to the Government, and is admirably suited to the purpose as the channel near the island is never closed by ice, and the island can be approached at all stages of the tide. An estimate for this purpose is included in the annual estimates.

Wood's Hole, Massachusetts.—The building occupied by the lampist has been repaired. To put this useful depot in good order and efficient condition, an appropriation of $5,000 is asked for, and is submitted in the estimates.

[7.]

THIRD DISTRICT.

The third district extends from Gooseberry Point, Massachusetts, to include Squam Inlet, New Jersey, and embraces all the aids to navigation on the sea and sound coasts of Rhode Island, Connecticut, and New York, Narragansett and New York Bays, Providence and Hudson Rivers, Whitehall Narrows, and Lake Champlain.

Inspector.—Commodore James H. Strong, United States Navy, to June 30, 1873. Commodore Stephen D. Trenchard, United States Navy, since June 30, 1873.

Engineer.—Col. I. C. Woodruff, Corps of Engineers, Bvt. Brig. Gen. U. S. A.

In this district there are:

Light-houses and lighted beacons	117
Light-houses and lighted beacons finished and lighted during the year ending July 1, 1873	6
Light-houses for which appropriations were available, but which were not finished on the 1st of July, 1873	9
Light-ships in position	6
Light-ships for relief	3
Fog-signals operated by steam or hot-air engines	8
Day or unlighted beacons	39
Buoys actually in position	465
Buoys for relief and to supply losses	283
Steam-tenders for supply and for inspection, "Putnam" and "Cactus"	2
Steam-tender for engineer purposes, "Mistletoe"	1
Supply-steamer for supplying the light-houses of the Atlantic and Gulf coasts, "Fern"	1

The numbers preceding the names of stations correspond with the light-house list of the Atlantic, Gulf, and Pacific coasts, and the northern and northwestern lakes of the United States, issued January 1, 1873.

LIGHT-HOUSES AND LIGHTED BEACONS.

The Whale, Narragansett Bay, Rhode Island.—In the last annual report it is stated that " This is a reef of rocks awash at all stages of the tide, and a dangerous obstruction to navigation in the approach to the west channel of the Narragansett Bay. This channel is habitually used by the daily line of Providence steamers which pass the locality during the night, carrying large numbers of passengers and valuable freights, and it is recommended that a light and fog-bell be erected on the ledge. The estimate of the engineer of the district for the structure is $35,000, which is embraced in the estimates of the board."

The recommendation is renewed, also the estimate for the structure, namely, $35,000.

122. *Beaver Tail, Rhode Island.*—The first-class fog-signal, a Daboll trumpet, two twenty-four-inch engines, authorized, was completed and put in operation at the close of the month of October, 1872.

The signal was operated during four hundred and·ninety-three and one-half (493½) hours of fog, throughout the past year.

124. *Newport Harbor, Goat Island, Rhode Island.*—The fog-bell authorized was erected, and the striking apparatus put in readiness for use on the first of March, 1873.

—. *Muscle Bed, Narragansett Bay, Rhode Island.*—A beacon-light and fog-bell have been erected. The light was exhibited and the fog-bell was ready for operation on the 1st of August, 1873. The illuminating-apparatus is dioptric of the 6th order of the system of Fresnel, and shows a fixed red light over an arc of 270°. The focal plane is 31 feet above the sea, and the light can be seen in clear weather at a distance of $10\frac{7}{10}$ nautical miles. The bell is struck by machinery at intervals of 20 seconds.

131. *Conimicut, river Providence, Rhode Island.*—The dwelling for the keeper, authorized by the appropriation made by the last Congress, is in progress under contract; on its completion the site of the present dwelling on Nyatt Point will be sold at public auction, as provided in the act making the appropriation for the new dwelling,

132. *Bullock's Point, river Providence, Rhode Island.*—The beacon-light authorized was erected and the light was exhibited on the 4th of November, 1872. It is on a shoal off the point on the east side of the channel. The pier is of granite and the illuminating-apparatus is dioptric of the 6th order of the system of Fresnel, and shows a fixed red light.

A dwelling for the keeper is recommended. The estimated cost of the dwelling, together with that of enlarging the foundation, is $15,000.

133. *Sabin's Point, river Providence, Rhode Island.*—The structure, embracing pier and dwelling of granite, has been completed, and the light first exhibited on the 4th of November, 1872.

It is situated on a shoal off the point, in 8 feet of water, near the eastern side of the channel. The pier on which it is built and the dwelling are of granite. The illuminating-apparatus is dioptric, of the 6th order of the system of Fresnel, and shows a fixed white light.

134. *Pumham Rock, river Providence, Rhode Island.*—The boat-house and landing-wharf authorized have been completed. The light was changed from white to red on the 1st of October, 1872.

135. *Fuller's Rock, river Providence, Rhode Island.*

136. *Sassafras Point, river Providence, Rhode Island.*—These beacon-lights are on opposite sides of the river and are distant about one mile.

The purchase of a site and the erection of a dwelling for the keeper, are recommended, as very great difficulty is experienced in securing a suitable person to attend the lights at the compensation fixed for such beacons. It is supposed that $5,000 would be adequate for the object, and it is therefore recommended. The light at Sassafras Point was changed from white to red October 1, 1872.

137. *Point Judith, Rhode Island.*—The first-class steam fog-signal authorized has been erected and put in operation. The apparatus is a syren, in duplicate, receiving the steam from the same boiler.

The number of hours of fog during the year is five hundred and forty-eight, during which the signal was in operation.

138. *Block Island, Rhode Island, (northerly.)*—The grading and paving for the protection of the dwelling and the site against the sand-drifts have been completed, and the measure has proved effectual in arresting the waste of the sands in the vicinity of the structure.

139. *Block Island, (southerly,) Rhode Island.*—The plans for the light-house and first-class steam fog-signal have been prepared, but the difficulty of obtaining to the title, and consequent delays, have prevented the commencement of the structures. The site was finally purchased in the month of July, and preparations are in progress for the erection of the fog-signal, which will be completed during this season. Measures will be taken to place the light-house under contract, so that the structure may be begun early in the spring.

141. *Montauk Point, New York.*—The first-class fog-signal, two twenty-four-inch engines and Daboll trumpet, authorized, has been erected, and was put in operation on the 1st of May, 1873.

142. *Stonington Harbor, Connecticut.*—Very extensive general repairs are needed, and an appropriation of $1,500 is asked for the purpose.

146. *New London Harbor, Connecticut.*—The fog-signal, second-class, two eighteen-inch engines and Daboll trumpet, authorized, has been commenced, and the building has been enlarged for its housing. The signal will be ready for operation early in October.

The fog-signal was in use two hundred and eighty-two and one-half (282½) hours during fog, but the duration of fog was much greater, for the former signal was out of repair, and was not sounded.

148. *Race Rock, Long Island Sound, New York.*—The work was discontinued for the remainder of the season early in the month of September, when adverse weather was experienced.

The plan was modified with the view of a concrete foundation in place of the riprap; and work under the new contract was commenced early in the month of May, since which the contractor has made considerable progress, having completed the laying of the facing or dimension-stone. The preparations for the laying of the concrete foundation are progressing, derricks are being erected, breakwater of riprap laid, &c.

149. *Little Gull Island, Long Island Sound, New York.*—The duplicate syren of the second class was erected and prepared for use in the month of September, 1872.

The draught of the chimney of the duplicate was found defective, and necessary alteration to remedy the defect has been made.

The number of hours of fog during the year is five hundred and thirty-four, (534,) during which the syren was in operation.

In the last annual report it is stated that "This station needs an appropriation of $5,000 for completing the landing, reference to which was made in the last annual report.

"There is special need for the facilities of a landing for the reason that the shelter from the sea is so limited that the difficulty of landing supplies of the station, including a large quantity of coal for the steam fog-signal, is unusually great. The recommendation for the appropriation of $5,000 for completion of the landing is renewed."

The recommendation is again submitted.

152. *Long Beach Bar, Long Island, New York.*—The breakwater for the protection of the iron screw pile light-house has been completed, and danger from the flow of ice is not apprehended.

154. *Saybrook, Lynde Point, Connecticut.*—The fog-bell frame needs rebuilding. This and the general repairs of the station will require an appropriation of $1,500, which is included in the estimates.

155. *Calves Island, Connecticut.*

156. *Brockway's Reach, Connecticut.*

157. *Devil's Wharf, Connecticut.*—The protection of the foundations of these lights has been carried to completion.

160. *Faulkner's Island, Long Island Sound, New York.*—In the last annual report it is stated that "the wasting away of the clay bank continues slowly during the freezing and subsequent thawing of the soil. The beach requires to be protected at an estimated cost of $2,500, which is recommended to be appropriated." The recommendation is renewed.

161. *New Haven Harbor, Connecticut, Southwest Ledge.*—The appropriation of $50,000 for commencing a light-house on this ledge has been applied to the foundation of the structure, which was decided by the board should be an iron tube 24 feet in diameter, filled with concrete, and surrounded by riprap. This foundation is under contract, and it is to be completed by the 1st of May, 1874.

There will be required $50,000 additional for the structure, for which an estimate is submitted.

163. *Stratford Point, Connecticut.*—In the last annual report it is stated that "the buildings of this station are very old and unfit for occupation. An estimate for a suitable dwelling, over which the tower may be placed, was submitted in the last annual report. It is recommended that the amount be appropriated, viz, $15,000." The recommendation is renewed.

164. *Stratford Point Shoal, Long Island Sound, New York.*—An appropriation of $50,000 was made for the commencement of a light-house to supersede the light-ship at this station.

The nature of the shoal has been examined by boring into the shoal, the result of which is considered favorable for the iron tubular foundation, or concrete as may be finally determined.

The amount of the existing appropriation will suffice for the foundation, which will carry the work above high water.

An additional appropriation of $50,000 will be required to continue the structure, and an estimate is submitted.

166. *Bridgeport Harbor, Connecticut.*—The better protection of the iron screw pile light house against the floating ice is deemed necessary, and a coping of heavy stones to resist the ice is proposed, for which there is required the amount of $5,000, for which an estimate is submitted.

167. *Black Rock, Connecticut.*—In the last annual report it is stated that "the tower and keeper's dwelling (erected in 1808) are in an advanced state of decay, and need rebuilding. The new structure may be planned with the tower over the keeper's dwelling." The recommendation is renewed, and an estimate is submitted.

168. *Penfield Reef, Connecticut.*—The riprap foundation and pier, including the landing, and all of granite, have been completed, and the contractor for the dwelling and tower, also of granite, has commenced this portion of the structure. The light will, doubtless, be exhibited early during the coming winter season.

170. *Eaton's Neck, New York.*—The supply of fresh water for the steam fog-signal was found to be failing very rapidly, and it became necessary to drive an artesian well and build an accessory cistern. The well has been driven, and the supply of fresh water is found to be adequate to all the wants of the signal. The number of hours' duration of fog in which the signal was operated during the year is 494½.

171. *Lloyd's Harbor, New York.*—The jettee built for the protection of the site of the dwelling and light has not fully answered the purpose for which it is intended.

The abrasion continues, and threatens the destruction of the site. The light subserves only a local purpose. The amount of $2,000 for the protection of the site is recommended.

173. *Execution Rocks, New York.*—The number of hours' duration of fog for the year during which the signal was operated, was 284½.

175. *Hart Island, New York.*—The patent from the State of New York for the site of the light-house has not been obtained, and consequently the work is suspended. The contract for the structure has been conditionally awarded, and work will be commenced as soon as the patent is secured from the State.

178. *Blackwell's Island, East River, New York.*—On the 23d of September, 1872, there was exhibited for the first time a fixed red light from a handsome tower constructed by the department of public charities of the city of New York, and the light is maintained by it.

The illuminating apparatus furnished by the United States is dioptric, of the 4th order of the system of Fresnel, and the focal-plane is 54 feet above the sea.

182 and 183. *Highlands of Navesink, New Jersey.*—Fencing and grading of the grounds are much needed. An appropriation of $1,500 is, therefore, asked for the purpose.

185. *East Beacon, Sandy Hook, New Jersey.*—The abrasion of the beach threatened the destruction of the dwelling and tower. The encroachment of the sea was so rapid that the removal of the building was out of the question. Resort was then had to brush jettees, one of which was built on each side of the building; the result proved favorable; the accumulation of sand being very rapid in the vicinity of the building, but the abrasion continued to the westward. Under the appropriation of $20,000 for this protection, jettees of brush have been commenced, and three are in progress; a fourth will be commenced. The accumulation of sand increases with the progress of the work on the jettees. The number of hours of fog at this station during the year was 539¾; during which the signal, a syren, was in operation.

186. *West Beacon, Sandy Hook, New Jersey.*—The jettees of crib-work built some years since for the protection of this site needs rebuilding. There will be required for this purpose an appropriation of $8,000.

187. *Conover Beacon, New Jersey.*—The wooden tower is so far decayed that its rebuilding becomes a case of necessity. The estimate for the work is $3,000.

193. *Princess Bay, New York.*—The protection sea-wall under contract is still in progress. It is completed with the exception of the jettees, three in number, about 50 feet in length.

194. *Fort La Fayette, New York.*—The location of the fog-bell was finally decided to be on the sea-wall of the fort on the east side of the Narrows. The bell has been erected and was put in operation on the first day of August.

195. *Fort Tompkins, New York.*—The dwelling and tower surmounting the dwelling have been completed. The lantern remains to be

placed on the tower, and the light will be exhibited therefrom in a short time. The temporary light will then be extinguished.

197. *Fort Columbus, New York Harbor.*—The fog-bell was erected on the sea-wall on the northwest extremity of Governor's Island, and put in operation during the month of February, 1873.

198. *Bergen Point, New Jersey.*—The large bell struck by machinery has been substituted for the small one struck by hand.

203. *West Point, New York.*—The light was exhibited from the new beacon during the month of September, 1872. The apparatus is dioptric, of the 6th order of the system of Fresnel, and shows a fixed white light over 270° of the horizon. The focal-plane is 40 feet above the river.

204. *Esopus Meadows, New York.*—The light was exhibited from the new building during the month of August, 1872.

The supporting pier and the light-house are built of granite, near the west side of the river; the apparatus is dioptric, of the 5th order of Fresnel, and illuminates an arc of 270° of the horizon, with a fixed white light. The focal-plane is 58 feet above the river, and the light can be seen in clear weather 12 nautical miles. Proposals were solicited for the sale and removal of the old stone-dwelling, but none were received. Instructions have been given to have the building torn down, and the stone to be thrown around the base as riprap.

207. *Hudson City, New York.*—The pile foundation and pier are under contract. The plans for the dwelling and tower are being prepared, and the work will be put under contract in good season.

211-222.—*Hudson River Beacons, New York.*—The portable beacons were removed during the month of November and stored at Stuyvesant Depot. Stake-lights were placed temporarily until the close of navigation. Repairs, more or less, were required at the sites of the lights, owing to the abrasion of freshets. The beacons were replaced during the month of May, and repainted.

470. *Crown Point, Lake Champlain, New York.*—The improvements authorized by the appropriation have been made, and consist of a barn, and general repairs of the dwelling and grounds.

471. *Barber's Point, Lake Champlain, New York.*—The light was first exhibited at this station on the opening of navigation on the lake. The station being isolated, the keeper is obliged to keep a horse to procure supplies for family use, the nearest town being about two and a half miles. A barn, therefore, becomes necessary, for which an estimate of $1,000 is submitted.

473. *Juniper Island, Lake Champlain, Vermont.*—The bell-frame needs rebuilding, for which, and the general repairs of the station, an appropriation of $1,000 is submitted.

476. *Colchester Reef, Lake Champlain, Vermont.*—A gale of unusual violence, on the 15th and 16th of January, damaged the dwelling to some extent; and the shock of the waves was so great as to greatly alarm the keepers, and to cause the tower to sway so much that the lens was thrown from its pedestal and damaged. The ice also threatened the foundation; and it is known that this produces effects of a serious character. In order to anticipate casualty to the building, and to quiet alarm for its safety in storms and against ice, an appropriation of $5,000 is asked for riprapping with large stone the base of the structure.

477. *Bluff Point, Valcour Island, Lake Champlain, New York.*—After many vexatious delays in the search of title to the site, the owner of the land refused to convey the deed unless certain conditions were guaranteed to him, namely, the right to construct a wharf near the site, and to have the right of way across the light-house grounds.

These conditions were assented to, as the use of the wharf will also be secured to the United States. The purchase was concluded in April, and the contractor for the building was duly notified to commence the structure. The cellar has been opened in solid rock, and large portions of the materials are on the grounds.

480. *Cumberland Head, Lake Champlain, New York.*—The purchase of the land adjacent to the light, required to open the view of the light to the northward, has been concluded, and the land has been fenced. The necessary clearing of the trees to open the light will be made.

482. *Isle La Motte, Lake Champlain, New York.*—The recommendations for a dwelling at this station, at an estimated cost of $8,000 in the annual reports of past years, are renewed and are indeed urged.

REPAIRS.

At each of the following stations in the third district, repairs, more or less extensive, have been made during the year:

122. *Beaver Tail*, Rhode Island.
123. *Lime Rock*, Rhode Island.
124. *Newport Harbor*, Rhode Island.
125. *Rose Island*, Rhode Island.
131. *Conimicut*, Rhode Island.
132. *Bullock's Point*, Rhode Island.
133. *Sabin's Point*, Rhode Island.
134. *Pumham Rock*, Rhode Island.
135. *Fuller's Rock*, Rhode Island.
136. *Sassafras Point*, Rhode Island.
137. *Point Judith*, Rhode Island.
138. *Block Island*, Rhode Island.
140. *Watch Hill*, Rhode Island.
141. *Montauk Point*, New York.
142. *Stonington Harbor*, Connecticut.
146. *New London Harbor*, Connecticut.
149. *Little Gull Island*, New York.
152. *Long Beach Bar*, New York.
154. *Saybrook*, (*Lynde Point*,) Connecticut.
155. *Calves Island*, Connecticut.
156. *Brockway's Reach*, Connecticut.
157. *Devil's Wharf*, Connecticut.
160. *Faulkner's Island*, New York.
161. *New Haven Harbor*, Connecticut.
163. *Stratford Point*, Connecticut.
166. *Bridgeport Harbor*, Connecticut.
167. *Black Rock*, Connecticut.
170. *Eaton's Neck*, New York.
173. *Execution Rocks*, New York.
174. *Sand's Point*, New York.
179. *Great West Bay*, New York.
180. *Fire Island*, New York.
182–183. *Highlands of Navesink*, New Jersey.
185. *East Beacon Sandy Hook*, New Jersey.
187. *Conover Beacon*, New Jersey.
188. *Chapel Hill*, New Jersey.
190. *Waackaack*, New Jersey.
191. *Elm Tree Beacon*, New York.
193. *Prince's Bay*, New York.

196. *Robbin's Reef*, New York.
198. *Bergen Point*, New Jersey.
200. *Passaic Light*, New Jersey.
204. *Esopus Meadows*, New York.
205. *Rondout*, New York.
206. *Saugerties*, New York.
208. *Four-mile Point*, New York.
209. *Coxsackie*, New York.
210. *Stuyvesant*, New York.
212. *New Baltimore Dike*, New York.
213. *Five-Hook Island*, New York.
214. *Coeyman's Bar*, New York.
215. *Roha Hook*, New York.
216. *Schodack Channel*, New York.
218. *Cow Island*, New York.
219. *Parada Hook*, New York.
220. *Van Wie's Point*, New York.
221. *Cross Over*, New York.
222. *Cuyler's Dike*, New York.
454–469. *Whitehall Narrows.*
470. *Crown Point*, New York.
476. *Colchester Reef*, Vermont.
480. *Cumberland Head*, New York.

The following-named stations in the third district require repairs and renovations during the current and ensuing years:

132. *Bullock's Point*, Rhode Island.
135. *Fuller's Rock*, Rhode Island.
136. *Sassafras Point*, Rhode Island.
142. *Stonington Harbor*, Connecticut.
149. *Little Gull Island*, New York.
154. *Saybrook. (Lynde Point.)* Connecticut.
160. *Faulkner's Island*, New York.
163. *Stratford Point*, Connecticut.
166. *Bridgeport Harbor*, Connecticut.
167. *Black Rock*, Connecticut.
171. *Lloyd's Harbor*, New York.
182–183. *Highlands of Naresink*, New Jersey.
186. *West Beacon Sandy Hook*, New Jersey.
187. *Conover Beacon*, New Jersey.
154–469. *Whitehall Narrows.*
471. *Barber's Point*, New York.
473. *Juniper Island*, Vermont.
476. *Colchester Reef*, Vermont.
482. *Isle la Motte*, New York.

The following-named stations in the third district are not ment[?] elsewhere:

126. *Dutch Island*, Rhode Island.
127. *Poplar Point*, Rhode Island.
128. *Prudence Island*, Rhode Island.
129. *Bristol Ferry*, Rhode Island.
130. *Warwick*, Rhode Island.
144. *Morgan's Point*, Connecticut.
145. *North Dumpling*, Long Island Sound.

150. *Gardiner's Island,* New York. ·
151. *Plum Island,* New York.
153. *Cedar Island,* New York.
159. *Horton's Point,* New York.
162. *New Haven Long Wharf,* Connecticut.
165. *Old Field Point,* New York.
169. *Norwalk Island,* Connecticut.
172. *Great Captain's Island,* New York.
176. *Throgg's Neck,* New York.
177. *North Brother Island,* New York.
178. *Blackwell's Island,* New York.
184. *Sandy Hook,* New Jersey.
189. *Point Comfort Beacon,* New Jersey.
192. *New Dorp Beacon,* New York.
199. *Corner Stake,* New Jersey.
201. *Elbow Beacon,* New Jersey.
202. *Stony Point,* New York.
472. *Split Rock,* New York.
474–475. *Burlington Beacons,* Vermont.
478–479. *Plattsburgh Beacons,* New York.
451. *Point au Roche,* New York.
483. *Windmill Point,* Vermont.

LIGHT-SHIPS.

121. *Brenton's Reef, off Brenton's Reef entrance to Newport Harbor, Rhode Island.*

143. *Eel Grass Shoal, off Mystic, Connecticut, in Fisher's Island Sound.*

147. *Bartlett's Reef, off New London, Connecticut, in Long Island Sound.*—This vessel needs repairing at an estimated cost of $500.

158. *Cornfield Point, Long Island Sound, off mouth of river Connecticut.*—This vessel needs small repairs at an estimated cost of $300.

164. *Stratford Point, off Stratford Point, on Middle Ground, in Long Island Sound.*—This vessel will be superseded by a light-house.

181. *Sandy Hook, off entrance to New York Bay six miles from Sandy Hook and Highlands of Navesink Lights.*—On the 15th of February, 1873, the lights of this vessel were changed from white to red, complaints having been made that they were sometimes mistaken for the Highland (Navesink) lights. These lights are in good condition, except it is otherwise specified.

Relief Light-ships Nos. 17 and 20 are in good order for service.

Relief No. 23, formerly stationed upon Willoughby Spit Channel to Hampton Roads, Virginia, is being thoroughly repaired and refitted at a cost of $1,800.

Relief No. 14.—This vessel, from age and service, was, upon examination, found not worth repairs, and was, on the 7th of October last, sold at public auction, and the proceeds, $615, turned into the Treasury.

FOG-SIGNALS OPERATED BY STEAM OR HOT-AIR ENGINES.

122. *Beaver Tail, Rhode Island.*—A first-class Daboll trumpet, in duplicate.

137. *Point Judith, Rhode Island.*—First-class siren, in duplicate.

139. *Block Island, (southerly) Rock Island.*—First-class siren, in duplicate, (building.)

141. *Montauk Point, Long Island.*—First-class Daboll trumpet, in duplicate.

146. *New London, Connecticut.*—Third-class Daboll trumpet, in duplicate.

149. *Little Gull Island, New York.*—Second-class siren, in duplicate.

170. *Eaton's Neck, New York.*—Second-class siren, in duplicate.

173. *Execution Rocks, New York.*—Third-class Daboll trumpet, in duplicate.

185. *Sandy Hook, entrance to New York Harbor.*—First-class siren, in duplicate.

Light-Ship Fog-signal in Long Island Sound.—The immense number of passengers who are afloat nightly in vessels in Long Island Sound, between New York, Fall River, Stonington, Providence, and Norwich, and other eastern cities, and the great amount of fog on the sound, demand that one or more steam fog-signals be placed on the light-ships which lie in the track of these vessels, and an appropriation is asked of $5,000 for this purpose.

DAY OR UNLIGHTED BEACONS.

1. *East Lime Rock, east side of Newport Harbor.*—A square granite structure, surmounted by an iron spindle and red cage.

2. *South Point, Rose Island, Narragansett Bay.*—("Rose Island Spindle.") A square granite structure, surmounted by a spindle and cage-work keg, painted black.

3. *Halfway Rock, three-fourths of a mile southward of Prudence Island Point, Narragansett Bay.*—A spindle with square cage. Should be painted with horizontal stripes, for a channel on either hand.

4. *Warwick, or Spindle Rock Beacon, entrance to Greenwich Harbor, west channel of Narragansett Bay.*—Spindle with square cage-work day-mark, painted black.

5. *Pawtucket Beacon, Narragansett Bay, Providence River.*—A round granite base, whitewashed, surmounted by a spindle with a black ball.

6. *Pumham Beacon, Providence River, Rhode Island.*—A round stone base, whitewashed, with spindle, black ball and vane.

8. *Borden's Flats, opposite to Fall River, Rhode Island.*—A square granite beacon, with iron column and square day-mark of cage-work, painted black.

9. *Castle Island, near north end of Hog Island, Bristol Harbor.*—A round stone beacon, whitewashed, surmounted by a spindle and red ball.

10. *Allen's Rock, Warren River.*—A square granite base, and pyramid, one-eighth of a mile north of Adams' Point.

11. *White Rock Beacon, at the entrance of Wickford Harbor, Narragansett Bay.*—A round stone beacon, with iron column and square day-mark. This beacon has been damaged by ice, and needs repair.

12. *Watch Hill Reef Spindle, entrance to Fisher's Island Sound, from light-house, southwest by south three-fourths of a mile.*—An iron spindle on a rock which is bare at low water, surmounted by a square cage painted black.

13. *Sugar Reef Beacon, Fisher's Island Sound.*—Destroyed; to be replaced.

14. *Catumb Reef Beacon, Fisher's Island Sound.*—An iron-pile beacon with conical cage-work day-mark.

15. *East Spindle, entrance to Fisher's Island Sound by Lord's Channel.*—A spindle with square cage-work day-mark; being on starboard of Lord's Channel.

16. *West or Wicopesset Spindle Rock, entrance to Fisher's Island Sound*

by Lord's Channel—northwest of East Spindle, two-thirds of a mile.—An iron spindle, with square cage-work day-mark, painted black.

17. *Latimer's Reef Spindle, Fisher's Island Sound, one mile northwest of east point of Fisher's Island, and three-fourths of a mile southeast of Eel-grass Shoal light-vessel.*—An iron spindle bearing a square cage-work day-mark, painted with horizontal stripes.

18. *Ellis's Reef, Fisher's Island Sound, three-fourths of a mile northwest of Eel-grass Shoal light-vessel.*—An iron spindle with a square cage-work, painted black.

19. *Ram Island Reef Spindle, Fisher's Island Sound, one-half mile southeast of Ram Island.*—An iron spindle with square cage-work, painted black. The spindle is somewhat bent.

20. *Whale Rock Spindle, ("Spindle on the Whale,") entrance to the Mystic River.*—A stone beacon has been erected during the year.

21. *Crook's Spindle, Mystic River.*—An iron spindle with a quarter-keg on top. The spindle is bent over.

—. *Pawtucket Point Spindle.*—Hitherto this spindle has been kept at private expense. A letter from the collector at Stonington, praying that it be maintained by the Board, has been received.

22. *Black Ledge Beacon, entrance to New London Harbor.*—An iron shaft bearing a cage-work day-mark, formed by two cones connected at the vertices.

The spindle and day-mark have disappeared, and a buoy marks the ledge at present. A new stone beacon will be constructed under an existing appropriation therefor.

23. *Groton Long Point Beacon, Fisher's Island Sound.*—An iron spindle with cage-work in the form of an inverted cone, painted red.

24. *Potter's or Seaflower Reef Beacon, one mile northwest of North Dumpling light-house.*—Square granite beacon, without day-mark, erected during the past year.

25. *Saybrook Beacon, Connecticut River.*—A stone beacon, with globe, on Saybrook Bar.

26. *Hen and Chickens, Long Island Sound.*—An iron spindle bearing a square cage painted red.

27. *Branford Reef Beacon, Long Island Sound.*—A granite beacon, with iron shaft and black ball.

28. *Huncher Rock, or Black Rock Beacon, west side of entrance to Black Rock Harbor, Connecticut.*—An iron pile beacon, with cage on top.

29. *Southwest Ledge Spindle, entrance to New Haven Harbor, Connecticut.*—The new light-house on this ledge, to take the place of the one on Five-Mile Point, has been commenced. The site of the spindle, carried away by ice, is marked by a spar-buoy.

30. *Quixe's Ledge Spindle, entrance to New Haven Harbor.*—An iron spindle, with a cask on top, on a rock dry at half tide.

31. *Stratford River Beacon, entrance to Stratford River.*—A granite beacon, with iron column and day-mark.

32. *Outer Beacon, Bridgeport Harbor, Connecticut.*—A frustum of a square wooden pyramid, with a cask on top of a spar.

33. *Inner Beacon, Bridgeport Harbor, Connecticut.*—A wooden structure, like the outer beacon.

34. *Southport Beacon.*—Granite beacon, with iron column and day-mark.

35. *Southport Breakwater Beacon.*—A granite structure, with iron column and day-mark.

36. *Norwalk Beacon, southwest of Norwalk Island, Connecticut.*—A granite structure, with iron shaft and day-mark.

21 Ab

37. *Great Reef of Norwalk Island, entrance to Norwalk Harbor.*—A wooden spindle, with cage day-mark.

38. *Sand Spit Beacon, Sag Harbor, Long Island, New York.*—A square stone beacon and wooden tower.

39. *Oyster Pond Point, Plum Gut, entrance to Gardiner's Bay.*—A granite beacon in course of erection, the foundation being up to low-water mark.

40. *Success Rock Spindle, Long Island Sound.*—An iron shaft with conical cage-work.

41. *Romer Shoal Beacon, New York Bay.*—A granite structure in the form of a frustum of a cone, bearing a wooden mast and square cage day-mark.

42. *Mill Reef Beacon, opposite New Brighton, in Kill Van Kull.*—A sheet-iron beacon, filled in with concrete, and secured to a granite base. It is conical in shape, and supports an iron shaft with an iron cage on top.

43. *Stepping Stones, Long Island Sound, New York.*—A day-beacon of granite is urgently recommended for this obstruction, very dangerous in its character. One of the large steamers navigating the sound ran upon it recently. It is marked by a can-buoy, but it is difficult to retain marks of this kind in position, owing to the tows and vessels passing so near. Attention has been called to this danger by masters of steamers and others. The estimate for the granite beacon is $6,000.

BUOYS.

The buoyage of the district is in good condition. Nearly all the buoys in the bay of New York were carried off by the ice during the past winter, but were recovered.

Sixty buoys of all kinds were lost during the year, valued with their moorings at $2,987.28.

The grading of the grounds and the general repairs of the buildings at the general depot at Staten Island have been continued. The grounds in front and rear of lamp-shop and near the north gate have been graded and partly laid in grass. The engine-room of the lamp-shop has been enlarged and a duplicate boiler placed there as a reserve, and a suitable 6-inch drain to conduct to the cesspool the water coming from the springs in the bank and overflowing the floor of the boiler-room. A 12-inch drain has been laid to conduct the water from the roof of the oil-vault, and a 12-inch drain from the cellar of the office building, all connecting with the main 18-inch drain of the yard.

The original drains, being only 6-inch diameter, became clogged and unserviceable.

Flagging has been laid from the gate at the south entrance along the front of the shop, office, and store-house nearly to the north gate, on the ends of each of the buildings, and thence to the oil-vaults.

Steam radiators have been introduced into the office building for the more perfect heating of the rooms of the building. The steam is furnished by the boiler of the lamp-shop.

The front of the north wharf has been extended so as to make an equal projection with the south wharf, to arrest injury to the basin from the flow of the ebb-tide into the basin.

It is proposed to apply a portion of the new appropriation of $5,000 to the introduction of an elevator of approved kind into the lamp-shop building, to ensure a safer method of transferring the lens apparatus into the store-rooms.

Grading of the grounds will be continued, and flagging, so far as the funds will admit.

The appropriation will not be adequate for building the cisterns recommended in the last annual report. A further sum of $5,000 will be needed for the purpose and for the general repairs and preservation of the buildings, dwelling, grounds, &c. In view of enlarging the basin, either to embrace the whole or a part of the water-front of the depot, as may be deemed advisable, there will be required for commencing the enlargement the sum of $30,000.

The capacity for storage is at certain times found inadequate. The addition of a brick story to the oil-shed, and raising upon this story the present frame building, would, it is believed, relieve the storage-room. The brick story would furnish a better store-house for the oil received in barrels, and awaiting inspection and testing, than the frame building, which is too hot for such a purpose, causing leakage and loss of oil. The cost of such addition and change would be $20,000.

The total amount therefore required for the general depot is $55,000.

Lens apparatus received from France and shipped from light-house depot, Staten Island, from July 1, 1872, to June 30, 1873.

	First order.	Second order.	Third order.	Third-and-a-half order.	Fourth order.	Fifth order.	Sixth order.	Steamer lenses.	Pressed lenses.	Canal lenses.	Totals.
Received	2	2	3	2	13	14	11	3	1	5	56
Delivered	1	3	2	1	11	6	9	1	......	5	39
Total	3	5	5	3	24	20	20	4	1	10	95

List of boxes, barrels, bundles, packages, cans, and kegs received at and shipped from light-house depot, Staten Island, from July 1, 1872, to June 30, 1873.

	Boxes.	Barrels.	Packages.	Total.
Received	2,929	3,886	5,627	12,442
Delivered	2,949	3,921	6,235	13,105
Total	5,878	7,807	11,802	25,547

List of cases containing illuminating apparatus received at and shipped from light-house depot, Staten Island, from July 1, 1872, to June 30, 1873.

	Lamps, &c.	First order.	Second order.	Third order.	Third-and-a-half order.	Fourth order.	Fifth order.	Sixth order.	Steamer lenses.	Pressed lenses.	Canal lenses.	Total.
Received	22	50	85	43	24	53	42	14	8	6	14	361
Delivered	......	47	80	23	11	33	14	27	10	2	15	262
Total	22	97	165	66	35	86	56	41	18	8	29	623

List of articles manufactured and repaired in lamp-shop, at light-house depot, Staten Island, from July 1, 1872, to June 30, 1873.

	Lenses.	Lamps.	Lamp burners.	Miscellaneous articles.	Totals.
Manufactured	3	160	245	296	704
Repaired	6	47	49	1,670	1,772
Total	9	207	294	1,966	2,476

GENERAL DEPOT OF THE LIGHT-HOUSE ESTABLISHMENT AT STATEN ISLAND, NEW YORK.

Buoys and appendages received at and shipped from light-house depot, Staten Island, from July 1, 1872, to July 31, 1873, inclusive.

	Can-buoys.			Nun-buoys.				Sinkers.				Ballast-balls.		
	First class.	Second class.	Third class.	First class.	Second class.	Third class.	Spar-buoys.	First class.	Second class.	Third class.	Stone.	First class.	Second class.	Third class.
Received	8			20							171			
Shipped	8	16	1	5	9	16	2				158	10	16	10
Total	16	16	1	25	9	16	2				329	10	16	10

[8.]

FOURTH DISTRICT.

The fourth light-house district extends from Squam Inlet, New Jersey, to and including Metomkin Inlet, Virginia. It includes the sea-coast of New Jersey below the Highlands of Navesink, the bay-coasts of New Jersey and Delaware, the sea-coasts of Delaware and Maryland, and part of the sea-coast of Virginia.

Inspector.—Com. W. H. Macomb, United States Navy, until his death, August 12, 1872; Capt. Reigart B. Lowry, United States Navy, from August 29, 1872, to June 30, 1873; Capt. Thomas G. Corbin, United States Navy, present inspector.

Engineer.—Col. I. C. Woodruff, Corps of Engineers, Brevet Brigadier-General, United States Army, until May 16, 1873; Lieut. Col. W. F. Raynolds, Corps of Engineers, Brevet Brigadier-General, United States Army, present engineer.

In this district there are:

Light-houses and lighted beacons	19
Light-houses finished and lighted during the year ending July 1, 1873	1
Light-houses for which appropriations were available, but which were not finished on the 1st of July, 1873	5
Light-ships, (in position)	2
Light-ships, (for relief)	1

Fog-signals operated by steam or hot-air engines 0
Day or unlighted beacons ....·... 0
Buoys actually in position... 110
Spare buoys for relief and to supply losses 116
Tenders (steam) for inspection, (Violet) 1
Tenders (steam) for construction and repairs, (Rose)............................ 1

The number preceding the names of stations correspond with those of the light-house list of the Atlantic, Gulf, and Pacific coasts of the United States, issued January 1, 1873.

LIGHT-HOUSES AND LIGHTED BEACONS.

223. *Barnegat, sea-coast of New Jersey.*—The semi-monthly measurements along the beach near the light-house have been continued, and no important changes of the water-lines are apparent, the works for protecting the beach having effected the object of their construction. The changes of the position of the sand-hill north of the dwelling are very marked. It has drifted toward the dwelling, and has already reached the store-house.

225. *Absecum, sea-coast of New Jersey.*—The semi-monthly measurements of the beach have been continued throughout the year. There have been but few changes in the water-lines since last report, the dangerous action having for the present, at least, ceased. The sand along the beach above high water has accumulated, and beach-grass is appearing on it.

The north channel into the inlet has become deeper, and is used almost exclusively. The south channel has filled up to about $5\frac{1}{2}$ feet over the bar at low water, while the north channel has about 8 feet at the same stage.

The authorities of Atlantic City have not yet furnished the deed from the owners of the property for the occupation of the land where it was proposed to construct jettees for the protection of the light-house site, and the appropriation therefor has reverted to the Treasury.

226. *Hereford Inlet, sea-coast of New Jersey.*—The site has been selected and bids have been received for the construction of the light-house. The cession of jurisdiction by the legislature of New Jersey to the Government of the United States has been granted.

232. *Mispillion, Delaware Bay.*—The structure authorized by the act of Congress re-establishing the light has been erected, and the light exhibited. It is in Delaware Bay near the mouth of Mispillion River, and was completed and lighted for the first time on the 15th of June, 1873. The light is a fixed white light of the sixth order of the system of Fresnel, and is shown from a wooden frame tower, connected with the dwelling of the keeper, both colored gray, with the exception of the lantern on the tower, which is black. The focal flame is 48 feet above the water.

233. *Brandywine Shoal Light-Station, Delaware Bay.*—This structure having stood for twenty-five years, and being one of the earliest examples of iron-pile light-houses, and subject since its construction to annual assaults by great fields of ice in the breaking up of the ice of the river and bay, it is an interesting as well as important point to know the effect of time and salt water upon it. This question being one which interested the Engineer Department of the Army, which is using iron quite extensively in the improvements in the Delaware, Lieutenant-Colonel Kurtz, in charge of these improvements, proposed to the light-house engineer of the district to unite their facilities and have an examination made for the mutual benefit of the two departments. Capt. M. R. Brown, Corps of Engineers, is stationed at Lewes, Delaware, under Colonel Kurtz's orders, and had in his service a diver and the other facilities required for making the proposed examination, but was without the means of reaching the locality; accordingly the tender Rose was ordered to report to Captain Brown for this duty.

The light-house was visited on the 30th and 31st of July, and seven of the house-piles and three of those of the ice-fender or breaker were examined. The results of this examination, as given by Captain Brown, are to be found in a table which accompanied the report of the engineer of the district. It seems evident, from the table, that the action on the iron has been quite irregular, some of the piles not having worn perceptibly, while others have diminished in diameter quite half an inch.

The following extracts from the report of Captain Brown will be of interest:

The platform of the light-house, we found, was more than 20 feet from the surface of the water, and it was at once apparent that we were obliged to work from a temporary platform, which we must build on horizontal braces about six feet from the surface of the water at mean stage of tide. Some heavy planks were found at the light-house, which were lowered and put in place as platforms, to serve as a base to hold the air-pump, &c., and to admit of some little convenience in working.

* * * * *

Not having much previous knowledge of the light-house I had somewhat underrated the scope and difficulty of the work involved in a thorough examination of the structure. The whole number of piles in the substructure is 77, and nearly all are covered with considerable metamorphosed iron, difficult in most cases to scrape off, and many with coral and other adhering substances, which add to the difficulty. The current here is quite strong, and around the piles is broken into numerous eddies. The water is about 9 feet deep at low water.

The horizontal braces at about the plane of low water have, in many localities, dropped to the bottom; the cast-iron collars which held them having broken, apparently by the weight of the superincumbent ice. In this way the lower system of braces is almost completely gone on the north side to an east and west line, just south of the north pile of the main structure, (1848.) They are also gone in the center of the south half of the octagon. Occasional braces, about one-third the original number, are out of place in the south end of the fender or ice-breaker, and, in fact, so few remain throughout the whole structure in this lower system that it is practically nearly useless, since the remainder are bent downward at various angles, as though by a weight, and they appear ready to follow soon the fate of the others.

These latter being supported just above the bottom by remnants of collars, rendered it difficult for a diver to walk about in a strong current; and since considerable time was required to move our temporary platform from one locality to another, it was apparent that we must measure piles so near to each other (in groups) as to necessitate few changes of the platform, in order to obtain results of any value in an inspection so limited in time as this was, for various evident reasons.

* * * * *

I judge that a thorough examination of the entire structure would consume two or three weeks of fair weather, and would probably yield results of considerable value and of great interest.

All of the piles are more or less perceptibly wanting in verticality, but very few of them seriously so. The two most remarkably inclined abnormally are marked X and Y on the diagram accompanying this report. They are so bent as to be inclined about 15° and 10°, respectively, to the vertical above water.

No great departure from a horizontal plane is noticeable in the platform of the light-house, but it appears to me that the southeast portion over one of the piles (X in the diagram) is slightly inclined downward to the southeast.

The light-house itself exhibits nothing abnormal. Many of the diagonal braces in vertical planes far above the surface of the water are so peculiarly corroded as to resemble, in a striking degree, the exterior bark of a red-oak tree, with deep seams and scales.

The notes on the diagram and tables seem to indicate all else not included in this report which your instructions and my limited opportunities appear to call for.

It is proper to say that the departure from verticality in the piles and the destruction of the lower system of braces referred to by Captain Brown took place soon after the structure was built. In 1855 it was decided·not to depend on the lower braces. Before that date there was no platform over the "fender" then consisting of 30 piles; in 1857 or 1858 the outer row of 38 piles was put down, thus more than doubling the strength. Then also the wooden superstructure and platform were put in, thus giving additional strength; since then the strength of the structure has been sufficient, and the only points to be guarded against are the decay of the wooden portions and the destruction by time of the iron.

236. *Cross Ledge Shoal, Delaware Bay.*—An appropriation of $50,000 for commencing a light-house to replace the light-ship was made at the last session of Congress. The survey of the site is now in progress.

237. *Mahon's River Light-Station.*—In October last repairs were made to the plank platform around the building. Sketches have been forwarded showing the abrasion of the marsh at this site. For several years the board has recommended the removal of the light-house to a more favorable site, and as the time cannot be distant when this must be done, it is not deemed necessary to make further repairs. The amount required for the new light-house, as given in previous reports, is $15,000, and the time required for its erection would be about six months.

—— *Ship John Shoal, Delaware Bay.*—An appropriation of $50,000 for commencing a light-house at this shoal was made at the last session of Congress. A survey of the site is now in progress.

—— *Bulkhead Shoal, Delaware River.*—An appropriation of $50,000 was made at the last session of Congress for commencing a light-house at this shoal. A survey of the site is now in progress.

—— *Pea-Pach Island, Delaware River.*—An appropriation of $8,000 for the erection of a light-house on or near the south end of the island was made at the last session of Congress. A survey of the site is now in progress.

REPAIRS.

At each of the following·named stations in the fourth district there have been repairs and renovations more or less extensive since the last annual report.

223. *Barnegat*, sea-coast of New Jersey.
228. *Cape May*, sea-coast of New Jersey.
220. *Cape Henlopen*, sea-coast of Delaware.
230. *Cape Henlopen Beacon*, entrance to Delaware Bay.
231. *Delaware Breakwater*, entrance to Delaware Bay.
234. *Maurice River*, New Jersey, mouth of Maurice River, New Jersey.
235. *Egg Island*, New Jersey, Delaware Bay.
238. *Cohansey*, New Jersey, Delaware Bay.
239. *Bombay Hook*, Delaware, Delaware Bay.
240. *Reedy Island*, Delaware, Delaware Bay.
241. *Christiana*, Delaware, mouth of Christiana River, Delaware Bay.
242. *Fort Mifflin*, Pennsylvania, Delaware River.
243. *Fenwick's Island*, sea-coast of Delaware.

The following are the names of light-stations in the fourth district not mentioned elsewhere in this report:

224. *Tucker's Beach*, sea-coast of New Jersey.
244. *Assateague*, sea-coast of Virginia.

LIGHT-SHIPS.

227. *"Five Fathom Bank," on Five Fathom Bank off the Capes of the Delaware.*—This ship is in good condition, but needs some minor repairs, which will be made at an early day.

236. *"Cross Ledge," on Cross Ledge Shoal in Delaware Bay.*—This vessel, needing extensive repairs was removed from her station and "Relief No. 18" was substituted in October last. The latter was forced from her station by ice drifts, December 24, 1872, and could not be replaced till February 12. She was again driven away on the 26th of February, and was replaced on the 11th of March.

Relief No. 18 is in good condition, and is now, temporarily, on Cross Ledge Shoal, Delaware Bay.

Winter Quarter Shoal.—Nearly half way from the capes of the Delaware to the capes of Virginia, six and a half miles from the nearest land, and directly in the track of our immense coast-trade, lies the danger known as Winter Quarter Shoal, which has caused many wrecks, and is a source of anxiety to the masters of all vessels passing that way. It is recommended that this shoal be marked by a light-ship, and an appropriation of $50,000 is asked for that purpose.

BUOYS.

The buoyage of the fourth district is in good order.

FOG-SIGNALS OPERATED BY STEAM OR HOT-AIR ENGINES.

There are no fog-signals operated by steam or hot-air engines in this district.

DAY OR UNLIGHTED BEACONS.

There are no day or unlighted beacons in this district.

DEPOT.

Christiana, Delaware.—A bulk-head has been constructed along the bank of the depot between the two wharves, and a portion of the space between the wharves has been excavated to serve as a winter harbor for the steam-tender and the relief light-vessels.

[9.]

FIFTH DISTRICT.

The fifth district extends from Metomkin Inlet, Virginia, to include New River Inlet, North Carolina, and embraces part of the sea-coasts of Virginia and North Carolina, Chesapeake Bay, and the James and Potomac Rivers.

Inspector.—Commodore Fabius Stanly, United States Navy.

Engineer.—Maj. Peter C. Hains, Corps of Engineers, Bvt. Lieut. Col., United States Army.

In this district there are—

Light-houses and lighted beacons... 70
Light-houses finished and lighted during the year ending July 1, 1873........... 3
Light-houses for which appropriations were available, but which were not finished
  on the 1st of July, 1873.. 7

Light-ships ....: 0
Fog-signals operated by steam or hot-air engines 0
Day or unlighted beacons 100
Buoys actually in position 634
Spare buoys for relief and to supply losses 376
Tenders (steam) Heliotrope (buoy-tender) and Tulip, (for engineer's construction and repairs) 2
Tenders (sail) Maggie (buoy-tender) and Spray, (engineer's tender for construction and repairs) 2

The numbers preceding the names of stations correspond with the light-house list of the Atlantic, Gulf, and Pacific coasts of the United States issued January 1, 1873.

247. *Cape Henry, on the south side of the main entrance to Chesapeake Bay, Virginia.*—The annual report of the Light-House Board contains the following statements in regard to the construction of a new tower and keeper's dwelling for this light-station:

The tower is a frustum of an octagonal pyramid, built on a raised foundation of loose stone, some thirty feet above the level of the sea. The masonry of the outside is a soft sandstone, with an inside brick cylinder, the latter having been built in 1857, at which time the station was last refitted. Of the eight faces of the tower, six of them show on the outside large cracks or openings, extending from the base upward. Four of them are apparently less dangerous than the other two, and alone would not warrant any great apprehensions of danger, but the latter, viz, those on the north and south faces, where the strength of the masonry is lessened by openings for windows, are very bad, extending from the base almost to the top of the tower. These cracks cannot be seen on the inside, on account of the brick cylinder, (which is of more recent construction than the outside masonry,) and doubtless terminate at the air-space, between the outer and inner walls. At present the tower is in an unsafe condition, and there is no way of repairing the damage satisfactorily, and a new one must be built. This old tower has done good service, having been built in 1791, and is now the oldest tower on the coast, south of Cape Henlopen ; but it has seen its best days, and now, from age, and perhaps defective workmanship, it is in danger of being thrown down by some heavy gale.

The light is of the second order, and cannot be seen as far at sea as its importance, in respect to location, demands. It is undoubtedly one of the first lights, in point of importance, on the coast. A new tower should be built at this station without delay, and the light made of the first order. A good site can be had near the present location, on Government land, and materials for building purposes can be landed without difficulty. It also should be noted that the keeper's dwelling is in a dilapidated condition, and at too great a distance from the tower to insure proper attendance. It is a frame building, and is now more than thirty years old. It is too small for the number of keepers at this station, and should be enlarged. At present it affords very poor protection to the keepers from inclemency of the weather in winter. A new dwelling is an absolute necessity for this station.

The above recommendation is renewed, and an appropriation of $50,000 is asked to commence the work.

248. *"The Thimble" Shoal, at the entrance to Hampton Roads, Virginia.*— The work on the structure, which at date of last annual report was in progress, was finished October 1, 1872, and the light exhibited for the first time on the night of October 15. At the same time the light-ship anchored near this shoal, but on the opposite side of the channel, was withdrawn. This light-house replaces the last light-ship in this district. The light is of the fourth order, and shows red flashes at intervals of 30 seconds. The station is provided with two fog-bells, one on the north, the other on the south side of the light-house, which are struck simultaneously by machinery at intervals of 5 seconds.

251. *Lambert's Point, on the shoal off Lambert's Point, Elizabeth River, Virginia.*—A few months after this light-house was completed, it settled about 14 inches on the west side, on account of an unequal distribution of supplies left at the station, and the soft character of the soil on which the screw-flanges rested. It was leveled, however, without difficulty and at little expense, by lowering those piles that had not settled, by means of the water-jet process. The light-house was then secured

in a level position by driving an extra pile at each corner of the structure, and relieving the main piles of a portion of the weight by means of struts connecting the two. The light-house is now firm.

253. *White Shoals, screw-pile light-house, James River, Virginia.*—This light-house had formerly a bell rung by hand for a fog-signal. During the past year it has been supplied with one of Stevens's fog-bell machines, which strikes the bell at intervals of ten seconds.

254. *Point of Shoals, James River, Virginia.*—This light-house had formerly a fog-bell rung by hand in foggy weather. It has been supplied with a machine which strikes the bell with two blows at intervals of 5 seconds, then after an interval of 20 seconds the two blows are repeated, and so on.

——. *Dutch Gap Canal, James River, Virginia.*—Plans and specifications have been prepared for a keeper's dwelling and two small beacons under the appropriation made therefor by Congress, and the necessary land for site purchased at a merely nominal price, from the city of Richmond. The cession of jurisdiction in this case comes under a general law, passed by the State, at the meeting of the last legislature, consequently no delay will be experienced, as is usually the case, by the necessity of having a special act passed. The keeper's dwelling is to be a plain frame structure, located on the high ground midway between the two beacons. The latter will be frame structures, boarded up and arranged with a room in each for supplies. The lights will be of the sixth order, one at each end of the cut. It is proposed to advertise for bids for their construction at once.

——. *Solomon's Lump, in Kedge's Strait, between Tangier Sound and Chesapeake Bay.*—The last annual report contained the following remarks and estimates relating to the necessity of establishing a light at this place, which are repeated:

In compliance with a resolution of the House of Representatives, an examination and report to Congress were made during last session, upon the necessity and expediency of establishing a light to mark the shoal known as Solomon's Lump, in Kedge's Strait, between Tangier Sound and Chesapeake Bay. Solomon's Lump is a point of land on the north end of Evan's Island. There is a shoal that extends out a considerable distance from this point in a northerly direction, and is a source of danger to vessels navigating Kedge's Strait at night. Near its extreme point is the regular channel. The shoal itself has not more than about 5 feet water on it, to a point near the red buoy, which marks its extreme northerly end. At night this buoy cannot be seen a sufficient distance to be of any use. The only light in this vicinity is that on Fog Point, about one and a fourth miles in a west southwest direction; but on account of its distance and location, it affords no security to vessels from going ashore on the foot of Solomon's Lump. The light at Fog Point was established in 1827, before the introduction of the screw-pile system of lighthouses, and though it has served to mark the entrance to Kedge's Strait for a very long time, it is of little value as compared with other positions that could have been selected for a screw-pile structure, which would not only have marked the entrance to the strait, but would have been a guide all the way through. A light established on the shoal on Solomon's Lump, near its extreme point, and of such water as at the shoal in the extreme end of the channel, would afford security to vessels, and ... entering Kedge's Strait ... a straight line, passing most of the ... as established, ... annual cost of ... .

An appropriation of $15,000 is asked for to establish a light-house off Solomon's Lump, to take the place of that at Fog Point.

270. ... Mary-
land.—At the date of last annual ... establishing a fog-signal at this station was recommended ... an appropriation for fog-signals. The signal is a bell ... struck by machinery

at intervals of ten seconds. It was finished and in operation November 2, 1872.

275. *Thomas Point Shoal, north side of the mouth of South River, Maryland.*—An appropriation of $20,000 was made during the last session of Congress for a screw-pile light-house to be built on the shoal that makes off from Thomas Point, Md., to take the place of the old light-house on land, which is in need of extensive repairs, and which, on account of its distance from the track of vessels navigating the bay, is of comparatively little use at any time, and perfectly useless in foggy and thick weather, as the light cannot be seen, and the distance is too great for a fog-bell to be heard. The location on the extreme point of the shoal is one of great exposure. In view of this fact, and with the experience of Love Point light-house during the winter of 1872–'73 before us, it was deemed expedient to change the plan of this light-house, and instead of building it on screw-piles, as was at first intended, to build it on a more solid structure, that could be depended on at all times to safely withstand the heavy ice-floes that form above it in the bay. A cast-iron tube filled with concrete was therefore decided on, similar to the one now being built for the front light of the Craighill Channel range, at the mouth of the Patapsco River. Plans for the light-house have been prepared and a careful examination of the locality made by the district engineer, with a view to determine the proper method of sinking the tube in position. The light-house will stand in 8 feet water, on the extreme easterly point of the shoal, which position is close to the main channel of the bay. Borings were made at the site selected, and the shoal, below about 1 foot of soft mud and shell, was found to consist of hard blue sand and shell, with a slight trace of mud to a depth of 20 feet. It is believed that a secure foundation can be had at a depth of 12 feet or less. The bearing capacity of the material on which the structure will rest has not yet been tested, but will be before the exact depth of the foundation is definitely fixed. The tube will be of the form of a frustum of a cone to a height of 12 feet from the bottom; above this, it will be cylindrical, the diameter of the base being 30 feet, that of the cylinder 24 feet. The shell will be built up in sections, bolted together through stout flanges and sunk in position by filling it with concrete. It will be protected on the outside from the scour of the tide by a riprap of loose stone. The keeper's dwelling will rest on this solid structure. It is supposed that the tube may be sunk in position by merely excavating the material from the inside, though it is possible that one or both of the pneumatic processes may have to be resorted to. This light-house will cost considerably more than one on screw-piles, and an additional appropriation of $25,000 is therefore required.

278. *Love Point Shoal, mouth of Chester River, Maryland.*—This light-house during the winter of 1872–'73 sustained considerable injury from fields of heavy, floating ice. Two of the ice-breaker piles were carried away, and two of the main columns of the light-house broken, so that it became necessary for a time to discontinue the light. Under an appropriation of $10,000 made at the last session of Congress, the light-house has been repaired and the structure protected by a riprap of loose stone placed around the light-house, forming an artificial island. The amount appropriated was not sufficient to carry the riprap as high as it should be. The location is one of the most exposed in the district, and it is therefore recommended that an additional appropriation of $5,000 be made to complete it.

279. *Craighill's Channel, range-beacons, upper or rear light, mouth of Pa-*

tapsco River, Maryland.—Owing to the lateness of spring and the severity of the winter of 1872-'73, considerable delay was experienced in locating this range line, as it had to be done with the utmost care on account of the length and the narrowness of the channel it is intended to mark. This made it possible for the work to be done only in very calm weather, in consequence of which work on the foundation of the structure did not commence until the month of April. Further delays were occasioned by unforeseen difficulties arising from the character of the ground on which the light-house rests. A careful examination showed that the soil on top was firm, hard sand, to a depth of two feet. Below this was a thin layer of sand and mud, mixed with stones, then soft mud to a depth of fifteen feet. A pile and grillage foundation became necessary to support the piers on which the columns of the frame-work rest, to build which it was necessary to construct a coffer-dam inclosing the entire work. The light-house stands in two feet of water, mean low tide. The coffer-dam, which was commenced the middle of April, was 60 feet by 60 feet, and consisted of two rows of sheet-piling about 18 inches apart, filled in with clay puddling and sustained in place by string-pieces nailed to piles driven at distances apart of 15 feet. The sheet-piling was put down with rapidity and satisfactorily by the water-jet process. The dam was then pumped out, and the foundation piles (after some delay owing to the breaking of the dam on two occasions during heavy gales) were driven and cut off. The grillage was finished in June, and work on the piers commenced. There are nine piers, built of Port Deposit granite. It was necessary to make them strong, as the ice is piled up very heavily here sometimes during the winter. The piers were finished in August.

The light-house will be an open frame-work of the form of a frustum of a pyramid of four sides, the corner columns being of cast iron resting on cast-iron disks, which are anchored to the masonry of the piers. The focal plane is to be 105 feet above ordinary tide. The keeper's dwelling will stand within the base of the pyramid, through which an inclosed stairway will pass, leading to the lantern. The cost of this structure was necessarily increased by the difficulties encountered in getting a secure foundation, and the appropriation that was made for the two range-lights (front and rear) will not be sufficient to complete them. It is necessary, however, to place both of them in a condition to resist the ice-floes of winter. The interests of commerce require that the range-lights of which this is one should be established without unnecessary delay, as the channel they will mark is the one now used by the largest class of vessels coming into the port of Baltimore.

In order, therefore, that commerce may not suffer from the want of these lights, it is designed to establish a temporary light on the unfinished structure until another appropriation can be made to complete the work, to do which will require for this light-house an appropriation of $10,000, which is earnestly recommended.

280. *Craighill's Channel, range-beacon, lower or front light, mouth of Patapsco River, Maryland.*—When the original appropriation for Craighill Channel range-lights was made, it was designed to build the front beacon on screw-piles. During the winter of 1872-'73, however, the ice formed so heavily in the Chesapeake Bay, in the vicinity of the proposed site of this light-house, that it was deemed advisable to change the plan and build a more solid structure that could, beyond all doubt, safely withstand the heavy ice-floes by which it will be assailed. It was therefore decided to place the keepers' dwelling, surmounted by a lantern, on a tubular foundation of cast iron filled with concrete ; the cast-

iron tube, between high and low water and for at least two feet above and below the space included between those limits, to be 2 inches thick, the other portions to be 1¼ inches thick. The tube consists of two parts, the lower portion, for a height of 12 feet, being in the form of a frustum of a cone 30 feet in diameter at the base, 24 feet at the top ; the upper portion to be a cylinder of the same diameter as the top of the frustum of the cone to which it is joined. The tubing will be cast in sections, each section being divided into twenty-four parts, joined together through flanges by wrought-iron bolts. The lower section of the tubing will be bolted to a grillage or flooring consisting of four layers of timber each 12 inches thick, forming a caisson, which will be sunk in position below the bottom of the bay, by filling it with concrete. Borings with an artesian-well apparatus were made after the site had been selected, (which was fixed upon in 17 feet water mean tide,) to determine the character of the soil on which the light-house is to rest. It was found that for a depth of 22 feet the soil is the softest kind of mud, so soft, in fact, that an ordinary pile, stood on end, would penetrate 20 feet under the action of its own weight. Below this alternate thin layers of sand, mixtures of sand, mud, and shell were found to a depth of 20 feet more, with no signs of a solid foundation within 60 feet of the water's surface. It was therefore determined to drive a cluster of piles, cut them off at a level of 27 feet below the surface of the water and lower the caisson on to them by filling it with concrete; and, in order to protect the light-house from lateral vibration and the scour of the tides, to build a rip-rap wall of loose stone around it. After duly advertising for bids, contracts were accordingly made for driving and cutting off the piles of the foundation ; building a pier from which the work of sinking it could be carried on; for the fabrication of the metal work forming the caisson and for sinking it in position. A circular space was first dredged out to a depth of 10 feet, in June, and the work of driving the piles for the foundation and temporary pier commenced in July. The iron work was also completed and delivered in that month. Owing, however, to rough weather, the work has been somewhat delayed. It is expected that the caisson will be in position by the middle of October. It is desirable that this light, taken in connection with the other one, just referred to and which forms the range for Craighill's Channel, should be established as soon as possible. It was therefore determined to place a temporary light on the caisson in its unfinished state, the appropriation not being sufficient to complete it.

The change in the character of this structure from what was first intended will add considerably to its cost, and an additional appropriation of $25,000 is therefore asked for.

As soon as the lights of the Craighill Channel range are established, the two lights at North Point will be discontinued.

—. *Shipping Point, Potomac River, Virginia.*—An appropriation of $9,000 was made by act approved June 10, 1872, for a light-house to mark the entrance to the anchorage in Quantico Creek, Virginia, drawings and specifications for which have been prepared. A general act was also passed by the State of Virginia, ceding jurisdiction over sites purchased or to be purchased by the United States for light-house purposes. The act approved March 3, 1873, authorized the Light-House Board to place the light-house provided for by the previous act anywhere in the near vicinity of Shipping Point that might be deemed proper. An examination of the river was accordingly made by the engineer and inspector of the district, both of whom agree that a light at Shipping Point would be of little, if any, use to navigation. Neither is there any place in the near vicinity of Shipping Point at which a light-house would be of use. The place most in need of a light-house in the Potomac River is at or near Matthias Point. It is suggested that the appropriation for Shipping Point be allowed to revert to the Treasury, and, in lieu thereof, that an appropriation of $20,000 be made for a light at the latter place. The wording of the act leaving it discretionary with the Light-house Board to locate the light-house at such place in the near vicinity of Shipping Point as they deem proper, conveys some latitude in regard to the location of the light-house, but it was not supposed that the act contemplated the possibility of its location 24 miles distant, which is the distance of Shipping Point from Matthias Point.

—. *Port Tobacco Flats, in the bend of Potomac River opposite Matthias Point.*—This is one of the most difficult places for experienced navigators, who are familiar with the river, to pass at night. Few places occur where experienced pilots cannot tell where they are by soundings; at this place, however, soundings run from 100 feet to 5 feet within a space of a hundred yards. The current, which is strong, sets directly on the flats, both at the flood and ebb tides, which renders it bad enough for sailing-vessels even by daylight, but at night the difficulty is much aggravated by the want of some guide to point out the dangerous spot. It is no uncommon sight to see a vessel aground on these flats. The United States naval steamer Frolic went ashore here during the summer of 1873, and remained for some time. It is recommended that an appropriation of $40,000 be made for a light-house at this place, with the proviso that the appropriation for a light-house at Shipping Point revert to the Treasury.

—. *Currituck Beach, midway between Cape Henry and Body's Island, sea-coast of North Carolina.*—An appropriation was made at the last session of Congress for a light-house at or near Poyner's Hill, midway between Body's Island and Cape Henry. This point was found to be near Whale's Head Hill, about two miles north of Poyner's Hill. Soon after the appropriation was made, a suitable site was selected and steps were at once taken to secure the necessary land. This has been accomplished, and work at the site can be commenced as soon as the necessary cession of jurisdiction is made by the State. The light-house will be a first-order sea-coast tower, to be built of brick, similar to the structure at Body's Island. The focal plane will be 150 feet above the level of the sea, and can be seen at a distance of eighteen nautical miles. Owing to the shallowness of the water in Currituck Sound, through which vessels carrying material will have to pass to land the same, the freighting of the material entering into the construction of the tower will be expensive, as it will be necessary to unload vessels some six or eight miles from the landing. It is proposed to do this with flat-boats that will not draw more than three feet water, loaded. This light has long been needed by the commerce of the country, and its necessity was recognized some time ago by Congress making an appropriation, which reverted to the Treasury. Its establishment will complete the system of sea-coast lights on the coast of North Carolina. An appropriation of $60,000 is asked for this work.

300. *Body's Island, sea-coast of North Carolina.*—At the date of last annual report this light-house was nearly completed. The light was first exhibited October 1, 1872, shortly after which a flock of wild geese flew against the lantern, breaking three panes of glass and considerably damaging the lens apparatus. It was found necessary to protect the lantern by a wire-screen which would break the force of the blow when

wild fowl fly against it. This was done, and no further trouble from this source has been experienced.

301. *Cape Hatteras, sea-coast of North Carolina.*—The tower at this light-station has been painted in spiral bands alternately black and white, there being four bands, two black and two white, each one making one and a half revolutions about the tower, the object being to render it more distinct at a distance, and consequently a better day-mark on this low, sandy coast. Some slight repairs were made at the station at the same time.

—. *Hatteras Inlet, Pamlico Sound, North Carolina.*—The want of a light at this entrance to the sounds of North Carolina has long been felt. It is the best inlet leading to and from those sounds, through which there is a large trade. Vessels bound to sea through this inlet have no guide to indicate to them at night their proximity to the entrance. With steamers it is not of so much importance, as they can regulate their time to arrive off the inlet at daylight, but the sailing-vessels must take advantage of the wind. At night they dare not approach the inlet, as a dangerous shoal, called Oliver's Reef, makes out into the sound, the position of which cannot be accurately determined, except by having it marked by a light-house. It is designed to place the light-house provided for by act approved March 3, 1873, on Oliver's Reef, north side of the entrance to Hatteras Inlet. An examination by the engineer of the district has been made, and the work will be commenced without unnecessary delay. The light-house will be on screw-piles, and show a fixed red light.

311. *Roanoke Marshes, on the east side of the narrow channel connecting Pamlico and Croatan Sounds, North Carolina.*—The following remarks touching this light-house were made in the last annual report in regard to rebuilding the structure:

It was built in 1860, on what was at that time a marsh, which was dry, or nearly so, at low water. The foundation consists of seven wood piles covered with cast iron; the latter, when the structure was first built, being screwed into the ground several feet. Since then the marsh has been washed away, so that there are now 10 feet water at the light-house. The piles being of wood, as soon as they were exposed by the washing away of the shoal below the depth covered by the cast-iron sleeve, were attacked by worms. In order to save the light-house from falling, three coppered piles were driven at each angle of the structure, capped by heavy squared timbers. A short time ago a raft drifted against the light-house, and carried away three of the copper piles above referred to. The house has settled some inches on the west side, and though the damage sustained by the striking of the raft has been repaired, it is not considered in a safe condition, nor can it be made so, except at great expense, for which an appropriation would be necessary. It will be cheaper in the end to build a new structure, and an appropriation for this purpose is recommended. The estimated cost of a light-house near the present site, but in about 6 feet water, is $15,000.

313. *North River, on a shoal at the mouth of North River, North Carolina.*—This station was supplied with a fog-bell and machine to strike it at intervals of 5 seconds.

316. *Cape Lookout, sea-coast of North Carolina.*—Under the appropriation made therefor, a new keeper's dwelling, which was much needed, was finished in April, 1873. At the same time repairs were made to the tower. The latter was then colored in diagonal checkers, to render it more distinct at a distance, and, consequently, more useful as a day-mark, for the same reason as at Cape Hatteras.

REPAIRS.

At each of the following-named light-stations in the fifth district there have been repairs and renovations, more or less extensive, made during the year.

247. *Cape-Henry*, on the south side of the main entrance to Chesapeake Bay, Virginia.

249. *Old Point Comfort*, on the north side of the entrance to Hampton Roads, Virginia.

265. *Jane's Island*, entrance to Little Annamessex River, Tangier Sound, Maryland.

266. *Somers' Cove*, entrance to Little Annamessex River, Tangier Sound, Maryland.

271. *Hooper's Straits*, on the shoal abreast of entrance to Honga River, Maryland.

272. *Cove Point*, four miles to the north of the entrance to Patuxent River, Maryland.

274. *Choptank River*, entrance to Choptank and Treadhaven Rivers, Maryland.

284. *Fort Carroll*, on Fort Carroll, in Patapsco River, Maryland.

293. *Piney Point*, on the east side of Potomac River, Maryland.

295. *Lower Cedar Point*, on the end of Yates's Shoal, west side of Potomac River, Virginia.

296. *Upper Cedar Point*, on end of shoal off Upper Cedar Point, Maryland.

299. *Bowler's Rock*, on the shoal of that name, Rappahannock River, Virginia.

309. *Pamlico Point*, on south side of entrance to Pamlico River, North Carolina.

The following are the names of the light-stations in the fifth district not mentioned elsewhere:

245. *Hog Island*, on west point of Hog Island, Great Matchepungo Inlet, Virginia.

246. *Cape Charles*, on Smith's Island, north side of entrance to Chesapeake Bay, Virginia.

250. *Craney Island*, on the west side of channel, near the mouth of Elizabeth River, Virginia.

252. *Naval Hospital*, on the wharf at the naval hospital, Elizabeth River, Virginia.

255. *Deep Water Shoals*, on the shoal above Mulberry Island, on James River, Virginia.

256. *Jordan's Point*, on Jordan's Point, James River, Virginia.

257. *Cherrystone*, on the shoal west side of entrance to Cherrystone Inlet, Virginia.

258. *Back River*, south side of entrance to Back River, Chesapeake Bay, Virginia.

259. *York Spit*, on easterly end of York Spit, entrance to York River from Chesapeake Bay, Virginia.

260. *New Point Comfort*, north side of entrance to Mobjack Bay, west side of Chesapeake Bay, Virginia.

261. *Wolf Trap*, on the east end of Wolf Trap Shoal, Chesapeake Bay, Virginia.

262. *Stingray Point*, south side of mouth of Rappahannock River, Virginia.

263. *Windmill Point*, on Windmill Point Shoals, north side of mouth of Rappahannock River, Virginia.

267. *Smith's Point*, on the shoal on southeast side of Potomac River, west side of Chesapeake Bay, Virginia.

268. *Fog Point*, on Smith's Island, opposite the mouth of Potomac River, Maryland.

269. *Clay Island*, northern extremity of Tangier Sound, at the mouth of Nanticoke River, Maryland.

273. *Sharp's Island*, entrance to Choptank River, Maryland.

276. *Greenbury Point*, on the north side of the entrance to Severn River, Maryland.

281. *Seven-Foot Knoll*, on a lump of that name at the mouth of Patapsco River, Maryland.

285. *Hawkins' Point*, on shoal near Hawkins' Point, Patapsco River, Maryland.

287. *Leading Point*, on Leading.Point, south side of Patapsco River, Maryland.

288. *Lazaretto Point*, north side of Baltimore Harbor, Maryland.

289. *Pool's Island*, on Pool's Island, near the mouth of Gunpowder River, Chesapeake Bay, Maryland.

290. *Turkey Point*, on a point separating the mouths of Elk and Susquehanna Rivers, at head of Chesapeake Bay.

291. *Fishing Battery*, on Fishing or Donoho's Battery, entrance to Susquehanna River, Maryland.

292. *Havre de Grace*, on Concord Point, near Havre de Grace, Maryland.

294. *Blackistone's Island*, near the entrance to Clement's Bay, Potomac River, Maryland.

297. *Fort Washington*, on the wharf at Fort Washington, Maryland.

298. *Jones' Point*, on west side of Potomac River, near Alexandria.

302. *Cape Hatteras Beacon*, near the southern extremity of Cape Hatteras Point, North Carolina.

303. *Ocracoke*, near the entrance to and on the north side of Ocracoke Inlet, North Carolina.

304. *Southwest Point Royal Shoal*, on the southwest point of Royal Shoal, near Ocracoke Inlet, North Carolina.

305. *Northwest Point Royal Shoal*, on the northwest point of Royal Shoal, in Pamlico Sound, North Carolina.

306. *Harbor Island*, on Harbor Island Bar, between Pamlico and Cove Sounds, North Carolina.

307. *Brant Island Shoal*, in southern part of Pamlico Sound, North Carolina.

308. *Neuse River*, on a shoal in east end of Piney Point, Neuse River, North Carolina.

310. *Long Shoal*, on the east point of Long Shoal, North Carolina.

312. *Croatan*, between Croatan and Albemarle Sounds, North Carolina.

314. *Wade's Point*, on the shoal, west side of Pasquotank River, North Carolina.

315. *Roanoke River*, near the mouth of Roanoke River, North Carolina.

LIGHT-SHIPS.

There are no light-ships in this district.

FOG-SIGNALS OPERATED BY STEAM OR HOT-AIR ENGINES.

There are no fog-signals operated by steam or hot-air engines in this district.

DAY OR UNLIGHTED BEACONS.

Names and positions of the day or unlighted beacons in the fifth district:

22 Ab

Smith's Point, south side of the mouth of Potomac River; old tower, colored white.

Bodkin's Point, south side of the mouth of Patapsco River; old tower, colored white.

Day's Point, half a mile from Day's Point, James River, Virginia; an iron shaft with cage on top.

Woodstock, entrance to Bell's Bay, &c., North Carolina; spar with barrel.

Hunting Quarter, Cove Sound, North Carolina, in mid-channel; spar with barrel.

Wilson's Bay, in Cove Sound, North Carolina, mid-channel; spar with barrel.

Piney Point, Cove Sound, North Carolina, mid-channel; two spars with barrels.

Yellow Shoal, Cove Sound, North Carolina, mid-channel; spar with barrel.

Bushes' Bluff Shoal, north side of entrance to the Elizabeth River, Virginia; an iron pile with cage on top.

There are, beside the above-named beacons, forty stake-beacons planted to mark channels in Cove Sound and other places.

There is an appropriation for three day-beacons in the Potomac River. It is designed to make them of iron. Drawings are now being prepared, and their construction will be taken in hand at an early day.

DEPOTS.

Lazaretto Point, Patapsco River, Maryland.—A number of spar-buoys and two iron beacons were made here during the year. Other buoys were repaired and painted, and a number of new sinkers made.

The wharf at this depot is in need of considerable repairs, which should be done without unnecessary delay. It is too small for the purpose, and should be extended so that a supply of coal could be kept there. The depot is much in need of a blacksmith's shop, which should be separate from the store-house, and in which small forging could be executed.

The estimate cost of repairs to the wharf and building a blacksmith's shop is $4,000, for which an appropriation is asked.

It should be further added in regard to the fifth district that there is a very large number of buoys to be cared for, and in the northern parts of the district there is always much complaint when they are shifted by the ice, in consequence of the delay, which cannot be prevented so long as the Light-House Establishment has but one steam-tender for the purpose. It is therefore earnestly recommended that an appropriation of $50,000 be made at the next session of Congress for a new steam-tender for buoy service in this district.

[10.]

SIXTH DISTRICT.

The sixth district extends from New River Inlet, North Carolina, to and including Cape Canaveral light-house, Florida, and embraces part of the coast of North Carolina, the coasts of South Carolina and Georgia, and part of the coast of Florida.

Inspector, Commander Charles S. Norton, United States Navy.

Engineer, Maj. Peter C. Hains, United States Engineers, brevet lieutenant colonel United States Army.

In this district there are—

Light-houses and lighted beacons	33
Light-houses finished and lighted during the year ending July 1, 1873	4
Light-houses for which appropriations were available, but which were not finished on the 1st of July, 1873	6
Light-ships, (in position)	4
Light-ships, (for relief)	1
Fog-signals operated by steam or hot-air engines	None
Day or unlighted beacons	44
Buoys actually in position	235
Spare buoys, (for relief and to supply losses)	39
Tender (steam) Atlantic, (buoy-tender)	1
Tender (sail) Mignonette, (used in engineer's constructions and repairs)	1

The numbers preceding the names of the stations correspond with those given in the "List of light-houses, lighted beacons, and floating lights of the Atlantic, Gulf, and Pacific coasts of the United States, published January 1, 1873."

——. *Orton's Point, west bank of Cape Fear River, North Carolina.*—There was a light formerly at this place, which was discontinued during the war, and has not been re-established. An inspection of the chart will almost of itself show its value.

For some distance above and below this point the river is quite wide, the banks are low, and shoals extend from the eastern shore about three-quarters of the distance across the river. There is good water close up to the west bank, and vessels going either up or down stream would have little difficulty in navigating at night if there was a light here to guide them.

The engineer of the district made a personal examination of this abandoned station in March. The light was formerly exhibited from a lantern on a keeper's dwelling, which had been built close up to the water's edge. The house is now in ruins. The walls and a portion of the flooring remain; but as the house was built on wooden piles, some of them have decayed, others have been eaten by the worms, and they no longer form a reliable support. It would cost more to repair the old house than to build a new one. It is, therefore, recommended that an appropriation be made to re-establish this light by building a new light-house on cast-iron piles close to the site of the old one.

The material in the latter can be used as a rip-rap protection to the shore, which has washed away somewhat under the abrasive action of the water. The light should be of the fifth order, illuminating an arc of 220°. The estimated cost of such a structure at or near this point is $15,000, for which an appropriation is asked.

——. *Campbell's Island, Cape Fear River, North Carolina.*—The re-establishment of this light, which was extinguished during the war, would render the navigation of this river at night comparatively safe. It is one of the most difficult places to pass at night that can be found on the river below Wilmington. The channel is narrow, the river wide; the shoals from the east and west banks approaching close to each other at the point where the course is changed. The establishment of a screw pile light-house at this point is practically the re-establishment of the light at Campbell's Island, and it is deemed of more importance at the present time than any other light on the Cape Fear River. Nothing remains of the old light-house. An appropriation of $15,000 is therefore asked for a light-house at or near Campbell's Island.

319. *Oak Island Beacons, at the main entrance to Cape Fear River, North Carolina.*—The recommendation of last year in regard to an

appropriation of $4,000 for the establishment of these beacons in order to secure a better range is renewed.   It is as follows:

These beacons mark the range over the bar at the Oak Island entrance to Cape Fear River.   They are, however, badly located, being so near each other that considerable deviation from the true course is necessary to make them appear to separate.   The front beacon is an open frame frustum of a square pyramid, resting on a rail tram-way, which allows of its being moved to the right or left, to suit the changes in the channel.   The rear light is placed on a wooden tower immediately over the center of the keeper's dwelling.   The shore-line at this place, as at many others on the southern coast, is not permanent, being washed away by the abrasive action of the sea.   The latter has gradually encroached upon the land till at present the high-water mark is only a few feet from the front beacon, which renders it in imminent danger of being destroyed in any southeasterly gale.   The two beacons being already so close together as to have their usefulness seriously impaired, the front beacon cannot be moved back any further.   To move both would be an expensive undertaking at this place, and would necessitate the discontinuance, for a time, of the lights; beside, there is no appropriation available.   It would be more satisfactory, and doubtless cheaper in the end, to build two new frame beacons, detached from the keeper's dwelling.   The pres-ent ones could then remain as they now are until the new ones are established.   By this means the change would cause no inconvenience to commerce, and such locations and relative elevation could be given them as would make them much more useful than they now are.

It is very important that this range be well maintained, as the channel which it marks is the most reliable, permanent, and the deepest of the several entrances to Cape Fear River.   An appropriation of $4,000 is therefore asked to re-establish the range.

322. *Cape Romain, on Raccoon Key, South Carolina.*—This tower is 150 feet high, built in the form of a frustum of an octagonal pyramid, resting on a concrete foundation.   In September, 1868, it was discovered that slight cracks had opened on the north and south faces, in which the windows are placed.   For a time these openings remained as they were when first discovered; since then additional cracks have opened on the west-erly faces, and the tower has settled considerably on that side, so much, in fact, as to require a re-adjustment of the lens.   The deflection of the tower is now 23½ inches from the vertical, and in all probability will in-crease; should it do so, the old tower will have to be replaced by a new one on a more secure foundation.   Careful and frequent observation will be made to determine this fact.

—. *Charleston Main Light, on the south end of Morris Island, South Caro-lina.*—The site of the old light-house at this station, which was destroyed during the rebellion, is on land owned by the Government, to which the State ceded jurisdiction many years ago.   It is proposed to locate the new structure, for which an appropriation was made at the last session of Congress, at or near the same spot.   The tower will be of brick, of the first order, 150 feet high, and of the form of a frustum of a right cone, resting on an octagonal base.   A contract was made for the iron work of the tower with the lowest bidder, after having advertised pub-licly for bids.   It is proposed to commence work on the foundation as soon as the sickly season is over.   An additional appropriation of $60,000 is asked for this work.

322. *Hunting Island Light, on the north end of Hunting Island, South Carolina.*—The site for this light-house has been selected at a point nearly a mile from the north end of the island.   This was deemed neces-sary, as the north point of the island is still washing away under the abrasive action of the sea.   The land at the north end is very low, how-ever, and is overflowed by high tides, which doubtless facilitates this action.   It is nevertheless believed that after a few hundred feet more are washed away it will cease, as the point of the island will then be protected from the action of the strong ebb tides by Harbor Island. In view, however, of the continued washing of the shore it was deter-

mined to make the light-house of cast iron, in sections, which can be taken down and removed in case of necessity, though it is not believed that such an emergency will arise.

A contract was made with the lowest bidder, after due public notice, for the fabrication of the metal work of the light-house, and a working party dispatched to the site to build a temporary wharf at and a road-way leading to the landing. Temporary quarters for workmen and store-houses for material have been erected. On account of the un-healthiness of the climate, however, this work has had to be suspended. A watchman has been left to take charge of Government property. It is proposed to resume operations about the 1st of November. An addi-tional appropriation of $20,000 is asked for this work.

334, 335. *Daufuskie Island Range Beacons, Calibogue Sound, South Carolina.*—The work of building the keeper's dwelling and range bea-cons was contracted for early in the spring, and was to have been com-pleted by the middle of May, but owing to unavoidable delays in the transportation of material to the site, and afterward by the sickness (in-cidental to the climate) of the contractor and his workmen, the time has been extended to the middle of September, when it is confidently ex-pected that the work will be entirely completed, and that the beacons will be lighted by the first of next October.

336. *Tybee, Entrance to Savannah River, Georgia.*—The following state-ment and recommendation for an appropriation of $50,000 for the com-mencement of a new tower at this station, in last annual report, is renewed. As then stated, "the tower is not in a safe condition, owing to the damage it sustained in the cyclone of 1871. This tower is very old, having been built in 1793. It is a frustum of an octagonal pyra-mid, built of Savannah brick. Five of its faces show dangerous cracks. As stated in a previous report, its great age and neglect during the war render it impracticable to properly repair it. An appropriation of $50,000 is therefore asked to commence the building of a new structure. This can be done without delay on Government land near the site of the present tower."

337. *Tybee Beacon, ranging with the main light, entrance to Savannah River, Georgia.*—The encroachment of the sea upon the southerly point of the island has made it necessary to remove the front beacon, a skeleton-frame structure. This has been done, and the beacon set back 400 feet to a safe position and placed on a new foundation. At the same time it was thoroughly repaired.

——. *Tybee Knoll, Savannah River, Georgia.*—Plans and specifications for the light-house authorized by the appropriation at last session of Congress, to take the place of the light-ship now stationed there, have been prepared, and a contract made for the fabrication of the iron-work and lantern. The light-house will be a square structure on five wooden piles incased in cast-iron sleeves, with two additional fender-piles, one up and the other down stream. The light will be of the fifth order. The station will be provided with a fog-bell struck by machinery.

349–350. *Amelia Island north range beacons, on the north end of Amelia Island, Florida.*—The front beacon has been moved about 200 feet north-ward, to range through a new channel that opened to the north of the old channel.

351–352. *Amelia Island main light, entrance to Fernandina Harbor, Florida.*—The keeper's dwelling, which was in a dilapidated condition, has received extensive repairs and renovations. The tower and beacon have also been repaired and renovated, the cost of these repairs being paid for out of the general appropriations for repairs and incidental expenses of light-houses. The plank walk between the tower and beacon is entirely worn out, and it is proposed to replace it with an earthen causeway.

355. *Saint Augustine, north end of Anastasia Island, Florida.*—As noticed in the last annual report, work on the new tower for this station had to be suspended for want of funds after the foundation had been carried up several feet above the ground. Work was resumed, however, as soon as the new appropriation became available. At the present date the tower has been built up to a height of 42¼ feet, and the first flight of stairs set. The material is all on hand for completing the tower, and the work will be pushed along with rapidity.

During the suspension of operations a small force was engaged in building jettees of coquina and brush to prevent the abrasive action of the sea. The experiment proved very satisfactory. The water had cut into the bank rapidly previous to the building of the jettees, so that only about 10 feet remained between the corner of the old light-house and high-water mark. The jettees not only stopped the washing away of the bank, but accumulated material to the southward of them so that the shore began to extend out into the sea again. Unfortunately coquina rock has not sufficient weight to prevent its being washed out of place during gales, occurring at the time of spring-tides, so that the present jettees are only temporary expedients, and should have a portion of the coquina replaced by some heavier material to render them permanent. A few hundred tons of granite is much needed for this purpose.

It is expected that the present appropriation will complete the tower and enable the light to be exhibited, but a keeper's dwelling will be required, as there are not sufficient or proper accommodations at the old light-house for three keepers—the number required to attend a first-order light-house—and the distance is too great from the new tower to insure proper attendance, even if the present dwelling were suitable. An appropriation of $20,000 is asked to build four jettees to protect the site, and a keeper's dwelling for the station.

——. *Mosquito Inlet, east coast of Florida.*—The following statement in the last annual report in regard to the establishment of a new light at this place is repeated :

In common with all the inlets and harbors on the east coast of Florida, this bar shifts constantly, so that no soundings can be relied on. The general effect of westerly winds is to reduce the depth of water, and that of northeasterly gales to increase it; thus the inlet may be opened or closed one or more times each year. The wrecks lying on or near the bar give a practical illustration of the uncertainty of the channel. For all practical purposes of construction of a light-house, it may, however, be safely assumed that the material can be delivered without any very serious difficulty or delay, although additional expense would be incurred by reason of the remoteness of the station and the small-sized vessels that would be required for transportation. As regards the necessity of a light at this point, it is manifest that the commerce passing through the inlet would not justify an expenditure by the United States for a light for merely local purposes, or at least that there are other points that may justly take precedence of it. But a light-house between Saint Augustine and Cape Canaveral lights is necessary, as one of a system of coast lights, and Mosquito Inlet is undoubtedly the proper site, as in the first place the light there would answer the double purpose of a harbor and coast guide, and in the second place, for a landing-place, both for the original construction and subsequent supply and inspection, which could be made with more safety and certainty there than at any other point along the open-sea beach. A tower 150 feet high, lighted by a first-order Fresnel lens, is recommended for this position, and for the commencement of its construction an estimate of $80,000 is submitted.

The distance from Saint Augustine to Cape Canaveral is ninety-five miles, of which there is an unlighted space of sixty miles.

356. *Cape Canaveral, on the northeast pitch of Cape Canaveral, sea-coast of Florida.*—This station has received extensive repairs and renova-

tions, of which it was much in need. The roofs of the keepers' dwelling and the kitchen have been shingled and provided with gutters. The veranda has been rebuilt and the plastering repaired. The tower, which is of iron, has been painted throughout, the outside being colored in horizontal bands, alternately black and white, which renders it visible at a greater distance, and consequently a better day-mark. The old tower was white.

REPAIRS.

At each of the following-named light-stations in the sixth district there have been repairs and renovations, more or less extensive, during the last year, viz:

317. *Federal Point*, New Inlet, entrance to Cape Fear River, North Carolina.

319–320. *Oak Island Beacons*, entrance to main channel, Cape Fear River, North Carolina.

321. *Georgetown*, entrance to Pedee River and Georgetown, South Carolina.

323. *Bull's Bay*, north end of Bull's Bay Island, South Carolina.

325–326. *Morris Island Beacons*, south end of Morris Island and entrance to Charleston Harbor, South Carolina.

327–328. *Sullivan's Island Beacons*, on Sullivan's Island, South Carolina.

336–337. *Tybee Light and Beacon*, entrance to Savannah River, Georgia.

339. *Cockspur Beacon*, on east end of Cockspur Island, Savanah River, Georgia.

340. *Oyster Beds Beacon*, on the oyster-beds, Savannah River, Georgia.

341. *Obstructions light*, on the obstructions, Savannah River, Georgia.

343–344. *Sapelo*, entrance to Doboy Sound, Georgia.

345–346. *Wolf Island Beacons*, entrance to Doboy Sound, Georgia.

347. *Saint Simon's*, entrance to Saint Simon's Sound, Georgia.

348. *Little Cumberland*, entrance to Saint Andrew's Sound, Georgia.

349–350. *Amelia Island north range beacons*, on the north end of Amelia Island, Florida.

351–352. *Amelia Island main light*, entrance to Saint Mary River and Fernandina Harbor, Florida.

355. *Saint Augustine*, (old light-house,) on Anastasia Island, entrance to Saint Augustine, Florida.

356. *Cape Canaveral*, on northeast pitch of the cape, Florida.

The following are the names of the light-stations in the sixth district not mentioned elsewhere:

329. *Fort Sumter*, on Fort Sumter, Charleston Harbor, South Carolina.

330. *Castle Pinckney*, on Castle Pinckney, Charleston Harbor, South Carolina.

331. *Combahee Bank*, on the southeast point of Combahee Shoal, Saint Helena's Sound, South Carolina.

332. *Fig Island Beacon*, on the east end of Fig Island, in Savannah River, Georgia.

LIGHT-SHIPS.

"*Frying-Pan Shoals*," *off Cape Fear, North Carolina.*—This vessel was extensively repaired in Wilmington, North Carolina, and towed to Charleston, South Carolina, October 29, 1872, where she remained as a relief till June 23, 1873, when she was taken to her present position, taking the place of Relief No. 32, which was temporarily on the station. The general condition of the vessel is good.

324. "*Rattlesnake Shoal,*" *off Charleston, South Carolina.*—The spar-deck is now being recalked, and the vessel is otherwise in good condition.

333. "*Martin's Industry,*" *off Port Royal, South Carolina.*—Is in good condition and needs no repairs.

338. "*Tybee Knoll,*" *on Tybee Knoll, mouth of Savannah River, Georgia.*—This vessel was placed on her station on September 6, 1872, relieving No. 33, which was towed to Charleston, and, by direction of the Treasury Department, was sold at auction, being unfit for repairs. She needs considerable repair, but will not be removed from her station for that purpose till the completion of the screw-pile light-house at Tybee Knoll, which will render the further use of a light-ship at that place unnecessary.

Relief No. 32.—On the night of the 6th of May, 1873, this vessel, then stationed on Frying-Pan Shoals, North Carolina, was run into by the Norwegian bark Mimi and considerably damaged. She was relieved by Light-ship No. 34 on June 24, and towed to Charleston, South Carolina, where the damages caused by the collision were repaired at the expense of the Mimi. Other repairs, not resulting from the collision, were put upon her, and she is now in good order and ready for service.

FOG-SIGNALS OPERATED BY STEAM OR HOT-AIR ENGINES.

There are no fog-signals operated by steam or hot-air engines in this district.

DAY OR UNLIGHTED BEACONS.

The following is a list of the unlighted beacons in the sixth district:

Bald Head, mouth of Cape Fear River, North Carolina; old tower discontinued on the establishment of the Frying-Pan Shoal light-ship.

Price's Creek, Cape Fear River, North Carolina, discontinued during the rebellion, not relighted.

Campbell's Island, Cape Fear River, North Carolina, discontinued during the rebellion; brick house with iron lantern.

Orton's Point, Cape Fear River, discontinued during the rebellion, open-frame beacon.

Fort Point, Georgetown, South Carolina, discontinued during the rebellion.

Cape Romain, South Carolina; old tower, near the present light-house.

Fort Ripley, iron screw-pile with cage, recently placed on the site of Fort Ripley, Charleston Harbor, South Carolina.

Battery Light, (White Point Garden,) Charleston; iron spindle; light discontinued during the rebellion.

Savannah City beacon, Georgia; iron spindle; light discontinued during the rebellion.

Saint John's River, Florida, old tower at the south side of entrance to river Saint John.

Cape Canaveral, Florida, old tower.

Dumb beacons at *Oyster Rocks,* river Savannah, near Cockspur Island, two iron-pile beacons.

Savannah River day-marks, two wooden beacons at Jones's Island and two on Long Island.

Saint John River, wooden piles planted along the river Saint John between its mouth and Jacksonville.

BUOYS.

The buoyage of this district is in very good condition.

DEPOTS.

Fort Johnson, Charleston Harbor, South Carolina.—Temporary repairs have been made during the past year, sufficient to keep the wharf standing until the contemplated change to Mount Pleasant can be made.

Mount Pleasant, Charleston Harbor, South Carolina.—The want of a light-house and buoy depot in this district has long been felt, that at Fort Johnson being only regarded as a temporary expedient, and not suitable for the purpose for various reasons, among which may be mentioned the difficulty of workmen and others in reaching it, except by special conveyance; bad location, being exposed to a heavy sea during the prevalence of northerly winds, and its proximity to the stone jetties built to prevent the abrasive action of the sea, rendering it frequently dangerous for a vessel to attempt to land.

A site was found at Mount Pleasant, which is reached by a ferry-boat from Charleston, is in a good harbor, and much more suitable in every way. Steps have been taken to secure a title, in conformity with the provisions of an act of the State legislature of South Carolina which enabled the United States to condemn land for light-house purposes when the owners thereof are unable to make a lawful conveyance.

It is proposed to build a wharf on iron piles. Borings have been made to test the character of the foundation, and work will be commenced as soon as the title is perfected. An appropriation of $20,000 for this purpose is included in the annual estimates.

[11.]

SEVENTH DISTRICT.

The seventh light-house district extends from Cape Canaveral, on the eastern coast of Florida, to Cedar Keys, on the Gulf coast, including the light-house at the latter point, but not at the former. It embraces nearly the whole peninsula of Florida, the whole of the Florida Reef, and the Tortugas Keys.

Inspector.—Commander Albert Kautz, United States Navy.

Engineer.—Lieut. Col. Chas. E. Blunt, Corps of Engineers, brevet colonel, United States Army.

In this district there are:

Light-houses and lighted beacons	11
Light-houses finished and lighted during the year ending July 1, 1873...........	0
Light-houses for which appropriations were available but which were not finished on the 1st of July, 1873	1
Light-ships	0
Fog-signals operated by steam or hot-air engines	0
Day or unlighted beacons...	60
Buoys actually in position	95
Spare buoys for relief and to supply losses....................................	68
Tenders (steam) Geranium, (buoy-tender) Arbutus, (used in engineer's constructions and repairs)..	1

The numbers preceding the names of stations correspond with those of the "List of light-houses, lighted beacons, and floating-lights of the Atlantic, Gulf, and Pacific coasts of the United States," issued January, 1873.

360. *Alligator Reef, Florida Reefs.*—This new structure, an iron-pile

light-house, has been brought nearly to completion during the year, and will be lighted early in the coming winter. It will meet the long-existing want of an additional guide in the now unlighted space between Carysfort Reef and Dry Bank light-houses, and will be a very important aid in the dangerous navigation along the Florida Reefs. It is erected in a very exposed position upon the northeast extremity of Alligator Reef, in five feet of water, but within two hundred yards of the deep water of the Gulf. The nearest land, Indian Key, four miles to the westward, has been used during the erection of the structure as a depot-quarters for the mechanics and laborers employed upon the work, and for machine-shop, smithy, &c. A new wharf was built at this key, upon which were landed the materials of the light-house when sent from the North, where the iron-work of the structure, with the keeper's dwelling and lantern, were manufactured.

The site, which covers an octagon of 56 feet diameter, was selected after careful borings. A temporary platform was erected upon this site, supported on mangrove piles shod with iron, and driven 5 feet into the bottom in partially indurated coral rock. A small landing-wharf or jettee for receiving materials was also built in connection with this platform. The platform being completed, the nine heavy cast-iron foundation-disks were accurately placed at the center and angles of the octagon, the surface of the coral rock being first smoothed and leveled for each disk. By an ingenious system of gauges the disks were set in their positions, with their proper relative distances. The talent and perseverance of the assistant engineer of the district have nowhere been more conspicuously shown than in the placing of these disks upon which the whole structure depended; the difficulties of the operation being enormously increased by the necessity of doing the work under water.

The foundation-piles pass through the centers of the disks and rest by shoulders upon them. These piles are of solid wrought iron, 26 feet long, and 12 inches in diameter, and pointed at their lower ends, the upper ends being lathe-turned and cut off in a plane at right-angles to the axis. The pile-driver used in driving them carried a hammer of 2,000 pounds, which was hoisted by the portable steam-engine which was used throughout the construction, and proved an invaluable aid, being easily moved about the platform. The piles were kept accurately vertical during the driving by purchases attached to their heads, which were moved according to the indications of a spirit-level applied to their tops. The penetration into the coral at each blow of the hammer, with an average fall of 18 feet, varied from one-half inch to one and a half inches, and about one hundred and twenty blows brought the shoulder of the piles into contact with the disks, giving them a depth in the coral-limestone rock of 10 feet.

The piles being driven, their tops were brought into one horizontal plane 11 feet above the water, by cutting off the necessary metal by a tool specially devised for the purpose. This done, the cast-iron sockets which fit on the heads of the piles and receive in their upper part the feet of the next series of columns, were put in their places. This second series consists of nine solid wrought-iron pillars 10 inches in diameter.

It is considered unnecessary to go any further into the details of the progress of the work, which, at the date of this report, has been carried to the base of the lantern. Great delays have occurred during the construction, owing to the exposed position of the light-house, the sea breaking heavily on the reef at times, rendering landing on the platform of men and materials impracticable, sometimes for several days in succession.

The completed structure will be similar, except in color, to the light-house upon "Dry Bank." The character of the light, however, will be different, being scintillating, flashing every five seconds, every sixth flash red. The focal flame will be 139 feet above the level of the sea, and will be visible from a deck 15 feet above the water eighteen nautical miles. The approximate position of the light is latitude 24° 51' 2" north; longitude 80° 37' 10" west.

363. *Key West.*—A new third-order lantern has been placed on this light-house, raising the tower and the focal plane 5 feet, and a great improvement has been recognized in the light by all approaching it. The wide sash-bars of the old lantern caused a marked diminution of the brilliancy of the light in certain directions.

—— *Fowey Rocks.*—The old light-house at Cape Florida (366) is so situated as to be almost useless as a guide to navigators, who are unanimous in the expression of the opinion that it should be replaced by a new one built at the dangerous locality called "Fowey Rocks." For the commencement of this new light-house an appropriation of $100,000 will be required.

REPAIRS.

No repairs have been made at any of the light-stations of the district during the year, owing to the entire working force of the district being engaged at Alligator Reef.

During the coming year repairs will be needed at the following stations:

358. *Carysfort Reef,* (repairs of iron-work and painting.)
361. *Dry Bank,* (painting.)
362. *Sand Key,* (renewal of stair-tower, water-tanks, painting, &c.)
366. *Dry Tortugas Harbor,* (new lantern.)

The renovations at Sand Key light-house must be of so extensive a character that a special appropriation of $20,000 is asked for them.

The following are the names of the light-houses of this district not heretofore mentioned in this report:

357. *Jupiter Inlet,* between Jupiter Inlet and Gilbert's Bar, Florida.
363. *Northwest Passage,* Key West, Florida.
365. *Dry Tortugas,* on Loggerhead Key, Florida.
367. *Egmont Key,* Tampa Bay, Florida.
368. *Sea-Horse Key,* Cedar Keys, Florida.

LIGHT-SHIPS.

There are no light-ships in the seventh district.

FOG-SIGNALS OPERATED BY STEAM OR HOT-AIR ENGINES.

There are no fog-signals operated by steam or hot-air engines in this district.

DAY OR UNLIGHTED BEACONS.

The line of iron day-beacons on the shoaler portion of the great Florida Reef, and marking out its general outline along the Gulf, has been completed during the year by the erection of thirteen beacons.

This line of beacons is in two series, one on points heretofore occupied and where beacons have been renewed, and a second in new positions. The first series is distinguished by letters from A to P, and the second by numbers from 1 to 8.

BUOYS.

The buoyage of this district is in excellent condition.

. [12.]

EIGHTH DISTRICT.

The eighth light-house district extends from Cedar Keys, Florida, to the Rio Grande, Texas, and embraces a part of the Gulf coast of Florida, and the coasts of Alabama, Mississippi, Louisiana, and Texas.

Inspector.—Commander Robert Boyd, jr., United States Navy.

Engineer.—James H. Simpson, colonel Corps of Engineers, brevet brigadier-general, United States Army, until December 31, 1872; A. N. Damrell, captain Corps of Engineers, brevet major, United States Army, until January 23, 1873; W. F. Raynolds, lieutenant-colonel Corps of Engineers, brevet brigadier-general, United States Army, until March 31, 1873; A. N. Damrell, captain Corps of Engineers, brevet major, United States Army, present engineer.

In this district there are—

Lights and lighted beacons.. 50
Lights finished and lighted during the year ending July 1, 1873............... 2
Light-houses for which appropriations were available, but which were not finished on the 1st of July, 1873.. 8
Light-ships, (in position)... 1
Light-ships, (for relief).. 0
Fog-signals, operated by steam or hot-air engines............................ 2
Day or unlighted beacons.. 15
Buoys actually in position.. 110
Spare buoys for relief and to supply losses................................. 132
Tenders (steam) Dandelion, (buoy tender) Ivy, used in engineer's constructions and repairs.. 2
Tenders (sail) Magnolia, (used in engineer's constructions and repairs,) Pharos, and Guthrie, (temporarily detailed for construction of Trinity Shoals and Timbalier light-houses).. 3

The numbers preceding the names of stations correspond with those of the list of light-houses, lighted beacons, and floating lights of the Atlantic, Gulf, and Pacific coasts of the United States, issued January, 1873.

LIGHT-HOUSES AND LIGHTED BEACONS.

370. *Dog Island, Saint George's Sound, Florida.*—As mentioned in the last annual report, the brick tower built here in 1838 was in imminent danger of destruction by the undermining of its foundation, caused by the encroachment of the sea on the south beach of the island. No funds being available to replace the light-house by the erection of a new one further inland, and the necessity for prompt action, to prevent the extinction of the light, being imperative, it was decided to remove the lens and lantern from their perilous position and place them on the top of the keeper's dwelling, (an ordinary square wooden building on iron screw-piles,) situated farther from the beach. This was accomplished by the party engaged on general repairs, and the light is now in a position of temporary security. As the beach wears away and approaches the present location of the light, so as to endanger it, the tower will have to be rebuilt on some more permanent site, and an appropriation will be requisite. It is presumed, however, that the light is safe for some time to come, and a discussion of the merits of the proper location and character of the new tower is consequently reserved for a future report.

—— *Saint Andrew's Bay, Florida.*—The amount of $22,000 recommended in the last report for the establishment of a light as a guide to the entrance to Saint Andrew's Bay has been granted by the act approved March 3, 1873. The commerce of the bay is not very important, the surrounding country being thinly inhabited; yet there is found here a harbor unexcelled by any on the Gulf coast for vessels of not more than 18 feet draught. The principal use of the light will be, therefore, as a guide to a harbor of refuge. A survey has been made of the entrance to the bay, in order to obtain data for determining intelligently upon the most suitable plan for the structure, its location with reference to its greatest value as a light, and the most secure position in regard to any contingent changes of the topography through the denuding action of the sea. Accordingly a design of a two-story wooden dwelling on brick piers, with tower supporting the lantern attached, has been made. The focal plan of the light (which will be of the fourth order) will have an elevation of 43 feet 8 inches above the ground, or nearly 60 feet above the water. The light-house will be situated on the main-land, facing the entrance, and in front of and a short distance from it will be placed two small beacon-lights, which will range two distinct channels into the bay, the main channel bearing toward the light north $22\frac{1}{2}°$ east, and the other north 20° west. It is proposed to immediately begin preparations for the work at an early day.

375. *Sand Island, off entrance to Mobile Bay, Alabama.*—At the close of the last fiscal year the tower had reached a height of 9 feet 6 inches above the grade-line; and a month later it was raised to 19 feet 6 inches, when the exhaustion of the appropriation caused the suspension of operations. Enough funds were reserved to pay for the brick, which had been engaged by contract; and the shipment of them, as well as that of iron-work, to the station, was continued after the removal of the working party.

As an appropriation of $20,000 was granted by the last Congress for the completion of the Sand Island light-house, operations were resumed in April, 1873, and the work was energetically prosecuted.

At the close of the month of July the tower was built up to a height of 113 feet above the grade-line. Its total height to the focal plane of the light will be 125 feet, or 132 feet above sea-level, and the visibility of the light will extend to a distance of seventeen and one-half nautical miles. A notice to mariners has been published, which advertises the exhibition of the light for the first day of the coming September.

The erection of a substantial wooden dwelling for the keepers is in progress. The Sand Island beacons described in the last annual report, to guide vessels clear of the neighboring shoals, will probably be established at a trifling cost, from the general appropriation for the station.

376. *Mobile Point, entrance to Mobile Bay, Alabama.*—The temporary sixth-order beacon, which for a number of years has done service here, has been replaced by a fourth-order iron tower, 30 feet in height, which, with the additional elevation of the bastion of Fort Morgan, upon which it stands, gives a height of 50 feet above sea-level to the focal plane. The light is fixed red. The iron-work of the tower was manufactured in Washington, and shipped to the station in November. Its erection on the brick and concrete foundation, which had been prepared for it, was completed in January, and on the 15th of February the old light was extinguished and that in the new tower exhibited.

377. *Dog River Bar and Choctaw Bar Channel, Mobile Bay, Alabama.*—The manner of tending these temporary range-lights was changed in December, by taking their care out of the hands of a contractor and

placing them under the immediate superintendence of the keeper of Battery Gladden light-house. For this service one of the launches formerly employed in the engineering operations of the district was detached and manned by two seamen. The change has been found to work well for the interests of the Light-House Establishment. The use of the beacons is to guide vessels through a narrow-dredged channel 45,000 feet long in Mobile Bay. Their arrangement and character is not of the best, as they were established hastily at the time of the commencement of the dredging operations, and only for temporary purposes. In the last annual report it was remarked that on the completion of the channel a change would be necessary. The time has now arrived to definitely propose a plan and recommend an appropriation. The channel does not follow a straight line from the deep water at the mouth of Mobile River to the curve of 13 feet water, at which place it ends, but there are several bends. To mark each angle with a light is an expensive manner of aiding its navigation. Experience in using the cheapest form of lights (common ships' lanterns, as at present) has showed that they are frequently liable to go out, especially in the winter season. To care for them by running from one to the other in a sail-boat is an uncertain method, as the winds are frequently contrary and the weather and sea rough. To maintain them through the provision of an especial keeper at each light would be an unwarrantable expense, both in the first cost of erecting a separate light-house provided with keeper's dwelling, at each station, and its future maintenance. It seems, then, that the most economical plan would be to mark the southern extremity of the channel with a conspicuous unlighted beacon, on cast-iron socket piles, surmounted by a hoop-iron wicker-globe about 6 feet in diameter. The parts of such a beacon are on hand, complete, except the globe. In front of Battery Gladden, a short distance off in the water, and bearing south 53° east from it, should be established a beacon on screw-piles, provided with a sixth-order light. It would be a simple framework in which to suspend the lens at a proper height above the water, and would be connected with a small wooden tower placed on Battery Gladden Island by means of an endless wire cable, to which would be attached the lens. The light would be lighted by the keeper of Battery Gladden light-house in the small tower on the island, and drawn out to the beacon in the water by means of crank and sheaves provided, as in the case of the pier-light at Oswego. In this manner the light could be tended in the stormiest season. The beacon just described and the Battery Gladden light would range a course which would strike through the outer dumb beacon at the entrance to the dredge-channel, six and two-third miles distant from Battery Gladden light-house, and vessels coming up the bay would be enabled by keeping the range to find the dumb beacon at the south end of the channel. (Battery Gladden light-house is situated near the head of the channel, but to the eastward of it, and the above described is the only way in which it could be brought into the service of its navigation.) The angles of the channel would next be marked by dumb beacons, consisting simply of five wooden piles, four placed at the angles and one in the center of a square, and having two faces of planking nailed to the diagonal corner piles. Between the principal turn-beacons piles should be driven, not very far apart, alternately on opposite sides of the channel, and marked in some distinguishing manner. By having them close enough a vessel could navigate the channel in almost any night. To carry out the above described system an appropriation of $8,000 is asked.

———*Grant's Pass, between Mobile Bay and Mississippi Sound, Alabama.*———

On the 27th of December, in the year 1864, a fifth-order light was established on the south side of the channel. The tower was of the temporary kind, still standing at Sand Island, with an elevation of 25 feet to the focal plane. It soon fell into decay by the action of the sea worms on the wood, and in 1866 was abandoned for want of funds to rebuild or repair it. For several years afterward a light was maintained by a private party, who has recently extinguished it. The Pass is a narrow channel, and affords the only water communication between Mobile Bay and Mississippi Sound. The re-establishment of the light would be a great benefit. It should be an ordinary wooden structure, on iron screw-piles, prepared for a depth of from 2 to 5 feet water. An appropriation of $20,000 is respectfully recommended.

—— *Horn Island Pass, Mississippi Sound, Mississippi.*—The appropriation of $22,000 asked for in the last annual report having been granted, a survey of the Pass and eastern end of Horn Island was made to decide upon a plan and location for the light-house. The result of the observations was, that a fourth-order wooden structure on iron screw-piles, similar to that at Cat Island, was found to be the most suitable for the objects intended. The plans being all ready, proposals for the iron-work were invited, bids were received and opened on the 2d day of July, and the contract for the iron-work of foundation and lantern awarded to a firm in Baltimore, to be completed on or before the 21st day of October next. The superstructure will be got out by hired labor, and the building erected by the same means. It will stand on the eastern end of Horn Island, a sandy point elevated 3 feet above the water. It is expected that before the next spring the light will be in operation.

386. *Saint Joseph's Island, entrance to Lake Borgne, Louisiana.*—The palmetto-pile breakwater proposed for this station has been built. It has three sides facing around from northeast to the southeast, and meeting each other at angles of 120°. It has a total length of 260 feet. No further danger is now apprehended from the denudation of the land around the light-house.

388. *Tower Dupré, at entrance of Mississippi and Mexican Gulf Ship-Canal, Louisiana.*—The small use made of this canal, with little prospect of any increase in the future, would not warrant the erection of a light-house, and it is therefore recommended that the project of building a light at either Proctorsville or Tower Dupré be abandoned. The balance of the appropriation for Proctorsville light-station has reverted to the Treasury.

390. *Point Aux Herbes, Lake Pontchartrain, Louisiana.*—The erection of a light-house at this point has not yet been undertaken, the title to the land on which it is proposed to build not having been acquired, though the officers of the Light-House Establishment have done all in their power to forward it. The plans are all ready.

——*Errol Island, Gulf of Mexico, Louisiana.*—A light to illuminate the dark space not covered by the lights at Chandeleur and Pass à l'Outre has been recommended in several annual reports. Errol Island seems to be the proper point, as it is almost exactly midway, or twenty-six miles from Chandeleur and Pass à l'Outre light-houses. The question of its establishment has received additional force since it is expected that the proposed Fort Saint Philip Ship-Canal will soon be undertaken. The canal is intended to form a never-failing means of access from the deep water of the Gulf to the Mississippi River, for vessels of the greatest draught. It will debouch into Isle au Breton Pass, southwest, twenty-three miles distant from the selected site of the light-house. The re-entrant position of the canal entrance debars its selection, as the

point for the establishment of a sea-coast light, while the situation of
Isle au Breton, just opposite, and seven miles farther seaward, would
not equally enough divide the dark gap, which the proposed light-house
is to fill. When the canal is built a light will be needed at its entrance.
The proposed light-house on Errol Island will be useful in the navigation of Chandeleur Sound, which is much used by coasters.

The light-house should be of the first or second order, and to insure
its existence, in the event of any future changes in the topography of
the island, like those of the past, an iron tower on screw-piles, the same
as those now building at Trinity Shoal and Timbalier Island, would be
a proper one, but the Board is of the opinion that the construction of a
light-house in this vicinity may be deferred till the canal approaches
completion.

400. *Southwest Pass, Mississippi River, Louisiana.*—The new tower to
take the place of the old one built in 1831 was, on the 1st day of July,
nearly finished; since that date the remainder of the work has been
completed and lighted. The iron-work for it was manufactured in Ohio
and shipped by sea to the site, arriving there in December. The construction was energetically prosecuted, and a long looked for aid to the
commerce of New Orleans will now guide vessels to the principal outlet
of the river Mississippi. The old brick tower had sunk several feet into
the soft ground, and had inclined 3 or 4 feet from the perpendicular.

For several years it had been in a dilapidated condition, and the
light was of an inferior order, compared with the importance of its position. The plan for the foundation of the new light-house was designed
after careful study of the treacherous nature of the soft alluvial formation of the Delta of the Mississippi. It is octagonal in shape, and 58
feet 8 inches lesser diameter. It consists, first, of 185 square piles driven
4 feet apart, to a depth of about 33 feet. At 6 feet below the tops of
the piles, which are 1 foot below low water, a horizontal course of 12-
inch square timbers are notched into the piles. Below the timbers a
mass of shell concrete 2 feet thick is rammed about the piles, and on
the timbers rests a floor of 3-inch plank. Above the flooring are a second and third course of timbers notched into the piles, and laid at right
angles with each other, and diagonally to the first course. A mass of
concrete is forced into the interstices of the timbers, and filled up to a
height of 4 feet above the third tier, bringing the top of the foundation
to about 18 inches above mean level of the water.

The superstructure is a skeleton iron tower, of the same character as
those now building at Trinity Shoals and Timbalier Island, and is bolted
strongly to the timbers of the foundation. It is composed of six series
of eight cast-iron columns, placed at the angles of an octagon, and
strongly braced and tied by wrought-iron rods. On the sixth series
stands the watch-room and lantern, the ascent to which is by means of
a stairway winding around the axis of the tower, and inclosed in a
riveted plate-iron cylinder. The keeper's dwelling rests on the first
series of columns. It is octagonal in plan, two stories in height, and is
built of riveted plate-iron, sheathed inside with wood.

402. *Timbalier, entrance to bay of Timbalier, Louisiana.*—A small portion of the iron-work for this light-house was shipped from New York,
and on its arrival at South West Pass, in June, was stored until the
preparations for its erection could be completed.

The lumber and material for the construction of the platform, necessary
to aid the work in its erection, was sent to the station by the light-house
tenders Guthrie and Magnolia and landed on the beach convenient to
the site. A working force was sent to the station early in July and the

building of the platform was commenced immediately on their arrival; it is proposed to urge the work forward with all possible dispatch. It is intended that the platform shall be large enough to hold the iron-work of the tower, and give sufficient room for the quarters of the working party, thus dispensing with the necessity of keeping large vessels moored close to the work.

Previous to the definite location of the site of the light-house a thorough survey of West Timbalier Island and the surrounding waters was made, as in the absence of any correct charts the nature of the bay of Timbalier was almost unknown.

The funds at present available for the erection of the tower are inadequate for its completion, and an appropriation of $15,000 to complete it is recommended.

404. *Southwest Reef, entrance to Atchafalaya Bay, Louisiana.*—An appropriation of $5,000 to protect the iron tower at this station from impending destruction is available. The first floor and gallery are 11 feet 9 inches above mean low water. Occasionally extraordinary tides, caused by southerly gales, visit the locality, rise nearly to the level of the floor, and cause the sea to beat with all its force against the lower part of the building. It is proposed to raise the tower off of its foundation, lengthen each of the four piles, which compose it, by bolting to them cast-iron columns, secured by a proper system of bracing, and lowering the tower again into place.

An appropriation of $15,000 has also been made for the establishment of a steam fog-whistle. The building containing the machinery will be supported on screw-piles, and be connected with the light-house by a passage-way. It is proposed to prosecute both works at the same time as soon as the material can be manufactured. An additional appropriation of at least $5,000 will be required for these two works.

405. *Trinity Shoal, off coast of Louisiana, Gulf of Mexico.*—The first-order iron tower for this station was shipped from New York, and stored at Southwest Pass in June, as in the case of the Timbalier light-house. The same plan of operations proposed to be pursued in the erection of the latter structure is laid out for Trinity Shoal, except that the platform will be but 100 feet square, and is intended to accommodate the workmen only, while the material will be kept on board a vessel anchored near. Greater difficulty is anticipated in putting down the platform, owing to the greater depth of water and the more exposed situation, it being twenty miles from the nearest land.

The material for the platform and the working party are now at the station, and the work of driving piles has already commenced, and will be continued as rapidly as the weather will permit.

As in the case of Timbalier, the present appropriation is insufficient to finish the tower; an additional sum of $20,000 is needed for that purpose.

406. *Calcasieu, entrance to river and Lake Calcasieu, Louisiana.*—Strenuous efforts were made to obtain a title to the site selected for the light-house, but without any definite result. The iron-work arrived in February, and for the above reason had to be stored at the depot at head of the passes, where it now remains. The old appropriation reverted to the Treasury on the 1st of July, 1873. A new appropriation of $15,000 is asked for the purchase of land for a site, and the transportation and erection of this light-house.

407. *Bolivar Point, entrance to Galveston Bay, Texas.*—The recommencement of operations at Bolivar Point, which had been suspended for want of funds, was undertaken in August last. A party was organ-

ized in New Orleans and sent to the station. By the end of October, the tower was finished, but the light could not be exhibited until the 19th of November, by reason of delay in the arrival of the lantern-glass. The two-acre lot on which the light-house and keeper's dwelling are built was inclosed by a picket-fence.

413. *Matagorda, entrance to Matagorda Bay, Texas.*—By reason of the exhaustion of the former appropriation, the work on the construction of this light-house was suspended July 31, 1872.

Additional funds having been granted, operations were again begun last May. A few days' work sufficed to complete the brick and concrete foundation, the iron-work on the tower was completed before the close of the present month, and the new light will be exhibited, for the first time, on the 1st day of September, as advertised in the printed "notice to mariners."

The design of the tower is very much like that at Bolivar Point, being conical in form and composed of cast-iron sections bolted together. The light will be of the third order, flashing every 90 seconds. A one and one-half story keeper's dwelling, of wood, is building near the light-house. The grounds have an area of ten acres, two of which will be inclosed by a picket-fence.

418. *Brazos Island Beacon, entrance to Brazos Santiago, Texas.*—The recommendation of an appropriation of $25,000 found in the last annual report for rebuilding this light-house is repeated. The present tower is one of several, hastily built, to serve temporary purposes, in place of those destroyed during the war. Those at Sand Island, Bolivar Point, and Matagorda, which were of a plan similar to that of Brazos Island, have been or are being replaced by suitable structures, and it is now desirable that this, the last of the kind, should give way to a more durable building. It has already been used a much longer time than was anticipated when it was erected, and in view of its condition something should be speedily done to render the light more surely permanent. The board is of the opinion, in view of the large amount of work to be done in the eighth district under existing appropriations, that an appropriation for this work should be deferred till another session of Congress.

REPAIRS.

At each of the following-named stations in the eighth district there have been repairs made, more or less extensive, during the past year:

369. *Saint Marks,* entrance to Saint Marks River, Florida.
371. *Cape Saint George,* Florida.
372. *Cape San Blas,* Florida.
373. *Pensacola,* entrance to Pensacola Bay, Florida.
407. *Sabine Pass,* entrance to Sabine River, Louisiana.
410. *Half-Moon Shoal,* Galveston Bay, Texas.
411. *Red Fish Bar,* Galveston Bay, Texas.
412. *Clopper's Bar,* Galveston Bay, Texas.
416. *Half-Moon Reef,* Matagorda Bay, Texas.
417. *Aransas Pass,* Texas.
418. *Brazos Island Beacon,* entrance to Brazos Santiago, Texas.
419. *Point Isabel,* Brazos Santiago, Texas.

It is proposed to make repairs at the following-named stations in the eighth district during the coming year:

379. *Round Island,* Mississippi Sound, Mississippi.
380. *East Pascagoula River,* Mississippi.

381. *Ship Island*, Mississippi Sound, Mississippi.
382. *Biloxi*, Mississippi Sound; Mississippi.
383. *Cat Island*, Mississippi Sound, Mississippi.
384. *Pass Christian*, Mississippi Sound, Mississippi.
385. *Morrill's Shell Bank*, Mississippi Sound, Mississippi.
387. *Rigolets*, Pleasanton's Island, Louisiana.
389. *West Rigolets*, east entrance to Lake Pontchartrain, Louisiana.
391. *Port Pontchartrain*, Lake Pontchartrain, Louisiana.
392. *Bayou Saint John*, Pake Pontchartrain, Louisiana.
393. *New Canal*, Lake Pontchartrain, Louisiana.
374. *Tchefuncti River*, Lake Pontchartrain, Louisiana.
395. *Pass Manchac*, Lake Pontchartrain, Louisiana.
396. *Chandeleur*, Chandeleur Island, Gulf of Mexico, Louisiana.
397. *Pass a l'Outre*, Mississippi River, Louisiana.
399. *Head of Passes*, Mississippi River, Louisiana.
401. *Barrataria Bay*, Louisiana.
403. *Ship Shoal*, Gulf of Mexico, off coast of Louisiana.
410. *Half-moon Shoal*, Galveston Bay, Texas.

The following are the names of light-stations in the eighth district, not mentioned elsewhere. They are in good condition and have not required attention in the past year and most probably will not need any in the coming year:

374. *Pensacola Bar Beacon*, entrance to Pensacola Bay, Florida.
378. *Battery Gladden*, Mobile Bay, Alabama.
398. *South Pass*, entrance to Mississippi River, Louisiana.
414. *West Shoal*, entrance to Matagorda Bay, Texas.
415. *East Shoal*, entrance to Matagorda Bay, Texas.

LIGHT-SHIP.

408. *Galveston, inside of Galveston Bar, Texas.*—This vessel, being in need of repair, was relieved by a chartered schooner, towed to New Orleans, docked, thoroughly repaired and refitted. She is now in good order.

FOG-SIGNALS.

Pass a l'Outre.—A 12-inch steam-whistle, in good condition.
Southwest Pass.—A 12-inch steam-whistle, in good condition.
Both of the above have had the supply-pipes of the whistles lengthened, to give increased range to the sound, the tall swamp-grass obstructing it. They are now frequently heard distinctly a distance of twelve miles.

Fog-bells have been ordered by the board and will be put up the coming year at the light-houses at *Half-moon Shoal, Red Fish Bar*, and *Clopper's Bar*, Galveston Bay, Texas.

Fog-bells to be rung automatically should also be placed on the light-houses to be erected at *Saint Andrew's Bay*, Florida, *Horn Island Pass*, Mississippi, and *Calcasieu*, Louisiana, from the appropriation for those stations.

Fog-bells are greatly needed at many light-stations on the west coast of Florida, and the coasts of Alabama, Mississippi, Louisiana, and Texas, and an appropriation of $5,000 is asked for the purpose.

DAY OR UNLIGHTED BEACONS.

The day beacons in the eighth district are all in good condition. Repairs have been made to the following named:

Beacons Nos. 1, 2, and 4, composed of four palmetto piles each, entrance to River Saint Mark's, Florida·

Stake Island, Southwest Pass, Mississippi River.—Iron-pile beacon surmounted by hoop-iron globe.

North Breaker Beacon, entrance to Galveston Bay, Texas.—An iron-pile beacon surmounted by a hoop-iron globe.

The palmetto beacons mentioned in the last report as about to be established in the upper part of Pensacola Bay have been placed. They are six in number; are placed, to mark lamps having less than 5 feet of water, in Santa Maria de Galvaez and Blackwater Bay. They are composed of seven palmetto piles each, grouped in a bunch and bolted together, the central pile projecting higher than the others and capped with a barrel.

BUOYS.

The buoyage of this district is in good condition.

DEPOTS.

Buoy and Coal Depot, Fort Pickens, Florida.—This depot was thoroughly repaired and placed in perfect order.

Coal Depot, Mobile Point, entrance to Mobile Bay, Alabama.—For the convenience of the steam-tenders in the service of the district, a coal platform, 50 feet square, and inclosed by a fence, was laid during the year, at a slight cost, and 278 tons of coal were stored on it. Its situation is not of the best for the purpose, as the wharf faces the north, and being at the southern shore of the bay is exposed to the accumulated force of the waves advancing thirty miles across it. It is only during calm weather or easterly and southeasterly winds that vessels can lay along side.

Buoy and Coal Depot, head of the Passes, Mississippi River.—An appropriation of $10,000 was granted by the act approved March 3, 1873, for the protection of the depot from the erosion of the shore.

Very recently the wharf, which for a long time threatened to give way, at last fell into the river. The great expense of building protective works and their limited duration by reason of the constant changes going on in the banks of the river, and the fact that the head of the Passes is out of the way of communication by either telegraph or mail, make it extremely advisable that the depot be changed to another locality. There seems to be no better one in this portion of the district than at the new light-house at Southwest Pass. The very substantial wharf built to aid the construction of the light-house is still there. It has a front of 67 feet and a width of 32 feet. From it a wooden pier about 700 feet long leads to the light-house. A crane and tramway, provided with trucks, are already there. By extending the wharf some 30 feet on one side would give a good coal-platform, while a buoy-shed, engineer's and inspector's store-rooms might be built on either side of the pier connecting the wharf and light-house. The wharf fronts on a sheltered bayou about three-quarters of a mile from the main channel of the Mississippi, free from all eroding action which has given such trouble at head of the Passes. The place is also in easy communication by mail and telegraph. The buoy-shed and store-house at head of the Passes could be taken down and re-erected at the new depot, and the lumber which is being used for the temporary platforms at Timbalier and Trinity Shoal could be made available when those works are finished. It is therefore recommended that the depot at head of the Passes be abandoned, and a new one established at Southwest Pass, and that the $10,000 already appropriated for the protection of the old depot be made available for the preparation of the new one, and an additional appropriation of $5,000 be made for the same purpose. The combined amount of $15,000 ought to establish a new, commodious and secure depot, better in every respect than the old one, and one which will probably never require protective works, whereas the old one, after the expenditure of the amount already appropriated for works of protection, will require an equal amount next year for a new wharf and general repairs, and a much larger amount within two years for securing it against the washing of the river, .a total of probably $30,000 or $40,000.

[13.]

TENTH DISTRICT.

The tenth district extends from the mouth of Saint Regis River, New York, to include Grassy Island light-house, Detroit River, Michigan, and embraces all the aids to navigation on the American shores of Lake Erie, Lake Ontario, and river Saint Lawrence.

Inspector.—Commodore Napoleon Collins, United States Navy.

Engineer.—Maj. G. L. Gillespie, Corps of Engineers, United States Army, until March 31, 1873; Maj. Franklin Harwood, Corps of Engineers, United States Army, present engineer.

In this district there are:

Light-houses and lighted beacons.. 57
Light-houses finished and lighted during the year ending July 1, 1873........... 2
Light-houses for which appropriations were available, but which were not
  finished on the 1st of July, 1873... 2
Light-ships 0
Fog-signals operated by steam or hot-air engines...................................... 0
Day or unlighted beacons... 1
Buoys actually in position... 83
Spare buoys for relief to supply losses... 51
Tenders.. 0

485. *Cross-over Island, Saint Lawrence River, New York.*—The tower and dwelling remain as reported last year. As a measure of economy the sooner a new tower and dwelling are authorized the better, as very expensive repairs will be shortly absolutely necessary to make the building tenable, and to maintain the light. As stated last year, the structure is not worth repairing, and it would be a waste of money to do so, excepting as a matter of pressing necessity. An appropriation of $14,000 is required for a new tower and dwelling.

488. *Rock Island, Saint Lawrence River, New York.*—The tower and dwelling are in a similar condition to that of Cross-over Island. A new tower is imperatively necessary. The dwelling might be repaired, but it is not considered economical in the end to do so, as it would only be postponing the building of a new one a few years, and it would probably cost less to build tower and dwelling together now. An appropriation of $14,000 is required for a new tower and dwelling.

495. *Fair Haven, Little Sodus Bay, Lake Ontario, New York.*—A title for the four-acre lot, mentioned in last annual report, was obtained in November, 1872, and sealed proposals for building the keeper's dwelling were publicly invited December 23, 1872. A contract was entered into February 13, 1873, and work was commenced in the middle of March. An elevated walk was built from the beach to the beacon.

496. *Big Sodus Beacon, (front,) New York.*—A wooden beacon was built in September and October, 1872, on the Light-house Crib at the head of west pier, and a fixed white light has been exhibited since Octo-

ber 29, 1872, from a sixth-order lens illuminating 360°. The former front "Range" beacon was removed from the middle of west pier. An elevated walk 1,150 feet long was erected from new beacon.

——. *Puttneyville, Lake Ontario, New York.*—A timber beacon showing a fourth-order light will be erected in the course of the year 1873–'74.

501. *Oak Orchard, Lake Ontario, New York.*—An elevated walk, extending 800 feet to the beacon, was built in the spring of 1873.

——. *Thirty-Mile Point, Lake Ontario, New York.*—An appropriation was made at the last session of Congress for a lake-coast light at this point. The plans have been prepared and the structure will be commenced at an early day.

——. *Olcott, Lake Ontario, New York.*—A timber beacon showing a fourth-order light will be erected during the summer and fall of 1873.

508. *Dunkirk Beacon, Lake Erie, New York.*—An elevated walk was built, extending 900 feet to the beacon. The beacon is old and needs renewing. An appropriation of $5,000 is required.

511–512. *Presque Isle Beacon, ranges Nos. 2 and 3, entrance to Presque Isle Bay, Pennsylvania,* were both rebuilt during the year. An appropriation of $8,000 is required.

514. *Peninsula Beacon, range No. 2, Lake Erie, Pennsylvania,* being in danger of being washed into the lake by its encroachments, a protection breakwater will be built in front of it during the summer and fall of 1873.

515. *Presque Isle, Lake Erie, Pennsylvania.*—An appropriation was made June 10, 1872, for a new tower and keeper's dwelling attached. Proposals were publicly invited in July for the delivery of the necessary building materials, but no acceptable offers were made, except for the stone of foundation, the water-table, and for the metal work of tower; the other materials had to be bought in open market, and the plans approved by the Light-House Board had so far to be altered as to substitute iron for stone in the cases of sills, outside steps, and tablet, and as to use of brick, instead of stone, above the water-table. These different dispositions delayed the work so much that ground could not be broken before September 2, 1872, and the progress of the structure was furthermore made slow by the difficulty of landing materials, the shore being so dangerous that in the calmest weather only approach is possible, and that no insurance company would take any risks in vessels or cargoes; and notwithstanding all the precautions taken and delays incurred, a scow with 6,000 bricks was lost.

The masonry of the dwelling being completed, and that of the tower nearly so, by the end of November the house was roofed, the tower covered, and the openings were boarded up, and the work was suspended December 8, 1872, until April 16, 1873.

The light-house was ready for exhibiting the light and for occupancy on July 1, 1873. The buildings consist of a tower with keeper's dwelling attached, built of brick on a limestone foundation.

The apparatus is a Fresnel lens of the fourth order, showing a fixed white light, varied with red flashes, (F. W. V. R.) at intervals of one minute, the height of focal plane above lake level being 57 feet. Arc of visibility is from E. S. E. ½ E. by northward to S. W. by W. The light will be exhibited on and after July 12, 1873.

516. *Conneaut, Lake Erie, Ohio.*—The keeper's dwelling was completed and accepted. The beacon-crib is in such a ruinous condition that extensive repairs are imperatively necessary, but inasmuch as these repairs would cost nearly as much as a new beacon at the head of west pier, a site much more suitable and more convenient of access to the

keeper's dwelling, which is on the opposite side of the river from the present beacon, will be placed there. An appropriation of $4,000 is required for a new beacon.

517. *Ashtabula, Lake Erie, Ohio.*—An appropriation was made March 3, 1873, for building a new pier-head beacon. As an extension of the west pier is contemplated, on the head of which the new beacon is to be placed, the construction of the same is deferred, and it is recommended to continue the appropriation to June 30, 1875.

519. *Grand River, Fairport, Lake Erie.*—The west pier of entrance to the harbor at this station is being extended 400 feet, and as the frame beacon is very old and needs renewing, it should be taken down and a new frame beacon should be erected at the pier-head of the new exten sion. An appropriation of $4,000 is required.

520. *Cleveland, Lake Erie, Ohio.*—The buildings were successfully completed, and the dwelling occupied by January 1, 1873. The light has been exhibited from the new tower since the opening of navigation of 1873. The station is now in fine order.

521. *Cleveland, Beacon No. 1, Lake Erie, Ohio.*—Being in a ruinous state, and having settled considerably to the east, should be rebuilt. Complaints have been made of the insufficiency of the pier-lights at this place, and it has been suggested that a fixed red light of the fifth or sixth order should be placed at the pier-head in lieu of the pair of common lanterns which are now there. The matter will have the attention of the board. An appropriation of $10,000 is required.

523. *Black River, Lake Erie, Ohio.*—This station has no keeper's dwelling. An appropriation of $4,000 was asked for last year for the construction of a frame dwelling similar to the one at Ashtabula, Ohio, but was not granted. On account of the considerable rise in the price of real estate in the village, an appropriation of $5,000 is required, and is earnestly urged as a measure of economy, as the place is growing rapidly and the value of property steadily increasing.

525. *Huron, Lake Erie, Ohio.*—The title-papers being accepted by the Attorney-General in August, the contractors collected materials immediately and began the construction of the keeper's dwelling in September. After serious delays, occasioned particularly by sickness of the workmen, the dwelling was completed in January, and occupied on February 1, 1873.

——. *Sandusky Bay, Ohio.*—Access to the city wharves is had from Cedar Point over a shoal through which the United States has been dredging, and will shortly complete a channel over the most favorable ground, but which will have two turns or elbows at present marked by buoys. These buoys are continually in danger of being carried away by rafts or barges, and when this occurs the channel is left undefined, often resulting in serious delays to shipping. These turning-points should be permanently defined, and it is therefore respectfully recommended to establish two day-beacons of construction similar to that located at Dunkirk, N. Y. An appropriation of $12,000 is required.

533. *Maumee Outer range, (rear.)*—An appropriation of $12,000 was asked for last year (see last annual report) for erecting two day-beacons in the southwest channel. A board of engineer officers, engaged in making plans for the improvement of the channels, recommended in the early part of 1873, instead of these beacons, two iron light-houses, and an estimate was made for $40,000.

The reasons given in advocating the establishment of day-beacons in Sandusky Bay, are still more cogent in this instance, for scarcely a month elapses during the season of navigation without one or the other of the can-buoys being carried away, while the displacement of one or more of the spars is of weekly occurrence.

An appropriation of $14,000 would be required for two day-beacons in the outer range.

538. *Monroe, Lake Erie, Michigan.*—The keeper's dwelling is in a ruinous condition; has no foundation, except a few rotten logs, and has a very exposed position, now entirely unsafe.

The pier-head needs renewal, but cannot be touched without endangering the dwelling. its present position, there is a safe beach about 5 feet high above the water.

It is recommended to build a house there of the same model as at Oak Orchard or Fair Haven, New York, leaving the tower for the present, which is on a safe pile foundation.

An appropriation of $5,000 is required for building keeper's dwelling.

——. *Point Mouillé, Lake Erie, Michigan.*—Constant casualties have occurred, especially during the fall of 1872, by reason of vessels grounding on Bar Point, a dangerous shoal jutting out from the Canada shore. As this shoal is in Canada waters, the United States can take no measures there for the preservation of our commerce. Yet, last year, the pecuniary loss incurred there to citizens of the United States, if saved, would not only have sufficed to establish a light, but also to maintain it for several years.

The loss occurs in this wise: Vessels entering and leaving river Detroit, notwithstanding the aid of Bois Blanc (Canadian) and Gibraltar (American) lights, have no definite guide as to when to change their course to their destination on Lake Erie, or *vice versa* in going into the river Detroit. Hence many vessels, especially in heavy weather, turning too soon, come to grief on Bar Point Shoal.

It has been suggested that all this can be avoided by establishing off Point Mouillé (see topographical chart of west end of Lake Erie) a beacon-light in such a position that vessels rounding it can take their course either to or from Detroit with perfect safety.

The Board is informed that the beacon need stand in not more than 24 feet water on a foundation of compact sand and gravel.

The matter, which is deemed of importance, will have the immediate attention of the Board.

539. *Gibraltar, Detroit River, Michigan.*—An appropriation was made, June 10, 1872, for rebuilding the tower and dwelling; sealed proposals were publicly invited, in July, for the delivery of the necessary materials, but without result. Except the metal-work for the tower; the materials had to be purchased in open market.

A temporary tower was built, and a light from a steamer-lens was exhibited August 10, 1872.

The old tower was removed, as also the old dwelling, and the new buildings, a tower with dwelling attached, of brick, erected upon the light-house lot.

The buildings were completed in January, 1873, and the dwelling occupied February 1, 1873.

The focal plane of the new tower is 47 feet above the level of the river Detroit.

REPAIRS.

At each of the following-named stations in the tenth district there have been made repairs and renovations, more or less, during the year:

486. *Sister Island*, river Saint Lawrence, New York.
488. *Rock Island*, river Saint Lawrence. New York.
489. *Tibbett's Point*, Lake Ontario, New York.

490. *Galloo Island*, Lake Ontario, New York.
491. *Horse Island*, Lake Ontario, New York.
493. *Oswego*, Lake Ontario, New York.
498. *Big Sodus Bay*, Lake Ontario, New York.
499. *Genesee*, Lake Ontario, New York.
501. *Oak Orchard*, Lake Ontario, New York.
502. *Niagara Fort*, mouth of Niagara River, New York.
503. *Horseshoe Reef*, Buffalo, New York.
504. *Buffalo Breakwater*, north end Lake Erie, New York.
506. *Buffalo*, light-station and depot.
507. *Dunkirk*, Lake Erie, New York.
509. *Erie Harbor, Pennsylvania*, Lake Erie, Pennsylvania.
510. *Presque Isle, Beacon range*, Erie, Pa., No. 1-2.
513, 14. *Peninsula-Ranges* 1-2, Erie, Pa.
516. *Conneaut*, Lake Erie, Ohio.
517. *Ashtabula*, Lake Erie, Ohio.
518. *Grand River*, Lake Erie, Ohio.
521. *Cleveland Beacon*, Cleveland, Ohio.
524. *Vermillion*, Lake Erie, Ohio.
525. *Huron*, Lake Erie, Ohio.
526. *Cedar Point*, Lake Erie, Ohio.
527. *Cedar Point Beacon*, Lake Erie, Ohio.
531. *Turtle Island*, Lake Erie, Ohio.
532. *Maumee Outer range.*
534. *Maumee Middle range.*
536. *Maumee Inner range.*

Stations at which repairs in the tenth district will be made during the next year:

484. *Ogdensburgh*, river Saint Lawrence, New York.
486. *Sister Island*, river Saint Lawrence, New York.
487. *Sunken Rock*, river Saint Lawrence, New York.
490. *Galloo Island*, Lake Ontario, New York.
491. *Horse Island*, Lake Ontario, New York.
492. *Stony Point*, Lake Ontario, New York.
495. *Fair Haven*, Lake Ontario, New York.
498. *Big Sodus Bay*, Lake Ontario, New York.
499. *Genesee*, Lake Ontario, New York.
502. *Niagara Fort*, mouth of Niagara River, New York.
504. *Buffalo Breakwater*, (north end,) Buffalo, N. Y.
507. *Dunkirk*, Lake Erie, New York.
509. *Erie Harbor*, Lake Erie, Pennsylvania.
515. *Presque Isle*, Lake Erie, Pennsylvania.
516. *Conneaut*, Lake Erie, Ohio.
517. *Ashtabula*, Lake Erie, Ohio.
518. *Grand River*, Lake Erie, Ohio.
524. *Vermillion*, Lake Erie, Ohio.
525. *Huron*, Lake Erie, Ohio.
526. *Cedar Point*, Lake Erie, Ohio.
528. *Marblehead*, Lake Erie, Ohio.
529. *Green Island*, Lake Erie, Ohio.
530. *West Sister*, Lake Erie, Ohio.
531. *Turtle Island*, Lake Erie, Ohio.
532. *Maumee Outer range*, Lake Erie, Ohio.
534. *Maumee Middle range*, Lake Erie, Ohio.
536. *Maumee Inner range*, Lake Erie, Ohio.
540. *Mamajuda*, Detroit River, Michigan.
541. *Grassy Island*, Detroit River, Michigan.

LIGHT-SHIPS.

There are no light-ships in this district.

FOG-SIGNALS OPERATED BY STEAM OR HOT-AIR ENGINES.

There are no fog-signals operated by steam or hot air in this district.

DAY OR UNLIGHTED BEACONS.

Dunkirk Harbor, New York, in good order.

BUOYS.

The buoyage of the district is reported in good order.

DEPOT.

The depot at Buffalo, New York, is in good order, and fills all the wants of the district.

[14.]

ELEVENTH DISTRICT.

The eleventh district embraces all aids to navigation on the northern and northwestern lakes, above Grassy Island light-station, Detroit River, and includes Lakes Saint Clair, Huron, Michigan, and Superior, and the straits connecting them.

Inspector.—Commodore Alexander Murray, United States Navy.

Engineer.—To May 1, 1873, Maj. O. M. Poe, Corps of Engineers, Bvt. Brig. Gen., United States Army; after that date Maj. Godfrey Weitzel, Corps of Engineers, Bvt. Maj. Gen., United States Army.

There are in this district:

Light-houses and lighted beacons	100
Light-houses finished and lighted during the year ending July 1, 1873	5
Light-houses for which appropriations were available, but which were not finished on the 1st of July, 1873	15
Light-ships	0
Fog-signals, operated by steam or hot-air engines	7
Day or unlighted beacons	1
Buoys actually in position	145
Spare buoys for relief, and to supply losses	84
Tender (steam) Haze, buoy-tender and supply vessel, (common to tenth and eleventh districts)	1
Tender (steamer) Warrington, (used in engineer's constructions and repairs)	1
Tender (sail) Belle, (used in engineer's constructions and repairs)	1

The numbers preceding the names of stations correspond with the light-house list of the northern and northwestern lakes, issued January 1, 1873.

542. *Windmill Point, Michigan, entrance to Lake Saint Clair.*—This station was built in 1838 and refitted in 1867. It is an important station, as it is a guide to the whole commerce of the lakes to Lake Saint Clair and the Detroit River. Both tower and dwelling are old and dilapidated, and new structures are recommended at a cost of $18,000.

541. *Saint Clair Flats Beacon, Lake Saint Clair, Michigan.*—It having become evident that the crib which surrounds this beacon was settling and drawing with it the tower, a survey was made of its condition on the 18th May, 1873. It was found that the north corner of the crib was 1.51 feet lower than the south corner, and the tower at the focal plane was 5½ inches out of plumb. On the 5th August, 1873, another survey was made, and the north corner found to be 1,665 feet lower than the

south, and the tower 5.95 inches out of plumb. This shows considerable movement in about two and a half months. The drawings of this station show that the tower is founded upon piles driven very deeply, and the crib is built close against the tower on all sides. The only way in which this can be remedied is to rebuild the crib, and for this purpose an appropriation of $10,000 is asked.

545–546. *Saint Clair Flats Canal.*—The work of protecting the lower wing of the west dike of the canal, upon which No. 545 is founded, has been completed, and the station is now in a secure condition.

547. *Fort Gratiot Light-Station, Lake Huron, Michigan.*—The greatest necessity exists for a new dwelling at this station, the one now used having been built fifty-three years ago, and is no longer worth repairing. An estimate of $10,000 is submitted for the purpose.

——. A *lake coast-light between Fort Gratiot and Point Aux Barques, Lake Huron, Michigan.*—The recommendation contained in the annual reports for several years past, for a coast-light to divide the long distance between Fort Gratiot and Point Aux Barques, is respectfully repeated. No argument seems to be necessary to show the necessity for this light, and an estimate of $40,000 is submitted.

Port Austin, Lake Huron, Michigan.—The steps necessary to obtain the requisite site and begin the construction of the station have been taken.

549. *Tawas, (Ottawa,) Lake Huron, Michigan.*—This station was originally built on the end of Tawas Point, on the north shore of Saginaw Bay, Michigan. Since that time the point has steadily made to the southward and westward, and the extremity of it is now more than a mile from the light. No extensive repairs or improvements have been made, as the necessity for the removal of the light has long been foreseen. It is intended to guide into the harbor of Tawas, which, from its situation so near the mouth of the much-dreaded Saginaw Bay, is of great value, and much resorted to for refuge. The construction of a light on the extremity of the present point, if possible, would be quite expensive, and it is an open question whether some other disposition should not be made to meet the requirements of navigation. An estimate of $30,000 is submitted for a light or lights to guide into Tawas Bay, Michigan, leaving the proper arrangement to future discussion.

551. *Saginaw Bay, Lake Huron, Michigan.*—The present dwelling is very old and dilapidated. It was originally built of rubble masonry, and has been repaired until no longer worth repairing. Nothing short of a new dwelling will be economical, and an estimate of $8,000 for building one is submitted.

557. *Spectacle Reef, Lake Huron, Michigan.*—The important work at this place has been carried on during the year with all possible expedition and success. At the close of the month of June, 1872, six courses of stone had been cut and set, and the six succeeding courses had been prepared at the harbor and then transferred to the crib. Up to the 15th of August, the eleven succeeding courses of stone had been set in the tower. This brought the work up to the seventeenth course inclusive, completing the entire cut-stone masonry of the solid portion of the tower. At the close of the season of 1872, the masonry had been advanced to the setting of the fifth upper course inclusive, except one stone not delivered in time to be used, but which was subsequently received. During the month of October a cargo of stone was delivered, which completed the entire quantity of cut-stone required. The cutting of the stone had been continued at the harbor to the completion of the tenth upper course.

A severe gale in the month of September had done considerable damage, though only of a temporary character, exposing the east face of the crib where it had not been sheathed to protect it from the ice during the winter, sweeping away the temporary cribs, and nearly destroying the workmen's quarters. The quarters were rebuilt, other repairs made, and the sheathing completed as far as was intended, with the exception of the east side, which was left until the following season.

The gale which occurred on the night of the 28th of September continued during the following morning. It was from the northeast, and of unusual severity. Some idea of its violence, and the damage done, may be had from the description by the superintendent of construction, who states:

The sea burst in the doors and windows of the workmen's quarters, tore up the floors and all bunks on the side nearest the edge of the pier, carried off the walk between the privy and pier, and the privy itself, and tore up the platform between the quarters and the pier. Everything in the quarters was completely demolished, except the kitchen, which remained serviceable. The lens, showing a temporary light, and located on top of the quarters, was found intact, but out of level. Several timbers on the east side of the crib were driven in some four inches, and the temporary cribs were completely swept away. The north side is now so filled up that the steamer can no longer lie there. A stone weighing over thirty pounds was thrown across the pier, a distance of 70 feet; but the greatest feat accomplished by the gale was the moving of the revolving derrick from the northeast to the southwest corner. At 3 o'clock in the morning the men were obliged to run for their lives, and the only shelter they found was on the opposite (the west) side of the tower. The sea finally moderated sufficiently to allow them to seek refuge in the small cement shanty standing near the southeast corner of the crib. Many lost their clothing.

The position selected for the new quarters for the workmen was regarded as the most sheltered as it is inside the circular track, on the north side where the sea is not so heavy.

The temporary cribs having been carried away, the east face of the crib was left as much exposed as the others, and therefore the same protection by sheathing was required, but, owing to the lateness of the season, this could not be put on. The precaution was taken, however, to fill with stone those compartments of the crib, which have been occupied as boiler and coal rooms. The season's work at the station was brought to a close on the 31st of October, and with the exception of two men left to take care of the temporary light on the pier, the working party returned to Detroit. On the close of navigation the two men referred to were brought away, and two others left to take charge of the shore-station at Scammon's Harbor, until the ensuing spring.

During the month of April, 1873, a crane had been constructed for setting the stone in the upper courses of the tower, materials for the work had been ordered, and a working party organized and ready to leave for the site of the station. But owing to the unusually late opening of navigation through the Straits of Mackinac the workmen did not reach their destination until the 8th of May. Even at that date it was found necessary to remove great quantities of ice from the pier of protection, before work can be recommenced. The labor of cutting the stone at the depot at Scammon's Harbor was immediately resumed, and all the appliances and machinery, both at the harbor and at Spectacle Reef, were overhauled and put in working order. During the winter, the portion of the workmen's quarters remaining from the wreck caused by the gale of the previous fall, from which the temporary light had been exhibited, was carried away by the ice, and together with the lantern totally destroyed. This was not unexpected, and in view of the probable result, the lens had been removed and stored in a place of security. In the meantime, until a new tower and lantern could be built, a light from an ordinary hand-lantern was exhibited and answered the purpose.

The fog-signal was uninjured, and was sounded as usual whenever necessary.

At the close of the month of June the cutting and fitting of the upper courses of stone had been completed to the sixteenth course inclusive. On the reef, after the erection of the crane, the setting of the sixth and seventh and the greater part of the eighth upper courses was completed. This very nearly finishes the masonry of the tower to the height of 50 feet above the water level. Various minor details connected with the work have also been completed, so that there is still hope that with a vigorous pushing of the work, and if no unforeseen obstacle occurs, it may be finished by the close of the season; or perhaps, with the exception of some of the interior details, this gratifying result may be accomplished, and, with the funds now available.

Mackinac or vicinity, Straits of Mackinac, Michigan.—The approach to the town and harbor of Mackinac from the westward is quite difficult at night. For many years a light-house to mark this approach has been recommended, but as yet no appropriation since that of 1854 (which long since reverted to the Treasury) has been made. The exact location of the desired light is somewhat in doubt, and an appropriation of $15,000 for a light-house and fog-signal at Mackinac or vicinity, Straits of Mackinac, is respectfully recommended.

562. *Saint Helena, Michigan.*—The erection of a tower and dwelling, connected by a covered way, at this site, was begun about the middle of September, 1872, under appropriation made by act approved June 10, 1872. At the close of the season, November 9, the base of the tower and the masonry of the covered way were completed in readiness for the brick-work, and with the exception of one 6-inch course, the masonry of the main building was finished to the water-table. On the 9th of May, 1873, the work was resumed, and by the 30th of June the entire station was completed, except setting up the lens and some other minor details. Four men were left at the station to finish up, which will require but a short time.

——. *Little Traverse, Lake Michigan, Michigan.*—The recommendation contained in the last annual report for a light-house and fog-signal to mark this fine harbor of refuge, and make it available at all times, is respectfully renewed. It has been proposed, however, to substitute a steam fog-signal for the bell recommended last year; if this substitution is approved, the estimate of last year must be increased to $15,000.

——. *Frankfort pier-head light.*—A pier-head light has just been erected at this place. A keeper's dwelling, at a cost of $5,000, is recommended.

572. *Manistee, Lake Michigan, Michigan.*—The rebuilding of this station, destroyed by the great fire of October 8, 1871, was commenced in the month of July last and completed in September.

574.—*Père Marquette, Lake Michigan, Michigan.*—This station is still without a keeper's dwelling. The last two annual reports contained recommendations for an appropriation therefor, but none has yet been made. The estimate of $5,000 for the purpose is respectfully renewed.

——. *Pentwater, Lake Michigan, Michigan.*—A pier-head beacon-light has been erected at the outer end of the south pier at Pentwater, and connected with the shore by an elevated walk. The light was first exhibited on the 20th June, 1873. A keeper's dwelling at a cost of $5,000 is recommended.

575. *Petite Point au Sable, Lake Michigan, Michigan.*—The site for

this station having been selected, and other preliminaries completed, a working party was placed on the ground and operations commenced in April last. A dock has been built for landing material, provisions, &c., and temporary buildings erected for the accommodation of the party and protection of the material. Excavations for foundations of the tower and dwelling have been made, and piles driven for the foundation of the tower. The coffer-dam has been built, the water pumped out, and all in readiness to commence laying the concrete.

576. *White River, Michigan, Lake Michigan.*—This light marks the entrance to the White River, on the banks and near the mouth of which are two thriving places, Whitehall and Montague. Very large interests, especially in lumber, are centered here, and a larger light than the present pier light should be placed here. There is therefore recommended an appropriation for a new station at a cost of $15,000.

581. *Holland, Lake Michigan, Michigan.*—The appropriation of the necessary funds for a keeper's dwelling at this station was made by act approved June 10, 1872. The long delay in perfecting the title has, however, prevented the work being carried on at an earlier date. It will be taken in hand in a short time.

585. *Saint Josephs pier-head light, Lake Michigan, Michigan.*—The work of removing the beacon to the outer end of the pier, and the construction of an elevated walk, were brought to completion in November last.

588. *Calumet, Lake Michigan, Illinois.*—The difficulties in the way of obtaining title to the site of this station having at length been surmounted, the work of repairing and renovating the station was taken in hand during the month of May and completed before the 30th June, 1873.

589–590. *Chicago main and pier lights, Lake Michigan, Illinois.*—Cracks have developed in the foundation of the main-light, and extensive repairs may be necessary. The extent of the injury can only be determined by a close examination, which will be made at as early a day as practicable. Attendance upon the pier light is very difficult in bad weather. It has been suggested to use ordinary illuminating gas, controlled from the main light, and thus avoid the necessity for visiting it when the weather is bad. It is doubtful whether such an experiment would be successful, since it failed under less unfavorable circumstances at Cleveland, because of condensation and freezing.

591. *Grosse Point, Lake Michigan, Illinois.*—Proposals for the construction of a second-order station at this point were invited by advertisement, and opened on the 13th August, 1872. The lowest bid was accepted, and articles of agreement were duly entered into. The work of excavation for the foundations of the tower, covered way, and dwelling, was commenced in September, and by the close of the season's work in November, the stone-work of the dwelling had been brought up to the grade, and the drains partially made. After some vexatious delays, attributed by the contractor to the inclemency of the weather, work was suspended for the winter, except the delivery of material. In April work was resumed, and during this month and the month of May good progress was made, the piles having been driven and the concrete laid for the foundation of the tower and the stone-work begun, while the brick-work of the dwelling was carried nearly to completion, as well as the roofs of the verandas, kitchens, and woodsheds, and a portion of the roof of the main building. By the 30th June, the tower was completed as far as the setting of the last course of the water-table, the passage-way and the oil-room finished to the roof, and the outside of dwelling nearly completed, having received one coat of paint. The blinds were all hung, the upper floors laid, the ceilings lathed, and the partitions of the main stairs built, and all the drains completed.

——. *Racine Point, Lake Michigan, Wisconsin.*—The recommendation contained in the last three annual reports, that a lake coast-light and fog-signal be established on Racine Point is respectfully renewed, and an estimate of $40,000 submitted therefor. This work is much needed, not only to satisfy the demands of the general commerce of Lake Michigan, but to aid in indicating the position of a very dangerous outlying reef upon which several wrecks have occurred.

596. *Racine pier-head light, Lake Michigan, Wisconsin.*—The erection of a pier-head beacon, and elevated walk to connect it with the shore, was begun in July, 1872, and a light exhibited for the first time on the 5th of September following.

597. *Milwaukee pier-head light, Lake Michigan, Wisconsin.*—The work of erecting a beacon at the outer end of the north pier, at the harbor of Milwaukee, and connecting it with the former beacon, was commenced in August, 1872. The beacon was completed and a light exhibited from it on the evening of October 30, and the elevated walk was finished in November.

—— *Twin River Point, Lake Michigan, Wisconsin.*—The requisite site for a light-house at this point has been selected, and all the preliminaries completed. As soon as the title to the site has been perfected, which will doubtless soon be done, the construction of the buildings will be commenced, and completed as soon as possible.

—— *Sturgeon Bay ship-canal, Lake Michigan, Wisconsin.*—At the Lake Michigan end of this important work a light and fog-signal should be established. The canal is being pushed vigorously, and there is no doubt that it will be completed as soon as a light-house can be built; and an appropriation of $40,000 for the purpose is recommended.

—— *North Bay, Lake Michigan, Wisconsin.*—By act of Congress approved July 15, 1870, an appropriation of $7,500 was made for the purpose of establishing a light or lights to enable vessels to enter this harbor, and a price for the site required was agreed upon with the owner. But it was found impracticable for him to make a good title before the 30th of the following June, when the appropriation reverted to the Treasury. It is recommended that the amount be re-appropriated, and another attempt made to obtain title.

——. *Poverty Island, Lake Michigan, Michigan.*—All the requisite preliminaries have been completed, and the erection of a light-house at this point, under the act of March 3, 1873, will be commenced before the close of this season.

614 and 615. *Grassy Island, Green Bay, Wisconsin.*—Both beacons, as well as the walk connecting them, were completed in October, 1872, and lighted for the first time November 15.

619. *Big Sable, Lake Superior, Michigan.*—The site has been selected, title obtained, plans approved by the board, and the construction of the buildings will be begun early in July of this year, and completed as soon as possible.

——. *Stannard's Rock, Lake Superior, Michigan.*—Preparations are being made to begin the survey and examinations provided for at this place by act of March 3, 1873, and the survey will be completed as soon as possible. There can be no doubt as to the practicability of building a light-house to mark this dangerous rock, and it can be done now cheaper than at any future time, as the costly apparatus and machinery used at Spectacle Reef is now available for use elsewhere, and being especially adapted to works such as this must be can be at once transferred. The rock is nearly twenty miles distant from the nearest land, and forty from a suitable harbor, and the tower will probably be located in water of about 11 feet in depth, facts which indicate a structure of the most substantial and costly kind known in light-house engineering. Because of the uncertainties attending such a construction, no detailed estimate of the probable cost can be given, but it is perfectly safe to say that it will not be less than $300,000. Large as this sum appears to be, it is believed that the outlay is fully warranted by the necessities of the Lake Superior navigation, and an appropriation of $200,000 is recommended with which to begin the work.

——. *L'Anse, Lake Superior, Michigan.*—The site of the proposed light-house at this place, provided for by act approved March 3, 1873, has been selected, and the owners have promised to perfect the title as soon as possible, after which no unnecessary delay will take place in erecting the requisite structures and exhibiting the light.

Eagle Harbor, Lake Superior, Michigan.—The attention of the board has been called by the Chief of Engineers of the Army to the necessity of range lights to enter this harbor, and it will take early steps to determine the amount necessary for the purpose.

——. *Portage Lake Ship-Canal, Lake Superior, Michigan.*—As soon as the title to the site required has been conveyed to the United States the construction of the buildings will be commenced and the light established as soon as possible, an appropriation having been made for the purpose.

——. *Outer Island, Lake Superior, Wisconsin.*—Under the appropriation made by act of March 3, 1873, the construction of the building required at this new station will be begun during the present season and pushed to completion as soon as possible.

——. *Sand Island, Lake Superior, Wisconsin.*—The remarks of last year's report concerning the necessity for a light-house on this island, and the estimates therefor, are respectfully renewed.

642. *Du Luth, Lake Superior, Minnesota.*—After much delay the keeper's dwelling and as much of the elevated walk as can be built at present were completed during the month of May. Owing to the damage sustained by the pier in a storm, last fall, it is not in fit condition to receive the beacon, and work has been suspended until the repairs to the pier are completed, when the contractor will be required to finish the beacon. Meanwhile a temporary light is exhibited from the outer end of the north pier of the canal.

——. *Rock Harbor, (Isle Royale,) Lake Superior, Michigan.*—The necessary examinations and measurements of the old tower and other buildings at this station have been made with a view to their renovation and the re-establishment of the light. The act of March 3, 1873, provides "for a light-house on Isle Royale, Lake Superior." The site for this has not yet been selected, but the matter will receive attention as soon as the isolated locality can be reached.

——. *Passage Island, Lake Superior, Michigan.*—The annual report for the last two years has contained a recommendation for a light-house on Passage Island, together with an estimate of cost, but no appropriation has yet been made. The recommendation and estimate ($18,000) are respectfully renewed. Some arguments have been advanced to show that the appropriation for a light-house on Isle Royale might be used for the purpose, but with these the board does not agree, as Passage Island is an entirely distinct island, at a distance of three and one-half miles from the most easterly point of Isle Royale.

PIER-HEAD LIGHTS.

The work of establishing pier-head lights is being continued as rapidly as circumstances permit. As the erection of these lights depends upon the extension of the harbor improvements it is not practicable to make an estimate in detail, but the amount of $15,000 in the aggregate will certainly be required in this district for this purpose.

REPAIRS.

Repairs of greater or less extent have been made or are in process of execution at the following stations:

545. *Saint Clair Flats Canal*, (lower light.)
547. *Fort Gratiot.*
548. *Point aux'Barques.*
549. *Tawas*, (Ottawa.)
551. *Saginaw Bay.*
553. *Thunder Bay Island.*
554. }
555. } *Presque Isle Ranges.*
556. *Presque Isle.*
558. *Detour.*
——. *Detour Fog-Signal.*
559. *Bois Blanc.*
560. *Sheboygan.*
563. *Waugoshance.*
564. *Skilligallee.*
569. *Mission Point.*
572. *Manistee.*
576. *White River.*
584. *Saint Joseph.*
586. *Michigan City.*
588. *Calumet.*
589. *Chicago.*
593. *Kenosha.*
610. *Eagle Bluff.*
611. *Chamber's Island.*
613. *Tail Point.*
617. *Point Iroquois.*
618. *White Fish Point.*
——. *White Fish Point Fog-Signal.*
624. *Marquette.*
635. *Eagle Harbor.*
639. *La Pointe.*
641. *Minnesota Point.*

Repairs and improvements are required at the following stations and will be made during the ensuing year:

548. *Point aux Barques.*
550. *Charity Island.*
553. *Thunder Bay Island.*
554. }
555. } *Presque Isle Ranges*
556. *Presque Isle.*
558. *Detour.*
559. *Bois Blanc.*
560. *Cheboygan.*
561. *McGulpin's Point.*

24 Ab

BUOYS.

Buoys marking the channel in Detroit and Saint Clair Rivers, and buoys marking the dangers to navigation in the Straits of Mackinac and adjacent waters, are regularly attended to by the light-house and buoy tender Haze, placing them on the opening of navigation each year and removing them at the close, stowing the buoys belonging to the Straits of Mackinac and adjacent waters at light-house depot, Scammon's Harbor, and those belonging to Detroit River and Straits of Saint Clair at light-house depot, Detroit. All other buoys in the district are attended by contract.

DEPOT.

Under the act of June 10, 1872, the work on the light-house depot at Detroit has progressed during the year. A dwelling for the store-keeper was built, and inclosed by a fence, and is occupied. A board fence was erected along the western side of the basin, between that and the adjoining glue-factory. Towards the close of last season the walls of the third story of the store-house were finished to receive the brackets, and covered with a temporary roof to protect it from the weather while operations were suspended for the winter.

In April, 1873, the work was resumed, the temporary roof removed, and the construction of the fire-proof roof of iron and slate carried to completion. Floors of wood were laid in some of the rooms, great care being exercised to see that the space between them and the supporting arches was completely filled with sand well rammed in. The landing-pier is completely worn out. It has been repaired until the supporting piles are no longer safe. No heavy weight can now be landed upon it, and an appropriation of $8,000 for building is urgently recommended. The supply of oil for the entire lake region is landed at this depot, and as the system of lights on the lakes increases, the importance of this depot increases. Designed less than five years ago, upon a scale which was then deemed ample, it is already apparent that some extension of the buildings and conveniences will be required before many years, in order to secure all the benefits of the depot.

FOG-SIGNALS.

The five steam fog-signals which have been in use in the district during the year have given great satisfaction. Five more have been ordered for points, as follows: Marquette, Skillagallee, Manitou Island, Outer Island; and Huron Island.

Similar signals are needed at the following points, viz: McGulpin's Point, Grand Haven, Port du Mort, Pottawatomie, Gull Rock, and Granite Island; and an appropriation of $25,000 for the purpose of establishing them is recommended.

TENDERS.

As previously reported, the Haze, (screw-steamer,) used as a supply-vessel for both the lake districts and buoy-tender for a portion of the eleventh district, is old and nearly worn out. For the last two years she has been used solely for inspection, delivering supplies, and in taking care of the larger buoys of the eleventh district. She has a very light frame, and it is not deemed best to recommend any extensive repairs. She was not built for the light-house service, but was purchased in an emergency; and while of excellent model and great economy in consumption of fuel, has a light frame, and has deteriorated to such an extent that it is recommended she be rebuilt; and for this purpose an appropriation of $30,000 is respectfully recommended.

SURVEYS OF LIGHT-HOUSE SITES.

The pressure of other duties has prevented as rapid a prosecution of this work as is desirable. The surveys completed since last report are Tawas, (Ottawa Point,) Saint Joseph, and Holland. In addition, a number of preliminary surveys, in connection with light-houses now building or to be built, have been made. It is intended to continue the work in accordance with a settled plan of the Board as rapidly as practicable.

[15.]

TWELFTH DISTRICT.

CALIFORNIA.

This district embraces all aids to navigation on the Pacific coast of the United States between the Mexican frontier and the southern boundary of Oregon, and includes the coast of California.

Inspector.—Commander Charles J. McDougal, United States Navy, until December 1, 1872; Capt. James H. Spotts, United States Navy, present inspector.

Engineer.—Maj. N. Michler, Corps of Engineers, brevet brigadier-general, United States Army.

In this district there are—

Light-houses and lighted beacons	16
Light-houses finished and lighted during the year ending July 1, 1873	1
Light-houses for which appropriations were available, but which were not finished on the 1st of July, 1873	5
Light-ships	0
Fog-signals, operated by steam or hot-air engines	6
Day or unlighted beacons	1
Buoys actually in position	40
Spare buoys for relief and to supply losses	26
Tender Shubrick, common to twelfth and thirteenth districts, used for inspectors' and engineers' purposes	

The numbers preceding the names of stations correspond with those of the "Light-House List of the Atlantic, Gulf, and Pacific Coasts of the United States," issued January 1, 1873.

421. *Point Fermin, on west side of San Pedro Bay, California.*—A site was selected and a reservation laid off for a light-house. Proceedings have been instituted by the United States attorney, district of California, for the purpose of condemning, under the laws of said State, the land upon which to build; but as yet no result has been reached. An appropriation, made June 10, 1872, of $20,000, is available for the establishment of a light and fog-signal at this point.

422. *Point Hueneme, entrance to the Santa Barbara Channel, California.*—As in the preceding case proceedings of condemnation of the site selected and surveyed are still progressing. An appropriation, made June 10, 1872, of $22,000, is available for constructing a light-house at this locality.

425. *Piedras Blancas, sea-coast of California.*—An appropriation, made June 10, 1872, of $75,000, is available for a first-order light and fog-signal at this point. A detailed survey during the early part of this year was made, and a map prepared of the locality; the height of which differing from previous information of the Board, necessitated a change in the design, which was published in the last annual report of the Board.

426. *Point Pinos, sea-coast of California.*—No information has been furnished this Office in regard to the decision of the Supreme Court in the case of the suit for condemnation of land for right of way to the light-house at this station, and which was referred to in the last annual report.

429. *Pigeon Point, sea-coast of California.*—The work on the light-house at this station was resumed in July, 1872, and completed in October. It was illuminated for the first time on the 15th of November, 1872.

——. *Point Montara, sea-coast of California.*—This Point is about midway between Pigeon Point and the Golden Gate, and within a few miles of Point San Pedro. An appropriation of $15,000 is available for a steam fog-signal here. The locality was examined and a site selected; a survey of the latter was made, and the map is being prepared by the district engineer.

434. *East Brother Island, San Pablo Bay, California, opposite Point San Pablo.*—In consequence of the apparent increasing litigation to gain possession of a site on the main-land for light-house purposes, an examination was made of the East Brother Island to ascertain if it would be a suitable locality. A special report was made by the district officers in regard to its advantages, and the selection was approved by the Board. Proposals were invited for building a light-house and a fog-signal building; for making the necessary excavations, and executing the grading; also, for building a retaining-wall. The lowest bid was accepted, and the work was commenced near the end of July.

435. *Mare Island, entrance to Straits of Karquines.*—The light-house of this station was completed by the 15th of July, although it was not quite ready for lighting at that date. An attempt was made to obtain water by digging a well, but without success. The point south of the dwelling was cut down and graded, a retaining-wall, built of rock to above high-water mark, forming a plateau for fog-signal. Inclines have been constructed from this plateau and from the plane of the dwelling to the boat-landing; windlasses, provided with turn-table and car, were set up on each. The erection of the necessary building for the fog-bell, and the sinking of a well for the weight of the machinery, still remains

to be done. A substantial picket-fence has been erected along the lines of the light-house reservation from the precipitous bluff on the east to that on the west.

436. *Point Reyes, sea-coast of California.*—An appropriation of $10,000 was made June 10, 1872, for rebuilding and re-establishing the steam fog-signal at this station. Men and material were shipped on board the tender Fern and landed at Drake's Bay, for the purpose of erecting a new building and constructing a new coal-chute. Machinists were also sent to repair the machinery, which had suffered much damage. Large shelving pieces of rock and bowlders had to be removed by drilling and blasting. The cistern requires to be cemented; cracks in the water-shed, supposed to have been caused by an earthquake, had also to be closed up; the old retaining-wall had to be pulled down and rebuilt from the foundation. Owing to the constantly shifting sand around the dwelling, it became necessary to cover the surface around it with boards. The fog-signal could not be put in operation until a sufficiency of water had been collected in the cistern after the commencement of the rainy season.

Fort Ross, sea-coast of California, midway between Point Reyes and Point Arena.—In June an attempt was made to examine a reservation for a light-house, which many years ago was made by the President, but owing to the dangerous anchorage it was not deemed safe to remain at anchor a sufficient length of time to accomplish that object. Another attempt will be made by an overland route.

437. *Point Arena, sea-coast of California.*—On the 27th of June the light-station at this point was inspected, and by direction of the board an examination of the reservation was made to ascertain whether the amount of land reserved by the President at Point Arena is in excess of the wants of the light-house service.

Mendocino City, Bay of Mendocino, California.—By direction of the board examinations for light-house purposes were made at the "south point of entrance to the harbor of Mendocino City," and of a "point four and a half miles to northward of Mendocino City," surveys have been made of the localities; the necessary maps will be prepared and a special report made in regard to both.

Shelter Cove, sea-coast of California, forty-five miles north of the Bay of Mendocino.—In June an attempt was made to land at this point to examine a proposed light-house site, but a heavy swell made it too dangerous to attempt a landing.

438. *Cape Mendocino, sea-coast of California.*—There is a settlement of the ground, caused by an earthquake, in the ravine to the north of the tower, the limits of which are well defined by a continuous crack in the earth. The south line of this crack passes through one end of the cement retaining-wall and within 15 feet of the tower; this has been filled up with concrete and well rammed. Granite posts were cut and sent there to be planted at the corners of the reservation to mark its limits. A suit, Buhne vs. Chism, to eject the light-house keepers at this station—a suit involving the title to the site—was decided on the 10th of October in favor of the United States.

439. *Humboldt, sea-coast of California, entrance to Humboldt Bay.*—An appropriation of $10,000 is available for a steam fog-signal at the entrance to Humboldt Bay, and the district officers have selected a site on the present reservation.

REPAIRS.

At each of the following named stations repairs more or less extensive have been made during the year:

420. *Point Lima.*—Sea-coast of California.
423. *Santa Barbara.*—Sea-coast of California.
424. *Point Conception.*—Sea-coast of California.
426. *Point Pinos.*—Sea-coast of California.
428. *Ano Nuevo.*—Sea-coast of California.
437. *Point Arena.*—Sea-coast of California.
438. *Point Mendocino.*—Sea-coast of California.
427. *Santa Cruz.*—Sea-coast of California, entrance to Monterey Bay.
431. *Point Bonita.*—Sea-coast of California, north side of the Golden Gate.
439. *Humboldt.*—Sea-coast of California, entrance to Humboldt Bay.
430. *Faralones.*—Off the Golden Gate, entrance to San Francisco Bay, California.
432. *Fort Point.*—San Francisco Bay, California.
433. *Alcatraz Island.*—San Francisco Bay, California.

The following are the names of light-stations in the twelfth district which are not mentioned elsewhere in this report:

440. *Humboldt Bar Bell-Boat.*—Off entrance to Humboldt Bay.
441. *Trinidad Head.*—Sea-coast of California.
442. *Crescent City.*—Crescent City Harbor, California.

FOG-SIGNALS OPERATED BY STEAM OR HOT-AIR ENGINES.

Point Conception.—A 12-inch steam-whistle.
Ano Nuevo Island.—A 12-inch steam-whistle.
Pigeon Point.—A 12-inch steam-whistle.
Point Reyes.—A 12-inch steam-whistle.
Point Arena.—A 12-inch steam-whistle.
Point Montara.—A 12-inch steam-whistle, (to be erected.)
Humboldt Bay.—A 12-inch steam-whistle, (to be erected.)
East Brother Island.—A 10-inch steam-whistle, (to be erected.)
Point Bonita.—A first-order steam-syren.

DAY OR UNLIGHTED BEACONS.

Fauntleroy Rock.—Crescent City Harbor, California.

The setting of the spindle for the day beacon in the Fauntleroy Wash Rock in the roadstead, off the town of Crescent City, was completed during the year.

BUOYS.

The buoyage of the twelfth district is in excellent condition.

DEPOT.

Yerba Buena Depot, San Francisco Bay, California.—A light-house depot on this island has been completed with the exception of placing the derrick in position; this will be done when the latter is received from the East. The wharf has been constructed and a railway laid upon it; the piles, previous to being driven, having been subjected to the Robbins creosote process for preservation. A watchman's house and a large store-house have been built adjoining the main building.

THIRTEENTH DISTRICT.

This district embraces all aids to navigation on the Pacific coast of the United States north of the southern boundary of Oregon. It extends from the forty-first parallel of latitude to British Columbia, and includes the coasts of Oregon and Washington Territory.

Inspector.—Commander Charles J. McDougal, United States Navy, until December 1, 1872; Capt. James H. Spotts, United States Navy, present inspector.

Engineer.—Maj. H. M. Robert, Corps of Engineers, United States Army.

In this district there are—

Light-houses and lighted beacons	10
Light-houses and lighted beacons finished and lighted during the year ending July 1, 1873	0
Light-houses for which appropriations were available but which were not finished on the 1st of July, 1873	3
Light-ships	0
Fog-signals, operated by steam or hot-air engine	1
Unlighted or day beacons	0
Buoys actually in position	49
Spare buoys for relief and to supply losses	23
Tender (steam) Shubrick, common to the twelfth and thirteenth districts	1

The following numbers which precede the names of stations correspond with those of the "Light-house List of the Atlantic, Gulf, and Pacific Coasts of the United States," issued January 1, 1873.

446. *Cape Foulweather, sea-coast of Oregon.*—The keeper's dwelling was completed in September, 1872. Notwithstanding the delays connected with transportation, the light-house would have been completed and the light exhibited as early as January, 1873, but for the fact that a part of the lantern had been lost at sea in transportation from the East, a fact not discovered in time to prevent the delay. Duplicates of the missing pieces have at length been received, and the light will be exhibited on the 20th of August, 1873.

—— *Point Adams, south side of the entrance to Columbia River, Oregon.*— The site for the light-house and steam fog-signal to be erected at this place has been selected by the district officers. The plans have been prepared and the machinery has been shipped from the East. The fog-signal may be in operation by early spring of 1874, and the light exhibited by November following.

447. *Cape Disappointment, mouth of Columbia River, Territory of Washington.*—A neat substantial oil-house has been erected at this station during the past year to take the place of the old oil-house, which was useless.

449. *Cape Flattery, entrance to the Straits of Fuca.*—The entire dwelling needs renewal, except walls and roof. One house-cistern needs rebuilding; the light-house buildings should be inclosed by a fence; a dry store-room should be built; a boat, boatways, and tramway are required to enable keepers to safely and conveniently land supplies. Estimated cost of above repairs, $5,000.

The present dwelling is not fit to be occupied, as the walls are damp and moldy nearly all the year, and it is totally inadequate for the accommodation of the four keepers at this station. A comfortable dwelling, similar to those at Cape Disappointment and Cape Foulweather, is greatly needed, and it would enable a better class of keepers to be retained here than would be willing to occupy the present dwelling. If a dwelling were erected, the old dwelling, without extensive repairs, would serve as store-room, and $18,000 would provide for necessary repairs (as above) and double dwelling for keepers.

451. *New Dungenness, Territory of Washington.*—A steam fog-whistle will be erected this season to replace the fog-bell.

—— *A light in Puget Sound.*—Congress at its last session appropriated $25,000 for a light at Point-no-Point, Territory of Washington, or such other point in Puget Sound as the Light-House Board might select. A report has been received from the district officers, recommending a site on Foulweather Bluff entrance to Hood's Canal, but the board have not yet determined in regard to it.

REPAIRS.

Repairs more or less extensive have been made at the following-named stations during the year:

449. *Cape Flattery*, entrance to the Straits of Fuca.

450. *Ediz Hook*, Straits of Fuca, Territory of Washington.

451. *New Dungeness*, Straits of Fuca, Territory of Washington.

453. *Admiralty Head*, east side of Admiralty Inlet, Territory of Washington.

Stations at which repairs are required to be made during the next year:

450. *Ediz Hook*, Straits of Fuca, Territory of Washington.

452. *Smith's or Blunt's Island*, inside the Straits of Fuca, Territory of Washington.

453. *Admiralty Head*, Admiralty Inlet, Territory of Washington.

The following are the names of light-stations in the thirteenth district, not mentioned elsewhere:

443. *Cape Blanco*, sea-coast of Oregon.

444. *Cape Arago*, (Gregory,) sea-coast of Oregon.

445. *Yaquina Bay*, Oregon.

448. *Shoalwater Bay*, Territory of Washington.

LIGHT-SHIPS.

There are no light-ships in this district.

DAY OR UNLIGHTED BEACONS.

Sand Island, mouth of Columbia River, Oregon.—An unlighted beacon, for which $1,000 will be required, is needed at this point, as the low beach and shifting nature of the island render it somewhat dangerous in hazy or foggy weather.

—— *Silvie de Grace Rock, about two miles above Astoria, Oregon, near the south shore of Columbia River.*—The channel of the Columbia is quite narrow at this point and the current rapid. Vessels must run close to this rock to keep the channel, and the position of the rock has heretofore been shown by the wreck of the Silvie de Grace, now nearly destroyed. The erection of a permanent unlighted beacon, at a probable expense of $2,000, is recommended.

FOG-SIGNALS OPERATED BY STEAM OR HOT-AIR ENGINES.

Cape Flattery.—A 12-inch steam-whistle.

BUOYS.

The buoyage of this district is in good condition.

DEPOT.

The construction of a buoy-depot at the mouth of the Columbia has been urged by the district officers. The buoys are now kept on an open wharf, at Astoria, where they are exposed to the weather and other causes of injury, and where the interruption by rain of painting is liable to detain the light-house tender. A project has been made for a depot large enough to provide for all storage and repairs under shelter.

JOSEPH HENRY,
Chairman.

REPORT OF THE SUPERVISING ARCHITECT.

TREASURY DEPARTMENT,
Office of Supervising Architect, October 1, 1873.

SIR: I have the honor to submit the following, being my eighth annual report of the business transacted by this office, and of the progress and condition of the public works under its charge.

Sites have been purchased for the public buildings at Covington, Ky., Dover, Del., Evansville, Ind., Fall River, Mass., Port Huron, Mich., and Parkersburgh, W. Va.; the property necessary for the extension of the public building at Indianapolis, Ind., and additional land adjoining the public buildings at Madison, Wis., and Springfield, Ill., the original lots having been found too small. The sites for the buildings at Hartford, Conn., and Lincoln, Nebr., which were presented by those cities, have been examined, found satisfactory, and accepted. It has been found impossible to purchase suitable sites for the proposed buildings at Cincinnati, Ohio, Utica and Albany, N. Y., or the addition to the site of the post-office and treasury building at Boston, Mass., at fair prices; proceedings in condemnation have consequently been instituted in each case, and are now in progress. A part of the site for the new post-office and court-house at Philadelphia, Pa., was purchased on satisfactory terms, but some of the owners having refused to dispose of their property for a reasonable sum, proceedings in condemnation have been instituted in those cases. Negotiations have been entered into with a view to procuring suitable sites for the proposed buildings at Atlanta, Ga., Jersey City, N. J., Little Rock, Ark., Memphis, Tenn., and Pittsburgh, Pa., and are now in progress.

The site of the old custom-house at Plymouth, N. C., has been sold, the building having been destroyed during the war and no necessity existing for a public building in that place. The marine hospitals at New Orleans, La., and Natchez, Miss., have been offered at public auction, but not sold, no satisfactory bid having been made.

Plans have been commenced, and are now well advanced, for the public buildings at Philadelphia, Pa., Cincinnati, Ohio, Parkersburgh, W. Va., Evansville, Ind., Dover, Del., Grand Rapids, Mich., and for the marine hospital at San Francisco, Cal. Preliminary surveys of the sites selected in other cities have been made, and the plans will be commenced at an early day.

The custom-house at Saint Paul, Minn., is now complete and occupied; it is a commodious and substantial building, and has been found, in spite of the charges of extravagance in size and construction, no larger or better than is demanded by the business of that city. The lot on which the building is erected is, however, too small, and I would earnestly recommend that an appropriation be obtained for the purchase of sufficient additional property to provide the necessary isolation and protection. The public building at Astoria, Oreg., has been completed, furnished, and is now occupied. It has been constructed, in a permanent and substantial manner, of undressed stone, and will undoubtedly be ample for all future wants of the Government in that city. It gives me great pleasure to report that the marine hospital building at Chicago, Ill., has been completed, as well as the grading and fencing of the grounds. It is now occupied, and is pronounced by the supervising surgeon to be the best arranged, best lighted, and best ventilated hospital in the country, and is undoubtedly one of the most substantial and thoroughly constructed buildings of the class ever erected.

The extension, remodeling, and repairs of the custom-house at Baltimore, Md., are completed. The building now provides accommodations for all branches of the public service in that city, excepting only those for the courts and officers of the judiciary. Should the business of the custom-house continue to increase, additional space will soon be needed, and as the Merchants' Bank is a part of the building, I desire to renew my recommendation that it be purchased. The increase of the business of the post-office at Norfolk, Va., has rendered it necessary to remove the United States public stores from the custom-house and post-office building in that city, in order to provide the additional space required; this has been done, and the entire building refitted and furnished, and it is now in better condition than when first completed. The public building at Mobile, Ala., which was in bad condition and much in need of improvement, has been thoroughly remodeled and repaired. The best portion of it was occupied by a large but useless staircase which has been removed, and much valuable space gained without detracting from the convenience of the structure, besides rendering it practicable to re-arrange the post-office, which has been done in a most satisfactory manner; it was also destitute of furniture, which has been supplied, and is now in excellent condition. The public building at Galveston, Tex., has been remodeled and refurnished, and is now in better condition than when first completed. The great increase of public business in that city made it necessary to rent a building for the use of the custom-house, the post-office requiring the entire first floor, and the courts and offices of the judiciary the remainder. The business of the port is rapidly increasing, and as it is the most important on the Gulf of Mexico, I would recommend to the favorable consideration of the Department the propriety of erecting a suitable and substantial brick building for the use of the custom-house, appraisers' and United States public stores in that city. The public building at Saint Augustine, Fla., which was erected by the Spanish government prior to the acquisition of that State, has been repaired, and is now in as good condition as the nature of the case would permit, and provides satisfactory accommodations for the custom-house, post-office, and courts.

The remarkable increase in the financial department of the New York post-office rendered it necessary to provide accommodations for that branch of the service in the second story of the new post-office building. To accomplish this the rooms intended for the offices of the judiciary in that story were appropriated, which of course made it necessary to provide for them elsewhere. This could only be done by the addition of a fourth story to the building, which was authorized by the act approved March 3, 1873. Orders were immediately given for the preparation of the necessary granite, which has been cut, delivered, and is now in place. The work at this time is in such condition that I feel no doubt of the completion of the roof during the present season, or that it will be occupied by the post-office by the 4th of July, 1874, and be entirely completed during the coming year. The great size of this building and its construction, which has been entirely experimental, have rendered it impossible to estimate its cost with the accuracy that would otherwise have been attained. It is, however, so far completed that it may be safely stated that its cost will not exceed $6,500,000 exclusive of fencing, grading, sewerage, machinery, furniture, and fixtures, or $7,000 000 inclusive of these items. This amount will undoubtedly appear enormous to persons who have not investigated the subject, but, when compared with the size of the building and with the cost of other great structures erected by the Government or by State or municipal authorities, it will be found to be a cheap structure. The building will be, when completed, larger than any granite or marble building yet commenced by the Government outside of the District of Columbia, and is not only the largest post-office building in the world, but will have unequaled facilities and accommodations for the transaction of business. Being satisfied that an under-ground way through the city of New York must sooner or later be constructed, and that in no other manner can quick and ample transit be assured, and that such connection between the various railroads centering in New York and the post-office is indispensable, I have made provision by which the mails can, in such an event, be received and delivered in the basement in the same manner as will be the case in the new post-office at St. Louis. It has also been so arranged that the various newspaper offices can, at a very trifling expense, arrange for the delivery of their issues in that portion of the building, and thereby save much valuable time as well as expense. The magnitude of the building may be inferred from the following statement of labor and material expended in its construction to the present time, viz: 94,000 cubic yards excavations, 8,000 cubic yards concrete, 5,500 cubic yards rubble, 15,000,000 bricks, 50,000 barrels cement, 15,000 cubic yards sand, 500,000 cubic feet granite, 6,000 tons wrought and cast iron, 350,000 feet, board-measure, rough lumber, 5,000 pounds lead, and over 1,000,000 day's labor, exclusive of that expended on contracts for iron work, &c.

I feel confident that when completed and occupied, the most prejudiced will admit that the money has been honestly and judiciously expended, and that the building is worthy of the commercial metropolis of the United States.

It was expected that the post-office and treasury building at Boston, Mass., would have been so far completed that it could be occupied by the post-office during the coming winter. Of this there is at present, I regret to say, no prospect, though it will undoubtedly be completed early next spring. Every effort has been made to hasten its progress, and I can offer no other excuse for the failure than the embarrassment, confusion, and delays that have followed the great fire. The building covers one-half of the block bordered by Devonshire, Congress, Milk, and Water streets; the remainder was occupied by buildings that were destroyed by the fire, which injured the granite-work of the building in close proximity, and in direct contact with the flames to the amount of $100,000. The streets adjoining were very narrow, Milk street being but 38 feet and Water street 39 feet in width. No material damage was, however, sustained by the destruction of the buildings on the opposite sides of the streets, showing conclusively that had it been surrounded by streets of the ordinary width it would have suffered no damage whatever. As it was it proved to be the only building that presented an impassable barrier to the fire, and undoubtedly saved millions of dollars to the city of Boston. In this connection it may be proper to remark that the general plans and estimates of this office were considered very extravagant by many prominent citizens of Boston, who failed to comprehend the possibility of such a conflagration or the danger therefrom.   One of these gentlemen was so strongly impressed with the extravagance of the Supervising Architect's ideas that he not only volunteered his advice to the Department in an elaborate communication, in which he expressed the opinion that buildings erected by him in that city were sufficiently fire proof for all practical purposes, and that a large amount would be saved by following his example; failing to convince the Department, he endeavored to impress his views upon the committee of the House of Representatives appointed to investigate the manner of construction of that building, and of the new post-office in New York.   The fire proved most disastrous to his theories, the buildings to which he referred offering no more resistance to the conflagration than buildings of the most ordinary construction, showing conclusively that, had his advice been followed, the loss to the Government would have amounted to millions of dollars, as the building would have been completed and occupied by the Post-Office and Treasury Department, and must inevitably have been destroyed.   It has, however, furnished an admirable illustration of the value of such opinions and advice.   The site for this building was, it will be remembered, purchased, not by the Department, but by a commission appointed by Congress, which consisted of the mayor and postmaster, the assistant treasurer, the president of the board of trade, the Hons. Alpheus Hardy and Daniel Davis, of Boston, and though it was, in the opinion of the postmaster, Gen. William L. Burt, entirely inadequate in size, (in which opinion this office concurred,) the views of the majority prevailed.   The result has justified the opinion of the postmaster, the building being of no more than half the capacity required.   This is so apparent that the purchase of the remaining portion of the block has been authorized, as heretofore stated.

The work on the foundation and basement of the new public building in Chicago, Ill., is now nearly completed, and good progress has been made with the superstructure.   The cut stone for the building is from the quarries at Buena Vista, Ohio.   The material thus far received is of the best quality and the workmanship unequaled.   The principal difficulties in the erection of the building have been overcome, and much greater progress will, it is hoped, be made during the next season.   I desire, however, to call the attention of the Department to the importance of erecting the Adams-street front, for which no appropriation has yet been made.   It is of great importance that this front should be erected simultaneously with the remainder; and as the entire building will be required, I would strongly recommend that an appropriation be obtained for the commencement of that wing. Should this be done, a considerable saving in cost as well as time will be made, and the entire building can be placed under roof at an early day.

The new mint at San Francisco, Cal., is nearly completed, and will be ready for occupancy as soon as the machinery is put in place.   The building itself could be finished at an earlier date, but, inasmuch as it would increase the expense of the work to do so, and as no time would be gained thereby, I have deemed it better to conduct the work in such a manner that the completion of the building and of the machinery will be as nearly simultaneous as possible.   It gives me pleasure to report that, though constructed on so much larger a scale than was generally thought necessary, it has proved to be no larger than is now required by the actual necessities of the Government. Indeed, but for its size, the Department would have been unable to adopt the improved machinery and apparatus with which it is to be supplied. The work on the building has been done in a substantial manner, and it is undoubtedly a cheap as well as a permanent structure. I deeply regret, however, that the material furnished by the contractor for the cut-stone work is not the kind contracted for, nor equal thereto in any particular. Of this I was not aware until after the death of the superintendent and the appointment of his successor, at which time the contract was completed. The stone has been cut in a satisfactory manner, and had the material been according to the sample, and been properly set, no cause for complaint would have existed. Under these circumstances I have felt it my duty to refuse any further payment to the contractors, and to submit the case for such action as you may deem necessary.

The entrance story of the custom-house at New Orleans, La., has at last been completed, and is now occupied by the post-office and the appraisers' department, for which purposes it provides ample accommodations. The main cornice, the interior stairs, the roof, the iron-work of the central and entrance halls have been finished. It has, however, been found impossible, from the peculiarity of the case, to make accurate estimates of the cost of completing the building. Much of the material on hand, which it was expected to use in the construction, was unsuitable and worthless; it was also necessary to remove a much greater amount of work than was contemplated and to perform a larger amount than was anticipated. The building is, however, well advanced toward completion, and, should the necessary appropriation be made can be finished at an early day. In this connection I have the honor to report that the modifications in the design of the building made thus far have been successful, and to recommend that authority be obtained to make such additional changes as are necessary to make the exterior harmonious and uniform. The expense will not be great, and will add both to its comfort and convenience, as well as its appearance, and make it an imposing if not an elegant structure. I do not hesitate to express the opinion that the magnitude and substantial character of the building would justify the additional appropriation. The change in the plan from a granite to a cast-iron cornice, authorized by the act of March 3, 1871, though effecting a saving of $245,416.30, rendered a considerable amount of granite useless which had already been completed. Claims for this work, including interest and damages on the contract for granite work, amounting to $125,365.84, have been presented to the Department. A compromise has, however, been made, subject to the approval of Congress, by which the claimants agree to accept $43,327.85, being the actual contract price of the work performed, less the cost of transportation to New Orleans, and on payment of the same to surrender all claims for damages arising under the contract. This arrangement is, in my opinion, a fair one, and advantageous to the Government, and I would recommend that an appropriation to the amount necessary to effect a settlement be obtained.

On the 20th of June, 1870, I submitted plans for the completion of the custom-house at Charleston, S. C., which contemplated the omission of the dome and the side porticos, and the modification of the east and west porticos in such a manner that, while increasing the capacity and value of the building, it reduced the cost of completion and, instead of injuring, improved its architecture. These plans and estimates were based upon the drawings on file in this office and the property returns of the former superintendent, and were carefully prepared therefrom, and believed to be correct. Soon after commencing work it was found that important changes had been made by the commission under whose direction the work had been performed, of which the Department was not aware, and which greatly increased the expense of completion; that a large portion of the marble appearing on the property returns of the superintendent was not to be found, having in all probability been removed during the war, and that the portion remaining had been damaged by the bombardment of Charleston, and from other causes, to a much greater extent than was anticipated. It has also been found necessary to take down and rebuild a large portion of the exterior walls in order to remedy errors and defects in the original construction. These and other causes have increased the cost of the work $187,388.84 beyond the amount estimated. Claims amounting to $59,176.64, the existence of which was unknown to the Department, have been presented, adjusted, and settled for the sum of $22,118.91, for which an appropriation should be made. The progress of the work has been entirely satisfactory, has been well and economically managed, and the cost of the work reduced to the lowest point, the excess over the estimate being due entirely to the causes above specified. The improvement in the appearance of the building and the reductions in the cost of completing have been all that was anticipated, the difference in favor of the modified plan being not less than $500,000. The building will, when completed, furnish suitable accommodations for the custom-house, including the appraisers' stores, for the collector of internal revenue, the assistant treasurer, and the officers of the judiciary, thereby enabling the Department to dispose of the court-house building in that city, which is but a temporary structure and cannot be expected to last many years.

The public building at Columbia, S. C., will be an elegant and substantial structure, of granite which is obtained in the immediate vicinity. The cutting was commenced by day's labor, and for a time proceeded in a satisfactory manner. The former superintendent, proved unable to control the cost of the work, and was accordingly removed. It was, however, found impossible to remedy the effects of his mismanagement, and to reduce the cost of the work to a proper price; a contract was accordingly made for its completion, which is now proceeding in a satisfactory manner, and the building will undoubtedly be placed under roof early in the coming season.

The progress of the public building at Knoxville, Tenn., has been satisfactory. The work is of excellent character, has been economically and judiciously conducted, and will be completed early the coming season within the amount of the appropriation.

The public building at Omaha, Nebr., is now inclosed and will be ready for occupancy at an early day. The work has been performed in a substantial manner, and at fair prices. The building is elegant and convenient, but perhaps open to the criticism that it is too good for the locality. I am of the opinion, however, that it is not desirable to erect inferior buildings in cities of the prospective importance of Omaha, and feel confident that the future of the town will justify the action of the Department. The building will be a credit to the Government, an ornament to the city, and provide ample and convenient accommodation for the transaction of the public business not only in the present but for the future.

The custom-house, court-house, and post-office building at Portland, Oreg., is a handsome and well-built structure of blue freestone, and occupies a commanding site in the pleasantest part of the city, but is, unfortunately, so far removed from the business portion that it is not, in my opinion, a good location for a custom-house, and it should not be occupied for that purpose. It is, however, no larger than is required for the proper transaction of the business of the post-office, the courts, the internal revenue, and other Government offices. I would, therefore, recommend that for the present the custom-house be continued in its present locality, and that a plain, substantial, fire-proof brick building be erected for the use of the customs department, including the appraisers' and the United States public stores. I am aware that this recommendation may seem extravagant, but it should be borne in mind that Portland is not only the second city on the Pacific coast, but is rapidly increasing in commercial importance and is probably the only port in the State of Oregon for which such provision will ever be required.

The extension of the public building at Indianapolis, Ind., is in progress and will be completed at an early date. It will, however, be impossible to complete it within the limit fixed by law. The extension has been of the size required ; the design was, of course, fixed by the original building, and the work has been done at the least possible cost. I therefore recommend that the necessary appropriation be obtained at an early day.

Work has been commenced on the government building at Saint Louis, Mo., which will be three stories in height, with a basement, sub-basement, and attic. The basement and sub-basement and a portion of the first story will be of Missouri red granite, the remainder of gray granite from Hurricane Island, Me. The building will have a frontage of 232 feet on Olive and Locust streets, and 177 feet on Eighth and Ninth streets, with a total height of 96 feet to the upper cornice and 184 feet to the top of the dome. Arrangements have been made with the Saint Louis Tunnel and Bridge Company by which the mails on all lines entering Saint Louis by that route will be received and delivered directly into the building. This arrangement will, it is believed, effect a large saving in the expense as well as much valuable time, as it will insure the delivery of the mails at the earliest possible moment and enable the Department to defer closing them until the train is leaving the depot. The progress on this work has been, up to the present date, very unsatisfactory. A contract for the foundation-stone, the sub-basement piers, and area walls was awarded to the Saint Louis Marble Company on the 2d of September, 1873, but to the present time the Department has been unable to procure any material from them and will undoubtedly be compelled to award the contract to other bidders. Every effort will be made to advance the work, and it is trusted that the obstacles in the way to its rapid prosecution will soon be removed.

The plans and estimates submitted for the appraisers' stores at San Francisco, Cal., contemplated a substantial, but not fire-proof, brick building three stories in height, the entrance story and basement to be used for the purposes of an appraisers' store, and the upper stories for offices of the United States courts, of the judiciary, the collector of internal revenue, the pension agent, and all other Government officers in that city, except those now accommodated in the custom-house and post-office building. During my last visit to San Francisco I carefully investigated the subject, and am satisfied that the necessities of the Government will compel the erection of a post-office building in that city at an early day, the custom-house building in which the post-office is situated being entirely inadequate to meet the requirements of both departments, and though suitable for a custom-house, it is not a desirable location for a post-office or for the United States courts, being near the wharves and remote from the business center of the city. It therefore appears to me that it would be far preferable to complete the present building as an appraisers' and United States public store, for which purposes it is admirably adapted, and would, if completed on this plan, yield a handsome income to the Government, and at the same time afford protection to the revenue that can be attained in no other manner. I also desire to call attention to the fact that the act approved February 12, 1873, re-organizing the mints of the United States, relieved the assistant treasurer from all duty in connection therewith. It will, therefore, be necessary to provide accommodations for that officer either in the custom-house, the appraisers' stores, or in the old mint building, which will be vacated at an early day. As the business of the custom-house and of the assistant treasurer is more intimately connected than any other branches of the Government business, it is very desirable that the treasurer should be provided with accommodations in the same building. The removal of the post-office would provide the additional accommodations now imperatively demanded by the customs department, and also sufficient space for the transaction of the business of the treasurer. If this cannot be done I would recommend that the old mint building be fitted up as soon as vacated for the use of the assistant treasurer, the location being a good one and the building reasonably well adapted for the purpose. I would, therefore, respectfully suggest that, before completing the building on the present plan, it would be well to investigate the subject and determine whether the erection of a post-office building is or is not a necessity.

Work has been commenced upon the public building at Hartford, Conn., and it is hoped that the basement story will be completed during the present season, though the progress of the work has been retarded by the operations of the act of July 12, 1870, which rendered it impossible to proceed with the preparation of material for the superstructure, and will consequently delay the completion of the building another year. The basement will be of Quincy granite, but no selection has been made of the material for the superstructure. This building being erected on a triangular piece of land, is, of necessity, irregular in shape. The extreme length is 109 feet, and the extreme width 91 feet.

Work has been commenced upon the public building at Trenton, N. J., and the basement story will be completed during the present season. The building will be 118 feet by 63 feet, three stories in height, with a basement and attic, the latter being intended for files and storage. The exterior of the building will be of sandstone from the quarries of the Clough Stone Company at Amherst, Ohio. The floors of the first story will be of brick arches turned on iron beams. The limitation on the cost of the building will, if insisted upon, render it necessary to construct the remaining floors and roof of the building of timber, which, it appears to me, would not be economy, and I recommend that an appropriation be obtained for the completion of the building as a fire-proof structure.

Work has been commenced upon the public building at Raleigh, N. C. It has, however, been found extremely difficult to procure either material or labor at reasonable rates, and as a consequence very little progress has been made. Negotiations are, however, in progress that warrant the belief that these difficulties will be overcome and that good progress will be made during the coming season. The building will be 116 feet by 63 feet, three stories in height, and will be constructed of pressed brick with stone trimmings.

The public building at Rockland, Me., has been commenced. It will be, when completed, 81 feet by 61 feet, two stories in height, with basement and attic, and will be constructed of undressed granite with hammered trimmings, the first floor of iron beams and brick arches, and the remaining floors and the roof of timber construction. The appropriation is in this case sufficient, there being, in my opinion, no necessity for making buildings of this class fire-proof.

The proposed new public building at Port Huron, Mich., has been commenced. Considerable difficulty has, however, been experienced in obtaining suitable material. But little progress has been made with the work, and no decision has been reached in regard to the material of which the building will be constructed. It will be 113 feet by 62 feet, two stories in height, with an attic and basement, and will have a fine cupola, from which a full view of the river and harbor can be obtained.

The alterations in the custom-house at Boston, Mass., which were authorized during the last session of Congress, have been commenced, and are now well advanced toward completion. The improvement has been even greater than was anticipated, and has satisfied me that the building can be made, by additional changes, for which I have prepared plans, a reasonably comfortable and convenient structure. The heating is very imperfect, and there is practically no ventilation whatever. These defects should also be remedied. I strongly recommend that the appropriations necessary to complete the improvements on this building be obtained.

It has been found necessary to remodel the post-office and custom-house building at Pittsburgh, Pa., in order to provide the accommodations immediately necessary. The improvements are well advanced, and will, when completed, afford considerable relief, and greatly increase and improve the accommodations of the building. The building is, however, far too small, and as the various branches of public business in that city are increasing very rapidly, I strongly recommend that an appropriation be obtained for commencing the new building at an early date.

The improvement and repairs of the public building at Toledo, Ohio, have been commenced ; the upper story has been fitted for the use of the United States district courts, which now hold sessions in that city. The increasing business of the post-office has rendered it necessary to assign to its use the entire basement, and to remove therefrom the furnaces, fuel-rooms and closets, and to erect a suitable building for the latter purposes.

The building will be placed in thorough repair and the entire space utilized. It is, however, entirely too small and should be extended, or a new one erected, at an early day—the latter being, in my opinion, the more desirable plan.

The court-house at Baltimore, Md., has been repaired and the arrangement of the interior and the ventilation improved. The inconvenient and unsightly inclosed stairway and portico on the Fayette street front, and the equally unsuitable portico on the North street front, have been removed, and a fine portico erected with the old material on the latter front, which has greatly improved its appearance and added to the convenience of the building.

I desire to call attention to the fact that the appropriations for the erection of the proposed new public buildings at Nashville, Tenn., Atlanta, Ga., Fall River, Mass., Covington, Ky., Evansville, Ind., Little Rock, Ark., Utica, N. Y., and Jersey City, N. J., are not sufficient, and that it is impossible to comply with the restrictions on their cost, except by erecting buildings inadequate in size and unsuitable for the purposes intended. The cost of buildings cannot be reduced below the actual market value of the material and labor necessary to furnish the required

25 Ab

accommodations; and it appears to me unjust to hold the Department responsible for the cost of public buildings when the limitations on their cost are fixed without proper information of the necessities of the case, and in advance of the preparation of estimates, or when the cost has been restricted to a sum much less than the estimates submitted, therefor, which have been prepared after a careful investigation of the necessities of the public service, the material available, and the cost of the same. As an illustration: the limitation on the cost of the proposed building at Nashville, Tenn., is less than one-half of the lowest estimate that could justly be made for any building that would answer the purpose, and but little more than one-third of the cost of such a building as should be erected in that city. An appropriation was first made for this building in the year 1856, but no action was taken beyond the purchase of a lot, which was so entirely unsuitable, both in size and location, that it was exchanged in 1870 for a large and desirable piece of property, which the Government now owns. I recommend that authority be obtained to expend a reasonable amount of money, and that provision be made for the commencement of this necessary and very important structure. The cost of the public building at Evansville, Ind., including the site, is limited to $200,000, but it has been found impossible to purchase a site for less than $100,000, in addition to a considerable sum which was contributed by the citizens of that place to make up the deficiency. Only $100,000 therefore remains for the building, or about one-third of the amount required. In Fall River, Mass., the cost of the proposed building and site is limited to $200,000. After the most careful examination and protracted negotiations it was found impossible to purchase a site in any way suitable for less than $103,200. I believe that an additional amount of land should be purchased, and am satisfied that a suitable building cannot be erected for less than double the available appropriation. The appropriations for the buildings at the other cities are equally inadequate and must be increased. The experience of the Department has shown that, so far from a saving being effected by the erection of small and unsuitable buildings, the result on the contrary is waste.

On entering upon the duties of this office I found it in charge of one hundred and twenty buildings, exclusive of temporary structures. Of these, eighty-eight only had been erected by the Government as permanent buildings; of these, twelve, costing $748,000.91, having been found unsuitable, have been sold for $291,336.19. Authority has been granted for the sale of four others for the same reasons; three of these, costing $828,611.94, have been offered at public auction but not sold, the highest bid amounting to but $55,660. Of the remaining seventy-two buildings, eight have been condemned as entirely inadequate and unsuitable, and the erection of new ones authorized in their stead. Five others have been condemned, but no provision has yet been made for replacing them. It will therefore be seen that out of eighty-eight buildings that have cost $27,741,328.86, twenty-nine, costing $3,820,961.47, have been already condemned as unsuitable for the Government. This exhibit, bad as it is, does not fully state the facts of the case, as of the remaining fifty-nine buildings not less than five have been extended and thirteen remodeled, and at an early date six others must be extended, two remodeled, and five replaced by other structures, showing that out of eighty-eight buildings erected without proper regard to the necessities of the public service, as previously explained, but thirty-three could be considered in any sense of the word permanent and suitable structures. Of these a large number are in towns of comparatively little importance. Indeed, of the buildings erected or commenced by the Government in the ten principal cities of the United States prior to 1865, but four can be considered of permanent value, namely: the custom-house at Boston, Mass., the treasury building at New York, the court-house at Baltimore, Md., and the custom-house at New Orleans, La.; a statement which appears to me to show conclusively the impolicy of erecting buildings without taking into consideration the necessities of the future or the necessities of the public service. I would, therefore, respectfully suggest that in cases where it is not considered desirable to appropriate the amount necessary to erect suitable and permanent buildings, it would be more advantageous to defer action and rent temporary accommodations until such time as the finances of the Government may warrant the appropriation of the necessary amount.

The marine hospital at New Orleans, La., has been offered three times at public auction without obtaining a reasonable offer therefor. It is at present partially occupied by the city of New Orleans as a hospital for its insane and as an asylum for its paupers; and is, in its present condition, a disgrace to the Government as well as the city. I have heretofore called attention to the fact that the location was not a suitable one, nor the building desirable for hospital purposes; and that it would cost far more to complete it than to erect a suitable pavilion hospital. It has, however, cost a large sum of money, and would, if completed, be an ornament to the city—to which it is undoubtedly worth more than to any private individual or association, or the Government. But as the financial condition of the city, in the opinion of its officers, precludes the purchase of the property at its estimated value, I would respectfully recommend that the property be transferred to it on such terms as its financial condition may appear to warrant. It appears to me very desirable that immediate action should be taken, as it is rapidly falling into decay, and should be completed, sold, or transferred to the city without delay.

Considerable difficulty has been experienced in selecting a site for the marine hospital at San Francisco, Cal., suitable for the purpose and unobjectionable to the military authorities. This difficulty has, it is believed, been overcome by the selection of a site at Mountain Lake, on the Presidio reservation. Arrangements have also been made for the commencement of work as soon as the transfer of the property is completed.

I desire to renew my recommendation that authority be obtained to sell the marine-hospital property in Pittsburg, Pa. The location is unsuitable, the building unfit for hospital purposes and in bad condition, unless sold it must be extended and repaired, which would cost as much as a new pavilion hospital in a suitable locality.

The marine hospital at Detroit, Mich., is also a badly arranged and inconvenient building, without ventilation, and so radically defective that it would cost more to remodel and re-arrange it than to erect a suitable building. The property is now a part of the city of Detroit, is valuable, and I believe could be sold for a sum sufficient to obtain a suitable site and erect a satisfactory building.

The marine hospital at Louisville, Ky., is too small. It is, however, built on a large and desirable lot, and can easily be extended and made one of the best and most valuable hospitals in the possession of the Government. As Louisville will, in all probability, remain one of the principal depots of marine patients, I would earnestly recommend this improvement to the favorable consideration of the Department.

I desire once more to call attention to the quarantine warehouse below New Orleans, and to the station at Philadelphia, known as the Lazaretto, both of which involve considerable expense to maintain. It does not appear to me that there is any greater necessity for such buildings at those points than at others, and that if necessary there, they are equally so at each of the principal ports. Indeed, an appropriation for a quarantine warehouse at the port of New York was made December 16, 1864, but was carried to the surplus fund, the amount being considered inadequate for the purpose. It appears to me, however, that, as quarantine is a State and not a national institution, the States should furnish the necessary means to carry out their own legislation, and that the Department should not be called upon to furnish warehouses for the storage of goods quarantined under State regulations. I would therefore recommend that authority be obtained to dispose of the buildings in question, or that some definite system be adopted.

I desire to call attention to the fact that the continued growth in the business of the Treasury Department renders it indispensably necessary that action be taken in regard to the rebuilding of the east front of the Treasury building. The Statistical Bureau has been removed from the building since the date of my last report, but the space so obtained has been absorbed without providing any material relief, and the removal of some of the larger and more important bureaus cannot be long delayed. It may seem an exaggeration, but it is nevertheless a fact, that the Treasury building has not more than half the capacity that is required to accommodate, in a proper manner, all of its different bureaus. Of these, however, the Second and Sixth Auditers and the Coast Survey are well provided for in other buildings, and need not, at this time, be considered. The rebuilding of the east and center wings would add very materially to the size of the building, increasing the accommodations in that portion about one-third. It may be added that a decision of this question, whether favorable or adverse, should be made at the earliest possible moment, inasmuch as it seriously affects the interests of a large number of property-owners who are naturally unwilling to improve their property until a decision is made, as it necessarily involves a change in the line of Fifteenth street, between Pennsylvania and New York avenues, as I have heretofore explained. I would also recommend that authority be obtained for the erection of a building for the accommodation of the Note-Printing Bureau and for the records of the Department, plans and estimates for which were submitted at the last session of Congress. Should this be authorized it would provide, in addition to the improvements heretofore indicated, sufficient space for all the legitimate wants of the Department for many years to come, and is, in my opinion, an improvement second in importance to none now under consideration by the Department.

I desire once more to call attention to the necessity for increased accommodations for the customs department in New York City. The apprehensions expressed in my previous reports have been verified, it having been found necessary to rent buildings for the accommodations of a portion of the officers and clerks. The present custom-house building is not half the size necessary for the proper transaction of the business of that port. The officers and employés of the Department are packed into rooms destitute of ventilation and deficient in light. It is, under such circumstances, impossible for them to perform their duties in a prompt, accurate, and satisfactory manner, and I have no hesitation in expressing the opinion that a great portion of the delays and errors in the transaction of the public business in that city is attributable to the unsuitable character and insufficiency of the accommodation. The building was not erected for a custom-house, and cannot be made convenient or suitable for the purpose. It is, at best, but a temporary expedient, and should be considered as such. I therefore desire to renew my recommendations that immediate steps be taken to secure, if possible, from the city of New York, the whole of the Battery, or such portion thereof as may be found necessary after a careful investigation of the subject, believing, as I do, that there is no other spot in the city of sufficient capacity, or so well adapted to the purpose, or that can be obtained at a reasonable price. I am aware that the project involves a large expenditure, but it should be remembered that more than two-thirds of the entire customs revenue of the country is collected at this port, and that it would not, at the highest estimate, require more than the revenue collected in two weeks to erect a suitable building; in addition to which the custom-house property, the assay-office property, and the old post-office site could be sold for a sum which would go very far toward defraying, if it did not meet, the entire expenditure. In this connection I desire to renew my recommendation that a suitable appraisers' store be erected in the same locality, believing, as I do, that it is of the utmost importance to concentrate, as far as possible, the entire customs department in one locality. I desire to call special attention to the urgent necessity that exists for immediate action in regard to the barge-office in New York. A fine granite dock and pier was erected some years since, but no appropriation has been made for the building. The surveyor of the port reports that it is impossible for him to enforce the revenue laws in a proper manner with the means at his command, and strongly urges the immediate erection of the building. I have examined the question fully and concur with the views expressed by the surveyor, and would recommend that an appropriation be obtained to carry them into effect. I have, heretofore, called attention to the unsuitable and unsatisfactory character of the accommodations provided for the appraisers' department in the city of New York, and to the excessive rental demanded and necessarily paid for the same. The lease having expired, proposals were invited for the rental to the Department of a suitable building, and, after a careful and exhaustive examination of the properties offered, the block of buildings bounded by West, Hubert, Washington, and Laight streets was selected. The buildings in question are probably better adapted to the wants of the Government than any other in the city of New York, and can be made entirely suitable by a comparatively moderate expenditure. The locality, though not, in my opinion, equal to the battery, is a good one, and convenient to or readily accessible from every foreign steamship line sailing from New York, and is in every respect superior to the building now occupied. I had previously called the attention of the Department to the great danger to be apprehended from fire in the building at present occupied. These apprehensions were verified on the 20th of July last, when the upper stories and a large amount of valuable goods were destroyed; a danger which will be avoided in the new building, which is fire-proof.

The public building at Pensacola, Fla., requires immediate enlargement and repairs to meet the ordinary wants of the Government in that city. I have caused a careful examination of the matter to be made, and have prepared an estimate of the cost of the alterations and repairs necessary to put the building in proper condition, and strongly urge that authority be obtained to proceed with the work. The building is at present occupied by the customs department, the court-house, and the post-office, neither of which has sufficient room for the proper transaction of its business. Indeed, the building is no larger than could be used to advantage by the custom-house alone, and as there appears to be no possibility of renting suitable accommodations in the city, I earnestly recommend it to the favorable consideration of the Department.

An appropriation of $150,000 toward the purchase of a site for the public building at Albany, N. Y., was made on condition that the city should contribute, if necessary, an equal sum. It has been found impossible, after careful investigations and protracted negotiations, to purchase any suitable property for the amount of the appropriation, or to obtain any effective co-operation from the city authorities. I recommend that the Department be authorized to purchase a suitable site, as there appears to be no prospect that the city will take any satisfactory action.

I have also to call attention to the necessity for extending the custom-house at Detroit, Mich. It is much too small, and the necessities of the service demand that provision should be made for its extension to at least double its present capacity.

I desire to call attention to the fact that, while the business of this office has increased beyond all expectation, it is not in arrears, and that all claims that have arisen have been promptly settled. At the time I assumed the duties of this office, the unsettled claims, many of which dated from 1842, amounted to upwards of $2,000,000, of which claims amounting to $1,509,360.31 have been carefully examined, and, after long and arduous investigation, adjusted by the allowance of $482,129.12. In this connection I desire to call the attention of the Department to the fact that, though the annual expenditures of this office have increased since 1865 from $742,316.16 to $9,084,550.46, (exclusive of an unexpended balance of $3,962,190.70,) the claims for extras and additional compensation have steadily diminished and are now nearly nominal; and that, while suits in the Court of Claims were formerly frequent and usually successful, no suit has been brought against the Government for work performed under my administration, and that the comparative cost of work has, at the same time, been decreased. Great difficulty was formerly experienced in making contracts for material and labor at advantageous rates and in enforcing the same. This was particularly the case in regard to the contracts for stone work, which were usually extravagant in price and the subject of disputes and litigations which, as a rule, resulted adversely to the Government. The experience of the last four years has demonstrated that the system recommended by me in my previous reports, and now in operation on the public buildings at New York, Boston, Chicago, Saint Louis, and on the new State, War, and Navy Department's building in this city, and popularly known as the percentage system, is the fairest and most equitable yet devised as the basis for contracts in which labor is the principal factor, and in which the quality of the work is determined by the amount of labor expended, or which cannot be accurately specified, or, as a consequence, exacted, such as stone-cutting, plumbing, and other similar work; and it has proved, in spite of the predictions, misrepresentations, and clamor of interested parties, to be the fairest and most economical system for such contracts that has been devised. Prior to the adoption of this system such contracts were the inevitable and usually prolific sources of controversies, claims, and protracted litigation, in many instances the claims amounting to more than the original contract, while the work was, as a rule, unsatisfactory in character and extravagant in cost. In this connection a few illustrations may possibly be of interest.

The custom-houses at Buffalo and Oswego, N. Y., were erected, under contract, by O. B. and O. S. Latham. The item of cut-stone work for both buildings amounted to but $54,962. The former building was, however, subsequently extended, which increased the value of the cut-stone work, at contract prices, to $69,121.60, which was accordingly paid, but failed to satisfy the contractors, who applied to the Court of Claims for relief, basing their claims on the following allegations: That they were the lowest bidders for the custom-house at Buffalo, and as the stone submitted with their proposal was unsatisfactory to the Department, that they voluntarily agreed to furnish the same stone that was offered by the next lowest bidder, Mr. C. A. Jones, of Rochester, N. Y., (whose bid was but $16,293 in excess of theirs;) that in executing their contract they found the stone in question was harder to procure and more costly and difficult to work than the stone on which they based their bid; that their contract did not require them to lay the stone on the quarry-bed, (though it did require them to lay and cut it to the satisfaction of the superintendent;) that they were required to finish a portion of the stone with patent axe-work, and that the ashler in the rear of the building was changed from random to specific lengths. The Court of Claims, after a protracted investigation, allowed them the additional sum of $31,397.69, their equitable right to which may be inferred from the remarks of Chief Justice Casey in referring to this award, on a subsequent occasion, in which he used the following language:

We have carefully considered the additional testimony submitted by the claimants on the subject of an allowance for a change of stone on the ground of representations alleged to have been made by Major Bowman to the claimants at the time of the letting of the Buffalo house. The evidence has failed to convince us that the claim is well founded. The conversation detailed took place between Major Bowman, Mr. Latham, and Mr. C. A. Jones, and it is impossible to say whether Mr. Latham, in agreeing to adopt the Peninsula stone, acted upon the opinion of Major Bowman or Mr. Jones, or, discarding both, was guided by his own judgment in the premises. Nor is it of any moment to inquire how he arrived at his conclusion. It was well known to Mr. Latham that Major Bowman was a public officer, having specific duties to perform and limited powers to exercise, and that it came neither within the range of his duties nor the scope of his authority to furnish information to bidders in relation to the cost and facility of obtaining the material out of which the building was to be constructed. If the bidder sought for it from him, or he voluntarily gave it, whether true or not, could affect the Government no more than the same representations made by any other individual.

We have, too, the singular fact that on the 7th of April, 1856, after the claimants had procured a large amount of Peninsula stone, and had a considerable quantity of it cut and dressed for the Buffalo house, they entered into a contract for building the Oswego custom-house of the same material. If it was difficult to procure and expensive to work, they must then have been fully aware of these facts. They had also been informed the previous September, that they would be required to lay this stone on the quarry-bed. Taking all the circumstances together we are unable to find anything in this record to support the claims for an allowance for a change of stone upon the ground of fraud, misrepresentation, or mistake. If we were to follow the opinion and theory of the witnesses for the plaintiff alone, it would result in an award for the claimants, according to the statement presented by their counsel, as items alleged to be proved by the opinions of their witnesses, of $256,608.33. This is claimed as extra compensation upon work which the claimants originally contracted to perform, and furnish the material, for $69,121.60. And this, too, it will be remembered, without any change having been made in the size of the building, the kind or amount of material, the plan or arrangement of the structures, or the general character and style of the work; but for placing the same material in the building in a different position, scaling it to regular systematic sizes, and placing on about one-half the exterior surface a different finish from that provided by the contracts and specifications. This result is attained by assuming the speculative values of the witnesses as the actual cost of the work, and deducting therefrom the amount received under the contract, leaving the difference we have stated above. Upon this statement it will naturally strike any intelligent mind that either the contract price was too small or the extras claimed are too large.

A number of the plaintiffs' principal witnesses are re-examined, and, without professing or attempting to give any new facts or data, restate their opinions and calculations in new phrases and in greater detail. Some of this testimony, we are compelled by law, is in a very objectionable form, consisting of affirmative answers in monosyllables to leading direct questions, proposing different aspects of the general theory upon which the case had been previously submitted. * * * * The witnesses on the other side testify that, in their opinion, the difference in the two modes of performing the work was but trifling, and that a few thousand dollars would meet the whole expense. When we find gentlemen of the highest skill in their professions and trades, and whose characters stand unimpeached, differing to the amount of $250,000 in their estimates and opinions upon this case, it must necessarily impair our confidence in the value of said testimony.

This statement of the learned Chief Justice shows conclusively that the award of the court was not based upon its convictions, but upon a weight of testimony which it could not legally ignore. The award of the court failed, however, to satisfy the contractors any more than the decision of the Department, and they appealed to Congress, which overruled the decision of the Court of Claims and increased the allowance to $74,583.37, which was paid to them on March 9, 1863. It would naturally be supposed that such an allowance for extras on contracts amounting to $60,121.60 would have satisfied any one. It did not, however, satisfy these enterprising contractors, who returned to Congress with a claim for $25,625.22, being the difference between the amount recommended by the Committee on Claims in the House of Representatives and the amount approved by the Committee on Claims of the Senate and appropriated by Congress. This claim was, however, rejected, and the stone-contract was supposed to be settled. Such was not, however, the opinion of the contractors, who again applied to the Court of Claims for the sum of $43,631.26, being the difference between the currency in which the appropriation for their relief was paid them and coin, to which they claimed to be entitled by their contract. This demand was rejected, the opinion being delivered by the Chief Justice in the following language:

An award made by Congress upon a claimant's demand should be paid in the kind of money then used. Such an act cannot relate back to the contract or be construed to make an assignment of a special kind of money. All the work done under the contracts had been paid for. Nor was the suit upon which the award was made based upon them, but upon the whole work as a quantum meruit. The report of the damages in this case was made on the 5th day of May, 1862, after the passage of the act authorizing Treasury notes, and a payment in that currency would, we think, have discharged the debt. ($31,397.00.) But what makes the case still stronger against the claimants, in our opinion, is that, being dissatisfied with our views and the principles upon which we assessed and by which we measured the damages, they induced Congress to reverse our finding and assess their damages on a quantum meruit. This gave them more than double the amount they were entitled to under the rule of damages fixed by the court. But it also put the contracts entirely out of the case.

It was supposed that this decision would be final, and that the Department had at last succeeded in paying for the stone-work of the custom-houses at Buffalo and Oswego. This does not, however, appear to be the case, the contractors having since the date of my last report again presented their little bill to the Department. The account stands as follows:

Original contracts and extras	$69,121.60
Extra compensation allowed by Congress	74,583.37
Total amount actually paid	143,704.97
Claims still pending	69,596.48
Total value of stone-work at claimants' value	219,301.45

Is it under the circumstances surprising that gentlemen who have once transacted business with the Government on such a basis are opposed to a system of contracts under which such claims could by no possibility arise?

Another illustration, of a different character, may be found in the contract for the granite-work of the custom-house at New Orleans, La., an extract from which will suffice, and is as follows:

And the party of the first part agrees to pay or cause to be paid for 90,500 superficial feet of ashler at 97¼ cents per superficial foot; and for all other granite required to complete said building agreeably to the design of the architect, prices with reference to the weight, form, and finish of such other granite shall be found to bear the same relation to the then market value or price thereof that 97¼ cents per superficial foot, the contract price for the aforesaid ashler, shall be found to bear to the then market value or price of similar ashler after such other granite shall have been received at the levee at New Orleans.

This contract appears to have been prepared either as a mathematical puzzle or to provide a basis of settlement that could not be controlled or supervised by the accounting officers of this Department. If the latter, it was undoubtedly a success, more especially as there was no market value for similar granite at New Orleans, the custom-house being the only granite building in that city.

The following extract from the contract for the marble-work of the custom-house at Charleston, S. C., though not open to the objections of the previous one, is an illustration of the complicated and intricate methods adopted to determine the value of labor and material, and is selected as a fair specimen of that class of contracts:

That the said party of the first part hereby covenants and agrees to pay to the said party of the second part therefor, agreeably to the stipulations of the aforesaid articles of agreement, the following sums, viz: For all plain, straight, square ashler not exceeding 6 inches bed or build, one dollar and thirty-eight cents per superficial foot, ($1.38,) and for each additional inch of bed or build of said ashler an additional sum of fifteen cents per superficial foot, and all plain work shall be considered of ashler; for columns cut plain, in pieces of not less than 5 feet and not exceeding 7 feet in length, five dollars and twenty-five cents ($5.25) per superficial foot, and for fluted columns five cents per superficial inch; for molded capitals and bases, seven (7) dollars per superficial foot; for Ionic capitals, eight dollars and fifty cents (8.50) per superficial foot; for cornice and its architrave and frieze, seven (7) dollars per superficial foot; for floor-tiles, wrought and finished, of a thickness not exceeding 2 inches, ninety-two (92) cents per superficial foot; for roof-tiles sawed in slabs not exceeding three inches in thickness, one dollar ($1) per superficial foot for entire upper surface measure, and forty (40) cents per superficial foot for cutting on the same; for all circular and beveled work forty per centum additional upon the prices for straight work; and for all moulding and panelling, also all carving and ornamental work not herein otherwise provided for, such additional sums shall be paid as the Supervising Architect or the duly authorized agent of the party of the first part shall ascertain to be its fair cost, increased by fifteen per cent. The number of superficial feet in chamfered or beveled quoins, and other stone that shows face or faces, head or heads, shall be determined by the longitudinal vertical section of the face and head or other cut part that shows, for which we are to be paid 93 cents per superficial foot for the first 8 inches of bed or build, and an additional sum of fifteen cents per superficial foot for each additional inch of bed or build, the number of which is also to be ascertained from the longitudinal vertical section as above.

For chamfers 2 inches on and 2 inches in, sixty cents per lineal foot.

For all ornamental work, to be first made up as plain work, then the cost of the ornamental work, viz, carving and molding, paneling, &c., to be increased by fifteen per cent.

For all straight steps and platforms we are to be paid ninety-three cents per superficial foot for the first 8 inches of bed or build, with fifteen cents per superficial foot additional for each aditional inch of bed or build, that is, as we have calculated them. An inspector to be appointed by the Treasury, to inspect and measure the stone at the quarry.

This contract, unlike the one previously quoted, may not be considered a fraudulent one, but it is undoubtedly extravagant, and, as such, has been canceled, as explained in a previous report. It is, however, noticeable in other respects, viz, that the contract was evidently drawn by the contractors and not by the officers of the Department, as is evidenced by the frequent use of the word "we," which could not properly appear in such a document; and that the value of the work being necessarily determined by a professional measurer, it was beyond the power of the Supervising Architect, or of the accounting officers of the Department, to revise the accounts or control the cost of the work. It will be seen that under this and similar contracts the prices were actually fixed without recourse to the Department by a subordinate of the Supervising Architect, whose dictum on similar expenditures in this district was also made final by the act of August 31, 1852, to which I desire to call attention as a remarkable illustration of a class of enactments which, while apparently imposing additional safeguards, offer inducements for fraud and render detection practically impossible.

I desire once more to call attention to the act of July 12, 1870, in regard to unexpended balances on public works, and to say that a careful and thorough test of the law has justified all of the objections heretofore made thereto, and has demonstrated that the only manner in which its conditions can be complied with is by the suspension of work at the close of the fiscal year, and until the accounts can be settled and adjusted. It should be remembered, also, that the fiscal year terminates on the 30th of June, in the midst of the building season, and that such a course would involve an enormous cost and be of no benefit whatever. The operation of this law has directly increased the cost of work and the duties of this office. It has complicated the accounts; it has necessitated an increase in the number of clerks who examine and adjust them, and, unless repealed or modified in this particular, will render the accounts for works extending over many years so complicated as to make it impossible to settle them within any reasonable time, and has, in addition, rendered it difficult to exercise a proper supervision over the cost of the work. It has, also, in many instances compelled a suspension of work, though the amount necessary for the completion of the building had been appropriated. It is also oppressive, the Department being in many instances unable to pay creditors whose accounts are adjusted—whose claims are just and indispensable—even when ample funds have been appropriated for the purpose. I therefore earnestly recommend that the repeal of so much of the law as relates to public improvements be obtained, feeling assured that the interests of the Government will be promoted thereby.

In conclusion I desire to call the attention of the Department to the enormous amount of business that has been transacted in this office during the past fiscal year, and the inadequate force authorized for the purpose, as well as the insufficiency of the salaries paid. The hours of the Department in all other bureaus are from 9 o'clock a. m. to 3 o'clock p. m. The hours in this bureau have been necessarily extended until 4 o'clock, and in the case of the principal officers and clerks have seldom terminated before 6, and often at a much later hour.

I desire once more to call attention to the eight-hour law, believing it to be alike injurious to the best interests of the Government and to the workmen themselves. It frequently happens that mechanics and laborers employed by the Government and those employed by contractors are required to work on the same building, and at the same time. Those employed by the Government work but eight hours, while those employed by the contractors work ten hours per diem. This causes much feeling, and it needs no argument to prove that it is unjust, and that the mechanic who performs ten hours' work is taxed for the benefit of the more favored workman who has friends and influence sufficient to obtain employment for him on Government work. It is also in direct violation of the principles of civil-service reform, inasmuch as it converts the employment of mechanics and laborers from a business question of competency and industry to a question of political patronage and personal influence. I do not hesitate to say that it has cost the Government millions of dollars, without benefiting the mechanic or laborer in the slightest degree, or, as far as I am advised, any other persons than perambulating and paid agitators, or the claim-agents who have instigated litigations and claims for their own benefit. The law has been fairly and fully tested; the experience of this Department, as well as of private establishments, has shown that it is not only impossible for a man to perform as much labor in eight hours as in ten, but that he absolutely performs less work per hour under the eight-hour system. It is a matter of neither interest nor importance to me whether mechanics and laborers perform eight or ten hours' work, provided the hours of labor are the same on public as on private works. It is, however, impossible to conduct work in a proper manner under a system that increases the compensation of mechanics and laborers employed by the Government 20 per cent. above market-rates, and thus makes them a favored class, without, as I have previously shown, obtaining any advantage therefrom. I would therefore recommend that such modification of the law be obtained as will entitle all persons employed by the Government to the highest market-rates for their labor and the benefit of all local rules and regulations in regard to the hours of labor, or otherwise. If this rule is, however, to be the permanent policy of the Government, and its mechanics and laborers are to be compensated at the rate of 20 per cent. above the highest market-rates, I see no reason why officers, clerks, and other employés of the Government should not be paid by the same rule. Under the present system gentlemen of education who occupy positions of trust and great pecuniary responsibility in the different bureaus actually receive less than mechanics' wages, and are discriminated against in favor of men who, as a rule, exhibit little interest in the performance of their duties and have no responsibility whatever. It is also a fact that many mechanics receive, under the present system, not only more than their foremen and master-mechanics, but more than the superintendent of the work on which they are engaged, the latter classes being allowed no compensation for extra labor performed.

In conclusion I desire to tender to the Secretary my most sincere thanks for the kindness with which I have been treated, and the support I have received, without which it would have been impossible for me to perform my duties. I also desire to express my appreciation of the manner in which the chief clerk, A. G. Mills, esq., has performed the very arduous duties of his office, and of the efficient assistance he has rendered me, and to express my entire satisfaction with the manner in which the labors of this office have been performed by the gentlemen connected with it, and to tender them my sincere thanks for the services they have rendered, and for the hearty co-operation I have received from them.

Respectfully submitted,

A. B. MULLETT,
Supervising Architect.

Hon. WM. A. RICHARDSON,
Secretary of the Treasury.

REPORT

OF

THE SECRETARY OF WAR.

WAR DEPARTMENT,
November 24, 1873.

Mr. PRESIDENT: I deem it proper in the commencement of this report to make a statement of the estimates of appropriations for the Department for the next fiscal year, comparing them with the appropriations for the current year, and giving the reasons for the change.

The estimates for military purposes for the year ending June 30, 1874, were $33,826,378.78. The estimates for the same purpose for the year ending June 30, 1875, are $34,410,722.89; the excess of the next year over the current one being $584,344.11. The appropriation for military purposes for the year ending June 30, 1874, were $32,917,971.37.

It has been the custom of Congress from time to time to reduce the estimates of the Department. I have endeavored, aided by the officers of the Department and of the Army, to keep the expenditures within the limit prescribed by Congress, but experience has shown that the amounts previously asked for, based on data carefully prepared by the chiefs of bureaus, after ample consideration, were necessary for the management of the Department.

In addition to the usual estimates already named, the following are submitted for such action as Congress may deem proper to take:

Armament of forts $1,449,550
Estimates for engineer purposes.. 20,459,396

It will be observed that among the estimates for the War Department for the next as well as the preceding years, many appropriations are asked for which should not be classed under those for the support of the Army proper: For instance, those for the observation and report of storms; the Freedmen's Hospital; the settlement of claims for horses lost in the military service; the collection and payment of bounty to colored soldiers; military telegraph lines in different parts of the country; refunding to States expenses incurred in raising volunteers; signal stations at light-houses; arming and equipping the militia; and numerous other subjects of like character, demand expenditures which cannot legitimately be charged as being for the current uses of the military establishment.

A critical examination of these expenditures, some of them authorized by Congress without any recommendation on the part of this Department, will show that the total expenditures are largely in excess of the amount absolutely necessary for the actual requirements of the Army itself.

. I refer especially to this subject in order that it may be understood that a great part of the money appropriated for this Department by Congress is for expenditures similar to those named, and should not be considered as required for the support of the Army, but arises from the trusts imposed upon the military branch of the Government in the execution of works of internal improvement, for the benefit of the people.

The act of March 3, 1873, for the establishment of a military prison, made no appropriation to meet any of the expenses necessary to carry it into effect. In order, however, that no time might be lost, a preliminary board, composed only of Army officers, was constituted to collect information and material for commencing more definite labor upon the plan so soon as Congress should appropriate the means. This board, in its investigations, has succeeded in doing even more than was anticipated; and, fortunately, two gentlemen from civil life, who have devoted much time and zealous study to the subject of reformatory prison discipline, have been found willing to give a share of their time gratuitously, until the appropriation shall be made, to the work of preparing a plan and regulations for the military prison. This has enabled me to carry out the provisions of the second section of the act, by appointing the board therein prescribed. Their report will form the subject of a future special communication to Congress.

It is very difficult, under existing laws, to supply the Army with field-musicians, two of which are allowed to each company. As this is an essential part of the military establishment better facilities for obtaining musicians should be afforded, by the passage of an act to authorize the enlistment of boys not under twelve years of age, always with the consent of parents or guardians. This provision did exist until, probably through inadvertence, the law of 1864, against enlistment of minors, put an end to it.

It is unnecessary to allude to notorious cases of efficient service by music boys, even on the field of battle, to illustrate their perfect competency for all the duties required of musicians. While they make the best musicians, they generally, at more advanced age, have become most valuable non-commissioned officers as the fruit of their early training. This plan has, too, the merit of being a most useful charity, for it would provide for many sons of old soldiers, living and dead, who now are without aim or object in life, and in danger of becoming worthless men, but who, if enlisted, would have the benefit not only of tuition in music, but also in the useful common branches of education taught at the depot school.

The subject of the discharge of minors who have enlisted in the Army has ever been a perplexing one. The most stringent prohibitions have been laid upon recruiting-officers, and whenever a minor has passed from the rendezvous to the depot, and is there detected by the examining board, he is sure to be at once discharged. In spite of every precaution a large number of young men, minors in the eye of the law, but actually men who have been practically their own masters for a considerable time, do pass themselves as of full age, freely take the oath to that effect, as embodied in the contract of enlistment, and are transported, at considerable expense, to regiments. Here, on the least dissatisfaction, or after commission of some crime involving punishment, they forthwith write to the parents, who have hitherto, perhaps, bestowed but little care upon them, and a moving appeal is made to the Department for their discharge. Since the passage of the act of May 15, 1872, the Department has judged that it had no discretion left, and when the proof of minority is clear, and the consent of parent or guardian has not been obtained, discharge is invariably given. Since the passage of the act referred to, and up to June 30, 1873, 296 applications for discharge from this cause have been received. Great expense to the Government, as well as frequent evasion of punishment, and consequent disorganization of necessary military discipline, is thereby caused; nor is the ostensible object of the parents to recover the child effected, because the latter is discharged hundreds of miles from home, and even if disposed to return, which is seldom the case, has not the pecuniary means. The recruiting-officers are charged with the expenses of enlistment of minors when clearly guilty of want of due care; but it is exceedingly difficult in many instances to ascertain the true age of a man, even with such critical examination as recruits are subjected to. Thus, while the Government is imposed upon, under an oath, by the recruit, while it, in good faith, feeds, clothes, transports to a regiment, and often pays him, it is by present legislation left without protection or remedy against the fraud. The recruit obtains all the benefit, sometimes is transported to a region where he wishes to settle, and then obtains a discharge with perfect impunity for his fraud.

It is suggested that some action be taken toward the passage of a positive law to provide for the punishment of recruits who have deceived the recruiting-officers by falsely swearing to their age or physical condition. In my judgment he should be immediately turned over to the proper tribunal, and the United States law-officer in whose district the recruit may have committed the offense should be required to prosecute him for the false oath he has taken and for the great expense he has given the Government.

The practice, which prevailed to a considerable extent, of Army officers visiting the seat of Government during the session of Congress, attempting to influence legislation by interviewing members of Congress, and presenting business which should only be brought to their attention through the head of the Executive Department, became such a serious evil that on March 15, 1873, I caused an order to be issued directing that no officer, either active or retired, shall, directly or indirectly, without being called upon by proper authority, solicit, suggest, or recommend action by members of Congress for or against military affairs. The necessity for this order was apparent. Members of Congress have frequently brought the subject to my attention, and have made complaint, very justly, of the persistent efforts made with them personally to influence their views on legislation. The order, as it itself says, is not intended to preclude officers from illustrating or expounding a measure before Congress which may have received the favor or sanction of the President, Secretary of War, or the General of the Army. The experience of officers when so used is and will be viewed as valuable, but it was and is intended to restrain officers from urging their views in an improper manner upon members of Congress, and in consuming the time of those intrusted with the necessary legislation of the Government. That order will be enforced so far as it lies within my power and authority to accomplish it.

I had the satisfaction during the spring, in company with the Lieutenant-General of the Army, to make a tour of inspection through the Department of Texas, and to visit many of the posts located on the frontier in that region.

My attention was particularly directed to the efficiency and good conduct of the troops there stationed. Situated as many of the posts are, remote from the comforts of civilization, it was a matter of great satisfaction that discipline was observed, and that all the requirements of good military service were strictly carried out. At several of these posts where both white and colored soldiers were stationed, the general good conduct and fine military appearance of all the troops composing the garrisons were prominent to a marked degree.

In section 24 of the act of July 15, 1870, the pay of officers of the Army was established, and provision was made that the sums therein specified should be in full of all commutation of quarters, fuel, forage, servant hire and clothing, longevity rations, and all allowances of every name and nature whatever, and should be paid monthly by the paymaster. Further legislation is necessary to define the scope of this provision, whether it is intended to include certain things, such as transportation in kind of officers' servants, transportation of officers' horses and baggage, authorized in regulations before its passage, but not held to be emoluments, or does it have reference simply to the money allowances then received by officers of the Army. If the former construction is to be given it, it then really discontinues the allowance of servants altogether, which all former laws and regulations have encouraged, and would often unfit an officer for effective service by depriving him of transportation for authorized horses and baggage that often could not be purchased or obtained at his new station. All these have been furnished by the Government from its foundation, and for its own interests, primarily, the benefit to the officer being but incidental, and while it is presumed that the clause referred to intended to embrace in a salary all that had been included in money allowances, in providing for the compensation of officers of the Army, a distinct enunciation of its meaning by Congress is desirable. I deemed it necessary, on the 25th day of February, 1873, to issue the following order in connection with this subject, which will continue as the rule unless further legislation is had:

The payment of rent, or any allowance for fuel or quarters of officers' servants, is hereby prohibited until more specific legislation shall sanction it.

During the past year the five Inspectors-general of the Army have been exclusively subject to the orders of the Secretary of War and the General of the Army, and have made careful and thorough inspections of the South, the Departments of Texas, of the Missouri, of the Gulf, of Arizona, of Dakota, and of the Columbia, excepting Alaska. In the Departments of Arizona, Texas, Dakota, and the Columbia, thorough examination was made into the condition of the personnel and material of the Army at all the remote and widely-dispersed posts, stations, and depots within the limits of those departments, (with the exception of Alaska,) embracing one hundred and seventeen military posts, garrisoned by eighteen regiments of infantry, seventeen companies of artillery, and eight regiments of cavalry. Besides this, other minor inspections and investigations have, from time to time, been made by the officers of this corps, involving voluminous reports, which have been made without any expenditure for clerical assistance. Scrutinizing examinations have been made by the Inspectors-general of the accounts of all officers who have made important disbursements of public money during the year. The funds received and expended by them, with the balances reported due the United States, have been carefully verified by official statements received from the Treasury Department and depositories, and under this system it is hardly possible that a defalcation or fraud on the part of disbursing officers of this Department can escape timely detection.

The assistant inspectors-general have been attached to the headquarters of the various military divisions, and they, as well as several officers who have been temporarily assigned to duty in some of the remote departments as acting assistant inspectors-general, have been actively and usefully engaged in the duties pertaining to their positions.

Since the close of the war, in the Quartermaster's Department, much time and labor have been bestowed upon the examination and settlement of the accounts of officers for disbursements made during the rebellion and since its close. Most of these accounts have been adjusted, and the accounts of disbursing officers of that Department are now examined promptly as received. Within the past two years I have caused the forms and methods of 'business in this Department to be simplified, to the advantage of the service and the relief of officers.

Much difficulty is experienced in keeping the expenses of the Quartermaster's Department within the amounts appropriated by Congress, and so apparent was it during the past fiscal year that the appropriation for barracks and quarters would not admit of any expenditure from that appropriation beyond the payment of rent of offices and hire of quarters for troops, that it was found necessary early in the spring to entirely arrest any work upon the repair and construction of barracks and quarters. Notwithstanding this necessary and sharp measure, which involved much inconvenience to the troops, crowded into buildings much in need of repair, or cantoned in tents and huts too much exposed to the inclemency of the weather, the liabilities have to a small amount exceeded the sum appropriated.

It is necessary that I should ask the attention of Congress to the difficulties of keeping accounts, and of paying for supplies and services, which arise under the operation of the act approved July 12, 1870. The act in its operation requires every disbursing officer to keep a separate and distinct set of accounts under every head of appropriation, and to keep a balance of money on hand to meet the demands under each head, thereby compelling officers to keep to their credit at depositories much larger balances than heretofore. A remedy for this is to make the appropriation for the Quartermaster's Department under one head as a single appropriation, requiring, as now, that the estimates upon which the appropriation is based shall be submitted in detail. No benefit can arise in practice from the system of keeping separate heads of appropriation in this Department, while its existence gives many occasions for error and mistakes, and is a burden upon the officer who is required to disburse the public money, as well as upon the Treasury. The evils of the present system are fully set forth in the report of the Committee on Expenditures in the War Department, made to Congress at its last session.

As many lieutenants of the line are often required to assume the labors and responsibilities of acting assistant quartermasters, it is recommended that an allowance of $10 per month be made by law to officers so detailed, as a moderate compensation to them for the risk as well as the labor in disbursing public money and keeping and distributing stores.

Of the fifty railroads which, at the close of the war, under executive orders, purchased from this Department railroad material to the appraised value of over $7,500,000, thirty of them have paid their debts in full. The remaining twenty are still in our debt to the amount of $4,658,924.07. The total amount collected from these sales, with interest and expenses, has thus far been $5,116,605.53.

I recommend the passage of a law which will enable the Department to collect from the Post-Office Department the postal earnings of several of these delinquent railroads. The bonds of the roads given at the time of purchase pledge them to use these earnings in liquidation of their debts, but they refuse or persistently neglect to give to the Post-

26 Ab

master-General the necessary formal orders to turn over the funds to this Department.

Ten thousand dollars was appropriated during the last year for the prosecution of the work on the artesian well at Fort D. A. Russell. Since then considerable progress has been made in that work. It has now reached a depth of 1,005 feet. The work has now for some hundreds of feet been carried through a stratum of clay, and there is good reason to hope that when the clay is pierced the water will be reached, and a strong flowing well developed. From the importance to the people of the Territories of Colorado, Wyoming, Montana, and Dakota, which a series of flowing wells would have upon the development of their material interests, I recommend that an appropriation be made to continue the present experiment.

Under the provisions of the appropriation act approved March 3, 1873, advertisement was made for bids to provide head-stones for the graves of deceased soldiers in the national cemeteries. Eighty bids were received and opened in public by the Quartermaster-General on the 6th of September.

The advertisement called for bids for furnishing head-stones of gray granite and white marble of a specified quality, as these materials, in my judgment, best fulfilled the requirements of the law in respect to "decency, durability, and cheapness."

A careful examination of the bids resulted in an award of contract for granite head-stones for the National Cemetery at Fredericksburgh, Va. For all the other national cemeteries contracts have been awarded to the four lowest bidders for white marble head-stones. The responsibility of the bondsmen of these contractors is required to be certified to by the United States district judge, or by the collector of internal revenue of the district in which they reside.

A small slab, four inches thick, has been prescribed for the known, and a block six inches square for the unknown dead. The former will number about 148,000, and the latter about 105,000.

Particular care has been taken to have these head-stones *permanent* when once erected. The entire cost of the slabs and blocks, under the contracts as awarded, should they be entered into by the successful bidders, will amount to $770,045.48.

Should, however, any of the parties to whom awards have been made fail to enter into the contracts prescribed, none of the contracts will be executed unless the whole work can be contracted for within the appropriation of $1,000,000, the limit prescribed by the law.

The appropriation of $100,000 made by Congress in the act approved March 3, 1873, for the erection of a depot at San Antonio, Tex., has not been expended, nor have any decided steps looking to the erection of the buildings contemplated been taken. A personal visit to San Antonio last spring, and consultation with the Lieutenant-General of the Army and other responsible officers, having satisfied me that no necessity exists for the expenditure of the money, and that the small force that will hereafter be required at that place could, economically, be provided for by rented or leased buildings. I recommend that the sum appropriated be used for the rent or purchase of such sites of posts in Texas as may be found to be actually needed for military purposes.

The report of the Commissary-General shows that the average cost of the Army-ration for the year has been seventeen cents and forty-eight hundredths, showing a trifling increase in cost over that of the previous year.

It is recommended that an act be passed authorizing the issue of tobacco to enlisted men of the Army, as a component part of the Army-ration, as near as may be in amount to that authorized to be sold to them.

Under the act approved March 3, 1873, to provide for the better care and protection of subsistence supplies, there have been appointed one hundred and forty-nine commissary-sergeants, who have been assigned to military posts. A considerable number of them have been in the performance of their duties a sufficient time to evidence to the Department the benefit that was anticipated from a body of experienced and worthy non-commissioned officers being in charge of this class of public property.

The Surgeon-General reports the following distribution of the first part of the Medical and Surgical History of the War, viz:

Sent to congressional committees as specimens....	12
Sent Senators	1,000
Sent Representatives	2,000
Sent Library of Congress	50
Damaged and imperfect copies	70
To be issued by Surgeon-General's Office.................................	1,868
Total number of copies printed	5,000

The second part of the work is now going through the press as rapidly as possible.

The recommendation made in former years is renewed, that the catalogue and tablets of the anatomical section of the Army Medical Museum be published in a style similar to Morton's Crania Americana. A bill for this purpose passed one house of Congress during the last session, but failed to become a law.

I am compelled to repeat the statement made in previous reports that very serious and increasing injury has resulted to the service from the continued prohibition of appointments and promotions in the Medical Corps. Thoroughly educated medical men, in selecting the Army as an occupation, are actuated by the reasonable prospect of promotion, but to render it impossible for them ever to advance in rank is to deter many desirable men from becoming candidates. I call attention most earnestly to the statement of the Surgeon-General as to the pressing necessity for such legislation as will secure to our officers and soldiers the efficient attendance in wounds and sickness which the Government should provide, and which will make a position in the Medical Corps of the Army now, as formerly, an object of ambition to the best educated and best qualified young men in the profession. There are now 64 vacancies in that corps, viz : 2 assistant medical purveyors, 5 surgeons, 56 assistant surgeons, and 1 medical store-keeper. In my judgment it is absolutely necessary for the welfare of the service that the corps be opened to appointment and promotion.

The Paymaster-General strongly urges the necessity of providing by legislation for an increase of the present force of paymasters, now much reduced by the operation of the act of March 3, 1869, prohibiting new appointments and promotions in certain staff corps and departments. The number of paymasters authorized by the Army organization act of July 28, 1866, was sixty. There are now but forty-four in service. The Paymaster-General recommends that the number be fixed by law at fifty-two, and that the sixth section of the act of March 3, 1869, be repealed, and promotions and new appointments be allowed.

Experience has shown that it is just that a greater period than thirty days be allowed to an officer on leave of absence without reduction of pay. Thirty days barely suffices to enable an officer to travel from and to his remote station in the West.

It is apparent that the act approved May 15, 1872, concerning the pay of enlisted men and establishing a system of deposits, has proved of much benefit to the soldier. The number of desertions has not been reduced to as great an extent as had been hoped, but still that number was five hundred less than in the year ending June 30, 1871. It would be difficult to devise legislation better calculated to encourage re-enlistments, reward faithful service, and diminish desertion, and it is believed its ultimate effect will be to heighten the tone of the whole enlisted force of the Army.

It appears from the report of the Paymaster-General that the average amount of deposits per company made by enlisted men during the past fiscal year was $482.26. The largest amounts of deposits per company were made in the Departments of Arizona and Columbia. In these departments there was the greatest amount of field operations. It may be safely inferred, then, that more deposits will be made by the enlisted men in time of war than in time of peace; and this leads to the conclusion that had a wise system of deposits been in operation in our volunteer Army during the rebellion, the Government would have had the handling of many millions of dollars for several years. During the last years of the war there were about 14,000 companies of troops employed, which would give, at the rate of $1,500 deposited by each company, $21,000,000 per annum.

The Corps of Engineers has been actively engaged upon the defensive works of our coasts ; upon river and harbor improvements, and the surveys for them, and for the protection of the navigable waters of the

United States against deterioration, whether from bridging or other causes; upon the geodetic and hydrographic survey of the lakes; upon surveys for the defenses of the coasts; upon military surveys and recon-noissances in the interior; upon geographical and geological explora-tions; upon public buildings and grounds in the District of Columbia; upon the construction of light-houses, and upon the demarkation of the boundary between the United States and Great Britain.

The works projected and approved for the modification and strength-ening of our sea-coast defenses and fortifications have been advanced with a rapidity consistent with economy and efficiency, and the works for our principal harbors now contain quite a number of platforms ready for their armaments of guns of the largest calibers. Heavy guns mounted in covered positions, along the shores of the inlets to our har-bors, must always be the basis of any successful defense, and the works projected and in course of construction should be prosecuted to comple-tion, and be suitably armed.

The Battalion of Engineers numbers 308 enlisted men, and is stationed at the Military Academy for instruction of cadets, and at Willet's Point, New York Harbor, where it forms the school of torpedo defense of the channels to our harbors, and the guards and workmen for the care and distribution of engineer-equipments. During the past summer a num-ber of detachments have served with advantage in the geographical and geodetic explorations. The appropriations asked for the engineer depot and post are recommended to Congress, and the recommendation for one chief musician and two principal musicians for the battalion ap-proved.

With the small appropriations granted for trials with torpedoes, the investigations upon this subject have been continued, to the benefit of our system of submarine mines. This accessory for the defense of our harbors in recent years has developed into one of great importance among the maritime powers, and to investigate the recent electrical methods and systems of torpedoes, as well as to procure certain materials, two officers of engineers were sent during the summer to Europe. The results of their mission are the collection of valuable information on this subject, and a saving of expenditure to the Government.

The river and harbor improvements mentioned in my last annual re-port have been continued, and the works and surveys connected there-with have been carried on during the past year with vigor. Detailed information in regard to each specific improvement, and the results of surveys directed to be made by the river and harbor appropriation acts, may be found in the report of the Chief of Engineers.

The improvement of our rivers and harbors consists, chiefly, in giving increased width and depth to existing channel-ways and basins, and protecting them, or in creating new channels and basins and giving them protective works. The operations to this end comprise the removal of obstructions of various kinds, such as rock in place and bowlders, bars of clay, sometimes indurated; of gravel, sand, and other alluvial matter; of rafts, often extending from the surface of the river nearly to the bottom, formed by masses of drifting trees, or the accumulation of slabs, edgings, and sawdust; of timber and other constructions placed in channel-ways to obstruct or close them; the construction of dikes, dams, wing-dams, and revetments, and the building of canals, break-waters, and piers, all tending to promote the general interests of commerce and navigation, by furnishing increased facilities of communication and giving greater security to trade.

The condition of the public works and grounds of Washington, and the progress made in their construction, repair, and improvement, are very creditable to the officer in charge. The improvements exhibit good taste, with much economy of expenditure. Many vacant and unimproved reservations have become attractive places of public resort, at little expense.

In accordance with the proviso attached to the appropriation for the improvement of the channel of the Delaware River at or near the Horse-shoe Shoals, a board of engineers was convened; and in view of their report upon the feasibility and expense of the plan proposed for the prevention and removal of the obstruction, it has been determined to defer final action upon the proposed plan until after the method adopted by the local authorities is fully tested, and it is found that the means used by them will not be sufficient to maintain an open channel during the winter months.

Section 3 of the river and harbor act of March 3, 1873, directed that a report be made upon the practicability of bridging the channel between Lake Huron and Lake Erie, without material injury to the interests of navigation, and upon the number and character of vessels navigating that channel. The subject has been committed to a board of experienced engineer officers, who are now engaged upon it. It is expected that their report will be received during the early part of the session of Congress.

The removal of the wreck in the channel-way off Sandy Hook, required by the act approved January 3, 1873, was completed March 6, leaving a clear depth of 25½ feet at mean low water.

Under the authority granted by the act approved January 23, 1873, a contract was closed for the construction of an iron hull for a light-draught snag-boat for use on the Mississippi, Missouri, and Arkansas Rivers, and it is expected that the boat will be ready for service during the present season.

The Lake Ontario Shore Railroad Company submitted a project for a bridge across the Genesee River, and in accordance with the provisions of the second section of the act authorizing its construction approved March 3, 1873, certain modifications in the plan were required, and of these the president of the railroad company has been notified.

In carrying out the provisions of recent acts of Congress authorizing the construction of bridges, my attention has been called to the fact that certain bridges have been built, and that one is now being constructed across navigable waters of the United States without any authority of law; and further, that certain parties claim the right to bridge, and that one of those parties is now constructing a bridge under authority claimed to be derived from acts granting right of way for railroads through public lands and granting lands to aid in the construction of a road chartered by State authority. In view of the provisions of the more recent acts of Congress requiring the Secretary of War to maintain a supervision over the location and construction of bridges crossing navigable waters of the United States, in order that the interests of navigation shall be protected, I feel it my duty to invite the attention of Congress to this subject and to suggest such general legislation as may be deemed necessary for the preservation of the great natural channels of commerce.

In this connection I have respectfully to recommend that the act authorizing the construction of a bridge across the Arkansas River at Little Rock, Arkansas, approved May 31, 1872, be repealed, for the reason that a bridge constructed in compliance with its terms would materially obstruct and impair the navigation of the river. A previous act of Congress (that of July 1, 1870) contains all the provisions for bridging this river at Little Rock essential to the preservation of the channel.

The survey of the lakes has been continued with success during the season. The survey of Lake Michigan has been pushed forward nearly to completion, and that of the Saint Lawrence River has been extended nearly to Lake Ontario. Other portions of the survey are in satisfactory progress; new surveys of special localities have been made, the longitude of important points determined by telegraph; assistance to the geographical and geological survey of adjacent States rendered; and meteorological and lake-surface observations continued through the entire lake region.

The main field operations of the geological exploration near the fortieth parallel, between the Sierra Nevada and eastern slope of the Rocky Mountains, were completed in November last, and the maps and results are being prepared for publication at an early day. Special examinations, giving important results, have been made of noted geological structures, and of the evidences of glacial action in the Sierras.

The geographical and geological surveys and explorations west of the one-hundredth meridian in Nevada, Utah, Colorado, New Mexico, and Arizona, have been prosecuted with great vigor and success. The field labors terminated in December, after which the work of preparation of the maps and observations for publication was continued in the office in this city. The field operations of the present season, embracing, in addition to the usual observations in the various branches of the survey, the erection of a field astronomical observatory at Ogden, Utah, and the determination of an astronomical base, commenced June 1, with an efficient organization.

The officers of the Corps of Engineers on detached duty at the headquarters of general officers commanding military divisions and departments have rendered valuable services in preparing such maps and sketches and making such surveys and reconnaissances as were required by their commanding officers. Besides these regular duties, several special reconnaissances have been made, yielding important information. Among these the reconnaissance of the lava-beds and surrounding country, the scene of operations against the Modoc Indians; the survey of the Yellowstone River, as far up as practicable; the reconnaissance of the head-waters of the Rio Grande and Southwestern Colorado; and the reconnaissance to discover an approach to the Yellowstone Lake Basin from the south or southeast, thus opening a new and shorter route to the National Yellowstone Park and the mining regions of Montana, together with the results of astronomical observations to determine the positions of important points, are particularly referred to in the report of the Chief of Engineers.

The commission appointed by the President, in accordance with the act approved March 3, 1873, to examine and report on a system of irrigation in the San Joaquin, Tulare, and Sacramento Valleys, California, met and organized in San Francisco in May, and proceeded at once to examine the valleys in question and the streams emptying into them. By the end of June they had made satisfactory progress. They are still engaged in this labor, and in the collection of information to enable them to render a full report upon the subject of investigation.

A complete set of the published maps and reports of the Engineer Department, together with sets of photographic views of remarkable natural features of the western country, and models of important engineer work of river and harbor improvement, and of armament, were prepared and forwarded through the commissioner appointed by the President to represent the United States at the Vienna Exhibition, with authority to present them, at the close of the exhibition, to the engineer department of the Austrian army.

The estimates of the Chief of Engineers are submitted separately, as presented by that officer, viz:

Fortifications and other works of defense	$3,376,000
Public buildings and grounds and Washington aqueduct	1,118,056
Surveys	480,000
Engineer depot at Willet's Point, N. Y	20,800
Office expenses	29,260
Improvement of rivers and harbors	15,464,540
Total	20,488,656

No steps have been taken by me to carry out the provisions of the act of March 3, 1873, authorizing the survey, plat, and sale of the cemetery grounds upon the Fort Gratiot military reservation in Michigan, as the formal preliminary action of the city authorities of Port Huron has not yet been completed.

The report of the Chief of Ordnance calls attention to the many potent arguments so often presented in favor of the repeal of the law prohibiting promotions in the corps which he represents. He refers to the hardship and humiliation to which officers of merit and long service have been subjected since the passage of that law, by being deprived of their deserved promotion, the only reward held out in their profession for years of duty well performed. Their claims to promotion appeal strongly to the attention of Congress.

A board of experienced officers, of which Gen. A. H. Terry was president, was convened in September, 1872, for the selection of a breech-loading system for the muskets and carbines of the military service. After an exhaustive trial of all the systems presented, the board selected the Springfield breech-loading system as the one, of all those brought before it, which is best calculated to meet the demands of our military service.

The report of the board was approved, and the Springfield system of breech-loader will henceforth be used for the muskets and carbines of the Army. At the same time the caliber of all small-arms for the service—rifles, carbines, and revolvers—has been fixed at .45 of an inch. It is now a question of grave importance whether new arms of the accepted system shall not be made at once in sufficient quantities for a reserve supply in case of war, and to this end an appropriation of $500,000 has been asked for the next fiscal year for the manufacture, together with the materials now on hand, of about 35,000 arms.

The annual appropriation of $200,000 for arming and equipping the militia, an amount fixed by Congress during the early part of the century, is now found inadequate, by reason of the great increase of population, to supply the wants of the whole body of the militia, and it is therefore recommended that the appropriation for that purpose be increased in a manner proportioned to the increase of the population since the passage of the act of 1808, providing for the distribution of arms to the militia of the country.

I feel great hesitation in recommending increased appropriations at this time, but I deem it my duty to say that the armament of our sea-coast defenses, which involves the question of the defense of our principal sea-board cities from attack, in case of war with a naval power, is a subject demanding the earnest attention of Congress. The principal cities on our coast are in a very defenseless state, and the tedious and costly work of preparation cannot be commenced on the breaking out of a war, with the hope of accomplishing any adequate result. The work must be done in time of peace, without waiting for an uncertain period in search after perfection in gun-constructions. The importance of this subject increases with the earnest and continued efforts on the part of all nations to supply their forts with the most improved armament, and should war find this country without a proper defense against iron-clads and their great guns, the responsibility cannot rest on this Department, as the importance of the subject has often been brought to the attention of Congress. An appropriation of $1,449,552 is estimated for by the Chief of Ordnance for the next fiscal year for the purchase of smooth-bore guns and for carriages, which sum will provide for one-sixth, only, of the guns and carriages that will be required for fortifications which will be ready by the 30th of June, 1874. This amount is not embraced in the regular estimates of appropriations for the Army, as heretofore alluded to, but it is a subject of great importance, and the question of these appropriations is respectfully submitted.

The heavy rifled guns selected for fabrication and test under the act approved June 6, 1872, are now in process of manufacture, and will be completed during the winter. Valuable information and experience are to be gathered in the trial of these guns, the result most probably leading to the early adoption of an effective rifle of suitable caliber for the service; and in this connection 1 would recommend the purchase of a suitable proving ground for the proper trial of these experimental heavy guns.

The cheapness of cast iron, and the marked progress attained in the manufacture of gunpowder in the past year, induces a recommendation that an appropriation of $75,000 be granted, to be applied in the fabrication and trial of 12-inch cast-iron rifled cannon, that the capabilities of the metal for rifle constructions of large caliber may be put to the fullest test, in the hope that its practical utilization for this purpose may be conclusively assured or denied.

The powder in the hands of the Department is, on account of the want of proper storage-room, concentrated in large part in the magazines of our sea-coast fortifications, where, under the searching influences of the salt air, it is rapidly undergoing deterioration. For its better preservation a large powder-depot should be established in some region where neither public nor private interests would be endangered by its proximity, and an appropriation of $100,000 is recommended for the purchase of a suitable site and the commencement of magazines.

The abolition of some of the smaller arsenals, and the application of the proceeds of their sale to the erection of a large arsenal of construction on the Atlantic coast, is again urged on strong economical grounds, and it is recommended that a law be passed authorizing the Secretary of War to make sale of any of the smaller arsenals at such times as would be most advantageous to the Government, and to apply the proceeds as suggested.

The sale of Kennebec arsenal, Detroit arsenal, Pikesville arsenal, and the small lot or tract at Sag Harbor, Long Island, now no longer needed for public purposes, is recommended.

By the act of Congress approved June 10, 1872, the Secretary of War was directed to sell the Mount Vernon arsenal, Alabama, pursuant to a recommendation made for its disposal as a part of the public domain. Subsequent to such recommendation the exigencies of the service required that the property should be used by the Quartermaster's Department for military purposes, and the period when such necessity shall cease to exist is very indefinite. Under these circumstances the repeal of so much of the act of June 10, 1872, as relates to the sale of this property is recommended.

That portion of the same act which directs the sale of the Apalachicola arsenal should, in my opinion, be repealed, for the reason that the property was granted to the State of Florida in 1870, by the act approved December 15 of that year, under the name of the Chattahoochee arsenal.

The Department feels much embarrassment arising from conflicting claims founded on alleged infringements of patent-rights in the construction of breech-loading guns at the national armory. Officers of the Ordnance Corps, in the execution of their official duties, are seriously annoyed by private actions for damages, instituted by persons claiming to hold valid patents which have been infringed in the productions of the Government armory, and some legislation seems to be required in order to enable the Department to dispose of the claims.

The fifth section of the act of July 12, 1870, which provides "That all balances of appropriations contained in the annual appropriation bills and made specifically for the service of any fiscal year, and remaining unexpended at the expiration of such fiscal year, shall only be applied to the payment of expenses properly incurred during that year, or to the fulfillment of contracts properly made within that year, and such balances not needed for the said purposes shall be carried to the surplus fund: *Provided*, That this section shall not apply to appropriations known as permanent or indefinite appropriations," is injurious to the interests of the Government where permanent buildings are to be erected, and appropriations for this purpose should be allowed to run for three years instead of one, as now limited by that act. It is recommended that the act be modified accordingly.

Systematic and continuous instruction of the Army in military signaling and telegraphy has continued during the past year at the school of instruction and practice at Fort Whipple, Va., and in the Department of the Missouri, and the special attention of some of the most powerful foreign goverments has been directed to these branches of military science, and they have taken pains to procure the minute details of our equipment and apparatus.

Recruiting for the signal-service has been successfully conducted, the standard of acquirement being maintained by special examination of those enlisted. After selection and enlistment, the men are at once placed under a course of drill and instruction, and after a second examination those especially designated for duty at stations are drilled, examined, instructed, tested by practice, instructed in the higher branches of the service, and again examined and tested before being intrusted with the management of stations of observation.

The Chief Signal-Officer renews his recommendation for the establishment by law of a permanent Signal Corps, or for such legislation as will secure a permanency for its details. He insists that the extent of the service and its now material importance should commend this subject to the attention of Congress.

The whole number of stations from which regular meteoric reports are now received is ninety-two, of which seventy-eight are in the United States, eleven in Canada, and three in the West Indies.

The regular telegraphic reports from Havana began on August 6, from Kingston, Jamaica, on September 18, and from Santiago de Cuba on September 29. Three other points in the islands of Porto Rico, Guadeloupe, and Barbados, will be equipped as soon as observers can be designated. It is a matter of regret that there is no international arrangement with the authorities of any of these islands, nor is there, at present, any return of weather-telegrams provided for or officially requested, Steps are in contemplation by which it is hoped the necessary arrangements will be effected.

The display of bulletins and weather-charts at stations, the supply of prompt and gratuitous information to the press, and the exhibition of day or night signals at times of probable special danger, for the benefit of shipping and commercial interests, have been continued.

A plan has been adopted whereby synopses of reports and probabilities have been forwarded to many points in the interior not reached by telegraph, and this plan has given satisfaction to the farming and interior population reached.

There are nineteen special river stations from which reports of the depths of water in the principal rivers of the United States are daily made by telegraph, at particular seasons, during which danger from freshets may be anticipated. River reports are also made from twenty of the regular stations.

These data are widely published and distributed along the line of the rivers, and contribute to the convenience and safety of the river commerce, by the constant and accurate knowledge given of the depth of water in the channels.

The benefits resulting from these reports, now in the second year of their issue, have been fully acknowledged by the various interests they have advanced.

The total number of special river-bulletins issued has been twenty-three thousand two hundred and ten. Eight thousand nine hundred and eighty-two printed copies of the weather-report are displayed daily.

Steps have been taken to carry out the legislation of the last Congress authorizing the establishment of signal stations at light-houses, and such of the life-saving stations on the lake or sea coasts as may be suitably located for that purpose, and to connect the same with such points as may be necessary for the proper discharge of the duties of the signal service, by means of a suitable telegraph-line, in cases where no lines are in operation. The plan in contemplation proposes the establishment of signal stations at life-saving stations and light-houses along the ocean-coast of New Jersey, from Sandy Hook to Cape May, a distance of twenty-five miles from each other. A line connecting the stations at life-saving stations and light-houses along the coast from Norfolk, Va., to Cape Hatteras, N. C., a distance of one hundred and thirty-seven miles, and on one of the most dangerous coasts of the United States, is being constructed. It is expected that the above-mentioned lines will be completed during the present year.

The ascertained comparative accuracy of the deductions from reports styled " probabilities ". has been more clearly presented in this than in preceding years. The percentage of verifications has been mathematically computed for each of the geographical districts mentioned in the reports. With a more rigid and scrutinizing mode of calculation than was before adopted, the percentage of verification has improved. The analysis of the year's work indicates clearly, at once, the wisdom of judiciously increasing the number of stations.

The Department acknowledges, as in previous years, the general support of the popular opinion of scientific men, and of the press, in its efforts to successfully carry on this work. Errors have occurred, but it has been generally recognized as inevitable that some must occur in the present condition of science. The great utility of the work is no longer doubted. It has achieved results, the promise of which, a few years ago, could hardly be hoped for.

It is mentioned in connection with this subject that arrangements have been made with the meteorological officers of Russia, England, and Turkey, to commence on January 1, 1874, an exchange with the United States of the daily reports taken simultaneously at the different stations throughout the great extent of the Russian and Turkish Empires, the British Islands, and the United States. The co-operation of the systems of other nations is expected.

My annual inspection of the affairs of the Military Academy and Corps of Cadets, in June last, disclosed a very creditable state of discipline, and an attention to study very commendable in the cadets.

One of the effects of the act of Congress approved February 2, 1872, increasing the congressional representation of the several States, was to increase the Corps of Cadets from 293 to 342. This is of marked advantage to the Academy, which, on account of the falure of many of the candidates for admission to pass the necessary examination, has not, in a long series of years, instructed the number of young men that was allowed by law to be educated at West Point. Examinations for admission are held twice yearly, in May or June and in September, and when a candidate not possessing the requisite qualifications fails to pass, as a large portion of those presenting themselves have done, their districts remain unrepresented during the period embraced between the date when they fail and the next examination, and the United States loses a cadet for the same period.

The report of the Board of Visitors, which this year had an opportunity of witnessing the examination of the candidates, comments upon the large proportion of those failing to those admitted; during the past year there were 119 candidates admitted and 87 rejected; of the latter number 13 only were rejected by the medical board; and at the semi-annual examination in January next it is more than probable that a considerable number of those admitted in June and September last will also fail. These facts furnish a strong commentary upon the present mode of selecting candidates for a military education at West Point.

The large number of those failing to meet the present standard clearly shows that due regard has not, in many cases, been paid to selecting those whose attainments qualify them for admission. If the members of Congress were a little more rigid in requiring those they propose nominating to be thoroughly conversant with the rudiments of a common-school education, their friends would escape the mortification and expense attendant on their rejection.

The Board of Visitors were thorough in their investigation into the affairs of the academy last June, and the attention of Congress is invited to the recommendations contained in their report.

A new set of regulations for the government of the Corps of Cadets has been prepared, and will very shortly go into execution.

The increase of the Military Academy band, the only one now provided for by law, which is very small and the pay of which is wholly insufficient to attract to or retain in the service competent musicians, when they can secure much larger salaries in the principal cities of the Union, is again urgently recommended to the attention of Congress. This subject was alluded to in my last annual report, and a bill was introduced to increase the number and compensation of the musicians, which, it is understood, passed one house of Congress, but was not taken up in the other. Its re-introduction and passage is earnestly recommended.

During the last session of Congress, the Committee on Expenditures of the War Department made an exhaustive report of the workings of this portion of the executive branch of the Government, and prepared a bill for a full and complete reorganization of the clerical force of the War Department.

I would earnestly represent that this Department has been peculiarly unfortunate as regards the rates of compensation paid its employés. It is hoped, therefore, that the report of the Committee on Expenditures of the War Department, above referred to, may receive careful consideration at the hands of Congress, and that action be taken upon the recommendations of the committee as to the required organization of the clerical force.

When from illness or other cause the Secretary of War is obliged to be temporarily absent, there is no person in the Department authorized by law to sign the money requisitions upon the Treasury and other papers necessary for its current business. In almost all the other Departments of the Government one or more assistant secretary is provided by law, who is authorized to perform such duties in the absence of the head of the Department. There is no assistant secretary for the War Department; and in order that inconvenience to individuals as well as to the Government may not arise from delay caused by such absence, I recommend the passage of a law which will permit the Secretary of War to authorize the chief clerk, in case of illness or other temporary absence of the head of the Department, to sign requisitions and other papers deemed necessary for immediate signature.

I again refer to the fact that by joint resolution of Congress the Secretary of War was required to appoint a competent person to arrange and prepare for publication the official documents relating to the rebellion and the operations of the Army during the war, and to submit a plan of said publication and estimates of the cost thereof to Congress at its then next session. A person was appointed to assume this work, who was to receive a compensation of $2,500 per annum. Although the appointment was made at that time, no acceptance was filed, and no action was taken toward the arrangement and publication of the records.

As the appointment, under previous legislation, cannot now be made, for the reason that the act prescribed that payments should cease in two years after its passage, this legislation should be revived and the Secretary of War authorized to make the appointment. This is a great national work, of much historical value, and constant daily observation and experience renders it evident that early steps should be taken to collect and prepare these vast and important materials for publication.

WM. W. BELKNAP,
Secretary of War.

PAPERS

ACCOMPANYING

THE REPORT OF THE SECRETARY OF WAR.

REPORT OF THE GENERAL OF THE ARMY.

HEADQUARTERS OF THE ARMY,
Washington, D. C., November 7, 1873.

SIR: I have the honor herewith to submit a statement showing the organization and actual strength of enlisted men in the Army, compiled from the official returns up to the latest date, and invite your attention to the recapitulation, showing 25,535 enlisted men of cavalry, artillery, and infantry, and 3,970 non-combatants, the whole aggregating 29,505, or 495 less than the number, 30,000, limited by law. In the active regiments the number of men sick and on the necessary details about the posts will fully equal 25 per cent., so that the actual strength for military service does not exceed 19,654 men.

In order that the Regular Army should fulfill its arduous duties on the frontier, as also form the model on which to shape the volunteer and militia forces of the United States, I earnestly recommend that Congress be asked to fix the limit of the enlisted force at such a figure as will give 30,000 men for the regiments of the line, and to provide specifically for the non-combatant detachments, such as the Engineer Battalion, the Ordnance Department, West Point detachments, Signal Department, ordnance and commissary sergeants, in the same manner as has been done for the hospital stewards.

The artillery regiments have an organization different from the infantry, viz, twelve batteries to a regiment. But of these only one is equipped and instructed as a battery of artillery, the other eleven companies of each regiment being armed with muskets, and instructed as infantry. In order to simplify the organization, and to apply the new tactics (now approaching completion) to all arms of service alike, with your approval I have ordered that the word "battery" apply technically to such only as are provided with horses and guns, and all others to be called companies. Some of the artillery officers think that the act of July 28, 1866, entitles them to the name "battery," whether they have guns or not, and it might be well to ask a modification of the law, so as to read "battery or company" for the artillery regiments, to correspond with the words "troop or company" used for the cavalry in the same act.

The number of regimental commissioned officers on duty, or belonging to the several departments and divisions, number in the aggregate 1,532; present for duty, 1,234; absent on leave or detached, 298.

The foregoing does not include the thirty-one second lieutenants recently appointed from civil life, now under orders to join their regiments.

I now inclose the annual reports of the division and department commanders, copies of which have been submitted to you as received.

The military divisions embrace the whole area of the United States, and these reports include the acts of all of the Regular Army, leaving nothing to be added by way of history of the events during the past year.

The reports of all the department commanders, with the exception of that of the Department of Columbia, not yet received, are also herewith sent.*

No part of the Army is under my immediate control, and the existing Army regulations devolve on the Secretary of War the actual command of the military peace establishment, and all responsibility therefor, so that I forbear making any further recommendations or report.

I have the honor to be your obedient servant,

W. T. SHERMAN, *General.*

Hon. W. W. BELKNAP,
Secretary of War.

Statement showing the organization and strength of enlisted men in the Army.

RECAPITULATION.

Regiment.	Number of men.	Regiment.	Number of men.
First Cavalry*	864	Seventeenth Infantry ¶	526
Second Cavalry	885	Eighteenth Infantry	516
Third Cavalry	921	Nineteenth Infantry	476
Fourth Cavalry	873	Twentieth Infantry	559
Fifth Cavalry	995	Twenty-first Infantry	547
Sixth Cavalry	876	Twenty-second Infantry **	544
Seventh Cavalry	1,040	Twenty-third Infantry	575
Eighth Cavalry †	784	Twenty-fourth Infantry	596
Ninth Cavalry ‡	701	Twenty-fifth Infantry	595
Tenth Cavalry	808		
First Artillery §	619		25,535
Second Artillery	722	Non-combatants:	
Third Artillery	593	Engineer Battalion	316
Fourth Artillery	663	Permanent and recruiting parties, music boys, and recruits not available for assignment.	963
Fifth Artillery	609		
First Infantry	422		
Second Infantry	487	General-service men on duty in the Bureaus of the War Department, Army, division, and department headquarters, &c.	477
Third Infantry	481		
Fourth Infantry	614		
Fifth Infantry	544		
Sixth Infantry	583	Ordnance Department	425
Seventh Infantry	589	West Point detachments	215
Eighth Infantry	507	Signal detachment	432
Ninth Infantry	507	Hospital stewards ††	391
Tenth Infantry	630	Ordnance sergeants	111
Eleventh Infantry	502	Available recruits at depots	488
Twelfth Infantry	551	Commissary sergeants	152
Thirteenth Infantry	508		
Fourteenth Infantry	600	Total non-combatants	3,970
Fifteenth Infantry ‖	502		
Sixteenth Infantry	531	Total	29,505

* Two hundred recruits ordered October 21, 1873; 100 recruits left October — 1873.
† Two hundred and twenty recruits ordered October 29, 1873.
‡ All disposable recruits ordered September 10, 1873.
§ Thirty recruits ordered to Battery K October 7, 1873.
‖ One hundred recruits ordered October 29, 1873.
¶ Eighty recruits ordered October 29, 1873.
** Sixty-five recruits ordered October 29, 1873.
†† Not included in the 30,000 authorized by law.

REPORT OF LIEUT. GEN. SHERIDAN.

HEADQUARTERS MILITARY DIVISION OF THE MISSOURI,
Chicago, October 27, 1873.

COLONEL: For the information of the General of the Army, I have the honor to submit my annual report of operations within this military

27 Ab

division during the past year, accompanied by the reports of subordinate commanders.

The organization of the division remains unchanged since my last report, and consists of four departments, viz: The Department of Dakota, commanded by Brig. Gen. Alfred H. Terry, consisting of the State of Minnesota and the Territories of Dakota and Montana; the Department of the Platte, commanded by Brig. Gen. Edward O. C. Ord, composed of the States of Iowa and Nebraska and the Territories of Utah and Wyoming; the Department of the Missouri, commanded by Brig. Gen. John Pope, including the States of Missouri, Kansas, and Illinois, and the Territories of Colorado and New Mexico; and the Department of Texas, commanded by Brig. Gen. Christopher C. Augur, embracing the State of Texas and the Indian Territory.

It will be seen that the Military Division of the Missouri includes most of the Western States and all the Territories east of Arizona, California, and Idaho, from British Columbia on the north to the Gulf of Mexico on the south. Within these limits, which include more than one million square miles of frontier country, are included great agricultural, pastoral, mining, and mercantile interests, and also 99 tribes of Indians, numbering about 192,000 persons, the majority of whom are wild and many of them hostile.

To give protection to the citizens of the frontier against these Indians and to guard the long line of our Mexican border against robberies by Mexican citizens and Indians living in Mexico; to explore unknown territory and furnish escorts to surveying-parties for scientific purposes and for projected railroads; to assist and guard the railways already built and other commercial lines of travel; to aid in the enforcement of the civil law in remote places; and to do generally all that is constantly required of our Army in the way of helping and urging forward everything which tends to develop and increase civilization upon the border, and at the same time to protect the Indians in the rights and immunities guaranteed them under existing treaties, has been the work of the troops in this military division for the past year, and that work has been successfully accomplished.

The effective military forces within the division—a detailed account of which will be found in the roster appended, marked A—consist of eight regiments of cavalry and seventeen regiments of infantry, aggregating 16,459 officers and enlisted men, who are distributed as follows: In the Department of Dakota, cavalry, 1,126; infantry, 3,022; in the Department of the Platte, cavalry, 1,502; infantry, 2,704; in the Department of the Missouri, cavalry, 1,558; infantry, 1,564; and in the Department of Texas, cavalry, 2,491; infantry, 2,492. This force is divided among 70 military posts, which cover the frontier from Montana on the north to the mouth of the Rio Grande on the south.

During the past year there has been only one change among the department commanders. Maj. Gen. Winfield S. Hancock was relieved from the command of the Department of Dakota on the 3d of December, 1872, by direction of the War Department, and assigned to the command of the military division of the Atlantic, and Brig. Gen. A. H. Terry was assigned to duty in his place.

Early last spring, in consequence of repeated attacks by the Indians on the post of Fort Abraham Lincoln, I deemed it necessary that a regiment of cavalry should be transferred to the Department of Dakota, in order that these Indians might be followed and punished, if they again renewed their attacks. On application to headquarters of the Army, the Seventh Cavalry was ordered from the Military Division of the South to the Department of Dakota, and, by direction of Gen. A. H. Terry, stationed at Forts Rice and Abraham Lincoln. This transfer was very fortunate, as it afterwards transpired that the authorities of the Northern Pacific Railroad desired to continue their surveys, and also that it had been determined by the Government to locate the northern boundary line, and the services of mounted troops became absolutely necessary for these purposes. As soon as the directors of the Northern Pacific Railroad had definitely settled upon their plan of operations for the summer, I deemed it necessary that some point upon the Yellowstone should be found near which to establish a depot for supplies, and by an agreement with Captain Coulson, agent of the contractor for Government transportation on the Missouri River for 1873, to furnish a steamboat to go from Fort Buford up the Yellowstone River, I sent Maj. George A. Forsyth, of my staff, to ascend that river, if possible, and fix upon some point near the mouth of the Powder River for this depot. This trip up the Yellowstone was successfully made as far as that point, and a convenient place found for a supply depot, in case one was required. Further explorations have also established the fact that the Yellowstone is navigable for light-draught boats for a considerable distance above the mouth of Powder River, and it is thought that boats can now be run up nearly or quite to the mouth of Big Horn River. Upon the completion of this duty, Major Forsyth returned to Fort Rice, where the expedition was being organized for the protection of the surveying parties of the Northern Pacific Railroad; and, upon his report, Brig. Gen. A. H. Terry, commanding the Department of Dakota, ordered the establishment of a depot of supplies for the Yellowstone expedition at or near Glendive Creek, where it empties into the Yellowstone, the point at which it was assumed that the surveying parties of the Northern Pacific Railroad would run their line across the river.

This expedition, under command of Col. David S. Stanley, Twenty-second Infantry, left Forts Rice and Abraham Lincoln on the 16th of June, returning to its point of departure on the 21st of September, and succeeded in accomplishing the purposes for which it was intended, for the details of which reference is made to the reports of Brig. Gen. A. H. Terry and the sub-reports of Col. D. S. Stanley and Lieut. Cols. George A. Custer and Luther P. Bradley.

The survey of the northern boundary line has been progressing satisfactorily to all concerned throughout the summer, and the troops are now en route for their winter-quarters at Fort Totten, Dak.

In the Department of the Platte, the troops were increased by the transfer of the Fourth Infantry from the Military Division of the South. In this department all of the troops have been kept actively employed in covering the advanced settlements in Nebraska, in Western Kansas along the line of the North Fork of the Republican River, in Wyoming Territory between Forts Fetterman and Laramie, and along the line of the Union Pacific Railroad. For a detailed account of the operations in this department, I respectfully refer to the accompanying reports of Brig. Gen. E. O. C. Ord and his subordinates.

Nothing of unusual interest has occurred in the Department of the Missouri. The troops have been kept actively employed in the field for the purpose of intimidating roving bands of Indians, who might be tempted to commit depredations upon settlers and interrupt lines of travel. Brig. Gen. John Pope, in his report, gives a clear and comprehensive statement of his year's work, to which reference is respectfully made.

In the Department of Texas there has been a great deal of trouble along the northern line of the State, and also along the line of the Rio Grande. The troubles on the northern frontier of Texas have been principally from Indians coming from the reservations in the Indian Territory; and I respectfully request that some definite authority be given me to punish these raiding parties of Indians upon their return to their reservations. I believe it is the only way in which the evil can be cured.

The people living along the line of the Rio Grande have been heretofore frequently plundered by raiding parties of Indians and Mexicans from Mexico. I am happy to state that these depredations have diminished very materially since the punishment administered by Col. Ranald S. Mackenzie, Fourth Cavalry, upon a raiding band of Kickapoo and Lipan Indians. For the details of Colonel Mackenzie's attack on the Lipans and Kickapoos, as well as for a very complete statement of military affairs in Texas, I respectfully refer to the accompanying reports of Brig. Gen. C. C. Augur.

It has been found necessary to make extensive repairs at many of the posts within this division during the year, but only one new post, the cavalry barracks near Fort Abraham Lincoln, has been erected. Considerable money has also been expended in the completion of the posts at Beaver City, Utah, and at Fort Clarke, Tex. In this connection I beg leave to call the attention of the General of the Army to the fact that, while the troops within this division will be quite comfortably quartered during the winter, they will be inconveniently crowded at some of the posts within the Departments of Dakota and of the Platte. Provision will have to be made for thorough repairs at Forts Laramie, Wyo., McPherson, Nebr., and Camp Douglas, Utah, during the ensuing summer.

The necessity of keeping Indians on their reservations is becoming more apparent every day, with the westward growth of the settlements and the rapid progress and development of the mining and cattle grazing interests in the State of Nebraska and the Territories of Wyoming and Colorado. During the last twelve months, depredations by roving bands of Indians, who, as a general thing, come from some one of the various Indian reservations within the limits of this command, have been exasperatingly frequent. They have attacked our posts, killed and wounded our citizens and carried off their cattle, and, when pursued by our troops, taken refuge within the line of their reservations and coolly boasted of their atrocities. It seems to me that a rigid rule should be made, forbidding their absence from their reservations, and in case they disregarded it, authority should be given the military to follow on the reservation, search out, capture and punish all whom it can be shown have been absent from their agencies, and off the reservations.

I respectfully recommend the erection of a large military post near the base of the Black Hills, at some good point to be selected hereafter. In this way we could secure a strong foothold in the heart of the Sioux country, and thereby exercise a controlling influence over these warlike people.

My thanks are due to Generals Pope, Terry, Ord, and Augur, who command the four Departments of this Military Division, for an intelligent administration of their commands, and for the exercise of a rigid economy in their estimates for, and expenditures of, public funds during the last fiscal year.

I am, colonel, very respectfully, your obedient servant,

P. H. SHERIDAN,
Lieutenant-General Commanding.

Col. WILLIAM D. WHIPPLE,
Asst. Adjt. Gen., U. S. A., Washington, D. C.

REPORT OF BVT. MAJ. GEN. JOHN POPE.

HEADQUARTERS DEPARTMENT OF THE MISSOURI,
Fort Leavenworth, Kans., October 6, 1873.

COLONEL: I have the honor to submit the following report of affairs in this department for the past year:

I am glad to be able to say that, with very trifling exceptions, I have no difficulties nor troubles with Indians anywhere in the department to report. The exceptions are: 1st, the murder of three surveyors, by a party of Cheyennes, on the Cimmarron River, in March last. The point where these murders were committed was beyond the limits of this department, but I deemed it necessary, in view of the fact that the scene of the trouble was nearer and more accessible to this place than to the headquarters department of Texas, to take immediate measures to prevent any further occurrence of that kind, and I accordingly placed two companies of the Sixth Cavalry at a point southwest of Wichita, on the Arkansas River, to scout continually the southern line of Kansas as far as the Cimmarron, and three companies of the same regiment at Fort Dodge—one company of which was directed to scout the country south and southeast from the post. Since then no trouble with Indians of any kind has occurred in that region.

2d. The usual small troubles (much more trifling in character and fewer in number) have occurred in the southern part of New Mexico with the Apaches on the reservations of Tulerosa and Fort Stanton, but by the active operations and judicious management of Major Price, Eighth Cavalry, who has general command in Southern New Mexico, and who has been continually moving about through that country with four, and at times five, companies of his regiment, difficulties and depredations have been kept within very narrow limits, and have now almost altogether ceased.

The policy in the department has been rather to prevent than try to punish Indian depredations, by adopting early in the spring, and maintaining until winter set in, such precautionary measures as seemed most efficient, and the results have been eminently satisfactory, and are plainly manifest in the undisturbed condition of the department and in the entire absence of alarm or uneasiness on the part of the frontier settlers, who have ceased entirely to feel alarmed themselves or to alarm other people. Instead of keeping the troops at the military posts, only to be sent out on receipt of news of Indian depredations, the entire cavalry force has been kept in the field since the early spring, moving about from place to place, a few miles every day, without special object in their marches, except water and grass for animals. Instead of permitting the Indians to wander about, as has been their custom, all through the summer, to commit depredations whenever the opportunity offered, the troops have themselves been kept on the march, so that the Indians could not know where they were or at what moment or when they might come in contact with them. In this manner the necessity of watching has been thrown upon the Indians and not, as hitherto, upon the troops shut up at the posts for a large part of the season, and the result has been that the Indians have been very cautious and have in the main kept very close to the region assigned them as reservations.

The greatest danger now in this department arises from what seems to me the unfortunate practice of granting permission to Indians, of whatever tribe, to leave their reservations, and on pretext of hunting or really for that purpose, to roam in considerable bands all through the frontier settlements of Kansas and Colorado. I do not consider such a practice just to the white settlers, and it is certainly unsafe both to them and to the Indians.

I dwelt at such length on this subject in my last report that I deem it unnecessary to discuss it here, more especially as I know that the division commander entertains the same opinion as I do on the subject and is as fully acquainted with the reasons.

There was at one time uneasiness about those bands of the Utes, upon whose reservations white men, miners, and prospectors had largely intruded, but no outbreak has occurred, and I presume such arrangements have now been made as will render any difficulty with those Indians unlikely.

I deem it unnecessary to enter into any consideration of the question of shelter for troops or the repair of posts now occupied by them, as such matters have been fully represented in regular correspondence concerning them.

It is proper, however, to state, as the result of actual experience, that a yearly sum ought to be appropriated to keep the military posts in repair. It is not to be supposed that such frail structures as are always built for the accommodation of the military forces of the United States doing duty on the remote frontier, (except the ordnance corps,) can be kept in repair without the expenditure of a considerable sum annually, nor does it seem the best or most efficient way of doing this to forward estimates to Washington for the smallest details of such matters. It certainly would seem better to assign a certain sum annually for repairs of all important permanent posts, so that these posts at least might be always kept in good order. The hardships and hard work which troops on the frontier must endure, and do, and which they cheerfully undergo, certainly entitles them to habitable quarters during the severe winters of this region, and whatever expenditure of money is necessary to secure this for them ought, if possible, to be made both for the sake of justice and of good policy.

I trust, therefore, that some provision will be made, however small, to assign at the beginning of every fiscal year a fixed sum, to be determined in any manner which may seem most suitable, to keep in repair all the posts in each military department in the gross or for each post separately, so that the trifling work which needs to be done nearly every day may be done when the necessity arises, and without waiting the long delay of sending to and receiving back from Washington small estimates for such purposes.

The sums thus required would be enough if furnished at the time, but are quite insufficient after a delay of two or three months.

It is my agreeable duty to bear testimony to the very efficient and judicious action of Major Price, Eighth Cavalry, in his dealings with the Indians in the southern part of New Mexico, as also of Major Alexander, Eighth Cavalry, commanding in the Ute country. Both these officers have been very active and very successful in keeping peace and in protecting the frontiers.

Lieut. Col. J. R. Brooke, Third Infantry, commanding Camp Supply, and Maj. R. I. Dodge, Third Infantry, commanding Fort Dodge, are entitled to the same justice at my hands.

The camp of the Sixth Cavalry near Fort Hays, under command of Col. James Oakes of that regiment, has also fully satisfied the objects for which cavalry was stationed in that region.

Orders will be sent in a few days to withdraw all the troops in the field to winter-quarters at the posts from which they were detached, and by November 10 it is expected that the execution of the orders will be completed.

After that date there is little, if any, fear that Indians will be found on the great plains.

We have been subjected to much inconvenience and some embarrassment by the absence of so many field officers from their regiments, and it is hoped that some of those now on detached service may be ordered to rejoin their regiments at the earliest convenient time.

Concerning the administration of the department in its various details, I refer to the reports of the chiefs of the staff departments inclosed, and in relation to the same matters, I ask attention to the recommendations made in my previous reports, which are again commended to the consideration of the proper authorities.

It is, perhaps, not improper for me to specify two subjects which seem to me to be worthy of attention:

1st. Concerning the recruiting service and the detail of officers for that duty. The tour of duty of officers assigned to recruiting service begins and ends on the 1st of January, the tour of such officers lasting two years. I suggest that the time of reporting for and being relieved from such duty be fixed at May 1 or July 1, instead of January 1. Officers detached for recruiting service from remote posts, far from railroads, and ordered to report January 1, in the depth of winter, find it, in many cases, impracticable or exceedingly difficult, without much suffering, to obey the order, unless, indeed, they leave their posts several months earlier than would be necessary to make the journey, and officers relieved from recruiting duty on the 1st of January, in like manner, find it, at times, absolutely impracticable in many cases to join their proper stations at that season of the year, and are therefore obliged either to ask leave of absence or delay in obeying the order, until the season is suitable to travel to remote posts. In this manner many officers are kept away from duty at their posts for several months, when, by fixing the time of joining recruiting stations, or being relieved from that duty, at May 1 or July 1, no such necessity would arise. I do not know what are the reasons for preferring the 1st of January for beginning and terminating recruiting-service details, but, unless they are very important, the interests of the service on the frontier would be greatly benefited by the suggested change.

2d. It would be greatly to the advantage of the Army on the frontier if the annual appropriations for building and repairing shelter for the troops could be made available on the 1st of February of each year instead of the 1st of July. It has not seemed practicable to distribute the sums approved on requisitions for the posts on the frontier so that they can reach such posts before the autumn, generally too late in the season to be applied to building before the following spring. By having the money assigned for such purposes early in the spring, the whole season in which building or repairing can be best done, would be available for the purpose, and the troops need not, as is now the case, suffer more or less all winter because of the impracticability of using the funds actually allowed during that season of the year. Whether this change can be made, or whether it be judicious to make it, must be left to higher authority, and I simply offer the suggestion for consideration.

I would also suggest the advisability of retransferring to this department that portion of the Indian country between the southern line of Kansas and the Canadian River, including Fort Gibson. I think the division commander agrees with me that the defensive arrangements of this department require that the department commander should have jurisdiction over that region.

The various staff departments have been conducted with efficiency and good judgment, as I think the results show.

We are rapidly acquiring thorough knowledge of all the country em- braced in the limits of the department, and most excellent maps, through the various scouting parties, in each of which an officer or an engineer soldier has made careful surveys and sketches under detailed instruc- tions from department headquarters.

I transmit inclosed a roster of the department and a field return of the troops serving in it.

I am, colonel, respectfully, your obedient servant,

JNO. POPE,
B'v't Maj. Gen., U. S. A., Commanding.

Official:

R. WILLIAMS,
Assistant Adjutant-General.

Lieut. Col. J. B. FRY, *Asst. Adjt. Gen.,*
Headquarters Military Division of the Missouri.

NOTE.—Since the above report was written, a party of two hundred Cheyennes left their reservation south of Camp Supply, and passing far to the west of all the posts entered the southern part of Colorado west of Fort Lyon, and went up as far as the Kansas Pacific Railroad at River Bend. The Indians were not hostile, and beyond stealing some cooking utensils and killing a few cattle they did no damage. Finding that their presence excited such immediate attention from the citizens as well as the troops, they hastened back toward their reservation.

Full report of the matter having been made to the division comman- der so recently, it seems unnecessary to enter into details here. As the Indians belonging to this party are individually known they can be arrested and punished at any time on their reservation. They have not committed any acts demanding such condign capital punishment as (I see from the papers) the Secretary of the Interior recommends; nor have they done anything that is not done every year by some of the reservation Indians, against the perpetrators of which severe measures have been discountenanced, not to say denounced. Only in February last a party of Cheyennes, some of whom were without doubt the same Indians who were on the late expedition into Colorado, went up the Canadian River from their reservation with the same purpose, (viz, to fight the Utes,) and in returning began to depredate on the settlements near Bascom. They were attacked by troops from that post and several killed. This act, which seems to be recommended in the present case, when it is too late for execution, was the occasion of remonstrance by the Interior Department, and a manifest intention was shown to throw the blame of any further depredations by the Cheyennes upon the mili- tary who did it. If the Interior Department really wishes the Chey- ennes recently in Colorado punished, they have only to consent to their arrest when they get back to their reservation. I can easily and promptly do this and save unnecessary bloodshed among innocent peo- ple.

REPORT OF MAJ. GEN. IRWIN McDOWELL.

HEADQUARTERS DIVISION OF THE SOUTH,
Louisville, Ky., October 6, 1873.

SIR: I have the honor to submit to the General of the Army the following report of the military operations and the military service in this division (reconstituted December 11, 1872, and consisting of the Departments of the South and the Gulf) for the year commencing October 1, 1872:

DEPARTMENT OF THE SOUTH.

October 1, 1872.—The posts of Lincolnton and Rutherfordton, N. C., were discontinued, and Company C, Seventh Cavalry, was ordered from Lincolnton to Charlotte, N. C., and Company C, Fourth Artillery, was ordered from Rutherfordton to Raleigh, N. C., where it arrived October 17, 1872.

October 16, 1872.—Company H, Seventh Cavalry, was sent from Nashville, Tenn., to Livingstone, Sumter County, Ala., to protect citizens at the election, and returned November 10, 1872.

October 21, 1872.—Company E, Eighteenth Infantry, sent from Atlanta, Ga., to Seales Station, Russell County, Ala., and ordered back November 8, 1872. One commissioned officer and twenty-five men, Company A, Seventh Cavalry, were ordered from Elizabethtown, Ky., to report to United States marshal. One commissioned officer and fifteen men of Company H, Seventh Cavalry, detached from Livingstone, Sumter County, to Carrollton, Pickens County, Ala., ordered back November 10, 1872.

October 22, 1872.—Company B, Second Infantry, was sent from Atlanta, Ga., to Demopolis, Marengo County, Ala., and Company I, Second Infantry, was sent from Chattanooga, Tenn, to Eutaw, Greene County, Ala. Both returned to their posts November 10, 1872. One commissioned officer and twelve enlisted men of Company A, Eighteenth Infantry, were ordered from Atlanta, Ga., to Macon, Ga., at request of the United States marshal, and ordered back November 10, 1872.

October 29, 1872.—Company E, Third Artillery, was ordered from Fort Pulaski to Savannah, Ga., during the election.

November 1, 1872.—One officer and ten men were placed en route for each of the following places in Alabama from Chattanooga, Tenn.: Abbeville, Henry County, Second Lieut. A. McIntyre, Second Infantry. Columbia, Henry County, First Lieut. J. Ulis, Second Infantry. Ordered back November 10, 1872.

One officer and ten men placed en route for each of the following places in Alabama, from Nashville, Tenn.; Ozark, Dale County; Greenville, Butler County; Rutledge, Crenshaw County; Troy, Pike County. Ordered back November 10, 1872.

November 6, 1872.—Headquarters, and Light Battery C, Third Artillery, were placed en route for New York City, in compliance with General Orders No. 88, War Department, Adjutant-General's Office, of 1872.

November 12, 1872.—Light Battery K, First Artillery, arrived in the department from the Department of the East, in compliance with General Orders No. 88, War Department, Adjutant-General's Office, of 1872, and took post at Charleston, S. C.

November 15, 1872.—Headquarters, staff, band, and Company H, First

Artillery, arrived in the department pursuant to General Orders No. 88. War Department, Adjutant-General's Office, of 1872, and took post at Charleston, S. C., relieving Company I, Third Artillery, which was placed en route for the Department of the East.

November 17, 1872.—Company D, First Artillery, arrived in the department from the Department of the East pursuant to General Orders No. 88, War Department, Adjutant-General's Office, of 1872, and took post at Savannah, Ga., relieving Company K, Third Artillery, which was placed en route for the Department of the East.

November 20, 1872.—Maj. John Hamilton and Companies B and C. First Artillery, arrived at Fort Pulaski, Georgia, from the Department of the East, relieving Companies E and H, Third Artillery, which were placed en route for New York City, in compliance with General Orders No. 88, War Department, Adjutant-General's Office, of 1872.

November 22, 1872.—Maj. J. C. Tidball and Companies F and I, Second Artillery, arrived at Raleigh, N. C., from the Division of the Pacific.

November 30, 1872.—Captain Weir and thirty enlisted men of Company D, Seventh Cavalry, were placed en route for Montgomery, Ala., on the request of the governor of Alabama, based on the representations of the sheriff of Montgomery County.

December 5, 1872.—Company K, Sixteenth Infantry, was relieved from duty at Saint Augustine, Fla., and ordered to Frankfort, Ky. Company I, Seventh Cavalry, was relieved from duty at Shelbyville, and ordered to Lebanon, Ky.

December 6, 1872.—Company L, Seventh Cavalry, was relieved from duty at Yorkville, S. C., and ordered to Shreveport, La., (Department of the Gulf,) and Company M, Seventh Cavalry, was relieved from duty at Unionville, S. C., and ordered to Oxford, Miss., (Department of the Gulf,) by order of the General of the Army.

December 11, 1872.—I assumed command of the Division and Department of the South, relieving Brig. Gen. A. H. Terry from command of the latter, in compliance with General Order 100, War Department, Adjutant-General's Office, of 1872.

December 16, 1872.—Company A, Sixteenth Infantry, was sent from Louisville to Frankfort, Ky., pursuant to paragraph 4th, Special Order 310, War Department, Adjutant-General's Office, of 1872; the Fourth Infantry was placed en route for Little Rock, Ark., in the following order: 16th, Company H; 18th, Company F; 19th, Company I; 21st, Company D; 23d, Company A; 24th, Company E; 25th, Company B; 26th, Company C; January 7, 1873, Company K; January 14, 1873, Company G.

December 18, 1872.—Company L, Seventh Cavalry, placed en route for Shreveport, La., in compliance with paragraph 4, Special Order 310, War Department, Adjutant-General's Office of 1872.

December 23, 1872.—Company K, Sixteenth Infantry, was sent to Frankfort, Ky., from Saint Augustine, Fla.

December 25, 1872.—Company M, Seventh Cavalry, from Unionville, S. C., placed en route for Oxford, Miss., in compliance with Special Order 310, War Department, Adjutant-General's Office, of 1872.

December 26, 1872.—Company I, Second Infantry, was ordered from Chattanooga, Tenn., to Lancaster, Ky.

December 30, 1872.—Company I, Seventh Cavalry, abandoned the post of Shelbyville, and went to Lebanon, Ky.

January 6, 1873.—One officer and twenty men of Company F. Seventh Cavalry, from Taylor Barracks, Ky., placed en route for Livingstone, Rockcastle County, Ky., to assist United States marshal in serving process of United States court.

January 17, 1873.—The post of Laurensville, S. C., ordered abandoned, and Company I, Eighteenth Infantry, ordered to Columbia, S. C., where it arrived January 26, 1873. Company G, Seventh Cavalry, ordered to Newberry, S. C., and arrived there January 23, 1873.

January 21, 1873.—The post of Chester, S. C., ordered abandoned, and Company H, Eighteenth Infantry, placed en route for Columbia, S. C. Detachment of cavalry sent to Yorkville, S. C., and arrived January 29, 1873.

January 26, 1873.—Detachment of Company A, Seventh Cavalry, ordered back to Elizabethtown, Ky., from Huntsville, Ala.

January 29, 1873.—At the request of United States Marshal Murray, Company A, Sixteenth Infantry, was sent to Lexington, Ky., from Frankfort, Ky., and ordered back February 7, 1873.

February 3, 1873.—Headquarters and band, Fourth Infantry, left Frankfort, Ky., for Little Rock, Ark.

February 15, 1873.—Commanding officer post of Atlanta, Ga., was directed to place one officer and twenty men en route for Moultrie, Colquitt County, Ga., at request of United States Marshal Smyth, of Georgia. They returned to Atlanta, Ga., April 16, 1873.

February 17, 1873.—Company D, Seventh Cavalry, was ordered from Opelika to Livingstone, Sumter County, Ala., by direction of the President.

March 3, 1873.—Company A, Sixteenth Infantry, was placed en route for Lebanon, Ky,

March 13, 1873.—Company D, Seventh Cavalry, arrived at Memphis, Tenn., from Livingstone, Ala.

March 15, 1873.—Company E, Seventh Cavalry, arrived at Memphis, Tenn., from Unionville, S. C.

March 17, 1873.—Company K, Seventh Cavalry, arrived at Memphis, Tenn., from Yorkville, S. C.

March 18, 1873.—Company M, Seventh Cavalry, arrived at Memphis, Tenn., from Oxford, Miss.

March 20, 1873.—Company C, Seventh Cavalry, arrived at Memphis, Tenn., from Charlotte, N. C. Company B, Seventh Cavalry, arrived at Memphis, Tenn., from Spartanburg, S. C.

April 2, 1873.—Headquarters, staff, band, and Companies A, F, H, and I, Seventh Cavalry, left Louisville, Ky., en route for Department of Dakota.

April 3, 1873.—Companies G and D, Seventh Cavalry, left Memphis, Tenn., for Department of Dakota.

April 4, 1873.—Companies E and K, Seventh Cavalry, left Memphis, Tenn., for Department of Dakota.

April 5, 1873.—Companies B, C, L, and M, Seventh Calvary, left Memphis, Tenn., for Department of Dakota.

May 20, 1873.—The post of Spartanburg, S. C., ordered abandoned, and garrison (Company D, Second Infantry) sent to Atlanta, Ga., June 2, 1873, arrived June 7, 1873.

June 11, 1873.—The post of Taylor Barracks, Louisville, Ky., abandoned, Company E, Sixteenth Infantry, placed en route for Lancaster, Ky., to relieve Company I, Second Infantry, the latter, when relieved, to proceed to Atlanta, Ga. Garrison at Nashville was temporarily removed to White Creek Springs on account of cholera.

July 10, 1873.—Charleston Arsenal, S. C., was ordered discontinued, and the arsenal (to be hereafter known as Charleston Barracks) to form part of the post of Charleston.

August 19, 1873.—The post of Sumter, S. C., ordered to be abandoned, and Company F, Eighteenth Infantry, to proceed to and take station at Columbia, S. C.

September 4, 1873.—The post of Charlotte, N. C., discontinued, and Company D, Second Artillery, ordered to take post at Charleston Barracks, S. C.

September 20, 1873.—The garrison of Mobile, Ala., headquarters, staff, band, and Companies G and K, Second Infantry, temporarily moved to Mount Vernon, Ala., in consequence of yellow fever. The movements of troops in this department were made in aid of the United States civil officers, to enforce the processes of the United States courts, and collect the internal revenue. In all cases the troops fulfilled the duty on which they were sent. Soon after assuming command of the division I made an inspection of all the posts in this department, and in the interests of discipline, military instruction, and economy, abandoned such of them as the nature of the public service permitted, and concentrated the troops, as far as practicable, at such points as enabled them to be maintained at the least cost and greatest comfort. Fourteen of the military posts of the department were thus abandoned, at an annual saving of over $100,000 on account of the Quartermaster's Department alone. For the purpose of making a further reduction in expense, of avoiding the necessity of repairing old temporary quarters built on hired ground, and of exchanging an unhealthy for a healthy post, I made a special inspection in person in the month of August last of the late Mount Vernon Arsenal, Ala., (now directed to be called Mount Vernon Barracks,) with the view of preparing economical and judicious estimates of alterations necessary to convert, at an early day, bare workshops into quarters, and an arsenal into barracks, that I might send there the troops now at Mobile. I trust the War Department may soon be able to sanction the estimates for these alterations, and grant authority for sending in estimates for a hospital. The place (I cannot yet say the barracks) at Mount Vernon is now occupied by the garrison from Mobile, it having sought refuge there from the yellow fever now afflicting the South. The late Charleston Arsenal, hereafter to be called Charleston Barracks, is now occupied by a single company. I propose soon to inspect the post with the view of submitting estimates for such alterations as will enable me to place there two, or at least one more company, and thus further reduce the sum we are now paying for hire of quarters.

The deputy quartermaster-general attached to this department (whose report is herewith) states the United States to be indebted through the Quartermaster's Department, in the Department of the South, for the fiscal year ending June 30, 1873, as follows:

Incidental expenses	$12,529.29
Barracks and quarters	11,197.16
	23,726.45

He further states that as this amount was not for material furnished, but for personal services, it is the decision of the War Department that the creditors cannot be paid from the appropriations for this year, and must now look to Congress for relief.

The sum of $12,529.29, for what is known as "incidental expenses," is made up of small sums due to, mostly, poor people; $4,471.49 being to clerks authorized by the War Department; $683 to colored scavengers at five different posts; $1,881 to blacksmiths for shoeing the artillery, cavalry, and quartermasters' horses at eighteen different posts; $4,196 to soldiers at twenty-three posts for extra duty, pay allowed by law when on constant hard labor for more than ten days; $1,320 to persons at twelve posts for rewards, allowed by law, for apprehension of deserters.

The sum of $11,197.16 is mostly due for rent of buildings and grounds

for barracks and quarters at twelve different posts—those still occupied—it having been thought best to pay in full at those which I caused
to be abandoned. I am safe in saying that everything has been done
to insure as little liability under these heads as possible; that, in fact,
it would have been much greater but for the reduction I have made in
the number of posts. I am assured, and believe, that the various post
assistant and acting assistant quartermasters have been prompt in sending in their estimates, and that these have been by the deputy quartermaster-general promptly sent to the Quartermaster-General's Office.

I have no question, also, that the funds were remitted to the extent
the appropriation permitted, and were distributed as soon as possible.
I only dwell on this subject because of the hardship I know it has
caused many deserving people, and of the discredit it has brought on
the service, and to show that the indebtedness is not due to any want
of vigilance or fault on my part, or of those under me.

I send herewith the reports of the chiefs of the several staff departments at department headquarters of the operations under their charge
during the part year.

DEPARTMENT OF THE GULF.

I submit herewith the report of Col. W. H. Emory, commanding the
department, for an account of the movement of troops and the state of
the service in his command.

The duty devolving on the officers and men and their commander in
this department during the past year has been of the most delicate,
important, and frequently embarrassing kind, and it gives me pleasure
to state that it has been discharged with tact, fidelity, and, in all cases,
with effect.

I have the honor to be, very respectfully, your most obedient servant,
IRWIN McDOWELL,
Maj. Gen. Commanding Division of the South.

The ASSISTANT ADJUTANT-GENERAL,
Headquarters of the Army, Washington, D. C.

REPORT OF MAJ. GEN. J. M. SCHOFIELD.

HEADQUARTERS MILITARY DIVISION OF THE PACIFIC,
San Francisco, Cal., November 3, 1873.

SIR : I have the honor to submit to the General of the Army the inclosed reports of operations in this military division during the past
year.

The Division of the Pacific embraces the three Departments of Arizona, California, and the Columbia.

The Department of Arizona, commanded by Bvt. Maj. Gen. George
Crook, lieutenant-colonel Twenty-third Infantry, since appointed briga-
dier general, has been the theater of active operations against hostile
Indians—operations characterized by consummate skill displayed in the
plans of the departmental commander, and by gallantry and untiring
energy of the officers and men engaged. With few exceptions the
lately-hostile Apaches have been forced to submit to authority, and are
now living quietly upon the reservations assigned them.

Since the close of General Crook's campaign it has been found possible to diminish somewhat the cavalry force in that department, which
had been increased to insure his success.

Increased development and security have diminished the cost of supplies for the troops.

The military telegraph to Prescott and Tucson, now nearly completed, beside its great military advantages, will facilitate commercial business and promote further development of the Territory.

The condition of Arizona is more hopeful than at any former period, and great credit is due for this improvement to the department commander and his subordinates.

I respectfully refer to General Crook's report and the accompanying documents for full and detailed information upon all matters connected with his command.

The Department of the Columbia has been the scene of a conflict more remarkable in some respects than any before known in American history. All the details of the Modoc war are so fully known to the Government and to the public, through reports heretofore made, that it would be superfluous to repeat them here.

The Department of the Columbia is now commanded by Bvt. Maj. Gen. Jefferson C. Davis, colonel Twenty-third Infantry, who succeeded to that command upon the death of the lamented General Canby.

General Davis's annual report has not yet been received at these headquarters.

The Department of California, under my immediate command, has enjoyed uninterrupted peace during the past year. Nearly all the troops, including the artillery, were engaged in the campaign against the Modocs, and some of them have since been employed in guarding the prisoners and in conducting them to their destination in the Department of the Platte.

The inclosure marked A gives the strength and distribution of the troops serving in the department.

The reports of the chiefs of staff departments, also inclosed, show the details of transactions in their separate departments.

Some changes in the stations of troops, rendered expedient by the progress of events, will hereafter be made the subject of special report, accompanied by estimates of the expenditures necessary to accomplish them.

Very respectfully, your obedient servant,

J. M. SCHOFIELD,
Major-General.

The ASSISTANT ADJUTANT-GENERAL,
Headquarters of the Army, Washington, D. C.

REPORT OF MAJ. GEN. W. S. HANCOCK.

HEADQUARTERS MILITARY DIVISION OF THE ATLANTIC,
New York City, September 30, 1873.

SIR: I have the honor to submit for the information of the General of the Army my annual report for the division.

I was assigned to that command and to that of the Department of the East by General Order No. 100, Headquarters of the Army, November 25, 1872, and pursuant to these orders assumed command December 16, 1872.

General Order No. 105, Headquarters of the Army, Adjutant-General's Office, December 7, 1872, transferred the headquarters of this division from Philadelphia, Pa., to New York City.

The organization of the division has not been changed since date of last annual report. Its aggregate in troops at date of last returns was as follows :

Department of the East, 178 officers; enlisted men, 1,531; Department of the Lakes, 78 officers; enlisted men, 603; total, 256 officers, 2,134 enlisted men.

I refer to my inclosed report, as commander of the Department of the East, for a detailed statement of operations in that command during the past year, and also refer for a similar purpose to inclosed annual report of the commander of the Department of the Lakes.

The attention of the General of the Army is respectfully invited to the remarks and recommendations contained in the concluding portion of my report, as commander of the Department of the East, relative to the urgent necessity for a military prison in that command, and which might serve as well for Department of the Lakes, and concerning the erection of some new buildings at certain posts in New York Harbor.

Having recently visited and inspected all the posts in the Department of the Lakes, I am able to concur in the remarks and recommendations of the commanding general of that department.

In reference to the reservation at Fort Gratiot, I may add, in addition to my approval of the views expressed in his report, that I think it unfortunate that the ground between the fort and the inlet of the straits should have been ceded by Congress, and that with all the guards that may be thrown around the deed of cession, I believe, for military purposes, the value of the reservation has been much impaired. I think, also, it would be better that the part of the light-house reservation authorized to be sold should be reserved for military purposes, as since the obstruction of the old reservation caused by the grant to the railroad company, I am not sure that it might not be as well to make that the defensive point instead of the present position.

I submit herewith a list of the military reservations in this division, showing when and how the land was secured to the Government, and how occupied at this date.

Fort Mackinac is an excellent place for the cantonment of troops intended for service on the upper lakes. It has no other importance at this date, as it cannot be made to protect the straits on which it is situated.

Plattsburg Barracks may also be used for the quartering of troops, but can serve no other military purpose not provided for by Fort Montgomery.

Carlisle is only important as a cantonment.

David's Island might advantageously be made a cantonment for the troops intended to occupy the forts in the East River, when completed.

As all of the reservations named in the accompanying list, save Fort Wilkins, Copper Harbor, Lake Superior, (now abandoned, and not important to the military service,) are deemed to be useful, it would in my judgment be better to retain all, with that exception.

I inclose herewith reports of the chiefs of the several staff corps at these headquarters.

The assistant inspector-general, having been absent for some time on a tour of inspection, has not been able to furnish his annual report. It will be transmitted to your office as soon as practicable after his return to these headquarters.

I am, sir, very respectfully, your obedient servant,

WINF'D S. HANCOCK,
Maj. Gen., U. S. A., Commanding.

The ASSISTANT ADJUTANT-GENERAL,
Headquarters of the Army, Washington, D. C.

REPORT OF THE ADJUTANT-GENERAL.

WAR DEPARTMENT,
Adjutant-General's Office, October 7, 1873.

SIR: My report of October 7, 1872, referred to the *re-established* business of the late Bureau of Refugees, Freedmen, and Abandoned Lands, and recited the regulations for conducting it. The said regula tions have proved well adapted to their object, and the results obtained are, in a high degree, satisfactory.

In addition to the disbursing offices established under War Department General Orders No. 79, of 1872, it has been found expedient to establish others: At Fort Monroe, Virginia; Forts Macon and Johnston, North Carolina; Charleston, South Carolina; and Savannah, Georgia, for the payments to claimants residing at and near to those points, thereby enabling them to receive the amounts due them, with comparatively little expense to themselves and a considerable saving to the Government.

For the thirteen offices now open, the force employed is, 13 commis sioned officers, 30 clerks, and 10 messengers and janitors.

The officers in charge of the offices at Forts Monroe, Macon, and Johnston, Charleston, and Savannah, attend to their ordinary post and company duties in addition.

The *discovery* of claimants who, since filing their claims, have changed their places of residence, many of them to other States, has, in many instances, proved extremely difficult, but through diligent effort on the part of the disbursing officers, who have availed themselves of all prac ticable means to attain that end, they have succeeded in ascertaining the whereabouts of a considerable number, and in securing to them the amounts awarded in settlement of their claims.

It was also ascertained that numerous claimants were living at points remote from either of the established paying districts, and that to secure payment to them through any one of the disbursing officers would be impossible, without entailing expenses largely disproportion ate to the amounts involved. A plan was therefore submitted which led to an arrangement, by the Secretary of War with the Postmaster-General, for the payment of such claimants through the postmaster at or nearest to their respective places of residence. A number have already been paid in this way, and the system is found to work favora bly. As a further aid to the "discovery of the claimants," a circular letter, copy herewith, A, dated March 18, 1873, was sent to certain Sen ators and Representatives. Resort was also had to advertising.

Early in the month of December, 1872, it was discovered that claims borne upon the records of the late Bureau of Refugees, Freedmen, and Abandoned Lands as *paid*, were, in fact, unpaid, while others borne as *unpaid* had actually been paid. It therefore became necessary to at once subject said records to a careful examination and comparison with those of the accounting officers of the Treasury, in order that all neces sary emendations might be made and the work of payment be safely proceeded with. This labor occupied about one month, during which period all payments were necessarily suspended. Until the discovery of the errors referred to, the disbursing officer stood in constant danger of making duplicate payments, or of rejecting just claims.

By the act of March 3, 1873, entitled "An act to place colored persons who enlisted in the Army on the same footing as other soldiers as to bounty and pension," a very large number of colored ex-soldiers have become entitled to bounty, of which they had hitherto been deprived by reason of their having been "slaves" April 19, 1861. Claims under said act are filing in the Office of the Second Auditor of the Treasury, and a few certificates in settlement have already been received at this office. When such claims come, as they undoubtedly will, to be numerously settled, the labors of this office will, of course, be proportionately enlarged.

The missing and defective records of the late Bureau have, to a limited extent, been supplied by the late Commissioner, eighteen packages, containing records of various descriptions, including books of "Letters received," "Letters sent," and "Indorsements," "Bounty registers," files of letters, claims, soldiers' discharges, &c., having been received. The bulk, however, of those indicated to the late Commissioner by letter of January 18, 1873, has not been produced.

The discontinuance, under the circular of August 8, 1872, of the *prosecution* of claims for bounties or other moneys due to colored soldiers and others, has resulted favorably to the Government by a large saving of expenses.

Correspondence has been had with the late Commissioner from time to time, relative to subjects involved in his administration of the late Bureau.

I respectfully submit, as a part of this communication, my reports dated February 20, 1873, August 4, 1873, and September 23, 1873, (now before the War Department,) which relate, respectively, to the condition of the affairs of the late Bureau, and the responsibility and accountability of the late Commissioner.

The tabular exhibits herewith, submitted by the chief disbursing officer, will indicate the financial operations during the fiscal year ending June 30, 1873, and to August 31, 1873.

Very respectfully, general, your obedient servant,
THOMAS M. VINCENT,
Assistant Adjutant-General.

The ADJUTANT-GENERAL OF THE ARMY,
Washington, D. C.

Approved and respectfully submitted to the Secretary of War.
E. D. TOWNSEND,
Adjutant-General.

Report of the recruiting service from October 1, 1872, to October 1, 1873.

WAR DEPARTMENT, ADJUTANT-GENERAL'S OFFICE,
Washington, October 14, 1873.

Recruiting for cavalry, artillery, and infantry has been carried on during the past year in the principal northern and western, and in a few of the southern cities. Owing, however, to the limited sums appropriated for this service for the last fiscal year, several rendezvous which might have been maintained in small towns as branches to those located in the large cities have been discontinued. On the same account it was found necessary to diminish the number of enlistments by raising the standard of height for artillery and infantry recruits, in order to keep down the expenses of the recruiting service. From this cause the regiments became reduced in number at the very season for active operations, and the Department had not the means to strengthen them.

The appropriation for the present year, reduced upon the original estimate made by this Office, will towards the close of the year again run

28 Ab

short. Meantime, however, every effort will be made to fill the regiments to the standard allowed.

Two rendezvous for organizations on the Pacific coast are maintained under the supervision of the commanding general, Military Division of the Pacific, but the number of men there enlisted is insufficient to keep up the strength of the organizations in that section of the country.

There is a rendezvous for the Corps of Engineers in New York City, under charge of an officer of that corps.

With the exception of those stationed on the Pacific coast, and those recruiting for the Battalion of Engineers, all recruiting officers enlist for the colored regiments.

A few officers located in cities where there are stations for the signal-service also enlist men for that arm of the service.

E. D. TOWNSEND,
Adjutant-General.

Statement showing the number of enlistments and re-enlistments in the Regular Army from October 1, 1872, to October 1, 1873; compiled from reports forwarded to this Office by superintendents of the recruiting service, &c.

Regiments, &c.	Number enlisted and re-enlisted.	Regiments, &c.	Number enlisted and re-enlisted.	Regiments, &c.	Number enlisted and re-enlisted.
General service	4,131	Ninth Cavalry	41	Eleventh Infantry........	34
Mounted service	3,419	Tenth Cavalry	131	Twelfth Infantry........	10
Engineer Battalion......	177	First Artillery	60	Thirteenth Infantry	9
Ordnance Department...	105	Second Artillery	88	Fourteenth Infantry	8
Military Academy	37	Third Artillery	105	Fifteenth Infantry	19
Artillery School.........	1	Fourth Artillery	65	Sixteenth Infantry........	83
Signal Corps	209	Fifth Artillery	56	Seventeenth Infantry	3
Ordnance sergeants......	2	First Infantry	73	Eighteenth Infantry	14
Hospital-stewards	21	Second Infantry	47	Nineteenth Infantry	151
First Cavalry	26	Third Infantry	62	Twentieth Infantry	20
Second Cavalry	72	Fourth Infantry	53	Twenty-first Infantry....	27
Third Cavalry...	45	Fifth Infantry	88	Twenty-second Infantry...	2
Fourth Cavalry	25	Sixth Infantry	0	Twenty-third Infantry..	7
Fifth Cavalry	7	Seventh Infantry.....	11	Twenty-fourth Infantry..	1
Sixth Cavalry	70	Eighth Infantry	34	Twenty-fifth Infantry....	9
Seventh Cavalry	114	Ninth Infantry	39		
Eighth Cavalry	34	Tenth Infantry	13	Total...............	9,881

NOTE.—Of the recruits enlisted for mounted service, 693 were for colored cavalry.

E. D. TOWNSEND,
Adjutant-General.

WAR DEPARTMENT, ADJUTANT-GENERAL'S OFFICE,
Washington, October 4, 1873.

REPORT OF THE INSPECTOR-GENERAL.

WAR DEPARTMENT, INSPECTOR-GENERAL'S OFFICE,
Washington, October 10, 1873.

SIR: The inspection service of the Army during the past year has been performed in conformity with the requirements of General Orders No. 87, series of 1872, the five inspectors-general having been exclusively subject to the orders of the Secretary of War and the General of the Army.

My own duties, for the most part, have been confined to the charge of the Inspector-General's Office, at the headquarters of the Army, receiving and examining inspection reports, and extracting therefrom all matters of interest to, or requiring action by, the Secretary of War, the

General of the Army, and the heads of the different bureaus of the War Department; and it is believed that much important information has thus been communicated which would not otherwise have come to the knowledge of those officials.

Inspectors-General D. B. Sacket, E. Schriver, N. H. Davis, and J. A. Hardie, during the autumn of 1872 and the winter of 1872 and 1873, made careful and thorough inspections of the Department of the South, a part of the Department of Texas, the entire Department of the Missouri, and the Department of the Gulf.

Early in the spring of 1873 these officers, under orders from the Secretary of War, commenced the inspection of the Departments of Arizona, Texas, Dakota, and the Columbia, thoroughly examining into the condition of the *personnel* and *matériel* of the Army at all the remote and widely dispersed posts, stations, and depots within the limits of those departments—excepting Alaska—and embracing one hundred and seventeen military posts, garrisoned by eighteen regiments of infantry, seventeen companies of artillery, and eight regiments of cavalry. This laborious service involved many thousands of miles of wagon-travel, for the most part over unsettled sections of country infested by hostile savages, and occupied each officer from seven to nine months.

Besides this, other minor inspections and investigations have, from time to time, been made by these officers, thus occupying all their time, and involving voluminous reports, which have been made without the expenditure of a dollar for clerical assistance.

Inspector-General Hardie, at the request of the general commanding the Military Division of the Pacific, and by authority of the Secretary of War, previous to inspecting the Department of the Columbia, visited the headquarters of the expedition against the Modoc Indians, and made certain inspections and reports for the division commander.

In a letter from General Schofield to Colonel Hardie, dated April 21, 1873, is the following:

In order that the public service may derive the fullest benefit from your tour of inspection in the Department of the Columbia, I request that your inspections may be extended to all branches of the military service, so far as it can be done without interfering with the plans or wishes of the department commander; and that all errors, faults, or defects you may discover be pointed out to the officers concerned, and corrected at once as far as practicable.

The instructions that may thus be given to young and inexperienced officers is one of the greatest benefits expected from your visit to the frontier posts.

*   *   *   *   *   *   *

Substantially similar requests were made of the other inspectors-general by the commanders of the departments of "Texas," "the South," "the Gulf," "Dakota," "Arizona," and "the Columbia," and in accordance with their instructions from the War Department, prompt reports were made directly to those commanders, upon all matters which were deemed of interest to them, or which required their action, and it is believed that those reports received immediate action at the hands of the department commanders.

The inspectors-general report that the commanders of the departments above named rendered great assistance to them in the execution of their duties, by directing that the most ample facilities should be afforded them to investigate every branch of the service at all the posts and stations within their respective commands. The inspectors' reports also show that the officers generally gladly availed themselves of the opportunity afforded by their visits to ask instruction relative to the correct interpretation of doubtful points of law, regulations, and orders and upon other mooted questions regarding the proper performance of military duties; and it seems to me reasonable to presume that the extended and diversified experience of these officers, both in the staff and line of the Army, eminently qualify them to give suitable answers to questions of this character, as well as sound advice and instruction to young and inexperienced officers.

This, besides promoting social harmony, will doubtless tend to produce uniformity in the manner of performing military duty in different departments and localities, and will unquestionably fortify and encourage zealous and competent officers in their action, and thus greatly conduce to the discipline and efficiency of the Army.

Assistant Inspectors-General R. Jones, A. Baird, and E. H. Ludington have during the year been attached to the head-quarters of the military divisions of "the Pacific," "the Missouri," and "the Atlantic," respectively. Their reports show they have been actively and usefully engaged in the duties pertaining to their positions, and, it is believed, to the entire satisfaction of their commanding officers.

Col. J. V. Bomford, Eighth Infantry; Lieut. Col. J. P. Hatch, Fourth Cavalry, and Capt. G. B. Russell, Ninth Infantry, for a portion of the year acted as assistant inspectors-general, but have been relieved.

Maj. W. H. Lewis, Seventh Infantry; Maj. A. W. Evans, Third Cavalry, and Capt. W.W. Sanders, Sixth Infantry, are respectively attached to the head-quarters of the Departments of Dakota, Arizona, and the Gulf, as acting assistant inspectors-general.

In compliance with the requirements of the system instituted by the Secretary of War, in General Orders No. 87, series of 1872, scrutinizing examinations have been made of the accounts of all officers who have made important disbursements of public money during the year. The funds received and expended by them, with the balances they reported due the United States, have been carefully compared and verified by official statements obtained from the Treasury Department and depositories.

If this system continues to be strictly carried out in accordance with the order, it is believed that few losses will occur to the United States, as it seems hardly possible that a defalcation can be concealed or overlooked for any great length of time, and it is gratifying to state that no embezzlement and but three cases of misapplication of funds have been reported during the year, the latter being small sums which probably will not result in any loss to the Government.

The inspectors report that in some cases the monthly balances of public funds on deposit, with the numbers and amounts of checks drawn, are not regularly furnished disbursing officers by the depositories, which prevents verifying their check-book balances with those of the depositories.

The inspection reports show that the troops have been well supplied with clothing during the year, although the new-pattern uniform has not yet reached some of the more distant posts. Subsistence supplies have been abundant and of good quality, but at a great many posts complaints have been made that large excesses of officers' and canned stores have accumulated and become damaged by age to such an extent as to render it necessary to sell them at much less than cost. At some of the posts three and four years' supply of certain perishable articles are reported on hand. Whether this surplus resulted from over-estimates or from the stores being furnished in excess of requisitions, or from the changes of troops, I am unable to say, but this condition of things has resulted in losses to the United States, and may, it is believed, be to a large extent avoided in the future if the post commissaries and post commanders, with the officers who fill the requisitions, are held to a rigid accountability that they call for and supply no more than is necessary.

Complaints have been made to the inspectors by the officers at many posts that their predecessors, on being relieved, have carried away files of orders, books, and other records which properly pertain to the posts; which practice should be promptly corrected by orders.

Inspector-General Davis states, in his annual report, that post quartermasters do not generally keep a proper morning report, accounting for their employés, public animals, and forage and fuel received, issued, and remaining on hand; this he regards as an important report, which, if properly kept, would avoid some discrepancies which might otherwise occur.

The inspections during the year have also disclosed the fact that at several posts large deficiencies of forage have existed, which the officers responsible have in some instances claimed resulted from great shrinkage in the dry atmosphere of the plains. There are good reasons for believing, however, that in some cases these deficiencies have arisen from want of proper care on the part of quartermasters in weighing and receiving the forage from contractors or predecessors.

Public animals picked up astray or coming into possession of quartermasters otherwise than by regular transfer, as well as forage rentered surplus by short issues, have not in all cases been taken up and accounted for until the attention of the authorities was called to the facts by the inspectors.

These irregularities are, however, exceptional, the inspection reports indicating that the officers performing the duties of quartermasters are generally improving in zeal and efficiency; that better care is taken of public property, and more regard manifested for economy and other interests of the service than heretofore.

All the facts above stated have been reported by the inspectors to department commanders, who have, it is believed, taken prompt measures to investigate and correct the irregularities.

To prevent soldiers under charges from being confined for long periods previous to trial, it is suggested that post commanders be invested with authority to present for trial, before general courts-martial, cases not of an unusual character, that have arisen subsequent to the ordering of the court, without the charges being first referred to department commanders, which, at some remote posts, consume six weeks' time, and frequently involve the necessity and expense of convening another court-martial.

Notwithstanding the fact that the condition of the soldier in our Army has been greatly ameliorated, and his pay and allowances increased, by recent regulations and legislation, and although the aggregate number of desertions in the past fiscal year has been about five hundred less than during the previous year, yet the desertions have continued to such an extent as to still constitute an evil to the service of the greatest magnitude. Many remedies have been suggested as preventive for this, one of the most heinous of military crimes, which involves not only an entire disregard of soldierly honor, but a deliberate act of perjury; yet nothing seems to have had the desired effect. But few deserters have been apprehended on the frontier, for the reason that in many localities they have been protected by the citizens, who do not generally appreciate the turpitude of the crime.

One of the inspectors-general has suggested a remedy which appears to me worthy of consideration. It is, that desertion be constituted by legislative enactment as a felony cognizable by the civil courts of criminal jurisdiction, the offenders to be arrested by marshals and deputies. like other criminals, but this jurisdiction to be concurrent with military courts.

This, it is believed, would have the effect of educating and impressing the public mind with a proper sense of the criminality of the offense, and prevent evil-disposed persons from harboring deserters.

It would, in my judgment, greatly augment the efficiency of the Army were more instruction given to recruits previous to sending them to organizations from the recruiting depots.

Since the reduction of the Army to the existing standard, urgent calls for recruits to fill vacancies in the different regiments upon the frontier have generally prevented them being kept at the depots more than a week or two, and they frequently join their companies knowing nothing of the use of arms, or even the position of a soldier. Whereas if they were properly instructed for three months at the recruiting depots they would be proficient in the company exercises.

The majority of the troops are now doing duty in the Indian country, where they are not only required to perform service as arduous and hazardous as in time of war, but they are often compelled to procure material for and build their own quarters, which, with their other indispensable fatigue duties, consumes so much of their time that it is frequently impossible to give them much systematic military instruction at the military posts on the frontier.

Besides, the exigencies of the service very often leave but one commissioned officer with a company, and his time is so much taken up with scouting, escorting, and his other multifarious duties, that he can give but little attention to drills or other military teaching.

I deem it proper to remark here that the adoption of the new code of Army Regulations, recently submitted to Congress for approval, will provide remedies for most of the irregularities and evils that have been mentioned.

The old Army Regulations of 1863, which, under the act of July 28, 1866, are to continue in force until the adoption of a new code, do not meet the existing exigencies of the service. Indeed, they have been so altered and amended by laws and orders, that it often requires considerable study and research to determine their actual signification Besides, this edition is now exhausted, with but few tattered copies extant, so that, unless something is done soon, it may be truly said that our Army have no regulations.

The officers, for the most part, are exceedingly desirous that a new code which they can comprehend should be speedily promulgated. In view of this, and the additional fact that the regulations now before Congress will settle many mooted military questions that have never been touched upon in former editions, and this in accordance with opinions of the best military minds we have ever had in service, and as in my judgment they are in other respects eminently adapted to the existing necessities of the service, I beg leave again most respectfully to recommend the early action of Congress upon them.

Respectfully submitted.

R. B. MARCY,
Inspector-General.

The ADJUTANT-GENERAL OF THE ARMY.

REPORT OF THE JUDGE-ADVOCATE-GENERAL.

WAR DEPARTMENT, BUREAU OF MILITARY JUSTICE,
Washington, D. C., October 1, 1873.

SIR: In compliance with instructions of circular of the 13th ultimo, I have the honor to submit for your consideration the following statement of the business of this Bureau since the date of my last annual report, of October 1, 1872:

1. Number of records of military courts received, reviewed, and registered, 16,088.

2. Number of special reports made upon court-martial proceedings, and applications for remission of sentences, and upon the miscellaneous questions of law, &c., referred for the opinion of the Bureau, 823.

3. Abstracts of proceedings of trials furnished to the proper officials of the War and Treasury Departments, 1,737.

4. The copies of records furnished under the ninetieth article of war to parties tried by military courts have amounted to 7,723 pages.

The amount of business thus performed during the past year varies little from that reported for the year preceding.

The work of systematically arranging, indexing, &c., the voluminous official papers of the late Provost-Marshal Baker, heretofore reported as in progress, has been completed during the current year.

Respectfully submitted.

J. HOLT,
Judge-Advocate-General.

Hon. W. W. BELKNAP,
Secretary of War.

REPORT OF THE QUARTERMASTER-GENERAL.

QUARTERMASTER GENERAL'S OFFICE,
Washington, D. C., October 10, 1873.

SIR: I have the honor to submit the annual report of operations of the Quartermaster's Department during the fiscal year ending 30th June, 1873.

*   *   *   *   *   *   *

At the close of the fiscal year the balances remaining in the hands of officers and not needed to discharge liabilities incurred during the fiscal year, and payable out of these balances, were called in and transferred to officers who found themselves deficient in funds to pay for supplies and services purchased or rendered under orders of their commanders.

This money, scattered all over the United States and Territories among some three hundred disbursing officers, has not yet been all brought into the Treasury, and the process of settlement of outstanding accounts is still going on. It appears that these balances thus collected will not be sufficient to pay for all the supplies purchased and services rendered, and a deficiency estimate has accordingly been submitted. It amounts to:

Regular supplies	$206,000
Incidental expenses	241,000
Army transportation	592,000
Barracks and quarters	127,000
Total	1,166,000

The principal deficiency is in the appropriation for transportation; but there are also deficiencies in regular supplies, incidental expenses, and barracks and quarters.

It is impossible for any human intelligence to predict the exact nature and cost of the military operations of a nation during a period of twelve months, which begins nearly twelve months after the estimate is made.

The average ordinary general expenses of the Army do not differ greatly from year to year, but the separate items differ greatly, as changes are more or less frequent in the stations of the troops, and as new posts are established and new districts occupied.

The estimates of this office are based upon experience, and when reduced it is not always possible for the War Department to so regulate the military movements and to control the cost of articles given by law and regulations to the troops in certain definite quantities as to keep within the appropriation.

The law gives to officers and men certain fixed supplies of clothing, of quarters, of transportation, and when the appropriations are deficient, the officers find themselves in the dilemma of failing to provide what the law requires them to supply, or of incurring liabilities beyond the amount of the appropriations. Whichever course is taken violates law.

The forms and methods of keeping and making accounts and returns in the Quartermaster's Department have been improved and simplified by the issue of General Orders No. 64, October 25, 1871; No. 68, November 4, 1871; No. 7, February 21, 1872, and No. 98, November 14, 1872. These four orders publish in compact form the existing regulations for making returns of money and of property, and those which govern the system of transportation of military material and of troops.

They have now been in operation, the two former for nearly two years, and the latter for one year, and the annual reports of officers doing duty in the Quartermaster's Department are bearing almost unanimous testimony to the advantages in simplicity and intelligibility of the forms and system now in use and established by these general orders.

I regret to see in the system of regulations recommended to the War Department by a board of officers, and, under the law of July 15, 1870, communicated to Congress, a proposition to transfer from the Quartermaster's Department to the Commissary Department a large portion of the duties of this Department.

The Quartermaster's Department has always had as one of its special duties the transportation of all military stores. It is organized and trained especially to this duty, and there can be no doubt that simplicity, and economy, and efficiency in military operations are best secured by committing such an important branch of the service to some one military department. Hence, I consider as likely to be very injurious, should it be adopted, the proposition to transfer to the Subsistence Department the transportation and storage of subsistence supplies.

The proposition is that the Subsistence Department shall be responsible for and have control over the transportation of its supplies; that commissaries, in addition to purchasing and issuing as heretofore, shall contract for all transportation of their supplies, wherever rail or water transportation can be contracted for or hired; that, when supplies are to be transported to posts away from rail or water, the commissary shall make requisition on the quartermaster, at the point where such supplies leave rail or water, for Government wagons and teams for their transportation. If the quartermaster cannot furnish these, the commissary to hire wagons or contract for the delivery of the supplies at the place of destination; and at points of transshipment, if there are no suitable store-houses, the commissary to hire or build such as are needed. This, if adopted, will transfer to the commissary a large part of the duties of the quartermaster. It will establish two great parties competing against each other at all important strategic points for transportation. The officer of each department will have as a first duty the success of his own department of the service, the fulfillment of the orders he receives. If there is but one steamboat, the quartermaster and the commissary will compete for its control, and the prices of freight will advance.

If there is a scant supply of wagons, of mules, or of oxen, the same competition will spring up. Instead of one department dealing with the owners of the steamboat, the railroad, the wagon, the inland mule or ox-train, there will be two, each acting in the interest of the same party, the United States, but competing and bidding against each other. So, too, instead of one department and one set of officers, as heretofore, constructing or renting the requisite store-houses, there will be two competing for the lease, and as the quartermaster will have no footing in the commissary store-houses there will be two store-houses erected or hired at the expense of the Treasury instead of one. Responsibility, too, will be divided and weakened. The commissary is to do these things after his goods leave the railroad or steamer in case the quartermaster is unable to furnish the wagons and has no spare store-houses.

There are other provisions in the draft of these regulations, as printed by Congress, H. R. Report 85, which make radical changes in the positions of large numbers of officers.

The Quartermaster's Department has been recognized by law, and by regulations and orders, as a part of the general staff of the Army. In it promotion and rank are regulated as a part of the staff. These proposed regulations propose to change all this, and to remand certain most important departments of the staff to a separate and anomalous condition as parts of a special staff or administrative service or supply-branches of the service.

The experience of many years in this country, and observation of the course of military events here and elsewhere, which in the life-time of this generation have been on a very great scale, both at home and abroad, have conclusively vindicated the system of this country which gives to all officers of the staff of the Army on whose intelligence, skill, and zeal the application and support of the physical and moral power of the soldier depend, military rank and military responsibility. This principle has been lately introduced even into the Navy. It secures a higher order of service, greater zeal, intelligence, ardor, and integrity, and now the draft of new regulations proposes to cripple and weaken this system by driving these several corps of intelligent officers out of the position and standing in which they have won honor to themselves, done credit to the Army, and good service to their country in time of its greatest need.

While the system of reports and accounts has been simplified by the action of the War Department in the publication of these general orders, legislation has introduced into all the accounts of this office, and of hundreds of disbursing officers, a serious difficulty and complication. Each officer of the Quartermaster's Department who disburses money has occasion to expend it under several of the different heads of appropriation. Though he may have a large sum of money to his credit and subject to his check, he may be unable to pay a just bill for forage or for services because he has none of that particular appropriation on hand. This increases nearly nine-fold the entries in his accounts. It often occasions delay in payment of the public creditor, and by complicating the accounts increases the liability to errors and disallowances. Both the officer and the public creditor suffer, and the Treasury suffers in many ways, as each disbursing officer must have a working balance under each head of appropriation; the total amount lying to his credit, unused, in the public depository must be much greater than if, out of any sum to his credit, he was allowed to pay any just account. The remedy for this evil—and it is a great one—would be the making of the appropriations for the Quartermaster's Department under a single title.

While the total gross sum needed for the service of this Department can be estimated for any ordinary year with considerable accuracy, it is not possible to secure absolute accuracy in each of the million items which go to make up the sum total, or in the several divisions under which it has been customary to present these estimates to Congress. It would be much better to appropriate for the Quartermaster's Department in one gross sum equal to the aggregate of the estimate, and thus simplify accounts and secure the prompt and certain payment of the public creditor. All dealers now charge something for the risk of delay which experience shows them that the present system too often causes.

The report of the officer in charge of the branch of this office which examines the accounts of disbursing officers sets forth in detail the inconvenience and injury to the service arising from this system, and the report (H. R. No. 87, Forty-second Congress, third session) by the Committee on Expenditures in the War Department, printed by the House of Representatives, also very forcibly presents the case.

The following table, which gives the balances remaining in Treasury on account of the Quartermaster's Department on the 30th June, 1873, will show the complication of accounts caused by the requirement of the law to treat each head of appropriation under each year as a separate and distinct appropriation, to be drawn upon and accounted for separately. There are forty-three separate appropriations.

Balances of appropriations undrawn by the Quartermaster's Department, July 1, 1873.

	Prior to July 1, 1870.	1870–1871.	1871–1872.	1872–1873.	1873–1874.
Regular supplies	$363,400 86	$82,069 05	$80,203 98	$1,628 55	$4,500,000 00
Incidental expenses	154,582 71	63,330 62	128,223 05	3,813 40	1,300,000 00
Purchase of horses	51,773 50	12,231 29	22,109 73	7,692 96	350,000 00
Barracks and quarters	125,124 02	45,075 91	79,902 32	32,952 33	1,700,000 00
Transportation of the Army	801,844 32	8,597 38	684,684 14	156,541 92	4,462,666 50
Transportation of officers' baggage	29,882 66				
Clothing of the Army	76,312 66	47,160 55	26,488 90	4 53	1,045,637 92
Stoves	34,493 27	21 00	40 00		
National cemeteries					275,000 00
Clocks for permanent posts	522 00				
Hospitals				15,473 49	100,000 00
Expenses of sales				9,157 57	
Head-stones				183,886 25	1,000,000 00
Monument at Salisbury, N. C.				10,000 00	
Preservation of clothing					50,000 00
Total	1,637,936 00	259,505 40	1,030,712 12	421,191 00	14,812,134 42

The number of money-accounts and of property-returns examined during the past year is not so great as in previous years. This is due in great measure to the increased difficulty of the settlement under the act of 3d June, 1870. But at this time all accounts and returns for years prior to 1873 have been examined, and nearly all those for first quarter of 1873 have been examined. Those for the second quarter of 1873 are now in course of examination, and the examination of those for the third quarter, which has just closed, will be commenced before all are received from officers. The work of examination may therefore be said to be up to date.

The Quartermaster's Department is charged with the duty of providing the means of transportation, by land and water, for all troops and all material of war. It furnishes the horses of the artillery and cavalry, and horses and mules for the trains. It provides and distributes clothing, tents, camp and garrison equipage, forage, lumber, and all material for camps and for shelter of troops and of stores. It builds barracks, hospitals, store-houses; provides wagons and ambulances and harness, except for cavalry and artillery horses; builds or charters ships, steamers and boats, docks and wharves; constructs and repairs roads, railways, and bridges; clears out obstructions in rivers and harbors when necessary for military purposes; provides, by hire or purchase, grounds for military encampments and buildings; pays, generally, all expenses of military operations not by law expressly assigned to some other department; and, finally, it provides and maintains military cemeteries, in which the dead of the Army are buried.

Food, arms, ammunition, medical and hospital stores are purchased and issued by other departments, but the Quartermaster's Department transports them to the place of issue, and provides store-houses for their preservation until consumed. The corps of officers upon whom all these duties fall has been reduced by time until it is not able to fill well every post at which an officer of activity and ability is needed. Its ranks should be now opened to promotion and appointment.

Many officers of the line, finding themselves charged with heavy responsibility as acting assistant quartermasters, and having insufficient assistance, at frontier posts, ask that the enlistment of post quarter-master-sergeants may be allowed by law. Such non-commissioned officers, selected for experience and fidelity shown in actual service, would be very useful. They would remain at posts in charge of the property when the garrison changed, and thus would preserve knowledge and responsibility now often lost through the frequent change of officers. Such officers also ask that some compensation may be granted them for the risk which they incur in the disbursement of public money, and for the responsibility involved in the care of large amounts of public property.

I have the honor to renew the recommendation heretofore made, that an allowance of $10 per month be made in addition to the pay of every line-officer who is detailed by proper authority as acting assistant quartermaster of a military post, when such detail is properly reported to and approved by the War Department. Such an allowance is only just, and it would relieve the service from the feeling that heavy duties are imposed by such detail without any recognition or compensation. Such duties are important, and they should be sought by good officers, not imposed upon the slothful or unwilling.

About three hundred and eighty officers of the line act every year for some portion of the time as acting assistant quartermasters.

The officers of the regular establishment of the Quartermaster's Department, all of whom have served through the late war and have had much experience, are stationed at the more important depots and posts. Yet many posts, involving heavy responsibility in money and property, and calling for good judgment, integrity, and zeal, are occupied by subalterns of the line, on duty as acting assistant quartermasters.

INSPECTION BRANCH.

To this branch of this office are committed the keeping of records of stations and duties of officers, of correspondence, the examination of reports of inspection, of reports of boards of survey, the filing and preservation and distribution of orders and circulars. Through this branch of the office about 180,000 papers pass and are recorded yearly. Lists of the officers of the Quartermaster's Department, and of officers of the line who have served in the Quartermaster's Department during the year, with their stations and duties, will be found attached to this report.

INDEBTED RAILROAD COMPANIES.

At the close of the war, under executive orders of 8th August and 14th October, 1865, there were sold on credit to various railroad companies, principally in the South, railroad material to the appraised value of..	$7,556,033 95
There remained due and unpaid from certain of these railroads on 30th of June, 1872	4,734,442 43
During the past fiscal year, interest and expenses accrued upon this debt to the amount of	101,573 95
Payments during the year, on account, have amounted to	151,303 44
On the 30th June, 1873, the debt uncollected amounted to	4,658,924 97
exclusive of the sum of $25,788.87 due from the New Orleans and Ohio Railroad, which debt is lost by the bankruptcy of the company. The total collections on account of this debt, to 30th June, 1873, amount to	5,116,605 53

The earlier collections, being reimbursements of the Quartermaster's Department for property originally purchased with its appropriations, were applied to its service, reducing the amounts of the annual estimates for appropriations; but since the passage of the law of May 8, 1872, requiring all proceeds of sales of public property to be deposited in the Treasury, to credit of miscellaneous receipts, these collections have taken that course. Fifty railroads originally availed themselves of the privileges of the executive orders. Thirty of them have paid their debts in full with interest. Twenty now remain in debt to the United States on this account.

A full statement of these accounts accompanies this report; to it reference is made for detailed information.

Against some of the roads greatly in default suits have been commenced in the United States courts.

Since my last report the suit against the Nashville and Decatur Railroad has been compromised and settled by the Secretary of War, under authority of the act of 3d March, 1871, (16 Stat., chap. 119) for the sum of $70,000, of which $6,000 was paid in cash, the balance to be paid in ten years from 1st July, 1872, with interest, semi-annually, at the rate of 5 per cent. per annum, secured by bond and lien upon the property of the company, guaranteed by the Louisville and Nashville Railroad, and by decree of the United States circuit court affirming the liability, and to be enforced by execution in case of default.

Other suits are yet unsettled, for details in reference to which I refer to the report of Major Ludington, the officer in charge of the transportation branch of this office, which accompanies this report.

Some of the roads largely indebted to the Government, and which have given bond for the application of their postal earnings to the payment of their debt, refuse or persistently neglect to give the order for the payment of their earnings, which, in the judgment of the Post-Office Department, is necessary, before the money can be thus applied. Some of these earnings have thus, under the law, lapsed into the Treasury; other considerable amounts are locked up. They are not turned over to the roads, but not being turned over to this Department it cannot credit the debt account of the railroads with them.

Some provision of law for the collection of this money and settlement of the debt, so far as it will go, is desirable.

TRANSPORTATION.

The General Order No. 98, of 1872, establishing the improved system of transportation, has been distributed to officers of the Army and to all railroads and transportation companies having dealings with this office. It is found to be satisfactory to the officers and to the public with whom they deal.

The total movement of transportation during the year, thus far reported, amounts to 72,860 persons, 8,148 beasts, and 164,125,223 pounds of material.

The cost of railroad transportation during the year amounts to $1,235,579.43, of which accounts for $921,514.87 have been settled or transmitted by this office to the Treasury for settlement.

The movement over the Pacific Railroad has been:

Name of railroad.	No. of persons moved.	No. of beasts moved.	Freight in pounds.
Union Pacific....................................	6,166	1,763	21,697,106
Central Pacific of California....................	3,034	63	2,444,211
Kansas Pacific..................................	1,951	390	5,711,947
Sioux City and Pacific..........................	223	36	3,544,054
Total	11,374	2,252	33,397,318

The cost of this service is estimated at:

For the Union Pacific Railroad..	$445,501 00
For the Central Pacific Railroad	136,598 07
For the Kansas Pacific Railroad..	149,797 00
For the Sioux City and Pacific Railroad	2,402 44
Total value of service of the Pacific railroads during the year......	734,298 51

Until the passage of the act of 3d March, 1873, one-half the earnings of these roads for military transportation was paid in cash, on proof of service, and the other half was retained by the Treasury to be used in payment of the interest on the United States bonds issued to them. Since the passage of that law the whole of these earnings have been withheld by the Secretary of the Treasury, but it is charged against the appropriations for transportation of the Army.

The earnings of the Pacific railroads in the previous fiscal year, ending June 30, 1872, were $800,857; in the year ending June 30, 1871, $767,047.99.

WAGON AND STAGE TRANSPORTATION.

By wagon we moved during the year 756 passengers, 32,004,635 pounds of material; by stage, 1,380 passengers, 3,648 pounds of material. The cost of wagon transportation was $997,943.44; of stage transportation, $59,319.29.

Thirty-two contracts for wagon transportation are reported during the year.

The existing contract for wagon transportation from the line of the new Atchison, Topeka and Santa Fé Railroad, and from the Kansas, Pacific and Denver and Rio Grande Railroads, to posts in the Department of Missouri, and in Texas and New Mexico, and to Camp Apache, Arizona, is at the rate of 90¾ cents per 100 pounds per one hundred miles. This is a considerable reduction from the previous contracts, which averaged $1.17½.

The existing wagon contract rates in Texas generally show a material reduction in price, attributable to the extension of railroads into the interior, the shortening of the wagon routes, and the avoidance of the routes through the heavy soils and wet climate of the coast.

On the Pacific coast the rates have slightly increased.. The demand for transportation due to the Modoc war, carried on during the rainy season, will account for this increase. That campaign was very destructive to the means of transportation.

WATER TRANSPORTATION.

By water the movement has been of 37,789 persons and 2,026 beasts, and 55,467,201 pounds of stores. The cost of this, so far as the bills have been settled, was $760,973.58.

Three small steamers and two schooners owned by the United States have cost during the year $37,413.19. Twelve vessels have been hired or chartered during the year, at a cost of $43,056.76. Both these sums are included in the aggregate cost of transportation by water, reported above.

During the past fiscal year accounts and claims for transportation service rendered in previous years have been paid, or transmitted from this office to the Treasury for payment, amounting to $652,409.17.

CONTRACTS FOR REGULAR AND MISCELLANEOUS SUPPLIES.

During the year 614 contracts for supplies were reported to this office, as follows: For forage, 230 contracts for 20,318,814 pounds of oats or barley, 19,372,472 pounds of corn, 30,744 tons of hay, 439,000 pounds of bran; 11 for 2,508 tons of straw; 30 for 22,011 tons of coal; 144 for 84,022 cords of wood; 37 for 49,075 bushels of charcoal; 4 for construction of quarters; 47 for transportation; 7 for horses and mules; 12 for clothing, camp and garrison equipage; 16 for national cemeteries, and many for miscellaneous supplies and services.

FORAGE, STRAW, AND FUEL.

The issues of these supplies have been: Corn, 588,488 bushels; oats, 939,690 bushels; barley, 172,870 bushels; hay, 48,588 tons; fodder, 116 tons; straw, 3,292 tons; bran, 55,084 bushels. Of wood, the issue was 130,786 cords; of anthracic coal, 16,937 tons; of bituminous coal, 15,300 tons.

ANIMALS.

One thousand nine hundred and thirty-eight horses, costing $255,- 460.19, were bought during the year. The average cost in California was $110.11; in the Department of the Columbia, $115; Department of the Missouri, $126.36; in Texas, $132.40; Dakota, $139.

In addition to occasional purchases of horses to supply losses, 1,200 remounts were authorized this spring for the several cavalry regiments, as follows: For First Cavalry, none; Second Cavalry, 175; Third Cavalry, none; Fourth Cavalry, 175; Fifth Cavalry, 150; Sixth Cavalry, 100; and Seventh, Eighth, Ninth, and Tenth Cavalry, each 150. Those for the Second, Sixth, Seventh, and Tenth Regiments were purchased in Missouri, Iowa, and adjoining States; those for the Fifth, in California; those for the Fourth, in Texas; those for the Eighth, at Leavenworth and in Colorado, and those for the Ninth, at points designated by the general commanding Department of Texas. These purchases were made by boards of officers assembled by the department commanders, each board consisting of a quartermaster and one or two officers of the regiment for which the horses were intended. The boards moved through the districts assigned for their operations; published their wants by posters, and purchased from farmers and stock-raisers direct, without intervention of middlemen. The result has given satisfaction, and the system secured good horses at fair prices.

MULES.

Two thousand three hundred and ninety-seven mules were purchased for the trains at a cost of $328,033.02. The greater number of these were bought for the expedition to escort the Northern Pacific Railroad surveying party from Fort Abraham Lincoln, on the Missouri, to and beyond the Yellowstone River. The average cost of mules was $137.

One thousand and fifty-one horses were sold for $46,624.43; 200 mules, for $9,313.06. The proceeds, $55,937.49, have been deposited in the Treasury to the credit of miscellaneous receipts.

Four hundred and twenty-four horses and 489 mules are reported to have died, and 158 horses and 100 mules to have been lost or stolen during the year, and the number in service at the close of the year was 10,130 horses and 10,425 mules.

ARMY WAGONS AND HARNESS.

There are reported in service 3,107 wagons, 125 spring-wagons, 240 ambulances, 23,411 sets of wagon-harness, 2,148 sets of ambulance-harness, all serviceable.

The stock of wagons in the Army has suffered by use and age. Even those kept in store have deteriorated by dry-rot and by attacks of insects, to which hard timber is liable, so that many of those in use were unreliable and unfit to be used on a long march. The Yellowstone expedition, in Department of Dakota, was outfitted with a new train, and many new wagons have been sent to other departments to replace those which had failed or threatened to fail.

Five hundred and fifty new wagons were purchased during the year. Two hundred and fifty, purchased in open market to meet the emergency of the immediate outfit of the Yellowstone expedition, cost $175 each. Contracts were made for the others, giving more time for the manufacture, at $149.50 each.

The train-wagon used for many years in the operations of the United States Army before the war is of excellent design and construction. In the very dry climate of the higher plains, and in the deserts of the Colorado and Gila, exposed to a scorching heat, and in an atmosphere without moisture, the timber shrinks and cracks. The wagon-builders of this country have for several years been experimenting with metallic hubs, many of which have been patented. Of some of the best of these, many thousands are now annually made and put into use. I believe that some of them will prove to be better fitted for use in the extremely dry climates than wood, and samples of each of those which appeared to be best have been purchased and distributed to posts in the most trying climates for trial. The change is an important one, and will not be made, generally, unless the result of these trials is conclusive in favor of some one of the metallic hubs.

HORSE-SHOES AND SHOEING-MATERIAL, SMITHS' AND SADDLERS' TOOLS

Under the provisions of General Orders No. 2, War Department, Adjutant-General's Office, January 2, 1873, the supply of tools and of shoes for shoeing cavalry and artillery horses was transferred from the Quartermaster's Department to the Ordnance Department, and large quantities of these materials and tools purchased by the Quartermaster's Department have, under that order, been transferred to the officers of the Ordnance Department.

The Quartermaster's Department must still keep smiths and tools for repair of its wagons, and for shoeing the draught animals, at every post, and when there are, as is frequently the case, no enlisted farriers with a body of cavalry, its officers are still called upon to provide for shoeing their horses. Thus two establishments are kept up throughout the military service to do the same thing, which appears not to be an efficient or economical arrangement.

EPIZOOTIC.

The epidemic catarrh which traversed the continent during the past year, visited, it is believed, every military post, and attacked a great majority of the horses and mules of the military establishment. It appeared early in New York and its vicinity, and a method of treatment adopted by Brevet Major-General Ingalls, assistant-quartermaster general, upon the advice of the veterinary surgeons of New York, was printed and distributed to military posts:

HEADQUARTERS DEPARTMENT OF THE EAST,
OFFICE CHIEF QUARTERMASTER,
New York City, October 28, 1872.

[Circular.]

The attention of officers and agents in charge of public animals belonging to the Quartermaster's Department in the Department of the East is called to the "epizootic catarrh" now prevalent among horses. They are directed to observe the following rules for the treatment of this disease, and to report results to this office at the end of the present month, and every ten days thereafter, until the disease disappears.

It is assumed that the stables are always kept clean, dry, and well ventilated, with plenty of fresh air and sunlight, when possible. It is also assumed that the horses are never overworked, but properly exercised at all times, whether sick or well, and that they are fed with wholesome forage, regularly groomed, and kept warm.

RUFUS INGALLS,
Col. and Asst. Q. Gen., Brt. Maj. Gen., U. S. A., Chief Quartermaster.

Rules for the treatment of the disease.

On the first appearance of the disease give the horse a thorough steaming with hot boiled oats, placed in a bag, and so fastened to the head that the steam from the oats will be inhaled. Repeat this until the discharge from the nostrils is free and of a natural color. Then take leather, or, what is better, carbolic disinfectant, in grains like large-sized cannon-powder, place it in a shallow pan, and burn it where the horse will be obliged to breathe it.

If the throat is sore, (which generally will be the case,) apply frequently hot vinegar, rubbing it well with the hand, and wrap the throat in flannel, dipped in vinegar. Sponge out the nostrils frequently with warm vinegar. Blanket well, night and day, but not enough to produce sweating, and give plenty of fresh, clean bedding.

Give several bran mashes, with from one-half to one ounce of powdered niter in each, and use linseed-meal or flax-seed in the oats. Use tepid water in the mash.

The hay and oats should be moistened with water—preferably tar-water.

Most cases if taken in time will yield to the above treatment; but should the attack be very severe, accompanied with considerable fever, and very sore throat, instead of the vinegar, an embrocation of equal parts of linseed-oil, turpentine, tincture of cantharides, and hartshorn should be rubbed in night and morning.

Powell's embrocation is very good.

Give as a drench, night and morning, the following:

Spirits of nitric ether.. 1 ounce.
Laudanum.. 4 drams.
Nitrate of potassa .... 3 drams.
Water.. 1 pint.
Mix.

Should the horse refuse his feed, offer him frequently thin gruel, with a handful of pulverized slippery-elm bark, and licorice-root stirred in it.

When convalescing, exercise gently daily, and stimulate the appetite with the following ball:

Extract of gentian .... 6 drams.
Powdered ginger .... 2 drams.
Mix.

A handful of wood-ashes mixed with a little salt, thrown into the feed-trough for the horse to lick up, will be relished by him and be beneficial.

At a later date the Secretary of War communicated to this office the following simple prescription, with directions to communicate it to all officers of the Army in charge of public animals:

One teaspoonful of chlorate of potash twice a day to four horses, put in a pail of water, and let each horse drink his proportion.

These two prescriptions were thus made known. The losses by death from the disease were very small, but the operations of supply were everywhere delayed and deranged as long as the disease prevailed. It was very hurtful, during its prevalence, among the animals employed in hauling supplies to the troops operating against the Modocs, and for a time it dismounted the cavalry in that campaign, as also in Arizona.

THE YELLOWSTONE EXPEDITIONS.

, In the summer of 1872 an expedition left the Missouri River to escort a party of engineers to explore a line for the Northern Pacific Railroad to the valley of the Yellowstone. This march showed that the wagon-trains, composed of wagons purchased during the war, had outlived their usefulness, and for the larger expedition organized in the month of June of the present year, it was necessary to procure a large number of new wagons and many mules. One hundred and fifty new wagons were supplied, which, with about fifty reported to be good and available in Dakota, completed the train; 1,058 mules were purchased and forwarded to Fort Abercrombie, where the mules were broken, organized into trains, fitted with harness, and supplied with teamsters, under the direction of Captain Dandy, assistant quartermaster, during the months of April and May. This train consisted of two hundred and two 6-mule teams and wagons, nine spring-wagons, with four mules each, two 6-mule artillery teams, and twelve riding mules for the wagon-masters.

One 6-mule wagon and one 4-mule spring-wagon and their teams, and nine saddle-horses, were also supplied for the use of the scientific commission, which, under authority of the Secretary of War, accompanied the expedition into this wild country.

29 Ab

The organization of this train was a laborious and difficult work, and its completion in so short a time is creditable to the officer in charge.

The following is an extract from the annual report of Capt. G. B. Dandy, assistant quartermaster, Fort Abraham Lincoln, Dak., who organized the trains:

On the 21st of April I received instructions from the chief quartermaster of the department relative to organizing army-wagons for service with the proposed Yellowstone surveying expedition. I was at that time in charge of the depot of transportation at Fort Abercrombie, consisting of three hundred and sixty-five mules and seventy wagons, which was further increased by the addition of ten hundred and seventy-five mules and one hundred and sixty wagons to be organized and added to the depot-train.

On the 27th April the mules and wagons, with the necessary harness for fitting out one hundred and fifty 6-mule teams for service with the exploring and surveying party of the Northern Pacific Railroad west of the Missouri River, commenced arriving at Breckenridge, Minn., fifteen miles from Fort Abercrombie. The last shipment of animals and material arrived on the 26th of May. The teamsters were hired in Saint Paul, with the exception of fifty hired on my recommendation at Fort Leavenworth, Kans. These latter were the only men sent me having any experience in the management of 6-mule teams, and many of the men employed at Saint Paul were vicious or worthless characters. About 25 per centum of the mules sent to me from Saint Louis were very wild, and required throwing or placing in the stocks to shoe. Many had to be thrown in order to harness them; and there were many other difficulties in the way of organizing this mass of raw men and material for efficient service in so short a time. The train, however, was completely shod and equipped and en route to the Yellowstone on the 29th May. It consisted of two hundred and two 6-mule teams, nine 4-mule teams for spring-wagons, two 6-mule teams for artillery, and some 12 riding mules for wagon-masters. In addition, there were one 6-mule team, one 4-mule spring wagon and team, and nine riding-horses provided for the use of the scientific party accompanying the expedition. Special attention was paid to fitting the train amply with spare parts, and blacksmiths', saddlers', and wheelwrights' supplies.

MODOC CAMPAIGN.

Summary of expenditures, indebtedness, &c.

Disbursements as reported by Captain Hoyt	$120,881 20
Ascertained indebtedness, as reported by Captain Hoyt	70,990 03
Transportation of 754,257 pounds from San Francisco, at 15 cents	113,138 55
Grain from Camp Halleck, consumed, cost at camp Halleck	5,000 00
Transportation of grain from Camp Halleck, consumed, rough estimate	25,000 00
	335,009 78

Items of expenditure not yet definitely reported to this office:
Cost of stores in San Francisco.
Cost of transportation of ordnance stores, &c., from Benicia arsenal; weight unknown.
Cost of transportation to Fort Klamath of over 200,000 pounds of grain and other supplies and stores remaining at the close of the campaign.

BARRACKS AND QUARTERS—MILITARY BUILDINGS.

During the year the construction of one hundred and twenty new buildings has been authorized, at an estimated cost of $245,544.87.

They are barracks for men, quarters for officers, stables, store-houses, guard-houses, bake-houses, &c. They are at military posts distributed through the following States and Territories: California, Louisiana, Florida, Michigan, South Carolina, North Carolina, Tennessee, Texas, Kansas, New York, Maryland, Oregon, Nevada, Kentucky, Georgia, Nebraska, Pennsylvania, Minnesota, Maine, Iowa, Connecticut, Virginia, Dakota, New Mexico, Montana, Washington, Arizona, Utah, Colorado, the Indian Territory, and the District of Columbia.

WHARVES.

The expenditure of $18,111.32 in repair and construction of wharves at various posts has been authorized.

REPAIRS.

Upon special estimates submitted to the Secretary of War, repair and alterations of military buildings to the amount of $228,796.49 have been authorized. Many small repairs, making in the aggregate a large sum, were also made under authority of local commanders, without special reference to the War Department for authority.

NEW POSTS ESTABLISHED.

The construction of two new posts in Arizona has been authorized—one near Tucson and one near the mouth of the San Carlos River These posts are designed for garrisons of four companies each.

The orders of the Secretary required the labor of the troops to be employed when possible, and limited the expenditure upon the two posts to $35,000.

The post near Tucson is Camp Lowell; that on the San Carlos is New Camp Grant, and they take the places of Tucson Depot and Old Camp Grant, which latter was in a very unhealthy, malarious location.

Erection of huts for one company of infantry at Otter Crossing, on the line of the Northern Pacific Railroad, was authorized in October, 1872.

A post known at first as Fort Cross, now named Fort Seward, has been erected on the James River, Dak., on the line of the same railroad.

Fort Abraham Lincoln has also been built at the Missouri crossing of the railrod.

New posts have been commenced at Tulerosa, N. Mex., and at Beaver City, Utah.

FIRE-PROOF BUILDING AT JEFFERSONVILLE.

This building has been occupied. The stores, heretofore in wooden buildings scattered over a large space, in constant danger of fire and depredations, involving heavy expense for protection against both these dangers, have been all removed to the new building, properly classed and arranged for easy access, and safe against damp and fire.

An elevated reservoir, kept by a steam-pump constantly filled with water from a pool within the depot, affords the means, through pipes and hose, of instantly subduing any fire occasioned by incendiary attempts or by spontaneous combustion.

A single watchman in the tower has constantly in view the door of every store-room. The cost of watching and guarding the property is thus greatly reduced.

The old buildings have been demolished and the materials sold.

DEPOT BUILDINGS AT SAN ANTONIO.

In the act of 3d March, 1873, (sundry civil appropriation bill,) is an appropriation of $100,000 for erection of depot buildings at San Antonio, including shops, offices, and commissary and quartermaster store-houses, upon grounds presented to the United States by the city of San Antonio.

Under the instructions of the Secretary of War none of this appropriation has been drawn from the Treasury or expended.

The construction of this depot will be of great advantage to the military service, which now pays a rent bill of over $20,000 for various buildings for military purposes in the city of San Antonio.

*　　*　　*　　*　　*　　*　　*

BUILDINGS TRANSFERRED FROM THE QUARTERMASTER'S DEPARTMENT.

Seven buildings at Clark's Point, Me., and thirteen at Fort Washington, Md., have been transferred to the Engineer Department, and the State arsenal at Savannah, Ga., held by the United States since the occupation of that city by the army of General Sherman, has been given up to the State.

GROUNDS SURRENDERED, SOLD, ETC.

Under the act of 25th February, 1873, the land at Wilmington, Cal., occupied by the United States, was ordered to be reconveyed to those who had originally conveyed it to the United States; the buildings thereon erected by the United States being first removed or sold. The buildings have been sold at public auction, and the land will be duly restored to its original owners.

Application has been made for the restoration to the donors of certain lands at Omaha, originally conveyed to the United States in consideration of the sum of $10, for the purpose of erection thereon of headquarters' offices and quarters for the department staff. The site is not a convenient one for the purpose, and the matter of reconveyance is before the Secretary of War.

The barracks at Houlton being no longer in use the buildings were sold at public auction, and Congress, by act of March 14, 1872, authorized the Secretary of War to sell the site, reserving to the county of Aroostook so much thereof as may be necessary to preserve the meridian monuments thereon erected by consent of the War Department: *Provided*, The land so granted to the county shall not exceed in value $500. The land not thus reserved, amounting to nearly 25 acres, was duly sold at auction, on 19th June, 1873, for the sum of $350. A deed to convey the portion reserved, whose value is much less than $500, is before the War Department for execution.

The act (17 Stat., p. 614) for procuring title to sites of military posts in Texas, approved 3d March, 1873, has not yet enabled the Department to perfect any title. A board of officers is now in session in Texas for the purpose of endeavoring to execute the law. This office has furnished the board with copies of all records bearing upon the subject which can be useful to them.

ARTESIAN WELLS.

An artesian well sunk at Madison Barracks, N. Y., under authority given in October, 1870, is a success. It affords an unfailing supply of good water. Its depth is 99 feet; the cost was $550. Two more are needed, and their construction has been authorized.

By the law of June 8, 1872, the Secretary of War was authorized to expend $10,000, or so much thereof as might be necessary, in boring for water at Fort D. A. Russell, near Cheyenne Depot, Wyoming. The site of this post is on the dry plains, at the base of the Rocky Mountains, 6,000 feet above the sea-level.

As no one could be found willing to contract to sink a well to water in this unexplored soil, the tools were purchased by the United States, and a skillful and experienced person was employed to direct the operation. After boring to a depth of 410 feet through drift, the first well was abandoned, having caved in and injured its tubing to such a degree that it was considered cheaper to begin a new well than to attempt to sink the first deeper. The expenditure to the time this first well was abandoned was $8,195.38.

The new well has been sunk through the same strata to a depth of 717 feet, and the expense has amounted to $6,164.62. The last 152 feet of this well are in impervious strata of clay, and as there is a large extent of country within forty miles rising to a height of 2,000 feet above the site of the well, there is good ground for the hope that beneath these strata, impervious to water, a gravel or fissured rock, saturated with water, may be found.

The exploration will be of value, if successful, by showing that water can be obtained; and if unsuccessful, by preventing others from throwing away money in future. I have, therefore, advised that it be continued until the stratum is pierced, or until the difficulties of penetrating deeper become insuperable.

The expenditure thus far has been $14,360; but the cost per foot of the second well has been much less than that of the first. This is due to the knowledge gained in the first boring. Boring began on the 27th of November, 1872. On the 16th of May, 1873, at a depth of 410 feet, this well was abandoned. Expenditure to this date, $8,195.38. Second well begun on the 22d of March, 1873, and the following are the results:

Strata.	Depth of each stratum.	Total depth.	Date.
	Feet.	*Feet.*	
Gravel, clay, and sand	75	75	Mar. 31, 1873
Soapstone	20	95	April 1, 1873
Soapstone and mixture of fine gravel	65	160	April 4, 1873
Gravel and mixture of clay	50	210	April 5, 1873
Red shale	190	400	April 8, 1873
Red shale, with gravel and indurated clay	20	420	April 10, 1873
Granite	10	430	April 12, 1873
Soapstone	20	450	April 13, 1873
Soapstone, very soft	62	512	April 16, 1873
Gravel and quicksand	28	540	June 12, 1873
White indurated clay	18	558	June 30, 1873
Quicksand	7	565	Aug. 5, 1873
White indurated clay	15	580	Aug. 15, 1873
White indurated clay, a little harder	35	615	Aug. 19, 1873
White indurated clay, a little harder	52	667	Aug. 21, 1873
Blue clay	3	670	Aug. 21, 1873
Clay, black, with indications of coal	5	675	Aug. 23, 1873
Blue clay	18	693	Sept. 9, 1873
Clay	7	700	Sept. 13, 1873
Blue clay	17	717	Sept. 15, 1873

The sum of $14,360 has thus far been granted for artesian wells at this post. On September 6, 1873, it was reported that $13,000 had been expended. It is, therefore, reasonable to suppose that the balance of the funds ($1,360) has been, or was very nearly, exhausted by September 15, 1873; which would make the cost of the second well thus far $6,164.62.

POSTS ABANDONED.

During the year the posts of Taylor Barracks, Ky.; Old Camps Grant, and Lowell, and Crittenden, Ariz.; and Fort Phœnix, Mass., have been abandoned.

FIRES.

Some 5,000 buildings are under the care of this Department. Most of them are of rude and temporary construction, and very liable to fire.

Seven fires at military posts have been reported during the year.

Such provision to contend against fires as it is possible to make at the military posts has been made. The fire-extinguisher, which by action of sulphuric acid on a solution of bi-carbonate of soda in a close vessel throws a small stream of water some forty feet, has been extensively distributed, and has saved a great quantity of property at military posts. A small, portable hand force-pump, known as Johnson's, has lately been tried in this city with such satisfactory results that it has been adopted as a part of the fire-apparatus to be supplied to military posts.

MILITARY RESERVES.

Seven military reserves have been declared by the Executive during the year: Fort Whipple, Va., 26th July, 1872; Camp Harney, Oreg., 2d December, 1872; Sibley Island, Dak., 11th February, 1873; Fort Abraham Lincoln, 11th February, 1873; Fort Boise, Idaho, 9th April, 1873; Beaver City, Utah, 12th May, 1873, and a reserve of timber-land for military purposes in Arizona, 20th June, 1873.

PUBLICATIONS.

A list of military posts, with short descriptions of the buildings, the situation, and the resources of the vicinity, has been published and distributed.

A short tract on construction in pisé and in concrete, the former extracted from Cresy's Dictionary of Civil Engineering, the latter furnished by the acting assistant quartermaster at Sidney Barracks, has been also published and distributed. Both of these methods of building are better than adobe, and there are few locations in which the unskilled labor of a garrison will not be sufficient to erect all necessary walls of the quarters, store-houses, and stables in one of these styles, with very little expense, if directed by intelligent officers.

The appropriation for barracks and quarters did not prove sufficient to meet the urgent demands made upon it, and toward the close of the fiscal year all new construction and repairs were arrested by order of the Secretary of War for want of funds. Still the rents and regular expenses which it was not possible to terminate have exceeded the amount available and given rise to a deficiency estimate.

POST CEMETERIES.

As the wilderness is settled, the military posts on the old emigrant routes are abandoned. At those occupied for many years are cemeteries containing the graves of soldiers who fell in protecting the emigrant from the savage, and the graves also of pioneers who lost their lives in settling the wilderness.

As the cost of properly and permanently inclosing these cemeteries in some positions is very great, arrangements have been made to remove the bodies. Those at old Fort Kearney and Sedgwick are to be removed to Fort McPherson, where they will be re-interred, and a permanent cemetery will be inclosed.

We have reports from 113 post cemeteries, which will be duly recorded and preserved.

NATIONAL MILITARY CEMETERIES.

The number of interments in the national military cemeteries by last year's report was 317,962. One hundred and forty-eight Union soldiers have been added to the list during the year. None have been removed. The number of the known is 170,187; unknown, 147,823.

A new national cemetery is being established at Fort McPherson, Nebr., to which the bodies of those who have fallen in the Indian fights of that frontier and been buried at neighboring posts, abandoned with the progress of settlement, are to be removed.

The cemetery established on the occupation of the city of Mexico by the Army of the United States has, under a law approved on 3d March, 1873, been designated a national military cemetery, and placed under the guardianship of the Secretary of War and subjected to the laws regulating other national military cemeteries. Reports and estimates of necessary improvements have been received from the consul-general of the United States, and their execution, approved by the Secretary of War, has been commenced. One of them is the sinking of an artesian well to supply water for irrigation, necessary in that dry and elevated position.

During the year brick-inclosing walls have been completed or are now building at the cemeteries of Newbern and Raleigh, N. C., Beaufort and Florence, S. C., and Memphis, Tenn.; stone walls at Danville, Glendale, Seven Pines, and Staunton, Va., at Salisbury, N. C., and Forts Leavenworth and Scott, Kans.

Superintendents' lodges have been completed during the year or are being erected at Danville, Glendale, and Seven Pines, Va., at Raleigh and Wilmington, N. C., Camp Nelson, Logan's Cross-Roads, and Lebanon, Ky., Memphis, Chattanooga, Fort Donelson, and Knoxville, Tenn., and at Fort Smith, Ark.

There remain to be provided for permanent inclosures at Andersonville, Ga., Fort Gibson, Indian Ter., Grafton, W. Va., and Fort McPherson, Nebr., and permanent lodges at Grafton, W. Va., Beverly, N. J., and Fort McPherson, Nebr.

The superintendents employed at the several cemeteries have had the aid of more labor during the past year, and an improvement in the keeping of the cemeteries is reported. The work of drainage is being prosecuted at those where it is most needed, as rapidly as the means allowed by Congress will justify.

A handsome stone gateway has been built at the Nashville cemetery, on the same design as that at Arlington, but of a local limestone of a different color.

Four civil engineers have been employed and stationed at central points in order to superintend the work of contractors upon permanent inclosures, and lodges and drainage, and to lay out such works.

HEAD-STONES.

The law of 3d March, 1873, (chapter 229, section 1, 17 Statutes,) appropriates $1,000,000 for erection of head-stones on certain conditions. Advertisements and specifications, copies of which accompany this report, have been published. The Secretary had decided that the head-stones should be of white marble or granite, four inches thick, and of widths and lengths described in the specifications herewith.

The list of graves requiring head-stones does not embrace those not in separate national military cemeteries, nor the unknown at Salisbury, for which cemetery a special provision of law directs a single monument of granite to be erected. The difference in the printed list from the number herein reported is due to the omission of 12,112 at Salisbury, and of those buried in lots in city and village cemeteries not known as national.

On the 6th September, 1873, eighty bids, received in response to the advertisements, were opened in this office. The prices varied greatly, as did the material offered; but fourteen bids, understood to agree substantially with the specifications, appeared to come within the total sum of $1,000,000, to which the cost is limited by law.

All are still before the Secretary of War for award under the law. No decision has as yet been communicated to this office.

CLAIMS FOR QUARTERMASTER'S STORES, UNDER THE ACT OF 4TH JULY, 1864.

On 1st July, 1872, there were on file in this office 10,351 claims under this act, amounting to $6,857,006.56. One thousand nine hundred and sixty-three were filed during the year, amounting to $2,024,725.16. Total on file, 12,314, for $8,881,731.72.

Six hundred and forty-two have been reported to the Third Auditor for settlement during the year. Amount claimed, $615,212.42. The amount allowed on these is $296,775.90; less than 50 per cent. Three hundred and twenty-five have been rejected; amount, $443,689.75. Total disposed of, 967 claims, amounting to $1,058,902.17, upon which $296,775.90 only has been proved to be just and allowable under the law. At the same rate the 11,347 claims yet on file will be probably settled for about one-third of their face, and of the $7,822,829.55 which they claim, it is probable that about $2,600,000 will be proved to be justly due.

For detailed information in regard to several other classes of claims which come under the cognizance of the Quartermaster General, reference is made to the report of the assistant, Major Ludington, in charge of that part of this office.

Various tables and abstracts also accompany this report, which give information in the business of this office important to preserve for future reference.

CLOTHING AND EQUIPAGE.

The President of the United States having adopted a new uniform for the Army, its manufacture was begun by this office. But the appropriation made before the change of uniform, and based upon estimates looking to the use of material in store, was not sufficient to provide uniforms of the new pattern for 30,000 men. The manufacture and distribution were therefore arrested until, on the 1st of July, 1873, the appropriation of the present fiscal year became available. Nearly all the troops have now received the new uniform. The old-pattern clothing stored in the Philadelphia depot has, in compliance with the law, been sold at public auction, the sales amounting to $490,094.31. The surplus of such clothing distributed at military posts throughout the country is being reported for sale as fast as the new uniform takes its place.

The sale of a large quantity of clothing stored at the Western or Jeffersonville depot, on the Ohio, is deferred until next season.

A great improvement in the shoes and boots of the Army has been made by the introduction of those whose sole is attached to the upper-leather by screws of brass wire. Reports are almost unanimous to the effect that these boots and shoes last longer, and are a better protection to the feet, than the sewed or pegged boots heretofore used.

Nearly all military posts have been supplied with single bedsteads; the head and foot trestles are of iron, supporting slats of wood, easily removable. They are much liked, are easily kept free from vermin, can be stacked in piles during the day so as to give room for circulation on the floors of the barrack-room, while at night they enable the men to sleep singly and thus put an end to much discomfort, unavoidable with the two and three story wooden bunks so long used in barracks.

MOTH AND MILDEW PROOFING—PROCESS OF GEORGE A. COWLES & CO.

The sum of $350,000, appropriated for the purpose by Congress, has been expended in treating the woolen and cotton material in store, according to the above process, in order to render it proof against moth and mildew. To complete its application to all material which will need it during the next fiscal year will require the sum of $100,000, for which an estimate has been submitted.

The appropriation for clothing and equipage for the past fiscal year was $900,000. The expenditures by this office were $858,412.07.

Forty-one thousand nine hundred and fifty-three dollars and thirty-three cents were transferred, by order of the Secretary of War, to the Ordnance Department, to which the manufacture and supply of knapsacks and haversacks has been transferred.

Four hundred and fifty-six thousand nine hundred and eighty-six dollars and eighty-two cents were received during the year from sales of clothing, including $18,832.56 derived from sales of clothing and material to officers for their personal use.

The National Asylum for Disabled Volunteers was entitled under the law to a large quantity of the old-pattern clothing. The president of the asylum obtained the authority of the Secretary of War to draw the equivalent of this clothing in shoes. One hundred and fifty-one thousand two hundred and forty-nine pairs of pegged shoes were delivered to the asylum from the stock in depot.

The clothing returns of officers of the Army are promptly examined and settled as received.

Full statements of the operations of the clothing and equipage branch of this office will be found at the close of this report, attached to the report of Major Bingham, quartermaster, on duty in this office during the year.

EXPLORING EXPEDITIONS.

The party under command of Lieutenant Wheeler, of the Corps of Engineers, engaged in the exploration of the territory west of the one hundredth meridian, has been supplied with animals, wagons, and forage, for transportation of escort, of supplies, and of its collections. Such quartermasters' stores as are needed by the civilians employed upon this expedition are sold to them at cost price.

The geologic and geographic exploration of Professor F. V. Hayden, United States geologist, has also been aided, under special authority of the Secretary of War, by sale of partially unserviceable animals and equipments.

The expedition for marking the boundary between the United States and Canada, west of the Lake of the Woods, under the charge of Commissioner Archibald Campbell, has also received aid and assistance from the Quartermaster's Department as heretofore.

During the month of November, 1872, under the order of the Secretary of War, I passed over the transportation routes from the East to the western end of Lake Superior and to the Red River of the North, at Fargo, the crossing of the Northern Pacific Railroad, and at Breckenridge, the terminus of the Saint Paul and Pacific Railroad. I had also intended to visit the depot of military transportation service on the Missouri River, then at Sioux City, as well as the crossing of the Missouri by the North Pacific, at Fort Abraham Lincoln; but I found the roads southwest of Saint Paul and west of the Red River blocked with snow and the routes impassable. I proceeded by the Kansas Pacific Railroad to Denver and to Cheyenne, and thence returned to this city. The extension of these roads greatly aids this department in its operations; but as the troops are moved further to the west and occupy posts within the mountain ranges, the total cost of transportation is not reduced. The field of operations is changed, but remains as extensive and as costly as before.

The officers who have been on duty in this office during the fiscal year are: Col. Robert Allen, who was on duty here during the whole of the preceding fiscal year, and was ordered, on the 11th March, 1873, to the headquarters Military Division of the Pacific, at San Francisco, where, since March 22, 1873, he has been on duty as chief quartermaster of that division.

Maj. J. D. Bingham has taken charge of those branches of the office (finance and inspection) vacated by this assignment of Colonel Allen, in addition to his former duties, except those of the cemeterial branch, to which, since June 25, 1873, Capt. A. J. McGonnigle has been assigned.

Maj. M. I. Ludington has continued on duty in this office.

All these officers have shown their usual zeal and intelligence in the performance of their respective duties, and their assistance has been very valuable.

The other principal stations of the Quartermaster's Department, during the fiscal year, have been filled as follows, viz:

Col. Robert Allen, assistant quartmaster general, chief quartermaster Military Division of the Pacific, at San Francisco, from March 22, 1873.

Col. D. H. Rucker, assistant quartermaster general, chief quartermaster Military Division of the Missouri, Chicago, Ill.

Col. Rufus Ingalls, assistant quartermaster general, chief quartermaster Department of the East, in charge of the general depot of the Quartermaster's Department at New York City, and, from 25th November, 1872, also chief quartermaster Military Division of the Atlantic.

Col. L. C. Easton, assistant quartermaster general, chief quartermaster Military Division of the Atlantic to 25th November, 1872, and in charge of the Philadelphia depot of the Quartermaster's Department—the principal depot of clothing and equipage of the Army—throughout the year.

Col. Stewart Van Vliet, assistant quartermaster general, from October 18, 1872, chief quartermaster Military Department of the Missouri, at Fort Leavenworth.

Lieut. Col. S. B. Holabird, chief quartermaster Department of Texas.

Lieut. Col. James A. Ekin, chief quartermaster Department of the South; also, from September 26, 1872, in charge of the Jeffersonville depot of the Quartermaster's Department, and, from December 11, 1872, chief quartermaster Military Division of the South.

Lieut. Col. A. R. Eddy, on duty at the Philadelphia depot to August 17, 1872; from August 27 and 28, 1872, depot quartermaster at San Francisco, chief quartermaster Department of California, and chief quartermaster Military Division of the Pacific, of which last duty relieved by Col. Robert Allen on March 22, 1873.

Lieut. Col. Rufus Saxton, to May 28–31, 1873, chief quartermaster Department of the Columbia, at Portland, Oreg.; from June 23, 1873, chief quartermaster Department of the Lakes, at Detroit, Mich.

Maj. A. J. Perry, chief quartermaster Department of the Platte, Omaha, Nebr.

Maj. J. G. Chandler, in charge of depot at Fort Leavenworth, and, from July 1 to October 18, 1872, acting chief quartermaster Department of the Missouri.

Maj. C. G. Sawtelle, to July 15, 1872, chief quartermaster Department of California, and depot quartermaster at San Francisco; from August 15, 1872, to close of the fiscal year, assistant to the depot quartermaster at Philadelphia, and chief quartermaster third quartermaster's district Department of the East.

Maj. J. J. Dana, chief quartermaster Department of Arizona, at Prescott.

Maj. James M. Moore, from September 1, 1872, depot quartermaster at Cheyenne.

Maj. William Myers, in charge of depot, at Washington, D. C.

Maj. B. C. Card, to April 18, 1873, depot quartermaster at San Antonio; from May 1, 1873, chief quartermaster Department of Dakota, at Saint Paul.

Capt. E. B. Grimes, depot quartermaster at Saint Louis.

Capt. A. F. Rockwell, in charge of depot at Yuma, on the Colorado, Ariz., relieved Capt. J. G. C. Lee, who had completed a full tour of duty in Arizona.

Capt. C. H. Hoyt, in charge of general depot at Jeffersonville, Ind., to September 26, 1872, and of construction of buildings to November 21, 1872. From December 23, 1872, disbursing officer District of the Lakes, at Camp Warner, Oregon; from February 26, 1873, to close of the fiscal year, chief quartermaster of the Modoc expedition.

Capt. John F. Rodgers, military store-keeper at Jeffersonville, Ind., to April 8, 1873; from December 21, 1872, he was also on duty at the Philadelphia clothing depot, so remaining to the close of the year.

These officers have administered the offices of the Government committed to their charge with ability and zeal.

One assistant quartermaster, Capt. Henry Inman, was cashiered on July 24, 1872; one military store-keeper, Capt. N. D. A. Sawyer, was cashiered on November 30, 1872; and another, Capt. G. H. A. Dimpfel, was wholly retired on August 16, 1872.

Lieut. Col. C. H. Tompkins was suspended by sentence of a court-martial for one year from the 4th January, 1873.

The work of the Department, extending over the whole territory of the United States, has been satisfactorily conducted by the officers of its establishment, aided by about three hundred subalterns detailed from the line as acting assistant quartermasters.

The personal annual reports received from these officers are filed among the records of the Department. They contain much valuable information in relation to the wants and supplies of the service, and bear testimony to the intelligence and fidelity of their writers. To the acting assistant quartermasters, upon whom the burden of the greater part of the detailed work of issue to troops and of care of public supplies falls in consequence of the insufficient number of officers of the regular establishment, this office is much indebted. I have spoken elsewhere on the legislation which I believe to be necessary to do them justice, and to give them assistance much needed in the performance of their laborious and responsible duties.

The principal active operations which have taxed the resources and the officers of this Department during the year, have been the operations against the Apaches in Arizona, who have been reduced to a state of comparative quiet; the campaign against the Modocs in California and Oregon, finally successful, and the organization and conduct of the trains of the expedition to the Yellowstone, which made a successful march of seven hundred miles into an uncultivated and in great part barren wilderness, and returned without serious loss of material, having accomplished its purpose.

In connection with this expedition, the Yellowstone River was for the first time navigated by steamboats, which met the troops at their crossing near Powder River and rendered essential service.

In these important active operations, Lieutenant-Colonel Eddy, chief quartermaster Department of California, and Captain Hoyt, the latter present with the troops in the Modoc campaign, Maj. J. J. Dana, chief quartermaster Department of Arizona, Maj. B. C. Card, chief quartermaster Department of Dakota, and Capt. G. B. Dandy, who personally organized the Yellowstone train, rendered valuable service.

I have the honor to remain, very respectfully, your obedient servant
M. C. MEIGS,
Quartermaster General, Brt. Maj. Gen., U. S. A.
Hon. W. W. BELKNAP,
Secretary of War.

List of papers accompanying the annual report of the Quartermaster General for the fiscal year ending June 30, 1873.

I. Report of Maj. J. D. Bingham, quartermaster, United States Army, of the inspection branch of the Quartermaster-General's Office during the fiscal year ending June 30, 1873.

A.—Report of officers on duty in the Quartermaster's Department during the fiscal year.

B.—List of line officers on duty as acting assistant quartermasters, and of the stations at which they have served during the fiscal year.

C.—Report of the stations and duties of officers of the Quartermaster's Department July 1, 1873.

II. Report of Maj. J. D. Bingham, quartermaster, United States Army, of the finance branch of the Quartermaster General's Office during the fiscal year ending June 30, 1873.

III. Report of Maj. J. D. Bingham, quartermaster, United States Army, of the operations of the accounting branch of the Quartermaster General's Office during the fiscal year ending June 30, 1873.

IV. Report of Maj. J. D. Bingham, quartermaster, United States Army, of the operations of the clothing branch of the Quartermaster General's Office during the fiscal year ending June 30, 1873.

Accompanying papers:

A.—Statement showing the quantity of clothing, camp and garrison equipage, and clothing materials in the hands of officers June 30, 1872, the quantity purchased, manufactured, sold, lost, and issued during the fiscal year, and quantity remaining on hand for the supply of the Army on June 30, 1873.

B.—Statement showing expenditure on account of clothing, camp and garrison equipage, during the fiscal year.

C.—Statement of amounts received from sales of surplus serviceable, unserviceable, damaged, and irregular articles of clothing, &c., sold at the principal clothing depots; also of the amounts derived from sales to officers, &c., during the fiscal year.

D.—Statement of the amounts received and expended on account of clothing and equipage during the fiscal year.

E.—Statement of returns of clothing, camp and garrison equipage, received, examined, and transmitted to the Treasury Department, and of letters received and written, during the fiscal year.

F.—Statement showing number of claims received and acted upon, on account of clothing and equipage, during the fiscal year.

V. Report of Maj. M. I. Ludington, quartermaster, United States Army, of the operations of the regular supplies, transportation, and barracks and quarters branch of the Quartermaster General's Office, during the fiscal year ending June 30, 1873.

A.—Statement of the indebtedness of southern railroad companies for railway material for the fiscal year.

B.—Statement of troops and stores transported during the fiscal year.

C.—Abstracts of contracts for wagon transportation received at the Quartermaster General's Office during the fiscal year.

D.—Abstract of contracts for water transportation entered into by the Quartermaster's Department during the fiscal year.

E.—Statement of vessels chartered, impressed, and employed during the fiscal year.

F.—Statement of vessels owned or purchased by the Quartermaster's Department during the fiscal year.

VI. Report of Capt. A. J. McGonnigle, assistant quartermaster, United States Army, of the operations of the cemeterial branch of the Quartermaster General's Office during the fiscal year ending June 30, 1873.

REPORT OF THE COMMISSARY-GENERAL OF SUBSISTENCE.

OFFICE COMMISSARY-GENERAL OF SUBSISTENCE,
Washington City, October 10, 1873.

SIR: I have the honor to submit the following report of the operations of the Subsistence Department of the Army for the fiscal year terminating June 30, 1873:

During the year subsistence supplies for the Army have been procured, distributed, stored, and sold or issued to officers, enlisted men, civilian army employés, and others whose connection with the Army entitles them to such supplies, by the methods required by law and Army Regulations, and under appropriate requisitions and orders of a general or special nature, no changes having taken place during the year in the sources of such supplies, except such as necessarily follow their increasing production and decreasing, cost at points nearer the troops to be supplied.

Responsible officers of the Subsistence Department stationed at the headquarters of the several geographical divisions and departments as chief commissaries, acting constantly under the knowledge and approval of their respective commanding generals, are charged, under conformity with the laws and regulations and the orders or decisions of the Secretary of War or Commissary-General, with the procurement, distribution, care, and issue of the necessary supplies.

During the fiscal year ending June 30, 1873, there were reported to this Office 205 advertisements inviting proposals for supplies, 305 contracts for fresh meat, 62 contracts for complete rations, 127 contracts for miscellaneous articles, and 298 contracts, consisting of written proposals and acceptances.

The average price of fresh beef per contracts made during the year was as follows, in the several States and Territories:

States or Territories.	Cents per pound.	States or Territories.	Cents per pound.	States or Territories.	Cents per pound.
Maine	13.62	Alabama	9.12	Dakota Territory	9.00
Massachusetts	14.00	Mississippi	10.50	Wyoming Territory	8.43
Rhode Island	11.75	Louisiana	9.00	New Mexico Territory	8.33
Connecticut	10.00	Texas	5.04	Colorado Territory	7.12
New York	11.69	Tennessee	8.68	Utah Territory	7.97
Pennsylvania	10.54	Kentucky	8.68	Montana Territory	9.15
Maryland	10.81	Illinois	7.95	California	11.70
District of Columbia	12.20	Michigan	10.85	Oregon	7.38
Virginia	11.93	Missouri	5.50	Arizona Territory	13.87
North Carolina	11.16	Minnesota	8.83	Washington Territory	9.14
South Carolina	10.72	Nebraska	7.35	Idaho Territory	11.82
Georgia	8.37	Kansas	8.68	Nevada	13.67
Florida	8.66	Indian Territory	7.12		

Making the average contract price for the year 9.81 cents per pound net, being 5¼ mills less than for the previous year.

The average cost of the complete ration for the fiscal year ending June 30, 1873, at ten of the principal points of purchase was as follows:

Months.	New York, N. Y.	Baltimore, Md.	Louisville, Ky.	Saint Louis, Mo.	Saint Paul, Minn.	Omaha, Nebr.	Fort Leavenworth, Kans.	Chicago, Ill.	New Orleans, La	San Francisco, Cal.
1872	Cents.	Cents.	Cents.	Cents.	Cents.	Cents.	Cents.	Cents.	Cents.	Cents.
July	15.97	21.57	14.58	15.69	16.31	16.13	16.57	15.90	17.15	22.63
August	15.97	19.16	14.17	16.22	16.29	16.81	16.61	16.07	17.97	22.88
September	16.20	19.15	14.46	16.11	16.28	17.92	14.18	15.75	19.45	22.34
October	16.73	18.91	14.71	16.87	16.41	19.03	18.93	15.69	20.00	21.71
November	17.01	18.92	15.10	15.90	15.97	19.41	18.83	15.29	19.44	22.50
December	16.49	18.25	14.62	16.62	16.58	19.13	19.04	14.38	17.82	21.62
1873										
January	15.50	19.17	14.55	15.26	16.72	17.14	17.55	14.70	18.32	21.52
February	16.75	20.58	15.36	16.26	16.12	18.65	16.00	14.21	20.52	21.42
March	18.31	20.58	16.02	16.31	15.84	18.63	18.52	16.17	17.70	22.48
April	16.60	20.33	15.68	15.46	16.57	18.76	18.01	15.41	17.53	22.49
May	17.45	21.49	15.50	16.66	17.14	18.25	17.64	14.59	18.10	22.67
June	17.30	19.08	15.46	16.61	16.61	16.06	16.88	13.95	18.55	22.16
Average	16.69	19.67	15.02	16.16	16.40	17.82	17.64	14.96	18.55	22.8

Making the general average for the year seventeen cents and forty-eight hundredths per ration, showing an increase of thirty-four hundredths of a cent over the average of the previous year.

Under the requirements of section 6, act of March 3, 1865, the Subsistence Department has during the year furnished tobacco for sale to the enlisted men of the Army at cost price, to the amount of $152,489.40, the average monthly sale being $12,707.45.

It is respectfully requested that tobacco be furnished to the enlisted men of the Army by issue as a component part of the regular ration, instead of by sale, and that the ration of tobacco be, as near as may be, the same amount as is at present authorized to be sold to them, viz. 16 ounces per month.

Under the provisions of section 16 of the act of June 30, 1834, and paragraph 1202, Revised Regulations for the Army, 1863, subsistence supplies to the value of $19,925.68 have, in the discretion of commanding officers, been issued gratuitously to Indians of the various tribes visit ing military posts, or in their respective nations, no part of which amount is returned to the appropriation for the subsistence of the Army.

During the fiscal year there were received from 415 officers of the Army on duty in the Subsistence Department, who were responsible for subsistence funds or supplies,

3,143 returns of provisions.

1,089 returns of commissary property.

3,231 accounts current.

7,463 total accounts and returns; of which all have been examined and forwarded to the Third Auditor of the Treasury for final settlement, with the exception of 876, which await examination in this Office.

Under the act of June 23, 1870, as extended by the act of June 7, 1872, authorizing the proper accounting officers of the Treasury, in the settlement of certain accounts of disbursing officers of the Army and Navy, to allow such credits for over-payments and for losses of funds, vouchers, or property, as they may deem just and honorable, when recommended, under authority of the Secretaries of War and Navy, by the heads of the military and naval Bureaus to which such accounts respectively pertain, credits have been recommended in the cases of 370 disbursing officers in the sum of $107,236.77, making the total number of officers relieved under the operation of the acts cited 767, in the total amount of $216,557.56.

Up to, and including, the 27th day of September, 1873, 6,096 claims, amounting to $3,312,757.68, had been submitted for examination under the third section of the act of July 4, 1864, for subsistence alleged to have been taken or furnished during the war for Army use in States not in rebellion; 105 of these, accompanied by regular vouchers given by the officers when purchasing the stores, have been recommended for payment, in the aggregate sum of $9,152.75, by the Third Auditor of the Treasury, as purchases under contract, while 1,301 others (aggregating $431,443.31) have been recommended to him for settlement under the act, in the aggregate amount of $308,295.79; and 4,443, amounting to $2,682,644.18, have been examined and disallowed.

Up to the 30th of September, 1873, there have been received and paid 6,525 certificates for commutation of rations to Union soldiers (prisoners of war) and their heirs, as authorized by the joint resolution of July 25, 1866, and section 3 of the act of March 2, 1867, amounting to $287,318.

Under the act of March 3, 1873, to provide for the better care and protection of subsistence supplies, by selecting from the sergeants of the line of the Army, who shall have faithfully served therein five years, as many commissary sergeants as the service requires, not to exceed one for each military post or place of deposit of subsistence supplies, there have been selected and appointed 149 commissary sergeants, who have been assigned to the same number of military posts; a considerable number of whom have been in the performance of their duties a sufficient length of time to show that they have performed them in a highly satisfactory manner, and already to give evidence that the benefit to the service that was anticipated would result from having such a body of experienced and worthy non-commissioned officers will be fully realized. These commissary sergeants have been selected from those sergeants of the line of the Army eligible under the law, who have an honorable record and are recommended by their company and regimental commanders; such recommendations in the majority of cases being accompanied by testimonials of character, capacity, and honorable service in the line as soldiers and non-commissioned officers by officers under whom they have served.

*   *   *   *   *   *   *

I have the honor to be, very respectfully, your obedient servant,

A. B. EATON,
Commissary-General.

The Hon. the SECRETARY OF WAR.

REPORT OF THE SURGEON-GENERAL.

WAR DEPARTMENT, SURGEON-GENERAL'S OFFICE,
Washington, October 1, 1873.

SIR: I have the honor to submit the following statement of finances and general transactions of the Medical Department of the Army for the fiscal year ending June 30, 1873:

FINANCIAL STATEMENT.

The funds subject to the requisitions of the Medical Bureau during the year ending June 30, 1873, were:

I. Appropriation for the relief of sick and discharged soldiers, under the act approved July 5, 1862:

Balance remaining July 1, 1872	$11,914 17
Disbursed during the year	1,556 43
Balance June 30, 1873	10,357 74

II. Appropriation under the act of March 3, 1869, to enable the Secretary of the Treasury to settle the accounts of disbursing officers:

Balance remaining July 1, 1872	$15,850 26
Transferred during the year	9,191 40
Balance June 30, 1873	6,658 94

III. Appropriation under act of March 3, 1873, to enable the Secretary of the Treasury to settle the accounts of disbursing officers ... $275,000 00

No disbursements.

IV. Appropriations for the Medical and Hospital Department of the Army for the time prior to July 1, 1870:

Balance remaining July 1, 1872		$1,248,215 66
Refunded by the Pay Department		200,000 00
Received from sales		45 55
Received from other sources		6 95
		1,448,268 12
Disbursed during the year	$224,488 54	
Carried to surplus fund	500,000 00	
Balance June 30, 1873	723,779 58	
		1,448,268 12

V. Appropriation for the Medical and Hospital Department for the fiscal year ending June 30, 1871:

Balance remaining July 1, 1872	$32,035 19
Deposited by Lt. Col. R. Murray May 15, 1872; covered into the Treasury September 30, 1872	212 66
	32,247 99

Disbursed during the year............................. $1,975 12
Balance June 30, 1873................................... 30,272 87

                                                             $32,247 99

VI. Appropriation for the Medical and Hospital Department for the
fiscal year ending June 30, 1872:
Balance remaining July 1, 1872.............................. $25,361 21
Deficiency appropriations of March 3, 1873.................. 8,000 00
Amount received from sales................................. 124 75
Received for property lost or damaged...................... 63 98
Received from all other sources........................... 6 22

                                               33,556 16

Disbursed during the year........................... $26,552 28
Balance June 30, 1873............................... 7,003 88

                                               33,556 16

VII. Appropriation for the [Medical and Hospital Department for the
fiscal year ending June 30, 1873:
Appropriation under act of June 6, 1872............................ $300,000 00
Disbursed during the year.................................. 252,303 20

      Balance remaining June 30, 1873..................... 47,696 80
Required for unsettled bills.................................. 32,400 00

VIII. Appropriation for support of the Army Medical Museum and
Library of the Surgeon-General's Office, under act of June 6,
1872.. $10,000 00
Disbursed during the year.................................. 8,859 26

      Balance June 30, 1873, required for unsettled bills.... 1,140 74

IX. Appropriation for completing the Medical and Surgical History of
the War, under act of June 8, 1872............................ $60,000 00
Disbursed during the year.................................. 12,706 12

      Balance remaining June 30, 1873..................... 47,293 88

X. Appropriation by act of June 6, 1872, for furnishing appliances to
disabled soldiers... $10,000 00
Disbursed during the year.................................. 1,198,62

                                               8,801 38

XI. Amount expended under the act of May 28, 1872, to provide for furnishing trusses to ruptured soldiers............................. $7,936 17

Number of artificial limbs allowed during the fiscal year:

In kind.		By commutation.
Arms......	4	300
Legs......	41	90
Feet.....	1	23
Apparatus	10	847
	56	1,260

HEALTH OF THE ARMY DURING THE FISCAL YEAR ENDING JUNE 30, 1873.

The monthly reports of sick and wounded received during the year
represent an annual average mean strength of 24,844 white and 2,520
colored troops.

Among the white troops, the total number of cases of all kinds reported
as taken on the sick-list was 48,767, being at the rate of 1,963 per
1,000 of mean strength. (That is very nearly two entries on the sick

30 Ab

report during the year for each man.)   Of the whole number 41,398, or 1,666 per 1,000 of strength, were taken on sick report for disease, and 7,369, or 297 per 1,000 of strength, for wounds, accidents and injuries.

The average number constantly on sick report during the year was 1,219, or 49 per 1,000 of strength ; of these 978, or 39 per 1,000 of strength, were under treatment for disease, and 241, or 10 per 1,000 of strength, for wounds, accidents, and injuries.

The total number of deaths reported was 412, or 17 per 1,000 of mean strength.   Of these 246, or 10 per 1,000 of strength, died of disease, and 166, or 7 per 1,000 of strength, of wounds, accidents, and injuries.   The proportion of deaths from all causes to cases treated was 1 death to 118 cases.

Eight hundred and ninety-four white soldiers are reported to have been discharged on "surgeon's certificate of disability," being at the rate of 36 per 1,000 of mean strength.

The reports from the colored troops give the following figures, which do not include the white officers.

The total number of cases of all kinds reported was 4,305, or 1,708 per 1,000 of mean strength.   Of these 3,625, or 1,438 per 1,000 of strength, were cases of disease, and 680, or 270 per 1,000 of strength, were wounds, accidents, and injuries.

The average number constantly on sick report was 122, or 48 per 1,000: of whom 94, or 37 per 1,000, were under treatment for disease, and 28, or 11 per 1,000, for wounds, accidents, and injuries.

The number of deaths from all causes reported was 53, or 21 per 1,000 of strength.   Of these 46, or 18 per 1,000 of strength, died of disease, and 7, or 3 per 1,000, of wounds, accidents, and injuries.   The proportion of deaths from all causes to cases treated was 1 death to 81 cases.

The number of discharges on "surgeon's certificate of disability" reported was 60, or 24 per 1,000 of mean strength.

WORK PERFORMED IN THE RECORD AND PENSION DIVISION.

The number of official calls for information from the Record and Pension Division is somewhat less than during the previous years, but still continues to be large.   During the fiscal year terminating June 30, 1872, as stated in my last annual report, 19,237 applications were received, of which 4,827 remained unanswered at the close of the year. From that time to June 30, 1873, the total number of new applications for information received was 16,601, of which 11,080 were from the Commissioner of Pensions, 5,125 from the Adjutant-General of the Army, and 396 from miscellaneous sources.   These new cases added to the 4,827 cases remaining on hand at the commencement of the year made 21,428 to be disposed of.

Search was made and replies furnished to the proper authorities in 19,875 of these cases, viz: 13,422 to the Commissioner of Pensions. 6,005 to the Adjutant-General of the Army, and 448 to miscellaneous applicants, leaving 1,553 unsearched cases on hand on the 30th of June. 1873.

As during previous years, the applications for information continue to refer chiefly to the cause of death or discharge from service and the hospital history of soldiers dead or disabled during the war of the rebellion.   This information is used in the adjustment of pension and other claims, and serves both as a protection to the Government against fraudulent claims, and as an aid in establishing the merits of worthy ones. It is thought that hereafter the amount of such work required of this Office will slowly but steadily diminish.

DIVISION OF SURGICAL RECORDS.

At the date of the last annual report there were entered on the registers abstracts of 207,135 surgical cases and of 39,291 surgical operations, or an aggregate of 246,426 surgical histories. During the year 12,738 cases of wounds and injuries, and 743 cases of operations, have been entered, making the aggregate 219,873 cases of wounds and 40,034 cases of operations, or a grand total of 259,907.

Supplementary information was added, results determined, &c., in 15,612 of these cases from the files of the Office, and in 2,683 cases the remote results of injuries were ascertained from the pension records.

Four thousand six hundred and sixteen reports, letters, and indorsements were received, indexed, and filed, and, in addition to routine acknowledgments, 566 letters were written.

ARMY MEDICAL MUSEUM.

Medical section.

Specimens in museum July 1, 1872	1,125
Specimens in museum July 1, 1873	1,168
Increase	43

Microscopical section.

Specimens in museum July 1, 1872	5,533
Specimens in museum July 1, 1873	6,095
Increase	562

Section of comparative anatomy.

Specimens in museum July 1, 1872	1,200
Specimens in museum July 1, 1873	1,270
Increase	70

There were embraced in the—

Surgical section.

Of specimens in the museum July 1, 1872	6,093
Of specimens in the museum July 1, 1873	6,272
Increase	179

Anatomical section.

Of specimens in the museum July 1, 1872	917
Of specimens in the museum July 1, 1873	995
Increase	78

Miscellaneous section.

Specimens in museum July 1, 1872	130
Received 12; transferred 8.	
Specimens in museum July 1, 1873	134
Increase	4

Fifteen casts of pathological specimens and two volumes of photographs were placed at the disposition of Prof. J. B. S. Jackson, to be presented to the museum of Harvard University.

From this it will be seen that although having attained an almost unprecedented size and value, this national collection continues to increase in importance and is becoming more generally appreciated and utilized. During the year 22,560 visitors registered their names.

MEDICAL AND SURGICAL HISTORY OF THE WAR.

The distribution of the first part of the Medical and Surgical History of the War having been authorized by Congress, about 1870 copies were available for issue from this Office as shown by the following statement:

Sent to congressional committees, as specimens	12
Sent to Senators	1,000
Sent to Representatives	2,000
Sent to Library of Congress	50
Damaged and imperfect copies	70
To be issued by Surgeon General's Office	1,868
Total number of copies printed	5,000

· The delivery of copies from the Government Printing Office commenced in February, 1873, and they have been distributed as fast as received.

The demand for the work has been very great, and the number of copies placed at the disposal of this Office proves insufficient to supply those who as ex-medical officers, having rendered satisfactory service through the war, may be considered as properly entitled to it.

The second part of the work is now going through the press as rapidly as possible.

The interest felt by the medical profession of the country in the attempt to establish a national medical library worthy of the name, in connection with the Army Medical Museum, has steadily increased, as shown by letters received and by numerous presentations of books and pamphlets during the year. The library now contains about 25,000 volumes and 15,000 pamphlets, and although still very incomplete when compared with similar national collections in Europe, is at present the largest in this country. A new catalogue is now being printed which will, it is believed, be a valuable contribution to medical bibliography.

I would respectfully renew the recommendation made in my annual reports of 1870 and 1872, "that the necessary legislation be procured to enable me to publish an edition of one thousand of the Catalogue and Tables of the Anatomical Section of the Army Medical Museum, in a style similar to Morton's *Crania Americana*." A bill for this purpose (H. R. 3453) passed the House, and was before the Military Committee of the Senate at the close of the last session of Congress, thus failing to become a law.

*   *   *   *   *   *   *

I am compelled to again repeat the statement made in previous reports that very serious and increasing injury has resulted to the service from the continued prohibition of appointments and promotions in the medical corps. The inducements of pay and rank, as at present established, are not sufficient to make the service attractive or remunerative to physicians already engaged in practice; and though, through the prerequisite rigid examination of candidates, it has heretofore been found possible to secure a high grade of talent and qualification, it is upon the younger portion of the profession, the recent graduates, that we must depend in filling up existing vacancies. As a large proportion of applicants fail to pass satisfactory examinations (which require in each case from three to six days) it will be the work of several years to restore the corps to the necessary standard of numbers as provided for in the act of Congress approved July 28, 1866. Although ambition to pass the Army medical board brings forward many of the most promising graduates of the medical colleges, additional inducements of rank, pay, and promotion are becoming more and more necessary, not only to make the number of candidates equal to the needs of the service, but to retain the most desirable of them in the service under their frequent inducements to accept advantageous offers in civil life. The action of the American Medical Association, representing the medical profession of this country, regarding the unequal position of medical officers of the Army—as compared to that of other staff corps—is based upon actual investigation of the subject, and presents to Congress all the facts in the case.

I can only urge most earnestly upon your attention the pressing and absolute necessity for such legislation as will secure to our officers and soldiers the efficient and reliable attendance in wounds and sickness which the Government should provide, and will make a position in the medical corps of the Army, now as formerly, an object of ambition to the best educated and best qualified young men in the profession.

At the date of my last report there existed fifty-nine vacancies in the medical department, viz: two assistant medical purveyors, four surgeons, fifty-two assistant surgeons, and one medical store-keeper. During the past year one surgeon and one assistant surgeon have died, and three assistant surgeons have resigned; leaving at present sixty-four vacancies in the corps, viz: two assistant medical purveyors, five surgeons, fifty-six assistant surgeons, and one medical store-keeper.

J. K. BARNES,
Surgeon-General, U. S. A.

To the Hon. the SECRETARY OF WAR.

REPORT OF THE PAYMASTER-GENERAL.

PAYMASTER-GENERAL'S OFFICE,
Washington, October 10, 1873.

SIR: I have the honor to submit my annual report of the transactions of the pay department of the Army for the last fiscal year ending 30th June, 1873.

Tabular statements herewith inclosed show in detail the fiscal operations of the department for that year, summarily stated as follows:

RECEIPTS AND DISBURSEMENTS.

Balance on hand at beginning of fiscal year, (July 1, 1872)		$2,289,221 94
Received during fiscal year from Treasury		14,008,477 95
Received from soldiers' deposits		209,850 38
Miscellaneous receipts		221,079 32
Total		16,728,629 59
Disbursed to the Army	$11,056,522 35	
Disbursed to the Military Academy	176,010 97	
Disbursed on Treasury certificates	1,936,230 16	
Total disbursements	13,108,763 48	
Surplus funds deposited in Treasury	1,188,467 30	
Miscellaneous receipts deposited	218,407 00	
Balance in hands of paymasters June 30, 1873, to be accounted for in next report	2,152,991 81	
Total		16,728,629 59

The most important matter which it is my duty to bring before you is the imperative necessity of more paymasters. The sixth section of the act of 3d March, 1869, forbids any appointments and promotions in the staff of the Army until further legislation. The thirty-first section of the act of 7th July, 1838, forbids the detail of officers of the Army as acting paymasters. Thus the Pay Department has not the resources of the Quartermaster's or Subsistence Departments; for details for temporary duty in those departments have always been made, as also for any of the other departments of the staff.

There are now sixteen vacancies in the Pay Department under the organization provided by the act of 28th July, 1866, two in the rank of lieutenant-colonel and fourteen in the rank of major, five of these vacancies occurring since my last annual report. The duties of paying the troops during the last year have been performed in as satisfactory a manner as could be expected, considering the reduced number of paymasters. I shall do but simple justice to them when I say that they have faithfully and efficiently discharged their duties, oftentimes in very remote and exposed regions on the frontier. One excellent officer has been lost at sea and two attacked by robbers (fortunately foiled in their audacious attempts) during the last year, which facts exhibit the dangers incident to their tours of duty. The War Department should have it in its power to give respite and relief to many on remote stations, which can only be accomplished by an increase of the number of paymasters. But without reference to those considerations, an increase is needed for the absolute wants of the service.

I recommend that the number of paymasters be now established at fifty-two instead of sixty as provided by law in the eighteenth section of the act of 28th July, 1866, and a repeal of the interdict upon future appointments and promotions. It is but just that the power of promotion should be restored to the Executive; for what is an army or a staff corps good for, in which the principle of promotion is not recognized?

I recommend that a greater period than thirty days be allowed to an officer on leave of absence without reduction or pay. Thirty days barely suffices to enable an officer to travel from remote departments to the East and return. By the eleventh section of the act of 20th June, 1864, it was enacted that "leave of absence for other cause than sickness or wounds may be allowed an officer by order of his proper commander, without deduction from his pay and allowances: *Provided,* That the aggregate of such absence shall not exceed thirty days in any one year." A previous act (of 3d March, 1863) provided that the reduction should be one-half the pay and allowances of the officer.

The only other legislation concerning the Pay Department which I recommend is, that the pay of paymasters' clerks should be increased. It is now $100 per month. A large share of their duties is discharged in regions where the journeys are arduous and very dangerous—regions, too, having many attractions to draw them from our employment. The superior pay enjoyed by clerks of the Quartermaster's and Subsistence Departments has often worked to the injury of the Pay Department. Expert clerks of this Department have resigned and gone into those Departments. This is but the natural effect of inadequate compensation and of the existing inequalities.

The acts of 15th May, 1872, concerning the pay of the enlisted men, and establishing a system of deposits, have signally ameliorated their condition. But they have not yet reduced the number of desertions as much as we had hoped. Still the number of desertions in the Army, in the fiscal year ending 30th June, 1873, was five hundred less than in the previous year, and one thousand less than in the year ending 30th June, 1871. It would be difficult to devise legislation better calculated than those acts to encourage re-enlistments, reward faithful service, and diminish desertions. It may require the experience of several years to develop their full effect upon the rank and file of the Army. Some of the company commanders represent that the interest given for deposits should have been established at 6 per cent., instead of 4 per cent., per annum.

‑ I append to this report a table exhibiting the average amount of deposits per company during the fiscal year ending June 30, 1873, in the various military departments. From this it appears that the largest amount of deposits per company was in the Department of Arizona, viz, $1,583; next, in the Department of the Columbia, $717 per company. In these departments there was the greatest amount of field operations, the troops being in campaign against the Apaches and Modocs.

This shows, as I expected, that in time of war the most deposits will be made by the enlisted men. During the civil war such a system would have given the Government the handling of many millions for years. During the last years of the war there were at least about 14,000 companies of troops employed. This, at the rate of $1,500 deposited by each company, would have made $21,000,000 per annum.

During the year ending 31st August, 1873, $246,643 (or an average exceeding $20,000 per month) have been deposited, the use of which the Government will have for an average period of about two and one-half years.

Respectfully submitted.

BENJ. ALVORD,
Paymaster-General United States Army.

The Hon. the SECRETARY OF WAR.

REPORT OF THE CHIEF OF ENGINEERS.

OFFICE OF THE CHIEF OF ENGINEERS,
Washington, D. C., October 20, 1873.

SIR: I have the honor to present for your information the following report upon the duties and operations of the Engineer Department for the fiscal year ending June 30, 1873.

OFFICERS OF THE CORPS OF ENGINEERS.

The number of officers holding commissions in the Corps of Engineers, United States Army, at the end of the fiscal year, was 106 on the active list, and 5 on the retired list; the latter, under the law of January 21, 1870, not being available for duty.

Since my last report the corps has lost, by death, two of its most distinguished officers—Col. Sylvanus Thayer, who died September 7, 1872, and Col. Hartman Bache, who died October 8, 1872. Neither of these officers, at the time of their decease, was upon the active list of their corps, but their services in former years were connected with the most important and distinguished duties of their branch of the Army. The Military Academy at West Point is an enduring monument to the eminent services of Colonel Thayer in its organization and administration; while the name of Colonel Bache is indissolubly connected with the in troduction of the refined methods of survey which have been applied to our harbors and rivers, and with the plans for their improvement.

But one officer has resigned, namely, Second Lieut. Edward S. Holden, who resigned March 28, 1873, to accept appointment as professor of mathematics in the Navy.

There have been added to the corps, by promotion of graduates of the Military Academy, four lieutenants, whose commissions date from June 13, 1873.

On the 30th of June, 1873, the officers were distributed as follows:

On duty, office of the Chief of Engineers, including the chief	4
On duty, projection and construction of fortifications	6
On duty, construction of fortifications and light-house duty	2
On duty, construction of fortifications and river and harbor works, and surveys for same	24
On duty, construction of river and harbor works and surveys for same	16
On duty, construction of river and harbor works and light-house duty, and surveys for same	7
On duty, survey of northern and northwestern lakes	6
On duty, explorations of country west of one hundredth meridian	3
On duty, with battalion of engineers	12
On duty, public buildings and grounds, District of Columbia	1
Off duty, sick	2
Detached, on duty with the General of the Army, generals commanding divisions, departments; light-house establishments; Military Academy; and survey of northern boundary-line under State Department	19
Recent graduates of the Military Academy, on leave of absence	4
Total	**106**

The officers detached were on duty as follows:

Col. I. C. Woodruff, engineer third light-house district	1
Lieut. Col. William F. Raynolds, engineer fourth light-house district	1
Maj. O. M. Poe on staff of the General of the Army	1
Maj. George H. Elliot, engineer secretary to the Light-House Board	1
Maj. J. W. Barlow, on staff of lieutenant-general commanding Military Division of the Missouri	1
Maj. P. C. Hains, engineer fifth and sixth light-house districts	1
Maj. George L. Gillespie, on temporary duty under orders of Lieutenant-General Sheridan	1
Capt. William J. Twining, on duty, under Department of State, upon the joint commission for the survey and demarkation of the boundary-line along the forty-ninth parallel, in accordance with act of Congress approved March 19, 1872	1
Capt. G. J. Lydecker, on staff of major-general commanding Military Division of the Pacific	1
Capt. William Ludlow, on staff of commanding general Department of Dakota	1
Capt. W. A. Jones, on staff of commanding general Department of the Platte	1
First Lieut. J. F. Gregory, on duty under Department of State, upon the joint commission for the survey of the boundary-line along the forty-ninth parallel, in accordance with act of Congress approved March 19, 1872	1
First Lieut. Ernest H. Ruffner, on staff of commanding general Department of the Missouri	1
Second Lieutenant F. V. Greene, on duty, under Department of State, upon the joint commission for the survey of the boundary-line along the forty-ninth parallel, in accordance with act of Congress approved March 19, 1872	1
Capt. C. W. Raymond, Capt. A. M. Miller, Capt. T. H. Handbury, First Lieut. E. W. Bass, First Lieut. S. E. Tillman, on duty at the Military Academy	5
Total	**19**

In the duties devolving upon the corps by law, and its organization, the employment of a number of scientists and civil assistants has been necessary, and among them are Gen. J. H. Wilson, member of board of engineers upon improvement of Des Moines and Rock Island rapids, and improvement of the Illinois River; and Mr. Clarence King, geologist in charge of geological exploration of the fortieth parallel.

TORPEDOES.

By the act of February 21, 1873, a sum of $300,000 was appropriated for "torpedoes for harbor defenses, and preservation of the same." The project for the expenditure of this fund was approved by the Secretary of War on the 24th of May, 1873. It contemplated the use of nearly the whole of the appropriation for the purchase of the electrical cable which is employed for firing the several torpedoes, and which it is difficult to obtain upon emergencies. Only a sufficient sum was reserved for the preservation and storage of the cable when procured, and the purchase of some twenty sets of electrical apparatus. To make these purchases, and at the same time to obtain the latest information concerning electrical apparatus, experiments, conditions of service, and of the systems of torpedo defenses in use in England and on the continent of Europe, Majors Thomas L. Casey and Henry L. Abbot were, upon my recommendation, ordered by the Secretary of War to proceed to Europe for the above purposes on the 1st of July, and to return about the 1st of October. They have accomplished this duty, and their report in full is now being prepared. So much, however, has already been preliminarily reported as to assure the Department of the excellent character of our own methods, and of the economy and advantage to the Government which has resulted from sending these officers upon this special duty.

ASSISTANCE RENDERED TO THE SURVEY OF STATES.

The results of the observations of the Lake Survey and its maps have been made available to the States of Michigan, Wisconsin, and Minnesota, for the preparation of topographical and geological maps of those States.

The latitude and longitude determinations made in connection with the military and geographical surveys, as well as the maps of those surveys, were also made available for the same purposes.

The land-office surveys of those States, connected with the astronomical and geodetic determinations of the lake, military, and geographical surveys, and their topographical maps, as well as those of the river and harbor improvement surveys, provide valuable material for the preparation of very creditable maps.

To the extent indicated above, it has been considered this Department could properly go, defraying the expenses of the determination of points in the interior, which were of use in correcting and improving the military map of the Western Territories, from the appropriation for military surveys; and the expense of the connection of the land-office and State surveys with the triangulation of the lake survey, from the appropriation for that survey. But any considerable further extension of aid, such as the determination of one or more points in each county, which is desired by the State authorities, could not be made without the sanction of Congress.

If this sanction be obtained, all the requisite assistance can be furnished without any large increase of expense to the lake survey, in consequence of the efficient organization, excellent working methods, and valuable data which it possesses, and can readily apply to any other similar and adjacent work.

Such a course seems highly desirable, as aiding a praiseworthy effort to produce reliable maps of these States, and as conducing to an accuracy which it is important they should possess.

As other States will probably desire similar assistance, it is respectfully suggested that provision be asked for, annually, sufficient to furnish, in the manner above indicated, such requisite geodetic work in any of the States adjacent to the great lakes or the Saint Lawrence River, as may, by appropriate legislation, provide for a geological or topographical survey of their territory. The application of the States in question, with estimates of cost of executing the necessary astronomical and trigonometrical work, will form the subject of a special communication at an early day.

MAPS OF CAMPAIGNS AND BATTLE-FIELDS.

The survey of the battle-fields in the Shenandoah Valley, Virginia, by Maj. G. L. Gillespie, under the direction of Lieut. Gen. Sheridan, was commenced in May last. An office was established at Winchester, Va., and two parties were organized to make a detailed topographical survey of the field of the engagement near that city, after which the battle-fields of Cedar Creek and Fisher's Hill will be surveyed in the same manner, and accurately mapped.   *   *   *

The maps of the Atlanta campaign are being recompiled in this office for publication.

The map of the battle-field of Gettysburg, by Maj. G. K. Warren, is now nearly ready for publication.

GEOLOGICAL EXPLORATION OF THE FORTIETH PARALLEL FROM THE SIERRA NEVADA TO THE EASTERN SLOPE OF THE ROCKY MOUNTAINS.

Mr. Clarence King, United States civil engineer, in charge.

The geological and topographical exploration of the belt of territory, nearly one hundred miles wide; lying along the line of the Pacific Railroad, has been completed. Special examinations were made during the year to solve important questions in glacial geology.

The principal field operations ceased in November, when those assistants that were necessary to work up the results and prepare the maps for publication were removed to New York.

The report of the field-work up to the close of operations is appended.

   *   *   *   *   *   *   *   *

The finished maps of the belt surveyed, five in number, are well advanced towards completion, three of them being now ready for the engraver. The preparation of the remaining volumes of the report, and the completion of the maps, with the publication of both, will be carried on and probably be accomplished in the present fiscal year.

In connection with a geological examination of Green, Bear, and Vermillion cañons, a special examination of the so-called "Diamond Fields" in the vicinity of the latter cañon was made by Mr. King in the month of November, which disclosed the existence of a great fraud in connection therewith. His interesting report of the examination and result is appended.   *   *   *

GEOGRAPHICAL AND GEOLOGICAL SURVEYS AND EXPLORATIONS WEST OF THE 100TH MERIDIAN, IN NEVADA, UTAH, COLORADO, NEW MEXICO, AND ARIZONA.

Officer in charge, First Lieut. George M. Wheeler, Corps of Engineers, having under his orders First Lieutenants R. L. Hoxie and William L. Marshall, Corps of Engineers.

The commencement of the fiscal year found the various parties about taking the field from the rendezvous camp near Salt Lake City. One astronomical party occupied the Mormon observatory at Salt Lake City during the season, while series of observations for latitude and longitude were made by two other astronomical parties at Beaver and Gunnison, Utah Territory; Pioche, Nev.; and Cheyenne, Laramie, and Fort Steele, Wyoming Territory. Observations at Green River, Wyoming Territory, were commenced, but not completed.

Two main topographical parties extended their season's survey from the limits of the survey of the fortieth parallel, on the north, to include portions of the Great Salt Lake, Sevier Lake, and other interior basins, and of the valley and basin of the Colorado in and around the lower of the grand cañons, embracing an area of more than 50,000 square miles, lying in Western and Southwestern Utah, Eastern and Southeastern Nevada, Northern and Western Arizona.

The field parties terminated their labors early in December, when those members who were retained for office-work returned to Washington to prepare the maps and arrange the observations, collections, and other data necessary to exhibit the results of the expedition.

The field-work of this season was resumed in June with an organization of three main topographical parties and five astronomical parties. The area proposed to be examined embraces a portion of Colorado, of Utah, Eastern Arizona, and Western New Mexico. From the early start and efficient organization excellent results are anticipated from the season's work. Lieutenant Wheeler submits an estimate for continuing the exploration, of $90,000 00

For engraving and printing the plates illustrating the six volumes of his report 25,000 00

Total 115,000 00

RECONNOISSANCES AND EXPLORATIONS.

The officers of the Corps of Engineers on detached duty at headquarters of general officers commanding divisions and departments have been engaged during the past year in preparing such maps and sketches and making such surveys and reconnoissances as were required by their respective commanding officers.

Maj. J. W. Barlow, on duty with the Lieutenant-General of the Army, commanding the Military Division of the Missouri, was employed during the year in the compilation and preparation of a new map of the Western Territories, the new additional material for which was derived from various reliable sources, the principal of which were the surveys and reconnoissances of exploring parties under direction of engineer officers, and the reports and sketches of scouting parties of troops. The first sheet has been published and the second and third are nearly ready for the engraver. A small map of the Territories to accompany a memoir describing the military posts and reservations in the military division has been prepared and published. Major Barlow states that there is great demand for accurate maps of the West, and suggests that a liberal expenditure should be made to carry on systematic surveys.

Maj. N. Michler, from June 30 to November 1, 1872, and Capt. G. J. Lydecker, for the remainder of the fiscal year, were on duty with the commanding general, Military Division of the Pacific. The latter in the months of April and May of this year made a *reconnoissance of the* lava beds and surrounding country—the scene of operations against the Modoc Indians, his report of which is appended. * * *

Capt. D. P. Heap, from June 30, 1872, to January, 1873, and Capt. William Ludlow, for the remainder of the fiscal year, were on duty at the headquarters of the Department of Dakota. In June Captain Ludlow accompanied the Yellowstone expedition for the purpose of *surveying the Yellowstone River as far up as practicable*, and also the military reservations of Forts Buford and Rice.

Capt. W. A. Jones, on duty with the commanding general, Department of the Platte, has during the year completed one sheet of the military map of the department, including the State of Nebraska, and commenced the second sheet, including Wyoming Territory. A survey of the military reservations of Fort Fetterman, Wyo., and of Beaver City, Utah, has been made. On June 2d of this year Captain Jones started with a party organized for a *reconnoissance of the country about the headwaters of the Snake, Green, Wind, Big Horn, Gray Bull, Stinking Water, Clark's Fork, and Yellowstone rivers*, for the purpose of discovering an approach to the Yellowstone Lake Basin from the east or southeast, thus opening, if possible, a new and shorter route to the National Yellowstone Park. He has recently returned, having found and crossed the mountains by two practicable routes, one from the headwaters of the Stinking Water, and another from the headwaters of the Wind River. A wagon-road can be readily opened by the last-named route, which will furnish a direct line of communication from the Union Pacific Railroad at Point of Rocks, through the Yellowstone Park to Fort Ellis, and the mining region of Montana.

Lieut. E. H. Ruffner, on duty with the commanding general, Department of the Missouri, has during the year continued the collection of data for the construction of a detailed military map of the department, by means of instructed engineer soldiers attached to scouting parties and marches of troops; and has commenced the survey of the boundary lines of the military reservation at Fort Tularosa and of the Indian reservation. A military *reconnoissance about the headwaters of the Rio Grande and into Southwestern Colorado* was started in May, to be continued during the field season.

Observations for the determination of the latitude and longitude of Denver, Col., and the longitude of Fort Hays and Fort Wallace, Kan., and Pueblo, Col., have been made. The results are appended in addition to Lieutenant Ruffner's annual report.

The completion of the military road from Santa Fé to Taos, New Mexico, provided for by the act of March 3, 1873, was placed in charge of Lieutenant Ruffner, assisted by Lieutenant Morrison, Sixth Cavalry, acting engineer officer of the district of New Mexico. These officers have made a personal reconnoissance of the route, and presented a project for the work, which has been approved, and the work ordered to be prosecuted in accordance thereto.

ESTIMATES OF AMOUNTS REQUIRED FOR MILITARY AND GEOGRAPHICAL SURVEYS, EXPLORATIONS, AND RECONNOISSANCES.

For continuing military surveys for works of defense on the Atlantic and Pacific coasts; for surveys and reconnoissances by officers on duty with the commander of the army, and commanders of military divisions and departments; and for explorations and surveys of Territories west of the one hundredth meridian of longitude, an appropriation of $75,000 will be required.

For engraving and printing the plates illustrating the report of the geographical and geological survey west of the one hundredth degree of longitude, $25,000 will be required.

COMMISSION ON IRRIGATION OF THE JOAQUIN, TULARE, AND SACRAMENTO VALLEYS, CALIFORNIA.

By act of Congress, approved March 3, 1873, the President was " authorized to assign two engineers of the Army and one officer of the Coast Survey, now stationed on the Pacific coast, for the purpose of examining and reporting on a system of irrigation in the San Joaquin, Tulare, and Sacramento Valleys, of the State of California; and for that purpose the officers so assigned may associate with themselves the chief of the geological survey of California, and also one other civilian distinguished for his knowledge of the subject."

By direction of the President, Lieut. Col. B. S. Alexander, and Maj. Geo. H. Mendell, Corps of Engineers, and Prof. George Davidson, Assistant in the Coast Survey, were appointed members of the commission. Professor Whitney, chief of the geological survey of California, and Mr. R. Maitland Brereton were invited to join the commission, but both declined the invitation.

The commission, in accordance with instructions, met and organized in San Francisco in April, and in May commenced a personal examination of the valleys in question, and rivers that empty into them. By the end of June the board had examined both sides of the San Joaquin and Tulare Valleys, the lands already irrigated, and the rivers rising in the Sierra Nevada Mountains, such as the Kern, Kings, San Joaquin, Merced, Tuolumne, Stanislaus, Calaveras, and Cosumnes, following them well up into the foot-hills, and in some cases to the cañons through which they escape from the mountains.

The board has since continued its examinations of rivers and lakes and the collection of information and data to enable them to report fully upon the subject of investigation placed in their hands.

CONTRIBUTIONS TO THE VIENNA EXHIBITION.

In accordance with the directions of the Secretary of War, a complete set of the published maps and reports of all kinds, including the professional papers of the Corps of Engineers; four volumes of photographic views, obtained by exploring expeditions of remarkable geographical features, in remote sections of the Western Territories; plans of important works of river and harbor improvement, and of important experiments in engineering; and models of the works in progress at Hell Gate, and of King's improved counterpoise gun-carriage; were prepared and forwarded by the channels prescribed by the commissioner appointed by the President to represent the United States at the universal exhibition, in accordance with the act of Congress of June 10, 1872. At the close of the exhibition the works contributed are, by the authority of the War Department, to be presented to the engineer department of the Austrian Army.

SALE OF CEMETERY GROUNDS UPON THE FORT GRATIOT MILITARY RESERVATION IN MICHIGAN.

The act of March 3, 1873, authorizes the Secretary of War to survey, plat, and sell the present cemetery grounds upon the Fort Gratiot Military Reservation in Michigan, subject to certain restrictions provided in the act.

Nothing has, as yet, been done in the Engineer Department to carry out the provisions of this act, as the preliminary action of the city of Port Huron, provided by the statute, has not been taken.

OFFICE OF THE CHIEF OF ENGINEERS.

In the labors of the office I was assisted on the 30th of June by the following officers in charge of the several divisions:

FIRST AND SECOND DIVISIONS.—*Fortifications, battalion, and engineer depots, lands, armaments, personnel, &c.*, Maj. T. L. Casey.

THIRD DIVISION.—*River and harbor improvements, &c.*, Maj. J. G. Parke.

FOURTH AND FIFTH DIVISIONS.—*Property accounts, estimates, funds, survey of the lakes, explorations, maps, instruments, &c.*, Lieut. Col. J. G. Foster.

Very respectfully, your obedient servant,

A. A. HUMPHREYS,
Brig. Gen., Chief of Engineers,
Commanding Corps of Engineers.

Hon. WM. W. BELKNAP,
Secretary of War.

REPORT OF THE CHIEF OF ORDNANCE.

ORDNANCE OFFICE, WAR DEPARTMENT,
Washington, October 10, 1873.

SIR: I have the honor to submit, for the information of the Secretary of War, the following report of the principal operations of the Ordnance Department during the fiscal year ended June 30, 1873, with such remarks and recommendations as the interests of that branch of the military service seem to require.

The fiscal resources and disbursements of the Department during the year were as follows, viz:

Amount of appropriations in Treasury June 30, 1872..	$2,689,308 62
Amount in Government depositories to credit of disbursing officers on same date......................	336,958 65
Amount of deposits in Treasury not reported to the credit of the appropriations on same date...........	478,383 86
Amount of appropriations from July 1, 1872, to June 30, 1873, including the fixed annual appropriation for arming and equipping the militia......	2,111,149 40
Amount transferred from the Quartermaster's Department, from "clothing of the Army," for the manufacture of knapsacks, haversacks, canteens, &c	41,953 33
Amount transferred from Engineer Department, balance of appropriation for railroad-bridge at Rock Island	19,690 43
Amount of appropriation of "sales of stores and materials" assigned to the Ordnance Bureau..........	5,000 00
Amount of appropriation for "Allowance for reduction of wages under the eight-hour law," on accounts audited and allowed during the year................	129,142 43

Amount received since June 30, 1872, on account of
damages to arms in hands of troops, from sales of
arms to officers, and of condemned stores, and from
all other sources not before mentioned $476,166 46

Total 6,287,753 18

Amount of expenditures since June 30, 1872 .... 2,161,517 16
Amount in Government depositories June 30, 1872, since
covered in as miscellaneous receipts, on account of
sales of ordnance stores 469,174 51
Amount of deposits in Treasury not reported to the
credit of the appropriations June 30, 1873 .... 450,195 44
Amount turned into the "surplus fund" June 30, 1873. 500,920 37
Amount in Government depositories to credit of dis-
bursing officers June 30, 1873 .... 497,471 27
Amount of appropriations in Treasury June 30, 1873 .. *2,208,474 43

Total 6,287,753 18

The operations at the several arsenals during the year have consisted
of caring for and preserving ordnance and ordnance stores, manufacturing and altering iron sea-coast carriages, metallic ammunition, and
other supplies, preparing for the manufacture of the new-model breech-
loading arms for the troops, erection of public buildings under special
appropriations, and supplying with arms, &c., the militia of the States
and Territories, experiments, &c.

PERSONNEL.

I have again to renew my recommendation, made in the last three
annual reports from this office, that the law of March 3, 1869, prohibiting promotions and appointments in the Ordnance Department, be
repealed. It is hardly necessary to recapitulate the many potent arguments so often presented in favor of this very just measure. The
hardship and humiliation to which officers of merit, experience, and
long service have been subjected during the past four years by the
deprivation of their deserved promotion—the only reward held out in
the profession for years of duty well performed—should no longer be
permitted, and it is earnestly requested that the attention of Congress
be specially called to this matter, that the act approved March 3, 1869,
be repealed.

SMALL-ARMS.

The act making appropriations for the support of the Army for the
year ending June 30, 1873, and for other purposes, approved June 6,
1872, provides:
"For manufacture of arms at the National Armory, $150,000: Pro-
vided, That no part of this appropriation shall be expended until a
breech-loading system for muskets and carbines shall have been adopted
for the military service, upon the recommendation of the board to be
appointed by the Secretary of War, which board shall consist of not

---

* Of this sum $989,632.66 pertain to appropriations prior to July 1, 1873, and can
only be used in liquidating liabilities incurred prior to that time, and $1,049,984.27 of
the balance belongs to the appropriation for arming and equipping the militia, leaving
only the sum of $168,857.50 available for expenditures in the current year.

less than five officers, as follows: One general officer, one ordnance officer, and three officers of the line; one to be taken from the cavalry, one from the infantry, and one from the artillery: *And provided further,* That the system, when so adopted, shall be the only one to be used by the Ordnance Department in the manufacture of muskets and carbines for the military service; and no royalty shall be paid by the Government of the United States for the use of said patent to any of its officers or employés, or for any patent in which said officers or employés may be directly or indirectly interested."

In conformity with the above provisions, a board, of which Brig. Gen. A. H. Terry was president, was convened in the city of New York on the 3d day of September, 1872, and concluded its labors and made its report on May 5, 1873. (The report and accompanying papers are herewith submitted.) After an exhaustive examination and trial, during a session of eight months' duration, of over one hundred arms, including those adopted by the first military powers of Europe, the board

"*Resolved,* That the board recommend that the Springfield breech-loading system be adopted for the military service of the United States, in accordance with the provisions of the act of Congress entitled 'An act making appropriations for the support of the Army for the year ending June 30, 1873, and for other purposes,' approved June 6, 1872."

This report, having been referred to this Bureau, was returned to the Secretary of War with the recommendation that it be approved, and it was so approved on May 20, 1873, thus complying, in its spirit and letter, with the requirements of the law.

It was also recommended, and approved by him, that all small-arms—rifles, carbines, and revolvers—should hereafter be of caliber .45 inch. This was in accordance with the opinion of the board of ordnance officers, composed of Majors Benton and Treadwell and Lieutenant Prince, whose exhaustive report of the trials and experiments made at the National Armory and at the Frankford Arsenal, for the determination of the best caliber for accuracy, penetration, and for giving the least load to the soldiers with the greatest efficiency, is appended in connection with the report of General Terry's board, by which the caliber was recommended for the infantry arm.

The Springfield Armory is now engaged in the manufacture of rifles and carbines, on the new model, for the military service; and, in accordance with the recommendation of General Terry's board, as modified by my indorsement and the approval of the Secretary of War, 10,000 of these arms will be supplied with the Rice trowel-bayonet, with the Chillingworth handle, for experimental trial in the field.

In our estimates for the next fiscal year $500,000 have been asked for continuing the manufacture of arms. This sum will not, with the material on hand, permit us to make more than 35,000 arms, a number the least that should be provided annually to meet current wants and possible future demands. It is not presumable that the new system of breech-loader, selected after such exhaustive tests of all inventions brought before the board, will soon be superseded by any more valuable and efficient system; and it is a grave question of public policy, deserving serious consideration, whether the new arm that has been adopted, after such intelligent and careful trial by a competent board, ought not to be manufactured in such quantities for a reserve supply in case of war as will place us in this part of our national armament on a footing with other first-class powers.

ARMING AND EQUIPPING THE MILITIA.

In this connection, as bearing most vitally on the effectiveness of the armed force of the nation in time of war, the wants of the whole body of the militia is again presented for legislative action. The annual appropriation of $200,000 for arming and equipping the militia, fixed by the act of April 23, 1808, is entirely inadequate at the present time, with a population increased from eight to more than forty millions. As a consequence, some of the richer States of the Union have had to make appropriations of money to provide the arms, &c., necessary to supply such deficiency, although the intention of Congress, as expressed in the law of 1808, was that the money so appropriated should supply the " whole body of the militia." If $200,000 were not deemed too much in 1808, when arms, &c., were cheap, as compared with the improved and costly mechanism now admitted to be a necessity, surely an increase of the appropriation to $1,000,000 annually is the least that is required to fully meet the wants of the " whole body of the militia" and carry out the express wishes of Congress.

It is believed that all issues of arms and other ordnance stores which were made by the War Department to the States and Territories between the 1st day of January, 1861, and the 9th day of April, 1865, under the act of April 23, 1808, and charged to the States and Territories, having been made for the maintenance and preservation of the Union, are properly chargeable to the United States, and the Secretary of War should be authorized to credit the several States and Territories with the sums charged to them respectively for arms and other ordnance stores which were issued to them between the aforementioned dates, and charged against their quotas under the law for arming and equipping the militia: *Provided*, That each State and Territory before receiving credit for the issues charged to them shall return the property to the Ordnance Department free of charge to the United States, or give satisfactory evidence to the Secretary of War that it was expended or otherwise disposed of in the public service during the rebellion. It is recommended that legislation to this effect be asked of Congress.

HEAVY ORDNANCE.

In my last report attention was specially invited to the absolute necessity of provision being made for the armament of our sea-coast defenses. The importance of the subject increases with the earnest and continued efforts on the part of all nations not only to improve the quality of their guns, but in providing, in quantities, those that have given best results in experimental trials. It is not the part of wisdom to wait for ultimate perfection in gun constructions, which may never be attained, or for the first rumbling of approaching strife, when guns are needed in the fortresses and not in the founderies, to commence the tedious and costly work of construction. In the modern quick and decisive settlement of differences by the arbitrament of arms there is no time for preparation after the declaration of war; and a nation may sink beneath the powerful blows of a well-armed adversary in less time than it takes to manufacture a single gun. It thus becomes the duty of this Bureau to bring to the attention of the War Department and of Congress the paramount importance of a subject upon which the successful defense of the country largely depends. This duty has been performed in years past; and should war with any naval power find our harbors open to the attack of iron-clads and their heavy guns, without proper provision having been made for a successful defense, the responsibility will not rest on this Bureau, which has, with almost disagreeable importunity, placed the matter squarely before the country, and asked for appropriations.

The statement, "Armament of the fortifications," appended, is based on information received from the Chief of Engineers, and shows that the number of guns, of all kinds, required to arm our forts, as far as yet determined, amounts to a total of 4,181. To completely arm all the forts, when the character of their armament is hereafter fully determined, will largely increase this total. Of these 4,181 guns, 2,801, including those on hand, will be needed on the 30th next June. There are on hand, at the forts and arsenals, 1,659 guns, leaving 1,142 required during the next fiscal year.

These guns, carriages, and necessary projectiles should be provided with all possible dispatch; but as no rifle of large caliber has yet been adopted for our service, our present wants can be best met by providing the smooth-bores, which are admitted to be the most efficient known. These are positive demands upon this Department for our coast defenses; not for an undefined future, but for the actual present.

It is, therefore, with all confidence in the justness and necessity of our wants, that an estimate of $1,449,552 has been made for the armaments of our forts for the next fiscal year, being about one-sixth of the money-value of the absolute requirements; and this estimate has been so reduced because it is believed that the whole manufacturing industry of the country is not equal to a larger production. The estimate has been made specifically, giving the minimum number of guns that ought to be at once provided for one or more forts that protect each of our most important harbors, that the subject, in its detail and its entirety, may be fairly stated and clearly understood.

Another consideration should not be disregarded. The moneys appropriated by Congress during the past two years for fortifications average $1,368,000. It would be difficult, if not impossible, to determine the actual cost of each fort per gun, depending, as this must, upon the material of its construction—an earth-work being comparatively cheap as compared with brick or stone or the more costly iron-clad walls—but it is fair to conclude that the guns and carriages, especially guns of steel, like Krupp's, or of wrought iron, like the Woolwich, with wrought iron carriages, do cost as much as the fort which they arm and defend. The price given by Krupp's agent on July 2, 1872, for a 12-inch steel gun and its carriage, delivered at the works in Essen, was $48,500 gold. An armament composed entirely of such guns would, it is believed, cost more than the most expensive fort of modern construction.

While, therefore, liberal appropriations are made annually for fortifications, there seems to be strong reason for appropriations of equal magnitude for the armament, when the fact is undeniable that a fort without its proper armament is worse than useless—an inert mass of expensive material, without power of attack or defense.

The heavy rifled guns recommended for trial by the board of officers convened under the provision of the act of Congress approved June 6, 1872, making an appropriation for "experiments and tests of heavy rifled ordnance," are now in process of manufacture. The delays incident to the preparations necessary for constructions of such novel character have had to be overcome; but it is believed that the four guns now being made will be completed and ready for trial during the winter. No doubts are entertained that much valuable information will result from the trials, which may possibly lead to the early adoption of a suitable rifle-gun of large caliber. Experiments on a large scale, with this end in view, have been prosecuted in other countries for years, and are still being conducted with persistent energy and skill and large expenditure of money; but a solution of this important question has not yet been reached—not one of such a satisfactory character as to make further expensive trials and experiments no longer necessary before final adoption.

It is respectfully recommended that an appropriation of $75,000 be asked of Congress for the manufacture and trial of cast-iron 12-inch rifles for experimental purposes. The very great improvement in the character of our gunpowder recently made will justify such an expenditure for the purpose of determining definitely whether cast iron cannot be successfully used in the manufacture of guns of the largest caliber for efficient service. This recommendation is made in the spirit of judicious economy; for, if cast iron can be made as available for rifles as for smooth-bores, the cost of our guns will be thereby reduced at least one-half or two-thirds, as compared with wrought-iron or steel constructions. The reason for this recommendation may be briefly stated as follows: Large-grain powder for heavy guns was first adopted by this Department in 1861, at a time when other nations continued the use of small-grain. This great improvement in the mode of manufacture was the result of careful study and experiment by the late General Rodman, who successfully used it in his first 15-inch gun. This, and his invention of the "perforated-cake" powder, which has been adopted by and is now in use in both Russia and Germany, and the "pebble" powder, similar to our "mammoth," adopted by England, created that revolution in the manufacture of gunpowder, based upon purely scientific principles of combustion and evolution of gases, that has enabled all nations to increase the size of their ordnance.

The necessity for strength in any gun construction depends upon the amount of strain that is brought upon it, and this strain is affected by the method and rate at which the gases are evolved in the burning of the powder-charge, and the rate at which the powder-space behind the shot is enlarged by the gradual movement of the shot through the bore. It is evident that if, by any proper manipulation of the powder in manufacture, the size and form and density of grain can be so determined and adjusted as to confine the strain within certain limits, the strength of the gun to resist such a strain need not reach the maximum requirements of steel, but may be found within the well-known capabilities of our best cast iron.

It must not be overlooked that the resistance of the projectile plays a no less important part in the development of strain in rifled guns, and this resistance becomes destructive when increased, either by the lack of uniformity in the expansion of the sabot in taking the grooves, or by its wedging in the gun from upsetting or breaking of the body of the projectile. It is believed, however, that the shot as now made will overcome these objections by the more perfect adjustment of the parts to the work to be performed, thus giving a uniform resistance to the efforts of the powder.

Recent trials from a 15-inch smooth-bore gun with a new experimental powder, with charges of 100 pounds of powder, and shot of 450 pounds, gave higher velocities with greatly diminished pressures, and a degree of uniformity of action seldom attained by the ordinary granulated mammoth. Each grain or pellet of this powder was formed in dies by pressure. The experiments clearly indicated that it can be manufactured in large quantities, of a uniform quality.

No doubts are entertained that similar results will follow from its use in large rifles, that is, increased initial velocity with marked diminution of pressure. It is in view of these facts that this Bureau is desirous to test cast iron to its fullest extent by experiment, in the hope that it may lead to its practical utilization for the construction of heavy rifled guns.

RIFLING AND VENTING EXPERIMENTAL RIFLE-GUNS.

The determination of the best method of rifling and venting the heavy guns now being made under the act of June 6, 1872, and the character of the powder, projectiles, and carriages to be provided for their trial, was confided to a board of ordnance officers, composed of Lieutenant-Colonel Laidley and Majors Crispin and Baylor, which convened in the city of New York last April. The report of their investigations and recommendations are herewith submitted.

GUN-CARRIAGES.

The very important subject of gun-carriages for fortifications has engaged the attention of this Department. Under General Orders No. 106, of December 13, 1872, a board of officers convened in New York in January last to examine and report upon such plans and models of such depressing and other carriages for heavy ordnance as it might deem worthy of trial. The report of the board, which includes an examination of more than fifty plans, is herewith submitted. Its recommendations have received the approval of the Secretary of War; "carriages provided with air-cylinders (pneumatic buffers)" and the "center-pintle chassis for mortar-carriages" are adopted for the military service. The other recommendations of the board will be carried out whenever funds are available for the purpose.

The object of adapting pneumatic buffers to gun-carriages is for the purpose of absorbing the recoil of the gun when fired. Recent experience seems to prove that in addition to the accomplishment of this object, the buffers perform their work so freely and smoothly as to solve the very difficult problem of platform constructions, which under the old methods of checking the recoil were often shattered by the shock and strain incident to a defective system.

An examination of these several reports will show that every facility was given to inventors, and others interested, to submit their devices, plans, &c., that while the interests of the United States might be best subserved by the widest range of study and examination on the part of the boards, individuals might also have every opportunity for a patient and intelligent hearing on the merits of the inventions presented.

NEW POWDER AND POWDER-DEPOT.

By the last act making appropriations for the support of the Army, authority was given the Secretary of War "to exchange the unserviceable and unsuitable powder on hand for new powder," and under the Secretary's orders steps have been taken by this Bureau to procure a supply under favorable terms.

The rapid deterioration of powder, often under the most favorable circumstances, renders its care and preservation a constant expense to the United States. The want of proper storage has forced this Department to concentrate large quantities of it in our forts, where, through the searching influences of the salt air, its deterioration, begun during the rebellion, has continued with great rapidity.

This experience is the best and strongest argument in favor of a powder-depot, to be located in some retired mountainous region, where it might be free from the worst atmospheric influences and not endanger either public or private interests by its proximity.

One hundred thousand dollars is the least that should be appropriated for the purchase of a site and commence the erection of magazines, and such an appropriation is earnestly recommended.

BREECH-LOADING FIELD-CANNON.

The act making appropriations for the support of the Army for the year ending June 30, 1873, provides "For constructing and testing Moffat's breech-loading field-pieces, eight thousand dollars." A Moffat gun is now in process of construction by this Department, under the personal supervision of the inventor, and will very soon be ready for trial. It is the intention to try it in comparison not only with our muzzle-loading field-pieces, but with a breech-loading field-gun, which, with its carriage, ammunition, &c., complete, was recently presented to the War Department by the government of Germany. It is believed that this trial will enable the Bureau to decide on their relative merits by giving us a mass of practical information and results never before obtained in this country.

GATLING GUNS.

The last Army appropriation bill, approved March 3, 1873, provides "For experiments and tests of two Gatling guns of large caliber for flank defense of fortifications, five thousand dollars." Upon the recommendation of this Bureau, a board of one engineer, one ordnance, and one artillery officer was convened last June to take this matter under consideration and make the "experiments and tests" required by the law. Their preparations are now nearly completed, and a report on the results of their labors may be shortly expected. Fifty Gatling guns of caliber .45 inch, for which an appropriation has been made, have been contracted for, and it is expected will be placed in service in the early spring for the use of the troops on the frontier. These guns are of such dimensions and weights as to be easily transported on pack-animals. Their efficiency can only be tested by actual use; but it is thought that they will be far more effective in Indian warfare than the mountain-howitzer heretofore in use.

REVOLVERS.

The general and constant demand from the field for revolvers using the metallic ammunition, together with the urgent necessity for some improved weapon to replace the revolvers previously used in service using the paper or linen cartridge, caused early efforts to be made to reach a solution of this very difficult problem. After trials in the field of two kinds, and experimental trials of improved models, this Bureau recommended for approval the purchase of a sufficient number of the Colt's to supply the cavalry arm of the service. They are now being made, and it is hoped that the whole number will be in the hands of troops before the next spring.

ATLANTIC ARSENAL.

My recommendation, made in previous reports, for the establishment of a large arsenal of construction, a powder-depot, and a proving-ground for heavy guns on the Atlantic coast, is again renewed. This very essential requirement can be best subserved, without a dollar of appropriation, by authorizing the sale of such of the arsenals east of the Mississippi as are no longer of any use to the country, and applying the proceeds of such sales to the purchase of a site and the erection of buildings. The concentration of manufacture in one establishment is the strongest argument in favor of economy and efficiency. The keeping in repair and preservation the many arsenals rendered useless since the war makes an important item in our estimates, and large amounts are thus expended that could be profitably used in manufactures. A general law should be passed giving the Secretary of War discretionary power for their sale at such times as would prove most advantageous to the Government, and the proceeds to be applied as suggested. It would be but placing the money value of these establishments, now no longer needed, into a more valuable and profitable investment, with a great annual saving in expenses, and economy in manufacture; and, in this connection, it may be pertinent to say that the act of June 6, 1872, providing for experiments and tests of heavy rifled ordnance, cannot be executed in the spirit of the law with our present facilities of a proving-ground. To efficiently and satisfactorily test a gun it is absolutely necessary to fire it for accuracy. The Department has now a range of less than 1,000 yards; it should have one of six miles, and it is believed that a suitable one can easily be obtained with but a small expenditure of money. It is therefore recommended that Congress be asked to make an appropriation for this purpose in the interests of the national defense.

SALES OF ARSENALS.

The law of June 10, 1872, authorizing and directing the sale of Rome, Champlain, and North Carolina arsenals, and the old arsenal-site at Augusta, Ga., has, in respect to each of those places, been carried into effect, the property realizing satisfactory prices. The Mount Vernon Arsenal, directed by the same act to be sold, has been, by order of the Secretary of War, turned over to the Quartermaster's Department for the use of troops. A modification of the law should therefore be requested, in view of the disposition made of this property.

The title of the United States in the captured lands and tenements at Shreveport, La., Marshall and Jefferson, Tex., and in Marion and Davis Counties, Tex., was found upon investigation not to be of sufficient marketable value to warrant proceedings under the above law, and under the sanction of the Secretary of War the interest of the United States to the Shreveport property has been relinquished to the owners, and the same course offered to be taken with respect to the Marion and Davis County property. On account of failure of title to the other property in Texas, no action has been taken in respect to the same by this Bureau.

The law also authorized and directed the sale of the Apalachicola Arsenal, in Florida. As this property was, by the "act donating Chattahoochie Arsenal to the State of Florida for educational purposes," approved December 15, 1870, directed to be transferred to the board of internal improvements of the State of Florida, the direction for its sale by the act of June 10, 1872, is thought to have been an oversight by Congress. Attention should be invited to the subject, that the matter may be cleared of ambiguity.

I have to recommend that authority be asked of Congress for the sale of Kennebec Arsenal, Augusta, Me., Detroit Arsenal, Dearbornville, Mich., Pikesville Arsenal, Pikesville, Md., and the property at Sag Harbor, N. Y., belonging to this Bureau, but now no longer needed for public purposes.

The several arsenals above named have in past years been of great value and importance, but the present facilities for intercommunication between the most remote portions of the country render their retention an expense, without corresponding benefit.

In this general connection, I have to add that the Charleston Arsenal has, by direction of the Secretary of War, been turned over to the Quartermaster's Department within the past year for the use of the troops, and that the ordnance depot at Omaha, Nebr., has been broken up and discontinued.

PATENT CLAIMS.

I have the honor again to invite attention to the necessity of some legislation providing for the adjudication and settlement of patent claims that are constantly urged against this Department. I quote from my previous reports:

The chief difficulties which this Department had to contend against in producing a good breech-loading musket have arisen from the impossibility of making any improvement which is not immediately claimed under some one of the many patents which have been granted for improvements in fire-arms, and from the extreme eagerness and strong efforts of some inventors, and all other parties interested in patents, to have their improvements used by the Government. Many persons claim to hold patents for improvements which are used in the conversion of the Springfield muskets; in some instances several parties have claimed to hold patents for the same thing, and it is believed that every improvement is claimed by more than one inventor. The Bureau has declined to acknowledge the validity of any patents for improvements used in the conversion of the Springfield rifled musket, knowing that it was not competent for it to decide the question, and believing that the proper course for patentees to take was to establish satisfactorily the validity of their claims, and then apply to Congress for compensation for the use of the patents.

These difficulties have continued to embarrass this Department, and to affect injuriously the interests of the Government, and it is respectfully suggested whether a law may not be devised which, while affording protection to all inventors in the rights secured to them by patents, will enable the Government to use unrestrictedly any improvement which it may be desirable for it to use. I have no desire to see any inventor deprived of any of his rights, without just compensation; but I am so fully convinced that some law protecting the Government against improper claims of inventors and owners of patents should be passed that I feel it my duty to bring the matter particularly to your notice, in the hope that something may be done to secure so desirable an end. Such a law would relieve this Department of much annoyance and embarrassment, and would tend, in my opinion, to increase to a considerable degree the efficiency of the public service.

It is respectfully suggested that a law be passed which will authorize officers in charge of public works to make use of all inventions or improvements whatever applicable to the work under their charge, and which will provide that when a claim for damages is made by any person for an invention or improvement so used, at least —— days' notice shall be given, requiring all parties claiming said invention or improvement to present their claims, with the evidence in support of the same, to some special judicial tribunal authorized to try the same, whose duty it shall be to decide who is the party entitled to damages or remuneration, and to fix the amount which should be paid by the United States for the use of the invention or improvement; their decision to be final, so far as the United States are concerned, and the amount declared to be due from the United States to be paid out of the appropriation for which the work done is paid.

The claim to which I had the honor to refer in my last annual report as having been decided adversely against the commanding officer of Springfield Armory has, upon the recommendation of this Office and the approval of the Secretary of War, been referred to the accounting officers of the Treasury, and allowed. This claim, therefore, is now settled: but other claims against the minor portions of the Springfield breech-mechanism remain as yet unadjudicated and unliquidated, and are a source of embarrassment to this Bureau. Two suits are now pending having reference to alleged infringements in the mechanism of the arm, the one against the commanding officer of the Springfield Armory, and the other against the United States.

A recent opinion of the Attorney-General, upon inquiries propounded by the Secretary of War, touching the general subject of claims arising out of infringement of private patent-rights in the Government shops, estops this Bureau from further consideration of claims arising out of the past use of such patents. The only extent to which this Bureau is therefore enabled to go, under these circumstances, is to throw its aid in favor of the officers of the Department who may be involved in private civil suits for alleged infringements, and thereby endeavor to break down, if possible, the claims which justly should be brought against the United States. The bringing of these private suits this Bureau is powerless to prevent, and the liquidation of damages, when adjudged, should not be borne by the officers of the Department. I have, therefore, to renew my recommendation above quoted for the appointment of some tribunal who shall be specially empowered to adjust and settle all the remaining claims, conflicting or otherwise, which exist against the arm. The justness of this recommendation is apparent from a consideration of the attitude in which this Bureau is placed with respect to its officers, as well as a consideration of the interests of parties who have equitable claims against the arm.

APPROPRIATIONS FOR PUBLIC BUILDINGS.

The first section of the act of July 1, 1870, has proved injurious to the interest of the Government, which applied to the appropriations for the erection of arsenals and other public buildings under the control of this Department.

E. Statement of ordnance, ordnance stores, &c., distributed to colleges from July 1, 1872, to June 30, 1873, under the joint resolution of May 4. 1870.

I have the honor to be, very respectfully, your obedient servant,
A. B. DYER,
Chief of Ordnance, U. S. A.

The ADJUTANT-GENERAL,
United States Army.

REPORT OF THE CHIEF SIGNAL-OFFICER.

WAR DEPARTMENT,
OFFICE OF THE CHIEF SIGNAL-OFFICER.
Washington, D. C., November 1, 1873.

SIR: Instruction in military signaling and telegraphy has continued during the past year at the Signal-School of Instruction and Practice at Fort Whipple, Va.

One of the officers at the Military Academy at West Point is designated as instructor of military signals and telegraphing, but no report has been received from him, and it is not known what proportion of study and practice is allotted the several branches under his charge. Experience leads to the belief that the whole time of a skilled and industrious officer would be occupied by a course of instruction of the cadets at West Point, which should insure to them that proficiency in military signaling and telegraphy requisite to maintain equality in these branches with the officers of European services, or to be of any practical value to the Army of the United States. The recommendation made in previous reports that more special instruction at the Military Academy should be provided for, with a merit value affecting the standing of the cadets, is renewed, and it is also suggested that, to secure accuracy and uniformity, the officer to be in future charged with that instruction should have passed the course at Fort Whipple. There has been a partial instruction in the Department of the Missouri, under the charge of Second Lieut. Philip Reade, Third United States Infantry, and acting signal-officer of that Department. Although this officer has not had the advantage of the course provided at Fort Whipple, his industry and zeal have been attended with good results. His reports show fifty-five officers to have been fully, and ninety-seven partially, instructed, and one hundred and two enlisted men fully, and three hundred and ten partially, instructed during the year.

The only full and regular course of instruction, that at Fort Whipple, has continued to be under the immediate direction of First Lieut. C. E. Kilbourne, Second United States Artillery, acting signal-officer, who has proved faithful and efficient. The report of commissioned officers instructed, (six in number,) with their respective amounts of field-practice, is given in Papers 1 and 2, hereto attached. The number of private soldiers instructed, as candidates for promotion to the grade of observer-sergeant, has been sixty-seven, and of those instructed as assistants to observer-sergeants, one hundred and twenty-seven. The details of their instruction, examination, promotion, and duty are presented in Papers 3 and 4.

The Signal School of Instruction and Post of Fort Whipple, Va., has, during the year, assumed a character of permanence which has been much desired. New barracks, a mess-hall, a guard-house, and stables have been erected; and two buildings for officers' quarters, a building for the purposes of instruction, and a wagon-shed for the field-telegraph train, are in progress of construction. The hospital has proved ample for the requirements of the command, and has been well managed under the charge of Acting Assist. Surg. L. W. Ritchie. A large amount of work has been performed in the leveling and preparation of the ground occupied by the old fortifications. To complete the equipment of the post, in addition to the need for a commissary and quartermaster store-house, a wagon-shed for quartermaster wagons, and stabling for necessary public animals, a pressing want is felt for officers' quarters, those now provided not being sufficient for the number of officers regularly on duty and under instruction. The Fort has become of interest to, and is frequently visited by, distinguished American citizens and officers of foreign governments. It is desirable that the War Department, always considered responsible for its existence, should provide for it as a creditable and representative post. The care of the Secretary of War has been already directed to the comfort of the enlisted men. His favorable consideration is now asked to secure the requisite accommodation for the officers and the protection of the public property.

The field-telegraph train has been greatly improved, and drills with it are regular and satisfactory, having been under the special direction of First Lieut. R. P. Strong, Fourth United States Artillery, acting signal-officer, who has, during the year, been in immediate charge of the post, and has shown much energy in the performance of the duties confided to him. The other drills of the signal-service detachment, with signal equipments, and with, as well as without, arms, have been thorough, and through increased facilities as well as numbers discipline has been advanced. The system of duty and practice at Fort Whipple gives the military training necessary for the duties of the signal-service, and it imparts the accurate understanding of the special branches for which it has been established. It is the sole place in the United States where either commissioned officers or enlisted men can be completely instructed and tested in a branch of the military profession now recognized to be of prominent importance in time of war, and of no less utility in time of peace.

The study of military signaling and telegraphy requires that the student shall have the example and illustration of a skilled master. It would be unwise, in providing for the instruction of the Army, to ignore the thorough and well-appointed school already established, and to expect much benefit from the mere issue of text-books and equipments, where teacher and taught are alike ignorant. The plan, at one time suggested, that post-adjutants should become instructors, has proved a failure.

During the past year a number of officers have applied to be instructed at Fort Whipple; but the absence of any arrangement for details has prevented, for the time, a favorable consideration of their requests. It is desirable that a system of details should be established. The proper discharge of the duties of the field signal-service simply, i. e., those embracing only such knowledge of military signaling and telegraphy as is constantly requisite at our frontier posts and for Indian wars, in time of general peace, or in the field during war, requires a special tuition of at least sixth months' duration, and officers of every regiment and company ought to pass through the course as a part of their requisite military study. The signal-service is an armed organization, and often needs the disciplined use of arms. Drills with arms, the movement of armed bodies, and the care of troops are as constituent a portion of the duties at Fort Whipple as at any post of the Army, and the officers ordered there need lose nothing of their military practice. It is recommended that six officers, to be selected by the Secretary of War, upon the recommendation of their regimental and departmental commanders, be detailed for instruction in the duties of the "field" signal-service alone, as distinguished from the full duties of that service. These officers to rejoin their commands upon the completion of the course, their places to be supplied through other details, published in advance, in the manner customary in details for artillery instruction. The time of instruction would average about six months.

The officers so to be detailed should, however, be held to be of a class distinct from those charged with the full duties of the signal-service. The full duties of the signal-service include those applicable to peace as well as to war, and to attain proficiency in them the whole time of an officer, during years of study and application, is requisite. They comprise the duties of the field signal-service above described, and also all the duties of the service in relation to the display of warning signals, giving notice in advance of storms and floods. The latter involve the study of meteoric indications, and the practice and habit of controlling the organization spread over the United States; of managing the taking, telegraphing, receipt, collocation, and publication of reports from the different stations; of deducing correct results from them, and of giving necessary warnings, by signals or otherwise, when danger threatens. The value of the officer constantly increases with the experience had in the observation of storms, the study of meteoric indications, and the correct ordering of signals. To fulfill it reliably, the employment of a selected officer, once placed upon this duty, must be permanent. Provision should be made for such permanent employment for the same reason as it is made for the permanent employment of officers of the engineers and of ordnance. It will be fatal to the service if it is attempted to perform its duty by temporary details. The detail of officers for the duties of the full signal-service, as distinguished from the field signal-service, should, therefore, be regarded as almost necessarily permanent, and it should be made with the expectation of being permanent, until such time as Congress shall provide an established organization, to prevent the accidents and imperfect working to which a temporary service is always liable. The urgent need of such legislation is again presented for the consideration of the Secretary of War.

In the last annual report mention was made of the hardship involved in the fact that the officers detailed for the duties of this service were subjected to the misconstruction, and sometimes to the injustice, of those from whose commands they are involuntarily separated. Applications are frequently pressed to bring about the relief of officers, by persons wholly ignorant of their duties, which, if successful, would seriously embarrass the execution of the work required by law. It ought not to remain possible, through neglect of legislation, that the whole machinery of the signal-service should stop in an hour, as might already have happened had not the wise discretion of the Secretary of War been exercised to prevent so great a misfortune. Justice would seem to require that a service which has existed, and with admitted good result to the United States, for now thirteen years as a temporary service, and on which officers have served continuously through details of ten years' duration, in peace and in war, living and dying in this service alone, should be held to have established a claim to permanency. With interests now depending upon its daily work as great as can by any possibility rest upon any other branch of the service, there is no day but upon which it may be embarrassed, or even fatally crippled, by the removal of its skillful men at the junctures at which their services are most needed. The War Department, while held rigidly responsible for the failures of the service, has not yet been granted the legislation to provide for its proper discharge.

Recruiting for assignment to the signal-service has been conducted under the direction of the War Department, that the recruiting officers of the general recruiting service at designated stations should enlist and order to this office such men, they passing the required physical examination, as may be presented to them by the recruiting observer-sergeants of the signal-service. While the popularity of the service has been remarkable, its requirements are not always understood by those who apply to be enlisted. So much trouble has been occasioned to the Secretary of War by recruits complaining of the military duties considered by this office essential, that a series of circulars and instructions, shown in Papers 5 and 6, and paragraph 144 of Paper 7, hereto annexed, have been prepared and so brought to the notice of every applicant for enlistment, the recruiting sergeant, and the recruiting officer, that misapprehension seems to be impossible. The recruits are divided into classes, those for the "full" and those for the "field signal-service." The first mentioned are such as, in the judgment of the observer-sergeant, after examination by him, are fitted by education and intelligence for the full duties of the signal-service, including not only the duties connected with field-signals and telegraphy, but the duties of observers at stations of observation. These men are placed on duty at Fort Whipple, Va., as private soldiers of the signal-service detachment there stationed, for at least two months, after which they have the privilege on their own application, their conduct being good, of appearing before a board of officers as candidates to be placed under the tuition necessary to be assistants to observers on stations. Passing this examination the soldier continues the course, still performing his military duties until such time as he is reported by the instructor competent to be an assistant. He may then be detailed on duty as an assistant to an observer on station. After six months' service satisfactorily rendered as such assistant, during which time he recites regularly to the observer in charge, and upon a favorable report, he may be ordered to Fort Whipple to be placed under the additional special instruction given to candidates for the grade of observer-sergeant. This additional instruction lasts about two months, during which the candidate must serve on four tours of guard duty. Upon its completion he is ordered before a board of officers convened at this office for final examination on the special subjects of the instruction, and also before another board convened at Fort Whipple for report on his proficiency in the drill (with and without arms) and duties of the signal service detachment, and his understanding of the military duties and responsibilities of sergeants in the signal-service, this examination embracing the more essential of the Articles of War, Army Regulations, and customs of the service applicable to the duties of the grade above mentioned. On passing both of these boards, the candidate, as vacancies occur, is promoted to be sergeant in the signal-service, but, as a rule, is obliged to serve one month at Fort Whipple before being ordered on station, during which period, in addition to his other duties, he takes, under the direction of the instructor, such observations and makes such records and reports as may keep him familiar with the duties of an observer.

Applicants who, in the judgment of the recruiting observer-sergeant, are not fitted by education and intelligence for the full duties of the signal-service, but who are of such ability and character as to render them qualified for its field duties, *i. e.*, those of field-signals and telegraphy, as distinguished from those including the duties of observer-sergeant, are presented to the recruiting officer for enlistment to and assignment to the "field signal-service." The recruits so enlisted are not precluded from eventual advancement to the full duties of the signal-service and promotion, in case they prove fit and worthy.

A division is also made, after enlistment, among the private soldiers, by which those of good conduct, who pass specified examinations in elementary education, military signaling and telegraphy, and the duties and drill (with and without arms) of soldiers of the signal-service detachment, are announced as privates of the first class, and wear the special designation in uniform provided for them in General Orders 92, War Department, Adjutant-General's Office, dated October 26, 1872.

The propriety of legislation which will establish, as a special grade, that of the observer-sergeants of the signal-service, is urged upon the consideration of the Secretary of War. Very many of these men have enlisted with the hope that Congress will, in an organization of the signal-service, improve their position. This hope ought to become a realization. The great majority of the men of this service have enlisted for it directly under the promise, authorized by the Secretary of War, that they shall not be transferred to any other branch of the Army. They neither have nor would have enlisted under the general recruiting regulations, and without the promise above referred to the work intrusted to this office could not have been done.

In this connection it is proper to add that the action of the President in the promotion of observer-sergeant Theodore Smith to a lieutenancy in the Army, for good conduct, has been highly beneficial to the service.

The systematic course by which the enlisted men are selected, drilled, examined, instructed, tested by practice, instructed in higher branches, again examined and again tested before being intrusted with the management of stations, has thrown much labor upon the several boards of examination. The preliminary board, convened at this office for the examination of applicants to be placed under the first course of instruction, is composed of Bvt. Lieut. Col. Garrick Mallery, acting signal-officer and assistant, Bvt. Capt. H. W. Howgate, acting signal-officer and assistant, and Second Lieut. David J. Gibbon, acting signal-officer. This board has held a session on every Thursday during the year, and has examined (including re-examinations) three hundred and one applicants.

Of the civilians, whose enlistment depended upon the result of their examinations, eighteen were accepted, a much larger number being rejected. The proportion of those already enlisted, whose examinations were satisfactory, has exhibited the good judgment of the observer-sergeants who selected them, one hundred and twenty-one having passed the board, while but fourteen are in the list of failures, some of whom may yet pass on another examination.

The board convened at this office for the examination of candidates for promotion to the grade of observer-sergeant is composed of Bvt. Lieut. Col. Garrick Mallery, acting signal-officer and assistant; First Lieut. C. E. Kilbourne, acting signal-officer and instructor at Fort Whipple; and Bvt. Capt. H. W. Howgate, acting signal-officer and assistant. This board meets from time to time, as the instructor at Fort Whipple reports candidates ready for examination, and has examined during the year fifty-two candidates, of whom all but two have passed and been promoted.

The board convened at Fort Whipple for examination in the general duties of soldiers and non-commissioned officers, and the special drill of the signal-service is composed of First Lieut. George S. Grimes, Second United States Artillery; First Lieut. C. E. Kilbourne, Second United States Artillery; and First Lieut. C. C. Wolcott, Third United States Artillery, all acting signal-officers.

The morning report of Fort Whipple for September 30 includes sixteen non-commissioned officers and one hundred and thirty-one privates as present. Of these, seven non-commissioned officers and thirty-seven privates are under special instruction.

The work done at this office has become of large amount, comprehending many details. Never ceasing for a moment, it is necessary that reliefs of officers and enlisted men shall be so arranged that each shall take up his duty at a particular point and perform it in the manner prescribed. At once the greatest expedition and minuteness are required, both of which can only be obtained by a number of persons working at the same time on different parts of the same general duty, with a system of checks and counter-checks to prevent error, or at once to detect its cause and the responsibility for it. The experience thus far obtained has resulted in the issue of regulations and rules for the government of the office, (Paper S,) to which attention is invited.

Bvt. Lieut. Col. Garrick Mallery, acting signal-officer and assistant, has continued during the year to have charge of records, general correspondence and orders, with the superintendence of enlistments and other details specially assigned to him. The various duties in his care have been faithfully discharged.

The correspondence of the office in its several divisions is extensive, forty-six thousand four hundred and thirty-two letters having been sent, and two hundred and seventeen thousand five hundred and seventy-five received during the year, the record of which is classified in Paper 9. The aggregate of the correspondence is two hundred and sixty-four thousand and seven letters and documents sent and received, exclusive of publications and telegrams. The numerous requests for information on subjects, some only indirectly connected with the duties of this office, require of themselves much attention.

The office is in communication with many foreign correspondents. The following-named below in order of time are some of those who have, at their request, been regularly furnished with copies of the weather maps and bulletins, viz, Robert Scott, esq., director Meteorological Office, London, England; Professor Buys Ballot, director Meteorological Institute of the Netherlands, Utrecht, Holland; Professor H. Mohn, director Royal Meteorological Institute of Norway, Christiania, Norway; Capt. N. Hoffmeyer, director Royal Meteorological Institute of Denmark, Copenhagen, Denmark; Professor Dr. Prestel, Emden, Germany; Monsieur Marie Davy, chef de la division météorologie de l'Observatorie physique central de Montsouris, Paris, France; Monsieur Harold Tarry, vice-president Meteorological Society of France, Paris, France; Imperial German Naval School at Kiel, Germany; His Majesty the King of Würtemburg, Stuttgart, Germany.

First Lieut. Henry Jackson, acting signal-officer and assistant, has continued to discharge the duties of property and disbursing officer with skill and industry. Seven thousand nine hundred and eighty-nine accounts have been examined and settled in the property division, excluding those of officers of the Army responsible for signal property.

which number four hundred and seven. Six hundred and six instruments have been purchased, and six hundred and twelve issued. (Paper 10.) Lieutenant Jackson has also continued the collection of statistics to complete the lists of elevations above sea-level, requisite for the accurate reduction of meteorological observations. There have been added this year sixty-three levels of lines of railroads received from railroad engineers, seven lines of levels received from civil engineers, fourteen levels collected from other sources.

The library of the office has been increased to two thousand four hundred and seventy bound volumes, exclusive of two hundred and thirty pamphlets, and one hundred and two maps and charts. The works are selected wholly for their value to the scientific branches connected with the duties imposed upon it, and many of them have been obtained without expense to the United States through the system of exchanges established. Paper 11 is a list of the foreign contributions to the library.

The act of Congress approved March 3, 1873, entitled "An act making appropriations for sundry civil expenses of the Government for the fiscal year ending June thirtieth, eighteen hundred and seventy-four, and for other purposes," contained the following proviso: "Provided that the chief signal-officer may cause to be sold any surplus maps or publications of the signal-office, the money received therefor to be applied toward defraying the expenses of the signal-service, an account of the same to be rendered in each annual report of the chief of the signal-service." This account is presented in Paper 12, being exclusively for the amounts received for the sale of maps.

Until recently, the office has not been able so far to increase the issue of its publications as to allow of any considerable surplus, nor have persons interested yet become generally aware of their privilege to obtain, at a trifling expense, the publications which before had been applied for and necessarily refused. It is believed that the above provision will lead in future to a wide distribution of meterological knowledge without expense to the United States.

Bvt. Capt. H. W. Howgate, acting signal-officer and assistant, has continued to have general charge of instruction and general supervision of the observer-sergeants and assistants to observers at stations, and of the receipt, record, and publication of the weather reports, which duties, together with others specially assigned to him, have been performed with marked devotion and ability.

*　　*　　*　　*　　~

SPECIAL RIVER-STATIONS.

Since the date of the last annual report nineteen stations have been selected on the principal western rivers and their tributaries, at which regular river observations are made and reported to this office by telegraph. These stations are independent of those occupied by enlisted men of the signal-service, and the observations are limited to the rise and fall of the rivers in which they are located, the state of the weather, and the direction of wind at the time of report. Each station is in charge of some well-known citizen, who takes sufficient interest in the service to make the observations regularly and correctly, and the general result of the past year's experience has been satisfactory in demonstrating both the practicability and the usefulness of the work. The reports are sent over all the river circuits, and dropped at each of the regular stations on the principal rivers. The following table shows the names of the several stations, the rivers upon which they are located, the name of the observer, and the date at which each began reporting:

	Stations.	Rivers.	Names.	Commenced reporting.
1	Freeport, Pa	Alleghany	David Alter	April 17, 1872
2	Hermann, Mo	Missouri	Edward Kehr	April 24, 1872
3	Jefferson City, Mo	do	Louis C. Lohman	May 14, 1872
4	Oil City, Pa	Alleghany	J. D. Thompson	April 22, 1872
5	Brownsville, Pa	Monongahela	J. Allen Hubbs	June 6, 1872
6	Evansville, Ind	Ohio	A. C. Pushee	April 21, 1872
7	Confluence, Pa	Youghiogheny	M. Tannehill	April 21, 1872
8	New Geneva, Pa	Monongahela	H. T. Davenport	April 14, 1872
9	Lexington, Mo	Missouri	Z. S. Mitchell	April 24, 1872
10	Kansas City, Mo	do	H. A. M. Vaughan	April 21, 1872
11	Brunswick, Mo	do	G. D. Kennedy	May 1, 1872
12	Little Rock, Ark	Arkansas	C. H. Conradt	April 14, 1872
13	Plattsmouth, Nebr	Missouri	A. L. Child, M. D	April 20, 1872
14	Marietta, Ohio	Ohio	J. H. Best	April 13, 1872
15	Saint Joseph, Missouri	Missouri	A. L. Kerr	May 8, 1872
16	Warsaw, Ill	Mississippi	D. H. Cox	May 7, 1872
17	Paducah, Ky	Ohio	Capt. C. Bachman	May 1, 1872
18	Booneville, Mo	Missouri	W. H. Young	April 24, 1872
19	Le Claire, Iowa	Mississippi	J. P. Disney	June 2, 1872

From July 1 to the present date, only one report per week from each station has been received by telegraph; but the observations have been kept up regularly at all of them, and reported weekly by mail on the established form adopted by the office. The regular daily telegraphic reports will be resumed October 1 and continue until the close of navigation renders them unnecessary. The instructions issued to these special stations, with the cipher in which the reports are transmitted, and the location of the " bench-marks " at all the river-stations, both regular and special, have been previously submitted to you and approved. Other instructions will be issued from time to time, as occasion requires.

*

CANADIAN STATIONS.

Regular telegraphic reports are now received from eleven stations in the Dominion of Canada and other British provinces.

*   *   *   *   *   *   *

There are seventy-eight stations now established in the United States and in regular operation, being an increase of thirteen during the year. The plan on which these have been designated was minutely described in the last annual report.

For the exact study of the phenomena of the upper portions of the atmosphere, and to determine more accurately the proper reductions to be made for great elevations, temporary stations have been established at favorable points. In addition to the regular station on the summit of Mount Washington, New Hampshire, three others, one at the base, and two dividing the interval between the base and the summit, were in operation between June 1 and July 31, (Paper 15.) The summit of Mount Mitchell, North Carolina, was occupied as a station during the months of June, July, and August, and the base of that mountain was also occupied during August, (Paper 16.) For similar reasons the difficult task of establishing a permanent telegraphic station on the summit of Pike's Peak, Colorado, at an elevation of 14,216 feet, has been accomplished, and the station is now in operation. A telegraphic line seventeen miles in length has been built to connect the summit with Colorado Springs, and a road has been made by which it is easily accessible. A substantial building has been erected on the crest of the peak. By the care of the honorable the Secretary of War proper steps have been taken to declare a portion of the mountain to be a Government reservation.

*   *   *   *   *   *   *

The reports now received by comity of exchange with the Dominion of Canada are from eleven stations, four having been added during the year. Return reports are telegraphed to Prof. G. T. Kingston, of Toronto, chief of the meteorological bureau of the Dominion, at his request. Separate reports have also been received from Prof. Charles Smallwood, director of the Montreal Observatory. Warnings are given to the meteorological bureau of the Dominion whenever the conditions known at this office are such as to indicate unusually dangerous weather on the lower lakes or eastern provincial coasts, in a manner and by a special arrangement of cipher agreed upon. The immediate value of this international system to both countries is now frequently shown, while its future good results, political and practical, will increase by time, and with the more thorough interchange which will follow the extension of both services.

After much delay arrangements have been completed by which telegraphic reports, regarded as essential for meteoric indications, are obtained from the West India Islands. The regular telegraphic reports from Havana, Cuba, began on August 6, from Kingston, Jamaica, on September 18, and from Santiago de Cuba, on September 29. Three other points in the islands of Porto Rico, Guadeloupe, and Barbados will be equipped as soon as observers can be designated. The arrangements are, in brief, that the observers at the stations are residents of the locality, specially recommended for their fitness, and the instruments are furnished by this office, which also pays for telegraphing the reports. The West India and Panama Telegraph Company transmits reports at one-third its regular rates, and is to be commended for its liberality. There is no international arrangement with the authorities of any of these islands, which fact is greatly to be regretted, nor is there at present any return of telegraphic reports provided for or officially requested. Mr. Adolf Strauss, of Havana, has rendered much assistance in procuring these reports.

The system of telegraphing the rise and fall of water in the principal rivers, commenced during the year 1872, has been extended. In addition to the regular stations, twenty in number, upon the Mississippi River and its confluents, which furnish the river-report in addition to that of the meteoric changes, nineteen other stations have been selected on the principal western rivers and their tributaries, from which special river-reports are received by telegraph.

These stations are independent of those occupied by enlisted men of the signal-service, and the observations are limited to the rise and fall of the rivers, the state of weather, and the direction of wind at the time of report. Each station is in charge of some well-known citizen, who is compensated for making the observations regularly and correctly. The general result of the past year's experience has been satisfactory, in demonstrating both the practicability and usefulness of the work. These reports are bulletined at each of the regular stations on the principal rivers.

The observations are required to be taken daily and forwarded by telegraph at certain seasons of the year when danger from freshets may be anticipated. At other seasons the observations are taken daily and reported weekly by mail, on forms furnished by this office. In the present year daily telegraphic reports have been had from each station from the date of its establishment to July 1st. They will be resumed October 1st, and continued until the close of navigation renders them unnecessary. Paper 18 contains the instructions issued to these special stations, with the cipher in which the reports are transmitted, and Paper 19 the location of the "bench-marks" at all the river-stations, both regular and special. The advantage already gained to the river commerce through their publication has been gratefully acknowledged. It is now attempted by this office to analyze these reports as received, in connection with the reports of other phenomena, and to prepare for publication a synopsis of the rise and fall of water, stating the present condition of the rivers reported upon and that probably to follow. A continued study of this subject will, it is hoped, allow of prognostics to protect river commerce, and the districts whose safety depends upon levees, from the disasters occasioned by freshets, as well as to give warnings useful for the navigation which is affected by the stage of water. The charts prepared by Lieut. Henry Jackson, acting signal-officer and assistant, attached to Paper 18, illustrate graphically the fluctuations during the year in the following rivers, viz, the Mississippi, Missouri, Ohio, Red, and Cumberland.

The whole number of stations of observations from which this office now receives its stated reports is ninety-two, of which seventy-eight are the regular stations in the United States, eleven belong to the Canadian system, and three to that commenced for the West Indies.

Applications have been received for the establishment of one hundred and forty-nine stations, which, with the present appropriations, cannot be supplied. Paper 25 exhibits a list of these stations.

The number of observer-sergeants on duty at this date is eighty-eight. The assistants to observers at stations number ninety-three.

Justice to the two civilian clerks provided by law for this office requires the renewal of the recommendation contained in the last annual report, that they should receive a more adequate compensation, which would be accomplished by an amendment of section 19 of the act of Congress approved March 3, 1863, changing the words "class two" to "class four." The services of these clerks are valuable. Their laborious duties can to some extent be estimated by reference to the appropriate heads in Paper 8. On examination of the classification of clerks in the several bureaus of the War Department, it is ascertained that no duties similar in character and equal in amount to those performed by the two clerks of the signal-service, are paid for at so small a rate as that provided for them ten years ago, when the work of the office was comparatively small.

The comparison and testing of meteoric instruments for the purpose of establishing standards has been continued, as also the study and experiment to provide improved apparatus for the equipment of stations. An electrical self-recording river-gauge, devised by Second Lieut. D. J. Gibbon, acting signal-officer, especially for use at river-stations, is still being tested, as is also one more recently devised by First Lieut. H. H. C. Dunwoody, acting signal-officer and assistant. The electrical self-recording attachment to the anemometer, devised by Lieutenant Gibbon, heretofore adopted by this office, has been improved by him, through the addition of electrical machinery connecting it with the wind-vane, by which the direction, as well as the velocity, of the wind is continuously given. A description of this instrument is given in Paper 7. Lieutenant Gibbon has also devised a self-recording barometer, the fluctuations of which are recorded continuously by means of electricity. This instrument has advantages in simplicity and cheapness.

The instrument-room at this office has been under the general charge of First Lieut. H. H. C. Dunwoody, acting signal-officer and assistant. Paper 20 gives a detailed report of the instruments compared and corrected for station-work, and tested for other purposes during the year.

The telegraphic service connected with the office has been, since January 1st last, under the special charge of Mr. James A. Swift, electrician, whose duties have been well performed. Seven hundred and sixty-eight thousand and sixty-six cipher words of weather-reports have been received by telegraph at, and three hundred and nineteen thousand nine hundred and ninety-two sent from, this office during the year. Three thousand seven hundred and twenty-one telegraphic messages, other than weather-reports, but connected with that work, have also been received, and three thousand four hundred and eighty-six sent. Eighty-three thousand one hundred and thirteen mailed reports have been examined and compared with telegraphic copies, and filed for future reference. The auditing of the bills of telegraph companies is also under the supervision of the electrician.

In the regular discharge of the duties of the office three telegraphic reports are received daily, each report averaging eight hundred and sixteen cipher words. The average time of transmission from the moment the instruments are read at the several stations until the reports of those observations are received at this office, has been eighty-five minutes.

The office has still to regret that its telegraphic facilities are not as complete as the best discharge of the duties in its care would require. The hope is entertained that this source of difficulty will be removed.

The preparation of the deductions, known as the Synopses and Probabilities, from the meteoric data recorded at this office, and the editing of the regular publications, the "Weekly Weather Chronicle," "Monthly Weather Review," "Synopses, Probabilities, and Facts," have been during the year in immediate charge of Prof. Cleveland Abbe, assistant; First Lieut. Robert Craig, acting signal-officer and assistant; Prof. Thompson B. Maury, assistant; and First Lieut. H. H. C. Dunwoody, acting signal-officer and assistant. The duties have been performed by them in rotation, each having care of the preparation of the deductions for the period of one month, and for the succeeding month supervising the publications above mentioned. The services of these officers upon these and other special details assigned them have been marked by fidelity.

A regular course of study and practice is pursued by officers at this office in preparation for these duties. As a portion of this course the following writings are required to be carefully read in the order named, viz: Loomis's Treatise on Meteorology; Practical use of Meteorological Reports and Weather-Maps; Instructions to Observer-Sergeants; Smithsonian Directions for Meteorological Observations; Buchan's Handy Book of Meteorology; Piddington's Horn Book; Espy's Philosophy of Storms; Fitz Roy's Weather-Book; Martin's Rotary Theory of Storms; Ley's Laws of the Winds; Espy's First Meteorological Report; Espy's Fourth Meteorological Report. In connection with these works, and reference had to others in the library of the office, the officer is required to make studies of the daily weather-maps noting thereon the atmospheric conditions as indicated by the reports, with the variations in pressure, temperature, humidity, wind-direction, &c., and the consequent changes as exhibited from day to day. The study of text-books and publications on the subject of meteorology is not considered sufficient for purposes of the education in view, without constant comparison of the reports in their sequence, and the charting of them as received, with the advice and correction of officers experienced in the duty. The charting of weather-maps is thus practiced until the officer becomes thoroughly familiar with the process, after which the preparation of deductions from the tri-daily reports is commenced and made a continuous study. Special attention is given to the subject of cautionary signals, with reference to the direction and velocity of wind considered dangerous at the various cautionary-signal stations.

The tri-daily Synopsis and Probabilities have been issued from this office in the manner explained in previous reports with unfailing regularity at 10.30 a. m., 6.30 p. m., and 1 a. m., daily, no case of omission or serious delay having occurred during the year.

The display of bulletins and weather-charts at stations, the supply of prompt and gratuitous information to the press, and the exhibitions at designated stations of day or night signals at times of supposed special danger, have been continued. The total number of tabulated bulletins issued and distributed at the several lake, sea-coast, and river ports, and inland cities have been one hundred and forty-three thousand and ninety-seven, excluding the special river-bulletins, which have amounted to twenty-three thousand two hundred and ten. The total number of weather-charts issued and distributed has been three hundred and twenty thousand seven hundred and seventy, and the press-reports (exclusive of the publication of the Synopses and Probabilities) have been twenty-three thousand two hundred and twenty-four.

The attention of the office has, during the past year, been frequently directed to the fact that the publication of the deductions known as Probabilities alone, as given in many of the journals, is not a sufficient exhibit of the data supplied. It ought to be understood that these deductions given alone constitute but an inferior portion of the information furnished. The plan of the office has been, from the beginning, to publish for public use, and tri-daily, four principal papers: 1st. The tabulated bulletins, exhibiting tri-daily the observations as read at each station; 2d. A chart presenting these data chartographically; 3d. A Synopsis; and 4th. A Probability. Each of these papers ought to be read with reference to the others, and if such reading is made with the use of local instruments and some knowledge of meteoric laws, it will be found that the instances are few in which important meteoric changes occur without some warning given of their approach. The tabulated bulletins are prepared for the press at most of the principal cities. The Synopsis is invariably transmitted to the several press associations, together with the Probabilities, the former condensing the facts upon which the opinions stated in the latter are based. The publication of the Probabilities alone causes the forecasts to appear as mere oracles, and not, as they are designed to be, scientific inferences or deductions from meteorological data actually recorded.

The office has continued, under the direction of the Secretary of War, its exertions to solve for the special benefit of agricultural interests the problem of giving promptly the information contained in the daily weather-reports to the many farming and other communities not now reached by telegraph, and for which the copies published by the press do not arrive in time for use. The plan adopted has been to divide the territory of the United States into districts, each district having a distributing point at or near the center, from which two printed copies of the Synopses and

Probabilities are forwarded by mail to all post-offices within the districts and which can be reached by rail, steamer, or mail-coach by 4 p. m. of the same day. These reports are designed to exhibit the probable condition of the weather in the district, including not only notice of storms generally considered dangerous, but, when possible, giving indication of dry weather, light rain, extremes of temperature, and frost.

On December 7 last a request was made by the Chief Signal-Officer to the honorable the Postmaster-General, with the approval of the honorable the Secretary of War, for his favorable action upon the plan indicated, and was responded to by the Postmaster-General on December 11, with assurance of the co-operation of the Post-Office Department, and the information that he had issued an order instructing all postmasters receiving the above-mentioned reports by mail to post them immediately in the frames supplied for that purpose by this office. So soon as the necessary arrangements could be made, the plan went into operation. The following list shows the stations taken up as distributing points, the time when the special work commenced at each, and the number of post-offices supplied from it.

Station.	Commenced.	Number of offices supplied.
1. Washington	January 3, 1873	146
2. New York	February 25, 1873	607
3. Cincinnati	April 7, 1873	753
4. Chicago	June 14, 1873	798
5. Detroit	July 21, 1873	337
6. Buffalo	July 25, 1873	153
7. Boston	July 15, 1873	403
8. Springfield	July 28, 1873	71
9. Memphis	August 25, 1873	59
10. New Orleans	September 15, 1873	30
11. Pittsburgh	October 1, 1873	298
12. Saint Louis	September 1, 1873	435
13. Montgomery	September 20, 1873	43
14. Nashville	September 4, 1873	96
15. Bangor	September 30, 1873	160

The correspondence on this subject is contained in Paper 21, to which is attached a chart exhibiting the distributing districts contemplated, as well as those established. The co-operation of the War and Post-Office Departments thus described now provides for the regular distribution daily of eight thousand nine hundred and eighty-two copies of the weather report to four thousand four hundred and ninety-one different post-offices, and will still be extended as rapidly as possible. The whole number of these special bulletins printed and distributed is eight hundred and ninety-five thousand and fourteen. The Synopses and Probabilities, as deduced from the midnight observations, are telegraphed at once from the central office at Washington to each of the distributing stations, and there printed in large type by the enlisted men of the signal-service, addressed to the several postmasters, and mailed according to a systematic arrangement, which takes advantage of every moment to reach each point with the greatest speed. The success already attained in the practical working of this plan, and the obvious satisfaction it has given to the public, should be a subject of gratification to the War and Post-Office Departments, as it is to this office. The thanks of the Department are due the honorable the Postmaster-General for the facilities furnished, and under him to Mr. George S. Bangs, superintendent of the railway mail-service, for his personal as well as official assistance. By the different modes of publication adopted for the service, each of which has been arranged with definite purpose, and including that had through the public press, it is estimated that the information emanating from this office reaches daily one-third of the households in the United States.

For the purpose of rendering the office better acquainted with the wants of the agricultural community, many agricultural societies have, at the request of the Chief Signal-Officer, appointed permanent committees to correspond and confer with the office. One hundred and seventeen of these organizations are now in correspondence, (Paper 22,) and notice has been given by others that committees will soon be appointed by them. A list of similar committees appointed by the boards of trade and chambers of commerce, forty-four in number, is in Paper 23.

It has been a duty of the office to publish the information obtained by it in the form of collated statistics. The Weekly Weather Chronicle, which was briefly alluded to in the last annual report as commenced, has been enlarged and improved. Each copy exhibits a general summary of the meteoric changes over the whole region from which reports are received, during the seven days previous to the day of publication, as well as for each separate day. A special reference is made to the river-reports. (Paper 24).

During the year nine thousand four hundred and two copies have been gratuitously distributed to committees of agricultural societies and boards of trade, to scientific persons in this country and abroad, and to the press.

The Monthly Weather Review, the publication of which was commenced in January last, reviews the facts for each month concerning storms, winds, rain-fall, air, river, and ocean temperatures, and the rise and fall of rivers. It is accompanied with charts showing the tracks of low barometric pressure, the isobars, isotherms, and prevailing winds for the month. The number of copies of this publication issued during the year has been six thousand seven hundred and ninety-six. Paper 25 includes the reviews issued since the date of the last annual report.

The Daily Bulletin has been prepared as a monthly publication for each month, from and including September, 1872. Each volume exhibits the several reports from synchronous observations at the various stations at the regular hours, viz, 7.35 a. m., 4.35 p. m., and 11 p. m., Washington mean time, with the weather-chart on a reduced scale for each observation in immediate connection not only with the Synopsis and Probabilities issued for each observation, but the "Facts" succeeding the latter being collated in detail from the reports of the observers made at the next regular observation following the issue of each Probabilities. This publication exhibits the data upon which this office has been compelled to act in making its tri-daily announcements, and presents for general use the information gathered. This work is not only a contribution of data valuable to meteoric science, but aims to show impartially and in detail the successes and failures of the office.

The publications of the office thus referred to amount in the course of the year to many volumes. The scope of an annual report permits this brief reference to them only.

At the request of Prof. Spencer F. Baird, United States commissioner of fish and fisheries, the work of the observers at the stations favorably located for the purpose has been increased, by requiring observations to be taken daily of the water temperatures in the different rivers and harbors. The reports of these observations are made on a special form, (Paper 24.) These reports have not yet been continued sufficiently long to permit of safe deductions, but promise to have useful results in the solution of problems beyond the important objects of pisciculture throughout the United States for which they were at first instituted.

An additional duty was imposed upon the Secretary of War by the provision of the act of Congress approved March 3, 1873, entitled—

An act making appropriations for sundry civil expenses of the Government for the fiscal year ending June thirtieth, eighteen hundred and seventy-four, and for other purposes, as follows:

Be it enacted by the Senate and House of Representatives of the United States of America in Congress assembled, That the following sums be, and the same are hereby, appropriated for the objects hereinafter expressed, for the fiscal year ending June thirtieth, eighteen hundred and seventy-four, namely:

* * * * * * * *

For contingencies of life-saving stations on the coast of the United States, fifteen thousand dollars. And that the Secretary of War be and hereby is authorized to establish signal-stations at light-houses, at such of the life-saving stations on the lake or sea coasts as may be suitably located for that purpose, and to connect the same with such points as may be necessary for the proper discharge of the signal-service by means of a suitable telegraph line in cases where no lines are in operation, to be constructed, maintained, and worked under the direction of the Chief Signal-Officer of the Army, or the Secretary of War and the Secretary of the Treasury; and the use of the life-saving stations as signal-stations shall be subject to such regulations as may be agreed upon by said officials; and the sum of thirty thousand dollars is hereby appropriated to carry into effect this provision.

In discharge of this duty a telegraph line has been completed ten miles in length, from Seaville to Peck's Beach, N. J., connecting at Seaville with the line of Western Union Telegraph Company. The material is ready, and the work is in progress on the construction of a line from Sandy Hook to Barnegat Inlet, N. J., a distance of fifty miles, connecting with the Western Union line at Long Branch. These connections will allow of signals being displayed at the life-saving stations established at Sandy Hook, Long Branch, Barnegat, Atlantic City, Peck's Beach, and Cape May. The plan in contemplation proposes the establishment of signal-stations at life-saving stations and light-houses along the ocean-coast of New Jersey, from Sandy Hook to Cape May, at distances of twenty-five miles from each other. A line is in process of erection from the village of Rockport, Mass., to Thatcher's Island light-house, a distance of three miles and a half, of which one mile and a half will be cable.

A line connecting the stations at life-saving stations and light-houses along the coast from Norfolk, Va., to Cape Hatteras, N. C., a distance of one hundred and thirty-seven miles, and on one of the most dangerous coasts of the United States, is in construction. It is expected that the above-mentioned lines will be completed during the present year. Attention is invited to the fact that the whole work now done in the erection of these lines, and to be done hereafter in operating them, has been done and is to be done by the officers and men of the signal-service of the Army. By no other agency could so large an amount of line so situated be constructed with the small appropriation provided.

It is not necessary to dwell upon the benefits to result from the work of the stations thus provided for. Not only will the meteoric information regularly received be greatly increased in amount and value by that taken on the sea-coast and at the actual sea-level; but storm-warnings visible at a sufficient distance from shore to allow often of the proper means to be taken for safety, can be given to vessels approaching dangerous coasts, while on the occurrence of inevitable disaster assistance can be summoned at once from the neighboring life-saving stations, and information regarding the occurrence be transmitted to underwriters and others interested. Communication can readily be held by signal

and telegraph with vessels of the naval and merchant marine from
Washington and from other cities, and the coast will be provided with
a vidette system, invaluable in time of possible war. The expense of securing these advantages to the country is comparatively trifling, the
observer-sergeant of the signal-service at each station being charged
with the telegraphic operations, and the necessary lines being constructed, maintained, and worked under the direction of the Chief Signal-Officer by enlisted men of the signal-service. It is to be hoped that
Congress will, by future appropriation, allow the extension of this special work to the lake and sea coasts, where the life-saving and light-
house systems are deemed necessary, affording thus coast-service un-
paralleled in the world. The thanks of the Chief Signal-Officer are due
to Mr. S. I. Kimball, the chief of the Revenue-Marine Bureau, who has
tendered rooms in each of the selected station-houses of the life-saving
service for the observer-sergeant of the signal-service, and has provided,
by the erection of a flag-staff on the new buildings, for the proper display of signals.

At the request of Hon. Francis A. Walker, Superintendent of the
United States Census, for the contribution by this office of charts to
form part of the statistical atlas of the United States, the compilation
of which is, by law, in his charge, such are now in course of preparation, showing, for the year 1872–'73, the following meteorological details,
viz : The isobarometric lines; the number of times each direction of
wind is recorded; the average hourly velocity of each wind; the maximum recorded velocity of each wind; the total annual movement of the
wind; the distribution of storms or storm frequency.

While responding, when possible, to all requests made for statistical
and other information, the thanks of the Chief Signal-Officer must be
rendered to many scientists, in this country and abroad, for their valuable assistance. Especial acknowledgment is to be made to Prof. John
Tyndall, of the Royal Institution, London ; Sir William Thomson, professor of natural philosophy in the University of Glasgow; Dr. Fred.
Patterson, of San Antonio, Tex.; Rev. James Rankin, D. D., president
of Hobart College, Geneva, N. Y.; and Mr. M. F. Stevenson, Gaines-
ville, Fla., have contributed regular or occasional reports of value. The
agent of the Pacific Mail Steamship Company at New York has forwarded a large number of marine records on forms furnished by this
office, and since July, 1872, regular monthly meteoric reports have been
received from the commanding officer of the United States receiving-
ship Vermont, stationed at the Brooklyn navy-yard. Capt. J. Sangster,
of the bark Express, of Annapolis, Nova Scotia, has presented a log-book
showing records of voyages from June, 1872, to February, 1873, and
one hundred and thirty-eight logs of vessels have been collected by the
observer-sergeants stationed along the Atlantic and Pacific coasts; in
procuring which the sergeants at Wilmington, N. C., and San Francisco,
Cal., have been most active. It is much to be regretted that so few of
the forms prepared for the purpose of being filled up with reports or
observations made at sea, and widely distributed, have yet been returned to this office. The accurate reports of storms on the oceans,
whether passing from or advancing upon the coasts of the United States,
are of much importance for study, even when not in time for immediate
deductions.

An interesting contribution to meteoric knowledge, prepared by Prof.
O. Abbe, assistant, from the records of the office, will be found in Paper
32, showing a chronological list of the auroras observed at the respective

signal-service stations from November 11, 1870, to July 31, 1873, inclusive.

On June 12, 1871, Observer-Sergeant Frederick Meyer, Signal-Service, United States Army, was, at the special request (approved by the Secretaries of War and of the Navy) of Capt. C. F. Hall, commander of the north polar expedition, authorized by Congress, ordered to report to him for duty in connection with that expedition with a complete set of meteorological instruments and signal equipments furnished by this office. The orders and instructions of Sergeant Meyer, and a report prepared by him since his return, are included in Paper 27.

The following table, prepared by First Lieut. Robert Craig, acting signal-officer and assistant, gives the lowest observed readings of the low barometers, with number of areas traced for each month, from October 1, 1872, to September 30, 1873, inclusive:

Oct., 1872, eight areas of low barometer, varying from .... 29.35 to 29.85.
Nov., 1872, nine areas of low barometer, varying from .... 29.08 to 29.74.
Dec., 1872, twelve areas of low barometer, varying from .... 29.17 to 29.93.
Jan., 1873, ten areas of low barometer, varying from .... 29.07 to 29.66.
Feb., 1873, nine areas of low barometer, varying from .... 29.04 to 29.49.
March, 1873, eleven areas of low barometer, varying from .... 28.80 to 29.52.
April, 1873, ten areas of low barometer, varying from .... 29.27 to 29.62.
May, 1873, nine areas of low barometer, varying from .... 29.28 to 29.63.
June, 1873, ten areas of low barometer, varying from .... 29.26 to 29.95.
July, 1873, thirteen areas of low barometer, varying from .... 29.44 to 29.68.
Aug., 1873, twelve areas of low barometer, varying from .... 29.49 to 29.79.
Sept., 1873, eleven areas of low barometer, varying from .... 29.21 to 29.76.

The charts appropriate to these areas will be found among those attached to Paper 25.

As the severe storms of the 14th August, in New Jersey, and the 24th and 25th of the same month, in Nova Scotia, were, from the want of stations at requisite points, and also from temporary failure of the telegraph, not fully presented for study in the regular tri-daily maps of this office, and yet possessed features worthy of special attention, Professor Abbe, assistant, was directed to collate in reference to it such information as could be obtained from the logs of vessels and similar sources. The detailed results of his work are given in Paper 28.

Both of these storms had their origin and much of their course beyond the limits of the United States, and beyond the scope of the observations taken at the regularly-established stations. The presence of similar cyclones passing near the coasts of the United States, and which are likely to be encountered by vessels sailing from the sea-coast ports, will, it is hoped, be recognizable by the observations to be taken at the series of stations now in process of establishment at the life-saving stations along the coasts. The telegraphic communication to be established with the Bermuda Islands will be of utility in this connection.

A valuable report by Prof. I. A. Lapham upon disasters to shipping upon the great American lakes, from the 1st of January to the 1st of September, 1873, is hereto annexed, as Paper 29.

On May 26, last, Observer-Sergeant James Mackintosh, Signal-Service, United States Army, was ordered to proceed to the district traversed by the violent tornado which passed through Iowa and Illinois on May 22, and to make a full report of its origin, path, and attendant phenomena. (Paper 30.)

The storm of April 14–18 presented features of peculiar interest. A description of the storm, with charts of its course as traced, prepared by Observer-Sergeant Theodore Smith, Signal-Service, United States Army, is herewith, (Paper 31.)

The stations on the sea and lake coasts, especially designated as cautionary-signal stations, at which the display of signals is ordered for the benefit of commerce, are the following, thirty in number, viz: New Orleans, Mobile, Jacksonville, Savannah, Charleston, Wilmington, N. C., Norfolk, Cape May, Baltimore, New York, New Haven, New London, Wood's Hole, Boston, Portland, Me., Eastport, Oswego, Rochester, Buffalo, Erie, Cleveland, Toledo, Detroit, Alpena, Grand Haven, Chicago, Milwaukee, Escanaba, Marquette, and Du Luth.

During the year orders have been issued for the display of the cautionary signals, described in previous reports, in anticipation of eighty-eight probable storms. In seventy cases the storms anticipated manifested their effects at one or more of the stations at which the signals were ordered; the signals thus giving warning to shipping and other interests which would otherwise, perhaps, have been dangerously exposed.

The order for each cautionary signal is special, and issued under the following rules: The display is ordered at a signal-station whenever the officer in charge of that duty considers it probable that there will be experienced within twelve hours at that station, or within one hundred miles thereof, and on any navigable stream, a wind dangerous to navigation. Dangerous winds on the navigable waters are, for the order in question, considered to be those reaching a velocity of twenty-five miles per hour, as registered by the anemometer on the land, provided that the temperature be decidedly above freezing. For temperature decidedly below freezing, and for foggy weather, winds are to be considered dangerous when the velocities are registered so low as twenty miles. The direction of the wind is not taken into consideration for the present. If at the tri-daily report next following the ordering of the signals it appears that the danger is not so imminent as was apprehended, the signal is to be ordered down. It is not to be displayed for an indefinitely long time. The immediate area referred to by the respective cautionary signals is as defined on the map of cautionary-signal stations at the office of the Chief Signal-Officer, which may be generally described as a circle, with a radius of one hundred miles, the station being the center. When any warning is given for points upon the lakes, the other lake-stations are notified of the warning. Each station is also notified when the signals are ordered down at any other station.

As in preceding years, where there has been error of display it has been on the side of caution. While on occasions the signals ordered may have proved unnecessary, and are so reported unverified, on the other hand no extensive storm has occurred in the regions included in the system of cautionary signals without warnings of its approach having been displayed in at least part of its course. While neither the indications upon which signals are certainly to be displayed, nor modes of verifying the display, have been as yet accurately arrived at, the public confidence exhibited in the heed given to the warnings when they are shown has evidenced their general utility.

Pursuant to the arrangements with Prof. G. T. Kingston, of Toronto, chief of the Dominion Meteorological Bureau, to which reference was made in the last annual report, forty dispatches, giving warning of approaching storms, have been sent to the Bureau under his charge.

* * * * * * * *

The percentage of verification for each geographical division or subdivision named has been for the year as follows:

New England	...	Ohio Valley	76.42
Middle States	...	Western Gulf	74.40
South Atlantic	...	Upper Lakes	75.95
Lower Lakes	...	Northwest	74.00
Eastern Gulf	...		

These percentages have been obtained by a careful analysis of the deductions as announced each day for each geographical division or subdivision mentioned, and the comparison of them with the facts subsequently obtained from the weather-reports for that date. A numerical value is given each item, as temperature, pressure, wind-direction, &c., mentioned in each deduction and verified; the sum of these values divided by the number of deductions exhibiting the average of verification for any period with approximate accuracy.

The aggregate percentage of verification ranges higher in New England, the Middle States, the South Atlantic, and the Lower Lake Region, than in the West, Southwest, and Northwest.

With a more rigid and scrutinizing mode of calculation than was before adopted, the percentages have improved upon those of the preceding year; the analysis of the year's work indicating at once the wisdom of increasing the number of stations and the regions in which they should be established. The percentage of verifications for each district exhibits a proportion to the number of stations from which reports having reference to the atmospheric conditions in the district under consideration have been received. It is thus to a certain extent mathematically demonstrated that the rules applied for the deductions of the forecasts are practically correct, and that with increasing facilities the percentage of verifications can be annually increased. It is not known that a demonstration of this character has been before attained.

In pursuance of invitations issued by the Austrian government, a congress of persons charged with meteoric duties was convened in Vienna in the month of September last, at which the Chief Signal-Officer was present under instructions from the Secretary of War. The proceedings of this congress cannot fail to be of importance as tending to establish a uniformity in methods of conference and of action. The opportunities it afforded of personal meeting and observation among the representatives from different countries must be productive of beneficial effects. The concurrence of the congress by a unanimous vote in a proposition to the effect that it is desirable, with a view to their exchange, that at least one uniform observation of such character as to be suitable for the preparation of synoptic charts should be taken and recorded daily and simultaneously at as many stations as practicable throughout the world, is regarded as of especial importance in reference to duties of the character of those now undertaken by the United States.

With the study of synoptic charts, the field of which may, with proper co-operation, on land and at sea, be made almost world-wide, there is reason to anticipate the discovery of facts relating to atmospheric phenomena and to the origin and movement of storms not hitherto recognized. It is to such co-operation effort will be directed. It is gratifying to state, in this connection, that arrangements have already been made with the meteorological offices at St. Petersburg, London, and Constantinople to commence the exchange by mail on January 1, 1874, of one daily simultaneous report taken over the vast territorial extent of the Russian and Turkish Empires, the British Islands, and the United States. (Paper 33.) The co-operation of the systems of other nations, of scientific associations, societies, and individuals is sought for and expected. With a work in view, not for the sole benefit of any country or people, but reaching to the good of all, there is ground to hope a world's assistance.

In the review of the year's duties there is found encouragement for the future. While the office has had to encounter many difficulties, the details of which would be out of place in this report, there has been the assurance that its labors have not been without a value generally recognized. The office acknowledges, as in preceding years, the general support of the popular opinion, of scientific men, of the press, and of the War Department. Without this aid the work achieved would have been impossible. Whenever errors have occurred, it has been recognized as inevitable that some must occur in the present condition of science. Success has been generously commended. The evidences of interest and progress in similar duties are extending in all countries. Their utility is no longer questioned, and effort at home and abroad turns only toward their development. The field becomes world-wide with the promise of results a few years ago hardly to be hoped for. There will be needed time and labor; there must often be disappointment; but the public good to follow is certain.

I am, sir, very respectfully, your obedient servant,

ALBERT J. MYER,
Brig. Gen., (Bvt. Ass'g'd,) Chief Signal-Officer, U. S. A.

REPORT

OF

THE SECRETARY OF THE NAVY.

———————

NAVY DEPARTMENT,
Washington, November 29, 1873.

SIR : The following report of the Navy Department and the naval service for the past year is respectfully submitted :

There are now in the Navy 165 vessels, carrying, exclusive of howitzers, 1,269 guns, which is a reduction, since my last annual report, by sale and otherwise, of 13 vessels. A general enumeration of these vessels presents : 63 steamers, other than iron-clads and tugs, carrying 826 guns ; 29 sailing-vessels, 322 guns ; 48 iron-clad vessels, 121 guns ; and 25 tugs, used for navy-yard and freight purposes. Of this number there are at present in commission for sea-service, distributed on the several foreign stations and on our own coast, 46 vessels, carrying 407 guns. The cruising or active force of the Navy, as these may be called, and which is controlled by the appropriations made and the seamen authorized by law, is about the same as last year, the places of those vessels which have been put out of commission within the past twelve months, from expiration of the cruises or for other causes, having been supplied by commissioning and sending to sea a corresponding number of others.

The list will show a force slightly decreased in numbers by the sale of some useless vessels, which were, while we retained them, only a source of expense, and it is somewhat weakened also in strength by the condemnation and laying up of several of our white-oak cruisers which have reached the limit of their cruising-life and can no longer be used with safety on the seas.

Many of the ships now on the Navy list, and which serve to swell the number to the figures above given, are far from being such as are really needed, and their true condition, which has been often officially represented to Congress, can be fully understood and appreciated by reference to the reports of the Bureaus which are herewith submitted.

In the meanwhile, however, we have been engaged in completely repairing six of our live-oak cruising-ships, which are now in various stages of forwardness at the several navy-yards. These are all of moderate size, and none of them sufficiently advanced to be of present use, but they are adapted to the wants of our cruising Navy, and will in a few months add materially to its strength and efficiency.

The eight new sloops of war authorized by the last Congress are all in process of building—one-half at the various navy-yards, three under contract in private yards, and the remaining one under private contract in the navy-yard at Kittery. The building of these ships, with their engines and machinery, is progressing rapidly, and the work, widely distributed at more than a dozen naval stations and private establishments, is contributing to the remunerative employment of several thousands of workmen, and to the maintenance of the very large number of persons dependent upon their labor for support and education. It is not without gratification that I am able to report that, besides the great value and importance of this work to the service, we have also been able so to utilize the liberality of Congress, as to contribute materially to the business interests of the country and to the support and comfort of many producing and dependent people.

The valuable work thus begun should not be discontinued, but the Department should be provided with a moderate amount of funds and authorized to commence each year to build a certain number of tons, to supply regularly the regular yearly expenditure of naval force which will of necessity occur.

IRON-CLADS.

The work of putting our iron-clad force in efficient condition, referred to in my last report, has been proceeded with as fast as the means necessary for the extraordinary work could be spared from the current appropriations for the support of the Navy. The wisdom of this action needs no illustration from me at this time; without it we would have been left not only powerless to assert our own rights, but almost defenseless against arrogance or aggression; but the expenditure required has crippled our working Bureaus in their general work, and it is necessary that this should be re-imbursed to them if they are to proceed steadily and efficiently.

CRUISING STATIONS.

The stations have been unchanged during the year. As now established, they are designated as the European, the Asiatic, the North Atlantic, the South Atlantic, the North Pacific, and the South Pacific. Over these, embracing the frequented waters of the globe, are scattered a cruising force of less than forty vessels, which by their presence are relied on to encourage our citizens, and, if required, to protect them and their property in all lands to which by their inclination or interests they are drawn.

THE EUROPEAN STATION.—Rear-Admiral A. Ludlow Case commands the naval force on the European station, having succeeded Rear-Admiral James Alden at Villefranche June 2, when the latter transferred his flag from the Wabash to the Brooklyn and returned home, arriving at New York July 10.

The vessels have been actively cruising during the year, and have visited ports of Great Britain, Holland, Germany, France, Portugal, Spain, Italy, Austria, Greece, Turkey, Syria, Egypt, Tunis, Tripoli, Algiers, and Africa, the islands of the Mediterranean, &c.

The disturbances in Spain which called a part of this force to that coast in July last have continued to require the presence of two or three vessels, which have given particular attention to the ports where there were American citizens and interests. They have been under instructions to give full protection to such, and to carefully abstain from interfering in any way with the affairs of the country or its people, except for the protection of our citizens and their property. The position of our commanding officers in that quarter has at times been extremely delicate, requiring the exercise of sound discretion and intelligent action.

In the appendix which accompanies this report will be found a summary of the movements of the vessels on this station and on the others.

THE ASIATIC STATION.—Rear-Admiral Thornton A. Jenkins, who was at the date of the last report, and is still, in command of the force on this station, will soon be relieved by Rear-Admiral E. G. Parrott, who sailed in the mail-steamer of the 1st of November from San Francisco.

Undisturbed friendly relations between our country and the great empires of the East have made the duties and services of our officers and vessels on the Asiatic station peaceful and agreeable. At the same time an increasing commerce, the opening of new avenues of trade, the surveying of uncertain and intricate channels, and the determining and fixing of dangers to navigation have afforded them useful employment, and given an importance and interest to the station surpassed by no other. The vessels have repeatedly visited the ports of China and Japan, penetrated their rivers as far as treaty stipulation and navigation would permit, and with scarcely an exception were received everywhere with good feeling. They have also extended their visits to Singapore, Bankok, Calcutta, and Manila.

The Colorado arrived at New York in March, and the Alaska in February, from this station, and their places were taken by the Hartford and Yantic.

THE NORTH ATLANTIC STATION.—Rear-Admiral G. H. Scott, who is at present in command of the force on the North Atlantic station, relieved Rear-Admiral Joseph F. Green at Key West, May 15, and the latter returned to Boston in the Powhatan, arriving May 27, and hauled down his flag.

The force on this station was reduced in the spring and summer by ordering north, as a necessity, some of the vessels, which were much in need of repairs and whose crews needed a change, having been long in the tropics. The Shawmut and Nipsic, two of the smaller but active class of vessels, came north in June, and the Richmond was about the same time, transferred to the North Pacific station. The Kansas was until July co-operating with the Nicaragua surveying expedition, but, at the same time, her repeated visits to Aspinwall enabled her to give full protection to our interests in that quarter.

Notwithstanding this reduction, important and useful cruises have been made, and our flag has been shown at almost all the commercial ports, or where there were American interests, in the Gulf and on the Caribbean Sea; many of them have been visited repeatedly, viz: St. Thomas, Santa Barbara, San Domingo, Port au Prince, Jacquemel, St. Nicholas Mole, Cape Haytien, Gonaives, Aux Cayes, San Juan, (Porto Rico,) Gaudeloupe, St. Pierre, La Guayra, Puerto Cabello, Curaçoa, Santa Martha, Carthagena, Aspinwall, Greytown, Vera Cruz, Kingston, Havana, Matanzas, Nuevitas, Santiago de Cuba, Guantanamo, and Bermuda.

Assistance has been offered, and extended when required, to our commerce and citizens, the commanding officers have been in constant communication with our ministers and consular representatives, our interests on the Isthmus have been watched, and a vessel, almost constantly stationed on either side, has been in readiness to protect the railroad if occasion should demand. Convoy has been afforded to the merchant service when menaced and threatened with unlawful seizure and violence.

In addition to these appropriate and legitimate duties of our ships of war on the North Atlantic station, they have been engaged, as occasion permitted, in important hydrographic surveys both on our own and neighboring coasts, securing important data for the benefit of commerce, and have aided, to a limited extent, submarine telegraphic enterprise.

THE SOUTH ATLANTIC STATION.—The force on this station is under the command of Rear-Admiral James H. Strong, who took passage in the steamer of September 23 from New York, and relieved Rear-Admiral William R. Taylor at Rio de Janeiro, October 24, hoisting his flag on the Lancaster. Rear-Admiral Taylor is returning home by mail-steamer.

Nothing has transpired to require an increase of the force on this station, which is now, and has been for several years past, at the lowest possible figure.

The Monongahela, which sailed from Newport on November 12, has taken the place of the Ticonderoga, which has already started for home. The vessels on this station, few in number, have been sufficient for all purposes, as the relations between our country and the countries with which the command has intercourse have been pleasant and friendly; and ample security has been extended by the authorities to American citizens engaged in commercial pursuits or sojourning in that quarter.

The usual cruising has been carried out, and the ports of commerce on the coast visited by the larger vessels on the station, while the Wasp has ascended the navigable streams of Uruguay and Paraguay, facilitating the movements of our diplomatic representatives and encouraging American residents in the interior.

Merchantmen in distress, whether of our own or other nationality, have received every assistance in the power of our vessels to afford; and it has been their good fortune to relieve several during the year. While not engaged in other more important business, the time has been usefully improved by contributing valuable hydrographic results by surveys conducted under instructions from the Bureau of Navigation.

THE NORTH PACIFIC STATION.—Rear-Admiral A. M. Pennock commands the naval force on the North Pacific station, with the Saranac as his flag-ship and San Francisco as his headquarters. His flag was transferred from the California June 28, and the latter vessel was put out of commission.

The movements of the vessels on this station have, during the year, extended to the Sandwich Islands, our possessions on the northwest coast, and the coast of Mexico and Central America.

The death of His Majesty the King of the Sandwich Islands, information of which was received late in December, and the changes which would naturally follow so important an event, suggested the propriety of the admiral visiting Honolulu, and he proceeded to that port at once, arriving January 15. In the mean time a new King had been chosen, a new ministry selected, and the government in the course of harmonious action. The Hawaiian flag was promptly saluted, and a gratifying exchange of visits and courtesies immediately followed. Later, His Majesty visited the California, and upon the invitation of the admiral availed himself of the opportunity of visiting some of the islands of his dominion by a passage in the Benicia, which was temporarily made the flag-ship of the station. Rear-Admiral Pennock returned to San Francisco in May, and in July proceeded on a northern cruise. Victoria, Esquimault, Sitka, Port Townsend, Olympia, Seattle, and Steilacoom were visited, as well as some other places of less importance.

Interviews were held with the Indians of Alaska, many of the chiefs of which visited the ship, and the occasion was availed of to impress them with the importance of maintaining the friendship of our people; and also to reconcile differences which had long existed between the principal tribes, which they were anxious to settle. The flag-ship returned to San Francisco September 29, and on the 7th of October following proceeded to the Sandwich Islands.

Other vessels of this command have shown the flag at ports in Costa Rica, Nicaragua, San Salvador, Guatemala, Honduras, Mexico, and Colombia, at all of which our commercial relations were undisturbed and the feeling of the officials and citizens represented to be of the most friendly character.

THE SOUTH PACIFIC STATION.—Rear-Admiral John J. Almy succeeded Rear-Admiral Charles Steedman in the command of the naval force on the South Pacific station, at Panama, September 22, hoisting his flag on the Pensacola.

This station includes the islands and waters of the Pacific south of the
33 Ab

equator, as far west as the one hundred and fiftieth meridian, and the coasts and sea-ports of Australia; but in consequence of the disturbed condition of the State of Panama, where there have been serious outbreaks, and the prosecution of important hydrographic surveys, the visiting of these distant quarters has been omitted during the year.

Within the limits of this station only two occasions have arisen where it has been necessary to land a force from our vessels for the protection of American citizens and property, and on each of those occasions the landings were made on the same territory, at the request or with the permission of the authorities, or under an admission, on their part, of their inability to promise the security and protection due from them.

Rear-Admiral Steedman, on arriving at Panama, May 7, found hostilities in progress between the opposing parties contending for possession of the government of the State of Panama, and, at the request of the United States consul and a number of influential American and other foreign citizens, sent on shore a force of two hundred sailors and marines, with four pieces of artillery, which were equally divided between the city and the railroad-station. This force was landed from the Tuscarora, which had prepared for responding to the signal for protection the evening before the arrival of Rear-Admiral Steedman, and from the flag-ship Pensacola. It was withdrawn from the city on the 11th, and from the depot on the 22d May, all differences having been settled.

The second landing was made September 24, under the order of Rear-Admiral Almy, the revolutionary movements having been renewed. A force of one hundred and thirty men, well armed and equipped, with howitzers, was stationed at the depot, and it was afterward increased to one hundred and ninety men, and detachments posted to protect the American consulate, and other American houses and American property. The authorities on this occasion gave notice of their inability to give the protection guaranteed by treaty. The landing parties were from the Pensacola and Benicia, the latter vessel belonging to the North Pacific station. Hostilities ceased October 8, and the force was withdrawn, excepting a detachment of thirty men, which was left a few days longer to guard the depot and the railroad should the troubles revive.

The landing of these detachments during the two emergencies, while quieting the fears of foreign residents, secured the safe transit of the passengers and their effects, and of the freight and specie of four lines of steamers, two of which were not of our nationality, depending on this road for prompt transportation.

The officers and men who composed the landing parties received the commendation of their respective commanders-in-chief for the creditable and admirable manner in which they discharged their duty. The commercial ports on the west coast of South America have been visited by the vessels of the South Pacific station, and some of them by vessels en route to the North Pacific station. With the exceptions above mentioned their proceeding have not been different from those common to our cruisers frequenting the waters of friendly nations; and the exchange of courtesies between our officers and the authorities and other residents appears to have been mutually gratifying.

MISCELLANEOUS.

In addition to the vessels which have constituted the regular force of the several stations, others have been usefully employed on special or separate service.

The Portsmouth has been engaged in surveying reported dangers and islands in the Pacific, on the highways of commerce, the existence or position of which has not been clearly established or definitely fixed. The Narragansett has been examining the route pursued by our merchant steamers along the Californian and Mexican coasts, for the promotion of safer navigation. The Tuscarora has conducted a series of soundings along and off the northwest coast, to determine a suitable bed for a submarine telegraph-cable between the United States and Asia; the Michigan has cruised on the lakes for the assistance of the merchant marine, or for any other emergency; the Juniata has visited the Greenland coast in search of the Polaris; the Blue Light has been at the disposal of the United States Commissioner of Fish and Fisheries on the coast of Maine; the Guard and Supply have carried out the articles of American exhibitors to the Vienna exposition; and the Constellation and Fortune have made the usual summer cruise with the cadet midshipmen and cadet engineers respectively.

In addition to the regular service, we still supply from the number authorized by law for the Navy the men and officers for the Coast Survey, and officers for light-house duty.

We have also completed, during the past year, two further surveys of the great Isthmus, and have made constant and extensive ocean soundings and surveys in the interest of science and commerce.

INTEROCEANIC CANAL.

The expeditions organized under the authority of Congress for the survey of the Darien and Nicaragua routes, with the view to the construction of an interoceanic canal, have completed the duties intrusted to them, and the reports of Commander Thomas O. Selfridge and Commander E. P. Lull, who respectively conducted the surveys, are herewith submitted.

The return of these expeditions, with full reports of their results, seems to leave little more to be done in the direction of isthmus surveys; and in the now completed explorations, most creditable to all engaged in them, the Department feels assured that the resolutions of Congress which led to the same have been carried out in the spirit in which they were conceived.

The results of these two last surveys may be summed up as follows:

DARIEN SURVEY.—The favorable report of Commander Selfridge of the survey of the Isthmus of Darien, in 1871, rendered it desirable to explore more thoroughly the region of the Napipi, and to definitely settle how far the surveys to the south could be profitably carried on in the valley of the Atrato.

Commander Selfridge was accordingly ordered to organize another expedition, which arrived in Panama in January last. The Tuscarora, Commander Belknap, of the Pacific fleet, was ordered to co-operate with it, and form a base for the desired surveys.

It is very gratifying that the expedition has been so successful as to materially improve upon the route already discovered and surveyed, and has marked out a line for this great enterprise that can be constructed within the limit of an expenditure more moderate than could have been expected, when compared with the immensity of the undertaking, and the great benefits that cannot fail, upon its completion, to occur to our commercial interests.

Briefly stated, the route selected by Commander Selfridge includes one hundred miles of river navigation of the Atrato, which has been carefully sounded, and found to be fully capable of being navigated by the largest class of ocean-steamers. Between Atrato and the Pacific a canal or artificial cut is made but twenty-eight miles in length. The canal for twenty-two miles of this distance passes through a plain, with a gradual rise of 90 feet. There will then remain six miles to the Pacific, of which there are a moderate open cut and three miles of tunneling. It is estimated that the work will cost between $50,000,000 and $60,000,000, and that it can be completed within ten years.

A careful survey and soundings of the Atrato resulted in the fact that, though capable of navigation for steamboats, even in its lowest stage; to Quibeto, the head of ship-navigation was reached but a short distance above the line selected for the canal.

Surveys of the interior settled the fact that it would not be profitable to explore south of the Napipi; not only because the westerly trend of the coast made the area that would have to be canalized broader in extent, but also that it was traversed by numerous streams, forming the water-shed of mountainous ridges that would have to be cut transversely. Moreover, the Cordilleras, which present a marked depression near the head-waters of the Napipi, increase rapidly in altitude as you proceed south.

The health of the expedition has been as satisfactory as the preceding ones.

These surveys, which include the whole Isthmus of Darien, have not resulted in the loss of a single life through climatic causes. Much of this immunity from disease in a sickly climate and an arduous duty is due to the provident care and well-laid plans of the officers in command.

NICARAGUA SURVEY.—The Nicaragua surveying expedition, in charge of Commander E. P. Lull, sailed from the United States in December, 1872, and returned in July last. The results of its labors prove the existence of a practicable route for an interoceanic ship-canal, having

Lake Nicaragua at its summit level. It is proposed to connect the lake with the Pacific by a canal 16.33 miles in length, beginning at the mouth of the Rio del Medio, and terminating at Brito. The first 7.50 miles will require an excavation averaging 54 feet in depth, and will be the most expensive part of the whole work. The profile for the rest of the distance is lower than the proposed level of the surface of the water; embankments will be built up with the material excavated. Ten locks and one tide-lock will be required between the lake and the sea. There will be fifty-six miles of lake navigation; 26 feet of water can be carried within 1,350 feet of the mouth of the Rio del Medio. On the east side a channel will have to be deepened, from 6 to 8 feet, for nine miles. The bottom is a firm mud without a single rock.

Slack-water navigation in the San Juan, from its head to the mouth of the San Carlos, is considered perfectly feasible; and it is proposed to improve the river by four dams, one each at Castillo Rapids, Balas Rapids, Machuca Rapids, and at the mouth of the San Carlos, at all of which places excellent locations for dams exist. A short section of canal with one lock will be required to get around each of the upper three dams. From just above the fourth dam to Greytown an independent canal will be required, 41.90 miles in length, of which thirty-six miles will require an excavation less than the prism of the canal; the remaining four miles are made up of short reaches, where the line cuts through hills. Seven locks, besides those abreast the dams, will be required, and should be located in the hills in order to take advantage of the natural rock foundation. Some improvement will be required in places in the river-bed, for which the amount has been computed and the cost estimated.

The total length of the proposed canal is 61.74 miles, of which 47.37 miles are in excavation and embankment. The average depth of excavation throughout is but 9 feet above the prism of the canal. No tunnel is required. The harbor of Greytown has been partially destroyed by a silt which comes from the San Carlos, and others of the lower tributaries of the San Juan, and the branch of the river leading to Greytown has become so much filled up that it is now, at the lowest stage of the water, but 324 feet wide and 6 inches deep at the fork. It is proposed to shut off this branch entirely and send all the silt-bearing water through the Colorado mouth, which empties into the sea eighteen miles from Greytown, and to admit to the harbor only the water of the canal, which being drawn from the main river above the mouth of the San Carlos will be perfectly clean. The harbor then once cleared out, will leave nothing to deteriorate it again.

A short breakwater will be required to protect the entrance from the surf, also one at Brito, both of which are included in the estimate for the work.

Careful gauges at the lowest stage show that Lake Nicaragua will supply thirty-eight times the maximum possible demand of water.

The climate is considered perfectly healthy for temperate people who adopt the simplest sanitary precautions. Part proof of this is that not a man has been lost in either of the expeditions lately operating in the country, though constantly subjected to severe labor and exposure.

THE POLARIS.

In my annual report of November 25, 1871, I communicated the latest information then known of the proceedings of the expedition toward the north pole, in mentioning the departure of the Polaris from Upernavik, Greenland, on the 18th August, 1871.

From that time no tidings from the Polaris were received until the 9th of May, 1873, when, by a telegraphic dispatch, the consul of the United States at Saint John's, Newfoundland, apprised the Department of State that nineteen persons, late of the Polaris, had been rescued from the floating ice in Baffin's Bay, by the British sealing-steamer the Tigress, and that they had safely arrived at that port.

The Department dispatched the United States steamer Frolic from New York to Saint John's to receive these persons and to bring them to Washington. The Frolic accomplished this mission without delay, and on the 5th of June arrived at the navy-yard, having on board two of the officers, eight of the crew, and nine Esquimaux, five of whom were children, all in good health.

For the reasons stated in my report to you of the 17th of June last, I deemed it advisable that I should hold an examination of these persons, and, accordingly, with my associates named in that report, such examination was carefully made, and the result communicated to you in our joint report of June 16. Both of these reports and the testimony of the witnesses, with the diaries of several of them, are published in the appendix to this report, and present a most interesting history of the voyage and discoveries of the Polaris up to the time of their accidental separation from these hardy mariners on the night of October 15, 1872, and of their own subsequent sufferings and adventures during the one hundred and eighty-seven dreary days of their drift among the ice.

Of the Polaris herself nothing more was known until September 19, 1873, when the arrival of the British sealing-steamer Arctic, at Dundee, Scotland, with six of the officers and three of her crew on board, was telegraphed to the Department of State by the United States consul at that port, with the further information that the remaining officer and the other two seamen would soon follow ; all hands of the Polaris having been picked up by the British whaling-steamer Ravenscraig on the 23d of June, south of Cape York, off the Greenland coast, while on their way in boats to the southward, the Polaris having been abandoned as a wreck.

As mentioned in my report to you of the 16th of June last, the Juniata, under Commander Braine, and the Tigress, under Commander Greer, were dispatched from New York as soon as they could be prepared for such service to search for the Polaris, and this duty was promptly and faithfully performed; but, happily, the British whaling-ships were on their cruising-ground early enough to rescue the whole party almost as soon as their boats rounded Cape York.

From the captain, officers, and crew of the Ravenscraig, Arctic, and Intrepid, all British sealing-steamers, these survivors of the Polaris received the kindest and most hospitable welcome and the most generous treat-ment, and I take great pleasure in recommending that a suitable acknowledgment be made to them for their humane and generous conduct.

On the arrival in this country of these nine persons, they also were brought to Washington and examined by myself and the same asso-ciates as on the former occasion. Awaiting the return of the three re-maining persons, this investigation has not been completed as yet, and the report is withheld until an opportunity offers to do so, when it will be submitted and printed.

To these reports, to the narrative of the expedition which will be prepared in due time for publication, to the scientific history of the re-sults obtained in that department, and to the map in course of construc-tion, I must leave the full development of all matters connected with this most interesting voyage toward the northern pole, made under the flag of the United States.

I may, however, state in general terms that the cruise of the Polaris has been decidedly the most successful of arctic expeditions. The geo-graphical knowledge of the arctic regions has been largely advanced. The ship herself, in two months after her departure from New York, attained the latitude of 82° 16′ north, a position far beyond the limits of all previous navigation toward the pole, and the exploration of Cap-tain Hall and of the officers, and of the scientific gentlemen upon the land, have all that singular interest which accompanies the exami-nation of regions heretofore unknown to civilized man.

The only death which occurred during the expedition, from first to last, was that of its commander, Capt. Charles F. Hall.

A very particular questioning of every one of the officers and crew of the Polaris and of the scientific corps (except the three persons as yet unexamined) has completely satisfied my associates and myself that his death occurred from purely natural causes; that his medical treat-ment was judiciously adapted to his case, and that he was tenderly nursed and cared for to the last.

The evidence has also made it manifest that Captain Hall was always faithful to the trust reposed in him in assigning him to the command of the expedition; that he was kind, firm, and humane in the exercise of his authority; that he was earnest in his desire and in his attempts to reach a high northern latitude, and if practicable, the pole itself, and that his untimely death was an irreparable loss to the expedition.

It is also apparent that Captain Buddington, who succeeded to the chief command on the death of Captain Hall, proved himself to be a good seaman, and that in all the dangerous positions in which the Polaris was placed, his conduct as her commander, was skillful and judicious, the natural result of a good judgment and of long experience at sea and in command in northern latitudes.

The domestic history of the expedition, as developed by investigations, was, on the whole, as harmonious as might have been expected. Obedience was maintained, and good order was generally preserved on board.

The ship herself proved to be exceedingly strong, and capable of resisting a very heavy pressure of ice. Had she been of less strength she would have been crushed and wrecked on occasions prior to October 15, 1872. The testimony is clear and unanimous on this subject, and is also conclusive on another vital point, that she was well found in provisions and stores for an arctic voyage. Her steam-machinery worked satisfactorily, and was in good order when she was run aground, on the 16th October, 1872, the day after she broke adrift from the ice-floe.

The injuries she received on the night of the 15th October, in addition to former hurts, proved fatal, and she was with great difficulty kept afloat until she could be beached on the next afternoon. During that day, notwithstanding that a lookout was kept for the missing people upon the ice, nothing was seen of them from the ship; and if they had been seen she could not have gone to their rescue.

The Polaris was beached in a sinking condition, at Life-boat Cove, near Littleton Island, in latitude 78° 23', a place visited by Kane and Hayes, in former years.

Friendly Esquimaux soon made their appearance with dogs and sleds and aided greatly in transporting stores from the ship to the shore, and kindly relations were kept up with these people to the last.

Constructing a house out of material supplied by the Polaris, the winter and spring were passed in comparative comfort. When the sun appeared in February the building of the boats, from the planks of the Polaris, was begun, and they were completed in time for the whole party to embark in them, with all of the records and specimens they could carry, as soon as the state of the ice would permit.

On the 3d of June last they abandoned their house, leaving nothing in it of any value whatever, and after an adventurous, but not very dangerous, voyage of 20 days, were picked up by the Ravenscrag, as before stated.

SEARCH FOR THE POLARIS.

The rescue of a portion of the officers and crew of the Polaris, and their return to St. John's, N. F., by the Tigress, a whaler of the Arctic Seas, and through whom intelligence of the disaster to the Polar expedition and of the death of its lamented commander was received.

gave hope that, although perilously situated, the remainder of the officers and crew, and the vessel itself, might, by prompt measures, be restored to their friends and country. As soon, therefore, as all necessary facts and information could be obtained, steps were taken to send out immediately an expedition to search for the vessel and party. The Tigress, which was well suited for such a purpose, far more so than any vessel we possessed, was procured for this service, brought to New York, and equipped, officered, and manned as soon as possible. At the same time the Juniata was made ready to proceed to the coast of Greenland and facilitate the movements of the Tigress, by carrying coal and other supplies, for which the latter had not sufficient capacity, and prosecute the search herself as far as was prudent for a vessel not built or strengthened for arctic navigation. Commander D. L. Braine was in command of the Juniata, and Commander James A. Greer was assigned to the command of the Tigress.

The orders to the Tigress were to make her way, if necessary, by every means possible and in the face of every danger, to the spot where the Polaris was last seen; those to the Juniata, which vessel was not so well fitted to encounter the ice, were to advance no farther in that direction than she could do without incurring more than ordinary risk and danger, and to aid in every possible way the special object of the Tigress. The orders in each case were promptly and ably executed, and on this hazardous and laborious service the officers and men exhibited commendable zeal and energy. The movements and proceedings of the vessels and commanders were as follows:

The Juniata, Commander D. L. Braine commanding, which sailed from New York June 24 for the arctic regions in search of the Polaris, returned to that port October 24. Some necessary changes were made in her condition, such as the reduction of her armament and complement of men, the sheathing of her bows, &c., to increase her carrying capacity and strengthen her to contend against the ice. She was coaled to the utmost to supply the Tigress and meet her own consumption, and after rather a hazardous passage, amidst fogs and icebergs, reached Fiskenaes, Greenland, July 14, having touched on the way at St. John's, N. F. She continued her voyage along the coast to the northward, stopping at Sukkertoppen and Holsteinborg, at which latter place the necessary dogs, skins, &c., for the use of the officers and men of the Tigress were procured, and reached Godhavn, island of Disco, July 21. Leaving there July 29, she pushed on through innumerable icebergs and rocks, and arrived at Upernavik July 31, at which port the governor stated that within his recollection of over thirty-five years no vessel of half the size of the Juniata had ever been.

From this place the steam-launch Little Juniata, under command of Lieutenant-Commanding Geo. W. De Long, with other officers and men, all volunteers for the occasion, equipped with sixty days' provisions and fifteen days' coal, sailed August 2 for Cape York, in search of the Polaris and her crew, performing one of the most extraordinary voyages on record, and returning August 12. Off Tessiusak she communicated with the Tigress. August 13 the Juniata left Upernavik and proceeded south to Godhavn to meet the Tigress, which had been previously supplied and coaled. The time here waiting the arrival of the Tigress, or news from her, was profitably spent in searching for coal. The whaleboat and the launch were employed in this service, under competent officers, and several veins of coal of a bituminous nature were found running longitudinally through the mountains in latitude 69° 45' north, longitude 52° 20', from which supplies were procured. The Tigress arrived at Godhavn August 25; was again coaled; and on the 31st August the Juniata sailed for St. John's, N. F. Here she prepared for a renewed search for the officers and crew of the Polaris, and sailed again for the arctic regions September 18. The same evening telegraphic intelligence, received by the United States consul at St. John's, Mr. T. M. Mulloy, from Dundee, reported the arrival of the Polaris party at the last-named port, and with great promptness and discretion he immediately chartered a steamer, overtook the Juniata, and she returned to St. John's. She awaited the arrival at that port of the Tigress, October 17, and then returned to New York as above stated.

The Tigress sailed from New York July 14, touched at St. John's, and arrived at Godhavn August 6. She coaled and left August 8, and reached Upernavik August 10. She there received from the Juniata skins, coal, &c., and proceeded northward the following day, communicated with the Juniata's launch off Cape York, skirted the shore as closely as navigation would permit, examined North Star Bay, Northumberland Island, Hartstene Bay, without success, and August 14, one month after leaving New York, discovered at Littleton Island the camp which the Polaris people had occupied the previous winter. From the natives then in possession of it, information was obtained of the departure in June, all in good health, of Captain Buddington and party southward in boats constructed from the ill-fated Polaris, which subsequently sunk. Such papers, instruments, &c., as were found in the camp, and were of any consequence or value, were secured by Commander Greer, and the next day the Tigress stood toward the south. She passed Cape York, anchored in Melville Bay, communicated with the authorities at Tessiusak, and arrived at Godhavn August 25. She was again coaled by the Juniata, and immediately resumed the search. She ran over to the west coast, thence southward to the entrance of Cumberland Sound, back to the coast of Greenland, in the vicinity of Ivigtut and Fiskenaes, searched in Davis Strait as long as her coal lasted, and then proceeded to St. John's, at which port she arrived October 16, and learned of the rescue and arrival in Scotland of Captain Buddington and party. She left St. John's October 30 and reached New York November 9.

The Department takes this occasion to express its indebtedness to the officials of the Danish government in Greenland for their uniform courtesy to the officers of the United States Navy connected with the recent expeditions to the Polar Seas, and for the facilities extended to those expeditions to promote their success.

TRANSIT OF VENUS.

The liberal appropriations made by Congress for making observations on the transit of Venus have been in part expended for the purchase of instruments. Five points will be occupied in the southern and three in the northern hemisphere. These observations are of so much scientific importance that it is my intention, under any eventuality now considered, to furnish naval transportation to the several parties designated, and such other facilities as may be practicable.

HYDROGRAPHIC OFFICE.

This office is steadily and surely progressing in its usefulness in the interests of navigation; as its issues of charts and books increase they are gradually taking the place of foreign publications, and some of its works are now much sought for abroad. The Pacific survey, originated in this office, under the Bureau of Navigation, will, as executed, be a great benefit, not only to the commerce of the United States, but to that of the world, and secondary to the survey, much information will be acquired in the various branches of natural science. The establishment, by electric telegraph, of the longitudes of the islands of the West Indies and the points on the northern coast of South America to which the cable has been laid by a party organized and instructed at this office, will make a most desirable addition to geographical knowledge and to navigation. I refer you to the report of the hydrographer to the Chief of the Bureau of Navigation, and recommend that two additional small vessels be employed in surveys, one in the West Indies, the other in Asiatic waters; in this we not only take, in common with other maritime nations, a part in the exploration of the channels of commerce, but give at the same time practical experience to the junior officers of the Navy in a most important branch of their profession.

Again I would call your attention to my recommendations in my previous reports, and I urgently recommend that an appropriation be made for the purchase and fitting a building permanent and suitable for the Hydrographic Office. I do not consider the rented building, at present occupied, as either suitable or safe in its present condition.

NAVY-YARDS.

I beg to renew the recommendations made in my annual reports of former years, in reference to our navy-yards, and to urge that their resources may be increased and developed to meet the emergencies of those wars to which even the most peace-loving nations are liable, and which are best averted by a readiness for action should they be thrust upon us.

At the most of our navy-yards little could be done during the past year beyond making the repairs necessary to keep them from falling to decay.

At Mare Island, our only naval establishment on the Pacific, the new dry-dock, and the iron-working shop for construction, are well in hand and will add largely to its resources. We have great naval interests on the Pacific, and I cannot too strongly express the hope that Congress may strengthen them by liberal appropriations to develop this admirably placed arsenal.

League Island.—At League Island, in obedience to the injunction of Congress, the work of removing to it the material and stores of the old Philadelphia navy-yard has begun. The heavy ordnance, shot, and cannon, the anchors and chain-cables, and a portion of the ship-building timber are already transferred. A massive machine-shop and storehouse for yards and docks has been built, and the foundation of a still greater establishment for construction has been begun. It is conclusively determined that there is no difficulty in finding a perfectly secure foundation at moderate cost, and that such a foundation at League Island will be no more costly than at New York or Norfolk, or other of our sea-board navy-yards. It is time that we should cease to have two navy-yards at Philadelphia, and that the narrow and cramped yard so much needed by the city for its commerce should be transferred to the grand and better site bestowed by Philadelphia, and accepted by Congress with its implied obligations. I beg to renew my recommendation that Congress may cause the old navy-yard to be valued, and that it advance the sum expected to accrue from its sale, instructing the Navy Department to expend the amount thus appropriated, within four years, on such buildings and improvements at League Island as shall authorize the abandonment of the old yard. The Treasury may then, by its sale, be reimbursed for the money advanced to create the new establishment.

New York.—I am impelled by recent experience to say that I trust that no legislation may interfere with the preservation of the New York navy-yard in its present site and in its integrity. The present moment shows in the clearest manner how invaluable this yard is to the Navy in utilizing in a time of emergency the vast naval resources of construction, equipment, and repair which its central position enables it to draw from the ship-yards, docks, machine-shops, and stores of the great city that surrounds it, teeming with a population of skilled artisans.

Pensacola.—I think it very important that the Pensacola navy-yard, burnt during the rebellion, but with many of its improvements unharmed, should be in some degree rebuilt. In the event of complications in, or near, the Gulf of Mexico or West Indies, it would be a station of vast importance.

New London.—I again call attention to the obligations of the Government in regard to the naval station at New London, in Connecticut.

We are the owners, by gift from the State, of a large and valuable property at this place, which has never been utilized for want of adequate means appropriate for the purpose. The considerations in favor of this site have been frequently presented, and I will only add that all that we have done there in the past has been done so well and so cheaply as to give an earnest for the future, and induce the belief that a well-found and supplied naval station at this point would be extremely valuable to the service and to the country.

ORDNANCE.

The report of the Chief of the Bureau of Ordnance, though brief, is highly interesting and satisfactory, especially with reference to the great advancement made in the manufacture of gunpowder and the perfection attained in the production of a suitable cartridge for small-arms.

The operations of this most important branch of our naval service have been closely confined within the appropriations, the narrow limits of which prevented any elaborate experiments being made in testing the manifold improvements which occupy the attention of ordnance men abroad.

The Bureau has, nevertheless, been extremely vigilant in collecting the necessary data to enable it to proceed intelligently in the solution of any of the great questions relating to naval armament whenever Congress may grant the requisite authority and supplies. In the mean time its resources are sufficient for the armament of every ship which can at present be placed in commission. Nothing in its economy appears to have been neglected, and it only remains to increase its efficiency by a liberal appropriation. Otherwise nothing, practically, can be done to keep pace with the movements of European navies.

Unquestionably the efficiency of a man-of-war is measured by the power of her battery, and the respect paid to our flag is in a direct proportion to the number and caliber of the guns which defend it.

I most earnestly recommend that ample provision be made for the support of this Bureau in order that nothing may interfere with its efforts to arm our ships with the most powerful guns.

NAVAL PENSION FUND.

Statement of the number and yearly amount of pensions of the Navy on the rolls November 1, 1873, and the amount which was paid during the last fiscal year.

	On the rolls November 1, 1873.	Yearly amount of pensions on the rolls November 1, 1873.	Amount paid for pensions during fiscal year ending June 30, 1873.
Navy invalids	1,484	$155,310 75	$160,971 98
Navy widows and others	1,799	290,516 00	302,936 71
Total	3,283	445,826 75	463,908 69

ESTIMATES AND EXPENDITURES.

The appropriations made by Congress for the fiscal year which ended June 30, 1873, including the amount of the special appropriation made last winter, and expended before the date named, were in the whole $20,589,601.57, and the actual expenditures for that period, viz, from July, 1872, to June 30, 1873, chargeable to these appropriations, including the expenditure during the time named of the special appropriations above referred to, amounted to $19,552,272.16, or something more than a million less than the whole amount appropriated. The appropriations made for the current year commencing July 1, 1873, amount in the aggregate, including the special appropriation for the new sloops of war, (less the small amount expended before June 30, 1873,) to the sum of $23,147,857.68. The amount of these appropriations for the current year drawn, up to the first of the present month, is $10,008,182.63, which, reduced by the amount remaining in the hands of the paymasters and agents of the Government, will leave about $6,500,000 as the amount actually expended from the current appropriations during the working months of this year.

A detailed account of the monthly expenditure of the Navy appropriations for the fiscal year 1872–'73, and for the present year (1873–'74) to November 1, will be found in the Appendix.

ESTIMATES.

Pay of officers and seamen of the Navy	$6,500,000 00
Pay of civil establishment in navy-yards	343,215 50
Ordnance and Torpedo Corps	651,344 71
Coal, hemp, and equipments	1,500,000 00
Navigation, navigation supplies	122,500 00
Hydrographic work	59,800 00
Naval Observatory, Nautical Almanac, &c	59,050 00
Repairs and preservation of vessels, &c	3,505,000 00
Steam-machinery, tools, &c	2,200,000 00
Provisions	1,587,600 00
Repairs of hospitals and laboratories	50,200 00
Surgeons' necessaries	40,000 00
Contingent expenses of various departments and bureaus	468,600 00
Naval Academy	129,707 40
Support of Marine Corps	1,105,911 25
Naval Asylum, Philadelphia, &c	69,307 00
Maintenance of yards and docks	860,000 00
	19,252,235 86

And to these is added the sum of $864,589.28 for current repairs of buildings, docks, and incidental expenses in navy-yards, &c.

These estimates are less than those of last year by rather more than $2,000,000, but they do not include any extraordinary expenditure for the permanent improvement of the Navy, nor the amounts necessary either for the repair of our iron-clad fleet, nor for the continued prosecution of some of the great works necessary to the proper condition of our naval establishment.

———

The foregoing is a general report of the condition, situation, and movements of the United States Navy for the past year, and until the commencement of the present month. Since that time, however, events have taken place which make it proper that the Navy should be put at once upon a footing for active service. It is by no means the province of this Department, as such, to take part in the conduct or discussion of any diplomatic question, nor should its attitude, at a time when serious international difficulties are possible, be held to indicate anything more than a determination on the part of a military department of the Government to be prepared for action, should the necessity for action arise. This is the present condition of public affairs, and such is the attitude of the Navy Department.

I have felt it to be my duty, under existing circumstances, to take promptly every means in my power to put our available force in the best possible condition for immediate and active service. All the power and means of the Department are now devoted to this end, greatly aided at every point by the enthusiastic activity of officers of every grade of the service.

Difficult of accomplishment as our purpose at first seemed, difficulties and even apparent impossibilities, are found to fade away before determination and organized activity, and the Navy is already in such a condition, that those to whom our interests and honor are now intrusted, may be relieved from the embarrassments of a situation, where just determination might be disregarded, because thought to be powerless, or decent consideration be mistaken for fear.

It is neither necessary nor proper that I should enter here into the details of our preparations; suffice it to say, that a respectable force of war-vessels and monitors is already on the sea, and concentrating at the station nearest the scene of our possible difficulties; that our whole available iron-clad fleet is in hand, and every wooden war-vessel that will float, in active preparation at the various naval stations. These will be ready for sea, fully fitted, as fast as proper crews can be provided for them; and if the necessity for action should come, before the time for it arrives, all that there is of the American Navy, which can be put afloat on the Atlantic Ocean, will be in condition and position to take its proper part.

Inadequate as this force may reasonably be deemed to the responsibilities and pretensions of a government like ours, and greatly at disadvantage as we certainly will be, in respect of number and character of vessels in a contest, with the fleets of any respectable naval power, I believe that the activity, skill, science, and experience of our Navy will be found equal to any difficulty which courage dares to meet or energy will avail to conquer. They are thoroughly imbued with the spirit, educated in the details, and experienced in the warlike duties of their profession, skilled in the use of all the terrible weapons which science has provided for modern warfare, and of a mood to meet any crisis without shrinking from danger. Thus prepared and in this spirit, they are ready to meet any of their country's adversaries with the means with which their country provides them.

In taking the action above referred to, the Navy Department has already incurred considerable expense, and has been forced to assume some responsibilities unusual in time of peace, but, convinced of the wisdom of prompt and decided action, I have not shrunk from these responsibilities, nor hesitated, with your approval, to make warlike preparations, in the interests of peace and of humanity. I confidently rely for support in this attitude upon the patriotism and good sense of the American people and their representatives, who cannot fail to remember that our naval condition is the result of causes which have been constantly pressed upon their consideration, but which have failed to receive full attention, doubtless on account of more pressing present requirements and obligations; and who will also clearly realize that duties constantly postponed are certain to be more difficult and much more expensive, when performed in haste, under the pressure of imperious necessity.

The Department has had no necessity to overstep its appropriations, even if it were lawful to do so, but the pressing demands of the present will consume now, what was provided for the service of the year, in several of the working Bureaus. These must be promptly relieved if their work is to go on.

The occasion has shown clearly, I think, that our Navy, as it exists, should at least be put in a condition for active service, and in any event a moderate appropriation for this purpose ought at once to be made. And if war should by any possibility come, we must be liberally provided to utilize the means we have and to provide others to meet the emergency.

GEO. M. ROBESON,
Secretary of the Navy.

The PRESIDENT.

THE REPORT OF THE SECRETARY OF THE NAVY

MOVEMENTS OF VESSELS IN COMMISSION.

EUROPEAN STATION.

The vessels on the European station are: Wabash, (flag-ship,) 45 guns; Congress, 16 guns; Alaska, 12 guns; Shenandoah, 11 guns; Wachusett, 6 guns.

The Brooklyn and Plymouth have returned from the station during the year. The former was put out of commission at Boston July 18, and the latter at Portsmouth June 28.

All the vessels above named, except the Alaska, left Cadiz October 30, 1872, and separated the same evening. Their movements, respectively, have been as follows:

The Wabash, then bearing the flag of Rear-Admiral James Alden, arrived at Gibraltar November 1, left on the 5th; arrived at Tangier the same day, left on the 9th, and arrived at Cartagena on the 13th. She sailed from the latter port on the 23d, and, in company with the Wachusett, reached Villefranche on the 26th. She sailed from Villefranche January 15, 1873, and the next day, with the Brooklyn and Wachusett in company, arrived at Spezia. Thence she proceeded, about January 25, to Naples and to Malta, arriving at the latter place March 3. About the 12th of March she sailed with the Wachusett for the Levant and the Archipelago. Having visited Alexandria, she left that port April 2, and on the 5th arrived at Piræus. She proceeded thence to Syra, sailing April 19 and arriving same day; left there on the 23d, arrived at Leghorn May 1; sailed on the 22d, and reached Villefranche the following day. June 2, Rear-Admiral Alden was relieved by Rear-Admiral A. Ludlow Case.

Bearing the flag of Rear-Admiral Case, the Wabash sailed from Villefranche June 12, for Trieste, and after touching at Genoa, Palermo, Messina, and Syracuse, arrived July 6. From Trieste she sailed July 21, and on the 24th arrived at Corfu. August 5 she left Corfu for the Spanish coast, touched at Messina from the 7th to the 8th, and reached Cartagena on the 14th. She remained on the coast of Spain until October 27, giving attention to our interests at Cartagena, Barcelona, &c., and then proceeded to Villefranche for provisions, &c., arriving on the 31st.

The Congress arrived at Gibraltar October 31, 1872, from Cadiz, left November 5; arrived at Malta on the 15th, left on the 21st; arrived at the Dardanelles on the 25th, left there the 30th, and arrived at Jaffa on the 8th of December. She sailed from Jaffa December 13, touched at Beirut, Port Said, Alexandria, and Messina, and arrived at Naples January 16, 1873. She left Naples February 16, and the next day arrived at Spezia. From Spezia she proceeded, March 7, to Villefranche; arrived the following day. Sailed again the 16th, touched at Marseilles and Malaga, and reached Gibraltar on the 24th. April 22 she took the store-ship Guard in tow, and left for Trieste, at which latter port she

34 Ab

arrived May 3, having touched on the way at Brindisi. She left Trieste May 10, touched at Messina on the 13th, and on the 17th reached Ville-franche. June 6 she sailed from Villefranche for the north of Europe, to visit some of the ports of Ireland, England, Germany, Holland, and France. She returned to the Spanish coast in October, and has been cruising in that quarter since.

The Brooklyn arrived at Cartagena November 3, 1872, from Cadiz, left on the 4th; arrived at Palermo on the 18th, left on the 20th; arrived at Messina on the 22d, left on the 24th, and arrived at Naples the next day. She left Naples on the 10th of December, visited Spezia, and arrived at Villefranche on the 27th. * * * January 22, 1873, she sailed from Spezia; arrived at Naples on the 24th, left on the 19th of February; arrived at Villefranche on the 21st, left on the 28th for Barcelona; arrived March 2, left on the 21st; arrived at Gibraltar on the 24th, and on the 31st sailed from the last-mentioned port with the Supply in tow, for Trieste, arriving there April 10. She left Trieste April 24, touched at Naples, and arrived at Villefranche May 7th. On the 2d of June she left Villefranche, bearing the flag of Rear-Admiral Alden, for the United States, touched at Gibraltar and Bermuda, and arrived at New York July 10, whence she was sent to Boston and put out of commission July 18.

The Shenandoah arrived at Tangier October 31, 1872, from Cadiz, left on the 4th November; arrived at Gibraltar the same day, left on the 10th; arrived at Algiers on the 15th, left on the 19th; arrived at Tunis on the 22d, left on the 27th; arrived at Malta on the 29th, and left there December 2 for Milo and Athens, reaching the latter port on the 10th. She sailed on the 26th for Syra and Smyrna. January 8, 1873, she left Smyrna, touched at Syracuse, Port École, Civita Vecchia, and Leghorn, and arrived at Spezia on the 29th. March 3 she sailed for Ville-franche, arrived the next day; left the 7th; arrived at Barcelona on the 9th, left May 6; touched at Port Mahon, from 7th to the 17th, and reached Villefranche on the 19th. June 7 she sailed from Villefranche to visit Barcelona and other ports on the coast of Spain. She remained on the coast until November 5, looking after American interests at Malaga, Barcelona, Tarragona, Cartagena, &c., and then proceeded to Nice to prepare for a cruise to Egypt and Syria.

The Wachusett left Cadiz October 30, 1872, in company with the flag-ship, and continued with her till she reached Villefranche November 26, having touched at Gibraltar, Tangier, and Cartagena. She left Ville-franche December 8, visited Marseilles and Barcelona, and returned January 1, 1873. She again sailed, in company with the flag-ship, Jan-uary 15, visited Spezia, Naples, Malta, Alexandria, Port Said, (took the admiral to Jaffa, and returned to Alexandria,) Piraeus, Malta the second time, Palermo, Barcelona, and returned to Villefranche May 17. June 7 she sailed from Villefranche, visited Majorca, Marseilles, Ajaccio, Messina, Corfu, and Brindisi, joined the flag-ship at Trieste, and accom-panied her to Corfu. From Corfu she was sent to the coast of Spain, and has been in that quarter ever since, visiting Santander, Ferrol, Coruña, Cartagena, Cadiz, and other ports.

The Plymouth arrived at Malaga November 1, 1872, from Cadiz, left on the 3d; arrived at Barcelona on the 9th, left on the 16th; arrived at Toulon on the 18th, left on the 26th, and arrived at Villefranche on the 28th. She sailed from the last-named port December 16, touched at Genoa, and arrived at Spezia on the 21st. From Spezia she pro-ceeded, January 22, 1873, to Lisbon via Villefranche and Gibraltar, and arrived there February 10. She left Lisbon on the 17th of February for the United States via the coast of Africa and the West Indies. The following places were visited by her: Canary Islands in February; ports Porto Praya and Porto Grande, Monrovia, and Cape Palmas, in March; Elmina, Cape Coast Castle, Fernando Po, Gaboon River, and St. Paul de Loando in April. She left St. Paul de Loando April 28, was at Bridgetown, Barbadoes, 1st to 6th June, and arrived at New York June 18; whence she proceeded to Portsmouth, N. H., and was put out of commission June 28.

The Alaska was put in commission at New York, August 6, 1873, from which port she sailed August 28, touched at Newport, and arrived at Cadiz September 25, since which time she has been stationed on the Spanish coast.

THE NORTH ATLANTIC STATION.

Rear-Admiral Gustavus H. Scott relieved Rear-Admiral Joseph F. Green of the command of this station at Hampton Roads May 15, and is now in command.

The following vessels are now or have been attached to the station at some time during the past year: Worcester, (flag-ship,) 15 guns; Canandaigua, 10 guns; Powhatan, 17 guns; Richmond, 14 guns; Pawnee, 2 guns; Wyoming, 6 guns; Shawmut, 3 guns; Nipsic, 3 guns; Terror, 4 guns; Saugus, 2 guns.

The movements of the vessels above named have been as follows:

The Worcester, bearing the flag of Rear-Admiral Green, having visited St. Thomas, St. John's, Porto Rico, Samana Bay, and Havana, arrived at Key West November 29, 1872. She remained there until February 3, 1873, and sailed for Matanzas, arriving the following day. She left Matanzas February 11, and arrived at Havana the same day. Left Havana the 26th, and arrived at Key West February 27. March 17 she sailed again on a cruise to the southward, arrived at Bridgetown the 2d and left the 5th of April; arrived at St. Pierre, Martinique, April 7, and left the next day for Puerto Cabello; arrived on the 12th, and sailed the same day for Santiago de Cuba; arrived at Santiago de Cuba April 18, and remained until the 22d; arrived at Kingston 24th, left on the 25th, and arrived at Key West May 5.

May 15 Rear-Admiral Scott relieved Rear-Admiral Green, and the latter proceeded in the Powhatan to Boston, where he hauled down his flag May 28.

The Worcester remained at Key West until July 5, when she came to Norfolk for repairs. August 25 she left the navy-yard for Bermuda; arrived there on the 21st. She sailed from Bermuda September 4, arrived at Hampton Roads on the 10th, off the anchorage on the 13th; went to the yard on the 20th, repaired, and sailed again from Hampton Roads for Key West November 18, and arrived there the 23d.

The Canandaigua sailed from Key West December 12, 1872, on a cruise to the southward; arrived at Samana December 24, left on the 26th; arrived at St. Thomas on the 28th, and left January 5, 1873. She was at Pointe à Pitre from the 9th to the 14th of January; at La Guayra from the 17th to the 20th; at Porto Cabello the 21st and 22d; at Curaçoa from the 24th to the 30th; at Santa Martha from the 1st to the 4th of February. February 10 she left Carthagena and arrived at Aspinwall on the 12th; left on the 14th, and reached Havana the 26th. She remained at Havana until March 4, and the following day reached Key West. March 25 she proceeded to Matanzas; remained there until the 31st, and the same day arrived at Havana. She left Havana April 5, touched at Matanzas, remaining there until the 10th, and arrived at Key West on the 11th. May 10 she left for Vera Cruz, via New Orleans, or the Southwest Pass, to convey the United States minister to his destination. The minister was disembarked at Vera Cruz on the 25th of May, and on the 31st the Canandaigua sailed for Key West, and arrived there June 9. On the 19th of June she sailed for Aspinwall and arrived the 29th. She remained there until August 3, when she proceeded to Kingston, Jamacia, for the benefit of the health of the crew, arriving on the 9th. She left Jamaica September 11, touched at Key West, and reached Hampton Roads, September 25, and was sent thence to Philadelphia for repairs.

The Wyoming sailed from Key West December 14, 1872, landed the United States consul-general to Cuba at Havana, and proceeded thence on a cruise to the southward. She reached San Juan January 2, 1873, and left on the 9th for San Barbara de Samana; thence she proceeded to Santo Domingo City, and Jacmel and Aux Cayes, and arrived at Kingston on the 19th. From Kingston she went to Port au Prince, also to Gonaives, Nicola Mole, and arrived at Santiago de Cuba February 4th. She left there on the 9th, touched at Matanzas, and reached Key West on the 19th. March 15 she proceeded to the Mexican coast, where she remained until June 4, and returned to Key West June 14. From Key West she came to Hampton Roads, arriving July 10, and went up to the yard on the 25th. August 6 she sailed for Aspinwall via Bermuda and Kingston; arrived at Bermuda August 28, sailed September 2; arrived at Kingston September 9, left on the 20th, and arrived at Aspinwall September 25, where she remained until November, when she went to Santiago de Cuba.

The Nipsic, from November, 1872, to January, 1873, was visiting the ports of Santo Domingo. January 7 she left Samana for Silver Bank Passage to examine shoals in the vicinity. She subsequently visited Cape Haytien, Guatanamo, and Havana, and arrived at Key West February 2. She left Key West February 13, on surveying service, on which she was engaged to 13th March, when she proceeded to San Juan for supplies, &c. April 10 she left for Samana, arrived on the 12th, left on the 14th, searched for Silver-Bank Passage Shoal, Clarion Shoal, Ciudado Reef, visited Matthew Town, and arrived at Nuevitas May 6. She proceeded thence to Key West via Matanzas, and arrived May 16. June 23 she left for Hampton Roads, thence for New York, and was put out of commission July 26.

The Shawmut was under repairs at Key West until March 5, when she sailed for and arrived at Havana the next day. She left Havana for Matanzas, March 26, and arrived the same day. She remained at Matanzas until April 28, when she proceeded to Key West. June 23 she left Key West for Hampton Roads; arrived on the 30th. July 30 she arrived at Washington, and has since been under repairs.

The Saugus left Philadelphia November 28, 1872, arrived at Key West February 13, via Norfolk and Savannah, and has since been at anchor in that harbor.

The Terror, having been relieved by the Saugus, left Key West May 17 in tow of the Powhatan, arrived off the Delaware River May 24, and came up to Philadelphia, where she was put out of commission June 10.

The Pawnee arrived at Key West February 8, 1873, from Pensacola, and has been stationed there since that time.

The Richmond was commissioned at Philhdelphia November 18, 1872; sailed, December 15, for Norfolk, arrived there the 19th; left Hampton Roads January 31, 1873; reported for duty on the station at Key West February 11, where she remained until the 23d, and proceeded to survey a supposed shoal near Jupiter Inlet. She returned to Key West March 9, left the 13th, arrived at San Juan, Porto Rico, the 22d; left the 28th, surveyed a shoal in the vicinity of Bolandar Head, and arrived at San Domingo City the 31st. She left San Domingo the same day, proceeded to Kingston, Jamaica, arrived there April 3, left the 5th for Santiago de Cuba, and arrived on the 7th. She remained there until the 12th, and effected the release of certain American seamen who were being tried, then proceeded to Guantanamo Bay; thence to Port au Prince and Cape Haytien. She left the latter place April 15, arrived at Havana on the 19th, left on the 21st, and arrived at Matanzas same day. She left Matanzas on the 29th, and arrived at Key West on the 30th. May 10, having been detached from the station, she left Key West for the North Pacific station, arrived at Rio de Janeiro July 7, sailed on the 26th, and reached Valparaiso October 4. She left the latter port October 25 for San Francisco.

The Powhatan, with the Saugus, left Philadelphia November 28, 1872, and arrived at Key West, via Norfolk and Tybee Roads, February 13, 1873. During the month of April she was employed a few days in assisting the telegraph company. May 6, she went over to Havana, returned on the 8th, and on the 17th left for Boston, via the capes of the Delaware, with the Terror in tow; arrived off the capes May 24, and at Boston May 28. July 25 she left Boston for Hampton Roads, and arrived on the 29th. In August she proceeded to Halifax, and returned to New York in September. In November she was ordered to Philadelphia, which port she left the 25th of that month with the Manhattan for Key West, but returned and took a second departure December 5, the last time from Wilmington.

THE SOUTH ATLANTIC STATION.

The vessels on this station are: Lancaster, (flag-ship,) 22 guns; Ticonderoga, 11 guns; Wasp, 1 gun.

The Ticonderoga is about sailing for the United States. Rear-Admiral William Rogers Taylor was relieved by Rear-Admiral James H Strong, at Rio de Janeiro, October 31.

The movements of the vessels have been as follows:

The Lancaster having completed repairs about the middle of November, 1872, left Rio de Janeiro on the 25th of that month for the La Plata. January 18, 1873, Rear-Admiral Taylor transferred his flag temporarily to the Wasp and made a visit to Buenos Ayres, Rosario, and Colonia, and returned to Montevideo February 9. The Lancaster in the mean time made a cruise to the south, returning about the 9th of February. She remained in the vicinity of the La Plata until the latter part of May, visiting Moldanado, Montevideo, St. Catharines, and Santos, and arrived at Rio de Janeiro June 11. She remained at Rio under repairs until August 28, when she proceeded on a cruise northward, arriving at Bahia September 16, leaving there the 29th and returning to Rio de Janeiro October 7. October 31, Rear-Admiral Taylor was relieved, as above stated.

The Ticonderoga sailed from Montevideo December 30, 1872, for Rio de Janeiro, where she arrived January 22, 1873. She left Rio January 28, for Santos and St. Catharines, and arrived at Montevideo from the last-named port March 14. She remained in the vicinity of the La Plata until about the middle of April, when she proceeded to Rio de Janeiro, arriving May 28. June 30 she proceeded southward again—visited Montevideo, Buenos Ayres, St. Catharine's, Santos, and returned to Rio de Janeiro October 20, from which port she expected to sail for the United States.

The Wasp, in November, 1872, visited Moldanado and Rio Grande de Sul, and was used by Rear-Admiral Taylor temporarily to visit, in January, Rosario, Buenos Ayres, and Colonia, from which service she returned to Montevideo February 9. In April she went to Colonia and returned to Montevideo May 3. She remained there, having new tubes put in her boilers, until fall. When last heard from, October 6, she was at Asuncion, having conveyed the United States minister up the Paraguay.

THE NORTH PACIFIC STATION.

The vessels on the North Pacific station are: Saranac, (flag-ship,) 11 guns; Benicia, 12 guns; Richmond, 14 guns.

The California was put out of commission at San Francisco July 3, and the St. Mary's, which returned from the station, at Norfolk, June 17.

The movements of the several vessels have been as follows:

The California, bearing the flag of Rear-Admiral Pennock, arrived at Honolulu January 15, from San Francisco, where, on account of affairs at the Sandwich Islands, she remained until May 7, then returned to San Francisco, arriving May 25. Rear-Admiral Pennock having transferred his flag to the Saranac, hoisting it June 28, the California was put out of commission as above stated.

The Richmond arrived at San Francisco December 4, from the North Atlantic station, and reported for duty on this station.

The Saranac arrived at San Francisco November 23, 1872, from Panama and intermediate ports. She sailed again in January, 1873, for the Mexican and Central American coasts. In February she visited Mazatlan, San Blas, and Acapulco, and in March, Punta Arenas, Corinto, and La Union, and returned to Acapulco March 16. April 25 she arrived at San Francisco, and June 28, Rear-Admiral Pennock transferred his flag to her. She left San Francisco July 5, on a northern cruise, and arrived at Esquimault on the 12th, left there on the 16th for Sitka, via the inland passage, anchored at numerous places on the way, and reached Chilcat Village, head of navigation, on the 30th. Leaving Sitka August 19, she returned the same route, visited Port Townsend, Seattle, Steilacoom, Olympia, and reached San Francisco September 29. October 7 she sailed for Honolulu and arrived on the 19th.

The Benicia arrived at Honolulu January 4, 1873, from San Francisco, and remained at the Sandwich Islands until the latter part of March. While there the flag was temporarily transferred to her. April 7 she arrived at San Francisco, filled up with stores, made some repairs, and sailed May 5 for Panama. She touched at some of the Mexican and Central American ports, and arrived at Panama August 12. In the latter part of September and early part of October she co-operated with the flag-ship of the South Pacific station, by landing a force at Panama for the protection of American citizens and property.

The St. Mary's sailed from San Francisco, November 23, 1872, for the Atlantic States. She arrived at Valparaiso January 23, 1873, left there February 20, arrived at Barbadoes April 28, touched at St. Thomas, and arrived at Norfolk June 3, where she was put out of commission as above stated.

The Narragansett arrived at Callao January 1, sixty-five days from Sydney, Australia. She made certain repairs and alterations at Callao, sailed March 20, and arrived at Panama April 2.. From Panama she proceeded to Lower California, and has been engaged in surveys in that vicinity.

THE SOUTH PACIFIC STATION.

The vessels now on this station are, the Pensacola, (flag-ship,) 22 guns; Omaha, 12 guns; Onward, 3 guns.

The Tuscarora was early in the year on the station, but was withdrawn for special service.

The movements of the vessels have been as follows:

The Pensacola, flag-ship of Rear-Admiral Charles Steedman, arrived at Talcahuano December 4, 1872, from Payta; left there on the 12th, and arrived at Valparaiso on the 14th of December. She remained at the last-mentioned port until March 20, when she proceeded to Coquimbo, arriving on the 22d. She left Coquimbo April 1, and arrived at Callao on the 9th; left Callao on the 22d for Panama, touching on the way at Payta, and arrived May 8. At Panama she landed a force for the protection of American citizens and their property during the revolution. She sailed from Panama June 2, arrived at Payta on the 10th and at Callao on the 18th, where she remained until the 9th of July, and then proceeded to Coquimbo. In September she left for Panama, where on the 22d of that month Rear-Admiral Steedman was relieved by Rear-Admiral John J. Almy. Shortly after the latter took command of the station, a second landing of men was made from the Pensacola for the same purpose as in the first instance. The Pensacola remained at Panama until October 23, when she proceeded south, bound for the coast of Chili.

The Omaha, which sailed from Philadelphia October 8, 1872, to join the station, arrived at Valparaiso February 6, 1873. March 20 she left Valparaiso in company with the flag-ship, and arrived at Coquimbo on the 22d. She remained at Coquimbo until April 7, when she proceeded to Callao, via Iquiqui, and arrived on the 21st. June 2 she left Callao for Panama, and arrived on the 15th. On the 25th of June she sailed for Guayaquil, thence to Coquimbo and Valparaiso. She was at Callao August 30.

The Tuscarora left Valparaiso October 30, 1872, for Callao, and on the 24th December sailed from the latter port for Panama, to co-operate with the Darien surveying expedition. She arrived at Panama January 1, 1873, and was engaged in this service until May 17, when she sailed for San Francisco, via Acapulco. She was at Acapulco from May 26 to June 1, and arrived at San Francisco June 25. She was subsequently engaged in surveying on the northwest coast, to determine a suitable route for a submarine cable, and returned to San Francisco from this service November 6.

The Onward has been permanently stationed at Callao.

ASIATIC STATION.

The following vessels comprise the force now on the Asiatic station: Hartford, (flag-ship,) 18 guns; Iroquois, 6 guns; Lackawanna, 10 guns; Saco, 3 guns; Palos, 6 guns; Monocacy, 6 guns; Ashuelot, 6 guns; Yantic, 3 guns; Idaho, 7 guns.

The movements of the vessels on this station during the past year have been as follows:

The Colorado left Hong-Kong November 21, 1872, arriving at Singapore on the 28th, and on the 2d of December sailed for the United States, touching at Anjer and Cape Town, and arrived March 12, and was put out of commission March 25, 1873.

The Hartford arrived at Point de Galle, Ceylon, via Suez Canal, on February 20; from thence to Penang, and, leaving March 3, arrived at Singapore on the 6th; from thence to Manila, arriving March 22; thence to Hong-Kong, arriving 30th March. On the 3d of April, Rear-Admiral Jenkins changed his flag to the Hartford from the Lackawanna. The Hartford left Hong-Kong for Amoy 30th April, arriving May 2; leaving the same day, arrived at Shanghai on the 10th; remained at Shanghai until July 12, when she left for Wusung; and in a few days sailed for Nagasaki, arriving on July 21; remained in Nagasaki until October 4, then sailed for Woosung, arriving on the 6th. On the 12th October entered the Yang-tse River, arriving at Chin-Kiang on the 14th; will reach Kiu-Kiang to-morrow, and will proceed to Hankow; from Hankow she will return to Shanghai, and thence to Hong-Kong, to arrive there about the 1st of December.

The Lackawanna left Hong-Kong, in company with the Colorado, November 21, 1872, arriving at Singapore on the 29th; sailed from Singapore December 6, calling at Pulo Penang, and remained four days; sailed thence to Calcutta, arriving December 20; sailed from Calcutta January 3, 1873, touching at Penang, and arrived at Singapore January 15; thence to Bangkok, arriving January 29. On February 8 sailed for Saigon, arriving on the 13th; thence on the 18th for Manila, arriving on February 26; sailed from Manila March 1, arriving at Hong-Kong 4th March, remaining until the 20th; in company with the Monocacy visited Macao and Whampoa, the Monocacy carrying my flag to Canton; returned to Hong-Kong on April 2, and sailed for Yokohama on the 10th, arriving on the 20th; remaining a short time in Yokohama, sailed for Nagasaki, visiting Kobe en route, and arriving at Nagasaki June 1; on June 12, in company with Yantic and Saco, sailed for Shanghai, arriving on the 15th; on the 18th of July sailed from Shanghai for Che-foo, arriving on the 22d, remaining two days; made short visits to Teng-chu-fu, Taku, and Ninghai; thence to Nagasaki, arriving August 2; sailed from Nagasaki to Wadwostok, Russian Siberia, arriving 28th, and left 31st August; thence to Hakodadi, arriving September 3; arrived, probably, at Yokohama about October 15, and is at this date on her way to or at Nagasaki.

The Iroquois, having been under repairs at Shanghai, left March 12, for Nagasaki, arriving on the 15th; thence on the 21st March to Kobe; thence on the 2d April to Yokohama, arriving on the 4th. Left Yokohama April 29, arriving at Shanghai May 4. Remained in Shanghai until July 22, when she sailed for Nieu-chwang; remaining there from July 28 until August 9th; thence to Nenghai, 10th August; Taku Bar, 11th to 13th August; Teng-chu-fu, 13th to 17th August; arriving at Che-foo August 18. On September 9 sailed for Shanghai, arriving on the 11th and leaving on the 17th; arrived at Chin-Kiang, Yang-tse River, on the 19th, and on the 15th October left for Shanghai.

The Saco, having been under repairs at Shanghai, sailed from thence on the 1st March for Nagasaki, arriving on the 5th; left on the 8th for Kobe, arriving on the 11th; left on the 17th for Yokohama, arriving 19th of March. Again left Yokohama May 1; in Kobe from 6th to 8th, arriving in Nagasaki on the 10th. In company with Lackawanna and Yantic sailed June 12 for Shanghai, arriving on the 15th. Left Shanghai June 30th, arriving at Taku Bar July 4, and proceeded to Tien-tsin; remained there until August 22; in Che-foo from 24th to 27th August, arriving at Nagasaki 31st August. Left Nagasaki September 8, visiting Kobe en route, and arrived at Yokohama 15th September, where she still remains.

The Yantic sailed from Zanzibar January 23, arriving at Seychelles on February 1, and leaving on the 14th; Point de Galle, from 5th to 9th of March; Pulo Penang, 22d and 23d of March; Singapore, 25th March to 2d of April, reaching Hong-Kong 15th of April. Left Hong-Kong May 18, calling at Amoy, 21st to 25th of May; Foo-chow, 26th to 29th May, reaching Nagasaki 5th of June. On the 12th of June, in company with Lackawanna and Saco, sailed for Shanghai. Left Shanghai June 30, calling at Nagasaki from 3d to 6th of July, Kobe 8th to 9th, arriving at Yokohama on the 11th. Sailed from Yokohama September 16, Kobe 19th to 20th September, reaching Nagasaki on the 22d. Sailed for Shanghai October 4, arrived on the 6th. She is under orders to go to Hong-Kong, and thence proceed to visit Manila and the ports in the Philippine Islands to the southward of Manila, Ilo-Ilo, Zebu, &c., and the Sulu Sea; to visit Brunai, capital of Borneo, Batavia, Singapore, Acheen, Penang, and Malacca.

The Ashuelot left Tien-tsin on July 3, arriving at Nagasaki on the 10th. Sailed from Nagasaki August 5, calling at Kobe on the 8th, arriving at Yokohama on the 14th, and remains at Yokoska, Japanese government dock-yard, under repairs.

The Monocacy left Shanghai for the ports on the Yang-tse River on November 13; in Chin-Kiang from 14th to 16th; in Kin-Kiang, 18th to 20th, reaching Hankow on the 21st. Remaining until the 28th of December, started down the river; Kin-Kiang 29th to 30th, 1872; Chin-Kiang from 1st to 15th of January, 1873, arriving at Shanghai on the 17th. Left Shanghai February 8, calling at Foo-chow, 11th to 15th February; Amoy, 16th to 19th; Swatow, 20th to 24th, reaching Hong-Kong February 25. Left, in company with Lackawanna, for Macao March 20 to 24, thence to Canton, the Lackawanna remaining at Whampoa. Left Canton April 1, arriving at Hong-Kong on the 2d. Sailed from Hong-Kong April 27; calling at Swatow 28th to 29th; Amoy, 30th April to 3d of May; Foo-chow, from 5th to 11th of May; Ningpo, from 13th to 16th, reaching Shanghai on the 17th. Sailed from Shanghai on July 16; Nagasaki, July 20. Left Nagasaki 24th, Kobe, 26th, arriving at Yokohama July 28, and went to Yokoska, where she is under repairs, which will be completed about November 1.

The Palos sailed from Ningpo January 22, reaching Shanghai on the 23d, leaving on the 26th to visit the ports on the Yang-tse River. On account of low water did not reach Hankow until April 4; remained until May 12, and, visiting the treaty-ports on her way down, reached Shanghai May 12. Leaving Woosung July 18, arrived at Nagasaki on the 22d. Sailed August 6, calling at Kobe 8th and 9th, arriving at Yokohama on the 11th, and went to Yokoska on the 12th, where she is under repairs at Japanese government dock-yard. She is expected to be ready for service by the 1st of November, and will be sent to Tien-tsin, on the Peiho River, for the winter.

The Idaho was towed by the Yantic on the 25th of July from Yokohama to Yokoska, and is stationed at the latter place.

The Alaska arrived at New York from this station February 14, and was put out of commission February 26.

MISCELLANEOUS.

The Supply was put in commission at New York February 8, 1873, to carry out American contributions to the Vienna Exposition. She sailed March 5, and arrived at Trieste April 10, having been towed from Gibraltar by the Congress. She arrived at New York November 22, (on return from this service,) and was put out of commission December 3.

The Guard was commissioned at New York February 1, 1873, for the same service as the Supply, and sailed March 22. She reached Trieste May 3, having been towed by the Congress from Gibraltar. She has not returned.

The Kansas, on special service connected with the Nicaragua survey, left Hampton Roads December 3, 1872, and arrived off Greytown December 20. She returned to New York from this service July 23, 1873. While on the Central American coast she was frequently at Aspinwall, protecting American interests in that quarter. November 14 she sailed from New York for Santiago de Cuba.

The Portsmouth, specially fitted out for surveying service in the Pacific, sailed from New York late in December, 1872, and arrived at Talcahuano, Chili, March 20, 1873. She proceeded thence to Valparaiso and Honolulu, arriving at the latter port May 23. She has been engaged in surveying and in examining reported dangers in the Pacific, making Honolulu her headquarters. She was at that port October 7, and expected to sail, October 9, on a surveying cruise.

The Constellation, with the cadet-midshipmen on board, left Annapolis, June 9, on a practice-cruise; passed the capes of the Chesapeake June 20, and came to anchor off Newport, R. I., July 29. She passed the remainder of the summer in that vicinity and in the adjacent waters of Long Island Sound and Gardiner's Bay, and, September 6, sailed for the Chesapeake. She reached the inside of the capes September 9, and on the 29th of that month returned to the Academy.

The Fortune was commissioned at the Washington navy-yard June 20, and on the 24th proceeded to Annapolis, where the cadet-engineers were received on board, and left again July 5. She visited Wilmington, Del., Chester, Philadelphia, New York, Cold Spring, West Point, and Boston, and returned to Annapolis, via Washington, September 27.

The Juniata was put in commission at Boston, February 10, 1873; went around to Newport, and thence to New York, arriving at the latter place May 7. She was assigned to special service in connection with the search for the Polaris, and her movements are detailed in the Secretary's report. November 19 she sailed from New York for Cuba.

The Ossipee was commissioned at New York October 10, 1873; left there, November 14, for Newport, thence for Hampton Roads, arriving on the 20th. With the Mahopac in tow, bound to Key West, she passed the capes November 23.

The Mahopac was commissioned at Norfolk, November 21, 1873, and left Hampton Roads on the 20th for Key West.

The Manhattan was commissioned at Philadelphia, November 19, 1873, and in company with the Powhatan started for Key West on the 25th. She returned to Wilmington, after passing the capes of the Delaware, December 1, and sailed again December 3.

The Monongahela was put in commission at Portsmouth, N. H., September 22, 1873; left there, October 2, for Newport, and sailed from the latter place for the Pacific November 12.

The Gettysburg was commissioned at Washington November 6, 1873, taking the place of the Tallapoosa.

The Plata was commissioned at Philadelphia November 22, 1873, and sailed on the 25th for Key West.

The Mayflower sailed from Portsmouth, N. H., November 22, for Boston, New York, Norfolk, and Key West.

The Bluelight, engaged on special service under the United States commissioner on fish and fisheries, left Washington June 29 for the coast of Maine. She returned to Portsmouth, N. H., September 6, and was put out of commission September 15.

REPORT OF BOARD OF VISITORS OF NAVAL ACADEMY.

UNITED STATES NAVAL ACADEMY.
June 2, 1873.

SIR : The Board of Visitors appointed "to attend the Academy during the May examination, for the purpose of witnessing the examination of the graduating and other classes, and of examining into the state of the police, discipline, and the general management of the institution," have the honor to present the following report :

The board entered upon its duties on the morning of May 20, all the members, with a single exception, being present. After the customary formal reception by the Superintendent and officers of the Naval Academy, the board organized by the choice of Rear-Admiral Charles H. Davis, U. S. N., as president, Bvt. Maj. Gen. Joseph J. Reynolds, U. S. A., as vice-president, and William H. Hackett, esq., as secretary.

For the purpose of observing as carefully as possible the stated examinations, the board appointed a standing committee, whose duty it should be to assign the members from day to day to attendance at the various class-rooms. This arrangement secured the presence of from one to three members at each examination, and, on one day, the board in a body attended successively all the examinations in progress. Standing committees were also charged with the duty of examining the general condition and management of the Academy, as respects the grounds and buildings, the system of police and discipline, the course of study and methods of instruction, and such other matters as might from time to time suggest themselves.

These committees examined in detail and with great care the several matters referred to them, and the results of their investigations were in all cases presented to the meetings of the board, and there fully discussed. The board is able to say, therefore, with entire confidence, that its conclusions are based upon as careful observation and reflection as could be bestowed upon so important subjects within the limited time allowed. The Superintendent and his entire corps of assistants placed within reach of the board every possible facility for the performance of the duties assigned to it, and it may be stated, in general, that the present condition of the Academy is in every important respect exceedingly prosperous and satisfactory.

The board is glad to believe that any prejudices against the Academy, which may have formerly existed, have passed away; or that, if they still exist, it is only in cases where the real facts are imperfectly understood.

All the appointments of the place are in excellent order. The grounds are kept in the most neat and tasteful condition ; the arrangements for the various kinds of drill and exercise are admirably adapted to the instruction of the cadets in a knowledge of their duties, as well as to maintain a high standard of physical health ; and the course of study land methods of discipline are thorough and successful.

The suggestions and recommendations that have been agreed upon, to be presented in this report, are accordingly made, not so much as criticisms upon the present organization, as indications of some particular directions in which the system already established may be made stil more successful and efficient. While there have been differences of opinion among the members of the board on some important subjects, the conclusions here presented have been adopted with substantial unanimity, and on one point, at least, there has been a most cordial and emphatic agreement, viz, that the Academy should be supplied with the very best equipment in men and appliances that can be furnished. No economy could be more unwise than that which would withhold from a national institution like this anything that could increase its vigor and efficiency. Whatever the exigencies of the future may require of the military arm of the United States service, it seems inevitable that the Navy should steadily increase in relative importance, both as an arm of defense along our extended coast-lines, and as a means of maintaining our widening intercourse with other parts of the world. It seems the obvious dictate of good judgment, therefore, that the officers who are to be intrusted with the responsible duty of directing this branch of the service should receive the most thorough training, theoretical and practical, that the resources of the country can supply.

In order to present the conclusions of the board as briefly and clearly as possible, they may be grouped under a few distinct headings.

I.—THE GROUNDS AND BUILDINGS.

These, as has been already indicated, are as well kept as could be desired. The chapel, the library, the new mess-hall, and some others of the buildings, are well adapted to the purposes for which they are intended, though it seems desirable, as previous boards have recommended, that the laundry and water-closets should be removed from the basement of the mess-hall, as soon as the purchase of additional ground, for which provision has already been made by a law of Congress, shall be completed. A few additions to the buildings, however, are imperatively needed at once.

1. *A new armory.*—The building now used for this purpose is in every respect unfit. It is so low on the ground that it has been found necessary to overlay a second floor upon the first, in order to keep it approximately dry; but this does not prevent the upper floor from being perceptibly damp for weeks together; moreover, the main walls are so insecure that one of them has to be supported by props, and there is a general appearance of shakiness about the structure, which is only partly concealed by an abundance of paint.

2. The growing wants of the department of steam-enginery require some enlargement of the building occupied by it. This is one of the most important and successful departments of the institution, and the board is unanimously of opinion that its needs should be supplied in the most liberal spirit. It is understood, from plans prepared under the direction of the Navy Department, and submitted to the board, that the necessary room can be secured at a comparatively trifling expense, by making some simple additions to the present building, without essential modification of its plan or appearance.

3. The accommodations for the department of physics and chemistry are altogether insufficient. The instructors in these subjects, and in mechanics, are obliged to use the same lecture-room, which can only be done at great and almost daily inconvenience; and the laboratory for the use of students in analytical chemistry can accommodate only eight at a time. The supply of apparatus, too, is entirely inadequate. The present appropriation for this purpose ($250) ought to be at least quadrupled. A better and better-ventilated lecture-room, a larger and better-equipped chemical laboratory, and a physical laboratory fitted up with an ample supply of the most approved apparatus, are absolutely necessary to save this department from being a discredit to the Academy and the Government.

4. The board emphatically concurs in the recommendation which has been made in former years, that some provision be made for a swimming-school. The importance of this seems sufficiently obvious, without a word of argument.

5. The board is also of opinion that the proposed purchase of additional grounds, which has already been referred to, is a measure of importance to the Academy, if it can be consummated on reasonable terms. An undesirable neighborhood will thereby be removed from immediate proximity to the Academy, the water-front will be considerably extended, and room will be secured for marine barracks, in place of the present structures, which are entirely unfit for the purpose, with other buildings that may from time to time be required.

II.—THE COURSE OF STUDY.

The board has been most favorably impressed with the excellence of the methods of instruction here pursued, and the satisfactory result attained. The whole course of study is arranged with a view of securing one practical end, the training of good officers for the Navy. The academic studies are accordingly taught with constant reference to their applications, and the practical exercises are conducted as models of practice in actual service, as well as illustrations of fundamental principles.

No one can examine the matter carefully without a high appreciation of the work that the Academy is doing, both in the way of furnishing the service with a body of accomplished and efficient naval officers, and of developing, with remarkable success, a system of education which combines in due proportion the theoretical and the practical.

An educated man, as the phrase ordinarily goes, may not be a good officer, and a good officer is not necessarily an educated man; but the graduates of the Naval Academy can scarcely fail to be both. In a few particulars the board is of opinion that the course of study, without the introduction of any radical changes, might be considerably improved.

1. It is found, for instance, that a good many cadets drop out of the Academy at the close of the first year, from inability to keep up with their class. During the last ten years about fourteen hundred cadets have entered the Academy, five hundred of whom have left before the middle of the second year. These are boys who are not thoroughly grounded in a knowledge of arithmetic, or have not studied algebra at all before entering the Academy. The rule seems to be that boys who are not well prepared in these two points are unable to go on successfully with the studies laid down for the first year (fourth class) of the course in the Academy. It would be, on every account, undesirable to lessen the amount or lower the standard of work required in that year; and the board therefore strongly recommends that arithmetic, elementary algebra, English grammar, and descriptive geography be added to the requirements for admission. This would but slightly raise the nominal standard; and it would exclude very few, if any, who are likely to maintain a respectable standing in the course as now organized. As the case now is, the requirements for admission, annually announced, are a standing invitation to boys to enter the Academy whose preparatory training is not such as to make it probable that they can succeed in completing the course. A wrong is thus done to the Government as well as to the individual concerned, and the board proposes only that the full amount of preparation which is really needed shall be distinctly stated.

2. The board also recommends that cadets be appointed a full year in advance, whenever it is possible, as is now done at the West Point Academy. This would enable candidates to make their preparations more thorough, and thus greatly diminish the risk of subsequent failure and mortification.

3. By a law of Congress, enacted at its last session, it is provided that the course of study for the class entering the Academy in 1873, and subsequently, shall be six years instead of four. It has been thought

by some that the two additional years should be spent in service at sea: but, after a careful consideration of the subject, this board earnestly recommends that one of the years be spent in additional study at the Academy. The principal reason for this recommendation is, that the cadet-midshipmen are already receiving about three months of sea-practice every year, and therefore do not, in the opinion of those best qualified to judge, need so much additional service before entering the grade of midshipmen: while there are many subjects, either altogether omitted from the present course, or but little studied, in which more instruction is very desirable. The amount of French and Spanish now taught is insufficient. It is important that the knowledge of modern languages, once acquired, should be retained and increased by constant use, either by continuing the instruction through every year of the course, or by pursuing, in text-books written in these languages, some of the subjects taught in the higher classes. Much more time should be devoted also to the study of international law with a more suitable text-book than Kent's first nine Lectures' and constitutional law. In ethics no instruction whatever has been given for some time past, and in order to remedy this deficiency, as it is understood the Superintendent proposes to do the coming year, some other study of perhaps equal importance must be displaced. The same may be said respecting the law of naval courts martial, which now is not studied at all, but the importance of which, to the complete education of a naval officer, is obvious. The elements of mental science, logic, and political economy ought also to be studied; and more time is needed for history in general, and military and naval history in particular. It is, however, plainly impossible to introduce these various subjects, or any of them, into a course already overcrowded. The only resource is, either to omit some important subjects that are now pursued, or else to extend the time. The board carefully considered the former alternative, with a particular view to the question whether some portion of the studies in higher mathematics might be spared or be dropped from the course. The result of the examination was, however, that a man in so composed that it is rather than less, time could be profitably devoted to these studies, and that no time could be cut out without seriously injuring the success and usefulness of the rest of the system. The whole science of naval the department of navigation is based in the greater part of the higher mathematics; so that to spare any time from that branch would be prejudicial to the success of the rest with great loss of ...

tion of the Secretary of the Navy.   The progress made in steam-enginery during the last fifteen years is such that the books now in use are no longer sufficient, and since it is found necessary for the Government to train up its own engineers, it seems desirable that they be instructed in the most approved methods.

5. There is one other recommendation respecting the organization of the Academy which the members of the board agree in considering of greater importance, if possible, than any of those already presented. It is that the heads of academic departments should be placed upon a more permanent footing, and so liberally remunerated that the very best talent in the country could be secured for these places. The heads of such departments as mathematics, chemistry, physics, mechanics, astronomy, international and constitutional law, and others that may perhaps be designated as departments of research, ought to be men of the greatest ability and eminence, whose lives are devoted to the sole business of investigating and teaching their particular subjects. In these days of rapid advancement in every branch of scientific knowledge, no man, however able, can keep fully abreast of discovery, even in his own field, if he is liable to alternations of service on sea and on land. The board wishes distinctly to say that these remarks are intended to be the statement of a general principle, and not, in any sense, a criticism on the ability or success of the gentlemen now holding these positions in the Academy. All of them are believed to be doing their work well, and some of them with exceptional excellence and success. But these would probably be the first to admit that their work would be more satisfactory to themselves and more productive of large results, if it were the pursuit of a life-time rather than a brief tour of duty. It is probably no exaggeration of the truth to say that the one measure which more than any other would enhance the success of the Academy, would be the establishment of a few permanent, well-paid professorships, capable of attracting the very highest order of talent and service.

6. With respect to religious instruction, the condition of the Academy is not all that could be desired. The subject has been considered by the board with the most serious attention; and while they are free to admit the serious difficulties involved in it, a large majority believe that a decided improvement might be effected by a change in the method of appointing the chaplain. It is recommended that, instead of detailing a naval chaplain for a brief term of duty at the Academy, a clergyman be selected, well known for learning, ability, eloquence, and piety, and with special fitness for wielding an influence over young men, and that the position be placed by law upon such a footing as will secure for it men possessing these qualifications in the highest degree.

III.—SANITARY CONDITION.—DISCIPLINE AND DRILL.

With respect to the general condition of the Academy in the matters of health, police, discipline, and drill, the board need only repeat the emphatic commendation already expressed. The health of the cadets is probably as good as that of any similar body of young men in the world. During the last year there have been no deaths, and but very little sickness. The various kinds of exercise secure the double result of preserving a robust physical condition and furnishing a practical training-school. The prescribed routine could hardly be improved upon in these particulars, and every visitor is struck with the appearance of manly vigor and self-possession which the cadets, singly and collectively, present. The board witnessed exercises in nearly every important kind of military and naval drill with very great gratification. The skill, and promptness, and accuracy exhibited were alike creditable to the intelligence of the young men and the faithfulness of their instructors.

The discipline of the Academy, on which all else depends, is in a state of efficiency which leaves nothing to be desired. It is scarcely possible to speak in too high terms of the patience, fidelity, and success with which Superintendent Worden discharges the laborious duties of his position. There seems to be no detail of administration which does not pass under his watchful and careful eye, and nothing which affects the welfare of the institution is too insignificant to enlist his attention. There is in the management of affairs a judicious blending of strictness with a kindly interest in the personal welfare of the cadets, which results in securing a very high standard of discipline and efficiency.

The board has been especially impressed with the earnestness with which the Superintendent has appealed to the honorable instincts of young men, in a series of orders directed against various petty barbarisms, at the same time that he has kindly, but firmly, warned them of the inevitable consequences of a continued course of ill-conduct.

The best commentary on the wisdom of the methods adopted is to be found in the present state of the institution, as it has been already described.

It would be unjust not to mention, in this connection, the ability and faithfulness of the Superintendent's adjutants, the commandant of midshipmen, the heads of departments, and their various assistants. They constitute together a body of men who reflect credit upon the institution and the Government. Some of them bear honored wounds, and others the seeds of disease contracted amid the hardships and perils of an exacting and laborious service. But it may be doubted whether the service which they are now rendering to the country is less important or valuable than that which they were lately called upon to perform amid the sterner scenes of actual war.

In conclusion, the board desires to express its conviction that the more generally the people of the country become acquainted with the affairs of the Naval Academy the more cordially will they insist upon maintaining it at the highest possible standard; and in order that it may be habitually and directly brought to the attention of their representatives, it is respectfully suggested that it might be well to have each House of Congress represented in the Board of Visitors.

It is recommended, also, that the regulations of the Academy relating to police and discipline be carefully revised, and then enacted into law by Congress.

All of which is respectfully submitted.

C. H. DAVIS,
Rear-Admiral and President.
J. J. REYNOLDS,
Col. Third Cav., Bvt. Maj. Gen., Vice President.
ALVAH SABIN, *Vermont.*
DAVID A. WALLACE, *Illinois.*
G. W. ATHERTON, *New Jersey.*
THOMAS H. DUDLEY, *New Jersey.*
WILLIAM H. HACKETT, *New Hampshire.*
CHAS. G. ROGERS, *Tennessee.*
ALVA A. KNIGHT, *Florida.*
DON A. PARDEE, *Louisiana.*
GEO. HENRY PREBLE,
Captain, United States Navy.
CHARLES H. BAKER,
Chief Engineer, United States Navy.

UNITED STATES NAVAL ACADEMY,
Annapolis, Md., October 27, 1873.

SIR: I have the honor to submit the annual report of the Superintendent of the Naval Academy.

The estimates for the support of this institution for the fiscal year ending June 30, 1875, were transmitted to the Department on the 27th August last.

The number of students in the several classes at the beginning of the academic year 1872-'73 was 262, viz: 233 cadet-midshipmen; 35 cadet-engineers, and 4 Japanese students, as follows:

		Members.
Cadet-midshipmen—first class	29	
second class	34	
third class	49	
fourth class	115	
		227
Cadet-engineers—first class	15	
second class	20	
		35
Total		262

The course of studies prescribed by the regulations was pursued as usual until the 20th day of May last, when the annual examination of the several classes commenced, and was continued, in the presence of the Board of Visitors, until the 31st of the same month, when it was concluded.

The first, or graduating, class of cadet-midshipmen was composed of 20 members, including Zuu Zow Matzmulla, the first Japanese student educated under the resolution of the Senate and House of Representatives of the United States, approved July 27, 1868. These gentlemen received their certificates of graduation as midshipmen on the 31st of May. The first class of cadet-engineers, 5 in number, also received their certificates of graduation at the same time, when they were all detached from the Academy, with orders to report their respective places of residence to the chief of the Bureau of Navigation and officer of detail, Washington, D. C.

Mr. Zuu Zow Matzmulla, the Japanese student, was then detached with instructions to proceed to Washington and report to the honorable the Secretary of the Navy for transfer to the authorities of the empire of Japan.

On June 2, all of the members of the present second class of cadet-midshipmen were, under the regulations, granted leave of absence, and on the 4th, the several classes, viz, late second and now first class, 29 members; late fourth and now third class, 56 members; and the transfers to the present fourth class, 16 members, making a total of 101 cadet-midshipmen, were embarked for the practice-cruise on the United States ship Constellation, Commander A. P. Cooke, commanding.

The examination of candidates for admission to the Academy as cadet-midshipmen commenced on the 5th of June, when 83 presented themselves for examination, 6 of whom were withdrawn, and 1 left pending the examination, and 32 were rejected by the academic board, and 44 were found duly qualified and admitted.

The Constellation sailed from her anchorage June 9, and from the outer roads on the 12th, touched at Hampton Roads, leaving the capes, crossed the Gulf Stream, and cruised to the westward of the Bermudas; recrossed the Gulf Stream, and cruised north along the coast between

Montauk Point and the capes of the Delaware ; touched at Newport, R. I., cruised in the vicinity and adjacent waters of Long Island Sound and Gardiner's Bay ; from thence sailed for and cruised in Chesapeake Bay, and arrived in Annapolis Roads on the 27th of September.

The steamer Fortune was detailed and fitted at the navy-yard at Washington, D. C., as a practice-vessel for the practical instruction of the cadet-engineers, and being reported ready to receive her officers, I ordered Lieut. Commander Alexander H. McCormick, United States Navy, to the command fo her, and the other officers detailed for her to proceed to Washington and report to the commandant of the navy-yard on the 16th of June, for duty.

The Fortune was put in commission on June 20th, and on the 24th she got under way for and arrived in Annapolis Roads on the 25th. On the 2d of July the cadet-engineers, 18 in number, were embarked, and on the 5th she proceeded on the practice-cruise, touched at Wilmington, Del., Chester and Philadelphia, Pa., New York City, Cold Spring, and West Point, N. Y., Boston and Charlestown, Mass., and at Washington, D. C., on her return. During her stay at these places the cadet-engineers were treated with much consideration, and, in charge of an officer, visited and inspected all the iron-foundries, rolling-mills, machine-shops, steam and marine engine works, as well as the several navy-yards, &c., and arrived in Annapolis Roads on the 27th of September.

The examination of candidates for admission as cadet-engineers commenced on the 15th, and was concluded on the 25th day of September. During that time 48 presented themselves for examination ; 1 was rejected by the medical board, 1 withdrawn pending the examination, and 46 examined, and a report of their proficiency, arranged in order of general merit, was prepared and transmitted to the Department. These young gentlemen were, like the candidates of the last two years, subjected to a thorough competitive examination, but taking into consideration the ages at which they presented themselves, I regret to be compelled to repeat the language of my last two reports, that they did not, on examination, exhibit that proficiency generally which young men of their ages should have acquired. Of the number examined the first 16 were appointed cadet-engineers and received into the Academy on probation.

In this connection I would respectfully recommend that hereafter all the candidates for this corps be required to report on the 15th day of September for examination, instead of the 15th and 25th, as at present prescribed. This would greatly expedite the examination and enable the board to conclude it before the examination of candidates for admission as cadet-midshipmen commenced, and also give to the Department time to appoint the cadet-engineers, and have them here by the 1st day of October of each year.

I beg leave also to state that the experience of the last two years has clearly demonstrated the insufficiency of the time allotted to the course of studies at present prescribed for the classes of cadet-engineers; and, in consideration of the difficulty of obtaining young men duly qualified for admission under the existing regulations, and in order that these students may be given the full advantage of the facilities for instruction offered by the Academy, I recommend that one more academic year be added to the present course of studies now prescribed by law, and that the course be thus modified for three instead of two academic years, as at present.

I would also recommend that a larger and more suitable steamer, of the most approved type of machinery, be detailed for the practical instruction of the cadet-engineers. The Fortune is imperfectly equipped and entirely too small for the accommodation of the classes to be embarked in her.

On the 20th September, the examination of candidates for admission as cadet-midshipmen was renewed; 106 presented themselves for admission, 5 of whom were rejected by the medical board, 51 by the academic board, 1 was withdrawn pending the examination, and 49 were found duly qualified and admitted, making the number found qualified and admitted in June and September, 93, and 1 Japanese student; and the total number of students in the Academy on its re-opening, 276, viz, 236 cadet-midshipmen, 37 cadet-engineers, and 3 Japanese students.

I have also to recommend that hereafter all candidates for admission to the Academy as cadet-midshipmen be required to report for examination between the 5th and 8th of June, and between the 20th and 23d of September, of each year, instead of the 5th and 15th of June, and the 20th and 30th of September, as at present prescribed. This would greatly expedite the examination, give ample time for it, and enable the academic board to conclude it, and be ready, on the arrival of the practice-ship from her summer cruise, to take up and conclude the re-examination before the beginning of the next academic year, viz, 1st of October.

During the last academic year, five candidates for admission to the United States Marine Corps, as second lieutenants, presented themselves for examination, three of whom were found duly qualified for appointment, and two were rejected under the regulations governing their admission.

That the Department may be fully informed relative to the particulars of the cruise of the Constellation and the Fortune, I transmit herewith copies of the reports of Commander Augustus P. Cooke and Lieut. Commander Alexander H. McCormick, the commanding officers of these vessels.

In conclusion, permit me to refer the Department particularly to that portion of the reports of Commander Cooke and Lieut. Commander McCormick, relative to their officers, and to express my gratification at the able and zealous manner in which they performed their duty, and to reiterate my approval of confining the practice-ships to our own coast, where the students can have greater advantages for practical instruction, rather than sending them on long, and, when the weather is unfavorable, tedious passages, thereby rendering their arrival here by the beginning of the next academic year quite uncertain.

I am, sir, very respectfully, your obedient servant,
JOHN L. WORDEN,
Rear-Admiral, and Supt. Naval Academy.

Hon. GEORGE M. ROBESON,
Secretary of the Navy, Washington, D. C.

BUREAU OF EQUIPMENT AND RECRUITING.

NAVY DEPARTMENT,
BUREAU OF EQUIPMENT AND RECRUITING,
Washington, October 25, 1873.

SIR: I have the honor to submit herewith the annual report of the operations of this bureau, together with the estimates for the fiscal year ending June 30, 1875.

During the past fiscal year 75 vessels have been either partially or wholly equipped at the several navy-yards, at an expenditure, including labor and material, of $832,794.54.

Thirty-seven thousand four hundred forty-five and one-fourth tons of coal have been purchased, at home and abroad, at a cost of $400,071.76, and 200¾ tons of manila hemp have been purchased, costing $72,832.50.

The rope-walk at the Charlestown navy-yard has supplied the wants of the service with hemp and manila rope; 304¾ tons of hemp of both kinds have been manufactured into rope. The bureau expects soon to have the wire-rope machinery in operation, for the manufacture of wire rope.

The equipment-shops at the Washington navy-yard have supplied all the wants of the service for anchors, chains, galleys, &c.

The complement of men allowed (8,500) has not been exceeded within the year. During the summer enlistments fell off and reduced the number of men on hand to 7,500. At present recruiting is more active, and the complement is filling up.

Every year's experience in enlisting men for the naval service makes the difficulty of procuring men the more apparent, and the necessity of providing by law for the establishment of a system of apprenticeship adapted to the wants of the Navy more and more requisite.

The former recommendations of the bureau as to furnishing enlisted men with an outfit on entering the service, and as to apprehending deserters after the time of their enlistment has expired, and causing them to serve out their lost time, as is the case in the Army, are respectively renewed.

I have the honor to be, very respectfully, your obedient servant,
WM. REYNOLDS,
Chief of Bureau.

Hon. Geo. M. Robeson,
Secretary of the Navy.

BUREAU OF YARDS AND DOCKS.

Bureau of Yards and Docks, Navy Department,
Washington, D. C., November 13, 1873.

Sir: I have the honor to submit the annual report of the Bureau of Yards and Docks, with estimates for improvements, repairs, and contingent expenses for the next fiscal year.

I beg leave to renew the recommendations offered in my last annual report, and especially to urge caution should an effort be made to alienate a portion of the navy-yard at New York. It is our most valuable navy-yard, admirably placed, and our great resource in time of war. Its marsh-lands are being rapidly filled up, without cost to the Government, by private persons using them as a dumping-ground for the earth taken from the excavations of the city, and I trust that no heed may be given to the speculators who approach Congress with specious recommendations, hoping to make their profit out of the sale of land invaluable to the Navy.

At Philadelphia, in obedience to the will of Congress, a large quantity of material has been removed from the old navy-yard to the new one at League Island; the cannon, the shot and shells, the anchors and chain-cables, and a portion of the timber, are already transferred; the foundation of the great iron-plating shop for construction is in progress, and the large and carefully-built store-house, workshop, and machine-shop for yards and docks are nearly completed.

An area equal to that of the old navy-yard has been filled and raised to the permanent grade adopted for the new yard.

No difficulty is found in securing a perfectly solid foundation for the new buildings at a moderate cost, and if Congress will have the old yard carefully valued, and appropriate a sum equal to this value to be expended in renewing on League Island the present establishment at Philadelphia, the old yard might soon be abandoned to its purchasers and the Treasury re-imbursed for the money advanced.

Since my last annual report I have carefully examined the navy-yard at Mare Island, and I beg to renew the statements and recommendations I made in my report of last year.

It is of especial importance that liberal appropriation should be made for the quay-wall on the water-front, not only to afford ample wharf-room for our ships, but to prevent the filling of the channel by mud.

A clear, unbroken quay-wall, carefully placed, will cause the tide to scour the navy-yard front, and thus prevent the deposit of earth now so fruitful of mischief and expense.

The system of hydraulic mining prevalent in California has loaded the rivers with earth, and has greatly increased the mud-deposit on our water-front.

The excavation of the dry-dock has been nearly completed, and the laying of masonry is about to begin.

A board of civil engineers is now in session at Mare Island, studying the most economical and best plan for developing and improving the resources of this admirable site for our great Pacific navy-yard.

In February last a board, of which Rear-Admiral John Rodgers was the senior member, made a careful examination of the navy-yard at Pensacola, and strongly recommended that some of the buildings destroyed during the war should be rebuilt, and that the navy-yard should not be removed from its old site. This yard would be of great importance in the event of our needing a large squadron in the Gulf of Mexico or West Indies, and I concur in the recommendations of the board, and respectfully urge that a liberal appropriation be made to put the navy-yard in good working order as a second-class yard.

A proper naval prison at one of our navy-yards is greatly needed. Our sailors and marines under sentence of courts-martial are crowded into cells at the marine barracks in a manner contrary to the humane spirit of the age, and ruinous to that hope of reform which well-regulated prisons encourage. Two men are of necessity placed in a cell not large enough for one, badly ventilated and drained, and generally insecure. Such confinement produces indecency and vicious habits, and I cannot too strongly urge an ample appropriation to remedy such a crying evil.

Our prisoners now pass their time in wretched idleness, but, under a better system, their labor would provide for their support, and perhaps lead to reformation. Lieutenant-Colonel Broome, of the Marines, has, under the direction of this bureau, examined the prisons of the Northern States, and has carefully and intelligently stated the need of the Navy in this particular, and the best method of meeting it. His excellent report is already in your hands.

* * * * *

EMERGENCIES AT NAVAL STATIONS.

Under this appropriation, as hereinbefore stated, there has been expended at the several navy-yards and stations, during the fiscal year ending 30th June, 1873, the sum of $27,963.12. These expenditures were made at Kittery, Charlestown, Brooklyn, Washington, Norfolk, Pensacola, Mare Island, League Island, Mound City, and New Orleans, for objects of pressing necessity, and for which no special appropriation had been made.

Estimates are submitted for the fiscal year ending 30th June, 1875, for "contingent at naval stations," which is the title given by Congress to this appropriation, for the sum of $50,000.

"GENERAL MAINTENANCE OF YARDS AND DOCKS."

The objects coming under this head were formerly estimated for under the head of "contingent," but at the last session of Congress the heading was changed to the present more appropriate one.

The amount expended at the several navy-yards and stations, under the head of "contingent," during the fiscal year ending the 30th June, 1873, is $879,528.75.

Estimates are submitted for the fiscal year ending 30th June, 1875, for necessary expenses for the same objects, but coming under the head of "general maintenance of yards and docks," amounting to $860,000.

I am, sir, very respectfully, your obedient servant,

C. R. P. RODGERS,
Chief of Bureau.

Hon. GEO. M. ROBESON,
Secretary of the Navy, Washington, D. C.

BUREAU OF NAVIGATION.

NAVY DEPARTMENT,
Bureau of Navigation, October 25, 1873.

SIR : I have the honor to submit the following report of the Bureau of Navigation for the past year, together with estimates for its support, and for the expenditures that will probably be required in that division of the naval service committed to its immediate charge, for the fiscal year ending June 30, 1875. Included in this report, and transmitted herewith, are the reports and estimates of the several officers under its cognizance.

NAVIGATION.

The Laurent octant, of which mention was made in my previous report as having been deemed worthy of trial, has been found sufficiently useful in night observations to warrant its being supplied to all our sea-going ships-of-war.

The errors of the compass, due to a ship's iron, have been found of sufficient importance, even on board our wooden ships, to receive special attention in the Navy for some time past; but when the ship, in addition to the iron carried in her machinery and equipment, is iron-built, the importance of this subject becomes specially manifest. In reality, the adaptation and treatment of the marine compass on board all our modern ships, whether of the Navy or of the merchant-service; the means for most readily finding the compass-errors, and of applying correctors whenever deemed expedient; and the study of the ship's magnetic characteristics, with the practical inferences deducible therefrom, are questions which had assumed so great importance within a comparatively brief period as to appear to justify, during the past year, bringing the matter to your notice in a special communication, and in recommending that a suitable officer of the Navy be placed in immediate charge of this duty under the supervision of the Bureau. You responded favorably to these suggestions, and detailed Professor B. F. Greene, of the Navy, as superintendent of compasses. Professor Greene, who has been occupied with this work since the 1st of April last, submits a first report of his operations, appended hereto, to which I ask your attention.

HYDROGRAPHY.

Since my last report a considerable extension has been given to hydrographic work in various directions.

The Wyoming, commanded by Commander F. H. Baker, has made a very good running survey of the east coast of Mexico, from the Rio Grande to the mouth of the Coatzacoalcos.

Other vessels have executed partial surveys in the West Indies, and others again on the east coast of South America.

The Portsmouth, commanded by Commander J. S. Skerrett, is now upon her field in the North Pacific Ocean, and has examined all the supposed possible dangers lying between the Sandwich Islands and our west coast. This vessel is now employed to the westward of those islands.

The Narragansett, commanded by Commander George Dewey, has made a good running survey from San Diego to Cape Corrientes, and is now at work within the Gulf of California, upon the completion of which survey she will join the Portsmouth.

All the results of these surveys, when received, are verified at the Hydrographic Office, prepared for publication, and published as rapidly as practicable. A liberal yearly appropriation is necessary to keep this work in progress, and is demanded by every consideration of public interest.

Besides these general surveys, much miscellaneous work is now being done, in special surveys of islands, harbors, and portions of coast-lines, within the limits of the several foreign naval stations, and in ascertaining the positions of reported dangers, or in disproving their existence.

A resolution of Congress, authorizing the employment of a vessel-of-war in making deep-sea soundings in the Pacific Ocean, caused the Department to detail the Tuscarora, commanded by Commander George E. Belknap, for that purpose. Excellent results are being obtained; and, although the season of the year has been unfavorable, soundings of great accuracy appear to have been taken for a distance of one thousand miles, from Puget Sound towards the Aleutian island of Atcha, gradually increasing depths to three statute miles.

The Fortune is being fitted, and is designed to proceed to the West Indies, for the determination of longitudes by means of the telegraphic lines now established, and for other observations in that region, to render the navigation of those waters less dangerous.

The surveys for an interoceanic ship-canal by the Napipi route have been continued to the Pacific during this year, with marked advantage, via the Doguado, one of the streams which form the Napipi. It is supposed that this survey completes the examination of all the water-sheds between Panama and the region lying south and east of that point, embracing all the lines, in fact, that gave promise of a favorable result.

The surveys via Lake Nicaragua for the same object have also been completed, and are, like the other surveys, in a high degree satisfactory.

It is perhaps advisable to advert to the general plan pursued in both surveys, in order to establish the fact that no other lines are as favorable for the construction of a ship-canal, within the limits designated, as those that are indicated. This plan has been to examine, locate geographically, and level up all the water-courses of both coasts, until having arrived at such altitudes and such distances apart of the several water-sheds of the two oceans as would settle the question of practicability of the points examined relatively to those which have been thoroughly surveyed.

The work on these surveys has been extremely laborious, tasking the highest qualities of the officers and men employed; and it is gratifying to this Bureau at their close to call officially to your notice the great merits of Commanders T. O. Selfridge and Edward P. Lull, the officers in charge of these two surveys, and the junior officers, who worked with great zeal and intelligence.

In connection with these surveys, it is proper to add that, on the east coast, the Kansas, Commander Allen V. Reed, was employed in aiding the survey under Commander E. P. Lull, and on the Pacific side, the Tuscarora, commanded by Commander George E. Belknap, aided the party under Commander T. O. Selfridge, furnishing a base of supplies, and men to assist in the field and execute the necessary hydrographic work.

The appended report of the Hydrographer gives special information in relation to the several subjects connected with the publication of charts, sailing-directions in various parts of the world, corrected lighthouse lists, and tide-tables. A careful examination of it will show how actively the Hydrographic Office has been employed, and how useful it will be to our commerce, as its publications become more numerous.

In connection with this Office it may be well to state that the appropriations asked for are, in part, rather apparent than real, considered as a tax upon the Treasury, since all the moneys received from the sale of charts and other hydrographic publications revert to the Treasury.

I beg leave again to invite your attention to the increasing necessity of a more suitable building for the Hydrographic Office than the one now occupied. Aside from the insufficiency of room in the present building, there is constant danger of losing by fire the very valuable original data already collected, and steadily increasing, which could not be replaced in case of accident but by the same labor and expense through which they were obtained.

NAVAL OBSERVATORY.

By the report of the Superintendent of the Naval Observatory, it will be seen that there has been no cessation in the efforts of the superintendent and other officers to increase its usefulness and maintain its position. The appendices of the late volumes fill up the gaps of hitherto unreduced and unpublished observations in years past, and bring up the work of the Observatory nearly to date. The officers of the Observatory, with commendable zeal, have, in addition to their routine work, devoted much time to the details of the preparation for the observations of the approaching transit of Venus; some of their number forming the majority of the commission authorized by Congress for that purpose. The preparatory work for making the observations is, in fact, well-nigh complete.

The large dome of the great equatorial telescope is completed, and ready for the instrument, which will probably be mounted during the month of October, thus supplying one of the greatest wants of the Observatory, and making it an institution deserving the continued fostering care of the Department.

NAUTICAL ALMANAC.

The report of the Superintendent of the Nautical Almanac sets forth the progress of the work under his charge.

It will be seen that the larger Ephemeris, which includes that computed for the meridian of Washington, meets with an increasing demand from all parts of the United States. More than 1,400 copies have been required for sale and distribution during the past year. Of the part for navigators, comprising that computed for the meridian of Greenwich, more than 4,000 copies have been sold.

The Nautical Almanac is now well up to more than three years in advance of date of publication.

NAVY-SIGNALS.

The International Signal-Code, of which mention was made in my report of last year as being in course of publication by this Bureau, has been stereotyped, and a limited edition printed, which is now in the hands of the binder. These books, after supplying the Navy with a sufficient number of copies for its own use, will be placed on sale in the principal nautical stores of the maritime ports for the use of such of our merchantmen as may desire to have the code at the mere cost of paper, printing, and binding. It is to be hoped that the masters of our merchant-ships will provide themselves with copies of this book, and with the necessary signal-flags, to enable them to hold communication, not only with the Navy and coast-stations of the United States, but, in time of need, with the ships and signal-stations of other maritime countries.

A new tactical signal-book for the Navy has been prepared, and is now ready for publication, requiring no distinctive flag for its use. As soon as practicable another signal-book for general service will be prepared to replace that now in use. In connection with this subject, it may be added that a key has been arranged for use, whenever desired, which will render the acquisition of our signal-books of no value to an enemy if it should ever fall into his hands.

The Army-signal method, admirable as it is for communicating with one or more parties in front, is of doubtful value in naval tactics, since it will often require to be read properly when seen from all quarters at the same time. In view of this, experiments are in progress for the use of chronosemic signals. The flash system, also, is under investigation. In the mean time the use of the Coston night-signals and of the day-flags will be regarded as in general sufficient for tactical purposes, employing the Army method as usual whenever specially available.

I am, sir, very respectfully, your obedient servant,

DANIEL AMMEN,
Chief of Bureau of Navigation.

Hon. GEO. M. ROBESON,
Secretary of the Navy.

BUREAU OF ORDNANCE.

BUREAU OF ORDNANCE, NAVY DEPARTMENT,
November 1, 1873.

SIR: I have the honor to submit the annual report of this Bureau, with accompanying estimates for the fiscal year ending June 30, 1875.

While engaged in the ordinary duties of preparing ships for sea-service, supplying their requisitions while abroad, and preserving the public property under its charge, the Bureau has not been unmindful of the very important questions connected with the armament of ships of war, nor of new means for offense and defense, in order that we may keep pace with the work of other nations.

The appropriations for experimental purposes were so far limited as to prevent the Bureau from making full investigation of many devices and theories which have either originated here, or were brought to public attention abroad.

A very large amount of information, nevertheless, has been collected, and arranged for future reference whenever opportunities may be afforded for experiment; and within the scope of the expenditures allowed by Congress much has been done in the way of preliminary inquiry.

The small battery near Annapolis is gradually being brought into working order, and during the next season will be in readiness for efficient experimental work.

It has been supplied with the best apparatus for observing ranges and velocities; it can also afford heavy practice against armor-plating, when required.

The solution of the powder question in respect to the relation of velocities to pressures, first prominently brought forward by General Rodman, remains the most important, and therefore receives special attention. It is one in which theories are of no avail. Experiment alone can determine the qualities required in different guns, and I have pleasure in informing the Department that the most satisfactory results have been obtained in this direction.

While seeking to obtain the highest velocity due to a given charge of powder, care must be taken to reduce to a safe limit the rupturing force, and to make them uniform in their action. To this end a series of experiments in the manufacture of powder, particularly the large-grained for heavy cannon, were instituted by my predecessor, and continued under my direction, at the Annapolis battery, in conjunction with the mills of the Messrs. Dupont, near Wilmington, Del. These have enabled us thus far to produce a powder which gives with substantial uniformity in the 15-inch a velocity of 1,800 feet, with a pressure of not more than 30,000 pounds per square inch upon the bore of the gun. These experiments have not only shown that the size of the grains should vary with the caliber, but have determined the limits of density, and have shown the importance of certain details in the manufacture hitherto neglected. This improvement upon the old manufacture may be understood from the fact that the samples of a lot of mammoth-grain powder (5 barrels taken indiscriminately from 1,000) fired July 8, 1872, gave (in charges of 100 pounds) irregular velocities and pressures, respectively, of 1,468 feet by 31,000 pounds; 1,500 feet by 57,500 pounds; 1,504 feet by 43,500 pounds, &c.

The effect of such variable propelling forces and strains upon the ranges and endurance of cannon may be readily imagined. They are extremely prejudicial to guns of any kind, but particularly dangerous to the cast-iron ordnance of our Navy. Wherefore it may be said that their safety is insured proportionately with the uniformity attained in the action of the powder used in them; the object being high velocities and low pressures. The best results are obtained with grains of definite form, regular surface, and uniform density. A simple method of securing this, which I proposed, has been adopted. Charges made of these hexagonal grains, weighing 100 pounds, were fired from a 15-inch smooth-bore gun, on the 20th of August, 1872. They gave velocities and pressures, respectively, of 1,644 feet by 28,500 pounds; 1,635 feet by

32,500 pounds, and 1,611 feet by 32,000 pounds. In the solution of this important question a friendly rivalry is maintained by the Army authorities, an example of which is shown in the following extract from an official report just made, and kindly sent me by the Chief of Ordnance. In this instance a 12-inch cast-iron rifle was used in firing the hexagonal grains.

*   *   *   *   *   *   *

In connection with the work upon powder for large cannon, I have also instituted experiments with the finer grains for the metallic cartridges of small-arms. In these experiments are embraced the details relating to the development of a perfected system of ammunition for the breech-loading small-arms of the Navy, and to serve also for the Gatling guns, which now form part of the equipment. The failures experienced by our seamen and marines, under very trying circumstances, in the Corea, from defective ammunition, drew attention to the absolute necessity of having a cartridge upon the keeping-qualities of which, in the moist and heated atmosphere of a ship's hold in tropical climates, the utmost reliance could be placed.

To this end my predecessor, Admiral Case, directed a searching examination of the subject to be made without delay, and from various specimens of cartridges, selected the solid-head cases, made by the United States Cartridge Company, at Lowell, Mass., for trial; not only because they exhibited excellent workmanship, but that they seemed to have the best method of reloading, an essential element in naval small-arm ammunition. With the limited quantity required for naval purposes, this Bureau does not consider it expedient to set up machinery for its manufacture, but prefers to rely on the competition of private establishments. Therefore it detailed an officer to maintain a special supervision and inspection of the work in every stage of its progress, from the preparation of the sheets of metal to the finished cartridge, ready for service. This duty has been performed in the most satisfactory manner, the people of the factory aiding the Bureau with signal ability; and the success of these joint efforts was shown in some recent practice made from a Gatling gun, during which 100,000 of these cartridges, brass cases, with solid heads, containing 70 grains of powder and a bullet of 450 grains, were fired with the following results:

Failed to extract after the cartridge exploded   0
Burst heads..   0
Failed to explode on first effort, and from all causes...........................   46

In no instance was there an escape of gas in the rear.

During the whole of the trial the gun was not impeded by any failure of a cartridge. On the first day 4,000 cartridges were fired with extreme rapidity, in 15' 8"; and on the second day, 60,000 in succession, without stopping to clean the gun. After the sixty thousandth round no appreciable difference was observed in the working of the gun, nor in its ability to deliver its fire with certainty and satisfactory accuracy. Cartridge-cases which had been reloaded 100 times each were found to be in excellent condition.

It will be observed that the percentage of failures to explode is extremely small; and no heads were burst; nor did any cartridge fail to extract, which is the most important element in a metallic case required for use in both the rifle and Gatling gun.

THE GATLING GUN

Exhibited qualities of precision, rapidity of fire, and endurance exceedingly remarkable. So much has been said concerning these pieces that it would be idle to repeat the details. . The general opinion among ordnance men is, that it will never entirely supplant the guns of light batteries, nor the boat-howitzers of the Navy. As an auxiliary, however, to the latter on board ship, and in dangerous boat operations, such as disembarking or embarking bodies of men in the face of an enemy, its value cannot be overestimated.

During the experiment at Annapolis, above recited, several modifications in the feed-drums, or cases, were suggested, by which the rapid delivery of the cartridges in firing might be facilitated. These will be supplied as soon as they can be made, and then tested in service.

In the artillery operations of the Franco-German war, breech-loading rifled field-pieces were used by the latter in all the battles which occurred; and there is little doubt of their having performed an important part in every engagement in which they were brought into play.

Whether, under similar circumstances, an equal number of muzzle-loaders, properly served, might not have done as well, is perhaps an open question. It is sufficiently obvious, however, that there are many advantages peculiar to breech-loaders which warrant their use in naval light artillery, as well as for heavy guns of a battery. Therefore the Bureau is now engaged in preparing for experimental firing two guns, both intended to use metallic cartridge-cases, which, in its judgment, are preferable for naval guns of small caliber. One of these is to be made after the designs of Mr. B. B. Hotchkiss, of New York, as a gun of the kind has already been subjected to trials in France with satisfactory results.

The advantage of using a cartridge-case lies in having a gas-check renewable at every round; and in the guns in question the arrangements of the breech for loading, closing, and extracting the empty cases are very simple.

TORPEDO STATION.

The report of examination of officers under instructions in torpedo service at Newport, made in compliance with the Department's orders, of date the 26th June, 1873, is hereto appended. It gives a very clear impression of the condition to which this particular branch of the ordnance service has been brought under the system inaugurated by my predecessor.

The necessity of maintaining this station, and utilizing it as a school in which officers may be trained in the details and exercises of torpedo warfare, needs no argument. It is, however, to be regretted that but one commanding officer has availed himself of its advantages, others being apparently content to take their instruction at second-hand from junior officers under their command. For this reason it has not reached all the development of which it is susceptible. Recent advices from our ships composing the European fleet inform me that no difficulties are experienced in firing improvised torpedoes in rapid succession. The items of appropriations for torpedo purposes are strictly observed in the expenditures.

The more pressing demands of the service, I regret to say, has caused the withdrawal of the Constellation from duty as the ordnance practice-ship.

The Department having discontinued the station of Mound City, Ill., all the ordnance property of any value has been transferred from thence to the navy-yard at Pensacola, where the improvements for ordnance purposes authorized by the act of May, 1872, are very nearly completed.

Finally, the Bureau is about to take the preliminary steps for the removal of the naval magazine in this city, as authorized and appropriated for by Congress at its last session.

The accompanying estimates have been carefully prepared and revised, and are believed to be as low as the necessities of the ordnance service will permit. I may remark, however, that whenever Congress may think proper to authorize the construction of heavy rifled-guns, and their equipment, the Bureau will be prepared with the necessary plans; and the inventive genius and mechanical skill of our people will doubtless be found sufficient for the task.

I have the honor to be, with high respect, your obedient servant,

WILLIAM N. JEFFERS,
Chief of Bureau.

Hon. GEORGE M. ROBESON,
Secretary of the Navy.

BUREAU OF MEDICINE AND SURGERY.

NAVY DEPARTMENT,
Bureau of Medicine and Surgery, November 1, 1873.

SIR : Herewith I have the honor to submit the report of the operations of this Bureau for the past year, with such suggestions as, in my opinion, are calculated to promote the efficiency of the medical service of the Navy.

NAVAL HOSPITALS.

During the summer the usual visit of inspection was made to several of the principal hospitals of the Navy, and to the United States Naval Laboratory, at Brooklyn.

The hospital at Portsmouth, N. H., stands within the navy-yard, and is an old and dilapidated building, in all respects inadequate to the pur poses for which it is used. It should at once be demolished, and a suitable structure erected elsewhere. An advantageous site can be obtained beyond the limits of the yard, and a small though commodious hospital built at a moderate cost. For this object an appropriation of $65,000 would be required. If, on examination, a good site could be found on ground now belonging to the Government, a somewhat smaller sum would suffice.

The Quarantine Hospital on Wood's Island, at the entrance to the harbor of Portsmouth, has been put in good order, at a cost of $2,000, and is now ready for the reception of the class of patients for whom it was designed. Being constructed on a mere ledge of rocks, its situation has been regarded as precarious; and though believed to be well secured by its present fastenings, it has once been nearly washed away, and the occurrence of an unusually heavy gale would excite solicitude for its safety. For this reason, if the preceding suggestion for the erection of a new hospital should be carried into effect, provision, at the same time, might be made, without much if any additional cost, for the construction of a quarantine building at a suitable distance from the former.

The hospital at Chelsea, Mass., having of late years had but little expended on it, except to meet demands of the most pressing kind, is now in want of considerable repairs; but it is not believed that any special appropriation will be needed for this purpose.

The hospital at New York is far from being in as good condition as could be desired. It is the most important establishment of the kind belonging to the Navy, and to maintain its efficiency will soon need general renovation and extensive repairs.

So little has been expended on the Norfolk hospital since its recovery by the Government that it has fallen into a dilapidated state, and is now in urgent need of repairs to preserve it from decay. A year ago a thorough inspection of the building and appendages having been made by a board composed largely of experts, the cost of the repairs found by them to be absolutely necessary was estimated by the civil engineer of the Norfolk navy-yard—himself a member of the board of inspectors—to amount to $32,649.55. Although it is not proposed to recommend the expenditure of so large a sum, this estimate by a practical man who had acquainted himself with the details of the work to be done, is mentioned here to show the actual condition of the establishment, as well as the pressing need of something being done for its preservation.

The hospital at Philadelphia requires no special appropriation, but can be kept in its present condition out of the resources ordinarily at the disposal of the Bureau.

I respectfully beg to renew a suggestion made by my predecessor, in his report of last year, that an appropriation of $50,800 is required to construct surgeon's quarters, drains, roads, water-pipes, &c., at the naval hospital, Mare Island, California.

The hospital at Pensacola, Fla., having been destroyed at the outset of the rebellion, the wants of the station since have been supplied, though to a very imperfect extent, by the use of a small wooden building hastily put up in the navy-yard during the war.

The building has long been felt as an inconvenience by the other departments of the yard, and on every account is unfit to be maintained any longer in its present position. Pensacola is necessarily a most important station in the Gulf of Mexico ; and, from the preponderance of our national interests in the adjacent waters, may at any moment become of still greater importance. A commodious hospital is greatly needed at this point, and I therefore urgently recommend that immediate steps be taken for its erection. For this purpose the sum of $100,000 will be required.

The naval hospital at Yokohama, Japan, being constructed of perishable materials, constantly calls for repairs.

Its enlargement will also soon become a matter of prime necessity. Being designed for the reception of merchant as well as naval seamen, our increasing commercial interests in those seas will not much longer be satisfied with the accommodations it now affords. To meet present, and provide for future wants, the small sum of $5,000 will be required.

Last year the sum of $25,000 was appropriated by Congress for " repairs and improvements of hospitals;" but my own observation, supplemented by the experience of medical officers in charge, convinces me that it was much too small. The sum now estimated for this purpose, though an increase on that of last year, will only be sufficient to execute necessary repairs, and to place these receptacles for the sick and wounded of the Navy on a respectable footing.

Without the least extravagance in fitting up, it is gratifying to know that most of the naval hospitals are now reasonably well provided with appliances for the care and comfort of the sick, so that no unusual expenditure will be required on this head. It is true the grounds and cemeteries of all of them would be improved by an increased expenditure at each, but although in this respect they are far behind our civil establishments, I do not propose applying to this end the money so imperatively needed for objects of greater importance.

NAVAL HOSPITAL FUND.

The financial condition of the Bureau demands, as I no doubt it will receive, your earnest consideration.

The naval-hospital fund, on which dependence is placed for the maintenance of hospitals, is nearly exhausted. The annexed table, marked C, explains its condition. While on October 1, 1872, it amounted to $73,910.04, on October 1, 1873, it had declined to $18,663.35. The difference, $55,246.69, represents the drafts, in excess of newly accruing credits, made on the fund last year for the support of hospitals. As the average annual disbursement for this object during the years 1869-'70-71-'72 was $127,913.95, to maintain the same unavoidable scale of expenditure, an appropriation will hereafter become necessary. To make up this deficiency for the remainder of the present fiscal year, $50,000 will be required, and for next year $100,000.

A few words of explanation will show why the fund has become so greatly reduced. On the 1st of January, 1869, the naval-hospital fund amounted to the large sum of $421,044.12. This, with additions regularly made to it from year to year, under the act of February 26, 1811, would long have been ample for the support of hospitals. During the years 1869, 1870, 1871, 1872, the sum of $217,852.80, belonging to the fund, was applied to the construction of the hospitals at Mare Island and Annapolis. Add to this the amount taken out of it annually for ordinary hospital purposes, and it will be seen that its exhaustion was necessarily only the work of a few years.

MEDICAL CORPS.

The present condition of the medical corps of the Navy is well calculated to excite uneasiness as to its future. There are now thirty vacancies in the grade of assistant surgeons, and resignations are still pending. Already the Bureau finds considerable embarrassment in procuring medical officers for the duty to be performed. But few candidates for admission present themselves before the medical board, and of these not more than one-fourth are found qualified for a commission. This result is not owing to any unusual strictness in the examinations, but to the want of the necessary qualifications on the part of candidates. The proof of this is seen in the written portions of the examination, which the rules of the Department wisely require to be lodged with the Bureau. While it is far from being assumed that boards are infallible, a perusal of this work in most instances carries with it convincing vindication of the soundness of their judgment. The facilities for obtaining medical degrees are so great that the possession of a diploma is no longer, *per se*, an evidence of merit. Hence the duty devolves on the board to exercise great vigilance in scrutinizing the pretensions of those coming before it. Then, too, the emphatic words of the Department, announcing that "the health and lives of the officers and men of the Navy are objects too important to be intrusted to ignorant or incompetent persons," are a continual reminder to the board "not to report favorably upon any case admitting of a reasonable doubt." An obvious reason exists why assistant surgeons in the Navy should possess high qualifications, even higher than medical men practicing on shore. In difficult cases the latter has the privilege of consulting with older and more experienced practitioners, while the former is often left to depend on his own resources alone.

The experience of naval medical boards shows that, although a candidate may not always come up to the established standard, yet he may give such proofs of general aptitude that his failure is obviously more due to want of opportunity than of capacity. If this omission could in any way be supplied, a valuable and much needed acquisition might be secured to the Navy.

This leads me to speak of a want which is beginning to make itself seriously felt throughout the service, viz, of a school of instruction, under the control of the Department, for candidates of the description mentioned, as well as for assistant surgeons preparing for their second examination. The course of instruction would be for a limited period, and should be conducted under the guidance of medical officers of the Navy. The proper place for such a school would be at New York or Philadelphia, where there are large naval and civil hospitals, with museums and facilities for the study of practical anatomy.

England, with all her educational advantages, finds military service so peculiar in its demands on medical men, that at Netley she has laid the foundations of a school through which, hereafter, her army and navy surgeons must pass. A school on a much more moderate scale would suffice for the present wants of our service.

NAVAL LABORATORY.

During the past year the naval laboratory at New York, under its present excellent management, has furnished the Navy with a full stock of the best medicines. In this respect there is little left to be desired. The opportunity which the laboratory would afford of acquiring a practical knowledge of pharmacy, and, to a more limited extent, of chemistry, is an additional reason why the proposed school should be established in New York.

BUREAU PUBLICATIONS.

The publications of the Bureau during the year comprise two volumes of medical and surgical essays; and, though on a modest scale, these have been extensively sought after, and are believed to possess considerable intrinsic value. In addition to these, the Bureau has in course of preparation a comprehensive medical and surgical work, which, when completed, will place within the reach of the profession an amount of valuable information now buried in journals and reports, which hitherto have never seen the light. When the manuscript is ready for the press, a small appropriation will be required to defray the expenses of publication. As the fruits of our enlarged experience during the war can thus be made available to the world at large, it is not doubted that the liberality which, in similar instances, has characterized the action of Congress, will sanction this new contribution to humanity and science.

Respectfully submitted.

J. BEALE,
Chief of Bureau.

BUREAU OF PROVISIONS AND CLOTHING.

BUREAU OF PROVISIONS AND CLOTHING,
November 3, 1873.

SIR: I have the honor to submit herewith estimates marked A, B, C, D, and E, and schedules marked F, G, H, I, and K, for the fiscal year ending June 30, 1875.

I am, very respectfully, your obedient servant,
JAS. H. WATMOUGH,
Acting Paymaster-General, U. S. N.

Hon. GEO. M. ROBESON,
Secretary of the Navy.

BUREAU OF STEAM ENGINEERING.

NAVY DEPARTMENT,
Bureau of Steam Engineering, Washington, 1873.

SIR: In obedience to your order of ———, I have the honor respect-fully to submit the annual report of this Bureau, with estimates for the several navy-yards; for repairs to the machinery of vessels of the Navy afloat; for the repair, preservation, and refitting of such as are required for service at sea; for stores and materials; and for the civil establish-ment in this Bureau and the navy-yards.

MACHINERY REPAIRED, UNDER REPAIR, AND TO BE REPAIRED.

During the year past the machinery of the following named vessels has been repaired and refitted for active service: Monongahela, (2d rate,) at the Kittery Navy-yard; Juinata, (3d rate,) at the Charlestown Navy-yard; Alaska, (2d rate,) Ossipee, (3d rate,) Kansas, (3d rate,) and Tigress, at the Brooklyn Navy-yard; Canandaigua, (2d rate,) Pilgrim, (tug,) and Pinta, (tug,) at the Philadelphia Navy-yard; Gettysburg, (4th rate,) and Fortune, (tug,) at the Washington Navy-yard; Mahopac (iron clad,) Jean Sands, (tug,) and Standish, (tug,) at the Norfolk Navy-yard; Saranac, (2d rate,) Benicia, (2d rate,) and Kearsarge, (3d rate,) at the Mare Island Navy-yard; and the Manhattan, (iron clad,) under con-tract with William Cramp & Sons, Philadelphia.

The Ashuelot, (3d rate,) Monocacy, (3d rate,) Saco, (3d rate,) and Palos, (4th rate,) having been retained on the Asiatic station, extensive repairs were required upon their boilers; which have been executed in the machine shops of private establishments principally at Shanghai, China, and at the Government dock-yard at Yokoska, Japan. Extensive repairs are now required to the boilers of the Iroquois, (3d rate.)

The machinery of the Tennessee, (2d rate,) at New York, under con-tract with John Roach, is very nearly completed, being now ready for trial under steam.

The machinery of the following-named vessels is under repair: Ply-mouth, (2d rate,) Speedwell, (tug,) and Blue Light, (tug,) at Kittery; Franklin, (1st rate,) and Brooklyn, (2d rate,) at Charlestown, and Shaw-mut, (3d rate,) at Washington; Canonicus, (iron clad,) under contract with "The Harlan & Hollingsworth Company," Wilmington, Del.; and the Nahant and Wyandotte (iron-clads,) under contract with the "Dela-ware River Iron Works," while entirely new machinery of the compound type is being constructed for the Nipsic, (3d rate,) under contract with William Wright & Co., Newburgh, N. Y. The machinery of the following-named vessels is to have extensive repairs, and new boilers are to be put on board; Congress, (2d rate,) Lancaster, (2d rate,) Pensacola, (2d rate,) Nyack, (3d rate,) Wyoming, (3d rate,) and Tallapoosa, (4th rate). The hull of the Nevada, (2d rate,) having been condemned the machin-ery has been removed and advertised for sale.

MACHINERY PARTIALLY COMPLETED AND COMPOUND ENGINES.

With reference to the disposition of the machinery on hand stored in the several navy-yards, and that partially completed, (50 inches by 42 inches engines, Quinnebaug class,) the board of engineer officers appointed by the Department, under date of February 8 and May 3 of last year, have submitted their report. This report contains, in addition to conclu-sions and suggestions as to the disposition of the above machinery, the results of thorough investigations of the theory and practice of the

36 Ab

compound engine.   The tables are formed upon data believed to be absolutely reliable.

*   *   *   *   *   *   *

Compound engines have never been used in vessels of the United States Navy, but have, however, been largely introduced in steamers of the commercial marine, and from the most reliable data the Bureau has been able to obtain, the method of using steam of high pressures and expanding in separate cylinders (one or more in number, depending upon the power to be transmitted,) is more economical and advantageous in its *practical* application than by the former method in single-cylindered engines with the pressures heretofore used in such cylinders.

50 INCH BY 42 INCH ENGINES—QUINNEBAUG CLASS.

The uncompleted engines (known as 50 inch by 42 inch) stored at several of the navy-yards, for which an appropriation was made by the last Congress to convert into compound engines and complete for the Marion, Vandalia, Swatara, Quinnebaug, Galena, and others, are well advanced towards completion.   One pair at the navy-yard, Brooklyn, are nearly ready for erection on board the Swatara, and the other pair will be ready for the Quinnebaug in about two months.   The delay in the latter has been in consequence of the failure to obtain iron of the proper quality for construction of the boilers.   At the Charlestown navy-yard two pairs of these engines are nearly ready for erection, one for the Marion at Portsmouth, and the other for the Vandalia at Charlestown.   Designs are in hand for two pairs of the same size and power for the Galena at Norfolk and the Mohican at Mare Island, the boilers for which have already been commenced.

MACHINERY FOR STEAM-VESSELS OF WAR.

The desire of the Department, in constructing the machinery for the new sloops-of-war authorized by act of Congress, approved February 10, 1873, was, that it should be of the very best type and design which the experience and practice of the day should have demonstrated to be the most perfect and best adapted to the propulsion of said vessels; and in order to avail itself of the experience and suggestions of the engineering profession of the entire country, proposals were solicited by advertisement for designs with the necessary specifications for the machinery required in vessels of 620 and 450 tons.   All the information required by the designers in adapting the machinery to the vessel, power to be developed, &c., was furnished by the Bureau to such as applied therefor.   The merits of the plans presented were to be determined by a board of competent engineers, and a reasonable compensation was to be paid for such designs as were adopted, either as a whole or in part.

*   *   *   *   *   *   *

It will thus be seen that no design presented was considered by the board, as a whole, preferable to those emanating from this Bureau, and upon this recommendation the designs of the Bureau were adopted, proposals to construct and erect the machinery and boilers were received, and the same placed under contract as follows: With the

Atlantic Works, Boston, Mass., one pair engines, 800 horse-power, for $175,000; contract dated August 16, 1873.

Atlantic Works, Boston, Mass., one pair engines, 800 horse-power, for $163,000; contract dated August 16, 1873.

James Murphy & Co., New York, one pair engines, 800 horse-power for $175,000; contract dated September 11, 1873.

John Roach, New York, one pair engines, 560 horse-power, for $120,000; contract dated September 11, 1873.

Woodruff Iron Works, Hartford, Conn., one pair engines, 800 horse-power, for $175,000; contract dated October 4, 1873.

A contract was also made with W. Wright & Co., Newburgh, N. Y., for the construction and erection of one pair engines, same design, 800 horse-power, for the Nipsic, for $175,000; contract dated September 11, 1873.

All of the above are to be completed within six months from date of their respective contracts, and erected on board vessels within three months from the time that they shall be notified that the vessel is ready, after such completion.

INTERNAL CORROSION OF NAVAL BOILERS.

By careful analysis made at the naval laboratory, Brooklyn, the rapid corrosion of boilers in steam-vessels of the Navy using surface-condensers, has been found to be caused by oleate of copper formed in the condenser, from which it passes into the boilers, where it is slowly transformed into oleate of iron, deriving the iron from different parts of the boiler with which it comes in contact, and precipitating its copper. The oleate of copper adhering to the iron under the conditions of high pressures and temperatures, the deposition of copper and the absorption of the iron begin.

To prevent this rapid deterioration of steam-boilers, an apparatus has been devised and patented by Mr. W. C. Selden, of New York, which has been introduced in several steamers of the merchant marine. This invention consists in a method of arresting the destructive agents formed in the condenser, and preventing their introduction into the boilers. It has been introduced in a few of the steamers of the Navy, and the reports as to its value and efficiency for the purposes for which applied are highly favorable, promising great success in prolonging the life-time of boilers to which it may be applied.

SCREW-PROPELLERS.

In many cases the original screws of four blades were removed from our naval steamers, and screws of two blades substituted. These changes were determined upon by the Department, with a view to rendering such vessels more efficient while under sail alone, by the supposed decreased resistance opposed to the vessel by screws of two blades, rather than those with four. In all cases where this change has been made, reports are received of the inefficiency of the two-bladed screw, as compared with those of four blades with which these vessels were originally fitted. With equal propelling-surface, no advantage whatever can be derived from using a screw of two instead of four blades, while under sail alone, because, when screws are uncoupled and revolving freely, screws of four blades oppose no greater resistance to the vessel than one of two. When fixed and held stationary, in a vertical position behind the stern-post, the loss of speed due to the resistance of the screw, expressed in percentages of the speed, has been determined by careful experiments to be 18.29 per cent., while the four or two bladed screw revolving freely by pressure of the water gives a resistance of only 9.96 per cent., being very nearly two to one in favor of the revolving screw.

The shocks caused to the vessel by the blades passing the stern-post are diminished as the number of blades is increased; the four-bladed screw producing less vibration in the ship than one of three, and one with three blades less than one with two.

The propelling efficiency of a screw is entirely independent of the number of its blades, but is wholly dependent upon the area, the pitch, the fraction of the pitch used, and the area of the circle described by the blades.

To diminish the shocks and vibration more or less incidental to the use of the screw-propeller, the largest amount of clearance admissible for the screw between the stern and rudder-posts should be given. It is obvious, then, that a port intended for a screw whose area is contained in four blades cannot receive a screw of two blades having the same area, pitch, and fraction of the pitch, for that screw must be just double the length of the former in the line of its axis. Consequently, the two-bladed screws which were substituted for those of four blades were necessarily constructed of less propelling areas, as the port-openings of the vessels could not be enlarged. Hence, the inefficiency of the screws substituted as reported.

ENGINEER FORCE ON SHIPBOARD.

In the quarterly reports of the steam departments of vessels in commission come many complaints of the inefficiency of this force under its present organization. In some cases the machinists have been trustworthy and reliable, but in many others they have been the opposite, leading us to believe that the position given them in the service is not of sufficient importance to induce the class of men that is really needed to perform this duty to accept these rates.

Except in certain cases, *firemen* no longer exist on our vessels of war, and their places are taken by men known as "seamen, engineer force," and "ordinary seamen, engineer force." It was expected that the old firemen would enlist under these new rates and regulations, and at first, to a certain extent they did. That time, however, seems to have passed, and these rates are now frequently given to men who know little or nothing about the duties of firemen. From one ship a statement is made that one of the "ordinary seamen, engineer force," had never been at sea, and that he had never before used firing-tools. A large proportion of these reports make similar statements regarding the inefficiency of these men as firemen, and also the short time they are allowed below in the engineering department, being called on deck for various drills at all hours of the day.

I would respectfully suggest that as many first and second class firemen as would together be able to do duty as oilers and properly fire all the furnaces, be shipped for duty in the steam department only, and that, when steaming, landsmen be taken from deck for coal-heavers.

The estimates for the year will be found in the accompanying papers.

Very respectfully, your obedient servant,

WM. W. W. WOOD,
Chief of Bureau.

Hon. GEO. M. ROBESON,
Secretary of the Navy.

BUREAU OF CONSTRUCTION AND REPAIR.

NAVY DEPARTMENT,
BUREAU OF CONSTRUCTION AND REPAIR,
November 5, 1873.

SIR: I have the honor to forward, in compliance with your instructions, the estimates for appropriations for the annual expenditures for the fiscal year commencing July 1, 1874, coming under the cognizance of the Bureau of Construction and Repair.

Estimates in tables marked A and B are for the pay of employés attached to this Bureau, and at the several navy-yards, as authorized by law.

Estimate in table marked C is for the preservation of vessels on the stocks and in ordinary; purchase of materials and stores of all kinds; labor in navy-yards and on foreign stations; preservation of material; purchase of tools; wear and tear and repair of vessels afloat, and general maintenance of the Navy; incidental expenses and foreign postage.

Estimate in table marked D is for the preservation of live-oak timber upon Government lands reserved for naval purposes.

I beg leave to call your attention to the inclosed list of vessels which have been repaired during the past year, by which it will be seen that a very large number in proportion to the whole are deteriorating, and their days of usefulness are rapidly passing away.

It may be seen by official statistics that the loss of vessels by wear, tear, and the disasters of the sea is equal to 10 per cent. per annum, and that that percentage must be supplied in new vessels every year to keep the original number up.

Although Government vessels are built generally of more durable materials than those of the merchant marine, the causes for deterioration in the former are greater than in those of the latter; consequently, if that percentage is not supplied in new vessels to the Navy, there is either a diminution in the number of vessels, or the number can only be kept up by extensive and costly repairs, the course pursued heretofore. But the expenditure would produce a better result if the number of vessels equal to this loss were constructed every year, as it would afford an opportunity for adopting all the improvements of the day, and thus, in proportion to the number, equal other nations in the efficiency of our Navy.

The eight steam-sloops authorized by act of Congress are in process of construction, and their completion will be hastened with due regard to economy.

The vessels built under the act above named will meet the pressing wants of the Government required of that particular class, but in any emergency, when especially a demand has to be made for redress, or for the immediate protection of the rights of our citizens abroad, naval vessels of more formidable character are required.

A number of the most available iron-clads have been repaired, and are nearly ready for sea, but a number of the most power require very extensive and expensive repairs, which, owing to the limited amount of past appropriations, have not been made. These double-turreted iron-armored vessels should be repaired immediately, as their services may be needed in any sudden emergency.

Large and powerful sea-going iron-clads, whose power for resistance and attack may be graded from their origin to that of the latest and most approved of the present day, seem to form the principal strength of all important maritime nations; and of which those of the monitor type are considered the most formidable, inasmuch as they present less surface for iron plating in proportion to their displacement than that of any other form. Of the above type there are a number which can be improved and repaired, making very efficient vessels, and which, until the power of ordnance, the resistance of practical iron armor, and the effect of the submerged torpedo is fully developed, would, it is thought, be sufficient.

Foreign nations seem to be gradually comprehending the future of a transition of naval iron-clads to the *swift*, invulnerable torpedo-vessel, whose power to destroy any of the most formidable and reliable vessels of war is not disputed.

The torpedo appears to be the most terrible and destructive implement of warfare ever brought into use upon the ocean, and many objections are urged against its barbarous effect, yet there seems to be no difference, in a moral point of view, in sinking a vessel and all on board with it than by the shot of a 20-inch gun, fired behind an invulnerable breastwork.

With the device for using torpedoes, already well demonstrated, a sufficient number of these invulnerable swift vessels need only to be built to carry on a successful warfare with any nation known; and our harbors can easily be protected from an enemy without the expensive fortifications now in process of erection.

Very respectfully, your obedient servant,

I. HANSCOM,
Chief of Bureau.

Hon. GEORGE M. ROBESON,
Secretary of the Navy.

MARINE CORPS.

HEADQUARTERS MARINE CORPS,
Washington, October 28, 1873.

SIR: I have the honor to report that I recently made a thorough inspection of the principal marine stations, and it gave me pleasure to find the troops in a most excellent state of discipline and efficiency, and the public property under their immediate charge in good order and well cared for. The duties of marines at the several navy-yards being chiefly confined to guarding the public property, there is little occasion for that active military duty which perfects the soldier in his profession; yet the equipment, drill, and high state of discipline of the several commands were all that could be desired, and gave assurance that if ever required for more active duty, the country would not be disappointed in them. At the stations where there are permanent barracks, the quarters and grounds were in the best condition, and will require merely the ordinary repairs during the coming year to keep them so. At Annapolis and Pensacola, the troops still occupy temporary buildings belonging to the Navy proper, which have heretofore, perhaps, answered the purpose very well, yet they are but very lightly-built structures, and cannot be much longer used for the purpose without extensive repairs. At Norfolk the men are still quartered on board the old ship St. Lawrence, which vessel I found very much in need of repairs, the decks being in such a leaky condition that, during wet weather, she is a very uncomfortable place of abode for the troops. It will require a considerable outlay to place this vessel in good order, as she requires a general and thorough overhauling. I have annually, for several years past, referred to the want of a good and permanent barracks at this station, and recur to the subject again with the hope the Department may deem it proper to invite the attention of Congress to the subject at the approaching session. This yard has again become one of the principal naval stations, and, in my judgment, should have a large and efficient force of marines at all times in readiness for service in permanent quarters within the yard, or immediately adjacent thereto. It is believed that a good and proper site within the present boundaries could be spared, without interfering with the naval operations of the yard.

The general monthly return of the corps, transmitted to the Department a few days ago, shows that there are at present 2,331 enlisted men in the corps, of which number about 1,000 are on board vessels in commission, and the remainder at the several shore stations. The corps is now 170 men short of its complement, but as recruits are readily obtained, it will soon be up to its authorized strength. Desertions have not been so numerous during the past year as heretofore, yet still a large number leave the service in this manner. The special attention of commanding officers has been called to this subject, and I am satisfied that every effort, consistent with the good of the service, has been made by them to check the evil. Recruiting officers have been enjoined to enlist none but men of good moral character and habits, so far as can be ascertained; the regulations with regard to pay, rations, clothing, &c., have been strictly conformed to, and every possible indulgence granted to the men; yet, notwithstanding all this, the crime still continues painfully frequent, and is beyond any remedy that I can apply.

The public attention seems to have been directed recently to the band of the Marine Corps, and it is now become to be generally regarded as a national band. Being at the seat of Government, it is at all times under the immediate orders of the Department, and its services are called for on all occasions of public ceremony, civic, as well as military. It is, therefore, very desirable that it should be placed upon a more respectable footing as regards its organization, pay, &c. Its numbers should be increased, and the pay fixed at such a rate that the services of first-class musicians could be at all times commanded. In deference, therefore, to the general desire of the public, I cordially commend the subject to the consideration of the Department.

The estimates for the support of the corps for the coming fiscal year have been confined to the absolute wants of the service, and are rather less in amount than those submitted for the last year.

I am, very respectfully, your obedient servant,

J. ZEILIN,
Brigadier-General and Commandant.

Hon. Geo. M. Robeson,
Secretary of the Navy, Washington, D. C.

DARIEN EXPEDITION.

REPORT OF THE SURVEY OF THE ISTHMUS OF DARIEN FOR 1873, BY COMMANDER THOS. O. SELFRIDGE, UNITED STATES NAVY.

Navy-Yard, Boston, *June* 12, 1873.

Sir: I have the honor to lay before you my report of the operations of the expedition under my command for the further survey of the Isthmus of Darien.

In obedience to your order I commenced the necessary preparations in December last; and on the steamer of January 1 "for Aspinwall," were embarked the officers detailed to accompany me: Lieutenants Collins, Eaton, Sullivan, and Assistant Paymaster Ring, with the necessary provisions, material, and instruments. I was myself prevented by illness from leaving for the Isthmus until the following steamer on January 10.

From the reports and maps of the expeditions of 1870 and 1871, it will be seen that the survey of the Darien Isthmus had been completed as far south as the Napipi River, and the appearance of the country in the valley of the latter, as far as our time permitted us to explore, gave the promise of most excellent results. We were encouraged, therefore, in the hope that a more extensive and detailed exploration would justify the time employed, and return a gratifying success.

It will not be out of place here to repeat what has been the general plan of all these surveys, for it is upon this basis that I feel confident in deciding that no portion of Darien possible for a ship-canal has been left unvisited.

The density of the tropical growth is such that any survey cut blindly through its forests would indicate but little knowledge beyond a few hundred feet aside of the surveyor's path. It became a question, then, what course to adopt, and I was led to this plan by the advice of Commodore Ammen, who has given much time and matured thought to the great problem of a ship-canal, and may be regarded as the pioneer of the work which I have been so fortunate as to be called upon to carry out.

With the simple law that water seeks always the lowest level, it follows that, having obtained the elevation of a water-course or river, you have the lowest level of the whole region drained by such rivers. And I would endeavor to particularly impress this feature of these surveys, for upon it rests the assumption that there is no portion of the Darien Isthmus as favorable for the construction of the ship-canal as the valleys of the Napipi and Doguado.

An examination of the general map of the Isthmus will show that the Cordilleras skirt the Atlantic coast as far as Cape Tiburon, and not only from the deck can no pass be seen, but the examination of the little rivers proved conclusively that they drained only the Atlantic slope, a fact that received an additional corroboration from the reports of Indians and traders.

There is but one exception, the Mondinga River, which empties into San Blas Bay at the narrowest part of the Isthmus. Here the Cordilleras recede, and the dividing range being afterward, as appeared, hid by an intervening ridge through which the Mondinga, by a series of falls, had forced itself, seemed very much depressed, and for a long time gave sanguine hopes of success.

The Pacific slope, as shown on the general map of the Isthmus, is drained by two large rivers, the Chucunagua and Bayamo, both rising in a transverse spur of the Cordilleras, and therefore indicating that only in the region adjoining their lower portions could be found a sufficiently low elevation for our purpose. A careful study of the Isthmus map indicates pretty thoroughly those portions where explorations should be conducted, and have all been examined by the spirit-level or carefully recorded barometrical observations.

The Cordilleras, as has been remarked, recede from the Atlantic coast at Cape Tiburon, and running about south-southwest strike the west coast at Cape Marzo, at which point, and as far as Solam Point, the dividing range rises almost perpendicularly from the ocean. The Atrato now becomes the drainer of the eastern slope, as is the river Tuyra that of the western.

It was reasonable to hope that the valley of the latter, with a line leaving it at a moderate elevation and running east so as to strike the great river Atrato at a low level and but a short distance from the sea, would be found adapted to our wants. But such was not the case, owing to no very high elevations, but to the hilly nature of the country bordering upon the Tuyra, which made the estimate of excavation enormous.

Continuing south we come to the valley of the Truando, which, thoroughly surveyed by the combined Army and Navy expeditions of Michler and Craven, required no further explorations.

The next point that presented itself, on account of the very short distance between the Atrato, which is to this point navigable for the largest ships, and the Pacific, was the valley of the Napipi. The severe labors imposed upon the members of the expedition of 1871 left me no time to examine thoroughly this river, though my reconnaissance of it left such favorable impressions that I was not willing to abandon it, and had given me a conviction that here was the favored spot for the location of the great enterprise.

Information received from what was then supposed reliable sources, also pointed to the next tributary south of the Napipi, known as the Bojoya, as being generally lower than the Napipi.

Here, then, lay the work of the expedition of 1873, and its completion would exhaust the profitable region to be explored, and enable me to report to the Department that the surveys of the Darien Isthmus for an interoceanic canal were finally and entirely finished.

As our operations would be carried on from the Pacific shore, you were pleased to detail the Tuscarora, Commander Belknap, to co-operate with me, and he did all in his power to render the expedition successful.

The region to be explored being confined in extent, did not require as large supplies of provisions, materials, and laborers as upon former expeditions, though the work, being of the same nature, was equally harassing. I had supplied generally the same kind of food as before, adding, however, the article of corn-meal put up in tin canisters, which, from its nutritious properties, and the variety of ways in which it could be cooked, even with our rude camp apparatus, was greatly relished, and I can heartily recommend it as a valuable article of food to any future explorers.

I proposed to use the gradienter only upon our surveys. This unique instrument, described in a former report, furnished by Wurdeman, of Washington, proved to be all that I had expected, and enabled us to keep our parties down to the minimum in numbers, a very necessary requirement when every article and every pound of food had to be carried on the backs of our sailors, there being no inhabitants except a few scattering Indians.

It not being possible to obtain any natives at Panama, and it having been represented to me that they could perhaps be procured at a little town called Valle, about thirty miles south of Cupica Bay, at the mouth of a small river called the Bahia, we sailed from Panama on Thursday, January 23. The wet season had proved very late, and up to this time the rains had not entirely ceased.

Valle comprises only a few huts, inhabited by Indians and a few peons who are employed by the head-men of the place, a mulatto named Gonzaloz, in collecting "tagua," or ivory-nuts, which is the sole article exported from the place. It required a great deal of palaver to engage even a man to go with us, the Indians being afraid, and the peons were mostly away; and it was not till Tuesday, the 28th, that we were able to leave, having engaged three negroes, two Indians, and a castaway sailor. No better proof of the general healthiness of this part of the coast can be given, than the fact that this sailor, named Paul, and a German whom we found here, had lived in this place six years and had never had but a single attack of fever.

COMMENCEMENT OF OPERATIONS.

As has been here stated, the objective point of the expedition was the easternmost indentation in the coast line, and it was also desirable to anchor as near as possible to the head-waters of the Bojaya River, the survey of which would occupy the largest portion of our time and force.

The most eastern point was not hard to find, but it was impossible for us to tell which was the nearest position to the Cuia or Bojaya Rivers. On this account we sailed first to Limon Bay, where I landed one of our peons named Alvarez, and his *companero*, with orders to go down the Napipi, then to cross over to the Cuia River and obtain an Indian guide to show them the trail over the hills to the Pacific.

The Tuscarora then steamed about seven miles south of Limon Bay to the most eastern point, near the mouth of a small river called Chiri-Chiri, which gives the name to the bay in which we anchored.

Desiring to lose no time, I sent Lieutenants Eaton and Sullivan out with our best Indian, Richardo, to endeavor to find the trail leading over the divide. Upon their return they reported the Indian had been able to find the trail, though it was very blind, and that in an hour's walk from the ship they had struck the head-waters of a river which I supposed then was the Cuia, but which proved to be the Doguado.

Without waiting any further intelligence from Alvarez, I ordered Lieutenant Collins to organize his party No. 1, consisting of himself and Midshipman Galt, with four sailors and four macheta-men. They landed January 31, with two weeks' provisions, established Camp No. 1 at the mouth of the Chiri-Chiri, and commenced work in the afternoon from bench-mark No. 1, cut on a cocoanut-tree growing on the beach at the edge of high water.

Party No. 1 at the end of the first day struck the foot of the dividing ridge, and the line was run up a very steep spur over the Indian trail, rising in many places at an angle of 70°, and so steep that often the foresights would not be over 5 feet in length.

The following week Camp No. 2 was established on the Doguado, and the provisions and material were transported to it after a great deal of hard work on account of the extreme steepness of the ascent.

The divide between the sea and the Doguado at its highest point was found to be 758 feet, though more to the northward, near the head-waters of the Chiri-Chiri, it was evidently much lower, but we could not level over it on account of the steepness of the hill-sides.

In the mean while Alvarez had returned from the Cuia, with an Indian named Pedro. From him I was enabled to obtain a better-defined knowledge of the country. I found that the river near the coast was called the Turcando, and that it joined the Cuia at a point about twelve miles distant from the beach.

In a personal reconnaissance I found it would be impossible to carry the survey over the Indian trail beyond Camp No. 2, as it led over a ridge 1,900 feet high, and there was but one place where water could be procured in a distance of eight miles. I therefore ordered Lieutenant Collins to strike an east-southeast course from Camp No. 2 to the Turcando, and, as the position of the river was uncertain, to send out reconnoitering parties, in which duty he was assisted by Lieutenant Sullivan, to find the lowest ascent.

The work of transporting their camp material and provisions with that of the survey over this very rugged country was so severe on this little party that it became necessary to strike the river as soon as possible, where I hoped to be able to use canoes for the purpose of transportation. Some peons I dispatched to bring light canoes up the

Turcundo came back and reported that on account of impassable falls it was impossible to do so.

Not knowing how far I should have to work down the Turcundo to get to our canoes, I at first made up my mind to abandon the line and commence again on the Indian trail. Still I was loth to do this, because nothing is more discouraging to men engaged in this work than to turn back and go over ground gained only by severe labor.

Upon visiting party No. 1 at their camp on the Turcundo, and after receiving a report of a reconnaissance of the river below, I determined to allow the survey to go on. As it turned out, a very fortunate conclusion, for my after-experience of the Indian trail over the country to the Cuia proved that a survey of it would have been painfully slow and laborious, owing to the very rugged country and the lack of water.

Upon my return to the ship, party No. 2 was organized, composed of Lieutenant Eaton, in charge, Lieutenant Sullivan, Midshipman Miles, and four sailors, with the necessary number of natives.

It had been my original intention to have had two parties under the above lieutenants, but the difficulty of supplying them with provisions and keeping up communication when widely separated compelled me to consolidate our means, an arrangement, as it proved, which was decidedly for the best.

While these several operations were in progress I dispatched a native carrier across the Napipi trail to my agent, Don Carlos Lemos, at Vijia, to send me a number of canoes and men to the junction of the Ciua and Turcundo Rivers. These Atrato men are athletic, industrious, and docile, and were, by far, the best help that I have employed on the Isthmus. In the event of building a canal probably one thousand of them could be gathered for that purpose, and kept up to this strength. Being excellent woodsmen, they would be invaluable in the first operations of clearing the country, building roads, and preparing the ground for the necessary railway.

To subsist party No. 2 it became necessary to make a depot at the mouth of the Turcundo, where was our camp known as Camp Relief.

Let it be remembered there were no roads in this wilderness, no maps, our topographical knowledge very limited, until by degrees we were able to map down the different ridges, rivers, and valleys. The only path was an Indian trail, rarely used, and so blind as only to be picked out by the natives of the forest. Like all such paths it led over the highest ground, making the transportation of our provisions and material a work of painful labor, and, to add to all, water was to be obtained at rare intervals. About thirteen hundred pounds was to be transported, and for this purpose Commander Belknap organized a provision-train of some sixty-five men. Including their own provisions this gave each man a load of about thirty pounds, and in a most inconvenient shape, as all our provisions were necessarily packed in water-tight kegs and boxes.

Party No. 2, Lieutenant Eaton in charge, and the provision party under Lieutenant Hubbard left the ship at noon February 19, and camped for the night at Camp No. 2 on the Doguado. The next day Lieutenant Eaton reached Camp Relief at the junction of the Cuia and Turcundo Rivers. But though this distance was but twelve miles, it took two days to get over the provisions, and the men toward the last were so worn out that they were obliged to lay down their burdens every few minutes and rest.

On the third day after their departure the provision party came straggling back, a few at a time, and their appearance was a sufficient sign of the difficulties of transportation in this rugged wilderness.

An accident happened to one of the men, named Turner, of the provision party, which filled us with grave apprehensions. Becoming.too exhausted to move on to camp, he laid down on the trail. During the night, becoming rested, he attempted to regain the camp and lost his way. As soon as the fact was known at the ship a party of natives and Indians were dispatched in search, stimulated by a large reward. The search was kept up a week without any success beyond finding some of his tracks. Finally, after being given up as dead, he was brought alongside by a native after an absence of thirty-five days. It appeared he wandered for three weeks in the woods, subsisting entirely on roots, when he finally reached the sea-shore. Here, when almost exhausted, he was found by one of the natives of Cupica Village, who cared for him until he was in a condition to return.

The operations of the survey being now well under way and requiring no longer a personal supervision, I proposed to make, in person, an extended reconnaissance of the whole ground, and a running survey of the river Atrato as far as Quibdo, some one hundred and twenty miles above the Vijia Funte, up to which point the Atrato survey had been carried the year previous; for which purpose I left the ship February 25, accompanied by two Indians as guides and provision bearers, crossed the hills, and reached Camp Relief, the head of navigation, after a toilsome march of a day and a half. Here I embarked in a canoe with Lieutenant Collins, and proceeding down the Cuia and Bojaya Rivers arrived at the Atrato after a passage of ten days.

I was much disappointed at the aspect of the country bordering on the Cuia. Not only was the intervening region between its head-waters and the Pacific much more mountainous than the corresponding country of the Napipi, but high ranges of hills were met with, first on one bank and then on the other, not seen at all in the valley of the Napipi, and gave me no doubt of the better adaptability of the latter, though it was left to the slower operations of the regular survey to map out the difference more closely.

Arriving at the little town of Vijia Funte, on the right bank of the Atrato, I made arrangements to embark the next morning in a large canoe, better adapted for a trip that was to last several days.

Traveling in a narrow canoe, when prolonged beyond a few days, becomes painfully laborious; even more so than a march of a corresponding distance, because one is obliged to remain in a cramped position during the day, and at night his rest must be on the split-palm floor of a native's hut.

Progress up stream is necessarily slow, and therefore there is no time to waste in putting up a tolerable shelter for the night. Propelled by the vigorous thrust of the Atrato canoe-men, and by making an early start, we averaged about thirty miles per day. Such a rate would not be possible against the current of the Atrato River, which averages from one to two and a half miles per hour, did not the boatmen avail themselves of slack-water and eddies by keeping the canoe close to the bank; and with long forked poles, called *poleneos*, it is pushed up stream, using only the paddle to direct its course. It required three days and a half to reach Quibdo, a distance of one hundred and twenty miles above Vijia Funte.

We were most hospitably received, the whole population turning out *en masse* to see *los Americanos del Norte*, their curiosity intensified to see the men whom, in their ignorance, they supposed were to build the canal at once and make Colombia the first country and Quibdo the chief city of the world, as they fondly hoped.

Two days were spent at Quibdo for a much-desired rest, and we left on our return, drifting down with the current, taking soundings every five minutes, while the traverse of the river was taken at the same time by angling between the points and noting the time of passing, the velocity of the current being found by experiment. The Atrato was found capable of ship-navigation but a few miles above Vijia, but navigable for the largest steamboats within two miles of Quibdo, where occurred the first approach to a rapid, the river spreading out with but three feet in the channel.

Our return was not marked with any particular event, and we reached the Tuscarora after an absence of nearly three weeks.

The exposure incident to so long a journey in an open canoe, together with the unhealthy condition of the Atrato Valley, caused both myself and Lieutenant Collins to be taken with a severe attack of fever, which incapacitated us for some weeks. In my absence the valley of the Murindo had been surveyed by Lieutenant Hubbard.

last bench-mark of party No. 3, which had been ordered in. This would give me three different lines of level to determine the height of the junction of the Napipi and Doguado, run by separate observers, and would prove a most excellent test of the general accuracy of the survey.

After these orders were carried out, Lieutenant Eaton was directed to bring his party back over the old Napipi trail to Limon Bay.

All the operations of the survey centering at Chiri-Chiri Bay, where the Tuscarora had removed since February 1, having been finished, we sailed for Limon Bay and arrived at our old anchorage of 1871.

Party No. 2 having completed the work above assigned them, returned to the ship at Limon Bay April 17, after an absence of seventy days.

This was the last party in the field, and their return completed the survey for this section of the Isthmus.

The survey of the Bojaya exhausted the limit of profitable territory to be explored for a ship-canal, and there now remained no portion of the Isthmus, beyond what had been unvisited, of the Darien that orographically or otherwise presented any favorable features; the Tuscarora accordingly returned to Panama, and the members of the expedition returned to the United States.

EXAMPLE OF ACCURACY OF THE SURVEY.

The position and height of the junction of the Doguado and Napipi has been determined by three separate parties, on three different lines, and affords a good illustration of the accuracy of our work.

One line by Lieutenant Collins, from Limon Bay and down the Napipi from its head-waters, gave an altitude of 140 feet.

One by Lieutenants Collins, Eaton, and Sullivan, from Chiri-Chiri Bay across to the Turcundo, down this river and the Cuia, across the Cuia to the Napipi, up the latter to the mouth of the Doguado, gave 136.5 feet.

One down the Doguado from its head-waters to its mouth gave the height of the latter 132 feet.

Here are three lines embracing nearly sixty miles of leveling, run by different parties, of a rough and mountainous country, and having an extreme difference of 8 feet. The mean, 136 feet, was taken for the true height, as shown on the profile.

The position of the same point as established by these separate parties did not vary but 1,000 feet, a hardly appreciable quantity on the map that accompanies the report of the expedition.

SUMMARY OF WORK PERFORMED BY THE DARIEN EXPEDITIONS OF 1870–1871, AND 1873.

In the northwestern portion, all the country contiguous to and the valleys of the following rivers have been surveyed either with the spirit-level or closely recorded observations of mercurial barometers: Mandinga, Samagundi, Necalagua, Carti, Centisiuegua, Bayamo, and Marmoni.

Hydrographic survey of the Gulf of San Blas, and Bayamo or Chepo Rivers to junction with Marmoni: In Central Darien, by same process, what is known as Cullen or Streim route, being the same as reported upon by Gisborne; the Caledonia or Aglamate; Aglasanigua River, called the Washington, to the mouth of the Alga; the Sassardi, Morti, Sucubti, Chucunaqua, Savanna, and Lava Rivers.

Hydrographic surveys of Caledonia and Sassardi Harbors, and Savanna and Lava Rivers: In Southern Darien, the river Atrato, from Quibdo to sea, two hundred and eighty miles. The river Tanela, known as De Puydt route. What is known as the Gorgoza, Lachaune, or Tuyra route, comprising Tuyra, Paya Cue, Terculegna, Cacurica, and Peranchita Rivers; also the valleys of the Napipi, Daguado, Murindo, Turcundo, Cuia, and Bojaya Rivers.

Hydrographic survey of Darien Harbor, Gulf of Darien, known as Columbia Harbor, and Chiri-Chiri Bay: Astronomical points were established on the Atlantic coast at Aspinwall, Cape San Blas, Isla del Oro, (Caledonia Bay,) Isla del Muerto, (Darien Harbor.) Pacific side: Panama, Chiprgana, and Purogana.

In the survey of the above, the following table will indicate concisely the amount of work performed each year:

Year.	Miles measured.	Miles leveled.	Miles surveyed: estimated.	Miles leveled by barometer.	Miles of line established.	Points established in triangulation.	Miles of lines of sounding.
1870.....	342	211	311.5	57	123.5	134	790.-
1871.....	32	61	81	81	100	50	230
1873.....	120.3	96.3	110.7	14	10	15	15
Total....	494.5	368.3	503.2	152	233.5	199	1035.-

DESCRIPTION OF THE PROPOSED CANAL ROUTE VIA THE NAPIPI AND DOGUADO VALLEYS.

Much has already been said of the nature of the country, and the difficulties to be encountered in the valley of the Napipi, in my previous report. But as the value of this route depends so entirely upon the capacity of ship-navigation of the river Atrato up to the point we leave it and cross to the Pacific Ocean by an artificial cut, I will again allude to it before proceeding to discuss the general features of the new proposed line.

Our knowledge of the Atrato is based upon a complete line of soundings run by Commander Lull the whole distance from the mouth of the Napipi to the mouth of the Atrato. For the whole distance from the Napipi to the ocean there is not so much as a rock or hill to be seen on the banks of the Atrato, a sufficient evidence of the alluvial nature of the country through which it flows, and a sufficient explanation of its great depth, now known for the first time, which seems to open to us a comparatively easy solution of the problem of a ship-canal.

No one who has visited this river and floated upon its surface as I have can but be struck with the grandeur of this mighty flow of water, and can but feel that it has been designed by the Almighty to bear a more important part in the great economy of the world's progress than the carrying of the little crafts which are now its sole navigators.

That the Atrato is entirely and wholly capable of ship-navigation to the point to which we wish to leave it, is a fact that no longer admits of any doubt.

From ocean to ocean, then, the only barriers are the half-mile of sand-bar at the Atrato's mouth, and the twenty-eight miles intervening at the mouth of the Napipi, between the Atrato and the Pacific, through which an artificial cut or canal must be made.

BAR OR OBSTRUCTIONS AT THE MOUTH OF THE ATRATO.

The Atrato spreads itself out into a delta at least twenty miles in length, and empties itself by thirteen mouths into the sea.

The great difficulty that has been met in the permanent improvement of the mouths of all the rivers that empty into the Gulf of Mexico is the shifting character of the sands, caused by the action of the sea-swell, and which require the constant use of the dredge, while a storm of a single night may open a channel entirely different from the one in use.

While nearly all the mouths of the Atrato are exposed to this same influence, that one known as the Uraba is an exception, as it empties into an almost land-locked harbor, the surface of which is hardly ruf-fled. This fact gives the character of its bar a permanence which none of the others possess in the same degree. Specimens of boring at a depth of 18 feet below the surface indicated that it is composed entirely of a black and white sand, whose geological proportions are the same as the hills from which the tributaries of the Atrato flow.

I was also struck by the fact that, as soon as we crossed the bar to a point where the overflow was restrained by the growth of plants, then did the depth commence to increase, and as soon as the flow was confined by banks compact enough, to sustain vegetation, the water at once deep-ened to five fathoms. This action of nature, in my mind, was conclusive proof that, if the current was confined by artificial banks and the inclosed distance dredged to the required depth, that there would be a perma nent channel, requiring no further outlay to keep open.

From the ten-fathom line to a depth of five fathoms, in the Uraba branch, it is about 2,500 feet. There would be required for a double row of piling the whole of this distance 10,000 trees 30 feet long and 1 foot or more diameter. Trees of the variety known as the Cedrón Guallaco or Trintago, Chacajo, and Insivé, can all be cut on or near the Atrato and its tributaries. These varieties are all hard and very dura-ble, of a specific gravity less than water, and could be therefore floated to the desired spot and driven at a cost not exceding $5 per pile.

For a channel 300 feet wide and a depth of 26 feet of water, there would require to be removed 640,000 cubic yards of material. The ex-pense, therefore, of the required improvement at the mouth of the Atrato may be summed up as follows:

10,000 piles, at $5 each	$50,000
640,000 cubic yards material, at 50 cents per cubic yard	320,000
	370,000
25 per cent. increase, for contigencies	92,500
Total	462,500

FROM THE MOUTH OF THE NAPIPI TO THE PACIFIC.

The new proposed route for the canal, as surveyed in 1873, embraces a portion of the same line as surveyed and reported upon in 1871. It starts from the Atrato, about three miles below the mouth of the Napipi, and runs almost due west, and never at a distance of more than half a mile from the river till near the mouth of the Dognado. Up to this point there are no rivers to cross, and but four small hills, none over 60 feet in height. The canal then bends with a gentle curve toward the river, and crosses the Napipi just below the junction of the Dognado. It follows close to the right bank of the latter, in a general southwest direction, and enters the Pacific Ocean at the mouth of a small stream called the Chiri-Chiri, which gives the name to the bay which will form the western terminus.

The total length of the whole is twenty-eight miles. That portion of the line that follows the valley of the Napipi has been already described, and it is only necessary to remark that as a locality there could be nothing better desired, being one continuous plain with a gradual rise of 90 feet.

From the mouth of the Dognado the country continues flat for two miles, with a gradual rise of 60 feet. We now strike broken country, with here and there small hills, increasing in height to 400 feet at about three and a half miles from the Pacific, at which point the tunnel commences and is continued for three miles, passing under the divide, which is about 660 feet above the sea. Beyond the western end of the tunnel, we have the valley of the Chiri-Chiri.

The head-waters of the Dognado is a charming country, embracing a large extent of table-land, well watered and timbered, and abounding in game. Here will be a beautiful and healthy spot for the hospitals, swept by rarefied breezes at an elevation of 600 feet above the sea.

HARBORS.

The magnificent harbor at the mouth of the Atrato, named by the expedition Columbia Harbor, has already been described in a previous report. Ten miles deep by five wide, with a uniform depth of ten fathoms, completely land-locked and easy of access, it has no superior.

On the Pacific the western terminus is on the bay of Chiri-Chiri. It is open to the west and southwest, but its shores are bold and clear of reefs, and has good holding-ground of clay in 20 fathoms about three-fourths of a mile from the beach.

To protect the mouth of the canal from the ocean-swell I propose to construct two short breakwaters. Their cost will be but trifling, because they will be made of the *débris* dumped from the western face of the tunnel, which will be the easiest and cheapest way to get rid of it.

An American sailor who had lived many years on the coast told me that he had never seen it blow on the sea so heavy but that our ship, the Tuscarora, could have laid at single anchor; that he never knew of any gales, but that there were in the fall some squalls from off the land from the north and northeast.

LENGTH AND DIMENSIONS.

As has been said, we use the Atrato River, which is free from all obstructions, except the bar at its mouth, for one hundred and fifty miles. The artificial cut, or canal, to be excavated is twenty-eight miles in length; of this twenty-two miles are over a plain, three miles of moderately deep cutting, and three miles of tunneling.

The dimensions of the proposed canal are a depth of 25 feet, and a width at bottom, of earth, of 50 feet, and in rock of 60 feet, giving a working surface width of 70 feet, which is about the size of the Suez Canal; the sides sloping in earth, 2 horizontal to 1 perpendicular, and in rock, 1 horizontal to 4 perpendicular.

The tunnel will be 112 feet high and 60 feet wide, leaving 87 feet in the clear above the water-surface.

Three sidings will be constructed six miles apart, 2,000 feet in length, for vessels whose size will not permit them to pass each other on the canal.

Four plans of construction are proposed, as follows: Plan A, as given in the profile, with a summit-level of 120 feet, requiring altogether twenty locks; plan B, with the same summit-level, but with the bottom of canal carried but 15 feet below the grade-line, the required depth obtained by embankment 12 feet high; plan C, with a summit-level of 80 feet, requiring twelve locks; plan D, which contemplates a through cut from the Atrato River, in which case the canal would be filled from the latter river, and but three locks required at the Pacific terminus.

The only advantage of the latter would be the superabundant supply of water and the saving of time in passing through the locks; while on the other hand it would be more expensive, would not permit the draining of the canal if desired for repairs, and, moreover, being necessarily very much below the bottom of the Napipi, would have to receive the surface drainage of the country through which it passed, which in the rainy reason might become a very great objection.

For myself I prefer plan B, as presenting the minimum of cost, and the moderate number of locks would add but little to the time necessary to pass from ocean to ocean.

The proposed size of the locks are a total length of 427 feet and a width of 54 feet, giving a clear length of 400 feet and a lift of 10 feet.

WATER-SUPPLY.

The water to fill the canal will be drawn entirely from the Napipi River, which at the summit-level will include also its two principal tributaries the Murindo and the Doguado Rivers. Its volume has been carefully, measured by cross-sections, and its flow at the point at which it will be tapped was about, April 1, 520,000 cubic feet per hour, which date may be considered the close of the dry season, as the rainy season commences during April and continues till the middle of June. From the marks on the trees indicative of high water, and an estimated velocity of two miles per hour, the volume of the Napipi at its highest stage is calculated to equal 8,000,000 cubic feet per hour. We are safe in allowing an average flow through the year of 3,000,000 per hour.

The survey across the country, which included a line of levels from the Cuia River to the Napipi, demonstrates that an aqueduct but three and a half miles long is necessary to utilize the flow of the Cuia, which in the dry season amounts to 450,000 cubic feet per hour, and which united with the Napipi will give a total supply of 23,280,000 cubic feet per day. This is a quantity far in excess of the demand required for a tonnage of three times the present amount that is estimated will use the canal, after making a liberal allowance for leakage, &c.

Should the time ever come that it would become necessary to build extra pairs of locks to accommodate a traffic beyond the resources of the canal to transport, we have the large river Opogado, which is about ten miles distant from the Napipi.

Experiments for evaporation at the mouth of the Atrato gave an average amount of about one-fifth of an inch every twenty-four hours.

37 Ab

This is a much smaller quantity than has been allowed in northern climates, but the difference is easily accounted for in the constant moist condition of the atmosphere of the Atrato Valley.

It is certainly a curious incident that the amount of evaporation as found in Captain Shufeldt's report upon the survey of Tehuantepec should have been found to be 0.19 of an inch, but 0.01 inch different from that obtained by our experiments; and therefore the evaporation in the tropics may be accurately set down at not more than two-tenths of an inch.

As will be seen farther on, in the construction of this work, after passing the first lock up to which the back-water from the Atrato will flow, the canal will be cut entirely through rock, care being taken to keep the bottom at such a distance below the grade-line as to accomplish this. On this account there can be no loss from filtration, an element in most canals that absorbs a large fraction of the water-supply.

The class of vessels that will frequent the canal are mostly of a large size. But the locks as proposed are long enough to take in at once two ships of 1,000 tons register each, one astern of the other.

Twenty lockages a day will represent a tonnage of 20,000 tons, provided each lock is filled by one or two vessels equal to 2,000 tons register; or during the year a total of 7,300,000 tons, which is three times the amount that it is calculated would at present use the canal.

With thirteen hours' daylight, and supposing that three lockages can be made in an hour, 40 lockages will represent the total amount that the canal is capable of accommodating. This would represent a carrying capacity of the canal for the year of 15,000,000, or six times the present amount of trade.

Therefore there is no doubt for the present, or at the time the canal is completed, but that the flow of the Napipi alone would be sufficient to supply the canal.

We have, therefore—

FLOW OF THE NAPIPI.

	Cubic feet.
Close of dry season	520,000
	24
Supply for twenty-four hours	12,480,000

DEMAND.

	Cubic feet.
Leakage, at 3,000 cubic feet per minute	1,320,000
Evaporation, twenty-four miles of canal	288,000
Waste	1,000,000
Twenty lockages a day, equal to 20,000 tons per day	4,611,600
	10,219,600
Supply	12,480,000
Excess	2,260,400

Applying the total capacity of the canal, which, for reasons above stated, cannot probably exceed 40 lockages, through both summit-locks, we have a total:

	Cubic feet.
Forty lockages	9,223,200
Leakage, &c	5,608,000
	14,831,200
Napipi and Cuia Rivers combined flow at close of dry season	23,280,000
Excess	8,448,800

With these results there can be no doubt of a sufficiency of water for every requirement of the canal upon this route.

For the purpose of collecting the total flow of the Napipi in twenty-four hours when necessary, and to more quickly fill the summit-locks, a reservoir, of a capacity of 20,000,000 cubic feet, will be constructed between the canal and Napipi above the summit-level.

COST AND EXCAVATION.

For the purpose of obtaining the exact amount of excavation, from which can be calculated a close estimate of cost, we divide the work into four divisions, which are subdivided into twenty-seven parts.

The area of the prism at the end of each part is calculated, and the mean taken, which is multiplied by the length of the part in feet, to obtain the cubical contents. Theoretically this is correct, but practically it will give too large a quantity; but this is preferable to having too small an estimate, and allows for irregularities of ground.

To obtain the total cost of the excavation of the canal we allow 33 cents per cubic yard in earth, $1.25 and $1.75 per cubic yard in rock, and $5.35 for tunnel-work.

These estimates of cost have been furnished me by Benjamin H. Latrobe, esq., the distinguished engineer of the Baltimore and Ohio Railroad, and are believed to be fully equal to the necessities of the case.

It is proposed to employ almost entirely coolies or Chinese labor. Though the Chinese cannot do as much per capita as northern laborers, they work with more steadiness, and they could be procured, clothed, and fed at a cost not exceeding $16 per month. The Chinese are extremely quick at learning, and very shortly they would be equal to skilled labor in the handling of mining implements. They are now employed in large numbers upon the railroads of Peru and Costa Rica, and make, I am told, excellent miners, of which nature most of the work upon the canal partakes.

PLAN A.

Division No. 1.—This extends from the Atrato River to the summit-level, or from A to T, a distance of 103,900 linear feet, or about 19.7 miles, and includes eight locks, six of 10 feet, and two of 11 feet lift. This division will require a total excavation of 5,328,493 cubic yards of earth, and 7,801,998 of rock.

5,328,493 cubic yards of earth, at 33 cents	$1,758,403
7,801,998 cubic yards of rock, at $1.25	9,752,498
Estimated cost of single lock, $175,000; 8 locks	1,400,000
Total	12,910,901

Of the above estimated cost of a single lock, $50,000 are for gates and machinery. This division is excavated as far as B in earth, the remainder in soft rock and earth. The deepest cut will be 56 feet, and the average about 35 feet.

Division No. 2.—It extends from lock No. 8 to east face of tunnel, or from T to T, a distance of 25,640 feet, or about 4.9 miles, in which there are to be excavated 691,329 cubic yards of earth, and 4,937,619 cubic yards of rock. Owing to the harder character of the rock, and the deeper extent of the cut, the cost per cubic yard is increased to $1.75 per yard. We have, then, for total cost of this division—

691,329, at 33 cents	$228,139
4,937,619, at $1.75	8,640,833
Total	8,868,972

The deepest cut in this division is at the east face of the tunnel, and amounts to 223 feet, the least 35 feet; but the average depth will not exceed 75 feet.

Division No. 3.—This division is a tunnel 5,233 yards in length, a fraction less than three miles. Its dimensions are 112 feet in width; its sides are perpendicular for 63 feet, and the remaining 49 feet an arch. The number of square yards in a linear yard are 633.

In estimating the cost of this work, supposing the rock to be self-sustaining, I have allowed a cost of $5.25 per cubic yard. Adding to this 25 per cent. additional, as shown in the general summing up, it would give $11 per cubic yard for the first 40 feet in height, and $500 per yard for the running rectangular space—an ample sum, when compared with the cost of tunnels now under construction. The total cost of division No. 3 amounts to $17,731,232.

I have already spoken at length in my previous report of the popular prejudice against tunnels, and there is little now to be said. Tunneling is becoming now a general resort of engineers; and with the improved power-drills, and enormous force of nitro-glycerine, it is no longer looked upon as a subject to be avoided.

The very size of this ship-canal tunnel is in its favor, as the work will cost less, yard for yard, than railroad work, from the increased facilities that its dimensions give in removing the blast.

There would be three shafts probably sunk, giving eight faces to work upon, whose united length would not exceed 962 feet.

It should not be forgotten that this feature of a tunnel will permit the excavation of the most costly portion of the line to be carried on uninterruptedly, day and night; while, on portions of this or any other canal constructed in the tropics, much delay and annoyance will be caused by the great rain-fall of the wet season.

Division No. 4.—This division, which terminates at the Pacific, or from A to C, is 4,400 feet in length. There will be required about 67,882 yards of earth, and 395,993 rock, of excavation. It includes the system of twelve locks, and which would follow one immediately after the other, and possibly one of them might have to be placed in the mouth of the tunnel.

Nothing more than an approximate estimate can be given for the cost of the locks in this work. But as they are excavated in the solid rock, of which the cost is allowed, the greater portion of the expense will be in the gates, machinery, gate-walls, and miter-sills. Blocks of concrete or béton can be substituted for dressed granite at much below the cost of the latter, and it is believed the sum allowed for the locks will cover their cost.

Cost of Division No. 4.

67,882, at 33	$22,401
395,993, at $1.25	494,991
12 locks, at $150,000 a lock	1,800,000
Total	2,317,392

Total divisional cost.

Division No. 1	$12,910,901
Division No. 2	8,868,972
Division No. 3	17,731,232
Division No. 4	2,317,392
Total	41,828,497

To utilize the whole daily discharge of the Napipi in the dry season it is proposed to construct a reservoir to hold 20,000,000 cubic feet.

This would require an excavation, supposing the banks raised 10 feet above the surface, 1,000 feet long by 800 feet broad, and 15 feet deep—a total of 440,000 cubic yards, which, at $1.25 per yard, would give as cost of reservoir, $550,000.

An aqueduct to connect the Cuia and Napipi Rivers would be 6,060 yards in length. Allowing $100 per linear yard for excavation and piping, it would give cost of aqueduct, $606,000.

Five hundred thousand dollars are allowed for culverts; one million dollars for construction of a narrow-gauge railroad to be used in the transportation of supplies, and as a tramway to remove the *débris;* also for the purchase of the necessary steamers on the Atrato, which would not probably exceed two in number. One million is also allowed for the crossing of the Napipi River by the canal, and the necessary sluice-ways and conduits to the reservoir.

We have, therefore, the following—

SUMMARY OF EXPENSES.

Cost of excavation	$41,828,497
Cost of reservoir	550,000
Cost of aqueduct between Cuia and Napipi Rivers	606,000
Cost of culverts	500,000
Cost of railroad, narrow gauge	1,000,000
Crossing the Napipi River by canal	1,000,000
Grubbing and clearing	500,000
Sea-wall, Chiri Chiri Bay	200,000
Wall, Atrato River and eastern mouth of canal	25,000
Executive department	120,000
Engineer department	375,000
Pay department	90,000
Quartermaster's department	135,000
Commissary department	120,000
Hoisting and pumping engines	875,000
Medical department	80,000
Improvements at mouth of Atrato River	462,500
Twenty-five per cent. added for contingencies	12,116,749
Total	60,583,746

The above amount placed to the credit of the medical department is too small. But there will probably be a yearly revenue of $50,000 from rents of land and buildings, which would be appropriated to the support of the hospitals.

PLAN B.

This differs from the preceding so far that the bottom of the canal is carried but 15 feet below the grade-line, and embankments are formed on each side, some 15 feet high, to retain the waters of the canal; but this will only apply to division No. 1; the others necessarily remain an ordinary cut. In other respects it does not differ from plan A, except requiring one more lock.

The advantage of this plan is the minimum of cost of division No. 1, which by this method amounts to $3,891,609; or, applied to the summary of expenses as given under plan A, would place the total cost of the canal at $53,937,247.

PLAN C.

This plan employs but four locks to the summit level, and eight locks down.

Its advantage is in tapping the Napipi River lower down and having an increased supply of water, and less delay in passing through but half the number of locks.

The excavation will be necessarily much greater, and the tunnel will be 1,900 feet longer than by plans A and B.

The Napipi will yield, at the point tapped on this plan, 200,000 cubic feet per hour more than when taken as in plan A. The total cost of excavation will amount to $64,220,670, and total cost of canal in this plan will be $72,518,795.

PLAN D.

This differs from all the above in the fact that it purposes to do away altogether with locks, except the three at the western terminus, to equalize the difference of level between the Atrato, at the point the canal leaves it, and the Pacific Ocean. It will be, therefore, a straight cut and filled from the Atrato, which has a volume in the dry season of at least 1,600 cubic feet per second.

Necessarily the excavation will be larger and the tunnel will be increased 3,900 feet, making the whole length of tunnel 3.71 miles.

The cost of excavation by this plan will amount to $81,815,320, and total cost of canal as an open cut will amount to $90,113,445.

HEALTH.

The health of the expedition of 1873 has been unexceptionably good. There were a few cases of intermittent fever, but they yielded readily to treatment.

But one man connected with the survey was lost, and he by drowning in the Atrato.

Though the work of the survey of the Isthmus of Darien has been of the most arduous nature, and necessarily required constant exposure, yet on all the expeditions, extending through three years, not a man has been lost by climatic causes, nor have the personnel of the expedition returned with impaired health.

Experience and observations have taught me that Europeans of regular habits, and abstemious in their diet, with the proper care of wearing light woolen clothing next to the skin, can live many years on the Isthmus of Darien without permanent injury to themselves.

It is a satisfaction to know that the Isthmus of Darien is no longer a doubtful land. That as far as its adaptibility for a ship-canal, that it has been thoroughly explored.

The United States has now, through the various expeditions fitted out for the purpose, the whole data to decide upon the feasibility of a project that has been the dream of centuries; and the best location for an enterprise the greatest and most important the world has yet seen.

To show the vast commerce that will flow through it, and the saving of time and distance over the old routes of Cape Horn and Cape of Good Hope, the following tables are given, as called for from the Secretary of the Treasury, by the House of Representatives, in February, 1872:

Trade of the United States with the following countries.

Countries.	Entered.		Cleared.		Total.	
	No.	Tonnage.	No.	Tonnage.	No.	Tonnage.
West coast of Mexico	60	29,551	72	20,853	132	51,407
West coast of Central America	29	5,626	19	4,210	48	9,846
West coast of South America	145	193,389	132	166,055	283	359,444
Sandwich Islands	59	32,819	64	40,822	123	73,641
Islands Pacific	7	1,547	4	757	11	2,294
Australia, New Zealand	84	64,034	50	29,889	134	93,443
China	90	42,658	44	34,084	143	88,742
Japan	47	30,380	19	11,400	66	43,560
Dutch East Indies	23	12,908	14	14,564	37	26,473
California*	100	100,000	100	155,022		250,022
Total tonnage from the United States through canal						869,006

* For year ending June 30, 1872.

Trade of Great Britain for 1870 with the following countries.

Countries.	Entered.		Cleared.		Total.	
	No.	Tonnage.	No.	Tonnage.	No.	Tonnage.
United States Pacific coast *	150	308, 625	.....	70, 639	.....	379, 264
West coast of Mexico	15	5, 572	4	1, 057	19	6, 629
West coast of Central America	19	8, 196	13	6, 368	32	14, 564
Islands of the Pacific	18	15, 580	5	2, 846	23	17, 426
Chili	146	86, 281	212	125, 264	358	211, 545
Peru	257	224, 131	139	114, 589	396	338, 720
Equador	6	1, 970	6	1, 768	12	3, 738
Japan	8	3, 667	53	33, 148	61	36, 815
Australia and New Zealand	243	220, 889	338	320, 872	581	541, 771
Total tonnage from Great Britain through canal						1, 550, 472

* For year ending June 30, 1873.

Total tonnage of Germany with above countries 146, 049
Total tonnage of France with above countries 169, 259

Total tonnage that would use the canal:

United States 969, 006
Great Britain 1, 550, 472
Germany 146, 049
France 169, 259

Total 2, 834, 786

In the above estimates no account is taken of the trade of Great Britain with China and East Indies, much of which, outward bound, would seek the canal.

Comparison of times and distances between the old routes, via Cape Horn, and Cape of Good Hope, and the Isthmus of Darien.

SAILING-VESSELS.

Outward.

	Present route.			Via canal.		Gain.	
From—	To—	Distance.	Days.	Distance.	Days.	Distance.	Days.
		Miles.		Miles.		Miles.	
New York	Hong-Kong	14, 930	110	12, 480	83	2, 450	27
Do	Shanghai	15, 200	115	12, 200	81	3, 000	34
Do	Yokohama	15, 750	119	11, 550	79	4, 200	40
Do	Manila	13, 700	108	12, 260	80	1, 440	28
Do	Batavia	12, 170	105	13, 425	87	....	18
Do	Sidney	12, 220	105	10, 480	75	2, 740	30
Do	Valparaiso	9, 760	93	6, 510	52	3, 250	41
Do	Callao	11, 100	105	6, 710	53	4, 390	52
Do	Honolulu	14, 500	121	7, 400	54	7, 100	67
Do	San Francisco	14, 840	130	7, 470	58	7, 370	72

Return.

		Present route.		Via canal.		Gain.	
Hong-Kong	New York	14, 660	110	11, 875	87	2, 785	23
Shanghai	do	16, 000	113	11, 305	80	4, 695	33
Yokohama	do	16, 070	114	10, 370	77	5, 700	37
Manila	do	14, 010	109	12, 035	83	1, 975	21
Sidney	do	13, 410	110	10, 390	70	3, 080	40
Valparaiso	do	9, 780	90	4, 965	42	4, 815	48
Callao	do	11, 120	100	3, 690	32	7, 430	68
Honolulu	do	15, 760	110	8, 055	63	7, 705	47
San Francisco	do	14, 970	125	5, 980	50	8, 990	75

TABLE FOR STEAMERS.

From—	To—	Time.	Distance.	Remarks.
		Days.	Miles.	
New York	Sidney	40	9,970	
Do	Hong-Kong	48	12,165	Via Honolulu.
Do	Manila	47	12,805	Do.
Do	Shanghai	46	11,605	Do.
Do	Yokohama	43	10,675	Do.
Do	Batavia	51	13,000	
Do	Honolulu	29	7,155	
Do	Callao	15	3,500	⎱ The same time and distance on the
Do	Valparaiso	21	5,000	⎰ return passage.
Do	San Francisco	25		
RETURN.				
Sidney	New York	42	9,970	
Hong-Kong	do	46	11,735	Great circle route.
Manila	do	48	12,325	Do.
Yokohama	do	43	10,315	Do.
Honolulu	do	29	7,300	
Batavia	do	54	13,190	

In conclusion, it is a pleasure to recommend to the favorable notice of the Department Lieutenants Collins, Eaton, and Sullivan, who volunteered to accompany me on the present expedition.

The frequency with which their names appear on the pages of these reports indicates the positions of honor and trust which they have so worthily filled, and is the best evidence of the zeal and ability which they have always displayed.

To Commander Belknap and officers of the Tuscarora I am indebted for valuable assistance and co-operation, without which it would have been impossible for me to have carried on the survey.

Trusting I have met with the expectations of the Department in the execution of the original orders to survey the Isthmus of Darien for a ship-canal, delivered to me in January, 1870, I have the honor to be, sir, very respectfully, your obedient servant,

THOS. O. SELFRIDGE,
Commander, United States Navy.

Hon. GEO. M. ROBESON,
Secretary of the Navy, Washington, D. C.

NICARAGUA EXPEDITION.

WASHINGTON, D. C., *October* 25, 1873.

SIR: I have the honor to submit the following report of the work performed and the result obtained by the United States surveying expedition lately operating in Nicaragua:

The following naval and civil officers were attached to the expedition, viz:

Naval officers.—Commander Edward P. Sull, commanding expedition; Lieutenant Commander G. C. Schulze, Lieut. Wm. W. Rhoades, Lieut. Eugene H. C. Leutz, Lieut. Jacob W. Miller, Lieut. Jefferson F. Moser, Master John M. Hauley, Master J. B. Briggs, (United States steamer Kansas,) joined the expedition April 9; Master K. Niles, Ensign Jas. H. Bull, First Asst. Engineer Geo. M. Greene, Asst. Surg. John M. Bransford, Commander's Clerk Augustin S. McCrea, jr.

Civil officers.—Chief civil-engineer, A. G. Menocal; civil engineer, J. Foster Crowell; mineralogist, J. E. Cropsey; draughtsmen, A. Pohlers and W. V. W. Reilly.

In addition to these there were attached to the expedition several young men, with petty-officers' ratings, detailed for duty as rod-men, chain-men, and pole-men.

The following instruments and other articles of outfit were either on hand or provided, viz:

Instruments, &c.—Two engineers' transits, three levels, two gradienters, two surveyors' compasses, two delicate pocket aneroid-barometers, four mercurial mountain-barometers, one boring-apparatus for testing excavations, one current-meter, surveyors' chains and pins, watches, pocket-compasses, sounding leads and lines, drawing instruments and materials, field-glasses, &c., transit and level books, sounding-books, and necessary stationery, &c.

General outfit.—Axes, hatchets, machetas, shovels, and picks; camp-kettles and frying-pans; and for each officer and man one shelter-tent, one India-rubber blanket, one knapsack, one haversack, one canteen, one pair of leggings, one hammock, and one mosquito-net.

Five months' provisions for sixty men were prepared, put up in packages of from 35 to 60 pounds each, and so securely as not to be liable to injury from exposure to heat and moisture, and consisted of the following, viz: bacon, soup and boulli, tomato-soup, hard bread, rice, beans, sugar and coffee.

The instructions of the Department, issued in February, 1872, to Commander A. F. Crossman, and, after the death of that officer, carried out in part by Commander Chester Hatfield, required an exploration within the limits of the State of Nicaragua, to discover if possible a practicable route for an interoceanic ship-canal.

GEOGRAPHICAL DESCRIPTION.

Nicaragua, in shape a quadrilateral of very unequal sides, lies between latitude 10° 40' north and 15° 20' north, and between longitude 83° 00' west and 87° 40' west. Lake Nicaragua lies in the southwest part of the state, is about ninety miles long, and from thirty-five to forty-five miles wide. It is separated from the Pacific by a narrow strip of land at one place, viz: between Virgin Bay and San Juan del Sur, but twelve miles wide. To the northward and westward of Lake Nicaragua, with a surface-level from twenty-two to twenty-eight feet higher, lies the smaller Lake Managua, connected with the former by the Rio Tipitapa, through which, however, there is no visible flow of water at the present time, though Lake Managua has no other outlet. Lake Nicaragua discharges its waters through the river San Juan, which, leaving the lake at its southeast extremity, flows in a generally east-southeast course to the Caribbean.

The Cordillera is divided in the northern part of the state. One branch, extending to the eastward, sends its multitudinous spurs to the coast and to the banks of the San Juan, while the other, passing to the westward of the lakes, sinks in some places into a mere range of hills. This is particularly the case near Leon, and again near Rivas. The bulk of the population and wealth of the country is in the departments bordering upon the Pacific.

The valley of the San Juan is entirely uninhabited, with the exception of the little villages of San Carlos and Castillo Viejo, clustering around the forts of the same names, and here and there a small plantation or a wood-chopper's station. Fort San Carlos is at the outlet of the lake, and Castillo Viejo some thirty-seven miles down the river, abreast the second rapids, to which, as well as the village, it gives its name.

THE PROBLEM AND ITS SOLUTION.

A glance at the map will show that any project for a canal through Nicaragua must involve the lake of the same name, not only because its water is needed at the summit-level, but because it lies in the narrowest part of the country, measuring from sea to sea.

It is quite clear that a line, more or less practicable, exists between the lake and the Caribbean, following the valley of the San Juan, and that this line is not only the lowest, but the shortest, which does exist between the two; the shortest, because the lake shore approaches nearer the coast at its outlet than at any other point, and the lowest, because if any other existed lower or as low, then would there be another outlet. This line, however, would be of no value unless a practicable line also existed between the lake and the Pacific. The attention of the explorer is therefore naturally first turned in that direction. Fortunately a great deal was already known in regard to that part of the country; and at least one line, i. e., that from the mouth of the Rio Lajas to Brito, surveyed in 1850–'51 by Col. O. W. Childs, had been reported upon very favorably. The first work done by Commander Hatfield's party was, in accordance with the Department's directions, to re survey this line. Child's description was found to be correct in the main, and his route was ever after taken as a standard of comparison for all others.

Commander Hatfield also examined, and found impracticable, the line starting from the mouth of the Rio Sapoa, ascending to the divide by the valley of that river, and terminating in Salinas Bay, on the Pacific; this line is generally regarded as the boundary between Nicaragua and Costa Rica. He had also partially examined a line indicated by Colonel Sonnenstern, the State Engineer of Nicaragua, following the valley of the Ochomogo, and having for its objective point on the Pacific the mouth of the Rio Escalante. The Ochomogo empties into the lake some thirty miles north of the mouth of the Lajas. The advent of the rainy season prevented Commander Hatfield's completing the work here, and also prevented the examination of another line to which his attention had been directed, in the immediate vicinity of Child's route, and which it was hoped would prove superior to it.

SAILING OF THE EXPEDITION.

The expedition of the present year sailed in the United States steamer Kansas, Commander A. V. Reed, from Hampton Roads, Virginia, on the 3d of December, 1872, and arrived off Greytown, (or San Juan del Norte, Nicaragua, December 20. We succeeded in landing without accident, and proceeded, as soon as possible, to Virgin Bay, to complete the work on that side of the lake. Arriving January 3 at Virgin Bay, we found Midshipmen Keeler, Winslow, and Hughes, United States Navy, who had been left with a steam launch and a few men to do some hydrographic work in the lake, as the calm weather of the rainy season was particularly favorable for it. These young officers were under orders to the United States, to be examined for promotion, and we were thereby deprived of their services, which would have been very valuable.

COMMENCEMENT OF OPERATIONS.

Two parties had been organized before reaching Virgin Bay, and were ready to go into the field at once. They consisted of the following, viz:

Party No. 1.—Lieut. E. H. C. Leutze, in charge Civil Engineer J. F. Crawell, in charge of the transit instrument, Lieut. Jacob W. Miller, in charge of level; four petty officers; rod-men, pole-men, chain-men, &c.; one seaman; two Caribs.

Party No. 2.—Lieut. William W. Rhoades, in charge; First Assistant Engineer George M. Greene, with the transit instrument; Lieut. Jefferson F. Moser, with level; Mr. J. E. Cropsey, mineralogist; four petty officers; rod-men, pole-men, and chain-men; three seamen.

In addition to these there were required for each party twelve natives to be employed as macheteros or choppers, muleteers, and cooks. These, with pack and saddle mules, were obtained without trouble, through the kind offices of Messrs. Pedro and José Chamorro, leading merchants of Rivas; one an ex-senator, the other an ex-minister of finance of the state. Through the kindness of these gentlemen we were saved much trouble and delay in obtaining help and in supplying our other needs, and I shall ever hold them in grateful remembrance.

Don José Chamorro was, shortly after our arrival, specially commissioned by his government to aid us, but it was impossible for him to do more than he had already been doing voluntarily.

To Lieutenant Rhoades's party was assigned the work of examination of the route already referred to, which it was hoped would prove to be superior to that of Childs's. This line began at the north of the Rio del Medio, followed up its valley, crossed the divide, and descended to Brito by the valley of the Rio Grande; a small portion of it coinciding with Childs's line.

Lieutenant Leutze's party was directed to complete the examination of the Ochomogo line. Master K. Niles, with three men, was sent to Brito to establish a tide-gauge.

An American gentleman, Mr. Ran Runnels, formerly United States consul at San Juan del Sur, but now residing at Virgin Bay, kindly placed at our disposition a cottage which he owned, to be used as a store-room, draughting-room, and quarters for officers; while the cuartel, or barracks, was given to us by the agent of the government as a hospital, &c. We fortunately had but little use for it in that capacity, however. To Mr. Runnels and his estimable family we were, and had been since the landing of the first expedition, constantly indebted for hospitality and assistance of every kind in their power. The commanding officer accepted an invitation to become their guest, and received every kindness and attention which their thoughtfulness could devise. They will long continue to occupy a warm place in the heart of every officer in the expedition.

Lieutenant-Commander Schulze, the executive officer, was placed in charge of the commissariat, as the keeping up of supplies required one of the most experienced officers. The commanding officer and the chief civil engineer were left free to move from party to party as occasion demanded.

The parties began work January 7; party No. 2 establishing their bench-mark at the lake-level, party No. 1 taking up the line on the Ochomogo, at the point where it was abandoned the previous year. Observations were taken daily at a lake-gauge at Virgin Bay, to show the amount of fall in the level of the water.

As the medio-line gave great promise at the outset, party No. 2 were directed to make their survey with great care and with considerable detail. The traverse was run with an engineer's transit and chain, and cross-sections were taken at every 500 feet, extending 500 feet either way. The levels were taken at every 200 feet or less. In the party operating upon the Ochomogo, a surveyor's compass was substituted for the transit; in other respects the instruments were the same. The line being less promising, and, in fact, scarcely promising at all, a close re-connaissance, rather than a detailed survey, was required. A few days served to show that this line was altogether impracticable. The level had reached 87 feet above the lake, although the end of the traverse was still at a distance of some miles from the divide. Reconnaissances were made in several directions by Messrs. Leutze, Menocal, Miller, and Crowell to find a lower pass than that they were now approaching, elevations being carefully measured by the aneroid barometer. It was found that the lowest pass was 225 feet above the lake-level, with a long slope on either side, making a very bad profile. There was, of course, no need of further examination. The line was accordingly abandoned, and the party removed to the banks of the Rio Gil Gonzales, some eighteen miles south of the Ochomogo, and whose valley was the only other locality where there was a possibility of finding a practicable route.

I might here add of the Ochomogo line that it had merely been indicated by Colonel Sonnenstern, as one of the localities which should be examined.

In the mean time party No. 2 were making excellent progress, the line developing well, and, except that it was longer than had been expected, (the lake-shore lines not having been correctly laid down on the maps,) it was proving quite as good as had been hoped.

On the 15th of January Colonel Sonnenstern, by order of his government, joined the expedition, giving us from that time till we left the country the benefit of his thorough acquaintance, not only with the territory but the people, and also of his personal services at all times when needed.

EXAMINATION OF NAPOLEON'S ROUTE.

Louis Napoleon, while a prisoner at Ham, wrote a pamphlet, in which he indicated a route for a ship-canal, which, after reaching Lake Nicaragua by the Valley of the San Juan, ascended by the Rio Tipitapa to Lake Managua, leaving which at its northwestern extremity it continued to the port of Realejo. The only object in carrying the line in this direction was to secure the harbor of Realejo as the Pacific terminus, opposed to which advantage were the disadvantages of the greater distance and the difference of level of the two lakes. The Department, in its instructions, deemed it proper that such examination should be made of this line as should show whether or not its advantages outweighed its disadvantages.

As the parties were now well under way with their work, the commanding officer, with Mr. Menocal, Colonel Sonnenstern, and Mr. Hawley, set out to make a reconnaissance covering the route just described. At Granada we were met by Mr. Hollenbeck, an American merchant doing business in Greytown, and president of the Nicaragua Steam-Navigation Company, (whose vessels navigate the San Juan and Lake Nicaragua,) and who, for his own purposes, desired to go over the ground which we proposed to examine.

The expedition had already been indebted to Mr. Hollenbeck for many favors, and he now added to these by offering us the joint use of a small metallic life-boat, which we gladly accepted. Mr. Hawley was seized with a sharp attack of fever, and was unable to proceed.

Colonel Sonnenstern, with our horses and mules, went by land to the head of the Lake Managua, where he was to indicate a landing by erecting a signal. The rest of us, embarking in the life-boat, proceeded to the Estero of Panaloya, sounding as we went; through the Estero to the river Tipitapa, ascending the latter until the rapids (so called, for no water flows over the rocky bed) were reached; then putting the boat onto an ox-cart, which we found at the hacienda of Pasquiel, we sent it to the upper lake; at the same time making a paced traverse from the spot where the boat was hauled out to where it was again launched, and measuring the difference of levels between the two lakes by aneroid barometers—one observer remaining at the level of the lower lake, and the other going to that of the upper one, so that we had simultaneous observations at the two points.

Embarking again, we continued our line of soundings to the head of Lake Managua, where we joined Colonel Sonnenstern, having been three days and a half on the way since leaving Granada. Colonel Sonnenstern now showed us all the low passes from the lake toward the coast, and a careful examination was made of each of the heights, being measured as before by simultaneous pairs of observations, one observer at the water's edge, at the lake side, and the other going over the line. The conclusions arrived at were as follows, viz:

To carry the canal through Lake Managua and on to Realejo or to the Gulf of Fonseco; first, there would have to be dredged a channel at least sixteen miles in length from deep water in Lake Nicaragua to the foot of the rocky portion of the Rio Tipitapa, the depth of water being now, on the average, 10, and in the deepest places but 12, feet; thence an independent canal of four miles, with three locks to lift from the level of Lake Nicaragua to that of Managua, there being a difference of level varying from 22 to 28 feet between the two lakes. Next a channel two miles in length to deep water in Lake Managua, to be dredged, the water now gradually deepening in that distance from 4 feet to 5 fathoms.

From Managua City to the western end of the lake the cordillera extends in an unbroken wall, gradually lessening in height from about 1,200 feet till it looses itself in a high plain.

Several lines were run from the lake shore to a distance of from three to five miles, leading as has been said, through the passes indicated by Colonel Sonnenstern. We found long gradual slopes with heights varying from 80 to 200 feet above Lake Managua, which of course gave, taking the mean difference of level between the two lakes, from 105 to 225 feet above lake Nicaragua, nor were we quite sure when the lowest of these levels was found that the summit had been reached.

The least distance from the lake to Realejo is some thirty miles, so that even if the profile were much better than it is, the line bears no comparison with Child's route on account of the distance alone, without considering the six additional locks, three ascending and three descending, required. We found one other objection, which would of itself be fatal to the line; the geological formation of that part of the country is entirely volcanic. A line of volcanoes, nine in number, and all more or less active, extends from the lake towards Realejo; nearly parallel to, and in close proximity with, the proposed line of canal. While writing these pages news comes of the outburst of one of them, Monotombo, (whose base is washed by the waters of the lake,) accompanied by a shock of earthquake which was felt slightly as far as Virgin Bay, a distance of eighty miles. The soil and the underlying rock are so extremely porous that even in the wet season no streams flow into the lake from that side, all the rain that falls being drank up by the earth. We examined all the wells that we met, and found them from 100 to over 300 feet deep. If a canal were built through this region it would be impossible to keep it full unless it were made artificially water-tight from one end to the other, which would involve a cost equal to that of the excavation. For all of these reasons we regard the route as utterly impracticable.

In a survey made by Mr. John Baily many years since, that gentle man professed to have found a pass with but 56 feet above the lake level, but the most of his statements are found to be entirely unreliable, and this is no doubt like the rest. For example, he finds Lake Nicaragua to be 121 feet above mean tide in the Pacific, while the true difference of level is but 107 feet. Many of his other statements have been proved to be equally incorrect.

One valuable discovery resulted from our reconnaissance, which was the existence of a lime-stone quarry near Tipitapa, from which a high order of natural hydraulic lime is produced.

Returning by land, we stopped for a couple of days at Managua. We made an official visit to the president, who expressed great interest in the enterprise in which we were engaged, and offered on the part of his government all the assistance in its power. This offer we found the authorities everywhere not only instructed but fully disposed to make good, while the people, particularly the more intelligent classes, were equally well disposed towards the expedition.

While at Managua we were visited by several of the ministers of state, senators, members of congress, and other prominent gentlemen, and were serenaded by the national band, under the immediate direction of the president of congress, who was accompanied on the occasion by the minister of foreign affairs.

We were enabled on our way back to obtain a great deal of useful information in regard to the country and its resources.

On arriving at the Rio Gil Gonzales, we found that Lieutenant Leutze's party had demonstrated the impracticability of the line following the valley of that river, and on our entering their camp we met Messrs. Leutze and Crowell returning from the last of several reconnaissances which had been made by themselves and Mr. Miller, to find a practicable pass across the divide.

The Gil Gonzales, before reaching the lake, loses itself in a swamp, which, though it gave encouragement in one sense, promising comparatively low ground, made it extremely laborious to get the levels and traverse to the lake. After this was accomplished, however, the work became comparatively easy, though the elevation rose quite rapidly, and soon proved that no practicable line was to be found, though, of course, it was not abandoned until each of its tributaries had been followed up to an inadmissible altitude. There being no other locality not already known, which gave any promise, the party was ordered in to headquarters, while we proceeded to visit Lieutenant Rhoades. We found that his line had reached within four miles of Brito, and had developed as well as had been hoped for it. The officers and men, like those of party No. 1, were all well, though nearly everybody in each party was suffering with innumerable itching sores, upon all parts of the person, produced partly by dietetic, and possibly by climatic causes, but mainly by the bites and stings of insects and the poisonings of different vines and plants; principally among the former were the *garapatas*, a vicious species of wood-tick, which swarm almost every leaf and plant growing near the ground, and are of every size from that of a pin-point to that of a large split pea; transferring themselves by thousands to one's clothing and thence to the person, they bury their heads under the skin and are extremely hard to rid of. Frequently beating the clothing with a switch will rid one of a great many of the little pests, but it was seldom that any one passed a whole day without finding a greater or less number upon his person. Although the region in which the parties were operating contained several estates more or less cultivated, yet by far the greater part of each line was through an unbroken virgin forest, the rank tropical vegetation in many places forming a perfect jungle; occasionally were met large areas filled with the terrible pica-pica, as it is called by the natives; it is a tall bush loaded with a kind of bean, whose pods are covered with a down consisting of minute barbed needles; these are detached from the bush at the least shake given to it, and alighting upon the person produce perfect torture, seeming to penetrate through the clothing as easily as into the unprotected parts of the skin; the sensation produced is exactly like that of fire. It was sometimes found impossible to cut through the pica-pica at all, and slight deflections of the line were caused by it several times. It is only at certain seasons that the pica-pica is so troublesome, and our parties unfortunately experienced it at its worst.

On the 15th of February Mr. Rhoades's party reached Brito, and Mr. Greene and Lieutenant Moser connected their traverse and levels, respectively, with Mr. Niles's tide-guage.

A few days were then spent in making detailed surveys of some particular localities. The traverse as already examined having been plotted, and the proposed line of the canal laid down on the map, it was found that it would be necessary, if possible, to turn in four or five places the channel of the Rio Grande, and also that particular information was needed at two or three other points, for which purpose the special surveys were directed. At the same time Mr. Hawley, with a few men, was sent with the boring apparatus to test the character of the excavations likely to be met.

A party consisting of Lieutenants Leutze and Miller, Mr. Crowell, Mr. McCrea, and three men, was also sent to run the levels between Lakes Nicaragua and Managua, in order to ascertain the exact difference of level.

By February 22 all the parties had returned, having completed their work, and preparations were made to transfer the expedition to the valley of the San Juan. For reasons which will be given under the appropriate head, the route just surveyed and known as the Rio del Medio line was regarded as showing a better combination of favorable conditions than any other line, and to be entirely practicable, not only in an engineering but also in a commercial sense.

On applying to the Messrs. Chomorro for the amount of the indebtedness of the expedition for the hire of men, animals, &c., I was informed by them that they had been directed by the government of Nicaragua to pay on its account all expenses for such objects incurred by the expedition; this very handsome offer I did not feel at liberty either to accept or decline, without communicating it to your Department. In answer to my communication, I was directed to decline the offer with the Department's thanks, not only for that, but for all the assistance which had been given us by the government and authorities of Nicaragua. This order I communicated to the minister of foreign relations, who caused it to be published in the official gazette.

Our friend Mr. Hollenbeck having been notified that we were ready, sent the lake steamer to Virgin Bay for us; we embarked in her and proceeded to the mouth of the Zavalo, a tributary of the San Juan, which it joins just above Toro Rapids. Arriving March 4, 1873, we named our encampment "Camp Grant."

Although the river San Juan had several times been surveyed with more or less care, the surveys had always been confined to the river proper, and previous to our visit nothing was known of the adjacent country beyond what could be seen from the river banks. When it is considered that there is seldom a spot where the eye can penetrate two rods' distance, it will be seen how extremely limited the information was.

The Department's instructions required that the river should be examined with a view to such improvement, wherever possible, as should fit it for ship navigation, and that a location should be sought in its valley for an independent canal between those points where it should be found that the river could not be used.

GENERAL DESCRIPTION OF THE SAN JUAN RIVER.

Descending the San Juan we find it a broad open river for twenty eight miles, when we reach the first, called the Toro Rapids : these are some two miles long; next we have a stretch of clear river for seven miles, then the second or Castillio Rapids, less than a quarter of a mile in extent, and taking their name from the fort upon an adjacent hill; seven miles farther we reach the Mico and Balas, coming so close together as really to form continuous rapids; their extent is not quite one mile ; four miles farther down we come to the Machuca Rapids, the last which we find; their length is about two miles.

For twenty miles from the foot of Machuca the river has a depth varying from 20 to 60 feet, with but little current ; this section is called by the natives Agua Muerte, or dead water. At the foot of the Agua Muerte, the San Carlos is received into the river, and is the first considerable tributary met; above this, although every valley has its little stream, often deep enough to give a good wetting to our parties, yet the most of these are insignificant. The Zavalo and the Paco Sol are the largest of the upper tributaries, but have but little effect upon the main river. Opposite and below the mouth of the San Carlos, which comes from a long distance up in the Costa Rica hills, the San Juan changes its character altogether, and is filled with shoals and sand-bars. Twenty-four and a half miles below the San Carlos is the confluence of the Serepiqui, a river of similar character and size, and also coming from Costa Rica. Thirteen miles farther, we come to the forks of the Colorado ; here the main river divides into two branches, the principal of which, the Colorado, flows to the eastward and empties into the sea ; the less, called the Lower San Juan, passes more to the northward, and is divided up into numerous mouths, one of which, the Tanso, discharges its waters into the sea, the others into the lagoon which was once the harbor of Greytown.

About four miles above the forks, a small caño, called the San Juanillo, leaves the main river and flows in a direction generally parallel to the lower San Juan, which it finally rejoins near Greytown.

Most persons who are acquainted with the tropical regions agree in the opinion that, as a rule, slack-water navigation in tropical streams is almost if not quite impossible, on account of their being subject to sudden and violent freshets. The San Juan having its origin in a body of water of so large area as Lake Nicaragua, and being fed, as said above, by insignificant tributaries in its upper portions, is not there subject to these freshets. Below the confluence of the San Carlos, which drains a large extent of mountainous country, the San Juan partakes of the character of other rivers in the same region ; farther on it will be seen that we propose the use of the river only above the mouth of the San Carlos, and an independent canal from there to the sea. At the present time the freshets of the San Carlos, by backing up the waters of the San Juan, affect the rises in the latter even as high as the foot of Machuca Rapids. This backing up will, however, be entirely overcome by the dam, which is estimated for, to be located just above the mouth of the San Carlos.

A rapid examination of the river, made while on our way to Virgin Bay, had convinced us that the navigation from its head to Castillio Rapids could be so improved as to fulfill the conditions required ; it was therefore determined to begin at the latter place the survey for an independent canal-route.

The organization of parties Nos. 1 and 2 continued pretty much as before, except that Master Hawley took the level in Lieutenant Leutze's party, relieving Lieutenant Miller, who was placed in charge of a separate party to make a survey of the river proper. Master Miles, Ensign Bull, and Mr. Brown, a young English gentleman, who accepted the vacant position of first-class apothecary, were assigned to Mr. Miller's party as assistants.

Colonel Sonnenstern was the bearer of instructions from the government to Colonel Sandoval, commandant of the fort of Castillio, to let us have as many soldiers as could be spared from duty to act as machetoros. Colonel Sandoval was able to let us have but eight men, just half as many as we needed, and after trying in vain for nearly a month to get more, either on the river or from Greytown, Colonel Sonnenstern went to Granada, where he procured a full supply. In the mean time the parties had to work short-handed, adding no little to the severity of the labor.

The section of the country adjacent to the river, between the Castillio and the Machuca Rapids, is exceedingly broken, many of the mountain spurs extending to the very water's edge. This section of the work bid fair to prevent more difficulties in locating a canal, and consequently required a more careful examination than any other. I concluded to keep the two parties together until past Machuca, giving to Mr. Rhodes's party the main line, and to Mr. Leutze's the special surveys of the several rapids, and of the probable locations of dams ; and also the running of offsets from the main line to the river bank.

It will be seen further on how admirably, upon the result of the survey of this section, the engineering skill of Mr. Menocal has solved that part of the problem which gave us most discouragement while the survey was progressing.

The country was so much more broken than had been supposed that a canal built through it would be enormously expensive, while it seemed as if the improvement of the river would be still more so. A happy combination of the two methods, however, has overcome the difficulties, and the section, instead of being the most expensive and troublesome, bids fair to be the least so.

A bench-mark was established on the left bank of the river about one-half mile above Castillio Rapids, and the work was fairly begun on the 6th of March. The parties made their first encampment in some farm buildings, but ever after had to rely upon their shelter-tents. These were of very light canvas, water-proofed, and afforded very fair protection from rain. Officers and men soon became so skillful in building houses with these that they were able to make themselves comparatively comfortable.

The line led through an unbroken virgin forest, so interlaced with parasites and undergrowth as to be almost impenetrable, and in most places altogether so without the vigorous use of the macheta, making it necessary to cut a trail for every foot of advance, passing sometimes three or four times a day over hills of greater or less height and through streams in every valley. Although at this season of the year we had reason to expect the dryest weather, scarcely a day passed without one or more showers, which converted the overlying stratum of clay into a stiff, clingy mud, particularly upon the hill-sides, where it was less covered with vegetable deposit. The labor upon the west side of the lake had seemed to be, and was, very severe, but it was looked back upon as very light in comparison to what was now endured, more particularly as the parties, always organized with the minimum number consistent with efficiency, were now, as has been mentioned, short, one five men and the other three. I might mention that no servants were allowed to officers, from commander down, as the small appropriation made it necessary to economize in every way possible. Indeed, after leaving the vicinity of Castillio Viego, the officers were obliged even to wash their own clothing, being out of the reach of anybody who could be hired for the purpose.

It would be impossible for me to express my appreciation of the untiring energy and zeal displayed by both officers and men, and of the cheerfulness with which they submitted to the hardships and discomforts of the seventy-six days spent in running the line to Greytown.

A general compass-course was taken from the map, and followed as nearly as the conformation of the ground would permit; constant reconnaissances on either side being made to take advantage of any low ground, which by diminishing the profile would compensate, or more than compensate, for the increase in length caused by deflections. This required a great deal of judgment, and was usually done by Mr. Menocal when present, and at other times by the officer in charge of the party, though there was ample employment for the latter without this extra duty; in fact it would always be better to have at least four officers in each party, so that when the officer in charge was absent upon a reconnaissance there would be another to lead the line without calling the officer in charge of either the transit or of the level to divide his attention between that duty and his own.

Mr. Menocal remained with party No. 2 until the line reached Machuca, and was indefatigable in his labors, saving many a mile of useless work by examining the country ahead of the instruments, though with every precaution the line would occasionally get into a nest of hills and spurs impossible to pass, when it would become necessary to retrace a greater or less distance and take a new departure, a most disheartening operation to a party with a long distance ahead and a limited time to accomplish it in.

With every exertion, under the existing circumstances, a mile a day was good progress, while in some few cases of unusually rainy days not more than 2,000 feet were made.

The line was so near the river that it was always convenient to locate the camps on its banks. This was a fortunate circumstance, as the only means of transportation was by boats or upon men's shoulders. A flat boat, lent to us by Mr. Hollenbeck, and a large canoe, were used for shifting camps, which was done whenever the line extended so far that it was inconvenient to walk back at night. At first a new camp was made for about every four miles of survey, but later not more than one for each eight miles, the new camp always being carried some distance ahead of the end of the line.

The Messrs. Hollenbeck, Runnels, and Chomorro, and Colonel Sonnenstern under his familiar title of " Don Max," were all remembered in giving names to the encampments.

After a few days at the level, Mr. Hawley was taken with a severe attack of fever and obliged to give up; he was, however, sent to Greytown to relieve Mr. Reilly in charge of the bulk of our provisions which had been left there in store. Requisition was made upon Commander Reed of the Kansas for another officer and also for five seamen ; in the mean time Lieutenant Leutze took charge of the level in addition to all his other duties. About the same time Lieutenant Commander Schulze was prostrated by a sunstroke, and so severe was the shock upon his system that the surgeon advised his being sent north as the only chance of recovery. Messrs. Schulze and Hawley had been a great deal in the West Indies of late, both serving in the first two expeditions under Commander Selfridge in Darien; neither was in a fit state of health to go on the present expedition, and we were deprived of the services of two experienced and zealous officers at at the very time when they were most needed. Mr. Hawley was very useful in his new position, however, which compensated largely for his loss in the field.

While the topographic parties were progressing toward Machuca, Lieutenant Miller made his preparations for beginning the survey of the river proper, fitting out for the purpose a little flotilla consisting of a flat-boat borrowed of a Colonel Hanger at the mouth of the Zavalo, a dinghy belonging to the Kansas, a balsa designed by Commodore Ammen, United States Navy, and a canoe; the flat-boat was designed to carry provisions and equipments, and also to be used as quarters for the officers and part of the men, and was fitted up with awnings and bunks; the rest of the men lived in the other boats.

The survey of the river was directed to be done with the gradienter, an instrument combining the functions of the transit and level, and also fitted with a micrometer-attachment, by which distances are obtained by measuring the angle subtended by a rod upon which two triangles are fixed 12 feet apart. The level was to be run from the lake to Castillo, where it was to be connected with Mr. Moser's initial bench-mark, in order that we might have a connected line of levels from the lake to the sea. On the 29th of March an officer came up the river from the Kansas with five seamen, two of whom were sent to Mr. Leutze, and the other three to Mr. Miller, making his party complete. About the same time Colonel Sonnenstern arrived from Granada with a number of natives, who were distributed between the two topographic parties, making them also of full strength.

In the hydrographic party the following distribution of work was made : Lieutenant Miller, with the balsa, took charge of the gradienter, recording the courses and distances and sketching in the topography. Master Niles, with the dinghy, took and recorded the soundings. Ensign Bull, with the canoe, took charge of the level and gradienter rods, and recorded the levels.

The work was done as follows: A bench-mark was established at the water's level on the wharf of the Navigation Company, at San Carlos ; the rods were set to the bench-mark, the gradienter set up, and back observations taken for course, distance, and height of instrument. The rods were then sent to the opposite bank of the river and somewhat down stream, where four observations were taken for course, distance, and height of station. Next, the instrument was carried down a convenient distance, but on the same side of the river, and back-sights were again taken as before. A line of soundings was run from instrument-station to rod-station, and thence to the next instrument-station, and so on. Mr. Browne, with the flat-boat, dropped down each day to a point abreast the last station, where a convenient place on shore was sought for building a fire, and the cook set to work to prepare dinner.

By the time that was accomplished, which was generally about sunset, the boats were anchored in the middle of the river, to avoid as much as possible the mosquitoes, which came out in swarms as night approached. Dinner dispatched, all hands were generally ready to spread their mosquito-nets and go to bed. Before daylight in the morning everybody was astir, breakfast and the midday luncheon were cooked at the same spot which had served the night before, and the traverse was again started.

From San Carlos to the mouth of the Zavalo, the banks of the river are low and swampy, though the water was at about its lowest stage —earlier in, the work could scarcely have been done at all—heavily fringed with grass, and overgrown with trees, brush, and parasites. The last are always particularly luxuriant near the water, and assume the most fantastic and often beautiful shapes, forming screens and bowers of dense foliage of all colors and varieties, very charming to the eye, though anything but agreeable to those who have to cut through it to find a setting for an instrument or rod and an outlook to the opposite bank, and who often find themselves covered with ants and other insects by the time they have finished.

The topographic parties reached Machuca April 2. It was now determined to divide the remainder of the work into two sections, giving to Lieutenant Leutze's party the line from the mouth of the river Serepiqui to Greytown, and to Lieutenant Rhoades's that from Machuca to the initial point of Mr. Leutze's section.

Mr. Leutze and party, accompanied by Mr. Menocal, started in the flat-boat on the 3d and arrived on the following day at the Serepiqui, established their camp some two miles below its mouth, and commenced their line at once.

On the 9th of April Master J. B. Briggs, of the Kansas, joined Mr. Leutze, and was placed in charge of the level.

My first intention had been to run the line for a canal continuously from Castillo to Greytown, leaving it to be decided afterward how much of it should be used, and how much of the river itself, a little further examination convincing us that with slight improvement the Agua Muerte could be made fit for ship-navigation; and the time being very limited I determined to let Mr. Rhoades bench off where he now was, April 16, about four miles below Machuca, and to recommence opposite the mouth of the San Carlos, directing Mr. Miller on his arrival to take up the level and connect Mr. Moser's two bench-marks.

By April 19 Mr. Rhoades and party had established a camp and commenced their new line.

At a good stage of water the river-steamers run from Greytown to the foot of Castillo Rapids, around which the cargoes are shifted by a tramway to another boat which carries them above the Toro Rapids, where they are again shifted to the lake-steamer. As the dry season advances the river-boats are first prevented from going nearer to Greytown than the forks of the Colorado, and soon after are unable to go above Machuca Rapids. A small flat-bottomed steamer of about fifteen tons burden is then brought into requisition to navigate the rapids, and even she has great difficulty in doing so. This state of affairs occurs at the very time when the freights on the lake and river are heaviest; when the coffee and indigo crops are being moved, together with large quantities of India rubber and hides. No little nerve is required in navigating the rapids at this season of the year, as the tortuous channels make it very dangerous to property if not to life. The river is strewed with the wrecks of steamers that have been lost in the last twenty years. Without the constant personal exertion of Mr. Hollenbeck, the steam-navigation company would have been brought to a.stand-still this year; and as it was, on account of the necessarily irregular trips of the boats, it became sometimes a difficult matter to keep our parties supplied with provisions, though Mr. Hollenbeck did everything in his power to aid us. I was obliged, on one occasion, to carry a load to Mr. Rhoades by canoe, a distance of sixty miles, against the strong current of the river, arriving just in time to save the party from being out of almost everything.

Lieutenant Miller's party reached the head of Toro Rapids with their survey by April 26, after which, the river-banks becoming higher and firmer, they commenced to have somewhat easier work per mile, but compensated for it by making more miles a day.

We were now beginning to experience the weather that we had expected earlier in the season, showers becoming more rare day by day, contrary to the predictions of the inhabitants, who had expected an early return of the wet season. All the parties were in consequence making exceptionally good progress, and were straining every nerve to complete the work before it should be interrupted by the rains.

Mr. Rhoades's section between the San Carlos and Serepiqui was developing very favorably for the canal, but was passing through a great deal of swamp, which made the work very severe; indeed, had it not been for the very dry weather it would have been impossible, in many places, for Messrs. Green and Moser to set up their instruments at all. The party were availing themselves of the sand-banks left dry by the falling waters as locations for camps. These were very pleasant, being clear and free from vegetation, while the breeze had free access, making them much cooler than while surrounded by trees; but to pay for these every officer and man suffered more or less from the inigua, or jigger, as it is sometimes called, and the mosquito-worm. These, or rather their germs, are both deposited under the skin by insects, the former generally located in the feet, where the young are developed in large numbers inclosed in a sack. If these are not extracted or destroyed they produce ugly sores. The most of us before leaving the country became quite skillful in removing them, and following the native rule of putting a little of the ash or juice of tobacco in the cavity which had been occupied by the sack, none of our number suffered any ill consequences from them. The mosquito-worm is much more troublesome. It attacks all parts of the person. The worm grows rapidly, and its gnawing is quite painful. The method used by the natives to extract it is to lay over the skin, for a few minutes, a piece of tobacco saturated in oil, after which it can generally be squeezed out without trouble. Calomel instead of tobacco is more efficacious still, and will sometimes succeed when the other fails. Mr. Greene removed two by it from his head where they had been annoying him for several days. The theory is, that the tobacco or the calomel makes the worm come to the surface.

I was never able to discover exactly what insect it was that produced either of these. The jigger is supposed to be deposited by a small sand-fly, and the worm, as its name indicates, by a peculiar kind of mosquito.

Insects, lizards, &c., had been so common from the first that the most of them had ceased to be annoying. Mosquitoes at night, and in the swamps at all times; and by day wasps, hornets, and congo-flies, particularly a large yellow species, which drew the blood every time it alighted upon the skin; no one could become enough used to it to produce indifference; our parties had plenty of opportunity if it had been possible. Garapatas, though not uncommon, were so much less plentiful than they had been on the west side as not to be taken into account. On the other hand mosquitoes which, except in the swamps, had never troubled us there, were here in countless swarms. Another of the pests of nearly every camp was the alligator-ant, which attains a length of nearly an inch, and whose bite is as painful as the sting of the hornet, and apparently even more poisonous. Hartshorn was always carried by some member of the parties as a remedy for bites and stings. Among the many favors which had been bestowed upon us by Mr. Runnels and his family, of Virgin Bay, was a present to each officer of a cedron-bean, said to be a certain remedy for the bites of venomous snakes or the sting of tarantulas; fortunately we never had occasion to test its merits, though there were many narrow escapes. Parasite vines of all sizes and colors, and festooned in every imaginable form, were so common that a snake hanging from a limb of a tree would often be unnoticed by the officers and sailors, though never by the macheteros, who seemed to be on the constant lookout for them. Occasionally one of the former would suddenly feel himself seized and jerked back, and would find that the keen eye and the strong arm of one of the natives had rescued him from an enemy that he himself had not seen, though perhaps looking directly toward it and not a yard from it.

Toward the last of April, Mr. Leutze's line had reached the San Juanillo, and was extending down its valley toward Greytown; the ground was very swampy, with heavy cutting, while the river itself at its head was impassable even for the smallest canoe, being full of drift-wood, and at that season having scarcely any water. After extending the line some three miles from the main river, returning each night to the camp which was still on the banks of the latter, it became impossible to proceed farther without obtaining a nearer camping-ground, as the six miles' walk going and coming was a fair day's work of itself. As it was quite impossible to transport the camp equipage, provisions, &c., to the end of the line, even if there had been a suitable location for a camp, it was concluded to cut a trail through, striking the main river some distance lower down, (the two streams, near their forks, running at an acute angle with each other.) This picket proved to be over a mile long, passing over several steep-sided hills, fortunately none of them very high, and through swampy ground in their valleys. It was some improvement in point of distance, however, and the camp was shifted down to where the picket struck the river-bank. The line was now extended some three miles farther on a compass-course, leading over hills, across runs, through swamps and mire, across several sloughs, and across three lagoons. Some of the streams could be forded, others had to be bridged by felling trees across them; logs had to be dragged and laid to make a footway across the sloughs, and generally the best that could be done made but a precarious one. Each time the party passed over the line it would be found that much of the work had to be done over again. The lagoons were overgrown with a tall, thick water-grass; this was beaten down until a sort of floating island was made, when by stepping lightly and quickly over it, the party succeeded in getting across, not without an occasional mishap attended with a good wetting and no little danger, as it was impossible to swim, and next to impossible for one to aid another.

It was hoped every hour as the line advanced that the San Juanillo would again be intersected and found navigable, when it was proposed to move the camp to its banks, by taking the boats down the lower San Juan to the junction, and up the former stream to the camping-place.

After going about three miles, a sluggish stream flowing to the south-ward and eastward was crossed. According to the best maps in our possession this should have been the desired river; it was still too shallow for the boats, and too muddy to be waded; so full of logs and other obstructions that even if the bottom had been hard it would have been a tremendous task to follow its bed. There was nothing left to do but to try and strike the stream again, lower down. Lieutenant Leutze and Mr. Crowell, with the macheteros, now spent one day cutting a trail to intersect the river. A mile and a half was run, showing no signs of it, and finally coming into a nest of hills; the party now returned to the main line, and extended that for 3,000 feet, when the lateness of the hour compelled them to start for camp. The work accomplished, together with the walk from the camp and back, had made a very severe day's labor, but there was worse to come. Mr. Leutze now resolved to cut through on the compass-course which he had been following, until the river was reached, and to run the instruments over it afterwards. Accordingly, on the morning of May 3, he, with Mr. Crowell and the macheteros, set out before daylight. The end of the line was nearly five miles from camp, and the trail, made worse each time it was passed over, was exceedingly heavy. On reaching it the men were divided into two reliefs, and working an hour each at a time. The line was advanced 13,600 feet, passing for a couple of miles over the same swamp and mire, after which it intersected seven different hills, from 80 to 150 feet high, with very steep sides; then a valley was followed for some distance, whose water-course had to be forded in numerous places; next, a wide shallow stream was reached. This obstacle at first seemed insurmountable; the stream was too shallow to be crossed by swimming; its muddy bottom afforded no footing, and its width precluded the usual method of bridging by felling a tree across it. Finally all hands set to work to cut and bring branches. These were thrown into the water, and confined in place by logs until sufficiently firm to bear a man's weight; then some of the number occupying that which was already laid, built further in the same manner, till a sort of causeway extended from bank to bank. The party then crossed over, but so little sustaining-power was there in the structure that the last man was nearly up to his waist in water before he reached the bank.

The party now proceeded on a short distance farther, when they suddenly came out upon the shore of a beautiful lagoon. The map showed a nest of lagoons in the vicinity, all connected with the San Juanillo, but whether this was one of them or not could not be told. Hoping that it might be, a signal was erected at the end of the picket and the party turned their steps homeward. Mr. Leutze hung up his blue flannel shirt upon the signal to make it more conspicuous. They reached the camp some time after dark, some of the number so exhausted that it was feared they would not be able to reach it at all. The day had been intensely hot, the breeze being entirely cut off by the dense vegetation. Myriads of insects filled the air; the yellow congo and the mosquitoes seemed unusually vicious. The fifteen miles of tramping, wading, climbing hills, scrambling over fallen trees and through the jungle would have been a severe day's work, alone, without the additional labor of cutting and road-building.

The limits of this report make it impossible to give anything like a detailed account of the labors of the different parties or of individual officers, but the above will give an idea of them, though candor compels me to say that the last day here described never had quite an equal; indeed, a very few such would have broken down the strongest of our people. Throughout the expedition the officers not only directed but led the work, no matter how hard or disagreeable it might be, and were most cheerfully followed by the petty officers and seamen. Especially deserving of mention were Messrs. John Quevedo, Charles H. Mays, Paul Hoffmann, John Buck, Joseph C. Bruner, and Henry Butz, who enlisted with petty officers' ratings to do duty in the expedition as rodmen, polemen, and chainmen, and exhibited great zeal and intelligence in the performance of their duties.

A couple of days after the events above narrated, Messrs. Leutze and Crowell went to Greytown, where they procured the services of an excellent guide, well acquainted with the Juanillo lagoons, and who, from their description, recognized the lagoon which they had found as the Silico, named from the Silico palm which grows upon its borders: to this he guided them. The route led up the San Juanillo for about four miles, then through a small creek and into the lakelet; here, to their joy, the signal was found. A great many fallen trees, branches, &c., had to be cut away before even a canoe could be forced through the creek. They now selected a place for a camp and returned to Greytown. A couple of days later they had brought the party around, established themselves in their new camp, and set to work to run the instruments and chain over the trail which had been cut, as described. First, however, several reconnaissances were made to see if the seven hills could be avoided without too great deflection. It was found that they could not be, and the line was accepted as it had been orignally run.

May 13, the commanding officer, accompanied by Colonel Sonnenstern, went in the Kansas to Monkey Point, examining carefully the intermediate coast for harbors, or locations where harbors might be formed, making surveys of the angles in the shore-line at Punta Gorda and at Monkey Point to see if either of these could be utilized; both, however, proved hopeless for the character of harbor required for a canal terminus. The country between Greytown and Monkey Point was very broken, except the alluvial formation which extends only a little over one-half of the distance. Colonel Sonnenstern, who, in 1866, had passed over the route between San Miguelito, on the lake, and the mouth of the Roma River, had declared the country to be utterly impracticable even for a railroad, which was then projected; but, although having every confidence in the opinion of that gentleman, the commanding officer thought it better to make such a personal reconnaissance in that direction as would fulfill the instructions of the Navy Department.

By May 22 all the parties had arrived in Greytown—the work in the interior complete. The weather for the last month had been magnificent, and more had been accomplished than during the previous two months. On the 20th the weather changed entirely, bringing heavy and frequent showers.

Several of the officers and men who had held out to the last day of the work, now, that the strain was relieved, were attacked with fever. Mr. Rhoades was among the number. None of the cases were at all serious, and were mainly due, probably, to overwork, and to sharp wettings during the last two or three days on the line.

There now remained only some hydrographic work to be done to supplement a survey of the harbor made the previous year, and to get the steam-launch down from the lake, the low stage of the water in the river not having permitted it before. As it was hoped that there might have been a rise, or soon would be, a small party under Mr. Leutze, accompanied by Mr. Browne, was sent after the launch. The commanding officer, Colonel Sonnenstern, and Dr. Bransford went up the river at the same time to attend to other matters, part of which was to pay off at Castillo the soldiers who had served as macheteros, and also deliver and pay for the use of some canoes which had been employed by the expedition.

In getting the launch over Tero Rapids, she was unfortunately grounded in about the worst part of it, involving two days' labor for all hands in the water. We even had the doctor overboard up to his neck; although this was not exactly in his department, the doctor was always ready for hard work when it could be made useful. The cultivation which Mr. Leutze and Mr. Browne had each given to his muscle worked greatly to our advantage also. Our friend Mr. Hollenbeck finally came to our rescue, after we had, with only partial success, exhausted our own means. Coming by in the steamer Panaloya, he tied her up to the bank, took our line to his capstan, and, after two or three hours' work, succeeded in getting the boat off. He then piloted her safely over the rapids through a channel known to himself.

At Castillo Mr. Leutze rigged sheers and hoisted out the launch's boiler, Colonel Loudoval with his soldiers, manning the falls of the tackle. Everything else was removed from the boat that could be, but as she still drew some four feet, it was found impossible to get her over the rapids. No rise had as yet taken place, though considerable rain had fallen. Mr. Hollenbeck promised to send the boat down the river by some of his people, as soon as there was a sufficient rise. We therefore left her in charge of a watchman, and returned to Greytown. On our arrival I found awaiting us orders from the Department, directing me to send a number of the officers home by mail steamer, and the remainder of the expedition by the Kansas. The former arrived in New York July 3, and the Kansas with her party, July 20. I am happy to say that not an officer or man was lost from any cause.

A full and detailed report is in course of preparation, with maps, plans, profiles, and diagrams, designs for locks, dams, culverts, &c., and for breakwaters and other proposed harbor improvements, with the estimated cost of each, and will all be forwarded to the Department as soon as completed.

The work was constantly checked as much as possible. So long a traverse required extreme care to prevent its swinging out more or less. As has been said, this work was immediately intrusted to Messrs. Greene and Crowell, in the topographic parties, and to Mr. Miller, in the hydrographic. Offsets were frequently run from the main line to the river bank, and were connected by Mr. Miller with his traverse. These gentlemen also sketched in the topography.

The levels from the lake to the sea, an aggregate distance of one hundred and nineteen miles, were run by three different officers, viz, Lieutenant J. F. Moser and Master J. B. Briggs, on the main line, with intermediate sections by Lieutenant Miller, upon the river-banks. These, compared with the line on the Pacific side, showed the height of the lake to be absolutely the same above mean tide of either sea. When the character of the ground passed over is considered, this coincidence seems quite remarkable, and shows with what extreme care the work was executed.

Too much cannot be said in praise of Lieutenants Rhoades, Leutze, and Miller, the commanders of parties, for the intelligence, judgment, and zeal with which they performed their multifarious and often perplexing duties. Lieutenant Miller speaks in the highest terms of his assistants, Messrs. Niles, Bull, and Browne.

Mr. McCrea, commander's clerk, volunteered for the duty of rodman, and continued to perform it until taken down with fever.

Dr. Bransford, in addition to treating the sick in the most successful manner, was indefatigable in collecting specimens of plants, animals, insects, &c., and in acquiring a knowledge of the peculiar diseases of the country, and what differences of treatment were found necessary in the case of the natives and of foreigners, for this purpose treating gratuitously all who applied to him. His report will doubtless be very interesting to medical men.

Mr. A. G. Menocol, the chief civil engineer, by his thorough knowledge of his profession and his constant personal exertions, as much as possible accompanying that party, who, for the time being, were operating in the most difficult section of country, contributed enormously to the success of the expedition. Indeed, with so able and zealous a set of officers there was but little left for the commanding officer to do except to keep the parties in supplies, and failure was impossible. I beg to add that these remarks are not made, as so often is the case, for the sake of saying something agreeable, but as giving expression to a conviction which was of great comfort to me during the progress of the work. As I could not be with each of the parties all the time, it was very pleasant to know that the work went on quite as well when I was not present as when I was, and possibly better.

THE PROPOSED CANAL AND IMPROVEMENTS.

The surface of Lake Nicaragua is 107 feet above mean tide in either sea. It is proposed to make this the summit level of the canal, and to connect the lake with the Pacific by canal, and with the Caribbean Sea by a combination of canal and slack-water navigation.

WESTERN DIVISION.

The first section of the proposed canal toward the Pacific leaves the lake at the mouth of the Rio del Medio, and extends for a distance of 7.58 miles, with an average depth of cutting of 54 feet. This section is by far the most expensive part of the whole work. The second section extends from the end of the first to Brito, a distance of 8.75 miles, making the total distance from lake to sea 16.33 miles. The line has been laid down as nearly as possible to correspond to the lowest profile. It consists, however, of straight reaches and of curves which are arcs of circles. The smallest radius admitted is 2,200 feet. The excavation in the second section will be, throughout, less than the prism of the canal; in other words, the proposed surface is higher than the profile of the ground. The material taken out will be used to build up embankments. There will be ten descending locks, all in this section, and located in the straight reaches. There will be at Brito a tide-lock.

LAKE NAVIGATION.

From the mouth of the Rio del Medio to the head of the San Juan the distance is about 56 statute miles. Twenty-six feet of water can be carried to within 1,350 feet of the mouth of the Rio del Medio. On the east side a channel will have to be deepened from 6 to 8 feet for a distance of nine miles. The bottom is a firm mud, easily removed by the dredge.

EASTERN DIVISION.

SLACK-WATER NAVIGATION.

It is believed, for reasons which have already been given, that slack-water navigation in the upper part of the San Juan is entirely practicable.

It is proposed to improve the river by the construction of four dams, the first at Castillo, the second at Balas, the third at Machuca, and the fourth near the mouth of the San Carlos. Most excellent locations for dams exist and have been selected at the first three places, with solid rock foundations, shallow water, and a wide-channel-way in proportion to the general width of the river, thus subjecting the dams to the minimum risk from the force of the water. The location at San Carlos would be called good, except in comparison with the others, which are exceedingly favorable.

Some improvement in the bed of the river will have to be made here and there by dredging and blasting out rocks. This has been estimated for, the amount of excavation being computed.

To get around the dams there will be required sections of canal of the following lengths, respectively, each containing one lock, viz, at Castillo, 0.78 mile; at Balas, 1.57 miles; and at Machuca, 1.16 miles.

CANAL.

From the mouth of the San Carlos to Greytown, a canal of 41.9 miles in length is proposed. This line has been laid down to correspond with the lowest profile, except when the increase of length required to make it do so was too great to be compensated for by the diminution in the depth of excavation. The curves, as in the western division, are all arcs of circles. The least radius is 2,500. The profile is so favorable that 36.96 miles out of the 41.90 will require excavation less than the prism of the canal, the material being used for embankments. The remaining distance is made up of several short reaches where the line cuts through hills.

Seven locks in addition to those abreast the dams will be required, making ten in all. These will be located in the hills just mentioned, in order to take advantage of the rock foundation, the advantage of which will be enormous.

The total length of canal will thus be 61.74 miles; of this, 47.37 miles will be in excavation and embankment combined, leaving but 14.37 miles in which the excavation is greater than the prism of the canal. 6.50 miles of the deep cutting is in one section, i. c., in the first of the western division; the rest is composed of the cuts through hills and parts of the sections around the dams. In all cases on the east side there will be convenient places of deposit for the material taken out close at hand; where embankments are made the whole of the material removed will be placed directly abreast the place from which it is taken.

The eminent American engineer, Mr. J. C. Trautwine, estimates that where excavation costs 19 cents per cubic yard when deposited within 25 feet, it will, if carried one mile in carts, cost 57.09 cents, and if carried two miles, will cost 95.57 cents per cubic yard. This exhibit of the rapid rate of increase in cost will show how immense is the advantage in a work of such magnitude of having the place of deposit so close at hand.

It happens that the section of the western division requiring the deep excavation is located in the best cultivated part of the country and where there are most roads. A little exercise of judgment on the part of the person directing the work will enable him to get rid of the most of his material even there without carrying it any great distance. The crest of the divide is but a few yards wide and the descent is quite rapid on either side. By commencing the work at different elevations turnouts will be found near at hand.

In comparing the relative merits of any two proposed routes for a canal, nothing can be less satisfactory than the mere statement of their relative lengths without also stating the average depth of excavation; thus, were the sides vertical, then would a canal ten miles long, with an average depth of 40 feet, be equal to one twenty miles long, with a depth of but 20 feet; but, in fact, the banks must always have an outward slope, in order to be self-sustaining; the least slope admissible in canals of the character here considered is in earth 1½ feet to 1, or, as both sides are the same, the cross-section widens 3 feet for every 1 foot of increased depth. The canal here estimated for has an average depth of cutting of but 9 feet above the prism, or the proposed water surface; the 61.74 miles are equal to but twenty-two miles of one whose average depth above the water-surface is 40 feet.

In estimating the cost of the work, 35 cents per cubic yard has been allowed for earth, and from $1.25 to $1.50 in rock. In computing the amount of rock, care has been taken to allow for more than is likely to be met, in order to be on the safe side.

It will be seen that prisms of two different widths are estimated for, the reduced is proposed for those portions which require deep cutting, and, except that the proposed depth of water is one foot greater, does not differ materially from the dimensions proposed for the Darien Canal. The wider is proposed for all the rest of the canal, i. e., for those portions where excavation and embankment are to be used. The difference in the shape of the prism for earth and for rock is due to the different slopes required.

DIMENSIONS OF CANAL PRISM.

Reduced.

	In rock.	In earth.
Width at bottom	50 feet.	50 feet.
Width 10 feet above bottom	90 feet.	
Width at surface of water	106 feet.	128 feet.

Broad.

	Earth.
Width at bottom	72 feet.
Width at surface of water	150 feet.
Width 10 feet above surface	180 feet.

The depth of water throughout is 26 feet.

The dimensions of the locks are: length between miter-sills, 400 feet; width of chamber, 72 feet.

It will be seen that the Rio del Medio route has been chosen in place of that known as Childs's. The reasons for this are as follows: First, the distance by the former is 2.60 miles less than by the latter; this advantage is about compensated for by a greater summit-height. Second, the valley of the Rio Las Lajas is exceedingly tortuous, giving curves of so small radius that it would be impossible to locate the canal in them, and to cut off the bends would carry the excavation through numerous hills which extend to the river-bank. The third and most potent reason is, that the Las Lajas line intersects no less than five considerable streams, which would have to be taken into the canal and would cause great inconvenience. On the other hand, the Rio del Medio line receives but one stream, and that under so favorable conditions that it can, without trouble and at moderate cost, be sent under the bed of the canal, by means of a culvert which will be found to be estimated for.

HARBOR AT BRITO.

On the right bank of the Rio Grande there is a high rocky hill which juts out into the sea in the form of a promontory for a distance of 1,600

. feet. The sides are steep-to. There are, near the outer extremity, 18 feet of water at low tide, close alongside the rocks.

The left bank of the river terminates in a sandy beach, bearing to the south-southwest. An angle is thus formed in the coast which we propose to convert into a harbor by running a breakwater from the end of the point in a southwest direction for a distance of 1,600 feet. The outer end will be in 6 fathoms of water. The rock can be blasted right at hand and dumped into the sea, being allowed to take its own slope. The bottom is a firm sand, but no doubt overlies a bed of rock, judging from the formation of the coast. The deep water extends to within 200 feet of the beach, where some dredging will have to be done.

HARBOR AT GREYTOWN.

A commodious and excellent harbor once existed at Greytown. The strip of sand which formed its outer limits has now extended across what was the entrance, and has converted the harbor into a lagoon. This has been gradually silting up, until there are islands where twenty years ago there was water enough to float a frigate.

The silt which has been destroying the harbor is a volcanic sand, so light as to be held in almost complete suspension by rapidly flowing water; it is the material of which the whole delta of the San Juan has been mainly formed; and, indeed, the entire alluvial district in the vicinity.

A quantity of sand taken from the outer beach at Punta Arenas (as it is still called) was recently submitted, with some from the sea-beach at Monkey Point, thirty-two miles north of Greytown, to Professor Henry, of the Smithsonian Institute. Under his direction the two specimens were examined and compared by the mineralogist of the institute. As will be seen, they were found to be quite different in composition and structure, showing clearly that the sand from Punta Arenas was not thrown up by the sea, but deposited by the river.

The constituents and peculiarities are as follows, viz:

No. 18.	No. 19.
Sand from Punta Arenas.	*Sand from Monkey Point.*
Constituents:	Constituents:
Quartz, a small quantity.	Quartz, chiefly.
Tourmaline.	Tourmaline.
10 per cent. magnetic sand.	3 per cent. magnetic sand
Feldspar, small percentage.	Feldspar, small quantity.
Hornblende, probably.	Fragments of marine shells.
Color, dark grayish-brown.	Color, light grayish-brown.
Grains fine, but coarser than No. 19.	Grains very fine.
No fragments of shell in this specimen.	This sand has evidently been subject to the action of water longer than No. 18.

The question is, can the harbor of Greytown be restored?

The first idea which seems to present itself to every mind as a solution to this problem is, that if the water of the Colorado be turned into the Lower San Juan by a dam placed across the head of the former, this will scour out the harbor and keep open its entrance.

Before we had fully examined the subject, this idea was very generally shared by the officers of the expedition. Its utter impracticability soon demonstrated itself.

For several years the Lower San Juan has been filling up and the Colorado widening and deepening. Just below the forks, the former is now, at the lowest stage of the water, but 324 feet wide and 6 inches deep; the latter is 1,200 feet wide and 10 feet deep. Its banks and bottom are of the silt already described. It is doubtful whether it would be possible to dam the Colorado at all; but if it could be done, the water would be more apt to cut around or under the structure than to make for itself a channel through the Lower San Juan.

A committee of the National Academy of Sciences in 1867 proposed, as a partial remedy for the decay of the river and harbor, the dredging out of the channel of the Lower San Juan and the construction of a wier from Leaf's Island to Concepcion Island. The latter of these is in the main river, near its right bank and above the forks. The former has now become joined to the angle or point of the main land, between the two branches. Concepcion Island is 2,000 feet from the point. The strongest part of the current runs between the two. The island is constantly cutting away at one place and forming at another, being composed entirely of silt banked around drift-logs which have lodged in the shoal water.

The wier, if indeed it could be constructed at all, with such a combination of unfavorable conditions, viz, the depth and strength of the water, and the yielding character of the bottom, would be quite as likely to fail in, as to effect, the object in view, i. e., the turning of the current into the lower San Juan, unless the latter was dredged out to a sufficient width and depth to prevent, by drawing it away, the water from cutting around the dam. This would have to be done for a distance of thirteen miles. I confess myself to have been very much discouraged when these facts and convictions impressed themselves upon my mind.

A thorough examination of the river made subsequently, showed us that all the silt comes from the San Carlos and from other Costa Rican Rivers, having their confluences lower down. This is the reason why the San Juan, below the mouth of the San Carlos, is filled with shoals and sand-bars. Before this fact had been established, other considerations, already detailed, had forced us to the conclusion that this part of the river could not be used, and that a canal must be built instead.

It is quite clear that, so long as the silt-bearing water is permitted to flow into the harbor, although, by adding to the current, it may assist in scouring at the entrance, it will certainly deposit in the still places, and indeed all over the broader parts of the harbor. Our plan is therefore to cut off the lower San Juan, and send all the water of the San Juan and its lower tributaries through the Colorado mouth, admitting to the harbor only the waters which come through the canal and through the San Juanillo, which will be perfectly clean. The harbor will then have to be dredged out to the proper size and depth. After which there will be nothing to again destroy it. A breakwater or jettee is estimated for to protect the entrance from the surf. The narrow strip of bare sand which divides the bay, if bay it may be called, from the sea, now shifts with every strong breeze that blows, and should be made permanent by covering it with mangrove and tough water-grasses. This might require several years for its accomplishment, but could be done with proper care. The planting should be done at the beginning of the rainy season, and those portions that did not take hold should be supplemented the next year, and so on till the work was complete.

ESTIMATES

The following are the estimates of the cost of various parts of the work, and are believed to be ample in each case, viz:

Clearing and grubbing..	$310,000
13,270,271 cubic yards of excavation in rock, at from $1.25 to $1.50 per cubic yard	18,217,300

28,237,401 cubic yards of excavation in earth, at 35 cents per cubic yard..	$1,131,025
3,231,500 cubic yards dredging, east side. at 35 cents per cubic yard......	19,441,289
941,541 cubic yards of embankment, at 15 cents per cubic yard..........	1,191,231
Dredging channel in lake to deep water, east side........................	1,705,379
Dredging channel in lake to deep water, west side	464,100
Dam at Castillo	290,000
Dam at Balas	430,900
Dam at Machuca	318,142
Dam at San Carlos	550,000
Dredging, &c., in river, viz, 3,530,667 cubic yards earth, at 50 cents, and 942,410 cubic yards rock, at $3..............................	4,092,573
20 locks...	8,000,000
1 tide-lock at Brito	421,306
Breakwater at Brito	213,330
Breakwater at Greytown	700,000
Dredging at Greytown, cubic yards	1,700,000
Dredging, &c., at Brito.	700,000
Diversion of Rio San Carlos..................................	400,381
Diversion of Rio Grande in five places	175,025
Crossing the Rio Zola.......................................	87,725
Culverts, west side	70,230
Culverts, east side	380,000
Side-drains, west side......................................	42,240
Side-drains, east side......................................	110,000
Total..	....
Add 25 per cent. for contingencies.........................	....
Grand total	....

WATER-SUPPLY.

Lake Nicaragua has a surface area of 2,700 square miles, and drains a territory of not less than 8,000 square miles. It would therefore seem unnecessary to consider the question of water-supply, except to show that it has not been forgotten.

Careful gauges of the San Juan River at numerous points were taken by Lieutenant Miller and party, using a delicate current-meter for the purpose. The least water found, and at about the lowest stage, was 11,390 cubic feet per second, or 984,096,000 cubic feet per day; against this supply we have the following as the maximum demand: Allowing forty lockages a day, or counting the ascending and descending, say eighty per day, without deducting the displacement of the vessels, which in descending we have the right to do, we have—

	Cubic feet.
80 lockages per day..	2,240,000
Allowing 1,000 per cent. for leakage, filtration, waste, and evaporation...	22,400,000
Total demand	24,640,000
Total supply	984,096,000
Excess of supply over demand	954,456,000

Or, to put it in another form, there is a supply equal to thirty-eight times the maximum possible demand.

CLIMATE, HEALTH, ETC.

The year in Nicaragua, as in the rest of the Isthmus, is divided into two seasons, the wet and the dry; the latter begins about the end of November, and lasts until May or June, when the rains begin, and continue with more or less force during the remaining months of the year.

Unlike the more southerly portions of the Isthmus, the rains here begin earlier and last longer near the Atlantic coast than in the interior. The annual rain-fall differs in different parts of the country, and in the same part differs for different years. No regular system of meteorological observations, continuing from year to year, has ever been established, as far as I have been able to ascertain. The present expedition found at Virgin Bay an aggregate fall of .47.79 inches from July 1, 1872, to March 1, 1873. As this period included the whole of the wet season the result probably does not differ very widely from the average annual rain-fall in that section. In the valley of the San Juan it is probably twice as great. This will, of course, be greatly modified in the event of extensive clearing at any future time.

Nicaragua lies wholly within the trade-wind belt, and during the dry season, when the trades " blow home," the climate is certainly delightful. In the vicinity of Rivas the thermometer seldom stands higher than 82° Fahrenheit in the shade, at mid-day; at night it often falls to 68°. In the valley of the San Juan it is somewhat warmer, but even there one can rarely sleep comfortably at night without a woolen blanket.

There is a very general impression abroad that the whole American Isthmus is exceedingly unhealthy, and this, as I conceive, very incorrect idea is entertained by many intelligent persons who have spent longer or shorter periods upon the Isthmus. It is true that in former years a large percentage of foreigners who remained there for any length of time died or were broken down in health, but nine out of ten of these cases were due to dissipation, or to the neglect of the simplest sanitary precautions, or generally to both. Dissipation will certainly kill much more surely and quickly in the tropics than in a temperate climate, and to just that extent and no more was the climate responsible for these cases. There have been during the last four years three exploring expeditions in Darien and two in Nicaragua. There have been as high as three hundred men employed at once, counting ships' companies, subjected to severe labor and exposure. Not a single officer or man has been lost from climatic disease. Under Providence, I ascribe this entire immunity to death and serious disease, partly to the following of a few sanitary rules, which anybody may do without inconvenience, but mainly to the strictly temperate lives led by officers and men (some voluntarily and some per force) while operating upon the Isthmus.

The percentage of deaths due to climatic causes alone, I am fully convinced, is smaller than in any other part of the world.

The prevailing diseases are few in number, simple in character, and generally yield most readily to treatment, unless the patient's blood is vitiated by alcohol.

Cleanliness, temperance in eating and drinking, sleeping under shelter and in dry clothing, wearing flannel next the skin at all times, avoiding heavy night-dews, and avoiding bathing immediately after meals or while much heated, are all the precautions necessary to preserve health; and with these any foreigner will be as safe upon the isthmus as anywhere else.

INHABITANTS, PRODUCTS, ETC.

The population of Nicaragua is variously estimated at from 250,000 to 300,000, and consists of whites, Indians, and negroes, and of mixed bloods in all degrees. Many of the Indians are civilized, and among their number are some of the worthiest citizens of the State. There are several tribes, however, in as savage a state as when the country was first discovered. These occupy the northeastern part of the territory.

The state is politically divided into departments. Of these the departments of Rivas, Granada, and Leon, bordering upon the Pacific, contain the bulk of the population and wealth.

The most numerous class of the inhabitants is formed by the Ladinos,* a mixture of white and Indian. Next to these, probably, are the pure Indians. The least numerous of all are the whites.

The laboring classes, both among the civilized Indians and the mixed races, are honest, docile, hardy, and not averse to hard work when occasion requires it, but so few are their natural wants (they have no artificial ones) and so easily supplied that they generally have no need of it. I estimate that, in the event of the construction of a canal, Nicaragua and the neighboring States would supply from 3,000 to 5,000 laborers; but this is very difficult to get at with any degree of accuracy, particularly in view of the probability that many new industries would be developed, each with its demand for operatives. Agriculture and grazing especially would receive an immense impetus.

The average wages of farm-hands and other out-door laborers, at the present time, is $16 per month, and the cost of subsistence at the present rates is $6 per month.

Nicaragua is full of undeveloped sources of wealth, some of these have been experimented with in a limited degree, but nothing to a beginning of its full capacity. Indigo, coffee, and cacao, all of excellent quality, are cultivated and exported to some extent. Sugar is raised, but the machinery used in its manufacture is of the rudest character and the article produced of very poor quality, though the cane is rich enough to rival the best in the world. Corn, beans, rice, yams, cassava root, quiquisque, a superior kind of yam, tobacco, plantains, bananas, oranges, limes, pine-apples, mangoes, watermelons, cantelopes, tomatoes, cocoanuts, nisperas, peppers, and numerous other fruits and vegetables grow in all parts of the country, and almost spontaneously. Near Greytown the delicious bread-fruit is raised, though hitherto no one has succeeded in producing it in the interior.

Of the domestic food-animals are beeves, hogs, goats, sheep, turkeys, ducks, common fowls, &c.

The forests are filled with game, among which are deer, wild hogs, tapirs, armadilloes, rabbits, turkeys, pheasants, ducks, mountain hens, pigeons, and many others. The manitee is found in the rivers and lagoons, and is highly esteemed as an article of food. The rivers and adjacent seas abound in fish of many varieties. Turtle are taken on the coasts. The country can abundantly supply all the subsistence which would be required in the event of a canal being constructed. Many articles yield two crops a year, others yield perpetually. Even the rude cultivation now given to the ground produces abundant returns. With the introduction of improved machinery and implements, and proper system, the yield might be augmented indefinitely; and it seems altogether probable that, with the increased facilities of transportation that must follow a large influx of people, added to the improvements above spoken of, prices will remain where they now are, even with the largely increased demand.

Abundance of valuable timber for construction, cabinet-work, dyewoods, &c., are found in all parts of the country, among others are mahogany, rose-wood, lignum-vitæ, cedar, moran-nispera, roble, ceiba, madera-negra, ron-ron, laurel, melon-tree, madroño, fustick, Brazil-wood, granadillo, cortes or iron-wood, guapinel, pochote, guanacoste, espanel, and others. The espanel is said to be impervious to the teredo navalis. The India rubber tree is found in many parts of the country, and furnishes a rapidly growing article of export.

Cochineal has been cultivated to some extent.

----

* This word is used with a different signification in some parts of Spanish America.

39 Ab

Medicinal plants and trees abound, though very little use is made of them so far.

There are many plants whose fibres are valuable; among these are cotton, pita, piñuela, tule, palm, and cocoa-nuts. Hats, cordage, hammocks, and some other articles are made with rude appliances.

Rock, limes, and clays needed for construction are to be had in great abundance. It is proposed to use concrete in place of dimension stone in the construction of locks, dams, &c. Material for this can be had immediately at hand in every case.

Gold and silver are found in paying quantities. The richest mines now being operated are in the department of Chontales on the east side of the lake. This region has been so little explored as to make it altogether improbable that a tithe of its mineral wealth has been discovered.

An inter-oceanic ship-canal across the American isthmus has been so long a subject of discussion among statesmen, merchants, and navigators, its desirability so often proved by able pens, the enormous saving of distance, cost, and risk which it would give to the commerce of the world so carefully tabulated, that there seems to be nothing left to prove except its feasibility; this I believe we shall be able to do from the information now in our possession, and that the line which has just been examined through Nicaragua presents by far a better combination of favorable conditions than any other route which has as yet been examined.

I have the honor to be, sir, very respectfully, your obedient servant,

EDWARD P. LULL,
Commander United States Navy,
Commanding Nicaragua Surveying Expedition.

Hon. GEORGE M. ROBESON,
Secretary of the Navy, Washington, D. C.

POLARIS EXPEDITION.

[Telegram No. 1.]

SAINT JOHN'S, NEWFOUNDLAND, *May 9, 1873.*

To SECRETARY OF STATE, *Washington, D. C.:*

Sealing steamer Walrus just arrived; reports steamer Tigress picked up on the ice off Grady Harbor, Labrador, on 30th April, fifteen crew of United States Polaris and five Esquimaux. Captain Hall died last summer. Tigress hourly expected. Will give further particulars.

T. N. MOLLOY,
United States Consul.

[Telegram No. 2.]

SAINT JOHN'S, NEWFOUNDLAND, *May 9, 1873.*

To SECRETARY OF STATE, *Washington, D. C:*

Just returned from Bay Roberts, Captain Tyson having reached north latitude 82.16; reached winter quarters in September, 1871, in latitude 81° 38″, longitude 61° 44″. Captain Hall died of apoplexy 8th October, 1871; was buried about half mile southeast of ship's winter quarters. Crossed Kane's polar sea, said to be a strait about fourteen miles wide with appearances of open water north. Left winter quarters August 12, 1872; got on beam ends 15th same month; thence drove south to 77, 35 in ship, when, owing to heavy pressure of ice, vessel was thrown up, and while landing stores, &c., vessel broke away from her mooring, and part of crew now here were drifted away south. Vessel last seen under steam and canvas making for harbor on east side of Northumberland Island. Polaris is without boats; lost two in a northern expedition; two landed on ice with Captain Tyson; one burnt to make water for crew; the other now in Bay Roberts. Crew lost vessel on 15th October, 1872; were picked up last April by Tigress in latitude 53.30, having been 197 days on ice. No lives were lost when last on board ship. She made no more water than during past winter and fall, but had received heavy injury to stem, causing her to leak badly. Names of crew here are Captain Tyson, Frederick Meyer, John Heron, W. C. Kruger, Frederick Jamka, William Nindeman, Frederick Authing, Gustavus Linguist, Peter Johnson, William Jackson, the Esquimaux Joe, Hannah, and child, Hans Christian, of Kane's expedition, wife, and four children, (youngest only eight months old.) Polaris is in charge of Captain Buddington. Crew have lived on a few ounces daily, and latterly on raw seals, eating skins, entrails, and all for the past two months, and are all in fairly good health. Captain Tyson does not expect Polaris will get clear before July, if in condition to come home. There were fourteen left on board, with plenty of provisions, and, if vessel be not fit to come home, they can easily construct boats for their safety. All provided for in Bay Roberts; will come here Monday.

T. N. MOLLOY,
United States Consul.

[Telegram No. 3.]
SAINT JOHN'S, NEWFOUNDLAND, <i>May</i> 12, 1873.</div>

To ACTING SECRETARY OF STATE, <i>Washington, D. C.</i>:

No direct steamer for the United States. Tigress owners offer to convey Polaris crew to New York free of charge, if Government will charter her to go in search of missing portion of expedition; consider her most suitable steamer in every respect; could leave on Wednesday. Do crew come under head of destitute seamen? Which Department do I draw on for expenses? Are Esquimaux to be forwarded? Steamer Nestorian may call on Thursday on way to Halifax, if coast clear of ice. Passage to Halifax $20 each.

T. N. MOLLOY,
United States Consul.

[Telegram No. 4.]
SAINT JOHN'S, NEWFOUNDLAND, <i>May</i> 12, 1873.</div>

To SECRETARY OF NAVY, <i>Washington, D. C.</i>:

Tigress just arrived; all landed; shall send further particulars to night.

T. N. MOLLOY,
United States Consul.

[Telegram No. 5.]
SAINT JOHN'S, NEWFOUNDLAND, <i>May</i> 12, 1873.</div>

To SECRETARY OF STATE, <i>Washington</i>:

All Polaris crew just landed; all cared for; wait answer for further proceedings.

T. N. MOLLOY,
United States Consul.

[Telegram No. 6.]

SAINT JOHN'S, NEWFOUNDLAND, *May* 13, 1873.

TO SECRETARY OF NAVY, *Washington :*

Crew of Polaris want $20 each besides clothing and boarding. Captain Tyson and Fred. Meyer, of signal-office, want funds also. Say amount I can advance on each account. Esquimaux and crew, on sick-list to-day. Harbor blocked with ice.

T. N. MOLLOY,
United States Consul.

[Telegram.]

NAVY DEPARTMENT,
Washington, May 13, 1873.

UNITED STATES CONSUL,
Saint John's, Newfoundland :

Take care of Polaris crew. Draw on Department or on Jay Cooke, McCulloch & Co., London, as most advantageous, notifying Department by telegram. Will telegraph how they can come home when determined.

GEO. M. ROBESON,
Secretary of the Navy.

UNITED STATES CONSULATE,
St. John's, Newfoundland, May 13, 1873.

SIR : I have the honor to inclose herewith a copy of a communication received from the owners of the steamship Tigress in reference to an offer to the Government to convey to New York the crew of the steamship Polaris, and also a tender of the said ship, with terms, in the event of the Government intending to search for the missing members of the expedition.

I also have the honor to inclose copies of telegrams sent, connected with this circumstance of the disaster to the expedition, for the information of the Department, and I have made the necessary arrangements for the proper treatment of the crew, having advanced them what I considered requisite for their comfort under the trying circumstances in which they have been situated. Since their landing yesterday, there has been a material reaction as regards their health, and 1 find, from both medical and my own observation, that most of them begin to feel the injurious result of their long sufferings and hardships which they have endured, several of them giving way, and fear will not be well enough to proceed home for at least a fortnight. At present there is no conveyance offering to take them direct to the United States, and although the mail-steamer Nestorian is due to-night or in the morning, by which this is intended, via Halifax, yet, from the coast being blockaded with ice, and the wind prevailing from the east, pressing the ice on the shore, there is very little probability of the Nestorian getting in here, and will likely have to pass by to Halifax without coming in.

In the event of the Government requiring a steamer, there are several here well adapted for a northern voyage, and which could be purchased or hired for a month or years.

I sent a telegram yesterday stating that the crew wanted money, (account of wages,) also Captain Tyson and Fred. Meyer, of the signal station. Already advanced $300, and given it to Captain Tyson to be divided among them, and have taken his receipt for the same, the particulars of which shall be sent forward in due course. Captain Tyson and Meyer have intimated that they will require about $1,200 between them.

The next Allan line steamer from Liverpool is due here about the 26th instant, and will go direct to Baltimore, by which the crew can go, unless you order otherwise in the mean time.

I have the honor to be, most respectfully, your obedient servant,

THOS. N. MOLLOY,
United States Consul.

Hon. SECRETARY OF THE NAVY,
Washington, D. C.

UNITED STATES STEAMER FROLIC, (4th rate,)
Navy-Yard, Washington, June 5, 1873.

SIR: I have the honor to report that, in obedience to your order of the 15th May, this ship, under my command, left New York on the evening of May 16, passed through Hell Gate, and arrived at Saint John's, New-foundland, at 6 o'clock on the morning of the 22d.

The weather was generally good during the passage, but on the night of the 19th, while passing Sable Island, it became so thick that I was obliged to direct speed to be reduced on account of the fog, as well as on account of passing a dangerous place. This prevented the ship from arriving at her destination on the 21st.

Cape Saint Mary and Cape Pine were sighted just after noon of the 21st, and Cape Race was rounded at 6 p. m. of that day.

Before reaching Cape Race, five large icebergs were passed, and during the following night one hundred and twenty were passed, including three floes of ice, the smallest of which I estimated to be about half a mile in diameter and the largest three or four miles. To avoid this ice the ship was kept well in-shore, which is steep-to. The ship was kept at low speed until day-light, as no one on board had been to Saint John's before, and no one was acquainted with the coast. I was unable to procure a Newfoundland pilot at New York.

The ship does not carry enough coal to burn more per diem than was used on the passage, and the complement of the ship is so small that there are not men enough to keep more fires going. On the passage east, twelve of the fourteen furnaces were kept going, and when in her best trim no more than ten knots were made.

Upon the arrival of this ship at Saint John's, I sent a letter to the United States consul at that port, asking for those persons rescued from the Polaris. The consul called upon me at once and stated verbally that the rescued people would be delivered before the ship sailed.

* * * * * * *

The day of our arrival was a religious holy-day, on which no labor could be had. The 24th being a national holiday, little could be done, and on Sunday no coal could be procured.

The intervention of these days delayed the ship. She had not received her coal until the evening of Tuesday, and sailed at 4 a. m. of Wednesday.

I did not leave Saint John's the latter part of the day on account of thick weather and ice, the latter this ship not being able to combat.

On the afternoon of the 27th I received nineteen persons of the crew of the Polaris, the list of whom is substantially the same as that furnished by the Department.

After passing Cape Race, at noon of the 28th, we were in a dense fog for fifty-three hours, except for a short time on the night of the 29th.

The speed was consequently lowered on that account, as well as from the fact of having a strong head wind and heavy sea.

Distance was lost by cleaning the tubes, which the Cardiff coal fre quently obstructed. No anthracite coal could be had at Saint John's, and there were but two lots of Cardiff coal, one of which was purchased. Native coal, I do not think, would have lasted the passage.

Sails were used to the best advantage. The Esquimaux are in two families, two male adults and the rest women and children. These are kept aft, and are occupying officers' apartments.

*   *   *   *   *

While at Saint John's I inspected, by request, the British steam-ship Tigress, and found, as far as I could judge, the representations of Messrs. Harvey & Co. to be correct as to her strength and construction. A copy of the letter from these gentlemen I forward.

Should it be the intention of the Department to dispatch a vessel to the polar regions, the Tigress is, in my opinion, the best one suited for that purpose.

To conclude, I regard the Frolic as one of the best and easiest sea-boats I have ever been on board of, and I believe her to be as strong as ships built of iron usually are.

For a passage of a week or more the bunkers do not carry enough coal for a consumption of more than about nineteen tons per diem, which, under favorable circumstances, will send the ship about two hundred miles.

The fact of not bringing back the boat of the Polaris is explained in my correspondence with the United States consul at Saint John's. This ship arrived at this port at 1.15 p. m. of this day.

I forward copies of correspondence.

I have the honor to be, very respectfully, your obedient servant,
                                   C. M. SCHOONMAKER,
                                   Commander United States Navy.

Hon. GEO. M. ROBESON,
      Secretary of the Navy.

                                   SAINT JOHN'S, *May* 10, 1873.

DEAR SIR : You are already aware that the steamer Tigress has re-turned to Bay Roberts, having rescued nineteen of the crew of the Polaris.

If it is the purpose of your Government to send in search of the other members of the expedition, we beg, on behalf of the owners of the Tigress, to say that she will be at their service, and is probably as suit-able a vessel as any that could be built for that purpose.

We will undertake to convey the persons already on board her to New York, and then deliver the steamer up to your Government, who may appoint their own officers, engineers, and crew, send her to the Arctic regions, and then deliver her up to us in New York, when it suits their convenience, in as good order as when they received her.

If they deliver her up to us in New York during the present year, (1873,) to pay the Tigress for services already rendered, and probable loss of a trip of seals by leaving the ice to bring home these people, and for her use until delivered up to us in New York, $30,000, American currency; if she should be caught and have to winter in the Arctic re-gions and not be delivered up to us until 1874, $60,000; if she should be lost during the voyage, the Government to pay $60,000 for her, and hire up to the date of their acquainting us with her loss.

She is well found in everything necessary for encountering an Arctic voyage, having last year been for the whale season in Cumberland Inlet or Baffin's Bay.

The vessel, as you know, is eighteen months old, fully sparred, and plenty of sail, compound engines, burning six to seven tons of soft coal in twenty-four hours for a speed of eight knots; would require docking and provisions only to proceed on the voyage.

We are, dear sir, yours truly,

HARVEY & CO.

T. N. MOLLOY, Esq.,
American Consul.

P.S.—You might acquaint your Government of the probable value of some of the second [sealing] trips brought in this year.

The above copy of Mr. Harvey's letter was furnished me by T. N. Molloy, esq., United States consul at Saint John's, Newfoundland, May 27, 1873.

C. M. SCHOONMAKER,
Commander.

UNITED STATES STEAMER FROLIC,
Saint John's, Newfoundland, May 22, 1873.

SIR: I have been dispatched in command of this ship to this place to receive the party from the Polaris, including the Esquimaux, on board for transportation to the United States. I request you to deliver them to me for that purpose as soon as practicable, wishing to return at once where coal can be obtained.

You will please inform me if any stores or conveniences will be required for the health and comfort of these persons besides what is usually carried on board men-of-war, in order that I may procure the before leaving.

Very respectfully, your obedient servant,

C. M. SCHOONMAKER,
Commander United States Navy.

T. N. MOLLOY, Esq.,
United States Consul, Saint John's, Newfoundland.

UNITED STATES CONSULATE,
Saint John's, Newfoundland, May 22, 1873.

SIR: I have the honor to acknowledge the receipt of your communication of 22d instant; and, in reference to the boat belonging to the Polaris, she is now at Bay Roberts, and I have directed her to be delivered up to me by first conveyance from that place; but if not here in time to be sent by the Frolic under your command, shall keep her here until future orders from the Navy Department.

The canoe belonging to Joe Eberbing (the Esquimaux) will be sent on board, with three rifles and two bags of furs.

I have the honor to be, most respectfully, your obedient servant,

THOS. N. MOLLOY,
United States Consul.

C. M. SCHOONMAKER,
Commander, Commanding United States Steamer Frolic.

UNITED STATES STEAMER FROLIC,
Saint John's, Newfoundland, May 22, 1873.

SIR: I wish to inform you that I will receive on board and carry to the United States the boat and canoe which were brought to this port by a part of the crew of the Polaris.

Very respectfully, your obedient servant,
C. M. SCHOONMAKER,
Commander, Commanding.

T. N. MOLLOY, Esq.,
United States Consul, Saint John's, Newfoundland.

UNITED STATES CONSULATE,
Saint John's, Newfoundland, May 27, 1873.

SIR: Agreeably to your communication of the 22d instant I have the honor to deliver up to you the party rescued by the sealing-steamer Tigress, Captain Bartlet, belonging to the United States steamer Polaris of the Arctic expedition, and also inclose herewith the names of the party as registered in this consulate.

I have the honor to be, most respectfully, your obedient servant,
THOS. N. MOLLOY,
United States Consul.

C. M. SCHOONMAKER,
Commander, Commanding United States Steamer Frolic.

List of persons rescued belonging to the Polaris, of the Arctic expedition.

George E. Tyson.
Frederick Meyer.
William Jackson.
J. W. C. Kruger.
Peter Johnson.
Hans Hendrick, wife and four children. }
Joe Eberbing, wife and daughter.   } Esquimaux.

Frederick Jamka.
William Nindemann.
John Heron.
G. W. Lindguist.
Frederick Authing.

Saint John's, Newfoundland, May 27, 1873.

THOS. N. MALLOY,
United States Consul.

UNITED STATES STEAMER FROLIC, (4th rate,)
Navy-Yard, Washington, June 5, 1873.

SIR: I respectfully forward the list of passengers of this ship for the passage from Saint John's, Newfoundland, to this station. (Form No. 10.)

I have the honor to be, very respectfully, your obedient servant,
C. M. SCHOONMAKER,
Commander United States Navy.

Hon. GEO. M. ROBESON,
Secretary of the Navy.

Forwarded by—

L. M. GOLDSBOROUGH,
Rear-Admiral, Commanding.

List of officers or others arrived as passengers in the United States steamer Frolic. Dated at Washington, D. C., the 5th day of June, 1873.

Names.	Rank.	Remarks.
George E. Tyson....	Assistant navigator.	The names in this list are the same as furnished by the United States consul at Saint John's, N. F. This list is substantially the same as the one furnished by the Department. The list comprises that part of the crew of the Polaris who were rescued from the ice by the British steamer Tigress. These persons were received on board for passage to the United States at Saint John's, N. F., on May 27, 1873.
Frederick Meyer....	Meteorologist.	
William Jackson...	Cook.	
J. W. C. Kruger.....	Seaman.	
Peter Johnson......	Seaman.	
Frederick Jamka ...	Seaman.	
William Nindemann.	Seaman.	
John Heron.........	Steward.	
L. W. Lindguist.....	Seaman.	
Frederick Authing..	Seaman.	
Hans Hendrick, wife and four children..	} Esquimaux.	
Joe Eberbing, wife and daughter.....		

C. M. SCHOONMAKER,
Commander, Commanding.

PROCEEDINGS OF THE JUNIATA IN THE SEARCH FOR THE POLARIS.

NAVY DEPARTMENT, *June* 19, 1873.

SIR: The Juniata is to proceed to Greenland to obtain tidings of the Polaris, to communicate with her, and to aid in her rescue. The steamer Tigress will shortly follow. Whenever the Juniata is ready for sea you will go direct to Saint John's, Newfoundland, fill up with coal, stowing as much on deck as can be conveniently carried, and, without further loss of time, make the best of your way to the port of Godhavn, on the island of Disco, on the west coast of Greenland, having due regard to the safety of your ship while navigating through a region in which more or less ice is usually to be met with at this season of the year. On arriving at Godhavn, communicate with the Danish authorities at that place, to whom you are furnished with letters of introduction, and ascertain if any intelligence has been received of, or from, the Polaris since October, 1872, when she was last seen, under Northumberland Island, in about the latitude 77° 13′ north, longitude 72° west.

Acting upon whatever information you may receive, or, in the absence of any, you will endeavor, with the aid of the Danish authorities, to open communication with the Polaris, by means of the Esquimaux, without delay. Any other measures for procuring intelligence of the Polaris, or for her relief and rescue, that may commend themselves to your best judgment, you are authorized to take, *except endangering your own ship and men within the ice.* Should, however, the navigation of Baffin's Bay be sufficiently open, as it at times is, to pursue it to the northward in an ordinary ship, you will carry the Juniata up the coast to Upernavik, and farther, if practicable, with safety, keeping a lookout for the Polaris, and for her people on the way. Should you be so fortunate as to rescue them, you will return to Godhavn, discharge all your obligations at that place, leave the requisite information for the Tigress, and return with all dispatch to New York; otherwise you will not leave Godhavn, to return homeward, until the last moment of the navigable season in the fall.

Upon falling in with the Tigress you will aid her in her search to the northward, as far as you can proceed together, unless you have already rescued the party; and when you part company if she has to go on to the north, make the best arrangements you can for awaiting her return, either at Upernavik or at Godhavn, beyond any risk to the Juniata from the ice. The Tigress is to push on for Northumberland Island if the Polaris, or her people, are not met with lower down; and, in that case, is not to fail to reach the island, even if she may have to winter in its vicinity. If the Polaris is reached she is not to be abandoned, if it is possible to bring her out; but, if she cannot be saved, her officers and men, and everything of value, are to be removed to the Juniata, or to the Tigress, as may be most convenient. If rescued she is to come homeward under the convoy of both the Juniata and Tigress, until clear of all danger from the ice, when you will hasten your own arrival at your destination, leaving the Tigress to convoy the Polaris into port.

The coal and stores which were landed at Godhavn by the Congress, for the Polaris, are to be used to the best advantage. Coal may, perhaps, be obtained at or about that port, if needed. Communicate with the Department whenever an opportunity offers.

At Saint John's you will fill up the Juniata with soft coal, such as is requisite for the use of the Tigress. This coal you will supply the Tigress with at Disco, or leave it there for her. In the execution of the duty to which you are assigned by these orders, much must be left to your judgment; and the Department here reminds you that in no event must you put your vessel, or the lives on board of her, in any jeopardy from the ice, for which the Juniata has not been built, or repaired, or specially fitted. Inclosed herewith is a letter from the Danish minister to the Danish authorities in Greenland, asking them to render you all assistance and co-operation with the expedition under your command.

Respectfully,

GEO. M. ROBESON,
Secretary of Navy.

Commander D. L. BRAINE, U. S. N.,
Commanding United States Steamer Juniata,
United States Navy-Yard, New York.

NAVY DEPARTMENT,
Washington, July 10, 1873.

SIR: Should the Tigress join company with the Juniata, her commander is directed, as usual, to show his instructions to his senior officer, and the Department desires you to assist in carrying out these instructions in every way, and particularly to facilitate his progress to the northward by every means in your power, keeping in mind the fact that the Tigress is fitted and ordered to make her way, if necessary, to the point where the Polaris was last seen, by every means possible and in the face of every danger, while you are ordered only to advance as far in that direction as you may be able to go without subjecting your ship to more than ordinary risk and danger, and the fact that the Tigress is fitted to encounter the ice, while you are not. Should you be in company when you meet the ice, or enter the latitudes where it may be dangerous, you will not detain her with you if her commander thinks it proper to push on, but will allow her to proceed at his own discretion, having informed him where he may expect to find or communicate with you on his return to Godhavn.

Your orders in respect to the Juniata are full and complete, and the Department further depends upon you to advance and further in every way the special object for which the Tigress is fitted out, and to facilitate her advance northward as the special expedition upon which the Department relies for the relief and rescue of the Polaris, her officers and crew, should they prove to be beyond the reach of assistance by the ordinary naval means which may be afforded by the Juniata under her orders. As the officers and crew of the Tigress have been selected with special reference to the circumstances of the case, you will not interfere in any way with her *personnel*, except at the request of her commander or under the pressure of imperative professional necessity; and should she be fortunate enough to rescue the Polaris and afterwards join you, you will permit her to convoy her home.

Reminding you that the season of operations is necessarily short, and that every necessary measure at your command must be taken in the most prompt and effective manner,

I remain, your obedient servant,

GEO. M. ROBESON,
Secretary of the Navy.

Commander DANIEL L. BRAINE,
Commanding U. S. Steamer Juniata, (By U. S. Steamer Tigress.)

No. 25.]   UNITED STATES STEAMER JUNIATA, (3d rate,)
Off Battery, New York, June 24, 1873.

SIR: I have the honor to report to the Navy Department that, in obedience to its orders of the 19th and 23d instant, I have sailed with this vessel under my command this day from this port in search of the Polaris.

I am, sir, very respectfully, your obedient servant,

D. L. BRAINE,
Commander U. S. N., Commanding Juniata.

Hon. GEORGE M. ROBESON,
Secretary of the Navy, Washington, D. C.

No. 30.]   UNITED STATES STEAMER JUNIATA, (3d rate,)
Saint John's, Newfoundland, July 9, 1873.

SIR: I have the honor to report the arrival of the United States steamer Juniata, under my command, at this port, June the 30th, and this being the first opportunity of communicating by mail, I avail myself of it. Your telegraphic dispatch of the 29th of June was duly received.

Since my arrival here, I found that several sheets of the thin sheet-iron placed on the bows of this ship at New York had washed off. After consultation with the ice-pilot, I have had the bow properly sheathed and prepared for meeting the ice through which I may have to run the ship between here and Upernavik.

*   *   *   *   *   *   *

I beg leave to report that our national holiday was duly observed as such by decorating the ship with flags and a holiday for the crew.

Having made all the preparations for sea, I shall sail this day for Greenland, in search of the Polaris upon my way, and in obedience to your written and telegraphic orders.

The health of the officers and crew, I have the pleasure to say, is excellent.

I am, sir, very respectfully, your obedient servant,
D. L. BRAINE,
Commander U. S. N., Commanding U. S. Steamer Juniata.

Hon. GEORGE M. ROBESON,
Secretary of the Navy, Washington, D. C.

No. 31.]   UNITED STATES STEAMER JUNIATA, (3d rate,)
Holsteinborg, Greenland, July 19, 1873.

SIR: I have the honor to report, since my letter of the 9th instant, written from Saint John's, New Foundland, that on July 14 I arrived off Fiskenaes, but, being unable to get a pilot, I proceeded to Sukkertoppen, which port I entered on the 17th instant, and found that no dogs were to be procured. July 18, sailed, and arrived at Holsteinborg the same day.

I have this day, through the courtesy of Governor Frederick Larssen, procured eighteen dogs, also one hundred and fifty seal-skins to make clothing for the men and officers of the Tigress, and I shall sail, weather permitting, to-day for Disco, where I will land the soft coal for the Tigress, and then proceed to Upernavik in the execution of your orders.

As yet, and I have news from Disco up to the 10th instant, no tidings have been received from the Polaris.

The ice is reported very heavy in Omenak Fiord and at and above Upernavik.

The health of all the officers and crew of this vessel is excellent.

I have the honor to be, very respectfully, your obedient servant,
D. L. BRAINE,
Commander U. S. N., Commanding U. S. Steamer Juniata.

Hon. GEORGE M. ROBESON,
Secretary of the Navy, Washington, D. C.

P. S.—This letter is sent per Danish brig Constance, via Copenhagen, Denmark.

———

No. 32.]   GODHAVN, DISCO ISLAND, GREENLAND,
July 29, 1873.

SIR: I have the honor to report, since my last communication of the 19th instant, I have proceeded, with the United States steamer Juniata under my command, to this port, where I have just landed about seventy tons of Cardiff coal for the use of the Tigress, the same carefully bagged and placed in the store-house. I also landed a quantity of lumber, which, I have no doubt, will be of great use to her. I have also landed the eighteen dogs purchased at Holsteinborg, besides twelve additional ones procured here, and I leave here directions to have them all delivered to the Tigress. I would here note that I find all the stores left here by the Congress and Polaris apparently to be in good order. I have also taken from the store-house $55\frac{550}{2240}$ tons of anthracite coal for the use of this ship.

My previous communication was dated July 19, Holsteinborg, and was sent per Danish brig Constance, via Copenhagen. The seal-skins which we procured at that port, from which we sailed July 21, 1873, are now being prepared here, to be made into clothing for the officers and men of the Tigress. I found it impossible here to procure any furs for the same purpose, but at Upernavik I am in hopes to obtain all that I desire.

It is my intent this day to sail for Upernavik, where I will endeavor to obtain information of the Polaris by sending out Esquimaux, with liberal offers of money or other articles as inducements for them to go, if possible, to obtain information of her whereabouts, so I may impart the same to the commander of the Tigress immediately upon her arrival. Should I not have the desired information, and the navigation is open to the northward, I will then accompany the Tigress as far to the northward as it is prudent for this ship to go; and I would here state that I am informed that, although this last winter in these regions has not been so mild as the two preceding ones, it has by no means been severe, and it is very likely the ice of Baffin's Bay has been adrift the whole winter through.

When we separate it is my intention, as far as present information warrants, to return to Upernavik, and remain there as long as open navigation will permit, say until August 30, upon which date I will proceed to Godhavn, Disco Island, and remain at that port until September 20 or 30, and then proceed to Holsteinborg, where I propose to wait until the latter part of October, at which point, by the following proposed means, I have hopes to bring you intelligence of what the Tigress may have accomplished, and the whereabouts of the Polaris or her officers and crew. I will arrange with Commander Greer, if the Tigress be frozen in to the northward of Upernavik, that he will send Esquimaux with information to Upernavik; from that point Esquimaux will bring it to Godhavn, Disco Island, and from there to me at Holsteinborg, from which port I will sail for Saint John's, Newfoundland, proceeding under sail, as my coal will probably be exhausted by that date.

I have the honor to report that we have been received with much courtesy and kindness at this place, and every facility afforded us by Mr. Müldrüp, the assistant governor, in the absence of the governor, Mr. S. T. Krariip Smith. The health of the officers and crew of this ship is excellent. The original of this was sent per Danish bark Thorwaldsen, via Copenhagen.

I am, sir, very respectfully, your obedient servant,

D. L. BRAINE,
Commander U. S. N., Commanding U. S. Steamer Juniata.

Hon. GEORGE M. ROBESON,
Secretary of the Navy, Washington, D. C.

No. 34.]   UNITED STATES STEAMER JUNIATA, (3d rate,)
Off Upernavik, Greenland, August 10, 1873.

SIR: I have the honor to report, since my last communication from Godhavn, island of Disco, Greenland, under date of July 29, 1873, I have proceeded to this place with the United States steamer Juniata under my command, arriving July 31.

I will now proceed to give you in detail up to this date all that I have done at this place in carrying out your orders of June 19, 1873.

The seal-skins procured at Holsteinborg, and prepared at Disco, were landed the day of my arrival, and, with others procured here, will be made up into clothing for the officers and crew of the United States steamer Tigress, and be finished, I hope, before her arrival, so no delay may occur in their proceeding to the northward. I have ordered the clothing under advice from the authorities here, as otherwise the Tigress would be delayed two weeks or more in procuring it.

After consultation with Governor Rudolph, of this place, (who has rendered me every facility in forwarding the expedition in search of the Polaris,) I found it impossible to arrange with the Esquimaux to proceed to the northward in search of the desired information of the officers and crew of that vessel.

Governor Rudolph informed me that the navigation to the northward was and had been unusually open this year, and free of floe-ice; that, indeed, as he expressed it, "there had been no winter." He assured me if I dispatched a steam-launch he could furnish her with a thoroughly competent Esquimaux pilot, who is a dog-driver and hunter also. I then decided to send the large steam-launch of this vessel, (and I may here state that, anticipating a search to the northward, in obedience to your orders, would have to be successfully accomplished under steam, I had the steam-launch prepared by sheathing her with wood, placing iron on her bows, and an iron guard or frame around her propeller,) to skirt the fast ice of the coast, to obtain all the information she could, and return by August 15, 1873, or before the Tigress would probably reach Upernavik. She was supplied with a most thorough outfit to make the reconnaissance. August 2, 1873, Lieut. George W. De Long, navigator of this vessel, was assigned to command her, and she was named the Little Juniata; lieutenant, Charles W. Chipp; ensign, Sidney H. May; pilot, Henry W. Dodge; boatswain's mate, Richard Street; machinist, Frank Hamilton; William King, seaman extra; and Martin T. Maher, ordinary seaman, and an Esquimaux pilot, named Jacob, formed the officers and crew, who, previous to starting, were each furnished with complete suits of fur clothing. The steam-launch was provisioned for sixty days full and one hundred and twenty days half ration; had coal for seventeen days' full steaming, and she sailed on August 2 for Tessuisak, from which point she sailed August 3 to the northward. At this date, August 10, she has not yet returned, but the weather has been excellent, and I feel confident she will soon be here.

At this place I met Inspector S. T. Krariip Smith, of Disco, who furnished me with the following information: Early in June, 1873, two English steam whale-ships, named the Eric, Captain Walker, and the Arctic, Captain Adams, on board of the latter, Commander A. H. Markham, of the royal navy, stopped at Disco, and Inspector Smith told them the news of the rescued party, and, with great forethought, requested them to look along the ice for the Polaris, or her officers and crew, in their passage to the northward, which the captains of these vessels kindly promised to do. Hence, if they skirt the ice to the westward, in Baffin's Bay, which they have probably done by this time, and the Little Juniata looks along the coast, the Tigress can proceed in the most direct and expeditious route to Northumberland Island; and I am sanguine that, with these three modes, the ship or her officers and crew will be rescued from their perilous position, although as yet nothing has been heard from them at this point.

I have further to state that another vessel, the Ravenscraigh, has proceeded to the northward on a whaling voyage, and has also been requested to keep a lookout for the Polaris.

Upon inquiry I am informed that it will be impossible to get the Esquimaux of this place to proceed in a kayak to Godhavn, Disco, after September 1; hence it will be impossible for me to get information from this place after that date, unless I am successful in inducing the governor of this place to send one of his sailing-vessels to that point. I have it in my mind, and may probably order our large steam-launch, upon her return to this point, to await for news until a certain day in September, and bring it to me at Disco, if so obtained. Should the Tigress successfully return, she can, of course, convey the launch to Godhavn.

After leaving this point it is my intent to obtain, if possible, coal from the mines on the island of Disco, opposite to Rittensbek. I shall also, if the inspector, Governor S. T. Krarüp Smith, consents, send a 50-ton sailing-craft to the westward of Godhavn, to search along the pack-ice for the Polaris, which vessel he thinks may be inclosed in it and drift-ing to the southward.

   *   *   *   *   *   *   *

Should I not get the desired coal on Disco Island upon my return to the United States, I may probably have to stop at Iviktout, with the double object, first, to obtain information of the Polaris, should she have got out of the pack-ice in the neighborhood of Holsteinborg or Suk-kertoppen, as Inspector Smith informs me she would probably go to Ivik-tout; secondly, to obtain coal for this vessel, and in order to know what facilities there are for procuring the same, and to obtain information of the Polaris. Upon the advice of Inspector Smith, I shall in a few days dispatch an Esquimaux in a kayak to Sukkertoppen, Holsteinborg, and Iviktout, to return to Godhavn, Disco, with information on these two points, viz, as to whether the Polaris has been heard from at those two places, and whether coal can be procured at Iviktout.

I am happy to state that we have thus far successfully navigated, with very imperfect charts, through dense fogs amongst innumerable icebergs and unknown islands and rocks, and had several very narrow escapes, arising from the dense fog, although we have thus far been favored with continuous daylight. The ship is in good order, but short of coal.

I cannot definitely state when I will sail for Saint John's, Newfound-land, as so much depends on the success or non-success of the Tigress or the Little Juniata, or the sudden appearance of the Polaris herself; but you may rest assured that your orders will be carried out, as far as it is in my power, with great earnestness. The health of the officers and crew is excellent.

I send this communication via Iviktout, Greenland, and the original via Copenhagen, Denmark, per Danish bark Thorwaldsen.

I am, sir, very respectfully, your obedient servant,

                    D. L. BRAINE,
Commander U. S. N., Commanding U. S. Steamer Juniata
                    and Senior Officer Present.

Hon. GEORGE M. ROBESON,
    Secretary of the Navy, Washington, D. C.

P. S.—I deem it my duty to mention that Lieut. Commander Edgar C. Merriman volunteered to go with the steam-launch and search for the United States steamer Polaris to the northward of this place, but Lieu-tenant De Long having previously volunteered, I had promised him, if I sent her, he should be the officer assigned for that duty.

                    D. L. BRAINE,
                    Commander U. S. N.

No. 35.]   UNITED STATES STEAMER JUNIATA, (3d rate.)
                Off Upernavik, Greenland, August 12, 1873.

SIR: I have the honor to inform you that the United States steamer Tigress, Commander James A. Greer, U. S. N., commanding, arrived here August 10. She was filled up with coal from the Juniata, and provided with everything she required.

David M. Howell, machinist, and Thomas Hovington, seaman, condemned by medical survey, (sick,) were received from her; also, S. Harding, (seaman,) complained of by Commander Greer as a skulk and worthless; and in their places I have transferred from this vessel to the Tigress the three following named, who are excellent men: Thomas Craven, machinist; Peter Newman, seaman; and Peter Brown, landsman, accompanied by their necessary transfer papers.

At 5.15 p. m. the 11th of August the Tigress steamed away north for Tessiusak in the performance of your instructions. We all gave her our heartiest good wishes and cheers. I will wait at this place until the 20th instant in hopes to hear from the Tigress.

I inclose herewith, for the information of the Department, a copy of the orders issued by myself, as senior officer present, to Commander Greer previous to the sailing of the Tigress from this port.

The original of this was sent via Iviktout, Greenland, to reach an American vessel returning to the United States.

I am; sir, very respectfully, your obedient servant,
D. L. BRAINE,
Commander U. S. N., Commanding U. S. Steamer Juniata,
and Senior Officer Present.

Hon. GEORGE M. ROBESON,
Secretary of the Navy, Washington, D. C.

UNITED STATES STEAMER JUNIATA, (3d rate,)
Off Upernavik, Greenland, August 11, 1873.

SIR: Having reported the United States steamer Tigress under your command ready in every particular for the search for the United States steamer Polaris, you will be pleased to sail immediately and carry out the instructions of the honorable Secretary of the Navy.

The steam-launch of this vessel sailed from this place August 2, 1873, upon a reconnaissance to the northward, to obtain information, if possible, of the Polaris for the Tigress, with instructions to return in fifteen days, or by the 17th of August, if possible.

You will, upon your route toward Cape York, be pleased to keep a lookout for her, as she may have valuable information for you; and should you fall in with, render her, her officers and crew any assistance they may require; and should she be able to prosecute her voyage of return, be pleased to direct her commanding officer to do so with all despatch to this place, where I shall await him until August 20, at which date I shall leave for Waigatt Strait, to obtain, if possible, coal for this ship. From that point I go to Godhavn, Disco Island, where I shall await the return of the Tigress, under your command, until the latest navigable moment of this year, when I will sail for Saint John's, Newfoundland. You will be pleased to communicate with the above places, should you return this year.

With the sincere hope and wish you may be successful in your search for the United States steamer Polaris, her officers and crew,

I am, very respectfully, your obedient servant,
D. L. BRAINE,
Commander U. S. N., Commanding U. S. Steamer Juniata,
and Senior Officer Present.

Commander JAMES A. GREER, U. S. N.,
Commanding United States steamer Tigress,
Off Upernarik, Greenland.

No. 36.]   UNITED STATES STEAMER JUNIATA, (3d rate,)
                 Godhavn, Disco Island, Greenland, August 16, 1873.

SIR : I have the honor to inclose herewith the report of Lieut. George W. De Long, United States Navy, who commanded the search expedition sent from this ship to Cape York in search of the United States steamer Polaris, her officers and crew, to carry information to them, if found, of coming relief, and also to obtain information for the United States steamer Tigress, so she might proceed direct as possible and carry out your orders.   •

Lieutenant De Long and party encountered very heavy ice near Cape York, and turned to the southward August 9, 1873, in obedience to my orders, (a copy of which I herewith inclose.) August 12, 1873, the steam- ·
launch (Little Juniata) met the United States steamer Tigress off Tessui sak and imparted to her commanding officer, up to August 9, 1873, valuable information of the condition of the ice, both going to the northward by the coast-line, and returning through Melville Bay.

I· beg leave to commend the officers and men who were with Lieutenant De Long upon this extra-hazardous expedition to the favorable consideration of the Navy Department; the former are deserving of acknowledgment and, praise, and in addition thereto, I recommend for the latter medals of honor for fidelity, zeal, and obedience.

I beg leave to report I sailed from Upernavik August 13, 1873, and ar rived at this port August 15, where I shall wait to obtain information from both the Tigress and Polaris, or, in case of their arrival here, to accompany them to the United States, in obedience to your orders of June 19, 1873.

The health of the officers and crew of this vessel is, I am happy to say, excellent.

In conclusion, I trust all that has been done by me to carry out your orders will meet with your approbation.

This letter goes forward by the Danish brig Thorwaldsen, via Copenhagen, Denmark, and a duplicate of the same via Iviktout, Greenland, per an American vessel.

I have the honor to be, sir, very respectfully, your obedient servant,
                                             D. L. BRAINE,
          Commander U. S. N., Commanding U. S. Steamer Juniata,
                                        and Senior Officer Present.

Hon. GEORGE M. ROBESON,
     Secretary of the Navy, Washington, D. C.

P. S.—I also inclose a track-chart of the steam-launch track.   I would also state that previous to our leaving Upernavik the ice formed in the fresh-water ponds on shore, and that here at this date we have had storms of snow and sleet, which seem to me to be indications of the approach of an early and severe winter.

                                        D. L. BRAINE.

————

                 UNITED STATES STEAMER JUNIATA, (3d rate,)
                       Upernavik, Greenland, July 31, 1873.

SIR : The Little Juniata, the largest steam-launch of this ship, has been carefully strengthened with outer planking, also with an iron stem-plate, and her propeller guarded with an iron frame.   She is thoroughly equipped, arranged, and provisioned for sixty days, under your supervision, for a search for the United States steamer Polaris along the fast

40 Ab

in-shore ice to the northward of this place toward Melville Bay. You will assume command of her, and at the first appropriate moment proceed to carry out said search as far as it is positively prudent to advance to the northward.

In navigating these northerly and almost unknown waters much must be left to your discretion, and your movements must be controlled by the short time the United States steamer Juniata will remain at Upernavik, which is until August 25, 1873.

You are enjoined to advise with the ice-pilot furnished you, who has twice passed over the waters you are about to navigate, and wintered in the Arctic frozen regions.

The Little Juniata is not to be jeopardized or pushed into the ice-packs if you meet them; nor is she or the lives of those on board to be involved in any way it is possible to avoid, for you must remember that the United States steamer Tigress, a vessel equipped and prepared for ice-cruising, will soon proceed up Baffin's Bay into Smith's Straits, to search for the Polaris, up to the point she was last seen (Northumberland Island) in October, 1872, and you are reconnoitering previous to her going, possibly to pass an Arctic winter in 77° north.

Should you find the Polaris, or her officers and crew, you will return with dispatch to Upernavik, at which place the Juniata will remain up to the date previously mentioned; and you are not, under any circumstances within your control, to be absent from this ship beyond fifteen days, for which time you have coal, at a daily consumption of 500 pounds.

Should you not find the Polaris by the time you have consumed one-half of your coal, you are to return to Upernavik, and sooner if you meet any formidable ice obstructions.

Should the United States steamer Tigress leave Upernavik before you return, she will be directed to keep a lookout for you, and should you meet her under any circumstances that warrant it, you will remain with her if her commander deems it most prudent you should do so; but should the Little Juniata be able to prosecute the voyage of return to Upernavik, I wish you to do so, and be at that place on or before August 25, 1873.

Should you not be at Upernavik by that date, I will leave there coal and provisions sufficient for your return to Godhavn, Disco Island, where I expect to remain until September 20 or 25, or the latest days previous to the close of navigation by the ice in those waters.

With hopes your search will prove successful and you may find the Polaris, or gain some tidings of her, or be the means of conveying through the Esquimaux to those on board the news of the vessels now in search of her, I sincerely wish you success in your undertaking.

I assure you I shall wait with great interest your return to this ship from the hazardous duty for which you and those associated with you have volunteered.

You will be accompanied by Lieut. Charles W. Chipp, U. S. N.; Ensign Sidney H. May, U. S. N.; Pilot Henry W. Dodge; Richard Street, boatswain's mate; Frank Hamilton, machinist; William King, seaman extra; Martin T. Maher, ordinary seaman.

I am, most sincerely, yours,

D. L. BRAINE,
Commander U. S. N., Commanding U. S. Steamer Juniata,
and Senior Officer Present.

Lieut. GEORGE W. DE LONG, U. S. N.,
Commanding the Steam-Launch Little Juniata.

UNITED STATES STEAMER JUNIATA, (3d rate,)
Upernavik, Greenland, August 12, 1873.

SIR: I have the honor to submit to you this my report of an expedition in the steam-launch Little Juniata, under my command, to the northward as far as Cape York, in search of the missing steamer Polaris, which expedition left this ship on the 2d instant and returned at 8 o'clock this evening.

The expedition was prepared by your order, and the necessary detail of arrangements (such as strengthening the boat with wooden sheathing, fitting a stem-plate of iron, an iron frame or guard for the screw, purchase of canned provisions in sufficient quantities to last eight people sixty days, the internal fittings of the boat with reference to stowage of fuel, &c., the arms and ammunition necessary, spars, sails, and spare machinery) was by you committed to my care and carried forward under my personal supervision during the stay of the ship at St. John's, Newfoundland, and Disco Island, Greenland.

The party consisted of the following-named persons in addition to myself: Lieut. Charles W. Chipp, United States Navy; Ensign Sidney H. May, United States Navy; Mr. Henry W. Dodge, ice-pilots Frank Hamilton, machinist; Richard Street, boatswain's mate; Martin T. Maher, ordinary seaman; William King, ordinary seaman, engineer'; force; and Jacob Lynghe, Esquimaux, who accompanied us as an interpreter and coast-pilot between Upernavik and Cape Shackelton.

On Saturday, August 2, at 12.55 p. m., the boat being in readiness, provisioned, and supplied with four tons of anthracite coal, I received your final orders and shoved off from the ship, with the dingy containing twelve hundred and seventy-eight pounds of coal in tow, and, heartily cheered by the ship's company, proceeded on our voyage to the northward, under steam, with a fine breeze from the southwest.

I immediately organized the party and divided them in two watches, one in charge of Lieutenant Chipp, and consisting of himself, Mr. Dodge, Hamilton, and Street, and the other in my own charge, and composed of the remaining four of the party, the Esquimaux being for the present excluded.   This arrangement of watches was kept up during our entire absence, the officers and men working alike, and turning in and out with each other.

At 3.30 the same afternoon we passed the small settlement of Kingitok, about twelve miles to the northward, and working our way among countless icebergs and through narrow passes between islands, arrived without accident at Tessuisak at 11 o'clock that night, and, in obedience to your orders, left the dingy at that place to be brought back by a Danish boat, landed six hundred pounds of coal from her for our use on returning, took the remainder into the launch, and were ready to depart at midnight. The weather, however, had set in bad, blowing fresh from the southwest, with a thick fog, and I deemed it prudent to wait until morning, or until there was some chance of working through the fog with safety.

Tessuisak is a small place of some half dozen Esquimaux huts, besides the house in which the chief trader, Jensen, resides.   Jensen is the Dane who accompanied Dr. Hayes on his several expeditions as a dog-driver and hunter, and is apparently an excellent man, speaking English well, and willing and anxious to be of service to Americans, of whom he speaks in the most enthusiastic terms.   At his hands we received a warm welcome and such hospitalities as his recent arrival and consequent unsettled condition would permit.   Tessuisak has a small harbor, but it is nearly always full of icebergs, and we were forced to anchor among them, too close for comfortable contemplation, and with the chance of any one of them turning over upon us. The night being rainy and comparatively warm, (45°,) many icebergs broke up, and the cracking and breaking and turning over and over continued during our entire stay.

At 10 a. m., Sunday, August 3, the fog having lifted to some extent, we got under way and steamed away to the northward, passing in between Brown Island and the main land, working our way among icebergs, and keeping close in to the main land to keep in smooth water and to be ready to slip in and anchor should a fog overtake us. At 4 p. m. had passed Cone Island and Wedge Island to the westward, and sighted Cape Shackelton and the Horse's Head, a prominent island off this cape, right ahead. Passed to the eastward of the island, and at 8 p. m., having Cape Shackelton close aboard, determined the position of the boat to be in latitude 73° 42' north, longitude 57° west.

I had calculated before leaving the ship that we should be enabled, with an expenditure of five hundred pounds of coal per day, to make an average speed of four knots per hour under a steam-pressure of twenty pounds, and with the view to keeping the feed-water for the boiler as fresh as possible, a steam-pipe had been carried from the boiler to the water-tank, for the purpose of melting fresh-water ice which we should pick up on the way and put in the tank. We found upon trial thus far that the expenditure of steam to melt the ice was too great to keep up our proposed speed; and I concluded to supply the boiler with salt water, which of course we had to dip up from the water outside. Running with salt water increased our expenditure of fuel, and I now feared that instead of coal for fifteen days, as originally calculated, we would have only enough for eight days. With our sails we may be able to do better should we be favored with fair winds. This day we had light northerly winds, smooth sea; average temperature of the air, 45°; of the water, 41°.

At 4 a. m., Monday, August 4, passed inside of the Duck Islands, Baffin's Island bearing true southeast; weather thick, breeze coming up fresh from northward and westward, and cloudy, with indications of coming fog. This state of affairs continuing, at 3 p. m. I kept the boat away to the eastward, made sail, and stood in for a headland which, from its position and my calculation of the boat's run, I assume to be Wilcox Head, in about latitude 74° 40' north. In getting under the headland, the fog continuing, we made the boat fast to an iceberg, and waited for a clearing up. At 5 p. m., the fog clearing, we slip from the berg and round the headland to the northward. My object in keeping in close to the shore now, though we were working through icebergs, was to get a sight of the Devil's Thumb, a remarkable pillar of land north of Wilcox Head, and from which I intended to take a fresh departure for crossing Melville Bay. But on rounding Wilcox Head we saw nothing of the Devil's Thumb, and I imagine I might have been deceived in the boat's position in the afternoon. Our accommodations were so limited, the boat had to carry so much, and the difficulty, not to say danger, of getting outside of the boat, was so great that the log could not be hove with any accuracy, and our reckoning was at the best not the most reliable. The currents set us out of our reckoning frequently, sometimes being to the northward and sometimes to the southward.

It is well to note here, for the information of any who may get into Allison Bay, that the chart is wrong in leaving it to be imagined that the bay is free except as to icebergs. It is filled with small islands, running along about fifteen miles from the glacier line, and extending from Cape Seddon nearly fifteen miles to the southward, toward Wilcox Head. It was the presence of these islands which confused us in reference to Wilcox Head.

Discovering another high headland to the northward of the supposed Wilcox Head, I stood on, getting in tolerably open water; and having a smooth sea and no wind, with clear sky, we headed for this new highland. On going below at 8 p. m. I directed Lieutenant Chipp to call me when nearly up with this headland, or in case of any change in the weather. At 10 p. m. Lieutenant Chipp called me, a fog having shut in, the land being entirely obscured, and much ice being encountered in the shape of pack-ice and icebergs, and some new ice an inch in thickness. I immediately put about and attempted to retrace our way, which we succeeded in doing for several miles, but finally, owing to the increasing thickness of the fog, we missed our track, and were brought to a standstill in the pack. As far as we could see we were caught in solid ice, about from one to two feet thick, with large hummocks and icebergs surrounding us. By steady ramming of the ice and working a clear space about us, we occasionally made small cracks in the floes, and succeeded in forcing our way a little at a time, getting occasionally in open patches of water, and among loose ice, and making two or three miles before being brought up again by solid ice. I had headed the boat to the westward on losing our way in the ice, and I knew that every foot we made in that direction was toward the open water. The temperature was from 30° to 32°, the rigging was covered with ice, and the new ice was rapidly forming around us and increasing in thickness. I did not dare to stop for a clearing up of the fog, lest we should be firmly frozen in, and so kept the boat under way with full steam pressure, grinding through the ice where we could, ramming it wherever there was a chance of success, and following every little lead to the westward.

In all this I was guided by Mr. Dodge, the ice-pilot, whose previous experience in the Arctic regions enabled him to give me good advice, and upon whose judgment in this emergency I relied, and handled the boat accordingly. The plan of keeping to the westward proved a wise one, for at 8.30 a. m. we were rewarded by coming into quite large spaces of open water, and at 9 a. m., were pleased to detect a little swell, giving indications of our approach to the open sea beyond. By 10 a. m. we were quite clear of the pack after our twelve hours of uneasiness, and with no more damage to our little craft than a slight scratching and splintering of our strengthening plank, occasioned by the new ice through which we forced during the night.

I immediately headed the boat to the northwest true, (northeast magnetic,) and the fog clearing up by noon, we sighted at 2 p. m. three islands on our starboard quarter, the Sabine Islands, marked on the chart as being in latitude 75° 28′ north, longitude 59° 55′ west. At the same time made out the glaciers beyond to the northeast, a large number of icebergs, and a curious looking hill with two peaks, which no doubt is the Cape Walker marked on the chart, or land in its immediate vicinity. Generally speaking, the chart is inaccurate to a great extent to the northward of Cape Shackelton—the coast-line as we found it being nearly always a glacier line. To the best of our ability to see and judge, the ice-pack was tolerably solid from these Sabine Islands to the coast, showing that we were not far removed from the edge of the Melville Bay pack. The entire bay was dotted with clusters of icebergs.

Between 4 and 6 p. m. we were favored with a light fall of snow, the thermometer standing at 42°, with a light southeast wind and swell.

Knowing that everything that could be accomplished by the boat must be done in fine weather, and that it would be well to keep a hold on the land as much as possible, owing to the uncertainty of our position and the inaccuracy of the chart, I determined to push on with greater speed, in order to be near the land as possible, which was at its nearest point about fifty miles distant, and to this end fired up afresh, making a large hole in our fuel.

At 8 o'clock the next morning, Wednesday, August 6, we had no land in sight ahead, but we found ourselves on the edge of the ice-pack, with a thick fog shutting in and no signs of a lead through. At about 11 a. m. land showed itself abeam, bearing northeast true, in the shape of two high hills, which Mr. Dodge recognized as the Peaked Hill, marked on the chart as being in latitude 76° 18' north and longitude 62° west. Just as we sighted this land Mr. Dodge discovered a lead in the pack to the westward; but the fog shutting in thicker than ever, we were unable to follow it, and I decided to anchor to an iceberg rather than risk the boat on the edge of the pack. We accordingly made our ice-anchor fast at 1 p. m., but discovering the berg to be full of cracks and looking very much like breaking up, I shifted our anchorage to a small ice-cake and banked fires.

At this point I took an account of fuel remaining, and calculated that it was very nearly half gone. We had accomplished this distance without any more serious mishap than our danger of being firmly caught in the ice in Allison Bay. Cape York was only forty miles off, and the people of the Polaris might be there waiting for relief. In the foggy state of the weather burning coal without advancing would be a waste of fuel, and I decided to let the fire go out under the boiler, hoping to accomplish something under sail should the fog lift, or a chance present itself of getting open water to the northward. Accordingly, in the morning of Thursday, August 7, we let the fire die out. The thermometer was at this time at 38°, but we suffered no additional inconvenience on that account.

During the forenoon it promised several times to clear up, the sun showing itself occasionally for a few moments, but with little or no effect on the fog. Becoming tired of inaction, we slipped from the ice at 9.45 a. m., and, making sail, stood to northwest with a light southeast wind and swell.

At noon I determined the position of the boat to be in latitude 75° 52' north, longitude 64° 05' west, by our dead reckoning, and the last bearing we had of the land in the neighborhood of the Peaked Hill. At 4 p. m. came in sight of the ice-pack again, and immediately hauled the boat up to west-northwest true. Discovering a lead in the pack to the northward and westward, stood into it for about five miles, until Mr. Dodge pronounced it a false lead, the ice closing in ahead about four feet thick, some being last year's ice and some older. Brought by the wind and beat out of the lead. At 8 p. m. the wind freshened from south-southeast, and we commenced to work to the westward, as much as possible keeping clear of the ice. At midnight hauled alongside of an iceberg to fill up with fresh-water ice for drinking and cooking. Moderate sea.

At 1.30 a. m., Friday, August 8, sighted high land bearing northwest by north true, and trending away to the northward in an apparently low neck. This, Mr. Dodge pronounces our anxiously looked for Cape York; and at 2.30 a. m., having worked clear of detached pieces of floe-ice, stood in toward the land, which we calculated to be about eight miles distant. At 3 o'clock a. m. the fog shut in again thick and we lost sight of Cape York, at the same time the wind freshened to a gale from southeast and I was compelled to bring the boat by the wind and reef down as snug as possible. At this time had we been in open water, Cape York could have been reached without any difficulty, but as far as we could see to the northward the ice was in a solid pack three to four feet thick, and we were struggling along on the edge of it looking for a lead, and working to the westward in so doing. To the northeast the ice was also in a firm pack, with icebergs and hummocks close enough together to prevent the opening of the ice to any extent. At noon I established the position of the boat in latitude 75° 48′ north, longitude 66° 50′ west.

In the afternoon the southeast gale had caused a fearful sea, and working as we were on the edge of the ice-pack, our situation became one of great danger. The wind had started the Melville Bay pack out from the land to the northward and westward, making a regular bight, in which we were fairly placed.. We had to carry sail in order to keep the boat under control. Steam would have been of no use, since the little Juniata could not for one moment have steamed against such a gale. Lying to was not to be thought of, lest we should drift to the pack and be ground to pieces. The prospect at this time was a terrible one. Icebergs near us, 100 feet in height, had the spray from the sea thrown over their tops. On approaching the edge of the pack-ice, we could see a scene of great confusion. The bordering ice would be broken in large pieces and hurled upon the more solid ice, only to be displaced by fresh pieces torn adrift by the gale and rolled over and over upon the face of the pack. The fate of the boat and the party appeared certain. We were half buried in the seas at times, shipping quantities of water and deluging everything in the boat. It rained in torrents. Had our sail split or our mast gone, nothing could have been done. Providentially everything held, and we were enabled to keep the boat under some control. The fog was very thick, making it extremely difficult to see the ice-pack each time, until we were fairly alongside of it, in which case we had to wear ship at once without delay, not knowing in so doing whether we could clear this grinding and crushing mass of ice or not.

This state of affairs continued until 10 o'clock on the morning of Saturday, August 9, at which time there came a lull. We had then been in this heavy gale thirty hours, and were in a very cold and exhausted state. Everything was completely saturated with water, and we had so much water in the boat that I feared she had sprung aleak. The Little Juniata behaved wonderfully well, and did more than such a small craft could have been expected to do. With our fire-room flooring covered with water, the coal-bunkers half full of the same, every locker in the boat afloat, all our baling would have made no impression on this bulk of water, which was constantly increased by the seas shipped at every one of the fearful plunges of the boat and the showers of spray thrown over us.

We hailed with great relief this lull in the wind which gave promise of a breaking up of the gale, and fearing for the safety of the boat, should the wind subside, leaving this fearful sea running, we attempted to get fire lighted under the boiler. This was no easy matter, and for a while seemed impossible. The matches we had taken with us were wet and useless. The tinder was likewise saturated and of no avail. After several hours' work we succeeded in getting a friction-match dry enough to ignite, Ensign May having warmed and dried it by keeping it next his body for that purpose, and with this match we lighted a candle in a lantern, which was almost immediately extinguished by a gust of wind. By a repetition of the same process, Mr. May secured another lighted match, and this time we succeeded in keeping our candle alight. We attempted then to build a fire, but every stick of wood was soaking wet. By taking cotton waste and junk, wet as they were, and pouring oil plentifully over them, we succeeded at last in lighting our fire.

During this time the wind had moderated and hauled to the southwest. I calculated the boat to have been in latitude 75° 48′ north, longitude 68° 30′ west, on the port tack, (wind at southeast true,) and longitude 67° 10′ west on the end of each starboard tack. We had been running on a line nearly east and west during the gale, making about twenty-five miles on each tack before wearing ship, and obliged to go over nearly the same ·ground on account of icebergs, luffing to the wind as occasion served or required.

At this point I was forced to the conclusion that prosecuting the search any longer was out of the question. My orders read positively to return when the fuel was half expended, and on no account to risk the boat in the ice-pack. The fuel was half gone, and what was left was in such a condition as to lead to very grave doubts as to its being reliable for steaming on the return. As far as we could see to the northward and eastward was pack-ice, and it was in this direction that our port lay. I did not know how close to the middle pack we had been blown during the gale, and I feared if the wind came out in the northwest, we would not only be·blown down upon the Mellville Bay pack, but be followed by detached portions of the middle pack and caught firmly between the two. Again, if we had succeeded in working our way through a lead in toward the land, and had reached it, we had not fuel enough to work our way back through the pack-ice, supposing that a northwest wind had not closed us in for the year.

Up to this time we had seen nothing of the Polaris or of her people Had they been at Cape York, it would not have added to their chances of safety had our little party increased their number, with the ice effectually closing our means of exit. Anxious as we were to find them. and tell them of relief coming, I could not further risk our party being caught in the ice in an open boat, with the season closing, new ice forming, and only fuel enough to keep us warm for a few days. I did not know how far the United States steamer Tigress was behind us, nor what our chances would have been of her rescuing us had we been frozen in. The weather was uncertain, another gale like our previous one was by no means unlikely, and my orders expressly forbade me to jeopardize the lives of the party by putting the boat in the pack-ice.

Reluctantly, therefore, I was compelled to announce that the search must be given up, and headed the boat to the southeast on our return, having steam enough to go ahead at 4 p. m. Having gone up on the in-shore track, I concluded to return by the off-shore or mid-channel track, in hopes that we might see something of the Polaris or her people, but in this we were not gratified.

The wind continued hauling to the westward, soon reducing the southeast swell, and creating a swell from the northwest. Before this we went along at a good rate, the weather clearing gradually, the ice-pack disappearing astern.

Sunday, August 10, opened clear and pleasant; so continuing till past meridian. For the first time since leaving the ship I succeeded in getting observations, and established the boat's position at noon in latitude 74° 45′ north, longitude 59° 37′ west, having run nearly one hundred and fifty miles during the preceding twenty-four hours.

At 1 p. m. sighted the Devil's Thumb, bearing true northeast by north, distant about sixty miles, verifying our position at noon with tolerable accuracy. The weather here became cloudy and squally from west-southwest, with snow, hail, and rain. Wind shifting again at 4 o'clock to southwest, with moderate sea, and so continuing till 9 p. m., from which time to midnight we had light, variable airs.

Monday, August 11, opened clear and pleasant, with freshening breezes from northeast. At 4 a. m. sighted land on port bow, which I recognized as Cape Shackelton, and at 5.30 a. m. sighted the Duck Islands on port beam. This day and the day previous we had considerable trouble with our fires. Knowing that we were short of fuel we economized as much as possible, and were sometimes rewarded by the engine stopping itself for want of steam.

At noon got our latitude by meridian altitude of the sun to be 73° 38' north, or on the parallel of the Horse's Head, which now showed itself on our port beam. We then headed in for Brown Island, off Tessuisak, favored with a fine breeze from north-northwest with long swell, which led me to think that the weather had been unsettled after our departure from Cape York. At midnight we were inside of Brown Island, heading in for Tessuisak.

At 1 a. m., Tuesday, August 12, sighted Jensen's house, and discovered a steamer, apparently at anchor, in the harbor. She immediately thereafter steamed out toward us, and coming alongside of us proved to be the United States steamer Tigress, Commander James A. Greer, from Upernavik the previous evening. I boarded her, and communicated to Commander Greer the result of our reconnaissance, imparting to him the circumstances of wind, weather, ice, and other details relating to his coming journey, up to 4 o'clock on the afternoon of Saturday, August 9, at which time we left the neighborhood of Cape York. I exhibited to him my chart, showing our track going and returning; reported to him the prevalence of pack and new ice in Allison Bay, and respectfully recommended him to strike to the northwest from Cape Shackelton, instead of looking for the Devil's Thumb.

I also offered him the services of our entire party and boat, expressing our willingness and readiness to accompany him to the northward in his search for the Polaris, which services, to our great regret, he declined. Receiving from him his mail and dispatches for you, I left the Tigress at 2 a. m., she immediately steaming to the westward to round Brown Island, and the Little Juniata steered in for her anchorage in front of Jensen's house.

The people of the Tigress were all well, in good spirits, and enthusiastic as to their success, which we heartily wished them in spite of our disappointment.

At 8.40 a. m., having received on board the six hundred pounds of coal left with Jensen on the 2d, and having received from him some seal blubber, in case we ran out of coal, we got our anchor and steamed away, passing among the same islands, and through the same channels, as in going north, and, favored with fine weather and smooth sea, reached the ship without any mishap at 8 p. m. to-day, and were warmly received and welcomed back by you and the other officers assembled at the gangway.

It now remains for me to hope, in submitting this report to your consideration, that my conduct in the affair will meet with your approbation, and that though we were unsuccessful in the endeavor to find the Polaris or her people, no means were left untried that the nature of the difficulties met with and the limited ability of our boat would allow.

I believe the Little Juniata to have accomplished more than was expected of her in reaching the parallel of 75° 52' north, there successfully working through a gale of great violence, and running nearly seven hundred miles while away from the ship. With the limited chances for keeping a reckoning, owing to the thick, foggy weather, and the constant discomfort of being in wet clothing, with every article in the boat drenched by the rains or by the waves breaking over her, I fear that this report will not prove as satisfactory for navigation purposes hereafter as would be desired.

I have made this report to you in detail, omitting no circumstance, however slight, that a fair general idea might be obtained of the circumstances of Arctic navigation in an open boat, even at this the most favorable season of the year.

From our experience I have no hesitation in saying that pack-ice is to be experienced from Allison Bay in-shore to Cape York, and for some miles to the westward of that place; that its location with reference to the shore is dependent on the winds, which are at best uncertain; that a lead in the pack with one wind may as surely be a trap in which a boat can be caught in another wind; that at this season even, new ice an inch in thickness will form in a single night, as per our experience in Allison Bay on August 4; that even the edges of the pack-ice were three feet and more in thickness, making it extremely difficult, if not impossible, for a powerful steamer to work her way through in safety; that a gale of wind in this region is always attended with danger if in the neighborhood of pack-ice. It may be that we are giving no new information on this subject, but our experience may be of service to some future expedition in which a reconnaissance may be made in boats.

I have to commend to you in the most favorable terms, Lieutenant Chipp, Ensign May, and Mr. Dodge. To the coolness and good judgment of Lieutenant Chipp I am indebted for much assistance in carrying on the work of the expedition, and for the zeal manifested in circumstances of great personal discomfort and in the face of dangerous difficulties, he could not have been excelled. Ensign May also performed his duty with ability and zeal, untiring in his work to the end. Of Mr. Dodge and his valuable assistance I have before spoken, and it gives me great pleasure to certify to his practical knowledge of the ice and its location, and the best ways of avoiding it, as well as to the cheerfulness and readiness with which he bore his part of the labors of handling the boat, tending fires, steering, &c., as well as going without rest repeatedly when our proximity to the ice made it necessary for me to have him on deck at all times, to profit by his information and previous experience.

I have to call to your favorable notice Frank Hamilton, machinist, Richard Street, boatswain's mate, Martin T. Maher, ordinary seaman, and William King, ordinary seaman, engineer's force, all of whom volunteered for the expedition, and who performed their duties well, being animated by the same zeal as the officers in reaching Cape York, as long as there was a chance of our being of service to the Polaris or her people. And I respectfully request that you will make such mention of these men to the honorable Secretary of the Navy as their voluntary services in a hazardous expedition may seem, in your judgment, to have entitled them.

Throughout this trip the officers and men worked alike and fared alike, and as we are unanimous in our regret that as far as finding and relieving the Polaris was concerned we failed, we beg to assure you we are of one voice in volunteering for any subsequent expedition from this ship or from the United States, in which our efforts can be made useful, or our experience in the Little Juniata of any effect.

I cannot close this report without commenting upon the great interest taken in the matter by yourself, the provision made for our comfort, and your thoughtful care that nothing should be wanting to insure our safety and the success of the expedition.

I have the honor to be, captain, very respectfully, your obedient servant,

GEORGE W. DE LONG,
Lieutenant U. S. N., late Commander Little Juniata.

Commander D. L. BRAINE, U. S. N.,
Commanding United States Steamer Juniata.

No. 37.]   UNITED STATES STEAMER JUNIATA, (3d rate,)
Godhavn, Disco Island, Greenland, August 18, 1873.

SIR: I have the honor to inclose herewith, for the information of the Navy Department, a copy of a communication received by me from Commander James A. Greer, United States Navy, commanding United States steamer Tigress, and which contains the latest intelligence of that vessel since her sailing from Upernavik for the northward. The original of this was sent via Iviktout, Greenland.

I am, sir, very respectfully, your obedient servant,

D. L. BRAINE,
Commander U. S. N., commanding U. S. Steamer Juniata,
and Senior Officer Present.

Hon. GEORGE M. ROBESON,
Secretary of the Navy, Washington, D. C.

TIGRESS, OFF TESSUISAK, *August* 12—10 m.

We have just arrived, my dear Braine, and I send this by the pilot. Please send the inclosed to the United States by the first good opportunity. If you desire to see icebergs, take a run up as far as Kingitoke and your curiosity will be satisfied. I had my first bump to-day; could not be helped, as it was a choice between rocks and bergs. No damage done; sensation novel. Hear nothing of De Long.

Yours, very truly,

JAMES A. GREER.

Commander BRAINE,
Commanding United States Steamer Juniata,
Upernavik Greenland.

My confounded engine got on center again; ran easily on a smooth rock; backed off with no damage. Governor Jenson is going to pilot us clear of the island. I have just met De Long on his way back; I send this by him at 1.30 m. All well.

Yours, &c.,

JAS. A. GREER.

UNITED STATES STEAMER JUNIATA, (3d rate,)
Harbor of Saint John's, Newfoundland, September 13, 1873.

SIR: I have the honor to report the arrival at this place of the United States steamer Juniata, under my command, ten days from Godhavn, Island of Disco, Greenland:

August 31, at 9.30 a. m., I sailed from Godhavn, taking a course down the middle of Davis Strait, passed Cape Walsingham and Cumberland Sound, Frobisher's and Hudson's Straits, crossing the track of whalers on their return. Most of the passage from Godhavn here was performed under sail alone and in very stormy weather, and here I would beg leave to state that from August 10, at Upernavik, at which date we had our first snow, until our departure from the Greenland coast, the weather was boisterous, with heavy gales, with ice, hail, and snow, the latter falling 10 to 18 inches of a night, with all the indications, as stated by the residents of Godhavn, of an early and unusually severe winter.

· I beg leave to refer to my letter No. 36, under date of August 16, 1873, wherein I informed the Department of my intent, under your instructions, to wait at Godhavn for the United States steamers Tigress and Polaris.

I had sent to the Waigatt mines our steam-launch, Ensign J. D. Keeler in charge, with the intent of getting coal for this ship, the Tigress, and Polaris; when, August 25, at 3 a. m., the Tigress arrived at Godhavn, having been, between August 11 and 25, to Littleton Island, (latitude 78° 25′ north, longitude 73° 46′ west,) and found (Commander Greer reports) the camp of the Polaris, near said island, upon the main land; for particulars of which I refer you to Commander Greer's report, which I herewith inclose; also copies of telegrams sent from here.

About meridian, August 25, the Tigress, having in the meantime been coaled by me, sailed to make further search along the Labrador coast for the officers and crew, whom she had not as yet rescued.

Before sailing, Commander Greer was informed by me that at Iviktout, Greenland, about latitude 61° north, arrangements had been made by which he could obtain a supply of coal, (he was furnished with a chart of that harbor,) and I advised him to take advantage of it, for, with that coal, he could continue his search to the northward and westward. When he left Godhavn, Disco Island, he had coal for twenty-eight days' full steaming, and if he were to use it continuously his supply should not be-exhausted until September 22. Before Commander Greer, in the Tigress, left Godhavn, Island of Disco, on the 25th of August, I suggested to him that he had better return to Godhavn and again meet the Juniata; he informed .that he did not intend to return to Godhavn; did not need the services of the Juniata any more; did not desire me to remain there any longer with the view to assist him in any way, and that he intended to proceed to Saint John's, Newfoundland, after his search was concluded to the west side of Baffin's Bay and Davis Straits.

After the Tigress sailed I waited at Godhavn nearly six days, in the meantime recalling the officers and men who were at the coal mine.

The Department's telegraph dispatch (in response to the one sent by me of the Polaris, as reported by the Tigress) was received September 11.

I am coaling with dispatch, and in a day or two will complete the required repairs to the engines and boilers of this vessel, and shall sail in search of the crew of the Polaris, in obedience to the Department order " to continue the search."

I am happy to state that the health of the officers and crew of this vessel is excellent.

I am, sir, very respectfully, your obedient servant,
D. L. BRAINE,
Commander U. S. N., commanding U. S. Steamer Juniata,
and Senior Officer Present.

Hon. GEORGE M. ROBESON,
Secretary of the Navy, Washington, D. C.

[Telegram.]

SAINT JOHN'S, NEWFOUNDLAND, *September* 10, 1873.

Hon. GEORGE M. ROBESON,
Secretary of the Navy, Washington, D. C., United States.

Juniata arrived to-day; met Tigress at Upernavik; coaled her. She sailed August 11 for Littleton Island. Tigress met Juniata steam-launch, Lieutenant De Long, off Tessuisak, who had been to Cape York in launch and returned. At Disco met Tigress again; again coaled her. August 25, Commander Greer reports: "Camp of Polaris found August 14 off Littleton Island, (latitude 78° 23' north, longitude 73° 46' west;) crew of Polaris all well; had gone south two months before in two whale boats made of ship. Polaris sank one month after. Kept careful lookout, going north and coming south; no signs. Stopped at all settlements; no news. Crew of Polaris probably on board of whaler from Cape York. Tigress left Disco August 25 for Labrador coast, to continue search as long as coal and season permit."

D. L. BRAINE,
Commander United States Navy.

———

[Telegram sent from Saint John's, Newfoundland, September 11, 1873.]

Commodore WILLIAM REYNOLDS, U. S. N.,
Acting Secretary Navy, Washington City, United States.

"Dispatch received; will coal and sail immediately; should I meet Tigress will instruct her continue search of Polaris crew, still missing."

D. L. BRAINE,
Commander United States Navy.

———

[Telegram from St. John's, N. F.]

GEORGE M. ROBESON,
Secretary Navy, Washington:

Juniata not fit or fortified sufficiently to proceed north at this late season. Captain Braine bound to sail at once. At the recommendation of experienced sealing masters of this port, would advise not to proceed. Five steamers now whaling north, and looking for them. Orders to come home after 5th September, fearing chance of being frozen up.

THOS. N. MOLLOY,
United States Consul.

———

[Telegram.]

NAVY DEPARTMENT,
Washington, September 13, 1873

Consul MOLLOY, *St. John's, N. F.:*

Telegram received. The Department hopes Juniata has gone north, in compliance with her orders.

WM. REYNOLDS,
Acting Secretary of the Navy.

[Telegram.]

NAVY DEPARTMENT, *September* 10, 1873.

Commander D. L. BRAINE,
    Commanding United States Steamer Juniata, St. John's, N. F.:
Dispatch received. Continue to search for crew of Polaris.

WM. REYNOLDS,
    Acting Secretary Navy.

[Telegram.]

Commodore WM. REYNOLDS,
    Acting Secretary Navy, Washington City, U. S.:
Dispatch received. Will coal and sail immediately. Should I meet
Tigress, will instruct her continue search if Polaris crew still missing.

D. L. BRAINE,
    Commander United States Navy.

ST. JOHN'S, N. F.

[Telegram.]

GEO. M. ROBESON,
    Secretary Navy, Washington, U. S.:
Yesterday started north to search as ordered. Midnight overhauled
by steamer Safety. Polaris crew rescued by English steamer Arctic.
Telegraphed from Dundee, Scotland; reported by American Consul
Molloy to me. Returned to port this day.

D. L. BRAINE,
    Commander United States Navy.

ST. JOHN'S, *September* 19, 1873.

[Telegram.]

NAVY DEPARTMENT,
    Washington, September 19, 1873.

United States Consul MOLLOY,
    St. John's, Newfoundland:
Dispatches of yesterday and to-day received. Thanks for your attention.

WM. REYNOLDS,
    Acting Secretary of the Navy.

[Telegram.]

ROBESON,
    Secretary Navy, Washington, U. S.:
Steamer Hector, whaler, arrived from Uiantibek Harbor, Cumberland
Inlet. Sailed thence September 17. Tigress left above place 16th, going
to Poiktout, Greenland, for coal, thence to track of homeward-bound
whalers. Greer told Captain Hector, if he did not get information of
Polaris or people, will be at St. John's about middle of October.

D. L. BRAINE,
    Commander United States Navy.

ST. JOHN'S, *September* 25.

[Telegram.]

SECRETARY NAVY, *Washington, D. C.*:

Whaling steamer Hector arrived. Report Tigress at Uiantihek, Cumberland Sound. All well 15th September. Will cruise to end of October to intercept Scotch whalers.

MOLLOY,
United States Consul.

DEPARTMENT OF STATE,
Washington, September 19, 1873.

SIR : A telegram has just been received from Mr. William Reed, vice-consul of the United States at Dundee, Scotland, stating that the "Polaris expedition arrived here destitute. Crew saved, awaiting orders; telegraph." There being no fund at the disposal of this Department from which the wants of these seamen can be relieved, I have the honor to request you to advise me of the action to be taken in the matter.

I have the honor to be, sir, your obedient servant,
J. C. B. DAVIS,
Acting Secretary.

Hon. GEORGE M. ROBESON,
Secretary of the Navy.

NAVY DEPARTMENT, *September* 19, 1873.

SIR : I have the honor to acknowledge the receipt of your letter of this date, in relation to the arrival of the crew of the Polaris at Dundee.

The Department would be glad if you will telegraph at its expense to the United States consul at Dundee to make proper provision for the comfort of the people of the Polaris and send them to the United States by the first steamer, and draw on this Department for the amount expended on this account.

Very respectfully,

WM. REYNOLDS,
Acting Secretary of the Navy.

Hon. J. C. B. DAVIS,
Acting Secretary of State.

DEPARTMENT OF STATE,
Washington, September 19, 1873.

SIR : Upon the receipt of your letter of this date respecting the arrival of the crew of the Polaris at Dundee, I telegraphed to the vice-consul there as follows: "Provide for the people of the Polaris and send them to the United States by first steamer. Draw on Secretary of Navy for expenses."

Since that telegram was sent the following has been received from General Badeau, consul-general at London, which I communicate for your information, viz:

Polaris expedition arrived at Dundee. Buddington and scientific men want money. Shall it be supplied ?

I have the honor to be, sir, your obedient servant,
J. C. B. DAVIS,
Acting Secretary.

Commodore WILLIAM REYNOLDS,
Acting Secretary of the Navy.

NAVY DEPARTMENT, *September 20, 1873.*

SIR: I have the honor to acknowledge the receipt of your letter of the 19th instant, in relation to a telegram from the consul-general at London, respecting the survivors of the Polaris expedition.

I will thank you to authorize the consul to supply the officers with two hundred or three hundred dollars each, and the men from fifty to one hundred dollars apiece, as they may desire, on account of their pay, and draw on the Department for the amount.

Very respectfully,

WM. REYNOLDS,
Acting Secretary of the Navy.

Hon J. C. B. DAVIS,
Acting Secretary of State.

DEPARTMENT OF STATE,
Washington, September 20, 1873.

SIR: I have the honor to acknowledge receipt of your letter of this date respecting advances to be made to the officers and men of the Polaris.

The following telegram has been sent to the consul-general at London:

Supply officers with two or three hundred dollars each, and men from fifty to one hundred dollars each, on account of their pay, and draw on Secretary of Navy, unless consul at Dundee has already done so under instructions of yesterday.

I have the honor to be, sir, your obedient servant,

J. C. B. DAVIS,
Acting Secretary.

Commodore WILLIAM REYNOLDS,
Acting Secretary of the Navy.

[Telegram.]

NAVY DEPARTMENT, *September 19, 1873.*

Commander BRAINE,
Juniata, St. John's, N. F.:

Await at St. John's arrival of Tigress, and then return to New York.

WM. REYNOLDS,
Acting Secretary Navy.

No. 45.]   UNITED STATES STEAMER JUNIATA, (3d rate,)
Harbor of St. John's, Newfoundland, September 14, 1873.

SIR: I have the honor to inclose herewith to the Department for your information copies of reports made to me by Ensign J. D. Keeler, and Second Assistant Engineer H. E. Rhoades, attached to this ship, in regard to the coal-mines at Waigatt Strait, Disco Island, Greenland, to which an expedition was sent to obtain coal for this ship.

Very respectfully, your obedient servant,

D. L. BRAINE,
Commander United States Navy,
Commanding U. S. Steamer Juniata, and Senior Officer Present.

Hon. GEORGE M. ROBESON,
Secretary of the Navy, Washington, D. C.

UNITED STATES STEAMER JUNIATA, (3d rate,)
Godhavn, Disco Island, August 30, 1873.

SIR: I have the honor to submit the following report of the cruise of the steam-launch Little Juniata, to obtain information respecting the possibility of procuring coal on this island, from the mines in the Waigatt, distant about ninety miles from this place, and to mine coal for this ship, if possible.

In obedience to orders received from yourself, I took charge of the steam-launch .Little Juniata, having on board the following officers: second assistant engineer, H. E. Rhoades; gunner, M. K. Henderson; captain's clerk, G. J. Marbury; pilot, H. W. Dodge; and twelve men, with mining implements and provisions for fifteen days; and at 6.15 p. m. on the 23d of August I left this vessel, having in tow the Danish sloop Three Sisters, with the intention of bringing her back loaded with coal, provided we could mine successfully, and if she was not detained by the Danish authorities at Rittenbenk. I arrived at that place at 3 a. m., August 25, and at 5.30 a. m. went on shore and communicated with the governor of the place. I found that the sloop would be delayed for some hours, as she had cargo to discharge, and therefore made arrangements with the governor to have the sloop follow me as soon as her cargo was landed, and at 11.45 a. m. of the same I got under way and stood for the settlement Njaiasusak, having in tow a small schooner, with eleven Esquimaux on board, whom I had engaged to assist me in mining, and one of whom, the governor assured me, knew the location of the mine. I left a quantity of provisions in the sloop, with Mr. Marbury in charge. As we were leaving the harbor, we met a sloop from Egedisminde, and upon hailing her was informed by her captain that he had orders to report to the governor of Rittenbenk for our use in transporting coal.

At 8 p. m. we arrived off Njaiasusak, came to anchor, and communicated with the trader of the station, from whom I learned that we could procure more Esquimaux help from his station if we should need it.

There being indications of bad weather, upon learning that there was no harbor near the mine, I set an anchor-watch, and arranged for the remainder of the crew to sleep on shore. The next day, at 10.25 a. m., I got under way and started for the mines. Owing to our inability to speak the Esquimaux language, we were unable to communicate freely with our pilot, who, it afterward appeared, had been misled by depending upon the assumed knowledge of some of the natives, hunters at Njaiasusak.

At 3 p. m., by the advice of the pilot, we came to anchor about sixteen miles above Njaiasusak, and accompanied by second assistant engineer, H. E. Rhoades, and the pilot, I went on shore, but we failed to find indications of coal in any quantity. I then asked the pilot if he knew the place where the Three Sisters had taken her last cargo of coal. He answered affirmatively, and I then ordered him to take me to that place, which he did, and at 6.15 p. m., August 26, we came to anchor about six miles above Njaiasusak. Accompanied by Mr. Rhoades, I went on shore again and found several veins of coal that had been partially opened by the natives. The inspection proving satisfactory, I immediately landed implements, provisions, and men, and organized camp. The vein in which we decided to commence mining is quite near the beach, and about one hundred feet above the level. I afterward opened another vein, also near the beach, as I found that by so doing I could work my men to better advantage. We commenced work at 5.30 a. m., August 27, and having removed sand and rubbish,

41 Ab

at 7 a. m. commenced taking out coal. After having worked nine hours I found that we had taken out and placed upon the beach, ready for embarking, fifteen tons of coal. The force employed was eleven men (two of them natives) mining, and nine Esquimaux (men and women) engaged in bagging the coal and carrying it to the beach.

Owing to the slowness or incapacity of the captain of the sloop, she had not yet arrived at the mines, and I was therefore obliged to content myself with having the coal already for shipment.

The implements which we employed in mining were picks, shovels, and chisel-bars, and I found them fully efficient for the work. At 8.40 a. m., August 28, I received orders from yourself, per kayak, to return to this vessel with all dispatch. I immediately struck my camp and embarked men and implements in the steam-launch, carrying only sufficient provisions to enable me to reach the ship, and embarking all the coal I possibly could, amounting to thirty-eight bags, fourteen of which remained in the launch when we reached the ship. The remainder of my provisions I embarked in the schooner and sent to Rittenbenk, consigning them to the care of the governor of that place, and made all haste to reach this place, where we arrived at 12 meridian, August 29, having been absent from the ship five days and eighteen hours. The veins of coal which we worked were of from 15 to 30 inches in thickness, and I noticed that the coal became of better quality as we worked into the hill. I believe that a force of one hundred men could easily mine and embark fifty tons of coal per day in ordinary weather, for I think that, except in gales of wind, the surf is never so heavy as to prevent ship's boats from landing and carrying off loads; if necessary, a small wharf could be easily constructed, as there is plenty of stone near by. In case of heavy weather, a vessel using steam-power could easily find a lee from wind of any direction. The harbor of Rittenbenk is only forty miles from the mine, bearing about E.S.E., (true) the land on the N.E. side of the Waigat is very high and would afford a protection against N.E. winds, even at a long distance from the shore; the width of the Waigatt at this point is about twenty-five miles. Flakkenbenk, the S.E. point of Disco Island, forms a protection against winds from N.W., and Rittenbenk harbor is perfectly protected from S.E. gales.

I noticed a constant current to the northward and westward setting through the strait, and found the whole of the Waigat, as far as I could observe, entirely clear of pack and floe-ice, although icebergs were quite numerous.

Native help may be easily obtained, and at reasonable rates, the usual price being one-half of a Danish dollar (about 28 cents,) per day, and rations.

The only shelter we had or needed at the mines were the canvas tents we took from this ship, and all enjoyed the most perfect health. In conclusion, I have the honor to express it as my opinion that coal can be procured at the Waigat mines in sufficient quantities, and with reasonable outlay of time and labor.

I am, sir, very respectfully, your obedient servant,

JOHN D. KEELER,
Ensign United States Navy.

Commander D. L. BRAINE, U. S. N.,
Commanding United States Steamer Juniata, (3d rate,)
Godharn, Disco Island, Greenland.

UNITED STATES STEAMER JUNIATA, (3d rate,)
Godhavn, Disco Island, Greenland, August 30, 1873.

SIR : I have the honor to submit the following report of my observations of the coal recently mined by the expedition sent by you in the steam-launch Little Juniata to the coal-mines, on the north side of this Island, and about ninety miles distant from this place.

At 6.15 p. m. of the 26th instant we arrived at the coal mine about six miles beyond Njaiasusak, a small settlement or hunting station. Ensign J. D. Keeler, who was in command of the expedition, and myself went on shore to prospect, and found three veins of coal that had been barely opened by the Esquimaux. The best vein of the three was about 2½ feet in thickness, running longitudinally through the mountain, only a few feet back from the beach, and about 100 feet above the level.

On top of this vein of coal were three strata, viz : one stratum of sand about 6 feet thick, another of black plate clay about 3 feet thick, and another of sand about 6 feet in thick_ess. The latter was immediately on top of the coal, very hard and occupied at least one-third of our time in removing it from the coal.

At 7 a. m. of 27th we commenced work, and in nine hours took out about fifteen tons of coal, and piled it on the beach, ready for embarkation in the sloop as soon as it arrived. The tools we used, which proved efficient and sufficient, were a dozen common pick-axes, a half dozen chisel-bars, and a dozen shovels, using the latter only for removing the sand. The mining was done by nine of our men and two Esquimaux, and the coal carried in bags, made of hide, by nine other Esquimaux to the beach. In the afternoon we divided our party into two separate gangs, and worked upon two separate veins, both veins being near at hand.

Next morning we found that the strata overlaying the coal had broken away and slid down, filling up our working ledge, which sand had to be removed before we could continue work. This was done after a half-hours' labor, and we resumed work upon the vein. As we advanced into the vein I noticed that the coal gradually assumed a blacker and brighter hue, indicating the presence of bitumen, and some lumps were sprinkled with small particles of resin. The vein was also growing thicker, being at this time over 3 feet in thickness. Up to this time we had only gone about 4 feet into the vein longitudinally.

At 8.45 a. m. of the 28th instant, Ensign Keeler received orders from you, brought by two kayaks from Godhavn, for the expedition to return to Godhavn as soon as possible, as you only awaited our arrival to depart from that place. The sloop had not arrived up to this time, and we had no means for transporting the coal which we had mined to Godhavn, consequently we were obliged to leave all that would not go into the launch on the beach. This we were very loth to do, but there was no help for it. After depositing our tents, implements, &c., into the launch, we found we had only room for about two tons of coal, which we brought with us. Our twelve men, six officers, and two Esquimaux, in addition to the other things, sunk the launch pretty deep. Our water-tanks, with the exception of two compartments holding about forty gallons of water, were converted into coal-bunkers, consequently we were obliged to use salt-water for our boilers, which necessitated frequent blowing to get rid of the saline matter left behind, after the steam had been generated from the water.

The expenditure of fuel to heat the double quantity of water used, which stood at a temperature of 42° F, was necessarily greater than it would have been had we used fresh-water, which this boiler was built for the use of.

We made the run from the mines to the ship, a distance of ninety miles, in exactly fifteen hours, burning about one and a quarter tons of coal, during which time we kept up a regular pressure of steam of twenty pounds to the square inch, with the furnace door open a part of the time, and at no time allowed the saturation to go above $\frac{3}{5}$. We were unable to perform any careful experiments of the coal on the trip, but the following observations of its steaming qualities, made by me, I most respectfully submit to you.

The coal, when taken out of the mine, was chiefly in lumps, but it is so friable in its structure that about half of it broke into small particles while transporting it to the launch from the mine. It is comparatively easy to ignite, it burns freely, and forms very little clinker, and I found that the small particles burned nearly as well as the lumps. By weight, I should judge that it required about one-fourth more of this coal consumed in any given time to produce a mechanical effect equal to the best Welsh coal. It is bituminous in its nature, it produces very little smoke, of a brownish color, and requires very little labor in stoking; and the best results are obtained from a thick and level fire.

During our leisure time at the mines we prospected the immediate vicinity and found other veins, which indicated good coal and quantities of it. The coal is so easily mined that our force of twenty-one people could have removed and carried to the beach at least one hundred tons of coal within five days, with the tools which we used.

I am, sir, very respectfully, your obedient servant,

HENRY E. RHODES,
Second Assistant Engineer, U. S. N.

UNITED STATES STEAMER JUNIATA, (3d rate,)
Harbor of St. John's, Newfoundland, September 28, 1873.

SIR: I have the honor to inclose herewith, for the information of the Department, a copy of my orders, given to Commander James A. Greer, commanding the United States steamer Tigress, at Godhavn, Disco Island, Greenland, on August 25, 1873, as senior officer present, and which I judged are in conformity with the instructions of the honorable Secretary of the Navy, to myself.

I am, sir, very respectfully, your obedient servant,

D. L. BRAINE,
Commander U. S. N., Commanding
U. S. S. Juniata, (3d rate) and Senior Officer present.

Hon. GEORGE M. ROBESON,
Secretary of the Navy, Washington, D. C.

UNITED STATES STEAMER JUNIATA,
Godhavn, Disco Island, Greenland, August 25, 1873.

SIR: I am pleased to acknowledge the receipt of your communication of this date, with the satisfactory information that, with the United States steamer Tigress, under your command, you successfully reached Littleton Island, Smith Sound, Arctic region, where you state that you obtained information that the crew of the Polaris passed last winter, and departed to the southward, some time in June, 1873. You also feel convinced that the officers and crew of the Polaris have been picked up by some of the whalers that this year passed Cape York. You will, therefore, be pleased to carry out the instructions of the honorable Secretary of the Navy by "renewing your search" on the west side of Davis Straits, until you find the officers and crew of the Polaris, or you gain satisfactory information of them, or you feel satisfied that you have done all in your power to carry out the orders of the Navy Department, from which I quote as follows: "Prosecute your search after parting company with him, (Commander Braine,) according to your own discretion under your orders." Wishing you success,

I am, very respectfully, your obedient servant,

D. L. BRAINE,
Commander, Commanding United States
. Steamer Juniata, and Senior Officer present.

Commander J. A. GREER,
Commanding United States Steamer Tigress.

P. S.—As you do not desire me to remain here any longer, with the view of assisting you in your search for the officers and crew of the United States steamer Polaris, I will sail from this port for St. John's, Newfoundland, about September 1 or 5, 1873, or as soon as the coaling party have returned from the coal-mine.

D. L. BRAINE,
Commander, United States Navy.

NAVY DEPARTMENT, *October 9, 1873.*

SIR: The Department has received your letter of the 28th ultimo, No. 50, and the copy therewith inclosed of the orders given by you to Commander J. A. Greer, commanding the United States steamer Tigress, in conformity with the instructions of the Department.

Very respectfully,

GEO. M. ROBESON,
Secretary of the Navy.

Commander D. L. BRAINE, U. S. N.,
Commanding United States Steamer Juniata.

UNITED STATES STEAMER JUNIATA, (3d rate,)
St. John's, Newfoundland, October 16, 1873.

SIR: I have the honor to report that the United States steamer Tigress, under the command of Commander James A. Greer, arrived in this port this afternoon, at 3 o'clock.

Agreeably with the telegraphic instructions I have received from the Navy Department, I have remained with this vessel under my command at this port until the arrival of the Tigress, and now, in accordance with the Department's orders, propose to sail with this vessel under my command for New York about the 20th instant, weather permitting.

I am, sir, very respectfully, your obedient servant,

D. L. BRAINE,
Commander U. S. N., Commanding Juniata, Senior Officer present.

Hon. GEO. M. ROBESON,
Secretary of the Navy, Washington, D. C.

[Telegram.]

NAVY DEPARTMENT, *October* 17, 1873.

Proceed to New York with Juniata.

GEO. M. ROBESON,
Secretary of Navy.

Commander BRAINE,
Care of United States Consul, St. John's, Newfoundland.

CONSULATE OF THE UNITED STATES OF AMERICA,
Dundee, October 22, 1873.

SIR: The Ravenscraig steamer, which picked up the fourteen men of the United States steamer Polaris off Cape York, arrived here on Saturday with the rough boat which the men had made during last winter, and by which they escaped from the ice. In the name of the United States, I claimed said boat as the property of the Navy Department, being in my opinion valuable as a relic of the north polar expedition. The captain denied my claim thereto, and stated (what I was not then aware of) that he was presented with the boat by Captain Buddington, Chester, and each and all of the men of the Polaris, and that it was now his property.

However, the owner of the Ravenscraig, Ninian Lockhart, esq., of Kirkcaldy, and the captain, very graciously (while repudiating the Navy Department's right to the boat) made a free gift of it to the Smithsonian Institution at Washington, and it will, I understand, be sent there along with the three men of the Polaris, (Bryan, Manch, and Booth,) who arrived at this consulate to-day in the Erick whaler.

I telegraphed you this afternoon that these three men had safely arrived, and would be forwarded to New York by the Georgia steamship, of the State Line Steamship Company, sailing from Glasgow on Friday, 1st.

Let me repeat that this company deserves thanks for their attention, and repeated offers to convey the Polaris crew to New York. The moment they heard of the arrival of Bryan, Booth, and Mauch they telegraphed me that the Georgia was at their service, and I accepted their generous offer to convey these men (along with the boat referred to) in the saloon of their steamer to New York free of charge. They will probably reach New York on Wednesday week, 5th or 6th November. All of them are in good health, and I have supplied them with clothing and money, same as I did to the others.

Captain Allen and the surgeon, Dr. Souttar, of the Ravenscraig steamship, who picked up the fourteen men, have personally sustained heavy expenses in providing from their own wardrobes clothing to all the men. On investigation I find that Captain Allen gave clothing to Captain Buddington, Mr. Chester, and other men, to the value of ten pounds sterling, while the surgeon, Dr. Souttar, distributed a great number of articles of his own clothing to Dr. Bessels and others, which would exceed six pounds in value. You may have some idea of the amount of clothing so furnished, when I mention that, when picked up, the fourteen men of the Polaris were, many of them, pretty much clothed with bear-skins, seal-skins, and other like articles. I would, therefore, recommend that, in addition to the thanks of the Navy Department being conveyed to Captain Allen and his crew for the rescue of the

Polaris people, as well as Dr. Souttar, for his kindness, they should be re-imbursed for their personal outlays of clothing by the Government. I wished these two gentlemen (Captain Allen and Dr. Souttar) to state to me what claims they had, but they declined to do. so, saying that they would rather prefer the Department itself to recognize their efforts in whatever way the Department thought proper.   They mentioned to me, however, that by receiving the men, and having them on board, they missed the opportunity of catching whales, (by which their wages are regulated,) and only returned to Dundee with one fish.

Mr. Lockhart, the owner of the Ravenscraig, has, in answer to my request to be furnished with his claim for the board of the fourteen seamen of the Polaris, from 23d June last, (when they were picked up,) just waited upon me.   He says that he cannot properly estimate what remuneration he is entitled to therefor, as he gave the men the free use of everything on board, which they availed themselves of.

Like Captain Allen and Surgeon Souttar, he prefers, he says, to leave his remuneration entirely in the hands of the Navy Department, feeling satisfied that the Government of the United States will not fail to recompense him for the loss he has sustained in his vessel returning home with only one fish, caused, he alleges, by receiving the Polaris's men, and having them on board, and providing for their wants, and getting them sent to Dundee.

It is not my duty to offer any suggestions to the Department as to the course to be pursued; but, as Her Britannic Majesty's government and the British press and people are anxiously watching what remuneration or recognition will be made by the United States Navy to the owners, captain, surgeon, and crew of the Ravenscraig, for their various kindnesses to the Polaris crew, and for rescuing them, I am sure that Congress, on the recommendation of your Department, will not fail to generously consider their claims, and award them ample recompense for their labors and outlays.

I have the honor to remain, your obedient servant,

WILLIAM REID,
United States Vice-Consul.

Hon. GEORGE M. ROBESON,
Secretary of the Navy, Washington, D. C.

No. 72.]   UNITED STATES STEAMER JUNIATA, (3d rate,)
Navy-Yard, Brooklyn, N. Y., November 10, 1873.

SIR: Referring to paragraph No. 1093, United States Naval Regulations, authorized by act of Congress May 17, 1864, I have the honor to again call the attention of the Department to the cases of the following-named men, reported by me in my letter No. 36 to the Department, under date of August 16, 1873, as deserving of medals of honor, for extraordinary service rendered as volunteers, in forming the crew of the steam-launch Little Juniata, in her cruise from Upernavik to Cape York, Greenland, and return, and whose names I think the Department may have overlooked.

I would again ask that, if consonant with the views of the honorable Secretary, the medals of honor and the accompanying gratuity, designated by the act of Congress above referred to "under the head of extraordinary heroism in the line of their profession," may be allowed these men, viz: Richard Street, boatswain's mate; Frank Hamilton, machinist; William King, seaman, extra; and Martin T. Maher, ordinary seaman.

Very respectfully, your obedient servant,

D. L. BRAINE,
Commander U. S. N., Commanding U. S. Steamer Juniata.

Hon. GEORGE M. ROBESON,
Secretary of the Navy, Washington, D. C.

UNITED STATES STEAMER JUNIATA, (3d rate,)
Off Battery, New York, November 1, 1873.

SIR : I have the honor to make the following report of the cruise of the United States steamer Juniata, under my command, whilst prosecuting the search in the Arctic regions for the United States steamer Polaris, her officers and crew; all under your orders dated June 19, 1873.

The Juniata sailed June 24, from the port of New York, deeply laden with a deck-load of coal and a reduced complement of men. We arrived at St. John's, Newfoundland, June 30, and, after sheathing her bows to meet the ice, and coaling ship to her utmost capacity with a heavy deck-load of coal for the United States steamer Tigress, July 9, 1873, we sailed for the Arctic regions. Amid dense fogs we prosecuted the voyage toward Greenland, having several very narrow escapes from collisions with icebergs.

July 14 we arrived off Fiskernaes, where we met large quantities of ice, and had to pick our way very carefully through it. After several hours' delay off this port, and making the usual signals and failing to obtain a pilot, we stood to the northward along the coast and had several very narrow escapes (owing to fogs) from rocks and icebergs which lined the coast.

July 17 arrived at the port of Sukkertoppen, Greenland, after considerable difficulty. Being unable to procure dogs at this place, in accordance with your instructions, after exchanging official visits with the Danish Governor Larsen, I sailed at 4 a. m. on the 18th for Holsteinborg, at which place I arrived the same day at midnight.

Through the courtesy of Governor Frederick Larsen, with whom I exchanged official civilities, I procured at Holsteinborg eighteen Esquimaux dogs and one hundred and fifty seal-skins for the use of the officers and men of the Tigress.

On July 21 I left Holsteinborg for Godhavn, island of Disco. While at the last-named port I landed about seventy tons of Cardiff coal in bags for the Tigress, also the dogs purchased at Holsteinborg, and in addition twelve others purchased for the same object at this last port. At this part of the Greenland coast, I may state that our cruise became of the most interesting character, having passed a belt of ice off Fiskernaes, also many bergs which had been swept by the current setting around from the east coast of Greenland, and thence north up the west coast.

Our necessitated stay at Godhavn of one week, enabled the officers to prosecute most interesting explorations in regard to Arctic mosses, flowers, and ferns on the mountains hereabout; also to observe an immense number of icebergs in Disco Bay, which had broken off from the glaciers back of Jacobshaven Fiord, thence passing out of the bay to the westward of the island of Disco, and drifting to the northward with the current, there being over a thousand in sight at one time, and others moving up through Waigatt Strait to the northward of the island of Disco, in connection with those already mentioned, came from Tussukats glaciers to the northward of Prindsen Island.

In conversation with the assistant governor, A. F. Muldriep, who, in the absence of the inspector, S. T. Krarup Smith, was in official charge of Godhavn, and the esteemed lady, the wife of Inspector Smith, of North Greenland, I first learned of the deposits of coal on Disco Island, at Nomsook Peninsula, on Amenak Fjord; but, as my object was to reach Upernavik with all dispatch, I could not at the time make an examination of the coal veins.

July 29, I sailed for Upernavik, and on the passage to that point, where we arrived July 31, we encountered many immense icebergs, whose altitudes were often 200 feet and upward; we had several narrow escapes from them, and on the morning of July 31, whilst pursuing our voyage, owing to the large variation of the compass 85″ westerly and upward and the local deviation together with the inset of the tides in the fiords, the ship was placed in a most perilous situation, we having run into the midst of a group of very high mountainous rocks. The rocks first reported close aboard we barely sheered clear of, only to find others on both bows and beam, and also in the direction in which we had come. After drifting about for half an hour and using our steam we fortunately found an anchorage in 85 fathoms of water, the general depth around us having been 200 fathoms and more. Here we lay close to the rocks, 2,000 feet in height, for several hours until the fog lifted, when we were fortunate again to get to sea; and that afternoon, after winding our way through an innumerable number of bergs, we anchored in the port of Upernavik.

Governor Rudolph and myself exchanged courtesies immediately, and he informed me that a ship of even half the size of the Juniata had never been there, certainly during the period of his official stay, extending over thirty-five years. He warned me of the great danger of remaining there, and recommended me to immediately place the ship in what is called the Danish Harbor, where the Royal Greenland Trading Company's vessels are loaded. I followed his advice and anchored in this harbor, which can more properly be designated as a pocket, and where a vessel is protected from the prevailing gales of that period on that coast, which blow from southwest, true. Here we moored head and stern with our heaviest cables. From this point I dispatched our largest steam-launch, the little Juniata, under command of Lieut. George W. DeLong, United States Navy, who had associated with him (they all being volunteers) the following-named officers and men: Lieut. Charles W. Chipp, Ensign Sidney H. May, Mr. Henry W. Dodge, ice-pilot; Richard Street, boatswain's mate; Frank Hamilton, machinist; William King, seaman extra; and Martin T. Maher, ordinary seaman.

With the Little Juniata most carefully equipped, with sixty days' provisions and fifteen days' coal, August the 2d, she sailed for Cape York, to prosecute the search for the Polaris, her officers and crew. After performing what Governor Rudolph considered one of the most extraordinary voyages on record, along the fast ice, through the innumerable icebergs, pack and hummock ice of Melville Bay, to Cape York, latitude 75° 56′ north, longitude 68° 18′ west, (for full particulars of her cruise, I have the honor to refer you to Lieutenant DeLong's report, a copy of which I forwarded to the Department,) he returned to the ship at Upernavik, August 12, having met the Tigress off Tessuisak, her commanding officer, Lieutenant DeLong, having imparted to Commander Greer what I considered important information in regard to the open water at that time between Cape York and Tessuisak, no doubt thereby facilitating the voyage of the Tigress to the northward and westward on her search.

Having had several falls of snow between the 2d and 12th of August, and being warned by Governor Rudolph of the peril of a stay here of a ship of the size of the Juniata, ice having also formed in the ponds 200 feet above the level of the sea, and ever since my arrival finding it necessary to stretch hawsers across the harbor to keep out the ice, and having to use our guns with solid shot to break up the small bergs drifting down against the ship, and having delivered to the Tigress the seal-skin clothing, coaled, and dispatched her from this point, the necessity was apparent that I should proceed to my next point of rendezvous with the United States steamer Tigress, viz, Godhavn, island of Disco. Thence I sailed August 13, and having very clear weather arrived at Godhavn August 15, where I expected to await until the last of the season, October 15, 1873, the arrival of the Tigress, or news from her, and from which place I dispatched a kyack seven hundred and fifty miles down the coast to Iriktout, latitude 61° 10' north, longitude 47° 10' west, with a request to the authorities there that they would reserve all the coal they could for the use of the Tigress, and at her arrival in which place afterward she obtained 190 tons.

With the expected leisure time before me at Godhavn, I immediately availed myself of the means at my command to prosecute a search for coal, expecting, should the Tigress be successful, that she, and perhaps the Polaris, might need it for their return home. The inspector of North Greenland, S. T. Krarup Smith, being absent at Egedismindie, a distance of seventy miles from this point, I dispatched the whale-boat, in charge of Ensign John D. Keeler, my clerk, G. J. Marbury, and gunner, M. K. Henderson, with a crew of six men, to that place, asking him for the use of any small vessels he might have at his disposal, to bring coal from the mine to the ship at Godhavn. The voyage was successfully made in three days through a gale of wind, and the duty so well performed that I assigned Ensign Keeler to the command of the steam-launch Little Juniata, having associated with him Second Assistant Engineer Henry E. Rhoades, also the officers who had been with the whale-boat, to the coal-mine on the northeast part of Disco Island.

They prosecuted the search successfully, and found several veins of coal running through the mountain longitudinally, the position of the mine being latitude 60° 45' north, longitude 52° 20' west.

The mines are a short distance back from the beach, and about 100 feet above the level of the sea. Enclosed please find photograph of a sketch of the same.

On top of these veins of coal were three strata, viz. one stratum of sand, another of black silicate clay, and one of sand, this latter immediately on top of the coal. The coal is easily obtained; the tools used were pickaxes, chisel-bars, and shovels, the mining being done by nine of our men ; the coal carried in bags to the beach. As the mining advanced into the mine, the coal assumed a brighter and blacker hue, indicating the presence of bitumen, and some lumps were sprinkled with small particles of resin, the veins growing thicker as the mining proceeded. The coal proved frail in its structure, not bearing much handling, and was obtained in lumps. It was experimented with for fifteen hours' steaming in the Little Juniata, using salt water. It ignites easily, burns' freely, and forms very little clinkers. The fine coal burns nearly as well as the lump. A regular pressure of steam was kept up 20 pounds to the square inch, with the furnace doors open part of the time, and at no time was the saturation above $\frac{2}{3}$. By weight I judge it requires about one-fourth more of this coal to be consumed in any given time to produce a mechanical effort equal to the best Welsh coal. This coal is bituminous in its nature. It produces very little smoke, of a brownish color, and requires but little labor in stoking. The best results as obtained are from a thick and level fire.

While in this locality, several veins were found which indicated good coal and large quantities of it; so easily was the coal mined that our men, nine in number, would have removed and carried to the beach at least 100 tons in eight days with the tools which we used.

I inclose herewith a chart of this and the immediate coal-regions on the west coast of Greenland.

I should here say, in this connection, that the anchorage and holding-ground off the coal-mines worked by us is good, with a depth of from 10 to 20 fathoms, and I deem it perfectly feasible to mine the coals at this point successfully and in large quantities of quality as stated above.

The unexpected arrival of the Tigress at Godhavn, August 25, where I again coaled her, and from whence she sailed the same day to prosecute her search to the westward and northward, caused me to recall the coaling party, though only a small quantity of this coal was brought from the mines, 35 tons of coal being left on the beach for want of means of transportation. I have sixteen bags of this coal, about 150 pounds to the bag, which will be sent to the Washington navy-yard, under the instructions of Engineer-in-chief W. W. W. Wood, Chief of the Bureau of Steam-Engineering, to be tested.

August 31, I sailed for St. John's, Newfoundland, where I arrived September 10, having performed the voyage of over twelve hundred miles almost entirely under sail alone, keeping a careful lookout for whalers in Davis Strait on the way.

On my arrival at St. John's I telegraphed information to the Department of the Tigress finding deserted camp of the Polaris officers and crew at Littleton Island, and that they had started to the southward early in June, 1873, in two whale-boats made of ship.

Here I received telegraphic orders to continue the search for the officers and crew of the Polaris, and after coaling the ship, filling the bunkers and taking a heavy deck-load of coal, I sailed to the northward September 18, in obedience to orders. At midnight of that day, when sixty-five miles to the northward of St. John's, I was overhauled by the English steamer Cabot, the United States consul to St. John's, Mr. T. N. Molloy, on board, who gave me the gratifying information of the safety of the officers and crew of the Polaris, who had arrived that day at Dundee, Scotland, in the English whale steamer Arctic. I immediately returned to St. John's, when I received telegraphic instructions to "await here the arrival of the Tigress."

October 16, 1873, the Tigress arrived at St. John's, and October 19, 1873, I sailed, in obedience to telegraphic orders, from St. John's for New York, at which port I arrived October 25, 1873.

I beg leave to inclose also a tracing of a chart showing the tracks of the United States steamers Juniata, Tigress, and steam-launch Little Juniata, in the prosecution of the search in the Arctic regions for the Polaris, her officers and crew, during the months of July, August and September, 1873.

I send to the Department a book containing specimens of flowers, ferns, mosses, and plants gathered in Greenland, with the latitude specified, also the elevation above the level of the sea.

In conclusion, it is with great pleasure I refer to the spirit which prevailed among the officers and crew of the Juniata, the zeal, energy, alacrity, and willingness of all to face every danger which we encountered, the spirit of emulation to prosecute the search at all hazards with the limited means at our command, the continuous volunteering for all kind of duty, enables me to speak of all in the highest terms of praise, and permits me to commend them to you as worthy of the Department's consideration when they are needed for duty calling for a high order of professional skill and confidence.

I am, sir, very respectfully, your obedient servant,

D. L. BRAINE,
Commander U S. N., commanding U. S. Steamer Juniata.

Hon. GEORGE M. ROBESON,
Secretary of the Navy, Washington, D. C.

NAVY DEPARTMENT, *October 30, 1873.*

SIR: The Department has this day authorized Vice-Admiral Rowan to grant two weeks' leave to the officers and one week's leave to the crew of your vessel, in such parties and at such times as you may suggest.

This is granted in consideration of the arduous services in the Arctic regions, from which you have just returned.

Respectfully,

GEO. M. ROBESON,
Secretary of the Navy.

Commander D. L. BRAINE, U. S. N.,
Commanding U. S, Steamer Juniata, New York.

UNITED STATES STEAMER JUNIATA, (3d rate,)
Navy-Yard, New York, November 1, 1873.

SIR: I have the honor to acknowledge the receipt of the Department's communication of the 30th ultimo, and with pleasure thank the honorable Secretary of the Navy for his appreciation, as expressed therein, of the services of the officers and crew of the ship under my command, during her voyage in the Arctic region in search of the Polaris, her officers and crew, during the months of July, August and September, 1873.

I have the honor to be, sir, very respectfully, your obedient servant,

D. L. BRAINE,
Commander U. S. N., commanding U. S. Steamer Juniata.

Hon. GEORGE M. ROBESON,
Secretary of the Navy, Washington, D. C.

PROCEEDINGS OF THE TIGRESS IN THE SEARCH FOR THE POLARIS.

NAVY DEPARTMENT,
Washington, July 10, 1873.

SIR: The Tigress has been purchased and commissioned by the Navy Department, and prepared in all respects to go the rescue of the Polaris, her records, officers and crew. She was built of extra strength for voyages amongst the ice, and has been materially strengthened since her purchase by the Department, in order to render her better adapted for the service she is now to undertake. You have been appointed to her command, and you will, as such commander, carefully carry out the following instructions:

When entirely ready for sea, you will proceed directly to St. John's, Newfoundland. At that place you will fill up with coal adapted for her use, taking as much in her bunkers and on deck as you can safely carry. Thence you will make the best of your way to Godhavn, on the island of Disco, on the west coast of Greenland, taking for that purpose the most open navigable route and keeping a lookout, as you proceed, for the Polaris and for the Juniata. If you fall in with the Juniata, at this or any other time, you will communicate with her, show your instructions to Commander Braine, and deliver to him the inclosed orders. Should you meet the Polaris alone, you will render every assistance necessary and afford her convoy direct to New York. Otherwise, on arriving at Godhavn, you will ascertain from the Danish authorities whether any information has been received from the Polaris or her crew; and you will probably there find letters from the Juniata, giving you information as to her movements, and such news and information of the Polaris expedition as she may have obtained.

After procuring such information, and supplying, as far as possible, all your wants at Godhavn, you will leave with the Danish authorities a report to the Department of your proceedings thus far, (requesting their transmission to the United States by the first opportunity,) and you will then proceed northward to Northumberland Island, keeping a careful lookout for any signs of those of whom you are in search, going by the way of Upernavik and Tessuisak, unless by falling in with the Polaris, or with some of her officers and crew, before reaching these points, or by reason of the receipt of some positive and reliable information concerning them and their situation, your further progress is rendered unnecessary.

If, however, you do not fall in with the Polaris or her people on the way, or no such positive and certainly reliable information reaches you, you are to push on, by every means in your power, for the position in which the ship was last reported by those of her crew who were rescued by the Tigress, namely, under Northumberland Island, in latitude 77° 35' north, and continue your search until you find them or obtain satisfactory information concerning them and the ship, or until you are compelled to abandon it by want of means, subsistence for yourself and crew, or by other reasons entirely beyond your control. If the Polaris, wherever found, can be brought home, she is not to be abandoned, but you will take charge of her, and, putting proper officers and crew on board, bring her to New York. If she cannot be saved by any means in your power, then her officers and men, her records, scientific and nautical, and everything of value that can be removed, will be transferred to the Tigress and brought by her to the United States.

The Department desires that you will endeavor to rescue and bring home—

First. The officers and crew of the Polaris;

Secondly. The records, scientific and nautical; and,

Thirdly. The ship.

Each of these to be saved in the order named, at the sacrifice, if necessary, of the others later in order of importance.

It is the hope of the Department that in prosecuting this search you will not be detained by the ice or by any other cause so long as to prevent your return during the autumn of the present year. If, however, circumstances compel you to winter in a northern latitude, you will take every precaution to secure the Tigress in a safe anchorage, promoting in every way the health and comfort of those under your command during the dangerous and trying months which must ensue, keeping up your watchfulness during the winter, and when the season opens again renewing your search and prosecuting it until prudence constrains you to return homeward, by no means remaining in the Arctic latitude after the navigation closes next year unless, on your judgment as an educated and responsible naval commander to whom is intrusted a Government ship with its officers and crew, you should think that the objects of your expedition and all the circumstances of the case fully justify you in such course.

Mr. Tyson, late of the Polaris, goes with you as ice-master and pilot. His knowledge of the navigation of Davis Strait, the result of much experience in those waters, and his recent service on the Polaris further north, will render his presence on board the ship of great value.

A competent assistant is also supplied to meet with the possibility of accident to or disability of Mr. Tyson. Six of the seamen of the Polaris, rescued with Mr. Tyson, will also form part of your crew, and may be considered as excellent hands in the service in which you are engaged.

The Esquimaux Hans and his family will be received on board of the Tigress, comfortably cared for, and landed at Godhavn, Upernavik, or such other port as he may desire, which may not interfere with the objects of your expedition; or, if he is willing, and you desire it, he may be retained to assist in your search at the same pay he is now receiving. If discharged, Hans is to be paid off in full. "Esquimaux Joe" will also accompany you, to be employed as you may find his services available, and to return with you to the United States. You will find him most trustworthy, and valuable as a hunter and sledge-driver, and can rely upon his fidelity and experience.

While you are in company with the Juniata you will of course be under the orders of the senior officer present, subject, however, to the orders of the Department, and when separated from that ship you will carry out your instructions to the best of your own ability and discretion, having due regard to the object for which the Tigress has been commissioned, fitted, and placed under your command—that is, to penetrate through the ice, if necessary, to Northumberland Island, to rescue the Polaris, her records, and people, or to ascertain their fate, and to return either this year or next, as may be possible, to the United States.

If it should be your good fortune to rescue the Polaris, you are authorized to put your own officers on board, and to convoy her to New York; but you will touch at such places of rendezvous on your return southward as may have been appointed for you to meet the Juniata; and, failing to meet her at any of them, you will proceed to Godhavn, where the Juniata is finally, under the orders of the Department, to await your arrival as long as the navigation remains open this season: and, in this event, you will be subject generally for your further instructions to the senior officer present, who will, however, allow you to bring in the ship you have rescued, and will not interfere with your orders for that purpose unless the interests of the service shall specially require it.

If, however, on your arrival at Godhavn, on your return homeward, either this year or next, you do not find there a senior officer, you will discharge all the obligations you may have incurred at that place, embark such of the stores and coal as remain there, and, if you have the Polaris in company with you, leave her there should prudence demand it, and if not, convoy her to New York, making from this port a report of your return, and of the particulars of your voyage, to the Department.

Special orders have been given to Commander Braine, commanding the Juniata, directing him to facilitate by every means in his power your advance northward, as the expedition specially fitted and intended to encounter the ice; and advising him that it is upon your specially fitted ship and selected crew that the Department relies to meet and overcome the dangers and difficulties of an Arctic voyage, to which the Juniata is not to be voluntarily exposed; and further directing him to permit you to prosecute your search after parting company with him according to your own discretion, under your orders, and to convoy the Polaris home, should you rescue her; and directing him not to interfere with the *personnel* of your ship, except at your request or under the pressure of imperative professional necessity.

Full reports of the examination of the portion of the crew of the Polaris rescued from the ice will be furnished you, with all the information resulting therefrom.

Relying upon your zeal, discretion, and professional knowledge and spirit, the Department bids you God-speed, and commends you and your comrades, and the result of your difficult and dangerous enterprise, to His overruling and all-wise providence.

Very respectfully, your obedient servant,
GEO. M. ROBESON,
Secretary of the Navy.

UNITED STATES STEAMER TIGRESS,
Navy-Yard, New York, July 14, 1873.

SIR: I have the honor to transmit a list of "passengers" of this vessel.

Very respectfully, your obedient servant,
JAS. A. GREER,
Commander, Commanding.

Hon. G. M. ROBESON,
Secretary of the Navy, Washington, D. C.

FORM No. 10.—PASSENGERS.

List of officers or others about to sail, as passengers, in the United States steamer Tigress. Dated at New York, the 14th day of July, 1873.

Names.	Remarks.
Hans Christian, wife, and 4 children.	Bound to Greenland.

Very respectfully,

JAS. A. GREER,
Commander, Commanding

UNITED STATES STEAMER TIGRESS,
Off Pollock Rip, July 16, 1873—7 a. m.

SIR: I have the honor to inform you that this vessel sailed from the navy-yard, New York, at 5.10 p. m., July 14. The weather has been pleasant and the sea smooth, giving us no chance to test the qualities of the vessel. All on board are well. I send this by the sound pilot. Three of the seamen of the Polaris, viz, G. W. Lindquist, J. Kruger, W. Nindermann, are on board. The others did not report on board.

Mr. Stickney, I presume, has informed you of his action as to paying the men. I filled up our complement from the Vermont. We have on board 11 officers, 32 men, and 7 Esquimaux.

Very respectfully, your obedient servant,
JAS. A. GREER,
Commanding.

Hon. G. M. ROBESON,
Secretary of the Navy, Washington, D. C.

————

UNITED STATES STEAMER TIGRESS,
St. John's, Newfoundland, July 23, 1873.

SIR: I have the honor to inform you that we arrived here this morning, after a passage of eight and a half days from New York. We had one moderate gale, of a few hours' duration, in which the vessel showed herself to be a good sea-boat. As a steamer she may be classed as a "five-knot" one.

The engineer proposes to make a change in the furnaces, which may increase the speed. I expect to sail for Disco in two days. We saw our first icebergs off Cape Race. All hands are well.

I send this by the mail-steamer, which leaves to-day.

Very respectfully, your obedient servant,
JAS. A. GREER,
Commander, Commanding.

Hon. G. M. ROBESON,
Secretary of the Navy, Washington, D. C.

————

UNITED STATES STEAMER TIGRESS,
St. John's, Newfoundland, July 26, 1873.

SIR: I have the honor to inform you that, having filled up with coal and other stores, we sail to-day for Disco.

I have exchanged with the governor the courtesies usual at this place. All are well.

Very respectfully, your obedient servant,
JAS. A. GREER,
Commander, Commanding.

Hon. G. M. ROBESON,
Secretary of the Navy, Washington, D. C.

UNITED STATES STEAMER TIGRESS,
Godhavn, Disco Island, August 8, 1873.

SIR: I have the honor to inform you that we arrived at this place on the 6th instant, ten and a quarter days from St. John's, Newfoundland, after a somewhat boisterous passage, during which the vessel showed her good qualities as a sea-boat.

By some changes made in the furnaces we have been able to obtain a speed which will authorize me to class the Tigress as a 6-knot steamer under favorable circumstances.

The Juniata sailed for Upernavik July 29, having taken all the anthracite coal which was here, and leaving for this vessel about sixty-five tons of Cardiff coal, which will not fill up by twenty-five tons.

As fuel is essential to this vessel for carrying out the wishes of the Department, I intend, when I meet the Juniata, to request Commander Braine to supply us with anthracite coal sufficient to fill our bunkers.

Owing to the short-handedness of the crew, and the impossibility of obtaining a sufficient force from Godhavn, the handling of the coal here has caused a detention of a day.

I beg to call your attention to the fact that there is now no coal on the Greenland coast. Should we be so fortunate as to fall in with the Polaris this season, and be able to reach a Danish settlement, she will be, (no matter how seaworthy,) in all probability obliged to remain there until supplied with coal next year. Should this vessel be obliged to spend a winter in the ice, the need of a supply of coal, to be in readiness for us on our return to the southward, will be apparent.

Mr. Smith, the inspector of North Greenland, is absent, but I have been courteously received by Mr. Müldrüp, the governor of Disco Island.

At St. John's two men deserted, viz, George Gray, (quartermaster,) and William Bayes, (carpenter's mate.) I shipped at that place one seaman, one man since rated carpenter's mate, and one machinist to take the place of a man who is physically disabled. I propose, in due form, and with Commander Braine's consent, to send him and one of the seamen who has proved to be worthless on board of the Juniata.

All hands are well, with the exception mentioned.

We sail for Upernavik this afternoon. I will have this letter sent (leaving a duplicate here) by a vessel which sails for Denmark soon.

  * * * * * * *

Very respectfully, your obedient servant,

JAS. A. GREER,
Commander, Commanding.

Hon. G. M. ROBESON,
Secretary of the Navy, Washington, D. C.

UNITED STATES STEAMER TIGRESS,
Off Upernavik, Greenland, August 11, 1873.

SIR: I have the honor to report that this vessel arrived here yesterday, thirty-nine hours from Godhavn, island of Disco.

The Juniata is here. Commander Braine has done everything in his power to facilitate our departure, and I expect to sail this afternoon for Tessiusak and the northward.

42 Ab

Thomas Harrington (captain of top) broke his leg at Godhavn. He and two other men have been transferred to the Juniata. Commander Braine has furnished men to take their places.

I cannot find at this place the copy of the agreement made with Hans Christian. I have paid him off in accordance with the terms mentioned by Captain Hall in one of his letters to the Department, viz, "fifty Danish dollars per month," for twenty-three and a half months, equal to $640.09 in American gold.

I have received from the Juniata thirty-seven and a half tons of anthracite coal.

There are on board of this vessel 45 persons, viz, 12 officers, 32 men, (including the apothecary,) and "Esquimaux Joe."

All hands are well.

Very respectfully, your obedient servant,

JAS. A. GREER,
Commander, Commanding.

Hon. G. M. ROBESON,
  Secretary of the Navy, Washington, D. C.

UNITED STATES STEAMER TIGRESS,
Off Godhavn, Island of Disco, Greenland, August 25, 1873.

SIR: I have the honor to report that this vessel sailed from Upernavik, North Greenland, on August 11, 1873, at 5.10 p. m., a Danish pilot being on board.

At 11.45 p. m. arrived at Tessiusak. On approaching the anchorage, and while forging ahead slowly, the engine caught on center. Let go the anchor, but failing to bring the vessel up, she ran lightly upon a smooth rock. Backed off in a few minutes; no damage done. Governor Jauses came on board, having no information. I accepted his services as pilot to clear us of the islands.

August 12, at 1.15 a. m., stopped and communicated with the Juniata's steam-launch. Obtained no information about Polaris.

At 1.45 a. m. discharged pilots, parted company with steam-launch, and stood to the northward.

August 13, at 10 a. m., passed Cape York. Heavy pack-ice prevented our getting very close, yet we were near enough to clearly observe any signals that might have been made. A bright lookout was kept at all times.

From Cape York skirted the shore as closely as safe navigation would permit. This was also done upon our return. At 9 p. m. examined North Star Bay.

August 14, examined Netihk Harbor; skirted Northumberland Island. Being convinced that this was not the place where the separation of the party on "ice-floe" and Polaris occurred, continued on for Capes Parry and Alexander. Examined Hartstene Bay. At 9 p. m., having passed Littleton and McGary Islands, feeling quite sure that this was the place we were seeking, stood well in and lowered a boat.

Discovered (one month and four hours after leaving New York) a camp, which, upon examination, proved to be the one which was occupied by crew of Polaris last winter. It is now occupied by Esquimaux, who seem to be quite intelligent. From them I learned that they came from Pond's Bay, on a hunting expedition, and found the Polaris secured to the rocks, the crew living on shore. That they had built two boats out of material taken from the vessel, fitted them with oars and sails, and about one moon or so ago, or when the ducks began to hatch, (which I think was about the middle of June,) they all being well, had gone to the southward. Also, that Captain Buddington, the head man, before he departed told him (the chief.Esquimaux) that he could have the vessel.

A gale of wind came on some time after the departure of the crew; the vessel broke adrift, (I saw the broken hawsers,) and, drifting about a mile and a half toward the passage between Littleton Island and the main land, sank. The native said he saw her go down, and regretted her loss very much. He went with Lieut. Commander H. C. White to the place, but two small (comparatively speaking) ice-bergs, with a heavy floe about them, covered it, having doubtless "grounded" upon the wreck, which caused their detention at the spot, as there were 7 to 11 fathoms of water around it.

At the camp a comfortable wooden house had been constructed, having in it bunks, mattresses, furniture, galley, &c.

The natives had two tents, made out of canvas, evidently from the Polaris. A rough carpenter's bench, with many shavings about it, was in the camp. Provisions, instruments, books, and stores of various kinds were scattered around the small camp in every direction, and all in quite bad condition.

I caused to be brought on board all the manuscript matter, including a mutilated log-book, all the books which were not torn to pieces, some fire-arms and broken instruments, the ship's bell, and some medical stores. The provisions and other stores were of no earthly value, and I did not bring them off. A cairn or place of concealment for papers and records was sought for, but none could be found.

The weather was quite threatening, thick, squally, and snowing at times, with an ice-pack to the northward, extending as far as the eye could reach across Smith Sound.

At 2.15 a. m., August 15, I stood to the southward, keeping a lookout for the people. The position of what I call "Camp Polaris" is, as taken from the chart, latitude 78° 23' north, longitude 73° 46' west.

At noon, August 16, passed Cape York near enough to have seen signals. Found much ice about it, and stood for Melville Bay.

August 19, at 2.30 p. m., communicated with Governor Jauses, at Tessiusak; obtained no news. At 9.30 p. m., anchored at Upernavik; nothing had been heard there of the crew of the Polaris. Remained at Upernavik, overhauling and repairing machinery, until August 23, 2 p. m., when we sailed for this place, arriving here August 25, 2 a. m., being almost positively assured in my own mind that the crew of the Polaris have been taken on board a whaler. The following-named are known to have passed to the northward this year, viz: Asuk, or Asik, of Dundee; Arctic, believed to be of Dundee; and seven others whose names I have not been able to learn, and they all (those that have been spoken) expected to sight Cape York.

I have concluded, in accordance with my instructions from the Department "to make a thorough search for the crew," to go to the west side of Davis Strait, skirting the pack until I find a chance to get through, then to work to the northward in search of the whalers, who, on their return voyage, follow the western shore. The search will be continued as long as prudence will justify, taking into consideration the condition of the ice and our supply of fuel, (which will be used economically.) I will then proceed to St. John's, Newfoundland. We have now on board 155 tons of coal.

I expect to sail to-day. All hands are well. Appended is a chart showing "Camp Polaris."

Very respectfully, your obedient servant,

JAS. A. GREER,
Commander, Commanding.

Hon. G. M. ROBESON,
Secretary of the Navy, Washington, D. C.

P. S.—Since writing the above, I have received from Commander Braine, of the Juniata, 13 tons of coal.

JAS. A. GREER.

Forwarded.

D. L. BRAINE,
Commander U. S. N., Commanding Juniata,
and Senior Officer Present.

UNITED STATES STEAMER TIGRESS,
Niantihk, Cumberland Sound, September 15, 1873.

SIR : I have the honor to inform you that this vessel sailed from God-havn, Disco, on August 25. We stood for the west side of Davis Strait, and on the 26th, in latitude 67° 30′ north, longitude 60° 15′ west, fell in with the pack, as it extended well to the north and east. I skirted it to the south and west, going into every lead that indicated a passage. When in the neighborhood of Cape Searle, found that the ice was packed tight to the shore; worked out, and tried to get into Exeter Bay, with same result. Having been informed that the Scotch whalers at times ran into Cumberland Sound at the close of their season, and being short of coal, I determined to come to this place.

South of Cape Walsingham we had a heavy gale, which lasted three days, during which it was necessary to lie to under steam and sail.

We arrived here on September 4, and have, when the weather would permit, been engaged in getting on board stone ballast.

*   *   *   *   *   *   *

I expect to sail to-morrow for Tonhik, Greenland. After obtaining at that place, all the coal possible, I will sail for the narrow part of Davis Strait, and cruise for the purpose of intercepting some one of the whaling fleet.

The Tigress may be expected at St. John's, Newfoundland, in the latter part of October. All are well.

Very respectfully, your obedient servant,

JAS. A. GREER,
Commander, Commanding.

Hon. G. M. ROBESON,
Secretary of the Navy, Washington, D. C.

UNITED STATES STEAMER TIGRESS,
Toigtut Sound, Greenland, October 4, 1873.

SIR : I have the honor to inform you that this vessel sailed from Niantihk, Cumberland Sound, on September 16. After a boisterous passage and one very heavy gale, we reached this place on September 27, having stopped a day at Sanernt on account of a head gale.

The authorities here have been very courteous, and have done everything in their power to assist us.

From Mr. S. Fritz, the very obliging agent of the Kryolith Company, I have obtained 190 tons of coal. In accordance with his desire, (as he does not know what the company will charge,) I have given him receipts for the coal, which he will forward to the New York agent of the company, Mr. C. Ed. Habicht, 68 Broadway, who will present the bill to the Department.

We, as usual, have much work to do to the machinery. For several days before our arrival here we were obliged to work high pressure, which reduced our speed very much.

We have heard nothing of the crew of the Polaris. I expect to sail to-day for the northward, keeping a lookout for the whalers. I shall cruise as long as the season will justify, and then proceed to St. John's, Newfoundland.

On the day that we left Niantihk, I supplied the American schooner Helen F., of New London, Conn., (which was in need of them,) with a few stores at Government prices. All hands are well.

Very respectfully, your obedient servant,

JAS. A. GREER,
Commander, Commanding.

Hon. G. M. ROBESON,
Secretary of the Navy, Washington, D. C.

[Telegram.]

ST. JOHN'S, NEWFOUNDLAND, *October* 17, 1873.

Hon. GEORGE M. ROBESON,
Secretary of the Navy, Washington, D. C., United States:

Tigress arrived. All well. Sail for New York in a week. Met no whalers. Had a bad time in Davis Strait.

JAS. A. GREER,
Commander, Commanding.

UNITED STATES STEAMER TIGRESS,
Navy-Yard, New York, November 10, 1873.

SIR: I have the honor to inclose a list of passengers brought to the United States in this vessel.

Very respectfully, your obedient servant,

JAS. A. GREER,
Commander, Commanding.

Hon. GEO. M. ROBESON,
Secretary of the Navy, Washington, D. C.

FORM No. 10.—PASSENGERS.

List of officers or others about to sail as passengers in the United States steamer Tigress, dated at St. John's, New Foundland, the 30th day of October, 1873.

Name.	Remarks.
Louis Moisette ..	A distressed American citizen, sent home by United States consul at St. John's. He served as a ward-room boy, and was of no expense to the Government.

JAS. A. GREER,
Commander, Commanding.

P. S.—The above-mentioned man came to New York in the Tigress.

JAS. A. GREER.

PROTECTION TO AMERICAN CITIZENS AND PROPERTY AT PANAMA.

South Pacific Station,
United States Flag-Ship Pensacola,
Bay of Panama, U. S. C., May 13, 1873.

Sir: I have the honor to inform the Department that as soon as I had dropped anchor at this place, on the 7th instant, Commander Belknap, of the Tuscarora, called upon me and reported that the parties contending for the possession of the government of the state of Panama had commenced hostilities, and at that time fighting was going on between them. That he had been called upon by our consul to furnish protection to the citizens of the United States and the railroad depot, and had promised to send a force on shore at such time as the consul should designate, and a certain signal would be made on shore in the event of the force being needed.

I approved of Commander Belknap's course, and gave orders to Captain Upshur, of this vessel, to have in readiness, to send on shore at a moment's warning, a force of one hundred men and two pieces of artillery.

At about 5 p. m. the signal as agreed upon was made, when the force above mentioned was promptly sent to the railroad depot for its protection and the immense quantity of property therein stored. The officer in command of this force, Lieut. T. B. M. Mason, United States Navy, was ordered to confine himself alone to the protection of the railroad depot and property, and not to enter the town.

An hour later I received a communication from the United States consul, Mr. Long, a copy of which is herewith transmitted, marked A, calling upon me to send an armed force of one hundred and fifty marines into the town for the protection of himself and others.

As it was near night when the request reached me, I deemed it unwise to comply with it, as I could not feel justified in landing and marching through a strange city at night the force asked for; and, besides, I considered that I had no right to land men on the soil of a friendly power without the consent of the authorities.

The day following, a deputation of gentlemen, bearing a letter signed by the most respectable and influential American and foreign citizens of Panama, and accompanied by a letter from the United States consul, (copies of which are enclosed, marked B, C,) requesting that for their protection and that of their property I would place in the town an armed force of one hundred men, stating at the same time that the chiefs of the contending parties had given their consent that this should be done. It was also represented to me that the moral effect of the presence of a respectable force from this squadron would tend materially to inspire confidence and prevent any lawlessness on the part of evil-disposed persons.

In compliance with this request, I increased the force then on shore to two hundred marines and blue-jackets, with four pieces of artillery, to be equally divided between the city and the railroad station.

Captain Upshur placed this force under the immediate command of Lieut. Commander P. F. Harrington, of this vessel, and Lieut. Commander Theo. F. Jewell, of the Tuscarora, as will be seen by his letter to me, a copy of which is inclosed, marked D.

On the 9th instant a truce was asked for by the Correoso party, with a view to burying their dead, which was granted. Subsequently an appeal was made to the foreign consuls by both parties to use their influence toward a cessation of hostilities, but they declined doing so, deeming it prudent to abstain from any interference.

The Correoso party then agreed to disarm, naming an hour, which was postponed from time to time, but eventually there was a surrender of their arms, and now all is quiet.

The political affairs of this state are in such a muddle that I am wholly unprepared to give any lucid explanation of the causes which have led to this last *émeute*. I send herewith editorials from the Panama Star and Herald, the local paper of the Isthmus. The statements, so far as I can judge, are correct.

The killed and wounded in the strife foot up one hundred, more than half of whom were killed.

It gives me pleasure to state that the conduct of our officers and men, with a few exceptions among the latter, has been most commendable.

* * * * * * *

Very respectfully, your obedient servant,
CHAS. STEEDMAN,
Rear-Admiral, U. S. N., Commanding U. S. Naval Force,
South Pacific Station.

Hon. GEORGE M. ROBESON,
Secretary of the Navy, Washington, D. C.

A.

UNITED STATES CONSULATE,
Panama, May 7, 1873.

SIR: A deplorable state of matters in Panama requires the presence of not less than one hundred and fifty marines to protect American interests during the night. I have informed both parties of my intention to appeal to you for ample protection.

I have the honor to be, your obedient servant,
OWEN M. LONG,
United States Consul.

Rear-Admiral STEEDMAN,
Commanding United States Naval Forces, South Pacific.

P. S.—During the night the signal for additional aid will be three rockets, followed, after a short interval, by three more.

B.

UNITED STATES CONSULATE,
Panama, May 8, 1873.

SIR: I beg leave to introduce to you the gentlemen who are bearers of this communication. They represent the various interests centered in business in this city. Many of the names are those of Americans who have their families and fortunes in this city. They can give you a thoroughly accurate statement of the present condition of affairs in this city.

I have the honor to be, with respect and esteem, your obedient servant,
OWEN M. LONG,
United States Consul.

Rear-Admiral CHAS. STEEDMAN,
Commanding United States Naval Forces, South Pacific.

C.

PANAMA, *May* 9, 1873—8 a. m.

SIR: The undersigned, foreign residents in Panama, beg to acquaint you of the fact that since 12 noon yesterday a contest has been going on in this city between the federal troops stationed here for the protection of the transit, and the state forces; that indiscriminate firing, endangering the lives of all residents, has continued since the hour before mentioned; that both parties threaten that sooner than surrender, they will fire the town; and that even if this threat be not carried out, it is to be feared that great excesses will be committed by either party which may be victorious; that the lives and property of the whole of the undersigned will be seriously imperiled if such excesses are committed; that the landing of an armed force of any foreign power here is of more value as a moral force than any other step that can be adopted; and that they therefore beg you, as commander of the only foreign force here, and the chief naval representative of the United States of America, with which power Colombia has treaties providing for such emergencies, to at once send such a force on shore as shall put a stop to such perilous and anomalous state of affairs.

H. SCHUBER,	D. GOLDSMITH & Co.,
JAS. BOYD,	S. L. ISAAC and ASH,
F. EDMUNDS,	G. W. PIERCE,
D. M. CORWINE,	S. L. LANGSBURGH & Co.,
GEO. REICKER,	HENRY EHRMAN,
H. M. KEITH,	BOSTON ICE COMPANY,
	And many others.

Rear-Admiral CHARLES STEEDMAN,
  Commanding United States Naval Forces, South Pacific.

D.

SOUTH PACIFIC STATION,
UNITED STATES FLAG-SHIP PENSACOLA,
  Panama, U. S. C., May 13, 1873.

SIR: In obedience to your order, I have to report that a force of one hundred blue-jackets and marines, with two howitzers, were landed from this vessel and Tuscarora on the 7th instant, at the railroad station, with orders to protect the buildings and property therein stored, and that subsequently, by your further orders, one hundred additional men and officers were landed, with two howitzers. This force was placed under the command of Lieut. Commander P. F. Harrington, and equally divided, one hundred being left at the depot, under the immediate command of Lieut. Commander T. F. Jewell, of the Tuscarora, and one hundred placed within the city, a detail from the division being sent to the United States consulate for its protection, the whole under the command of Lieut. Commander P. F. Harrington.

The moral effect of the presence of this force was, as you had foreseen, to inspire confidence, affording security to the lives and property of American and other foreign merchants and residents, and exercised a measurable restraint over the belligerents.

Hostilities between the contending parties having ceased on the 10th, it was deemed expedient to keep our force *in statu quo*; however, the civil authorities of the town being re-established on the day following, a request was made that our people be withdrawn from the city, which was complied with, but a sufficient force continued at the railroad depot. I therefore withdrew from the town and returned to the United States steamer Tuscarora her men and officers. I have left at the railroad station sixty men and two howitzers, under the command of Lieut. T. B. M. Mason.

In closing this report, I beg leave to call your attention to the thorough, satisfactory, and able manner in which our operations on shore have been conducted, all the more delicate from the fact that we were neutrals. To Lieut. Commander P. F. Harrington and Lieut. Commander T. P. Jewell, and to the officers and men under their command, great praise is due for the intelligent, earnest, and complete manner in which the duty you have given them has been performed. It has excited much remark on shore, and met with universal commendation. Lieut. Commander P. F. Harrington and Lieut. T. B. M. Mason, and the officers and men of the ship, forming very much the largest part of the force on shore, have come more directly under my observation, and it gives me great pleasure in mentioning the zeal and discipline they have manifested under circumstances well calculated to try both officers and men, and gives ample proof that the crew of a well-organized ship can, when required so to do, perform on shore all the duties of a well-trained soldier.

Very respectfully,

J. H. UPSHUR,
Captain and Chief of Staff.

Rear-Admiral CHARLES STEEDMAN, U. S. N.,
Commanding United States Naval Force, South Pacific Station.

SOUTH PACIFIC STATION,
UNITED STATES FLAG-SHIP PENSACOLA, (2d rate,)
Bay of Panama, U. S. of C., October 6, 1873.

SIR: In my dispatch No. 1, dated the 22d of September, 1873, I informed the Department that I had on that day relieved Rear-Admiral Steedman, in command of the United States naval force on the South Pacific station.

I was not long permitted to be idle and without something to do. A revolution had been brewing in Panama and vicinity for some weeks.

* * * * * *

On the 24th of September affairs seemed to be approaching a crisis. In the afternoon of that day, I landed a force of one hundred and thirty men, well armed and equipped with howitzers and rifles, under competent officers, and stationed them at the Panama Railroad depot for its protection, and to be ready to furnish escorts on the railroad trains to Aspinwall to guard the passengers and specie which were being daily transported over the road.

The President of Panama had previously notified the United States consul that, under the present circumstances, he was unable to give the Panama Railroad that protection and safeguard guaranteed in the treaty.

This movement was quite opportune, as that night at midnight the "ball opened," and the conflicting forces commenced firing upon each other, about two miles outside of the city, but it did not prove serious to either party.

The firing was resumed and continued at intervals the following day, and has continued up to this time of writing.

I afterward increased the force on shore to one hundred and ninety men, stationing detachments to protect the American consulate and other American houses and American property.

There are now four lines of steamers communicating with Panama, viz, the American, (two lines, the San Francisco and the Central America,) English, and the French, whose passengers, freight, and specie have to be transported over the Panama Railroad. By care, attention, and hard work, the American naval force has securely protected the transit and passengers, and their effects have been, up to this time, transported over the railroad without any delay.

The United States ship Benicia, Capt. A. G. Clary, of the North Pacific squadron, happened in here very opportunely, and the ship and officers have done good service in rendering me important aid.

Lieut. Commander J. D. Graham, the executive officer of the Benicia, has commanded the forces stationed at the city, and Lieut. Commander Allen D. Brown, the executive officer of the Pensacola, has command of the forces at the railroad. Both of these officers have performed their duty with good judgment and efficiency.

* * * * * * *

*October 8.—Later.—*On the 6th instant hostilities ceased, the outside or besieging party, under General Correoso, withdrawing a few miles into the interior, being deficient in ammunition and other supplies. This enables us to move about without the fear of being hit by bullets from one party or the other.

In course of time revolutionary movements will, perhaps, be again the order of the day.

There is not the necessity for keeping so large a force on shore, and I have withdrawn all but thirty men to the ships.

A small force is still required, at least for a few days, as a precautionary measure at the railroad depot, and to guard the road in case of the re-appearance of the revolutionary forces.

The mail-steamer is just in from San Francisco, and I shall see that the passengers, mails, specie, baggage, and freight are all conveyed without molestation over the road to Aspinwall to-day.

I am, sir, very respectfully, your obedient servant,

JOHN J. ALMY,
Rear-Admiral, U. S. N., Commanding United States
Naval Force, South Pacific Station.

Hon. GEORGE M. ROBESON,
Secretary of the Navy, Washington, D. C.

MERITORIOUS SERVICES AND CONDUCT.

UNITED STATES STEAMER COLORADO, (1st rate,)
FLAG-SHIP ON THE ASIATIC STATION,
Hong-Kong, China, November 5, 1872.

SIR: I have the honor to forward to the Department a copy of a letter from Commander R. R. Wallace, commanding, reporting an act of distinguished gallantry done by Lieut. Commander Douglas Cassel, United States Navy, executive officer of the United States steamer Ashuelot.

Knowing from my own recent observation of the Pei-Ho River, at Tien-Tsin, the great personal peril which Lieutenant-Commander Cassel unhesitatingly incurred in jumping into the always rapid, and, at the time of the occurrence, the swollen and turbulent current, to rescue from drowning one of the ship's company, I beg leave to represent his act as of the most honorable, manly, and courageous kind.

But for Lieutenant-Commander Cassel's very prompt, self-reliant, and self-forgetful action, the carpenter's mate, who had fallen overboard while in the discharge of his duty at general quarters, would inevitably have been drowned; and but for his coolness, resolution, and strength, Lieutenant-Commander Cassel himself might have met the same fate.

I have the honor and pleasure to respectfully commend Lieutenant-Commander Cassel's heroic action to the special notice of the honorable Secretary.

Very respectfully, your obedient servant,
THORNTON A. JENKINS,
Rear-Admiral, U. S. N., Commanding U. S.
Naval Force on the Asiatic Station.

Hon. GEO. M. ROBESON,
Secretary of the Navy, Washington, D. C.

UNITED STATES STEAMER ASHUELOT, (3d rate,)
Tien-Tsin, China, October 14, 1872.

SIR: I have the honor to inform you that during exercises at general quarters this morning the carpenter's mate was sent over the side to plug a shot-hole. The lanyard to the slings was not well secured, and, as soon as a strain was brought on it, it sundered, and he fell overboard. He would have been drowned, (as he had on a heavy pair of canvas-slings, tools, &c., which rendered him helpless,) but for the prompt assistance of Lieut. Commander Douglas Cassel, who jumped overboard and succeeded in getting him on the port quarter-post, and kept him there until a boat could be got to them. Mr. Cassel's gallant conduct is worthy of the highest praise. Had he missed the quarter-post, they would both have been drowned, as the current was so strong it would have been impossible to have kept afloat, loaded down as they were, long enough to get a boat to them.

I am, sir, very respectfully, your obedient servant,
R. R. WALLACE,
Commander, Commanding.

Rear-Admiral THORNTON A. JENKINS,
Commanding United States Naval Force on Asiatic Station.

NAVY DEPARTMENT, *January 6, 1873.*

SIR: I take great pleasure in furnishing you with a copy of dispatch, dated the 29th of November last, received by the Department from Rear-Admiral Thornton A. Jenkins, commanding the United States naval force on the Asiatic station; also, with a copy of a report which accompanied it, relative to your heroic conduct in saving from drowning the carpenter's mate of that vessel, who fell overboard into the river Pei-Ho, near Tien-Tsin, during exercise at general quarters.

It is very gratifying to the Department to receive and place on its files such evidence of the self-sacrificing spirit and devotion of the officers of the Navy, and any acknowledgment which it could make of it would scarcely be so satisfactory to you as the appreciative and complimentary letter of the commanding officer of the station.

This instance of your coolness and courage gives additional luster to your history as recorded in the official reports of your services in the face of the enemy at the capture of the Corean forts.

Very respectfully,
　　　　　　　　　　　　　　GEO. M. ROBESON,
　　　　　　　　　　　　　　　　Secretary of the Navy.

Lieut. Commander DOUGLAS CASSEL,
　　United States Steamer Ashuelot, Asiatic Station.

———

UNITED STATES STEAMER OMAHA, (2d rate,)
At Sea, lat. 37° 6′ S., long. 52° 2′ W., January 7, 1873.

SIR: I have to report the death of John Owens, rated a carpenter, on board of this vessel.

The death of the above-named John Owens occurred on the 7th day January, 1873, at sea, and in the line of duty.

While at work on the fore-topsail yard the standing part of the runner gave way, letting the yard down by the run, and jerking Owens overboard, after striking the rail of the pivot-gun port with such force as to break it. As he floated by the after part of the ship, Lieut. Seth M. Ackley seized a rope and sprang overboard to his assistance, succeeding in getting hold of him, but unable to retain it or the rope on account of the vessel's headway. The man sinking, Mr. Ackley swam to the life-buoy, and was brought on board by life-boat, uninjured.

I would respectfully call the attention of the Department to Mr. Ackley's gallant attempt to save life.

Very respectfully, your obedient servant,
　　　　　　　　　　　　　　JNO. C. FEBIGER,
　　　　　　　　　　　　　　　　Captain, Commanding.

Hon. GEORGE M. ROBESON,
　　Secretary of the Navy, Washington, D. C.

———

NAVY DEPARTMENT, *May 2, 1873.*

SIR: Your commanding officer, Captain Febiger, has very properly considered it his duty to report to the Department your gallant conduct on the 7th of January last, in endeavoring, at the imminent risk of your life, to rescue one of the crew of the Omaha from drowning.

One who is capable of such an act of chivalry, or rather of philanthropy, backed by intrepidity, does not need the applause of the world. Providence takes care to give a due and sufficient reward. But it is the duty of the Department to assure you, and leave it on record, that your generous disregard of self is known and appreciated.

Very respectfully,
　　　　　　　　　　　　　　GEO. M. ROBESON,
　　　　　　　　　　　　　　　　Secretary of the Navy.

Lieut. SETH M. ACKLEY, U. S. N.,
　　United States Steamer Omaha, South Pacific Station.

WASHINGTON, D. C., *January* 26, 1873.

SIR: I beg leave to call the attention of the Department to the gallantry, good conduct, and good judgment displayed by Lieut. W. H. Brownson upon the occasion of the boat expedition under his charge from the Mohican, as detailed in my report under date of June 19, 1870, and respectfully to suggest that a few words of commendation from the Department to Lieutenant Brownson and the officers and men of the expedition, indicating the appreciation of the Department of the successful performance of a dangerous and difficult service, would be an encouragement and a satisfaction to themselves and an incitement to others in their career in the service.

I have the honor to be, very respectfully, your obedient servant,

W. W. LOW, *Captain.*

Hon. GEO. M. ROBESON,
  Secretary of the Navy, Washington, D. C.

NAVY DEPARTMENT, *March* 3, 1873.

SIR: The Department is always pleased in appropriately acknowledging the meritorious services of the officers and seamen of the Navy, and regrets to find, on recurring recently to the circumstances of the destruction of the piratical cruiser Forward, in Tencapan River, January 17, 1870, that it omitted to express to you, and through you to those who composed the expedition under your command, its appreciation of the good judgment, good conduct, and gallantry displayed on the occasion.

It therefore gives it pleasure, even at this remote day, to supply the omission, and to say that the reports of Commander Low, who commanded the Mohican, and of yourself, indicate that promptness, discretion, and bravery marked the expedition from its inception to its termination.

Having, in the appendix to my annual report of 1870, expressed the satisfaction of the Department with the result of the expedition, and published in full the detailed reports concerning it, it is deemed unnecessary to mention here, by name, those who shared with you its dangers and honors, and those who lost their lives in protecting the flag and commerce of the country. Their fidelity and gallantry are unextinguishably recorded in those reports, which have become a part of the nation's history.

To you and all others concerned in the expedition, the Department expresses its grateful acknowledgments.

Respectfully,

GEO. M. ROBESON,
  Secretary of the Navy.

Lieut. W. H. BROWNSON,
  Naval Academy, Annapolis, Md.

No. 280.] UNITED STATES NAVY-YARD, NEW YORK,
  Commandant's Office, November 8, 1873.

SIR: 1 have the honor to forward herewith, for the favorable consideration of the Department, a letter from Lieutenant Schetky, addressed to Captain Low, and by him referred to me, commending the conduct of John Dempsey, ordinary seaman, belonging to the crew detailed for the Kearsarge.

I respectfully suggest that a medal of honor would be a suitable recognition of Dempsey's gallantry and good conduct.

I am, very respectfully, your obedient servant,

S. C. ROWAN,
Vice-Admiral, Commanding.

Hon. GEO. M. ROBESON,
Secretary of the Navy, Washington, D. C.

UNITED STATES RECEIVING-SHIP VERMONT,
Navy-Yard, Brooklyn, November 6, 1873.

SIR: I have the honor to report the following case of good conduct and bravery on the part of John Dempsey, ordinary seaman:

While on board the United States tug Rocket, waiting transfer to the Pacific mail-steamer Grenada, for transportation to Mare Island, California, having been drafted for the United States steamer Kearsarge, James Hayes, ordinary seaman, accidentally fell overboard, and being unable to swim, was in danger of drowning. John Dempsey, without hesitation, sprang overboard and supported Hayes until a line could be passed him, when both were safely landed on board the tug.

Very respectfully, your obedient servant,

O. A. SCHETKY,
Lieutenant United States Navy.

Capt. W. W. LOW, U. S. N.,
Commanding U. S. Receiving-Ship Vermont, Navy-Yard, Brooklyn.

No. 61.] OFFICE COMMANDER-IN-CHIEF SOUTH PACIFIC STATION,
UNITED STATES FLAG-SHIP PENSACOLA, (2d rate,)
Bay of Coquimbo, Chili, August 22, 1873.

SIR: It is with pleasure I forward the inclosed copy of a report made by Capt. John H. Upshur, detailing the gallant conduct of Patrick Regan, ordinary seaman, in saving a shipmate from drowning, and beg that the Department may be pleased to notice his conduct.

Very respectfully, your obedient servant,

CHARLES STEEDMAN,
Rear-Admiral United States Navy,
Commanding United States Naval Force, South Pacific Station.

Hon. GEORGE M. ROBESON,
Secretary of the Navy, Washington, D. C.

SOUTH PACIFIC STATION,
UNITED STATES FLAG-SHIP PENSACOLA,
Harbor of Coquimbo, Chili, July 30, 1873.

SIR: I am pleased to call your notice to the brave and honorable conduct of Patrick Regan, ordinary seamen of this ship, in saving a shipmate from drowning.

During the prevalence of a "norther" at this port this morning Peter Linguist, ordinary seamen, fell from the lower boom, when attempting to come on board from one of the ship's boats. As he rose from the water the boat struck him on the head and stunned him. He had large top-boots on, and was otherwise heavily clothed, and, becoming insensible, Linguist was drowning.

At that moment Regan observed the accident from the gun-deck, and he at once jumped out of a port, and swam to the rescue, and had the happiness to save the man's life.

Though in humble life, the man Regan has been truly noble, and I am sure you will commend his conduct.

Very respectfully, your obedient servant,

J. H. UPSHUR,
Captain, Commanding.

Rear-Admiral CHARLES STEEDMAN, U. S. N.,
Commanding United States Naval Force, South Pacific Station.

NAVY DEPARTMENT, *Washington, October 6, 1873.*

SIR : Rear-Admiral Steedman, commanding the United States naval force on the South Pacific station, forwarded to the Department, August 22 last, a report made by Capt. J. H. Upshur, commanding the flag-ship Pensacola, of your brave and honorable conduct in saving a shipmate from drowning.

The Department is pleased to hear of your heroic, humane, and successful efforts, which will be mentioned in a general order.

A medal of honor will be given you.

Very respectfully,

WM. REYNOLDS,
Acting Secretary of the Navy.

Mr. PATRICK REGAN,
Ordinary Seaman, United States Steamer Pensacola,
South Pacific Station.

No. 52.] UNITED STATES FLAG-SHIP LANCASTER, (2d rate,)
Rio de Janeiro, Brazil, October 24, 1872.

SIR : I have the honor to inclose herewith a copy of a letter from Captain Caldwell, of this ship, in regard to the gallant conduct of James A. Rodney, ordinary seaman, and John O'Brien, seaman, who jumped overboard to assist a man who fell from aloft and was severely injured. In my opinion, the conduct of the former probably saved the life of the injured man.

I beg leave to suggest to the Department the propriety of noticing, in some public manner, the conduct of the two men named above.

I am, sir, very respectfully, your obedient servant,

WM. ROGERS TAYLOR,
Rear-Admiral, U. S. N., Commanding United States Naval Force,
South Atlantic Station.

Hon. GEO. M. ROBESON,
Secretary of the Navy.

UNITED STATES FLAG-SHIP LANCASTER, (2d rate,)
Rio de Janeiro, Brazil, October 22, 1872.

SIR: I have respectfully to report that while furling sail Charles Beckman, seaman, fell from aloft, struck a gun in his descent, which inflicted a severe wound on his head, and then tumbled overboard. Immediately on his striking the water, James A. Rodney, ordinary seaman, very gallantly jumped overboard and brought the wounded man to the grab-rope, and supported him there until a boat could be sent to his assistance. John O'Brien, seaman, also jumped overboard and rendered timely assistance.

Very respectfully, your obedient servant,

C. H. B. CALDWELL,
Captain.

Rear-Admiral WM. ROGERS TAYLOR, U. S. N.,
Commanding United States Naval Forces, South Atlantic Station.

I hereby certify that the above is a true copy.

JOHN F. BUST,
Clerk South Atlantic Station.

UNITED STATES STEAMER, POWHATAN, (2d rate,)
Norfolk Harbor, Virginia, December 27, 1872

SIR: I have the honor to bring to the notice of the Department the gallant conduct of Joseph B. Noil, seaman, (negro,) one of the crew of this vessel.

The circumstances are as follows: On yesterday morning the boatswain, I. C. Walton, fell overboard from the forecastle, and was saved from drowning by Joseph B. Noil, seaman, who was below on the berth-deck at the time of the accident, and hearing the cry "Man overboard," ran on deck, took the end of a rope, went overboard, under the bow, and caught Mr. Walton, who was then in the water, and held him up until he was hauled into the boat sent to his rescue.

The weather was bitter cold, had been sleeting, and it was blowing a gale from the northwest at the time.

Mr. Walton, when brought on board, was almost insensible, and would have perished but for the noble conduct of Noil, as he was sinking at the time he was rescued.

Very respectfully, your obedient servant,

PEIRCE CROSBY,
Captain, Commanding.

Hon. GEO. M. ROBESON,
Secretary of the Navy, Washington, D. C.

Respectfully forwarded.

C. H. DAVIS,
Rear-Admiral and Commandant.

UNITED STATES STEAMER POWHATAN, (2d rate,)
Key West, May 16, 1873.

SIR: I beg leave to bring to the notice of the Department the heroic conduct of Francis Gallagher, landsman. The facts are as follows: On the 29th of April, while swaying aloft top-gallant yards, the jack-block through which the fore-top-gallant-yard rope was run—carried away, striking Francis Gallagher, landsman, and Thomas Dyer, coxswain, who were at the time standing on the top-mast cross-trees, and injuring them severely. The latter, Dyer, lost his balance, and was in the act of falling, when Gallagher, notwithstanding he was severely hurt, by his great presence of mind, caught Dyer and held him until assistance could be sent.

Had it not been for the instantaneous action of Gallagher, Dyer would have, without doubt, been killed by falling to the deck.

Very respectfully, your obedient servant,

PEIRCE CROSBY,
Captain, Commanding.

Hon. Geo. M. Robeson,
Secretary of the Navy, Washington, D. C.

———

United States Flag-Ship Wabash, (1st rate,)
Ville Franche Harbor, November 13, 1873.

Sir: I have the honor to inform the Department that while this vessel was moored in Barcelona Harbor on the 5th of October, 1873, Patrick Sullivan, quartermaster, rescued from drowning Frank Westphale, ordinary seaman.

The circumstances were as follows: While one of the stern-boats was being hoisted the after-fall unhooked, and the boat fell about 20 feet to the water. There were two men in the boat at the time, one of whom, Westphale, was unable to swim. He made vain efforts to keep on the surface, and could just be seen beneath the surface struggling, but gradually sinking, when Patrick Sullivan went down the stern-ladder, dropped into the water, grasped him and held him until a rope was thrown him. About the same time a boat from Her Britannic Majesty's steamer Pallas, which was lying close to us, reached the spot.

I would also state that Frank Davis, one of the crew of the Pallas, seeing the men struggling in the water, jumped overboard and attempted to reach the spot in time to be of assistance.

I am, sir, respectfully,

S. R. FRANKLIN,
Captain, Commanding.

Hon. Geo. M. Robeson,
Secretary of the Navy, Washington, D. C.

———

REPORT OF ADMIRAL PORTER.

Washington, D. C., October 22, 1873.

Sir: I have the honor to state that since my last report ten ships of war have been inspected before going to sea and found to be properly fitted out, and in nearly every case an improvement over the previous year.

I do not know that anything more is to be desired in the manner of preparing vessels for sea, except that further facilities for saving life should be provided.

43 Ab

I have not yet heard of any ship in commission that had the means, in case of fire or other accident, of providing for the safety of her crew by boats or life-rafts, for it is quite certain that in the hurry of a fire or collision proper rafts could not be improvised.

The last thing at an inspection is to see what facilities a ship has for saving her crew, a much more important problem at present than in former times, when torpedoes were not used in naval warfare, yet, as I said before, in no instance has a United States vessel been found provided with the means of saving those on board, and our boats are, for this purpose, in many instances even inferior to those of ocean passenger steamers.

I have referred to this important subject in several reports to the Department, and again recommend that it receive the attention it merits.

No ship can carry boats enough to save her crew in a heavy sea, but life rafts can be fitted in such a way as not to encumber the vessel or injure her appearance, and with their aid the entire ship's company could be saved.

Some officers object to those life-saving appliances as unsightly, and make any excuse to leave them behind ; and the gutta-percha rafts are stored away in boxes unused, and without ventilation, until they become unserviceable.

I would therefore recommend that every vessel in the Navy should have a monthly exercise, to test the efficiency of the means at hand for transporting the crew, the result of which should be reported to the Department. I venture to say that at every trial some useful experience will be gained, and in case of the destruction of any of our ships by torpedoes, the good effects of such practical experiments would be seen.

The best life-rafts are those of Commodore Ammen, Mason & Rogers, Torrey's Gutta-Percha, and the Hammock Life-Preserver, the latter recommended by Mr. R. B. Forbes, a gentleman who, at his own expense, has undertaken experiments in life-saving apparatus which should properly be conducted by the Government.

These experiments of Mr. Forbes's have shown the way to save life at sea under all circumstances, and if the results are adopted they will prove very satisfactory to those who have to encounter the perils of the ocean.

Nine ships have been inspected on their return from sea, and all were found in creditable condition. This speaks well for the commanders and officers, who have had a pretty hard time in maintaining discipline among the cosmopolitan sailors who man our ships, with rules scarcely stringent enough even for times of peace.

CREWS.

In examining the quarterly returns of inspections, I find the universal excuse for deficiencies " shortness of crew," and although in some cases this excuse is hardly admissible, yet, on the whole, our ships' companies are about 15 per cent. below the complement, which should not be the case with vessels of war.

The calculations for our ships' crews have already been very closely made without, as in former times, allowing any supernumeraries. Consequently the loss of ten working-men will be felt even in the largest of our vessels, and a single man would be missed in a small one. Yet, if a commanding officer should experience defeat owing to the shortness of his crew, I fear he would meet with little sympathy on that account.

In my last report to the Department I nearly exhausted this subject; but as no remedy to the growing evil has yet been applied, I again beg leave to suggest that some legislation be procured from Congress for properly manning the Navy, both as regards numbers and material.

After careful study and many years' experience at sea, I adhere to the opinion heretofore expressed from time to time in my reports to the Department, that an apprentice system, based on the plan I lately submitted to you, should be adopted for the service.

It has hitherto been thought that our merchant-marine would be a school from which we could always recruit seamen, whereas the Navy is now actually the school from which merchants obtain their best men, and the wages in the mercantile marine are so much better than those in the Navy that no inducements held out by the latter are sufficient to keep men in the Government service.

Seamen naturally go where they can get the highest pay. They find the merchant service more remunerative and more desirable than the Navy, which men enter deeply in debt for an outfit which should be furnished them free of cost.

It is possible that, after adopting the apprentice system now existing in the British navy, we might at the end of five years' apprenticeship, still be furnishing men for the merchant service, but in time of war we would get them back again, and would then experience the benefit of having seamen educated in the Navy and attached to their country and flag.

In all probability a large number of apprentices would elect to remain in the naval service and enjoy the benefits arising from continuous employment.

At all events, no harm could result from the adoption of the apprentice system, and we should secure a larger number of native Americans than are at present in service, for frequently on the return of a United States vessel from a cruise, about the only nationality she has is in her officers and the flag flying at her peak.

My last report was very full upon this subject, and gave indisputable facts to corroborate what I now write.

BATTERIES OF VESSELS.

I beg leave to call your attention to a defect in some of the smaller vessels which has on several occasions been noticed by the inspecting-board, and which is obvious to naval officers generally; that is, the batteries are too heavy for the vessels and the guns too large for the breadth of beam. This applies more particularly to the nine-inch guns on board vessels of the Plymouth class, and those of smaller tonnage. The breadth of beam does not allow the working of the nine-inch guns to advantage, and in time of action they would be knocked to pieces against the coamings. Without referring to other disadvantages, I recommend that a suitable eight-inch gun be substituted for the nine-inch.

There is but little difference in the weight and range of the eight-inch shot, and its effects against a wooden vessel would be almost as destructive as the nine-inch. Neither gun would have any effect against an ordinary iron-clad unless accidentally striking some very vulnerable part.

Some of the vessels to which I have alluded could probably carry a couple more of the eight-inch guns in consequence of their lighter weight, owing to a decrease of caliber. The eight-inch gun could also be more rapidly handled with a smaller number of men, and in my opinion at ordinary range, ten eight-inch would be superior to eight nine-inch guns.

It is a disputed point with some officers what constitutes heavy guns, but an eight-inch should certainly be considered in that category, as it is one of the favorite pieces of the service, and only a few years ago but four of them were placed on board our largest frigates.

STEAM CAPSTANS.

In my last report I drew your attention to the want of steam capstans in the navy, and gave reasons for their use. I recommend their adoption in the ships now building, for no ships of war can be thoroughly efficient without them.

I also mentioned the necessity of building more buoyant steam-cutters, of models better adapted to a heavy sea, such as they are often obliged to encounter. The machinery and boilers of our cutters are now all that is required and are capable of driving boats of larger size.

ALLOWANCES OF OFFICERS.

Of late years some improvements have been made in the cabin allowances of our naval vessels, but the increase in the cost of living abroad causes officers to incur expenses far beyond their means, and at the end of a cruise they are often deeply in debt.

The pay of officers may appear liberal to those living in retired places, but when it is remembered that an officer has to provide for his family on shore during his absence from home, and accept and return the hospitalities of foreign officials without any allowance from Government, a different opinion must prevail.

Naval men are proverbially hospitable, and European governments, desiring their officers to be so, afford them the necessary means. The cabins are provided with the requisite furniture, and the tables fitted even to the smallest particulars. Our policy should be equally liberal. Such a system makes an officer very independent, enabling him to leave home, at a moment's notice, to join a ship in any part of the world, without encumbering himself with troublesome effects and going to an expense he can ill afford.

To show the difference between the pay of our own and foreign officers, I will compare the grades of rear-admiral in the navies of the United States and Great Britain.

The pay of an officer in the British navy is given for the support of himself and family, but to prevent the commander of a vessel being put to pecuniary inconvenience, thereby impairing his usefulness, the government allow table-money and other emoluments.

Thus, a rear-admiral or commodore of the first class receives $5,475, with an allowance of $8,210 for table-money, servants, &c., amounting in all to $13,685 per annum, or more than twice the full pay of one of our rear-admirals afloat.

This difference is still greater when it comes to the pay of higher officers. For instance, an admiral of the fleet receives $19,160, and a vice-admiral $15,510, beside other allowances.

In addition to the above, all commanding officers are allowed table-money for entertainments, which enables them to leave a sufficient amount of pay at home to support their families.

From this it will be seen how inadequate would be considered by other governments the pay of our commanding officers.

I doubt if we have an admiral, captain, or commander afloat who is not sorely pinched on account of the various calls upon his hospitality, and duty on shore is so much more agreeable and less oppressive that officers naturally hesitate to seek sea-service.

Some may urge that our officers abroad are not obliged to incur these expenses; but it would not look well for the commander of a United States vessel of war, after partaking the hospitalities of foreign officers, to get up his anchor and steam out of port to avoid reciprocating.

Courtesies between officers tend to cement the bonds of good feeling which nations should experience towards each other, and they should therefore receive the greatest encouragement.

On two occasions within my knowledge, the Department of State has paid out some $10,000 to enable the commanding officer of the European squadron to return civilities and do honor to our country, and these precedents it would be well to follow. It is not just that officers out of a pay only sufficient for the support of themselves and families should be subjected to any expense in returning hospitalities which are absolutely of a national character.

I speak in behalf of the Navy, having no personal interest in the matter, and trust that a liberal view will be taken of the subject and every possible allowance made to prevent our officers abroad from being placed in embarrassing positions and subjected to unnecessary expense.

This subject naturally belongs to Congress, but the Navy Department can in a measure regulate the matter of allowances and add to the comfort of commanding officers abroad as well as those in command of shore stations.

FLAGS.

A petition has been numerously signed by officers of the Navy, including myself, asking that the flags of Admiral, Vice-Admiral, and rear-admiral which were in use during the late war, together with the old broad pendant, be restored to the service to take the place of the flags now worn. The present flags are distasteful to the officers and men, and do not afford the distinction between grades that they were originally intended to effect.

There are traditions connected with the old flags that are dear to the officers and men who served in the war for the Union, and we do not wish to relinquish those familiar objects.

Admiral Farragut was allowed to retain the flag under which he had gained his renown, but at his death it was abolished, and the Navy now asks that it may be resuscitated. The younger officers now coming forward will look up to the old flag with more pride than to the one at present in use, which signifies nothing at all.

It was incorrectly supposed, at the time the change of flags was made, that I was responsible for it, but I never liked the new flag. The alteration was, however, deemed advisable by the chief of Bureau having charge of such matters, on the ground that the new flag would assimilate with the uniform system adopted by foreign nations. This was a fact, but as there was a national sentiment connected with the old flag, I think the substitution unadvisable.

The new flag having been tried for some years, and giving no satisfaction, the officers of the Navy petition strongly for the change, which I trust you will grant.

TORPEDOES.

The torpedo system has occupied my particular attention during the past year, and although much engaged in matters relating to the building of the new torpedo vessel, I have yet found time to investigate the experiments made in other quarters.

I am confirmed in my opinion that the torpedo system, although still in its infancy, is destined to play a most important part in future naval warfare, so that the nation most advanced in torpedo science will possess great advantages over all others.

To us, who seem to experience so much difficulty in maintaining a Navy, it is absolutely necessary that we should devòte more time and attention to the subject of torpedoes than other nations, and make a liberal outlay for this purpose.

I regret to say that there is much less interest displayed in this question, in our Navy, than its importance deserves, for I know of but two vessels that have gone to quarters and fired their torpedoes the same as if in action.

I am convinced that proper attention will not be given to this subject until special instructions are issued from the Department.

Although the theoretical instruction hitherto given at the torpedo station has been of a very interesting kind, I think a larger amount of practical experiments could be substituted for it with advantage. Officers would naturally feel more interest in actual practice than in mere theory. I have conversed with several who have been under instruction at the station, and although they express themselves pleased with the information they have gained, they seem on the whole not sorry to have (as they suppose) "finished with the business."

In my opinion, no one can make a good torpedo officer unless his heart is in the work, and hence I believe it well to make the duty as attractive as circumstances will admit.

At present the torpedo station is a theoretical school without sufficient practice, and the experiments are not altogether suited to impress the students with the importance of the work on which they are engaged. I am pleased to say, however, that some very good and useful practice has lately been had at Newport while fitting the Monongahela, which will do more to impress the officers and crew of that ship with the power of torpedoes than anything else could have done.

A number of officers would like to go to Newport for instruction, but some of the rules of the station seem to them inconsistent with the relations that should exist between seniors and juniors where the latter are superintendents and instructors.

Now, in foreign navies—in that of England, for instance—torpedo instruction is under the immediate supervision of a rear-admiral or other officer of rank, who has the opportunity of selecting the best talent in the service as assistant instructors. Two rear-admirals, ten commodores, and a large number of captains and commanders are now under instruction in the British navy, and seeing the difficulty in the way of our future progress, I recommend that a like course be pursued by us.

Among all the officers who have studied at the torpedo station, I have met with no one who had invented anything or proposed any improvement on what has been done before. I think this is because they are not sufficiently interested. It should be the policy to encourage an officer to use all his faculties to bring the torpedo system to perfection.

In my several visits to the torpedo-station during the present year, and during my sojourn there of two months, it was evident to me that the means of practical instruction were inadequate. There are only two or three small launches attached to the station, which are not at all suited for the work, and there is no course of instruction whatever for defense against torpedoes.

It is evident that to make the torpedo-school what it should be a more liberal expenditure is required, and the cost of one small ship of war annually for this purpose would be money well spent.

There should be added to the present means of instruction four large steel launches, each 50 feet in length and 10 feet beam, with double screws for quick manœuvering, and all other modern appliances; also the different kinds of torpedoes for harbor defense, the various nets and spars for the protection of vessels against torpedoes, and a good monitor from which to send off the Lay torpedo; for I do not believe ships will come close enough to port to be injured by that device, and we must consequently go off shore to attack them.

In addition to the above, there should be sections of ships, or iron buoys made equally as strong, to test the effect of the different torpedoes fired from the water level to 20 feet below. Specimens of all foreign torpedoes should be bought and tested, and preventives applied against their attack.

Such contrivances as prove good we should adopt into the Navy, and teach our officers how to encounter and use them under all circumstances.

I merely make these suggestions without going into details; but the liberal expenditure of money in this matter of torpedoes would no doubt give birth to many devices not thought of at present.

A great deal of importance has been given to the Harvey torpedo, the Fish torpedo, and the Lay torpedo, and the probability of their destroying ships under all circumstances.

No doubt these inventions are formidable to a certain extent; and a commanding officer, ignorant of the manner in which their attack should be met, would be in danger of losing his vessel; but with an understanding of the subject, and a vessel of equal speed, either of the torpedoes mentioned could be eluded and destroyed.

No towing, diving, or swimming torpedo yet invented is a match for a smart ship, properly armed, with her crew at the guns; and it is for this reason that I recommend the construction of so many large launches to teach officers how to maneuver in attacking and repelling the attacks of torpedoes or torpedo vessels.

Officers would soon find out the difficulty of destroying a ship, properly handled, by means of towing torpedoes, unless the latter were hidden, although it might be easy to blow up a vessel not on the alert, or one improperly handled.

A vessel of equal speed need have little fear of an opponent carrying either the Harvey or Fish torpedo; for these inventions can only be successfully used against ships taken by surprise or lying at anchor.

As a protection against such contrivances I would recommend that all our ships be supplied with 24-pound howitzers to fire at them over the stern and quarter when coming up, or down upon their decks when close on board. An intelligent commander would naturally bring either of these torpedoes astern of his vessel, which it is easy to do in daylight, no matter from what direction they may approach. If from ahead, he can turn on his heel. If from abeam, he can change his course eight points, and the Harvey torpedo-vessel, with all her reels and towing-lines, deck crowded with men, &c., would soon be *hors du combat* unless proof against shot, which could hardly be the case, for a torpedo boat must be light, and able to maneuver quickly.

In fights between two or more ships, as the vessels are always enveloped in smoke, these torpedoes will be extremely formidable, and it will require great ingenuity to guard against their attacks; but the practice I recommend of maneuvering in steam-launches will teach officers how to provide for every contingency.

Any ship can be arranged with a heavy net all around, from the bowsprit end to the end of the spanker-boom, which, fastened to her lower yards, (the yards resting on the gunwale,) can be kept triced up and dropped just before the Harvey or Fish torpedo gets within striking distance. The torpedo would explode 20 feet from the ship, doing no harm except to the net, which should be of nine-thread ratlin-stuff, with meshes sufficiently small to prevent the torpedo passing through the interstices.

Here, then, is a most important experiment to be tried.

The net-work is the only certain defense a ship can have against anything that dives, although it is a poor protection against a torpedo at the end of a bar, connected with a properly-constructed torpedo-vessel, with appliances for cutting through obstructions.

Such a torpedo-vessel will be the most dangerous to deal with, for there will be no chance to avoid her unless with superior speed. With iron decks and men all under cover, grape-shot would do little damage, and offering but a small target, solid shot would seldom strike the torpedo-vessel, especially at night or in a fog.

Yet all these matters are problems to be worked out only by actual experiment, and we are solving them too slowly.

In the late experiments conducted on board the United States steamer Monongahela, where a hulk was blown up by a spar-torpedo, the ship running for the quarter of the hulk, two large pieces of timber containing several bolts were thrown back on board the ship, together with some smaller fragments. To avoid casualties at such times every ship in the Navy should carry a rope-splinter netting as a portion of her regular outfit.

I feel that I am touching a delicate matter when I refer to the question as to how far naval jurisdiction extends in the protection of our coasts and harbors with torpedoes.

No matter how well drilled a soldier may be, he is never as much at home in a boat or on shipboard as a seaman, nor can an Army officer as well direct the management of a boat or vessel as an officer of the Navy. Torpedoes planted to defend the harbor should be laid down by men accustomed to boats and skilled in the management of lines and tackles. Along the open coast or on the ocean, torpedo duty must of necessity fall to the lot of the Navy.

During the late war the torpedo duty of the enemy afloat was in the hands of rebel naval officers, who managed it with great success, taking into consideration the small means at their command.

In time of war the duty of the soldier defending a harbor is behind the fortifications, to protect with the fire of his guns torpedoes planted to obstruct the channel, for torpedoes unprotected by guns on shore would be of little use, and guns on shore would not prevent the passage of vessels without torpedoes; but in handling torpedoes in boats, in all weathers, seamen alone can be relied upon.

The question then arises, will not the Navy, in the event of war, be called upon to protect our coasts by torpedoes, and ought there not to be a system adopted and provision made to meet future emergencies?

In some countries there is a torpedo-corps, composed of officers and men taken from the Navy, whose sole duty it is to look after the coast and harbor defenses.

I am strongly in favor of such a corps in our Navy, with a permanent head, the junior officers to serve a length of time equal to that served at sea or on other duty.

The organization of a suitable torpedo corps will necessarily be from the Navy, for the reasons I have stated, and as it will eventually become a very important part of our naval system, we should take advantage of the present opportunity and commence the establishment. It will be rather late when war breaks out to discuss a matter already plain enough to those who have examined the subject, for the enemy would pass the gates while the argument was going on.

In my opinion it is simply the duty of the Army to fire torpedoes from the stations after they have been planted. For this the Army should have the proper appliances, and every means for knowing the arrival of an enemy's vessel over a torpedo-nest.

I have said so much on this subject to show that to the Navy the most important torpedo appropriation, for operating on the water, should be made, and for those torpedoes used on land the appropriation should be given to the Army. Common sense would, indeed, point out that the defense of harbors and coasts, where there are often dangerous bars, reefs, and breakers, with any description of torpedoes in any way connected with a vessel, should be in the hands of the Navy.

A line should be drawn between the duty of the Army and Navy, where one terminates and the other commences, otherwise there will be confusion.

EXERCISES.

I would respectfully call your attention to the fact that the quarterly returns of exercises on shipboard are not as full as the regulations require, or as is desirable for the purpose of maintaining efficient drill. No ship can be a thorough man-of-war unless perfect in all exercises and ready for any emergency. A vessel going into action should be able to strip for the fight in a few moments, for with all her top hamper up and rigging rove she runs the risk of fouling her propeller should a mast be shot away, and crippling her guns by falling spars. Now that battles are fought under steam, there is no longer any necessity for spars aloft in time of action, but constant exercises are necessary to make a ship thoroughly efficient.

Upon one occasion, while in command of the Naval Academy, I saw a sloop-of-war with royal-yard across, rigging rove and sails bent, stripped to her lower rigging, and her rigging all tallied, in seventeen minutes, and this the work of young midshipmen without previous preparation. I have frequently seen the same thing done in half an hour, but I hardly think any of our ships now in commission can do as well.

The reasons assigned by commanding officers for not performing all the exercises do not always seem to me valid, and frequently no explanation at all is given of omissions.

Many complaints are made that the iron-work on board our ships gives way during the exercises, and this is offered as an excuse for not sending up and down top-masts and lower yards, for of course no commanding officer should risk the lives of men on doubtful hooks or bolts.

But there is a simple remedy for this, which is to have every bolt, bar, and hook tested to see what it will bear, and a test-mark put upon it.

When iron breaks it is always the case that it had previously been held together by only about one-fifth of its thickness, the fault of bad forging.

Ships stationed in the tropics have neglected their exercises on the ground of the excessive heat making them oppressive to the crews, but few of the evolutions occupy more than ten minutes, and if the crews are called to quarters daily, cast loose, run in and out the guns and secure, it will do no one any harm.

The sending up and down topgallant yards and masts requires not more than three minutes in the cool of the morning and evening, loosing and furling sails require at the most three minutes, and the sails are quite as well preserved on the yards as in a sail-room, where they are apt to mould and rot. I think these things will strike intelligent officers as they do me.

Upon the whole the exercises as far as they go, considering the shortness of our crews, are fairly performed, but in indorsing the reports of commanding officers, I am obliged to be governed by what is stated therein.

UNIFORM OF SEAMEN.

I notice that the clothing of our seamen does not yet conform to regulations, and that some officers alter it to suit their own taste, which they are not authorized to do.

The present uniform is appropriate, is as inexpensive as it can be made, and clearly indicates the several distinctions among the sailors; yet I have seen the boats' crew of a ship some time in commission wearing three different varieties of uniform, none of them regulation.

The only change I would recommend in the uniform is the abolition of the dungaree collar, now worn on the blue-flannel shirt, and the substitution of blue nankin on the collars of white frocks, in place of dungaree, which changes in washing to all the colors of the rainbow.

STEAM DEPARTMENT.

The seamen-firemen and seamen-coal-heavers substituted in place of the old rates of firemen and coal-heavers, do not like the duty assigned them when steam is raised. The work is unpopular because, as a rule, steam is seldom used, and the extra pay allowed for these occasions will not even compensate for the clothing worn out.

Firemen and coal-heavers being, as one may say, regular denizens of the lower regions in a ship of war, have stow-holes, or boxes, allowed them in which to keep their steaming and coaling clothes, but a seaman has only his bag, which contains his best apparel, and he cannot provide for this extra steam duty.

The result is that most of the seamen-firemen and seamen coal-heavers desert, and I would recommend that the system be changed. The duties are so distinct that it is out of the question to make a good fireman out of a sailor.

SCHOOL-SHIP.

Having visited the Naval Academy practice-ship during the past summer, I beg leave to submit a few remarks in relation to that vessel.

Although a fine ship of her class, I do not think her altogether adapted to the purpose for which she is used. The midshipmen are too much crowded together and thrown too much with the crew, which is not desirable.

When the Tennessee is finished she will make an excellent school-ship, and being provided with the best of engines, will afford the midshipmen and cadet-engineers a fine means of instruction in steam.

If she is kept constantly in commission with a picked crew, the ship will be a good school of discipline, and the importance of having everything on board a ship kept in order will be impressed upon the youthful mind. Besides, the midshipmen would, in such a ship, learn more of the routine of the navy in three months than they would in three cruises in a vessel hastily fitted out and with a green crew on board.

I herewith enclose reports of inspection of receiving-ships and the general condition of vessels of the monitor class. Those of this class that have been reconstructed on the plan I recommended are excellent vessels, much more comfortable and efficient than before, and they will be serviceable for many years to come.

I have the honor to be, very respectfully, your obedient servant,
DAVID D. PORTER,
Admiral.

Hon. GEORGE M. ROBESON,
Secretary of the Navy, Washington, D. C.

Washington, D. C., November 6, 1873.

SIR: As an addition to my report, I beg leave to submit the following in relation to monitors.

Since my last report the Saugus has been completely repaired as recommended, is now an excellent vessel, and is at sea.

The Manhattan has been repaired in a similar manner, and can be got ready for sea in a short time.

The Wyandotte and Nahant are being repaired, and will be finished in six months.

The Canonicus, being repaired in a similar manner, will be ready in three months.

When finished, all the above-named vessels will be much improved, and will last for many years with very few repairs.

The following named vessels of the Nahant class, now at League Island, should be repaired in the same manner as those before mentioned, as they have good hulls and machinery, although rotten in their woodwork: Nantucket, Catskill, Jason, Lehigh, Passaic. These vessels can be repaired in six months by giving the work to separate firms, and would cost $180,000 each.

I beg leave to renew my recommendation with regard to the Puritan. She has a fine hull, and if finished on the new plans will make an admirable monitor and ram.

I also recommend that the Terror, one of the finest vessels in the Navy, be rebuilt with an iron hull, which could be done in seven months.

At Boston navy-yard, the light draught monitors Shawnee and Wassuc should be repaired like the rest, at a cost of $140,000, each.

The Mahopac, at Norfolk, could be ready in a month at a cost of $1,000. She is a fine vessel since the alterations were made in her.

The monitor Amphitrite, at the Naval Academy, was originally one of the most formidable vessels in the Navy, and though deficient in steam power has a good hull and turret. She could, with an outlay of $180,000, be made a most powerful vessel.

The Dictator, at New London, also requires repairs without delay. She is one of the best vessels we have, and would make a powerful ram.

With the monitors thus repaired, we could defend our ports against any ordinary enemy, and the work I have proposed on these vessels would not be too much to undertake at one time.

RECEIVING-SHIPS.

I have examined into the condition of the receiving-ships, and find them kept in as good order by their commanding officers as circumstances will admit. Some of them, however, require a thorough overhauling and repairing to make them comfortable and efficient.

A suitable place should be provided on board for the examination of recruits, and for this reason, if for no other, the sick-bay should be placed on the gun-deck of a frigate, and the upper gun-deck of a ship of the line.

Bath-rooms should also be provided for the ablutions of recruits when they come on board. This is indispensable, as the recruits nearly always present themselves in a condition too filthy for physical examination.

The sick-bays should be enlarged, as none of them will now accommodate more than fifteen patients.

The receiving-ships are properly heated in winter, and in that respect are comfortable.

Respectfully submitted.

DAVID D. PORTER,
Admiral.

Hon. GEORGE M. ROBESON,
Secretary of the Navy.

REPORT

OF

THE SECRETARY OF THE INTERIOR.

DEPARTMENT OF THE INTERIOR,
Washington, D. C., October 31, 1873.

SIR: I have the honor to submit the following report of the operations of this Department during the past year, together with such suggestions as my experience has convinced me will promote the efficiency of the public service:

INDIANS.

The situation in the Indian service may be regarded as favorable and as a vindication of the propriety and practicability of the humane policy which was inaugurated at the beginning of your first presidential term, and which has governed the Department in the transaction of all business matters pertaining to the conduct of Indian affairs. That policy has for its main object and aim the restraint and elevation of the wild tribes of the frontier through firm but kind treatment. That progress has been made in the establishment of that policy, and in an improvement of the condition of Indians reached by it, is shown by the increased interest in educational matters, a growing willingness on the part of the Indians to engage in industrial pursuits, a desire for the division of lands, and an increase of stock and farm products.

THE INDIAN POLICY.

Preliminary to the annual exhibit of the affairs of the Indian service, so far as the control of the Department is concerned, and especially in view of certain occurrences of the past year in that service, and the very general discussion of the character and scope of the Indian policy, I deem it proper to indicate at this time more in detail what that policy was originally intended to accomplish, and the appliances through which it was sought to work.

The so-called peace policy sought, first, to place the Indians upon reservations as rapidly as possible, where they could be provided for in such manner as the dictates of humanity and Christian civilization require. Being thus placed upon reservations, they will be removed from such contiguity to our frontier settlements as otherwise will lead, necessarily, to frequent outrages, wrongs, and disturbances of the public peace.

On these reservations they can be taught, as fast as possible, the arts of agriculture, and such pursuits as are incident to civilization, through the aid of the Christian organizations of the country now engaged in this work, co-operating with the Federal Government. Their intellectual, moral, and religious culture can be prosecuted, and thus it is hoped that humanity and kindness may take the place of barbarity and cruelty.   Second ; whenever it is found that any tribe or band of Indians persistently refuse to go upon a reservation and determine to continue their nomadic habits, accompanied with depredations and outrages upon our frontier settlements, then the policy contemplates the treatment of such tribe or band with all needed severity, to punish them for their outrages according to their merits, thereby teaching them that it is better to follow the advice of the Government, live upon reservations and become civilized, than to continue their native habits and practices.   Third, it is the determination of this policy to see that all supplies of every kind, whether of food or clothing, purchased for distribution to Indians, upon reservations and remaining at peace with the Government, are procured at fair and reasonable prices, so that the Indian meriting such supplies may receive the same without having the funds of the Government squandered in their purchase.   Fourth ; it is the purpose of the Government, as fast as possible, through the instrumentality and by the advice and assistance of the various religious organizations, and by all other means within its power, to procure competent, upright, faithful, moral, and religious agents to care for the Indians that go upon reservations; to distribute the goods and provisions that are purchased for them by the benevolence of the Government ; to aid in their intellectual, moral, and religious culture, and thus to assist in the great work of humanity and benevolence, which the policy aims to accomplish.   Fifth ; it is the further aim of the policy to establish schools, and, through the instrumentality of the Christian organizations, acting in harmony with the Government, as fast as possible, to build churches and organize Sabbath-schools, whereby these savages may be taught a better way of life than they have heretofore pursued, and be made to understand and appreciate the comforts and benefits of a Christian civilization, and thus be prepared ultimately to assume the duties and privileges of citizenship.   These are the aims and purposes of the peace policy, briefly stated, and must commend themselves to every right-minded citizen as in keeping with the duty of a powerful and intelligent nation towards an ignorant and barbarous race providentially thrown upon it for control and support.

It was not, of course, to be expected that so radical a change in the management of widely-scattered bands of roving Indians, whose only restriction hitherto had been their own capricious inclinations, and who roamed at will over vast regions of country, could be effected without resistance on their part and a show of force on the part of the Government.   Such a result was never anticipated, even by the most sanguine friends of the new policy, and the various impediments which have from time to time intercepted and obstructed the operations of the Indian Bureau have not, therefore, discouraged the reasonable hopes of final success which its active friends have always entertained. Satisfactory progress towards the accomplishment of the ends sought to be attained by this policy has already been made, fully justifying the hope that it' will eventually achieve the end in view. ·

IMPEDIMENTS.

As the Department progresses in securing the adoption of this policy, the impediments are developed and modifications in details are suggested as necessary to give it greater efficiency and adaptability to the work in hand. Among these impediments is the practice, which has obtained for many years, of paying annuities to certain tribes, in money, in accordance with treaty stipulations, in lieu of goods and subsistence stores. It seems to be an unvarying result of such payments in money that the Indians are in worse condition in every respect than if they received payment in goods and supplies, and it appears in many cases that those receiving the most money are in the worst condition. Money seems to brutalize instead of civilizing, as they are ignorant of its value and unable to use it with any discretion. The result is, that in a short time after the receipt of the cash annuities they are often found in a state of great destitution. The recommendation of the Commissioner of Indian Affairs that such payments be hereafter made in goods and supplies, even if it be found necessary to modify the treaties to enable the change to be made, meets with my unqualified approval. In this connection I desire to refer particularly to certain moneys due to the Prairie band of Pottawatomies, as well as certain sums which are expected soon to be to the credit of the Kansas Indians, which, under existing treaty stipulations and laws, are required to be paid to said bands of Indians respectively. It is very desirable, in my opinion, that the sums here referred to should be held and regarded by the Government as funds for the civilization of these several bands of Indians; that it would be demoralizing, and therefore improper to pay said sums over to the Indians to be squandered.

I shall, therefore, present to the proper committees of each House of Congress, during the present session, bills providing that the sums of money here referred to be invested in Government bonds and placed to the credit of said Indians respectively, for the purpose of their civilization, to be used by the Commissioner of Indian Affairs for that object, both interest and principal, at such times and in such manner as the President of the United States may direct.

It is likewise detrimental to the substantial improvement of the race that they are compelled to hold their lands in common. Such community of interest operates as a premium upon indolence and unthrift, and places a discouraging burden upon those who are willing to work and who desire to acquire property. As fast as practicable, and whenever a disposition is manifested by an Indian to improve a separate tract of land and secure the comforts of a permanent home, a farm of suitable area should be set apart and secured to him for his exclusive occupancy and improvement, and he should be aided by donations of stock and farming implements, out of the annual appropriations for his tribe.

The first steps toward the permanent settlement of Indians in fixed homes is the establishment and rigid enforcement of regulations to keep them all upon reservations. This can only be done, at present, upon some of the reservations by a display of a sufficient military force near the reservation to punish all violations of such requirements. It is believed that many Indians who are subsisted by the Government persist in making forays upon white settlements and upon neighboring tribes, and then retreat to the refuge of their reservations where they can secure their spoils, and be fed and recuperated for fresh outrages. It will be found to be a measure of mercy to all if such Indians can be punished as they deserve.

INTERFERENCE WITH INDIANS ON RESERVATIONS.

Serious complaints are made to the Department relative to the presence, upon Indian reservations, of white men, who go there solely for the purpose of hunting buffalo, which are thus destroyed in large numbers. While I would not seriously regret the total disappearance of the buffalo from our western prairies, in its effect on the Indians, regarding it rather as a means of hastening their sense of dependence upon the products of the soil and their own labors, yet these encroachments by the whites upon the reservations set apart for the exclusive occupancy of the Indian is one prolific source of trouble in the management of the reservation Indians, and measures should be adopted to prevent such trespasses in the future, or very serious collisions may be the result. The Government has a two-fold object in confining Indians to reservations: to prevent their encroachments upon white settlers, and to isolate them as far as possible from association with white people. This cannot be accomplished if whites are allowed to trespass at will upon reservations. These remarks apply with greatest force to the so-called Indian Territory south of Kansas.

ENLISTMENT OF INDIANS.

The policy of enlisting friendly Indians as scouts and auxiliaries in punishing hostile tribes has obtained for some years in the Army, and Indians so serving have rendered valuable service, and received honorable mention in the reports of military officers, and have even been recommended as worthy of receiving certificates of merit for acts of special gallantry. It has been objected to such enlistments that they tend to intensify and perpetuate traditional inter-tribal feuds, and should, therefore, be avoided. Take for example the Rees and other tribes at the Fort Berthold agency, in the Territory of Dakota, in their relations to the neighboring bands of Sioux.   The valuable services of the former have been recognized by Generals Stanley and Crittenden, but these tribes have suffered in consequence by the depredations of the Sioux. I recommend a careful consideration of this subject as one of the utmost importance, but am not prepared to give it my approval, in view of the fact that its propriety is questioned by many of the most judicious friends of the Indian cause, whose opinions are entitled to great weight. If such enlistments are to be made, however, we should do all that is necessary to strengthen the tribes from which recruits are enlisted by liberal supplies and improved arms, thus enabling them not only to defend themselves more effectually, but to render more efficient service to the Government.   The complaint is now made by some of the friendly tribes thus circumstanced, that the bounty of the Government is dispensed in direct proportion to the hostility of a tribe, and that those which have been friendly from their own voluntary choice are left for the most part to their own resources.

The Sioux Nation is almost completely surrounded by tribes that are really friendly to the Government, and at the same time bitterly hostile to the Sioux. If these friendly tribes could be liberally supplied with improved fire-arms and ammunition, the present supremacy of the Sioux might in a few years be destroyed with but little aid from the Army, and quiet would prevail over the vast extent of country now roamed by that powerful nation.

HUNTING PRIVILEGES OF THE SIOUX.

Attention is invited to the eleventh article of the treaty of 1868 with the Sioux Nation, granting them certain hunting privileges within the State of Nebraska, and without the bounds of their reservation.   On account of the violation of the other provisions of that treaty by the Sioux, and the scarcity of game in the country referred to, the Government will, I think, be justified in abrogating that article, and I respectfully suggest such action.

REDUCTION AND CHANGE OF RESERVATIONS.

Satisfactory progress has been made within the year in the reduction of the area of existing reservations, in the exchange of reservations lying within the range of advancing settlements and railroad construction for other locations equally desirable for all purposes of Indian occupancy, as well as in bringing tribes upon reservations for the first time, and in the removal of other tribes to the Indian Territory.   All this is the legitimate result of the working of the existing policy, and the efforts of the Department in that direction have been unremitting. Several important negotiations have been concluded during the year looking to the change in the location of tribes and the reduction in the area of reservations.

It will be found by an examination of these negotiations that by the treaty with the Crows their reservation has been reduced by 4,000,000

44 Ab

of acres. Their present treaty appropriation, amounting to $130,000 per annum, expires with the present year, and by the terms of the negotiations under which they release the 4,000,000 acres of land above referred to, the Government will be required to pay them $50,000 per annum, a reduction of $80,000 per annum. In the negotiations with the Utes they relinquish between 4,000,000 and 5,000,000 acres of land, at an annual compensation of $25,000. Their present treaty appropriation, amounting to $20,000 per annum, expires with the present year. The net gains under the two negotiations in the annual expenditure of supporting these tribes amounts to $75,000, as compared with the expenditures of former years. The terms of these negotiations provide for the payment of the respective amounts named in such articles as the President may direct, which is in conformity with a suggestion made in a previous portion of this report, that further payments of annuities in money, to Indians, should cease. These negotiations will be submitted to Congress for action. The result, if ratified by Congress, will be to release a large area of valuable agricultural and mineral land, thereby enabling our white settlements to advance and occupy a desirable portion of the public domain. In this work the Department is greatly indebted to Hon. Felix R. Brunot, president of the Board of Indian Commissioners.

INCREASING DIFFICULTIES OF THE SERVICE.

While there have been no extensive Indian depredations during the year there may have been an apparent increase in the number of petty raids and depredations. These have, without doubt, been magnified and attributed to a supposed failure of the policy, or its want of adaptation to the management of all the tribes. If there really be an increase of these occurrences it is clearly attributable to other causes, and is not unexpected. Our relative position towards the Indians is materially changed within the last few years.

The progress of population, through the instrumentality of railroads and other facilities for travel, has brought the Indians and our frontier population into close proximity over an immense area of country hitherto uninhabited by civilized man, and entirely occupied by the Indian and the buffalo. Where difficulties arise between Indians and whites in our frontier settlements we can no longer, as heretofore, mitigate or avoid the trouble by removing the Indians into a country remote from civilization. We are now compelled to solve the question of preserving order and security between the Indians and whites through a vast region of country, not less than four thousand miles in length by twenty-five hundred in width, extending from the extreme northern and northwestern limits of Washington Territory to the Gulf of Mexico, and from the line which separates the United States from the British possessions in the North to the line which separates the United States from the territory of Mexico in the extreme southwest. Everywhere and in all places throughout this extensive region we are in constant danger of conflicts between our savage wards and our white citizens. The statement here made, if properly considered, will suggest to the reflecting mind how greatly increased are the difficulties of preserving peace, and securing everywhere the lives and property of our progressive and enterprising western settlers. We must look for and prepare to prevent, as far as possible, a clashing of interests where habits are so diverse.

Our civilization is ever aggressive, while the savage nature is tenacious of traditional customs and rights. The natural distrust of the Indians, embittered by generations of real or fancied imposition and wrong, coupled with the greatly increased facilities and temptations for hostile raids and petty outrages is probably more than Indian nature can withstand, and it will be difficult to avoid for a time an increase of such occurrences. This condition of things calls loudly for more efficient efforts to separate the Indians from the whites by placing them on suitable reservations as fast as circumstances will permit to avoid such collisions in the future.

THE MODOC WAR.

The most serious difficulty which the Indian Office and the Department have encountered during the year with any Indian tribe is that known as the Modoc war. As soon as I had reason to anticipate serious hostilities from the Modocs every possible effort was made by the Department and the Indian Bureau, co-operating with the War Department, to adjust the difficulty without bloodshed. So desirable was it to accomplish this end that it was deemed advisable to exhaust all possible measures calculated to secure peace. Unfortunately, however, so much excitement and so strong a desire for revenge were found to exist as to prevent the accomplishment of this object. It would be useless to attempt to trace here the causes which defeated these efforts and ended in the sad catastrophe with which the country is familiar. The final treachery of the Modoc chiefs, which culminated in the assassination of Maj. Gen. E. R. S. Canby, of the Army, and Rev. Edward Thomas, D. D., of California, one of the commissioners treating with him for a peaceful adjustment of the difficulties, and in the serious and dangerous wounding of A. B. Meacham, of Oregon, another member of the commission, rendered it necessary to inflict upon this tribe not only severe but exemplary punishment. This was accomplished, first, by the Army in totally subduing the Modocs and capturing most of the tribe, in the trial and conviction by court-martial, and finally in the execution of the most notorious and wicked leaders of the tribe. This being accomplished you deemed it advisable, if possible, to make this the occasion of furnishing to other Indian tribes an example calculated to deter them in future from the commencement of hostilities. To do this most effectually it was deemed best to remove the entire remnant of the tribe to this side of the Rocky Mountains, to break up its tribal relations and divide the members thereof among certain friendly Indians in the Southern superintendency. This work is now in process of accomplishment, the entire body having been removed to the location indicated. It is now the intention of the Government to separate the members of this tribe and place them with different bands of Indians, taking care in doing this not to separate families, and to keep together, as far as possible, women and children whose husbands and male relatives were destroyed in the conflict.

The Indian is greatly attached to his tribal organization, and it is believed that this example of extinguishing their so-called national existence and merging their members into other tribes, while in reality a humane punishment, will be esteemed by them as the severest penalty that could have been inflicted, and tend by its example to deter hostile Indians in future from serious and flagrant insurrections.

The experience which the Modoc difficulty has furnished the Indian Office will, it is believed, enable that office to take measures calculated to prevent the recurrence of like difficulties under similar circumstances.

THE INDIAN TERRITORY.

The condition of the so-called Indian Territory is practically unchanged during the year, although progress has been made in the permanent location of additional tribes therein. The lawless condition of the Territory, the growing insecurity of life and property, and the manifest indisposition of the tribes there resident to accept voluntarily any improved form of government whereby existing difficulties might be avoided, would seem to call for some legislation to effect an improvement in the status of the Territory. It is to be regretted that the Ocmulgee constitution, with the amendments heretofore suggested by you, was not adopted by the council of tribes to whom it was submitted, as I am well convinced that such action on their part would have been attended by the most beneficial results. Recent information induces the belief that the opposition heretofore offered to those amendments by the Indians will be withdrawn at the next meeting of their council, and that the constitution will be adopted as amended. If it shall not be adopted, and Congress shall not deem it advisable to erect a territorial government within the Indian Territory, I trust that the necessary legislation may be obtained to at least provide for the organization of a court or courts therein, under the jurisdiction, so far as the appointment of the judicial officers is concerned, of the Federal Government. The necessity which now compels the resort to a court in an adjoining State involves a burden of expense to litigants as well as to our Government which operates as almost a bar to justice, and produces a condition of anarchy throughout the Territory under which life and property are in jeopardy to an extent almost equal to that in territory occupied by tribes making no pretense of civilization.

MISSION INDIANS OF CALIFORNIA.

Attention is invited to the condition of the so-called Mission Indians of Southern California, as set forth in the interesting report of the special agent sent to investigate their condition, and which accompanies the report of the Commissioner of Indian Affairs. Their past history and present condition, the treatment they have received from their white neighbors and from the Government, offer the strongest reasons for legislation in their behalf that they may be enabled to secure to themselves homes and the protection of the law.

CO-OPERATION OF THE WAR DEPARTMENT, ARMY, INDIAN COMMIS. SIONERS, ETC.

I take pleasure in being able to say that this Department has had during the past year the cordial and earnest co-operation of the Secretary of War and the officers of the Army in carrying out its policy of dealing with the various Indian tribes. This, with the valuable aid and assistance which has been rendered by the Board of Indian Commissioners, and especially its President, Hon. Felix R. Brunot, and the various religious organizations by whom the Indian agents of the Government are selected, has materially aided the Department in its difficult and complicated labors. A continuance of this work, sustained by the other branches of the public service just referred to, will, I have no doubt, in a few years, result in greatly improving the moral and physical condition of the Indians, and in giving security to our frontier settlements from Indian depredations, as well as in laying a permanent foundation for the progress of our various Indian tribes in the pursuits of peace and civilization.

LANDS.

During the fiscal year ending June 30, 1873, public lands were disposed of as follows:

	Acres.
Cash sales	1,626,266.03
Located with military warrants	214,940.00
Taken for homesteads	3,793,612.52
Located with agricultural-college scrip	653,446.41
Certified to railroads	6,083,536.57
Certified to wagon-roads	76,576.82
Approved to States as swamp	238,543.65
Certified for agricultural colleges	10,223.29
Certified for common schools	76,909.17
Certified for universities	51,228.09
Certified for seminaries	320.00
Approved to States for internal improvements	190,775.76
Indian scrip locations	14,222.96
Total	13,030,606.87

This quantity exceeds that disposed of during the previous year by 1,165,631.23 acres.

The cash receipts were $3,408,515.50, a sum greater by $190,415.50 than that received the previous year.

The surveys amounted to 30,488,132.83 acres, an increase on the quantity surveyed the previous year of 1,037,193.28 acres. The total area of the land States and Territories is 1,834,998,400 acres, of which 616,554,895 acres have been surveyed.

The Commissioner states that the arrearages of work in his office have been diminished, and that its business is now, in most of its branches, in an advanced condition. This business is, however, steadily increasing *pari passu* with the tide of immigration to the frontier; and to keep it in a satisfactory state will require a thorough re-organization of the clerical force. I would respectfully and earnestly invite the attention of Congress to the Commissioner's suggestions on this head, as well as to those concerning the expediency of repealing the pre-emption laws and requiring settlers on the public lands to obtain title thereto under the homestead laws only.

The report of the Commissioner contains much valuable information; the principal rulings of the office and of the Department during the last fiscal year; circulars to carry into effect recent legislation relating to the public domain; all showing this important branch of the public service to be wisely managed by its energetic and capable head.

MENNONITES OF SOUTHERN RUSSIA.

I desire to invite the attention of Congress to a request from a colony of Mennonites, now and for several generations residing in Southern Russia, near the shores of the Black Sea and the Sea of Azov; for a modification of the existing land laws in certain particulars, to enable them to settle upon our public domain in a compact colony.

By a decree of the Russian government this people, numbering between forty thousand and fifty thousand persons, have been deprived of certain immunities which they have enjoyed ever since their first settlement in Russia, and the granting of which had originally induced them to leave their former homes in Prussia and settle in their present place of abode.

It is their desire to come to the United States and to occupy a portion of our public lands in a compact body, with no strangers to their religious faith within the exterior bounds of their possessions. Such exclusive occupancy they deem essential to enable them to carry out their peculiar system of farming, which to some extent involves a community of interest in and occupancy of the lands; and they also wish to avoid, as far as possible, the presence of any disturbing elements in their immediate neighborhood.

The deprivation of the immunities heretofore enjoyed by them does not take effect until the expiration of ten years from June, 1871, the date of the imperial decree. Within that time it is their desire to dispose of their property in Russia, and remove to a country where they may enjoy civil and religious liberty; and they have selected the United States as a place where they can most fully realize such freedom.

In order, however, to enable them to obtain possession of lands in a compact body, some concessions must necessarily be made from the present requirements of the land laws. I would respectfully suggest that the Secretary of the Interior be authorized to withdraw from sale or entry such lands as they may desire to occupy, for a term of years long enough to enable them to emigrate to this country and settle thereon, and to dispose of such lands to those persons among the emigrants who shall make the proper entry or purchase thereof in accordance with existing laws. Should they desire to settle within railroad limits, the authority should enable the withdrawal, in like manner, of the alternate sections belonging to the Government. It is possible that the entire body of emigrants may not desire to locate in one colony, but would prefer the selection of two or more colonies or locations. It would be well, therefore, to confer such discretion on the Secretary of the Interior as would enable him to meet their views in that regard. The entire area they will probably require will be about 500,000 acres.

POSSESSORY RIGHTS OF BRITISH SUBJECTS IN THE TERRITORY CONFIRMED TO THE UNITED STATES BY THE DECISION OF THE EMPEROR OF GERMANY.

The Secretary of State has called my attention to a communication from Sir Edward Thornton, the British minister, who, under instructions from his government, has asked the consideration of the case of those persons, subjects of Great Britain, who had settled upon the islands between the continent and Vancouver's Island, which were confirmed to the United States by the decision of the Emperor of Germany. And the Secretary of State, after calling the attention of the Department to this subject, has inquired whether he may be justified in saying to the British minister that this Department will be prepared to recommend to Congress any legislation on this subject at the approaching session, and also to ask, in case any legislation will be recommended, that, if there be no objections, he may be informed of the provisions which Congress will be asked to enact into a law.

The third article of the treaty of June 15, 1846, above referred to, is in the following words:

In the future appropriation of the territory south of the forty-ninth parallel of north latitude, as provided in the first article of this treaty, the possessory rights of the Hudson's Bay Company, and of all British subjects who may be already in the occupation of land or other property lawfully acquired within the said territory, shall be respected.

The construction placed upon this article of the treaty by those most familiar with its history is that the possessory rights of the Hudson's Bay Company, and all British subjects who were in the occupation of land or other property within said territory at the date of the treaty, are the only possessory rights to be respected. I have concluded to follow this construction.

I have therefore advised the Secretary of State that this Department will be prepared to recommend to Congress the passage of a law providing in substance as follows:

First. For the appointment of a commission to make, and report to the Secretary of the Interior, a list of the British subjects within said territory at the date of the treaty of June 15, 1846, with a description of the lands actually occupied by each at that time.

Second. That such parties shall have one year from the date of 'the filing of such report with the Secretary of the Interior in which to enter and pay for the lands so occupied by them, at the ordinary minimum price per acre where the lands are outside of railroad limits, and at double minimum price where the lands are within railroad limits. The entry to be according to legal subdivisions so as to include the improvements of occupants, and where two or more parties shall have improvements on the same smallest legal subdivision, that they may be entitled to make joint entry.

Third. That in case entry and payment are not made within one year from the time when the report of the commission is filed in the office of the Secretary of the Interior, all possessory rights under the treaty shall be considered forfeited, and the lands shall thereafter be deemed and treated as part of the public domain, to be disposed of as other public lands.

I have therefore respectfully to recommend the adoption by Congress of some measure which will embody the principles contained in my communication to the Secretary of State herein referred to.

Should Congress be of opinion that the construction of the third article of the treaty of 1846 which I have adopted is incorrect, and that it should be so interpreted as to embrace the possessory rights of all persons who were occupants of land or other property, lawfully acquired, at the date of the award of the Emperor of Germany, before referred to, it will be in their power to enlarge the scope of the measure which I here recommend so as to include this class of persons.

If grave doubts are found to exist in regard to the interpretation of this article, and if, in view of such doubts, it shall appear to Congress that some equitable provision should be made for such persons as may have acquired possessory rights within the territory after the date of the treaty of 1846, it will be in the power of Congress to make such provision for these equitable rights as in its wisdom may be deemed advisable.

Should such doubts arise, it may be proper, if any legislation is had for the protection of the equitable rights of persons coming into the territory after the date of the treaty, that it be limited so as to prevent any occupant of this class acquiring more than one quarter-section of land.

THE GROWTH OF TIMBER ON THE PUBLIC DOMAIN.

On the 3d of March last an act was approved entitled "An act to encourage the growth of timber on western prairies," the first section of which provides, "That any person who shall plant, protect, and keep in a healthy, growing condition, for ten years, forty acres of timber, the trees thereon not being more than twelve feet apart each way, on any quarter-section of any of the public lands of the United States, shall be entitled to a patent for the whole of the said quarter-section, at the expiration of said ten years, on making proof of such fact by not less than two credible witnesses: *Provided*, That only one quarter in any section shall be thus granted."

The Commissioner of the General Land-Office, in preparing rules and regulations under the sixth section of the above act, in order to carry its provisions into effect, refused to permit more than one entry of a quarter-section to be made by any one person.

It is claimed, on the other hand, that this act permits any person to make entry of as many quarter-sections as he sees fit.

While it may not be perfectly clear that the ruling of the Commissioner is according to the true legal interpretation of the act, it seems to me that it is in accord with the general purpose of Congress in disposing gratuitously of the public domain, and that to allow a contrary interpretation would be to encourage the incumbrance of the public domain, by entries of this character to a large amount, by persons whose circumstances enable them to make the necessary expenditures, whereby the public lands would be withdrawn from the free and easy settlement now secured to persons of moderate means; and that, in this manner, considerable inconvenience and injustice to pre-emptors and homestead-settlers would necessarily ensue.

I have deemed it best, therefore, to sustain the construction put upon the act by the Commissioner of the General Land-Office, and, in this manner, to invite the attention of Congress to the subject, so that, if deemed necessary, they may declare distinctly the right of any one individual to make as many locations as he sees fit under the aforesaid act.

PATENTS.

During the year ending September 30, 1873, there were filed in the Patent Office 20,354 applications for patents, including re-issues and designs; 283 applications for the extension of patents; and 519 applications for the registering of trade-marks. Twelve thousand nine hundred and seventeen patents, including re-issues and designs, were issued, 235 extended, and 965 allowed but not issued by reason of non-payment of the final fee; 3,274 caveats were filed, and 475 trade-marks registered. The fees during the same period from all sources amounted to $701,626.72, and the total expenditure to $699,449.69, making the receipts $2,177.03 in excess of the expenditure. The appropriation asked for the fiscal year ending June 30, 1875, is $693,500.

The excess of receipts over expenditures for said year is not, nominally, so great as during previous years.   This is explained by the following statement of the Commissioner:

The publication of the Official Gazette of the office requires an annual expenditure of $40,000, but a small portion of which is at present returned to the office by subscription.   It has been deemed advisable to publish an edition of 10,000 copies, although less than half of that number are now distributed.   Subscriptions, however, are being constantly received, and the back numbers are invariably called for.   The Commissioner expresses his conviction that the entire edition will be exhausted within a few years.   During said year the cost of printing the current drawings for the office has been paid from the appropriations made for the Patent Office.   Previously that expense had been defrayed from appropriations made for the Government Printing Office.   This expense, amounting to $40,000 annually, has thus been added to the regular expenditures of the office; but it is, in effect, only a transfer from appropriations made for the Government Printing Office to those for the Patent Office.   The sum of $60,000 has been expended in the reproduction of old drawings, but this amount appears to be no part of the current expenses of the office.   The Commissioner states that in a few years all of the old drawings will be reproduced in such quantities as will supply the future demand for them.   He considers the amount thus expended well invested, not only financially, but with reference to the intelligent advancement of the manufacturing interests of the country. The drawings are being sold for more than their actual cost, and it is believed that a greater amount will eventually be received from their sale than has been expended for their reproduction.

The items above referred to amount to $140,000, which sum has been added, during the year ending September 30, 1873, to the regular current expenses of the office in previous years, and has absorbed almost the entire amount of the excess of receipts over expenditures which would otherwise have existed.   ·

The Commissioner again earnestly invites attention to the great want of additional room for the proper transaction of official business, stating that it is utterly impossible to properly classify the work of the office, in order to insure its being economically and properly done, in the present crowded state of the files, records, and exhibits.

PENSIONS.

There are now borne upon the pension-rolls the names of 445 widows of soldiers in the revolutionary war, a decrease of 26 since the last annual report.   The names of 1,105 widows and children of soldiers who served in the wars subsequent to the Revolution and prior to the late rebellion, excepting the war of 1812, are borne on the rolls, being 52 less than the preceding year.

During the year ending June 30, 1873, there were examined and allowed 6,422 original applications of soldiers for invalid pension, at an aggregate annual rate of $413,344.50; 20,946 applications of soldiers for increased pension, at an annual aggregate rate of $920,930.25; and 251 applications of invalid pensioners for restoration to the rolls, at an aggregate yearly rate of $12,868.92. The number of claims for increased invalid pensions of soldiers is greatly in excess of previous years, owing to the liberal provisions of the act of June 8, 1872; 15,505 claims, or more than three-fourths of the number above named, having been admitted under said act. During the same period 3,949 original pensions to widows, orphans, and dependent relatives of soldiers were allowed, at an annual aggregate rate of $520,802.07; 545 applications of the same class for increase of pension were admitted, at a total yearly rate of $20,108.87; and 73 applicants of that class were restored to the rolls, at an aggregate annual rate of $8,034. The whole number of Army claims for pensions, original, increase, and restoration, and exclusive of those of the war of 1812, which were allowed during the said year, was 32,186, and the annual amount of pension thus granted was $1,896,088.61. At the close of the last fiscal year there were borne on the rolls the names of 99,804 invalid military pensioners, whose yearly pensions amounted to $9,627,240.09; and of 112,088 widows, orphans, and dependent relatives of soldiers, whose annual pensions amounted to $13,962,764.39; making the aggregate number of Army pensioners 211,892, at a total annual rate of $23,590,004,48. The whole amount paid during said year to invalid military pensioners was $10,564,825,51, and to widows, orphans, and dependent relatives, $15,388,644.75; a grand total of $25,953,470.26, which includes the expenses of disbursement.

During the same year there were admitted 129 new applications for invalid Navy pensions, at a total yearly rate of $15,421; 239 applications of the same class for increase of pension, at an annual aggregate rate of $11,086; 1 application of that class for restoration to the rolls, at an annual rate of $48; 124 original applications of widows, orphans, and dependent relatives of those who died in the Navy, at an aggregate yearly rate of $20,184; 31 applications of the same class for increase of pension, at a total annual rate of $1,500; and 6 applicants of that class were restored to the rolls, at an aggregate annual rate of $1,200. The total number of Navy claims, original, increase, and restoration, admitted during said year, was 530, the annual pension thereby granted amounting to $49,439. At the close of said year there were borne on the rolls of Navy pensioners the names of 1,430 invalids, whose yearly pensions amounted to $150,537.75; and of 1,770 widows, orphans, and dependent relatives, at a total yearly rate of $280,550, making the whole number of such pensioners 3,200, at an aggregate annual rate of $431,087.75. The total amount paid during the last fiscal year to Navy invalid pensioners was $160,971.98, and to widows, orphans, and dependent relatives, $302,936.71, a total amount of $463,908.69.

Prior to June 30, 1873, 39,331 claims of survivors and of widows of soldiers in the war of 1812 had been received, of which number 2,780 were filed during the last fiscal year. There were pending on the 30th day of June, 1872, 11,580 claims of this character, which, added to the number received during the succeeding year, makes a total of 14,360 claims which were before the office for adjudication during said year. Of these there were allowed during the year 3,186 claims of survivors, at a total yearly rate of $305,856; 2,242 claims of widows, at an aggregate yearly rate of $215,232; 16 claims of survivors and 6 of widows for restoration, at a total annual rate of 2,112; making the total number of claims of this character allowed during said year, 5,450, and the annual amount of pensions thus granted, $523,200. During the same period there were rejected 3,933 claims of survivors and 2,082 of widows a total of 6,015 claims. On the 1st instant there were pending 2,895 claims of this description, more than half of which are believed to be without merit, and will probably be rejected. The total amount paid during the year to survivors of the war of 1812 was $2,078,606.98, and to widows, $689,303.69, a total amount of $2,767,910.67, including the expenses of disbursement.

The number of original pensions of all classes granted during the past fiscal year was 16,405. During the same period there were dropped from the rolls, from various causes, 10,223 names, leaving a net addition to the pension-rolls during said year of 6,182 names. The whole number of pensioners of the Government on the 30th day of June, 1873, was 238,411, whose annual pensions amount to $26,259,284.23. The amount paid during said year for pensions of all classes, including the expenses of disbursement, was $29,185,289.62, being $984,050.38 less than the amount paid during the preceding year.

Three hundred and forty bounty-land warrants were issued during the year for 52,160 acres, being 15,880 less than the number of acres issued for the preceding year. During the same period 1,398 persons availed themselves of the benefits of the act of June 30, 1870, providing for artificial limbs and apparatus for resection, or commutation therefor, of whom 1,332 preferred the latter.

On the 30th day of June, 1873, there were on file, unadjusted, 32,054 claims for invalid pension, 29,615 claims of widows, orphans, and dependent relatives, and 3,004 claims of soldiers and of widows of soldiers in the war of 1812, making a total of 64,673 unadjusted claims, a decrease of 17,845 since the last annual report.

The Commissioner, in his report, refers to certain defects in the system which has obtained with respect to the establishment of claims for pension, and expresses the opinion that, until such defects are remedied by new legislation, there is no adequate security to the Government against dishonest claimants. The work of investigating frauds, committed by dishonest claimants and attorneys, has continued during the year, with its customary good results. The direct saving to the Government effected by these investigations is many times greater than the sum expended in making them, and sound policy dictates that they should be continued. While the efforts made by those charged with the duty of detecting frauds already committed are generally successful, it is apparent that they are powerless, under the present system of establishing pension-claims, to prevent their commission.

The act of March 3, 1873, provided for the appointment of a " duly qualified surgeon as medical referee," and of such other " duly qualified surgeons (not exceeding four)" as assistants to such referee. This legislation supplied a want which had long existed in the administration of the office. Inasmuch as in a large proportion of claims for invalid pension the question of title thereto is purely of a medical character, it had been found necessary in past years to organize a medical division in the office, but no direct provision therefor was made by law until the passage of said act. That division is now organized upon a legal basis, and is in the charge of a chief whose official position is established by law. An accomplished surgeon, who had previously been in charge of the medical division, was appointed medical referee, and his four assistants were selected from among those of the clerical force of the office who, upon a competitive examination, conducted with reference to the special qualifications required, were found to be the most competent for such positions. The certificates of the examining surgeons of pensions constitute a very important feature of claims of invalids, inasmuch as they prescribe in a great measure the rates of pension allowed. In order to guard against an improper expenditure of the public money, on the one hand, and to insure justice to claimants on the other, it is essential that such certificates should be the result of the best medical judgment attainable, and that they should be analyzed and corrected by the office, so as to secure proper and uniform rating of pensions. The roster of examining surgeons is constantly undergoing changes with a view to greater efficiency, and its members have been thoroughly instructed in respect to their duties. An evidence of the efficiency with which the medical division has labored in this direction is shown by the fact that only about five per cent. of the certificates of examination are at present returned for correction to the surgeons making them, whereas two years ago about forty per cent. thereof was returned for that purpose. The improvement in the character of such certificates, and the careful and intelligent supervision of them by the medical division, has resulted in a more uniform and equitable adjudication of claims for invalid pension than has ever been attained hitherto in the practice of the office.

The Commissioner suggests that the law in relation to pensions of Indians be amended in certain particulars, so as to enable the office to do justice to a class of persons whose equitable claims upon the bounty of the Government have been long delayed.

Owing to recent modifications of the pension laws, which compelled the re-adjustment of an unusual number of claims, the work of the office has been largely increased, and the biennial examination of pensioners, made in September last, also entailed upon its clerical force much additional labor. Some delay has thus been caused in the ordinary routine business of the office, but it is confidently believed that the force now employed will soon be equal to the demands made upon it. The biennial examinations above referred to were so recently made, that, at the date of the Commissioner's report, sufficient returns therefrom had not been received upon which to base an opinion as to the probable result with respect to the annual pension appropriation.

The Commissioner represents the necessity for a re-organization of the office by creating heads of divisions, whose duties shall be defined by law, and whose compensation shall be commensurate with the responsibility imposed upon them.

The amount that will probably be required for the pension service during the next fiscal year is $30,480,000. The same amount was asked for and appropriated for the current fiscal year. There would have been a considerable decrease in the amount now asked for had it not been for the new legislation contained in the act of March 3, 1873. Under that act widows of officers are entitled to additional pension on account of minor children by such officers, and a single minor child of a deceased soldier is also entitled to additional pension. In both of these cases, hitherto unprovided for, arrears of the additional pension are due since July 25, 1866. A considerable sum will also be required to satisfy claims on account of permanent specific disabilities for the increased rates provided for in said act.

EDUCATION.

During the past year this office has steadily pursued the course of work laid down for it by law. The library of the Bureau has received important accessions, especially of foreign educational reports and literature. About 7,000 volumes and 36,000 pamphlets, published by the Bureau, have been distributed during the past year.

In accordance with the expressed wishes of the Department of State and of the General Director of the Vienna Exposition, the Bureau of Education, during the winter of 1872–'73, took measures to procure and forward to the exposition specimens of school-books, charts, school furniture, educational reports, catalogues of libraries, and other appropriate matter. These were duly exhibited in Group XXVI of the exposition, with additional material collected by similar efforts; and the collection thus gathered in Vienna has, during the past summer, been an object of profound interest to the great assembly of educators, scientists, and intelligent observers who visited that city. As a recognition, in the words of the awards, of its "distinguished services in the cause of education, and for important contributions to the exposition," a grand diploma of honor (the highest prize given) was awarded to the Bureau.

Three other grand diplomas of honor, viz, to the State of Massachusetts, the city of Boston, and to the Smithsonian Institution, respectively, as well as many medals and diplomas of merit to various cities of the United States for their contributions to the educational department of the exposition, were awarded.

The Commissioner recommends an increase of the permanent force of the office commensurate with the increasing amount of work to be done, an appropriation for book-cases and record-cases, additional funds for the publication of circulars of information to meet the increasing demand for the same, the passage of a law requiring annual reports respecting the condition of education in the Territories for the information of Congress and the public, the setting apart of the net proceeds of public land-sales in behalf of public instruction, and the printing of a larger number of his annual report.

CENSUS.

The report of the Superintendent of the Census details the work of that office during the past year, in supervising the printing and publication of the voluminous reports of the ninth census; in adjusting under the act of Congress approved March 3, 1873, the accounts of assistant marshals at the eighth census in the Southern States; in conducting current correspondence; and in placing the records and files of the office in shape for use and reference at future censuses. It will be seen that the three quarto volumes, comprising the complete reports of the ninth census, as well as the compendium provided for by the concurrent resolution of Congress passed on May 31, 1872, have issued from the press since the date of the last annual report of this Department. Eight hundred and twenty-eight accounts of assistant marshals at the eighth census, which have for twelve years been suspended for proof of loyalty, have been adjusted, in a total sum of $164,341.53, and forwarded to the Treasury Department for payment. The force of the office has meanwhile been rapidly reduced. Now that the last of the great body of manuscript record brought into the Department by the enumeration of 1870 has been arranged, one clerk, it is believed, will suffice, as in the interval between the eighth and ninth censuses, to conduct all the correspondence and perform all the duties relating to this branch of the public service.

At the date of my last annual report the duties of the Superintendent of the Census under my appointment were discharged by the Commissioner of Indian affairs, Hon. Francis A. Walker, who had held the office of superintendent prior to his appointment to the Indian Bureau. On the resignation of Commissioner Walker, February 1, 1873, to accept a position in private life, I requested him to continue his charge of matters relating to the census, in order that the continuity of plan and procedure might not be unnecessarily interrupted. In compliance with this invitation Mr. Walker duly qualified, and has continued to act as

Superintendent of the Census until the present time, without salary, giving to the work so much of his time and attention as was required.

I respectfully renew my recommendation for a census to be taken in 1875, the results of which could be published in season for the centennial celebration of the Independence of the United States. The suggestion to this effect contained in the last annual report of this Department has received the cordial approval of a large portion of the press of the country. It is scarcely possible to doubt that authentic information respecting the increase in population and wealth during any term of five years would well repay its cost in directing our industrial development, as well as through the better information of Congress respecting the condition, wants, and capacities of the people. But there appears to me to be a peculiar fitness in thus ascertaining by official count our numbers and resources at the close of the first century of the national life, and exhibiting to the world, in this conspicuous manner, the wonderful effects wrought by the social, industrial, and political freedom which the people of the United States have enjoyed. I sincerely trust that this measure may receive the early and favorable attention of Congress.

RAILWAYS.

The subscriptions to the stock of the Union Pacific Railroad Company amount to $36,783,000, of which $36,762,300 has been paid. The receipts for the year ending 30th June, 1873, from the transportation of passengers were $3,786,208.20; of freight, $5,024,998.37; and from miscellaneous sources, $822,758.52; total, $9,633,965.09. The entire cost of the road and fixtures to said date was $112,259,336.53, and the operating expenses of the road for the last fiscal year (ending 30th June, 1873) were $4,697,999.50. The total bonded indebtedness of the company at the end of that year amounted to $75,427,512, of which $27,236,512 is due to the United States. The "floating debt" to same period (not including the company's note for $2,000,000 issued to the Hoxie contract) amounted to $1,940,239.73, and "exchange loans," £120,000.

The Central Pacific Railroad Company by consolidation (as heretofore reported) embraces, besides the original company of that name, also the Western Pacific, the California and Oregon, the San Francisco and Oakland, and the San Francisco and Alameda Companies. Stock to the amount of $62,608,800 has been subscribed, and $54,275,500 paid. The receipts for the year ending June 30, 1873, from transportation of passengers were $4,388,307.14, and of freight, $7,277,482.33; total, $11,665,789.47. The operating expenses of the road for the year were $5,349,425.21, leaving net earnings to the amount of $6,316,364.26. At the close of said year the indebtedness of the company amounted to $85,433,816.60, of which $27,855,680 was to the United States.

The stock subscription of the Central Branch Union Pacific Railroad

Company is $1,000,000, of which $980,600 has been paid in. The receipts for transportation of passengers for the year ending June 30, 1873, were $48,591, and for freight $71,071.91; total, $119,662.91. The expenses of the road and fixtures have been $3,723,700. The expense of the road for the fiscal year ending as above stated is $172,231.44. The company's indebtedness (in addition to the first-mortgage bonds, $1,600,000, and the Government loan, $1,600,000) is $303,058.45.

The amount of stock of the Kansas Pacific Railway Company subscribed is $9,992,500, and the amount paid is $9,655,950. Total amount of stock allowed by law, $10,000,000. The receipts for the transportation of passengers for the year ending June 30, 1873, are $1,393,633.96; for freight during same period, $2,285,038.52; miscellaneous earnings, $69.617.34; total, $3,748,289.82. The cost of construction and equipment of 639 miles of main line, and 33 miles of branch line (672 miles) has been $33,392.840.66. The total funded debt of the company is $27,452,100, of which $6,303,000 is due the United States. Other liabilities and indebtedness, $2,996,148.97; total, $30,448,248.97.

The amount of the stock of the Denver Pacific Railway and Telegraph Company subscribed and paid in is $4,000,000. The receipts for the year ending June 30, 1873, for transportation of passengers were $173,720.58; of freight, $149,012.42; and from miscellaneous sources, $13,215.25; total, $335,948.25. The cost of construction and equipment of the road to the date above stated was $6,493,800, and the indebtedness of the company to that date was $2,513,747.16.

Stock of the Sioux City and Pacific Railroad Company to the amount of $4,478,500 has been subscribed, of which $1,791,400 has been paid in. The receipts for the year ending June 30, 1873, from the transportation of passengers were $73,460.84; of freight, $169,507.36; of mails, $7,299.98; from express, $2,617.38; and from miscellaneous sources, $9,044.56; total, $261,930.12. The expenses during that period were $201,164.60, leaving net earnings, $60,765.52. The indebtedness of the company is $3,339,743.80, of which $1,628,320 is due to the United States. This road commences at Sioux City, Iowa, and extends to Fremont, Nebr., where it intersects the Union Pacific Railroad, a distance of $101\frac{77}{100}$ miles.

At the close of the fiscal year ending June 30, 1873, the amount of subscribed stock of the Southern Pacific Railroad Company of California was $13,189,400; of which $11,965,400 was paid. Explorations and examinations of former preliminary lines have been continued since the last report amounting to 750 miles; $114\frac{50}{100}$ miles of road have been permanently located, and $64\frac{50}{100}$ completed. Twenty miles of this latter distance is on the route from Tipton to Delano, and 50 miles (commencing at the San Fernando Pass via Los Angeles, thence toward San Bernardino, ending about 29 miles easterly from Los Angeles) on the line from Tehachapi Pass to Fort Yuma. Forty-two and one-half miles have been completed on the branch line in the Salinas Valley. The cost of the surveys to June 30, 1873, has been $105,000. The amount received for the transportation of passengers for the fiscal year was $469,789.63; of freight, $486,465.37; total, $956,255. The expenses of the road for the year were $458,739.14, leaving net earnings $497,515.86. The indebtedness of the company is shown by their report to be $8,050,000. The fourth section of 20 miles of this road was accepted by you on the 6th of August last, making the total number of miles miles accepted 90$\frac{26}{100}$.

Stock of the Texas and Pacific Railway Company has been subscribed to the amount of $2,000.000, of which $200,000 has been paid in. The bonds of the company consist of two kinds, viz, "First-mortgage six per cent. gold-construction bonds," and "First-mortgage land-grant" bonds. Of the former none have been issued. Of the latter, there have been issued in the purchase of consolidated roads, $4,000,000. The indebtedness of the company is shown by their report to be as follows: Capital stock, (as shown above,) $2,000,000; land bonds, $4,000,000; debt Southern Pacific Railroad Company to State of Texas, assumed by the Texas and Pacific Railway Company, $209,126.31; floating debt, $790,095.71; "Interest coupons on land bonds," $140,000; total, $7,139,222.02. The operating receipts and expenditures of the road for the year ending June 30, 1873, have been as follows: *Receipts*, from passengers, $104,392.44; freight, $223,211.99; United States mails, $5,328; miscellaneous, $448.43; total, $333,380.86. *Expenditures*, for conducting transportation, $51,994.43; maintenance of roadway, $111,044; cost of running and maintenance of motive power and cars, $62,370.20; general expenses, $31,153.56; total, $256,562.19. Receipts over expenditures, $76,818.67. There have been 109 miles of this road constructed, and 355 miles graded, bridged, and tied. Since the date of the last report of the company (June 30, 1872) the engineers in charge of the surveys have run over 8,000 miles of instrumental lines, and made 15,000 miles of reconnoissance, developing a country 1,500 miles long east and west, and 150 miles in width north and south, so thoroughly that the line of location from Red River to the Pacific can very nearly be determined. The lines of road surveyed and in part undergoing construction are as follows: *Southern division*, from Longview, Tex., to Fort Worth, 155 miles; *Jefferson division*, from Marshall to Texarkana, 69 miles; *Transcontinental division*, from Texarkana to Fort Worth, 237 miles; *Brazos division*, from Fort Worth to the one-hundredth meridian, about 175 miles; *Pecos division*, from the one-hundredth meridian to Rio Grande River, 412 miles; *New Mexico division*, from Rio Grande to the Pimas Villages, 388$\frac{85}{100}$ miles; *California division*, from Pimas Villages to San Diego, Cal., 444 miles; total distance, 1,880$\frac{85}{100}$ miles. The greatest altitude reached in crossing the continent is 6,355 feet.

The Atlantic and Pacific Railroad Company's report for the year ending June 30, 1873, shows that $19,760,300 of stock has been subscribed and paid in. Grading has been done in the Soledad Pass, Cal., and $8,013.72 expended in grading at this pass, to June 30, 1873. On June

29, 1872, the company leased for a term of 999 years the Pacific Railroad of Missouri, extending from Saint Louis, Mo., to Kansas City, Mo., including Carondelet Branch, (297¼ miles,) and assumed the leases to said Pacific Railroad of the following-named lines : Missouri River Railroad, 25¼ miles ; Leavenworth, Atchison and Northwestern Railroad, 21¼ miles ; Osage Valley and Southern Kansas Railroad, 25 miles ; Lexington and Saint Louis Railroad, 55¼ miles ; Saint Louis, Lawrence and Denver Railroad, 61 miles. The cost of the surveys of the Atlantic and Pacific Railroad to June 30, 1873, was $306,357.84. The amount received from passengers on the Atlantic and Pacific Railroad Division, was $303,357.84; on the Pacific Railroad of Missouri and leased-lines division, $1,073,981.02   total, $1,377,338.86. The amount received for freight on the Atlantic and Pacific Railroad Division was $945,711.69; on the Pacific Railroad and leased-lines division, $2,587,852.37 ; total, $3,533,564.06. The cost of the Atlantic and Pacific Railroad and fixtures, as appears from the accounts of the Treasurer, June 30, 1873, was $36,262,322.70. The running expenses of the road from 1st July, 1872, to June 30, 1873, were $692,529.16. The same expenses of the Pacific Railroad of Missouri and leased lines for that period, were $2,693,926.36; total for the fiscal year, $3,386,455.52.

The indebtedness of the company is as follows : Bonded debt of the South Pacific Railroad Company, secured by mortgage of lands, assumed, $7,190,000 ; Atlantic and Pacific Railroad Company's bonds dated 1st July, 1868—20 years—$2,945,500 ; Atlantic and Pacific Company's railroad and land-grant bonds, November 1, 1871, $1,190,000 ; same company's central division land-grant bonds, dated November 1, 1871, $797,922 ; same company's second mortgage railroad and land-grant bonds, dated November 1, 1871, $1,272,000 ; same company's scrip for bonds dated November 1, 1870, $1,718,438.36; total bonded indebtedness, $15,113,860.36 ; floating indebtedness, $2,758,025.38 ; total indebtedness, $17,871,885.74. Assets of cash, debts due company, and securities other than of this company, amounting to $1,340,070.31, on hand.

Stock of the Northern Pacific Railroad Company, to the amount of $100,000,000, has been subscribed, and certificates for 172,695 shares of $100 each have been issued. During the year 1873, the road was definitely located from the mouth of Heart River, on the Missouri, to the mouth of Glendive Creek, on the Yellowstone, a distance of 205 miles. The precise point of crossing the Missouri River has not yet been fixed by the company. The surveys necessary to complete a continuous line across the continent, which were left unfinished last year by reason of the open hostility of the Sioux Indians of Montana and Dakota, have, this year, been brought to a most satisfactory conclusion. A continuous line has been surveyed from Lake Superior to Puget Sound, and the data have been obtained for deciding the final location of the road between the above-named termini. The entire line of route has not as yet been definitely fixed upon. The company reports that "for climate, soil, quantity, and variety of mineral wealth, and all the elements necessary to the support of a dense population, there is no zone of similar extent and value between the Mississippi River and the Pacific Ocean' as that "of the region lying between and contiguous to parallels 46 and 47 north latitude." The whole amount expended on surveys from the beginning of the work to the 1st of July last is $1,058,873.74. The extent of line surveyed is 9,388 miles, and, in addition, 2,350 of river-reconnoissance. The amount received from passengers on the road (in Minnesota and in Washington Territory) is $153,551.97; for transportation of freight, $393,549.23, which includes a few days of the earnings of June, 1873, in Dakota. The expense of the road and fixtures has been $20,092,380.09, and the indebtedness of the company is $29,309,337.40. The word "expense," as used above, is said by the company " to mean the cost of the road proper and its fixtures" only. The company's report states that, on October 1, 1873, trains were running regularly, (both passenger and freight,) engaged in the general traffic from Lake Superior to the Missouri River, a distance of 453 miles, and from Kalama, on the Columbia River, northward, 65 miles toward Puget Sound. Beyond that, a distance of 25 miles of track has been laid, and 15 miles more nearly graded, which, when completed, (about the 1st of December, this year,) will make a continuous road from the Columbia River to Puget Sound, 105 miles. On the 6th of last January you accepted the first 228 miles of the Northern Pacific Railroad in Minnesota, (from its junction with the Lake Superior and Mississippi Railroad, near Thomson, to the Red River of the North;) and, on the 10th of September, 1873, 65 miles of the road in Washington Territory, " on its main line between the city of Portland, Oreg., and its western terminus on Puget Sound." The report of the commissioners appointed to examine the completed portion of the road (195 miles) in Dakota Territory has not yet been received.

On the 11th of March last you accepted $155\frac{35}{100}$ miles of the Missouri, Kansas and Texas Railway, from the $86\frac{76}{100}$ mile (south of the southern boundary-line of Kansas) to Red River, near Preston, Tex. Total number of miles accepted $242\frac{11}{100}$.

I accepted, on the 4th of September last, $84\frac{23}{100}$ miles of the Cairo and Fulton Railroad, lying between Little Rock, in Arkansas, and the southern boundary of Missouri. Application having been made for the examination of the portion of this road lying between Little Rock and Fulton, commissioners have been appointed for that purpose, but their report has not yet been received.

You accepted, November 4, 1872, the final portion ($50\frac{2}{4}$ miles) of the Burlington and Missouri River Railroad, in Nebraska, reported on by commissioners on the 30th October of that year. This makes a total accepted line in that State of $190\frac{2}{4}$ miles.

That portion of the Memphis and Little Rock Railroad from the west side of the Saint Francis River to a point opposite the city of Little Rock, on the north bank of the Arkansas River, called "Argenta"—91$\frac{7}{10}$ miles—was accepted by the Department on the 5th of last March.

GEOLOGICAL SURVEY.

The geological and geographical survey of the Territories of the United States, under the direction of this Department, and conducted by Professor F. V. Hayden, United States Geologist, has been continued during the past season with very satisfactory results. The section of country traversed by the survey lies in the central portion of Colorado Territory, lying between parallels 38° and 40° 20' north, and meridians 104° 30' and 107° west, comprising about 20,000 square miles. This area was divided into three districts, and the survey of each intrusted to a party of geologists and topographers. The northern district included the Middle Park; the middle district, the South Park; and the southern district, the San Luis Valley. The whole area, which is about 160 miles long by 130 wide, embraces the most interesting ranges of mountains and the largest group of lofty peaks yet explored on this continent. Besides the parties already referred to, three other parties were in the field, one of which carried on the primary triangulations from the summits of the most important peaks in the area of the survey. These several parties composed, altogether, a complete organization for the purposes of the survey.

A preliminary field-map was prepared last spring, based upon the land surveys made by this Department, which indicated those portions of our territorial domain which were least known, and which promised the most valuable results. The field-work was commenced about the middle of May last, and the parties have all returned from the scene of their labors. The results of the survey are very satisfactory, and the collections in geology, botany, and natural history are as extensive and valuable as those of former surveys.

The geologist in charge requests a deficiency appropriation, to enable him to continue and complete the work of the year, and assigns the following reasons for the occurrence of the necessity for such an appropriation, viz:

The geological survey of the unknown portions of the national domain, especially in the mountainous localities, and those remote from routes of ordinary travel, involves a large expenditure for what is known as an "outfit." In former surveys the materials composing the "outfit" have been sold at the close of the season, for a fair percentage upon their cost; but, at the close of the present season, it was found that the "outfit" could not be sold except at a great sacrifice. It was, therefore, deemed advisable to retain the "outfit" for use during the season of 1874, should Congress authorize a continuation of the survey. The estimated value of the materials of said "outfit" is $20,000, and the geologist in charge deems an appropriation for that amount necessary to the completion of this season's work.

In view of the importance to science and to the material interests of the country of the objects of the survey, I recommend the deficiency appropriation asked for, as well as the regular annual appropriation for its continuance,

THE YELLOWSTONE NATIONAL PARK.

I deem it incumbent upon me to refer to the present unprotected condition of the Yellowstone National Park. No appropriation has yet been made for the purpose of opening the park to the public and of enabling this Department to carry into effect the necessary rules and regulations for its government. I am informed that the park has been visited during the past summer by many persons, and that it has been despoiled by them of great quantities of its mineral deposits and other curiosities.

A superintendent of the park was appointed in May, 1872, but there being no appropriation from which his compensation could be paid, his services have, necessarily, been gratuitous, and he could not be expected, under such circumstances, to reside permanently in the park. Applications have been made by various parties for permission to erect buildings and to construct roads within the park. The act of March 1, 1872, confers upon me the necessary authority to grant leases for building purposes; but no leases have been granted, for the reason that sufficient information has not been obtained as to the responsibility of the several applicants. It appears to me to be eminently proper that early steps should be taken by Congress for the protection of this great national wonder from the vandalism of curiosity hunters. This Department should not be held responsible for the condition of the park, so long as there is no money under its control applicable to the ends contemplated by the act of March 1, 1872. The boundaries of the park should be properly surveyed and located, as many persons desire to enter and settle upon public lands contiguous thereto.

CAPITOL.

The architect reports various repairs and improvements made in the Capitol during the past year. There have been provided large coal-vaults for each wing of the building; a fresh-air duct for the heating apparatus of the Senate wing, and a passenger-elevator for the same wing. The galleries of the hall of the House of Representatives have been re-arranged, and new chairs and desks for that hall have been provided. The steam-boiler and heating-apparatus have been thoroughly repaired, and many committee-rooms have been refitted, painted, and improved. The architect recommends that while the defective portions of the rooms in the center building are being renewed, the improvements may be made in a fire-proof manner by replacing the present wooden rafters with iron ones; also, that the remodeling and finishing of the rotunda be made to harmonize with the vault and interior walls of the dome.

First street, which bounds the Capitol grounds on the west, has been paved from Pennsylvania avenue to Maryland avenue with cypress-wood pavement, and the curve at the southwest, from Maryland avenue to New Jersey avenue, is now being paved with granite blocks. Over one hundred thousand loads of earth have been deposited in the grounds south of the Capitol and on south B street. The Capitol grounds are now in a condition for laying out the interior walks and for planting, and the architect recommends the employment of a competent land-scape gardener, under whose direction the grounds may be properly laid out and ornamented.

The architect reports that the buildings of the reform-school for the District of Columbia are nearly completed. The main building is so far advanced that portions of it are used as work-rooms. It is expected that said building will be completed before Congress convenes. The family building has been occupied since the middle of last winter.

EXTENSION OF CAPITOL GROUNDS.

Congress, at its last session, appropriated the sum of $284,199.15 wherewith to complete the purchase, by the United States, of the property embraced in squares 687 and 688, lying adjacent to the square East of the Capitol. The whole of said appropriation has been disbursed through the supreme court of the District of Columbia, and the title to the entire property above described is now vested in the United States. Under authority conferred by the act of March 3, 1873, those of the buildings and other improvements on said property which were not required for public use have been sold at public auction, and the materials have nearly all been removed therefrom. It is expected that the two remaining buildings on square 688 will be removed, and that all the materials yet remaining on both squares will be cleared away, before the meeting of Congress. Litigation may be necessary in order to conclude the sale, at auction, of one of said buildings. I am unable, therefore, to report the exact amount which will have been received from the sale of said improvements. The amount thus far received is $19,357.44, from which the sum of $3,619.80 has been paid for advertising, auctioneer fees, extra clerical labor, services of commissioners of appraisement, and the other expenses incident to the purchase of said squares and the sale of said improvements. When the whole expenses shall have been paid, the residue, which will approximate the sum of $17,000, will be applied to the improvement of the extension, as provided for by law.

This addition to the grounds surrounding the Capitol will bring them into greater harmony with the noble proportions of that building than has hitherto been the case, and when they shall have been properly laid out and ornamented, they will form an appropriate setting for the National Capitol.

PNEUMATIC TUBE.

Congress, on the 10th day of June, 1872, appropriated the sum of $15,000 for the purpose of constructing a pneumatic tube to connect the Capitol with the Government Printing-Office, for the transmission of books, packages, &c., "the money to be expended under the direction of the Secretary of the Interior, and the work to be done under the supervision of the architect of the Capitol extension." Pursuant to this provision of law, a contract for the construction of such tube was awarded by said architect on the 20th of June, 1872, and the same was approved by this Department. It was stipulated, in said contract, that the tube should be completed and ready for use on or before the 30th day of June, 1873; but, on the 26th of March last, a resolution was adopted by the Senate, directing me to report to that body, at its next session, all the information in my possession in regard to the non-completion of the tube, the amount expended in its construction, and other circumstances connected therewith. To enable me to answer the resolution intelligently, I designated Joseph Henry, Secretary of the Smithsonian Institution, O. E. Babcock, Superintendent of Public Buildings, and A. M. Clapp, Congressional Printer, as a committee to examine the work done and report to me their views in relation thereto. A copy of their report, together with a detailed statement of all the circumstances connected with the construction of the tube, will be laid before the Senate at its approaching session. The first attempt to lay the tube was unsuccessful, owing to various causes. The contractor, however, is now making another endeavor to construct such a tube as will accomplish the purposes intended. and informs me that the tube will, probably, be completed before the 1st of January next. His present operations are conducted at his own expense, so that no further appropriation by Congress will be necessary to its completion.

BENEVOLENT INSTITUTIONS.

INSANE ASYLUM.

During the year ending June 30, 1873, there were under treatment at the Government Hospital for the Insane 762 patients, of whom 413 were from the Army and Navy, and 573 were males. Two hundred and one patients were admitted during said year; 66 were discharged as recovered, 24 as improved, and 7 as unimproved. The recoveries were 68 per cent. of the discharges including, and 46 per cent. excluding deaths. During the same period 45 patients died, leaving under treatment at the close of said year, 620 patients, of whom 468 were males. Sixty-nine of those treated during said year were private or pay-patients, of whom 24 were discharged, 4 were transferred to the list of indigent patients, and 41 remained under treatment at the close of the year. 3,348 persons, of whom 1,634 were native-born, have been treated in the hospital since it was opened. The general health of the hospital has been very good.

The expenditures for the past fiscal year amounted to $136,992.43. The amount received for board of private patients was $9,744.86, and that from the sale of live stock, &c., $2,247.57. The products of the farm and garden during the year were estimated as worth $17,763.25, and the value of the live stock, farm and garden implements, &c., belonging to the institution, is estimated at $16,418.20.

In addition to the regular expenditures for the support of the hospital, there has been expended the sum of $37,800 in the erection of an extension of the wards for the excited class of patients, and $6,000 for heating boilers. There are now owned by the United States and devoted to the objects of the hospital a little upwards of 419 acres of land; 360 acres are embraced in one nearly complete parallelogram, and the remainder comprises a single tract, conveniently situated for grazing, or for the cultivation of the staple annual crops. The tract of 185 acres, originally purchased for the hospital, and within which its buildings are situate, is inclosed by a wall nine feet high, excepting on the river front.

The board of visitors submit the following estimates for the year ending June 30, 1875, viz:

For support of the institution, $140,785; for repairs and improvements, $15,000; for completing the river wall, and raising the boundary walls at their intersection with the former, $8,748; for the erection, furnishing, and fitting-up of an extension of the center building of the hospital, $35,956; for a coal vault in the rear of the east wing, $2,500; for the erection, furnishing, and fitting-up of an extension of the west detached building for patients, $12,000, and to supply deficiencies for the current year, $11,366; a total of $226,355.

DEAF AND DUMB INSTITUTION.

On the 1st instant there were 108 pupils in the Columbia Institution for the Deaf and Dumb, 34 of whom were received since July 1, 1872. Of these 60 have been in the collegiate department, representing seventeen States and the District of Columbia, and 48 in the primary department. One hundred and eight pupils have been under instruction since July 1, 1872, of whom 92 were males. Three students, having passed satisfactory examinations in the entire course of studies, received the degree of Bachelor of Arts. The health of the institution was excellent, not one death having occurred during the year.

The receipts for the support of the institution, during the last fiscal year, exceeded the disbursements $821.39, as they did also for the improvement of the grounds, $1,626.19.

The board of directors report that, in completing the purchase of the Kendall Green property, toward which Congress, in 1871, appropriated the sum of $70,000, a balance of indebtedness remains, unprovided for, of $10,697.46. It had been hoped by the board that this amount could be raised by private subscription, but owing to the fact that the title to all the real estate of the institution is vested in the United States, this expectation, it is feared, will not be realized, as those who are called upon for subscriptions are disposed to decline aiding what has, practically, become a Government institution. No estimate of an appropriation for the amount is submitted by the board, but they invite attention to the indebtedness, representing the importance of securing the possession of this valuable property, and trust that Congress will be disposed to make an additional appropriation for the purpose.

The following estimates are submitted by the Board of Trustees for the ensuing fiscal year:

For support of the institution, salaries and incidental expenses, including $500 for books and illustrative apparatus, $49,500; and for continuing the work of erecting, furnishing, and fitting up of the buildings of the institution, in accordance with plans heretofore submitted to Congress, including necessary repairs to the completed portion thereof, $54,000; a total of $103,500. The directors state that the estimate of $54.000 for building purposes is greatly needed to complete the college building, and to provide for the erection of two houses for professors. The college building has been in an incomplete condition for nearly seven years, and requires enlargement for the increasing wants of the institution. The plans submitted with the ninth report of the institution showed the necessity of ultimately erecting six dwelling houses for its officers, as it was considered to be to the interests of the institution for its officers to reside on the premises. Two of such dwelling houses have been built, and it is desirable to erect two more at present.

COLUMBIA HOSPITAL FOR WOMEN.

During the last fiscal year 2,285 women received treatment at the Columbia Hospital for Women and Lying-in Asylum. Of these, 2,135 were received during the year, and 1,924 were out-door patients. Twelve hundred and seventeen were restored to health, 542 relieved, 104 discharged as incurable, 9 died, the results are not known in 296 cases, and 117 remained under treatment. Of the whole number treated, 401 were foreign born. The hospital has been remodeled, an additional story and a number of private rooms added, and a thorough system of sewerage, heating and ventilation of the building introduced. The wards and private rooms have been refurnished, and every comfort that can be desired for the sick has been supplied.

The estimates for the next fiscal year are as follows: For the support of the institution, $24,000, and for the erection of a stone wall around the western and northern portion of the grounds, with stone coping and iron railing, and for grading and graveling the grounds, $10,000; a total of $34,000. The directors state that the improvements estimated for are necessary from the fact that the grounds north of the hospital building are twenty feet above the proper grade, and must be graded and terraced to render them serviceable.

NEW JAIL.

Considerable progress has been made during the year in the construction of a jail in and for the District of Columbia, authorized by an act of Congress approved June 1, 1872, to be erected under the supervision of the supervising architect of the Treasury Department, after plans and designs to be prepared by him and approved by a board of commissioners, composed of the Secretary of the Interior, the governor of the District of Columbia, and the chief justice of the supreme court of said District.

At a meeting of said board, held October 22, 1872, certain general plans, designs, and specifications, prepared by said supervising architect, were approved; and at a subsequent meeting, viz, on April 15, 1873, the supervising architect submitted the full working plans and specifications for the jail, which were approved by the board. Under authority conferred by the board, the supervising architect has, at various times, advertised for proposals for such materials as were required in the construction of the jail, and contracts have been awarded to various parties, who were the lowest responsible bidders in each case, for rubble-stone, concrete, cement, sand, ironwork, and cut stone. In each instance the contracts referred to were authorized by the board of commissioners, and have been approved by at least a majority of its members. As the work progresses it will be necessary to award contracts for the necessary flagging, and for a galvanized iron cornice for the building.

The supervising architect reports that the foundation-walls have been laid, the superstructure built up to an average height of eleven feet, and about two-thirds of the necessary grading completed. He states that if no unforeseen difficulties occur, the building will probably be completed within the current fiscal year.

The architect represents that, although the plans for the jail were prepared in view of the amount appropriated for the purpose, viz, $300,000, unexpected and unavoidable expenses have been incurred in grading the site for the building, and in building a wharf on the Anacostia River, amounting to upwards of $15,000, which amount he considers to be not properly chargeable to the appropriation for the erection of the jail, and should be refunded thereto; otherwise, an additional appropriation will become necessary. He also states that in order to keep the cost of the jail within the amount appropriated, he was compelled to provide in the specifications for a galvanized iron cornice; for wooden joists and floors to warden's office and chapel wing, and for timber framing and boarding to the roof, with a tin covering to the same. He expresses the opinion that the building should be constructed in a fire-proof manner; that the cornice should be of stone, and the roof-covering of slate, and states that in order to accomplish these ends and insure a substantial fire-proof building, an additional appropriation of $100,000 will be necessary.

The supervising architect invites attention to the fact that the building, when completed, will be suitable, not only for the ordinary purposes of a jail, but, also, for those of a penitentiary; and, as the grounds surrounding it are of ample capacity, he strongly recommends that the necessary authority be obtained from Congress for its use as a penitentiary as well as a jail. He states that the additional expense would be comparatively small, as it would involve little more than the cost of the necessary work-shops, and the materials necessary for the construction of a wall to inclose the grounds, which could be entirely erected by the labor of the convicts. He is of the opinion that, if this suggestion were adopted, a large saving in the expense of the jail to the Government would be made, and that, in time, the use of convict labor would constitute a source of revenue to the District of Columbia. He also suggests the importance of providing a separate building for the detention and punishment of female prisoners, which should be under the exclusive charge of female officers. He states that experience has demonstrated that proper prison discipline is impossible when both sexes are confined in the same building, and that, if the reformation of female convicts be intended, they should be committed exclusively to the custody of their own sex. He recommends, therefore, that authority be asked of Congress for the erection of a house of correction for the punishment and reformation of female convicts.

The total expenditures on account of the construction of the jail, up to the 30th ultimo, amounted to $95,022.60, leaving an unexpended balance of the appropriation of $204,977.40.

TERRITORIAL PENITENTIARIES.

Congress, by an act approved February 22, 1873, appropriated the sum of $40,000, to be set apart and paid out of the net proceeds of the internal revenue in the Territory of Washington for the fiscal years severally ending on June 30, 1866, June 30, 1867, and June 30, 1868, for the purpose of erecting, under the direction of this Department, a penitentiary building in said Territory. The sum of $20,000 had been thus set apart and appropriated for the purpose by an act approved January 22, 1867, but that amount was found to be inadequate for the construction of a proper penitentiary, and an additional sum of $20,000 was asked for. The act of February 22, 1873, is amendatory of the former act, and provides the same amount for a penitentiary in Washington Territory as had been provided for such buildings in the other Territories.

A site for the building having been selected by the commissioners appointed by the legislative assembly of the Territory, and approved by this Department, immediate steps were taken for the erection of the building. Proposals were duly invited by public advertisement, and on the 26th of April last a contract for the erection of one wing of the building, in accordance with the plans adopted, was awarded to the lowest responsible bidder. Upon a careful comparison of the proposals it was found that but one wing of the penitentiary could be built within the amount appropriated. By the terms ot the contract the building is required to be completed by the 24th of November next, and the latest advices from the superintendent of construction indicate that such requirement will be fulfilled by the contractor. When the building is finished it will be delivered into the charge of the United States marshal for the Territory, pursuant to the provisions of section one of an act of Congress approved January 10, 1871. By a subsequent act approved January 24, 1873, Congress repealed so much of the former act as related to "placing the penitentiaries in the Territories of Montana, Idaho, Wyoming, and Colorado under the care and control of the re spective United States marshals for said Territories," and transferred the care and custody of said penitentiaries to said Territories respectively. Inasmuch as the erection of the penitentiary for Washington Territory was not provided for until after the passage of the latter act, and as no reference to said penitentiary is made therein, its provisions are not applicable to that penitentiary, and the building will necessarily remain in the custody of the United States marshal until Congress snall otherwise direct, as in the cases above mentioned.

PUBLIC DOCUMENTS.

Frequent application is made to this Department, by officers of the Government authorized to receive them, for volumes of the United States Statutes and Wallace's Reports of the Supreme Court, to complete deficient sets in libraries and to furnish offices newly created. As the supply of the earlier volumes of the United States Statutes and of Wallace's Reports is entirely exhausted, the Department is and has been for some time past unable to furnish them. I would suggest that a sufficient amount be appropriated to furnish these documents, in order that requisitions for them in future may be filled.

In this connection, I beg to call your attention to the fact that the existing laws regulating the distribution of the standard public documents, such as the United States Statutes at Large, Wallace's Reports of the Supreme Court, the Official Register, and the Pamphlet Laws, are somewhat vague and indefinite in specifying the officers of the Government who are entitled to them. The experience of late years has also demonstrated that the number of copies of the before-mentioned documents allotted to heads of Departments and Bureaus is altogether insufficient to meet the demands of the public business, and some ncrease should be made in these instances; especially should the number of copies of the United States Official Register ordered by law to be printed on the assembling of each new Congress be augmented to at least double the number now authorized, which is but 750 copies.

It is highly important that some action should be taken in this matter, with the view of collecting in one comprehensive act the duties assigned to this Department, in connection with the custody and distribution of public documents.

NEED OF ADDITIONAL ROOM FOR THE DEPARTMENT.

In closing this report I desire to invite special attention to the necessity for additional room for the accommodation of the several bureaus of the Interior Department. At the present time almost the entire clerical force of the Pension Bureau, with all its voluminous and valuable files and records, the entire Bureau of Education, and the Geological Survey, are located in buildings owned by private parties, and in the case of the former especially, in a building that is poorly protected from fire. The rapid growth in the business of the Patent-Office will, in a few years, if it does not already, require all of the room in the present Patent-Office building for its occupancy, and measures should be taken at an early day to provide for the accommodation of the other bureaus of the Department in a suitable fire-proof building.

I am, sir, very respectfully, your obedient servant,

C. DELANO,
Secretary.

The PRESIDENT.

· PAPERS

ACCOMPANYING

THE REPORT OF SECRETARY OF THE INTERIOR

REPORT OF THE COMMISSIONER OF THE GENERAL LAND-OFFICE.

DEPARTMENT OF THE INTERIOR,
General Land-Office, October 20, 1873.

SIR: I have the honor to submit the following as an abstract of my annual report for the fiscal year ending June 30, 1873, viz:

	Acres.
Disposal of public lands by ordinary cash sales	1,626,266.03
Military bounty-land warrant, locations under acts of 1847, 1850, 1852, and 1855	214,940.00
Homestead entries	3,793,612.52
Agricultural college scrip locations	653,446.41
Certified to railroads	6,083,536.57
Certified for wagon-roads	76,576.82
Lands approved to the States as swamp	238,548.65
Certified for agricultural colleges	10,223.29
Certified for common schools	76,909.17
Certified for universities	51,228.69
Certified for seminaries	320.00
Internal improvement selections approved to States	190,775.76
Sioux half-breed scrip locations	7,515.47
Chippewa half-breed scrip locations	6,707.49
Total	13,030,606.87
Disposals of previous year	11,864,975.64
Increased disposal	1,165,631.23
Cash receipts under various heads	$3,408,515 50

		Acres.
Total area of the land States and Territories		1,834,998,400
Surveyed within the fiscal year ending June 30, 1873	30,488,132	
Previously surveyed	586,066,763	
Total surveyed to June 30, 1873		616,554,895
Leaving yet to be surveyed		1,218,443,605

List of papers composing the annual report of the Commissioner of the General Land-Office.

1. Surveys of public lands, showing the progress made at the close of the last fiscal year, giving a statement of appropriations made for the surveying service during the same time, and submitting estimates for said service during the present fiscal year.
2. Surveys of Indian reservations.
3. Statement of progress of surveys on State and territorial boundaries.

4. Of pre-emption laws, and rulings under the same, recommending a repeal of the pre-emption laws.

5. Sioux Indian reservation.

6. Cherokee strip in Kansas.

7. Round Valley Indian reservation in Montana.

8. Homestead law; operations under the same, and recommending amendments.

9. Graduated lands; relief for suspended entries under recent confirmatory act of Congress.

10. Useless military reservations.

11. Offerings of public lands.

12. Educational land bounty.

13. Timber depredations; showing the action of this Office to preven the same.

14. Railroads; progress of transcontinental lines, and of roads in States and Territories to which subsidies in land have been granted.

15. Operations under the mining laws.

16. Coal lands; rules and regulations under the act March 3, 1873.

17. Private land claims.

18. List of surveyors-general and land-offices.

19. Reports of the surveyors-general, from A to Q.

Tabular statements accompanying Commissioner's annual report.

No. 1. Tabular statements showing the number of acres of public lands surveyed in the States and Territories at the close of the fiscal year ending June 30, 1873; also the total area of the public lands remaining unsurveyed at that date.

No. 2. Statement of public lands sold; of cash and bounty-land scrip received therefor; number of acres entered under the homestead law of May 20, 1862; of commissions received under the sixth section of said act; also, land located with scrip under the agricultural college and mechanic act of July 2, 1862, and commissions received by registers and receivers on the value thereof; and statement of incidental expenses thereon in the first half of the fiscal year commencing July 1, 1872, and ending June 30, 1873.

No. 3. Statement showing like particulars for the second half of the fiscal year ending June 30, 1873.

No. 4. Summary for the fiscal year ending June 30, 1873, showing the number of acres disposed of for cash; for bounty-land scrip; by entry under the homestead laws of May 20, 1862, March 21, 1864, and June 21, 1866, with aggregate of $5 and $10 homestead payments; homestead commissions; also, locations with agricultural college and mechanic scrip under act of July 2, 1862.

No. 5. Statement showing the quantity of swamp lands selected for the several States under acts of Congress approved March 2, 1849, September 28, 1850, and March 12, 1860, to September 30, 1873.

No. 6. Statement exhibiting the quantity of swamp land approved to the several States under acts named in table No. 5 to September 30, 1873.

No. 7. Statement exhibiting the quantity of swamp land patented to the several States under acts approved September 28, 1850, and March 12, 1860; also, the quantity certified to the State of Louisiana under act approved March 2, 1849.

No. 8. Statement showing the State selections under the internal improvement grant of September 4, 1841, to the 30th June, 1873.

No. 9. Exhibit of bounty-land warrant business under acts of 1847,

1850, 1852, and 1855, showing the issues and locations from the commencement of operations under said acts to June 30, 1873.

No. 10. Statement showing the selections made by certain States of lands within their own limits under the agricultural college and mechanic act of July 2, 1862, and supplemental acts of April 14, 1864, and July 23, 1866; also, the locations made with scrip under said acts.

No. 11. Statement exhibiting land concessions by acts of Congress to States for canal purposes from the year 1827 to June 30, 1873.

No. 12. Statement exhibiting land concessions by acts of Congress to States and corporations for railroad and military wagon-road purposes from the year 1850 to June 30, 1873.

No. 13. Estimate of appropriations required for the office of the Commissioner of the General Land-Office, for the fiscal year ending June 30, 1875.

No. 14. Estimates of appropriations required to meet expenses of collecting the revenue from sales of public lands in the several States and Territories for the fiscal year ending June 30, 1875.

No. 15. Estimates of appropriations for the surveying department for the fiscal year ending June 30, 1875.

No. 16. Estimates of appropriations required for surveying the public lands for the fiscal year ending June 30, 1875.

No. 17. Table showing the time when the various railroad rights attach to the lands granted so far as at present determined.

No. 18. Connected map of the United States from ocean to ocean, exhibiting the extent of surveys, land districts, seats of surveyors-general and district land-offices; also, localities of railroads of general interest.

During the fiscal year ending June 30, 1873, there were received 56,109 letters, and 48,965 were written and recorded. Forty-five thousand three hundred and seventy-eight patents were written and recorded.

It will be seen, by reference to the foregoing statements, that 30,488,132.83 acres of land were surveyed during the last fiscal year. The amount surveyed for the fiscal year ending June 30, 1870, was 18,165,278 acres. These figures show an increase of 12,322,844.83 acres in the annual survey since I assumed the control of the Office.

The disposals of public land under various heads, for the last fiscal year, amounted to 13,030,606.87 acres. The disposal for the fiscal year ending June 30, 1870, was 8,095,413 acres, showing an increase of 4,935,193.87 acres.

Notwithstanding this increase in the survey and sale of lands, which involves a corresponding increase in the work of this Office, I have thus far been able to transact the current business, and largely reduce the vast accumulation of unfinished work which I found on assuming control of the Office, and to which I have alluded in previous reports, and the work of the Office is now well advanced in most of its branches. The adjustment of *ex parte* homestead and pre-emption cases is now kept up to current dates. The number of contested cases awaiting adjustment has been much reduced, but, owing to the insufficiency of the clerical force, this class of work still remains somewhat in arrears.

When I took charge of the Office there was a large accumulation of California private land claims unadjusted. This accumulation has been removed and, at this time, only four cases are awaiting examination.

Notwithstanding the satisfactory progress thus far made in bringing up arrearages, the business of the Office is increasing so rapidly as to justify the conclusion that present arrearages cannot be brought up and the current business of the Office transacted promptly without a thorough

46 Ab

reorganization and increase of the clerical force of this bureau. I therefore respectfully, but earnestly, renew the recommendations made by me on this point in my last annual report.

I am, sir, very respectfully, your obedient servant,
WILLIS DRUMMOND,
Commissioner.

The Hon. SECRETARY OF THE INTERIOR.

DEPARTMENT OF THE INTERIOR,
GENERAL LAND-OFFICE,
Washington, D. C., October 20, 1873.

SIR: The surveys of public lands of the United States, for the fiscal year ending June 30, 1873, were as follows: Minnesota, 2,399,136.81 acres; Kansas, 3,464,229.04 acres; Nebraska, 4,417,397.66 acres; California, 1,226,784.73 acres; Nevada, 1,254,731.59 acres; Oregon, 1,319,140.68 acres; Washington Territory, 1,360,451.00 acres; Colorado Territory, 98,401.12 acres; Utah Territory, 45,593.83 acres; Arizona Territory, 302,900.15 acres; New Mexico Territory, 391,341.22 acres; Dakota Territory, 2,295,399.29 acres; Idaho Territory, 646,586.47 acres; Montana Territory, 1,473,917.75 acres; Wyoming Territory, 1,193,395.88 acres; Louisiana, 172,377.96 acres; Florida, 730,103.68 acres; Indian Territory, 4,996,243.97 acres; total, 30,488,132.83, which, added to the amount surveyed prior to that time, makes an aggregate of 616,554,895 acres, surveyed since the commencement of operations under the present system, leaving an estimated area of 1,218,443,506 acres unsurveyed.

The following table exhibits the progress of surveys and the disposal of public lands since the fiscal year ending June 30, 1863:

Fiscal year ending June 30—	Surveying districts.	Land-offices.	Cost of survey.	No. of acres surveyed.	No. of acres disposed of.
1864	10	53	$172,506 60	4,315,954	3,428,865 60
1865	10	54	170,721 40	4,161,772	4,513,720 00
1866	10	61	186,369 86	4,287,037	4,629,312 00
1867	12	63	423,416 22	10,804,311	7,041,114 00
1868	13	64	325,779 50	10,170,654	6,655,762 00
1869	12	66	497,471 00	10,822,812	7,666,151 00
1870	17	81	560,210 00	12,165,278	8,095,413 00
1871	17	83	683,910 00	22,016,607	10,765,705 00
1872	17	92	1,019,578 66	29,450,339	11,864,975 04
1873	17	90	1,217,731 67	30,488,132	13,030,606 87

This shows an increase of the number of surveyors-general from ten to seventeen, and of land-offices from fifty-three to ninety, and an increase in the annual survey from 4,315,954 acres to 30,488,132 acres, and an increase in the number of acres disposed of from 3,238,865.00 to 13,030,606.87, the amount disposed of during the year ending June 30, 1873.

The following appropriations for surveys were made by Congress for the present fiscal year: Florida, $12,000; Louisiana, $18,000; Minnesota, $50,000; Dakota Territory, $80,000; Nebraska, $60,000; Kansas, $60,000; Colorado Territory, $80,000; New Mexico Territory, $30,000; Arizona Territory, $20,000; Utah Territory, $25,000; Wyoming Territory, $50,000; Montana Territory, $60,000; Idaho Territory, $30,000; Nevada, $50,000; California, $90,000; Oregon, $70,000; and Washington Territory, $70,000,

The estimates for the ensuing fiscal year are as follows: Florida, $15,000; Louisiana, $22,000; Minnesota, $40,000; Dakota Territory, $80,000; Nebraska, $60,000; Kansas, $89,700; Colorado Territory, $80,000; New Mexico Territory, $40,000; Arizona Territory, $30,000; Utah Territory, $30,000; Wyoming Territory, $60,000; Montana Territory, $60,000; Idaho Territory, $40,000; Nevada, $60,000; California, $90,000; Oregon, $70,000; and Washington Territory, $70,000.

2.—SURVEYS OF INDIAN RESERVATIONS.

Pursuant to treaty stipulations and the sixth section of the act of Congress approved April 2, 1864, (Stats. at Large, vol. 13, p. 41,) which devolve the duty of surveying Indian reservations on the Commissioner of the General-Land Office, surveys were made during the last fiscal year as follows:

Date of treaty.	Indian reservations.	Locality of lands.	Extent of surveys in acres.	Contracts let by—	Remarks.
July 19, 1866 June 14, 1866 Mar. 21, 1866	Cherokee, Creek, and Seminole.	Indian Ter....	4,422,298 00	Comm'r General Land-Office.	
	Senecas	...do		Surveyor-general of Kansas.	Remarking boundaries.
Feb. 27, 1867	Pottawatomie.......	...do	573,945.16	Comm'r General Land-Office.	Survey into forty-acre tracts.
Feb. 22, 1855	Fond du Lac	Minnesota	12,194.73	Surveyor-general, Minnesota.	
Feb. 22, 1855 Oct. 2, 1863	Chippewas of the Mississippi and of the Red Lake.	...do		......do	Surv. of boundaries.
Oct. 2, 1863	Chippewas of the Red Lake, and Pembina Indians.	...do		......do	Do.
Mar. 11, 1863 Mar. 20, 1865	The Pillager, Winnebigoshish, and Leech Lake.	...do		......do	Do.
Mar. 19, 1867	White Earth.......	...do		......do	
Apr. 19, 1858	Yankton Sioux ...	Dakota		Surveyor-general, Dakota.	Survey into forty-acre tracts.
June 9, 1863	Nez Percé	Idaho	55,536.44	Surveyor-general, Idaho.	Survey into twenty-acre tracts.
	The Bannock and Fort Hall.	...do		......do	Survey of boundaries.
Sept. 30, 1854	La Pointe or Bad River.	Wisconsin ...	5,912.43	Surveyor-general, Minnesota.	Survey into eighty-acre tracts.
Feb. 18, 1867	Sac and Fox of Missouri.	Kansas and Nebraska.	14,411.02	Surveyor-general, Kansas.	Act of June 10, '72.
Mar. 15, 1854	Otoes and Missourias.	...do		Surveyor-general, Nebraska.	Do.
Sept. 24, 1857	Pawnee.........	Nebraska	48,430.06	......do	Do.
June 15, 1855	Warm Springs....	Oregon........	26,905.77	......do	
Nov. 15, 1865	Klamath.........	...do	89,032.21	Surveyor-general, Oregon.	
Oct. 14, 1864	Coast Range ...... Flathead, &c......	...do .... Montana......	9,005.44 215,907.08	......do .... Surveyor-general, Montana.	Act March 3, 1873.

3.—STATE AND TERRITORIAL BOUNDARIES.

1. *The eastern boundary of California.*—Partial returns have been made by Allexey W. Von Schmidt, contractor, showing the completion of that part of the line between the north shore of Lake Tahoe and the forty-second parallel of north latitude. He also reports the completion of that part of the line between Lake Tahoe and the Colorado River of the West, and that he is now engaged in the preparation of maps, &c.

2. *The northern boundary of Nevada.*—The field-work of this survey has been completed by Daniel G. Major, contractor, but the returns have not yet been received.

3. *The southern boundary of Wyoming.*—The survey of this line is being prosecuted in the field, but no returns have been received.

4. *The western boundary of Wyoming.*—Under the appropriation of $13,800, made by act of Congress approved March 3, 1873, the contract for the survey of this land has been let to Alonzo V. Richards.

5. *The western boundary of Kansas.*—The survey of this line has been completed, and the returns made and approved.

6. *The northern boundary of Nebraska.*—The contract for the survey of this line has been let, but owing to a fear on the part of the Indian Office that the prosecution of the work would excite the Indians and lead to difficulties, operations in the field have been delayed.

7. *The Washington and Idaho boundary line.*—The contract for the survey of this line was let on the 2d day of June, 1873, but no report of progress made by the contractors has been received.

8. *The northern part of the eastern boundary of New Mexico and the eastern part of the southern boundary of Colorado.*—Under the appropriation made by act of Congress approved March 3, 1873, the contract for the survey of these lines has been let to John J. Major, but returns have not been received.

4.—PRE-EMPTIONS.

The general pre-emption laws of September 4, 1841, March 3, 1843, March 3, 1853, and March 27, 1854, remain in force. The following act, entitled "An act for the relief of settlers on the late Sioux Indian reservation in the State of Minnesota," was approved February 24, 1873 :

Be it enacted by the Senate and House of Representatives of the United States of America in Congress assembled, That all actual settlers who have duly filed their declaratory statements under the pre-emption laws, with the register of the proper local land-office, upon the unsold lands now included within the limits of the late Sioux Indian reservation in the State of Minnesota, shall be allowed until the first day of March, anno Domini eighteen hundred and seventy-four, in which to make proof and payment for their claims.

March 3, 1873, "An act authorizing joint entry by pre-emption settlers, and for other purposes," was approved, and March 31 the following circular to the district land-office containing the law and instructions for its execution was issued by this Office:

DEPARTMENT OF THE INTERIOR,
General Land-Office, Washington, D. C., March 31, 1873.

To Registers and Receivers:

GENTLEMEN : Your attention is hereby called to the following act of Congress, approved March 3, 1873, and entitled "An act authorizing joint entry by pre-emption settlers, and for other purposes."

"*Be it enacted by the Senate and House of Representatives of the United States of America in Congress assembled,* That when settlements have been made upon agricultural public lands of the United States prior to the survey thereof, and it has been or shall be ascertained, after the public surveys have been extended over such lands, that two or more settlers have improvements upon the same legal subdivision, it shall be lawful for such settlers to make joint entry of their lands at the local land-office, or for either of said settlers to enter into contract with his co-settlers to convey to them their portion of said lands after a patent is issued to him, and after making said contract, to file a declaratory statement in his own name, and prove up and pay for said land, and proof of joint occupation by himself and others, and of such contract with them made shall be equivalent to proof of sole occupation and pre-emption by the applicant : *Provided,* That in no case shall the amount patented under this act exceed one hundred and sixty acres, nor shall this act apply to lands not subject to homestead or pre-emption entry.

"SEC. 2. That effect shall be given to this act by regulations to be prescribed by the Commissioner of the General Land-Office.

"Approved March 3, 1873."

Concerning your duties in the administration of the aforesaid act I have to advise you as follows, to wit:

When the survey in the field finds two or more settlers with improvements on the same legal subdivision, a joint entry thereof will be allowed as heretofore.

If they so elect, however, they may contract by and between themselves *only* that one of them may file for and enter the whole of such tract, and, after a patent is issued therefor to him, convey to the others their portion of said land.

Under the last-named provision it is necessary that the said contract be made *first*, and that the filing and entry shall both be made in pursuance thereof.

This contract must be made in writing, signed by all parties thereto, attested by two disinterested witnesses, and acknowledged before some officer authorized to take acknowledgments of deeds within and for the State where the land is situated. The character and authority of the officer must be verified by the seal of a court of record. You will make no reference to the contract until the party seeks to make actual entry, when you will require the original paper, or, if the same has been placed upon the records of the county, a duly certified copy thereof under seal will be sufficient.

You will require such proof of occupation by settlement, residence, and improvement, by each and every party to said contract, as would be sufficient under the former practice to justify a joint entry. Their good faith and compliance with law must be fully proven.

The proviso to section one is held to mean that not more than one hundred and sixty acres or a technical quarter-section, as allowed under the pre-emption laws, shall be included in any one entry. An inconsiderable excess, when the tract is bounded by regular quarter-section lines, will be permitted.

The act does not specify *what* improvements a settler must have on a legal subdivision, partly occupied by another, to entitle him to a joint entry. It is held, however, that each must have improvements of value, and not merely of a nominal character or extent, to warrant a proceeding under this act.

The pre-emption affidavit as written on page 17 in circular of August 30, 1872, will be amended, in cases where entry is made under this act, by inserting after the word "whomsoever," in the ninth (9th) line, the words "save under the act of March 3, 1873, and as specified in the contract herewith submitted in pursuance thereof."

You will in each case forward, with the entry papers, to this Office said original contract, or the certified copy from record as aforesaid.

You will perceive that the act refers only to pre-emptors on agricultural lands; and the word "homestead" in the last line of the proviso to the first section is used only in a descriptive sense. You will also observe that where either or any of the parties settle *after* survey no joint entry or proceeding under this act can be had.

Respectfully,

WILLIS DRUMMOND,
Commissioner.

Prior to said act, when two or more settlers were found, on survey in the field, with valuable improvements on the same smallest legal subdivision of forty acres, they were allowed, under rulings of the Department, to make joint entry of such tracts when such a course constituted the only equitable method of adjustment. Under this act settlers may unquestionably proceed with more certainty and avoid litigation, after issue of patent, in the matter of a division of the land so jointly entered.

An act entitled "An act to authorize pre-emptors or settlers upon homesteads on the public land to alienate portions of their pre-emptions or homesteads for certain public purposes," was approved March 3, 1873, and is as follows, to wit:

Be it enacted, &c., That any person who has already settled or hereafter may settle on the public lands of the United States, either by pre-emption or by virtue of the homestead law or any amendments thereto, shall have the right to transfer by warranty, against his or her own acts, any portion of his or her said pre-emption or homestead for church, cemetery, or school purposes, or for the right of way of railroads across such pre-emption or homestead, and the transfer for such public purposes shall in no way vitiate the right to complete and perfect the title to their pre-emptions or homesteads.

The periods within which settlers under the pre-emption laws must file their declaratory statements and make final proof and payment for their claims remain the same as at date of my last report.

The district land-officers are instructed to permit no pre-emption entry to be consummated until three months from and after the date of filing the township plat of survey in the district office shall have expired. Said period of three months is given pre-emptors who settle prior to the filing of the township plat, by statute, in which to file their declaratory statements.

The seventh section of the act of July 23, 1866, "An act to quiet land titles in California," has received new and more liberal construction by the Department proper. Said section provides—

That where persons in good faith and for a valuable consideration have purchased lands of Mexican grantees or assigns, which grants have subsequently been rejected, or where the lands so purchased have been excluded from the final survey of any Mexican grant, and have used, improved, and continued in the actual possession of the same according to the lines of their original purchase, and where no valid adverse right or title (except of the United States) exists, such purchasers may purchase the same, after having such lands surveyed under existing laws, at the minimum price established by law, &c.

In case of Sanford E. Wilson's application to purchase certain lands under said section, the Hon. Secretary of the Interior decided in substance—following the doctrine laid down by the Supreme Court of the United States in case of Myers vs. Croft, (13 Wallace, 291)—that the right of purchase secured thereby is alienable and descends to the heirs upon the death of the purchaser. Prior to said decision the contrary doctrine prevailed.

In case of L. H. Bascom vs. Moses Davis, in which Davis is a claimant under said seventh section, the Hon. Secretary of the Interior decides, in substance, that when parties bring themselves in other respects within the law, but fail to show use, improvement, and possession of all the land as according to the lines of their original purchase, they may purchase from the Government such portion of their original purchase as they have had in actual possession. These decisions constitute the precedents on which similar cases will hereafter be adjudicated.

Pursuant to my former recommendations, a bill for the repeal of the pre-emption laws received favorable action from both Houses of Congress at the last session, but at so late a date in the House of Representatives that the Senate was unable to act upon some slight amendments by the House, and it therefore failed to become a law.

The many frauds which occur under the pre-emption laws, almost universally in the interest of speculators; the fact that most liberal terms are provided under the homestead laws for such as desire to obtain title to the public lands in good faith for purposes of actual settlement and cultivation; that actual inhabitancy and improvement are worth more to the country than the excess of revenue derived from the sale to pre-emptors; that the policy of the Government is that these lands should be occupied, improved, and made to augment the productions of the country, and that under the pre-emption laws this object is substantially defeated, impel me, in view of the magnitude of the interests involved, to again urge the repeal of the several pre-emption acts, so that those who wish to obtain title to the public lands as actual settlers may be required to do so under the homestead laws.

5. SIOUX RESERVATION

The following act, entitled "An act for the relief of settlers on the late Sioux Indian reservation in the State of Minnesota," was approved February 24, 1873:

Be it enacted, &c., That all actual settlers who have heretofore filed declaratory statements under the pre-emption laws with the register of the proper local land-office upon the unsold lands now included within the limits of the late Sioux Indian reservation in the State of Minnesota, shall be allowed until the first day of March, anno Domini eighteen hundred and seventy-four, in which to make proof and payment for their claims.

6.—CHEROKEE STRIP IN KANSAS.

The act approved May 11, 1872, to carry out certain provisions of the Cherokee treaty of 1866, and for the relief of settlers on the Cherokee lands in the State of Kansas, recognized settlements existing at the date of said act, and such as should be made within one year thereafter. One year from the date of the approval by the Secretary of the Interior of the acceptance of the provisions of the act by the Cherokee national council, or a duly authorized delegation therefrom, was given for payment to settlers at the date of the act, and one year from date of settlement when the same was made subsequent to the approval of the act. By instructions from this Office three months from notice or settlement were allowed each claimant to file his declaratory statement. The period in which settlement was thus authorized expired May 11, 1873, and the time allowed for filing declaratory statements on the latest settlements ended August 11, 1873. Under said act there had been entered at the Independence and Wichita land-offices prior to September 1, 1873, 83,732.27 acres. There had been 1,416 declaratory statements filed at said offices August 11, 1873. The area of land embraced in said filings is not known. If each filing represents 160 acres, the total area filed for would be 226,560 acres. Inasmuch, however, as very many claims embraced less than 160 acres, the area actually covered by declaratory statements will doubtless be much less than said amount. The area which will be entered under the aforesaid provisions cannot be known prior to the receipt of the district land-officers' returns for May, 1874. But one town-site entry, that of Coffeyville, has been made on said lands.

7.—ROUND VALLEY INDIAN RESERVATION, IN MONTANA.

No entries have been made under the act of June 5, 1872, entitled "An act to provide for the removal of the Flathead and other Indians from the Bitter Root Valley, in the Territory of Montana."

By the terms of the act, Indians who at its passage were actually residing upon and cultivating any portion of said lands were allowed to remain in said valley and pre-empt without cost the land so occupied to the extent of 160 acres. The superintendent of Indian affairs in Montana not having furnished a list of said Indians so entitled, and whose claims must be ascertained before a disposition of lands to other claimants, the execution of the act is necessarily suspended.

The land has been surveyed, instructions furnished to the district land-officers, and nothing which this Office can do in the premises is wanting to carry the law into effect.

8.—HOMESTEAD LAW.

The demand for lands by actual settlers under the homestead law continues very large.

During the fiscal year ending June 30, 1873, 31,246 preliminary entries were made, covering an area of 3,752,347.26 acres. The number of final entries was 9,894, being an increase in final entries of 4,115 over the preceding fiscal year.

This law, with some slight amendments, would meet all the requirements and necessities of actual settlers, and I again respectfully renew my recommendation for a complete consolidation of all statutes respecting settlement rights into a general homestead law. A bill for that purpose met with favorable action from both Houses of the last Congress, but owing to a slight amendment, as to the time when it should take effect, by the House, on the last day of the session, in which the Senate had not time to concur, it failed to become a law.

9.—GRADUATED LANDS.

Since my last annual report Congress has passed the following act, confirming entries made under the act of August 4, 1854, graduating the price of public lands:

AN ACT to confirm certain entries of land therein named.

Be it enacted by the Senate and House of Representatives of the United States of America in Congress assembled, That all entries of public lands under the act to graduate and reduce the price of the public lands subject to entry to actual settlers and cultivators, approved the fourth day of August, eighteen hundred and fifty-four, made prior to the passage of this act, in which the purchaser has made the affidavit and paid or tendered the purchase money as required by said act, and the instructions issued and in force and in the hands of the register at the time of making said entry, are hereby legalized, and patents shall issue to the parties, respectively, provided that in case of tender the money shall be paid, excepting those entries under said act which the Commissioner of the General Land Office may ascertain to have been fraudulently or evasively made: *Provided,* That this act shall not be so construed as to confirm any of said entries which have heretofore been annulled and vacated by said Commissioner on account of fraud, evasion of law, or other special cause: *And provided further,* That nothing herein contained shall be so construed as to deprive any actual settler and cultivator of his right to any land on which he resided at the time of an entry by another person under the act to which this is an amendment.

Approved February 17, 1873.

Under this confirmatory act a large number of entries previously suspended, because of the failure of parties to make the required proof of settlement and cultivation, have been relieved from suspension, and patents are being delivered upon application in proper form.

10 USELESS MILITARY RESERVATIONS.

The act of Congress of February 24, 1871, provided for the disposition of the lands embraced in certain military reservations abandoned by the War Department, viz: Fort Lane, Oreg., estimated area 640 acres; Fort Walla Walla, Wash., 1,920 acres; Fort Jesup, La., 6,400 acres; Fort Sabine, La., 18,200 acres; Fort Smith, Ark., 306 acres; Fort Wayne, Ark., 11,680 acres; Fort Zarah, Kans., 3,068 acres; Fort Abercrombie, Minn., 6,993 acres; Camp McGarry, Nev., 75 square miles; Fort Sumner, N. Mex., 214 square miles; and so much of Fort Bridger, Wyo., as might be no longer required for military purposes.

At the date of my last annual report proceedings under said act were suspended .... of an appropriation to meet the necessary expenses.

The necessary ....

....

....

....

.... OF ...... LANDS.

....

....

President, at Saint Cloud, embracing the public lands in 113 townships, at Taylor's Falls, embracing the public lands in 10 townships; at Litchfield, embracing the public lands in 105 townships; and at Duluth, embracing the public lands in 49 townships.

12.—EDUCATIONAL LAND-BOUNTY.

The selections certified for common schools during the fiscal year ending June 30, 1873, amounted to 76,909.17 acres, and for seminaries 320 acres. The selections certified for agricultural colleges amounted to 15,976.21. The locations of agricultural college scrip by assignees of the States to which the same was issued, reported during the year cover an area of 653,446.41. Since my last annual report agricultural-college scrip representing 240,000 acres has been issued to the States of Arkansas and Florida. This exhausts the amount which Congress authorized.

13.—TIMBER DEPREDATIONS.

In administering the laws for disposing of the public lands, the depredations committed on the timber growing thereon has received attention. It is held that the United States, as owner of the lands, has all the legal means of protecting the timber which individuals enjoy in like cases. The act of Congress of March 2, 1831, as construed by the Supreme Court, makes the depredating on such timber a criminal offense, punishable with fine and imprisonment. The extent of the evil at an early period induced special efforts by the executive authority for its correction. In 1855 the matter was placed in charge of this Office for its supervision. The duty was imposed on the registers and receivers of the district land-offices to act as timber agents, without additional compensation, in their respective land-districts. When reliable information reaches them that spoliation of public timber is committed, their instructions require them to investigate the matter, to seize all timber found to have been cut without authority on the public land, to sell the same to the highest bidder at public auction, and deposit the proceeds in the Treasury. They are to bring the offense committed to the attention of the proper officers that the perpetrator may be arrested and held to answer as usual in criminal cases. In these proceedings, however, the purpose in view being merely to protect the rights of the Government, and not to indulge in vindictive prosecutions, due regard is had to the circumstances of each case; and, when these justify so doing, the district officers are authorized to compromise with the parties, on their paying any costs incurred and a reasonable stumpage for the timber, which is then released, and prosecution waived. By this course, although depredations continue, yet they are checked to some extent, and that without cost, it being made a rule that the expenses incurred shall not be permitted to exceed the money realized for the Treasury from the sales of timber seized, and stumpage paid in compromised cases.

14.—RAILROADS.

In the adjustment of land-grants for railroad purposes considerable progress has been made. In July, 1872, a division was organized to which all questions growing out of the adjustment of railroad grants are referred for examination. Prior to that time these questions had been adjusted in connection with other branches of business. This resulted in complications and delays which are obviated by the new arrangement.

The examination of settlers' claims in conflict with those of railroad companies forms a large part of the business of the new division.

Under the ruling of the Department made in 1871, known as the Boyd decision, this class of claims is largely increased.

By the former practice of treating all reversions of alternate sections within railroad limits as inuring to railroads, the only question relating to settlement likely to arise was determined by the date of its inception. If the settlement was made prior to withdrawal, and the requirements of the pre-emption law had been complied with, the claimant was permitted to acquire title. Upon his abandonment, at any period, of his right, the land passed to the use of the grant.

But since that decision the adjustment is no longer narrowed to the question of the right of the first settler, or homestead claimant, to consummate title. The time when the right of the railroad attached must be ascertained, and the right of the parties is to be determined by the exact status of the land at that time. If the party originating the claim still holds the right to consummate title, he is permitted to make an entry. If, however, he abandoned his claim prior to the time the railroad right attached, the lands are awarded to the railroad when it fully complies with the conditions of the grant. If the abandonment was subsequent to such time the land reverts to the United States and is again subject to appropriation under the pre-emption and homestead laws.

Hearings for the investigation of these conflicting claims have accordingly been ordered, and trials are in constant progress before district officers for their settlement. Upward of eleven hundred cases of conflict have been entered upon the dockets of this Office, of which about one-half have been decided during the year, and about one hundred have been examined and remanded for further hearing, the testimony not being sufficiently explicit to justify an award.

The Supreme Court of the United States, at the late December term, decided, in the case of the Kansas Pacific Railway Company vs. John H. Prescott, that the requirement of the act of July 2, 1864, providing for the payment of the costs of survey, extends to the lands granted by act of July 1, 1862, within ten miles of the Pacific Railroad and branches. Modified instructions to meet this construction of the law have been issued.

During the fiscal year ending June 30, 1873, 6,083,536 acres of land have been certified for railroad purposes, an increase over the amount certified the previous year of 2,528,649 acres.

The records of the Office show an aggregate construction of two thousand two hundred and seventy-eight miles of road, distributed as follows: in Michigan, one hundred and eighty-six miles; Wisconsin, eighty-nine miles; Iowa, fifty miles; Minnesota, seven hundred and twelve miles; Missouri, ninety-seven miles; Kansas, four hundred and sixty-four miles; Arkansas, two hundred and forty miles; California, forty miles; Colorado, two hundred and forty-five miles; Indian Territory, one hundred and fifty-five miles; total as above, two thousand two hundred and seventy-eight miles.

Portions of the roads included in the foregoing report of construction were actually completed prior to the commencement of the last fiscal year. This report will be understood as referring more particularly to the official record of construction, and to the acceptance by the proper

authorities, the evidence of which has been received at this Office since my last annual report, and consequently was not included therein.

During the previous year the reports show a constructed length of one thousand seven hundred and forty-three miles of road, a difference in favor of the latter year of five hundred and thirty-five miles.

The policy of extending aid to railroad enterprise by national legislation having been restricted by the caution of Congress during the last few years, the aggregate of definite location of new roads is not as great as in former years. The reports show the definite location of three hundred and twenty-three miles during the fiscal year, of which two hundred miles are of the Northern Pacific Railroad, in the Territory of Dakota.

In their appropriate place in this report will be found carefully prepared tables, showing the condition of the adjustment for the various land-grant roads up to the close of the fiscal year.

15.—OPERATIONS UNDER THE MINING LAWS.

Since the date of my last report the fifth section of the mining act. of May 10, 1872, has been amended, and the following circular issued:

"The following is an act of Congress approved March 1, 1873, (17 Stat., 483 :)

"'AN ACT to amend an act entitled "An act to promote the development of the mining resources of the United States."

"'Be it enacted by the Senate and House of Representatives of the United States of America in Congress assembled, That the provisions of the fifth section of the act entitled "An act to promote the development of the mining resources of the United States," passed May tenth, eighteen hundred and seventy-two, which requires expenditures of labor and improvements on claims located prior to the passage of said act, are hereby so amended that the time for the first annual expenditure on claims located prior to the passage of said act shall be extended to the tenth day of June, eighteen hundred and seventy-four.'

"By this legislation the requirements of the fifth section of the act of May 10, 1872, are changed by extending the time for the first annual expenditure upon claims located prior to May 10, 1872, to June 10, 1874.

"The requirements in regard to expenditures upon claims located since May 10, 1872, are in no way changed."

The following act of Congress was approved February 18, 1873, (17 Stat., 465 :)

AN ACT in relation to mineral lands.

Be it enacted by the Senate and House of Representatives of the United States of America in Congress assembled, That within the States hereinafter named deposits or mines of iron and coal be, and they are hereby, excluded from the operations of an act entitled "An act to promote the development of the mining resources of the United States," approved May tenth, eighteen hundred and seventy-two, and said act shall not apply to the mineral lands situate and being within the States of Michigan, Wisconsin, and Minnesota, and that said lands are hereby declared free and open to exploration and purchase according to the legal subdivisions thereof, as before the passage of said act; and that any bona-fide entries of such lands, within said States, since the passage thereof, may be patented without reference to the provisions of said act.

Previous to the date of said mining act of 1872, lands containing deposits of iron ore were disposed of for cash at private entry the same as agricultural lands. The language of the mining act, however, is so comprehensive as to justify the belief that it was the intention of Congress to include iron ore among the mineral deposits to be disposed of under its provisions. Congress by subsequent legislation appears to have placed this construction upon the act.

By the act approved February 18, 1873, it is provided that deposits of nitrate of soda in Michigan, Wisconsin, and Minnesota shall be excluded from the operation of the act of May 10, 1872. This is in effect saying that prior to that time deposits of mines of iron and lead subject to the operations of said act in these States, and that they remain subject to the operations in the States not specifically named. Lands chargeable only valuable on account of veins or deposits of iron than for agriculture can be entered only under the mining acts of Congress.

*   *   *   *   *   *   *

PRIVATE LAND CLAIMS.

CALIFORNIA.

Much difficulty has been experienced by this Office in determining questions of fact connected with the location of private land-claims in California, for the reason that under former practice and regulations testimony was taken and submitted in the form of ex-parte affidavits, which often served rather to confuse than explain the matters in controversy.

*   *   *   *   *   *   *

Among the rulings which have been made during the past year, and which affect a number of claims not adjudicated, are the following:

Rancho Guadalupe, Diego Olivera and T. Arellanes, confirmees.—In this case it was decided by this Office:

1st. That a newspaper dated and first distributed in the town of Santa Barbara, in Santa Barbara County, Cal., was published in Santa Barbara, although said paper was printed in San Francisco, Cal.

2d. Where a survey had become final by publication under the act of June 14, 1860, and a patent in accordance with such survey had been duly signed, sealed, recorded, sent to the United States surveyor-general for delivery, subsequently recalled, a new survey made, published in accordance with the provision of the act of July 1, 1864, (13 Stat., p. 332,) approved by the Commissioner of the General Land-Office, and a patent for such resurvey signed, sealed, recorded, transmitted to the United States surveyor-general for delivery, and recalled without the consent of the parties claiming possession thereof, that in such a case the first patent having been legally executed, was the patent to be delivered to the parties in interest, and that said first patent having been legally executed, there was no authority of law for the issue of the subsequent patent, which was void *ab initio*, and might properly be recalled by the Commissioner of the General Land Office.

Affirmed on appeal March 26, 1873.

Rancho La Brea, confirmed to Antonio Jose Rocha et al.—In this case this Office held that it had jurisdiction to examine the validity of the conveyances of a rancho, so far as to be enabled to decide who, under such conveyances, was entitled to select the quantity of land confirmed within larger exterior boundaries to the claimant or claimants by the board of land commissioners for California, or United States courts.

Affirmed on appeal March 21, 1873.

Rancho La Cachenegra, William Forster, confirmee.—In this case a portion of the rancho as granted, conflicted with the boundaries of the Rancho Cañada del Rincon, which had been confirmed and patented by the United States. Both ranchos were for quantity within a larger exterior and prior to confirmation the title in each case was confirmable only.

the claimant of neither having received juridical possession from the Mexican authorities. The record showed that the Rancho La Carbonera had the older grant, and under the doctrine of relation as laid down in Grisar *vs.* McDowell, (6 Wall., 380,) and Lynch *vs.* Bernal, (9 Wall., 315,) it had also the older confirmation. The Supreme Court of the United States having also ruled, in United States *vs.* Amijo, (5 Wall., 444,) that the right of selection could not be exercised so as to defeat the equitable prior rights of others, it was held by this Office that La Carbonera having the older grant and confirmation, had the prior equity, and was therefore first entitled to select its quantity of land, and that for the land thus selected within its exterior boundaries and interfering with the Rancho Cañada del Rincon a patent should issue reciting said interference.

Affirmed May 21, 1873.

Mission La Purisima, José Ramon Malo, confirmee.—In this case it was decided on appeal that the first section of the act of June 14, 1860, relative to the publication of notice of surveys for four weeks in two newspapers, required that for some part of the four weeks the notice should be simultaneously publishing in both newspapers.

* * * * * *

During the year ending June 30, 1873, the surveys of twenty-three private land-claims were received from the United States surveyor-general for California, and during the same period forty-two patents for similar claims were prepared by this Office, and transmitted, for delivery, to the parties in interest.

NEW MEXICO, COLORADO, AND ARIZONA.

I have the honor again to call attention to the condition of private land-claims in the remainder of the territory acquired by the treaty of Guadalupe Hidalgo, and also to similar claims located in the territory, acquired by the treaty commonly known as the Gadsden purchase. Some provision for the speedy adjustment of these claims should be made at an early day, so that parties, whose rights are guaranteed by treaty, may be enabled to obtain a United States title to their possessions, as in the case of like claims in California, and the United States be given an opportunity to show the invalidity of such claims as may now be held under fraudulent Mexican or Spanish grants.

* * * * * *

By a decision dated July 29, 1872, in the matter of John B. Chapman's donation claim in Washington Territory, it was held by this Office that, although settlement was made in good faith in June, 1851, and inhabitation and the other requirements of the law complied with up to June, 1852, yet the claimant, Chapman, had now no title thereto, either legal or equitable, it appearing by the evidence produced that at the date last named he left Washington Territory with the intention of abandoning his claim, and that for a period of nearly eighteen years thereafter he neither resided on nor asserted title to the tract thus abandoned. In affirming this decision, the Hon. Secretary of the Interior, in his letter of May 23d, 1873, remarks: "I agree with you in the conclusion at which you have arrived, (that Chapman abandoned his claim when he left the Territory in the summer of 1852, and forfeited all right therein he then had or might have acquired.")

* * * * * *

A large number of donation claims in the State of Oregon, and in Washington Territory, have been examined, and five hundred and four of such claims have been patented during the year ending June 30, 1873, and it is believed that before the close of the year ending June 30, 1874, the arrears of work on this class of claims in the General Land-Office will have been brought up to date.

I am, sir, very respectfully your obedient servant,

WILLIS DRUMMOND,
Commissioner.

The Hon. SECRETARY OF THE INTERIOR.

REPORT OF THE COMMISSIONER OF INDIAN AFFAIRS.

DEPARTMENT OF THE INTERIOR,
OFFICE OF INDIAN AFFAIRS,
November 1, 1873.

I have the honor, in accordance with law, to forward herewith the annual report of Indian affairs of the country.

In respect to the general question of civilization of Indians, the record of the year is a good one. In many of the agencies gratifying progress has been made, as shown in increased interest in the education of children, a disposition to labor, the desire for allotment of lands, and in the increase of stock and ordinary farm products, and other personal property. At other agencies serious efforts in the same direction have developed more decidedly the difficulties which lie in the way of progress. Among these hinderances six are specially noticeable.

FICTION IN INDIAN RELATIONS.

First. A radical hinderance is in the anomalous relation of many of the Indian tribes to the Government, which requires them to be treated as sovereign powers and wards at one and the same time. The comparative weakness of the whites made it expedient, in our early history, to deal with the wild Indian tribes as with powers capable of self-protection and fulfilling treaty obligations, and so a kind of fiction and absurdity has come into all our Indian relations. We have in theory over sixty-five independent nations within our borders, with whom we have entered into treaty relations as being sovereign peoples; and at the same time the white agent is sent to control and supervise these foreign powers, and care for them as wards of the Government. This double condition of sovereignty and wardship involves increasing difficulties and absurdities, as the traditional chieftain, losing his hold upon his tribe, ceases to be distinguished for anything except for .the lion's share of goods and moneys which the Government endeavors to send, through him, to his nominal subjects, and as the necessities of the Indians, pressed on every side by civilization, require more help and greater discrimination in the manner of distributing the tribal funds. So far, and as rapidly as possible, all recognition of Indians in any other relation than strictly as subjects of the Government should cease. To provide for this, radical legislation will be required.

EVILS OF PAYMENTS BY CASH ANNUITIES.

The second hinderance, growing directly out of the first, is found in the form in which the benefactions of the Government reach the Indian. In treaties heretofore made with many of the tribes, large sums are stipulated to be paid in cash annuities.   Facts show that ordinarily the Indians who have received the most money in this form are in the most unfavorable condition for civilization.   The bounty of the Government has pauperized them, and in some cases has tended to brutalize more than to civilize.   There are instances where for many years tribes have been receiving from $300 to $500 cash annually to each family of four or five persons, and in all such cases the Indians have made no use of the soil which they possess, and are annually reduced to extreme want within a short time after receiving annuities.   These Indians would probably have been far better off to have had only their lands, out of which they might have dug a living, if compelled by hunger, than to have received this bounty in a form that tends to perpetuate idleness and poverty.   I recommend that hereafter the appropriations to fulfill these promises for annuities of cash in hand be made for the same amounts, to be expended, in each case, under the direction of the Secretary of the Interior, for purposes of civilization of the tribe, reserving to the discretion of the Secretary the power to pay cash annuities whenever, in his judgment, it is found expedient.

If the objection should be made that this is a violation of a treaty stipulation, the answer is, that the Government is bound to consider the best interests of its wards.   And if, in previous years, wrong methods have been adopted, or if the present condition and exigencies require a different method of dealing with the Indians in order to secure their improvement and greatest good, then both justice and humanity require that the change be made.

A satisfactory experiment of this method has been made under a treaty with the Sisseton and Wahpeton Sioux, in accordance with which the moneys paid to these tribes, in payment for their lands sold to the Government, have been expended in goods and provisions, which have been issued to Indians only in return for labor on their part, the labor being, in most cases, for themselves; and thus a threefold benefit has been procured.   They have actually received the value of the money; they have received the products of their own labor, and, best of all, they have learned to labor.   If a similar use can be made of sums of money now paid to vagrant Indians, and practically squandered by them within a few days, a large incentive to industry will be gained.

WANT OF INDIVIDUAL PROPERTY-RIGHTS.

The third hinderance is found in the want of individual property-rights among Indians.   A fundamental difference between barbarians and a civilized people is the difference between a herd and an individual.   All barbarous customs tend to destroy individuality.   Where everything is held in common, thrift and enterprise have no stimulus of reward, and thus individual progress is rendered very improbable, if not impossible.   The starting-point of individualism for an Indian is the personal possession of his portion of the reservation.   Give him a house within a tract of land, whose corner-stakes are plainly recognized by himself and his neighbors, and let whatever can be produced out of this landed estate be considered property in his own name, and the first principle of industry and thrift is recognized.   In order to this first step, the survey and allotment in severalty of the lands belonging to the Indians must be provided for by congressional legislation.

LAW AMONG INDIANS.

The fourth hinderance is the absence of law for Indians.   The first condition of civilization is protection of life and property through the administration of law. As the Indians are taken out of their wild life they leave behind them the force attaching to the distinctive tribal condition. The chiefs inevitably lose their power over Indians in proportion as the latter come in contact with the Government or with white settlers, until their government becomes, in most cases, a mere form, without power of coercion and restraint. Their authority is founded only on "the consent of the governed," and only as they pander to the whims or vices of the young men of the tribe can they gain such consent. As a police restraint upon lawlessness they are of no avail, being themselves subject to the control of the worst element in the tribe. An Indian murdering another Indian is accountable only to the law of retaliation. The State authorities do not concern themselves in punishing the murders among Indians, even when such murder is committed under the shadow of their criminal courts.

I submit, for the consideration of the honorable Secretary, whether it is not necessary that crimes among Indians shall be defined by United States law; and made punishable before United States courts, or whether it may not be practicable to invest magisterial powers in agents and superintendents, by which they may summon a jury among the Indians or other persons residing at the agencies by authority of law, before whom any serious offense against law and order may be tried. Such a court would be the beginning of administration of justice, out of the workings of which would gradually grow a code of laws, which would cover these cases arising in the Indian country, and come to be enforced by a police among themselves.

At the same time, ample provision should be made for the prosecution of citizens who attempt to encroach upon the rights of Indians, or to debauch them by the sale of intoxicating liquors. The employment of detectives, through the Department of Justice, has worked satisfactorily, so far as the limited appropriation of last year has allowed. The difficulty of securing conviction of parties who are known to be engaged in selling whisky to Indians, makes the prosecution, when attempted by the agent alone, expensive and more frequently unsuccessful. In order to induce information and secure efficiency in these prosecutions, I recommend that such legislation be procured as will insure to the informant all fines arising from conviction under the law.

REFUSAL OF INDIANS TO REMAIN ON RESERVATIONS.

The fifth hinderance, the persistent refusal of a portion of some of the tribes to remain upon their reservation according to treaty, has been mainly experienced with five tribes, viz, the Sioux, Arapahoes, Cheyennes, Kiowas, and Comanches. A portion of the Arapahoes and Cheyennes are identified with the Sioux in their depredations. The remainder are living on a reservation in the Indian Territory.

SIOUX.

The actual depredations committed by the Sioux have been comparatively few, but a portion of the tribe have assumed a hostile attitude toward the Government by attacking the surveying expedition on the Northern Pacific Railroad. According to the best information of this office, the greater number of Indians engaged in these hostilities were a band of Northern Sioux, who have hitherto declined to treat with the Government, and with them a large re-enforcement from different agencies along the Missouri River, as also from Spotted Tail's and Red

Cloud's camps. There is no doubt that the majority of the Indians whom General Stanley encountered in Dakota have been at different times in the year on reservations, and have drawn rations from the Government, some occasionally and some regularly. It is to be regretted that these hostiles could not have been met and defeated by military force. Their actual punishment, in the loss of four or five warriors, was so slight that they seem to regard it at least a drawn fight, if not a victory on their side. The Sioux at Red Cloud and Spotted Tail agencies have also assumed impudent manners and made hostile threats, which have prevented the proper administration of agency affairs. It has been impossible for the agents to issue rations upon actual count of lodges, the Indians refusing to have a count made, and demanding the issue of rations upon the returns brought in by themselves. The agents, not having a force at hand to restrain the demands of the Indians, have been obliged to yield, and, as a consequence, there has often been over-issue, and the Indians have grown bold by successful resistance to authority. Such a course of treatment is unwise and unsafe.

Hitherto the military have refrained from going on this reservation because of the express terms of the treaty with the Sioux, in which it is agreed that no military force shall be brought over the line. I respectfully recommend that provision be made at once for placing at each of the Sioux reservations a military force sufficient to enable the agents to enforce respect for their authority, and to conduct agency affairs in an orderly manner. Also, that all Sioux Indians be required to remain on the Sioux reservation, and that any found off, or refusing to come in and treat with the Government, be forced in and brought to obedience by the military. I am confident that steady progress towards civilization is being made at the different agencies among the Sioux, and, if the turbulent element of this nation can be subdued, the question whether they can be induced to live quietly and to adopt habits of civilization, so as to become self-supporting, will be one only of time and patience.

If it should become necessary to reduce the hostile portion of these Sioux to submission by military force, the Government will find faithful and efficient allies in the several Indian tribes around, the Crows, Black Feet, Gros Ventres, and Arickarees. From these Indians a sufficient number of scouts can be enlisted to break the power of the Sioux Nation.

ARAPAHOES AND CHEYENNES.

The attempt is being made to induce the Northern Arapahoes and Cheyennes to join their respective tribes in the Indian Territory. Those now in the Territory are affiliated to such a degree as to be in one agency, and to occupy together the same reservation. They number 3,500. The union of the northern tribes with them would swell the number to 4,500. There is also a portion of the Cheyennes living upon the staked plains which have never yet come in. They subsist entirely on buffalo, and plunder in Colorado, Mexico, and Texas. Not a little of the raiding in Texas which has been charged upon the Kiowas and Comanches during the past year has been done by these Cheyennes. A company of surveyors, four in number, were murdered by them upon their reservation in June last. The demand made upon the tribe to surrender the murderers has not been complied with, and it is not impossible that, if the Government proceeds to enforce compliance, war will result.

47 Ab

KIOWAS AND COMANCHES.

The Kiowas and Comanches are affiliated in like manner as the Arapahoes and Cheyennes, occupying a common reservation with the same agency. The conduct of the Kiowas during the past year has been comparatively exemplary, under promise of receiving their chiefs Satanta and Big Tree. These prisoners were in the executive control of the governor of Texas, and, on account of the peculiar atrocity of the crimes of which they were convicted, there was strong opposition on the part of the citizens of Texas to their release. But the pledge of the Government having been given to the Kiowas, and the Kiowas having reason to expect its fulfillment because of their own good conduct for the year past, an appeal was made to the courtesy of the governor of Texas to relieve the Government from its embarrassment by the release of the prisoners; and a pledge was made that the Government would use every means to protect the border of Texas, and would require the Comanches to surrender a certain number of raiders from their tribe who have been depredating in Texas during the past summer. Governor Davis accepted the pledge of the Government, in lieu of the further retention of the chiefs as a means of procuring safety for the citizens of Texas, and Satanta and Big Tree were sent to their tribe. The following day the Comanches were brought into council and required to surrender five (5) of their raiders. The chiefs did not deny that some of their young men had been raiding in Texas, nor that they had been committing theft and murder, but they declared it to be impossible for them to arrest and surrender the marauders, and desired to have one more trial in the way of peace. This I declined to give, except on the conditions already made with the governor of Texas, that the raiders should be surrendered. Some of the Comanches then volunteered to accompany the cavalry into Texas to arrest some of their own tribe whom they knew to be engaged at that time in plunder. A cavalry force was at once sent out, with these Indians enlisted as scouts. But they were unable to find the raiders, and returned without any prisoners to surrender in compliance with the requirement made upon them. The conduct of the Comanches is especially flagrant because of their solemn pledge, made one year ago and renewed in July, not to raid any more, on which their captive women and children were surrendered to them.

But it is a serious problem how to punish the guilty ones without striking the innocent. It is also certain that, on the opening of hostilities, a large portion of the tribe would leave the agency and take to the plains, when the difficulty of reaching and controlling them by military force becomes greatly increased. It is believed, however, that there is no alternative. The reservation cannot be made a refuge for thieves and murderers. No policy can assume the name of peace and kindness that expressly provides for immunity of crime. If the military force cannot be made strong enough to follow these Indians whenever they leave the reservation, and strike them while in the act of depredating. then the whole tribe, on refusal to surrender guilty parties, must be held responsible. And while there will be a loss of results already reached in gathering around the agencies these Indians from the plains, and many innocent ones will perhaps suffer with the guilty, yet I am persuaded that vigorous treatment will be kindness in the end. An attempt to restrain and punish the turbulent element in these three different tribes, to be successful, will require a larger military force than merely to strike their camps, destroying them in part, and scattering the remainder on the plains; but the Government can better afford to use a larger force than to undertake a warfare after the savage method of indiscriminate slaughter of women and children.

INTERTRIBAL WARFARE.

Intertribal warfare presents a sixth hinderance in the way of civilization. In view of the hostilities among the different tribes of Indians, and the frequent attacks by some of the tribes, requiring a constant state of defense on the part of others, an order has been issued that no Indians be allowed to leave their reservation without permit from the agent, and the Secretary of War has been requested to direct the commanders of military posts to prevent Indians from passing from one agency to another without such permit; and if they find Indians marauding, or engaged in any hostile expedition against any other tribe, to strike them without parley. A satisfactory execution of this arrangement will probably require either an increased enlistment of scouts from friendly Indians, or an increased military force in the different portions of the Indian country.

On account of their massacre of the Pawnees during the last buffalo hunt in Nebraska, the Sioux have been forbidden to leave their reservation for such hunting. This prohibition is likely to cause complaint and dissatisfaction among the Indians, but the increasing annoyance and peril from wandering Indians in Nebraska seem to justify the office in making the violation of their treaty by the Sioux the occasion of prohibiting their hunting in Nebraska hereafter; and I recommend that this matter be laid before Congress, in order that this prohibition may be enforced, by declaring that that portion of the treaty of 1868, allowing them to hunt within a certain range of country where buffalo are found, be rendered null and void by the act of the Sioux in attacking the Pawnees, and also by their refusal to surrender the members of their tribe who are guilty, while marauding off their reservation, of the wanton murder of the Hall family.

ISSUE OF ARMS AND AMMUNITION.

In several instances tribes entirely friendly to Government and well disposed to civilization have been kept in terror by their marauding neighbors, and prevented from attempting civilized life during the year. In such instances, if the friendly Indians could have been armed they would have defended themselves without assistance from the United States, and I recommend that steps be taken to procure legislation authorizing the Secretary of War to issue arms and ammunition for the self-protection of friendly tribes, on the request of this office, such arms to be accounted for by the agent to whom they are delivered.

MANUAL LABOR SCHOOLS.

Upon no other subject or branch of the Indian service is there such entire agreement of opinion from all agents and persons, connected directly and indirectly with Indian civilization, as upon the necessity of labor schools for Indian children. It is manifest that barbarism can be cured only by education. Instruction in the day-school merely, except among Indians who are already far along in civilization, is attempted at great disadvantage on every hand. Indian children cannot come from the wigwam suitably clad for the school-room. If clothes are provided for them the supply must be frequently repeated. The habits also of wigwam life are entirely irregular. The Indian has no regular habits or hours. He eats and sleeps when and where he will or can, and no school attendance, which depends upon regular home habits of the parents or children, can be relied upon. It is also well nigh impossible to teach Indian children the English language when they spend twenty hours out of the twenty-four in the wigwam, using only their native tongue. The boarding school, on the contrary, takes the youth under constant care, has him always at hand, and surrounds him by an English-speaking community, and above all, gives him instruction in the first lessons of civilization, which can be found only in a well-ordered home.

Any plan for civilization which does not provide for training the young, even though at a largely increased expenditure, is short-sighted and expensive. A large expenditure for a few years in the proper direction will be more economical than a smaller expenditure perpetuated; and it is believed that at least one-half of the Indian children, now growing up in barbarism, could be put during the coming year in such processes of education in home schools, if the means were at hand for supporting such schools. Four or five years of this appliance of civilization cures one-half of the barbarism of the Indian tribe permanently. For these children thus trained, though many of them might lapse into nomadic ways, would never go back so far as to be dangerous or troublesome to the citizens of the Government, and within that length of time it is reasonable to be expected that the other tribes, whose children could not at first be obtained for such schools, will be brought within the reach of the Government, and thus be ready to receive their turn at this training process. I most earnestly recommend that this appropriation for education be made on a scale commensurate with the urgent necessities of the case.

CO-OPERATION WITH RELIGIOUS SOCIETIES.

The arrangement by which, in accordance with the direction of the President, all agents are appointed on the nomination of some religious body is working with increasing satisfaction. In proportion as these religious societies gain assurance that this plan of co-operation with the Government is likely to be permanent, they are generally entering heartily into operations that contemplate earnest educational and religious work in the respective agencies allotted them. They are also learning from experience what are the essential qualifications of an Indian agent, and also the serious nature of the responsibility to the Government which they assume in these nominations. The result is a greater care in the selection of men, and increased watchfulness over their official actions. Out of the sixty-five agents thus nominated there have been several failures during the year, from want of adaptation to the service, or from want of integrity. But in nearly every case the religious society represented by these men has been the first to make the discovery of unfitness, and to ask for a change of agents.

INADEQUATE SALARIES.

There is a serious complaint on the part of these religious bodies that they are not able, at the salary of $1,500, to find competent men willing to accept the service, and that when such men have been secured it has often been found impossible to retain them. The service has lost several of the most competent and reliable agents during the year from this cause. No man capable of managing the business of an agency ranging from $15,000 to $200,000 ought to be asked to give full service to the Government for $1,500 a year. I recommend that the salary of agents be increased to $2,000 per annum for the more eastern agencies, and $2,500 for those remote and inaccessible.

CONDITIONS OF PROGRESS.

In estimating the actual progress attained, under the operation of what has been termed the peace policy, it is necessary to keep in mind the constant change in the position of the Indians toward the white settlers. Tribes which a few years ago were so far removed from all white settlements as to render any annoyance or conflict between the two races improbable and almost impossible, have now, by the tide of emigration, been brought in close proximity to, and almost daily contact with, settlers. Naturally the difficulties in the Indian problem are largely increased by such contact. The clashing interests of both parties produce irritation and make complaints more numerous.

But the peace policy is not to be charged with these increasing troubles, nor to be connnected with them except by the inquiry as to what would probably have been the difficulties, in the same circumstances, under any other policy.

The question of the civilization of Indians reduced to its last analysis is twofold. First, whether the Government is willing to make sufficient appropriation to teach barbarous men how to live in a civilized way; and, second, whether the expenditure of such an appropriation can be fairly made through the administration of persons fitted to become their teachers. Without suitable provision for the necessary expenditures the best efforts of the best men will be comparatively futile; and with the most abundant provision that the resources of the nation can make, nothing will be accomplished worthy of the effort unless there can be found persons ready and fitted to go to these Indians, in the spirit of kindness and Christian love, with a faith in God and a faith in man strong enough to sustain them amid the degradation and perversities of barbarism, and cheer them on in the full conviction that no being made in God's image is incapable of improvement. No effort for lifting the poor and degraded can succeed which is not guided by the enthusiasm which comes from this faith. The agent and his employés will not give full work without it, and the Indian will not throw off his suspicion and wake out of his indolence until he feels this touch of human sympathy.

For this reason the Government is specially to be congratulated on the response which the Christian people of the country have made to the proposition of the President that they should take a certain supervision of Government labor for the Indians, by nominating agents and furnishing employés suitable to represent the Government in its beneficent efforts with these tribes, as well as in sending missionaries and teachers for religious labor among them.

THE INDIAN TERRITORY.

The affairs of this Territory will doubtless receive the serious consideration of Congress during the coming session. The practical absence of law as between the inhabitants of the Territory and the citizens of the United States; the general state of unthrift from lack of competition and every incitement to labor incident to ordinary life in this country; the unwillingness of the Indians to take their lands in severalty; the persistent refusal of the Choctaws to give negroes their rights as citizens of the Territory, together with the strong pressure from parties interested in railroad enterprises and investments in lands, will be quite likely to induce legislation of some kind for this country.

If the inhabitants of the Territory would adopt the Okmulgee constitution with the amendments suggested by the President, upon this a satisfactory government could be created for this country. Then if the Indians would have their lands surveyed and allotted to them in severalty, the first steps toward citizenship would be fairly taken. Every consideration of justice seems to require that the treaty obligation which the Government has assumed toward these nations shall be observed. No circumstances can be supposed to exist that will justify the nullification of these obligations, but if it is found, on careful examination, that the highest interests of both the United States and the Indian nations of this Territory require a change in their relations which is not provided for by the different treaties, then the question is fairly raised whether the Government may not assume the responsibility of making the changes in such form as shall secure every right which these Indians can reasonably ask for themselves, and as will also commend itself to the moral sense of the country. The attempt to administer justice for all the Territory through the United States courts at Fort Smith has been largely a failure, and sometimes worse. If the adoption of a territorial constitution by the Indians does not provide a remedy, then a United States court should be established, at some convenient point in the Territory, to take cognizance of all cases of complaint arising between the citizens of the United States and inhabitants of the Territory, and between members of the different tribes and nations in the Territory.

MISSON INDIANS IN SOUTHERN CALIFORNIA.

Special attention is invited to the report of John G. Ames, who was appointed a special commissioner to inquire into the condition and necessities of the Mission Indians in Southern California. These Indians, under the Mexican government, enjoyed civil and property rights, and were abundantly able to take care of themselves from the products of the soil. But under our Government these rights were not considered as transferred, and they now find themselves liable to have the lands which they have cultivated for generations taken from them by white settlers. It would seem that there is no alternative, in any just settlement with these Indians, but to secure for them, in the way proposed in the report of Agent Ames, the land to which they are entitled, or its equivalent, upon which they will be able to subsist themselves without help from the Government.

WEAVING.

The effort during the year to instruct the Indian women among the Chippewas in Wisconsin and Minnesota in the art of weaving has already succeeded so far as to make it certain that, by the introduction of looms among all Indians where the herding of sheep is practicable, a new industry may be brought within the reach of the Indians, which will be of large service in the slow process of civilization.

ARICKAREES, MANDANS, AND GROS VENTRES.

An attempt has been made to induce the Arickarees, Mandans, and Gros Ventres, who occupy the reservation at Fort Berthold, to remove to the Indian Territory, but they have declined to send a delegation to prospect for the tribe, and seem averse to removal from their present grounds, where they are exposed to raids from the Sioux, and their crops are alternately cut off by the grasshopper and the drought. Their crops generally this year are reported as a failure, and it is not unlikely that, without help through a deficiency appropriation, they will suffer severely during the winter. The Indians on these agencies deserve more from the Government than any other tribes in Dakota, on account of their fidelity to the Government and the faithful service rendered by them as scouts in compelling other Indians to keep the peace.

MINNESOTA CHIPPEWAS.

The wandering bands of Chippewas in Minnesota require the attention of the Government. There are two permanent reservations in the State, at Leech Lake and White Earth, and the different bands remaining among the settlements of Pembina and Otter-Tail should be gathered upon the White Earth reservation. For these bands the Government has acquired, by purchase from the Mississippi Chippewas, the right to settle upon this reservation; but in order to establish them there a special appropriation will be required. The appropriation of $10,000, made by last Congress for the removal of the Pembinas, being too limited for the purpose, has not been used.

The Mille Lac band of Chippewas in Minnesota remains in its anomalous position. They have sold their reservation, retaining a right to occupy it during good behavior. With this title to the soil it is not deemed expedient to attempt permanent improvements at Mille Lac, unless a title to the reservation can be returned to them on condition that they surrender to Government all moneys acquired in consideration of their cession of the Mille Lac reservation. If this cannot be done, their Indians should be notified that they belong at White Earth, and be required to remove. In their present location, on its present tenure, nothing can be done looking toward their civilization.

UTES.

In consideration of the condition of the scattered bands of different tribes of Utes in Nevada, Colorado, and Utah, it was deemed advisable to send a commission to inquire as to their numbers and the possibility of gathering them upon one or more reservations, where they would be more immediately under the care of the Government, and removed from the white settlers. Agent G. W. Ingalls and Major J. W. Powell were appointed on this commission. They seem to have adopted the exhaustive method, and the interesting report of their labors for the summer is herewith submitted, and attention invited to their recommendations, which are heartily indorsed by this office.

THE CAUSES WHICH LED TO THE MODOC WAR.

October 14, 1864, a treaty was concluded with the Klamath and Modoc tribes and Yahooskin band of Snake Indians in Oregon, by the first article of which said Indians ceded to the United States all their right, title, and claim to all the country claimed by them, and accepted a reservation described in said article by natural boundaries, upon which they agreed and bound themselves to locate immediately after the ratification of the treaty.

The ratification of this treaty was advised and consented to by the Senate, July 2, 1866, and the same was proclaimed by the President February 17, 1870. At the date of proclamation the Modocs were found on their reservation, where they remained until April, 1870, and then left for their camp on Lost River.

There is evidence that Captain Jack and his band were prepared at this time to remain upon the reservation and settle down in the way of civilization, if there had been ordinary encouragement and assistance, and if the Klamaths, who largely outnumbered Captain Jack's band, and who were their hereditary enemies, had allowed them so to do. This band began to split rails for their farms, and in other ways to adopt civilized habits; but the Klamaths demanded tribute from them for the land they were occupying, which the Modocs were obliged to render. Captain Jack then removed to another part of the reservation, and began again to try to live by cultivating the ground. But he was followed by the same spirit of hostility by the Klamaths, from which he does not seem to have been protected by the agent. The issue of rations seems also to have been suspended for want of funds, and for these reasons Captain Jack and his band returned to their old home on Lost River, where they became a serious annoyance to the whites, who had in the meanwhile settled on their ceded lands.

This annoyance led to serious apprehensions on the part of the military authorities, and under date of the 19th of March, 1872, the honorable Secretary of War transmitted to this Department copies of correspondence between the military in regard to the matter. A copy of this correspondence was sent to Superintendent Odeneal by the Indian Office, April 12, 1872, with directions to have the Modocs removed, if practicable, to their reservation; and if removed, to see that they were properly protected from the Klamaths.

The superintendent was then instructed, in case they could not be removed, to report the practicability of locating them at some other point. The superintendent reported on the 17th June that their reservation was the best place for them to be located, but that he did not believe it practicable to remove them without using the military for that purpose, and that if they should resist, he doubted whether there was force enough in the country to compel them to go. In reply, the superintendent was directed, July 6, 1872, to remove them to the Klamath reservation. The attempt to execute this order resulted in a conflict between the Modocs and the troops and the white settlers. For the purpose of examining into the same, and, if possible, to procure a peaceable solution of the difficulties, a commission was appointed by the Secretary of the Interior in January last. This commission, as finally composed, consisted of A. B. Meacham, late superintendent Indian affairs for Oregon, L. S. Dyar, agent for the Klamath agency, and Rev. E. Thomas, and by direction of the Secretary of the Interior, under date of March 22, 1873, they were put under the direction of General Canby. While engaged in a conference with Captain Jack, chief of the Modocs, and other representative men of the tribe, on the 11th of April, General Canby and Dr. Thomas were brutally murdered by these Indians, and Mr. Meacham severely wounded.

Thus ended the negotiations with the Modocs, who, after seven months' fighting, were subdued by the military, and Captain Jack and three of his principal men were tried by court-martial and executed. The remnant of this Modoc band has been transferred to the Indian Territory, and located for the present on the Quapaw Indian reservation, where they have gladly availed themselves of the privilege of putting their children in school, and have entered upon industrial life with such readiness and good will as to warrant the conclusion that if these Indians could have had this opportunity of gaining their support out of soil upon which an ordinary white man could get a living, and had received just treatment, there would have been no cause of trouble with them. The report of the commission, prepared by the surviving member, A. B. Meacham, is herewith submitted.

* * * * * * *

LEGISLATION RECOMMENDED.

ISSUES OF PATENTS TO ROBERT BENT AND JACK SMITH.

By a postscript to the treaty concluded with the Arapahoe and Cheyenne Indians February 18, 1861, these Indians gave to Robert Bent and Jack Smith 640 acres of land each, and requested the Government to confirm said gifts to said parties. No provision, however, for the issue of patents to these persons is contained in the treaty; and even the postscript cannot be considered as a grant in the absence of legislation. It is therefore recommended that the gifts be confirmed and the issue of patents authorized by act of Congress, in order that the wishes of the Indians may be carried out.

KANSAS OR KAW INDIAN LANDS IN KANSAS.

These lands having been appraised under the act of May 8, 1872, and a sale of those embraced in the "diminished reserve" having been attempted, but not enough having been sold to defray the expenses of the offering, the Department decided to set aside the appraisement and have a new one made. A commission having been appointed for this purpose, after reaching the lands the chairman reported that he did not deem the first appraisement too high. It was restored, and legislation by Congress is recommended as follows: That bona-fide settlers be allowed to purchase the same at the Topeka land-office, making payment of one-fourth of the appraised value at the date of settlement, and the remainder in three equal annual installments, giving security for the deferred payments.

AGREEMENT WITH THE CROW TRIBE OF INDIANS.

An act of Congress approved March 3, 1873, authorized negotiations with the Crow Indians for the cession of their reservation, or a portion thereof, in Montana, and the establishment of a smaller reservation for them. The necessity for such negotiation was found in the fact that the recent discovery of gold on the reservation had drawn many white persons there, with whom there was likely to be trouble; also in the fact that the Northern Pacific Railroad would likely pass through a portion of the reservation; whereas the policy is to have the reservations located at a distance from the public lines of travel. An agreement was concluded with said Indians by Special Commissioner Felix R. Brunot, chairman Board of Indian Commissioners, James Wright and E. Whittlesy, on the 16th of August last, by the terms of which the Crows cede their reservation and accept a reserve in Judith Basin. This agreement is made subject to the action of Congress, and its ratification is respectfully recommended.

ALLOTMENT OF CHOCTAW AND CHICKASAW LANDS.

The 11th article of the treaty concluded with the Choctaw and Chickasaw Indians April 28, 1866, sets forth that it is believed the holding of their lands in severalty will promote their general civilization, and tend to advance their permanent welfare ; and it is therefore agreed that the lands be surveyed and allotted, should the Chickasaw and Choctaw people, through their respective legislative councils, agree to the same. The lands of the Chickasaws have been surveyed at their request, and their legislative council has, through their executive authorities, requested this Department to allot their lands; besides, the Chickasaw people in public assemblages have passed resolutions petitioning the Government to the same effect. The Choctaw council, however, refuse to join the Chickasaws in making the request for allotments as contemplated by the treaty. It is deemed proper, therefore, that Congress should afford the necessary legislation to enable this Department to comply with the request of the Chickasaws, independent of the action of the Choctaws, in order that the object of the treaty may be carried out, at least so far as the Chickasaws are concerned.

PAWNEE INDIAN RESERVATIONS IN NEBRASKA.

By the treaty concluded with the Pawnee Indians September 24, 1857, a reservation was set apart for said Indians in extent 30 miles from east to west by 15 miles from north to south. Upon a re-survey of the eastern boundary-line of said reservation, it has been ascertained that the east and west lines are but 29¼ miles apart in place of 30 miles, thus leaving a deficiency in the proper area of the reservation of 4,800 acres. The Pawnees insist upon indemnity for said deficiency, and it is deemed just that Congress should provide for the same, at the rate of one dollar and twenty-five cents per acre, the minimum price of Government lands.

AGREEMENT WITH CŒUR D'ALÈNE INDIANS IN IDAHO.

In 1867 an Executive order was issued setting apart a reservation for the Cœur d' Alènes, but, being dissatisfied with the location, they never located thereon, and continued to roam over the tract of country claimed by them. For the purpose of extinguishing their claim to all the tract of country claimed by them, and of locating them on a reservation suitable to their wants as an agricultural people, an agreement has been made with them by Hon. J. P. C. Shanks, Gov. Bennett, of Idaho, and Agent J. B. Montieth, subject to ratification by Congress, which is respectfully recommended. Pending such action by that body, I have deemed it prudent to have set apart by executive order the tract of country described in said agreement as a reservation for said Indians, in order that white persons may be prohibited from settling there a and claiming compensation for improvements from the Government.

SILETZ RESERVATION IN OREGON.

By the terms of a treaty concluded with the Coo-umpqua, Sinselano, Alsea, and other Indians embraced within the Siletz agency, in Oregon, provision was made for a reservation for said Indians. The treaty, however, was never ratified, and, to secure to them the reservation, an Executive order was issued November 9, 1855, setting the same apart for Indian purposes. These Indians are well advanced in civilization, and earnestly desire allotments, with patents for the same. Congress should therefore provide for the allotment of their lands and the issue of patents to such of said Indians as desire to cultivate the soil.

OFFICIAL SEAL FOR THE BUREAU.

Much inconvenience is caused by the want of an official seal for the purpose of certifying copies of files and records frequently called for as evidence in the civil courts. As it is, the seal of the Department has to be used for the purpose of certifying to the official character of the Commissioner of Indian Affairs. I therefore recommend that Congress authorize the use of a seal by this office, and provide that papers authenticated therewith shall have the same validity as in case of the use of a seal by other bureaus.

I have the honor to be, sir, very respectfully,

Your obedient servant,

EDW. P. SMITH,

Commissioner.

The Hon. SECRETARY OF THE INTERIOR.

REPORT OF THE COMMISSIONER OF PENSIONS.

DEPARTMENT OF THE INTERIOR,
Pension Office, Washington, D. C., November —, 1873.

SIR: I have the honor to submit the following report of the transactions of this Bureau for the year ending June 30, 1873:

THE ROLL OF PENSIONERS.

There have been added to the pension-rolls during the past year, by the allowance of original claims, 6,422 Army invalid pensioners; 3,949 Army widow and dependent-relative pensioners; 129 Navy invalid pensioners; 124 Navy widow and dependent-relative pensioners; and, pensioned under the act of February 14, 1871, 3,186 survivors, and 2,243 widows of soldiers of the war of 1812. By restoration, under section 3, act of July, 27, 1868, 233 Army invalids; 59 widows and dependent relatives; 1 Navy invalid and 2 Navy widows and minors. By restoration, for incidental causes, 18 Army invalids; 14 Army widows and dependent relatives; 4 Navy widows; 16 survivors of the war of 1812, and 6 widows of soldiers of the war of 1812—making, in all, an addition of 16,405 new pensioners.

The losses have been to the invalid roll by death, recovery from disability, and failure to claim pension for three years, as required by section 3 act of July 27, 1868, 2,423; to the widows and dependent-relatives' roll by death, remarriage of widows and mothers, expiration of minors' pensions, and failure to claim within three years, 5,542; to the war-of-1812 roll by death, soldiers, 2,036; widows, 222—making a total loss from all causes of 10,223 pensioners.

The additions, 16,405—less the losses, 10,223—give a net gain of all classes of pensions of 6,182. This, added to the number on the rolls at the close of the preceding fiscal year, 232,229, gives a grand total of 238,411 pensioners of the United States on the 30th of June, 1873, classified as follows:

Army invalids	99,804
Army widows and dependent relatives	112,088
Survivors of the war of 1812	18,285
Widows of soldiers of the war of 1812	5,053
Navy invalids	1,430
Navy widows and dependent relatives	1,770
Total	238,411

The increase in the annual amount of pension.

Besides the increase to the annual amount of pension attendant upon the above addition of new pensioners to the rolls, the pensions of 20,946 Army invalids have been increased to the amount of $920,930.35 per annum; 239 Navy invalids to the amount of $11,066 per annum; 545 Army widows and minors to the amount of $20,106.67 per annum, and 31 Navy widows and minors to the amount of $1,500 per annum— an aggregate of 21,761 pensions increased, and an increase in the annual amount of pension by this increase of rate of former pensioners of $953,605.02 per annum.

The greatest increase in rates has been in the invalid classes, under the act of June 8, 1872, whereby the pensions of those specifically or extremely disabled pensioners, then receiving $15, $20, and $25 per month, were increased to $18, $24, and $31.25 per month, respectively. Under the provisions of this act, 15,505 Army and 180 Navy pensions were increased to the aggregate amount of $598,254.25.

The annual amount of the present roll of pensioners by classes.

The annual amount of the pensions of the Army invalid pensioners has increased since June 30, 1872, from $8,611,854.91 to $9,627,240.09, while the annual amount of the pensions of Army widows and dependent relatives has fallen from $14,530,778.39 to $13,962,764.39.

The annual amount of the pensions of Navy invalids has increased from $136,545.30 to $150,537.75; of Navy widows and dependent relatives, from $269,208 to $280,550; of survivors of the war of 1812, from $1,641,600 to $1,753,536; and of widows of soldiers of the war of 1812, from $290,592 to $484,656.

The great increase in the annual amount of the Army invalid pension, $1,015,385.18, is partially counterbalanced by the falling off in the annual amount of Army widows and dependent-relatives' pension of $568,014; but the still existing increase of $447,371.18 is raised by the increase in amount of Navy invalid pension, $13,992.45; of Navy widows, &c., $11,342; of survivors of the war of 1812, $111,936; of widows of soldiers of the war of 1812, $194,064, to an aggregate increase of $778,705.63 over the annual amount of June 30, 1872, ($25,480,578.80,) making the total annual amount of all pensions June 30, 1873, $26,259,284.43. But, as will be seen in the proper statement, the total disbursements on account of pensions for the fiscal year was $29,185,289.02, including the salaries and commissions paid to agents, fees to examining surgeons, commutations for artificial limbs, and expenses of the agencies.

Gains and losses.

The Army invalid roll has increased from 95,405 June 30, 1872, to 99,804 June 30, 1873; the Navy widows and dependent relatives from

1,730 to 1,770; the survivors of the war of 1812 from 17,100 to 18,266; the widows of soldiers of the war of 1812 from 3,027 to 5,053, while the roll of Army widows and dependent relatives has decreased from 113,518 to 112,088, and the Navy invalids from 1,449 to 1,430. An annual diminution of the widows and dependent-relatives' roll may hereafter be expected by reason of the termination of minors' pensions (of which there were on the 30th of June last 34,850) on account of the children reaching the age of sixteen years.

A very careful and interesting analysis of this roll has been made since the close of the fiscal year, from which it is found that of the 112,088 pensioners upon it, 21,862 were widows without minor children; 29,696 were widows with children to the number of 54,451 under sixteen years of age; 34,850 were minors' pensions, with 57,807 children receiving the benefits therefrom; 21,852 were dependent mothers; 2,025 were dependent fathers, and 56 were pensions to brothers and sisters of deceased soldiers.

A tabular statement will be found in the appendix giving the results of this examination.

During the fiscal year the gains and losses to the rolls in numbers and in annual amount of pension were as follows:

	Number.	Number.	Annual amount.
INVALID ROLL.			
Added—Army original pensions	6,422		$413,344 50
Army pensions restored under section 3, act July 27, 1868.	233		11,547 92
Army pensions restored, miscellaneous causes	18		1,321 00
Army pensions increased		a30,946	920,930 25
Navy original pensions	129		15,421 00
Navy pensions restored under section 3, act July 27, 1868.	1		48 00
Navy pensions increased		b239	11,086 00
	6,803	21,185	1,373,698 67
Losses by death, recovery from disability, &c.	2,423		344,321 04
Actual gain to invalid roll	4,380		1,029,377 63
WIDOWS AND DEPENDENT-RELATIVES' ROLL.			
Added—Army original pensions	3,949		520,802 07
Army pensions restored under section 3, act July 27, 1868.	56		6,474 00
Army pensions restored for miscellaneous causes	14		1,560 00
Army pensions increased		545	20,108 57
Navy original pensions	124		20,184 00
Navy pensions restored under section 3, act July 27, 1868.	2		240 00
Navy pensions restored for miscellaneous causes	4		960 00
Navy pensions increased		31	1,500 00
	4,152	576	571,828 64
Losses by death, remarriage, and expiration of minors' pensions.	5,542		1,128,500 64
Net loss to widows' roll	1,390		556,672 00
WAR-OF-1812 ROLL.			
Added—Soldiers' original pensions	3,186		305,856 00
Soldiers by restoration	16		1,536 00
Widows' original pensions	2,242		215,232 00
Widows by restoration	6		576 00
	5,450		523,200 00
Losses by death—Soldiers	2,036		
Widows	222		
	2,258		217,200 00
Net gain to war-of-1812 roll	3,192		306,000 00

a. 15,505 of these were increased under act June 8, 1872.
b. 180 of these were increased under act June 8, 1872.

Comparative statement of the number of pensioners. Annual amount of pension and expenditures June 30, 1872, and June 30, 1873.

The following comparative statement will exhibit the number of pensioners, with the annual amount of pension of each of the principal classes of pensioners, June 30, 1872, and June 30, 1873, together with the amount paid to each class during the fiscal year terminating on the above dates:

June 30, 1872.

Classes of pensioners.	Number.	Annual amount.	Paid to each class during the year ending June 30, 1872.
Invalid, Army	95, 405	$6, 611, 854 91	$40, 145, 145 40
Navy	1, 449	136, 545 00	149, 442 65
Soldiers, war of 1812	17, 100	1, 641, 600 00	1, 977, 415 54
Widows, Army	112, 518	14, 530, 778 39	17, 286, 136 62
war of 1812	3, 027	290, 502 00	335, 903 63
Navy	1, 730	269, 208 00	295, 186 57
	232, 229	25, 480, 578 30	30, 169, 341 00

June 30, 1873.

Classes of pensioners.	Number.	Annual amount.	Paid to each class during the year ending June 30, 1873.
Invalid, Army	90, 804	$6, 627, 240 00	$40, 564, 825 51
Navy	1, 430	150, 537 75	160, 971 90
Soldiers, war of 1812	18, 266	1, 753, 536 00	2, 078, 606 90
Widows, Army	112, 088	13, 962, 764 39	15, 365, 644 75
Navy	1, 770	290, 550 00	302, 936 71
war of 1812	5, 053	464, 656 00	649, 303 69
	238, 411	26, 239, 284 23	29, 185, 289 62

While the general rule of annual increase which has characterized the yearly disbursements of pensions during the past ten years has been maintained in the payments to certain classes of pensioners during the past year, the marked feature of the expenditures for the year 1872-'73 has been the large decrease in disbursements to the great class of widow and dependent-relative pensioners.

The amount paid to Army invalids was $419,680.02 greater than the year before; to Navy invalids, $11,529.13; to Navy widows, $7.750.14; to survivors of the war of 1812, $101,191.14, and to widows of soldiers of the war of 1812, $353,310.06, but, to more than offset this, the payments to Army widows and dependent relatives fell off $1,877,511.87, by which the total disbursements for pensions for the fiscal year ending June 30, 1873, were reduced to $29,185,289.62, being $984,051.38 less than the preceding year, ($30,169,341.)

＊   ＊   ＊   ＊   ＊   ＊   ＊

Of the unexpended balance of the appropriation for Army pensions there was in the hands of the pension agents on the 30th of June $1,031,985.71. (See table appendix.)

Of the unexpended balance of the appropriation for Navy pensions there was in the hands of the pension agents on the 30th of June $14,511. (See appendix.)

These balances have been covered into the Treasury under act of July 12, 1870.

The appropriations for the present fiscal year are as follows:

For Army pensions.. \$20,000,000
For Navy pensions.. 480,000

These appropriations would have been amply sufficient had no additional expenditure been imposed by new legislation. The act of March 3, 1873, by extending the provision for \$2 per month additional pension of act of July 25, 1866, to the children of officers and to single minors of privates, will increase very materially the amount paid to widow and minor pensioners, especially during the present fiscal year, as, upon the re-adjustment of the pension, arrears of increase from July 25, 1866, (or from commencement of original pension if subsequent to July 25, 1866,) are allowed. (The extent of this increase cannot be accurately estimated, but up to October 1, 1873, over eight thousand claims have been filed.)

By providing for the intermediate grades of \$12, \$13, \$14, &c., for certain classes of invalid pensioners now receiving but \$8, a further unexpected demand has been made upon the fund.

It is possible that the appropriation for "Army pensions" may be found sufficient, but the extremely small balance of the "Navy pension" appropriation remaining unexpended at the close of the past fiscal year indicates that with these new demands upon an appropriation of like amount for the present year it may be found insufficient.

Number of claims for pension arising from the war of the rebellion filed in the Pension-Office up to June 30, 1873, with the number allowed, rejected, and unadjudicated at that date.

A tabular statement was prepared for the last annual report from this office, showing the number of claims filed and allowed during each fiscal year since June 30, 1861, for wounds or injuries received, disease contracted in, or death resulting from, service in the war of the rebellion. The same statement is reproduced below, brought down to June 30, 1873.

Year ending June 30.	ARMY.				NAVY.			
	Number applications filed.		Number claims allowed.		Number applications filed.		Number claims allowed.	
	Invalids.	Widows.	Invalids.	Widows.	Invalids.	Widows.	Invalids.	Widows.
1862..	1,362	1,008	329	....	60	65	78	49
1863..	26,380	28,377	3,913	3,574	200	285	183	133
1864..	20,263	32,627	16,742	22,148	385	324	271	248
1865..	27,299	44,464	14,659	24,656	435	406	250	266
1866..	35,790	28,732	21,913	27,023	350	375	238	218
1867..	15,905	20,285	15,742	19,269	250	333	137	263
1868..	7,292	13,099	8,991	18,940	170	207	135	219
1869..	11,035	14,496	6,844	15,535	290	245	172	209
1870..	12,991	11,400	5,942	12,267	260	200	149	160
1871..	8,837	8,985	7,656	8,191	190	142	127	117
1872..	8,857	6,755	6,060	7,057	240	173	151	124
1873..	8,728	6,427	6,903	3,949	248	120	129	134
	184,748	210,627	114,294	168,600	3,188	2,940	2,020	2,100

Grand summary.

Total filed.. 401,503
Total allowed... 281,233
Total rejected.. 58,581
Total pending... 61,689

The maximum number of invalid claims filed during any one year was reached immediately after the close of the war, in 1866, during which year 35,799 were filed. Since then the percentage of this maximum number, filed during each succeeding fiscal year, down to June 30, 1873, has been as follows:

In 1867, 44 per cent.
In 1868, 20 per cent.
In 1869, 30 per cent.
In 1870, 36 per cent.
In 1871, 24 per cent.
In 1872, 24 per cent.
In 1873, 24 per cent.

It will be seen by this that applications for original pensions have settled down upon a basis of about 24 per cent. of the maximum year, or about three-tenths of one per cent. of the whole number of soldiers (2,688,523) who served in the late rebellion. This percentage will probably continue, without much diminution, for a period of years. It is probable that, as those who served during the rebellion advance in life, disabilities will develop with many who left the service apparently sound, which they will regard as having originated in the service; but in a large proportion of such cases their claim will not be susceptible of proof.

The maximum number of claims of widows and dependent relatives filed during any one year was reached in 1865, during which year 44,461 were filed. The percentage of this maximum number, filed during each succeeding fiscal year down to June 30, 1873, has been as follows:

In 1866, 64 per cent.
In 1867, 45 per cent.
In 1868, 29 per cent.
In 1869, 32 per cent.
In 1870, 25 per cent.
In 1871, 20 per cent.
In 1872, 15 per cent.
In 1873, 15 per cent.

Probably very few claims of widows and orphans of soldiers who died during the war remain to be presented. The claims growing out of the death of a soldier which are now being filed are principally those where death has occurred subsequent to the discharge of the soldier, (in a large proportion of cases the soldier having been in receipt of invalid pension,) and those of dependent relatives.

There is no reason to expect any considerable increase or diminution in the number of such claims which will annually be filed for some years to come.

THE AVERAGE PENSION.

The average pension to each of the following classes of pensioners was, on the 30th June last:

To Army invalids, $96.46 per annum—$8.04 per month.

To Army widows and dependent relatives, $124.56 per annum—$10.38 per month.

To Navy invalids, $105.27 per annum—$8.77 per month.

To Navy widows and dependent relatives, $158.00 per annum—$13.16 per month.

A careful and accurate examination of the entire invalid roll was made to determine the number of different rates paid to invalid pensioners, and the number of pensioners at each rate, and the result is presented in tables in the appendix, and is summarized as follows:

ARMY.

Number.	Rate.	Number.	Rate.	Number.	Rate.	Number.	Rate.
1	$40 00	4	$16 75	8	$10 62	71	$5 66
685	31 25	14	16 66	1	10 50	8	5 62
180	30 00	1	16 25	1	10 20	2,261	5 33
1	26 66	28	16 00	775	10 00	1,891	5 00
2	26 25	1	15 87	1	9 50	4	4 80
1	26 00	2,316	15 00	4	9 37	120	4 25
235	25 00	3	14 87	5	9 00	25,744	4 00
1	24 20	104	14 00	1	8 75	101	3 75
717	24 00	1	13 75	563	8 50	1	3 66
1	23 00	1	13 60	8	8 33	2	3 40
53	22 50	61	13 33	1	8 25	7	3 2
4	22 00	1	13 25	17,318	8 00	3,378	3 00
1	21 25	1	13 12½	436	7 50	3,004	2 66
873	20 00	24	13 00	341	7 00	1	2 50
2	19 00	268	12 75	1	6 75	2	2 33
59	18 75	99	12 50	61	6 66	1	2 12
1	18 50	1	12 25	2	6 50	7,972	2 00
1	18 33	225	12 00	1	6 40	1	1 87
15,010	18 00	2	11 66	16	6 37	5	1 60
14	17 50	84	11 33	14	5 25	2	1 50
484	17 00	164	11 25	13,863	6 00	20	1 33
1	16 87	4	11 00	2	5 75	49	1 00

Total number of Army pensions, 99,804.

NAVY.

Number.	Rate.	Number.	Rate.	Number.	Rate.	Number.	Rate.
1	$38 50	5	$14 25	3	$9 50	2	$3 75
17	31 25	4	14 00	9	9 00	5	3 50
2	30 00	1	13 75	1	8 50	1	3 33
6	25 00	3	13 50	240	8 00	1	3 06
21	24 00	4	13 25	14	7 50	31	3 00
18	20 00	2	13 00	9	7 00	19	2 66
1	19 00	20	12 50	5	6 66	1	2 62
1	18 75	7	12 00	1	6 50	4	2 50
175	18 00	2	11 50	147	6 00	1	2 37
2	17 50	1	11 25	6	5 33	77	2 00
2	17 00	2	11 00	1	5 25	2	1 87
2	16 00	7	10 75	54	5 00	1	1 50
4	15 75	3	10 50	5	4 50	1	1 33
50	15 00	50	10 00	371	4 00	3	1 00
1	14 50	1	9 75				

Total number of Navy pensions 1,430.

There are 88 different rates of Army pensions, and 58 of Navy pensions. Forty-three thousand four hundred and eighteen Army invalids are pensioned at $8 (total disability) and upwards, and 59,386 below $8 per month. Six hundred and sixty-eight Navy invalids are pensioned at $8 per month and upward, and 762 below the rate of total disability.

Widows of revolutionary soldiers.

The roll of widows of revolutionary soldiers has been reduced during the past year by the death of twenty-five of these pensioners and the dropping of the name of one.*

*   *   *   *   *   *

Below is given the number upon the rolls at the close of each year for five years last past:

June 30, 1869.. 887
June 30, 1870.. 727
June 30, 1871.. 634
June 30, 1872.. 471
June 30, 1873.. 445

* Polly Gibson, Nashua, N. H.

Artificial limbs and commutation therefor under the acts of June 17 and 30, 1870.

During the first fiscal year after the passage of the act granting artificial limbs or apparatuses, or in lieu thereof, commutation in money, once in five years to invalid soldiers disabled by loss of limb, or resection, there were issued 7,770 commutation orders, amounting to $468,350, and 1,248 bills, amounting to $90,350, were approved for bills for limbs furnished in kind.

During the second year the number of commutation orders issued was 438, amounting to $27,150, and the number of bills approved for limbs furnished in kind was 326, amounting to $23,025. These claims received the concurrent approval of the Surgeon-General and the Commissioner of Pensions.

There were other claims on which a perfect agreement was not had. By act of June 8, 1872, under which the adjudication of these claims was left solely with the Surgeon-General, during the fiscal year ending June 30, 1873, there have been issued 1,332 commutation orders, amounting to $70,550, and during the year there have also been paid 66 bills for limbs in kind, amounting to $4,200.

As the adjudication of these claims is now removed from the jurisdiction of the Commissioner of Pensions, it seems desirable that the pension appropriation should be relieved from the expenses attendant upon their allowance, and that a fund be placed at the control of the Surgeon-General for the purpose of paying the same.

Tabular statements.

Herewith will be found the usual annual tabular statements, with others which have been prepared expressly to accompany this report. They are as follows:

A. Number and amount of Army pensions allowed and increased in each State and Territory during the past fiscal year.

B. Amount paid to Army pensioners in each State and Territory during the last fiscal year.

C. Number and amount of Army pensions June 30, 1873, by States and Territories.

D. Balance of Army funds in the hands of pension agents.

E. Number and amount of Navy pensions allowed and increased in each State and Territory during the past fiscal year.

F. Amount paid to Navy pensioners in each State and Territory during the past fiscal year.

G. Number and amount of Navy pensions June 30, 1873, by States and Territories.

H. Balance of Navy funds in the hands of pension agents.

I. Statement of the number of Army, Navy, and privateer pensioners, with the amount paid each year from 1791 to June 30, 1873.

K. Tabular statement of the rates of invalid Army pensions, with the number of pensioners at each rate, June 30, 1873.

L. Tabular statement of the rates of invalid Navy pensions, with the number of pensioners at each rate, June 30, 1873.

PENSIONERS OF THE WAR OF 1812.

During the fiscal year the office has received the following number of claims for pension under the act of February 14, 1871: Survivors, 1,481; widows, 1,299; total, 2,780. There were re-opened during the year 310 survivors, 272 widows; total, 582. There were admitted during the year: survivors, 3,186; widows, 2,242; total, 5,428. The number rejected was: survivors, 3,933; widows, 2,082; total, 6,015. Total disposals: survivors, 7,119; widows, 4,324; aggregate, 11,443; leaving the following number of claims pending at the close of the year, viz: survivors, 1,487; widows, 1,523; total, 3,004. The following table shows the entire receipts of claims, and the disposal thereof, under the act in question, since its passage for a period up to October 1, 1873:

Total receipts... {	Survivors	29, 510
	Widows	10, 471
		39, 981
Total admissions {	Survivors	21, 108
	Widows	5, 630
		26, 738
Total rejections. {	Survivors	7, 048
	Widows	3, 448
		10, 496
Total disposals.. {	Survivors	28, 156
	Widows	9, 078
		37, 234
Claims pending. {	Survivors	1, 354
	Widows	1, 393
		2, 747

Statement showing cause for rejection of claims filed under act of February 14, 1871, for the fiscal year ending June 30, 1873.

Cause	Surviv'rs.	Widows.	Total.
Insufficient service..	2, 834	844	3, 678
Marriage subsequent to treaty of peace...................	....	410	410
Remarriage after death of soldier.........................	....	28	28
Consolidation and transfer................................	59	15	74
Miscellaneous...	1, 040	785	1, 825
	3, 933	2, 082	6, 015

As foreshadowed in my last report, the work of this division has been substantially brought to a close; nearly the whole of the large force that has heretofore been engaged thereon having either been dropped or assigned to other duties.

The claims yet pending are principally those not proven, and which for various reasons are incapable of being satisfactorily sustained by evidence.

New claims are being received at the average rate of 120 per month, and, as will be observed in the foregoing tabular statement, the total of claims received (40,041) is but ninety-two less than the number of persons estimated by this office as probably entitled at the date of the passage of the original act, viz, 40,133.

BOUNTY-LAND.

The whole number of bounty-land warrants issued during the year ending June 30, 1873, was 340, representing 52,160 acres, as follows:

Act of February 11, 1847—1 warrant, 80 acres	80 acres.
Act of September 28, 1850—1 warrant, 160 acres	160 acres.
Act of March 3, 1855—301 warrants, 160 acres	48, 160 acres.
Act of March 3, 1855—21 warrants, 120 acres	2, 520 acres.
Act of March 3, 1855—15 warrants, 80 acres	1, 200 acres.
Act of March 3, 1855—1 warrant, 40 acres	40 acres.

During the year there have been received 1,034 applications for bounty-land, of which number 437 have been rejected as identical with claims previously allowed.

During the ten years from 1864 to 1873, inclusive, warrants were issued as follows: In 1864, 1,812; 1865, 1,161; 1866, 406; 1867, 954; 1868, 1,077; 1869, 1,650; 1870, 1,758; 1871, 2,598; 1872, 443; 1873, 340.

It will be perceived that the number of warrants issued in the past year is less than during any other of the years mentioned. The principal cause of this reduction was the more careful adjudication of claims, induced by the discovery of frauds. Of suspended claims, under the several bounty-land acts, there are now on file 99,587.

The total amount of land for which warrants have been issued for military service since the organization of the Government is 74,052,811 acres, which, estimated at $1.25 per acre, the minimum price, is equal in value to $92,566,013.75, as shown by the annexed table:

	Acres.
Act of September 16, 1776, revolutionary	2,095,120
Act of February —, 1801, Canadian refugees	57,860
Scrip acts of 1830, 1832, 1833, 1835, and 1852	2,459,511
Act of August 10, 1790, Virginia military district, (Ohio)	3,669,848
Act of May 6, 1812, war of 1812	4,846,240
Act of March 5, 1816, Canadian volunteers	75,792
Act of February 11, 1847, Mexican war	13,207,880
Act of January 26, 1849, Mexican war, (special)	1,280
Act of September 28, 1850	13,165,880
Act of March 22, 1852	693,920
Act of February 28, 1855, war of 1812, (special)	160
Act of March 3, 1855	33,779,320
Total acres	74,052,811

In addition to this amount, there were issued under the act of February 11, 1847, in lieu of land-warrants, 2,729 certificates, amounting to $238,400, which, added to the amount above given as the minimum value of land granted, makes the total value of grants $92,804,413.75.

In the last annual report your attention was invited to the fact that the character of parol evidence filed in many claims for bounty-land was continually inducing suspicion of the validity of the claims; and I added: "Unjust and incomplete claims are bought by unscrupulous agents for trifling sums, and are completed by an abuse of a privilege granted by authority of the third section of the act of May 14, 1856, admitting parol evidence to establish a claim when no record exists. By stringent rules and regulations, this Bureau has sought to prevent these wrongs. But the only complete protection will be found in the repeal of the section to which reference has been made."

Experience, since the above suggestion was made, has confirmed the conviction that the position then taken was fully justified, and I do now earnestly ask that Congress be requested either to repeal said third section of act of May 14, 1856, (United States Statutes, vol. 11, p. 8,) or so to amend the same as to preclude the acceptance of parol evidence where record evidence of the service of the company (in which service by the claimant is alleged) exists.

It is also deemed advisable that the act of March 3, 1869, (United States Statutes, vol. 15, p. 336,) construing the act of June 3, 1858, (United States Statutes, vol. 11, p. 308,) so as to "authorize the legal representatives of deceased claimants, whose claims were filed prior to their decease, to file the proof necessary to perfect the same," should be so amended as to transfer the authority therein given from the legal representatives to the heirs or legatees of deceased claimants.

FRAUDS AND SPECIAL INVESTIGATIONS.

In the last annual report I dwelt at some length upon the subject of fraudulent pension claims. Attention was invited to the defects of the present system of determining the right to a pension, and the opinion was expressed that those defects rendered frauds so easy, and that consequently there was, in fact, so large a percentage of cases wrongfully established, as to challenge the careful consideration of Congress, and that some remedy should, if possible, be devised. The experience of the past year has confirmed and emphasized that view.

The principal weakness of the system consists, as was then stated, in accepting as a basis of adjudication *ex parte* affidavits, which the Government has no power to sift by cross-examination, while at the same time it has no means of research for adverse testimony. In my opinion there can be, under these conditions, no security to the Government against dishonest claims, and probably the proportion of such claims which will be successfully prosecuted will increase, rather than diminish, the dishonest attorneys becoming more skilled, and the temptation to fraud becoming greater, as the average value of pension is enhanced by the accumulation of arrears and growing liberality of legislation.

Frequently considerable time is necessarily consumed in obtaining such evidence of violation of the law as will warrant the institution of proceedings in the courts, and in such cases, among the obstacles to success in securing the punishment of offenders is the shortness of the period during which, under the statute of limitation, an indictment must be found. In view of this fact, I earnestly urge your attention to the propriety of recommending to Congress the necessity of an extension of the term of limitation to five years.

The special service, as at present organized, is necessarily mainly occupied with cases of suspected fraud, where pension has already been allowed. It is doing important, valuable, and successful work. Every effort has been made to increase its efficiency and to perfect its organization. The direct saving to the Treasury from its work is many times greater than the sum expended in maintaining it; and the indirect saving by repressing fraud is known to this office to be most satisfactory. But as a means of prevention of fraud it is entirely insufficient, and in my belief no remedy will be found to be adequate which does not subject all the parol proof offered in support of claims to the sifting process to which it is subjected in ordinary courts of law, and which does not empower the Government to inquire into the facts in each case independently of claimant and his attorney, and there is no doubt that the reduction of the roll which would result from the adoption of such methods would justify the cost of such a system, even though that cost should be very considerable.

MEDICAL DIVISION—EXAMINING SURGEONS.

· Since the date of my last report the number of examining surgeons has slightly decreased. During the year ending June 30, 1873, 25 have been dismissed on account of professional incompetency; 30 have been dropped because of change of residence; 43 have been dropped for various other reasons, including neglect of duty; 08 have resigned; 19 have died; and 176 have been appointed. The whole number at this date is 1,394.

Although there has been a slight decrease in their number, the area represented by the roster is considerably greater than at any time hitherto in the history of the office. The rapid settlement of the Western States and Territories, the population of which contains no inconsiderable element of those who served in the Army or Navy during the late war, has demanded the appointment of examining surgeons to meet the want thus created. In their appointment it has been the object to locate them so as to best serve the convenience of pensioners and claimants, and yet not to make any appointment in excess of the actual demand, it having been the constant experience of this office that such excess entails vexation and mischief, and not unfrequently attempts at fraud.

As hitherto in the conduct of the office, no effort has been spared to instruct the surgeons as to what is desired of them, and to incite them to increased care in conducting the examinations and in the construction of the certificates of examination.

There is every reason to believe that this has been attended by good results, since, while two years ago about 40 per cent. of the certificates were returned to the surgeons for correction or for greater detail, there are now not more than 5 per cent. returned to them, and these to such surgeons as, newly appointed, are not yet familiar with the requirements. This improvement in the character of the certificates of examination has resulted, it is firmly believed, in a degree of intelligence and accuracy in the adjudication of invalid claims not before attained.

As said in my report of 1872, the certificates of examination constitute a very important part of every invalid claim, and practically amount to vouchers for the disbursement of the pension appropriation, and I take pleasure in saying that at no time in the history of the office has the examination of invalid claimants been so thorough, nor the certificates thereof so accurate in the "particular description," as within the past year.

The act of Congress of March 3, 1873, codifying the laws in existence, as recommended in the last report, provided by its 38th section for the appointment of a "duly qualified surgeon as medical referee," and for the appointment of such other duly "qualified surgeons (not exceeding four) as the exigencies of the service may require," as aids to the medical referee. Immediately upon the passage of the act, Dr. T. B. Hood, who had been chief of the medical division, was appointed medical referee, and, after an examination in compliance with the civil service regulations of such character as to insure qualifications of a high grade, Drs. J. B. G. Baxter, N. F. Graham, William Grinsted, and W. L. Worcester, were appointed as his aids.

The records of this office contain matter relating to injuries and diseases, particularly those forms incident to military service, which, properly classified and tabulated, would be not only of professional and general interest, but of great practical value, as affording, in case of need, basis for intelligent calculation and legislation. From these facts, tabulated, could be studied many questions touching the rarer forms of gunshot wounds, and the relation of some of the commoner forms of a disease—consumption, for instance—to military service. Many other questions, such as the influence of war in unfitting any given mass of people of a country for manual labor, might be studied from them also—questions which, in their social bearing, are daily becoming more and more important, and of greater and greater interest to the scientist and statesman.

It was hoped to be able to present herewith a table bearing upon the average life of the invalid pensioner of the United States, but so extremely difficult was it found to collate the data that it was necessarily abandoned. There is presented, however, a short table exhibiting the average life, after being pensioned, of 684 invalid pensioners of the revolutionary war. Its value consists in that it relates to a class of persons concerning whom almost anything is interesting. It may be said the data from which it is constructed were collected from various sources, and that it is thought that all means of information touching the subject were exhausted.

State.	No. of pensioners.	Average duration of life from date of pension.		
		Years.	Months.	Days.
New Hampshire	17	14	3	2
Vermont	18	10	9	1
Massachusetts	94	11	3	19
Rhode Island	16	16	4	5
Connecticut	97	15	1	15
New York	83	11	4	7
New Jersey	36	11	1	10
Pennsylvania	190	9	7	6
Maryland	51	7	1	5
Delaware	18	12	4	......
Virginia	46	14	9	11
North Carolina	16	9	8	......
South Carolina	1	2	4	......
Georgia	1	9	9	......
	684	11	5	8

Disabilities and rating.

The existing method of rating disabilities is attended with great confusion and uncertainty, and is open to grave objections. This grows out of the purely technical use of the word "total" in its application to a disability which is not total. Prior to the act of June 6, 1866, the greatest sum which could be paid to any grade of rank was fixed by the amount representing the total of that grade. That act provided that a private, or any officer whose total was less than $20, should, for a disability which disabled him for "any manual labor," that is, wholly disabled him, be paid $20 per month, at the same time leaving the "totals" for each grade of rank, unchanged. It followed necessarily that the word total came to have two meanings for each of these grades, and that an officer below the rank of captain, who was totally disabled, could claim by rank or disability as he elected. It is found extremely difficult to instruct a newly-appointed surgeon, so that he will make the distinctions practised by the office, in preparing his certificates of examination. When told that a private's total is $8, and that still he is paid $24 dollars when totally disabled, he is at once confused, and asks what degree of disability is recognized as entitling a private to a "total rating." The difficulty lies in the shifting basis, and this applies equally to all, or nearly all, the ranks.

It is clear that the only remedy for the confusion growing out of the technical use of the word "total" would be such change as would fix a total (disability) for the performance of any manual labor, as the unit; any proportion of disability for any manual labor to be expressed by fractional rating. The subject is being fully considered, but as yet I do not feel able to do more than point out these objections, and to suggest the propriety of some change, without in the least indicating any detail.

PENSION CLAIMS OF INDIANS.

The present neglected condition of pension claims of the heirs of Indians of the Cherokee and Creek nations, who served in the Union army during the war of 1861, seems to me so wholly irremediable under existent laws, as to warrant the consideration of some further legislation for their relief. The preparation of these claims almost exclusively by one attorney, was in such disregard of the laws and departmental regulations thereunder, as to prompt investigation in the vicinage of the claimants, and said investigations, (the results of which are included in the report of Indian affairs committee, No. 96, second session forty-second Congress, and the report of the same committee, No. 98, third session forty-second Congress,) while they satisfied this office that the Indians themselves had not attempted fraud, induced the conclusion that the requirements relative to the execution of applications, and the character of evidence of marriage should be modified, and that the limitations as to time of filing, and the period for completion of the claims, not supported by record evidence as to cause of death, should be extended. Both these changes were made by provisions in the act of March 3, 1873.

The legal modifications to which reference is above made do not overcome the difficulties to which the Indian claimants are subjected by reason of their marriage customs, and the laxity of their regulations respecting records of births and deaths, as well as the loose manner in which the regimental and company records of the said soldiers were kept; and it seems hardly possible to alter the general pension law so as entirely to accomplish the removal of those obstacles. But I am of the opinion that the law might be so amended as to provide that where the records show enlistment, and there is proof of death during the term for which the soldier enlisted, from any cause incident to the service, further evidence, either record or parol, as to service and death, shall not be required; that some more specific and applicable requirement as to marriage might be established; and further, that evidence of the care and custody of minors, with such other proof as is available from the Indian records, shall be accepted as evidence of guardianship, with such distinction as may seem proper where the mothers have been the parties in charge.

The changes which have transpired in the Indian Territory since the origin of these claims, by reason of which the United States Government has virtually acquired a practical and political jurisdiction not heretofore had, seem to render the execution of these suggestions more feasible and desirable.

POLICY AND PROGRESS OF THE PENSION SYSTEM.

Believing that the general policy of the Government in providing for pensions to those who suffer by reason of service in the Army or Navy, and the progress which has thus far been made in liberalizing and in the execution of that policy, should be present, in a brief and comprehensive shape, to those who may desire any further changes thereof, and that a general review of the laws which have been enacted will best secure that presentation, the annexed has been prepared.

The resolutions of the Continental Congress, of August 26, 1776, and April 23, 1782, form the basis of the pension system of the United States.

INVALID PENSIONS.

The resolutions of August 26, 1776, provided that an officer or soldier of the Army so disabled in the service (in the Revolutionary war) as to be "incapable of afterwards getting a livelihood" should be paid, after cessation of pay for service, and during the continuance of such disability, one half his monthly pay; and that a commissioned officer, marine, or seaman of a ship of war or armed vessel, who should be disabled as above stated, should be paid in the amount and manner above provided, except that in case of loss of a limb in an engagement in which a prize should be taken, the amount of prize-money received by the party so disabled should be accounted as part of his half-pay.

It was also provided that applications should be made to the legislative bodies of the respective States in which the applicants resided; and, further, that should the disability not be total the pension should be such as might be deemed adequate by the legislature of the State in which he resided, not exceeding his half pay; and that such of said persons entitled to pensions as were capable of doing guard-duty, were to be formed into a corps of invalids, and so employed. By resolution of April 23, 1782, the pension was restricted to $5 per month, in lieu of all pay and emoluments, to all the sick and wounded of the army who preferred to be discharged, and so pensioned in lieu of service in the invalid corps.

By act of April 30, 1790, it was provided that any officer or soldier who should be wounded or disabled while in the line of his duty should be pensioned at such rate and under such regulations as should be directed by the President of the United States, not to exceed half-pay for officers nor $5 for privates per month. By act of March 23, 1792, these pensions were confirmed for life, or during the continuance of disability; and the payment of them, previously made by the respective States, was assumed by the United States. Said act also prohibited any pledge, assignment, or transfer of any right or interest in the pension. Act of February 21, 1795, provided that the right to pension should commence at the time of completion of testimony; and the act of March 3, 1795, continued the $5 pension to privates and the half-pay pension to commissioned officers, with proviso that all inferior disabilities should entitle the person so disabled to receive an allowance proportionate to the highest disability. Other acts were subsequently passed, not materially modifying the preceding, until the repeal of all former acts. This was done by the act of April 10, 1806. Said act of April 10, 1806, comprised the provisions of the act of February 21 and March 3, 1795, as above stated, restricted the highest pension to the half-pay of a lieutenant-colonel; provided for increase of those pensioned at lower rates to such sums as should be found just and proper by the testimony adduced, to exceed in no case the full pension provided by act of March 3, 1795. The benefits of the act of April 10 were, by act of April 25, 1808, extended to all persons who served after the Revolution, and before the passage of the last-named act.

The acts of January 11 and February 6, 1812, and that of January 29, 1813, provided for half-pay pension to soldiers of the war of 1812 in the same manner as had been provided for the soldiers of the Revolution. The act of April 24, 1816, increased the rates of pension to full-pay, as follows: First lieutenants to $17, second lieutenants to $15, third lieutenants to $14, ensigns to $13, non-commissioned officers, musicians, or privates, $8 per month, leaving that of officers of higher rank than above mentioned at half-pay as before.

The act of March 18, 1818, provided for all who had served for nine months or more in the war of the Revolution in the Army, and to those who served in the Navy, and should become indigent, if a commissioned officer, a pension of $20, and if of a lower grade, $8 per month during life. The pension was enlarged to full-pay to officers and soldiers of the continental line, May 15, 1828.

The act of June 7, 1832, gave all (except foreign officers) who had served for two years in the war of the Revolution, in the land or naval forces, full-pay pension, and to those who had so served at least six months an amount proportionate according to the length of their service.

The act of May 13, 1846, provided for pensions to the disabled volunteers of the war with Mexico, in accordance with the laws then existent and applicable to the war of 1812.

The general provisions for the pensions of various classes of invalids who were disabled in the wars above mentioned stood as heretofore stated until 1864 (April 1) when an additional annual stipend of $100 was granted to each surviving revolutionary pensioner for life, and in 1871 (February 14) the requirement of disability in claims on account of service in the war of 1812 was dispensed with, service of sixty days and proof of loyalty during the war for the suppression of the rebellion only being required, and a pension not to exceed $8 per month provided for then surviving officers and enlisted and drafted men of said war.

In July, 1861, an act, providing for employing volunteers for suppression of the rebellion, promised to those who should be disabled in said service the same rates of *full-pay* pension as were provided by act hitherto named for the invalids of the war of 1812 and the Mexican war.

In July, (14,) 1862, an act was passed re-enacting the provisions of the act of July 22, 1861, and specifying the rates of pension to invalids, the same as those of the act of April 24, 1816, with the additional specification of the exact amounts of full pension to be paid to those of higher rank than first lieutenant. Subsequently provision was made for pensions for particular disabilities at fixed rates, as follows: In 1864, (July 4,) for loss of both eyes, $25 per month, and for loss of both feet, $20 per month. In 1865 (March 3) pension for loss of one foot and one hand, at same rate as had been provided for loss of both feet, $20 per month. In 1866 (June 6) for loss of one hand or one foot, pension of $15 per month. In 1868 (July 27) to those who, having but one eye on entering the service, shall have lost the same, $25 per month.

In 1872 (June 8, to commence June 4) the above specific disability pensions were increased as follows: From $25 to $31.25, from $20 to $25, and from $15 to $18; and in 1873 (March 3) pension for loss of a leg above the knee, and such consequent disability as to preclude the use of an artificial limb, was specifically provided for at $24, and the loss of hearing likewise at $13 per month.

The above shows that the provisions for invalids' pensions have been, from time to time, but generally at long intervals, liberalized as to the requirements upon which claims should be based. In claims on account of service in the Revolution, first requiring service and disability, and without limitation as to time of filing claims, allowing only half-pay pension; seventeen years after, two years, limitation for filing was adopted, and two years thereafter the date of completion of the required proof was made the date of commencement of pension. Forty-two years passed before pension was granted on account of indigence, and fifty-two years elapsed before full-pay pension was allowed. In provisions for pensions of invalids in the war of 1812, no material change was made until the act of February 14, 1871.

In provisions for pensions for invalids of the war of Mexico, there has been no important change up to the present time. It is, however, proper here to state that the time of limitation of two years for filing, which governed the revolutionary claims, was extended to three years with reference to pensions of all wars by the act of July 14, 1862, with the renewal of the proviso that the commencement of pension should be from the date of completion of proof, and the time of filing was extended in 1868 (July 27) to five years.

Within three years after the first act providing pensions for invalids of the last war, provisions for specific disabilities were commenced, and have been continued from time to time, as heretofore stated.

In addition to the large increase on account of specific disabilities which has been provided since the commencement of the late war, numerous disabilities, for which, under the old laws, only ordinary pensions were granted, have been included among those which are ranked as equivalent to the specific disabilities, and for which much higher rates are provided.

From and after July 25, 1866, for all persons who had been or should be pensioned under acts prior to March 4, 1861, the same rates as those of same class pensioned under act of 1862 (July 14) and those subsequent were provided.

Pensions to widows, minors, and dependents.

The first extension of the pension provisions to widows and orphans was by resolution of August 24, 1780, which gave the half-pay pension for seven years to widows of officers who had died, or might die in the service, and to the orphans, if no widow survived the soldier, or upon the death or remarriage of his widow. An act passed March 16, 1802, fixing the military peace establishment of the United States, gave half-pay pension for five years to the widows and minor children of commissioned officers dying from wounds received in actual service. The act of January 11, 1812, providing for raising an additional military force, also provided for half-pay pension for five years to the widows and minor children of officers dying by reason of wounds received in actual service. By the act of August 2, 1813, five years' half-pay pension was granted to widows and orphans of privates.

No further action in favor of widows and orphans was had for nearly twenty-three years, when the act of July 4, 1836, was passed. Said act provided for half-pay pensions for five years to the widows and orphans of privates who died in the service after April 20, 1818, or in consequence of wounds received in the service after said date. This act also provided for payment to widows and orphans of the arrears of the invalid pensions under the following conditions: Where the service of the deceased was such as is specified under act of June 7, 1832, and he had died after March 4, 1831, and before the passage of the act of June 7, 1832, and also where the widow was married to him before the expiration of his service, the amount that would have accrued to him if he had survived the passage of said act, provided she still remained his widow. The act of March 3, 1837, also granted the arrears as aforesaid, on the same conditions, to the widows who had married after the decease of the husbands for whose services they claimed pension, provided they were widows at the time of the passage of the act, and the same to those whose husbands served until November 3, 1783; and the resolution of July 7, 1838, extended the grant of said arrears, on the same conditions, also, to those whose husbands should thereafter die. The same day, an act was passed restricting said provision for arrears to those who were married before January 1, 1794. (Said act also added to the prohibition against pledge or transfer of pension, that the same "shall inure wholly to the personal benefit of the pensioner.")

From March 4, 1841, to March 4, 1843, no pension was provided for widows in their own right, except to those included in the provisions of the act of July 4, 1836. August 16, 1842, the restriction relative to widows whose husbands died after the passage of the act of June 7, 1832, and before that of the act of 1838, was removed; and on the 23d of same month the bar to claims of widows who had remarried was removed provided they were widows at the time of application for pension. March 3, 1843, the five years widows' pensions were extended from March 4, 1836, to March 4, 1844, and in 1844 again extended to March 4, 1848. April 30, 1844, a provision was enacted that no pension should thereafter be granted to a widow for the same time during which her husband had received one; and on the 2d of February, 1848, an act was passed continuing pensions to the widows of the officers and privates of the Army of the Revolution during widowhood. On the 21st of July of the same year an act granting the benefits of the act of July 4, 1836, to the widows and orphans of officers and privates of the Mexican war twas passed. On the 29th of the same month an act was passed granting pensions to widows (of revolutionary soldiers and officers) who were married before 1800; and on the 11th of August of the same year it was enacted that the pensions of widows of officers, seamen, and other employés of the Navy, should be continued during widowhood.

In 1849 (February 22) the act of July 20, 1848, was so amended as to include the widows and minor children of persons who were wounded or contracted disease in the service, of which they died after their discharge and return to their homes; and by the resolution of September 28, 1850, said acts were made to include the widows and minor children of those who had died after the passage of said acts.

In 1853 (February 3) provision was made for pensions to widows of the revolutionary war married after the 1st of January, 1800, and for renewal of the pension for five years to widows and minor children of officers and soldiers of the Florida and Mexican wars, the war of 1812, and the Indian wars. In 1854 the above was amended so that no widow should be deprived of the benefits of it, provided she should be a widow at the time of application.

In 1858 (June 3) pensions to widows of all wars subsequent to the Revolution were extended to continue during widowhood.

The act of April 2, 1862, cuts off all claims for pension or increase of pension by children or descendants of those who served in the war of the Revolution, when the claim to pension was not established by those who served or by their widows.

The act of July 14, 1862, grants pensions to the widows, minor children, dependent mothers, and dependent sisters, of persons who died from any cause which originated in the military or naval service, and line of duty, after the 4th of March, 1861, at the rate to which their husbands and fathers would have been entitled under the same act. The act of June 6, 1866, extended the benefits provided by the act of July 14, 1862, for mothers and sisters, to the dependent fathers and dependent brothers.

The act of July 25, 1866, increased the pension of widows provided for by the act of July 14, 1862, $2 per month for each child under sixteen, by herself, of the person on account of whose service and death the widow was entitled to the aforesaid original pension; and also increased the pension to the minor children provided for by the act of July 14, 1862, by granting $2 per month for each of them, where there was more than one.

The act of July 27, 1868, provided for the increase of the pension of the widows by adding also $2 per month on account of each of the children by a former wife of the person, on account of whose service and death she was entitled to the original pension.

In the act of February 14, 1871, provision is made for pension at the same rate that is prescribed for the surviving officers and enlisted and drafted men of the war of 1812, to their widows who were married before the treaty of peace which terminated said war.

The addition to the expenditure in payment of pensions by reason of increase of rates, the including of so large a proportion of the pensioners among those entitled to the higher rates, and the extension of the benefits of the pension laws to so many classes of pensioners, have been so great as to warrant consideration in connection with any proposition for further increase.

GENERAL REMARKS.

There has been a decided increase in the general business of the office, resulting from the changes in legiation which required the re-adjustment of so large a number of claims, and the careful review of all the certificates of the recent biennial examination. This imposed unusual labor upon the clerical force, and necessitates unavoidable delays in the transaction of routine business. Greater satisfaction could be given the public if Congress would be pleased to make a small addition to the clerical force; but if reasonable time can be granted without working injustice to claimants, the present force will soon be adequate to the demands made upon the office.

I have ordered the preparation of a grand alphabetical roll of pensioners, which shall comprise, in a record relative to each pension which has been granted, the following features: Name of soldier; name and residence of the pensioner; number of pension certificate; act under which it was granted; commencement and termination of the pension; such changes as may have been made in it; and, so far as practicable. the disability, or cause of death, on account of which it was granted, The incomplete character of the roll, as heretofore kept, has been for years clearly manifest, and it is believed that the method adopted as above stated, after careful consideration, will secure a concise, correct, and available statement of every pension awarded by the Government.

The attention of Congress was invited in my last report to the necessity of a complete codification of the pension laws. Congress was pleased to act upon the suggestion then offered, and the office is now operating under the codified laws, approved March 3, 1873. The objects sought by this legislation have been in the main accomplished, and the confused mass of laws has been made uniform and consistent. The large and increasing number of instances in which claims for increase of invalid pensions having been once adjudicated, are immediately, or before a reasonable time has elapsed, renewed, and new adjustment urged, is a source of embarrassment to the office, and the question presents itself whether it might not be well to prescribe by law a definite period of time during which, after any adjudication of an invalid-pension claim, acquiesced in by the claimant, the rate of pension should remain as fixed in that adjudication.

Attention has been heretofore invited to the insecure condition of the Seaton House. I now respectfully refer to what I stated in my report of last year, so that Congress may be duly impressed with their responsibility in case any calamity should occur.

Experience constantly teaches us the manifest injustice of longer delay in reorganizing the Bureau by a system of positive law, definitely fixing duties by creating heads of divisions, and granting a compensation adequate to the responsibilities. This was proposed at the last session of Congress, but action was withheld on the ground that legislation would be had at the long session for a general re-organization of all the bureaus of the Government. It is to be hoped that an act, so necessary to the proper legal appointments of the public service, and reasonable justice to faithful and competent employés, will be considered and enacted at the coming session of Congress.

The operations of the civil service, so far as this Bureau is concerned, have been highly satisfactory. There is an increased demand for accuracy and efficiency in the manner in which the public work is performed. The demand is reasonable, necessary, and I might also add, imperative. The civil-service rules may be regarded as the product in this direction of the just sentiment of the country, and so far as my power extends they shall receive my willing co-operation as the head of the Bureau.

It may not be amiss to say, in this connection, that one of the great practical effects of the enforcement of these rules has been the marked cessation of importunate applications for position. On assuming the duties of the office of Commissioner of Pensions, fully one-fourth of the hours of official business was consumed by questions arising out of the matter of appointments and removals, and that generally, too, from sources which could not be disregarded. This embarrassment—and it was a most serious one—has disappeared, and my time can be freely given to more legitimate duties, to the great advantage of the public service.

It may also be added that the sentiment prevails among the many good men we have in the Bureau, that it is safer to maintain their position by reason of capacity and fidelity than to be at the mercy of political friends. And it is also apparent that, as these rules have become an established fact, they work out a certain logical result by inspiring the clerical force with the idea that their retention in office is now entirely dependent upon themselves, and they apply themselves with more care and fidelity to the performance of duty.

If Congress would go a step further, and provide adequate compensation for those who are charged with grave responsibilities, the movement for civil-service reform would be far more complete.

Very respectfully, your obedient servant,

J. H. BAKER, *Commissioner.*

Hon. C. DELANO, *Secretary of the Interior.*

REPORT OF THE SUPERINTENDENT OF THE CENSUS.

DEPARTMENT OF THE INTERIOR,
Census Office, Washington, D. C., November 15, 1873.

SIR: In compliance with the requirements of law, I have the honor to report the operations of this Office during the year just closed.

In the last annual report it was stated that all the statistical tables which it was proposed to embrace in the publications of the Ninth Census had then been completed. No small amount of labor, however, still remained to be done during the progress of these tables through the press. It has been the uniform rule of the Office that every page of figures should be added and proved in type, independently of previously ascertained totals. When it is considered that the three quarto volumes contain over 2,100 pages of tabular matter, having often as many as 22 vertical columns and 90 horizontal lines to the page, some impression may be obtained of the amount of labor involved in this effort to secure the highest attainable accuracy in the publication of the census. It has, of course, not been found practicable to eliminate every error from the material which was brought into the Office by the enumeration, or from the results as compiled in the Office, but certainly all who have taken part in the labors or responsibilities of the Ninth Census may well feel repaid for their exertions by the gratifying reception which these volumes have met from the people and the press of the country. In the revision of the statistical tables as they were put into type, this Office has been greatly assisted by the intelligent interest and kindly co-operation of the Congressional Printer, Hon. A. M. Clapp, who has afforded every opportunity consistent with other demands upon his office for the perfecting of this important national work, even to the last detail of publication. The several dates of issue for the three quarto volumes and the compendium were as follows: Population and social statistics, (quarto,) November 30, 1872; vital statistics, (quarto,) March 1, 1873; compendium, (octavo,) May 1, 1873; industry and wealth, May 9, 1873.

The revision of tabular statements has, however, not been the only work upon which the clerical force of the Office has been engaged during the year past. Each census brings into the Department an increasing mass of manuscript record, the usefulness of which, as record, is to depend wholly on the orderliness and compactness with which it shall be arranged for reference and consultation, after the compilation of general results for publication has been completed. The manuscript returns of the Ninth Census contain not only the name of every man, woman, and child in the United States on the 1st of June, 1870, in number 38,558,371, but nineteen entries, descriptive or merely affirmative or negative, against every such name. Moreover, every farm, factory, mill, or shop in the United States is returned by its location and the name of its owner, with from fifteen to fifty-two specifications of capital, stock, machinery, material, and product. In addition to the above, the statistics of mortality and what are known as the social statistics compose a body of manuscript larger than would have been required for the whole enumeration of the United States at the first two censuses, on the schedules then in use. The completion of the statistical tables of the census for publication leaves something like one million five hundred thousand pages in such place and order as the necessities of compilation required. Each of the five schedules must thereafter be brought together, sheet to sheet, township to township, county to county, State to State. The returns of each of the five classes must be prepared for binding by arranging the pages in numerical succession within the township, the townships in alphabetical order within the county, the counties in alphabetical order within the State. When this has been done, the record of the census is complete, 550 folio volumes of manuscript at 1870, of the average weight of 30 pounds.

The work, of which a rough description has here been given, has been carefully performed by skilled clerks, in order that the highest possible authority might be given to the record, and to secure the greatest ease and convenience of reference and consultation in the future.

Not less exacting have been the duties imposed upon the Office by the act of the last session providing for the payment of the assistant marshals of 1860, without proof of loyalty, as heretofore required.

By the act of March 3, 1873, making appropriations " for the legislative, executive, and judicial expenses of the Government for the year ending June 30, 1874, and for other purposes," the Secretary of the Treasury was directed to "pay to the census-takers of 1860, or their assigns, the sums set to their credit now in the Treasury of the United States, any provision of existing laws to the contrary notwithstanding." In this legislation it was assumed that the accounts of the unpaid census-takers at the Eighth Census were in the Treasury Department; but the fact was otherwise. During the continuance of the Census Office as organized for the purposes of the Eighth Census, the Treasury Department received no notification of services rendered in enumeration, except upon and after the payment of individual accounts for such services, the marshals and assistant marshals for that census having been paid directly by the disbursing clerk of the Census Office. Subsequently to the disbandment of the Census Office, accounts of assistant marshals were occasionally paid by the disbursing clerk of the Department of the Interior, upon requisitions issued by the Treasury; but it was only in cases where the accounts were complete for payment that they were forwarded to the latter Department. The great body of claims from the Southern States, being cut off from present payment by the requirements of law in respect to proof of loyalty, were held in the Department of the Interior awaiting authority and appropriation for their adjustment. The passage of the act of March 3, 1873, therefore, involved the careful re-examination of these accounts, their verification by the original census returns of 1860, and the identification of claimants. Blank forms for executing the necessary papers were immediately dispatched to the latest known addresses of the unpaid assistant marshals of 1860. Up to the present time, the accounts of 828 assistant marshals, reaching a total of $164,341.53, have been forwarded to the Fifth Auditor of the Treasury for his action.

The following table exhibits the number and aggregate amount of claims which have thus been adjusted for each of the judicial districts of 1860. It will be seen that three of the claims adjusted were from non-slave-holding States, the persons interested having, it may be presumed, been compromised by subsequent removal to States in rebellion; at any rate, not offering to make proof of loyalty while that requirement of law continued as a condition of payment:

Judicial districts.	Number of claims.	Amount of claims.	Judicial districts.	Number of claims.	Amount of claims.
Alabama, northern.....	31	$4,025 85	Missouri, eastern	8	$996 44
Alabama, southern	48	13,798 98	Missouri, western	20	3,041 30
Arkansas, eastern......	48	7,656 52	North Carolina	88	15,171 43
Arkansas, western	12	2,422 34	South Carolina.........	41	20,113 83
California, northern	2	1,212 78	Tennessee, eastern.....	26	4,285 43
Florida, northern	18	2,011 64	Tennessee, middle	24	4,965 66
Georgia	92	21,022 31	Tennessee, western	13	3,197 59
Kentucky..............	32	4,691 31	Texas, eastern	19	2,877 38
Louisiana, eastern	26	4,549 83	Texas, western.........	70	9,094 94
Louisiana, western.....	24	6,710 18	Virginia, eastern	111	18,634 93
Maine	1	33 06	Virginia, western	20	3,195 13
Mississippi, northern ..	25	5,704 43			
Mississippi, southern ..	29	5,696 04	Total	828	164,341 53

The First Comptroller of the Treasury having notified this Office of his decision that the term "census takers" in the act cited does not embrace United States marshals superintending the enumeration, but only assistant-marshals, the actual enumerators, no steps have been taken toward the adjustment of the claims of the unpaid marshals at the Eighth Census. The number of such marshals is 18. As no authority or appropriation exists for their payment, their accounts have not been taken up for final adjustment. The amount appearing as due them under the act of May 23, 1850, in connection with the Eighth Census, is in the neighborhood of $9,000. All but one of these claimants, however, appear on the books of the Treasury Department as debtors in larger sums to the United States, on account of moneys in their hands for the expenses of their offices at the outbreak of the rebellion, and not accounted for. It is, therefore, unnecessary to contemplate or provide for their payment as marshals in respect to the census, at this or any future time.

There still remain two United States marshals and twenty-three assistant marshals at the Ninth Census with whom no final settlement of account has been made. The total amount of the possible claims on these accounts is $5,270. Of the marshals unpaid, one has made no claim for compensation, having, as is understood, absconded; the other is reported by the Department of Justice as a defaulter to the United States in a much larger sum than his compensation would amount to for services in respect to the census. Of the assistant marshals indicated, four, claiming a total amount of $501.63, have failed to return their receipts for payment as required by the Treasury Department; five, claiming the total amount of $1,278.20, have been refused payment for fraud, or gross delinquency tantamount to fraud, and fourteen, claiming the total amount of $2,738.04, have failed of payment by reason of the refusal of the marshals of their respective judicial districts to furnish the pay certificates required as a condition of payment by the act of May 23, 1850. In the majority of cases this refusal of the marshal is based on the refusal or neglect of the assistant marshal to make copies of his returns as required by law. In each of the foregoing cases a statement of the reasons for refusing or delaying payment has been filed in the Department for reference, should any of the claimants appear at a future time. I see no reason, however, to believe that any considerable portion of these claims will ever be perfected for payment.

The balance of appropriation on account of the Ninth Census remaining unexpended at date is $1,450.90.

The clerical force of the Office has been reduced as rapidly as was consistent with the performance of the duties before enumerated. The following table exhibits the number and grade of clerks employed at each of the dates specified. In accordance with the universal custom of the Department, a short leave of absence was given each clerk on discharge, to afford means and opportunity for seeking other employment. It will, therefore, be understood that the actual service in the Census Office of these clerks ceased by an average term of one month earlier than would appear from the dates in the table:

| | Total. | Chief clerk. | Number of clerks of— | | | |
			Class 4.	Class 3.	Class 2.	Class 1.
1870—October	31	1	3	3	1	23
November	21	1	4	3	1	12
December	12	1	3	2		6
1871—January	7	1	2	1		3
February	7	1	2	1		3
March	5	1	2	1		1
April	5	1	2	1		1
May	5	1	1	1		1
June	5	1	1	1		1
July	1	1				
August	1	1				
September	1	1				

executive, and judicial expenses of the Government for the year ending June 30, 1874, and for other purposes," the Secretary of the Treasury was directed to "pay to the census-takers of 1860, or their assigns, the sums set to their credit now in the Treasury of the United States, any provision of existing laws to the contrary notwithstanding." In this legislation it was assumed that the accounts of the unpaid census-takers at the Eighth Census were in the Treasury Department; but the fact was otherwise. During the continuance of the Census Office as organized for the purposes of the Eighth Census, the Treasury Department received no notification of services rendered in enumeration, except upon and after the payment of individual accounts for such services, the marshals and assistant marshals for that census having been paid directly by the disbursing clerk of the Census Office. Subsequently to the disbandment of the Census Office, accounts of assistant marshals were occasionally paid by the disbursing clerk of the Department of the Interior, upon requisitions issued by the Treasury; but it was only in cases where the accounts were complete for payment that they were forwarded to the latter Department. The great body of claims from the Southern States, being cut off from present payment by the requirements of law in respect to proof of loyalty, were held in the Department of the Interior awaiting authority and appropriation for their adjustment. The passage of the act of March 3, 1873, therefore, involved the careful re-examination of these accounts, their verification by the original census returns of 1860, and the identification of claimants. Blank forms for executing the necessary papers were immediately dispatched to the latest known addresses of the unpaid assistant marshals of 1860. Up to the present time, the accounts of 828 assistant marshals, reaching a total of $164,341.53, have been forwarded to the Fifth Auditor of the Treasury for his action.

The following table exhibits the number and aggregate amount of claims which have thus been adjusted for each of the judicial districts of 1860. It will be seen that three of the claims adjusted were from non-slave-holding States, the persons interested having, it may be presumed, been compromised by subsequent removal to States in rebellion; at any rate, not offering to make proof of loyalty while that requirement of law continued as a condition of payment:

Judicial districts.	Number of claims.	Amount of claims.	Judicial districts.	Number of claims.	Amount of claims.
Alabama, northern.....	31	$4,095 85	Missouri, eastern	5	$685 44
Alabama, southern	48	13,798 94	Missouri, western	20	3,043 50
Arkansas, eastern......	46	7,656 56	North Carolina	86	15,171 43
Arkansas, western	12	2,429 34	South Carolina	41	20,113 65
California, northern	2	1,212 78	Tennessee, eastern	36	4,995 60
Florida, northern	18	2,011 64	Tennessee, middle	94	4,985 65
Georgia.................	92	21,029 31	Tennessee, western	13	3,197 29
Kentucky..............	32	4,691 31	Texas, eastern	19	2,577 50
Louisiana, eastern	36	4,549 53	Texas, western	70	9,054 94
Louisiana, western.....	34	6,710 18	Virginia, eastern	111	15,494 69
Maine	1	33 06	Virginia, western	89	3,186 19
Mississippi, northern ..	24	5,704 43			
Mississippi, southern ..	29	5,698 04	Total	828	164,341 53

The First Comptroller of the Treasury having notified this Office of his decision that the term "census takers" in the act cited does not embrace United States marshals superintending the enumeration, but only assistant-marshals, the actual enumerators, no steps have been taken toward the adjustment of the claims of the unpaid marshals at the Eighth Census. The number of such marshals is 18. As no authority or appropriation exists for their payment, their accounts have not been taken up for final adjustment. The amount appearing as due them under the act of May 23, 1850, in connection with the Eighth Census, is in the neighborhood of $9,000. All but one of these claimants, however, appear on the books of the Treasury Department as debtors in larger sums to the United States, on account of moneys in their hands for the expenses of their offices at the outbreak of the rebellion, and not accounted for. It is, therefore, unnecessary to contemplate or provide for their payment as marshals in respect to the census, at this or any future time.

There still remain two United States marshals and twenty-three assistant marshals at the Ninth Census with whom no final settlement of account has been made. The total amount of the possible claims on these accounts is $5,270. Of the marshals unpaid, one has made no claim for compensation, having, as is understood, absconded; the other is reported by the Department of Justice as a defaulter to the United States in a much larger sum than his compensation would amount to for services in respect to the census. Of the assistant marshals indicated, four, claiming a total amount of $501.63, have failed to return their receipts for payment as required by the Treasury Department; five, claiming the total amount of $1,278.20, have been refused payment for fraud, or gross delinquency tantamount to fraud, and fourteen, claiming the total amount of $2,738.04, have failed of payment by reason of the refusal of the marshals of their respective judicial districts to furnish the pay certificates required as a condition of payment by the act of May 23, 1850. In the majority of cases this refusal of the marshal is based on the refusal or neglect of the assistant marshal to make copies of his returns as required by law. In each of the foregoing cases a statement of the reasons for refusing or delaying payment has been filed in the Department for reference, should any of the claimants appear at a future time. I see no reason, however, to believe that any considerable portion of these claims will ever be perfected for payment.

The balance of appropriation on account of the Ninth Census remaining unexpended at date is $1,450.90.

The clerical force of the Office has been reduced as rapidly as was consistent with the performance of the duties before enumerated. The following table exhibits the number and grade of clerks employed at each of the dates specified. In accordance with the universal custom of the Department, a short leave of absence was given each clerk on discharge, to afford means and opportunity for seeking other employment. It will, therefore, be understood that the actual service in the Census Office of these clerks ceased by an average term of one month earlier than would appear from the dates in the table:

	Total.	Chief clerk.	Number of clerks of—			
			Class 4.	Class 3.	Class 2.	Class 1.
1872—October	31	1	3	3	1	23
November	21	1	3	3	1	12
December	12	1	3	2	....	6
1873—January	7	1	2	1	....	3
February	7	1	2	1	....	3
March	5	1	2	1	....	1
April	5	1	2	1	....	1
May	5	1	2	1	....	1
June	5	1	1	1	....	1
July	1	1	....	....	....	....
August	1	1	....	....	....	....
September	1	1	....	....	....	....

49 Ab

The ordinary salary of the Superintendent has not been drawn since the 1st of December, 1871. From that date till January 31, 1873, the Superintendent of Census was also Commissioner of Indian Affairs, receiving only the compensation affixed to the latter office. On my resignation as Commissioner of Indian Affairs, January 1, to take effect January 31, 1873, I received the following communication from the honorable Secretary:

> DEPARTMENT OF THE INTERIOR,
> *Washington, D. C., January* 31, 1873.
>
> SIR: I transmit herewith a commission appointing you to be Superintendent of the Census.
> You will observe that the word "emoluments" is erased from the commission, as at your express request the appointment is made "without compensation" for your services.
> If you accept the appointment, be pleased to signify the same, take and subscribe the inclosed oath of office, and transmit it to this Department.
> I am, sir, very respectfully, your obedient servant,
>
> C. DELANO,
> *Secretary of the Interior.*
>
> Hon. FRANCIS A. WALKER, *of Massachusetts.*

Under this letter of appointment I at once duly qualified, and have discharged the duties of the Office during the remaining portion of the year to the best of my ability, so far as was consistent with professional duties involving a residence in a city somewhat remote from the seat of Government. The work of the Superintendent of Census does not cease abruptly with the publication of the statistical reports. The remains of office-work are by no means trifling, while the publication of the reports of itself gives rise to an extensive correspondence. Where no positive objection exists, it is of course desirable that the person who has organized and administered the service to the point of the publication of the reports should conduct this correspondence and supervise the remaining details of administration, in order to secure the highest degree of continuity and consistency of plan and operation. It was in this view, as I understood it, that the honorable Secretary issued the appointment above recited, and it was for this reason that I cheerfully accepted the position. I shall be fully satisfied if I can believe that the public service has been in any, even the smallest, degree advantaged thereby.

I have the honor to be, sir, very respectfully, your obedient servant,

FRANCIS A. WALKER,
Superintendent.

Hon. C. DELANO,
Secretary of the Interior.

REPORT OF THE ARCHITECT OF THE CAPITOL EXTENSION.

ARCHITECT'S OFFICE, UNITED STATES CAPITOL,
Washington, D. C., November 1, 1873.

SIR: I have the honor to submit the following report relative to the Capitol building and grounds, and other public works under my supervision.

CAPITOL EXTENSION.

Since the date of the last annual report from this office various improvements have been made. Large coal vaults, each capable of containing one thousand tons of coal, have been constructed at both wings. To get rid of the coal-gas, which was often driven into the area from which the air from the exterior was taken, an underground air-duct, opening at the foot of the lower terrace of the western grounds, has been constructed. The openings of this duct being so far from the furnace-chimneys—the cause of defilement—will afford a supply of purer air at all times, and in summer a cooler air than could be obtained from the former inlet.

The steam-boilers of both wings, which were found defective from long use by the Government inspector, have been thoroughly repaired, and extensive repairs and improvements made to the heating-apparatus of the entire building; many rooms and corridors repainted and otherwise fitted up. The reporters' gallery of the Senate has been enlarged ; the galleries of the House of Representatives so re-arranged that the diplomatic and the members' galleries will be on the east, the ladies' gallery on the west, and the men's on the north side. New desks and chairs have been placed in same hall, so disposed as to dispense with the outer platform. As provided for by a resolution of the House, the bathing-room of the south wing has been extended and fitted up.

CENTER BUILDING.

This portion of the building has been kept in repair and likewise improved; the Senate bathing-rooms refitted with new tubs, pipes, and floors; the steam-heating apparatus of the Congressional Library put in good order.

The roof of this part of the building is constructed on wooden rafters, and is, in many places, so defective that a new covering of copper is demanded. In these repairs I recommend that they be made in a fire-proof manner. In fact, to avoid damage from fire, the whole roof should be reconstructed.

Attention is called to the unfinished condition of the rotunda, and inner portion of the dome. I recommend that its walls be encrusted with ornamental marbles; the pilasters and first cornice taken away, and the floor laid with encaustic tile. By omitting the first cornice, and letting the story terminate at the line of the second cornice, which cornice should be enlarged, the wall of the rotunda will have greater apparent height, and the anomaly of three cornices—similar members—so near each other, will be abolished.

Lofty doorways, with sculptured enrichment, should be made, and the vault of the rotunda decorated with painted enrichments. While these changes will entail a large expenditure, I consider them necessary to make a complete and harmonious finish to this the principal feature of the building.

CAPITOL-GROUNDS.

Squares 687 and 688, in accordance with the act approved March 3, 1876, have been purchased.

All the buildings on square 687 have been disposed of at public sale, or the material taken away and used for public purposes. Nearly all the buildings on square 688 have been disposed of in the same manner. It is expected that the two buildings yet remaining on that square may be taken down and the materials cleared away before the meeting of Congress. The cavities on these squares have been filled, and the surfaces graded to correspond with the grade of the pavement at the north and south of each square.

First street, at the foot of the Capitol, from Pennsylvania to Maryland avenues, has been paved with cypress-wood pavement, and the curve at the south, from Maryland to New Jersey avenues, is now being paved with granite blocks. Over one hundred thousand loads of earth have been deposited on the grounds at the south of the Capitol and on South B street this season.

Not having any practice or pretensions to skill as landscape gardener, I earnestly recommend that a first-class artist in this line may be employed to plan, plant, and lay out these grounds.

Attention is called to the eastern grounds, with the hope that authority may be given to grade them, to suit the requirements of the streets surrounding them, which have been cut down to the Government grades. In the event of cutting down the Eastern Park, I feel confident, and have the opinion of experts, that most of the trees necessary to preserve can be lowered into place without great risk of loss. My opinion is that these grounds should be treated as a lawn, and none but the best trees retained. The great number of trees in them, when in foliage, effectually screen the eastern (principal) front of the building from view from Capitol Hill. There are no vistas through which it can be seen entirely, nor is there any point of view from which this front can be seen to advantage, on account of the disposition of the trees in this park. Trees may be planted at the north and south of the wings, as they are now at the western grounds, where they are required to screen the rustic terraces, as well as for shade; but, in my judgment, the grandeur and extent of the main front will be revealed by taking out a large number of trees in the eastern grounds.

The plateau at the eastern front should be paved, and the side-walks around the grounds flagged next season. The funds on hand not being sufficient to pay the expense of a proper flag-pavement around these grounds, a narrow foot-walk of bricks has been laid for the season.

PNEUMATIC TUBE.

The attempt to lay the pneumatic tube from the Capitol to the Printing-Office building has been unsuccessful, owing in part to the unexpected difficulties met in getting the tube under the track of the Washington and Baltimore Railroad. To accomplish this the trench had to be sunk in some places fifteen feet, thus loading the tube with so great a weight of earth, that it was so forced out of shape that the sphere would not pass through. Mr. Brisbane expected, when he undertook this work, that North Capitol street, along which the tube was to be laid, would be filled and graded, so that the tube would be placed about three feet below the surface. If this could have been done, I have no reason to believe that the tube would not have worked successfully. Mr. Brisbane is now anxious to renew this work, at his own expense; but as he will have the same difficulties to overcome, I have doubts of his success, unless the tube is made much smaller than stipulated for in his contract. I am so convinced of the practicability of this mode of transportation, that I recommend, for the sake of durability, that the tube be made of iron.

REFORM SCHOOL.

The buildings at the Reform School are near completion. The main building is so far advanced as to be partly used by the boys as workshops. It is expected that it will be entirely finished, ready for occupancy, by the meeting of Congress. The family building has been occupied ever since the middle of last winter.

BOTANICAL GARDEN.

At the request of the Joint Committee on the Library, various improvements have been made, under my supervision, at the Botanical Garden.

The fence on Third street, from Pennsylvania to Maryland avenues, has been raised to suit the new grade of the street, and a brick fence constructed on First street, between the same avenues. Gateways have been erected at the principal entrance on both these streets. The conservatory has been extended and finished, by the erection of the octagon at the eastern end. Forcing-houses, work and packing shops, have been erected on the square bounded by Maryland avenue, B, Second, and Third streets, in order to extend the working capacity of the garden.

CITY-HALL.

At the request of the Attorney-General I have superintended the improvements recently made at the City-Hall. The western court-room has been improved by the introduction of another furnace for heating, and the ceiling of the same room has been pierced to obtain ventilation. The exterior has been repainted and the roof thoroughly repaired; several ceilings in the upper story, which were damaged by the leaks in the roof, have been plastered. Both court-rooms, the judges' and the jury rooms have been put in good condition.

As this building is now wholly the property of the Government, and as additional room is required for the courts and record-offices, I recommend that this building be extended to suit the wants of the public business.

COLUMBIA HOSPITAL FOR WOMEN.

The improvements authorized by Congress have been made, and the entire building is now ready for occupancy. Steam-heating apparatus has been put in, and boiler and fuel-vaults constructed this season.

To give this building a respectable appearance the grounds should be graded in some places, and the street-fronts terraced and fenced.

CAPITOL EXTENSION.

Amount expended from June 30, 1872, to June 30, 1873.

Amount paid on rolls of mechanics, laborers, salaries, &c.	$43,447 86
Amount paid for paint and painting	4,611 21
Amount paid for miscellaneous bills, such as lime, sand, cement, lumber, &c.	9,716 45
Amount paid for flagging and setting	2,200 00
Amount paid for iron and brass work	527 71
Amount paid for marble	135 19
Amount paid for hardware	1,891 95
Amount paid for gas-fitting and fixtures	109 65
Amount paid for tiling	422 70
Amount paid for stone-work	149 00
Amount paid for forage for horses	450 26
Amount paid for material for heating and ventilating	7,526 05
Amount paid for boiler and water-tank	8,330 00
Amount paid for fire-proof felting	742 50
Total	80,260 53

Cash account.

Amount available July 1, 1872	$7,000 00
Amount appropriated June 10, 1872	50,000 00
Amount appropriated March 3, 1873	91,000 00
Total	148,000 00
Amount expended from July 1, 1872, to July 1, 1873	80,260 53

Leaving on the 1st of July, 1873, an unexpended balance of . 67,739 47

GRADING AND PAVING STREETS AROUND THE CAPITOL AND FOR IMPROVING CAPITOL-GROUNDS.

Amount paid on rolls for labor	$17,082	02
Amount paid for earth for filling	8,154	28
Amount paid granite curb, (straight)	7,943	42
Amount paid granite curb, (circular)	1,538	90
Amount paid laying and jointing flagging	266	53
Amount paid laying brick pavement	270	00
Amount paid asphalt pavement	9,506	48
Amount paid Belgian pavement	8,955	73
Amount paid lumber	624	93
Amount paid stone and stone-work	648	81
Amount paid miscellaneous bills, such as lime, sand, cement, bricks, &c., &c.	6,607	55
	61,598	65

Cash account.

Amount appropriated June 10, 1872	$35,000	00
Amount appropriated March 3, 1873	125,000	00
Total	160,000	00
Amount expended from July 1, 1872, to July 1, 1873	61,598	65
Leaving on the 1st of July, 1873, an unexpended balance of	98,401	35

ELEVATOR IN SENATE WING OF THE CAPITOL.

Amount of L. Atwood's contract for machinery and car	$6,000	00
Amount paid on rolls of mechanics, laborers, &c	1,660	50
Amount paid for marble	417	31
Amount paid for engineer's expenses for traveling	174	40
	8,252	21

Cash account.

Amount appropriated March 3, 1873	$10,000	00
Amount expended from March 3, 1873, to June 30, 1873	8,252	21
Leaving on the 30th June, 1873, an unexpended balance of	1,747	79

ALTERING AND REFITTING HALL OF REPRESENTATIVES.

Amount paid for steam-trap	$300	00
Amount paid for model desks and chairs	323	60
	623	60

Cash account.

Amount appropriated March 3, 1873	$40,000	00
Amount expended from March 3, 1873, to June 30, 1873	623	60
Leaving on June 30, 1873, an unexpended balance of	39,376	40

CONSTRUCTING PNEUMATIC TUBE.

Amount paid to Albert Brisbane on account of contract	$12,000	00

Cash account.

Amount appropriated June 10, 1872	$15,000	00
Amount expended from June 30, 1872, to June 30, 1873	12,000	00
Leaving on June 30, 1873, an unexpended balance of	3,000	00

Respectfully submitted.

EDWARD CLARK,
Architect.

Hon. COLUMBUS DELANO,
Secretary of the Interior.

REPORT OF THE COLUMBIA INSTITUTION FOR THE DEAF AND DUMB.

COLUMBIA INSTITUTION FOR THE
INSTRUCTION OF THE DEAF AND DUMB,
Washington, November 6, 1873.

SIR : In compliance with the acts of Congress making provision for the support of this institution, we have the honor to report its progress during the year ending June 30, 1873.

NUMBER OF PUPILS.

The pupils remaining in the institution on the 1st day of July, 1872, numbered..	74
Admitted during the year......................................	17
Since admitted..	17
Total	108

Under instruction since July 1, 1872, males, 92; females, 16. Of these 60 have been in the collegiate department, representing seventeen States and the District of Columbia, and 48 in the primary department. A list of the names and residences of the pupils will be found appended to this report.

HEALTH OF THE INSTITUTION.

We are permitted to record a year of exemption from death, and also from any prevailing or even serious illness among our pupils and students. The few slight indispositions that have occurred yielded readily to the judicious treatment of our attending physician and the skillful nursing of the matrons.

CHANGES OF OFFICERS.

Professor James M. Spencer, who has for six years occupied the chair of mathematics in the college faculty, has resigned his position. It gives occasion for sincere regret to all the friends of the college that so valuable and successful an instructor should retire from his position, and Professor Spencer carries with him the best wishes of his associates and students for his success in whatever line of effort he may direct his energies.

Mr. Joseph C. Gordon, M. A., for three years a successful instructor in the Indiana Institution for the Deaf and Dumb, has been appointed to the professorship of mathematics and chemistry, entering upon the performance of his duties at the beginning of the current academic year.

RETURN OF THE PRESIDENT FROM EUROPE.

At the end of the period of absence granted him by the board of directors, President Gallaudet resumed his duties with health apparently fully restored by the rest and freedom from care secured in his temporary residence abroad.

While in Europe he visited a number of institutions for the deaf and dumb, but met with nothing which he deems worthy to be reported to the board. No facts came to his notice which served to change the conclusions set forth in his "Report on the Systems of Deaf-Mute Instruction pursued in Europe," presented to the board in October, 1867.

While he would by no means claim that the system in general use throughout the United States is free from defects in its practical workings, he is convinced that the principles on which it rests are sound, and that greater benefits can be secured to the mass of deaf-mutes through its agency than by any system which undertakes to make articulation its basis, assuming to teach all deaf-mutes to speak, and discarding the language of signs.

During the absence of the president the general direction of the institution was committed to Professor Fay; and the recitations coming under the charge of the president, in his capacity as professor of moral and political science, were conducted by Professor Porter. Both these gentlemen discharged the duties thus devolved upon them to the entire satisfaction of the board. And in this connection commendatory mention should be made of the faithfulness and efficiency of the entire corps of officers, all of whom, during the absence of the president, were ever ready to sustain acting President Fay, and to do whatever lay in their power to advance the interests of the institution and maintain good order in its several departments.

THE COURSE OF STUDY.

The courses of study pursued in the several departments have remained essentially the same as in previous years. The following schedules will show the branches taught and the text-books used in the respective classes:

IN THE PRIMARY DEPARTMENT.

During the first and second years of instruction: Elementary Lessons for the Deaf and Dumb, by Harvey Prindle Peet, LL. D.; First Lessons for the Deaf and Dumb, by John R. Keep, M. A.; the School Reader, part first, by Charles W. Sanders, M. A.

During the third and fourth years: Lessons for Children, by Mrs. Barbauld; Reading without Tears, part second, by Mrs. Mortimer; Felter's Primary Arithmetic; Primary Geography, by Fordyce A. Allen, M. A.

During the fifth and sixth years: Primary History of the United States, by G. P. Quackenbos, A. M.; Common School History of the World, by S. G. Goodrich; First Lessons in English Grammar, by Simon Kerl, M. A.; New Intermediate Geography, by S. Augustus Mitchell; Felter's Intermediate Arithmetic.

Instruction is given through the whole course in the structure of the English sentence, and in penmanship according to the Spencerian system.

IN THE COLLEGIATE DEPARTMENT.

Studies of the preparatory class.

Mathematics.—Eaton's Grammar School Arithmetic; Loomis's Treatise on Algebra, (through quadratic equations.)

Physical Geography.—Guyot's Physical Geography.

History.—Lossing's Common School History of the United States.

Natural Philosophy.—Peck's Ganot's Natural Philosophy.

English.—Kerl's Common School Grammar; Berard's History of England; original compositions.

Latin—Allen's Latin Grammar; Allen's Latin Lessons; Cæsar's Commentaries.

Studies of the freshman class.

Mathematics.—Loomis's Treatise on Algebra ; Loomis's Geometry.
English.—Kerl's Common School Grammar, (reviewed ;) Berard's History of England ; original compositions.
Latin.—Sallust ; Cicero's Orations ; Allen's Latin Grammar.
* *Greek.*—Boise's First Lessons in Greek ; Hadley's Greek Grammar ;
Xenophon's Anabasis. •

Studies of the sophomore class.

Mathematics.—Loomis's Conic Sections ; Loomis's Plane and Spherical Trigonometry and Surveying.
Botany.—Gray's School and Field Book of Botany.
Chemistry.—Cooley's Chemistry, with lectures.
Latin.—Virgil's Æneid ; Odes of Horace.
* *Greek.*—Homer's Iliad.
History.—Thalheimer's Manual of Ancient History ; White's Eighteen Christian Centuries.
English.—Trench's English Past and Present ; original compositions

Studies of the junior class.

Mathematics.—Snell's Olmstead's Natural Philosophy ; Loomis's Treatise on Astronomy.
Chemistry.—Laboratory Practice, with lectures.
Mineralogy.—Dana's Manual of Mineralogy.
Geology.—Dana's Text-book of Geology.
French.—Prendergast's Mastery Method ; Otto's French Grammar ; Souvestre's Philosophe sous les Toits ; Erckmann-Chatrian's Romans Nationaux ; Racine's Athalie.
* *Greek.*—Demosthenes on the Crown.
History.—Guizot's History of Civilization.
English.—Bain's Rhetoric ; original compositions.

Studies of the senior class.

Geology.—Dana's Text-book of Geology.
Physiology.—Hitchcock's Anatomy and Physiology.
German.—Prendergast's Mastery Method ; Whitney's German Grammar ; Whitney's German Reader ; Fouqué's Undine ; Lessing's Minna von Barnhelm ; Schiller's Wilhelm Tell.
Mental philosophy and logic.—Porter's Elements of Intellectual Science ; Jevons's Logic.
English.—Shaw's Manual of English Literature ; original compositions.
Moral philosophy and evidences of Christianity.—Haven's Moral Philosophy ; Butler's Analogy.
Political philosophy.—Perry's Political Economy ; Woolsey's International Law.
Æsthetics.—Bascom's Elements of Beauty.
Instruction in book-keeping and in drawing and painting is given to those who desire it.
Instruction in articulation is given to those who desire it, and are found to possess such natural aptness for correct vocalization as seems to justify the great expenditure of time and labor essential to any satisfactory progress.

---

* Optional.

ENLARGEMENT OF THE LIBRARY.

During the past year the library of the institution has been enlarged by the addition of 317 volumes, making the total number of volumes 1021. The nearness of the great libraries of the Government makes it unnecessary for us to emulate other colleges in the increase of our library. Our aim is, therefore, to choose our books, with the view of having at hand only such as are likely to be often needed by our students and officers.

COMMENCEMENT EXERCISES.

The commencement exercises, on the ninth anniversary of the college, were held on Wednesday, June 25, in the hall of the institution.

The address to the graduating class was delivered by the Hon. John Eaton, jr., Commissioner of Education. After speaking of the great advance which had taken place in public sentiment with reference to the deaf and dumb, resulting in the establishment of a college for their benefit, the Commissioner addressed a few earnest words to the graduates, reminding them of the responsibility resting upon them, not only as educated men, but as representatives of the only college for deaf-mutes in the world.

* * * * *

EXPENDITURES.

I. SUPPORT OF THE INSTITUTION.

The receipts and disbursements for the year now under review will appear from the following detailed statements:

Receipts.

Received from Treasury of the United States	$48 000 00
Received from board and tuition	1,774 42
Received from work done in shop	756 23
Received from students for books and stationery	341 05
Received from sale of live stock	156 00
Received from board of two horses	113 00
Received from sale of insurance scrip	40 00
Received from rent	15 00
Received from damage to grounds by cattle	11 95
Received from sale of wood	10 00
Received from sale of old wagon-truck	8 00
Received from sale of old fencing	4 00
Received from sale of old bureau	5 00
Received from sale of old stove	3 00
Received from sale of fodder	3 00
Total	51,240 65

Disbursements.

Expended for salaries and wages	$23,495 75
Expended for meats	4,394 66
Expended for groceries	3,944 93
Expended for fuel	3,450 00
Expended for butter	1,969 80
Expended for household expenses, including vegetables	2,064 62
Expended for bread	1,452 35
Expended for hardware, including materials for repairs on buildings	1,215 20
Expended for books and stationery	1,187 70
Expended for dry goods and clothing	994 57
Expended for lumber	928 58
Expended for gas	851 40
Expended for blacksmithing and general repairs	891 59
Expended for furniture	718 42
Expended for paints and glass	540 77
Expended for medicines and chemicals	344 98
Expended for medical services	340 00

Expended for harness and 1 carriage...	$394 87
Expended for seeds and implements...	261 94
Expended for printing and engraving...	181 09
Expended for 1 iron safe..	175 00
Expended for 1 mare..	150 00
Expended for awnings..	128 00
Expended for stone...	152 14
Expended for cow and calf..	80 00
Expended for carriage-hire..	14 00
To balance..	821 39
	51,240 65

II. Improvement of Grounds.

Receipts.

Balance from old account...	$384 60
Received from Treasury of the United States......................................	6,000 00
Total...	6,384 60

Disbursements.

Paid for grading..	$1,970 85
Paid for lumber...	772 67
Paid for labor..	1,265 73
Paid for drain-pipe..	271 88
Paid for 1 wagon..	149 00
Paid for paving...	133 75
Paid for 1 mowing-machine..	170 00
Paid for freight...	24 53
Balance due the United States from disbursing agent..............................	1,626 19
Total...	6,384 60

PURCHASE OF KENDALL GREEN.

The following statement of receipts and disbursements on account of the purchase of Kendall Green dates back to April 2, 1870, the time at which the institution gained control of the property, and includes all expenses and payments on account of said purchase:

RECEIPTS.

Received for rent of houses...	$749 71
Received for fruit sold..	146 48
Received from manual-labor fund..	865 05
Received by transfer from general-expense account...............................	4,134 25
* Received from private subscriptions..	9,875 00
Received from the United States, July 1, 1872...................................	70,000 00
Total...	85,770 49

* See Appendix.

DISBURSEMENTS.

Expended for record of deeds, stamps, &c..	$178 75
Expended for payment due July 1, 1870...	5,000 00
Expended for interest due July 1, 1870...	1,275 00
Expended for interest due January 1, 1871.......................................	2,400 00
Expended for interest due July 1, 1871...	2,400 00
Expended for payment due July 1, 1871...	10,000 00
Expended for interest due January 1, 1872.......................................	2,100 00
Expended for interest due July 1, 1872...	2,100 00
Expended for balance of purchase-money remaining unpaid July 1, 1872.....	70,000 00
Expended for labor..	251 00
Expended for sundry items of interest..	174 19
Paid in collecting private subscriptions...	589 01
Total...	96,467 95

It will be seen that a balance remains unprovided for of $10,697.46.

By borrowing a portion of the annual appropriation for the support of the institution, the board have been able to avoid the necessity of paying interest on this balance of indebtedness, except for a few days at the end of the fiscal year. This is, however, an .arrangement which ought not to continue indefinitely. The board had hoped to be able to raise by private subscription an amount sufficient to liquidate this small debt; but the fact that the title to all the real estate of the institution has been vested in the United States is likely to stand in the way of the realization of this expectation; for private parties object, when called upon, that they should not be asked to aid what has practically become a Government institution.

We have submitted no estimate to provide for this balance, but we venture to direct the attention of Congress to the fact of the indebtedness, and to ask if it would not be proper that an appropriation should be made.

The importance of securing, at the low price paid, so valuable an estate as Kendall Green can hardly be overestimated, and we are sure that no one who considers the present and prospective value of the property will fail to perceive the great advantages likely to grow out of its acquisition by the Government.

ESTIMATES FOR NEXT YEAR.

The following estimates of appropriations required for the service of the fiscal year ending June 30, 1875, have already been submitted :

For the support of the institution, including salaries and incidental expenses, and $500 for books and illustrative apparatus, $49,500.

For continuing the work on the erection, furnishing and fitting up of the buildings of the institution, in accordance with plans heretofore submitted to Congress, including necessary repairs on the completed sections of the buildings, $54,000.

The estimate for building purposes is greatly needed, to enable us to proceed with the work of completing the college-building, and to provide for the erection of two professors' houses.

The college-building has stood in an incomplete condition for nearly seven years. Until within the last two years the completed portion sufficed for the accommodation of our collegiate department.

It is now, however, much crowded, and no possibility exists of conveniently accommodating more students, while we have reason to expect increased numbers of applications for admission during several years to come.

Only two rooms in the college-building can be used for recitations, and we are compelled to conduct our class-room exercises in corners of the chapel-hall and in other places temporarily arranged in the central building, all of which are inconvenient and ill adapted for the purposes to which we are compelled to devote them.

The rooms available for students' dormitories ought not to be made to contain more than twenty-five students, while the number at present occupying them is forty-seven.

The interests of the institution make it very desirable that its officers and employés should reside on the premises. The plans submitted to Congress in our ninth report, that for the year 1866-'67, showed our need of erecting, ultimately, six dwelling-houses for the officers of the institution.

Of this number only two have thus far been built. Two more are required at the present time for the accommodation of instructors who have young and growing families, and who are compelled to submit to arrangements involving considerable inconvenience both to them and to the institution.

All of which is respectfully submitted by order of the board of directors.

EDWARD M. GALLAUDET,
President.

Hon. COLUMBUS DELANO,
Secretary of the Interior.

REPORT OF THE BOARD OF VISITORS OF THE GOVERNMENT HOSPITAL FOR THE INSANE.

GOVERNMENT HOSPITAL FOR THE INSANE,
Near Washington, D. C., October 31, 1873.

SIR: In behalf of the Board of Visitors the undersigned have the honor to submit the eighteenth annual report of the "condition and wants of the institution."

The number of patients remaining under treatment on the 30th day of June, 1872, was—

From the Army,	white	males			151	
" " "	colored	"			6	
" " "	white	" (discharged)			126	
" " "	colored	"			2	
" " "	white	" (civilians)			3	
" " "	colored	"	"		1	
" " "	white females	"			3	
						292
From the Navy,	white	males			31	
" " "	colored	"			1	
" " "	white	" (discharged)			3	
" " "	colored	"	"		1	
					36	
						328
From civil life,	white	males			82	
" " "	"	females			110	
					192	
" " "	colored males				15	
" " "	" females				26	
					41	
						233

Males, 422; females, 139; total... 561

The number of patients admitted during the year ending June 30, 1873, was—

From the Army, white males			40	
" " " " " (discharged)			35	
			75	
From the Navy, white males			9	
" " " " " (discharged)			1	
			10	
				85
From civil life, white males			58	
" " " " females			37	
			95	
From civil life, colored males			8	
" " " " females			13	
			21	
				116

Males, 151; females, 50; total.. 201

Seven patients were admitted a second time in the course of the year. There were, therefore, seven less persons than cases under treatment.

The whole number of patients under treatment in the course of the year 1872–'73, was—

```
From the Army, white males.................................................  191
   "      "     "    colored "...............................................    6
   "      "     "    white  "  (discharged)..............................  161
   "      "     "    colored "    "    .................................    2
   "      "     "    white  "  (civilians).............................    3
   "      "     "    colored "    "    .................................    1
   "      "     "    white females "   .................................    3
                                                                    ——— 367
From the Navy, white males.................................................   40
   "      "     "    colored "............................................    1
   "      "     "    white  "  (discharged)............................    4
   "      "     "    colored "    "    .................................    1
                                                                    ——— 46
                                                                         ——— 413
From civil life, white males..............................................  140
   "      "     "      "    females.......................................  147
                                                                    ——— 287
   "      "     "    colored  males.......................................   23
   "      "     "       "     females.....................................   39
                                                                    ——— 62
                                                                         ——— 349

   Males, 573; females, 189; total..........................................  762
```

The number of patients discharged in the course of the year, was—

```
Recovered, from the Army, white males.............................   11
   "        "    "    "      colored "............................    1
   "        "    "    "      white  " (discharged)...............    4
                                                             ——— 16
   "        "    "  Navy, white male...............................    1
                                                                  ——— 17
   "        "  civil life, white males............................   31
   "        "    "    "      "   females..........................   10
                                                             ——— 41
   "        "    "    "    colored males..........................    3
   "        "    "    "      "   females..........................    5
                                                             ——— 8
                                                                  ——— 49
                                                                       —— 66
Improved, from the Army, white males, (discharged)...............    3
   "        "    "  Navy, white males.............................    4
   "        "    "    "    colored "..............................    1
                                                             ——— 5
                                                                  ——— 1
   "        "  civil life, white males............................   10
   "        "    "    "      "   females..........................    5
                                                             ——— 15
   "        "    "    "    colored male...........................    1
                                                             ——— 16
                                                                  ——— 24
Unimproved, from the Army, white male, (discharged)..............    1
   "        "    "  civil life, white males.......................    2
   "        "    "    "    "      "   females......................    4
                                                             ——— 6
                                                                  ——— 7

   Males, 73; females, 24; total..........................................   97
```

The number of patients who died in the course of the year, was—

```
From the Army, white males............................................     7
    "      "      "    colored  "     ........................................     1
    "      "      "    white    "    (discharged) ..............................    11
                                                                                 ——   19
    "      "   Navy, white males...........................................     2
                                                                                      ——   21
    "      civil life, white males............................................     8
    "        "     "      "    females........................................    12
                                                                                 ——   20
    "        "      "   colored males..........................................     3
    "        "      "       "    female........................................     1
                                                                                 ——    4
                                                                                      ——   24
```

Males, 32; females, 13; total 45

The number of patients remaining under treatment on the 30th day of June, 1873, was—

```
From the Army, white males............................................... 173
    "      "      "    colored "  ....................................     4
    "      "      "    white    "   (discharged) ..............................  142
    "      "      "    colored "          "      ................................     2
    "      "      "    white    "   (civilians)..............................     3
    "      "      "    colored "          "      ................................     1
    "      "      "    white females    "       ................................     3
                                                                                  —— 328
From the Navy, white males.............................................    33
    "      "      "        "      "   (discharged)..............................     4
    "      "      "    colored "          "      ................................     1
                                                                                  ——  38
                                                                                      —— 366
From civil life, white males.............................................    89
    "      "      "      "    females .........................................   116
                                                                                  —— 205
    "      "      "    colored males...........................................    16
    "      "      "       "    females ........................................    33
                                                                                  ——  49
                                                                                      —— 254
```

Males, 468; females, 152; total 620

The use of the word "discharged" in the preceding tables designates persons formerly in the military or naval service of the country, and admitted by authority of the act of July 13, 1866; and those designated as "civilian" are civil employés of the Army admitted by order of the Secretary of War, under authority of the same act.

* * * * * *

The recoveries this year were 68+ per cent. of the discharges, 46+ per cent. of the discharges and deaths together, 33— per cent. of the admissions, and 9— per cent. of the whole number of patients under treatment. The ratio of recoveries to discharges was somewhat higher, and that of the deaths to the whole number under treatment slightly lower than the average of several preceding years, and both are more favorable, perhaps, than they are likely to be in the years that are to come. As, under the original organic act and that of July 13, 1866, all cases of mental disease, of whatever duration or complication, that arise, or have arisen, in the Army and Navy, and in the District of Columbia, may be, as the most of them, in fact, are, sent to this institution, in which, when once legally within its walls, the chronic cases find a home for the remainder of their lives; and as the reception of all cases of insanity, recent and chronic, entitled to treatment in this hospital, and the continued residence of chronics, have now taken place for such a length of time that the average proportion of recent and chronic cases has found its normal adjustment, and the number of recent and presumptively curable cases with which one year is begun is only equal to that which goes over to the next, it becomes a fact of very great economic and social interest and importance that the ratios of recoveries and deaths to the numbers and movements of the household of this establishment during the past year, present an approximate expression of the average curability and mortality of all the insanity, if under treatment in hospitals, that exists in our different American communities.

Near the close of the wide prevalence of small-pox in the District last autumn and winter, four cases of variolous disease occurred in the hospital. The disease was introduced into the institution by an attendant, who spent the 9th of February in Washington, and was seized with the premonitory symptoms on the 23d. The other three cases were patients in the same ward with the attendant, who were seized on the third, fifth, and seventh days after his attack, and it is probable that he brought with him from town some infected piece of clothing or pocket article that communicated the disease to the patients before his own case had reached an infectious stage. All of the patients, officers, and employés of the institution were vaccinated between the 1st and 3d of January, and by the immediate repetition of the vaccination and the strictest isolation of the cases as they occurred, the further spread of the disease was happily prevented. Two of the cases proved to be variola in the confluent form, and two the modified disease. One of the former died and the other three recovered. It is quite remarkable that in the large population of the hospital, which is constantly receiving accessions from all parts of the country, these are the only cases of variolous disease that have occurred in the institution since the close of the late war. A part of the vaccinations were made with virus direct from the cow, and a part with humanized matter, but the results throw but little light upon the relative potency of the two kinds of virus. They are thought to be of sufficient interest, however, to justify their presentation here in a tabular form.

Tabular history of two vaccinations of 724 persons, the first on the 1st to 3d of January, and the second on the 26th of February, 1873.

	Number that appeared to have had variola, or varioloid.	Number that showed vaccine scars.	Number that did not appear to have been vaccinated with effect.	Whole number of patients, officers, and employés vaccinated.
	35	627	97	724
Number of vaccinations that ran a regular course and yielded characteristic crusts	4	110	36	150
Number that produced only irritative local inflammation	10	301	24	335
Number that was wholly ineffective	21	197	21	239
Whole number of patients, officers and employés vaccinated	35	608	81	724

No suicide has occurred in the course of the year, and the general health of the patients has been excellent.

Chapel services were suspended during the summer months of 1872, while the general-assembly room was undergoing thorough repairs, including re-frescoing and the addition of about 50 per cent. to the original number of seats, but were maintained as usual during the remainder of the year. The exhibition of photographs by the camera and hydro-oxygen light, musical soirees, and dramatic and literary entertainments, have also been continued with much spirit, and contributed largely to the happiness and improvement of a household whose retirement from the ordinary associations of men is essential to its safety and welfare; and in the year under review, as in all the previous years of the history of this great institution of beneficence and charity, a diligent, earnest, and, in view of the many inherent difficulties of the work and the imperfections that attend the best of human endeavors, we think we may say successful, effort has been made by its officers to fulfill in the entirety of their spirit and letter the noble objects of its creation and maintenance, which Congress nearly two decades of years ago declared to be "the most humane care and enlightened curative treatment of the insane of the Army and Navy of the United States and of the District of Columbia."

Soon after the preparation of the last report, the hospital came into possession of the tract of 29 acres, 1 rood and $2_{\frac{4}{10}}$ perches of agricultural land, for the purchase of which Congress had made the requisite appropriation, and more recently the United States has received the gratuitous deed of one-third of an acre of land lying adjacent to the northern boundary of the enclosed grounds, and embracing a deep, narrow ravine, the control of which by the hospital authorities will enable them to prevent the undermining of the boundary wall at that point. There are now owned by the United States and devoted to the objects of the hospital a little upwards of 419 acres of land, about 360 of which form one nearly complete parallelogram. The remainder is a separate tract, conveniently situated for grazing or the cultivation of the staple annual crops. The original purchase of about 185 acres, within which the hospital edifices are situated, is enclosed by a brick and stone wall 9 feet high above ground, except on the river-front, where the wall is designed to be a "sea" or "retaining" wall, which does not obstruct the view of the external scenery. One-half of the river-wall has been built.

With the additions that have been made to the original purchase of land for its use, the hospital is most fortunate in its site. Perhaps it is not practicable, under any circumstances, to attain to a higher degree than has so happily been done here, the desideratum to the insane of liberty and privacy—of opportunity for unconstrained as well as agreeable and healthful exercises in the open air, without the many serious evils of exposure to the curious public; and the extent of the agricultural lands and their variety of soil and exposure afford the most available means for the economic employment of the chronic cases, and for producing in abundance and at moderate cost the fresh fruits and vegetables, and pure milk that are so essential to the health and comfort of all classes of the insane.

As the institution now has the use of all the land it needs, both for the special purposes of a hospital of this character and for agricultural purposes, and is not likely to receive any further acquisition of territory, the accompanying contour-line map of the entire grounds has been prepared from critical and elaborate surveys made in the course of the past summer.

The expenditures and receipts in the year, were:

50 Ab

EXPENDITURES.

Expended for	flour, meal, and crackers	$11,452 69
"	butter and cheese	7,900 86
"	meats, including hams	16,766 51
"	poultry and eggs	718 85
"	fish	2,044 59
"	groceries and ice	14,173 56
"	potatoes and vegetables	2,066 61
"	feed for stock	3,558 04
"	agricultural implements, seeds, and fertilizers ; also fruit-trees, vines, and shrubs	1,596 49
"	stock	1,596 93
"	repairs and improvements on buildings, cooking, heating, and lighting apparatus, water-supply, farm and garden lands and roads	9,292 87
"	repairs to carriage, harness, &c	887 95
"	furniture, glass, china, and hardware	4,967 57
"	boots, shoes, findings, &c	1,552 03
"	bedding	1,994 90
"	dry goods	3,744 46
"	books, stationery, and printing	512,53
"	fuel and lights	7,867 16
"	money refunded to private patients	475 29
"	return of eloped patients	35 00
"	postage	120 89
"	salaries and wages	41,658 14
"	medicines, surgical instruments, and liquors	1,607 61
"	recreations and amusements	313 25
"	miscellaneous supplies	87 65
	Total	136,992 43

RECEIPTS.

From the Treasurer of the United States	125,000 00
" private patients, for board	9,744 86
" pigs, hides, rags, &c., sold	2,247 57
Total	136,992 43

The rate paid for the board of private patients has ranged from $4 to $12 per week, according to the means of individuals and the accommodations required. The average rate paid has not varied materially from that of several recent years, and, so far from contributing anything to the support of the dependent classes, it has been barely sufficient to comply with that clause of the organic act which requires that independent or pay patients shall not be received at " less than the actual cost of their support." The low average rate received for the board and treatment of the private patients admitted to this hospital, is doubtless due in part to the fact that there are but few people of large wealth in the national district from which most patients of this class come, but there is as little doubt that it is also due in part to a general indisposition among all citizens in all parts of the republic, to pay a Government institution a profit upon any service it renders them. It is the same common sentiment that prevents the hospital from realizing all the income to which it is entitled by that provision of law which requires those patients admitted by order of the Hon. Secretary of the Interior to pay such a portion of the expenses of their board and treatment as they are able.

In addition to the disbursements for the support of the hospital, an appropriation of $37,800 was expended in the erection of an extension of the wards for the excited classes of patients, and $6,000 for heating boilers. The appropriation for the purchase of land was disbursed by the Department.

The new wards are at least as cheerful and pleasant as any others of the establishment, and great pains has been taken to adapt their construction, furniture and fittings to the care and comfort of the excited classes of patients.

The several sums asked in the last report were appropriated in full, except that, in consequence of a misunderstanding, it is believed, a reduction of $5,500 was made in the grant for the support of the house after the bill containing the amount of the original estimate had passed the House of Representatives.

* * * * * * *

The estimates already submitted for the year ending June 30, 1875, are as follows:

1. For the support, clothing, and medical and moral treatment of the insane of the Army and Navy and Revenue-Cutter Service, and of all persons who have become insane since their entry into the military or naval service of the United States, and who are in indigent circumstances, and of the indigent insane of the District of Columbia, in the Government Hospital for the Insane, $140,785.

At the close of the year ending June 30, 1873, there were under treatment in the hospital 621 patients, 41 of whom paid, on an average, the cost of their support, leaving 580 who were supported wholly by the Government. Under the acts of Congress providing for the care and treatment in this institution of several classes of insane persons at the expense of the Government, more patients were sent to it in July and August of the current year than the average monthly admissions in last year, and it is estimated that the average number of such patients that it will be necessary to provide for under existing laws in the year 1874-'75, will be not less than 600. Experience shows that the expenditure of $4.50 per week for the entire maintenance, including clothing and medical and moral treatment of each patient, with a careful economy in purchasing and disbursing supplies, in the management of the farm and garden, and in the staff of assistants and employés, is barely sufficient to afford all the comforts and advantages of treatment to which the insane supported by the Government are entitled, and that the rate cannot be properly lessened. At that rate the maintenance of an average of 600 patients during the year in question, will cost the amounts asked for that purpose.

2. To supply the deficiency in the amount ($125,000) appropriated to support the hospital during the current year, (1873-'74,) $11,366.

The estimates for the current year were based upon the supposition that there would be an average of 555 patients to be supported by the Government, under the requirements of existing laws, at an estimated cost of $130,500, but only $125,000 were appropriated for this object, as before stated in this report; and instead of an average of 555 non-paying patients, there were 580 at the beginning of this year, or 25 more than were estimated for; and there is the strongest probability that the average number of this class of patients through the year will be larger than at its beginning. The deficiency in the appropriation is $5,500, and the cost of maintaining 25 additional patients will be $5,866, and the sum of those amounts is the amount of this estimate.

3. For repairs and improvements, $15,000.

Additions to the original plan of the hospital and the increase in the number of patients under treatment, render it necessary to correspondingly increase the size of the ventilating fan and of the engine that drives it, and to furnish and fit up another kitchen. About one-third of the amount of this estimate will be needed for those purposes, and the remainder will be required for painting and repairs necessary to preserve public property, and for such improvements in the furniture and fitting up of the wards and in the facilities for the medical and moral management of the patients, as are suggested by experience and the progress of this branch of the healing art.

4. For completing the river-wall and raising the boundary-walls at their intersection with the latter, $8,748.

The river-wall has been built on just one-half the extent of the river front, at a cost of $10,000, but as the average depth of the water is less along the line of the remainder of the river front, it is estimated that this part of the work can be completed for $7,788, and that the cost of raising those portions of the boundary-walls that were originally extended into the river as water-fences and now intersect the front wall so that the former cannot be scaled from the latter, nor from the filling of earth behind it, will be $960, the two amounts making the sum of $8,748.

5. For the erection, furnishing, and fitting up of an extension of the center building of the hospital edifice, $35,956.

The center building of the hospital edifice contains the administrative offices of the establishment, the principal kitchens and store-rooms, the general-assembly room and the officers' quarters. The hospital was originally intended to accommodate a maximum of 350 patients, and the present center was planned for an institution of that size. The number of patients now under treatment exceeds 600, and is increasing, and more room is required for the assembling of the patients, both for worship on the Sabbath and for lectures, concerts, and exhibitions on other days of the week. The present assembly-room accommodates barely 350 patients and their attendants, and at least 100 of the inmates of the institution, whose mental condition is such that they would derive pleasure and benefit from being present on such occasions, are now unable to attend the Sabbath services and the entertainments on other days. Additional room is also much needed for all the other purposes for which the center building was designed and is used. It is proposed to add 45 feet to the rear end of the present structure, and by extending the assembly-room into the addition, nearly double its present capacity; and the two stories and a cellar below the addition to the assembly-room will afford the other rooms and accommodations that are needed.

6. For a coal-vault in rear of the east wing, $2,500.

The demand for increased accommodations has rendered it necessary to fit up two of the original coal-rooms for dining-rooms, and to use the remaining two as work-shops, and for some years it has been necessary to deposit the most of the coal used in heating the house, in a huge, unsightly pile a short distance outside of the windows of patients' rooms. By using the foundation walls of the house for two sides of the vault, it is estimated that convenient storage-room for 500 tons of coal can be secured for the moderate amount of the estimate.

7. For the erection, furnishing, and fitting up of an extension of the west detached building for patients, $12,000.

This building was erected in 1856 to accommodate 20 patients, and it may be extended so as to comfortably accommodate at least 44. The room is needed, and it can be obtained in no cheaper way, nor in any manner that will be more advantageous to the proper ward-separation of those classes of the insane whose "most humane care and enlightened curative treatment" is required alike by the laws of Congress and the public sentiment which those laws embody.

The members of the board of visitors have in the past year, as in all previous years since the organization of the board in 1855, made frequent and careful inspections of all departments of the hospital, and it affords them much pleasure to be able to certify that the general condition and management of the institution under their supervision are highly satisfactory, and to express their belief, founded upon personal observation, that the assistant physicians and principal heads of the several divisions of the hospital service have been earnest and faithful in the discharge of their respective duties, and devoted to the comfort and welfare of the patients.

Chapel services having been interrupted for some time for the improvement of the general-assembly room, two vacancies in the corps of chaplains, which occurred by reason of the removal of the incumbents from the district, were not filled by the appointment of other clergymen. The chapel and other religious services have been satisfactorily conducted. The chaplains and occasional visitors frequently express surprise at the quiet that generally prevails among the patients, and the close and apparently intelligent attention that is paid to all the exercises.

We should not fail to acknowledge the valuable services of several of the attendants of both sexes, who by their tact, patience, and kindness in their treatment of the inmates under their immediate care have won not only the high respect both of the officers of the institution and of the best of their own associates and friends, but the gratitude of many patients and of their relatives and friends.

We are, very respectfully, your obedient servants,

W. GUNTON,
President of the Board.
C. H. NICHOLS,
Secretary ex-officio.

Hon. COLUMBUS DELANO,
Secretary of the Interior.

REPORT

OF

THE POSTMASTER-GENERAL.

POST-OFFICE DEPARTMENT,
Washington, D. C., November 14, 1873.

SIR: The ordinary revenues of this Department for the fiscal year ended June 30, 1873, were $22,996,741.57, and the expenditures of all kinds $29,084,945.67. For the year ended June 30, 1872, the ordinary revenues were $21,915,426.37, and the expenditures $26,658,192.31. In 1873 there was an increase of revenue over 1872 of $1,081,315.20, or 4.93 per cent., and an increase of expenditures of $2,426,753.36, or 9.10 per cent. A comparison of 1873 with 1871 shows an increase in revenues of $2,959,696.15, or 14.42 per cent., and an increase of expenditures of $4,694,841.59, or 19.24 per cent. The increase or decrease in each item of receipt and expenditure during the fiscal year ended June 30, 1873, as compared with the years ended June 30, 1872, and June 30, 1871, respectively, is shown by table No. 2, accompanying the report of the Third Assistant Postmaster-General.

If, in addition to the ordinary revenues, the Department is credited with the amounts drawn and expended for subsidies to mail steamship-lines, ($725,000,) it will be seen that the amount drawn from the general Treasury under the appropriations to meet deficiencies during the year was $5,265,475, against $3,317,765.94 in 1872. To the deficiency for 1872, however, are to be added the standing appropriations for free matter, amounting to $700,000, which have since been repealed.

The estimated expenditures for the year ending June 30, 1875, are.... $33,929,912 00

The ordinary revenues, estimated at 13 per cent. over
1873 .... $25,908,817 00
Estimated revenue from money-order business........ 100,000 00
Estimated revenue from postal cards................. 1,034,732 00
Estimated revenue from postage-stamps supplied to
Departments 2,250,000 00

Making the total estimated revenues for 1875 .... 29,293,549 00

Leaving a deficiency to be appropriated out of the general Treasury of. 4,636,363 00

The foregoing estimates do not include the following special appropriations in the nature of subsidies:

For mail steamship-service between San Francisco and Japan and China,
under acts approved February 17, 1865, and February 18, 1867........ $500,000 00
For additional subsidy under act approved June 1, 1872.................. 500,000 00
For mail steamship-service between the United States and Brazil, under
act of May 28, 1864.. 150,000 00

For mail steamship-service between San Francisco and the Sandwich Islands, under act of March 2, 1867 .... $75,000 00

Total 1,225,000 00

Of the appropriations for deficiencies there were unexpended on June 30, 1872, the following amounts, viz:
For the fiscal year 1869–'70 .... $1,000,000 00
For the fiscal year 1870–'71 .... 2,618,396 00
For the fiscal year 1871–'72. .... 885,633 00
$4,504,029 00
Amount appropriated for the fiscal year 1872–'73 .... 5,700,970 00

A total of... 10,204,999 00
There were drawn during the last fiscal year, on account of payment, for previous fiscal years, the following:
Of the amount appropriated for 1869–'70 .... $152,225 00
Of the amount appropriated for 1870–'71 .... 978,000 00
Of the amount appropriated for 1871–'72. .... 535,000 00
Of the amount appropriated for 1872–'73 .... 3,600,250 00
5,265,475 00

Leaving the amount of appropriations for deficiencies undrawn and available for payments of indebtedness to June 30, 1873.............. 4,939,524 00
Against this sum there are chargeable sundry unliquidated accounts estimated as follows:
For balances to foreign countries............................ $116,200 00
For mail-service under contract and recognized, but not yet reported... 393,643 00
For mail-service still unrecognized....................... 157,000 00
666,843 00

Leaving, after settlement of all liabilities to June 30, 1873, a net balance of deficiency-appropriations of............................... 4,272,681 00

The number of adhesive postage-stamps issued during the year was 601,931,520, representing.. $16,681,189 00
Stamped-envelopes, plain, 65,014,600, representing..................... 1,722,512 00
Stamped-envelopes, "request," 52,201,250, representing............... 1,544,567 50
Newspaper-wrappers, 13,956,750, representing......................... 140,567 50
Postal-cards, 31,094,000, representing.................................. 310,940 00

The whole number of stamps, stamped-envelopes, newspaper-wrappers, and postal-cards was 764,198,120, of the value of.................... 20,399,776 00

The increase in the issue of stamps, stamped-envelopes, newspaper-wrappers, and postal-cards is exhibited by the following table:

Description.	Fiscal year ended June 30, 1873.	Fiscal year ended June 30, 1872.	Increase, amount	Increase, per cent.
Adhesive postage-stamps.................	$16,681,189 00	$15,840,649 00	$840,540 00	5.31
Stamped-envelopes, plain	1,722,512 00	1,663,196 50	59,315 50	3.56
Stamped-envelopes, requests	1,544,567 50	1,391,630 00	152,937 50	10.99
Newspaper-wrappers......................	140,567 50	175,152 50	*34,585 00	*19.75
Postal-cards.............................	310,940 00	....	310,940 00	....
Aggregate	20,399,776 00	19,070,628 00	1,329,148 00	6.97

* Decrease.

The number of packages of postage-stamps lost in the mails during the year was three, representing $59, and of stamped envelopes one, representing $8.45, and of postal cards none; being the smallest losses ever incurred during any year. This is undoubtedly owing to the fact that all packages of postage-stamps, stamped-envelopes, newspaper-wrappers, and postal-cards are registered, and illustrates in a most effective manner the security of the registry system.

CONTRACTS.

There were in the service of the Department, on the 30th of June, 1873, 5,930 contractors for the transportation of the mails on public routes.

There were, at the close of the year, 2,359 "special" offices, each with a mail-carrier, whose pay from the Department is not allowed to exceed the net postal yield of the office.

Of public mail-routes in operation there were 7,424, aggregating in length 256,210 miles; in annual transportation, 119,909,650 miles; and in annual cost, $13,635,341. Adding the compensation of railway post-office clerks, route-agents, mail-route messengers, local agents, mail-messengers, and baggage-masters in charge of registered packages, amounting to $2,525,693, the aggregate annual cost was $16,161,034. .

The service was divided as follows:

Railroad routes: Length, 63,457 miles; annual transportation, 65,-621,445 miles; annual cost, $7,257,196—about 11.06 cents per mile.

Steamboat routes: Length, 16,762 miles; annual transportation, 3,947,785 miles; annual cost, $799,645—about 20.25 cents per mile.

Other routes, upon which the mails are required to be conveyed with "celerity, certainty, and security:" Length, 175,991 miles; annual transportation, 50,340,420 miles; annual cost, $5,578,500—about 11.08 cents per mile.

There was an increase over the preceding year in length of routes of 4,812 miles; in annual transportation, 4,925,328 miles; and in cost, $1,063,077. Adding the increased cost for railway post-office clerks, route, local, and other agents, $318,749, the total increase in cost was $1,381,826.

The railroad routes have been increased in length 5,546 miles, and in cost $754,425, against an increase last year of 8,077 miles in length and $777,792 in cost.

RE-ADJUSTMENT OF PAY ON RAILROAD ROUTES.

About the 1st of February, 1873, circulars were sent out from the Department to the proprietors of railroad routes in the States of Maine, New Hampshire, Vermont, Massachusetts, Rhode Island, Connecticut, and New York, calling for returns of the amount and character of the mail-service they performed, with a view to the re-adjustment of their pay for the new contract term commencing 1st of July, 1873. The results are shown in Table E, which contains returns, also, as usual, from routes in other States. The passage of the act approved March 3, 1873, providing for a general re-adjustment of pay on railroad routes upon a showing of the state of the service to be furnished for a period subsequent to June 30, 1873, prevented the use of the returns made under the call of 1st of February, 1873, as data for determining the compensation for the new contract term in the States above named; and, in conformity with the requirements of the new law, the proprietors of all the railroad routes in the country have been called upon to submit new returns for thirty days, commencing 1st of October, 1873, this month being supposed to afford a fair average for the year. The re-adjustment to be predicated upon these new returns, (which are not yet at hand,) will take effect from the commencement of the current fiscal year. Payments have been made for the quarter ended 30th of September, 1873, but with the understanding that they are hereafter to be modified, if necessary, to agree with the character of the new returns. Table F exhibits the re-adjustment of the rates on 52 routes, and the adjustment of rates on 21 new routes, ordered within the year ended 30th of September, 1873, to take effect prior to the close of the last fiscal year. The rates were increased, it will be seen, on 44 routes and decreased on 8, the net increase in the amount of annual pay being $223,823.55. The 21 new routes included in the table are only a portion of the new routes put in operation, temporary rates, not exceeding the maximum fixed by law for routes of the lowest class, being allowed on the residue in the absence of the usual returns. The number of new railroad routes put in operation during the year ended June 30, 1873, was 61.

POST-ROUTE MAPS.

The work of the topographer has been continued and extended, with good results to all branches of the public service. A large map, in four sheets, on a scale of ten miles to the inch, of the States of Illinois, Missouri, and Iowa, with adjacent parts of Wisconsin, Minnesota, Nebraska, and Kansas, has been finished during the year, and many copies printed and distributed. The increasing demand, already beyond the capacity of the Department to satisfy, for this and the other maps previously published, and the many encomiums bestowed upon them for accuracy, clearness, and neatness of execution, attest the high esteem in which they are held.

FINES AND DEDUCTIONS.

The amount of fines imposed upon contractors and deductions made from their pay for failures and other delinquencies, for the year, was $75,277.53; and the amount remitted during the same period was $8,617.08; leaving the net amount of fines and deductions $66,660.45.

MAIL-BAGS, LOCKS, AND KEYS.

A table appended to this report exhibits in detail the number, description, and cost of mail-bags and mail-catchers, and of mail-locks and keys, purchased under contracts, during the last year. Of locked mail-bags, (used for letters,) there were 8,600; of tied mail-bags, (used for printed matter,) there were 86,650; and of mail-catchers, (used for exchanging mails with postal cars under full speed,) there were 300. The total cost of bags and catchers was $94,828.40. The total cost of mail-locks and keys, including repairs, was $28,018.76.

THROUGH MAILS.

The through-mail tables appended hereto exhibit an improvement in the service between New York and San Francisco, the average time westward, during the year ended 30th September, 1873, being 179 hours 4 minutes, a little less than seven and a half days, against 216 hours 23 minutes, or more than nine days, the preceding year; and the average time eastward, 174 hours 59 minutes, a little over seven and a quarter days, against 197 hours 45 minutes, or nearly eight and a quarter days, the preceding year. Between Washington and New Orleans the average time was about four hours more going south, and about three hours less going north, than during the preceding year, the time south being 81 hours 45 minutes, against 77 hours 39 minutes the preceding year, and the time north 72 hours 53 minutes, against 75 hours 38 minutes the preceding year. The usual full details will be found in the tables of the service on the lines running westward from Washington and New York to Cincinnati, Saint Louis, and Chicago.

MAIL DEPREDATIONS.

The number of recorded complaints for the past year of missing letters was 6,165, of which 3,980 were unregistered and 2,185 registered, containing in the former, as reported, in bonds, drafts, and currency, $309,123.53, and in the latter $70,421.91. Of the registered letters, 899 were accounted for, 313 are reported as actually lost, and 973 are still in the hands of special agents for investigation. During the year 302 persons were arrested for various offenses against the postal laws and regulations. Of these, 94 have been convicted, 20 have been acquitted, 193 are awaiting trial, and 95 have been discharged for want of proof sufficient to insure conviction. It is amazing that so many persons will persist in sending money through the mails, thereby subjecting themselves and the public to risk, and tempting the weak to dishonesty and ruin, when the Department provides the means of safe transmission by money-orders at an insignificant cost. Some of the most experienced officers in the service are of the opinion that Congress should adopt such legislation as will prevent the use of the mails for the conveyance of money in letters, and compel the registration of every valuable package.

RAILWAY POST-OFFICES.

A tabular statement hereto appended shows that the number of railway post-office lines in operation on the 30th of June, 1873, was 59, extending over 14,866 miles of railroad and steamboat routes—an increase of 2 lines and 749 miles over the preceding year. The number of clerks employed was 752, at an annual cost of $941,000—an increase of 103 clerks and $119,400. Upon 12,312 miles the service is performed daily; upon 2,533 miles twice daily, and upon 21 miles four times daily, equivalent in all to 17,462 miles each way daily. Counting all the lines both ways, the aggregate service is 34,925 miles daily.

FOREIGN MAILS.

The total number of letters exchanged during the year with foreign countries was 27,459,185, an increase of 3,096,685 over the number reported for 1872. Of this number, 14,332,674 were sent from and 13,126,511 were received in the United States.

The number of letters (single rates) exchanged in the United States and European mails was 19,585,514, an increase of 1,902,515 over the number reported for 1872.

The total postages on the letters exchanged with foreign countries amounted to $2,021,310.86, an increase of $150,053.61 over the amount reported for 1872.

The aggregate amount of postage (sea, inland, and foreign) on the letter-mails exchanged with the United Kingdom of Great Britain and Ireland, Germany, France, Belgium, the Netherlands, Switzerland, Italy, Denmark, Sweden, Norway, and Spain, was $1,406,507.50, an increase of $102,653.45 over the amount reported for 1872. The postages on letters *sent* exceeded the postages on letters *received* from the same countries, in the sum of $22,934.58, being 1.63 per cent. of the aggregate amount. The postages collected in the United States amounted to $865,511.47, and in Europe to $540,996.03; the excess of collections in the United States being $324,515.44, or 23 per cent. of the entire postage receipts on European correspondence.

Comparing the year 1873 with the year 1872, the rate of increase in the total number of letters exchanged with foreign countries was 12.7 per cent., and the rate of increase in the amount of postages thereon was 8 per cent. The increase in the number of letters exchanged with European countries was 10¾ per cent., and the increase of postages thereon amounted to 7⅞ per cent.

The total weight of mails exchanged during the year with European countries was 1,825,397 pounds, (over 912 tons,) an increase of 184,708 pounds, or 92 tons, compared with the previous year. The weight of letter-correspondence was 397,339 pounds, and of printed matter and samples, 1,428,058 pounds. The aggregate weight of mails *sent* to Europe was 899,580 pounds, and of mails *received* from Europe 925,817 pounds. The weight of letter-correspondence *sent* to Europe was 211,616½ pounds, and of letter-correspondence *received* from Europe 185,722½ pounds. The weight of printed matter and samples *sent* to Europe was 687,964 pounds, and of printed matter and samples *received* from Europe 740,094 pounds.

The cost of the United States transatlantic mail steamship service for the year 1873 was $226,745.77, being an increase of $6,440.07 over the cost of the same service for the year 1872. The payments made to the respective steamship lines conveying mails to Europe, receiving the sea-postages as full compensation for the service, were as follows:

The Liverpool and Great Western, (Williams and Guion line,) for 51 trips from New York to Queenstown...	$79,294 43
The Hamburg-American Packet Company, for 52 trips from New York to Plymouth and Hamburg, and four trips from New Orleans to France, Spain, and Hamburg...	57,958 88
The North German Lloyd of Bremen, for 77 trips from New York to South-ampton and Bremen, and also for conveying mails from Baltimore and New Orleans to Bremen..	33,573 74
The White Star line, for 33 trips from New York to Queenstown..........	29,831 97
The Inman line, for 16 trips from New York to Queenstown...............	14,641 70
The Canadian line, for 52 trips to Liverpool	6,055 13
The Cunard line, for 55 trips from Boston to Liverpool..................	4,977 37
The National line, for 2 trips from New York........................	390 49
The Baltic Lloyd line for 1 trip from New York to Stettin...............	12 07
Total	226,745 77

The United States postages on mails conveyed to and from the West Indies, Panama, and Central America, Brazil, Mexico, Bermuda, Nova Scotia, New Granada, and New Zealand, amounted to $137,517.68, and the cost of the sea conveyance thereof was $95,525.58. The United States postages on mails exchanged with Brazil, Japan, and China, the Sandwich Islands, New Zealand, and Australia, by means of the sub-sidized lines of direct mail-steamers, amounted to $49,829.38. The total cost of the United States ocean mail steamship service for the year 1873, (including $725,000 paid from special appropriation for steam-ship service to Japan and China, to Brazil, and to the Hawaiian Islands,) was $1,047,271.35.

A new contract has been executed with the Pacific Mail Steamship Company, for the additional monthly mail between San Francisco and Hong-Kong, (China,) via Yokohama, (Japan,) authorized by sections 3 and 6 of the act of Congress approved June 1, 1872, which discharges and releases from future responsibility the sureties for said company under the original contract, executed the 29th of August, 1872, and sub-stitutes new sureties in their stead. A copy thereof is hereto annexed.

The additional service authorized by the law of June 1, 1872, should have been commenced on the 1st of October, 1873, by American-built iron steamships of not less than 4,000 tons register. The company has, however, failed to comply with its contract, because, as is alleged, of unexpected difficulties, which retarded the building of the new steamships now being constructed for this service.

In the statement submitted by the company of the causes of its failure to place the new ships on the line on the 1st of October last, it appears that immediately after the passage of the act of Congress authorizing the additional monthly mail on this route, a contract was made for the construction of two iron screw-steamers of upwards of 4,000 tons register, the hulls of which are now nearly completed, and that the first of these ships will be launched early in December next.

In the month of May, 1872, the Pacific Mail Steamship Company commenced an additional monthly mail service between San Francisco and Japan and China, which has been maintained regularly, with three exceptions, to the present date; for which service the sea-postages on the mails transported have been allowed as full compensation, under the provisions of the general law fixing the rates of compensation for the sea-conveyance of mails; so that a regular semi-monthly mail service is now being performed on the line, although by steamers of less tonnage than that required for the additional monthly service. The company has requested that it may be permitted to continue the service as at present, until it can place the new ships of the required tonnage on the line. It is, doubtless, doing all it can, with its present resources, to comply, in good faith, with the requirements of the contract at an early day; but, as this service was specially authorized by act of Congress, upon certain prescribed terms and limitations, and the success or failure of the enterprise is a question fraught with important national interests, I have not felt at liberty either to annul the contract for the additional monthly service on account of the failure to commence the same on the day fixed by law, or to give any permission or assurance for a continuance of the contract and service as requested by the company. No good reason is, however, perceived why the company should not be permitted to continue the service as at present, until the new ships are completed and placed upon the line, with the understanding that it shall make no claim upon the additional subsidy, or any part thereof, but shall receive the sea-postage only, as heretofore, in full compensation for the additional service, until the contract shall be fully complied with.

Notice was given to this department on the 4th of March, 1873, by the United States, New Zealand and Australia Mail Steamship Company of the withdrawal of its steamers from the route between San Francisco, New Zealand, and the Australian Colonies, via the Sandwich Islands, the effort of said company to establish an American line of mail-steamships on that route having proved unsuccessful.

A postal convention has been concluded with the United Kingdoms of Sweden and Norway, establishing and regulating a direct exchange of correspondence with those kingdoms, at reduced postage charges.

This convention, a copy of which is appended, was carried into operation on the 1st of July, 1873.

A second additional postal convention has been concluded with Belgium, a copy of which is appended, reducing, on and after July 1, 1873, the single rate of letter postage from 10 to 8 cents, by closed mail via England, and to 6 cents by direct steamers.

An exchange of postal cards with Canada, and also with Newfoundland, has been established on the basis of a prepaid postage of 2 cents in full to destination in either direction, prepayment thereof to be made by affixing to the card an ordinary 1-cent postage-stamp of the country of origin in addition to the stamp printed or impressed thereon. Copies of the additional articles providing therefor are appended.

A similar arrangement has been concluded with the post-department of North Germany for the mutual exchange of United States and German postal cards, on prepayment of a postage of 2 cents on cards from the United States for Germany, and of one silber groschen on cards from Germany for the United States. The additional articles providing for such exchange are hereto appended.

A proposition to the British office for a like arrangement for an exchange of United States and British postal cards, has been declined by that office.

A postal convention, establishing and regulating an exchange of correspondence between the United States and the empire of Japan, by means of direct lines of steamships plying between the sea-ports of the two countries, has been formally agreed upon and executed with the chargé d'affaires of Japan at Washington, and is to be carried into effect six months after its ratification by the government of Japan.

The basis of a postal convention with France was agreed upon at Paris, in the month of October last, between Mr. Washburne, our minister to France, and the director-general of the French post-office, which fixed the single rate of international postage for letters at 8 cents (40 centimes) per each 10 grams or fraction thereof, to be divided equally between the two countries. The articles of this basis were transmitted to me for consideration, but before any action was taken upon them, the negotiations were transferred to Washington, and renewed through the Marquis de Noailles, envoy extraordinary and minister plenipotentiary of France, for the avowed object of obtaining such an increase of letter-postage as would guarantee to France her full interior letter rate of 20 centimes. The proposition to increase the single rate of letter-postage from 40 to 50 centimes, and other changes of the basis agreed upon at Paris relating to the standard weight for letters and a just division of the expenses of intermediate sea-transportation, were fully considered at several interviews had with the Marquis de Noailles, but without result. I objected to increasing the letter-postage, because of my earnest desire to establish a letter rate approximating in some degree to the much cheaper rates established between the United States and Great Britain, Germany, and other leading countries of Europe. I was also unwilling to accept the French domestic letter standard of 10 grams, because, being exceptional, and differing from our domestic standard of one-half ounce, which is also used in rating postage on letters exchanged with all other countries, it could not be applied at our post-offices without serious embarrassment and difficulty, resulting from mistakes in collecting the proper amount of postage, and consequent additional charges at destination. At length, finding· it impossible to conclude a satisfactory arrangement on the ordinary plan of optional prepayment of postage, and wishing to divest the subject of the perplexing questions of disagreement, I submitted the simple proposition for a postal convention on the plan of "compulsory prepayment, with no accounts," the main features of which were: An international letter-postage of 9 cents, and the nearest equivalent thereof in French money; prepayment obligatory, the mailing country to retain to its own use all the postage it collects, and the receiving country to deliver at destination free of charge; each country to levy and collect postage by the standard weight adopted for its domestic mails, and to defray the expenses of intermediate transportation of the mails sent to the other. In submitting this proposition, this Department yielded to France an increase of the rate of letter-postage and the advantage of rating and collecting her postage by the smaller standard of weight; and nothing can be urged against its adoption except the demand that this country shall use the exceptional French standard for rating letters. It has been submitted by the French minister to his government for instructions, and I trust it will be accepted, as it concedes all that, in my judgment, this Department can concede to effect a settlement of the vexed questions in controversy, a due regard being had to the interests and convenience of the American people.

APPOINTMENTS.

The report of the appointment-office shows the following:

Number of post-offices established during the year	2,462
Number discontinued	1,081
Increase	1,381
Number in operation on June 30, 1872	31,863
Number in operation on June 30, 1873	33,244
Number filled by appointments of the President	1,363
Number filled by appointments of the Postmaster-General	31,881

Appointments were made during the year—

On resignations	4,802
On removals	945
On changes of names and sites	193
On deaths of postmasters	386
On establishment of new post-offices	2,462
Total appointments	8,788
Number of cases acted on during the year	10,101

The number and aggregate compensation of special agents, route-agents, mail-route messengers, railway post-office clerks, and local agents in service during the year ended June 30, 1873, were—

47 special agents*	$155, 03
752 railway post-office clerks	941, 00
862 route-agents	824, 24
171 mail-route messengers	108, 74
110 local agents	82, 86

1,942 Total	2, 113, 90

The free-delivery system has been in operation during the year in fifty-two of the principal cities, with the following aggregate results :

Number of letter-carriers	1, 490
Mail-letters delivered	140, 958, 87
Local letters delivered	38, 340. 04
Newspapers delivered	43, 390. 65
Letters collected	137, 065, 69
Newspapers collected	15, 560, 373
Whole number of pieces handled	374, 915, 664
Amount paid carriers, including incidental expenses	$1, 422, 495. 4
Average cost per piece	3.8 mills
Amount of postage on local matter	$1, 112, 251 21

Showing the following increase compared with last year :

Letter-carriers	56
Mail-letters delivered	13, 860. 059
Local letters delivered	5, 336. 16
Letters collected	6, 703. 25
Amount paid carriers, including incidental expenses	$33, 567. 5
Postage on local matter	$204, 499. 5
Percentage of increase of receipts on local postage	.22
Percentage of increase in cost of service	.03

With this report ends the first decade of the free-delivery service in this country. The grounds mainly relied upon for its establishment and extension, namely, public convenience and the stimulus to correspondence, have been fully verified by experience thus far. This system, with its letter-boxes located at convenient points throughout the large postal centers, and its frequent deliveries and collections of mail-matter by carriers, has proved to be a virtual extension of the post-office to every house. The transaction of the postal business of large communities by a few men selected for the purpose is justified, in an economic point of view, by the time saved to the people, the saving of labor in post-offices, the facilities and stimulus given to correspondence, the frequency, promptness, and accuracy secured in the delivery of letters, and the reduction of the number of advertised and dead letters. While these benefits are most apparent in the larger cities, they are seen and appreciated in all places where the frequency of the mails, the density of the population, and the distance from the

---

* Other special agents charged to separate appropriations.

office make it inconvenient for citizens to call or send for their mail. The average of population to each carrier varies with the number of people to be served from the office, the extent of territory, and the frequency of the deliveries. The general average, however, is estimated at 3,690. The expense of the system at each office is paid out of the revenue of that office. It seems but fair, therefore, that this mode of delivery should be extended to all cities where the population, business, extent of territory, and frequency of the mails may authorize the requisite force and outlay. Just how far these elements should combine to warrant the extension of the system, it is difficult to determine; but I am of the opinion that it might be advantageously provided for cities having in their corporate limits a population of not less than ten thousand.

The following table shows the number of employés in the Post-Office Department; also the number of postmasters, contractors, clerks in post-offices, route-agents, railway post-office clerks, and other officers in service on the 30th June, 1872, and the 30th June, 1873, respectively:

Departmental officers and employés:

1872.		1873.
1	Postmaster-General	1
3	Assistant Postmasters-General	3
1	Superintendent of Foreign Mails	1
1	Superintendent of Money-Order System	1
1	chief of division of dead letters	1
1	chief clerk of Department	1
4	chief clerks of bureaus	4
334	clerks, laborers, watchmen, &c	342
346		354

Other officers and agents:

31,863	postmasters	33,244
5,544	contractors	5,930
3,754	clerks in post-offices	4,025
1,443	letter-carriers	1,499
764	route-agents	862
642	railway post-office clerks	752
146	mail-route messengers	171
95	local agents	110
59	special agents	63
44,655	Total in service	47,010

DEAD LETTERS.

The operations of the Dead-Letter Office are fully given in a tabular statement printed in the appendix, and may be epitomized as follows:

Number of domestic letters received, 4,133,928; number of foreign letters, 268,420; total, 4,402,348, representing an actual or nominal value of $5,795,764.11. Of this number 1,826,108, representing $5,377,923.27, were delivered to owners or writers; 31,388, representing $132,993.33, which could not be delivered, were filed for reclama-

51 Ab

tion; 11,370 remained either on hand not acted upon, or were outstanding in the hands of postmasters for delivery June 30, 1873, and representing $284,847.51; and 2,533,482, which either could not be delivered, or from various causes were worthless, were destroyed.

The number of applications for dead letters was 6,598, and in 2,075 cases the letters were found and forwarded to applicants or owners.

The amounts received during the year and deposited in the Treasury were—

From unclaimed dead letters..............................		$6,208 00
From proceeds of sales of waste paper.....................	$3,401 55	
From proceeds of sales of post-route maps.................	502 40	
From proceeds of sales of old carpets	293 56	
		4,143 51
Total deposited during the year...................		10,351 51

POSTAL MONEY-ORDER SYSTEM.

The number of money-order post-offices in operation during the last year was 2,775. On the 7th of July, 1873, 299 additional offices were established, and 5 were discontinued, making the whole number at present 3,069. Of the additional offices, seven were opened at sub-post-offices or stations in large cities, viz: one in Boston, one in Chicago, and five in Philadelphia.

The number of domestic money-orders issued during the year was 3,355,686, the aggregate value of which was...		$57,516,216 69
The number of such orders paid was 3,314,818, amounting in value to.............................	$56,900,351 23	
To which is to be added the amount of orders repaid to the remitters...................................	394,661 04	
Total of payments................................		57,295,012 27
Excess of issues over payments.......................		221,204 42

The amount of fees paid by the public to postmasters for the issue of money-orders was $354,602.25. These transactions show an increase over those of 1872 of $9,000,683.97, or 18.55 per cent., in the amount of orders issued; of $8,875,367.30, or 18.33 per cent., in the amount of orders paid; and of $4,316.59, or 1.23 per cent., in the amount of fees received. The average amount of the money-orders issued during the last year was $17.14, being $1.71 less than the average of the preceding year. The small increase in the fees received, as compared with the issues and payments of orders, is owing to the reduction, by the act of June 8, 1872, of the fee for orders not exceeding $10 from 10 cents to 5 cents. The diminution of the average amount of the order is to be attributed to the same cause, which stimulated the purchase of small orders issued at one-half the rate formerly charged.

Duplicate money-orders to the number of 14,521 were issued by the Department during the year, of which 14,256 were in lieu of original orders which failed to reach the respective payees in due time, because of change of residence or imperfect address, or because not called for, or because alleged to have been lost in transmission by mail. One hundred and forty-five duplicates were substituted for orders which became invalid, because not presented for payment within one year after issue; 31 for orders made invalid in consequence of having, contrary to law, more than one indorsement; 87 for orders mutilated or destroyed while in possession of the remitter or the payee; and 2 for orders lost by robbery of a post-office.

The increase in the number of duplicates during last year was 801, or about 5.84 per cent., being nearly 13 per cent. less than the ratio of increase in the orders issued.

The receipts and expenditures of the domestic money-order system, as adjusted and reported by the Auditor, were as follows:

Receipts:

Fees received for money-orders issued	$354,602 25
Amount received for premium on drafts	214 41
Total	354,816 66

Expenditures:

Commissions to postmasters and allowances for clerk-hire	$257,928 58	
Allowances for postmasters' remittances lost in transmission by mail	4,345 56	
Incidental expenses for stationery and fixtures	23,001 32	
Bad debts	957 20	
Total		286,232 66
Excess of receipts over expenditures		68,584 00

In compliance with the act of June 8, 1872, this sum has been placed to the credit of the Treasurer of the United States for the service of the Post-Office Department.

During the year 1872, the revenue amounted to $105,977.77, being larger by $37,393.77 than that of the last year. This decrease is due to the unusually small receipts from fees, as compared with the large increase of orders issued, resulting from the reduction above mentioned of the fee for orders of $10 and under from 10 to 5 cents. In 1872 the amount of orders issued increased 15 per cent., and the fees 18⅜ per cent.; but during the last year the increase of the fees was only 1.23 per cent., while the issues were augmented 18.55 per cent. The great increase of issues and payments during the last year involved additional expenditure for clerk-hire, stationery, and other incidental items, but produced no proportionate augmentation of receipts. The public, however, has derived substantial advantage from the additional facilities afforded by greatly reduced rates for the transmission of small sums by postal orders.

During the past year the aggregate amount of surplus funds accruing at the smaller post-offices from the sale of money-orders, and remitted by them to the larger offices designated as their depositories, was $43,885,826.68. Twenty-three of these remittances, amounting in the aggregate to $5,557.31, were reported as lost in transmission by mail, a sum larger by $1,509.31 than the reported losses of the previous year. Of this amount, the sum of $2,543.04 was allowed before the close of the year to the credit of the several postmasters who had remitted the same; credit claimed for a remittance of $200 was disallowed; the sum of $2,034.27 was recovered by special agents; and claims amounting to $780 are yet pending. The total amount allowed to postmasters during the last year for remittances lost in the mails was $4,345.56, of which the sum of $1,802.52 was on account of losses during the two preceding years. Of these former losses, the sum of $250 was charged to postmasters' accounts; the sum of $99 was recovered by special agents; and there remain unsettled cases to the amount of $560.

The drafts drawn by postmasters whose payments exceed their issues of money-orders against credits given them, from time to time, with the postmaster at New York, amounted to $5,004,800. Certain postmasters in the Pacific States and Territories, who required occasional assistance to meet their money-order payments, were furnished with funds to the amount of $52,034 by the postmaster at San Francisco, and to the amount of $23,587 by the postmaster at Portland, Oregon.

Out of the whole number of orders paid, viz: 3,314,818, it was claimed that payment of 22, amounting to $613.80, was fraudulently procured through forgery of the payee's signature, or by other unlawful or improper means, being at the rate of one fraudulent payment in every 150,673 payments.

Forty-nine cases of improperly-paid orders were investigated or undergoing examination during the year. Twenty-seven of them occurred during the previous year; and of these 12 were not brought to the knowledge of the Department until after the completion of the last annual report. In twenty-one instances the amount of the orders, the total value of which was $742.19, was recovered by special agents, and paid to the rightful owners. In six cases, amounting to $178.71, the paying postmasters were, after due investigation, held responsible for the erroneous payments. The amount of six improperly-paid orders, $252, was refunded by the Department, the paying postmasters not having been found at fault; and sixteen cases, of the aggregate value of $472.55, are still pending.

The rapid increase in the amount of the money-order business which closely followed the recent monetary disturbance and the general suspension of currency payments by the national banks is a circumstance not unworthy of notice. During the last week of September and the first three weeks of October, 1872, the number of orders issued at the fifty-six largest money-order offices was 36,744, amounting to $817,344.99, and the number of orders paid was 119,107, amounting to $1,981,724.47. During the same period of the present year, these offices issued 53,071 orders, of the aggregate amount of $1,211,297.41, and paid 163,577 orders of the total value of $3,055,696.02, showing the unprecedented increase of 48.19 per cent. in the amount of issues, and of 54.19 per cent. in the amount of payments. This statement clearly indicates the utility of the system to the public as a safe, convenient, and expeditious mode of making small remittances.

The number of international postal orders issued in this country on Switzerland was 2,801, amounting to $78,313.93, and the number from that country paid here was 600, amounting to $16,809.58; showing, in comparison with last year's business, a decrease of $7,265.99, or 8.49 per cent. in the issues, and an increase of $2,708.23, or 19.20 per cent. in the payments. The fees received amounted to $2,164, and the expenses to $24.86. It appears from the accompanying report of the Auditor, that, after the payment of all balances due Switzerland on the exchange of money-orders during the year, a net revenue of $5,152.76 accrued to the United States, of which the sum of $3,013.62 represents profits derived from the purchase, at advantageous rates, of bills of exchange in payment of gold balances.

The number of money-orders issued in this country for payment in the United Kingdom was 69,592, amounting to $1,364,476.32, and the number of British orders paid here was 10,486, of the aggregate value of $215,087.61. The fees received amounted to $40,504, and the cost of commissions to postmasters, clerk-hire, and incidental items was $15,487.18. An exact statement of the revenue of last year cannot, at present, be furnished by the Auditor, as a final settlement of the accounts of the last quarter has not yet been made by the accounting officers of both countries. The revenue for the year 1872 is reported by the Auditor at $23,321.92.

From the establishment of the exchange of postal money-orders between the United States and the German Empire, on the 1st of October, 1872, to June 30, 1873, 19,454 orders, amounting to $420,722.12, were issued in this country in favor of payees in Germany, and 11,613 orders from that country were paid in the United States. The fees received amounted to $11,662.80, and the sum paid for commissions, clerk hire, and incidental expenses, to $1,693.65.

MISCELLANEOUS.

An appropriation for the manufacture and delivery of postal cards having been secured by the act of January 8, 1873, immediate steps were taken to meet the public demand therefor. Unavoidable delays occurred in the preparation of the plates and in procuring suitable stock, but at length all obstacles were so far overcome that the delivery of the cards on requisitions was commenced on the 1st of May last. As predicted, they have been favorably received. They have supplied a public want, and have made a new and remunerative business for the Department. The issues foot up:

From May 1 to June 30.. 31,094,000
From July 1 to September 30 33,208,300

    Total in five months.. 64,302,300

These figures indicate that the estimate of 100,000,000 for the consumption of the first year will be more than realized.

The several acts for the repeal of the franking privilege became operative on the 1st of July last. The results of the first quarter of the current year are highly satisfactory, and have fully verified the predictions of the friends of the repeal. The confusion and delay in the distribution and transmission of the mails, caused by suddenly throwing, without notice or system, immense masses of free matter upon important postal routes, have been remedied, thus making it possible to effect a decided improvement in the organization and practical working of the service.

Section 4 of the act of March 3, 1873, making it the duty of the Postmaster-General to provide official stamps and stamped envelopes for the several Executive Departments, has been strictly complied with. The stamps and envelopes furnished have been executed in the highest style of art, and will compare favorably with those of any other country. From July 1 to September 30, of the current year, the following varieties, numbers, and values were issued :

POSTAGE-STAMPS.

To whom issued.	No.of denominations.	Number of stamps.	Value.
The Executive	5	5, 150	$896 00
The State Department................................	14	60, 495	30, 70 71
The Treasury Department	11	7, 642, 500	407, 000 00
The War Department	11	446, 500	17, 649 00
The Navy Department	11	247, 830	12, 859 00
The Post Office Department..........................	10	10, 054, 660	354, 532 00
The Interior Department.............................	10	1, 058, 475	50, 171 00
The Department of Justice...........................	10	65, 400	2, 900 00
The Department of Agriculture.......................	9	275, 000	20, 732 00
Making a total of	91	20, 055, 410	896, 213 72

STAMPED ENVELOPES, ETC.

To the War Department..............................	9	547, 100	10, 315 30
To the Post-Office Department	3	4, 936, 300	147, 007 00
Making a total of	12	5, 483, 400	157, 322 30

The stamps for the Departments other than the Post-Office do not differ materially from those for sale to the public, except that each Department has its own distinctive color and legend. The colors are: For the Executive, carmine: State Department, green ; Treasury, velvet-brown: War, cochineal-red : Navy, blue: Post-Office, black:

Interior, vermilion; Department of Justice, purple; and Department of Agriculture, straw-color.

In the stamps for the Post-Office Department the medallion head gives place to a numeral representing the value, with the words "Post-Office Department" above and the denomination expressed in words below. All the official stamps correspond in denominations with those issued for the public, except in the case of the State Department, for which four of higher value were made for dispatch-bags. These four are of the denominations of $2, $5, $10, and $20, respectively, are of larger size and printed in two colors, and bear a profile bust of the late Secretary Seward.

In presenting the financial results of the abolition of franking, I am for the present confined to the operations of the stamp division for the first quarter only of the current year. To make those operations more intelligible, the following comparative statement is submitted:

Comparative statement of the value of postage-stamps, envelopes, and newspaper-wrappers, (exclusive of postal-cards and official stamps,) issued during the quarter ended September 30, in each of the years 1868, 1869, 1870, 1871, 1872, and 1873.

Quarter ended—	Value of issues.	Increase.	
		Amount.	Percentage.
September 30, 1868	$3,411,421 50		
September 30, 1869	3,963,907 00	$552,485 50	16.2
September 30, 1870	3,797,513 25	*166,393 75	*4.2
September 30, 1871	4,420,135 50	622,622 25	16.4
September 30, 1872	4,659,987 50	239,852 00	5.4
September 30, 1873	4,911,102 50	251,115 00	5.4
Average percentage of increase from 1869 to 1873			7.8

* Decrease.

The aggregate of sales for the quarter may be arrived at thus:

Value of ordinary stamps, stamped envelopes, and newspaper-wrappers, issued during the quarter ended September 30, 1873, as above $4,911,102 50

Add value of postal-cards issued during same quarter 332,083 00

　Making a total of 5,243,185 50

An increase over the value of issues for same quarter of 1872 of $583,198, or a percentage of 12.5.

Add the value of official stamps and stamped envelopes issued to the close of quarter ended September 30, 1873, (less $1,159.56, cost of manufacturing envelopes) 1,052,356 70

　Making a total for the quarter of all issues of 6,295,542 20

An increase over the total value of issues for the same quarter of 1872 of $1,635,554.70, or a percentage of 35.1.

It cannot be expected that the sales of postal-cards or official stamps will average throughout the year the extraordinary sums above given for the first quarter. A general supply having been obtained, subsequent orders will be made only for the actual consumption. Hence in the estimates for 1875 the net sales of postal-cards have been placed for the ntire year at $1,034,732, and of official stamps at $2,250,000.

The large increase of receipts above stated is derived altogether from general and departmental matter and from postal-cards. Publications of the class heretofore printed and sent out by order of Congress have been almost entirely cut off since the 1st of July. Of the relief thus afforded some idea may be formed from the fact that during the three months next preceding that day there were forwarded from this city over a single route, the Baltimore and Ohio Railroad, in box-cars, independently of the amount conveyed in the regular mail-cars, 665,504 pounds of such publications, as appears from returns of the actual weight thereof taken by the company with the permission of the Department.

These facts, it is respectfully submitted, are ample to sustain the opinion, given in a special report to Congress under date of January 12, 1871, that the cost of free matter if charged with the regular rates of postage would amount to $2,543,327.72 annually; and it is hoped that they will be sufficient to prevent any attempt to revive an abuse which would impose the most grievous burdens upon the postal service at a time when that service is struggling to meet the growing wants of the country in its course of unparalleled development.

In my report for 1869 I had the honor to suggest a plan for the prepayment of postage on newspapers and other matter of the second class by weight of packages, rather than by the present system, which requires the manipulation of each particular paper and allows the payment of postage at either the mailing office or the office of delivery. A careful revision of the subject confirms me in the opinion that the postage on all such matter should be collected in advance at the mailing office. Collections are now made with great difficulty, and there is no provision whatever by which dishonesty or negligence can be detected. No stamps are used for the payment of such postage, and the Department is compelled to accept in full satisfaction whatever sums of money postmasters choose to charge against themselves. So execrably bad is this system that postal officers of high standing have estimated that not more than one-third of the postage properly chargeable on newspapers is accounted for and paid over. Furthermore, disputes are continually arising between postmasters and publishers as to whether the sheets they transmit come within the meaning of the term *newspaper*, and as to the number of their *bona fide* subscribers. In the hope of contributing to a more faithful collection of postages, the more prompt and efficient transmission of newspapers, the saving of labor in post-offices, and the general advantage, as well of the Department as of publishers and their patrons, I respectfully submit the following plan for prepayment of newspapers of the second class, and urge its adoption. Let all publishers, or their business managers or agents, be required at the beginning of every quarter to state under oath that, after diligent inquiry, they are satisfied that they will send in the mails to regular subscribers during the coming quarter not more than —— copies of the newspaper known as —— ——, [giving the number of copies and name of newspaper,] and let them be further required to pay in advance the postage prescribed by law, taking therefor duplicate receipts, one of which shall be transmitted to the Post-Office Department; and, to afford reasonable opportunity for an increase of circulation during the quarter, let the oath taken at the beginning of the next quarter embrace all additional copies for the last quarter, as well as the number to be sent during the then commencing quarter. On the other hand, let postmasters be required to return, within two weeks after the beginning of every quarter, correct lists of all the newspapers addressed to regular subscribers and dispatched in the mails from their respective offices, stating the number of copies of each newspaper, the average weight per paper, the number of issues per week, and the amount of money paid as postage therefor. Payment having been made in advance for the quarter no stamp or manipulation would be needed, but, when received into the office, every paper answering to the description given in the receipt would be treated as paid. The papers of persons subscribing after quarter-day would be forwarded immediately and paid for at the beginning of the next quarter. So marked would be the improvement in the collections under this plan, that I believe the Department could safely consent, in case of its adoption, to a reduction in newspaper rates of 40 per cent. on present prices. At the reduced rate, I am satisfied the Department would realize more revenue than now. I also believe that so great would be the saving of labor to newspaper proprietors in the preparation of their papers for the mail, and so decided their gain from the greater dispatch and freedom from mistakes in transmission and delivery, that they would find the new plan more advantageous to them than the present one. A similar plan could be adopted for magazines and periodicals of the second class.

I further recommend that on all matter of the third class the postage be made uniform at 1 cent for each two ounces or fraction thereof, and the maximum weight of packages increased to four pounds. If this recommendation be adopted, the postage on flexible patterns, samples of ores, metals, minerals, and merchandise, sample-cards, photographic paper, letter-envelopes, postal-envelopes, and wrappers, unprinted cards, plain and ornamental paper, card-board, or other flexible material, and on all other mailable matter not included in the first class, will be reduced from 2 cents to 1 cent for each two ounces or fraction thereof, and the weight of packages increased from twelve ounces to four pounds. On books the postage will be reduced from 2 cents to 1 cent for each two ounces or fraction thereof; and the weight of packages of woolen, cotton, or linen clothing addressed to any non-commissioned officer or private in the Army of the United States will be increased from two pounds to four pounds.

I also recommend that any person be permitted, without additional charge, to write a form of presentation in any book, pamphlet, magazine, periodical, or on any other matter of the third class, and also that the sender of any package be permitted, without additional charge, to write his or her name and address on the outside thereof, with the word "from" above or preceding the same, so as to inform the person addressed of the name of the sender, and to write briefly on any package the number and name of the articles inclosed.

The present mode of determining the salaries of postmasters, so far as it affects those not appointed by the President, is very defective. Formerly the salary of every postmaster was computed by commissions on the actual receipts of the office as returned to the Sixth Auditor. In 1864 the law was changed, and it was provided that salaries should be adjusted for two years in advance upon special returns for a stated time to be made by postmasters to the First Assistant Postmaster-General, it being urged in favor of the new method that it would save a large amount of clerical labor in post-offices, as well as in the Department. The change has worked well in presidential offices, and many of the elaborate and expensive accounts of former days have been discontinued; but in the smaller offices the effect has been far from beneficial. Unfortunately there are no criteria whereby the accuracy of salary returns may be tested, except the quarterly returns made to the Sixth Auditor, and upon these the Department is obliged to rely in every case of doubt or suspicion. It has been found, however, in practice, that while a comparison can readily be made of the accounts of presidential offices, which number only 1,363, great difficulties and delays attend a like scrutiny into the affairs of the 31,881 offices filled by appointment of the Postmaster-General; and yet there is more need of the utmost care in dealing with the latter class of offices, because of their large and rapidly-increasing number, and the better opportunity they present to those in charge of them for increasing their compensation by fraudulent or excessive returns. Moreover, it has been observed, as a general result of making each man his own accountant, that, while all are eager to supply data upon which they can claim an increase of salary, very few are willing to furnish information that will lead to a reduction.

I therefore recommend that the salaries of all offices of less importance than presidential offices; that is to say, all with a salary of less than $1,000, be henceforth adjusted by a resort in the first instance to the quarterly returns in the office of the Sixth Auditor. This action will dispense with much useless labor, prevent complaint, remove a temptation to fraud, and secure an adjustment of salaries upon the basis of actual receipts, whether more or less.

The events of the past few weeks have awakened a lively interest in a plan heretofore submitted, for securing the savings of the great body of the people by a pledge of the credit and faith of the United States. In my reports for 1871 and 1872 I urged the organization of institutions for that purpose, under the title of "Post-Office Savings Banks." The name was not well chosen. The institutions I have in view and recommend are not designed, and should not be permitted, to encroach upon the legitimate powers and duties of the national banks. They are totally distinct from the banks in their scope and character, in the machinery they employ, and in the ends they are intended to accomplish, and may be more accurately designated as Postal Savings Depositories of the United States.

The financial difficulties in which the country has been unexpectedly involved, and which still continue to oppress it, have demonstrated the necessity for some means of maintaining confidence in times of threatened disaster, and of gathering and wisely employing the immense wealth scattered among the people, to prevent panic and escape the ruin which inevitably follows in its track. That the people of the United States hold the reins of financial as well as political power clearly appears from the following tables, taken from the public debt statements, reports of the national banks, and from official accounts:

Treasury notes of all kinds, including fractional currency, in the Treasury, in the national banks, and in the hands of the public on June 30, 1869, 1870, 1871, 1872, and 1873.

Date.	Aggregate.	In the Treasury.	In national banks.	In the hands of the public.
June 30, 1869	$386,118,859 73	$37,097,818 89	$82,738,974 53	$268,282,066 31
June 30, 1870	395,984,940 48	28,945,067 19	96,758,465 39	270,281,407 90
June 30, 1871	396,679,380 06	9,533,363 15	124,298,373 22	262,847,643 69
June 30, 1872	398,444,131 52	15,321,689 87	125,063,881 12	258,058,560 53
June 30, 1873	432,609,332 94	*41,513,529 77	108,204,050 84	282,891,752 33

* Thirty-one million seven hundred and thirty thousand dollars of the currency in the Treasury June 30, 1873, represents special deposits for redemption of certificates of deposit issued under act of June 8, 1872, which certificates are held by the national banks as part of their reserve of lawful money.

National bank-notes held by the banks and the public on June 30, 1869, 1870, 1871, 1872, and 1873.

Date.	Aggregate.	On hand.	In the hands of the public.
June 30, 1869	$299,742,474 95	$17,915,295 95	$281,827,179 00
June 30, 1870	299,267,486 35	23,056,596 35	276,210,890 00
June 30, 1871	317,616,919 20	26,101,252 20	291,515,667 00
June 30, 1872	337,240,692 30	23,162,340 30	314,078,352 00
June 30, 1873	346,777,827 30	26,432,588 30	320,345,239 00

Recapitulation of currency in the hands of the public.

June, 1869.—Treasury issues	$268,282,066 31	
National bank notes	281,827,179 00	$550,109,245 31
June, 1870.—Treasury issues	270,281,407 90	
National bank notes	276,210,890 00	546,492,297 90
June, 1871.—Treasury issues	262,847,643 69	
National bank notes	291,515,667 00	554,363,310 69
June, 1872.—Treasury issues	258,058,560 53	
National bank notes	314,078,352 00	572,136,912 53
June, 1873.—Treasury issues	282,891,752 33	
National bank notes	320,345,239 00	603,236,991 33
Aggregate for 5 years		2,826,338,757 76
Average		565,267,751 55

On the 30th June last the public held, independent of the Treasury and the banks, $603,236,991.33. The amount of currency was then considered sufficient for all business purposes. In the month of August following a stringency began to be felt in the money market, and we have since witnessed the extraordinary spectacle of the banks suspending and declaring their inability to pay United States notes or bank-notes, or even fractional currency, to their depositors. Of course, under such circumstances, they could not continue to make their usual discounts for the accommodation of their customers. This can only be accounted for upon the theory of a general lack of confidence on the part of the people, and a consequent refusal to deposit, or invest, or even pay out in discharge of obligations the currency held by them. To meet this strange state of affairs, and to prevent a recurrence of the like in the future, many plans have been suggested—one involving an expansion of the currency, another compelling a return to specie payment, and still another providing for the issue by the Government of a convertible-bond at a low rate of interest—but all open to objections more or less serious. The opinion is universal that if there could be a general restoration of confidence there would immediately be let loose an ample circulation for the entire country. If, therefore, a plan can be devised that will afford to depositors equal security to that afforded to note-holders, but little doubt can be entertained that a general amelioration of the present condition will be effected. The immense sum of $600,000,000 held by the people in June last, with the large accessions since made thereto by heavy drafts upon the Treasury and the banks, will be brought out from its places of concealment and applied to its legitimate work of aiding in forwarding our crops and products to market and in sustaining our vast manufacturing and other business interests. In my judgment, a system of postal savings-depositories would powerfully contribute to this most desirable consummation. Throughout the plan for their organization and work two ideas predominate: first, the United States is to insure the safe return of principal and interest whenever demanded; and, secondly, the extensive machinery of the Post-Office is to be used to bring its advantages home to the great mass of the people. The details would be simple, safe, and efficient. Money-order offices, as agents of the Government, would receive deposits in small sums, ranging from one dollar upward to the limit fixed by law, which sums the postmaster would forward at short intervals to the nearest depository of the United States Treasury. A certificate, fixing the responsibility of the Government, would be issued immediately to the depositor by the postmaster, and notice thereof would be sent either to the Department or some established branch office, to the end that due entry thereof might be made and a more formal acknowledgment forwarded to the depositor. No depositor should be allowed in any one year to deposit exceeding $300; no greater accumulation of deposits should be permitted for any one depositor than $1,000; and no greater accumulation of deposits and interest should be allowed than $1,500. Meantime, however, the United States should contract to pay interest not exceeding 4 per cent., to be computed from the first day of the month following the deposit, and to stop upon the first day of the month in which any withdrawal might be made. Interest should be computed to the end of the fiscal year, and then, if not drawn, should be added to the principal. It would of course be necessary to keep an exact account of all such deposits, and of the expenses incident to the management thereof, in the Treasury Department; also to make provision for the payment of the amounts due depositors whenever and wherever they might desire to withdraw them; and to allow and credit to such accumulations a somewhat greater rate of interest than that paid depositors, so that all expenses might be paid out of the fund and the institution made self-sustaining. I am confident that the plan of operations thus generally sketched may be so amplified and guarded that the people could be efficiently served, and the Government saved from all loss or expense. The great ends to be attained are, first, absolute security; secondly, the utmost facilities for deposits, withdrawals, and transfers; and thirdly, perfect secrecy. A system thus organized and conducted would not only encourage economy and habits of saving on the part of all who might be in the way of earning small sums of money, but would tend largely to utilize and keep in circulation the immense amounts which are paid out for wages and in business, and give every depositor a direct interest in the stability of the Government. It would strengthen our national finances by pouring these accumulations into the Treasury, which, in turn, by judicious investments, could afford to monetary and banking institutions the very relief they now so eagerly seek. Thousands who doubt the security of the banks and savings institutions, whether private or organized under State laws, would cheerfully place their surplus money upon such terms in the keeping of the Government.

The extent of the benefits which will inure to the people and the Government from the establishment of this system will be best indicated by a statement of the amounts deposited in existing savings-banks in some of the States of the Union. With the means of information at my command, I am able to make only a partial statement under this head. Congress wisely provided, by the act of February 19, 1873, for an annual report to be made by the Comptroller of the Currency of the condition of all banks, banking companies, and savings-banks organized under the laws of the several States and Territories; but, on application to that officer, I have been informed that he has not yet succeeded in collecting the information necessary for such a report, and that in many of the States and Territories no returns are made by the savings-banks, either to the legislature or any State officer, and that thus they are left without any supervision whatever. I regret that I shall be deprived for the present of the experience and industry which will doubtless be applied to the discharge of the duty imposed by the law referred to.

In the table following, the returns for Massachusetts are brought up to the 26th of October, 1862; for Rhode Island, Maine, and New Hampshire, to the year 1869–'70; for Connecticut, to January 1, 1871; for the State of New York, to January 1, 1873; and for California, to July 1, 1872:

State.	No. savings-institutions.	Number of depositors.	Amount deposited.	Average to each depositor.
Massachusetts	172	630, 246	$184, 797, 313 92	$293 21
Rhode Island	25	67, 238	27, 067, 072 00	402 55
Maine	36	39, 527	10, 490, 368 00	265 40
New Hampshire	45	71, 336	18, 759, 461 00	262 25
Connecticut		178, 000	55, 000, 000 00	310 00
New York	150	822, 642	285, 286, 621 00	346 79
California		58, 713	47, 784, 372 00	
		1, 867, 802	629, 185, 207 92	

Thus seven States had, many months ago, 1,867,802 depositors, and $629,185,207.92 on deposit, an amount greater by $3,476,930 than all the deposits, including those of individuals, the United States, and United States disbursing officers, held by all the national banks of the United States, numbering 1,919, on the 3d day of October, 1872.

Objection has been made to the establishment of postal savings depositories upon the ground that they would interfere with and overthrow the present savings banks. I respectfully submit that this objection is without foundation. Savings banks were originally established by the benevolent and philanthropic to provide safe places of deposit for the small savings of laboring people, and in the beginning they were conducted without hope of either profit or reward other than that which comes from the consciousness of doing good. In so far as they have since been used for purposes of speculation, their managers have diverted them from their original design, and to that extent have abused the confidence reposed in them. Security is to be sought above all other considerations, and hence the spirit of speculation should be thoroughly eradicated from their administration. If savings banks are subjected to risks, and prostituted for purposes of gain for their managers, they should be overthrown. If, on the contrary, they continue to be well and profitably managed, and pay a greater rate of interest than that paid by the Government, they will in no wise be put to disadvantage, because every depositor will be left free to select his place of deposit.

Nor can the national banks raise a valid objection. They are organized to afford facilities to the community by lending money on personal security, dealing in exchange, issuing notes, and receiving deposits, not for permanent investment, but as temporary custodians. Bankers should own the capital they employ. When they attempt to do business on borrowed capital they are operating on a fictitious credit and become mere speculators. If they succeed in realizing more interest than they pay they make a profit by raising the price of money above its value. If they do not succeed in so doing, then, like other unfortunate speculators they fail, and their creditors become their dupes. Hence a law prohibiting the payment of interest by the banks would simply confine them to their legitimate business, and prevent them from assuming improper risks. With the Government it is totally different. Its obligations must be met by resorting either to loans or taxation, and in determining its choice of alternatives, the paramount consideration should be the best interests of the people, whose agent it is. Sound policy dictates that the Government should lose no opportunity of borrowing from its own people, at a low rate of interest, for the purpose of discharging an indebtedness abroad, or relieving industry and enterprise at home from the trammels of taxation. But when the Government can arrest panic, restore confidence, call forth the hoarded treasure of the country, and revive the pursuits of industry, by a simple pledge of the people's credit for the people's security, who will say that that pledge should not be given ?

Another objection is the tendency to centralization. To this I answer, that, if to establish postal savings depositories would be in violation of the Constitution, there is an end of the matter at once. If, on the contrary, such action would not be unconstitutional, then the only question is whether their establishment would on the whole be advantageous for the people and the Government. Since the National Government has assumed to organize and control the banking of the country, and has found warrant of law for undertaking the transmission of the people's money through the mails, it would appear that it is only discharging its whole duty and completing its financial work by providing for the safety of the small savings of the industrious and frugal poor. If, in addition, it can be shown that postal savings depositories will serve to fortify the national credit, make more equable the financial operations of the country, cultivate habits of thrift among the industrial classes, and illustrate the excellence of our institutions by protecting and augmenting the accumulations of self-denying toil, and thus in time merging the workman into the capitalist, the cry of centralization cannot be made to drown the voice of the people in their demand that the Government of the United States shall execute for their benefit the high offices enjoined upon it by the Constitution.

Another objection, more practical, if not more tenable, is based on an alleged increase of expenses and public officers. So far as the establishment of savings depositories would have any effect upon appointments its tendency would be to secure a better, class of officers in all respects. None but competent persons could discharge the duties of such institutions, and no man or party, having a reputation to sustain, would be willing to commit interests so important to unworthy hands. The Government would seek its principal agents and employés among experienced men, wherever they could be found. A numerous force of additional officers would not be required. Many persons already employed in the postal-service could be made to discharge a portion of the required duties. A force far less than that now needed in savings-banks would be sufficient, with the assistance of the machinery of the post-office, to accomplish the same amount of work, and this, together with a supervising bureau in the Post-Office Department, and the necessary accounting officers in the Treasury, is all that would be needed. The fact that the money-order office, during the past year, received, transmitted, and paid out nearly $00,000,000, shows how well that branch of the Post-Office discharges its duties. I am entirely satisfied that the character of the service would be elevated, and the work more cheaply and better done by Government officers, controlled at every step by law, and punishable by severe penalties in case of default or embezzlement, than is possible under the present irresponsible and inefficient mode in which savings-banks are conducted in many of the States.

But the argument by example is, perhaps, the most powerful. Let us, then, invoke the experience of other nations. The savings-bank, like many other products of Christian civilization, was perfected piecemeal. An institution of a kindred character was founded at Hamburgh as early as 1778, and first gave a demonstration of the power of small sums contributed by many, when aggregated, though, it is stated, its operations were confined to the granting of deferred annuities. An institution approaching nearer to the savings-bank, it is generally believed, was formed at Berne, Switzerland, in 1787. The idea, however, was fully developed in England, and the honor of its first practical application is divided among several persons, all of whom may claim to be benefactors of their race. In the year 1798 a friendly society for the benefit of women and children was established under the superintendence of Mrs. Priscilla Wakefield, and, before the year 1801, there had been combined with its main design a two-fold improvement, namely, a fund for loans and a bank for savings. In 1804 the savings-bank was more regularly organized, and Mr. Eardley Wilmot, M. P., and Mr. Spurling were appointed trustees. A prior claim, however, is raised on behalf of Rev. Joseph Smith, of Wendover, who, in 1799, circulated in his parish proposals to receive deposits during the summer and return the amount at Christmas with an addition of one-third as a bounty. The first publication in England of the idea of savings-banks, under the name of frugality banks, is also attributed to the celebrated Jeremy Bentham as early as 1797. The society next formed was opened, in 1808, at Bath, chiefly through the instrumentality of certain ladies, who received deposits from female servants. In 1810 the first savings-bank in Scotland was formed by Rev. Henry Duncan, minister of Ruthwell, Dumfriesshire; and, in November, 1815, the providence institution of Southampton was established, under the patronage of the Right Honorable George Rose. The seeds thus sown rapidly germinated, took root, and soon exhibited a vigorous growth. By the year 1817 there had been formed no less than seventy banks in England, four in Wales, and four in Ireland, by the voluntary association of benevolent persons. Parliament then took up the question, and, by two separate acts, recognized and organized banks for savings in England and Ireland, and, two years later, in Scotland. Thenceforth such institutions were under the protection and guidance of the law, and much labor was expended in the effort to protect them from peculation and fraud; notwithstanding all which, it has been stated by competent authority that between the years 1844 and 1857 frauds were perpetrated to the amount of £228,800. The effect was disastrous in the extreme. Confidence was destroyed, and the disposition to economize became a subject of ridicule. Attention is called to the following:

Table showing the amount of deposits and withdrawals, and the capital of savings-banks, in the United Kingdom at the end of each year, from 1841 to 1861, inclusive.

Year ended November 20—	Deposits.	Withdrawals.	Capital of savings-banks in the United Kingdom.
1841	£5, 694, 908	£5, 487, 723	· £24, 536, 971
1842	5, 789, 203	5, 656, 160	25, 406, 642
1843	· 6, 327, 125	5, 333, 015	27, 244, 266
1844	7, 166, 465	5, 716, 275	29, 653, 180
1845	7, 153, 176	6, 897, 042	30, 950, 983
1846	7, 300, 367	7, 255, 654	31, 851, 238
1847	6, 649, 008	9, 060, 075	30, 236, 632
1848	5, 862, 742	8, 653, 108	28, 114, 136
1849	6, 196, 883	6, 522, 760	28, 537, 010
1850	6, 363, 690	6, 760, 398	28, 930, 982
1851	6, 782, 059	6, 305, 566	30, 277, 654
1852	7, 281, 177	6, 684, 906	31, 754, 261
1853	7, 653, 590	7, 116, 330	33, 362, 260
1854	7, 400, 141	7, 956, 347	33, 736, 080
1855	7, 188, 211	7, 654, 133	34, 263, 135
1856	7, 741, 453	8, 023, 583	34, 946, 012
1857	7, 581, 415	8, 375, 095	34, 145, 567
1858	7, 901, 925	7, 839, 903	36, 220, 362
1859	9, 021, 907	7, 335, 349	38, 995, 876
1860	9, 478, 585	8, 258, 421	41, 258, 368
1861	8, 764, 879	9, 621, 539	41, 546, 475
Total	151, 298, 830	152, 313, 312	
Excess of withdrawals		1, 014, 482	

It is worthy of note that during the years 1847, 1848, 1849, and 1850 the withdrawals exceeded the deposits by amounts respectively of £2,411,067, £2,790,366, £328,877, and £396,638, and that in the years 1854, 1855, 1856, 1857, and 1861, also, the withdrawals largely exceeded

52 Ab

the deposits. The remarkable fact is also revealed that, taking the whole period between 1841 and 1861, when the increase in population in England and Wales was 4,190,496, when the exports increased from £51,545,116 to £125,102,814, and when the amount of wages paid must have been largely increased, the withdrawals actually exceeded the deposits by £1,014,482. The commercial crisis of 1847-'48, and the scarcity of money during the Crimean war, had, no doubt, a marked effect during some of the years recorded in the foregoing table; but the general result can be accounted for on no other theory than that the confidence of the masses had been weakened by the discovery of the enormous frauds above mentioned, the knowledge of the defects of the system, and the divided responsibility under which it was worked. It thus became apparent that a radical reform must be effected, otherwise the usefulness of savings-banks would be seriously impaired. After numerous failures a project for post-office savings-banks was finally brought to the attention of Sir Rowland Hill, who gave it his cordial approval. A plan having been finally matured by Mr. George Chetwynd, and approved by Mr. Frank Ives Scudamore, fixing the rate of interest at 2½ per cent., it was carried through Parliament under the powerful championship of Mr. Gladstone, and became the law of the land on the 17th day of May, 1861. The details being approved, and the necessary machinery provided, it went into effect on the 17th day of September following. The annexed table, covering its operations from that date until the 31st day of December, 1872, proves its steady and uniform growth and its triumphant success.

Operations of the British post-office savings-banks.

Period.	Number of post-office savings-banks.	Number of deposits.	Amount of deposits.	Total sum standing to credit of post-office savings-banks on books of national debt commissioners at close of the year.	Balance in hands of postmaster-general after allowing for charges of management at close of the year.	Total balance in hand applicable to payment of deposits at close of the year.
			£	£	£	£
From Sept. 16, 1861, to Dec. 31, 1862	2,535	639, 916	2, 114, 640	1, 659, 632	35, 609	1, 694, 304
1863	2, 901	642, 648	2, 651, 900	2, 396, 182	44, 413	2, 372, 330
1864	3, 093	1, 110, 702	3, 350, 000	4, 795, 063	5, 340	5, 001, 303
1865	3, 381	1, 302, 309	3, 719, 017	6, 392, 389	4, 307	6, 393, 693
1866	3, 507	1, 585, 671	4, 600, 637	8, 331, 176	26, 701	8, 306, 007
1867	3, 699	1, 506, 344	4, 643, 904	9, 807, 703	47, 690	9, 903, 338
1868	3, 813	1, 737, 308	5, 333, 630	11, 863, 052	Nil.	11, 690, 490
1869	4, 047	1, 906, 644	5, 787, 818	13, 735, 547	19, 306	13, 794, 690
1870	4, 098	2, 125, 903	5, 995, 121	15, 305, 049	152, 609	15, 403, 009
1871	4, 325	2, 302, 621	6, 064, 690	17, 308, 635	166, 609	17, 670, 673
1872	4, 607	2, 765, 845	7, 690, 916	19, 552, 804	202, 670	19, 669, 696

Every year shows an increase in the number and amount of deposits; and on the 31st day of December, 1872, the total balances applicable to the payment of depositors amounted to the sum of £19,860,874. The postmaster-general states, in his last annual report, that the cost of each deposit or withdrawal, including postage, is now about sixpence instead of about one shilling in the old savings-banks. No greater triumph was ever achieved in post-office management, with the single exception of that of Sir Rowland Hill in effecting penny-postage.

Post-office savings-banks encountered at every step the most implacable opposition, and were established only after a prolonged struggle. The same arguments were brought to bear against them that have been used against the adoption of a like system here. It was urged that they would be destructive of the old savings-banks; that the post-office would never be able to perform the additional important duties imposed upon it; that the government was undertaking a great risk; and that the scheme was centralizing in its tendency. They were opposed by Lord Colchester, an ex-postmaster-general, and by Lord Monteagle, of Brandon, once chancellor of the exchequer. A practical trial of twelve years has conclusively established the fallacy of all the arguments adduced against this beneficent measure.

The same system, somewhat simplified, has been put into operation in the British Australian colonies, in Queensland and in Canada, with like unvarying success. Mr. J. C. Stewart, superintendent of the post-office savings banks of Canada, writes, under date of October 25, 1873:

Post-office savings-banks work smoothly with us. We commenced five and a half years ago very much in the dark, and we have had to work out the system to a great extent unaided; but we learned to think out and reason out a system with which we are now well satisfied. There is nothing which prevents our extending it to every money-order office, save want of office accommodation at the head office.

Reason and philanthrophy being thus sustained by the prolonged experience of so many peoples speaking the English language, how can the success of similar institutions in the United States be longer doubtful? I believe that the financial perils through which we are now passing could have been mainly averted if these institutions had been open to receive deposits. The people of this country earn more and deposit more than those of any other. The State of New York alone exhibits an aggregate of savings-bank deposits equal to those of the whole United Kingdom of Great Britain and Ireland; and it is not extravagant to say that if a spirit of universal frugality could be encouraged by an assurance of good faith and absolute security, the savings of the American people would soon grow into such gigantic proportions that the voluntary loans of a single generation would exceed the whole of the national debt.

I am clear in the conviction that the establishment of postal-savings depositories will be found an eminently wise and practical measure;

and, in the hope of contributing something to that end, I will submit at an early day a form of bill embodying the necessary legislation.

A year ago I earnestly urged the assumption by Government of the control of the telegraph, and gave at some length my reasons for believing that such action would correct the defects of the present management and result in great benefit to the country. I also presented at the same time estimates of the cost of duplicating the lines and apparatus now in use. There is no need of repeating those reasons or estimates. I desire, however, to express my full confidence in the soundness of the former, and the approximate correctness of the latter, notwithstanding the efforts which have been made to invalidate them. Ample time has elapsed for a full and free discussion of the subject in all its bearings, but no points have been developed which have not already been considered. One fact is conspicuous and most significant, and that is, that the opposition to the postal telegraph comes almost entirely from the telegraph companies and those directly interested with them in sustaining their monopoly. Every intelligent disinterested observer who has seen the working of the Government systems abroad gives them the decided preference.

The necessity for an efficient and cheap mode of telegraphic communication, which shall be beyond the control of private monopolies, and within the means of all, is daily becoming more apparent. Under the present management the use of the telegraph by the masses of the people is almost prohibited, by reason of arbitrary rates, unnecessarily high charges, and a want of facilities. This assertion is verified by the testimony of the president of the Western Union Company, who stated before a committee of Congress that, out of forty millions of our population, only one million use the telegraph at all. This is certainly an anomalous condition of affairs among a people the first in the world for intelligence and business activity. It may, however, be regarded as settled that, while under the control of private companies, whose chief object is to make a profit for their stockholders, and whose skill and labor are expended in efforts to advance the prices of their stock, and to enforce the highest rates to which the public can be made to submit, the telegraph will never become a general medium of correspondence. A Government postal telegraph is the only means by which the full advantage of this great invention can be secured; for, wherever the telegraph is under government management, it is operated at its minimum cost, and the people receive the benefit in low rates of transmission and in greatly extended facilities.

Appended to this report are four tables, to which reference may be made for reliable information, derived from official sources, as to the condition, force, and operations of various government telegraphs in Europe. Table 1, kindly furnished by the director of the bureau of International telegraphs of Switzerland, gives condensed returns, showing the receipts, expenditures, and other details of European systems. Table 2 gives the number of messages (exclusive of press and news messages) forwarded from postal-telegraph stations in the United Kingdom during each month of 1871 and 1872; and tables 3 and 4 give a like statement for each week and month of the first three quarters of 1872 and 1873, respectively.

Nature furnishes an inexhaustible storehouse of electricity. The earth and the atmosphere constitute the never wearying media of its transmission. Its application to infinite uses is limited only by human knowledge and ingenuity. A single generation has filled the earth with wonder, and we are still on the mere threshold of investigation. Successive improvements have contributed so much to the simplification of telegraphic apparatus that the work of the operator is no longer a mystery. Private lines, connecting the residences of merchants and other business men with their stores and offices, are increasing in number and popularity; and so notable has been the advance that electricity is now called into daily requisition to meet the ordinary wants of domestic life.

For years past the attention of inventors and scientists has been attracted to the necessity for a more rapid and less expensive mode of transmission than the Morse, which requires the message to be spelled out by a slow and tedious process, at about the speed of an ordinary writer. One of the results of their investigations is the "automatic" or fast system, now in operation between New York and Washington. This system is capable of a speed of from 500 to 800 words per minute. The average of an expert Morse operator is not over 25 words per minute. Therefore, it is evident that if the automatic method can be made to accomplish what its advocates confidently predict for it, the capacity of a single wire for business will be increased nearly or quite thirty times. This increased capacity may be again doubled, or perhaps quadrupled, if the duplex apparatus, now used every day by established companies for sending messages simultaneously in different directions on the same wire, can be successfully combined with the automatic machine. There can be no doubt of the ultimate success of the automatic principle. Its battle with an incredulous public is almost won. As soon as it shall be thoroughly developed and applied in practice, the problem of cheap telegraphy will be definitively solved.

Experiments by the French electricians and inventors, D'Arlincourt and Meyer, in the direction of rapid autographic telegraphing, have resulted in marked improvements. By the autographic system a *fac simile* of the message written by the sender for transmission is reproduced at the distant office of delivery, thus enabling the receiver to verify the signature of his correspondent. Diagrams, maps, plans, tracings, or letters written in stenographic characters or in symbols, can also be transmitted by this instrument, and as the message or drawing to be sent is itself used as a medium of transmission, and the act of sending is entirely mechanical, errors very rarely occur.

In truth, there is no limit to the possibilities of electrical and telegraphic invention. Improved processes are constantly being discovered, new instruments devised, and new adaptations made; and in the near future the entire methods and machinery of telegraphic communication will be cheapened and familiarized to such an extent that the Government will be compelled to assume their control, in order to protect the people from extortion, and to secure for them the most improved and extended facilities at the lowest possible cost. In this wide field of operation no money-making privilege should be tolerated. As well might a charter be granted for the exclusive use of air, light, or water; as well might a price be set on the winds and waves, on rivers flowing to the sea, on seed-time and harvest, and on the power which causes the seed to germinate and the fruits of the earth to grow, as to restrict for the sake of profit the use of electricity, that most subtile and universal of God's mysterious agents. The electric telegraph should be the common messenger of the human race, and no man or association of men should be permitted to burden it with excessive charges. Surely the great republic will not hesitate longer to follow kingdoms and empires in recognizing and protecting the rights of the people.

There are now but two parties in the controversy over the postal telegraph—on one side the people, on the other the Western Union Telegraph Company. At a meeting of the directors, held on the 8th of October last, the president of the company, in his report, stated its policy, with commendable candor, in the following words:

The scale of rates fixed by competition on the most important routes, and between the principal cities, has been applied recently to the whole country east of the Rocky Mountains, so that the inducement to subscribe capital for the extension of competing lines, in order to secure the benefit of competing rates, no longer exists. At the rates now established it is impossible for any competing company to realize profits, and means of them are known to be, and all are believed to be, operating at a loss. As a result, the extension of competing lines has ceased, and it is not believed that capital can be found wherewith to inaugurate new enterprises in any quarter. The time is not distant, therefore, when the Western Union Company will be without a substantial competitor in the conduct of a business which, notwithstanding the enormous growth of the last seven years, still is in its infancy. With the increase of lines already provided and now in progress, the capacity of which the duplex apparatus hereinbefore spoken of will be able to double at small cost, it is believed that the constantly increasing volume of business, the growth of which will be stimulated by the present low and uniform rates, can be successfully handled with a less annual investment in new construction than has heretofore been necessary; so that with competition checked and in process of being extinguished, the percentage of expenses may be reduced, and the patience of the stockholders be rewarded at an early day by the resumption of regular dividends.

The Western Union Company has always contended for high rates, and enforced them with a strong hand. When new associations have been formed for the purpose of reducing rates, the Western Union has at once entered the lists to destroy its rivals, and in pursuit of victory has not scrupled to use any device which the powerful can employ against the weak. Failing to vanquish its adversary in the open field of fair competition, it has resorted to artifice, and triumphed by making gold its weapon. Thus it has acquired, by lease or purchase, the lines of the American Telegraph Company, the Illinois and Mississippi Company, the Chicago and Mississippi Company, and the California State Company; and during the past year it has obtained control of the International Ocean and the Pacific and Atlantic Telegraph Companies by buying up a majority of their stock. Its president has attributed a loss of profits in part to "a reduction of rates rendered necessary by the action of competing companies" along their lines, and in "other sections" to a similar reduction made "in order to equalize rates and thereby remove the inducement for competing lines to extend still farther," thus evincing a settled purpose to reduce rates only that it might exterminate competing companies already organized, or which it feared would be organized.

During seven years of this enforced abstinence from high dividends, it is admitted in the above-mentioned report that the company has realized "net profits" to the immense amount of $20,312,618; and that, after paying out of such profits for dividends to stockholders $4,857,239, for interest on the company's bonds $2,216,194, for its own stock $4,054,483, for stock of Gold and Stock Company $1,173,509, for bonds of Western Union Company, redeemed and canceled, $974,075, for real estate, exclusive of Broadway and Dey street property, $318,263, for patent of Page and Duplex apparatus $73,758, for sinking-fund $249,555, and other smaller sums, it managed with the residue to effect such extensions and purchases as increased its wires from 70,000 to 160,000 miles. After this admirable exposition of what has been accomplished by "net profits," it is to be regretted that there had not been placed by the side of it, for the gratification of a curious public, an equally lucid statement of the amount of cash capital paid in by the stockholders of the Western Union Company, and of the companies out of which it has been compounded. Elated as he must have been by a contemplation of the manner in which the "net profits" had swept away all opposition, present or prospective, President Orton might well say, in the language quoted from his report, that "the time is not distant when the Western Union Company will be without a substantial competitor in the conduct of a business which, notwithstanding the enormous growth of the last seven years, still is in its infancy."

What a pleasing prospect for the people! Here it is in brief: a powerful monopoly, unchecked by opposition or the fear of it in the future, has adroitly secured possession of the whole country, and now issues its proclamation that henceforth there will be no more competition, no more reductions of rates, but always "regular dividends."

But the president of the Western Union Company did not exhaust his candor in the quotation above made. He further declared:

The franks issued to Government officials constitute nearly a third of the total complimentary business. The wires of the Western Union Company extend into thirty-.

seven States and nine Territories within the limits of the United States, and into four of the British Provinces. In all of them our property is more or less subject to the action of the national, State, and municipal authorities, and the judicious use of complimentary franks among them has been the means of saving to the company many times the money-value of the free service performed.

In another part of the same report it is stated that the total complimentary business amounted during the last year to $58,000. Then, assuming the assertion last cited to be correct, the "judicious use" of complimentary franks to the amount of $19,333 secured such action or non-action, whichever the company desired, on the part of the officials of the United States and of thirty-seven States, nine Territories, and four Provinces, as was equivalent to " many times the money-value of the free service performed." Truly a most "judicious use" of patronage! For if the subsidizing process included only the principal legislative, executive, and judicial officers of the governments, States, Territories, and Provinces above mentioned, the average value of the "complimentary frank" to each person could not have exceeded $5, or $10 at the utmost. It is presumed that hereafter very few "officials" will be willing to accept any courtesy, great or small, from the Western Union Company, now that they have been informed that the company will place the recipients of its favors upon its roll of retainers and advertise them as such.

The telegraph should be made a part of the postal system without further delay. As Congress does not seem inclined to exercise the discretion given in the third section of the act of July 24, 1866, to appoint appraisers to value the " lines, property, and effects " of the companies now in operation, and as the Western Union Company appears to be unwilling to make a voluntary sale at a fair price, I recommend that provision be made by law for the immediate establishment of the postal telegraph, and for the construction of all such lines as may be needed, under the direction of competent officers of the Engineer Corps of the Army. The experience they acquired during the war of the rebellion would enable them to do the work in the most economical and satisfactory manner.

Very respectfully, your obedient servant,

JNO. A. J. CRESWELL,
Postmaster-General.

The PRESIDENT.

APPENDIX.

No. 1.—*Estimates for expenditures for the fiscal year ending June 30, 1875.*

FIRST ASSISTANT POSTMASTER-GENERAL:

For compensation to postmasters		$6,500,000
For clerks in post-offices		3,250,000
For payments to letter-carriers		2,000,000
For wrapping-paper		27,000
For wrapping-twine		48,000
For marking-stamps		9,000
For letter-balances		3,000
For rent of post-offices	$350,000	
For fuel	150,000	
For light	160,000	
For stationery and other miscellaneous items	60,000	
		720,000
Total for First Assistant's Bureau		$12,557,000

SECOND ASSISTANT POSTMASTER-GENERAL:

For inland transportation	$15,582,021	
For increase of compensation on railroad routes under act of March 3, 1873	525,000	
For railway post-office clerks	1,320,014	
For route-agents	929,035	
For mail-route messengers	160,000	
For local agents	110,383	
For mail-messengers	643,533	
For baggage-masters	1,000	
		$19,270,986
For mail depredations and special agents		160,000
For mail locks and keys		50,000
For mail-bags and mail-bag catchers		200,000
For preparation and publication of post-route maps		35,000
Total for Second Assistant's Bureau		19,157,986

THIRD ASSISTANT POSTMASTER-GENERAL:

For postage-stamps	$118,667	
For stamped envelopes and newspaper-wrappers	535,424	
For expenses of agency	10,200	
For postal-cards	168,270	
For expenses of agency	5,600	
		$838,161
For advertising		90,000
For registered-package envelopes and seals		42,680
For office-envelopes		69,500
For dead-letter envelopes		4,585
For ship, steamboat, and way letters		7,500
For office-furniture		6,500
For fees to United States attorneys, marshals, clerks of courts, and counsel necessarily employed by special agents of Post-Office Department, subject to approval by the Attorney-General		7,500
For engraving, printing, and binding drafts and warrants		3,000
For miscellaneous items		2,500
Total for Third Assistant's Bureau		1,071,926

SUPERINTENDENT OF FOREIGN MAILS:

For transportation of foreign mails	$325,000	
For balances due foreign countries	260,000	
Total for office of foreign mails		585,000
Grand total estimate for expenditures		33,929,912

Estimated amount provided by the Department, being its own revenue, accruing from postage and other sources...................................... $29,293,549

Amount to be provided from the general Treasury to make the receipts equal the expenditures, (deficiency)...................................... 4,636,363

Expenditures under special appropriations to be provided out of the general Treasury :

For mail-steamship service between San Francisco, Japan, and China $1,000,000
For mail-steamship service between United States and Brazil.. 150,000
For mail-steamship service between San Francisco and Sandwich Islands 75,000

Total 1,225,000
For official postage-stamps for use during the fiscal year................ 950,000

Total to be provided from general Treasury...................... 6,811,363

EDWARD W. BARBER,
Third Assistant Postmaster-General.

No. 3.—*Statement of payments made under sundry heads charged to miscellaneous accounts for the fiscal year ended June 30, 1873.*

For regular allowances to postmasters for rent, light, fuel, stationery, and miscellaneous items during the fiscal year ended June 30, 1873...................................... $498,791 32
Less amounts allowed and subsequently recharged to postmasters.. 1,050 70

Amount actually allowed and paid................................. $497,740 62
For extra allowances for same items for years 1868, 1869, 1870, 1872, and 1873.. 8,094 88
For preparing and publishing post-route maps.......................... 25,168 35
For registered-package envelopes.. 41,981 92
For envelopes for official use of postmasters........................... 45,449 01
For envelopes for return of dead letters to writers................... 1,899 22
For letter-balances.. 2,304 24
For twine, (cotton, $30,700.42; hemp, $8,464).......................... 39,164 42
For fees paid to United States marshals................................. 2,014 12
For fees paid to United States attorneys................................ 3,981 00
For fees paid to United States clerks of courts........................ 485 64
For engraving, printing, and binding drafts and warrants 1,621 88
For miscellaneous items... 86 50

Total.. 669,890 90

EDWARD W. BARBER,
Third Assistant Postmaster-General.

No. 4.—*Estimate of indebtedness of Post-Office Department on June 30, 1873, and not yet adjusted.*

Balances due foreign countries...................................... $116,200
Mail-service under contract or recognized, but not yet reported for payment. 393,643
Mail-service unrecognized.. 157,000

Total.. 663,843

EDWARD W. BARBER,
Third Assistant Postmaster-General.

Table of mail-service for the year ended June 30, 1873, as exhibited by the state of the arrangements at the close of the year.

[The entire service and pay on each route are set down in the State under which the route is numbered, though extending sometimes into other States, instead of being divided among the States in which the different portions lie.]

States and Territories	Length of route	Annual transportation and cost						Total annual transportation by celerity, certainty, and security.	Total annual transportation by steamboat.	Total annual transportation by rail road.	Total annual transportation.	Total annual cost.
		Celerity, certainty, and security.		By steamboat.		By railroad.						
	Miles.	Miles.	Dollars.	Miles.	Dollars.	Miles.	Dollars.	Miles.	Miles.	Miles.	Miles.	Dollars.
Maine												
New Hampshire												
Vermont												
Massachusetts												
Rhode Island												
Connecticut												
New York												
New Jersey												
Pennsylvania												
Delaware												
Maryland												
West Virginia												
Virginia												
North Carolina												
South Carolina												
Georgia												
Florida												
Alabama												
Mississippi												
Louisiana												
Texas												
Arkansas												
Missouri												
Tennessee												
Kentucky												
Ohio												
Indiana												
Illinois												
Michigan												
Wisconsin												
Iowa												
Minnesota												
Nebraska												

Table of mail-service for the year ended June 30, 1873, as exhibited by the state of the arrangements at the close of the year—Continued.

[The entire service and pay on each route are set down to the State under which the route is numbered, though extending sometimes into other States, instead of being divided among the States in which the different portions lie.]

States and Territories.	Length of routes.	Annual transportation and cost.						Total annual transportation by celerity, certainty, and security.	Total annual transportation by steamboat.	Total annual transportation by railroad.	Total annual transportation.	Total annual cost.
		Celerity, certainty, and security.		By steamboat.		By railroad.						
	Miles.	Miles.	Dollars.	Miles.	Dollars.	Miles.	Dollars.	Miles.	Miles.	Miles.	Miles.	Dollars.
Kansas	7,317	4,935	125,918			2,389	937,381	1,457,988		1,609,104	3,106,332	303,239
Nevada	2,136	2,064	180,112			32	3,741	758,494		32,299	790,786	183,853
California	10,878	7,166	535,032			1,651	998,063	2,411,445		1,967,818	4,061,807	916,125
Oregon	2,415	2,163	65,097	2,061	92,676			368,980	362,544		495,520	96,097
Washington Territory	3,345	1,478	116,780	252	31,000			250,876	126,360		458,004	179,456
Idaho Territory	1,175	1,175	105,509	1,867	62,676			346,890	107,127		346,890	105,509
Montana Territory	1,381	1,381	114,306					519,300			519,300	114,306
Dakota Territory	1,154	1,093	94,396			61	4,611	211,602		38,384	255,986	99,007
Wyoming Territory	163	163	11,541					39,416			39,416	11,541
Utah Territory	2,039	2,903	371,258			36	1,625	1,469,118		29,776	1,491,894	373,023
Colorado Territory	2,406	2,194	190,894			919	10,575	771,507		131,976	903,483	190,899
New Mexico Territory	1,812	1,812	319,417					692,348			692,348	319,417
Arizona Territory	1,539	1,539	92,397					597,996			597,996	92,397
Total	256,910	175,991	5,578,500	16,703	799,645	63,457	7,257,196	50,340,490	3,947,785	65,691,445	119,969,650	13,635,341
Railway post-office clerks												970,800
Route-agents												829,240
Mail-route messengers												106,740
Local agents												82,894
Mail-messengers												535,441
Baggage-masters in charge of registered packages												576
Aggregate												16,161,034

JOHN L. ROUTT,
Second Assistant Postmaster-General.

Statement of the number, description, and cost of mail-bags purchased by contract and put into service during the fiscal year ended June 30, 1873.

Number.	Description.	Size.	Price.	Cost.	Aggregate.
50	Leather mail-pouches	No. 1	$8 20	$410 00	
625	.....do	No. 2	6 45	4,031 25	
1,125	.....do	No. 3	5 50	6,187 50	
1,000	.....do	No.	4 35	4,350 00	
1,050	.....do	No. 5	3 20	3,360 00	
3,850					$18,338 75
600	Canvas mail-pouches	No. 1	4 85	2,910 00	
800	.....do	No. 2	3 90	3,120 00	
1,000	.....do	No. 3	3 45	3,450 00	
800	.....do	No. 4	2 89	2,312 00	
300	.....do	No. 5	2 65	795 00	
3,500					12,587 00
450	Leather horse mail-bags	No. 1	6 65	2,992 50	
500	.....do	No. 2	5 65	2,825 00	
300	.....do	No. 3	5 15	1,545 00	
1,250					7,362 50
43,000	Jute canvas mail-sacks	No. 1	57	24,510 00	
32,000	.....do	No. 2	46	14,720 00	
11,500	.....do	No. 3	15	1,750 00	
86,500					40,980 00
50	Cotton canvas mail-sacks	No. 2	74½	37 25	
50	Cotton canvas mail-sacks, (striped)		55	27 50	
50	.....do		25	12 50	
150					77 25
300	Mail-catchers		15 00	4,500 00	
500	Mail-catcher's sockets		50	250 00	
32	.....do		70	22 40	
					4,772 40
496,840	Mail-bag labels, (wooden)		01¼	6,210 50	
1,000	Mail-bag label-cases		25	4,500 00	
					10,710 50
					94,828 40

Number and cost of mail locks and keys purchased and repaired during the year ended June 30, 1873.

Number.	Description.	Price.	Cost.
40,000	New iron mail-locks	$0 58	$23,200 00
5,000	New brass mail-locks	74	3,700 00
1,000	New iron mail-keys	12½	125 00
500	New iron mail-keys	20	100 00
2,577	Old iron mail-locks repaired	20	515 40
2,322	Old iron mail-locks repaired	10	232 20
2,566	Old brass mail-locks repaired	65	196 30
893	Old iron mail-keys repaired	02	17 86
	Total cost		28,616 76

JOHN L. ROUTT,
Second Assistant Postmaster-General.

Table of mail-service for the year ended June 30, 1873, as exhibited by the state of the arrangements at the close of the year—Continued.

[The entire service and pay on each route are set down to the State under which the route is numbered, though extending sometimes into other States, instead of being divided among the States in which the different portions lie.]

States and Territories	Length of routes.	Annual transportation and cost.						Total annual transportation by celerity, certainty, and security.	Total annual transportation by steamboat.	Total annual transportation by rail-road.	Total annual transportation.	Total annual cost.
		Celerity, certainty, and security.		By steamboat.		By railroad.						
	Miles.	Miles.	Dollars.	Miles.	Dollars.	Miles.	Dollars.	Miles.	Miles.	Miles.	Miles.	Dollars.
Kansas	7,317	4,935	125,918			2,382	277,381	1,437,528		1,669,104	3,106,332	303,939
Nevada	2,136	2,064	180,119			52	3,741	738,494		39,292	790,786	183,853
California	10,878	7,166	536,032			1,631	296,093	2,411,445		1,967,618	4,061,807	916,125
Oregon	2,415	2,183	65,097	2,041	92,000			368,980	392,544		455,014	96,077
Washington Territory	3,345	1,478	116,780	232	31,000			250,876	135,380		346,980	179,456
Idaho Territory	1,175	1,175	105,599	1,807	62,676			346,780	107,127		519,390	105,490
Montana Territory	1,381	1,381	114,306					512,390			955,966	114,306
Dakota Territory	1,154	1,154	94,390					311,602			39,416	99,007
Wyoming Territory	183	163	11,541			61	4,611	39,416		38,364	1,691,894	11,541
Utah Territory	2,039	2,903	371,558					1,469,118			903,483	373,063
Colorado Territory	2,406	2,194	190,584			36	1,985	771,507		52,776	692,348	194,669
New Mexico Territory	1,813	1,813	319,417			219	10,575	692,348		131,976	257,996	319,417
Arizona Territory	1,532	1,532	92,397					257,996				92,397
Total	256,910	175,991	5,578,500	16,762	799,645	63,457	7,257,196	50,340,420	3,947,785	65,621,645	119,909,650	13,635,341
Railway post-office clerks												970,800
Route-agents												928,940
Mail-route messengers												106,740
Local agents												82,896
Mail messengers												538,441
Baggage-masters in charge of registered packages												516
Aggregate												16,161,034

JOHN L. ROUTT,
Second Assistant Postmaster-General.

Statement of the number, description, and cost of mail-bags purchased by contract and put into service during the fiscal year ended June 30, 1873.

Number.	Description.	Size.	Price.	Cost.	Aggregate.
50	Leather mail-pouches	No. 1	$8 20	$410 00	
625	......do...................................	No. 2	6 45	4, 031 25	
1, 125	......do...................................	No. 3	5 50	6, 187 50	
1, 000	......do...................................	No.	4 35	4, 350 00	
1, 050	......do...................................	No. 5	3 20	3, 360 00	
3, 850					$18, 338 75
600	Canvas mail-pouches	No. 1	4 85	2, 910 00	
800	......do...................................	No. 2	3 90	3, 120 00	
1, 000	......do...................................	No. 3	3 45	3, 450 00	
800	......do...................................	No. 4	2 89	2, 312 00	
300	......do...................................	No. 5	2 65	795 00	
3, 500					12, 587 00
450	Leather horse mail-bags......................	No. 1	6 65	2, 992 50	
500	......do...................................	No. 2	5 65	2, 825 00	
300	......do...................................	No. 3	5 15	1, 545 00	
1, 250					7, 362 50
43, 000	Jute canvas mail-sacks	No. 1	57	24, 510 00	
32, 000	......do...................................	No. 2	46	14, 720 00	
11, 500	......do...................................	No. 3	15	1, 750 00	
86, 500					40, 980 00
50	Cotton canvas mail-sacks....................	No. 2	74½	37 25	
50	Cotton canvas mail-sacks, (striped)..........	....	55	27 50	
50	......do...................................	....	25	12 50	
150					77 25
300	Mail-catchers...............................	....	15 00	4, 500 00	
500	Mail-catcher's sockets	....	50	250 00	
32	......do...................................	....	70	22 40	
					4, 772 40
496, 840	Mail-bag labels, (wooden)....................	....	01¼	6, 210 50	
18, 000	Mail-bag label-cases	....	25	4, 500 00	
					10, 710 50
					94, 828 40

Number and cost of mail locks and keys purchased and repaired during the year ended June 30, 1873.

Number.	Description.	Price.	Cost.
40, 000	New iron mail-locks...	$0 58	$23, 200 00
5, 000	New brass mail-locks..	74	3, 700 00
1, 000	New iron mail-keys..	12½	125 00
500	New iron mail-keys..	20	100 00
2, 577	Old iron mail-locks repaired	20	515 40
2, 322	Old iron mail-locks repaired	10	232 20
2, 566	Old brass mail-locks repaired	05	128 30
893	Old iron mail-keys repaired	02	17 86
	Total cost	....	28, 018 76

JOHN L. ROUTT,
Second Assistant Postmaster-General.

Recapitulation and comparative statement of the service of June 30, 1872, and June 30, 1873, showing the increase.

	June 30, 1872.	June 30, 1873.	Increase.
Number of lines of railway post-offices	57	59	2
Aggregate number of miles of the above	14,117	14,866	749
Number of miles of actual service performed daily	33,690	34,925	1,235
Number of miles of actual service performed annually	12,296,850	12,747,625	450,775
Number of head clerks at $1,600 per annum	267	283	16
Number of clerks at $1,300 per annum	329	379	50
Number of assistant clerks at $1,000 per annum	53	90	37
Making total number of clerks	649	752	103
With annual compensation amounting to	$821,600 00	$941,000 00	$119,400 00

JOHN L. ROUTT,
Second Assistant Postmaster-General.

Statements showing operations and results of foreign mail-service for the fiscal year ended June 30, 1873.

The postages on United States and European mails were as follows:

The aggregate amount of postage (sea, inland, and foreign) on the mails exchanged:

With the United Kingdom	$770,931 28
With the North German Union	477,196 38
With France	17,342 50
With Belgium	14,622 86
With Netherlands	22,112 39
With Switzerland	36,926 81
With Italy	37,430 15
With Denmark	29,815 95
With Norway	103 08
With Spain	26 10
Total postages	1,406,507 50

Being an increase of $102,653.45 over the amount reported for the previous year.

The postages on mails sent to Europe were as follows, viz:

To United Kingdom	$402,877 12
To North German Union	243,457 24
To France	6,899 90
To Belgium	7,704 48
To Netherlands	12,075 48
To Switzerland	17,708 00
To Italy	15,333 10
To Denmark	8,567 52
To Norway	62 10
To Spain	26 10
Total	714,711 04

The postages on mails received from Europe were as follows, viz:

From United Kingdom	$368,054 16
From North German Union	233,739 14
From France	10,442 60
From Belgium	6,918 38
From Netherlands	10,036 91
From Switzerland	19,218 81
From Italy	22,097 05
From Denmark	21,248 43
From Norway	40 98
Total	691,796 46

Postages collected in the United States	865,511 47
Postages collected in Europe	540,996 03
Excess of collections in the United States	324,515 44

Number of letters (single rates) sent from the United States	10,273,711
Number of letters (single rates) received from Europe	9,311,803
Total	19,585,514

Being an increase of 1,902,515 over the number reported for the previous year.

The excess of postages on mails sent from the United States to differ-

53 Ab

ent countries of Europe over that on mails received from the **same** countries was as follows:

United Kingdom	$34,822 96
Germany	9,718 10
Netherlands	2,038 57
Belgium	786 10
Spain	26 10
Norway	21 12
Total	47,412 95

The excess of postages on mails received over those on mails sent was as follows:

With France	$3,522 70
Italy	6,763 95
Switzerland	1,510 81
Denmark	12,680 91
Total	24,478 37

Nmber of letters and amounts of postage on mails conveyed to and from Europe by the respective steamship-lines.

Name of line.	Number of letters.			Amounts of postage on letter-mails.		
	Sent.	Received.	Total.	Sent.	Received.	Total.
North German Lloyd	1,800,379	2,431,210	4,231,589	$129,090 52	$186,578 48	$315,668 00
Hamburg line	2,765,366	1,185,424	3,950,790	192,424 99	91,166 50	283,591 49
Cunard line	223,393	3,246,489	3,469,882	15,238 23	230,661 24	245,899 47
Williams & Guion line	3,399,690	985	3,399,905	236,728 36	96 04	236,754 42
Inman line	554,646	2,370,314	2,924,960	39,559 28	175,843 71	215,402 99
White Star line	1,233,870	6,035	1,239,905	62,338 32	441 00	62,779 32
Canadian line	253,577	2,135	255,712	15,703 22	129 08	15,832 30
French line	26,007	64,457	90,464	2,600 70	6,447 70	9,048 40
National line	15,564		15,564	944 88		944 88
Baltic-Lloyd line	1,167	3,626	4,703	70 32	348 23	418 55
Transient steamers		1,096	1,096		108 60	108 60
Norwegian steamers		683	683		40 98	40 98
Red Star line	122	49	171	12 20	4 90	17 10
Total	10,273,711	9,311,803	19,585,514	714,711 04	691,796 46	1,406,507 50
Increase over 1872	859,585	1,042,930	1,902,515	52,395 85	50,257 60	102,652 65

Payments during fiscal year ended June 30, 1873, to ocean steamship lines transporting mails for the sea postages as compensation for the service.

Williams and Guion line	$79,204 42
Hamburg line	57,958 88
North German Lloyd line	33,573 74
White Star line	29,831 97
Inman line	14,641 70
Cunard line	4,977 37
Canadian line	6,065 13
National line	390 49
Baltic Lloyd line	12 07
	226,745 77
To Pacific Mail Steamship Company	$27,731 56
To West Indies, Mexico, Brazil, Bermuda, New Granada, and New Zealand	65,145 94
To Nova Scotia	2,648 08
	95,525 58
Total	322,271 35

Weight of correspondence exchanged during the fiscal year ended June 30, 1873, between the United States and countries of Europe with which the United States have concluded postal conventions.

Countries.	LETTER MAILS.						PRINTED MATTER AND SAMPLES.						Total weight of mails exchanged with European countries.	
	From the United States.		To the United States.		Total.		From the United States.		To the United States.		Total.			
	Grams.	Ounces.	Grams.	Ounces.	Grams.	Ounces.	Grams.	Ounces.	Grams.	Ounces.	Grams.	Ounces.	Grams.	Ounces.
United Kingdom	53,888,366	1,969,979½	45,678,105	1,816,869¾	88,566,471	3,806,840½	70,300,257	7,631,575¾	24,052,048	10,617,428	94,352,305	18,249,003½	152,888,776	22,055,844½
Germany	747,161		802,799		1,549,953		11,437,758		965,345		12,403,103		13,953,056	
France	683,877		556,860		1,240,737		2,008,524		1,932,551		3,941,075		5,181,812	
Belgium	1,250,561		819,165		2,069,726		1,677,979		1,263,668		3,141,647		5,211,373	
Netherlands	1,578,301		1,478,771		3,057,072		5,547,992		3,158,821		8,706,813		11,763,885	
Switzerland	1,307,077		1,404,410		2,711,487		3,833,721		2,047,352		5,881,073		8,592,560	
Italy	1,062,693		1,999,566		3,062,259		555,167		1,276,416		1,831,583		4,883,842	
Denmark	9,294		6,900		16,794		87,748		6,075		93,823		110,617	
Norway and Sweden	2,088				2,088								2,088	
Spain														
Total grams and equiv- alents in ounces	29,550,118	1,305,886¼½	32,716,469	1,154,689¼½	72,266,587	2,550,585½⁹⁄₂	95,649,146	3,375,838⅜	34,682,276	1,224, 0⅜	130,331,422	4,599,905½¹⁸	202,598,009	7,150,517½³³
Total		3,385,865¹⁷⁄₁₀	8,971,561¹⁷⁄₁₀		6,357,490⁴⁹⁄₇₀		11,097,487¹⁴¹⁄₁₀		11,841,509²⁹⁄₁₀		23,849,036¹⁷⁄₁₀		29,906,369¹⁷⁄₁₀	
Increase over 1872		406,889¹⁷⁄₁₀	590,055¹¹³⁄₁₁₀		736,946¹⁹⁄₁₁₀		968,573¹⁴⁄₁₀		1,295,812¹⁰⁄₁₀		2,298,385¹¹⁄₁₁₀		2,955,335¹⁴⁄₁₁₀	

Total operations of the Appointment Office for the year ended June 30, 1873.

States and Territories.	Post-offices.				Postmasters.			Total number of changes.
	Established.	Discontinued.	Names and sites changed.	Appointments on change of name and site.	Resigned and commissions expired.	Removed.	Deceased.	
Alabama	94	42	4	3	116	34	8	296
Alaska	...	1	...	...	...	...	...	1
Arizona	10	4	2	...	3	1	1	21
Arkansas	110	50	7	...	95	35	8	305
California	59	21	6	3	76	23	6	191
Colorado	23	10	8	5	27	3	...	71
Connecticut	16	3	2	...	31	9	6	67
Dakota	27	5	7	3	25	6	...	70
Delaware	7	3	3	1	5	2	1	21
District of Columbia	...	2	...	...	3	...	...	5
Florida	25	8	2	...	43	13	4	95
Georgia	79	40	5	1	102	20	10	256
Idaho	15	4	1	...	8	2	1	31
Illinois	90	36	28	9	280	29	18	481
Indiana	64	37	7	3	279	39	16	442
Iowa	61	56	25	10	250	30	10	432
Kansas	178	52	41	24	214	26	6	517
Kentucky	81	57	9	4	138	49	10	344
Louisiana	54	5	3	2	61	34	4	163
Maine	15	8	8	4	58	8	11	108
Maryland	22	6	11	7	65	10	6	120
Massachusetts	11	14	5	2	43	5	11	80
Michigan	60	33	15	8	153	29	21	311
Minnesota	76	34	9	2	133	34	8	294
Mississippi	62	5	3	3	64	18	7	150
Missouri	104	86	17	5	248	55	16	586
Montana	8	3	1	1	19	4	2	37
Nebraska	80	23	16	10	81	14	...	214
Nevada	20	8	5	1	14	2	...	49
New Hampshire	15	8	3	1	44	8	11	90
New Jersey	22	2	7	1	56	10	3	106
New Mexico	8	7	...	...	2	3	1	21
New York	62	25	18	5	229	91	33	473
North Carolina	107	48	11	5	124	37	11	332
Ohio	71	39	25	9	295	36	23	449
Oregon	29	10	13	7	62	6	1	121
Pennsylvania	111	36	27	16	400	42	26	642
Rhode Island	...	...	1	...	10	1	...	12
South Carolina	52	23	4	2	57	15	5	156
Tennessee	78	61	10	4	177	32	17	375
Texas	136	41	9	6	150	42	8	346
Utah	15	2	7	4	15	6	1	46
Vermont	5	1	...	...	41	7	4	58
Virginia	135	50	19	6	225	36	29	494
Washington	24	7	2	1	16	1	...	50
West Virginia	73	35	8	6	85	16	4	231
Wisconsin	56	27	10	8	160	21	16	290
Wyoming	6	3	1	1	10	1	...	21
Total	2,462	1,081	425	193	4,802	945	386	10,101

Table showing the increase and decrease of post-offices in the several States and Territories, also the number of post-offices at which appointments are made by the President and by the Postmaster-General, for the year ended June 30, 1873.

States and Territories.	Whole number of post-offices in the United States June 30, 1872.	Whole number of post-offices in the United States June 30, 1873.	Increase.	Decrease.	Number of postmasters appointed by the President June 30, 1872.	Number of postmasters appointed by the President June 30, 1873.	Increase.	Decrease.	Number of postmasters appointed by the Postmaster-General June 30, 1872.	Number of postmasters appointed by the Postmaster-General June 30, 1873.	Increase.	Decrease.
Alabama	635	687	52	....	11	14	3	....	624	673	49	....
Alaska	4	3	......	1	......	......	....	....	4	3	......	1
Arizona	31	37	6	....	1	1	....	....	30	36	6	....
Arkansas	565	625	60	....	5	5	....	....	560	620	60	....
California	592	630	38	....	20	23	3	....	572	607	35	....
Colorado	132	145	13	....	7	9	2	....	125	136	11	....
Connecticut	415	428	13	....	35	41	6	....	380	387	7	....
Dakota	77	99	22	....	1	2	1	....	76	97	21	....
Delaware	98	102	4	....	4	4	....	....	94	98	4	....
Dist. of Columbia	7	5	....	2	2	2	....	....	5	3	......	2
Florida	170	187	17	....	5	6	1	....	165	181	16	....
Georgia	548	587	39	....	20	22	2	....	528	565	37	....
Idaho	42	53	11	....	2	2	....	....	40	51	11	....
Illinois	1,738	1,792	54	....	110	122	12	....	1,628	1,670	42	....
Indiana	1,418	1,445	27	....	49	57	8	....	1,369	1,388	19	....
Iowa	1,309	1,314	5	....	54	65	11	....	1,255	1,249	....	6
Kansas	761	887	126	....	27	33	6	....	734	854	120	....
Kentucky	985	1,009	24	....	22	24	2	....	963	985	22	....
Louisiana	270	319	49	....	6	7	1	....	264	312	48	....
Maine	838	845	7	....	23	24	1	....	815	821	6	....
Maryland	553	569	16	....	9	12	3	....	544	557	13	....
Massachusetts	702	699	....	3	82	102	20	....	620	597	....	23
Michigan	1,101	1,128	27	....	56	63	7	....	1,045	1,065	20	....
Minnesota	702	744	42	....	18	19	1	....	684	725	41	....
Mississippi	443	500	57	....	17	22	5	....	426	478	52	....
Missouri	1,436	1,454	18	....	37	44	7	....	1,399	1,410	11	....
Montana	96	101	5	....	4	4	....	....	92	97	5	....
Nebraska	372	429	57	....	7	8	1	....	365	421	56	....
Nevada	70	82	12	....	7	8	1	....	63	74	11	....
New Hampshire	414	421	7	....	19	24	5	....	395	397	2	....
New Jersey	600	626	26	....	39	44	5	....	561	582	21	....
New Mexico	47	48	1	....	2	2	....	....	45	46	1	....
New York	2,757	2,794	37	....	146	152	6	....	2,611	2,642	31	....
North Carolina	838	897	59	....	11	10	....	1	827	887	60	....
Ohio	2,095	2,127	32	....	88	100	12	....	2,007	2,027	20	....
Oregon	220	239	19	....	2	5	3	....	218	234	16	....
Pennsylvania	2,964	3,039	75	....	106	116	10	....	2,858	2,923	65	....
Rhode Island	107	107	......	....	10	10	....	....	97	97	......	....
South Carolina	391	420	29	....	8	13	5	....	383	407	24	....
Tennessee	930	947	17	....	14	17	3	....	916	930	14	....
Texas	654	749	95	....	20	25	5	....	634	724	90	....
Utah	155	168	13	....	3	3	....	....	152	165	13	....
Vermont	471	475	4	....	18	19	1	....	453	456	3	....
Virginia	1,185	1,270	85	....	20	21	1	....	1,165	1,249	84	....
Washington	109	126	17	....	2	2	....	....	107	124	17	....
West Virginia	658	696	38	....	5	8	3	....	653	688	35	....
Wisconsin	1,128	1,157	29	....	43	45	2	....	1,085	1,112	27	....
Wyoming	30	33	3	....	3	2	....	1	27	31	4	....
Total	31,863	33,244	1,387	6	1,200	1,363	165	2	30,663	31,881	1,250	28

Statement of the operations of the letter-carrier system for the year ending June 30, 1873.

Name of post office.	State.	Number of carriers.	Delivered. Mail letters.	Local letters.	Newspapers.	Collected. Letters.	Newspapers.	Pieces handled. Aggregate.	Per carrier.	Cost of service. Aggregate, including incidentals.	Per piece.	Per carrier.	Amount of local postage.
Albany	New York	23	2,521,809	224,570	790,033	1,997,877	144,194	5,678,483	227,139	$21,796 69	3.8	$671 87	$7,106 38
Allegheny	Pennsylvania	9	783,500	69,299	443,752	362,909	30,645	1,710,535	190,060	7,474 31	4.3	830 48	4,363 61
Baltimore	Maryland	59	5,028,349	694,075	1,210,477	4,994,833	181,401	11,407,175	193,342	58,403 95	5.3	989 90	20,520 08
Boston	Massachusetts	70	6,704,679	2,173,386	1,677,124	9,597,880	649,719	21,096,779	300,097	67,599 59	3.2	964 71	64,841 31
Brooklyn	do	46	2,945,019	849,139	1,352,392	1,547,189	85,998	6,789,838	147,599	45,006 78	6.6	978 41	22,506 44
Buffalo	do	32	2,814,831	413,318	1,906,339	1,978,139	197,655	6,910,482	194,077	31,585 01	5.0	987 03	8,971 44
Cambridge	Massachusetts	7	542,333	44,180	113,803	143,559	7,911	853,795	935,229	3,251 65	4.5	989 371	983 40
Cambridgeport	do	4	420,075	25,366	190,348	192,817	4,318	832,913	904,661	3,291 65	3.9	812 66	581 40
Charlestown	do	4	364,254	98,141	222,594	284,748	19,957	1,129,604	894,661	3,481 41	3.9	899 98	679 74
Chicago	Illinois	111	14,420,442	2,473,265	3,193,490	19,923,970	5,128,651	45,138,684	406,655	108,873 98	2.4	980 66	47,783 74
Cincinnati	Ohio	50	4,782,360	743,277	1,061,410	3,571,445	280,683	10,472,703	209,454	51,945 81	4.8	1,034 91	98,109 12
Cleveland	do	36	2,985,703	352,235	1,091,347	2,946,785	199,668	6,706,698	537,944	94,130 38	3.2	928 09	8,497 02
Dayton	do	15	948,035	41,902	443,661	905,946	151,388	2,464,362	900,334	9,583 59	3.1	736 62	1,069 01
Detroit	Michigan	25	3,534,113	388,551	1,344,321	1,925,460	151,944	7,344,362	929,778	22,904 81	3.1	916 17	7,629 80
Erie	Pennsylvania	6	531,254	21,375	413,123	210,971	10,699	1,225,070	204,178	5,669 83	4.6	944 99	1,689 68
Harrisburgh	do	4	366,902	21,375	167,624	143,410	6,716	711,477	177,860	3,987 75	4.6	981 84	1,901 35
Hartford	Connecticut	11	875,700	112,504	344,743	449,787	24,396	1,814,132	164,981	8,339 40	4.0	757 21	5,513 82
Indianapolis	Indiana	11	2,022,143	208,640	635,026	143,539	933,230	4,544,006	239,161	15,708 97	3.4	898 79	3,963 70
Jersey City	New Jersey	6	684,513	65,321	164,057	982,292	33,241	1,229,424	204,904	5,500 00	4.4	916 66	1,638 97
Lancaster	Pennsylvania	5	407,530	25,619	170,876	126,868	745,392	746,392	148,656	4,219 75	3.2	849 55	589 07
Lawrence	Massachusetts	5	544,673	30,140	338,022	507,775	15,198	1,454,679	943,679	95,561 09	4.2	1,027 54	703 44
Louisville	Kentucky	26	2,967,639	339,160	731,110	9,005,844	185,166	6,945,975	940,365	95,561 00	2.6	985 11	6,000 40
Lowell	Massachusetts	6	642,663	34,680	959,427	639,049	94,981	1,649,660	981,613	4,402 00	2.6	733 66	1,089 40
Lynn	do	7	437,704	32,013	243,432	370,559	33,915	1,175,461	168,353	5,708 84	4.8	815 58	990 85
Manchester	New Hampshire	13	512,912	155,637	327,550	965,759	33,915	1,164,783	194,130	5,708 84	4.8	911 37	690 85
Memphis	Tennessee	12	1,413,701	155,637	329,523	905,104	131,338	2,944,670	194,130	8,116 32	3.9	750 36	1,531 12
Milwaukee	Wisconsin	22	2,414,300	166,762	663,284	1,406,842	131,338	4,732,366	914,653	21,257 75	4.5	966 80	5,195 00
Nashville	Tennessee	9	922,356	63,719	352,985	460,723	54,136	1,870,134	998,420	4,098 11	4.3	998 65	1,988 34
Newark	New Jersey	21	1,652,750	363,567	701,688	1,013,966	54,446	3,784,637	180,220	21,165 75	5.5	1,003 13	7,562 89
New Bedford	Massachusetts	11	451,948	21,532	922,222	523,073	13,789	2,664,546	180,719	4,331 94	4.4	864 25	1,008 42
New Haven	Connecticut	5	678,219	142,008	342,669	450,022	13,789	1,624,546	151,086	9,412 75	5.6	854 79	4,000 90
New Orleans	Louisiana	45	1,965,537	392,600	973,707	2,851,114	473,984	6,565,348	145,963	24,910 94	5.3	775 79	4,062 98
New York	New York	317	29,192,797	16,842,457	6,252,561	36,079,985	36,079,985	90,907,800	288,789	282,788 59	3.3	958 30	577,039 80
Philadelphia	Pennsylvania	177	14,925,773	7,425,136	5,680,950	15,014,644	2,374,704	47,025,817	907,942	184,781 95	3.8	1,043 85	166,009 03
Pittsburgh	do	24	1,964,624	996,827	744,709	1,574,644	41,363	5,676,048	204,361	19,290 40	4.1	963 76	6,000 05
Portland	Maine	10	528,621	39,146	384,661	743,191	47,161	1,730,649	172,386	9,299 80	4.6	829 80	8,899 43
Providence	Rhode Island	12	823,440	194,605	481,054	444,680	47,161	1,625,093	129,394	12,344 50	6.0	636 97	10,105 30
Reading	Pennsylvania	4	500,363	47,476	326,474	970,306	10,874	1,055,565	262,206	4,638 91	5.3	638 91	1,100 87
Richmond	Virginia	7	1,199,201	42,211	368,476	666,085	61,981	2,399,579	171,380	10,126 65	4.9	707 62	2,364 68
Rochester	New York	19	2,225,614	156,164	1,051,663	1,397,534	144,660	4,866,139	934,927	17,107 01	3.5	900 36	2,353 50

Saint Louis	Missouri	64	10,142,547	944,155	1,631,895	6,990,311	359,053	19,707,961	309,571	64,309 96	3.2	1,004 75	19,861 67
Salem	Massachusetts	6	355,803	37,603	503,727	979,139	13,531	869,703	144,865	4,910 46	5.6	818 41	889 13
San Francisco	California	24	1,290,991	277,355	466,961	3,079,733	296,795	4,350,344	181,964	25,095 94	5.7	1,045 66	10,163 48
Syracuse	New York	15	1,576,533	175,388	668,400	892,584	158,374	3,471,388	231,484	13,101 98	3.7	877 46	3,507 64
Trenton	New Jersey	4	447,991	37,900	182,777	953,714	19,881	964,413	241,103	3,457 08	3.5	864 57	1,180 64
Toledo	Ohio	10	1,026,829	63,563	423,505	953,843	140,903	2,606,643	990,864	9,124 90	3.4	912 42	2,043 98
Troy	New York	15	1,644,663	209,928	589,191	1,129,586	143,957	3,717,935	947,817	11,845 32	3.1	789 68	5,130 09
Utica	do	12	1,007,754	110,163	419,037	783,636	60,691	2,381,301	198,432	10,822 37	4.5	902 44	1,995 74
Washington	District of Columbia	30	1,962,648	312,949	874,034	1,461,968	184,536	4,803,137	160,105	29,332 58	6.1	977 75	7,216 99
Williamsburgh	New York	14	902,500	62,969	380,681	348,407	99,608	1,794,982	132,164	11,981 50	6.2	805 88	1,639 24
Wilmington	Delaware	10	711,523	85,630	280,977	354,877	16,674	1,448,901	144,890	8,278 57	5.7	897 56	3,059 08
Worcester	Massachusetts	10	611,334	75,096	284,665	341,237	11,746	1,334,978	133,687	6,061 33	6.0	896 13	3,596 16
Total		1,499	140,958,887	38,340,049	43,390,685	137,065,809	15,560,373	374,915,664		1,419,563 63			1,119,951 21

Salary of special agent of Post-Office Department paid out of the appropriation for letter-carriers — 4,720 35

Amount paid for letter-boxes at Des Moines, Iowa; Oswego, N. Y.; Scranton, Pa.; Wilkesbarre, Pa.; Quincy, Ill.; not included above — 211 50

Total					137,065,809				1,423,495 48			

REPORT OF THE AUDITOR OF THE TREASURY FOR THE POST-OFFICE DEPARTMENT.

OFFICE OF THE AUDITOR OF THE TREASURY
FOR THE POST-OFFICE DEPARTMENT,
October 20, 1873.

SIR: I have the honor to submit the following annual report of the receipts and expenditures of the Post-Office Department, together with the operations of this office in connection therewith, for the fiscal year ended June 30, 1873:

COLLECTION OF POST-OFFICE REVENUES.

The number of post-offices in operation during the year was 33,513, which are thus classified under the regulations adopted for the government of the Department, chapter 25, sections 352 to 368, inclusive.

The following-named offices, seventy-one in number, are denominated depositories, and are required by the Postmaster-General to receive and retain, subject to the drafts of the Department, the funds of certain adjacent offices, as well as the revenues of their own:

List of offices designated as depositories, with names of postmasters.

Albany, N. Y.	J. F. Smyth.	Milwaukee, Wis.	S. C. West.
Atlanta, Ga.	J. L. Dunning.	Mobile, Ala.	M. D. Wickersham.
Bangor, Me.	A. B. Farnham.	Montpelier, Vt	J. W. Clark.
Batavia, N. Y.	William Tyrrell.	Nashville, Tenn.	W. F. Prosser.
Binghamton, N. Y.	E. B. Stephens.	Newark, N. J.	William Ward.
Buffalo, N. Y.	J. M. Schermerhorn.	New Haven, Conn.	N. D. Sperry.
Cleveland, Ohio.	John W. Allen.	Ogdensburgh, N. Y.	R. G. Pettibone.
Columbus, Ohio.	James M. Comley.	Olean, N. Y.	J. G. Johnson.
Concord, N. H.	M. T. Willard.	Peoria, Ill	D. W. Magee.
Davenport, Iowa.	Edward Russell.	Pittsburgh, Pa.	J. H. Stewart.
Des Moines, Iowa.	J. S. Clarkson.	Plattsburgh, N. Y.	H. S. Ransom.
Detroit, Mich.	F. W. Swift.	Portland, Me.	C. W. Goddard.
Dover, Del.	J. B. Smith.	Portsmouth, Ohio.	O. Wood.
Dubuque, Iowa.	G. L. Torbert.	Providence, R. I.	E. S. Jackson.
Easton, Pa.	J. K. Dawes.	Quincy, Ills.	M. Piggott.
Evansville, Ind.	T. R. McFerSon.	Raleigh, N. C.	W. W. Holden.
Fort Wayne, Ind.	J. J. Kamm.	Richmond, Va.	E. L. Van Lew.
Geneva, N. Y.	Charles L. Hemiup.	Ripon, Wis.	H. S. Town.
Grand Rapids, Mich.	A. B. Turner.	Rochester, N. Y.	E. M. Smith.
Harrisburgh, Pa.	George Bergner.	Rutland, Vt.	J. B. Kilborn.
Hartford, Conn.	John H. Burnham.	Sandusky, Ohio.	A. C. Van Tine.
Huntsville, Ala.	J. D. Sibley.	Scranton, Pa.	J. S. Slocum.
Indianapolis, Ind.	W. R. Holloway.	Springfield, Ill.	J. L. Crane.
Kalamazoo, Mich.	J. A. Stone.	Springfield, Mass.	H. C. Lee.
Keene, N. H.	H. C. Henderson.	Steubenville, Ohio.	J. M. Reede.
Knoxville, Tenn.	William Rule.	Saint Paul, Minn.	J. A. Wheelock.
Lafayette, Ind.	J. L. Miller.	Syracuse, N. Y.	D. H. Bruce.
Lancaster, N. H.	John W. Spalding.	Urbana, Ohio.	D. C. Hilt.
Leavenworth, Kans.	J. Clark.	Utica, N. Y.	C. H. Hopkins.
Lexington, Ky.	S. W. Price.	Vincennes, Ind.	W. N. Denny.
Lima, Ohio.	C. Parmenter.	Wheeling, W. Va.	C. J. Rawlings.
Louisville, Ky.	L. M. Porter.	Williamsport, Pa.	Robert Hawley.
Lowell, Mass.	J. A. Goodwin.	Wooster, Ohio.	A. L. McClure.
Madison, Wis.	E. W. Keyes.	Worcester, Mass.	Josiah Pickett.
Meadville, Pa.	D. V. Derrickson.	Zanesville, Ohio.	J. J. Douglas.
Memphis, Tenn.	J. Deloach.		

The following depositaries and assistant treasurers receive and retain, subject to the warrants of the Post-Office Department, the funds of such post-offices as are instructed to deposit in their hands:

DESIGNATED DEPOSITARIES.

S. J. Holley	Buffalo, N. Y.	J. Cushman	Olympia, W. T.
E. W. Little	Santa Fé, N. M.	Thomas Steel	Pittsburgh, Pa
J. P. Luce	Louisville, Ky.	C. H. Lorde	Tucson, Ariz

ASSISTANT TREASURERS.

Thomas Hillhouse	New York, N. Y.	J. D. Geddings	Charleston, S. C.
George Eyster	Philadelphia, Pa.	W. E. Davis	Cincinnati, Ohio.
Peter Negley	Baltimore, Md.	J. D. Webster	Chicago, Ill.
F. Haven, jr.	Boston, Mass.	A. G. Edwards	Saint Louis, Mo.
B. F. Flanders	New Orleans, La.	William Sherman	San Francisco, Cal.

One hundred and eighty-seven post-offices are draft-offices, and during the year paid 18,898 drafts issued by the Postmaster-General, countersigned, entered, and sent out by the Auditor, for sums in the aggregate of... $2,754,891 63

Thirty-seven hundred and two offices are deposit-offices, a portion of which, during the year, deposited with the Treasurer and assistant treasurers of the United States the sum of......................... 4,339,628 21

The remaining deposit-offices deposited with the depositaries named above, the sum of $820,086.67, which is embraced in the $2,754,891.63 paid on the drafts of the Department by said depositaries and draft-offices.

Twenty-seven thousand nine hundred and twenty-one offices are collection offices, and paid on collection orders issued to mail-contractors the sum of.. 3,013,962 99

Forty-seven hundred and seventy-two offices are special and mail-messenger offices, and derive their mail supplies by the payment of the revenue of their offices therefor, amounting to.................... 514,116 08

The amount paid into the Treasury by postmasters for the use and purposes of the Post-Office Department during the fiscal year was..... 10,622,598 91

Revenue account of the Post-Office Department.

The receipts of the Department for the fiscal year ended June 30, 1873, were... $22,996,741 57

The amount placed in the Treasury for the service of the Department for the fiscal year, being grants in aid of the revenue under the following acts of Congress, were:

Under the third section of the act approved June 1, 1872, for mail-steamship service between San Francisco, Japan and China.................... $500,000 00

Under the third section of the act approved June 1, 1872, for mail-steamship service between the United States and Brazil.................... 150,000 00

Under the third section of the act approved June 1, 1872, for mail-steamship service between San Francisco and the Sandwich Islands.................... 75,000 00

Under the second section of the act approved March 3, 1869, for supplying deficiency in the revenue of the Post-Office Department for the fiscal year ended June 30, 1870.................... 152,225 00

Under the first section of the act approved March 3, 1871, for supplying deficiency in the revenue of the Post-Office Department for the fiscal year ended June 30, 1871.................... 978,000 00

Under the third section of the act approved March 3, 1871, for supplying deficiency in the revenue of the Post-Office Department for the fiscal year ended June 30, 1872.................... 535,000 00

Under the fourth section of the act approved June 1, 1872, for supplying deficiency in the revenue of the Post-Office Department for the fiscal year ended June 30, 1873.................... 3,600,250 00

5,990,475 00

Aggregate of revenue and grants.................................. 28,987,216 57

The expenditures of the Department for the fiscal year ended June 30, 1873, were... 29,084,945 67

Excess of expenditures.. 97,729 10

The net revenue of the Department from postages, being the aggregate of balances due the United States by postmasters on the adjustment of their quarterly accounts for the year, after deducting their compensation and expenses of their offices, was:

For the quarter ended September, 30, 1872	$3,158,463 32
For the quarter ended December 31, 1872	3,397,009 59
For the quarter ended March 31, 1873	3,618,911 48
For the quarter ended June 30, 1873	3,529,552 66
Total	13,703,937 05

The amount of newspaper and pamphlet postage paid in money, was:

For the quarter ended September 30, 1872	$264,722 72
For the quarter ended December 31, 1872	264,149 59
For the quarter ended March 31, 1873	276,113 22
For the quarter ended June 30, 1873	268,012 72
Total	1,072,998 19

The amount of letter-postage paid in money, was

For the quarter ended September 30, 1872	$81,861 94
For the quarter ended December 31, 1872	88,132 10
For the quarter ended March 31, 1873	95,658 47
For the quarter ended June 30, 1873	83,196 98
Total	348,849 49

The amount of stamps, stamped envelopes, and postal cards sold, was:

For the quarter ended September 30, 1872	$4,783,224 94
For the quarter ended December 31, 1872	5,004,483 06
For the quarter ended March 31, 1873	5,310,054 35
For the quarter ended June 30, 1873	5,227,055 15
Total	20,324,817 50

The number of quarterly returns of postmasters received and audited, on which the sum of $13,703,937.05 was found due the United States, was:

For the quarter ended September 30, 1872	31,012
For the quarter ended December 31, 1872	31,548
For the quarter ended March 31, 1873	31,818
For the quarter ended June 30, 1873	31,754
Total	126,132

MAIL TRANSPORTATION.

The amount charged to transportation accrued and placed to the credit of mail-contractors and others for mail transportation during the year, was:

For the regular service of mail-routes	$13,501,520 42
For the supply of special and mail-messenger offices	563,386 46
For the salaries of postal-railway clerks, route and other agents	1,830,894 38
For the salaries and per diem of the assistant superintendents of the postal-railway service	46,626 96
	15,942,428 22

Foreign mail transportation.

San Francisco and Hong-Kong, China	$500,000 00
San Francisco and the Hawaiian Islands	75,000 00
United States and Brazil	150,000 00
New York, Queenstown, and Liverpool	120,703 96
New York and England, France, Hamburg, and Bremen	94,483 25
New York and Havana, and New York and Vera Cruz	47,557 74
New York and the West Indies	11,248 10
New York, Panama, and San Francisco	21,610 95
New York and Rio de Janeiro	482 72
Portland, Detroit, Chicago, and England	6,065 12
Boston and England	4,977 34
Boston, Nova Scotia, and Prince Edward Island	970 88

Baltimore and Havana, and New Orleans and Havana....	$4,101 58	
New York and Stettin	12 07	
Baltimore and Bremen	51 27	
Portland and Nova Scotia	1,678 20	
New Orleans, Bremen, France, and Spain	451 70	
New Orleans, New York, and Havana, and Philadelphia and Havana	1,934 52	
New Orleans and Belize	1 89	
San Francisco, Japan, and China	3,502 87	
San Francisco, New Zealand, and Australia	5,869 85	
Expenses of Government mail-agent at Aspinwall	889 99	
Expenses of Government mail-agent at Havana	800 00	
Expenses of Government mail-agent at Panama	1,659 85	
		$1,054,053 89
		16,996,482 11
The amount credited to transportation accrued and charged to contractors for over-credits was	11,601 24	
Fines imposed on contractors	2,297 05	
Deductions from their pay	65,643 75	
		79,542 04
Net amount to the credit of mail-contractors and others		16,916,940 07
The amount actually paid and credited during the year, was		$16,833,682 58

Statement of collecting division showing balances collected from late postmasters.

During the year this division has had charge of accounts of 24,517 late postmasters during the period from July 1, 1870, to June 30, 1873.

Amounts collected on balances due from late postmasters who went out of office prior to July 1, 1872.

Collected by draft		$77,770 16
Collected by suit		26,097 93
Credited on vouchers		42,653 93
Charged to suspense		1 32
Charged to bad debts		24,415 31
Total		170,938 65
Amount collected by draft from contractors		$10,007 49
Number of changes of postmasters reported by appointment office during the fiscal year, was 8,930; and the balances due the United States upon the accounts of said late postmasters amount to		424,506 47
Of which there has been collected by draft	$79,292 71	
Charged to suspense	195 16	
Charged to bad debts	40 57	
Credited on vouchers	2 73	
		79,531 17
Total remaining due		344,975 30
Of which there remains in suit	$4,558 19	
Of which there remains not in suit	340,417 11	
		344,975 30
Amounts due late postmasters in fiscal year 1873		42,704 81
Amounts paid late postmasters on all accounts prior to July 1, 1873		27,067 11
Amounts due by late postmasters, for which suits were instituted during the fiscal year		55,714 56
Amount collected by suit during the fiscal year		51,435 34

The subjoined tables, numbered from 1 to 52, inclusive, exhibit in detail the transactions of the Department for the fiscal year.

I have the honor to be, very respectfully,

J. J. MARTIN, *Auditor.*

Hon. JNO. A. J. CRESWELL,
Postmaster-General.

Statement of the postal receipts and expenditures of the

States and Territories.	Letter postage.	Newspaper postage.	Waste paper and twine.	Stamps sold.	Emoluments.	Total receipts.
Maine	$4,534 52	$25,687 34	$118 82	$335,005 69	$20,354 62	$365,700 99
New Hampshire	1,758 00	16,971 31	135 19	210,457 24	9,908 55	239,239 85
Vermont	1,544 58	15,815 26	68 80	199,687 41	7,461 16	224,577 30
Massachusetts	21,590 83	56,916 44	601 11	1,612,131 91	91,416 72	1,782,657 01
Rhode Island	2,119 20	7,188 68	51 78	177,179 40	17,341 71	203,880 77
Connecticut	4,450 62	25,503 15	201 54	476,033 34	32,632 98	538,821 63
New York	119,410 76	145,089 60	1,589 48	4,395,807 86	173,757 03	4,835,654 79
New Jersey	7,563 80	23,313 95	143 75	426,446 32	23,968 32	481,336 14
Pennsylvania	27,938 40	90,698 35	933 94	2,099,042 56	77,039 52	2,295,652 73
Delaware	505 60	2,987 44	4 80	56,809 75	838 19	63,145 78
Maryland	8,544 62	16,208 45	97 36	400,363 49	8,432 54	433,646 46
Virginia	2,237 56	20,376 80	68 03	319,141 17	11,403 37	353,226 93
West Virginia	714 86	8,691 29	53 12	106,404 16	4,213 61	120,077 24
North Carolina	891 99	11,910 65	10 13	147,577 51	5,900 44	166,290 72
South Carolina	1,207 62	8,429 35	23 79	195,731 89	8,340 07	143,732 72
Georgia	2,294 91	16,959 30	108 73	263,474 08	23,229 45	306,065 90
Florida	1,581 01	2,350 96	1 85	43,579 36	3,541 87	51,055 25
Ohio	14,268 77	83,694 35	768 29	1,359,288 80	68,508 62	1,596,528 83
Michigan	21,856 23	49,665 49	328 80	671,552 19	50,060 05	793,462 76
Indiana	3,230 55	47,412 17	208 90	569,637 56	41,606 99	655,098 25
Illinois	24,568 77	83,272 89	1,760 78	1,625,741 90	91,133 40	1,896,477 74
Wisconsin	8,891 10	34,225 25	293 53	466,378 32	33,838 15	543,556 05
Iowa	5,705 20	40,794 06	148 43	541,196 61	48,606 46	636,450 76
Missouri	7,729 33	44,649 63	230 49	796,196 01	34,971 20	813,906 66
Kentucky	2,692 75	21,224 40	147 81	396,634 56	14,748 46	365,447 98
Tennessee	2,003 01	16,910 54	167 06	274,137 07	10,033 14	303,259 82
Alabama	1,301 66	10,296 19	46 34	157,454 82	14,966 85	184,065 86
Mississippi	852 39	10,074 91	27 68	137,346 81	11,922 06	160,223 65
Arkansas	675 66	6,029 22	5 91	77,545 77	6,796 37	91,052 93
Louisiana	9,099 48	8,572 63	20 15	196,988 59	21,384 18	235,357 96
Texas	4,681 89	19,679 51	46 71	249,287 11	26,110 02	299,805 24
California	13,044 47	30,082 88	150 90	494,489 43	43,496 36	581,194 04
Oregon	306 64	5,385 35	15 00	49,014 62	7,100 82	61,822 43
Minnesota	8,610 14	19,017 49	152 37	230,953 85	21,737 73	280,471 58
Kansas	1,616 97	16,337 46	24 78	243,983 83	24,857 82	286,820 86
Nebraska	1,311 58	6,804 01	17 32	151,436 13	9,756 13	169,327 17
Nevada	453 60	5,167 36	1 00	42,706 62	7,840 01	56,168 59
Colorado	517 69	3,908 36	12 00	62,838 18	14,584 76	81,861 01
Utah	547 53	4,205 90	29 20	41,986 50	5,483 57	52,252 70
New Mexico	27 99	474 75	4 25	11,629 68	1,012 75	13,149 42
Washington	152 23	1,931 80	4 25	15,217 26	1,754 27	19,059 90
Dakota	293 04	684 17	......	12,322 09	814 19	14,314 02
Arizona	41 41	279 19	......	7,389 78	543 75	8,256 13
Idaho	76 46	934 20	1 50	7,868 22	1,560 00	10,440 38
Wyoming	134 59	925 04	1 25	17,015 99	1,942 98	20,019 85
Montana	141 97	1,858 96	25	17,738 49	5,314 26	25,053 93
Alaska	10 89	8 98	......	36 00	......	55 87
District of Columbia	3,079 02	4,096 65	193 88	128,384 99	7,076 33	142,830 83
Deduct miscellaneous items	346,807 65	1,073,902 26	8,950 92	20,303,503 51	1,148,491 98	22,881,655 72
Add miscellaneous items	2,042 44		904 07	21,313 99	1,550 46	24,002 76
Total	348,849 49	1,072,998 19	8,950 92	20,324,817 50	1,150,042 38	22,905,658 48

NOTE.—The following items of expenditure and revenue, being of a general nature, are not embraced

Amount paid for foreign mails and expenses of government agents	$1,054,053 89
Foreign postage collected and returned to foreign governments	209,041 05
Ship, steamboat, and way letters	4,257 96
Wrapping-paper	23,494 49
Office furniture	2,352 61
Advertising	74,579 10
Mail-bags	92,778 36
Blank-agents and assistants	7,500 00
Mail locks, keys, and stamps	38,377 30
Mail depredations and special agents	157,963 26
Expenses of postage-stamps and stamped envelopes	653,921 76
Salaries and per diem of assistant superintendents of postal-railway service	46,696 96
Miscellaneous payments	171,099 38
Repairs to Post-Office building	11,735 15
Excess of expenditures brought down	3,704,305 45
	6,342,086 72

OFFICE OF THE AUDITOR OF THE TREASURY
FOR THE POST-OFFICE DEPARTMENT, *October* 20, 1873.

United States for the fiscal year ended June 30, 1873.

Compensation of postmasters.	Incidental expenses of post offices.	Compensation to letter carriers.	Compensation of route-agents, postal-railway clerks, mail-messengers, and supply of special offices.	Transportation by States.	Total expenses.	Excess of expenditures over receipts.	Excess of receipts over expenditures.
$146,695 78	$47,636 56	$9,299 60	$33,177 12	$106,164 54	$403,975 80	$18,274 81	....
101,331 42	15,393 10	5,468 94	16,817 68	70,306 41	209,947 06	....	$29,983 63
105,939 99	13,910 41	....	16,149 79	119,532 07	255,532 96	30,954 96	....
333,586 76	285,666 02	112,752 96	131,536 25	277,255 43	1,140,796 74	....	641,860 97
36,731 13	19,230 75	12,344 59	6,469 11	24,512 15	99,987 73	....	104,593 04
155,878 00	62,336 92	17,742 13	38,643 60	141,577 79	416,178 66	....	122,642 97
606,144 33	1,014,318 70	466,454 29	361,810 15	934,386 73	3,443,198 20	....	1,392,596 59
157,864 89	35,924 54	30,122 63	23,600 34	131,745 44	379,278 66	....	2,058 06
492,961 55	313,230 27	230,374 46	165,715 63	694,918 96	1,897,302 19	....	308,448 54
19,823 66	6,301 83	8,278 57	7,140 45	23,853 94	65,446 15	2,300 37	....
70,074 21	62,091 14	56,403 95	36,885 43	269,049 75	536,504 56	102,864 06	....
117,938 16	47,731 29	10,186 69	34,782 81	361,306 79	571,945 74	218,718 81	....
48,999 75	14,085 56	....	18,419 61	94,649 23	180,154 15	60,076 91	....
66,991 78	13,937 90	....	33,414 65	169,694 78	283,939 95	117,648 53	....
44,850 61	11,555 02	....	15,806 53	151,509 30	223,731 46	79,908 74	....
84,101 94	43,417 74	....	44,974 23	214,514 98	390,308 87	84,249 90	....
22,410 83	5,297 15	....	6,841 46	192,565 31	217,114 85	166,050 60	....
307,922 35	177,751 29	94,043 91	151,570 81	949,949 58	1,751,277 94	294,749 11	....
249,864 39	95,473 49	22,904 25	57,941 17	479,980 11	905,466 41	112,003 65	....
231,300 36	92,696 76	15,708 97	87,458 01	371,236 96	800,601 06	145,504 63	....
443,779 54	343,384 24	104,939 24	305,944 42	825,446 85	2,027,360 33	200,883 50	....
194,505 69	50,139 72	21,957 75	59,466 36	295,745 12	621,114 81	77,756 76	....
256,013 95	55,542 90	41 00	121,934 63	432,943 56	866,475 55	230,094 59	....
194,031 91	119,214 47	64,302 94	130,410 36	569,802 22	1,077,765 12	264,758 56	....
110,630 73	49,074 99	2,561 99	41,567 57	987,461 22	494,500 50	129,058 56	....
86,264 19	50,168 79	17,200 43	67,663 87	218,363 65	639,621 63	138,430 81	....
61,303 69	25,474 66	....	31,104 03	230,361 62	357,794 46	173,738 60	....
74,879 21	12,402 50	....	22,327 63	206,302 29	315,811 63	155,587 98	....
42,306 31	12,133 51	....	8,949 56	300,713 54	363,402 94	272,350 01	....
33,552 05	55,462 76	34,910 94	15,651 87	241,957 55	360,841 17	145,488 21	....
109,155 00	39,237 53	....	20,439 02	616,808 79	778,630 34	478,825 10	....
110,490 61	91,551 90	25,095 94	53,100 98	468,467 95	1,164,707 32	547,513 98	....
25,406 82	9,593 12	....	2,346 70	90,876 15	128,222 79	66,400 26	....
109,217 30	31,490 41	....	46,771 66	225,994 67	406,474 96	121,002 62	....
131,587 60	26,711 61	....	44,846 42	333,162 78	536,998 55	249,467 09	....
41,181 07	16,133 31	....	69,799 26	351,500 39	476,658 96	309,385 79	....
182,302 99	10,637 47	....	2,638 51	165,547 06	201,216 03	145,047 44	....
27,550 40	12,389 83	....	6,306 41	177,893 96	223,451 60	141,580 50	....
18,094 02	9,054 65	....	916 24	370,778 24	396,841 35	346,568 65	....
8,752 10	411 15	....	7 67	316,919 78	326,090 64	312,941 82	....
9,195 93	954 50	....	644 18	170,985 71	191,802 96	162,742 58	....
6,972 11	1,154 50	....	890 00	26,378 82	34,775 43	26,461 41	....
4,343 94	905 00	....	....	74,143 96	78,604 20	70,638 07	....
6,679 02	1,029 25	....	94 00	103,190 71	110,992 96	100,550 60	....
10,980 76	2,647 95	....	....	11,225 10	24,773 12	4,733 87	....
14,061 74	4,486 56	....	....	122,972 00	141,602 24	116,748 31	....
962 25	....	....	....	....	908 85	906 34	....
6,977 61	115,545 54	29,332 58	53,226 71	....	905,144 44	62,313 61	....
5,703,976 77	3,549,029 61	1,419,775 13	2,394,290 84	13,473,555 79	26,540,699 14	6,452,277 79	2,699,113 39
21,649 35	16,674 25	3,215 56	....	27,964 63	69,343 79	69,343 79	24,002 76
5,725,468 12	3,565,703 86	1,422,990 69	2,394,290 84	13,501,520 42	26,609,963	936,521,621 51	2,716,116 66

In the above statement, viz:

Receipts on account of dead letters	86,908 00
Receipts on account of fines	3,917 39
Receipts on account of miscellaneous	12,373 79
Receipts on account of money-order business	64,584 66
Excess of transportation accrued	162,790 53
Total excess of expenditures over receipts	6,088,204 10

6,342,666 72

J. J. MARTIN. *Auditor.*

Statement of the postal receipts and expenditures of the

States and Territories.	Letter postage.	Newspaper-postage.	Waste paper and twine.	Stamps sold.	Emoluments.	Total receipts.
Maine	$4,534 52	$25,687 34	$118 82	$335,005 69	$30,354 02	$395,700 99
New Hampshire	1,758 60	16,971 31	135 19	210,457 24	9,908 55	239,230 23
Vermont	1,544 56	15,815 26	68 89	199,687 41	7,461 16	224,577 38
Massachusetts	21,590 83	56,916 44	601 11	1,612,131 91	91,416 72	1,782,657 01
Rhode Island	2,119 20	7,188 68	51 78	177,179 40	17,341 71	203,880 77
Connecticut	4,450 02	25,503 15	201 54	476,033 34	32,639 08	538,881 62
New York	119,410 76	145,069 66	1,589 48	4,395,807 86	173,757 03	4,835,634 79
New Jersey	7,563 80	23,313 95	143 75	426,446 32	23,868 32	481,336 14
Pennsylvania	27,938 40	90,696 35	933 94	2,099,042 56	77,039 52	2,295,652 73
Delaware	505 60	2,987 44	4 80	58,809 75	838 19	63,145 78
Maryland	8,544 62	16,208 45	97 36	400,363 49	8,432 54	433,646 46
Virginia	2,237 56	20,376 80	68 00	319,141 17	11,403 37	353,226 00
West Virginia	714 86	8,691 29	53 12	106,404 16	4,213 81	120,077 24
North Carolina	891 99	11,910 65	10 13	147,577 51	5,900 44	166,290 72
South Carolina	1,207 02	8,429 35	23 79	125,731 89	8,340 07	143,732 72
Georgia	2,294 91	16,959 30	108 73	263,474 08	23,299 45	306,062 95
Florida	1,561 01	2,350 06	1 85	43,579 56	3,541 87	51,055 22
Ohio	14,268 77	83,604 35	768 29	1,359,288 80	68,508 62	1,526,528 82
Michigan	21,856 03	49,665 49	328 80	671,552 19	50,060 05	793,462 76
Indiana	3,230 55	47,412 17	208 90	562,637 56	41,606 99	655,096 25
Illinois	24,568 77	83,272 39	1,760 78	1,625,741 90	91,133 40	1,826,477 70
Wisconsin	8,891 10	34,225 25	223 23	466,378 32	33,838 15	543,556 60
Iowa	5,705 20	40,794 06	148 43	541,196 61	48,606 46	636,450 70
Missouri	7,729 33	44,649 63	230 49	726,196 01	34,971 20	813,006 08
Kentucky	2,692 75	21,294 40	147 81	326,634 56	14,748 46	365,447 98
Tennessee	2,003 01	16,910 54	167 06	274,137 07	10,033 14	303,250 82
Alabama	1,301 66	10,296 19	46 34	157,454 82	14,985 85	184,085 86
Mississippi	852 39	10,074 91	27 68	137,346 81	11,982 06	160,283 85
Arkansas	675 66	6,029 22	5 91	77,545 77	6,796 37	91,052 03
Louisiana	9,092 48	8,572 63	20 15	196,288 52	21,384 18	235,357 96
Texas	4,681 80	19,679 51	46 71	249,287 11	26,110 02	299,805 24
California	13,044 47	30,069 88	150 90	494,489 43	43,496 36	581,194 04
Oregon	306 64	5,385 35	15 00	49,014 62	7,100 62	61,822 43
Minnesota	8,610 14	19,017 49	152 37	230,953 85	21,737 73	280,471 58
Kansas	1,616 97	16,337 46	24 78	243,983 83	24,857 62	286,820 66
Nebraska	1,311 58	6,804 61	17 32	151,438 13	9,756 13	169,327 17
Nevada	453 60	5,167 36	1 00	42,706 62	7,840 01	56,168 59
Colorado	517 69	3,908 36	12 00	62,838 18	14,584 78	81,861 01
Utah	547 53	4,205 90	29 30	41,946 50	5,483 57	52,252 70
New Mexico	27 99	474 75	4 25	11,620 68	1,012 75	13,149 42
Washington	152 23	1,931 69	4 25	15,217 26	1,754 27	19,059 90
Dakota	293 04	684 17	....	12,322 69	814 12	14,314 02
Arizona	41 41	279 19	....	7,389 78	543 75	8,256 13
Idaho	76 46	934 20	1 50	7,868 22	1,500 00	10,440 38
Wyoming	134 59	945 04	1 25	17,015 99	1,942 98	20,019 85
Montana	141 97	1,858 96	25	17,738 49	5,314 26	25,053 93
Alaska	10 80	8 08	....	36 00	....	55 87
District of Columbia	3,079 08	4,096 65	193 88	128,384 20	7,078 33	142,830 83
	346,807 05	1,073,002 26	8,950 92	20,303,503 51	1,148,491 98	22,881,655 72
Deduct miscellaneous items	....	904 07	....	....	....	....
Add miscellaneous items	2,042 44	....	....	21,313 99	1,550 40	24,002 76
Total	348,849 49	1,072,998 19	8,950 92	20,324,817 50	1,150,042 38	22,905,658 48

NOTE.—The following items of expenditure and revenue, being of a general nature, are not embraced

Amount paid for foreign mails and expenses of government agents	$1,054,053 80
Foreign postage collected and returned to foreign governments	299,041 83
Ship, steamboat, and way letters	4,857 94
Wrapping-paper	23,494 40
Office furniture	2,352 61
Advertising	74,579 10
Mail-bags	92,778 36
Blank-agents and assistants	7,500 00
Mail locks, keys, and stamps	38,377 30
Mail depredations and special agents	157,963 98
Expenses of postage-stamps and stamped envelopes	653,921 76
Salaries and per diem of assistant superintendents of postal-railway service	46,698 94
Miscellaneous payments	171,099 34
Repairs to Post-Office building	11,735 15
Excess of expenditures brought down	3,704,305 43
	6,342,006 72

OFFICE OF THE AUDITOR OF THE TREASURY
FOR THE POST-OFFICE DEPARTMENT, *October 20, 1873.*

United States for the fiscal year ended June 30, 1873.

Compensation of postmasters.	Incidental expenses of post-offices.	Compensation to letter-carriers.	Compensation of route-agents, postal-railway clerks, mail messengers, and supply of special offices.	Transportation by States.	Total expenses.	Excess of expenditures over receipts.	Excess of receipts over expenditures.
$146,695 78	$47,638 56	$8,299 80	$33,177 12	$168,164 54	$403,975 80	$18,274 81	
101,331 42	15,323 10	5,468 24	16,817 89	70,306 41	209,247 06		$29,983 83
105,939 99	13,910 41		16,149 79	119,532 07	255,532 26	30,954 96	
333,586 78	285,666 02	112,752 26	131,536 25	277,255 43	1,140,796 74		641,860 27
36,731 13	19,230 75	12,344 59	6,469 11	24,512 15	99,287 73		104,593 04
155,878 00	62,336 92	17,742 13	38,643 80	141,577 79	416,178 66		122,642 97
666,144 33	1,014,318 70	466,458 29	361,810 15	934,396 73	3,443,128 20		1,392,526 59
157,884 89	35,924 58	30,122 83	23,600 34	131,745 44	379,278 08		2,058 06
492,961 55	313,230 27	230,378 46	165,715 65	694,918 26	1,897,202 19		398,448 54
19,893 66	6,301 23	8,278 57	7,189 45	23,853 24	65,446 15	2,300 37	
70,074 21	82,091 18	58,403 95	36,885 43	289,049 75	536,504 52	102,858 06	
117,938 16	47,731 29	10,186 69	34,782 81	361,306 79	571,945 74	218,718 81	
48,999 75	18,085 56		18,419 61	94,649 23	180,154 15	60,076 91	
66,901 78	13,927 90		33,414 85	169,694 72	283,939 25	117,648 53	
44,859 61	11,555 02		15,808 53	151,508 30	223,731 46	79,998 74	
86,101 98	43,417 74		44,274 23	214,514 92	390,308 87	84,242 90	
22,410 93	5,297 15		6,841 46	182,565 31	217,114 85	166,059 60	
397,922 35	177,751 29	94,083 91	151,570 81	929,949 58	1,751,277 94	224,749 11	
249,868 39	95,472 49	22,904 25	57,941 17	479,280 11	905,466 41	112,003 65	
233,300 36	92,896 78	15,708 97	87,458 01	371,236 96	800,601 08	145,504 83	
443,779 54	343,268 24	108,939 28	305,924 42	825,448 85	2,027,360 33	900,882 59	
194,505 86	50,139 72	21,257 75	59,466 36	295,745 12	621,114 81	77,758 76	
256,013 26	55,542 90	41 00	191,934 63	432,943 56	866,475 35	230,094 59	
194,031 91	119,218 47	64,302 26	130,410 36	569,802 22	1,077,765 22	264,758 56	
110,830 73	49,078 99	25,561 99	41,567 57	267,461 22	494,500 50	129,052 52	
86,264 89	50,168 79	17,200 43	67,663 87	218,383 65	439,681 63	136,430 81	
61,383 69	25,874 86		31,104 03	239,361 88	357,724 46	173,738 60	
74,879 21	12,402 50		22,327 83	206,202 29	315,811 83	155,587 98	
42,306 31	12,133 51		8,949 58	300,713 54	363,402 94	272,350 01	
33,552 05	55,468 76	34,910 94	15,651 87	241,257 55	380,841 17	145,483 21	
102,155 00	39,227 53		20,439 02	616,808 79	778,630 34	478,825 10	
110,490 61	91,551 90	25,095 94	53,100 92	888,467 93	1,168,707 32	587,513 22	
25,406 82	9,593 12		2,346 70	90,876 15	128,222 79	66,400 36	
102,217 30	31,490 41		46,771 88	225,994 67	406,474 26	126,002 68	
131,527 60	26,711 81		44,886 42	333,162 72	536,288 55	249,467 69	
41,121 07	16,133 31		69,799 26	351,599 32	478,652 96	309,395 79	
22,392 99	10,637 47		2,638 51	165,547 06	201,216 03	145,047 44	
27,559 40	12,389 83		6,208 41	177,293 96	223,451 60	141,590 59	
18,098 02	9,054 85		916 24	370,772 24	398,841 35	346,588 65	
8,752 10	411 15		7 67	316,919 72	326,090 64	312,941 22	
9,195 93	954 50		686 12	170,965 71	181,802 26	162,742 36	
6,972 11	1,134 50		290 00	26,378 82	34,775 43	20,461 41	
4,343 94	205 00			74,143 26	78,694 20	70,438 07	
6,679 02	1,029 25		94 00	103,190 71	110,992 98	100,559 60	
10,860 76	2,687 26			11,225 10	24,773 12	4,753 27	
14,061 74	4,868 56			122,872 00	141,802 24	116,748 31	
262 25					262 25	206 38	
6,977 61	115,545 54	29,332 58	53,288 71		205,144 44	62,313 61	
5,703,978 77	3,549,029 61	1,419,775 13	2,394,280 84	13,473,555 79	26,540,620 14	6,452,277 73	2,692,113 30
21,489 35	16,674 25	3,215 56		27,964 63	69,343 79	69,343 79	24,002 76
5,725,468 12	3,565,703 86	1,422,990 60	2,394,280 84	13,501,520 42	26,609,963 93	6,521,621 51	2,716,116 06

In the above statement, viz:

Receipts on account of dead-letters	$6,208 00
Receipts on account of fines	3,917 39
Receipts on account of miscellaneous	12,373 70
Receipts on account of money-order business	68,584 00
Excess of transportation accrued	162,799 53
Total excess of expenditures over receipts	6,088,204 10

Statement showing the transactions of the money-order office of the United States for the fiscal year ending June 30, 1873.

States and Territories	Number of orders issued	Balance from last year	Amount of orders issued	Revenue. Total fees received.	Revenue. Premiums.	Drafts and deposits received.	Balance due post-masters.	Transferred from— Postage fund.	Transferred from— Swiss fund.	Transferred from— British fund.	Transferred from— German fund.
Alabama	42,963	$18,018 53	$902,609 75	$5,319 45	$72 93	$389,746 19		$2,350 53	$652 25	$1,885 89	$2,545 77
Arizona Territory	3,902	8,995 75	156,422 80	807 85			$51 04	59 00		806 94	127 00
Arkansas	35,373	31,187 38	158,601 02	5,302 70		560,373 00	48 34	885 03		2,476 87	1,180 63
California	54,920	14,087 30	1,391,863 89	7,791 40		1,136,925 00	32 50	5,907 66	1,366 00	37,297 00	30,131 75
Colorado Territory	30,631	11,271 61	470,224 60	2,700 95		296,650 73		863 00	119 00	18,732 00	491 00
Connecticut	61,561	6,821 95	938,344 72	5,974 75		413,774 00		17,550 87	400 00	40,498 16	4,947 00
Dakota Territory	9,384	519 95	52,960 17	303 75				75 00		53 00	137 25
Delaware	7,651	1,278 37	132,043 83	834 00	2 87	10,025 00		2,370 00	116 00	2,963 58	120 00
District of Columbia	23,178	12,962 34	460,335 65	2,663 70		1,184,327 13			1,447 00	6,977 00	6,754 00
Florida	45,364	15,032 61	731,766 87	4,003 55		87,512 00		10 00	73 00	6,932 00	4,292 25
Georgia	44,541	46,455 15	464,719 13	3,299 90		921,535 43	24 36	441 00	15 00	5,516 58	311 50
Idaho Territory	4,297	6,051 96	143,330 00	761 50				513 00		7,100 00	
Illinois	365,033	106,379 20	5,410,194 97	34,848 90		4,928,960 70	156 01	46,951 75	4,970 96	115,948 49	94,039 70
Indiana	190,732	34,146 17	3,423,974 04	18,155 15		1,009,312 39	64 48	14,288 07	1,030 00	30,737 07	5,383 48
Iowa	210,340	34,643 50	3,112,403 49	20,210 15		1,104,629 96	71 35	11,509 97	661 22	8,570 87	5,635 69
Kansas	41,165	19,836 88	1,423,662 88	6,782 70	01	494,461 19	141 19	11,566 34	153 00	3,205 35	1,751 00
Kentucky	64,835	11,651 77	1,923,689 33	6,430 15		685,897 31	67 15	16,030 00	988 25	6,069 25	3,332 00
Louisiana	38,681	42,895 77	744,336 07	4,192 80		1,237,253 24	18 63	309 63	424 00	9,854 00	1,934 00
Maine	52,540	9,183 56	1,061,946 69	6,291 60		497,539 00	75 88	8,691 18		101,879 15	713 00
Maryland	42,702	7,662 14	756,393 33	4,608 90		994,371 00	46 13	4,901 96	394 00	8,169 73	13,989 71
Massachusetts	121,914	21,960 20	2,176,362 99	13,146 90		1,663,493 54	225 96	38,774 68	1,207 50	149,370 70	14,069 33
Michigan	128,731	43,117 70	2,924,096 59	18,238 10		1,538,563 50	118 81	24,641 15	1,852 00	35,391 93	7,578 84
Minnesota	77,628	21,517 96	1,278,850 08	7,984 90		543,252 00	2 99	4,517 44	455 00	4,653 00	2,177 02
Mississippi	15,747	15,747 13	1,097,461 06	6,562 20	6 43	1,000 00		553 95		9,498 17	701 10
Missouri	141,436	29,495 95	2,370,110 93	14,707 05		2,448,729 41	70 75	27,649 36	1,683 00	14,908 19	4,349 00
Montana Territory	5,914	8,574 97	144,109 33	835 90				314 52		2,077 00	1,374 28
Nebraska	37,317	3,461 63	685,668 60	4,151 65		917,020 01	29 88	14,571 67	87 00	4,744 28	653 80
Nevada	7,454	3,951 05	224,658 63	1,258 95					436 00	10,359 76	1,395 00
New Hampshire	38,996	3,536 53	635,335 13	3,951 30		76,475 00	57 38	57 33		16,933 49	1,314 95
New Jersey	45,318	7,874 45	766,359 42	4,713 30		92,825 00	468 85	32,242 41	1,400 00	73,349 68	8,339 00
New Mexico Territory	1,978	780 90	67,597 55	357 90				104 00		79 58	
New York	238,991	239,463 63	4,110,090 02	25,729 60		14,737,963 42	425 00	112,923 43	46,052 53	907,921 91	77,619 63
North Carolina	43,375	10,860 24	907,003 16	5,369 70		132,811 04	11 49	4,814 00	6 00	938 07	9,159 14
Ohio	270,486	43,397 81	3,195,519 38	18,012 10		2,778,020 84	688 37	49,316 96	3,048 00	73,757 30	98,745 79
Oregon	14,753	20,527 43	325,954 04	1,992 10		329,456 88	5 37	1,570 61	923 00	5,945 81	2,796 00
Pennsylvania	191,767	32,879 53	2,999,513 07	12,855 15	10 98	3,044,800 49	980 74	51,400 92	3,598 00	114,968 78	13,545 67
Rhode Island	18,920	3,119 89	330,680 85	2,065 85		189,958 00		1,130 00	198 00	39,848 13	1,108 00

Table exhibiting the receipts and expenditures of the Post-Office Department from July 1, 1836, to June 30, 1873.

Year.	Receipts.			Expenditures.
	Revenue.	Treasury grants.	Total.	
1837....................	$4,945,668 21	....	$4,945,668 21	$3,288,319 03
1838....................	4,238,733 46	....	4,238,733 46	4,430,662 21
1839....................	4,484,656 70	....	4,484,656 70	4,636,536 31
1840....................	4,543,521 92	....	4,543,521 92	4,718,235 64
1841....................	4,407,726 27	$482,657 00	4,890,383 27	4,499,527 61
1842....................	4,546,849 65	....	4,546,849 65	5,674,751 80
1843....................	4,296,225 43	....	4,296,225 43	4,374,753 71
1844....................	4,237,287 83	....	4,237,287 83	4,296,512 70
1845....................	4,289,841 80	....	4,289,841 80	4,320,731 90
1846....................	3,487,199 35	750,000 00	4,237,199 35	4,076,036 91
1847....................	3,880,309 23	12,500 00	3,892,809 23	3,979,542 10
1848....................	4,555,211 10	125,000 00	4,680,211 10	4,326,850 27
1849....................	4,705,176 28	....	4,705,176 28	4,479,049 13
1850....................	5,499,984 86	....	5,499,984 86	5,212,953 43
1851....................	6,410,604 33	....	6,410,604 33	6,278,401 68
1852....................	5,184,526 84	1,741,444 44	6,925,971 28	7,108,459 04
1853....................	5,240,724 70	2,255,000 00	7,495,724 70	7,982,756 59
1854....................	6,255,586 22	2,736,748 96	8,992,335 18	8,577,424 19
1855....................	6,642,136 13	3,114,542 26	9,756,678 39	9,968,342 20
1856....................	6,920,821 66	3,748,881 56	10,669,703 22	10,405,286 36
1857....................	7,353,951 76	4,526,004 67	11,881,956 43	11,506,057 93
1858....................	7,486,792 86	4,679,270 71	12,166,063 57	12,722,470 01
1859....................	7,968,494 07	3,915,946 49	11,884,430 56	11,458,083 63
1860....................	8,518,067 40	11,154,167 54	19,672,234 94	19,170,609 90
1861....................	8,349,296 40	4,639,806 53	12,989,102 93	13,606,750 11
1862....................	8,299,820 90	2,598,953 71	10,898,774 61	11,125,364 13
1863....................	11,163,789 59	1,007,848 72	12,171,638 31	11,314,206 84
1864....................	12,438,253 78	749,980 00	13,188,233 78	12,644,786 20
1865....................	14,556,158 70	3,968 46	14,560,127 16	13,694,728 28
1866....................	14,386,986 21	....	14,386,986 21	15,352,079 30
1867....................	15,237,026 87	3,991,666 67	19,228,693 54	19,235,483 46
1868....................	16,292,600 80	5,696,525 00	21,989,125 80	22,730,592 65
1869....................	18,344,510 72	5,707,115 30	24,051,626 02	23,698,131 50
1870....................	19,772,220 65	4,022,140 85	23,794,361 50	23,998,837 63
1871....................	20,037,045 42	4,126,200 00	24,163,245 42	24,390,104 08
1872....................	21,915,426 37	4,993,750 00	26,909,176 37	26,658,192 31
1873....................	22,996,741 57	5,990,475 00	28,987,216 57	29,084,945 67
Total	333,889,966 04	82,772,593 87	416,662,559 91	415,028,565 64

J. J. MARTIN,
Auditor.

OFFICE OF THE AUDITOR OF THE TREASURY
FOR THE POST-OFFICE DEPARTMENT, *October 20, 1873.*

Statement showing the transactions of the money-order office of the United States for the fiscal year ending June 30, 1873.

States and Territories	Number of orders issued	Balance from last year.	Amount of orders issued.	Total fees received.	Premiums.	Drafts and deposits received.	Balance due post-masters.	Postage fund.	Swiss fund.	British fund.	German fund.
				Revenue.				Transferred from—			
Alabama	42,963	$18,018 53	$902,609 73	$5,319 45	$72 93	$362,746 19		$2,350 53	$632 25	$1,865 89	$2,545 77
Arizona Territory	4,902	8,995 75	156,422 80	807 95			$31 04	59 00		806 34	197 00
Arkansas	35,273	31,187 30	958,601 62	5,362 77		503,373 00	46 34	885 03		2,476 87	1,180 75
California	54,920	11,047 30	1,391,963 89	7,791 40		1,136,595 00	32 50	5,907 66	1,366 00	37,297 00	30,131 75
Colorado Territory	39,695	11,571 63	476,214 69	2,700 95		296,650 73		863 00	119 00	18,732 06	491 00
Connecticut	61,561	6,821 93	938,344 72	5,974 75		413,774 00		17,550 87	400 00	40,498 16	137 25
Dakota Territory	22,364	1,275 38	52,460 17	303 35				75 00		53 00	137 00
Delaware	22,621	1,275 31	132,043 63	536 03		10,625 00		2,370 00	116 00	2,985 58	130 00
District of Columbia	123,178	12,992 54	460,335 65	2,663 70		1,164,387 13	2 67	73 00	1,447 00	6,977 00	6,754 00
Florida	44,511	13,032 63	711,766 13	4,003 25		87,512 00		15 00		6,282 00	930 00
Georgia	44,207	46,455 15	664,719 13	3,299 90		921,535 43	24 98	441 00		5,516 53	4,999 25
Idaho Territory	4,257	6,051 96	143,330 00	761 35				519 00		7,100 00	311 50
Illinois	365,033	106,379 20	5,410,168 97	34,848 30		4,998,960 70	156 61	46,951 75	4,970 96	115,943 49	94,039 70
Indiana	190,732	34,146 17	2,822,974 04	18,155 15		1,009,319 89	64 48	14,298 07	1,039 00	20,737 07	5,383 48
Iowa	210,340	34,613 50	3,112,493 49	20,210 15	01	1,162,829 98	71 33	11,509 97	661 22	8,570 87	3,655 00
Kansas	54,165	19,636 84	1,423,602 68	8,742 70		494,461 19	144 19	11,566 34	133 00	3,205 35	1,751 60
Kentucky	62,853	11,651 92	1,623,829 33	6,430 15		685,897 31	67 15	16,030 00	948 25	3,669 95	3,920 00
Louisiana	30,821	42,495 71	744,336 07	4,192 95		1,337,253 59	16 68	308 00	424 00	101,854 00	1,804 00
Maine	52,549	9,133 56	1,961,846 69	6,291 60		497,539 00	18 63	8,691 18		9,854 00	713 00
Maryland	42,707	7,662 74	756,323 33	4,008 30		994,371 94	73 88	4,401 96	394 00	101,679 15	19,989 71
Massachusetts	121,914	21,910 30	2,176,362 69	4,000 00		1,603,493 54	46 13	4,691 56	1,307 50	149,370 70	14,009 33
Michigan	157,711	43,117 90	2,924,096 50	14,238 10		1,532,563 50	118 81	34,641 15	1,959 00	35,291 93	2,578 86
Minnesota	77,623	11,517 96	1,670,850 42	7,984 20		1,000 00	9 99	553 44	455 44	4,653 00	2,177 00
Mississippi	54,399	15,747 13	1,057,661 06	6,562 10	0 43	917,020 01		27,553 95		2,498 17	701 10
Missouri	141,426	28,463 93	2,370,110 93	14,707 03		76,475 00	70 75	27,642 36	1,483 00	14,908 12	4,340 00
Montana Territory	24,816	4,574 97	148,109 33	835 00		92,885 00	28 88	314 52	67 00	4,744 39	1,374 00
Nebraska	37,317	1,444 73	685,664 09	1,254 25			37 38	14,571 67	436 00	2,077 00	633 00
Nevada	7,454	5,361 63	234,626 61	3,951 00			468 88			10,359 78	1,395 00
New Hampshire	44,996	5,536 53	635,335 13	3,713 30				7,733 45		16,933 48	1,314 95
New Jersey	45,316	1,474 45	766,350 42	357 90				24,262 44	1,400 00	74,340 48	8,333 00
New Mexico Territory	1,072	740 00	67,597 55					104 00		79 58	
New York	224,991	229,463 63	4,110,029 02	25,729 00	10 26	14,737,963 63	425 00	119,923 43	46,632 53	907,981 91	77,619 63
North Carolina	43,375	10,460 94	997,003 16	3,309 70		132,811 00	11 99	4,814 00	6 00	938 97	2,130 14
Ohio	979,446	43,397 43	3,943,319 34	56,012 15		2,774,620 04	648 37	49,316 36	9,044 00	73,757 30	98,745 79
Oregon	14,733	38,527 43	321,934 04	1,992 10		273,644 00	5 37	1,576 61	632 00	3,045 81	12,866 67
Pennsylvania	191,767	34,479 53	1,999,513 07	1,855 15		3,044,900 49	980 74	51,460 32	2,389 00	114,998 78	13,855 67
Rhode Island	18,991	2,119 89	410,688 82	4,005 82		189,928 00		1,139 00	988 00	38,048 12	1,106 00

South Carolina	30,087	6,773 94	594,888 98	3,941 40	124 79	325,804 95	10 99	150 00		1,998 00	894 00
Tennessee	75,979	34,948 30	1,530,137 56	9,056 15		1,729,418 76	17 53	2,989 54	3,477 00	6,658 00	1,957 00
Texas	45,954	31,971 74	1,080,105 60	6,133 90		19,886 00		8,678 61	469 75	9,157 18	6,661 01
Utah Territory	7,393	4,348 43	905,465 55	1,117 30		1,900 00	22 10	936 00	1,864 00	8,049 00	599 00
Vermont	39,325	6,000 30	639,847 53	3,989 50		68,250 00	50 66	631 13		6,936 30	928 00
Virginia	57,914	18,422 88	1,163,518 81	6,950 85		1,453,360 00		7,354 76	916 15	13,497 00	2,536 00
Washington Territory	5,436	3,799 75	149,627 17	825 45		8,199 00	4 33	597 19		1,396 00	389 00
West Virginia	93,561	5,506 78	431,059 18	2,661 35		52,700 00		1,481 00	41 00	3,783 99	1,127 00
Wisconsin	175,827	41,949 93	3,080,679 94	18,831 45		1,960,733 00	221 15	10,004 76	1,566 50	17,263 85	11,631 85
Wyoming Territory	5,550	696 96	145,434 09	806 00						948 00	66 00
Total	3,353,686	1,088,535 63	57,516,914 09	354,608 95	214 41	46,889,851 68	3,468 03	547,657 23	90,022 97	1,923,037 08	295,335 18

54 Ab

Number of letters exchanged between the United States and foreign countries during the fiscal year ended June 30, 1873.

Countries.	Number of letters.	
	Received.	Sent.
United Kingdom of Great Britain and Ireland	5, 718, 550	6, 114, 566
German Union	2, 728, 803	3, 443, 103
France	104, 413	68, 366
Belgium	64, 477	73, 165
Netherlands	89, 814	130, 760
Switzerland	181, 341	181, 214
Italy	133, 984	153, 072
Denmark	239, 648	118, 160
Norway and Sweden	683	1, 035
Spain		261
Panama	116, 990	110, 506
Mexico	17, 048	26, 170
Brazil	37, 027	52, 429
Honduras		229
Ecuador	1, 687	4, 666
Venezuela	1, 002	
New Granada	3, 582	3, 311
West India Islands	493, 497	344, 779
China and Japan	124, 466	92, 050
Honolulu, &c	41, 911	43, 796
Nova Scotia, Newfoundland, and Bermuda*	14, 895	5, 734
Canadian provinces	2, 942, 673	3, 375, 852
Total	13, 126, 511	14, 332, 674
Increase compared with last fiscal year	1, 606, 506	1, 676, 996

* Partial returns only.

J. J. MARTIN, *Auditor.*

OFFICE OF THE AUDITOR OF THE TREASURY
 FOR THE POST-OFFICE DEPARTMENT, *October* 20, 1873.

Amounts reported as due the steamers of the Dale or Inman line for services rendered during the fiscal year ended June 30, 1873.

Third quarter of 1872	$11,790 40
Fourth quarter of 1872	195 00
Second quarter of 1873	508 62
Total amount paid	12, 494 02

Amounts reported as due the steamers of the North German Lloyd, of Bremen, for services rendered during the fiscal year ended June 30, 1873.

Third quarter of 1872	$7,620 12
Fourth quarter of 1872	8, 314 46
First quarter of 1873	7, 813 39
Second quarter of 1873	9, 806 97
Total amount paid	33, 554 94

Amounts reported as due the steamers of the Canadian line for services rendered during the fiscal year ended June 30, 1873.

Third quarter of 1872	$1,696 36
Fourth quarter of 1872	961 77
First quarter of 1873	1, 711 69
Second quarter of 1873	1, 695 31
Total amount paid	6, 065 13

South Carolina	17,686	333,664 36	2,853 49	949 33	1,530 00	131 00	93 00	516,193 98	5 50	1,815 78	9,507 90	55 04
Tennessee	57,750	1,917,014 38	8,539 37	91 84	1,192 04	588 00	2,411 00	2,032,566 00	2,965 92	5,460 46	36,999 36	
Texas	15,068	449,776 24	8,975 30			742 31	2,979 21	644,467 83	19 25	2,430 11	43,179 66	
Utah Territory	2,757	65,987 29	734 00			420 00	781 78	132,910 00		402 50	3,288 81	
Vermont	95,854	455,683 71	3,471 05	985 00		394 78	102 85	971,039 40		2,468 73	7,777 65	65 25
Virginia	46,864	1,044,067 67	5,736 04	49 25		2,610 00	1,349 00	1,589,300 45	57 74	4,495 39	90,098 95	16 46
Washington Territory	1,916	71,893 56	1,488 90			320 44	140 00	88,954 00	7 75	454 85	1,779 09	
West Virginia	11,735	934,053 77	2,594 09	1 00	140 00	136 41	511 00	253,417 55	136 53	1,520 33	6,080 88	50 08
Wisconsin	119,331	2,459,117 06	22,174 23	1,173 78	2,896 61	6,349 07	98,044 83	2,599,943 00	158 96	11,643 54	56,592 68	123 87
Wyoming Territory	895	93,857 66	1,206 91			5 60	19 44	119,884 00		308 96	2,719 08	
Total	3,314,818	56,900,351 93	394,661 04	730,373 45	67,098 33	1,907,549 13	228,679 73	48,974,503 98	93,304 08	257,998 56	1,250,880 91	4,685 69

OFFICE OF THE AUDITOR OF THE TREASURY
FOR THE POST-OFFICE DEPARTMENT, *October 20, 1873.*

J. J. MARTIN, *Auditor.*

Number of letters exchanged between the United States and foreign countries during the fiscal year ended June 30, 1873.

Countries.	Number of letters.	
	Received.	Sent.
United Kingdom of Great Britain and Ireland........................	5,718,550	6,114,566
German Union...	2,728,893	3,443,103
France...	104,413	68,366
Belgium..	64,477	73,168
Netherlands..	89,814	120,760
Switzerland..	181,341	181,214
Italy..	133,984	153,072
Denmark...	239,648	118,160
Norway and Sweden...................................	683	1,035
Spain...	....	261
Panama..	116,990	110,506
Mexico..	17,048	26,170
Brazil..	37,097	52,429
Honduras..	....	299
Ecuador...	1,687	4,066
Venezuela...	1,002	....
New Granada...	3,589	3,311
West India Islands...................................	493,427	344,779
China and Japan......................................	124,466	92,089
Honolulu, &c...	41,911	43,798
Nova Scotia, Newfoundland, and Bermuda*..............	14,895	5,734
Canadian provinces...................................	2,962,673	3,375,852
Total...	13,126,511	14,332,674
Increase compared with last fiscal year.................	1,608,598	1,676,998

* Partial returns only.

J. J. MARTIN, *Auditor.*

OFFICE OF THE AUDITOR OF THE TREASURY
 FOR THE POST-OFFICE DEPARTMENT, *October* 20, 1873.

Amounts reported as due the steamers of the Dale or Inman line for services rendered during the fiscal year ended June 30, 1873.

Third quarter of 1872...	$11,790 40
Fourth quarter of 1872..	195 00
Second quarter of 1873..	508 62
Total amount paid...	12,494 02

Amounts reported as due the steamers of the North German Lloyd, of Bremen, for services rendered during the fiscal year ended June 30, 1873.

Third quarter of 1872...	$7,620 12
Fourth quarter of 1872..	8,314 46
First quarter of 1873...	7,813 39
Second quarter of 1873..	9,806 97
Total amount paid...	33,554 94

Amounts reported as due the steamers of the Canadian line for services rendered during the fiscal year ended June 30, 1873.

Third quarter of 1872...	$1,696 36
Fourth quarter of 1872..	961 77
First quarter of 1873...	1,711 69
Second quarter of 1873..	1,695 31
Total amount paid...	6,065 13

Amounts reported as due the steamers of the Hamburg-American Packet Company for ser-
vices rendered during the fiscal year ended June 30, 1873.

Third quarter of 1872	$10,524 27
Fourth quarter of 1872	14,520 20
First quarter of 1873	17,458 67
Second quarter of 1873	14,116 40
Total amount paid	56,619 54

Amounts reported as due the steamers of the Cunard line for services rendered during the fis-
cal year ended June 30, 1873.

Third quarter of 1872	$1,517 04
Fourth quarter of 1872	704 30
First quarter of 1873	546 06
Second quarter of 1873	1,975 25
Total amount paid	4,742 65

Amounts reported as due the steamers of the Liverpool and Great Western Steam Company
for services rendered during the fiscal year ended June 30, 1873.

Third quarter of 1872	$17,861 57
Fourth quarter of 1872	18,085 35
First quarter of 1873	18,824 56
Second quarter of 1873	19,825 94
Total amount paid	74,597 42

Amount reported as due the steamers of the Baltic-Lloyd for services rendered during the
fiscal year ended June 30, 1873.

Third quarter of 1872	$12 07

Amounts reported as due the steamers of the White Star line for services rendered during
the fiscal year ended June 30, 1873.

Third quarter of 1872	No service.
Fourth quarter of 1872	$10,095 23
First quarter of 1873	11,643 42
Second quarter of 1873	8,093 32
Total amount paid	29,831 97

Amount reported as due the steamers of the National line for services rendered during the
fiscal year ended June 30, 1873.

Second quarter of 1873	$390 49

Amounts reported as due the steamers of the Pacific Mail Steamship Company for the con-
veyance of mails between the United States and Panama during the fiscal year ended
June 30, 1873.

Third quarter of 1872	$7,556 18
Fourth quarter of 1872	5,970 83
First quarter of 1873	7,394 93
Second quarter of 1873	6,809 62
Total amount paid	27,731 56

Amounts reported as due the steamers conveying the mails between the United States and
the West India Islands, Mexico, Brazil, Bermuda, New Granada, and New Zealand, for
services rendered during the fiscal year ended June 30, 1873.

Third quarter of 1872	$14,485 59
Fourth quarter of 1872	19,643 39
First quarter of 1873	16,026 21
Second quarter of 1873	14,990 75
Total amount paid	65,145 94

REPORT

OF

THE COMMISSIONER OF AGRICULTURE.

DEPARTMENT OF AGRICULTURE,
Washington, October 26, 1873.

TO THE PRESIDENT:

The progress of events connected with the administration of this Department during the past year has served to exemplify, not only its practical usefulness, but its appreciation by the people, and especially by those who are interested in the pursuits of agriculture. The planters and farmers of the country seem to recognize this Department as a sentinel upon the watch-tower of agricultural interests; to mark whatever new ideas and principles may be developed in the minds of men upon that subject; and to discover and procure such new and useful seeds and plants as may enable them to keep pace with agricultural progress throughout the world.

There is no other duty which devolves upon me so acceptable, so agreeable, and withal so profitable, as the correspondence which I have sought to promote with agricultural colleges, societies, and individuals respecting improvements in the modes of cultivation and experiments in its practical operations. I mean no disparagement of any class of people when I say that the contrast between the character and quality of farming in different portions of our country is most remarkable. Whilst there is a great difference in the natural products of one section from that of another, which requires different modes of culture, yet there are certain fixed principles of the science of agriculture which are common to both, and the neglect of which can never be disregarded with impunity. The planters of our Southern States undertake to cultivate too much land with too little diversity of crop, thereby disabling themselves from obtaining that rotation so essential to successful farming. This undoubtedly grows out of their immediate necessities, the consequences of the late war, from which time only will relieve them. My attention has been strongly attracted to this state of things, and it has given me great satisfaction to sympathize with those who most need the helping hand of this Department of the Government. Whilst the people of the Northern and Middle States, apart from the consideration of the sacrifice of human life, were rather benefited by the war than otherwise, the people of the Southern States were greatly impoverished.

The Western States, now rapidly filling up with a population, many of whom have spent almost the last dollar of their means to reach their place of destination—they, too, have claims upon the consideration of the Government, which, I do not hesitate to say, have been largely administered to by this Department. It is a pleasing task to supply want when it can be done consistently with a proper discharge of duty. And I feel sure that the actions of this Department, as here indicated, will not be found fault with by any portion of a generous people. I may safely say, without the fear of contradiction, that there is no branch of industry in our whole country that is marching forward with so steady and certain a step to improvement as that of agriculture, and it gives me great satisfaction to know that the judicious recognition by Congress of the instrumentality of this Department has enabled me greatly to aid the effort and enterprise which have taken this direction. It is through this influence that the successful experiences or useful discoveries of any part of the world are communicated to our own people, whereby they are enabled immediately to profit.

I have taken great pains to impress upon the Southern planters the importance of turning their attention to the cultivation of jute, and in giving them special instructions with regard to its culture, manufacture, and use. By the instrumentality of this Department jute was first introduced into this country from Calcutta, and now its cultivation will probably become one of the established industries of the Southern States. In 1872 there was imported into this country in bales 41,851 tons, costing about $64 per ton in gold at the place of exportation, of which, adding duties, transportation, and exchange, the cost will be more than $4,000,000 for an article of consumption of which a superior quality can be profitably raised in many of the Southern States. Judging from the tone of letters received from parties engaged in the cultivation of this plant, I am assured that it will soon become a profitable industry to an extent now scarcely credible, and this too in a section of our country where diversity of product and certain profit is so desirable. Ramie, another most valuable plant, has been greatly retarded in its production, by the difficulty of separating the fiber; no machinery having been invented which will accomplish this work, although large rewards have been offered by the British government to inventors.

The failure of Congress at its last session to provide for the publication of the annual report has subjected the Department to great inconvenience. There are from one to four agents in every county of every State who monthly report the acreage, condition of the crop, and final result, which, when aggregated, tabulated, and published monthly, afford such information as keeps the subject of agricultural products out of the hands of speculators, and thereby protects the interests of producers. The only compensation which can be given for this most useful work is that we can supply such agents with our annual and monthly publications, and seeds for distribution to the farmers around them. This, as to the annual report, we have not been enabled to do. There is no work published in this country for which there is so great a demand as the annual report of this Department. The farmers of the country have been so long accustomed to receive it, that they cannot understand why there should be any intermission in its publication. The Senate, in their executive session, ordered twelve hundred copies to be printed for their use, which necessarily involved the composition and stereotyping of the work, leaving little expense to be incurred in supplying the usual number of copies for general distribution, which I trust that Congress when it meets may immediately order.

The Department is in the daily receipt of information from its agents and others with regard to the results from superior seeds and plants which have been distributed; from which it is very certain that, in wheat and oats alone, the increased production of each amounts to many millions of bushels. Farmers have been convinced of this; hence it has been the pleasure of Congress from time to time for several years to increase the appropriation for the seed department. I take this occasion to suggest that the work of this division should not be done in the building occupied by the Department. If a house were built for this purpose, it might be so constructed as, in a great measure, to exclude vermin, which infest the rooms now occupied. Such a building might be constructed for ten thousand dollars, the appropriation of which I recommend.

The following tabular statement will show the quantity and kind of seeds distributed by the seed division from the 1st July, 1872, to the 30th June, 1873.

Name of seed.	Varieties.	Senators and Members of Congress.	Agricultural societies.	Statistical correspondents.	Meteorological observers.	Miscellaneous applicants.	Totals.
Vegetable...............papers..	244	138, 103	119, 350	79, 330	10, 690	270, 161	617, 564
Flower......................do....	189	60, 965	4, 225	140	7, 140	154, 896	227, 296
Herbs......................do....	12	....	60	....	....	211	271
Tree and evergreen ....do....	74	30	32	179	....	3, 631	3, 872
FIELD SEEDS.							
Wheat...................quarts..	10	14, 317	24, 894	13, 975	....	10, 242	63, 356
Oats.......................do....	4	20, 214	15, 488	6, 210	....	4, 298	46, 210
Barley.....................do....	2	186	7, 406	1, 430	....	802	9, 694
Rye........................do....	2	....	2, 172	5, 976	....	839	8, 977
Buckwheat..................do....	2	1, 778	50	6, 398	....	314	8, 476
Corn.......................do....	2	896	4, 646	5, 989	....	1, 590	12, 851
Pease ....do....	1	553	176	2, 338	....	339	3, 406
Grass ....do....	7	2, 330	4, 540	5, 837	....	2, 409	15, 116
Clover ....do....	4	42	106	2	....	1, 316	1, 466
Sugar-beet.................do....	2	91	1, 737	214	....	948	2, 078
Mangel-wurzel... ....do....	4	96	1, 365	....	....	164	1, 632

Name of seeds.	Varieties.	Senators and Members of Congress.	Agricultural societies.	Statistical correspondents.	Meteorological observers.	Miscellaneous applicants.	Totals.
Rice................................do....	2	....	4	....	....	44	48
Sorghum........................do....	2	12	40	....	....	189	243
Broom-corn ....do....	1	....	....	....	....	29	29
Sunflower.....................do....	2	....	....	....	....	38	28
Vetches or tares ....do....	1	....	....	....	....	6	6
Tobacco.....................papers..	4	20,466	1,12	....	....	2,959	24,543
Osage orange.................do....	1	....	....	....	....	139	139
Tea seeds ....do....	1	16	30	....	....	145	191
Opium-poppy ....do....	1	40	....	....	....	461	501
Millet.......................quarts.	1	8	....	....	....	24	32
TEXTILES.							
Cotton.......................quarts.	....	52	26	1,034	....	362	1,474
Jute ....papers..	....	340	40	32	....	338	750
Ramie........................do....	....	....	....	....	....	255	255
Hemp.......................quarts.	....	24	4	....	....	5	39
Total amounts...............	....	260,559	187,449	129,014	17,760	456,104	1,050,836

I took occasion in my last annual report to note how admirably adapted and judiciously associated were the component parts of the Department to promote and care for the agricultural and horticultural interests of the country. Longer experience confirms this opinion.

The division of horticulture, pomology, and arboriculture is necessarily a very important one: the introduction and extension of utilizable plants, valuable for their commercial products, the testing of fruits and intelligent advisory dissemination of the various kinds of fruit-plants, are operations oftentimes slow in their fulfilment, as they are tardy in development, but valuable when completed. Years may elapse between the procuring of a plant and its final disposition. Fiber-plants and those of like character, whose ultimate value depends upon perfected chemical and mechanical manipulations, should not be too hastily laid aside.

In the Southern States, where many semi-tropical products may be cultivated, a great desire is being manifested to experiment with various crops not hitherto successfully cultivated there; this desire increases as a knowledge of the benefits of diversified culture extends. Such is the interest taken in this subject, that I have been repeatedly requested to recommend the establishment of stations or farms at different localities throughout the country, for the purpose, among other objects, of acclimating seeds and plants of tropical and semi-tropical kinds; to which I have always replied that I cannot acquiesce in the propriety of such a proposition, for, apart from the vast immediate expense which such establishments would require, and the host of officers and employés that it would necessitate, I had great doubt whether any profitable result would be attained. Whilst the human system may, to some extent, be acclimated to the endurance of heat and cold, and perhaps to resist causes of disease, it is very questionable whether any plant can be acclimated to any useful purpose out of its native element.

The improvement in the grounds of the Department, especially those of a permanent character, are being completed as rapidly as means allow. The planting of the arboretum proceeds slowly on account of the difficulty of procuring the rare species and varieties to which the wants of the collection are now reduced.

The arrangement and improvement of some of the streets of Washington have so affected the character of the lot heretofore used as a propagating garden, which lies between Four-and-a-half and Sixth streets, as to render it entirely useless for the purposes of this Department; it has, therefore, been abandoned, and plants, such as can be removed, have been transferred to the Department grounds and buildings prepared for them there.

The filling up of the canal and construction of a street upon part of its location has thrown out a strip of ground, about four acres, along the north side of the Department ground, which by an arrangement with the Commissioner of Public Buildings and Grounds, has been exchanged for the lot above referred to, and will be properly inclosed.

The importance of the entomological division is daily becoming more important. An illustration of the injuries done by insects to the farmers and planters will be found in the statement by the statistician of the Department, who estimates the loss of cotton by worms, the present season, at half a million of bales, which, at $75 per bale, represents a loss of $37,500,000. A loss of ten per cent. of the wheat-crop by the depredation of insects, which cannot be deemed an extravagant assumption, means this year a loss of twenty-five million of bushels, worth as many million dollars. This data leads necessarily to the conclusion that the observations and study of the entomologist is an important branch of agricultural knowledge. Some insects, as the western potato-bug, and others, have already been extensively destroyed, and the crops saved, by the use of Paris green and flour, and experiments are now being made to test its efficacy in destroying the much dreaded cotton caterpillar. A circular has been issued to ascertain how much has been accomplished in this direction during the present season, and as soon as answers shall have been received, the facts will be published in the reports.

During the past year an additional room has been fitted up, which will be devoted to an exhibition of economic entomology, and adapted to the rapidly increasing collection of beneficial and injurious insects, and arranged to illustrate some of the most prominent vegetable products and their enemies, giving at a glance all the injurious species preying upon that product, in their different stages. Here will be shown, too, the architecture of insects; their cases, nests, galls, cocoons, and specimens showing how all kinds of vegetable and animal substances are injured, eaten, mined, or otherwise destroyed by insects, so that the farmer may at once recognize them by their work. All of which will be classified according to the latest and best systems, and identified by their names, localities, &c., making the whole of great practical value to the student of entomology.

During the past year the work of the botanical division has been energetically prosecuted. The collections of several of the Government exploring expeditions have been received, as well as some from private individuals. Over 5,000 specimens have been added to the herbarium. Packages comprising several thousand specimens have been prepared and forwarded to men of science in Switzerland, Germany, Austria, and to the Imperial Herbarium of St. Petersburg; and many packages of duplicates are ready for distribution to scientific societies of our own country.

I respectfully suggest that this division should embrace a full collection of sections, of convenient size, of all the forest trees of our country, so arranged as to exhibit their natural character of bark, with longitudinal sections showing the appearance of the wood and its adaptation to purposes of economy in the arts—as, for building or cabinet work— each accurately named and accompanied with specimens of their fruit and leaves. Such a collection would have an especial value, as presenting, comprehensively, the richness of our country in the variety and qualities of our forest vegetation, and would offer a rare opportunity to students and men of science for instruction in this department of knowledge. And in connection with this subject I suggest that the approaching Centennial Exposition affords an additional argument for the preparation of such a collection of our forest specimens. Such a work will not be done by any private individual, and it seems to be peculiarly fit that this feature of our great country should be shown through the medium of this Department. This would require an appropriation by Congress not exceeding two thousand dollars.

An individual in Aiken, S. C., well known for his researches in fungi and the lower order of vegetation, is possessed of a large and valuable collection of specimens, the result of thirty years' accumulation, which he proposes to sell for one thousand dollars. It occurs to me that the opportunity of securing so valuable a collection should not be neglected, when it is considered that this field of study is so abstruse, and has been so little prosecuted, and that there are in the country so very few reliable and authentic collections.

The operations of the statistical division are, year by year, becoming more accurate and comprehensive. The crop-reporting system, though an unpaid service, is more efficient and reliable than any other means employed to ascertain the condition of growing crops. It is similar to that employed by associations and trade-boards, except that it is more extensive, regular, and prompt in communication, more systematic and thorough in detail, and more intelligent and practical in the material of its returns. There are now sixteen hundred counties, which include nearly all of much importance in production, represented each by a principal correspondent and board of assistants, selected from the most intelligent and public-spirited farmers. The work of the statistical division includes also the entire range of agricultural statistics, and embodies and epitomizes the facts of American agriculture, as created by systematic experiment, current practice, the work of agricultural organizations, and the movement of inter-continental and export trade. Nor does it neglect altogether the experience and practice of foreign countries, the extent of their production, and range of prices. Still more attention will be given to this field which has so intimate relation to our own agricultural prosperity, in affording a market for our surplus products, and in furnishing suggestions of economy and skill in practice and diversity and profitable extension in production. To this desirable end the statistician was sent to Europe the past summer to perfect exchanges, to establish relations of statistical reciprocity, investigate statistical methods, and thus increase and perfect the resources of the statistical division in this direction. The importance of foreign agricultural statistics is indicated by the constantly increasing value of our agricultural exports, which, in the fiscal year of 1872, amounted to the magnificent sum of $406,394,254, including $1,773,716 for living animals; $75,287,133 for animal products; $84,751,688 for breadstuffs; $182,988,835 for cotton and cotton products; $15,240,872 for wool in its various forms, and $46,352,010 for oils, vegetables, tobacco, and miscellaneous products of agriculture, either raw or extended.

There has been an increase of upwards of four hundred volumes to the library of the Department the past year. Of this increase, about two hundred volumes have been presented by the authors and by foreign agricultural and scientific associations, and from State boards of agriculture. The aggregate number of volumes is about 6,000.

We continue to receive transactions of all the leading agricultural societies of England, France, Germany, and Italy, as well as from several governments in Central and South America. To the courtesy of the Canadian government we are indebted for full reports on the agriculture, fisheries, public works, statistics, &c., of the Dominion. The library contains nearly complete sets of the transactions of the boards of agriculture of the leading States for the last twenty years. The boards of trade of the chief cities of the union have presented complete sets of their reports. All the associations referred to continue to forward their current volumes as fast as published.

In all the standard works on agriculture and its cognate branches of botany, geology, chemistry, and entomology, the library is now undoubtedly the most complete, in this country at least. It is in constant use by the clerks of the Department, and in fact is indispensable for reference in conducting its large correspondence.

Of the numerous pamphlets presented to the library, those possessing permanent interest or value are classified and bound together; such as, the reports of the dairymen's associations, and those of the State commissioners on the fisheries; those of a more miscellaneous nature are bound, those of each State by themselves, and lettered with the name of the State to which they refer.

The librarian is now engaged in the preparation of a catalogue of the library. This is a task which requires much time, labor, and knowledge. The full title of each book will be copied under the author's name; then a classification of subjects, and a cross-reference, comprising a short abstract, (generally in one line,) of the titles of all the books in the library referring to any particular subject. The great assistance of this arrangement to those engaged in the investigations and correspondence of the Department is obvious.

The shelving on the west side of the room, completed last year, is already nearly filled by the steady increase of the library. An appropriation of $500 was made last winter to carry the shelving and gallery across the south end; but this sum may be insufficient for the purpose. As this additional space will be indispensable, in the course of a year or two, for the natural increase of the library, I therefore respectfully suggest that an additional appropriation of $500 be made. This improvement would also add to the beauty and symmetrical appearance of the room, already so attractive as to be constantly noticed by visitors.

Among the most important additions to the library the past year, are "Sowerby's English Botany," in 11 volumes, comprising colored figures and descriptions of all the plants grown in Great Britain, and the "Flora Française," a similar work on the plants of France. These, and other works of a scientific character, are very expensive; and to purchase them and the various scientific periodicals of Europe and America, so as to keep abreast with the rapid progress of modern science, renders necessary the usual appropriation by Congress for the increase of the library.

The microscopic division of this Department was established a little more than a year ago, and has for its objects the investigation of all subjects relating to agriculture which require more minute observations in their examinations than can be made with the naked eye, whether they belong to the animal, vegetable, or mineral kingdom. Numerous letters of inquiry upon subjects of the character here referred to, had been received from time to time, by the Department, the responses to which had long urged the necessity of such a division. Thus far the microscopist has made some investigations into the organic structure and the mode of growth of plants, but his attention has been chiefly directed to their diseases, and especially to those which are supposed to originate from a class of very minute organisms called parasitic fungi, several thousand species of which are, as individuals, invisible to the naked eye, and appear as mere pigments of different colors scattered

INDEX.
